A
People
and a
Nation

BRIEF EDITION

i

A
People
and a
Nation

A History of the United States

BRIEF EDITION ▪ **FIFTH EDITION**

Mary Beth Norton
Cornell University

David M. Katzman
University of Kansas

Paul D. Escott
Wake Forest University

Howard P. Chudacoff
Brown University

Thomas G. Paterson
University of Connecticut

William M. Tuttle, Jr.
University of Kansas
and

William J. Brophy
Stephen F. Austin State University

Houghton Mifflin Company   Boston   New York

Associate Sponsoring Editor: Colleen Shanley Kyle
Senior Project Editor: Carol Newman
Senior Production/Design Coordinator: Carol Merrigan
Senior Manufacturing Coordinator: Marie Barnes
Senior Marketing Manager: Sandra McGuire

Cover designer: Jon Valk

Cover image: *Oklahoma Land Rush*, John Stewart Curry, 1989. U. S. Department
of the Interior.

Text photographs researched by Pembroke Herbert and
Sandi Rygiel/Picture Research Consultants.

Printed in the U.S.A.

Library of Congress Catalog Card Number: 98-72222

ISBN: 0-395-92131-7

1 2 3 4 5 6 7 8 9-VH-02 01 00 99 98

Brief Contents

Contents

1

Three Old Worlds Create a New, 1492–1600 *3*

2

Europeans Colonize North America, 1600–1640 *25*

6

A Revolution, Indeed, 1774–1783   *101*

7

Forging a National Republic, 1776–1789   *118*

8

Politics and Society in the Early Republic, 1789–1800   *137*

12

The American Social Landscape, 1800–1860   *213*

13

Reform, Politics, and Expansion, 1824–1844   *236*

14

Slavery and America's Future: The Road to War, 1845–1861   *257*

15

Transforming Fire: The Civil War, 1861–1865 *276*

16

Reconstruction: A Partial Revolution, 1865–1877 *299*

17

The Development of the West and South, 1877–1892 *319*

18

The Machine Age, 1877–1920   *336*

19

The Vitality and Turmoil of Urban Life, 1877–1920   *355*

25

The Great Depression and the New Deal, 1929–1941   *466*

26

Peaceseekers and Warmakers: United States Foreign Relations, 1920–1941   *488*

27

The Second World War at Home and Abroad, 1941–1945 *506*

28

Postwar America: Cold War Politics, Civil Rights, and the Baby Boom, 1945–1961 *526*

29

Foreign Relations Glacier: The Cold War and Its Aftermath, 1945–Present *549*

30

Foreign Relations Storm: Contesting Revolution and Nationalism in the Third World, 1945–Present *577*

31

Reform and Conflict: A Turbulent Era, 1961–1974 *604*

32

The End of the Postwar Boom: Stagflation, Immigration, and the Resurgence of Conservatism, 1974–1989 *624*

33

Anxiety and Anger: America in the 1990s   *646*

Appendix   *A-1*

Index   *I-I*

Maps

Charts

Preface to the Brief Fifth Edition

This text is a condensation and updating of the highly successful Fifth Edition of *A People and a Nation*. As with earlier brief editions, the authors have preserved the strengths of their full-length work—its readability, scholarship, comprehensiveness, and, most important, its dynamic blend of social, cultural, political, foreign relations, and economic history. This treatment of the whole story of United States history is especially suited for short courses or courses in which additional readings are assigned.

In preparing this brief edition, the authors have ensured that it reflects the changes in content and organization incorporated into the full-length Fifth Edition (see the Preface to the full-length edition, which follows). William J. Brophy, who prepared the condensation, collaborated closely with the six authors of the full-length edition to revise with great care; every line was scrutinized. We thus avoided deleting entire sections and attained our objective by paring down detail. Where two examples were used in the full-length edition, we deleted one; where many statistics were presented, we used a few. Although we abridged or deleted some excerpts from diaries and letters, we have retained many quotations and accounts of everyday life.

Creation of the Brief Edition

The brief edition is available in both one-volume and two-volume formats. The two-volume format divides as follows: Volume A contains Chapters 1 through 16, beginning with a discussion of three cultures—American, African, and European—that intersected during the exploration and colonization of the New World and ending with a discussion of the Reconstruction era. Volume B contains Chapters 16 through 33, beginning its coverage at Reconstruction and extending the history of the American people to the present. The chapter on Reconstruction appears in both volumes

to provide greater flexibility in matching a volume to the historical span covered by a specific course.

While the following Preface to the full-length Fifth Edition elaborates on specific content changes, in brief, the authors paid increased attention to the following: the interaction of the private sphere of everyday life with the public sphere of politics and government; grass-roots movements; religion; the emerging cultural globalism of American foreign relations; the development of the American West; and the relationship of the people to the land, including conflict over access to natural resources. These new emphases, as well as the up-to-date scholarship on which they are based, are retained in the Brief Fifth Edition.

Changes in This Edition

While each author feels answerable for the whole of *A People and a Nation*, we take primary responsibility for particular chapters: Mary Beth Norton, Chapters 1 through 8; David M. Katzman, Chapters 9, 10, 12, and 13; Paul D. Escott, Chapters 11, 14, 15, and 16; Howard P. Chudacoff, Chapters 17 through 21 and 24; Thomas G. Paterson, Chapters 22, 23, 26, 29, and 30; William J. Tuttle, Jr., Chapters 25, 27, 28, and 31 through 33.

A number of useful learning and teaching aids accompany the Fifth Edition of *A People and a Nation*, Brief Edition. They are designed to help instructors and students achieve their teaching and learning goals. *@history: an interactive American history source* is a multimedia teaching/learning package that combines a variety of material on a cross-platformed CD-ROM—primary sources (text and graphic), video, and audio—with activities that can be used to analyze, interpret, and discuss primary sources; to enhance collaborative learning; and to create multimedia lecture presentations. *@history* also has an

Study and Teaching Aids

accompanying website, located at *www.hmco.com/college/*, where additional primary sources, on-line resources for *A People and a Nation*, and links to relevant sites can be found.

The two-volume *Study Guide*, prepared by George Warren and Cynthia Ricketson of Central Piedmont Community College, includes an introductory chapter on studying history that focuses on interpreting historical facts, test-taking hints, and critical analysis. The guide also includes learning objectives, a thematic guide, lists of terms, multiple-choice and essay questions for each chapter, as well as map exercises and sections on organizing information of some chapters. An answer key alerts students to the correct response and also explains why the other choices are wrong.

A new *Instructor's Resource Manual with Test Items*, prepared by Donald Frazier of Texas Christian University, contains ten chronological resource units in addition to teaching ideas for each chapter of the text. Each chronological resource unit includes sections on geography, technology, physical and material culture, historical sites, documentary films, popular films, and music. The manual also includes for each text chapter an overview of material in the chapter, a brief list of learning objectives, a chapter outline, ideas for classroom activities, discussion questions, and ideas for paper topics. There are also more than 1,000 new multiple-choice questions, identification terms, and essay questions.

A *Computerized Test Item File* is available to adopters for both Windows and Macintosh computers. This program allows professors to create customized tests by editing and adding questions.

There is also a set of over one hundred fifty full-color *American History Map Transparencies*, available in two volume sets upon adoption.

A variety of *videos*, documentaries and docudramas by major film producers, is available for use with *A People and a Nation*.

Please contact your local Houghton Mifflin representative for more information about the ancillary items or to obtain desk copies.

Author teams rely on review panels to help create and execute successful revision plans. Many historians advised us on the revision of this fifth edition, and the book is better because of their

Acknowledgments

thoughtful insights and recommendations. We heartily thank:

James H. O'Donnell III, *Marietta College*
Linda Madson Papageorge, *Kennesaw State University*
William D. Young, *Johnson County Community College*
Monica Maria Tetzlaff, *Indiana University South Bend*
Ann DeJesús Riley, *Hartnell College*
Richard M. Ugland, *Ohio State University*
Regina Lee Blaszczyk, *Boston University*
Richard M. Chapman, *Concordia College*
Patrick J. Kelly, *University of Texas at San Antonio*

Finally, we want to thank the many people who have contributed their thoughts and labors to this work, including the talented staff at Houghton Mifflin.

For the authors, WILLIAM J. BROPHY

Preface to the Full-Length Fifth Edition

Some twenty years ago, when we first embarked on this textbook-writing adventure, most survey texts adequately covered American politics and diplomacy, important historical events, and the famous people at the top of the hierarchy of power, but something was missing: the stories of ordinary Americans. Our experience as teachers told us that, although a rich scholarship in social history had emerged, it was not yet being incorporated into survey texts. We set out to weave this significant dimension of American history into the traditional fabric of party politics, congressional legislation, wars, economic patterns, and local and state government. The response to our approach proved exceptionally gratifying.

As we wrote subsequent editions, always challenged by enriching scholarship, the task changed from "inserting" social history to integrating it fully into the historical narrative and treating social history not only as the study of the private lives of Americans but also as power relationships among competing groups that looked to the public sphere of politics and government to mediate their differences. In this new edition we especially worked to accomplish this new task. After all, like other teachers and students, we are always recreating our past, restructuring our memory, rediscovering the personalities and events that have shaped us, inspired us, and bedeviled us. This book represents our rediscovery of America's history—its diverse people and the nation they created and have sustained. As this book demonstrates, there are many different Americans and many different memories. We have sought to present all of them, in both triumph and tragedy, in both division and unity.

After meeting in frank and searching planning sessions, critiquing one another's work, and reading numerous evaluations of the fourth edition of *A People and a Nation*, we developed a plan for this edition. Guided by up-to-date scholarship, we

New Thematic Emphases

decided to place new emphasis on several themes and subjects that we had discussed in previous editions but believed needed more attention: the interaction of the private sphere of everyday life with the public sphere of politics and government; grassroots movements; religion; the emerging cultural globalism of American foreign relations; the development of the American West; and the relationship of people to the land, including conflict over access to natural resources. By reexamining every sentence, editing every paragraph, and condensing, reconfiguring, and reconceptualizing chapters (see below), we accomplished a thorough revision (reducing the book by one chapter) while including a considerable amount of fresh material for new emphases, examples, and interpretations.

As before, we challenge students to think about the meaning of American history, not just to memorize facts. Through a readable narrative about all of the American people, we invite students to take themselves back in time to experience what it was like to live in—and to make life's choices in—a different era. Chapter-opening vignettes that dramatically recount stories of people contending with their times help define the key questions of a chapter (two-thirds of the vignettes are new to this edition). Succinct, focused introductions and conclusions frame each chapter. Illustrations, graphs, tables, and maps tied closely to text encourage visual and statistical explorations. We do not detail historiographical debates, but we acknowledge interpretations different from our own, and in the "Suggestions for Further Reading" sections at the end of each chapter we cite works with varying points of view to demonstrate that the writing of history is very much infused with debate.

Especially successful in the fourth edition, and strengthened here, is the "How Do Historians

xxvii

Know?" feature, which explains how historians go about using evidence to arrive at conclusions. In this highlighted section, our discussion—coupled with illustrations—explores how historians can draw conclusions from a variety of sources: crafts, political cartoons, maps, medical records, diaries, tape recordings, postcards, census data, telegrams, popular art, photographs, and more. This feature also helps students to understand how scholars can claim knowledge about historical events and trends. More than half of these discussions are new to this edition.

"How Do Historians Know?"

A People and a Nation is comprehensive in its treatment of the many ways in which Americans have defined themselves—by gender, race, class, region, ethnicity, religion, sexual orientation—and of the many subjects that have reflected Americans' multidimensional experiences: social, political, economic, diplomatic, military, environmental, intellectual, cultural, and more. We highlight the remarkably diverse everyday life of the American people—in cities and on farms and ranches, in factories and in corporate headquarters, in neighborhood meetings and in powerful political chambers, in love relationships and in hate groups, in recreation and in the workplace, in the classroom and in military uniform, in secret national security conferences and in public foreign relations debates, in church and in prison, in polluted environments and in conservation areas. We pay particular attention to lifestyles, diet and dress, family life and structure, labor conditions, gender roles, and childbearing and child rearing. By discussing music, sports, theater, print media, film, radio, television, graphic arts, and literature—in both "high" culture and "low" culture—we explore how Americans have entertained and informed themselves.

How We Study the Past

The private sphere of everyday life always interacts with the public sphere of politics and government. To understand how Americans have sought to protect their different ways of life and to work out solutions to thorny problems, we emphasize their expectations of government at the local, state, and federal levels; government's role in pro-

viding answers; the lobbying of interest groups; the campaigns and outcomes of elections; and the hierarchy of power in any period. Because the United States has long been a major participant in world affairs, we explore America's descent into wars, interventions in other nations, empire building, immigration patterns, images of foreign peoples, cross-national cultural ties, and international economic trends.

Mary Beth Norton, who had primary responsibility for Chapters 1 through 8, further developed her comparative focus in Chapters 1 and 2, explaining the growth of contrasting American, African, and European societies in the colonial world, giving new attention to the Spanish borderlands. Chapter 3 includes new discussion of the introduction of slavery into English mainland colonies and comparisons with New France and the Spanish borderlands. Chapter 4 has been recast with new emphasis on intercultural interactions among Indians and Europeans and comparisons of families in New France, the Spanish borderlands, and the English colonies (including Indian and mixed-race families). Chapter 7 includes new material on economic/fiscal issues in the Confederation period.

Major Changes in This Edition

David M. Katzman, who had primary responsibility for Chapters 9, 10, 12, and 13, rewrote to emphasize the role of the federal government and debates over centralized political authority. New emphases are found in his discussion of the conquering of the West (including a new vignette featuring Lewis and Clark in Chapter 9) and the growth of a Mexican-American culture in the Southwest (Chapter 12). He also widened his presentation of ethnic diversity, mental health reform, family and marriage (including divorce laws and women's property legislation), and manifest destiny.

Paul D. Escott, who had primary responsibility for Chapters 11, 14, 15, and 16, introduced new material on the westward movement of slaveholders and slaves and attitudes toward centralized government, African-American soldiers during the Civil War, and Confederate relations with Indians in the West. A new chart details the unprecedented losses of the Civil War, and several new and rarely seen photographs capture the drama of the Civil War period on many levels.

Howard P. Chudacoff, who had primary responsibility for Chapters 17 through 21 and 24, added new material on and gave new thematic emphasis to land (and water) control, conflict over access to natural resources, and environmental management in a newly titled Chapter 17, "The Development of the West and South, 1877–1892." Multiracial composition and racial tensions in the West are highlighted in Chapters 17 and 19, and new material is also presented on home life—indoor and family amusements and the impact of engineers and technology on household life—in Chapter 19. Chudacoff also reworked the section on agrarian protest and Populism, especially in the Rockies and Far West, and reconceptualized Gilded Age politics, adding the religio-cultural dimension (Chapter 20). To his discussion of Progressive reform (Chapter 21), he added coverage of women's clubs, the National Consumer's League, and federal policy on resource conservation. In his new account of the 1920s (Chapter 24), he emphasized the clash between "tried-and-true" and "modern" values and added new references to lobbying as a major influence in political decision making.

Thomas G. Paterson, who had primary responsibility for Chapters 22, 23, 26, 29, and 30, gave added emphasis to the theme of cultural relations and the conditioning of the foreign relations decision-making environment by ideology and images of foreign peoples. For Chapter 22, he included new material on relations with Africa, Canada, China, Chile, and Hawai'i and on international environmental agreements. In Chapter 23, on the First World War, the role of women in the peace movement, African-American attitudes toward the war, the economic impact of the war, and treatment of the war dead also received added attention. In Chapter 26, newly titled "Peaceseekers and Warmakers: United States Foreign Relations, 1920–1941," Paterson integrated new material on the role of nongovernmental organizations such as the Rockefeller Foundation and the Americanization of Europe. As part of the restructuring of the post-1945 chapters in the text, Chapters 29 and 30

carry the foreign relations story to the present. These chapters, well cross-referenced, especially reflect the post–Cold War declassification of documents from foreign sources (Russian, Chinese, and German, for example). Here the reader will discover new examinations of the origins of the Korean War, the Cuban missile crisis, Japan's "economic miracle," covert activities of the Central Intelligence Agency, human rights, United States Information Agency propaganda, the Middle East peace process, Haiti, and the debate over foreign aid. In lengthy coverage of the Vietnam War, Paterson included new material on Ho Chi Minh's relationship with Americans in 1945, the Tonkin Gulf crisis, and the My Lai massacre.

William M. Tuttle, Jr., had primary responsibility for Chapters 25 and 27, and the post-1945 Chapters 28 and 31 through 33. In Chapter 25, he added new material on Social Security and the end of the New Deal. In Chapter 27 on the Second World War, readers will find new discussions of race and ethnic relations, women and children, and the decision to drop the atomic bomb. Tuttle substantially rewrote and reorganized the material on post-1945 domestic history, reducing the number of chapters covering this period by one. In a new Chapter 28 he interweaves the political, economic, social, and cultural history from 1945 to 1961, adding fresh material on Cold War politics, civil rights, and the baby boom. Chapter 31 takes the story from 1961 to 1974, shedding new light on the Equal Rights Amendment, women in the civil rights movement, *Roe v. Wade*, and Richard Nixon and the Watergate tapes. The next chapter incorporates recent studies on economic woes, the new immigration from Latin America and Asia, social polarization, and the rise of political and cultural conservatism in the 1970s and 1980s. Chapter 33, which concludes the book, is a new history of the 1990s, focusing on Americans' political disaffection and on their hopes and fears as they approach the twenty-first century.

The multidimensional Appendix, prepared by Thomas G. Paterson, includes a new, extensive table on the "Fifty States, the District of Columbia, and Puerto Rico." Here students will discover essential information on dates of admission with rank, capital cities, population with rank, racial/

ethnic distribution, per capita personal income with rank, and total area in square miles. Once again, the Appendix begins with a guide to reference works on key subjects in American history. Students may wish to use this updated and enlarged list of encyclopedias, atlases, chronologies, and other books when they start to explore topics for research papers, when they seek precise definitions or dates, when they need biographical profiles, or when they chart territorial or demographic changes. The table of statistics on key features of the American people and nation also have been updated and expanded, as have the tables on presidential elections, the cabinet members of all administrations, party strength in Congress, and the justices of the Supreme Court.

Many instructors and students who have used this book in their courses have found its many learning and teaching aids very useful. The most exciting addition to our ancillary lineup is *@history: an interactive American history source*.

Study and Teaching Aids This multimedia teaching/learning package combines a variety of material—primary sources (text and graphic), videos, audio, and links to Web sites—with activities that can be used to analyze, interpret, and discuss primary sources; to enhance collaborative learning; and to create multimedia presentations. *@history* provides instructors with an interactive multimedia tool that can improve the analytical skills of students and introduce them to historical sources.

The *Study Guide*, prepared by George Warren and Cynthia Ricketson of Central Piedmont Community College, includes an introductory chapter on studying history that focuses on interpreting historical facts, test-taking hints, and critical analysis. The guide also includes learning objectives, a thematic guide, lists of terms, multiple-choice and essay questions for each chapter, as well as map exercises and sections on organizing information for some chapters. An answer key alerts students to the correct response and also explains why the other choices are wrong.

A *Computerized Study Guide* is also available for students. It provides approximately 15 multiple-choice questions for each chapter and functions as a tutorial that gives students information on incorrect as well as correct answers. The computerized guide is available in Macintosh, IBM, and IBM-compatible formats.

"A new *Instructor's Resource Manual*, prepared by Donald Frazier, Marvin Schultz, and Bruce Winders of Texas Christian University and Robert Pace of Longwood College, contains ten chronological resource units in addition to teaching ideas for each chapter of the textbook. Each chronological resource unit includes sections on geography, technology, physical and material culture (artifacts), historical sites, documentary films, popular films, and music. The manual also includes for each textbook chapter a content overview, a brief list of learning objectives, a comprehensive chapter outline, ideas for classroom activities, discussion questions, and ideas for paper topics.

A *Test Items* file, also prepared by George Warren, provides approximately 1,700 new multiple-choice questions, more than 1,000 identification terms, and approximately 500 essay questions.

A *Computerized Test Items File* for IBM and Macintosh computers is available to adopters. This computerized version of the printed *Test Items* file allows professors to create customized tests by editing and adding questions.

A set of full-color map transparencies is also available to instructors on adoption. A variety of videos—documentaries and docudramas by major film producers—is available for use with *A People and a Nation*.

At each stage of this project, historians read drafts of our chapters. Their suggestions, corrections, and pleas helped guide us through our revisions. We could not include all of their recommendations, but the book is better for our having heeded most of their advice.

Acknowledgments

We heartily thank

Diane Allen, *Columbia Gorge Community College*
David E. Conrad, *Southern Illinois University*

Paige Cubbison, *Miami Dade Community College, Kendall*

Joseph A. Devine, Jr., *Stephen F. Austin State University*

Shirley M. Eoff, *Angelo State University*

Maurine Greenwald, *University of Pittsburgh*

Melanie Gustafson, *University of Vermont*

D. Harland Hagler, *University of North Texas*

Craig Hendricks, *Long Beach City College*

Robert Kenzer, *University of Richmond*

Timothy Koerner, *Oakland Community College*

Lisa M. Lane, *Miracosta College*

Larry MacLestch, *Mendocino College*

Jeff Ostler, *University of Oregon*

William Robbins, *Oregon State University*

Athan Theoharis, *Marquette University*

Lynn Weiner, *Roosevelt University*

Marianne S. Wokeck, *Indiana University–Purdue University of Indianapolis*

Gerald Wolff, *University of South Dakota*

Once again we thank the extraordinary Houghton Mifflin team who designed, edited, produced, and nourished this book. Their high standards and careful attention to both general structure and fine detail are unmatched in publishing. Many thanks to Jean Woy, editor-in-chief; Pat Coryell, senior sponsoring editor; Ann West, basic book editor; Jeffrey Greene, senior associate editor, Keith Mahoney, assistant editor; Carol Newman, senior project editor; Carol Merrigan, senior production/design coordinator; Charlotte Miller, art editor; and Florence Cadran, manufacturing manager.

For helping us in many essential ways, we also extend our thanks to Michael Donoghue, Jan D. Emerson, Steven Jacobson, Andrea Katzman, Eric Katzman, Sharyn Brooks Katzman, Walter D. Kamphoefner, G. Stanley Lemons, Pam Levitt, Shane J. Maddock, Jill Norgren, Aaron M. Paterson, Norman G. Radford, Zil-e-Rehman, Paul L. Silver, Peter Solonysznyi, Julee Stephens, Luci Tapahonso, Kathryn Nemeth Tuttle, Samuel Watkins Tuttle, and Daniel H. Usner, Jr. Some of these individuals sent us suggestions for improving *A People and a Nation,* and we took their recommendations seriously. We welcome comments from professors and students about this new edition, too.

For the authors, THOMAS G. PATERSON

A
People
and a
Nation

BRIEF EDITION

1

Three Old Worlds Create a New
1492–1600

At birth, she was called Malinalli. The Spaniards christened her Doña Marina. History knows her as Malinche, a name formed by adding the Aztec suffix *che*, a term of respect, to her original name. She has been celebrated as the symbolic mother of the modern Mexican people and maligned as a traitor to Mexico's ancient residents.

Born sometime between 1502 and 1505, Malinalli was the daughter of a village chief within the Aztec Empire. Her father died while she was young, and her mother soon remarried. To protect the inheritance of the son born to that second marriage, the mother sold her daughter into slavery. Eventually, Malinalli came to live with Mayan-speaking people.

In 1519, she was presented as a gift to the Spanish conquistador Hernán Cortés. Cortés, who first arrived in the Spanish West Indies in 1504, embarked for the mainland in search of wealthy cities rumored to exist there. Little did he know that Doña Marina would be one of the keys to his conquest of Mexico. She spoke the languages of both the Aztecs and the Mayas, learned Spanish, and became Cortés's translator and mistress. Accompanying Cortés on his travels in Mexico, Doña Marina did more than simply interpret words for him: she explained the meanings that lay behind the language, opening the Aztec world to the Spaniards.

The Aztecs and subsequent Mexican historians have blamed Malinche for betraying her own people. But who were her people? The

Aztecs, in whose empire she had been born and who had sold her as a slave? The Mayas, among whom she was raised? Or the Europeans, who relied on her translations?

Malinche's life history, and her dual image as betrayer of ancient Mexico and symbolic mother of the modern mixed-race nation, encapsulate many of the ambiguities of the first encounter between Europeans and Americans. Sold into slavery by her Aztec-connected family, she owed that people little loyalty. The Spaniards gave her respect, yet she did not become Spanish: Cortés never married her. Malinche was caught between two worlds, part of both and of neither, alternately praised and blamed for her actions. Many people from both sides of the Atlantic were to meet the same fate as they attempted to cope with the rapidly changing world of the fifteenth and sixteenth centuries.

As European explorers and colonizers sought to exploit the resources of the rest of the globe, peoples from different races and cultural traditions came into regular contact for the first time. All were profoundly changed by the resulting interaction. By the time Cortés and his troops invaded Mexico in 1519, the age of European expansion and colonization was already well under way. Over the next 350 years, Europeans would spread their influence across the globe. The history of the tiny colonies in North America that became the first components of the United States must be seen in this broad context of European exploration and exploitation.

When the Europeans arrived, the Americas were already populated by skillful plant breeders who had developed vegetable crops more nutritious and productive than those grown in Europe, Asia, or Africa. They had also invented systems of writing and mathematics and had created calendars fully as accurate as those used on the other side of the Atlantic. In the Americas, as in Europe, states rose and fell as leaders succeeded or failed at the goal of expanding their political and economic power. The Europeans' arrival in their world immeasurably altered the Americans' struggles with each other.

After 1400, European nations tried to improve their positions relative to neighboring countries

not only by waging wars on their own continent but also by acquiring valuable colonies and trading posts elsewhere in the world. In response, nations in Asia, Africa, and the Americas attempted to use the alien intruders to their own advantage or, failing that, to adapt successfully to the Europeans' presence in their midst. All the participants in the resulting interaction of divergent cultures were indelibly affected by the process. The contest among Europeans for control of the Americas and Africa changed the course of history on four continents. Although in the end Europeans emerged politically dominant, they did not control many aspects of the interactions.

 American Societies

Human beings probably originated on the continent of Africa, where humanlike remains about 3 million years old have been found in what is now Ethiopia. Over many millennia, the growing human population slowly dispersed to the other continents. About 30,000 years ago, a land bridge that scholars have called Beringia linked the Asian and North American continents at the site of the Bering Strait. Some of the peoples participating in the vast worldwide migration crossed this now-submerged land bridge.

Those forerunners of the American population are known as Paleo-Indians. The earliest confirmed evidence of their presence in the Americas dates to approximately 28,000 years ago. The Paleo-Indians

Paleo-Indians

were nomadic hunters of game and gatherers of wild plants. Spreading throughout North and South America, they probably moved as extended families, or *bands*. By about 11,500 years ago, the Paleo-Indians were making fine stone projectile points, which they attached to wooden spears and used to kill and butcher the large mammals then living in the Americas. But as the Ice Age ended and the human population increased, all the large American mammals except the bison (buffalo) disappeared. Scholars cannot agree whether overhunting or the change in climate caused their

Important Events

30,000–10,000 B.C.E.	Paleo-Indians began migrating from Asia to North America across the Beringia land bridge	1494	Treaty of Tordesillas divides land claims between Spain and Portugal in Africa, India, and South America
7000 B.C.E.	Cultivation of food crops begins in America	1496	Last of the Canary Islands falls to Spanish attack
c. 1000 B.C.E.	Olmec civilization appears	1497	John Cabot reaches North American coast
c. 300–600 C.E.	Height of influence of Teotihuacán		
c. 600–900 C.E.	Classic Mayan civilization	1513	Ponce de León explores Florida
1000 C.E.	Anasazi settlements in modern states of Arizona and New Mexico flourish as trading centers	1518–30	Smallpox epidemic devastates Indian population of West Indies and Central and South America
1001	Norse establish settlement in "Vineland" (Newfoundland)	1519	Hernán Cortés invades Mexico
1050–1250	Height of influence of Cahokia; prevalence of Mississippian culture in midwestern and southeastern United States	1521	Tenochtitlán surrenders to Cortés; Aztec Empire falls to Spaniards
		1534–35	Jacques Cartier explores St. Lawrence River
14th century	Aztec rise to power	1539–42	Hernando de Soto explores southeastern United States
1450s–80s	Portuguese explore and colonize islands in the Mediterranean Atlantic and São Tomé in Gulf of Guinea	1540–42	Francisco Vásquez de Coronado explores southwestern United States
1477	Publication of Marco Polo's *Travels*, describing China	1587–90	Sir Walter Raleigh's Roanoke colony vanishes
1492	Christopher Columbus reaches Bahama Islands	1588	Thomas Harriot publishes *A Briefe and True Report of the New Found Land of Virginia*

demise. In either case, the Paleo-Indians, deprived of their primary source of meat, had to find new ways of survival.

Consequently, by approximately 9,000 years ago, the residents of what is now central Mexico began to cultivate food crops, especially maize (corn), squash, beans, and peppers. In the Andes Mountains of South America, people started to grow potatoes. As knowledge of agricultural techniques improved and spread through the

Importance of Agriculture

Americas, vegetables and maize proved a more reliable source of food than hunting and gathering. Except for those living in the harshest climates, most Americans started to adopt a more sedentary style of life so they could tend fields regularly. Some established permanent settlements; others moved several times a year among fixed sites. All the American cultures emphasized producing sufficient food to support themselves. Although they traded goods, no society ever became dependent on another group for items vital to its survival.

Wherever agriculture dominated the economy, complex civilizations flourished. Such societies were able to accumulate wealth, produce ornamental objects, and create elaborate rituals and ceremonies. In North America, the successful cultivation of nutritious crops seems to have led to the growth and development of all the major civilizations: first the large city-states of Mesoamerica (modern Mexico and Guatemala), then the urban clusters known collectively as the Mississippian culture and located in the present-day United States. Each society reached its height only after achieving success in agriculture. Each later declined and collapsed after reaching the limits of its food supply. Even the powerful Aztec Empire that the Spaniards encountered in 1519 is thought to have been approaching the point at which it could no longer sustain its population.

The Aztecs were the heirs of a series of Mesoamerican civilizations, the history of which stretched back to the Olmecs, who about 3,000 years ago lived near the Gulf of Mexico in large cities dominated by temple pyramids.

Mesoamerican Civilizations

More than 1,000 years later, the Mayan civilization developed on the Yucatán Peninsula. The Mayas built large urban centers containing tall pyramids and temples. They studied astronomy, created the first writing system in the Americas, and developed a richly symbolic religious life. By the fifth century C.E. (Common Era), or about 1,500 years ago, the kings of the Mayan city-states started to war with each other, attempting conquest on a grand scale. Eventually, the constant fighting combined with overpopulation and resulting environmental stress to cause the collapse of the most powerful cities ending the classic era of Mayan civilization by 900 C.E.

The largest Mesoamerican metropolis was contemporary with, and a major trading partner of, the Mayas. Teotihuacán, founded about 300 B.C.E. (Before the Common Era)—some 2,300 years ago—in the Valley of Mexico, was one of the largest cities in the world in the fifth century C.E., with a population of over 100,000. The rulers of Teotihuacán gained their position chiefly through commerce; their trading network extended hundreds of miles in all directions. Teotihuacán also served as a religious center; pilgrims must have come long distances to visit the impressive Pyramid of the Sun and Pyramid of the Moon and the great temple of Quetzalcoatl—the feathered serpent, the primary god of central Mexico.

Teotihuacán's influence was felt so widely in Mesoamerica before its decline in the eighth century C.E. that some scholars have argued that this Mexican city-state also influenced societies farther north, in what is now the United States.

Moundbuilders, Anasazi, and Mississippians

The Moundbuilders of the Ohio River region, who flourished about two thousand years ago, just as Teotihuacán rose to prominence, constructed earthen mounds. But the Ohioan mounds were used as burial sites, not as bases for temple pyramids. Also, the Moundbuilders' economy, which was based on hunting and gathering, bore little resemblance to that of Mesoamerica. Trade goods from as far away as the Great Lakes and the Gulf of Mexico have been found in the mounds, but direct evidence of contact with Teotihuacán is lacking.

The same is true for sites inhabited by the Anasazi peoples in the modern states of Arizona and New Mexico. Pueblo Bonito in Chaco Canyon, a city that by 1000 C.E. consisted of many large adobe buildings constructed along the sides of the canyon, served as a major regional trading center. The Anasazi cultivated maize and other Mesoamerican crops, but they did not construct temple pyramids, nor did their towns resemble those built by their contemporaries in what is now Mexico. Accordingly, scholars have concluded that their contact with Mesoamerica was slight.

More likely, Teotihuacán and later Mesoamerican empires like that of the Aztecs had an impact on the development of the Mississippian culture, which flourished around 1000 C.E. in what is now the midwestern and southeastern United States. This civilization, like those to the south, was based on the cultivation of maize, beans, and squash. Not until about 700 to 900 C.E. were these crops grown successfully in the present-day United

Pueblo Bonito in Chaco Canyon in what is now the state of New Mexico. More than six hundred buildings were present on the well-defended site. The circular structures were kivas, used for food storage and for religious rituals.   David Muench photography.

States; soon after their introduction, large cities with plazas and earthen pyramids first appeared in the region. With a population of at least 15,000, the largest of the cities was Cahokia, near modern St. Louis. Until about 1250 C.E., Cahokia was a religious and trading center. Its main pyramid, today called the Monk's Mound, was in 1492 the third largest structure in the Western Hemisphere. Spanish explorers encountered other Mississippian peoples in present-day South Carolina, Alabama, and Georgia in the mid-sixteenth century. The Natchez, a society characterized by temple mounds and autocratic priestly rulers, survived in the lower Mississippi River valley until the 1720s.

The Aztecs' histories tell of the long migration of their people (who called themselves Mexica) into the Valley of Mexico during the twelfth century. The uninhabited ruins of Teotihuacán, which by then had been deserted for at least two hundred years, awed

Aztecs

and mystified the migrants. The Aztecs' primary god, Huitzilopochtli, was a god of war represented by an eagle. Aztec chronicles record that Huitzilopochtli directed the Aztecs to establish their capital at the spot on an island where they saw an eagle eating a serpent (thus symbolizing Huitzilopochtli's triumph over the traditional deity, Quetzalcoatl). That island city became Tenochtitlán, the center of a rigidly stratified society composed of hereditary classes of warriors, merchants, priests, common folk, and slaves.

The Aztecs conquered their neighbors and forced them to pay tribute in luxury items, raw materials, and human beings who could be sacrificed to Huitzilopochtli. The war god's taste for blood was not easily quenched. In the Aztec year Ten Rabbit (1502) at the coronation of Motecuhzoma II (Montezuma, to the Spanish), five thousand people are thought to have been sacrificed by having their still-beating hearts torn from their bodies.

How do historians know that the ruins of Teotihuacán "awed and mystified" the Aztecs when they arrived in the Valley of Mexico at least two hundred years after that city had been abandoned by its inhabitants? One striking indication of the Aztecs' attitude toward the earlier civilization is this beautiful greenstone mask with polished obsidian eyes, which was created at Teotihuacán. Archaeologists found it not there but rather in the ruins of the Aztecs' Templo Mayor, constructed in Tenochtitlán (the site of modern Mexico City) about a thousand years after the mask was sculpted. The temple had two sides, one dedicated to the war god Huitzilopochtli, the other to the rain god Tlaloc.

The place where the two sides met was at the heart of the Aztecs' most sacred site. There they buried this mask, which they must have found at Teotihuacán, about 20 miles from Tenochtitlán. Although we cannot know for certain what the Aztecs intended to accomplish by this gesture, it seems reasonable to conclude that they hoped to draw on the mysterious powers that the mask (and the civilization it represented) symbolized for them. Had they not been awed by it, they never would have buried the mask where they did. Michel Zabe-Thiriat.

The Aztecs believed that they lived in the age of the Fifth Sun. Four times previously, they wrote, the earth and all the people who lived on it had been destroyed. They predicted that their own world would end in earthquakes and hunger. In the Aztec year Thirteen Flint, volcanoes erupted, sickness and hunger spread, wild beasts attacked the Aztecs' children, and an eclipse of the sun darkened the sky. Did some priest wonder whether the Fifth Sun was approaching its end? Eventually, the Aztecs learned that their year Thirteen Flint was called 1492 by the Europeans.

North America in 1492

Over the centuries, the Americans who lived north of Mexico had adapted their once-similar ways of life to very different geographical settings, thus creating the diverse cultures that the Europeans encountered when they first arrived (see map).

Bands that lived in environments not well suited to agriculture because of inadequate rainfall or poor soil, for example, followed a nomadic lifestyle. Within the area of the present-day United States, these groups included the Paiutes and Shoshones, who inhabited the Great Basin (now Nevada and Utah). Because of the difficulty of finding sufficient food for more than a few people, such hunter-gatherer bands were small. Where large game was more plentiful and food supplies therefore more certain, as in present-day Canada and the Great Plains, bands of hunters were somewhat larger.

In more favorable environments, larger groups combined agriculture with gathering, hunting, and fishing. Those who lived near the seacoasts, like the Chinooks of present-day Washington and Oregon, consumed fish and shellfish in addition to growing crops and gathering seeds and berries. Residents of the interior (for example, the Arikaras of the Missouri River valley) hunted large animals

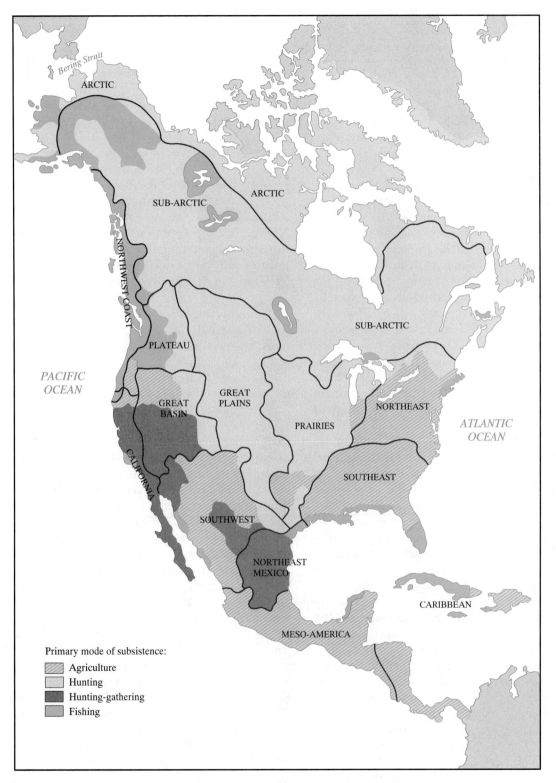

Primary mode of subsistence:
- Agriculture
- Hunting
- Hunting-gathering
- Fishing

Native Cultures of North America *The natives of the North American continent used the resources of the regions in which they lived. Coastal groups relied on fishing, residents of fertile areas engaged in agriculture, and other peoples employed hunting (often combined with gathering) as a primary mode of subsistence.*

while also cultivating maize, squash, and beans. The Algonkian-speaking peoples of what is now eastern Canada and the northeastern United States also combined hunting and agriculture.

Societies that relied primarily on hunting large animals assigned that task to men and allotted food processing, clothing production, and

Sexual Division of Labor in North America

child rearing to women. Before such nomadic bands acquired horses from the Spaniards, women—occasionally assisted by dogs—also carried the family's belongings whenever the band relocated. Such a sexual division of labor was universal among hunting peoples. Agricultural societies, by contrast, differed in their assignments of work to the sexes. In what is now the southwestern United States, the Pueblo peoples defined agricultural labor as men's work. In the East, Algonkian, Iroquoian, and Muskogean peoples allocated most agricultural chores to women, although men cleared the land. In all the farming societies, women gathered wild foods, prepared food for consumption or storage, and cared for children, while men were responsible for hunting.

The southwestern and eastern agricultural peoples had similar social organizations. They lived in villages, sometimes sizable ones with a thousand or more inhabitants. The Pueblos, descendants of the Anasazi, lived in large, multistory buildings constructed on terraces along the sides of cliffs or other easily defended sites. Northern Iroquois villages (in modern New York State) were composed of large, rectangular, bark-covered structures, or long houses. In the present-day southeastern United States, Muskogeans and southern Algonkians lived in large houses made of thatch. Most eastern villages were surrounded by wood palisades and ditches to aid in fending off attackers. The defensive design of such villages and of the western pueblos discloses the significance of warfare in pre-Columbian America.

In all these agricultural societies, each dwelling housed an extended family defined *matrilineally* (through a female line of descent). Mothers, their married daughters, and their daughters' husbands and children all lived together. Matrilineal descent did not imply *matriarchy*, or the wielding

of power by women, but rather served as a means of reckoning kinship. Extended families were linked into *clans*, also defined by matrilineal ties. The nomadic bands of the Great Plains, by contrast, were most often related *patrilineally* (through the male line).

American leaders governed largely through consensus, but political structures in the various groups differed considerably. Among Pueblo

Native American Politics and Religion

and Muskogean peoples, the village council was the highest political authority; no government structure connected the villages. The Iroquois, by contrast, had an elaborate political hierarchy incorporating villages into nations and nations into a widespread confederation. In all the North American cultures, political power was divided between civil and war leaders, who, unlike Europe's autocratic rulers, wielded authority only so long as they retained the confidence of the people.

The political position of women varied. Women were more likely to assume leadership roles among agricultural peoples than among nomadic hunters. Squaw sachems (female rulers) led Algonkian villages in what is now Massachusetts, but women were never chosen as heads of hunting bands of the Great Plains. Iroquois women did not become chiefs, yet clan matrons exercised political power. Probably the most powerful female chiefs were found in what is now the southeastern United States. In the mid-sixteenth century a female ruler known as the Lady of Cofitachequi governed a large group of villages in present-day western South Carolina.

Americans' religious beliefs varied, but all the peoples were *polytheistic*, worshiping a multitude of gods. One common thread was their integration with nature. Thus each group's most important beliefs and rituals were closely tied to its economy. The major deities of agricultural peoples were associated with cultivation, and their chief festivals centered on planting and harvest. The most important gods of hunters were associated with animals, and their major festivals were related to hunting. A band's economy and women's role in it helped to determine women's potential as religious leaders.

Women held the most prominent positions in those agricultural societies (like the Iroquois) in which they were also the chief food producers.

A wide variety of cultures, comprising more than 5 million people, thus inhabited mainland North America when Europeans arrived. The diverse inhabitants of North America spoke well over one thousand different languages. For obvious reasons, they did not consider themselves one people, nor did they—for the most part—think of uniting to repel the European invaders.

African Societies

Fifteenth-century Africa also housed a variety of cultures adapted to different geographical settings (see map). In the north, along the Mediterranean Sea, lived the Berbers, a Muslim people. (Muslims are adherents of Islam, founded by the prophet Mohammed in the seventh century C.E.) On the east coast of Africa, Muslim city-states engaged in extensive trade with India, the Moluccas (part of modern Indonesia), and China. Through the East African city-states passed a considerable share of the trade between the eastern Mediterranean and the Far East; the rest followed the long land route across Central Asia known as the Silk Road.

In the African interior, south of the Mediterranean coast, lie the great Sahara and Libyan deserts. Below the deserts, much of the continent is divided between tropical rain forests (along the coasts) and grassy plains (in the interior). People speaking a variety of languages and pursuing different economic strategies lived in a wide belt south of the deserts.

Most of the enslaved people carried to North America came from West Africa. The Europeans called this land of tropical forests and small-scale farming Guinea. The northern region of West Africa, or Upper Guinea, was heavily influenced by Islamic culture. As early as the eleventh century C.E., many of the region's inhabitants had become Muslims. Trade between Upper Guinea and the Muslim Mediterranean was sub-Saharan Africa's major connection to Europe and the Middle East.

West Africa (Guinea)

In return for salt, dates, silk, and cotton cloth, Africans exchanged ivory, gold, and slaves with northern merchants.

The people of the so-called Rice Coast of upper Guinea (present-day Gambia, Sénégal, and Guinea) fished and cultivated rice. The Grain Coast, the next region to the south, was thinly populated. Its people concentrated on farming and raising livestock. Both the Rice and the Grain Coasts—especially the former—supplied slaves destined for sale in the Americas, but even more enslaved people came from Lower Guinea.

In West Africa, land was not owned by individuals, but people could be; and the possession of slaves allowed the accumulation of wealth. Slaves—mostly debtors, wartime captives, criminals, or their descendants—were therefore essential components of the African economy. The first slave voyages diverted some of the thriving internal traffic in slaves to Europe or the Americas.

Many of the first slaves destined for sale across the Atlantic came from the Gold Coast, comprising thirty little kingdoms known as the Akan States. By the eighteenth century, though, it was the area farther east, the modern nations of Togo and Benin, that supplied most of the slaves sold in the English colonies. While seeking to enhance their positions by acquiring European trade goods, the Adja kings of the region, which became known as the Slave Coast, encouraged the founding of slave-trading posts and served as middlemen in the trade. Initially, those sent to the Americas came from the ranks of the already enslaved. By the early eighteenth century, however, after the demand for bondspeople in the American colonies had increased dramatically, African rulers appear to have warred on other groups primarily to obtain slaves for sale.

The societies of West Africa, like those of the Americas, assigned different tasks to men and women. In general, the sexes shared agricultural duties. Men also hunted, managed livestock, and did most of the fishing. Women were responsible for childcare, food preparation, and cloth manufacture. Everywhere in West Africa, women were the primary local traders.

Sexual Division of Labor in West Africa

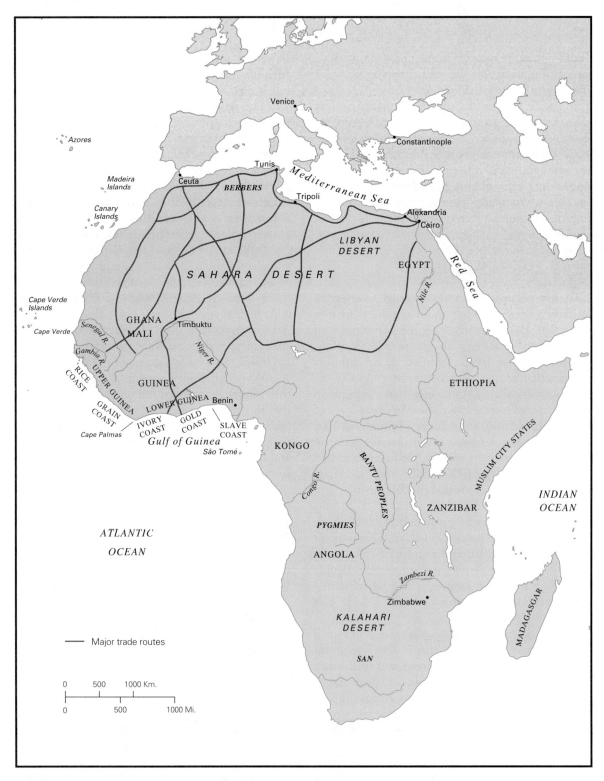

Africa and Its Peoples, c. 1400   *Even before Europeans began to explore Africa's coastlines, its northern regions were linked to the Mediterranean (and thus to Europe) by a network of trade routes.*

Despite different economies and the rivalries among states, the peoples of Lower Guinea had similar social systems. In Lower Guinea, each sex handled its own affairs: just as male political and religious leaders governed men, so females ruled women. In the Dahomean kingdom, for example, every male official had his female counterpart; in the Akan States, chiefs inherited their status through the female line, and each male chief had a female assistant who supervised other women.

Throughout Lower Guinea, religious beliefs likewise stressed complementary male and female roles. Both women and men served as heads of the cults and secret societies that directed the spiritual life of the villages. Young women were initiated into the Sandé cult, young men into Poro. Although West African women (unlike some of their Native American contemporaries) rarely held formal power over men, female religious leaders did govern other members of their sex within the Sandé cult.

West African Religion

The West Africans brought to the Americas, then, were agricultural peoples, skilled at tending livestock, hunting, fishing, and manufacturing cloth from plant fibers and animal skins. Both men and women were accustomed to working communally, alongside other members of their own sex. They were also accustomed to a relatively egalitarian relationship between the sexes, especially within the context of religion. In the New World, they entered societies that had little respect for their cultural traditions.

 European Societies

In the fifteenth century, Europeans, too, were agricultural peoples. The daily lives of Europe's rural people had changed little for several hundred years. Split into numerous small, warring countries, Europe was divided linguistically, politically, and economically, yet in social terms Europeans' lives were more similar than different. European societies were hierarchical: a few families wielded arbitrary power over the majority of the people. Europe's kingdoms accordingly resembled those of Africa or Mesoamerica but differed greatly from the more egalitarian, consensus-based societies then established in America north of Mexico.

Most Europeans, like most Africans and Native Americans, lived in small villages. European farmers, who were called *peasants*, owned or leased separate landholdings, but they worked the fields communally. Because fields had to lie fallow (unplanted) every second or third year to regain fertility, families could ensure food supplies only if all the villagers shared the work and the annual crop. Men did most of the fieldwork; women helped out chiefly at planting and harvest. Women's duties consisted primarily of childcare and household tasks, including preserving food, milking cows, and caring for poultry. If a woman's husband was an artisan or a storekeeper in a city, she might assist him in business. Since Europeans kept domesticated animals (pigs, goats, sheep, and cattle) for meat, hunting had little economic importance in their cultures.

Sexual Division of Labor in Europe

Unlike African and Native American societies, men dominated all areas of life in Europe. A few women—notably Queen Elizabeth I of England—achieved status or power, but the vast majority were excluded from positions of political authority. In the Roman Catholic Church and later in the new Protestant denominations, leadership roles were reserved for men. In short, European women generally held inferior social, economic, and political positions.

When the fifteenth century began, European nations were slowly beginning to recover from the devastating epidemic of plague known as the Black Death. Bubonic plague, spread by rats and fleas as well as by human contact, arrived in Europe from China, traveling with long-distance traders along the Silk Road. During the 1360s and 1370s, an estimated one-third of Europe's people died. That led to a precipitous economic decline and to severe social, political, and religious disruption because of the deaths of clergymen and other leading figures.

Black Death

As plague ravaged the population, England and France waged the Hundred Years War

(1337–1453), initiated because the English mon

Political, Economic, and Technological Change

archy claimed the French throne. The war interrupted overland trade routes through France that connected northern Europe to the Italian city-states and thence to Central Asia. Merchants in the eastern Mediterranean thus had to find new ways of reaching their northern markets. They solved that dilemma by forging a regular maritime link with the north to replace the overland route. The use of a triangular, or lateen, sail (rather than the then-standard square rigging) improved the maneuverability of ships. The perfection of navigational instruments like the astrolabe and the quadrant also allowed oceangoing sailors to estimate their position (latitude) by measuring the relationship of sun, moon, or stars to the horizon.

In the aftermath of the Hundred Years War, European monarchs relied on nationalistic feelings to consolidate their previously diffuse political power and to raise new revenues through increased taxation of an already hard-pressed peasantry. In England, Henry VII in 1485 founded the Tudor dynasty and began uniting a previously divided land. In France, the successors of Charles VII unified the kingdom. Most successful of all were Ferdinand of Aragón and Isabella of Castile. In 1469 they married and combined their kingdoms, thereby creating the foundation of a strongly Catholic Spain. In 1492, they defeated the Muslims, who had lived in Spain and Portugal for centuries, therefter expelling all Jews and Muslims from their domain.

The fifteenth century also brought technological change to Europe. Movable type and the printing press, invented in Germany in the 1450s, made information more accessible than ever before. Printing stimulated the Europeans' curiosity about fabled lands across the seas, lands they could now read about in books. The most important such work, Marco Polo's *Travels*, printed in 1477, noted that China was bordered on the east by an ocean. Polo's account led many Europeans to believe that they could trade directly with China in oceangoing vessels instead of relying on the Silk Road or the trade route through East Africa.

The European explorations of the fifteenth and sixteenth centuries were made possible by technological advances and by the growing strength of newly powerful national rulers. The primary motivation

Motives for Exploration

for exploratory voyages was each country's craving for easy access to desirable African and Asian goods—spices like pepper, cloves, cinnamon, and nutmeg (to season the bland European diet); silk; dyes; perfumes; jewels; and gold. A secondary motive was to spread Christianity around the world. The linking of materialist and spiritual goals might seem contradictory today, but fifteenth-century Europeans saw no conflict.

 ## Early European Explorations and the Columbus Voyages

Before European mariners could discover new lands, they had to discover the oceans. To reach Asia, seafarers needed not just the maneuverable vessels and navigational aids increasingly used in the fourteenth century, but also knowledge of the sea, its currents, and especially its winds. How did the winds run? Where would Atlantic breezes carry their ships?

Europeans learned the answers to these questions in the Mediterranean Atlantic, the expanse of the Atlantic that is south and west of Spain and is

Sailing in the Mediterranean Atlantic

bounded by the island groups of the Azores (on the west) and the Canaries (on the south), with the Madeiras in their midst (see map). Europeans reached all three sets of islands during the fourteenth century. The Canaries proved a popular destination for mariners from Iberia (the peninsula that includes Spain and Portugal). Sailing to the Canaries from Europe was easy, because strong winds known as the Northeast Trades blow southward along the Iberian and African coastlines. The problem was getting back. The very winds that had brought the Iberian sailor so quickly to the Canaries now blew directly at him.

Atlantic Winds and Islands *European mariners had to explore the oceans before they could find new lands. The first realm they investigated was the Atlantic winds and islands.*

What could be done? Some unknown seafarer figured out the answer: sailing "around the wind." If a mariner could not sail against the trade winds, he had to sail as close as possible to the direction from which the wind was coming without being forced to tack. In the Mediterranean Atlantic, that meant pointing his vessel northwest into the open ocean, away from land, until—weeks later—he reached the winds that would carry him home, the so-called Westerlies. Those winds blow northward along the coast of North America before heading east toward Europe.

This solution proved to be the key to successful exploration of both the Atlantic and the Pacific Oceans. Once a sailor understood the winds and their allied currents, he no longer feared leaving Europe without being able to return. Faced with a contrary wind, all he had to do was sail around it until he found a wind to carry him in the proper direction.

During the fifteenth century, armed with knowledge of the winds and currents of the Mediterranean Atlantic, Iberian seamen regularly visited its islands, all of which they could reach in two weeks or less. By the 1450s Portuguese colonists were employing slaves (probably Jews and Muslims brought from Iberia) to grow large quantities of sugar on Madeira, which developed into the world's first colonial plantation economy.

Islands of the Mediterranean Atlantic

After the Spaniards conquered the Guanche people in the Canaries in 1496, they devoted the land to sugar cultivation. Collectively, the Canaries and Madeira became known as the Wine Islands because much of their sugar production was employed to make sweet wines.

For Portugal's Prince Henry the Navigator, however, the islands were steppingstones to Africa. He knew that vast wealth awaited the first

Portuguese Trading Posts in Africa

European nation to tap the riches of Africa and Asia directly. Each year he dispatched ships southward along the African coast, attempting to discover an oceanic route to Asia. But not until after Prince Henry's death did Bartholomew Dias round the southern tip of Africa (1488) and Vasco da Gama finally reach India (1498).

Long before these voyages, West African states allowed the Portuguese to establish trading posts along their coasts. Charging the traders rent and levying duties on the goods they imported, the African kingdoms set the terms of exchange and benefited considerably from their new, easier access to European manufactures. The Portuguese gained too, for they no longer had to rely on the long trans-Saharan trade route. They earned immense profits by swiftly transporting African gold to Europe. Another valuable cargo was slaves. When they carried previously enslaved Africans back to the Iberian Peninsula, the Portuguese introduced black slavery into Europe.

An island off the African coast, previously uninhabited, proved critical to Portuguese success. São Tomé, located in the Gulf of Guinea (see map, page 12) was colonized in the 1480s. The soil of São Tomé proved ideal for raising sugar, and plantation agriculture there expanded rapidly. Large numbers of slaves were imported from the mainland to work in the cane fields, thus creating the first colonial economy based primarily on the bondage of black Africans.

By the 1490s, even before Christopher Columbus set sail to the west, Europeans had learned three key lessons of colonization from their

Lessons of Early Colonization

experiences in the islands of the Mediterranean Atlantic and the African coast. First, they knew that they could transplant their crops and livestock successfully to exotic locations. Second, they learned that the native peoples of unknown lands could be either conquered or exploited to European advantage. Third, they successfully developed a model of plantation slavery and a system for supplying nearly unlimited quantities of bound workers. The stage was set for a critical moment in world history, and the man of the hour was a sailor named Christopher Columbus.

Columbus was well schooled in the lessons of the Mediterranean Atlantic. Born in 1451 in the Italian city-state of Genoa, Columbus was

Christopher Columbus

by the 1490s an experienced sailor and mapmaker. Like many mariners of the day, he was drawn to Portugal and its islands, especially Madeira, where he commanded a merchant vessel. At least once he voyaged to the Portuguese colony on the Gold Coast. There he acquired an obsession with gold; and there he came to understand the economic potential of the slave trade.

Like all accomplished seafarers, Columbus knew the world was round. But he differed from other cartographers in his estimate of the earth's size: he thought that Japan lay only 3,000 miles from the southern European coast. Thus, he argued, it would be easier to reach Asia by sailing west than by making a difficult voyage around the southern tip of Africa. Experts scoffed at this crackpot notion, accurately predicting that the two continents lay 12,000 miles apart. When Columbus in 1484 asked the Portuguese authorities to back his plan to sail west to Asia, they rejected the proposal.

Ferdinand and Isabella of Spain, ruling a newly united kingdom and jealous of Portugal's successes in Africa, were more receptive to Columbus's ideas. Urged on by some Spanish noblemen and a group of Italian merchants residing in Castile, the monarchs agreed to finance the risky voyage. And so, on August 3, 1492, in command of three ships—the *Pinta*, the *Niña*, and the *Santa Maria*—Columbus set sail from the southern Spanish port of Palos.

On October 12, he and his men landed on an island in the Bahamas, which he named San Salvador. (Because Columbus's sketchy description of his landfall can be variously interpreted, two different places—Watling Island and Samana Cay—are today proposed as possible landing sites.) Later he went on to explore the islands now known as Cuba and Hispaniola, which their residents, the Taíno people, called Colba and Bohío. Because he thought he had reached the Indies, Columbus referred to the inhabitants of the region as *Indians.*

Three themes predominate in Columbus's log, the major source of information on this first encounter. First, he insistently asked the Taínos where he could find gold, pearls, and valuable spices.

Columbus's Observations Each time, his informants replied (largely via signs) that such products could be obtained on other islands, on the mainland, or in cities in the interior.

Second, Columbus wrote repeatedly of the strange and beautiful plants and animals. Yet Columbus's interest was not only aesthetic. "I believe that there are many plants and trees here that could be worth a lot in Spain for use as dyes, spices, and medicines," he observed, adding that he was carrying home to Europe "a sample of everything I can," so that experts could examine them.

Third, Columbus also described the islands' human residents, and he seized some to take back to Spain. The Taínos were, he said, very handsome, gentle, and friendly.

The Taíno People Columbus believed the Taínos to be likely converts to Catholicism. But he also thought that the islanders "ought to make good and skilled servants."

Thus the very first encounter between Europeans and America and its residents revealed a theme that would be of enormous significance for centuries to come: the Europeans' desire to extract profits from North and South America by exploiting their natural resources, including plants, animals, and peoples alike.

Christopher Columbus made three more voyages to the west, exploring most of the major Caribbean islands and sailing along the coasts of Central and South America.

Naming of America Until the day he died in 1506, Columbus believed that he had reached Asia. Even before his death, others knew better. Because the Florentine Amerigo Vespucci, who explored the South American coast in 1499, was the first to publish the idea that a new continent had been discovered, Martin Waldseemüller in 1507 labeled the land "America." By then, Spain, Portugal, and Pope Alexander VI had signed the Treaty of Tordesillas (1494), confirming Portugal's dominance in Africa and Brazil in exchange for Spanish preeminence in the rest of the New World.

The first mariners to explore the region of North America that was to become the United States and Canada followed a very different route.

Northern Voyages Some historians argue that European sailors may have found the rich Newfoundland fishing grounds in the 1480s but kept their discoveries a secret so that they alone could exploit the sea's bounty. Whether or not fishermen had crossed the entire width of the Atlantic, they had thoroughly explored its northern reaches. In the same way the Portuguese traveled the Mediterranean Atlantic, fifteenth-century English seafarers and others voyaged among the European continent, England, Ireland, and Iceland.

Five hundred years before Columbus, in the year 1001, the Norseman Leif Ericsson and other explorers from Greenland briefly established a settlement at a western site they named Vineland (now L'anse aux Meadows, Newfoundland) before attacks by local residents forced them to depart hurriedly. Therefore, the European generally credited with "discovering" North America is John Cabot. More precisely, it might be said that Cabot brought to Europe the first formal knowledge of the northern coastline of the continent.

In 1507 Martin Waldseemüller, a German mapmaker, was the first person to designate the newly discovered southern continent as "America." He named the continent after Amerigo Vespucci, the Italian explorer who realized that he had reached a "new world" rather than islands off the coast of Asia.   John Carter Brown Library at Brown University.

Cabot was a master mariner from the Italian city-state of Genoa who was in Spain when Columbus returned from his first trip to America. Calculating that England—which traded with Asia only through a long series of middlemen stretching from Belgium to Venice to the Muslim world—would be eager to sponsor exploratory voyages, Cabot sought and won the support of King Henry VII. He set sail from Bristol in late May 1497, reaching his destination on June 24. Scholars disagree about the location of his landfall (some say it was Cape Breton Island, others New-

John Cabot's Explorations

foundland), but all recognize the importance of his month-long exploration of the coast.

The voyages of Columbus, Cabot, and their successors finally brought the Eastern and Western Hemispheres together. The Portuguese explorer Pedro Alvares Cabral reached Brazil in 1500; John Cabot's son Sebastian followed his father to North America in 1507; France financed Giovanni da Verrazzano in 1524 and Jacques Cartier in 1534; and in 1609 and 1610 Henry Hudson explored the North American coast for the Dutch West India Company (see map). Although these men were primarily searching for the legendary, nonexistent "Northwest Passage" through the Americas, what

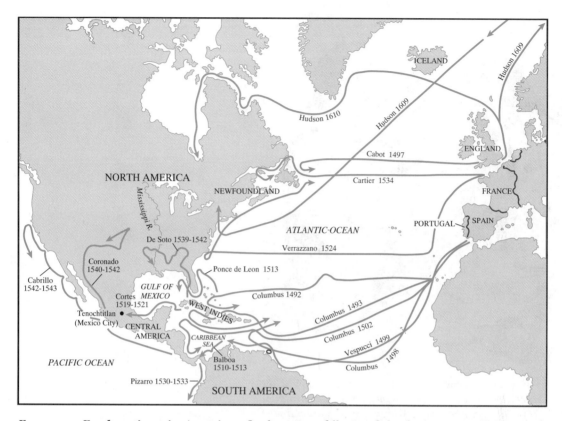

European Explorations in America *In the century following Columbus's voyages, European adventurers explored the coasts and parts of the interior of North and South America.*

they learned interested European nations in exploring North and South America.

Spanish Colonization and the Exchange of Diseases, Plants, and Animals

The Europeans' greatest impact on the Americas was unintended. Diseases carried from Europe and Africa by the alien invaders killed millions of Indians, who had no immunity to germs that had infested the other continents for centuries. The statistics are staggering. When Columbus landed on Hispaniola in 1492, more than 1 million

Smallpox and Other Diseases

people probably resided there. Fifty years later, only 500 were still alive. The greatest killer was smallpox. In 1518 a smallpox epidemic began in Hispaniola. When Cortés and his men carried the epidemic to the mainland, its impact on Tenochtitlán, the Aztec capital he besieged, was devastating. As an old Aztec man recalled, "Some quite covered [with pustules] on all parts—their faces, their heads, their breasts. . . . There was great havoc. Very many died of it." In the Aztec year Three House, on the day One Serpent (August 1521), Tenochtitlán surrendered. On the site of the Aztec capital, the Spaniards built what is now Mexico City.

Far to the north, where smaller American populations encountered only a few Europeans, disease also ravaged the countryside. A great epidemic, most likely chickenpox, swept through the villages along the coast north of Cape Cod from 1616 to 1618. The mortality rate may have been as high as

The Codex Florentino, *which has the fullest Aztec account of the Spaniards' conquest of Mexico, contains this image of an Indian afflicted with the smallpox that ravaged Tenochtitlán during the Spanish siege of the city.*   Biblioteca Medicea Laurenziana, Florence.

90 percent. Because of this dramatic depopulation of the area, just a few years later English colonists were able to establish settlements virtually unopposed.

The Americans, though, took a revenge of sorts. They gave the Europeans syphilis, a virulent venereal disease. The first recorded case of the new disease in Europe occurred in Barcelona, Spain, in 1493, shortly after Columbus's return from the Caribbean. Carried by soldiers, sailors, and prostitutes, it spread quickly through Europe and Asia, reaching as far as China by 1505.

The exchange of diseases was only part of a broader mutual transfer of plants and animals that resulted directly from European voyages. Many large mammals like cattle and horses were native to the connected continents of Europe, Asia, and Africa, but the Americas contained no domesticated beasts larger than dogs

Exchange of Plants and Animals

and llamas. However, the vegetable crops of the New World—particularly corn, beans, squash, cassava, and potatoes—were more nutritious and produced higher yields than those of the Old World, like wheat and rye. In time, the Native Americans learned to raise and consume European livestock, and the Europeans and Africans became accustomed to planting and eating American crops. As a result, the diets of all three peoples were vastly enriched.

The exchange of two other commodities significantly influenced European and American civilizations. In America, Europeans encountered tobacco, which was at first believed to have beneficial medicinal effects. Smoking and chewing the "Indian weed" became a fad in the Old World after it was planted in Turkey in the sixteenth century.

Also important was the impact of the horse on some Indian cultures. Horses brought to America by the Spaniards inevitably fell into the hands of Native Americans. Traded northward, descendants of these horses became essential to the life of the nomadic buffalo hunters of the Great Plains, who used horses for transportation and hunting. They also calculated their wealth in the number of horses owned and waged wars primarily from horseback. Women no longer had to carry the bands' belongings on their backs. Through the acquisition of horses, then, a mode of subsistence that had been based on hunting several different animals, in combination with gathering and agriculture, became one focused almost wholly on hunting buffalo.

The European and African invasion of the Americas therefore had a significant biological component, for the invaders carried plants and animals with them. Some creatures, such as livestock, they brought deliberately. Others, including rats, weeds, and diseases, arrived unexpectedly. And the same process occurred in reverse. When the Europeans returned home, they deliberately took back such crops as corn, potatoes, and tobacco, along with that unanticipated hitchhiker, syphilis.

Only in the areas that Spain explored and claimed did formal colonization begin immediately. On his second voyage in 1493, Columbus brought to Hispaniola seventeen ships loaded with twelve hundred men, seeds, plants, livestock, chickens, and dogs. The settlement named Isabela (in the modern Dominican Republic) and its successors became the staging area for the Spanish invasion of America.

Spanish Colonization

At first, Spanish explorers fanned out around the Caribbean basin. In 1513, Juan Ponce de León reached Florida and Vasco Núñez de Balboa crossed the Isthmus of Panama to the Pacific Ocean. Eight years later, the Spaniards' dreams of wealth were realized when Cortés conquered the Aztec Empire, seizing a fabulous treasure of gold and silver. Venturing northward, conquistadors like Juan Rodriguez Cabrillo (who sailed along the California coast), Hernando de Soto (who journeyed to the Mississippi River), and Francisco Vásquez de Coronado (who explored the southwestern portion of what is now the United States) found few of the products the Spanish coveted. By contrast, Francisco Pizarro, who explored the western coast of South America, acquired the richest silver mines in the world by conquering and enslaving the Incas in 1535. By 1550, Spain controlled the richest, most extensive empire Europe had known since ancient Rome.

Spain established a three-element model of colonization that other countries later attempted to imitate. First, the Crown maintained tight control over the colonies, establishing a hierarchical government that allowed little autonomy to New World jurisdictions. Second, most of the colonists sent from Spain were male. They married Indian—and later African—women, thereby creating the racially mixed population that characterizes much of Latin America to the present day. Third, the colonies' wealth was based on the exploitation of both the native population and slaves imported from Africa. The *encomienda* system, which granted tribute from Indian villages to individual conquistadors as a reward for their services to the Crown, in effect legalized Indian slavery. Yet in 1542 a new code of laws reformed the system, forbidding Spaniards from enslaving Indians. In response, the conquerors, familiar with slavery in Spain, began to import Africans in order to increase the labor force under their direct control.

Spanish wealth derived from American suffering. The Spaniards deliberately leveled American cities, building cathedrals and monasteries on sites once occupied by Aztec, Incan, and Mayan temples. Some conquistadors sought to erase all vestiges of the great Indian cultures by burning the written records they found. With traditional ways of life in disarray, devastated by disease, and compelled to labor for their conquerors, many demoralized residents of Mesoamerica accepted the Christian religion brought to New Spain by friars of the Franciscan and Dominican orders.

The friars devoted their energies to persuading Mesoamerican people to move into new towns and to build Roman Catholic churches. In such towns, they were exposed to European customs and to religious rituals newly elaborated in an attempt to assimilate Christianity and pagan beliefs.

Christianity in New Spain

For example, the friars deliberately juxtaposed the cult of the Virgin Mary with that of the corn goddess. These conversion efforts met with remarkable success as thousands of Indians residing in Spanish territory embraced Catholicism.

European Traders, Fishermen, and Early Settlements

Northern Europeans, denied access to the wealth of Mesoamerica by the Spanish and beaten to South America by the Portuguese (who founded a colony in Brazil in 1532), were initially more interested in exploiting North America's abundant natural resources than in the difficult task of establishing colonies on the mainland. Following John Cabot's report of a plentiful supply of fish along the North American coastline, European fishermen sailed into the area. By the 1570s, more than 350 ships were exploiting the bounty of the Newfoundland Banks each year, bringing back to their homelands a much desired and inexpensive source of nourishment.

European fishermen soon learned that they could supplement their profits by exchanging cloth and metal goods like pots and knives for the Native Americans' beaver pelts. At first the Europeans conducted their trading from ships sailing along the coast, but later they established permanent outposts on the mainland to centralize and control the traffic in furs.

Northern Traders

The Europeans' insatiable demand for furs, especially beaver, was matched by the Native Americans' desire for European goods that could make their lives easier and establish their superiority over their neighbors. Some bands began to concentrate so completely on trapping for the European market that they abandoned their traditional economies. The intensive trade in pelts also had serious ecological consequences. In some regions, beavers were completely wiped out. The disappearance of their dams led to soil erosion, especially when combined with the extensive clearing of forests by later European settlers.

Although their nation reaped handsome profits from fishing, English merchants and political leaders watched enviously as Spain's American possessions enriched Spain immeasurably. In the mid-sixteenth century, English "sea dogs" like John Hawkins and Sir Francis Drake began to raid Spanish treasure fleets sailing home from the West Indies. Their actions helped to foment a war that in 1588 culminated in the defeat of a huge invasion force—the Spanish Armada—off the English coast. As a part of the contest with Spain, English leaders started to think about planting colonies in the Western Hemisphere, thereby gaining better access to valuable trade goods and simultaneously preventing their enemy from dominating the Americas.

The first English colonial planners hoped to reproduce Spanish successes by dispatching to America men who would similarly exploit the native peoples for their own and their nation's benefit. In the 1580s, a group that included Sir Humphrey Gilbert and his younger half-brother Sir Walter Raleigh promoted a scheme to establish outposts that could trade with the Indians and provide bases for attacks on New Spain. Approving the idea, Queen Elizabeth I authorized Raleigh and Gilbert to colonize North America.

Sir Walter Raleigh's Roanoke Colony

Gilbert failed to plant a colony in Newfoundland, and Raleigh was only briefly more successful. In 1587 he sent 117 colonists to the territory he named Virginia, after Elizabeth, the "Virgin Queen." They established a settlement on Roanoke Island, in what is now North Carolina, but in 1590 a resupply ship could not find them. The colonists had vanished, leaving only the name of a nearby island carved on a tree.

Thus England's first attempt to plant a permanent settlement on the North American coast failed, as had earlier efforts by Portugal on Cape Breton Island (early 1520s) and France in northern Florida (mid-1560s). All three enterprises collapsed for the same reasons: inability to be self-sustaining with respect to food and hostile neighbors.

The explanation for such failings becomes clear in Thomas Harriot's *A Briefe and True Report of the*

New Found Land of Virginia, published in 1588 to publicize Raleigh's colony.

**Thomas
Harriot's
*Briefe and
True Report***

Harriot, a noted scientist who sailed on an exploratory voyage to Roanoke, was charged with describing the animals, plants, and people of the region for an English readership. His account revealed that although the explorers were almost wholly dependent on nearby villagers for food, they needlessly antagonized their neighbors by killing some of them for what Harriot himself admitted were unjustifiable reasons.

Harriot's *Briefe and True Report* depicted a bountiful land full of opportunities for a quick profit. The people already residing there would, he thought, "in a short time be brought to civilitie" through conversion to Christianity, admiration for European superiority, or conquest—if they did not die from disease, the ravages of which he witnessed. Harriot's prediction was far off the mark. European dominance of North America was to be difficult to achieve.

 Conclusion

The process of initial contact between Europeans and Americans that ended near the close of the sixteenth century had begun approximately 250 years earlier when Portuguese sailors first sailed into the Mediterranean Atlantic. That region of the Atlantic so close to European and African shores nurtured the mariners who, like Christopher Columbus, ventured into previously unknown waters. When Columbus first reached the Americas, he thought he had found Asia, his intended destination. Later explorers knew better but, except for the Spanish, regarded the Americas primarily as a barrier that prevented them from reaching their long-sought goal of an oceanic route to the riches of China and the Moluccas. Ordinary European fishermen were the first to realize that the northern coasts had valuable products to offer: fish and furs, both much in demand in their homelands.

The wealth of the north could not compare to that of Mesoamerica. The Aztec Empire dazzled the conquistadors with the magnificence of its buildings and its seemingly unlimited wealth. Nonetheless, the Spaniards destroyed the great temples and used their stones (and Indian laborers) to construct cathedrals honoring their God, rather than Huitzilopochtli. The conquerors employed first American and later enslaved African workers to till the fields, mine the precious metals, and herd the livestock that earned immense profits for themselves and their mother country.

The initial impact of Europeans on the Americas proved devastating. Flourishing civilizations were, if not entirely destroyed, markedly altered in just a few short decades. By the end of the sixteenth century, many fewer people resided on the continent than had lived there before Columbus's arrival, even taking into account the arrival of many Europeans and Africans. And the people who did live there—Indian, African, and European—resided in a world that was literally new—a world engaged in the unprecedented process of combining foods, religions, economies, styles of life, and political systems that had developed separately for millennia. Conflict and dissension permeated that process.

Suggestions for Further Reading

General

Alfred W. Crosby, *The Columbian Exchange: Biological and Cultural Consequences of 1492* (1972); Alfred W. Crosby, *Ecological Imperialism: The Biological Expansion of Europe, 800–1900* (1986); D. W. Meinig, *Atlantic America, 1492–1800* (1986); Herman Viola and Carolyn Margolis, eds., *Seeds of Change: Five Hundred Years Since Columbus* (1991).

Mesoamerican Civilizations

Brian Fagan, *Kingdoms of Gold, Kingdoms of Jade: The Americas Before Columbus* (1991); Eduardo Matos Moctezuma and David Carrasco, *Moctezuma's Mexico: Visions of the Aztec World* (1992); Linda Schele and David Friedel, *A Forest of Kings* [on the Mayas] (1990).

North American Indians

Brian Fagan, *Ancient North America: The Archaeology of a Continent* (1991); Francis Jennings, *The Founders of America: From the Earliest Migrations to the Present* (1993); Alvin Josephy, Jr., ed., *America in 1492* (1992); Lynda N. Shaffer, *Native Americans Before 1492: The Moundbuilding Centers of the Eastern*

Woodlands (1992); Colin F. Taylor, ed., *The Native Americans. The Indigenous People of North America* (1992).

Africa

Jacob Ade Ajayi and Michael Crowder, *History of West Africa* (1985); Paul Bohannon and Philip Curtin, *Africa and Africans* (1988); John Thornton, *Africa and Africans in the Making of the Atlantic World, 1400–1680* (1992).

Exploration and Discovery

Emerson Baker et al., eds., *American Beginnings: Exploration, Culture, and Cartography in the Land of Norumbega* (1994); Felipe Fernández-Armesto, *Before Columbus: Exploration and Colonization from the Mediterranean to the Atlantic, 1229–1492* (1987); Felipe Fernández-Armesto, *Columbus* (1991); Jerald T. Milanich and Susan Milbrath, eds., *First Encounters: Spanish Explorations in the Caribbean and the United States, 1492–1570* (1989); Samuel Eliot Morison, *The European Discovery of America: The Northern Voyages, A.D. 1500–1600* (1971); Samuel Eliot Morison, *The European Discovery of America: The Southern Voyages, A.D. 1492–1616* (1974); J. H. Parry, *The Age of Reconnaissance* (1963); J. H. Parry, *The Discovery of the Sea* (1974); William and Carla Phillips, *The Worlds of Christopher Columbus* (1992); David B. Quinn, *North America from Earliest Discovery to First Settlements* (1977); Paolo Emilio Taviani, *Columbus: The Great Adventure* (1991).

The Conquest of Mexico

Ross Hassig, *Mexico and the Spanish Conquest* (1994); Miguel León-Portilla, ed., *The Broken Spears: The Aztec Account of the Conquest of Mexico* (1992); Hugh Thomas, *Conquest: Montezuma, Cortés, and the Fall of Old Mexico* (1993).

Early European Settlements

Kenneth Andrews, *Trade, Plunder and Settlement: Maritime Enterprise and the Genesis of the British Empire, 1480–1630* (1984); Charles Gibson, *Spain in America* (1966); Karen O. Kupperman, *Roanoke, the Abandoned Colony* (1984); David J. Weber, *The Spanish Frontier in North America* (1992).

CHAPTER

2

Europeans Colonize North America
1600–1640

In August 1630, Fray Alonso de Benavides brought thrilling news to Madrid. Franciscan friars in the remote territory called New Mexico had successfully converted to Roman Catholicism at least eighty thousand heathens. In village after village, Indians had embraced baptism and built beautiful churches and schools with their own hands.

Fray Alonso supervised the New Mexico missions from 1626 to 1629. His account of the Franciscans' successes created a sensation in Europe. Alonso's *Memorial* not only was immediately published in Spanish but also was quickly translated into Latin, French, Dutch, and German. Fray Alonso undertook the arduous and successful journey to Spain to convince the king to increase his financial and administrative support of the Franciscan missions.

Yet de Benavides's report contained a troubling undercurrent. The colonial capital at Santa Fe, he noted, was inhabited by only about 250 Spaniards (along with another 750 Pueblos and mestizos). The soldiers were "few and poorly equipped," and the church had been "a miserable hut" before Fray Alonso ordered the construction of a new one. Furthermore, not all the local Indians had been receptive to the friars' message. The residents of Picurís pueblo, for one, had tried to murder the priests stationed there.

So, while praising the Spaniards' stunning successes in New Mexico, Fray Alonso revealed their equally striking weaknesses: more than a few

25

Native Americans staunchly combated their missionizing; both priests and soldiers lacked adequate financial resources; and the one tiny, impoverished European settlement was surrounded by tens of thousands of potentially troublesome Pueblos, Apaches, and Navajos. And there was an additional problem he did not describe: royal governors often clashed with the Franciscans in a struggle for primacy in the region.

By the time Fray Alonso arrived in Madrid in 1630, England, France, and the Netherlands had also founded permanent colonies in North America. No longer were the Spaniards the only Europeans on that vast continent. Just as Franciscans played a major role in the Spanish settlements, so too Jesuit priests were active in New France. The French and Dutch colonies, like the Spanish outposts, were peopled largely by European men. Like the conquistadors, French and Dutch merchants and planters hoped to make a quick profit and then perhaps return to their homelands.

In contrast to other Europeans, most of the English settlers came to America intending to stay. Especially in the area that came to be known as New England, they arrived in family groups. They recreated European society and family life to an extent not possible in the other colonies, where migrant men had to find their sexual partners within the Native American or African populations. Among the English colonies, those in the Chesapeake region and on the Caribbean islands most closely resembled colonies founded by other nations. Their economies, like those of Hispaniola or Brazil, soon came to be based on large-scale production for the international market by a labor force composed of bonded servants and slaves.

Wherever they settled, the English, like other Europeans, prospered only after they learned to adapt to the alien environment. The first permanent English colonies survived only because nearby Indians assisted the newcomers. The settlers had to learn to grow unfamiliar American crops. They also had to develop extensive trading relationships with Native Americans and with colonies established by other European countries. In need of laborers for their fields, they first used English indentured servants, then later began to import African slaves. Thus the early history of the region that became the United States and the English Caribbean can best be understood as a series of complex interactions among a variety of European, African, and American peoples and environments rather than as a simple story of English colonization.

New Spain, New France, New Netherland, and the Caribbean

Spaniards were the first Europeans to establish a permanent settlement within the boundaries of the modern United States, but they were not the first to attempt that feat.

Florida

Twice in the 1560s groups of French Protestants (Huguenots) sought to escape from persecution in their homeland by planting colonies on the south Atlantic coast. The first colony, in present-day South Carolina, collapsed when its starving inhabitants had to be rescued by a passing ship. The second, near modern Jacksonville, Florida, was destroyed in 1565 by a Spanish expedition under the command of Pedro Menéndez de Avilés. To ensure Spanish domination of the strategically important region (located near sea lanes used by Spanish treasure ships bound for Europe), Menéndez set up a small fortified outpost, which he named St. Augustine—now the oldest continuously inhabited European settlement in the United States. By the end of the sixteenth century a chain of Franciscan missions stretched across northern Florida.

More than thirty years passed after the founding of St. Augustine before conquistadors ventured anew into the present-day United States. In

New Mexico

1598, drawn northward by rumors of rich cities, Juan de Oñate, a Mexican-born adventurer, led a group of about five hundred soldiers and settlers to New Mexico. At first, the Pueblos greeted the interlopers cordially. When the Spaniards began to torture, murder, and rape the villagers to extort food and clothing,

● Important Events ●

1533	Henry VIII divorces Catherine of Aragon; English Reformation begins		**1620**	Plymouth colony founded, first permanent English settlement in New England
1558	Elizabeth I becomes queen		**1622**	Powhatan Confederacy attacks Virginia colony
1565	Founding of St. Augustine (Florida), oldest permanent European settlement in present-day United States		**1624**	Dutch settle on Manhattan Island (New Amsterdam)
1598	Juan de Oñate conquers Pueblos in New Mexico for Spain			English colonize St. Christopher, first island in Lesser Antilles to be settled by Europeans
1603	James I becomes king			James I proclaims Virginia a royal colony
1607	Jamestown founded, first permanent English settlement in North America		**1625**	Charles I becomes king
1608	Quebec founded by the French		**1629**	Massachusetts Bay colony founded
1609	Henry Hudson explores Hudson River for the Dutch		**1634**	Maryland founded
1610	Founding of Santa Fe, New Mexico		**1635**	Roger Williams expelled from Massachusetts Bay; founds Providence, Rhode Island
1611	First Virginia tobacco crop		**1636**	Connecticut founded
1614	Fort Orange (Albany) founded by the Dutch		**1637**	Pequot War in New England
1619	First Africans arrive in Virginia		**1638**	Anne Hutchinson expelled from Massachusetts Bay colony, goes to Rhode Island
	Virginia House of Burgesses established, first representative assembly in the English colonies		**c. 1640**	Sugar cultivation begins on Barbados
			1642	Montréal founded by the French

however, the residents of Acoma pueblo killed several soldiers. The invaders responded ferociously, killing more than eight hundred people. Not surprisingly, the other Pueblo villages surrendered.

Finding little wealth in New Mexico and learning that it was too far from the Pacific coast to assist in protecting Spanish sea lanes, many of the Spanish officials considered abandoning the isolated colony. Instead, in 1609, the authorities decided to maintain a small military outpost and a few Christian missions in the area, with the capital at Santa Fe (founded 1610). This was the constricted world in which Fray Alonso de Benavides arrived in 1626.

After Spain's destruction of France's Florida settlement in 1565, the French turned their attention northward. In 1608 Samuel de Champlain founded a trading post at an interior site that he named Quebec. He had chosen well: Quebec was the most easily defended spot in the entire St. Lawrence River valley, a stronghold that controlled access to the heartland of the continent. In 1642, the French established a second post, Montréal, at the falls of the St. Lawrence (and thus at the end of navigation by oceangoing vessels).

New France

Before the founding of Quebec and Montréal, French fishermen served as the major conduits through which North American beaver pelts reached France, but the two new posts quickly took over control of the lucrative trade in furs. In

The Founding of Permanent European Colonies in North America, 1565–1640

Colony	Founder(s)	Date	Basis of Economy
Florida	Pedro Menéndez de Avilés	1565	Farming
New Mexico	Juan de Oñate	1598	Livestock
Virginia	Virginia Company	1607	Tobacco
New France	France	1608	Fur trading
New Netherland	Dutch West India Company	1614	Fur trading
Plymouth	Pilgrims	1620	Farming, fishing
Maine	Sir Ferdinando Gorges	1622	Fishing
St. Kitts, Barbados, et al.	European migrants	1624	Sugar
Massachusetts Bay	Massachusetts Bay Company	1630	Farming, fishing, fur trading
Maryland	Cecilius Calvert	1634	Tobacco
Rhode Island	Roger Williams	1635	Farming
Connecticut	Thomas Hooker	1636	Farming, fur trading
New Haven	Massachusetts migrants	1638	Farming
New Hampshire	Massachusetts migrants	1638	Farming, fishing

an attempt to attract settlers, the colony's leaders offered land grants along the river to prospective settlers, including wealthy seigneurs (nobles) who were expected to import tenants to work their farms. Even so, more than twenty-five years after Quebec's founding, it had just sixty-four resident families, along with traders and soldiers.

One other important group was part of the population of New France: missionaries of the Society of Jesus (Jesuits), a Roman Catholic order dedicated to converting non-believers to Christianity. First arriving in the colony in 1625, the Jesuits, whom the Indians called Black Robes, initially tried to persuade indigenous peoples to live near French settlements and to adopt European agricultural methods as well as the Europeans' religion. When that effort failed, the Jesuits learned native languages and traveled to remote regions of the interior, where they lived in twos and threes among hundreds of potential converts.

Jesuit Missions in New France

Using a variety of strategies, Jesuits sought to undermine the authority of village shamans (the traditional religious leaders) and to gain the confidence of leaders who could influence others. Trained in rhetoric, they won admirers by their eloquence. Immune to smallpox (for all had survived the disease already), they explained epidemics among the Indians as God's punishment for sin. Perhaps most important, they amazed the villagers by communicating with each other over long distances and periods of time by employing marks on paper. The Native Americans' desire to learn how to harness the extraordinary power of literacy was one of the most critical factors in making them receptive to the missionaries' message.

Although the process took many years, the Jesuits slowly gained thousands of converts. The converts replaced their own culture's traditional equal treatment of men and women with notions more congenial to the Europeans' insistence on male dominance and female subordination. Further, they altered their practice of allowing premarital sexual relationships and easy divorce because Catholic doctrine prohibited both customs.

Jesuit missionaries faced little competition from other Europeans for Native Americans' souls, but French fur traders had to confront a direct challenge. In 1614, only five years after Henry Hudson sailed up the river that now bears his name, his sponsor, the Dutch West India Company, established an outpost (Fort Orange) on that river at the site of present-day Albany, New York. Like the French, the Dutch sought beaver pelts, and their presence so close to Quebec posed a threat to French domination of the region. The Netherlands, at the time the world's dominant commercial power, was interested primarily in trade rather than colonization, and New Netherland, like New France, therefore remained small. The colony's southern anchor was New Amsterdam, a town founded in 1624 on Manhattan Island.

As the Dutch West India Company's colony in North America, New Netherland was a relatively unimportant part of a vast commercial empire.

**New
Netherland**

Autocratic directors-general ruled the colony for the company; with no elected assembly, settlers felt little loyalty to their nominal leaders. Migration was sparse. Even a company policy of 1629 that offered a large land grant, or patroonship, to anyone who would bring fifty settlers to the province failed to attract takers. As late as the mid-1660s, New Netherland had only about five thousand inhabitants.

Despite their geographical proximity and their trading rivalry, New France and New Netherland did not come into armed conflict with each other. Yet their Indian allies did. In the 1640s, the Iroquois, who traded chiefly with the Dutch and lived in modern upstate New York, went to war against their northern neighbors the Hurons, who traded primarily with the French and lived in present-day Ontario (see map, page 30). Using guns supplied by the Dutch, the Iroquois largely exterminated the Hurons. The Iroquois thus established themselves as a major force in the region, one that Europeans could ignore only at their peril.

It was in the Caribbean, though, that France, the Netherlands, and England clashed most openly in the first half of the seventeenth century.

The Caribbean

The Spanish concentrated their colonization efforts on the Greater Antilles—Cuba, Hispaniola, Jamaica, and Puerto Rico. They left many smaller islands alone, partly because the mainland offered greater wealth for less effort. But other European powers coveted the tiny islands as bases from which to attack Spanish vessels loaded with American gold and silver. They also viewed them as sources of valuable tropical products, such as spices, dyes, and fruits.

England was the first northern European nation to establish a permanent foothold in the smaller West Indian islands (the Lesser Antilles). English people settled on St. Christopher (St. Kitts) in 1624, then later on other islands such as Barbados (1627). France was able to colonize Guadeloupe and Martinique, and the Dutch gained control of St. Eustatius (strategically located near St. Kitts). As a result of conflict among the European powers, most of the islands were attacked at least once during the course of the century, and some changed hands.

Why did other Europeans devote so much energy to gaining control of these tiny bits of land neglected by Spain? The primary answer to that question was sugar, one of the

**Satisfying
Europe's
Sweet Tooth**

most important components of the post-Columbian exchange of plants and animals. First domesticated in the East Indies, it was being grown in North Africa and southern Spain by 1000 C.E. Canary Island sugar canes were among the plants Columbus carried to Hispaniola on his 1493 voyage.

At the end of the sixteenth century, most American sugar was being produced in Brazil, part of which the Dutch controlled between 1630 and 1654. There the Dutch learned how to grow and process sugar cane, skills they then taught to the English on Barbados. In return, the Dutch expected to sell African slaves to West Indian planters and to carry to Europe barrels of molasses and rum, which was distilled from sugar. The

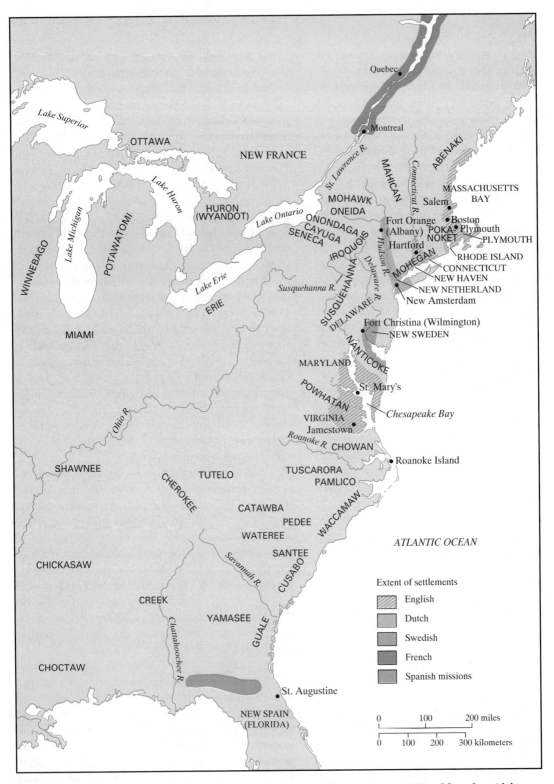

European Settlements and Indians in Eastern North America, 1650 *Note the widely scattered European settlements along the ocean and riverbanks, while America's native inhabitants controlled the vast interior.*

results must have exceeded their wildest dreams. The Barbados sugar boom in the 1640s was both explosive and lucrative. Planters, slave traders, and Dutch shipping interests alike earned immense profits. Indeed, for a hundred years sugar was the most important American commodity. In the eighteenth century, sugar grown by slaves in British Jamaica and French St. Domingue dominated the world market. Yet, in the long run, the future economic importance of the Europeans' American colonies lay on the mainland rather than in the Caribbean.

England Colonizes Mainland North America

The failure of Raleigh's attempt to colonize Virginia ended English efforts to settle in North America for nearly two decades. When the English decided in 1606 to try once more, they again planned colonies that imitated the Spanish model. Success came only when they abandoned that model and sent large numbers of men and women to set up agriculturally based colonies on the mainland. Two major developments prompted approximately 200,000 ordinary English men and women to move to North America in the seventeenth century and led their government to encourage that migration.

The first major development that led English folk to move to North America was the onset of dramatic social and economic change caused by

Social Change in England

the doubling of the English population in the 150-year period after 1530, largely as a result of the introduction of nutritious American crops into Europe. All those additional people needed food, clothing, and other goods. The competition for goods led to high inflation, coupled with a fall in real wages as the number of workers increased. Those with sizable landholdings benefited from the increased demand for food and clothing fibers, but landless laborers and those with very small amounts of land fell into unremitting poverty.

Well-to-do English people reacted with alarm to what they saw as the disappearance of tradi-

tional ways of life. Steady streams of the landless and homeless filled the streets and highways. Obsessed with the problem of maintaining order, officials came to believe that England was overcrowded. They concluded that colonies established in North America could siphon off England's "surplus population," thus easing social strains at home. For similar reasons, many English people decided that they could improve their circumstances by migrating from a small, land-scarce, apparently overpopulated island to a large, land-rich continent. Such economic considerations were rendered even more significant in light of the second development, a major change in English religious practice.

The sixteenth century witnessed a religious transformation that eventually led large numbers of English dissenters to leave their homeland. In

English Reformation

1533, Henry VIII, wanting a male heir and infatuated with Anne Boleyn, sought to annul his marriage to his Spanish-born queen, Catherine of Aragon. When the pope refused to approve the annulment, Henry left the Roman Catholic Church. He founded the Church of England and—with Parliament's concurrence—proclaimed himself its head. The English people welcomed the schism. At first the reformed Church of England differed little from Catholicism in its practices, but under Henry's daughter Elizabeth I, new currents of religious belief that had originated on the European continent early in the sixteenth century dramatically affected the English church.

The leaders of the continental Protestant Reformation were Martin Luther, a German monk, and John Calvin, a French cleric and lawyer. Combating the Catholic doctrine that priests must serve as intermediaries between laypeople and God, Luther and Calvin insisted that each person could interpret the Bible for himself or herself. Both Luther and Calvin rejected Catholic rituals and denied the need for an elaborate church hierarchy. They also asserted that salvation came through faith alone, rather than—as Catholic teaching had it—through a combination of faith and good works. Calvin, though, went further than Luther in stressing God's absolute omnipotence and emphasizing the need for people to submit totally to God's will.

Elizabeth I tolerated religious diversity among her subjects as long as they generally acknowledged her authority as head of the Church of England. Accordingly, during her long reign (1558–1603) Calvin's ideas gained influence within the English church. By the late sixteenth century, many English Calvinists—those who came to be called Puritans because they wanted to purify the Church of England—believed that the English Reformation had not gone far enough. Henry had simplified the church hierarchy; they wanted to abolish it altogether. Henry had subordinated the church to the interests of the state; they wanted a church free from political interference. And, unlike the inclusive Church of England, the Puritans believed that only the "saved" should be church members.

Puritans

Elizabeth I's Stuart successors, her cousin James I (1603–1625) and his son Charles I (1625–1649), were less tolerant of Puritans than she had been. As Scots, they also had little respect for the traditions of representative government that had developed in England. As adherents to the theory of the *divine right of kings*, the Stuarts insisted that a monarch's power came directly from God and that his subjects had a duty to obey him. A king's authority was absolute, they argued.

The First Stuart Monarchs

Both James I and Charles I believed that their authority included the power to enforce religious conformity among their subjects. Because Puritans were challenging many of the most important precepts of the English church, the monarchs authorized the removal of Puritan clergymen from their pulpits. In the 1620s and 1630s a number of English Puritans accordingly decided to move to America, where they hoped to put their religious beliefs into practice unmolested by the Stuarts or the church hierarchy.

However, the initial impetus for the establishment of what was to become England's first permanent colony in the Western Hemisphere came not from the Puritans but from a group of merchants and wealthy gentry. In 1606, envisioning the possibility of earning great profits by finding precious metals and opening new trade routes, the men established a joint-stock company, the Virginia Company, to plant colonies in America.

Joint-stock companies had been developed in England during the sixteenth century as a mechanism for pooling the resources of many small investors, primarily to finance trading voyages. For that purpose they worked well: no one risked too much money, and investors usually received quick returns. Joint-stock companies turned out to be a poor way to finance colonies, because the early settlements required enormous amounts of capital and, with rare exceptions, failed to return much immediate profit. Colonies founded by joint-stock companies consequently suffered from a chronic lack of capital.

Joint-Stock Companies

The Virginia Company was no exception to this rule. Chartered by James I in 1606, the company tried but failed to start a colony in Maine and barely succeeded in planting one in Virginia. In May 1607, the company dispatched 104 men and boys who established a settlement called Jamestown on a swampy peninsula in a river they also named for their monarch.

Founding of Virginia

The colonists were ill equipped for survival in the unfamiliar environment, and the settlement was afflicted by dissension and disease. Many were gentlemen unaccustomed to working with their hands; others were artisans with irrelevant skills like glassmaking. Having come to Virginia expecting to make easy fortunes, most could not adjust to the conditions they encountered. They resisted living "like savages," retaining English dress and casual work habits despite their desperate circumstances. Such attitudes, combined with the effects of chronic malnutrition and epidemic disease, took a terrible toll. Only when Captain John Smith, one of the colony's founders, imposed military discipline on the colonists in 1608 was Jamestown saved from collapse. But after Smith's departure the settlement experienced a severe "starving time" (the winter of 1609–1610). Although more settlers (including a few women and children) arrived in 1608 and 1609 and living conditions slowly improved, as late as 1624 only 1,300 of approximately 8,000 English migrants to Virginia remained alive.

That Jamestown survived was a tribute not to the English but rather to the Native Americans within whose territories they settled, a group of six Algonkian tribes known as the Powhatan Confederacy (see map, page 30). A shrewd and powerful leader, Powhatan was aggressively consolidating his authority over some twenty-five other small tribes when the Europeans arrived. Fortunately for the colonists, Powhatan at first viewed them as potential allies. He found the English colony a reliable source of items such as steel knives and guns, which gave him a technological advantage over his Indian neighbors. In return, Powhatan's tribes traded their excess corn and other foodstuffs to the starving settlers. The initially cordial relationship soon deteriorated, however. The English colonists kidnapped Powhatan's daughter, Pocahontas, holding her as a hostage in retaliation for Powhatan's seizure of several settlers. In captivity, she agreed in 1614 to marry a colonist, John Rolfe.

The relationship between the Jamestown colony and the coastal tribes was uneasy. English and Algonkian peoples had much in common: deep religious beliefs, a lifestyle oriented around agriculture, clear political and social hierarchies, and sharply defined gender roles. Yet the English and the Powhatans themselves usually focused on their cultural differences. English men thought that Algonkian men were lazy because they did not work in the fields, and that the women were oppressed because they did heavy fieldwork. Algonkian men, however, thought English men effeminate because they did "women's work" of cultivation.

Other differences between the two cultures caused serious misunderstandings. Although both societies were hierarchical, the nature of the hier-

Powhatan Confederacy

Theodor de Bry's America *depicted crucial events in the continent's history. This illustration is de Bry's version of the kidnapping of Pocahontas, Powhatan's daughter, in 1612. In the foreground, two other Native Americans are enticing Pocahontas to join the English; at right center, she is being led onto a ship; in the background, English raiders are burning the villages of Powhatan's people.* Library of Congress.

Algonkian and English Cultural Differences

archies differed considerably. Among the East Coast Algonkian tribes, people were not born to positions of leadership, nor were political power and social status necessarily inherited through the male line. Members of the English gentry inherited their position from their fathers, and English political and military leaders tended to rule autocratically. By contrast, the authority of Algonkian leaders rested on consensus. Accustomed to the European concept of powerful kings, the English sought such figures within the tribes. Often (for example, when negotiating treaties) they willfully overestimated the ability of chiefs to make independent decisions for their people.

Furthermore, the Algonkians and the English had very different notions of property ownership. In most Algonkian villages, land was held communally by the entire group. Rights to use the land might be transferred, but the land could not be bought or sold. English people, in contrast, were accustomed to individual farms and to buying and selling land. In addition, the English refused to accept the validity of Indians' claims to traditional hunting territories, insisting that only land intensively cultivated could be regarded as owned or occupied.

Above all, the English settlers believed unwaveringly in the superiority of their civilization. They expected Native Americans to adopt English customs and to convert to Christianity. They showed little respect for traditional Indian ways of life, especially when they believed their own interests were at stake. That attitude was clearly revealed in the Virginia colony's treatment of the Powhatan Confederacy in subsequent years.

The spread of tobacco cultivation upset the balance of power in early Virginia. In tobacco the settlers and the Virginia Company found the sal-

Tobacco: The Basis of Virginia's Success

able commodity for which they had been searching. John Rolfe planted the first crop in 1611. By 1630, Virginians were exporting 1.5 million pounds of cured leaves. The great tobacco boom had begun, fueled by high prices and substantial profits for planters. Although the price fluctuated wildly from year to year, tobacco became the foundation of Virginia's prosperity. The colony developed from a small outpost peopled exclusively by males into an agricultural settlement inhabited by both men and women.

Successful tobacco cultivation required abundant land, since the crop quickly drained soil of nutrients. Planters soon learned that a field could produce only about three satisfactory crops before it had to lie fallow for several years to regain its fertility. Soon eager planters applied to the Virginia Company for large land grants on both sides of the James River and its tributary streams.

Opechancanough, Powhatan's brother and successor, watched the English colonists steadily encroaching on the confederacy's lands and at-

Indian Uprising

tempting to convert its members to Christianity. Recognizing the danger, the war leader launched coordinated attacks all along the river on March

22, 1622. By the end of the day, 347 colonists (about one-quarter of the total) lay dead, and only a timely warning from two Christian converts saved Jamestown itself from destruction. The colony survived this war and the one waged by Openchancanough in 1644. His defeat in the latter ended the Powhatan Confederacy's efforts to resist the spread of English settlement.

Life in the Chesapeake: Virginia and Maryland

In 1624 James I made Virginia a *royal colony*—a colony ruled by the king through appointed officials. The king also allowed the Virginia Company's "headright" system to continue. Under this system

Headrights

(adopted in 1617), every new arrival paying his or her own way was promised a land grant of 50 acres; those who financed the passage of others received similar headrights for each person. To ordinary English farmers, many of whom owned little or no land, the headright system offered a powerful incentive to migrate to Virginia. To wealthy gentry, it promised even more: the prospect of vast agricultural enterprises worked by large numbers of laborers.

In 1619, the company had introduced a second policy that James was more reluctant to retain: it had authorized the landowning men of the

The House of Burgesses

major Virginia settlements to elect representatives to an assembly called the House of Burgesses. James at first abolished the assembly, but Virginians protested so vigorously that by 1629 the House of Burgesses was functioning once again. Only two decades after the first permanent English settlement was planted in North America, the colonists successfully insisted on governing themselves at the local level. Thus the political structure of England's American possessions came to differ from that of New Spain, New France, and New Netherland, all of which were ruled autocratically.

By the 1630s, tobacco was firmly established in Virginia as the staple crop and chief source of revenue. It quickly became just as important in the second English colony planted on Chesapeake Bay: Maryland, settled in 1634 and given by Charles I to the Calvert family as a personal possession, a *proprietorship*. The Calverts intended the colony to serve as a haven for their fellow Roman Catholics, who were being persecuted in England. Cecilius Calvert, second Lord Baltimore, became the first colonizer to offer freedom of religion to all Christian settlers; he understood that protecting the Protestant majority was the only way to ensure Catholics' rights.

Founding of Maryland

In everything but religion the two Chesapeake colonies resembled each other. In both colonies, planters spread out along the region's deep, wide rivers, which served as the means of transporting imported and exported goods. With little need for commercial centers and with a dispersed population, few towns existed in the Chesapeake.

Because the tasks associated with tobacco culture were labor intensive, planters faced the problem of finding increasing numbers of workers. Nearby Indians, their numbers reduced by war and disease, could not supply them. Nor could Dutch traders; although they did carry a few Africans to the Chesapeake beginning in 1619, they could more easily and profitably sell slaves in the West Indies. In the first half of the seventeenth century, therefore, only a few Africans, some of them free, arrived in the Chesapeake. By 1650 only about three hundred blacks lived in Virginia.

Need for Laborers

Chesapeake tobacco planters thus looked primarily to England to supply their labor needs. Because of the headright system (which Maryland also adopted in 1640), a prospective tobacco planter anywhere in the Chesapeake could simultaneously obtain both land and labor by importing workers from England. Through good management, a planter could use his profits to pay for the passage of more workers and thereby gain title to more land.

Because prevailing gender roles dictated that field laborers should be men, most migrants were male. They came as *indentured servants*—in return for their passage, they contracted to work for planters for periods ranging from four to seven years. Indentured servants accounted for 75 to 85 percent of the approximately 130,000 English migrants to Virginia and Maryland during the seventeenth century. Roughly three-quarters of the servant migrants were males between the ages of fifteen and twenty-four; only one in five or six was female. Most of the men had been farmers and laborers and were what their contemporaries called the "common sort."

English Migrants

For such people the Chesapeake appeared to offer good prospects. After fulfilling the terms of their indentures, servants were promised "freedom dues" consisting of clothes, tools, livestock, casks of corn and tobacco, and sometimes even land. Yet the migrants' lives were difficult. Servants typically worked six days a week, ten to fourteen hours a day. Their masters could discipline or sell them, and they faced severe penalties for running away. Even so, the laws did offer them some protection. For example, their masters were supposed to supply them with sufficient food, clothing, and shelter. Servants who were especially cruelly treated turned to the courts for assistance.

Conditions of Servitude

Servants and planters alike had to contend with epidemic disease. Migrants first had to survive the process the colonists called "seasoning"—a bout with disease (probably malaria) that usually occurred during their first Chesapeake summer. They then had to endure recurrences of malaria, along with dysentery, typhoid fever, and other diseases. As a result, approximately 40 percent of male servants did not survive long enough to become freedmen.

For those who survived the term of their indentures, however, the opportunities for advancement were real. Until the last decades of the seventeenth century, former servants were usually able to become independent planters ("freeholders") and to live a modest but comfortable existence. Some even assumed positions of political prominence. But after 1670, tobacco prices fell, good land grew scarce and expensive, and Maryland

How do historians know what seventeenth-century settlements looked like? Recent excavations at St. Mary's City, Maryland, founded as the capital and sole town of Calvert's colony in 1634, demonstrate the importance of cooperation between historians and archaeologists. St. Mary's City is one of only two major seventeenth-century English settlements in America not now buried under modern cities. (The other, Jamestown, was located in 1996, although for many years historians believed that it had been eroded into the James River.) The site of St. Mary's City was abandoned in 1696 when the colonial capital was moved to Annapolis; later the area was incorporated into a tobacco plantation. Working from written documents like deeds and wills, historians created hypotheses about the layout of the town. But when archaeologists began digging into the soil, they discovered what the documents had not revealed: the town plan was based on triangles intersecting at the town's central square. A modern artist's reconstruction of the town as it might have looked in 1685 shows portions of those triangles. At far right, top, is the Jesuit chapel, the first Catholic church in Anglo-America. At center is the square, with the large Country's House, the building once used as the capitol, on the left. (The new state house constructed in 1676 is off this map to the far left, at the point of a triangle at the same distance from the square as the chapel.) The artist needed both archival and archaeological data to produce this drawing. Historic St. Mary's City Commission.

dropped its legal requirement that servants receive land as part of their freedom dues. By 1700 the Chesapeake was no longer the land of opportunity.

Life in the early Chesapeake was hard for everyone. Farmers (and sometimes their wives) toiled in the fields alongside servants. Most people rose and went to bed with the sun, consumed a diet based on pork and corn, and lived in ramshackle dwellings with just one or two rooms. As a rule, planters devoted their income to improving their farms, buying livestock, and purchasing more laborers rather than to improving their standard of living.

Standard of Living

The predominance of males, the incidence of servitude, and the high mortality rates combined to produce unusual patterns of family life. Female servants normally were not allowed to marry during their terms of indenture because masters did not want pregnancies to deprive them of workers. Many male ex-servants could not marry at all because there were relatively few women. In con-

Chesapeake Families

trast, nearly every adult free woman in the Chesapeake married, and widows usually remarried within a few months of a husband's death. Yet because their marriages were delayed by servitude or broken by death, Chesapeake women bore only one to three children, in contrast to English women, who normally had at least five.

This low rate of natural increase meant that migrants would make up a majority of the Chesapeake population throughout the seventeenth century, with important implications for politics in Maryland and Virginia. Migrants composed the vast majority of the membership of Virginia's House of Burgesses and Maryland's House of Delegates (established in 1635). So, too, in each colony they dominated the governor's council, which was simultaneously the colony's highest court, part of the legislature, and executive adviser to the governor.

Chesapeake Politics

English-born colonists naturally tended to look to England for solutions to their problems, and they often relied on English allies to advance their cause. Because of the low birth rates and high mortality, no cohesive native-born ruling elite emerged until the early eighteenth century. Before that, the Chesapeake colonies' immigrant leaders engaged in bitter and prolonged struggles for power, which thwarted the ability of the Virginia and Maryland governments to function effectively. Thus the existence of representative assemblies failed to create political stability. Indeed, instability may have been the price of the region's demographic patterns.

The Founding of New England

The economic motives that prompted English people to move to the Chesapeake colonies also drew men and women to New England. But two factors combined to make New England different from the Chesapeake. First, the northern climate and landscape were more conducive to diversified small farms than to large production units yielding staple crops. Second, Puritans organized the New England colonies, and their church became the region's most important institution. Neither the Church of England nor Roman Catholicism held that significance in the Chesapeake.

Religion was a constant presence in the lives of pious Puritans. They believed that God predestined souls to heaven or hell before birth and that Christians could do nothing to change their ultimate fate. One of their primary duties as Christians, though, was to assess the state of their own souls. They devoted themselves to self-examination and Bible study, and families prayed together each day under the guidance of the husband and father. Yet even the most pious could never be absolutely certain they were numbered among the saved (or elect). Consequently, devout Puritans were filled with anxiety about their spiritual state.

Puritan Beliefs

Some Puritans (called Congregationalists) wanted to reform the Church of England rather than abandon it. Another group, known as Separatists, believed the Church of England to be so corrupt that it could not be salvaged. The only way to purify it, they believed, was to start anew, establishing their own religious bodies, with membership restricted to the saved, as nearly as they could be identified.

In 1620, some Separatists, many of whom had earlier migrated to Holland in quest of the right to practice their religion freely, received permission to settle in part of the territory controlled by the Virginia Company. Later that year, more than one hundred people, only thirty of them Separatists, set sail from England on the old and crowded *Mayflower.* Two months later, in November, they landed in America, but farther north than they had intended. Still, given the lateness of the season, they decided to stay where they were. They established their colony on a fine harbor, and they named their settlement Plymouth.

Founding of Plymouth

Even before they landed, the Pilgrims had to surmount their first challenge—from the "strangers," or non-Puritans, who had sailed with them to America. Because they landed outside the jurisdiction of the Virginia Company, some of the strangers questioned the authority of the colony's leaders. In response, the Mayflower Compact, signed in November 1620 while everyone was still on board the *Mayflower*, established a "Civil Body Politic" and a rudimentary legal authority for the colony. The settlers elected a governor and at first made all decisions for the colony at town meetings. Later, after more towns had been founded, Plymouth, like Virginia and Maryland, created an assembly to which the landowning male settlers elected representatives.

A second challenge facing the Pilgrims was survival. Like the Jamestown settlers before them, they were poorly prepared to subsist in the new environment. Their difficulties were compounded by the season of their arrival, for winter quickly descended on them. Only half of the *Mayflower*'s passengers were still alive by spring. But, again like the Virginians, the Pilgrims benefited from the political circumstances of their Native American neighbors.

Pokanokets

The Pokanokets (a branch of the Wampanoags) controlled the area in which the Pilgrims had settled. To protect themselves from the powerful Narragansetts of the southern New England coast, the Pokanokets decided to ally themselves with the newcomers. In the spring of 1621, their leader, Massasoit, signed a treaty with the Pilgrims, and during the colony's first difficult years the Pokanokets supplied the English with essential foodstuffs. The settlers were also assisted by Squanto, a Pokanoket who in the early 1610s had been captured by fishermen and taken to England, where he learned to speak English. Squanto became the Pilgrims' interpreter and a major source of information about the unfamiliar environment.

Massachusetts Bay Company

Before the 1620s ended, another group of Puritans—this time Congregationalists—launched the colonial enterprise that would come to dominate New England. The event that stimulated their interest in North America was Charles I's accession to the throne in 1625. Charles was more hostile to Puritan beliefs than his father had been. Because of Charles's actions, some non-Separatists began to think about settling in America. A group of Congregationalist merchants sent out a body of colonists to Cape Ann, north of Cape Cod, in 1628. The following year the merchants obtained a royal charter as a new joint-stock company, constituting themselves as the Massachusetts Bay Company.

The company quickly attracted Puritans of the "middling sort" who increasingly feared they no longer would be able to practice their religion freely in England. They remained committed to the goal of reforming the Church of England but concluded that they could better pursue that aim in America. In a dramatic move, the Congregationalist merchants boldly decided to transfer the company's headquarters to New England. The settlers would then be answerable to no one in the mother country and would be able to handle their affairs as they pleased.

Governor John Winthrop

The most important recruit to the new venture was John Winthrop, a member of the lesser English gentry. In October 1629, the Massachusetts Bay Company elected Winthrop as its governor. It fell to Winthrop to organize the initial segment of the great Puritan migration to America. In 1630 more than one thousand English men and women moved to Massachusetts—most of them to Boston, which soon became the largest town in British North America. By 1643 nearly twenty thousand compatriots had followed them.

Winthrop's was a transcendent vision. The society Winthrop foresaw in Puritan America was a true *commonwealth*, a community in which each person put the good of the whole ahead of his or her private concerns. It was also to be a society whose members all lived according to the precepts of Christian love. Although the ideal was beyond human reach, it long prevailed as a Puritan goal.

Ideal of the Covenant

The Puritans expressed their communal ideal chiefly in the doctrine of the covenant. They believed God had made a covenant—that is, an agreement or contract—with them when they were chosen for the special mission to America. In turn they covenanted with each other, promising to work together toward their goals.

The founders of churches and towns in the new land often drafted formal documents setting forth the principles on which such institutions would be based. The same was true of the colonial governments of New England.

The leaders of Massachusetts Bay likewise transformed their original joint-stock company charter into the basis for a covenanted community based on mutual consent. Under pressure from landowning male settlers, they gradually changed the General Court—officially the company's small governing body—into a colonial legislature. They also granted the status of freeman, or voting member of the company, to all property-owning adult male church members residing in Massachusetts. Less than two decades after the first large group of Puritans had arrived in Massachusetts Bay, the colony had a functioning system of self-government composed of a governor and a two-house legislature. The General Court also established a judicial system modeled on England's.

The colony's method of distributing land helped to further the communal ideal. Groups of families—often from the same region of England—applied together to the General Court for grants of land on which to establish towns. The men who received the original town grant had the sole authority to determine how the land would be distributed. First they laid out town lots for houses and a church. Then they gave each family parcels of land scattered around the town center: pasture here, a woodlot there, an arable field elsewhere. They reserved the best and largest plots for the most distinguished among them (including the minister).

New England Towns

When migrants began to move beyond the territorial limits of the Massachusetts Bay colony into Connecticut (1636), New Haven (1638), and New Hampshire (1638), the same pattern of town land grants was maintained. Only Maine, with coastal regions thinly populated by fishermen and their families, deviated from the standard practice.

Thus New England settlements initially tended to be more compact than those of the Chesapeake. Town centers grew up quickly, developing in three distinctly different ways. Some, chiefly isolated agricultural settlements in the interior, tried to sustain Winthrop's vision of harmonious community life based on diversified family farms. A second group, the coastal towns like Boston and Salem, became bustling seaports. The third category, commercialized agricultural towns, grew up in the Connecticut River valley, where easy water transportation enabled farmers to sell surplus goods readily.

The migration to the Connecticut valley ended the Puritans' relative freedom from clashes with their Native American neighbors. The first English settlers in the valley moved there from Newtown (Cambridge, Massachusetts), under the direction of their minister, Thomas Hooker. Connecticut was fertile, and the wide river promised ready access to the ocean. The site had just one problem: it fell within the territory controlled by the powerful Pequots.

The Pequots' dominance was based on their role as primary middlemen in the trade between New England Indians and the Dutch in New Netherland. The arrival of English settlers signaled the end of the Pequots' power over the regional trading networks, for their tributary bands could now trade directly with Europeans. Clashes between Pequots and English colonists began even before the Connecticut valley settlements were established, but their founding tipped the balance toward war. After two English traders were killed (probably not by Pequots), the English raided a Pequot village. In return, the Pequots attacked the new town of Wethersfield in April 1637, killing nine and capturing two of the colonists. To retaliate, a Massachusetts Bay expedition the following month attacked and burned the main Pequot town on the Mystic River. At least four hundred Pequots, mostly women and children, were slaughtered.

Pequot War

For the next thirty years, the New England Indians tried to accommodate themselves to the spread of European settlement. They traded with the newcomers and sometimes worked for them, but they resisted acculturation or incorporation into English society. The Native Americans clung to their traditional farming methods. Indeed, the only European agricultural practice they adopted was keeping livestock; in the absence of game, domesticated animals provided excellent sources of meat.

Although the official seal of the Massachusetts Bay colony showed an Indian crying "Come over and help us," most colonists showed little interest in converting the New England Algonkians to Christianity. Only a few Massachusetts clerics, most notably John Eliot, seriously undertook missionary activities. Eliot insisted that converts should reside in towns, farm the land in English fashion, assume English names, wear European-style clothing and shoes, cut their hair, and stop observing a wide range of their own customs. He understandably met with little success. At the peak of Eliot's efforts, only eleven hundred Native Americans lived in the fourteen "Praying Towns" he had established.

John Eliot and the Praying Towns

The Jesuits' successful missions in New France contrasted sharply with the Puritans failure to win many converts. Initially, Catholicism had several advantages over Puritanism. The Catholic Church employed attractive rituals, instructed converts that through good works they could help to earn their own salvation, and offered Indian women an inspiring role model—the Virgin Mary. In Montréal and Quebec, communities of nuns taught Indian women and children and ministered to their needs. Furthermore, the few French colonists on the St. Lawrence did not alienate potential converts by encroaching steadily on their lands (as did New Englanders). Perhaps most important, the Jesuits understood that Christian beliefs were to some extent compatible with Native American culture. Unlike Puritans, Jesuits were willing to accept converts who did not wholly adopt European styles of life.

Puritan and Jesuit Missions Compared

Life in New England

New England's colonizers adopted lifestyles that differed considerably from those of both their Indian neighbors and their European counterparts in the Chesapeake. Unlike the Algonkian bands, who usually moved four or five times each year to take full advantage of their environment, English people lived year-round in the same location. And unlike residents of the Chesapeake, New Englanders constructed sturdy dwellings intended to last. They used the same fields again and again, believing it was less arduous to employ manure as fertilizer than to clear new fields every few years. Furthermore, they had to fence their croplands to prevent them from being overrun by their cattle, sheep, and hogs. When New Englanders began to spread out over the countryside, the reason was not so much human crowding as it was animal crowding.

Because Puritans commonly moved to America in family groups, the age range in early New England was wide; and because many more women went to New England than to the tobacco colonies, the population could immediately begin to reproduce itself. Moreover, New England was much healthier than the Chesapeake. New England was even healthier than the mother country. Although adult male migrants to the Chesapeake lost about ten years from their English life expectancy of fifty to fifty-five years, their Massachusetts counterparts gained five or more years. Consequently, while Chesapeake population patterns gave rise to families that were few in number, small in size, and transitory, the demographic characteristics of New England made families there numerous, large, and long-lived. If seventeenth-century Chesapeake women could expect to rear one to three healthy children, New England women could anticipate raising five to seven.

New England Families

The nature of the population had other major implications for family life. New England in effect created grandparents, since in England people rarely lived long enough to know their children's children. And whereas early southern parents commonly died before their children married, northern parents exercised a good deal of control over their adult children. Young men could not marry without acreage to cultivate, and because of the communal land-grant system they were dependent on their fathers to supply them with that land. Daughters, too, needed the dowry of household goods that their parents would give them when they married. Yet parents needed their children's labor and often were reluctant to see them marry and start their own households. Generational conflict existed, but children had few alternatives and thus obeyed their parents' wishes.

Another important difference lay in the influence of religion on New Englanders' lives. Puritans controlled their governments. With the exception of Rhode Island, Congregationalism was the only officially recognized religion; members of other sects had no freedom of worship. Some non-Puritans voted in town meetings, but in Massachusetts Bay and New Haven, church membership was a prerequisite for voting in colony elections. All households were taxed to build meetinghouses and pay ministers' salaries. Massachusetts's first legal codes (1641 and 1648) incorporated regulations drawn from Old Testament scriptures into the laws of the colony; those codes were later copied by New Haven, Plymouth, New Hampshire, and Connecticut.

Impact of Religion

In addition, the Puritan colonies attempted to enforce strict codes of moral conduct. Colonists there were frequently tried for drunkenness, card-playing, even idleness. Couples who had sex during their engagement—as revealed by the birth of a baby less than nine months after their wedding—were fined and publicly humiliated. (Maryland, by contrast, did not penalize premarital pregnancy, only bastardy.) More harshly treated in both regions were men—and a handful of women—who engaged in behaviors that today would be called homosexual. (The term did not then exist.)

In New England, church and state were thus intertwined. Puritans objected to secular interference in religious affairs but at the same time expected the church to influence the conduct of politics and the affairs of society. They also believed that the state had an obligation to support and protect the one true church—theirs. As a result, though they came to America seeking freedom to worship as they wished, they saw no contradiction in their refusal to grant that freedom to others. Indeed, the two most significant divisions in early Massachusetts were caused by religious disputes and by Massachusetts Bay's unwillingness to tolerate dissent.

Roger Williams, a Separatist, migrated to Massachusetts Bay in 1631. He soon began to express some eccentric ideas: that the king of England had no right to give away land already occupied by Native Americans, that church and state should be kept entirely separate, and that Puritans should not impose their religious beliefs on others. Banished from Massachusetts in late 1635, Williams founded the town of Providence on Narragansett Bay. Because of Williams's beliefs, Providence and other towns in what became the colony of Rhode Island adopted a policy of tolerance toward all religions, including Judaism.

Roger Williams

The other dissenter, and an even greater challenge to Massachusetts Bay orthodoxy, was Anne Marbury Hutchinson. A skilled medical practitioner popular with the women of Boston, she was a follower of John Cotton, a minister who stressed the *covenant of grace*, or God's free gift of salvation to unworthy human beings. By contrast, most Massachusetts clerics emphasized the need for Puritans to engage in good works, study, and reflection in preparation for receiving God's grace. After teaching her ideas during childbed discussions (when no men were present), Hutchinson began holding women's meetings in her home to discuss Cotton's sermons. She emphasized the covenant of grace more than did Cotton himself, and she even adopted the belief that the elect could be assured of salvation and communicate directly with God. Such ideas had an immense appeal for Puritans. Anne Hutchinson offered them certainty of salvation instead of a state of constant anxiety.

Anne Hutchinson

Hutchinson's ideas were a dangerous threat to Puritan orthodoxy. So in November 1637, the leaders of the General Court charged her with having maligned the colony's ministers by accusing them of preaching the covenant of works, the idea that people could earn their own salvation.

For two days she defended herself cleverly against her accusers. But then Hutchinson triumphantly and boldly declared that God had spoken to her "by an immediate revelation," telling her that he would curse the Puritans' descendants for generations if they harmed her. That assertion assured her banishment to Rhode Island.

The authorities in Massachusetts Bay perceived Anne Hutchinson as doubly dangerous, for she threatened not only religious orthodoxy but also traditional gender roles. Puritans believed in the equality before God of all souls, but they considered actual women (as distinct from their spiritual selves) inferior to men. Christians had long followed Saint Paul's dictum that women should keep silent in church and be submissive to their husbands. Hutchinson did neither. A minister at her church trial told her bluntly: "You have stept out of your place, you have rather bine a Husband than a Wife and a preacher than a Hearer."

The New England authorities' reaction to Hutchinson reveals the depth of their adherence to European gender-role concepts. To them, an orderly society required the submission of wives to husbands as well as the obedience of subjects to rulers. English colonists intended to change many aspects of their lives, but not the sexual division of labor or the assumption of male superiority.

 ## Conclusion

By the middle of the seventeenth century, Europeans had unquestionably come to North America to stay, a fact that signaled major changes for the peoples of both hemispheres. Europeans killed Indians with their weapons and diseases and had but limited success in converting them to European religions. Contacts with the Native Americans taught Europeans to eat new foods, speak new languages, and recognize the persistence of other cultural patterns. The prosperity and even survival of many of the European colonies depended heavily on the cultivation of American crops (maize and tobacco), thus attesting to the importance of post-Columbian ecological change.

In America, Spaniards reaped the benefits of their South and Central American gold and silver mines, while French people earned their primary profits from Indian trade (in Canada) and cultivating sugar cane (in the Caribbean). Sugar also enriched the Portuguese. The Dutch concentrated on commerce—trading in furs and sugar as well as carrying human cargoes of enslaved Africans to South America and the Caribbean. Of these nations, only France and Spain went beyond the economic relationships they established with native peoples to attempt to Christianize them.

Although the English colonies at first sought to rely on trade, they quickly took another form altogether when so many English people of the "middling sort" decided to migrate to North America. To a greater extent than their European counterparts, the English transferred the society of their homeland to a new environment. Although New England and the Chesapeake differed in many ways, both were English in origin, and in the years to come both regions would be drawn into the increasingly fierce rivalries besetting the European powers. Those rivalries would continue to affect Americans of all races until after France and England had fought the greatest war yet known in the mid-eighteenth century and the Anglo-American colonies had won their independence.

Suggestions for Further Reading

General

David Hackett Fischer, *Albion's Seed: Four British Folkways in America* (1989); D. W. Meinig, *Atlantic America, 1492–1800* (1986); Gary B. Nash, *Red, White, and Black: The Peoples of Early America*, 2d ed. (1982); Mary Beth Norton, *Founding Mothers & Fathers: Gendered Power and the Forming of American Society* (1996); Paula Treckel, *To Comfort the Heart: Women in Seventeenth-Century America* (1996); Alden T. Vaughan, *Roots of American Racism* (1994).

New Spain, New Netherland, New France, and the Caribbean

Karen Anderson, *Chain Her by One Foot: The Subjugation of Native Women in Seventeenth-Century New France* (1991); Denys Delâge, *Bitter Feast: Amerindians and Europeans in Northeastern North America, 1600–64* (1993); Richard S. Dunn, *Sugar and Slaves: The Rise of the Planter Class in the English West Indies, 1624–1713* (1972); William J. Eccles, *France in America*, rev. ed. (1990); Donna Merwick, *Possessing Albany, 1630–1710* (1990); Sidney Mintz, *Sweetness and Power: The Place of Sugar in Modern*

History (1985); Marc Simmons, *The Last Conquistador: Juan de Oñate and the Settling of the Far Southwest* (1991); David J. Weber, *The Spanish Frontier in North America* (1992).

England

Susan Dwyer Amussen, *An Ordered Society: Gender and Class in Early Modern England* (1988); Peter Laslett, *The World We Have Lost*, 3d ed. (1984); Keith Wrightson, *English Society, 1580–1680* (1982).

Early Contact Between Europeans and Indians

James Axtell, *The Invasion Within: The Contest of Cultures in Colonial North America* (1985); Philip Barbour, *Pocahontas and Her World* (1970); William Cronon, *Changes in the Land: Indians, Colonists, and the Ecology of New England* (1983); Francis Jennings, *The Invasion of America: Indians, Colonialism, and the Cant of Conquest* (1975); Karen O. Kupperman, *Settling with the Indians: The Meeting of English and Indian Cultures in America, 1580–1640* (1980); Neal Salisbury, *Manitou and Providence: Indians, Europeans, and the Making of New England, 1500–1643* (1982); Timothy Silver, *A New Face on the Countryside: Indians, Colonists, and Slaves in South Atlantic Forests, 1500–1800* (1990); Peter Wood et al., eds., *Powhatan's Mantle: Indians in the Colonial Southeast* (1989).

Chesapeake Society and Politics

Lois Green Carr et al., *Robert Cole's World: Agriculture and Society in Early Maryland* (1991); David Galenson, *White Servitude in Colonial America: An Economic Analysis* (1981); James Horn, *Adapting to a New World: English Society in the Seventeenth-Century Chesapeake* (1994); Ivor Noël Hume, *The Virginia Adventure: Roanoke to James Towne* (1994); Gloria L. Main, *Tobacco Colony: Life in Early Maryland, 1650–1720* (1983); Edmund S. Morgan, *American Slavery, American Freedom: The Ordeal of Colonial Virginia* (1975); Alden T. Vaughan, *American Genesis: Captain John Smith and the Founding of Virginia* (1975).

New England Communities, Politics, and Religion

David D. Hall, *Worlds of Wonder, Days of Judgment: Popular Religious Belief in Early New England* (1989); Stephen Innes, *Creating the Commonwealth: The Economic Culture of Puritan New England* (1995); Stephen Innes, *Labor in a New Land: Economy and Society in 17th-Century Springfield* (1983); Sydney V. James, *Colonial Rhode Island* (1975); George Langdon, *Pilgrim Colony: A History of New Plymouth, 1620–1691* (1966); John Frederick Martin, *Profits in the Wilderness: Entrepreneurship and the Founding of New England Towns in the 17th Century* (1991); Edmund S. Morgan, *The Puritan Dilemma: The Story of John Winthrop* (1958); Darrett Rutman, *Winthrop's Boston* (1965).

New England Women and Family Life

David Cressy, *Coming Over: Migration and Communication Between England and New England in the Seventeenth Century* (1987); John Demos, *A Little Commonwealth: Family Life in Plymouth Colony* (1970); Lyle Koehler, *A Search for Power: The "Weaker Sex" in Seventeenth-Century New England* (1980); Edmund S. Morgan, *The Puritan Family*, rev. ed. (1966); Roger Thompson, *Sex in Middlesex: Popular Mores in a Massachusetts County, 1649–1699* (1986).

CHAPTER

3

American Society
Takes Shape
1640–1720

The hangman tightened the noose around the condemned man's neck and shoved him off the ladder. The rope broke, and the notorious pirate Captain William Kidd lay on the ground, dazed. The hangman repeated the procedure with a new rope. This time it held. The event happened on May 23, 1701, near the London docks. As a warning to others, Kidd's body was left dangling from a gibbet on the bank of the Thames.

William Kidd, born in Scotland, had made his home in New York, the port once known as New Amsterdam. The merchants there, being none too choosy about the source of their profits, eagerly provisioned pirates' ships and purchased goods pirated from ships plying the expanded trade routes. In the 1690s, Manhattan's economy depended on this illegal trade. For years Kidd and other pirates could count on New York's governors to ignore their activities in exchange for shares of the bounty.

Why was Captain Kidd condemned to die? His fatal enterprise began in London in early 1696, when he gained financial backing from several powerful and prominent English investors for a voyage to the Indian Ocean. After more than a year of buccaneering, Kidd returned to New York by way of the Caribbean, hoping to avoid prosecution for piracy by paying off his investors in full and by bribing colonial officials. Unfortunately for Kidd, one of his financial backers, the earl of Bellomont, had become governor of New York. Bellomont was waging a vigorous campaign against piracy and could not afford to protect Kidd. In addition, as governor he could claim one-third of any confiscated illegal cargo. Kidd's fate was sealed when Bellomont ordered his arrest and shipped him back to England for trial.

The saga of William Kidd illustrates above all the involvement of the English mainland colonies in a growing network of trade and international contacts. North America, like England itself, was becoming increasingly embedded in a worldwide matrix of exchange and warfare. The web woven by oceangoing vessels now crisscrossed the globe, carrying West Indian sugar to Europe, Africans to America, cloth and spices from the East Indies to Africa, and New England fish and wood products to the Caribbean. Formerly tiny outposts, the North American colonies had expanded their territorial claims and embarked on a deliberate course of economic development. In response, the English government for the first time began to adopt policies to systematize colonial administration, passing laws that regulated trade and reshaped the American governments.

Three developments shaped life in the mainland colonies between 1640 and 1720: the introduction of a system of chattel slavery, especially in the south Atlantic coastal regions; changes in the colonies' relationship with their mother country; and increasing conflicts with their North American neighbors, both European and Native American.

The explosive growth of the slave trade was of critical significance in the colonial economy. For slave trader and planter alike, slaves meant huge profits. The arrival of large numbers of West African peoples dramatically reshaped colonial society and fueled the international trading system. Moreover, the burgeoning North American economy attracted new attention from officials in London who attempted to supervise the American settlements more effectively and thus ensure that England benefited from their economic growth.

Neither English colonists nor London administrators could ignore other peoples living on the North American continent. As the English settlements expanded, they came into violent conflict not only with the powerful Indians of the interior but also with the Dutch, the Spanish, and especially the French. By 1720, war had become an all-too-frequent feature of American life.

The English Civil War, the Stuart Restoration, and the American Colonies

In 1642, England erupted into civil war. Disputes over taxation, religion, and other issues led to armed conflict between supporters of the Puritan-dominated Parliament and King Charles I. After four years of warfare, Parliament triumphed. Charles I was executed in 1649, and the parliamentary army's leader, Oliver Cromwell, assumed control of the government. Yet after Cromwell's death in 1658 Parliament decided to restore the monarchy if Charles I's son and heir would agree to restrictions on his authority. In 1660, Charles II ascended the throne, having promised to support the Church of England and to seek Parliament's consent for any new taxes. Thus ended the Interregnum (Latin for "between reigns") or Commonwealth period.

The Civil War, the Interregnum, and the reign of Charles II (1660–1685) had far-reaching significance for the Anglo-American colonies. During the Civil War and the Commonwealth period when Puritans controlled the English government, the migration to New England largely ceased. During the subsequent reign of Charles II, six of the thirteen colonies that eventually would form the American nation were either founded or came under English rule: New York, New Jersey, Pennsylvania (including Delaware), and North and South Carolina. All were proprietorships granted in their entirety to one man or to a group of men who held title to the soil and controlled the government. Charles II gave these vast American holdings as rewards to men who had supported him during the Civil War. Collectively, these became known as the Restoration colonies, because they were created by the restored Stuart monarchy.

One of the first to benefit was Charles's younger brother James, the duke of York. In 1664, Charles II gave James the region between the

New Netherland Becomes New York

Connecticut and Delaware Rivers, including the Hudson valley and Long Island. James immediately organized an invasion fleet. In late August the vessels anchored off Manhattan Island and demanded New

The Founding of English Colonies in North America, 1664–1732

Colony	Founder(s)	Date	Basis of Economy
New York (formerly New Netherland)	James, duke of York	1664	Farming, fur trading
New Jersey	Sir George Carteret, John Lord Berkeley	1664	Farming
North Carolina	Carolina proprietors	1665	Tobacco, forest products
South Carolina	Carolina proprietors	1670	Rice, indigo
Pennsylvania	William Penn	1681	Farming
Georgia	James Oglethorpe	1732	Rice, forest products

Netherland's surrender. The colony complied without resistance.

Thus England acquired a tiny but heterogeneous possession. In 1664, an appreciable minority of English people already lived in the colony. New York, as it was now called, also included sizable numbers of Indians, Germans, and Scandinavians, as well as a smattering of other European peoples. Because the Dutch had actively imported slaves into the colony, almost one-fifth of Manhattan's approximately fifteen hundred inhabitants were of African descent.

Recognizing the population's diversity, the duke of York's representatives moved cautiously in their efforts to establish English authority. The Duke's Laws, a legal code proclaimed in 1665, at first applied solely to the English settlements on Long Island, only later being extended to the rest of the colony. Dutch forms of local government were maintained, Dutch land titles confirmed, and Dutch residents allowed to maintain customary legal practices. Religious toleration was guaranteed by allowing each town to decide which church to support with its tax revenues. Much to the dismay of English residents of the colony, the Duke's Laws made no provision for a representative assembly. Like other Stuarts, James was suspicious of legislative bodies, and not until 1683 did he agree to the colonists' requests for an elected legislature.

The English takeover thus had little immediate effect on the colony. Its population grew slowly, barely reaching eighteen thousand by the time of the first English census in 1698. One of the chief reasons

Founding of New Jersey

the English conquest brought so little change to New York was that the duke of York in 1664 regranted the land between the Hudson and Delaware Rivers—East and West Jersey—to his friends Sir George Carteret and John Lord Berkeley. That grant deprived his own colony of much fertile land and hindered its economic growth. Meanwhile, the Jersey proprietors acted rapidly to attract settlers, promising generous land grants, limited freedom of religion, and—without authorization from the Crown—a representative assembly. New Jersey grew quickly; in 1726, it had 32,500 inhabitants, only 8,000 fewer than New York.

Within twenty years, Berkeley and Carteret sold their interests in the Jerseys to separate groups of investors. The purchasers of all of Carteret's share (West Jersey) and portions of Berkeley's (East Jersey) were members of the Society of Friends, seeking a refuge from persecution in England. The Society of Friends, also called Quakers, denied the need for intermediaries between individuals and God. They believed that anyone could receive the "inner light" and be saved and that all were equal in God's sight. They had no formally trained clergy; any Quaker, male or female, could speak in meetings or become a "public friend" and travel from meeting to meet-

• Important Events •

1642–46	English Civil War; end of first New England economic system based on furs and migrants
1649	Charles I executed
1651	First Navigation Act passed to regulate colonial trade
1660	Stuarts restored to throne; Charles II becomes king
1662	Halfway Covenant drafted in New England, creating category of partial membership in Congregational churches
1663	Carolina chartered
1664	English conquer New Netherland; New York founded New Jersey established
1670s	Jacques Marquette, Louis Jolliet, and Robert Cavelier de La Salle explore the Great Lakes and Mississippi valley for France
1675–76	King Philip's (Metacom's) War devastates New England
1676	Bacon's Rebellion disrupts Virginia government; Jamestown destroyed
1680–92	Pueblo revolt temporarily drives Spaniards from New Mexico
1681	Pennsylvania chartered
1685	James II becomes king
1686–89	Dominion of New England established, superseding all charters of colonies from Maine to New Jersey
1688–89	James II deposed in Glorious Revolution; William and Mary ascend throne
1689–97	King William's War fought on northern New England frontier
1692	Witchcraft oubreak in Salem Village; nineteen executions result
1696	Board of Trade and Plantations established to coordinate English colonial administration
1701	Iroquois adopt neutrality policy toward France and England
1702–13	Queen Anne's War fought by French and English
1711–13	Tuscarora War (North Carolina) leads to capture or migration of most Tuscaroras
1715	Yamasee War nearly destroys South Carolina
1718	New Orleans founded in French Louisiana
1732	Georgia chartered

ing to discuss God's word. The Quaker message of radical egalitarianism was not welcome in either England or Puritan New England.

The Quakers obtained their own colony in 1681, when Charles II granted the region between Maryland and New York to his close, personal friend William Penn, a prominent member of the sect. Although Penn held the colony as a personal proprietorship, he saw his province as a haven for his persecuted coreligionists. He offered land to all comers on liberal terms, promised toleration of all religions (though only Christians were given the vote), guaranteed Eng-

Pennsylvania: A Quaker Haven

lish liberties such as trial by jury, and pledged to establish a representative assembly. He also publicized throughout Europe the ready availability of land in Pennsylvania.

Penn's activities and the attraction of his lands for Quakers gave rise to a migration whose magnitude was equaled only by the Puritan exodus to New England in the 1630s. By 1689 Pennsylvania's population had reached twelve thousand—among them Welsh, Irish, Dutch, and Germans. Philadelphia, carefully planned to be the major city in the province, drew merchants and artisans from throughout the English-speaking world. From mainland and West Indian colonies alike came Quakers seeking religious freedom. Pennsylvania's lands were both plentiful and fertile, and the colony soon began exporting flour and other food-stuffs to the West Indies. Practically overnight Philadelphia acquired more than two thousand citizens and began to challenge Boston's commercial dominance.

A pacifist with egalitarian principles, Penn attempted to treat Native Americans fairly. Before selling land to European settlers, he purchased it from the Delawares (or Lenapes). He also established strict regulations for trade and forbade the sale of alcohol to Indians.

William Penn's Indian Policy

Penn's policies attracted Indians who moved to Pennsylvania near the end of the seventeenth century to escape repeated clashes with English colonists in Maryland, Virginia, and North Carolina. Most important were the Tuscaroras. Shawnees and Miamis moved eastward from the Ohio valley. By a supreme irony, however, the same toleration that attracted Indians also brought non-Quaker Europeans who showed little respect for Indian claims to the soil. In effect, Penn's policy was so successful that it caused its own downfall. The Scots-Irish, Palatine Germans, and Swiss who settled in Pennsylvania clashed repeatedly over land with groups of Indians who had also recently migrated to the colony.

The other proprietary colony, granted by Charles II in 1663, encompassed a huge tract of land stretching from the southern boundary of Virginia to Spanish Florida. The area had great strategic importance; a successful English settlement there would prevent Spaniards from pushing farther north. The proprietors named their new province Carolina in honor of Charles, whose Latin name was *Carolus*. The Fundamental Constitutions of Carolina, which they asked the political philosopher John Locke to draft for them, set forth an elaborate plan for a colony governed by a hierarchy of landholding aristocrats. But Carolina failed to follow the course the proprietors laid out. Instead, it quickly developed two distinct population centers, which in 1729 permanently split into two separate colonies.

Founding of Carolina

The Albemarle region that became North Carolina was settled by Virginia planters. They established a society much like their own, with an economy based on tobacco cultivation and the export of such forest products as pitch, tar, and timber. Because North Carolina lacked a satisfactory harbor, its planters continued to rely on Virginia's ports and merchants to conduct their trade. Although North Carolina planters held some slaves, they never became as dependent on slave labor as did the other population center in Carolina.

Charleston, South Carolina, was founded in 1670 by a group of settlers from the island of Barbados. The English migrants from Barbados brought with them the slaves who had worked on their sugar plantations and the legal codes that had governed those laborers, thereby shaping the future of South Carolina and the subsequent history of the United States.

 ## The North American Slave Trade and the Enslavement of Africans

Since England had no tradition of slavery, why did English settlers begin to enslave Africans around the middle of the seventeenth century? The answer to that question lies in a combination of the settlers' need for labor and the experience of other Europeans.

Although the English had not previously practiced slavery, other Europeans had. Both the Spanish and Portuguese had imported enslaved Africans as laborers into the islands of the Mediterranean Atlantic during the fifteenth century. They then extended that practice to their American possessions. No free people of any description were willing to toil for wages in the difficult and dangerous conditions of South American mines or Caribbean sugar plantations. To produce the profitable goods they had come to America to seek, Europeans needed bound laborers—people who, by law or contract, could be forced to work. Dutch, French, and English Caribbean planters eagerly purchased slaves from the 1640s on. Twenty years later, in the 1660s, when the supply of English indentured servants began to dry up, Chesapeake planters also turned to Africans.

In the early mainland English settlements, the few residents of African descent varied in status: some were free, some indentured, some enslaved.

Atlantic Creoles

All came from a population that historian Ira Berlin recently termed "Atlantic creoles"—people who participated in the new international system of trade and piracy. Often of mixed race, they were already familiar with Europeans and fitted easily into established niches in the many-faceted hierarchical social structures of the early colonies. Slave status was not clearly defined in law, and individuals moved back and forth across boundaries of freedom, indenture, and enslavement.

Before the 1660s, none of the English mainland colonies systematically categorized Africans as slaves. But after Chesapeake planters began to

Systematic Enslavement of Africans

import already enslaved Africans from Caribbean sugar islands and then to purchase slaves directly from Africa, that situation changed decisively. As increasing numbers of slaves arrived each year beginning in the 1670s, the enslaved population changed from acculturated creole to newly imported African, and most of the English colonies adopted codes to govern slaves' behavior. By the end of the century, African slavery was firmly established as the basis of the economy in the Chesapeake.

One of the most remarkable aspects of the adoption of the slave system was that the English enslavers never seem to have questioned—or even felt the need to justify with racist rationalizations—the decision to hold Africans and their descendants in perpetual bondage. That fact suggests the importance both of prior Spanish and Portuguese practice and of economic motives in leading to this momentous development. The English did not contend that Africans were inferior to other peoples. Accepting Africans' already enslaved status, English planters wanted to employ the bound laborers to their own advantage.

Between 1492 and 1770 more Africans than Europeans came to the Americas. The vast major-ity of them went to Brazil or the Caribbean: of at least 10 million enslaved people brought to the Americas during the existence of slavery, only about 260,000 had been imported by 1775 into the region that later became the United States. The magnitude of the slave trade raises three related questions. What was its impact on West Africa and Europe? How was the trade organized and conducted? What was its effect on the people it carried and on the region to which they were taken?

West Africa was one of the most fertile and densely inhabited regions of the continent, so the trade in human beings did not seriously depopu-

West Africa and the Slave Trade

late the area. Even so, because American planters preferred to purchase male slaves, the trade significantly affected the sex ratio of the remaining population. The relative lack of men increased the work demands on women and simultaneously encouraged *polygyny*.

In Guinea, the primary consequences of the trade were political and economic. Coastal rulers served as middlemen, allowing the establishment of permanent slave-trading posts in their territories and supplying resident Europeans with slaves to fill ships that stopped regularly at the coastal forts. Such rulers controlled both European traders' access to slaves and inland peoples' access to desirable European goods. The centralizing tendencies of the slave trade helped to create such powerful eighteenth-century kingdoms as Dahomey and Asante.

Europeans, however, were the chief beneficiaries of this traffic in slaves. The expanding network of trade between Europe and its colonies

Europe and the Slave Trade

in the seventeenth and eighteenth centuries was fueled by the sale and transportation of slaves, the exchange of commodities produced by slave labor, and the need to feed and clothe so many bound laborers. The sugar planters of the Caribbean and Brazil, along with the tobacco and rice planters of North America, eagerly purchased slaves from Africa, dispatched shiploads of valuable staple crops to Europe, and bought large quantities of cheap food, much of it from elsewhere in the Americas.

The European economy, previously oriented toward the Mediterranean and Asia, shifted its emphasis to the Atlantic Ocean. By the late seventeenth century commerce in slaves and the products of slave labor constituted the basis of the European economic system. The irony of Columbus's discoveries was thus complete: seeking the wealth of Asia, Columbus found instead the lands that ultimately replaced Asia as the source of European prosperity.

European nations fought bitterly to control the slave trade. The Portuguese had at first dominated the trade, but they were supplanted by the Dutch in the 1630s. The Dutch in turn lost out to the English, who controlled the trade through the Royal African Company, a joint-stock company chartered by Charles II in 1672. Holding a monopoly on all English trade with sub-Saharan Africa, the company transported more than 120,000 slaves to England's colonies in the Caribbean and on the mainland. Yet even before the company's monopoly expired in 1712, many individual English traders had illegally entered the market for slaves. By the early eighteenth century, independent traders were carrying most of the Africans imported into the colonies and earning huge profits.

The experience of the Middle Passage (thus named because it was the middle section of the so-called triangular trade among England, Africa, and the Americas; see page 58) was always traumatic and sometimes fatal. An average of 10 to 20 percent of slaves died en route. On voyages that were unusually long or plagued by epidemic diseases, mortality rates were much higher. In addition, some slaves died either before the ships left Africa or shortly after their arrival in the Americas. Their European captors also died at high rates, chiefly through exposure to diseases endemic to Africa. Once again, the exchange of diseases caused unanticipated death and destruction.

The Middle Passage

One of the most vivid accounts of the Middle Passage was written by Olaudah Equiano, who was eleven years old in 1756 when African raiders kidnapped him. Terrified by the light complexions, long hair, and strange language of the sailors, he was afraid that "I had gotten into a world of bad spirits." After a long voyage during which many Africans died of disease brought on by the cramped, unsanitary conditions and poor food, the ship arrived at Barbados. Equiano and his shipmates feared that "these ugly men" were cannibals, but experienced slaves came on board to assure them that they would not be eaten and that many Africans like themselves lived on the island. "This report eased us much," Equiano recalled, "and sure enough soon after we landed there came to us Africans of all languages." He was not purchased in the West Indies but was instead carried to Virginia, where he was soon sold and put to work on a tobacco plantation before being resold to a visiting ship captain.

The voyage Equiano described was typical, for most slave ships landed in the Caribbean before heading north to Virginia. So many Africans were imported so rapidly that by 1710 one-fifth of the Chesapeake population was of African descent. Slaves usually cost about two-and-a-half times as much as indentured servants, but they repaid the greater investment with a lifetime of service.

Slavery in the Chesapeake

Although planters with enough money could acquire slaves and accumulate greater wealth, the less affluent could not even buy indentured servants, whose price was driven up by scarcity. As time passed, Anglo-American society in the Chesapeake became more and more stratified—that is, the gap between rich and poor steadily widened.

Cultural values were also affected by the involuntary arrival of Africans. Without realizing it, Anglo-Americans in the Chesapeake adopted African modes of thought about the use of time and the nature of work. Africans were more accustomed than European migrants to life in a hot climate. Anglo-Americans soon learned the benefits of African patterns of time usage—working early and late, taking a long rest in the midday heat. And unlike New England's Puritans who scorned all

Slave traders tightly packed their human cargoes, attempting to carry as many people as possible on each voyage. This cutaway view of a typical vessel gives the ship's dimensions and shows the way slaves were transported in cramped quarters, with only small openings providing light and air. British Library.

leisure-time activities, Chesapeake dwellers came to recognize the importance of recreation.

Since Africans were included among the first colonists to come to South Carolina from Barbados in 1670, they composed one-quarter to one-third of the early population. The Barbadian slaveowners quickly discovered that Africans had a variety of skills well suited to the semitropical environment of South Carolina. African-style dugout canoes became the chief means of transportation in the colony, which was crisscrossed by rivers, and Africans' skill at killing crocodiles equipped them to handle alligators. Finally, Africans also adapted their traditional techniques of cattle herding for use in America.

African-Americans in South Carolina

Since meat and hides—not the exotic products originally envisioned—were the colony's chief exports in its earliest years, Africans contributed significantly to South Carolina's prosperity.

The similarity of South Carolina's environment to West Africa's, coupled with the large proportion of Africans in the population, ensured that more aspects of West African culture survived in that colony than elsewhere on the North American mainland. Only in South Carolina did enslaved parents continue to give their children African names; only there did a dialect develop that combined English words with African terms. (Known as Gullah, it still survives in isolated areas.) African skills remained useful, so techniques that in other regions were lost when the migrant generation died were instead passed down to the

How do historians know that enslaved Africans were able to preserve at least some aspects of their cultural heritage in colonial North America? Although most enslaved people were illiterate and therefore did not leave written records of their cultural beliefs or practices, African-Americans did create objects that showed their connections to their homeland even more vividly than could words on a page. Many such objects have been found in the United States. The drum on the left was constructed on the Gold Coast of Africa in the nineteenth century, that on the right in Virginia sometime before the middle of the eighteenth century. The similarities of style and decoration suggest strong cultural affinities between the two drum builders, although they were separated by three thousand miles of ocean and at least one hundred years. Photo: Trustees of The British Museum; Smithsonian Institution, Washington, D.C.

migrants' children. And in South Carolina, as in Guinea, African women were the primary traders.

Significantly, the importation of large numbers of Africans near the end of the seventeenth century coincided with the successful introduction of rice as a staple crop in South Carolina. English people knew little about the techniques of growing and processing rice, but people from Africa's Rice Coast (see Chapter 1, page 12) had spent their lives working with the crop. It seems likely that the Africans' expertise enabled their English masters to cultivate the crop profitably. After rice had become South Carolina's

Rice and Indigo

major export, 43 percent of the Africans imported into the colony came from rice-producing regions.

South Carolina later developed a second staple crop, and it, too, made use of slaves' special skills. The crop was indigo, much prized in Europe as a source of blue dye for clothing. In the early 1740s, Eliza Lucas, a young woman who was managing her father's plantations, began to experiment with indigo cultivation. Drawing on the knowledge of slaves and overseers from the West Indies, she developed the planting and processing techniques later adopted throughout the colony. Indigo was grown on high ground, and rice was planted in low-lying swampy areas; rice and indigo also had different growing seasons. Thus the two crops complemented each other perfectly.

After 1700, southern planters were irrevocably committed to slavery as their chief source of labor but northerners were not. Lacking large-scale agricultural enterprises, the rural North did not demand many bound laborers. In northern urban areas, though, European domestic servants were hard to find and slaves were often used. Slaves accounted for more than 10 percent of the population in some northern colonial cities (notably Newport, Rhode Island, and New York City).

Slavery in the North

The introduction of large-scale slavery in the South, coupled with its near absence in the rural North, accentuated regional differences that already had begun to develop in England's American colonies. To the distinction between diversified agriculture and staple-crop production was now added a crucial difference in the status of most laborers.

Relations Between Europeans and Indians

Everywhere in North America, European colonizers depended heavily on the labor of native peoples. In the Northeast, France, England, and the Netherlands competed for the pelts supplied by Indian trappers. In the Southeast, England, Spain, and later France each tried to control a thriving trade with the Indians in deerskins and Indian slaves. In the Southwest, Spain attempted to exploit the agricultural and artisan skills of the Pueblo peoples (see map).

After Fray Alonzo de Benavides departed for Madrid in 1629 (see Chapter 2), Franciscan friars continued their conversion efforts, with mixed success. The Pueblo peoples were willing to add Christianity to their own religious beliefs but not to give up their indigenous rituals. Friars and secular colonists who held *encomiendas* also placed heavy demands on the Indians. As the decades passed, Franciscans adopted brutal tactics in an at-

Popé and the Pueblo Revolt

tempt to wipe out all traces of the native religion. Finally, in 1680 the Pueblos revolted under the leadership of Popé, a respected shaman, and drove the Spaniards out of New Mexico. After Spanish authority was restored in 1692, Spanish governors stressed cooperation with the Pueblos, rather than confrontation, and no longer attempted to reduce them to bondage or to violate their cultural integrity. The Pueblo revolt was the most successful and longest-sustained Indian resistance movement in colonial North America.

When the Spanish expanded their territorial claims to the east and north, they followed the same strategy they had used in New Mexico, establishing their presence through military outposts and Franciscan missions. The army's role was to maintain order among the subject peoples and to guard the boundaries of the Spanish Empire from possible incursions, especially by the French. By the late eighteenth century, Spain claimed a vast territory that stretched from California (first colonized in 1769) through Texas (settled after 1700) to the Gulf Coast.

Spain's North American Possessions

Europeans along the eastern seaboard valued Indians as hunters rather than as agricultural workers, but they were no less dependent on Indian labor than were Spaniards in the Southwest. To obtain pelts and deerskins from indigenous peoples, Europeans had to supply trade goods the Indians wanted. Such commodities included ammunition, clothing, and alcohol (usually rum distilled from West Indian molasses). The demand for alcohol (a commodity introduced by the traders) made rum a key component of colonial commerce, and alcohol abuse hastened the deterioration of villages already devastated by disease and dislocation.

Also destructive of tribal communities was traffic in Indian slaves. Carolina Indians, especially the Creeks, profited from selling their captive enemies to the English, who either kept them as slaves or exported them to other mainland settlements or to the West Indies. There are no reliable statistics on the extent of the trade in

Indian Slave Trade in the Southeast

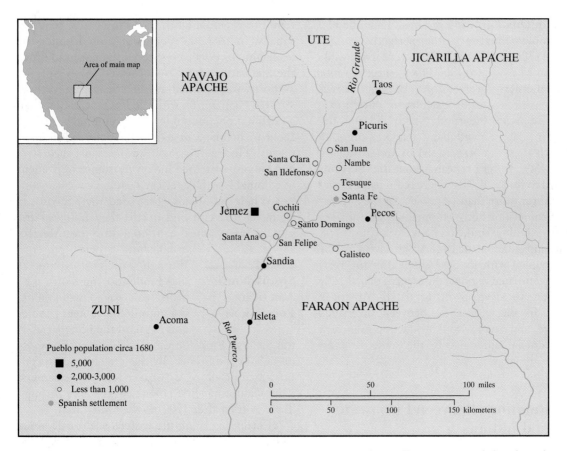

New Mexico, ca. 1680   *In 1680, the lone Spanish settlement at Santa Fe was surrounded and vastly outnumbered by the many pueblos nearby.*   Source: Adapted from *Apache, Navaho, and Spaniard*, by Jack D. Forbes. Copyright ©1960 by the University of Oklahoma Press. Used by permission.

Indian slaves, but in 1708 they composed 14 percent of the South Carolina population.

Bitter conflicts between the Carolina settlers and indigenous peoples also produced mass migrations. In 1711 the Tuscaroras, an Iroquoian people, attacked a Swiss-German settlement at New Bern, which had expropriated their lands without payment. The Tuscaroras were slave traders who often sold captured Algonkian enemies into slavery. Therefore the Algonkians joined the English colonists to defeat their enemy in a bloody two-year war. In the end, more than a thousand Tuscaroras were themselves sold into slavery, and the remnants of the group drifted northward, where they joined the Five Nations Iroquois in New York.

Tuscarora and Yamasee Wars

The slave trade's abuses led to yet another Indian war in Carolina. Colonial traders were notorious for cheating Native Americans, physically abusing them (including raping women), and selling friendly peoples into slavery. In the spring and summer of 1715, the Yamasees, aided by Creeks and others, retaliated by attacking English settlements. Refugees by the hundreds streamed into Charleston; the Creek-Yamasee offensive came close to driving the intruders from the mainland altogether. But colonial reinforcements arrived from the north, and Cherokees joined English settlers to fight the Creeks, their ancient enemies.

The war pointed up both the difficulty of achieving unity among the Indians and their critical dependence on European weapons. When the Creeks and Yamasees ran out of ammunition and could not repair their broken guns, their cause was lost. The Yamasees moved south to Florida, and the Creeks retreated to villages in the west.

That the Yamasees could escape by migrating southward exposed the one remaining gap in the line of English coastal settlements, the area between South Carolina's southern border and Spanish Florida. The gap was plugged in 1732 with the chartering of Georgia, the last of the colonies that would become part of the United States. Intended as a haven for English debtors by its founder James Oglethorpe, Georgia was specifically designed as a garrison province. Since all its landholders were expected to serve as militiamen to defend English settlements, the charter prohibited women from inheriting or purchasing land in the colony. The charter also prohibited slavery and the use of alcoholic beverages. Such provisions reveal the founders' intention that Georgia should be peopled by sturdy, sober yeoman farmers who could take up their weapons at a moment's notice against Indians or Spaniards. None of the original conditions of the charter were enforced, however, and all of them had been abandoned by 1752, when Georgia became a royal colony.

Founding of Georgia

In the Northeast, relationships were complicated by the number of European and Indian nations involved in the fur trade. The key players were the Iroquois, not one tribe but five—the Mohawks, Oneidas, Onondagas, Cayugas, and Senecas. (In 1722, the Tuscaroras became the sixth.) Under the terms of a defensive alliance forged early in the sixteenth century, decisions of war and peace for the entire Iroquois Confederacy were made by a council of tribal representatives. Each nation retained some autonomy, and none could be forced to comply with a council directive against its will.

Iroquois Confederacy

The Iroquois were unique among Native Americans, not only because of the strength and persistence of their alliance but also because of the role played by their clan matrons. The older women of each village chose its chief and could either start wars (by calling for the capture of prisoners to replace dead relatives) or stop them (by refusing to supply warriors with necessary foodstuffs).

Before the arrival of Europeans, the Iroquois waged wars primarily to acquire captives to replenish their population. The Europeans' coming created an economic motive for warfare: the desire to control the fur trade and gain unimpeded access to European goods. The war with the Hurons in the 1640s (see page 29) was but the first of a series of conflicts with other tribes known as the Beaver Wars, in which the Iroquois fought desperately to maintain a dominant position in the trade.

In the mid-1670s, just when they were achieving their goal, the French stepped in; an Iroquois triumph would have destroyed France's plans to trade directly with the Indians of the Great Lakes and Mississippi valley. Over the next twenty years the French launched repeated attacks on Iroquois villages. The English offered little assistance other than weapons to their trading partners. Their people and resources depleted by constant warfare, the Iroquois in 1701 negotiated neutrality treaties with France, England, and their Indian neighbors. For the next half-century they maintained their power through trade and skillful diplomacy rather than warfare.

The wars against the Iroquois Confederacy were crucial components of French Canada's plan to penetrate the heartland of North America. The plan included the explorations of Father Jacques Marquette, Louis Jolliet, and Robert Cavelier de La Salle in the Great Lakes and Mississippi valley regions in the 1670s. French officials hoped a trade route to Mexico would be found; La Salle sought to monopolize the fur trade by establishing trading posts along the Mississippi River.

French Expansion

Unlike Spaniards, French adventurers did not attempt to subjugate the Native Americans they encountered or even to claim the territory formally for France. Still, when France decided to strengthen its presence near the Gulf of Mexico by founding New Orleans in 1718—to counter both the westward thrust of the English colonies and the eastward moves of the Spanish—the Mississippi posts became the glue of empire (see map).

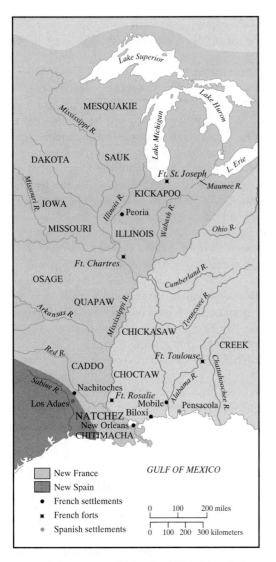

Louisiana, ca. 1720 *By 1720, French forts and settlements dotted the Mississippi River and its tributaries in the interior of North America. Two isolated Spanish outposts were situated near the Gulf of Mexico.* Source: Adapted from *France in America*, by William J. Eccles. Copyright ©1972 by William J. Eccles. Reprinted by permission of Harper-Collins Publishers Inc.

Most of the posts consisted of a small military garrison and a priest, surrounded by powerful Indian nations. The Indians permitted French soldiers and traders to remain among them because they wanted easy access to valuable European goods. The French, for their part, sought political as well as economic ends, attempting to prevent the English from encroaching too far into the interior. Their goals were limited; they neither engaged in systematic efforts to convert nearby Native American peoples to Christianity nor coveted substantial amounts of their land for agricultural purposes.

Matters were very different in the English colonies, where white colonists had an avid interest in acquiring more land. By the early 1670s, some Virginians were eagerly eyeing rich lands north of the York River that early treaties had reserved for Native Americans. Using as a pretext the July 1675 killing of an English servant by some Doeg Indians, the settlers attacked not only the Doegs but also the powerful Susquehannocks. In retaliation, Susquehannock bands raided frontier plantations in the winter of 1676. The land-hungry Anglo-Americans rallied behind the leadership of Nathaniel Bacon, a recently arrived planter, who wanted "to ruine and extirpate all Indians in general." Governor William Berkeley, however, hoped to avoid setting off a major war.

Bacon's Rebellion

Berkeley and Bacon soon clashed. After Bacon forced the House of Burgesses to authorize him to attack the Indians, Berkeley declared Bacon and his men to be in rebellion. As the chaotic summer of 1676 wore on, Bacon alternately pursued Indians and battled with the governor's supporters. In September Bacon marched on Jamestown itself and burned the capital to the ground. But when Bacon died of dysentery the following month, the rebellion collapsed. Even so, a new treaty signed in 1677 opened much of the disputed territory to English settlement.

More than coincidentally, New England—also colonized more than fifty years earlier—was wracked by conflict with Native Americans at precisely the same time. In each area, the colonists' original accommodation with the Indians no longer satisfied both parties.

In the half-century since the founding of New England, colonial settlement had spread far into the interior. In the process, the colonists had completely surrounded the ancestral lands of the Pokanokets (Wampanoags) on Narragansett Bay. Their chief, Metacom (known to the English as King Philip), was troubled by encroachments on Pokanoket lands and equally concerned about the impact European culture and Christianity were having on his people. Metacom led his warriors in attacks on nearby communities in June 1675.

King Philip's War

The Nipmucks and the Narragansetts soon joined Metacom's forces. In the fall, the three tribes jointly attacked settlements in the northern Connecticut River valley. In early 1676, they devastated well-established villages and even attacked Plymouth and Providence. Altogether, the alliance totally destroyed twelve of the ninety Puritan towns and attacked forty others.

New England's very survival seemed at stake. But the tide turned in the summer of 1676, as the Indian coalition ran short of food and ammunition. After Metacom was killed in an ambush in August, the alliance crumbled. Many surviving Pokanokets, Nipmucks, and Narragansetts were captured and sold into slavery in the West Indies. The power of New England's coastal tribes had been broken. Thereafter they lived in small clusters, subordinated to the colonists and often working as servants or sailors.

 ## New England and the Web of Imperial Trade

From the early years of colonization to the close of the seventeenth century, New England changed in three major ways. The population grew dramatically; the residents' relationship to Puritanism altered; and the economy developed in unanticipated ways.

By 1700, New England's population had quadrupled to reach approximately 100,000. Such an increase placed great pressure on available land, and many third- and fourth-generation New Englanders had to migrate—north to New Hampshire or Maine, south to New York, west beyond the Connecticut River—to find sufficient farmland for themselves and their children. Others abandoned agriculture and learned skills like blacksmithing or carpentry.

Population Pressures

The passage of time also brought changes in Puritanism, for two of the Puritans' fundamental beliefs came inevitably into conflict. Puritans practiced infant baptism, yet at the same time they insisted that only the saved could be members of their churches. No one foresaw the problem that confronted congregations in the 1660s: young people baptized as children married and had babies before undergoing the searching examination of their faith required to join a church. Could the offspring of such couples be baptized? The need to answer that question led in 1662 to the adoption of the so-called Halfway Covenant, which established a category of "halfway" membership in Puritan congregations. If previously baptized adults acknowledged the church's authority over them, the ministers declared, they could have their children baptized.

By the 1660s, women were far more likely than men to become either full or halfway members of Puritan congregations. This phenomenon prompted Cotton Mather, the most prominent member of a family of distinguished ministers, to deliver sermons outlining women's proper role in church and society—the first formal examination of that theme in American history. Mather advised American women to be submissive to their husbands, watchful of their children, and attentive to religious duty.

Women, Men, and Puritan Churches

But why had New England's men become more reluctant to acknowledge the church's authority over them? One historian hypothesizes that the connection between church membership and political obligation was critical. Believing that unchurched men were unlikely to be elected to office, male New Englanders may well have failed to join congregations because they wanted to avoid having to serve as constables or militia officers. Such jobs not only took them away from their farms and families but also could cause dissension in their neighborhoods. Others hypothesize that men in seaport towns like Boston and Salem became more worldly and less interested in religion as the economy of the New England colonies changed.

Initially, New England's economy rested on two foundations: the fur trade and the constant flow of migrants. Together, those had allowed New Englanders to acquire the manufactured goods they

New England's First Economy needed. The fur trade gave them valuable pelts to sell in England, and the migrants were always willing to exchange clothing and other items for the earlier settlers' surplus seed, grains, and livestock. But New England's supply of furs was quickly exhausted by excessive trapping, and the migrants stopped coming after the English Civil War began. Thus in the early 1640s that first economic system collapsed.

The Puritans then began a search for new markets and salable crops. They found the trade goods in fish, grain, and wood products. By 1643 they had also found the markets: the Wine Islands and the English colonies in the Caribbean, which lacked precisely the goods that New England could produce in abundance: cheap food (corn and salted fish) to feed to slaves and wood for barrels to hold wine and molasses (the form in which sugar was shipped).

Thus developed the series of transactions that has become known, inaccurately, as the triangular trade. The northern colonists sold their goods in the West Indies and elsewhere to earn the money with which

Atlantic Trading System to purchase English imports. There soon grew up in New England's ports a cadre of merchants who acquired—usually through barter—cargoes of timber and foodstuffs, which they then dispatched to the West Indies for sale. In the Caribbean, the ships sailed from island to island, exchanging fish, barrel staves, and grains

for molasses, fruit, spices, and slaves. Once they had a full load, the ships returned to Boston, Newport, or New Haven to dispose of their cargoes.

Most important, northerners distilled West Indian molasses into rum, a key component of the only part of the trade that could be termed triangular. Rhode Islanders took rum to Africa and traded it for slaves, whom they carried to the West Indies to exchange for more molasses to produce still more rum. With that exception, the trading pattern was not a triangle but a shifting set of two-way voyages (see map, page 59).

The New Englanders who ventured into commerce were soon differentiated from their rural counterparts by their ties to a wider transatlantic world and their preoccupation with material endeavors. As time passed, increasing numbers of Puritans became involved in trade. Small investors who owned shares of voyages soon dominated the field numerically if not monetarily.

The gulf between commercial and farming interests widened after 1660, when, with Stuart Restoration, merchants who were members of the Church of England (Anglicans) began to migrate to New England. Such men had little stake in the survival of Massachusetts Bay and Connecticut in their original forms, and some were openly antagonistic to Puritan traditions. As non-Congregationalists they were denied the vote, but they were still taxed to support the church. Further, Anglicans were forbidden to practice their own religion freely. They resented their exclusion from the governing elite, believing that their wealth and social status entitled them to political power. Congregationalist clergymen returned their hostility, preaching sermons lamenting New England's new commercial orientation. But the ministers spoke for the past, because by the 1670s colonial America, including New England, was part of an international trading network upon which Anglo-America's prosperity depended.

English officials seeking a new source of revenue after the disruptions of the Civil War realized that the colonies could make important contributions to England's economic well-being. Addi-

Mercantilism tional tax revenues could put England back on a sound fi-

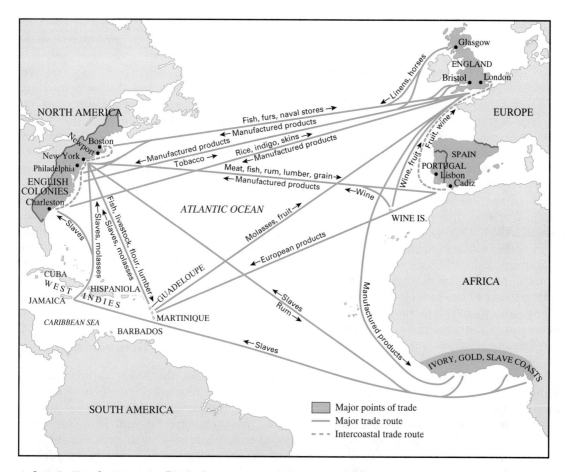

Atlantic Trade Routes   *By the late seventeenth century, the countries and colonies bordering the Atlantic Ocean were linked by an elaborate trade network. The most valuable commodities exchanged were enslaved people and the products of slave labor.*

nancial footing, and English merchants wanted to ensure that they—not their Dutch rivals—reaped the benefits of trading with the English colonies. Parliament and the restored Stuart monarchs accordingly began to draft laws designed to confine the profits of colonial trade primarily to the mother country.

England based its commercial policy on a series of assumptions about the operations of the world's economic system. Collectively, these assumptions are usually called *mercantilism*, though the term and the theory were formulated only a century later. The economic world was seen as a collection of national states, whose governments actively competed for shares of a finite amount of

wealth. Each nation's goal was to become as economically self-sufficient as possible while maintaining a favorable balance of trade with other countries by exporting more than it imported. Under the system, colonies could supply the mother country with valuable raw materials and serve as markets for the mother country's manufactured goods.

Parliament applied mercantilist thinking to the American colonies in laws known as the Navigation Acts. The major acts—passed between 1651 and 1673—established three main principles. First, only English or colonial merchants and ships could engage

Navigation Acts

in trade in the colonies. Second, certain valuable American products could be sold only in the mother country or in other English colonies. At first, these "enumerated" goods were wool, sugar, tobacco, indigo, ginger, and dyes; later acts added rice, naval stores (masts, spars, pitch, tar, and turpentine), copper, and furs to the list. Third, all foreign goods destined for sale in the colonies had to be shipped by way of England and were subject to English import duties. Some years later, a new series of laws established a fourth principle: the colonies could not export items (such as wool clothing, hats, or iron) that competed with English products.

The intention of the Navigation Acts was to center American trade on England. The mother country was to benefit from colonial imports and exports. England had first claim on the most valuable colonial exports, and all foreign imports into the colonies had to pass through England first, enriching its customs revenues in the process. Some colonies, like those in the West Indies and the Chesapeake, were adversely affected by the laws because they could not seek new markets for their staple crops. In others, the impact was less severe. The northern and middle colonies, for example, produced such nonenumerated goods as fish, flour, and barrel staves that could be traded directly to foreign purchasers as long as they were carried in English or American ships.

The English authorities soon learned that it was easier to write mercantilist legislation than to enforce it. The many harbors of the American coast provided ready havens for smugglers, and colonial officials often ignored the sale of illegally imported goods. Consequently, Parliament in 1696 enacted another Navigation Act. This law established in America a number of vice-admiralty courts, which operated without juries. Because American juries had already demonstrated a tendency to favor local smugglers over customs officers, Parliament decided to remove Navigation Act cases from the regular colonial courts.

England took another major step in colonial administration in 1696 by creating the fifteen-member Board of Trade and Plantations, which

Board of Trade and Plantations

thereafter served as the chief organ of government concerned with the American colonies. (Previously, no single body had that responsibility.) It gathered information, reviewed Crown appointments in America, scrutinized legislation passed by colonial assemblies, supervised trade policies, and advised successive ministries on colonial issues. Still, the Board of Trade did not have any direct powers of enforcement. It also shared jurisdiction over American affairs with the customs service, the navy, and the secretary of state for the southern department, the member of the ministry responsible for the colonies. In short, supervision of the American provinces remained decentralized and haphazard.

 ## Colonial Political Development and Imperial Reorganization

English officials in the 1670s and 1680s confronted not only resistance to the Navigation Acts but also a bewildering array of colonial governments. Massachusetts Bay and Plymouth functioned under their original charters. Neighboring Connecticut (including the formerly independent New Haven) and Rhode Island had been granted charters by Charles II in 1662 and 1663, respectively. Virginia was a royal colony, and New York also became one when its proprietor ascended the throne in 1685 as James II. All the other mainland settlements were proprietorships.

Still, in political structure the colonies shared certain characteristics. Most were ruled by a governor and a two-house legislature. In New England, the governors were

Colonial Political Structures

elected by property-holding men or by the legislature; in the Chesapeake and the middle colonies, they were appointed by the king or the proprietor. A council, either elected or appointed, advised the governor on matters of policy and sometimes served as the colony's highest court. The councils also served as upper houses of colonial legislatures. At first, councilors and elected representatives met jointly to debate and adopt laws affecting the colony. But as time passed, the fundamental differences between the two legislative groups' purposes and constituencies led them to separate. Thus developed the two-house legislature still used in almost all of the states.

Meanwhile, local political institutions were taking shape. In New England, elected selectmen initially governed the towns, but by the end of the century town meetings—held at least annually and attended by most free adult male residents—handled matters of local concern. In the Chesapeake colonies and both of the Carolinas, appointed justices of the peace ran local governments. At first the same was true in Pennsylvania, but by the early eighteenth century elected county officials began to take over some government functions. And in New York, local elections were the rule even before the establishment of the colonial assembly in 1683.

Thus by the late seventeenth century, Anglo-American colonists everywhere were accustomed to a considerable degree of local political autonomy. Those who owned property expected to have a voice in how they were governed—and especially how they were taxed. These expectations clashed with those of the crown. James II and his successors sought to bring order to the apparently chaotic state of colonial administration by tightening the reins of government and reducing the colonies' political autonomy. They began to chip away at the privileges granted in colonial charters and to reclaim proprietorships for the Crown. New Hampshire (1679), its parent colony Massachusetts (1691), New Jersey (1702), and the Carolinas (1729) all became royal colonies. The charters of Rhode Island, Connecticut, Maryland, and Pennsylvania were temporarily suspended but ultimately were restored to their original status.

The most drastic reordering of colonial administration targeted Puritan New England, which English officials believed was a hotbed of smuggling. Moreover, Puritans refused to allow freedom of religion to non-Congregationalists and insisted on maintaining laws that ran

Dominion of New England

counter to English practice. New England thus seemed an appropriate place to exert English authority with greater vigor. The charters of all the colonies from New Jersey to Maine (then part of Massachusetts) were revoked, and a Dominion of New England was established in 1686. Sir Edmund Andros, the governor, was given immense power: all the assemblies were dissolved, and he needed only the consent of an appointed council to make laws and levy taxes.

New Englanders endured Andros's autocratic rule for more than two years. Then came the dramatic news that James II had been overthrown in a bloodless coup known as the Glorious Revolution and had been replaced on the throne by his daughter Mary and her husband, the Dutch prince William of Orange. James II had levied taxes without parliamentary approval. He also had announced his conversion to Roman Catholicism. Through the Glorious Revolution, Parliament affirmed its supremacy and that of Protestantism. Meanwhile, New Englanders jailed Andros, proclaimed their loyalty to William and Mary, and wrote to England for instructions about the form of government they should adopt.

Glorious Revolution in America

In other American colonies, too, the Glorious Revolution was a signal for revolt. In Maryland the Protestant Association overturned the government of the Catholic proprietor, and in New York a militia officer of German origin, Jacob Leisler, assumed control of the government. Like the New Englanders, the Maryland and New York rebels saw themselves as carrying out the colonial phase of the English revolt against Stuart absolutism.

William and Mary, however, like James II, believed that England should exercise tighter control over its unruly American possessions. Consequently, the only American rebellion that received royal sanction was that in Maryland, primarily because of its anti-Catholic thrust. In New York, Jacob Leisler was hanged for treason, and Massachusetts (including the formerly independent jurisdiction of Plymouth) became a royal colony with an appointed governor. The province was allowed to retain its town meeting system of local government and to elect its council, but the new charter issued in 1691 eliminated the traditional religious test for voting and officeholding. An Anglican parish was set up in the heart of Boston.

Compounding New England's difficulties in a time of political upheaval and economic uncertainty was a war with the French and their Native American allies. King Louis XIV of France allied himself with the deposed James II, and England declared war on France in 1689. The conflict, which lasted until 1697, was known in Europe as the War of the League of Augsburg, but the colonists called it King William's War. The American war was fought chiefly on the northern frontiers of New England and New York.

In this period of extreme stress an outbreak of witchcraft accusations occurred in Salem Village (now Danvers), Massachusetts. Like their contemporaries elsewhere, seventeenth-century New Englanders believed in the existence of witches. Before 1689, 103 New Englanders, most of them middle-aged women, had been charged with practicing witchcraft, chiefly by neighbors who attributed their misfortunes to the suspected witch. Only a few of the accused were convicted, and fewer still were executed.

Witchcraft in Salem Village

The crisis began in early 1692 when a group of girls and young women accused some older female neighbors of having bewitched them. Before the hysteria spent itself ten months later, nineteen people (including several men, most of them related to convicted female witches) were hanged, one was pressed to death with heavy stones, and more than one hundred persons were jailed. The events at Salem Village can best be understood when seen in the context of political and legal disorder, Indian war, and religious and economic crises. These factors undermined the sense of security Puritan New Englanders had about their future.

Nowhere was that more true than in Salem Village, a farming town torn between old and new styles of life because of its position on the edge of the bustling port of Salem. And no residents of the village had more reason to feel insecure than those who issued the first accusations. Many had been orphaned in recent Indian attacks on Maine and

No seventeenth-century New Englander ever drew a picture of a witchcraft trial or execution, but an artist did record the hanging of several witches in England around 1650. The multiple executions of Salem witches in the summer of 1692 probably resembled this gallows scene.   Folger Shakespeare Library.

were living in Salem Village as domestic servants. Their involvement with witchcraft began as an experiment with fortunetelling as a means of foreseeing their futures, in particular the identities of their eventual husbands. As the most powerless people in a town apparently powerless to direct its fate, they offered a compelling explanation for the seemingly endless chain of troubles afflicting their province: it was under direct attack from the Devil and his legion of witches. Accordingly, it is not so much the number of witchcraft prosecutions that seems surprising but rather their abrupt cessation in the fall of 1692.

There were three reasons for the rapid end to the crisis. First, the accusers grew too bold. When they began to charge some of the colony's most distinguished and respected residents with being in league with the Devil, members of the ruling elite began to doubt their veracity. Second, the colony's ministers formally expressed strong reservations about the validity of the spectral evidence used against most of the accused. Third, the implementation of the new royal charter ended the worst period of political uncertainty, eliminating a major source of stress.

Over the course of the next three decades, Massachusetts and the rest of the English colonies in America accommodated themselves to the new imperial order. While resenting the officials sent to implement English policies, most colonists adjusted to the trade restrictions imposed by the Navigation Acts. They fought another imperial war—the War of the Spanish Succession, or Queen Anne's War—from 1702 to 1713, without enduring the stresses of the first. Colonists who allied themselves with royal government received patronage in the form of offices and land grants and composed "court parties" that supported English officials. Others, who were either less fortunate in their friends or more principled in defense of colonial autonomy, made up the opposition, or "country" interest. By the end of the first quarter of the eighteenth century, most men in both groups had been born in America and were members of elite families.

 Conclusion

The eighty years from 1640 to 1720 established the basic economic and political patterns that were to structure all subsequent changes in mainland colonial society. In 1640 there were just two isolated centers of English population, New England and the Chesapeake. In 1720, nearly the entire east coast of North America was in English hands, and Indian power east of the Appalachian Mountains had been broken. What had been a migrant population was now mostly American-born; economies originally based on the fur trade had become far more complex and more closely linked with the mother country; and a wide variety of political structures had been reshaped into a more uniform pattern. Yet at the same time the introduction of large-scale slavery into the Chesapeake and the Carolinas irrevocably differentiated their societies from those of the colonies to the north.

Meanwhile, the Spanish had expanded from the small outpost in Sante Fe, New Mexico, to Texas and California. As for the French, they dominated the length of the Mississippi River and the Great Lakes region. The extensive Spanish and French presence to the south and west of the English settlements meant that future conflicts among the European powers in North America were nearly inevitable.

By 1720, the essential elements of the imperial administrative structure that would govern the English colonies until 1775 were firmly in place. The regional economic systems originating in the late seventeenth and early eighteenth centuries also continued to dominate North American life for another century—until after independence had been won. And Anglo-Americans had developed the commitment to autonomous local government that later would lead them into conflict with Parliament and the king.

Suggestions for Further Reading

General

Wesley Frank Craven, *The Colonies in Transition, 1660–1713* (1968); W. J. Eccles, *France in America*, rev. ed. (1990); Jack P. Greene and J. R. Pole, eds., *Colonial British America* (1984).

New Netherland and the Restoration Colonies

Edwin Bronner, *William Penn's "Holy Experiment": The Founding of Pennsylvania, 1681–1701* (1962); Wesley Frank Craven, *New Jersey and the English Colonization of North America* (1964); Joyce Goodfriend, *Before the Melting Pot: Society and Culture in Colonial New York City, 1664–1730* (1992); Oliver Rink, *Holland on the Hudson: An Economic and Social History of Dutch New York* (1986); Robert C. Ritchie, *The Duke's Province: A Study of Politics and Society in Colonial New York, 1660–1691* (1977); Robert M. Weir, *Colonial South Carolina: A History* (1983).

Africa and the Slave Trade

Jay Coughtry, *The Notorious Triangle: Rhode Island and the African Slave Trade, 1700–1807* (1981); Joseph Inikori and Stanley Engerman, eds., *The Atlantic Slave Trade* (1992); Robin Law, *The Slave Coast of West Africa, 1550–1750: The Impact of the Atlantic Slave Trade on an African Society* (1991); Daniel C. Littlefield, *Rice and Slaves: Ethnicity and the Slave Trade in Colonial South Carolina* (1981); James Rawley, *The Transatlantic Slave Trade: A History* (1981); Barbara Solow, ed., *Slavery and the Rise of the Atlantic System* (1991).

Africans in Anglo-America

Douglas Deal, *Race and Class in Colonial Virginia: Indians, Englishmen, and Africans on the Eastern Shore During the Seventeenth Century* (1993); Allan Kulikoff, *Tobacco and Slaves: The Development of Southern Cultures in the Chesapeake, 1680–1800* (1986); Edgar J. McManus, *Black Bondage in the North* (1973); Peter H. Wood, *Black Majority: Negroes in Colonial South Carolina from 1670 Through the Stono Rebellion* (1974).

European–Native American Relations in the North

Russell Bourne, *The Red King's Rebellion: Racial Politics in New England, 1675–1678* (1991); John Demos, *The Unredeemed Captive: A Family Story from Early America* (1994); Matthew Dennis, *Cultivating a Landscape of Peace: Iroquois-European Encounter in Seventeenth-Century America* (1993); Michael Puglisi, *Puritans Beseiged: The Legacies of King Philip's War in the Massachusetts Bay Colony* (1991); Daniel Richter, *The Ordeal of the Longhouse: The Peoples of the Iroquois League in the Era of European Colonization* (1992); Richard White, *The Middle Ground: Indians, Empires, and Republics in the Great Lakes Region, 1650–1815* (1991).

European–Native American Relations in the South and West

Verner W. Crane, *The Southern Frontier, 1660–1732* (1929); Elizabeth A. H. John, *Storms Brewed in Other Men's Worlds: The Confrontation of Indians, Spanish, and French in the Southwest, 1540–1795* (1975); Andrew Knaut, *The Pueblo Revolt of 1680* (1995); James Merrell, *The Indians' New World: Catawbas and Their Neighbors from European Contact through the Era of Removal* (1989); Daniel H. Usner, Jr., *Indians, Settlers, and Slaves in a Frontier Exchange Economy: The Lower Mississippi Valley before 1783* (1992).

New England

Bernard Bailyn, *The New England Merchants in the Seventeenth Century* (1955); Christine Heyrman, *Commerce and Culture: The Maritime Communities of Colonial Massachusetts, 1690–1750* (1984); Richard Melvoin, *New England Outpost: War and Society in Colonial Deerfield* (1990); Amanda Porterfield, *Female Piety in Puritan New England* (1991); Laurel Thatcher Ulrich, *Good Wives: Image and Reality in the Lives of Women in Northern New England, 1650–1750* (1982).

New England Witchcraft

Paul Boyer and Stephen Nissenbaum, *Salem Possessed: The Social Origins of Witchcraft* (1974); Elaine Breslaw, *Tituba, Reluctant Witch of Salem: Devilish Indians and Puritan Fantasies* (1996); John Demos, *Entertaining Satan: Witchcraft and the Culture of Early New England* (1982); Peter Hoffer, *The Devil's Disciples: Makers of the Salem Witchcraft Trials* (1996); Carol Karlsen, *The Devil in the Shape of a Woman: Witchcraft in Early New England* (1987); Bernard Rosenthal, *Salem Story: Reading the Witch Trials of 1692* (1993).

Imperial and Colonial Politics

Robert M. Bliss, *Revolution and Empire: English Politics and the American Colonies in the Seventeenth Century* (1991); Lawrence W. Harper, *The English Navigation Laws: A Seventeenth-Century Experiment in Social Engineering* (1939); Richard P. Johnson, *Adjustment to Empire: The New England Colonies, 1675–1715* (1981); David S. Lovejoy, *The Glorious Revolution in America* (1972); Robert C. Ritchie, *Captain Kidd and the War Against the Pirates* (1986); I. K. Steele, *Politics of Colonial Policy: The Board of Trade in Colonial Administration* (1968); Stephen Saunders Webb, *Lord Churchill's Coup: The Anglo-American Empire and the Glorious Revolution Reconsidered* (1995); Stephen Saunders Webb, *1676: The End of American Independence* (1984); Stephen Saunders Webb, *The Governors-General: The English Army and the Definition of the Empire, 1569–1681* (1979).

CHAPTER

4

Growth and Diversity
1720–1770

Maturina, a free black resident of New Orleans, awoke with a start at 3 A.M. on June 2, 1782, to the shouts of her neighbor, a slave woman named Louisa. "Maturina, someone has stolen your hens!" Louisa yelled. Leaping from her bed, Maturina ran to investigate. She knew where to look for missing chickens. At dawn, Maturina went with her son and her brother Nicolas to the city market on the levee (river bank), where they soon encountered a man carrying her three fowls. By threatening him with prosecution, they learned that he had purchased the hens from a French grocer named La Rochelle. So the three confronted La Rochelle at his hut. Under questioning, the grocer reluctantly admitted that "it was a negro who had brought them to him to sell." Suspicious, Maturina searched La Rochelle's own hut, rousting out the thief, who was hiding within. He tried to escape, but Nicolas pursued and captured him. Brought before the authorities, the thief proved to be Juan, a runaway slave from the countryside.

That much of this action took place on the Mississippi River levee is not surprising. In the mid-eighteenth century, the crude market centered there was a focal point of New Orleans. To the levee came Indian traders, French and German farmers, free and enslaved Africans—all intent on buying and selling.

The lively markets in New Orleans and Anglo-American cities such as Boston and Philadelphia illuminate several key themes of colonial development in the mid-eighteenth century: population growth, ethnic diversity, the increasing importance of colonial urban centers, the creation of an urban elite that purchased food and clothing from other colonists, rising levels of consumption for all social ranks, and the new significance of internal markets. In the French and English mainland colonies, exports continued to dominate the economy. Yet expanding local populations demanded greater quantities and types of goods, and Europe could not supply all those needs. As a result, colonists came increasingly to depend on exploiting and consuming their own resources.

Ethnic diversity was especially pronounced in the small colonial cities, but even the countryside attracted settlers from a wide range of nations. Only the Spanish Borderlands and rural New England had few resident newcomers. The middle and southern Anglo-American colonies attracted by far the largest number of immigrants, both free and enslaved. Their arrival swelled the total population, altered political balances, and affected the religious climate by introducing new sects.

The ruling elites in the colonies paid little heed to the newcomers. In New France and New Spain, ordinary settlers were already denied any voice in their government, but even in Anglo-America elected and appointed leaders often refused to allow recent migrants from Europe adequate representation and government services. A series of violent clashes ensued after midcentury. By that time, native-born elites dominated the English colonies and contended with governors and other officials born in the mother country for control of the government machinery.

Intermarried webs of wealthy families developed in each of Europe's American possessions by the 1760s. Such well-off, educated colonists participated in transatlantic intellectual communities, whereas many colonists of the "lesser sort" could neither read nor write. The elites lived comfortably, while most colonists, whether free or enslaved, struggled just to survive. Such divisions were most pronounced in British America, where by 1750 the social and economic distance among different ranks of Anglo-Americans had widened noticeably.

Wealthy Anglo-Americans in particular were heavily influenced by the Enlightenment, the prevailing European intellectual movement of the day. The Enlightenment stressed reason and empirical knowledge, deliberately discarding superstition and instinct as guides to human behavior. Enlightened thinkers saw God as a distant presence who had ordered the world, setting forth natural laws that humans could discover through careful investigation and logical thought. Thus the religious revival known as the Great Awakening, which erupted in the English colonies in the 1740s, aroused much opposition from elites because that revival drew primarily on the Calvinist concept of a God that people could never fully comprehend.

In 1720, much of the North American continent still fell under Indian control. By 1770, settlements of Europeans and Africans ruled by Great Britain filled almost all of the region between the Appalachian Mountains and the Atlantic Ocean; and the British, thanks to their victory over France in the Seven Years War (see pages 86–88), dominated the extensive system of rivers and lakes running through the heart of the continent. Spanish missions extended in a great arc from present-day northern California to the Gulf Coast. Such geographic, economic, and social changes transformed the character of Europe's North American possessions.

 ## Population Growth and Ethnic Diversity

One of the most striking characteristics of the English mainland colonies in the eighteenth century was their rapid population growth. Only about 250,000 European- and African-Americans resided in the colonies in 1700; by 1775, 2.5 million lived there. Such rapid expansion appears even more remarkable when compared to the modest changes that occurred in Louisiana, New Mexico, California, and Texas. By the last quarter of the eighteenth century, Texas had only about 2,500 Spanish residents and California even fewer; the largest Spanish colony, New Mexico, included just 20,000 or so. The total European population of New France was about 70,000 in the 1760s, but only between Quebec and Montréal and in New Orleans were there significant concentrations of French settlers.

• *Important Events* •

1691	Locke's *Two Treatises of Government* published, applying Enlightenment thought to the realm of politics
1739	Stono Rebellion (South Carolina) leads to increased white fears of slave revolts
	George Whitefield arrives in America; Great Awakening broadens
1739–48	King George's War disrupts American economy
1740	Black population of Chesapeake begins to grow by natural increase, contributing to rise of large plantations
1741	New York City "conspiracy" reflects whites' continuing fears of slave revolts
1760s	Baptist congregations take root in Virginia
1760–75	Peak of eighteenth-century European and African migration to English colonies
1765–66	Hudson River land riots pit tenants and squatters against large landlords
1767–69	Regulator movement (South Carolina) tries to establish order in back country
1771	North Carolina Regulators defeated by eastern militia at Battle of Alamance

Although migration accounted for a considerable share of the growth in English America, most of the growth resulted from natural increase. Once the difficult early decades of settlement had passed, the American population doubled approximately every twenty-five years. Such a rate of growth was then unparalleled in human history. Among its causes were women's youthful age at the onset of childbearing. Since married women became pregnant every two or three years, women normally bore five to ten children. Because the colonies were healthful places to live (especially north of Virginia), a large proportion of children who survived infancy reached maturity and began families of their own. As a result, about half of the American population was under sixteen years old in 1775. (By contrast, only about one-third of the American population was under sixteen in 1990.)

Africans (about 278,000) constituted the largest racial or ethnic group that came to the mainland English colonies during the eighteenth century.

Newcomers from Africa and Europe

In the slaveholding societies of South America and the Caribbean, a surplus of males over females and appallingly high mortality rates meant that only a large, continuing flow of enslaved Africans could maintain the captive work force at constant levels. South Carolina, where rice cultivation was difficult and unhealthy, bore some resemblance to such colonies. But in the Chesapeake the number of black residents grew especially rapidly, because the new African workers were added to a population that began to sustain itself through natural increase after 1740.

The offspring of slaves were also slaves, whereas the children of servants were free. The consequences of this important difference between enslaved and indentured labor were not clear until after 1720. It then became evident that a planter who owned adult female slaves could watch the size of his labor force increase steadily—through the births of their children. Not coincidentally, the first truly large Chesapeake plantations appeared in the 1740s.

In addition to the new group of Africans, about 585,000 Europeans moved to North America during the eighteenth century, most of them after 1730 (see maps). Because some of these migrants (for example, convicts sentenced to exile by English courts) and all the slaves did not freely choose to come to the colonies, approximately one-third of the newcomers moved to America against their will.

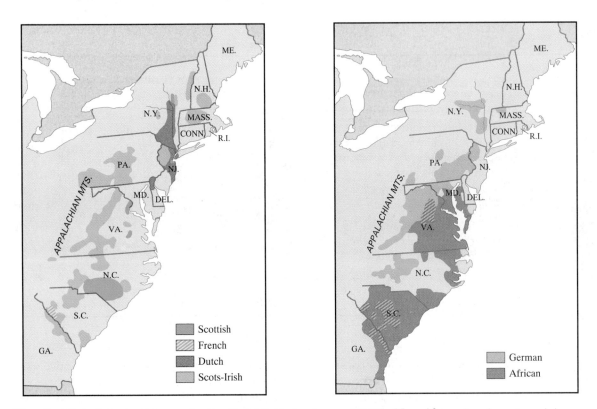

Non-English Ethnic Groups in the British Colonies, c. 1775 *Non-African immigrants arriving in the years after 1720 were pushed to the peripheries of settlement, as is shown by these maps. Scottish, Scots-Irish, French, and German newcomers had to move to the frontiers. The Dutch remained where they had originally settled in the seventeenth century. Africans were concentrated in coastal plantation regions.*

One of the largest groups of immigrants— nearly 150,000—came from Ireland or Scotland. About 66,000 were Scots-Irish, descended from Presbyterian Scots who had settled in the north of Ireland during the seventeenth century. Some 35,000 people came directly to America from Scotland. Another 43,000 migrated from southern Ireland. Fleeing economic distress and religious discrimination, they were also lured by hopes of obtaining land. Scots, Irish, and Scots-Irish immigrants often arrived in Philadelphia. They moved west and south, settling chiefly in Pennsylvania, Maryland, Virginia, and the Caroli-

Scots-Irish, Germans, and Scots

nas. Frequently unable to afford any acreage, they squatted on land belonging to Indians, land speculators, or colonial governments.

Migrants from Germany numbered about 85,000. Most emigrated from the Rhineland between 1730 and 1755, also usually arriving in Philadelphia. By the late 1700s, they and their descendants accounted for one-third of Pennsylvania's residents. But many other Germans moved west and then south along the eastern slope of the Appalachian Mountains, eventually finding homes in western Maryland and Virginia. Others sailed first to Charleston or Savannah and settled in the interior of South Carolina or Georgia. The Germans belonged to a wide variety of Protestant sects and therefore added to the already substantial religious diversity of the middle colonies.

The most concentrated period of immigration to the colonies fell between 1760 and 1775. Tough times in Germany and the British Isles led many to decide to seek a better life in America; simultaneously, the slave trade burgeoned. In those fifteen years alone arrived more than 220,000 persons—or nearly 10 percent of the entire population of British North America in 1775. Late-arriving free immigrants had little choice but to remain in the cities or move to the edges of settlement; land elsewhere was fully occupied.

Because of these migration patterns and the concentration of slaveholding in the South, half of the colonial population south of New England was of non-English origin by 1775. Whether the migrants assimilated readily into Anglo-American culture depended on patterns of settlement, the size of the group, and the strength of the migrants' ties to their common culture. For example, the Huguenots—French Protestants who fled religious persecution in their homeland after 1685—settled in tiny enclaves in American cities but were unable to sustain either their language or their religious practices. Within two generations they were almost wholly absorbed into Anglo-American culture. By contrast, the equally small group of colonial Jews maintained a distinct identity. In a few cities—notably New York and Newport, Rhode Island—they established synagogues and worked actively to preserve their culture. Members of the larger groups of migrants (Germans, Irish, and Scots) found it easier to sustain Old World ways. Countless localities were settled almost exclusively by one group or another.

Effects of Ethnic Diversity

Recognizing the benefits of keeping other racial and ethnic groups divided, the English elites on occasion deliberately fostered antagonisms. When the targets of their policies were European migrants, the goal was the maintenance of political and economic power. When the targets were Indians and Africans, as they were in South Carolina, the stakes were considerably higher. South Carolinians of English origin, a minority of the population, wanted to prevent Indians and Africans from making common cause against them. To foster antagonism, Anglo-Americans employed Indians to catch runaway slaves and used slaves as soldiers in Indian wars.

The elites probably would have preferred to ignore the English colonies' growing racial and ethnic diversity, but they could not do so for long and still maintain their power. When such men decided to lead a revolution in the 1770s, they recognized that they needed the support of non-English Americans. Quite deliberately, they then began to speak of "the rights of man," rather than "English liberties," when they sought recruits for their cause.

Economic Growth and Development

The dramatic increase in the population of Anglo-America served as a source of stability for the colonial economy and provided a firm basis for further growth. Again, a comparison to French and Spanish America reveals significant differences. The population and economy of New Spain's Borderlands stagnated. The isolated settlements produced few items for export (notably, hides and skins); residents were more likely to exchange goods illegally with their French and English neighbors than with the distant centers of Spanish Mexico or the Caribbean. French Canada exported large quantities of furs and fish, but monopolistic trade practices ensured that most of the profits ended up in the home country. The Louisiana colony required substantial government subsidies to survive, despite its active internal trade and some agricultural exports such as tobacco and rice. Of France's American possessions, only the Caribbean islands flourished economically.

British, French, and Spanish Colonies Compared

In British North America, by contrast, each year the rising population generated ever-greater demands for goods and services, which led to the development of small-scale colonial manufacturing and a complex network of internal trade. As the area of settlement expanded, roads, bridges, mills, and stores were built to serve the new communities. A lively coastal trade developed; by the late 1760s, 54 percent of the vessels leaving Boston harbor were sailing to other mainland colonies rather than to foreign ports. Such ships not only collected goods for export and distributed imports but also sold items made in America. The colonies thus began to move away from their earlier pattern of near total dependence on Europe for manufactured goods. For the first time, the American population was generating sufficient demand to encourage manufacturing enterprises. The largest indigenous industry was iron making; by 1775, American furnaces and forges were producing more iron than was England itself.

The major energizing, yet destabilizing, influence on the colonial economy nevertheless remained foreign trade. Colonial prosperity still depended heavily on overseas demand for American products like tobacco, rice, indigo, fish, and barrel staves; the sale of such items earned the colonists the credit they needed to purchase English and European imports. If demand for American exports slowed, the colonists' income dropped and so did their ability to buy imported goods.

Despite fluctuations, the economy grew slowly during the eighteenth century. That growth produced better standards of living for all property-owning Americans. In the first two decades of the century, households began to acquire amenities such as chairs and earthenware dishes. Diet also improved as trading networks brought access to more varied foodstuffs. Thus the colonists became *consumers*, in the sense that for the first time they could make choices among a wide variety of products and also could afford to buy items not absolutely essential for survival and subsistence.

Growth of Consumption

Yet the benefits of economic growth were not evenly distributed: wealthy Americans improved their position relative to other colonists. The native-born elite families who dominated American political, economic, and social life by 1750 were those who had begun the century with sufficient capital to take advantage of the changes caused by population growth. They were urban merchants, large landowners, slave traders, and the owners of rum distilleries. Their rise helped to make the social and economic structure of mid–eighteenth-century America more stratified than before.

Despite the increased stratification, there seems to have been relatively little severe poverty among free settlers in rural areas, where 90 percent of the colonists lived. But in the cities, families of urban laborers lived on the edge of destitution. In Philadelphia, for instance, a male laborer's average annual earnings fell short of the amount needed to supply his family with the bare necessities. Even in a good year, his wife or children had to do wage work; in a bad year, the family could be reduced to beggary. By the 1760s public urban poor-relief systems were overwhelmed with applicants for assistance, and some cities began to build workhouses or almshouses to shelter the growing number of poor people.

Urban Poverty

Within this overall picture, it is important to distinguish among the various regions: New England, the middle colonies, the Chesapeake, and the Lower South (the Carolinas and Georgia). Each region of the colonies had its own economic rhythm derived from the nature of its export trade.

In New England, three elements combined to influence economic development: the nature of the landscape, New England's leadership in colonial shipping, and the impact of imperial wars. New England's poor soil did not produce salable surpluses other than livestock, so wood products constituted a major cash crop. Farms were worked primarily by family members; the region had relatively few hired laborers. It also had the lowest average wealth per freeholder in the colonies. But New England had many wealthy men: merchants and professionals whose income was drawn from trade with the West Indies.

New England and King George's War

Boston, by the 1730s a major shipbuilding center, soon felt the effects when warfare resumed in 1739. British vessels clashed with Spanish ships in the Caribbean, setting off a conflict that became

How do historians know that the residents of colonial North America began to purchase luxury items in the eighteenth century and that those goods came from wide-ranging trade networks? Probate inventories—written records of what people possessed at the time of their deaths—are a useful documentary source. But perhaps even more revealing are the results of archaeological excavations at the sites of colonial settlements. The shards shown on the left were found at one of the first French outposts in Louisiana—Old Mobile, established in 1702 on Mobile Bay, in what is now Alabama. The pots, of which only these small pieces remain (see the complete example), represent the final stage in a long trade route originating in China. The Chinese sold ceramics to traders in the Philippines, which Spain controlled, in exchange for Mexican silver. Spanish ships then carried the porcelain across the Pacific to Mexico, where it was purchased at annual fairs in Acapulco, carried by mule train across Mexico to Vera Cruz, then shipped to Caribbean ports and to Spain itself. The three hundred or so residents of Old Mobile bought such items from the Spanish settlement at Pensacola in nearby Florida. A brief description in an inventory could not convey so much information nearly as vividly as do these small bits of pottery. Fragments: The Magazine Antiques. Pot: The Metropolitan Museum of Art.

known in America as King George's War. Nominally the war was fought to determine who would sit on the Austrian throne (in Europe it was called the War of the Austrian Succession), but one of its causes was European commercial rivalries over the lucrative West Indian trade. The war's first impact on Boston's economy was positive. Area seamen were used by the British as privateers to seize enemy shipping and merchants profited from military supply contracts.

But Boston suffered heavy losses of manpower. Massachusetts's most costly and successful expedition was its 1745 capture of the French fortress of Louisbourg (in modern Nova Scotia), which guarded the sea lanes leading to New France. Afterward, though, Massachusetts had to levy heavy taxes on its residents to pay for the expensive effort. For decades Boston's economy felt the continuing effects of King George's War. Widows and children were put on the relief rolls, taxes remained high, and the shipbuilding boom ceased with the war's end. As a final blow to the colony, Britain gave Louisbourg back to France in the Treaty of Aix-la-Chapelle (1748).

The middle colonies were more positively affected by King George's War and its aftermath because of the greater fertility of the soil in New York and Pennsylvania, where commercial farming was the norm. With the outbreak of hostilities, the middle colonies were able to profit from the wartime demand for grain and meat. After the war poor grain harvests in Europe

Prosperity of the Middle Colonies

caused flour prices to rise rapidly. Philadelphia and New York became agricultural export centers, but Boston, lacking a fertile hinterland, found its economy stagnating.

Increased European demand for grain had a significant impact on the Chesapeake as well. After 1745, some Chesapeake planters began to convert tobacco fields to wheat and corn. By diversifying their crops, they could avoid dependency on one product for their income. Tobacco still ruled the region and remained the largest single export from the mainland colonies. Yet the conversion to grain cultivation brought about the first significant change in Chesapeake settlement patterns by encouraging the development of port towns (like Baltimore) to house the merchants who marketed the new products.

Change in the Chesapeake

Like the Chesapeake, the Lower South depended on staple crops and an enslaved labor force. But in contrast to tobacco prices, which rose slowly through the middle decades of the century, rice prices doubled by the late 1730s. Because Parliament removed rice from the list of enumerated products (see pages 56–60) in 1730, South Carolinians were able to do what colonial tobacco planters never could: trade directly with continental Europe. Dependence on European sales had its drawbacks, however. When the outbreak of King George's War disrupted trade with Europe, rice prices plummeted, and South Carolina entered a depression. Still, prosperity returned by the 1760s. Indeed, the Lower South experienced more rapid economic growth in that period than did the other regions of the colonies. Partly as a result, it had the highest average wealth per freeholder in Anglo-America by the time of the American Revolution.

Trade and the Lower South

The varying economic results of King George's War and its aftermath on the English mainland colonies point up a crucial fact: they did not compose a unified whole. They were linked economically into regions, but they had few political or social ties beyond or even within those regions. Despite the growing coastal trade, the individual colonies' economic fortunes depended not on their neighbors in America but rather on the shifting markets of Europe and the West Indies.

Colonial Cultures

A seventeenth-century resident of England's American possessions miraculously transported to 1750 would have been surprised by what the historian Richard Bushman has termed "the refinement of America." Wealthy colonists spent their money ostentatiously. Most notably, they built large houses containing rooms specifically designed for such forms of socializing as dancing, cardplaying, or drinking tea. Sufficiently well-off to enjoy "leisure" time, they attended the theater, gambled at horseraces, and played games. They also cultivated polite manners, adopting stylized forms of address and paying attention to "proper" ways of behaving. Elite families in New Mexico, Louisiana, and Quebec also set themselves off from the "lesser sort."

Genteel Culture

Affluent men prided themselves not only on their possessions and their positions in the colonial political, social, and economic hierarchy, but also on their level of education and their intellectual connections to Europe. Many had been tutored by private teachers; some even attended college in Europe or America. (Harvard, the first colonial college, was founded in 1636.) In the seventeenth century, studies focused heavily on ancient languages and theology. But by the mid-eighteenth century, colleges broadened their curricula to include courses on mathematics, the natural sciences, law, and medicine. Accordingly, young men from elite or upwardly mobile families enrolled in college to study for careers other than the ministry. Colonial women, however, except for some in Canada and Louisiana who joined convents, were uniformly excluded from advanced education.

Education and the Enlightenment

The learned clergymen who headed colonial colleges in the eighteenth century were deeply affected by the intellectual current known as the Enlightenment. About the middle of the previous century, some European thinkers began to analyze nature in an effort to determine the laws that govern the universe. They employed experimentation and abstract reasoning to discover general principles behind phenomena such as the motions of planets and stars, the behavior of falling objects, and the characteristics of light and sound. Above all, Enlightenment philosophers emphasized acquiring knowledge through reason.

The Enlightenment had an enormous impact on educated, well-to-do people in Europe and America. It supplied them with a common vocabulary and a unified view of the world through which they endeavored to make sense of God's orderly creation. Thus American naturalists like John and William Bartram supplied European scientists with information about New World plants and animals so that they could be included in newly formulated universal classification systems.

Enlightenment rationalism also affected politics. John Locke's *Two Treatises of Government* (1691) challenged previous concepts of a divinely sanctioned political order. Governments, declared Locke, were created by men and so could be altered by them. If a ruler broke his contract with the people and did not protect their rights, he could legitimately be ousted from power by peaceful—or even violent—means. The aim of government was the good of the people, Enlightenment theorists proclaimed. A proper political order could prevent the rise of tyrants; even the power of monarchs was subject to God's natural laws.

Yet the world in which such ideas were discussed was that of the few, not the many. Most residents of North America did not know how to read or write. Books were scarce and expensive, public schools supported by tax levies were few and far between. European youngsters who learned to read were usually taught by their parents or older siblings. A few months at a private "dame school" run by a literate local widow might complete their education by teaching them the basics of writing and simple arithmetic. Enslaved African-American children were denied even that level of learning; teaching slaves to read and write was forbidden as too subversive of the social order. And only the most zeal-

Oral Cultures

ous Indian converts were taught Europeans' literacy skills.

Thus the cultures of colonial North America were primarily oral, communal, and—at least through the first half of the eighteenth century—intensely local. The major means of communication was face-to-face conversation. Information tended to travel slowly and within relatively confined regions. Different locales developed divergent cultural traditions, and racial and ethnic variations heightened those differences. Public rituals served as the chief means through which the colonists forged their cultural identities.

Attendance at church was perhaps the most important such ritual. In Congregational (Puritan) churches, seating was assigned by church leaders to reflect standing in the community. In early New England, men and women sat on opposite sides of a central aisle, arranged in ranks according to age, wealth, and church membership. By the mid-eighteenth century, wealthy men and their wives sat in privately owned pews; their children, servants, and the less fortunate were still seated in sex-segregated fashion at the rear or sides of the church. In eighteenth-century Virginia, seating in Anglican parishes also conformed to the local status hierarchy. In the city of Quebec, Catholic feast days were celebrated by formal processions of men into the parish church; each participant's rank determined his placement in the procession. By contrast, Quaker meetinghouses used an egalitarian but sex-segregated seating system.

Religious Rituals

Communal culture centered on the civic sphere as well. In New England, colonial governments proclaimed official days of thanksgiving and days of fasting and prayer. Everyone was expected to participate in the public rituals held in churches on such occasions. Monthly militia musters also brought the community together, since all able-bodied men between the ages of sixteen and sixty were members of the militia.

Civic Rituals

In the Chesapeake, important cultural rituals occurred on court and election days. When the county court was in session, men would come from miles around to file suits, appear as witnesses, serve as jurors, or simply observe the goings-on. Attendance at court functioned as a method of civic education; from watching the proceedings men learned what behavior their neighbors expected of them. Elections served the same purpose, for freeholders voted in public. An election official, often flanked by the candidates for the office in question, would call each man forward to declare his preference. The voter would then be thanked politely by the gentleman for whom he had cast his oral ballot.

Everywhere in colonial North America, the public punishment of criminals served not just to humiliate the offender but also to remind the community of proper standards of behavior. Public hangings and whippings expressed the community's outrage about crimes and restored harmony to its ranks. Judges often assigned penalties that shamed miscreants in especially appropriate ways. In New Mexico, for example, a man who had assaulted his father-in-law was directed not merely to pay medical expenses but also to kneel before him and to beg his forgiveness publicly, in front of the entire community.

The wide availability of consumer goods after the early years of the eighteenth century fostered new rituals centered on consumption. The rituals began with the acquisition of desirable and often nonessential items in specialty shops. By 1750 New York, Boston, Philadelphia, and New Orleans had many such stores. Even small and medium-size towns had one or two retail establishments by then. A colonist with money to spend would set aside time to "go shopping," a novel and pleasurable activity. The purchase of a desired object—for example, a ceramic bowl or a mirror—marked only the beginning of consumption rituals. Consumers would then deploy their purchases in an appropriate manner: hanging the mirror prominently on a wall of the house or displaying the bowl on a table or sideboard. Individual colonists clearly took personal pleasure in owning lovely objects, but they also could take pride in displaying their acquisitions (and thus their wealth and good taste) publicly to kin and neighbors.

Rituals of Consumption

Tea drinking played an especially important role in Anglo-American consumption rituals. From early in the eighteenth century, households with aspirations to genteel status sought to acquire the items necessary for the proper consumption of tea, including strainers, sugar tongs, bowls, and even special tables. And because of its cost, tea served as a crucial marker of status. Although poor households also consumed tea, they could not afford the fancy equipment used by their better-off neighbors.

Rituals also allowed the disparate cultures of colonial North America to interact with one another. Particularly important were the rituals that developed on what the historian Richard White has termed "the middle ground"—that is, the psychological and geographical space in which Indians and Europeans encountered each other.

When Europeans sought to trade with Indians, they came into contact with an indigenous system of exchange that stressed gift giving rather than formalized buying and selling. Although French and English traders complained constantly about the need to present gifts prior to negotiating for furs and skins, such a step was essential to successful bargaining. Over time, an appropriate ritual developed. A European trader arriving at a village would give gifts (cloth, rum, gunpowder, and other items) to Indian hunters. Eventually, those gifts would be reciprocated. To the detriment of Indian societies, rum became a crucial component of these intercultural trading rituals. With some reason, traders came to believe that drunken Indians would sell their furs more cheaply.

Intercultural Rituals

Rituals surrounding murders were also critical points of cultural interaction. Indians and Europeans both believed that murders required a compensatory act, but the two groups differed on what that act should be. Europeans sought primarily to identify the murderer and to punish, perhaps to kill, that person. Such "eye for an eye" revenge was for Indians only one of many possible responses. Compensation could also be accomplished by capturing someone who could take the dead person's place or—most important for maintaining peace on the frontiers— by "covering the dead," or providing the family of the deceased with goods that could compensate for the loss. Among the French and the Algonkians a ritual evolved in which frontier murders were investigated and murderers identified, but by mutual agreement deaths were usually "covered" by trade goods rather than by blood revenge.

Throughout colonial North America, therefore, rituals both cemented ties and established rank within communities. They also allowed those communities to interact peacefully with one another.

 ## Colonial Families

As Europeans consolidated their hold on the North American continent during the first three quarters of the eighteenth century, Native Americans were

Indian and Mixed-Race Families

forced to adapt to novel circumstances. Bands reduced in numbers by disease and warfare recombined into new units; for example, the group later known as the Catawbas emerged in the 1730s in the western Carolinas from the fragmentary remains of several earlier Indian nations. Likewise, Indian family forms were reshaped under pressure from European secular and religious authorities. Whereas many Indian societies had permitted easy divorce, English, French, and Spanish missionaries frowned on such practices; and those societies that had allowed polygynous marriages (including New England Algonkians) redefined such relationships, designating one wife as "legitimate" and others as "concubines."

Continued high mortality rates in traditional societies gave new importance to extended kin who could assume responsibility for surviving children. Family forms also were affected by European dominance and the accompanying changes in traditional modes of subsistence in an occupied region. In New England, for instance, many Algonkian husbands and wives were unable to live together because they were supporting themselves

by working separately for Anglo-Americans (perhaps wives as domestic servants, husbands as sailors). And in New Mexico, detribalized Navajos, Pueblos, and Apaches employed as servants by Spanish settlers clustered in the small towns of the Borderlands. Known collectively as *genizaros*, they lost contact with Indian cultures and instead lived on the fringes of Hispanic society.

Wherever there were relatively few European women in the population, sexual liaisons occurred among European men and Indian women. The resulting mixed-race population of mestizos and métis worked as a familial "middle ground" to ease other cultural interactions. In New France and the Anglo-American backcountry, such families frequently resided in Indian villages and were enmeshed in trading networks; often, children of these unions became prominent leaders of Native American societies. By contrast, in the Spanish Borderlands the offspring of Europeans and genizaros were treated as degraded individuals.

Family life among the many European migrants to North America was far more stable than that among Indian and mestizo peoples. Fami-

European- American Families

lies (rather than individuals) constituted the basic units of colonial society. Headed by European men or their widows, households were the chief mechanisms of production and consumption. Their members—bound by ties of blood or servitude—worked together to produce goods for consumption or sale. The head of the household represented it to the outside world, managing the finances and holding legal authority over the rest of the family—his wife, his children, and his servants or slaves. (At the time, *family* meant everyone who occupied one house, whether or not they were blood kin.) Such households were considerably larger than American families today. Most of those large families were nuclear—that is, they did not include extended kin like aunts, uncles, or grandparents.

In English, French, and Spanish America alike, the vast majority of European families supported themselves through agriculture. The scale and nature of the work varied: the production of tobacco in the Chesapeake required different sorts of labor from subsistence farming in New England or cattle ranching in New Mexico and Texas. As in the European, African, and Native American societies, household tasks were allocated by sex, discussed in Chapter 1.

The mistress was responsible for what Anglo-Americans called "indoor affairs." She and her female helpers prepared food, cleaned the house, did laundry, and often made clothing. These basic chores were complex and time-consuming. Preparing food, for instance, involved planting and cultivating a garden, harvesting and preserving vegetables, salting and smoking meat, drying apples and pressing cider, milking cows and making butter and cheese, not to mention cooking and baking. The head of the household and his male helpers, responsible for "outdoor affairs," also had heavy workloads. They had to plant and cultivate the fields, build fences, chop wood for the fireplace, harvest and market crops, care for livestock, and butcher cattle and hogs to provide the household with meat.

A European-American man's household could include African-American families as well as his own kin. More than 95 percent of colonial African-Americans were held in perpetual bondage. Although many of them lived on farms with only one or two other slaves, most lived and worked in a largely black setting. In South Carolina and Louisiana, a majority of the population was of African origin; in Georgia, about half; and in the Chesapeake, 40 percent.

Large plantations enabled the specialization of labor. Each had its own enslaved male blacksmiths, carpenters, and shoemakers, along with slave women who worked as seamstresses, cooks, dairymaids, and midwives. These skilled slaves—between 10 and 20 percent of the African-American population—were essential to the smooth functioning of the plantation. But most slaves, male or female, worked in the fields.

African-American Families

Because all the colonies legally permitted slavery, African-Americans had few potential refuges from bondage. Some recently arrived Africans stole boats to try to return home or ran off in groups to frontier regions to join the Indians. Some slaves from South Carolina and Georgia managed to reach Spanish Florida, where they were allowed to establish a free community on the outskirts of St. Augustine. Violent resistance had even less to recommend it than running away because European-American colonists, although in the minority in some areas, controlled the guns and ammunition.

Lack of rebellion, however, did not imply an absence of resistance to enslavement. Family ties often provided a key means for such resistance. Even though slaves were not allowed to marry legally, they established strong family structures in which youngsters usually carried their parents' and grandparents' names. Extended-kin groups protested excessive punishment of relatives and asked to live in the same quarters. The links that developed among African-American families who had lived on the same plantation for several generations served as insurance against the uncertainties of existence under slavery. If a nuclear family was broken up by sale, other relatives could help with child rearing and similar tasks. Among African-Americans, just as among Indians, the extended family served a more important function than it did among European-Americans.

Most slave families managed to carve out a small measure of autonomy, especially in their working and spiritual lives. Enslaved Muslims often clung to their Islamic faith. Other Africans converted to Christianity, finding comfort in the assurances that all people would be free and equal in heaven. On many plantations, slaves were allowed or required to plant their own gardens, hunt, or fish to supplement the minimal diet their masters supplied. In some regions, most notably South Carolina and Louisiana, enslaved people were allowed to accumulate personal property by working for themselves once they had finished their assigned tasks. Late in the century, some Chesapeake planters with a surplus of laborers began to hire out slaves to others, often allowing the workers to keep a small part of their earnings. Such accumulated property could buy desired goods or serve as a legacy for children.

Farmer Abraham's Almanac, published in Philadelphia in 1759, contained this crude woodcut showing women engaged in chores associated with dairying: at right, milking a cow; at left, churning butter. American Antiquarian Society.

Just as African- and European-Americans lived together on plantations, so, too, were both groups found in cities. Yet the few colonial cities were nothing but large towns by today's standards. In 1750 the largest, Boston, had just seventeen thousand inhabitants. Still, city life differed considerably from rural life. City dwellers everywhere, purchased foodstuffs and wood at markets and cloth in shops, instead of laboriously producing such items themselves.

Life in the Cities

City people also had much more contact with the world beyond their own homes than did their rural counterparts. By the 1750s, most major cities had at least one weekly newspaper that printed the latest "advices from London," news from other English colonies, and local reports. Newspapers were available at taverns and inns, so people who could not afford to buy them could catch up on the news. Even illiterates could do so, since literate customers often read the papers aloud. Contact with the outside world also had drawbacks: sailors sometimes brought exotic and deadly diseases into port.

 ## Politics and Religion: Stability and Crisis in British America

In the first decades of the eighteenth century, Anglo-American political life exhibited a new stability. Despite substantial migration from overseas, most residents of the mainland had been born in America. Men from genteel families dominated the political structures in each province, for voters (free male property holders) tended to defer to their well-educated "betters" on election days.

Throughout the Anglo-American colonies, political leaders sought to increase the powers of elected assemblies relative to the powers of the governors and other appointed officials. Assemblies began to claim privileges associated with the British House of Commons, such as the rights to initiate all tax legislation and to control the militia. The assemblies also developed effective ways of influencing British appointees, especially threats of withholding salaries. In some colonies (Virginia and South Carolina, for example), elite members of the assemblies usually presented a united front to royal officials; in others (like New York), they fought bitterly with each other. New York took the first steps on the road to modern American democracy. In an attempt to win hotly contested elections, the province's genteel leaders began to appeal to "the people," competing openly for the votes of ordinary freeholders. Yet in 1733 that same New York government imprisoned a newspaper editor, John Peter Zenger, who had too vigorously criticized its actions. Defending Zenger against the charge of "seditious libel," his lawyer argued that the truth could not be defamatory, thus helping to establish a free-press principle now found in American law.

Rise of the Assemblies

Eighteenth-century assemblies bore little resemblance to twentieth-century state legislatures. Only on rare occasions did they formulate new policies or pass laws of real importance. Members of the assemblies believed their primary function was to stop the governors or councils from enacting oppressive taxes, rather than to pass laws that would actively benefit their constituents.

By midcentury, politically aware colonists commonly drew analogies between their own governments and Great Britain's balance of king, lords, and commons—a combination that had been thought to produce a stable polity. Although the analogy was not exact, political leaders equated their governors with the monarch, their councils with the aristocracy, and their assemblies with the House of Commons. All three were thought essential to good government, but Americans viewed the appointed governors and councils as potential threats to colonial freedoms and customary ways of life. By contrast, colonists saw the assemblies as the people's protectors. And the assemblies in turn regarded themselves as representatives of the people.

Such beliefs should not, however, be equated with modern practice. The assemblies, firmly controlled by dominant families whose members were reelected year after year, rarely responded to the concerns of their poorer constituents. Although settlement continually spread westward, assemblies failed to reapportion themselves to provide adequate representation for newer communities— a lack of action that led to serious grievances among frontier dwellers. Thus it is important to distinguish between the colonial ideal of protecting the people's liberties and the reality of protecting wealth and privilege.

At midcentury, the political structures were confronted with a series of crises. None affected all the mainland provinces, but no colony escaped wholly untouched. The crises exposed the internal tensions building in the pluralistic American society, foreshadowing the greater disorder of the revolutionary era. Most important, they demonstrated that the political accommodations arrived at in the aftermath of the Glorious Revolution were no longer adequate to govern Britain's American empire.

One of the first and greatest crises occurred in South Carolina in 1739. Early one September morning, about twenty South Carolina slaves gathered near the Stono River south of Charleston. Seizing guns and ammunition from a store, they killed the storekeepers and some nearby planter families. Then, joined by other local slaves, they headed south toward Florida in hopes of finding refuge. By that afternoon, a troop of militia attacked the fugitives, who then numbered about a hundred, killing some and dispersing the rest. More than a week later, most of the remaining conspirators were captured. Those not killed on the spot were later executed.

Stono Rebellion

The Stono Rebellion shocked slaveholding South Carolinians and residents of other colonies as well, and British America stiffened its laws governing the behavior of African-Americans. The most immediate response came in New York City, which had suffered a slave revolt in 1712. There the news from the South, coupled with fears of Spain generated by the outbreak of King George's War, set off a reign of terror in the summer of 1741. Hysterical whites interpreted a biracial gang of thieves as malevolent conspirators who wanted to foment a slave uprising under the guidance of a supposed priest in the pay of Spain. By summer's end, thirty-one blacks and four whites had been executed for participating in the "plot." The Stono Rebellion and the New York conspiracy exposed Anglo-Americans' deepest fears about the dangers of slaveholding and revealed the assemblies' inability to prevent serious internal disorder. Events of the next two decades confirmed that pattern.

By midcentury, most of the fertile land east of the Appalachians had been purchased or occupied. As a result, conflicts over land titles and conditions of landholding grew in number and frequency as colonists competed for control of land good for farming. In 1746, for example, some New Jersey farmers clashed violently with agents of the East Jersey proprietors. The proprietors claimed the farmers' land as theirs and demanded annual payments, called quitrents, for the use of the property.

Land Riots in New Jersey and New York

The most serious land riots of the period took place along the Hudson River in 1765 and 1766. Late in the seventeenth century, several huge tracts in the lower Hudson valley had been granted to prominent colonial families. The proprietors in turn divided these estates into small farms, which they rented chiefly to poor Dutch and German migrants. After 1740, though, increasing migration from New England brought conflict to the great New York estates. The New Englanders squatted on vacant portions of the manors and resisted all attempts at eviction. In the mid-1760s the Philipse family sued the New Englanders, some of whom had lived on Philipse land for twenty or thirty years. New York courts upheld the Philipse claim and ordered squatters to make way for tenants with valid leases. Instead of complying, the farmers organized a rebellion against the proprietors. For nearly a year insurgent farmers terrorized proprietors and loyal tenants. The rebellion was put down only after British troops dispatched from New York City captured its leaders.

Violent conflicts of a different sort erupted just a few years later in the Carolinas. The Regulator movements of the late 1760s (South Carolina) and early 1770s (North Carolina) pitted backcountry farmers against wealthy eastern planters who controlled the provincial governments. Frontier dwellers, most of whom were Scots-Irish, protested their lack of an adequate voice in colonial political affairs. South Carolinians for months policed the countryside in vigilante bands, contending that law enforcement in the region was too lax and biased against them. North Carolinians, whose primary grievance was heavy taxation, fought and lost a battle with eastern militiamen at Alamance in 1771.

Regulators in the Carolinas

The most widespread crisis, however, was religious. From the late 1730s through the 1760s, waves of religious revivalism—today known collectively as the Great Awakening—swept over various parts of the colonies, primarily New England (1735–1745) and Virginia (1750s and 1760s). Orthodox Calvinists were eager to combat Enlightenment rationalism, which denied innate human depravity. In addition, many recent immigrants and residents of the backcountry had no prior religious affiliation, thus presenting evangelists with a potential source of converts.

First Great Awakening

The first signs of the Great Awakening appeared during 1734 and 1735 in western Massachusetts, in the Northampton Congregational Church. There the Reverend Jonathan Edwards, a noted preacher and theologian, taught that individuals could attain salvation only through recognition of their own depraved natures and the need to surrender completely to God's will. Such surrender, Edwards noticed, brought to members of his congregation an intensely emotional release from sin, which came to be seen as a single identifiable moment of conversion.

The effects of such conversions remained isolated until 1739, when George Whitefield, an English Anglican cleric, arrived in America. For fifteen months he toured the British colonies, preaching to large audiences from Georgia to New England. A gripping orator, Whitefield was the chief generating force behind the Great Awakening. Thousands turned out to listen—and to experience conversion. At first, regular clerics welcomed Whitefield and the American-born itinerant evangelist preachers who sprang up to imitate him. Soon, however, many clergymen began to realize that although "revived" religion filled their churches, it ran counter to their own approach to doctrine and matters of faith.

George Whitefield

Opposition to the Awakening heightened rapidly, causing large numbers of congregations to splinter. "Old Lights"—traditional clerics and their followers—engaged in bitter disputes with the "New Light" evangelicals. Already characterized by numerous sects, American Protestantism became further divided as the major denominations split into Old Light and New Light factions and as new evangelical sects—Methodists and Baptists—gained adherents. Paradoxically, the angry fights and the rapid rise in the number of distinct denominations eventually led to an American willingness to tolerate religious diversity.

The most important effect of the Awakening was its impact on American modes of thought. The revivalists' message directly challenged the colonial tradition of deference. Itinerant preachers, only a few of whom were ordained clergymen, claimed they understood the will of God better than did orthodox clerics. The Awakening's emphasis on emotion rather than learning undermined the validity of received wisdom, and New Lights questioned not only religious but also social and political orthodoxy.

Impact of the Awakening

Nowhere was this trend more evident than in Virginia. By the 1760s Baptists had gained a se-

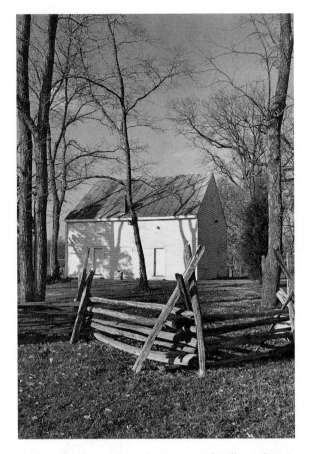

Built in the late eighteenth century and still standing in Fairfax County, Virginia, the Frying Pan Meetinghouse was one of the Baptist churches with a racially integrated congregation from its earliest years. The existence of such egalitarian religious bodies directly challenged the colony's hierarchical society.   Virginia Department of Historic Resources, VA.

cure foothold in Virginia; their beliefs and behavior were openly at odds with the way most genteel families lived. They rejected as sinful the horseracing, gambling, and dancing that occupied much of the gentry's leisure time. They addressed each other as "brother" and "sister" regardless of social status, and they elected the leaders of their congregations.

Virginia Baptists

Strikingly, almost all the Virginia Baptist congregations included both black and white members. Church rules applied equally to all members; interracial sexual relationships, divorce, and adultery were forbidden to everyone. In addition, masters were directed not to break up slave marriages through sale. Biracial committees investigated complaints about church members' misbehavior. Churches also excommunicated masters for physically abusing their slaves. Some other Baptists decided that owning slaves was "unrighteous" and freed their bondspeople.

 ## Conclusion

The Great Awakening thus injected an egalitarian strain into Anglo-American life at midcentury and further disrupted traditional structures of existence. Although primarily a religious movement, the Awakening also had important social and political consequences, calling into question habitual modes of behavior in the secular as well as the religious realm. In short, the Great Awakening helped to break Anglo-Americans' ties to their limited seventeenth-century origins.

Also important were the changes in the economy that enmeshed the colonies in an international network of trade, drawing them into European wars and creating the wealthy class of merchants and landowners who dominated colonial life.

By 1750 the colonies mixed diverse European, American, and African traditions into a novel cultural blend that owed much to Europe and North America. Colonists continued to identify themselves as French, Spanish, or British rather than as Americans. That did not change in Canada, Louisiana, or the Spanish Borderlands, but in the 1760s some Anglo-Americans began to realize that their interests were not necessarily identical to those of Great Britain or its monarch.

Suggestions for Further Reading

General

Jack P. Greene, *Pursuits of Happiness: The Social Development of the Early Modern British Colonies and the Formation of American*

Culture (1988); Peter C. Mancall, *Deadly Medicine: Indians and Alcohol in Early America* (1995); Stephanie G. Wolf, *As Various as Their Land: The Everyday Lives of 18th Century Americans* (1992).

New France and New Spain

Ramón Gutiérrez, *When Jesus Came, the Corn Mothers Went Away: Marriage, Sexuality, and Power in New Mexico, 1500–1846* (1991); Gwendolyn Midlo Hall, *Africans in Colonial Louisiana: The Development of Afro-Creole Culture in the Eighteenth Century* (1992); Dale Miquelon, *New France, 1701–1744* (1987); G. F. G. Stanley, *New France, 1744–1760* (1968); Daniel H. Usner, Jr., *Indians, Settlers, and Slaves in a Frontier Exchange Economy: The Lower Mississippi Valley Before 1783* (1992).

Anglo-American Society

T. H. Breen, *Tobacco Culture* (1985); Lois Green Carr et al., eds., *Colonial Chesapeake Society* (1988); Rhys Isaac, *The Transformation of Virginia, 1740–1790* (1982); Christopher Jedrey, *The World of John Cleaveland: Family and Community in Eighteenth-Century New England* (1979); Sung Bok Kim, *Landlord and Tenant in Colonial New York: Manorial Society, 1664–1775* (1978); Peter C. Mancall, *Valley of Opportunity: Economic Culture Along the Upper Susquehanna, 1700–1800* (1991); Gary B. Nash, *The Urban Crucible: Social Change, Political Consciousness, and the Origins of the American Revolution* (1979); Michael Zuckerman, *Peaceable Kingdoms: New England Towns in the Eighteenth Century* (1970).

Anglo-American Economics and Politics

Bernard Bailyn, *The Origins of American Politics* (1968); Patricia U. Bonomi, *A Factious People: Politics and Society in Colonial New York* (1971); Richard Bushman, *King and People in Provincial Massachusetts* (1985); Richard Bushman, *The Refinement of America: Persons, Houses, Cities* (1992); Cary Carson et al., eds., *Of Consuming Interests: The Style of Life in the Eighteenth Century* (1994); Stephen Innes, ed., *Work and Labor in Early America* (1988); John J. McCusker and Russell R. Menard, *The Economy of British America, 1607–1789* (1985).

Immigration to British America

Bernard Bailyn, *The Peopling of British North America* (1986); Bernard Bailyn, *Voyagers to the West* (1986); Bernard Bailyn and Philip Morgan, eds., *Strangers Within the Realm* (1991); R. J. Dickson, *Ulster Immigration to Colonial America, 1718–1775* (1966); David Dobson, *Scottish Immigration to Colonial America, 1607–1785* (1994); A. Roger Ekirch, *Bound for America: The Transportation of British Convicts to the Colonies, 1718–1775* (1987); Ned Landsman, *Scotland and Its First American Colony* (1985); A. G. Roeber, *Palatines, Liberty, and Property: German Lutherans in Colonial British America* (1993).

African-Americans

Thomas J. Davis, *A Rumor of Revolt: The "Great Negro Plot" in Colonial New York* (1985); Marvin L. Michael Kay and Lorin Lee Cary, *Slavery in North Carolina, 1748–1775* (1995); Allan Kulikoff, *Tobacco and Slaves: The Development of Southern Cultures in the Chesapeake, 1680–1800* (1986); Michael Mullin, *Africa in America: Slave Acculturation and Resistance in the American South and the British Caribbean, 1736–1834* (1992); William Pierson, *Black Yankees: The Development of an Afro-American Subculture in Eighteenth-Century New England* (1988); Mechal Sobel, *The World They Made Together: Black and White Values in Eighteenth-Century Virginia* (1987).

Anglo-American Women and Families

Cornelia Hughes Dayton, *Women Before the Bar: Gender, Law, and Society in Connecticut, 1639–1789* (1995); Joan Gundersen, *To Be Useful to the World: Women in Eighteenth-Century America* (1996); Barry J. Levy, *Quakers and the American Family* (1988); Marylynn Salmon, *Women and the Law of Property in Early America* (1986); Daniel Blake Smith, *Inside the Great House: Planter Family Life in Eighteenth-Century Chesapeake Society* (1980).

Anglo-American Education, Science, and the Enlightenment

Patricia Cline Cohen, *A Calculating People: The Spread of Numeracy in Early America* (1982); Lawrence A. Cremin, *American Education: The Colonial Experience, 1607–1783* (1970); Richard Beale Davis, *Intellectual Life in the Colonial South, 1585–1763* (1978); Henry F. May, *The Enlightenment in America* (1976); William Sloan and Julie Williams, *The Early American Press, 1690–1783* (1994); Raymond P. Stearns, *Science in the British Colonies of America* (1970).

Religion and the Great Awakening

Patricia U. Bonomi, *Under the Cope of Heaven: Religion, Society, and Politics in Colonial America* (1986); J. M. Bumstead and John E. Van de Wetering, *What Must I Do to Be Saved? The Great Awakening in Colonial America* (1976); Jon Butler, *Awash in a Sea of Faith: Christianizing the American People* (1990); Harry S. Stout, *The Divine Dramatist: George Whitefield and the Rise of Modern Evangelicalism* (1991); Patricia Tracy, *Jonathan Edwards, Pastor* (1980).

5

Severing the Bonds
of Empire
1754–1774

The two men must have found the occasion remarkable. The artist customarily painted portraits of the wealthy and high born, not of artisans. Moreover, the political sympathies of the painter, John Singleton Copley, lay primarily with Boston's conservatives, whereas the sitter, the silversmith Paul Revere, was a noted leader of resistance to British policies. Yet some time in 1768 Revere commissioned Copley to paint his portrait, and the result is one the greatest works of American art.

Copley portrayed Revere surrounded by the tools of his trade and contemplating a teapot he was crafting. Revere's pose and apparel convey an impression of thoughtfulness, virtuous labor, and solidity. The teapot, too, carries a message, especially in the year 1768. Simultaneously a reflection of a craftsman's skills and a prominent emblem of the new "empire of goods" in British America, it resonated with symbolism because, as shall be seen later in this chapter, tea boycotts were an important component of colonial resistance to Great Britain.

In retrospect, John Adams identified the years between 1760 and 1775 as the era of the true American Revolution. The Revolution, Adams declared, was completed before the fighting started, for it was "in the Minds of the people," involving not the actual winning of independence but a fundamental shift of allegiance from Britain to America. Not all historians would agree with Adams's interpretation, but none would

John Singleton Copley's portrait of Paul Revere is generally regarded as one of his masterpieces. Copley captured Revere's character as a hard-working, respectable artisan—a man unafraid of displaying his humble origins to the world. Museum of Fine Arts, Boston. Gift of John W., William B., and Edward H. R. Revere.

deny the importance of the events of those crucial years.

The story of the 1760s and early 1770s describes an ever-widening split between Great Britain and Anglo-America. In the long history of British settlement in the Western Hemisphere, considerable tension had at times marred the relationship between individual provinces and the mother country. Still, that tension rarely had been sustained for long, nor had it been widespread, except during the crisis following the Glorious Revolution in 1689. In the 1750s, however, a series of events caused colonists to begin to examine their relations with Great Britain. It all started with the Seven Years War.

Britain's overwhelming victory in that war, confirmed by treaty in 1763, forever altered the

balance of power in North America. France was ousted from the continent and Spain from Florida, events with major consequences for both the indigenous peoples of the interior and the residents of the British colonies. Indians could no longer play off European powers against one another and so lost one of their major diplomatic tools. Anglo-Americans, for their part, no longer had to fear the French threat on their northern and western borders or the Spanish in the Southeast.

The British victory in 1763, then, constituted a major turning point in American history because of its direct effect on all the residents of North America. It also had a significant impact on Great Britain. To win the war, Britain went heavily into debt. To reduce the debt, Parliament for the first time imposed on the colonies revenue-raising taxes in addition to the customs duties that had long regulated trade. That decision exposed differences in the political thinking of Americans and Britons.

During the 1760s and early 1770s a broad coalition of Anglo-Americans resisted new tax levies and attempts by British officials to tighten controls over provincial governments. The colonies' elected leaders became ever more suspicious of Britain's motives as the years passed. They laid aside old antagonisms to coordinate their response to the new measures, and they slowly began to reorient their political thinking. As late as the summer of 1774, though, few harbored thoughts of independence.

 ## Renewed Warfare Among Europeans and Indians

The English colonies along the Atlantic seaboard were surrounded by hostile, or potentially hostile, neighbors: Indians everywhere, the Spanish in Florida and along the coast of the Gulf of Mexico, the French along the great inland system of rivers and lakes that stretched from the St. Lawrence to the Mississippi. The Spanish outposts posed little direct threat, for Spain's days as a major power had passed. The French were another matter. Their long chain of forts and settlements dominated the North American interior, facilitating trading partnerships and alliances with the Indians. In none of the three wars fought between 1689 and 1748 was

• *Important Events* •

1754	Albany Congress meets to try to forge colonial unity Fighting breaks out with Washington's defeat at Fort Necessity	**1766**	Stamp Act repealed Declaratory Act insists that Parliament can tax the colonies
1756	Britain declares war on France; Seven Years War officially begins	**1767**	Townshend Acts lay duties on trade within the empire, send new officials and judges to America
1759	British forces take Quebec	**1768–70**	Resistance to Townshend duties takes form of boycotts and public demonstrations but divides merchants and urban artisans
1760	American phase of war ends with fall of Montréal to British troops George III becomes king		
1763	Treaty of Paris ends Seven Years War Pontiac's allies attack British forts in West Proclamation of 1763 attempts to close land west of Appalachians to English settlement	**1770**	Lord North becomes prime minister Townshend duties repealed, except for tea tax Boston Massacre kills five colonial rioters
		1772	Boston Committee of Correspondence formed
1764	Sugar Act lays new duties on molasses, tightens customs regulations Currency Act outlaws paper money issued by the colonies	**1773**	Tea Act aids East India Company Boston Tea Party protests the Tea Act
1765	Stamp Act requires stamps on all printed materials in colonies Sons of Liberty formed	**1774**	Coercive Acts punish Boston and the colony of Massachusetts as a whole Quebec Act reforms government of Quebec

England able to shake France's hold on the American frontier. Under the Peace of Utrecht, which ended Queen Anne's War in 1713, the English won control of such peripheral northern areas as Newfoundland, Hudson's Bay, and Nova Scotia (Acadia). But Britain made no territorial gains in King George's War.

During both Queen Anne's War and King George's War, the Iroquois Confederacy pursued a policy of neutrality and skillfully played the Europeans off against each other.

Iroquois Neutrality

When the Iroquois went to war, it was against their traditional southern enemies, the Catawbas. Since France repeatedly urged them to attack the Catawbas, who were allied with Britain, the Iroquois achieved desirable goals. They kept the French happy and si-

multaneously consolidated their control over the entire interior region north of Virginia. The campaign against a common enemy also enabled the confederacy to cement its alliance with the Shawnees and Delawares.

But even careful Iroquois diplomats could not prevent the region inhabited by the Shawnees and Delawares (now western Pennsylvania and eastern Ohio) from providing the spark that set off a major war. That conflict spread from America to Europe, proving decisive in the contest for North America. Trouble began in 1752 when Anglo-American fur traders ventured into the area known as the Ohio country (see map, page 87). The French could not permit their rivals to gain a foothold in the region: a permanent British presence in the Ohio country could challenge France's control of the western fur trade and even threaten its prominence in the

The Colonial Wars, 1689–1763

American Name	European Name	Dates	Participants	American Sites	Dispute
King William's War	War of the League of Augsburg	1689–97	England, Holland versus France, Spain	New England, New York, Canada	French power
Queen Anne's War	War of Spanish Succession	1702–13	England, Holland, Austria versus France, Spain	Florida, New England	Throne of Spain
King George's War	War of Austrian Succession	1739–48	England, Holland, Austria versus France, Spain, Prussia	West Indies, New England, Canada	Throne of Austria
French and Indian War	Seven Years War	1756–63	England versus France, Spain	Ohio country, Canada	Possession of Ohio country

Mississippi valley. Accordingly, in 1753 the French pushed southward from Lake Erie, building fortified outposts at strategic points.

In response to the French threat to their western frontiers, delegates from seven northern and middle colonies gathered in Albany, New York, in June 1754. With the backing of administrators in London, they sought two goals: to persuade the Iroquois to abandon their traditional neutrality and to coordinate the defenses of the colonies. They succeeded in neither. The Iroquois saw no reason to change a policy that had served them well for half a century. And although the Albany Congress delegates adopted a Plan of Union (which would have established an elected intercolonial legislature with the power to tax), their provincial governments uniformly rejected the plan—primarily because those governments feared a loss of autonomy.

Albany Congress

While the Albany Congress delegates deliberated, the war they sought to prepare for was already beginning. Virginia claimed ownership of the Ohio country, and its governor sent a small force westward to counter the French. But the Virginia militiamen arrived too late. The French had already taken possession of the strategic point— now Pittsburgh—where the Allegheny and Monongahela Rivers meet to form the Ohio, and they were busily engaged in constructing Fort Duquesne. The inexperienced young officer who commanded the Virginians attacked a French detachment and then allowed himself to be trapped in his crudely built Fort Necessity at Great Meadows, Pennsylvania. After a day-long battle (on July 3, 1754), twenty-two-year-old George Washington surrendered. He and his men were allowed to return to Virginia.

Washington had blundered grievously, setting off a war that eventually would encompass nearly the entire world. He also ensured that the Ohio valley Indians would for the most part support France in the conflict. The Indians took Washington's mistakes as an indication of Britain's inability to win the war, and nothing that occurred in the next four years made them change their minds. In July 1755, a few miles south of Fort Duquesne, a combined force of French and Indians ambushed British and colonial troops led by General Edward Braddock. Braddock was killed, and his men were demoralized by a devastating defeat. After news of the debacle reached London, Britain declared war

Seven Years War

European Settlements and Native Americans, 1750 *By 1750, Europeans had expanded the limits of the English colonies to the eastern slopes of the Appalachian Mountains.*

on France in 1756, thus formally beginning the conflict known as the Seven Years War.

For three more years one disaster followed another for Great Britain. The tide began to change in 1757 when William Pitt was named secretary of state. Under his leadership the British mounted the effort that won them the war in North America. By agreeing to reimburse the colonies for their military expenditures and placing troop recruitment wholly in local hands, Pitt gained wholehearted American support for the war effort. Earlier in the war, British officers had usually tried to coerce the colonies into supplying men and materiel to the army. In July 1758, British forces recaptured the fortress at Louisbourg. Then, in a surprise night attack in September 1759, General James Wolfe's soldiers defeated the French on the Plains of Abraham and took Quebec. Sensing a British victory, the Iroquois abandoned their policy of neutrality and allied themselves with Britain. A year later the British captured Montréal and the American phase of the war ended.

In the Treaty of Paris (1763), France ceded its major North American holdings to Britain. Spain, an ally of France toward the end of the war, gave Florida to the victors. Britain, fearing the presence of France on its western borders, forced the French to cede Louisiana to Spain. The British thus gained control of the fur trade of the entire continent. And no longer would the English seacoast colonies have to worry about the threat to their existence posed by France's extensive North American territories.

Because most of the fighting had occurred in the Northeast, the war had especially pronounced effects on New Englanders. Wartime service left a lasting impression on the New Englanders who served

American Soldiers

in the provincial army. For the first time, ordinary Americans came into extended contact with Britons—and they did not like what they saw. The provincials regarded the British troops as haughty, profane Sabbath-breakers who arbitrarily imposed overly harsh punishments on anyone who broke the rules.

The New England soldiers also learned that British troops did not share their adherence to principles of contract and consensus—the values that had governed their lives at home. Colonial regiments mutinied or rebelled en masse if they believed they were being treated unfairly, as happened, for example, when they were not allowed to leave at the end of their formal enlistments. One private in these circumstances grumbled in his journal in 1759, "Although we be Englishmen born, we are debarred Englishmen's liberty." Such men would later recall their personal experience of British "tyranny" when they decided to support the Revolution.

The overwhelming British triumph stimulated some Americans to think expansively about the colonies' future. People like the Philadelphia printer Benjamin Franklin, who had long touted the colonies' wealth and potential, predicted a glorious new future for British North America. Such men uniformly opposed any laws that would retard America's growth and after 1763 persistently supported steps to increase Americans' control over their own destiny.

 ## 1763: A Turning Point

The great victory over France had an irreversible impact on North America, felt first by the indigenous peoples of the interior. With France excluded from the continent altogether and Spanish territory now confined to the area west of the Mississippi, the diplomatic strategy that had served the Indians well for so long could no longer be employed. The consequences were immediate and devastating.

Even before the Treaty of Paris, southern Indians had to adjust to the new circumstances. After Britain gained the upper hand in the American war in 1758, Creeks and Cherokees lost their ability to force concessions by threatening to turn instead to France or Spain. In desperation, and in retaliation for British atrocities, Cherokees attacked the Carolina and Virginia frontiers in 1760. Though initially victorious, the Indians were defeated the following year by a force of British regulars and colonial militia. Late in 1761 the two sides concluded a treaty under which the Cherokees allowed the construction of British forts in tribal territories and opened a large tract of land to European settlement.

In the Ohio country the Ottawas, Chippewas, and Potawatomis reacted angrily when Great Britain raised the price of trade goods and ended traditional gift-giving practices. Britain also allowed settlers to move into the Monongahela and Susquehanna valleys, onto Delaware and Iroquois lands.

Pontiac, the war chief of an Ottawa village near Detroit, understood that only unity among the western tribes could prevent total dependence on and subordination to the victorious British. Using his considerable powers of persuasion, in the spring of 1763 he forged an unprecedented alliance among Hurons, Chippewas, Potawatomis, Delawares, Shawnees, and even some Mingoes (Pennsylvania Iroquois). Pontiac then laid siege to Fort Detroit while war parties attacked other British outposts in the Great Lakes region. Detroit withstood the siege, but by late June all the other forts west of Niagara and north of Fort Pitt (old Fort Duquesne) had fallen to the Indian alliance. But the alliance could not take the strongholds of Niagara, Fort Pitt, or Detroit. In early August, colonial militiamen soundly defeated a combined Indian force at Bushy Run, Pennsylvania. Conflict ceased when Pontiac broke off the siege of Detroit in late October. A treaty ending the war was finally negotiated three years later.

Pontiac's Uprising

Pontiac's uprising showed Great Britain that the huge territory it had just acquired from France would not be easy to govern. In October, in a futile attempt to assert control over the interior, the British ministry issued the Proclamation of 1763, which declared the headwaters of rivers flowing into the Atlantic from the Appalachian Mountains to be the temporary western boundary for colonial settlement (see map, page 87). The proclamation was intended to prevent clashes between Indians and colonists by forbidding whites to move onto Indian lands until tribes had given up their land by treaty. But many whites had already established farms or purchased property

Proclamation of 1763

west of the proclamation line, and from the outset the policy was doomed to failure.

Other decisions made in London in 1763 and thereafter had a wider impact in British North America. The hard-won victory created both problems and opportunities for the British government. The most pressing problem, Britain's immense war debt, had to be solved by King George III and his new prime minister, George Grenville.

George III had assumed the British throne in 1760. The twenty-two-year-old king was a man of mediocre intellect and an erratic judge of character. During the crucial years between 1763 and 1770, when the rift with the colonies was growing ever wider, he replaced ministries with bewildering rapidity. Moreover, the king often substituted stubbornness for intelligence, and he regarded adherence to the status quo as the hallmark of patriotism.

George III

The man he selected as prime minister in 1763, George Grenville, confronted a financial crisis: England's burden of indebtedness had nearly doubled since 1754. Grenville's ministry had to find new sources of funds, and the British people themselves were already heavily taxed. Since the colonists had benefited greatly from the wartime expenditures, Grenville concluded that Anglo-Americans should be asked to pay a greater share of the cost of running the empire.

Grenville did not question Great Britain's right to levy taxes on the colonies. Like all his countrymen, he believed that the government's legitimacy derived ultimately from the consent of the people, but he defined consent far more loosely than did the colonists. Americans had come to believe that they could be represented only by men for whom they or their property-holding neighbors actually voted. Grenville and his English contemporaries, however, believed that Parliament—king, lords, and commons acting together—by definition represented all British subjects, even colonists who could not vote.

Theories of Representation

According to this theory of government, called *virtual representation*, the colonists were seen as virtually, if not actually, represented in Parliament. Thus their consent to acts of Parliament could be presumed. By contrast, in the colonies members of the lower houses of the assemblies were viewed as specifically representing the voters who had elected them.

Events in the 1760s threw into sharp relief Americans' attitudes toward political power. The colonists had become accustomed to a central government that wielded only limited authority over them and affected their daily lives very little. In consequence, they believed that a good government was one that largely left them alone, a view in keeping with the theories of a group of British writers known as the Real Whigs. These writers stressed the dangers inherent in a powerful government, particularly one headed by a monarch. Real Whigs warned that political power was always to be feared, that rulers would try to corrupt and oppress the people, and that only the perpetual vigilance of people and their elected representatives could preserve their fragile yet precious liberty, which was closely linked to their right to hold private property.

Britain's attempts to tighten the reins of government and raise revenues from the colonies in the 1760s and early 1770s convinced many Americans that the Real Whigs' reasoning applied to their circumstances, especially because of the link between liberty and property rights. Excessive and unjust taxation, they believed, could destroy their freedoms. They began to interpret British measures in light of the Real Whigs' warnings and to see oppressive designs behind the actions of Grenville and his successors. In the mid-1760s, however, colonial leaders did not immediately accuse Grenville of an intent to oppress them. They at first simply questioned the wisdom of the laws he proposed.

Parliament passed the first such measures, the Sugar and Currency Acts, in 1764. The Sugar Act revised existing customs regulations and laid new duties on some foreign imports into the colonies. It also established a vice-admiralty court at Halifax, Nova Scotia, and included provisions aimed at stopping the widespread smuggling of molasses,

Sugar and Currency Acts

one of the chief commodities in American trade. Although the Sugar Act appeared to resemble the Navigation Acts, which the colonies had long accepted as legitimate, it broke with tradition because it was explicitly designed to raise revenue, not to channel American trade through Britain. The Currency Act effectively outlawed colonial issues of paper money. (British merchants had complained that Americans were paying their debts in inflated local currencies.) Americans could accumulate little sterling, since they imported more than they exported; thus the act seemed to the colonists to deprive them of a useful medium of exchange.

Because the Sugar and Currency Acts were imposed on an economy already in the midst of a postwar depression, it is not surprising that some Americans objected to them. But lacking any precedent for a united campaign against acts of Parliament, Americans in 1764 took only hesitant and uncoordinated steps. Eight colonial legislatures sent separate petitions to Parliament requesting the Sugar Act's repeal. They argued that its commercial restrictions would hurt Britain as well as the colonies and that they had not consented to its passage. The protests had no effect. The law remained in force, and Grenville proceeded with another revenue plan.

 ## The Stamp Act Crisis

The Stamp Act (1765), Grenville's most important proposal, was modeled on a law that had been in effect in Great Britain for almost a century. It touched nearly every colonist by requiring tax stamps on most printed materials. The heaviest burden fell on merchants and other members of the colonial elite, who used printed matter more frequently than did ordinary folk. Anyone who, for example, purchased a newspaper or pamphlet, made a will, transferred land, bought dice or playing cards, or borrowed money would have to pay the tax. Never before had a revenue measure of such scope been proposed for the colonies. The act also required that tax stamps be paid for with sterling, which was scarce, and that violators be tried in vice-admiralty courts, which operated without juries. Finally, such a law would break decisively with the colonial tradition of self-imposed taxation.

The most important colonial pamphlet protesting the Sugar Act and the proposed Stamp Act was *The Rights of the British Colonies Asserted and Proved*, by James Otis, Jr., a brilliant young Massachusetts attorney. Otis starkly exposed the ideological dilemma that was to confound the colonists for the next decade. How could they justify their opposition to certain acts of Parliament without questioning Parliament's authority over them? On the one hand, Otis asserted, Americans were "entitled to all the natural, essential, inherent, and inseparable rights" of Britons, including the right not to be taxed without their consent. On the other hand, Otis was forced to admit that under the British system, "the power of parliament is uncontrollable but by themselves, and we must obey."

James Otis's *Rights of the British Colonies*

Otis's first contention implied that Parliament could not constitutionally tax the colonies because Americans were not represented in its ranks. Yet his second point both acknowledged political reality and accepted the prevailing theory that Parliament was the sole, supreme authority in the empire. Even unconstitutional laws enacted by Parliament had to be obeyed until Parliament decided to repeal them. Otis tried to find a middle ground by proposing colonial representation in Parliament, but his idea was never taken seriously on either side of the Atlantic. The British believed that colonists were already virtually represented in Parliament, and Anglo-Americans quickly realized that a handful of colonial delegates to London would simply be outvoted.

Otis published his pamphlet before the Stamp Act was passed. When Americans first learned of the act's adoption in the spring of 1765, they were uncertain how to react. Few colonists publicly favored the law, but colonial petitions had already failed to prevent its adoption and further lobbying appeared futile. Perhaps Otis was right that the only course open to Americans was to pay the stamp tax, reluctantly but loyally.

Not all the colonists shared his views. One of them was a twenty-nine-year-old lawyer serving his first term in the Virginia House of Burgesses. Patrick Henry later recalled that he was appalled by his fellow legislators' unwillingness to oppose the Stamp Act. Henry decided to act. "Alone, unadvised, and unassisted," he wrote the Virginia Stamp Act Resolves.

Patrick Henry and the Virginia Stamp Act Resolves

Patrick Henry introduced his seven proposals near the end of the legislative session, when many burgesses had already departed for home. Henry's fiery speech led the Speaker of the House to accuse him of treason. (Henry denied the charge.) The few burgesses remaining in Williamsburg adopted five of Henry's resolutions by a bare majority. Although they repealed the most radical of the five the next day, their action had far-reaching effects.

The four propositions adopted by the burgesses repeated Otis's arguments, asserting that the colonists had never forfeited the rights of British subjects, among which was consent to taxation. The three rejected resolutions had gone much further. The one that was repealed claimed for the burgesses "the only exclusive right" to tax Virginians. The final two (those never considered) asserted that residents of Virginia need not obey tax laws passed by other legislative bodies (namely Parliament).

The burgesses' decision to accept only the first four of Henry's resolutions anticipated the position most Americans would adopt the following decade. Though willing to contend for their rights, the colonists did not seek independence. They rather wanted some measure of self-government. Accordingly, they backed away from the assertions that they owed Parliament no obedience and that only their own assemblies could tax them.

Continuing Loyalty to Britain

Over the next ten years, America's political leaders searched for a formula that would enable them to control their internal affairs, especially taxation, but remain under British rule. The chief difficulty lay in British officials' inability to compromise on the issue of parliamentary power. The notion that Parliament could exercise absolute authority over all colonial possessions was basic to the British theory of government. In effect, the Americans wanted British leaders to revise their fundamental understanding of the workings of their government. But that was simply too much to expect.

The ultimate effectiveness of Americans' resistance to the Stamp Act came not from ideological arguments but from the decisive and inventive actions of some colonists. In August 1765, the Loyal Nine, a Boston social club of printers, distillers, and other artisans, organized a demonstration against the Stamp Act. Hoping to show that people of all ranks opposed the act, they approached the leaders of the city's rival laborers' associations, based in Boston's North End and South End neighborhoods. The Loyal Nine convinced them to lay aside their differences to participate in the demonstration.

Loyal Nine

Early on August 14, the demonstrators hung an effigy of Andrew Oliver, the province's stamp distributor, from a tree on Boston Common. That night a large crowd led by a group of about fifty well-dressed tradesmen paraded the effigy around the city and threw stones at officials who tried to disperse them. In the midst of the mélée, the North End and South End leaders drank a toast to their successful union. The Loyal Nine achieved success when Oliver publicly promised not to fulfill the duties of his office. Twelve days later, a mob reportedly led by the South End leader Ebenezer MacIntosh attacked the homes of several customs officers. This time the violence drew no praise from Boston's respectable citizens; the mob completely destroyed Lieutenant Governor Thomas Hutchinson's townhouse.

The differences between the two Boston mobs of August 1765 exposed divisions that would continue to characterize subsequent colonial protests.

Americans' Divergent Interests

The skilled craftsmen who composed the Loyal Nine, and the merchants, lawyers, and other members of the educated elite preferred orderly demonstrations confined to political issues. For the city's laborers, by contrast,

economic grievances may have been paramount. Certainly, the wrecking of Hutchinson's house suggests a resentment against his ostentatious display of wealth.

Colonists, like Britons, had a long tradition of crowd action in which disfranchised people took to the streets to redress deeply felt local grievances. But the Stamp Act controversy drew ordinary urban folk into the vortex of transatlantic politics for the first time. Matters that previously had been of concern only to the gentry or to members of colonial legislatures were now discussed on every street corner.

The entry of unskilled workers, slaves, and women into the realm of imperial politics both threatened and afforded an opportunity to the elite men who wanted to mount effective opposition to British measures. The elite realized that crowd action could have a stunning impact. Anti–Stamp Act demonstrations occurred from Nova Scotia to the Caribbean island of Antigua. They were so successful that by November 1, when the law was scheduled to take effect, not one stamp distributor was willing to carry out his official duties. Thus the act could not be enforced. But wealthy men also recognized that mobs composed of the formerly powerless could endanger their own dominance of society. What would happen, they wondered, if the crowd turned against them?

They therefore attempted to channel resistance into acceptable forms by creating an intercolonial association, the Sons of Liberty. The first such group was created in New York in early November, and branches spread rapidly through the coastal cities. Composed of merchants, lawyers, prosperous tradesmen, and others, the Sons of Liberty by early 1766 linked protest leaders from Charleston, South Carolina, to Portsmouth, New Hampshire.

Sons of Liberty

The Sons of Liberty could influence events but not control them. In Charleston in October 1765, an informally organized crowd forced the resignation of the South Carolina stamp distributor. But the new Charleston chapter of the Sons of Liberty was horrified when in January 1766 local slaves paraded through the streets crying "Liberty." That was not the sort of liberty elite slave-owners had in mind. And in Philadelphia, resistance leaders were dismayed when an angry mob threatened to attack Benjamin Franklin's house. The city's laborers believed Franklin to be partly responsible for the Stamp Act, since he had obtained the post of stamp distributor for a close friend. But Philadelphia's artisans—the backbone of the opposition movement there and elsewhere—were fiercely loyal to Franklin. They protected his home and family from the crowd, but the resulting split between the better-off tradesmen and the common laborers prevented the establishment of a successful workingmen's alliance like that of Boston.

During the fall and winter of 1765–1766, opposition to the Stamp Act proceeded on three separate fronts. Colonial legislatures petitioned Parliament to repeal the hated law and in October sent delegates to an intercolonial congress. The Stamp Act Congress met in New York to draft a unified but conservative statement of protest. At the same time, the Sons of Liberty held mass meetings, attempting to rally public support for the resistance movement. Finally, American merchants organized nonimportation associations to pressure British exporters. By the 1760s, one-quarter of all British exports were being sent to the colonies, and American merchants reasoned that London merchants whose sales suffered severely would lobby for repeal. Since times were bad, American merchants also believed that nonimportation would reduce their bloated inventories.

In March 1766, Parliament repealed the Stamp Act. The nonimportation agreements had had the anticipated effect. But boycotts, formal protests, and crowd actions were less important in winning

Repeal of the Stamp Act

repeal than was the appointment of a new prime minister. Lord Rockingham, who replaced Grenville in the summer of 1765, had opposed the Stamp Act, not because he believed Parliament lacked power to tax the colonies but because he thought the law unwise and divisive. Thus, although Rockingham proposed repeal, he linked it to passage of the Declaratory Act, which asserted Parliament's ability to tax and legislate for Britain's American possessions "in all cases whatsoever." As they celebrated the Stamp Act's repeal, few colonists saw the ominous implications of the Declaratory Act.

Resistance to the Townshend Acts

The colonists had accomplished their immediate aim, but the long-term prospects were unclear. In the summer of 1766, another change in the ministry in London revealed how fragile their victory had been. The new prime minister, William Pitt, was ill much of the time, and another minister, Charles Townshend, became the dominant force in the ministry. An ally of Grenville, Townshend decided to renew the attempt to obtain additional funds from Britain's American possessions.

The taxes Townshend proposed in 1767 were to be levied on trade goods like paper, glass, and tea, and thus seemed to be nothing more than extensions of the existing Navigation Acts. But the Townshend duties differed from previous customs duties in two ways. First, they were levied on items imported into the colonies from Britain, not from foreign countries. Thus they were at odds with mercantilist theory (see page 59). Second, they were designed to raise money to pay the salaries of some royal officials in the colonies. That posed a direct challenge to the colonial assemblies, which derived considerable power from threatening to withhold officials' salaries. In addition, Townshend's scheme provided for the creation of an American Board of Customs Commissioners and of vice-admiralty courts at Boston, Philadelphia, and Charleston. Both moves angered merchants, whose profits would be threatened by more vigorous enforcement of the Navigation Acts.

The passage of the Townshend Acts drew a quick response. One series of essays in particular, *Letters from a Farmer in Pennsylvania* by the prominent lawyer John Dickinson, expressed a broad consensus. Dickinson contended that Parliament could regulate colonial trade but could not exercise that power to raise

John Dickinson's Farmer's Letters

revenue. By drawing a distinction between trade regulation and unacceptable commercial taxation, Dickinson avoided the sticky issue of consent and how it affected colonial subordination to Parliament. But his argument in effect obligated the colonies to assess Parliament's motives in passing any law pertaining to trade before deciding whether to obey it—an unworkable position in the long run.

The Massachusetts assembly responded to the Townshend Acts by drafting a letter to be circulated among the other colonial legislatures, calling

Massachusetts Assembly Dissolved

for unity and suggesting a joint petition of protest. Not the letter itself but the ministry's reaction to it united the colonies. When Lord Hillsborough, the first secretary of state for America, learned of the circular letter, he ordered Governor Francis Bernard of Massachusetts to insist that the assembly recall it. He also directed other governors to prevent their assemblies from discussing the letter. Hillsborough's order gave colonial assemblies the incentive they needed to join forces to oppose this new threat to their prerogatives. In late 1768 the Massachusetts legislature met, debated, and resoundingly rejected recall. Bernard immediately dissolved the assembly, and other governors followed suit when their legislatures debated the circular letter.

During the subsequent campaign against the Townshend duties, the Sons of Liberty and other American leaders made a deliberate effort to involve ordinary folk in the resistance movement. Most important, they urged colonists not to purchase or consume British products. The new consumerism that previously had linked colonists economically now linked them politically as well, supplying them with a ready method of displaying their allegiance.

As the primary purchasers of textiles and household goods, women played a central role in the nonconsumption movement. In Boston, more than three hundred matrons publicly promised not to buy

Daughters of Liberty

or drink tea. The women of Wilmington, North Carolina, burned their tea after walking

A Society of Patriotic Ladies (1775), attributed to Philip Dawes, an English printmaker. This grotesque caricature of female patriots shows the women emptying their tea into a chamber pot (at left) and flirting with their male counterparts (at center), while a neglected child sits below the table. The cartoon bears no resemblance to the actual event, the signing of an anti-British petition by female residents of Edenton, North Carolina.   Library of Congress.

through town in a solemn procession. The best known of the protests (because it was satirized in a British cartoon reproduced here), the so-called Edenton Ladies Tea Party, actually had little to do with tea. It was a meeting of prominent North Carolina women who pledged formally to work for the public good and to support resistance to British measures.

Women also encouraged home manufacturing. In many towns, young women calling themselves Daughters of Liberty met to spin in public in an effort to persuade other women to make homespun and thus end the colonies' dependence on British cloth. The young ladies from well-to-do families who sat publicly at spinning wheels all day, eating only American food and drinking local herbal tea were serving as political instructors. Many women took great satisfaction in their new-found role.

Even so, the colonists were by no means united in support of nonimportation and nonconsumption. If the Stamp Act protests had occasionally revealed a division between artisans and merchants on the one side and common laborers on the other, resistance to the Townshend Acts exposed a rift between urban artisans and merchants. The split was caused by changed economic conditions.

Divided Opinion over Boycotts

The Stamp Act boycotts had helped to revive a depressed economy by creating a demand for local products and reducing merchants' inventories. But in 1768 and 1769, merchants were enjoying boom times. They had no financial incentive to support a boycott, and they signed the agreements only reluctantly. In contrast, artisans supported nonimportation enthusiastically, recognizing that the absence of British goods would create a ready market for their own manufactures. They also used coercion to enforce nonimportation.

Such tactics were effective: colonial imports from England dropped dramatically in 1769. But the tactics also aroused heated opposition. Some Americans who supported resistance to British measures began to question the use of violence to force others to join the boycott. In addition, wealthier and more conservative colonists were frightened by the threat to private property inherent in the campaign. Moreover, political activism by ordinary colonists challenged the ruling elite's domination.

Americans were relieved when news arrived in April 1770 that the Townshend duties had been repealed, with the exception of the tea tax. A new prime minister, Lord North, had persuaded Parliament that duties on trade within the empire were bad policy. Although some colonial leaders argued that nonimportation should continue until the tea tax was repealed, merchants

Repeal of the Townshend Duties

quickly resumed importing. The rest of the Townshend Acts remained in force, but repeal of the taxes made the other laws appear less objectionable.

 ## Growing Rifts

On the very day Lord North proposed repeal of the Townshend duties, however, a clash between civilians and soldiers in Boston led to the death of five Americans. The origins of the event that patriots called the Boston Massacre lay in repeated clashes between customs officers and the people of Massachusetts. The decision to base the American Board of Customs Commissioners in Boston was the source of the problem.

From the day of their arrival in November 1767, the customs commissioners were frequent targets of mob action. During a 1768 riot sparked by the seizure of John Hancock's sloop *Liberty* on suspicion of smuggling, customs officers' property was destroyed. The British responded by assigning troops to maintain order in the city. For Bostonians, the redcoats were a constant reminder of the oppressive potential of British power.

Bostonians found themselves hemmed in at every turn. Guards on Boston Neck, the entrance to the city, checked all travelers and their goods. Redcoat patrols roamed the city day and night, questioning and sometimes harassing passersby. But the greatest potential for violence lay in the uneasy relationship between the soldiers and Boston laborers. Many redcoats sought employment in their off-duty hours, competing for unskilled jobs with the city's ordinary workingmen.

Violence erupted early on the evening of March 5, 1770, when a crowd of laborers began throwing hard-packed snowballs at soldiers guarding the Customs House. Goaded beyond endurance, the sentries acted against express orders and fired on the crowd, killing four and wounding eight, one of whom died a few days later. Resistance leaders idealized the dead rioters as martyrs for the cause of liberty, holding a solemn funeral and later commemorating March 5 annually with patriotic orations. Paul Revere's engraving of the

Boston Massacre

massacre was part of the propaganda campaign. (See How Do Historians Know? on page 97.)

Leading patriots wanted to ensure that the soldiers did not become martyrs as well. Thus when the soldiers were tried for the killings in November, they were defended by John Adams and Josiah Quincy, Jr., both unwavering patriots. All but two of the accused men were acquitted, and those convicted were released after being branded on the thumb. Undoubtedly the favorable outcome of the trials prevented London officials from taking further steps against the city.

For the next two years, a superficial calm descended on the colonies, but questions remained. The most outspoken colonial newspapers accused Great Britain of a deliberate plan to oppress the colonies.

A British Plot?   After the Stamp Act's repeal, the patriots had praised Parliament; following repeal of the Townshend duties, they warned of impending tyranny. The apparent isolated mistake—a single ill-chosen stamp tax— now appeared to be part of a plot against American liberties. Essayists pointed to the stationing of troops in Boston and the growing number of vice-admiralty courts as evidence of plans to enslave the colonists. Indeed, patriot writers played repeatedly on the word *enslavement*. Most white colonists had direct knowledge of slavery, and the threat of enslavement by Britain must have hit them with peculiar force.

Still, no one yet advocated complete independence from the mother country. Though the patriots were becoming increasingly convinced that they should seek freedom from parliamentary authority, they continued to acknowledge their British identity and their allegiance to George III. They began, therefore, to envision a system that would enable them to be ruled by their own elected legislatures while remaining loyal to the king. But any such scheme was alien to Britons' conception that Parliament held sole undivided sovereignty over the empire.

Although most of the duties had been repealed, the remainder of the Townshend Acts were still in force, and in the fall of 1772, the North ministry began to implement the section that provided for governors and judges to be paid from customs revenues. In early November, voters at a Boston town meeting established a Committee of Correspondence to publicize the decision by exchanging letters with other Massachusetts towns. Heading the committee was the man who had proposed its formation, Samuel Adams.

Samuel Adams   Samuel Adams was fifty-one in 1772, a decade the senior of most other leaders of American resistance. He had been a member of the Massachusetts assembly, an ally of the Loyal Nine, and a member of the Sons of Liberty. An experienced political organizer, Adams continually stressed the necessity of prudent collective action. His Committee of Correspondence thus undertook the task of creating an informed consensus among all the residents of Massachusetts.

Boston Committee of Correspondence   Such committees, which were eventually established throughout the colonies, represented the next logical step in the organization of American resistance. Until 1772, the protest movement was largely confined to the seacoast and primarily to major cities and towns. Adams realized that the time had come to widen the movement by involving the residents of the interior in the struggle. Accordingly, the Boston town meeting directed the Committee of Correspondence "to state the Rights of the Colonists and of this Province in particular," to list "the Infringements and Violations thereof that have been, or from time to time may be made," and to send copies to the other towns in the province.

The committee's statement declared that Americans had absolute rights to life, liberty, and property. The idea that "a British house of commons, should have a right, at pleasure, to give and grant the property of the colonists" was "irreconcileable" with "the first principles of natural law and Justice . . . and of the British Constitution in particular." The list of grievances complained of taxation without representation, the presence of unnecessary troops and customs officers on American soil, the use of imperial revenues to pay colonial officials, the expanded jurisdiction of vice-admiralty courts, and even the nature of the

How do historians know whether ordinary people were familiar with the ideas propounded by the leaders of the American Revolution? This is a difficult question to answer, because most of the evidence about the patriots' ideology comes from pamphlets and newspapers aimed at the well educated. People who could read at only a basic level might not have been able to understand the sophisticated criticisms of British policies advanced in such writings. But because an engraver made his point visually rather than verbally, anyone, even illiterate folk, could interpret an image like Paul Revere's masterful portrayal of the Boston Massacre. The label "Butcher's Hall" on the Customs House merely reinforces the patriot view of the incident on March 5, 1770. The British soldiers are shown firing on an unresisting crowd (not the aggressive, angry mob described at the soldiers' trial), and a gun with smoke drifting up from its barrel emerges from a window above the redcoats, suggesting the complicity of civilian officials in what the patriots interpreted as an outrageous act.   Photo: Library of Congress.

instructions given to American governors by their superiors in London. No mention was made of obedience to Parliament. Patriots—at least in Boston—had placed American rights first, loyalty to Great Britain a distant second.

In their responses, most towns aligned themselves with the city. From Braintree came the assertion that "all civil officers are or ought to be Servants to the people and dependent upon them for their official Support, and every instance to the Contrary from the Governor downwards tends to crush and destroy civil liberty." The citizens of Petersham commented that resistance to tyranny was "the first and highest social Duty of this people." Beliefs like these made the next crisis in Anglo-American affairs the final one.

 ## The Boston Tea Party

The only Townshend duty still in effect by 1773 was the tax on tea. Although a continuing tea boycott was less than fully effective, tea retained its explosive symbolic character. In May 1773, Parliament passed an act designed to save the East India Company from bankruptcy. The company, which held a legal monopoly on British trade with the East Indies, was of critical importance to the British economy (and to the financial well-being of many prominent British politicians). Under the Tea Act, certain duties paid on tea were to be returned to the company. Only designated agents were to sell tea, which would enable the East India Company to avoid colonial middlemen and undersell any competitors, even smugglers.

Tea Act

The net result of bypassing the middlemen would be cheaper tea for American consumers. Resistance leaders, however, interpreted the new measure as a pernicious device to make them admit Parliament's right to tax them, for the less-expensive tea would still be taxed under the Townshend law. Others saw the Tea Act as the first step in the establishment of an East India Company monopoly of all colonial trade. Residents of the four cities designated to receive the first shipments of tea ac-

cordingly prepared to respond to what they perceived as a new threat to their freedom.

In New York City, the tea ships failed to arrive on schedule. In Philadelphia, the governor of Pennsylvania persuaded the captain to sail back to Britain. In Charleston, the tea was unloaded, stored under the direction of local tradesmen, and later destroyed. The only confrontation occurred in Boston, where the town meeting on one side and Governor Thomas Hutchinson on the other rejected compromise.

The first of three tea ships entered Boston harbor on November 28. The customs laws required cargo to be landed and the appropriate duty paid by its owners within twenty days of a ship's arrival; otherwise, the cargo would be seized by customs officers and sold at auction. After a series of mass meetings, Bostonians voted to post guards on the wharf to prevent the tea from being unloaded. Hutchinson, for his part, refused to permit the vessels to leave the harbor.

On December 16, one day before the cargo would have been confiscated, more than five thousand people (nearly a third of the city's population) crowded into Old South Church. The meeting, chaired by Samuel Adams, made a final attempt to persuade Hutchinson to send the tea back to England. But the governor remained adamant. In the early evening Adams reportedly announced "that he could think of nothing further to be done—that they had now done all they could for the Salvation of their Country." Cries then rang out from the back of the crowd: "Boston harbor a tea-pot tonight! The Mohawks are come!" Within a few minutes, about sixty men crudely disguised as Indians, including Paul Revere and other artisans, assembled at the wharf, boarded the three ships, and dumped the cargo (342 chests of tea) into the harbor.

While supporters of the resistance movement rejoiced over the tea party, the North administration reacted with considerably less enthusiasm. In March 1774, Parliament adopted the first of four laws that became known as the Coercive, or Intolerable, Acts. It ordered the port of Boston closed until the tea was paid for, prohibiting all but

Coercive and Quebec Acts

coastal trade in food and firewood. Later in the spring, Parliament passed three other punitive measures. The Massachusetts Government Act altered the province's charter, substituting an appointed council for the elected one, increasing the governor's powers, and forbidding most town meetings. The Justice Act provided that a person accused of committing murder in the course of suppressing a riot or enforcing the laws could be tried outside the colony where the incident had occurred. Finally, the Quartering Act gave broad authority to military commanders seeking to house their troops in private dwellings. Thus the Coercive Acts punished not only Boston but also Massachusetts as a whole, alerting other colonies that their residents, too, could be subject to retaliation if they opposed British authority.

After passing the last of the Coercive Acts, Parliament turned its attention to much-needed reforms in the government of Quebec. The Quebec Act thereby became linked with the Coercive Acts in the minds of the patriots. Intended to ease strained relations with the former French colony, the Quebec Act granted greater religious freedom to Catholics—alarming Protestant colonists, who equated Roman Catholicism with religious and political despotism. It also reinstated French civil law and established an appointed council as the governing body of the colony. Finally, in an attempt to provide northern Indians with some protection against Anglo-American settlement, the act annexed to Quebec the area east of the Mississippi River and north of the Ohio River. That region, parts of which were claimed by individual seacoast colonies, was thus removed from their jurisdiction.

Members of Parliament who voted for the punitive legislation believed that the acts would be obeyed. To patriots, the Coercive Acts and the

Implications of the Coercive Acts

Quebec Act revealed Great Britain's deliberate plan to oppress Americans by denying them their rights and liberties. If the port of Boston could be closed, why not the ports of Philadelphia or New York? If the royal charter of Massachusetts could be changed, why not the charter of South Carolina? If certain people could be removed from their home colonies for trial, why not all violators of all laws? If troops could be forcibly quartered in private houses, did not that action pave the way for the occupation of all of America? If the Roman Catholic Church could receive favored status in Quebec, why not everywhere?

The Boston Committee of Correspondence urged all the colonies to join in an immediate renewed boycott of British goods. But the other provinces were not yet ready to take such a drastic step. They suggested that another intercolonial congress be convened to consider an appropriate response. Few people wanted to take hasty action; even the most ardent patriots remained loyal to Britain and hoped for reconciliation with its leaders. So the colonies agreed to send delegates to Philadelphia in September to attend a Continental Congress.

 ## Conclusion

During the preceding decade, momentous changes had occurred in the ways colonists thought about themselves and their allegiance. Once linked unquestioningly to Great Britain, they had begun to develop a sense of their own identity as Americans. They had started to realize that their concept of the political process differed from that held by people in the mother country. They also had come to understand that their economic interests did not necessarily coincide with those of Great Britain. Colonial political leaders reached such conclusions only after a long train of events, some of them violent, had altered their understanding of their relationship with the mother country.

In the late summer of 1774, the Americans were committed to resistance but not to independence. Even so, they had started to sever the bonds of empire.

Suggestions for Further Reading

General

Ian R. Christie and Benjamin W. Labaree, *Empire or Independence, 1760–1776: A British-American Dialogue on the Coming of the American Revolution* (1976); Marc Egnal, *A Mighty*

Empire: The Origins of the American Revolution (1988); Ronald Hoffman and Peter Albert, eds., *The Transforming Hand of Revolution: Reconsidering the American Revolution as a Social Movement* (1995); Merrill Jensen, *The Founding of a Nation: A History of the American Revolution, 1763–1776* (1968); Robert W. Tucker and David C. Hendrickson, *The Fall of the First British Empire: Origins of the War of American Independence* (1982).

Colonial Warfare and the British Empire

Fred Anderson, *A People's Army: Massachusetts Soldiers and Society in the Seven Years' War* (1984); Douglas Leach, *Roots of Conflict: British Armed Forces and Colonial Americans, 1677–1763* (1986); Robert C. Newbold, *The Albany Congress and Plan of Union of 1754* (1955); Alan Rogers, *Empire and Liberty: American Resistance to British Authority, 1755–1763* (1974); John Shy, *Toward Lexington: The Role of the British Army in the Coming of the American Revolution* (1965); James Titus, *The Old Dominion at War: Society, Politics, and Warfare in Late Colonial Virginia* (1991).

British Politics and Policy

James E. Bradley, *Popular Politics and the American Revolution in England* (1986); John Brooke, *King George III* (1972); Michael Kammen, *A Rope of Sand: The Colonial Agents, British Politics, and the American Revolution* (1968); Nancy F. Koehn, *The Power of Commerce: Economy and Governance in the First British Empire* (1994); P. D. G. Thomas, *Tea Party to Independence* (1991); P. D. G. Thomas, *The Townshend Duties Crisis* (1987); P. D. G. Thomas, *British Politics and the Stamp Act Crisis* (1975).

Native Americans and the West

Gregory Dowd, *A Spirited Resistance: The North American Indian Struggle for Unity, 1745–1815* (1992); Francis Jennings, *Empire of Fortune: Crowns, Colonies and Tribes in the Seven Years' War in America* (1988); Howard H. Peckham, *Pontiac and the Indian Uprising* (1947); Richard White, *The Middle Ground: Indians, Empires and Republics in the Great Lakes Region, 1650–1815* (1991).

Political and Economic Thought

Bernard Bailyn, *The Ideological Origins of the American Revolution* (1967); J. C. D. Clark, *The Language of Liberty, 1660–1832: Political Discourse and Social Dynamics in the Anglo-American World* (1994); J. E. Crowley, *This Sheba, Self: The Conceptualization of Economic Life in Eighteenth-Century America* (1974); Jay Fliegelman, *Prodigals and Pilgrims: The American Revolution Against Patriarchal Authority, 1750–1800* (1982).

American Resistance

David Ammerman, *In the Common Cause: American Response to the Coercive Acts of 1774* (1974); Richard D. Brown, *Revolutionary Politics in Massachusetts: The Boston Committee of Correspondence and the Towns, 1772–1774* (1970); Benjamin W. Labaree, *The Boston Tea Party* (1964); Pauline R. Maier, *The Old Revolutionaries: Political Lives in the Age of Samuel Adams* (1980); Pauline R. Maier, *From Resistance to Revolution: Colonial Radicals and the Development of American Opposition to Britain, 1765–1776* (1972); Edmund S. Morgan and Helen M. Morgan, *The Stamp Act Crisis: Prologue to Revolution* (1953); Bruce A. Ragsdale, *A Planters' Republic: The Search for Economic Independence in Revolutionary Virginia* (1996); Richard Ryerson, *The Revolution Has Now Begun: The Radical Committees of Philadelphia, 1765–1776* (1978); John W. Tyler, *Smugglers and Patriots: Boston Merchants and the Advent of the American Revolution* (1986); Richard Walsh, *Charleston's Sons of Liberty: A Study of the Artisans, 1763–1789* (1959); Hiller B. Zobel, *The Boston Massacre* (1970).

CHAPTER

6

A Revolution, Indeed
1774–1783

W hen John Provey and Richard Weaver appeared before the loyalist claims commissioners in London at the end of the Revolution, the commissioners were not impressed with their descriptions of losses and loyal service to the king. Such men had "no right to ask or expect any thing from Government," the commissioners declared. So Provey and Weaver were denied any assistance from the funds allocated by Parliament to compensate loyalists for the damages they had incurred by opposing the Revolution. Why were Weaver and Provey treated thus? They were African-Americans.

Provey, a former slave from North Carolina, had served in a black corps of the British army during the war; the freeborn Weaver had left Philadelphia with the British troops when they evacuated that city in 1778. Because they were denied the help they sought, they and their families, along with hundreds of other African-Americans, became dependent on charity.

Seeing no future for themselves in London, they both agreed to emigrate to West Africa, to the new colony of Sierra Leone. Provey died on shipboard, but Weaver made it to Sierra Leone and was elected the first governor of the tiny colony, composed largely of exiled African-American loyalists. Conflicts with a nearby ruler and with slavers who established a post near the settlement almost destroyed it. But in 1792 the future of the colony was assured by the arrival of an additional twelve hundred African-American refugees.

The little-known tale of the black loyalists who returned to the homeland of their ancestors is but one dramatic example of the disruptive effects of the American Revolution. The Revolution uprooted thousands of families, disrupted the economy, reshaped society by forcing many colonists into permanent exile, led Americans to develop new conceptions of politics, and created a nation from thirteen separate colonies.

The struggle for independence required revolutionary leaders to accomplish three tasks. The first was political and ideological: transforming a consensus favoring loyal resistance into a coalition supporting independence. Various means, including coercion, were used to enlist all European-Americans in the patriot cause. Fearing that Indians and blacks would side with Britain, the colonies' elected leaders hoped at least to ensure those groups' neutrality in the impending conflict. The second task involved foreign relations. To win independence, patriot leaders knew they needed international recognition and aid, particularly from France. Thus they dispatched to Paris the most experienced American diplomat, Benjamin Franklin, who skillfully negotiated the Franco-American alliance of 1778, which was to prove crucial to winning independence.

Only the third task directly involved the British. George Washington, commander-in-chief of the American army, soon recognized that his primary goal should be not to win battles but to avoid losing them decisively. The outcome of any one battle was less important than ensuring that his army survived to fight another day. Consequently, the story of the Revolutionary War reveals British action and American reaction, British attacks and American defenses. The American war effort was aided by Britain's focus on winning battles rather than on the primary goal of retaining the colonies' allegiance.

Government by Congress and Committee

When the fifty-five delegates to the First Continental Congress convened in Philadelphia in September 1774, they knew that many Americans would support any measures they adopted. That summer, open meetings held throughout the colonies had endorsed the idea of another nonimportation pact.

Committees of correspondence publicized these meetings so effectively that Americans everywhere knew about them. Since governors had forbidden regular assemblies to conduct formal elections, most congressional delegates were selected by extralegal local gatherings. Thus the very act of designating delegates to attend the Congress involved Americans in open defiance of British authority.

The colonies' leading political figures—most of them lawyers, merchants, and planters—attended the Philadelphia Congress. The Massachusetts delegation included both Samuel Adams and his younger cousin John, an ambitious lawyer. Among others, New York sent John Jay, a talented young attorney. From Pennsylvania came the conservative Joseph Galloway and his long-time rival, John Dickinson. Virginia elected Richard Henry Lee and Patrick Henry, both noted for their patriotic zeal, as well as George Washington.

First Continental Congress

The congressmen faced three tasks when they convened on September 5, 1774. The first two were explicit: defining American grievances and developing a plan for resistance. The third—outlining a theory of their constitutional relationship with Great Britain—proved troublesome. Radical congressmen, like Lee of Virginia, argued that colonists owed allegiance only to George III and that Parliament was nothing more than a local legislature for Great Britain, with no authority over the colonies. The conservatives—Joseph Galloway and his allies—proposed a formal plan of union that would have required Parliament and a new American legislature to consent jointly to all laws pertaining to the colonies. The delegates, who narrowly rejected Galloway's plan, also refused to accept the radicals' position.

Finally, they accepted a compromise position worked out by John Adams. The crucial clause that Adams drafted in the Congress's Declaration of Rights and Grievances read in part: "From the necessity of the case, and a regard to the mutual interest of both countries, we cheerfully consent to the operation of such acts of

Declaration of Rights and Grievances

• *Important Events* •

1774	First Continental Congress meets in Philadelphia, adopts Declaration of Rights and Grievances
	Continental Association implements economic boycott of Britain; committees of observation established to oversee boycott
1774–75	Provincial conventions replace collapsing colonial governments
1775	Battles of Lexington and Concord; first shots of war fired
	Second Continental Congress begins
	Lord Dunmore's proclamation offers freedom to patriots' slaves if they join British forces
1776	Thomas Paine publishes *Common Sense*, advocating independence

	British evacuate Boston
	Declaration of Independence adopted
	New York City falls to British
1777	British take Philadelphia
	Burgoyne surrenders at Saratoga
1778	French alliance brings vital assistance to the United States
1779	Sullivan expedition destroys Iroquois villages
1780	British take Charleston
1781	Cornwallis surrenders at Yorktown
1782	Peace negotiations begin
1783	Treaty of Paris signed, granting independence to the United States

the British parliament, as are bona fide, restrained to the regulation of our external commerce." Notice the key phrases. "From the necessity of the case" declared that Americans would obey Parliament only because they thought that doing so was in the best interest of both countries. "Bona fide, restrained to the regulation of our external commerce" made it clear to Lord North that they would continue to resist taxes in disguise, like the Townshend duties. Most striking of all was that such language—which only a few years before would have been regarded as irredeemably radical—could be presented and accepted as a compromise in the fall of 1774.

With the constitutional issue resolved, the delegates readily agreed on the laws they wanted repealed (notably the Coercive Acts) and decided to implement an economic boycott while petitioning the king for relief. They adopted the Continental Association, which called for nonimportation of British goods (effective December 1, 1774), nonconsumption of British products (effective March 1, 1775), and nonexportation of American goods to Britain and the British West Indies (effective

September 10, 1775, so that southern planters could market their 1774 tobacco crop).

To enforce the Continental Association, Congress recommended the election of committees of observation and inspection in every American locality. By specifying that committee members be chosen by all persons qualified to vote for members of the lower house of the colonial legislatures, Congress guaranteed the committees a broad popular base. The seven to eight thousand committeemen became the local leaders of American resistance.

Committees of Observation

Though created to oversee the boycott's implementation, the committees soon became de facto governments. They examined merchants' records and published the names of those who continued to import British goods. They also promoted home manufactures, encouraging Americans to adopt simple modes of dress and behavior to symbolize their commitment to liberty and virtuous behavior. Since expensive leisure-time activities were believed to reflect vice and corruption, Congress urged Americans to forgo dancing, gambling, horseracing, cockfighting, and other forms of "extravagance and dissipation." By enforcing these injunctions, the committees gradually extended their authority over many aspects of American life.

The committees also attempted to identify opponents of American resistance, developing elaborate spy networks, circulating copies of the Continental Association for signatures, and investigating reports of dissident remarks and activities. Suspected dissenters were first urged to support the colonial cause; if they failed to do so, the committees had them watched, restricted their movements, or tried to force them to leave the area. People engaging in casual political exchanges with friends one day could find themselves charged with "treasonable conversation" the next.

By early 1775, the regular colonial governments were collapsing. Only in Connecticut, Rhode Island, Delaware, and Pennsylvania did

Provincial Conventions

legislatures continue to meet without encountering patriot challenges to their authority. In every other colony, popularly elected provincial conventions took over the task of running the government. In late 1774 and early 1775, these conventions approved the Continental Association, elected delegates to the Second Continental Congress (scheduled for May), organized militia units, and gathered arms and ammunition. Unable to stem the tide of resistance, the British-appointed governors and councils watched helplessly as their authority crumbled.

Royal officials throughout the colonies became politically impotent. Courts were prevented from holding sessions; taxes were paid to the conventions' agents rather than to provincial tax collectors; sheriffs' powers were challenged; and militiamen would muster only when committees ordered. In short, during the six months preceding the battles at Lexington and Concord, independence was being won at the local level. Not many Americans fully realized what was happening. The vast majority still proclaimed their loyalty to Great Britain and denied that they sought to leave the empire. Among the few who recognized the trend toward independence were those who opposed it.

Choosing Sides: Loyalists, African-Americans, and Indians

The first protests against British measures had won the support of most colonists, but in the late 1760s and early 1770s, many Americans began to question the aims and tactics of the resistance movement. By 1774 and 1775 such people found themselves in a difficult position. Most of them objected to parliamentary policies, favoring some kind of constitutional reform. Nevertheless, if forced to a choice, these colonists sympathized with Great Britain rather than with an independent America. Their objections to violent protest, their desire to uphold the legally constituted colonial governments, and their fears of anarchy combined to make them especially sensitive to the dangers of resistance.

Some conservatives began in 1774 and 1775 to publish essays and pamphlets critical of the Congress and its allied committees. In Pennsylvania, Joseph Galloway published a tract attacking the Continental Congress for rejecting his plan of union. In Massachusetts, the young attorney Daniel Leonard, writing under the pseudonym Massachusettensis, engaged in a prolonged newspaper debate with Novanglus (John Adams). Leonard realized that the dispute was becoming less about American subordination to Parliament and more about whether the colonies would remain linked to Great Britain at all.

Some colonists heeded the conservative pamphleteers' warnings. About one-fifth of the Anglo-American population remained loyal to

Loyalists, Patriots, and Neutrals

Great Britain, actively opposing independence. With notable exceptions, most people of the following descriptions remained loyal to the Crown: British-appointed government officials; merchants whose trade depended on imperial connections; Anglican clergy everywhere and lay Anglicans in the North; former officers and enlisted men from the British army, many of whom had settled in America after 1763; non-English ethnic minorities, especially Scots; tenant farmers, particularly those whose landlords sided with the patriots; members of persecuted religious sects; and many of the backcountry southerners who had rebelled against eastern rule in the 1760s and early 1770s. All these people had one thing in common: patriot leaders were their long-standing opponents. Local and provincial disputes thus helped determine which side people would choose in the imperial conflict.

Active patriots, who accounted for about two-fifths of the population, came chiefly from the groups that had dominated colonial society, either numerically or politically. Among them were yeoman farmers, members of dominant Protestant sects, Chesapeake gentry, merchants dealing mainly in American commodities, city artisans, elected officeholders, and people of English descent. Wives usually but not always adopted their husbands' political beliefs. Although all these patriots supported the Revolution, they pursued divergent goals within the broader coalition. Some sought limited political reform, others extensive political change, and still others social and economic reforms.

About two-fifths of the white population fell somewhere between the loyalists and the active patriots. Some of those who tried to avoid taking sides were sincere pacifists, such as Quakers. Others opportunistically shifted their allegiance to whatever side happened to be winning at the time. Still others simply wanted to be left alone. The latter group made up an especially large proportion of the population in the southern backcountry, where Scots-Irish settlers had little love for either the patriot gentry or the English authorities.

To American patriots, those who were not for them were against them. By the winter of 1775–1776, the Second Continental Congress was recommending that all "disaffected" persons be disarmed and arrested. State legislatures passed laws prescribing severe penalties for suspected loyalists. Loyalists who were banished often had

their property confiscated and the funds from its sale used for the war efforts. Perhaps as many as 100,000 Americans preferred to leave their homeland rather than live in a nation independent of British rule. And patriots worried not only about loyalists but also about the reactions of Indians and slaves.

Bondspeople faced their own dilemma: how could they best pursue their goal of escaping slavery? Should they fight with or against their masters? No correct choice was immediately apparent. Some African-Americans joined the revolutionaries, but to most an alliance with Great Britain appeared more promising. Thus news of slave conspiracies surfaced in different parts of the colonies in late 1774 and early 1775. All shared a common element: a plan to assist the British in return for freedom. The most serious incident occurred in 1775 in Charleston, where Thomas Jeremiah, a free black harbor pilot, was brutally executed after being convicted of attempting to foment a slave revolt.

African-Americans' Dilemma

Fear of such acts made sugar planters in the British West Indian colonies more cautious in their opposition to parliamentary policies than were their counterparts on the mainland. On most of the Caribbean islands, slaves outnumbered their masters by six or seven to one. With the ever-present threat of slave revolt or foreign attack hanging over their heads, planters could not afford to risk opposing Britain, their chief protector.

Slavery affected politics in the continental colonies as well. In the North, with few resident slaves, revolutionary fervor was at its height. In Virginia and Maryland, where free people also constituted a safe majority, there was occasional alarm over potential slave revolts but no disabling fear. But South Carolina and Georgia, where slaves composed more than half of the population, were noticeably less enthusiastic about resistance. Georgia sent no delegates to the First Continental Congress and reminded its representatives at the second one to

Slavery and Patriotic Fervor

consider its circumstances, "with our blacks and tories [loyalists] within us," when voting on the question of independence.

The slaveowners' worst fears were realized in November 1775, when Lord Dunmore, the governor of Virginia, offered to free any slaves and indentured servants who would leave their patriot masters to join the British forces. Dunmore hoped to use African-Americans in his fight against the revolutionaries and to disrupt the economy by depriving planters of their labor force. But at most only two thousand African-Americans rallied to the British standard. Even so, Dunmore's proclamation led Congress in January 1776 to modify an earlier policy that had prohibited the enlistment of African-Americans in the regular American army.

Although slaves did not pose a serious threat to the revolutionary cause in its early years, the patriots turned rumors of slave uprisings to their own advantage. In South Carolina, resistance leaders argued that unity under the Continental Association would protect masters from their slaves at a time when royal government was unable to muster adequate defense forces. This strategy undoubtedly kept many fearful whites in the patriot camp.

Similarly, the threat of Indian attacks helped persuade some reluctant westerners to support the struggle against Great Britain. In the years since the Proclamation of 1763, British officials had won the trust of the interior tribes by attempting to protect them from land-hungry European-Americans. British-appointed superintendents of Indian affairs, John Stuart in the South and Sir William Johnson in the North, lived among and understood the Indians. In 1768, Stuart and Johnson negotiated separate agreements modifying the proclamation line and attempting to draw realistic, defensible boundaries between tribal holdings and European-American settlements. The treaties supposedly established permanent western borders for the colonies. But just a few years later, the British pushed the southern boundary even farther west to accommodate the demands of settlers in western Georgia and Kentucky.

By 1775, many Indian groups were impatient with European-Americans' aggressive pressure on their lands. Such pressure, when combined with their confidence in Stuart and Johnson, predisposed most Indians toward an alliance with Great Britain. Even so, the latter hesitated to make full and immediate use of these potential allies because Indian war aims and tactics were not compatible with those of the British. Accordingly, they sought from the tribes only a promise of neutrality.

Indians' Grievances

Recognizing that their standing with the tribes was poor, the patriots also sought the Indians' neutrality. In 1775 the Second Continental Congress sent a general message to the tribes describing the war as "a family quarrel between us and Old England" and requesting that they "not join on either side" since "you Indians are not concerned in it." A group of Cherokees led by Chief Dragging Canoe nevertheless decided that the "family quarrel" would allow them to settle some old scores. They attacked settlements along the western borders of the Carolinas and Virginia in the summer of 1776. But a militia campaign destroyed many of their towns. Dragging Canoe and his diehard followers fled to the west, establishing new outposts; the rest of the Cherokees agreed to a treaty that ceded still more of their land.

The fate of the Cherokees foreshadowed the history of Indian involvement in the Revolution. The British victory over France in 1763 had removed the Indians' strongest weapon: their ability to play the European powers off against one another. Successful strategies were difficult to envision under these new circumstances, and even if the interests of several neighboring tribes coincided, old enmities kept them from forming alliances. Consequently, during the Revolution many Indian nations avoided active involvement in the war.

Native Americans' Diverse Interests

Thus, although patriots could never completely ignore the threats posed by loyalists, neutrals, slaves, and Indians, only rarely did fear of these groups seriously hamper the revolutionary movement. The reality was that the practical impossibility of a large-scale slave revolt, coupled with tribal feuds and the patriots' successful campaign to disarm and neutralize loyalists, ensured that the revolutionaries would remain firmly in control as they fought for independence.

War Begins

On January 27, 1775, Lord Dartmouth, secretary of state for America, addressed a fateful letter to General Thomas Gage in Boston. Expressing his belief that American resistance was nothing more than the response of a "rude rabble without plan," Dartmouth urged Gage to take a decisive step.

Dartmouth's letter did not reach Gage until April 14. He responded by sending an expedition to confiscate provincial military supplies stockpiled at Concord. Bostonians dispatched two messengers, William Dawes and Paul Revere (later joined by Dr. Samuel Prescott), to rouse the countryside. So when the British vanguard of several hundred men approached Lexington at dawn on April 19, they found a ragtag group of seventy militiamen drawn up before them on the common. The Americans' commander ordered his men to withdraw, realizing they could not halt the redcoats' advance. But as they began to disperse, a shot rang out; the British soldiers then fired several volleys. When they stopped, eight Americans lay dead and another ten had been wounded. The British moved on to Concord, 5 miles away.

Battles of Lexington and Concord

There the contingents of militia were larger, Concord residents having been joined by groups of men from nearby towns. An exchange of gunfire at the North Bridge spilled the first British blood of the Revolution: three men were killed and nine wounded. Thousands of militiamen then fired from houses and from behind trees and bushes at the British forces as they retreated to Boston. By the end of the day, the redcoats had suffered 272 casualties, including 70 deaths. The patriots had suffered just 93 casualties.

By the evening of April 20, approximately twenty thousand American militiamen had gathered around Boston. Many soon returned home for spring planting, but those who remained dug in along siege lines encircling the city. For nearly a year the two armies sat and stared at each other across those lines. The redcoats attacked their besiegers only once, on June 17, when they drove the Americans from trenches atop Breed's Hill in Charlestown. In that misnamed Battle of Bunker Hill, the British incurred their greatest losses of the entire war: over 800 wounded and 228 killed. The Americans, though forced to abandon their position, lost less than half that number.

First Year of War

During the same eleven-month period, patriots captured Fort Ticonderoga, a British fort on Lake Champlain, acquiring much-needed cannon. Trying to bring Canada into the war on the American side, they also mounted an uncoordinated northern campaign that ended in disaster at Quebec in early 1776. Most significant, the lull in the fighting at Boston gave both sides a chance to regroup, organize, and plan their strategies.

Lord North and his new American secretary, Lord George Germain, made three central assumptions about the war they faced. First, they concluded that patriot forces could not withstand the assaults of trained British regulars. Accordingly, they dispatched to America the largest force Great Britain had ever assembled anywhere: 370 transport ships carrying 32,000 troops and tons of supplies, accompanied by 73 naval vessels and 13,000 sailors. Such an extraordinary effort, they thought, would ensure a quick victory.

British Strategy

Second, British officials and army officers treated this war as comparable to wars they had fought successfully in Europe. They adopted a conventional strategy of capturing major American cities and defeating the rebel army decisively without suffering serious casualties themselves. Third, they assumed that a clear-cut military victory would automatically bring about their goal of retaining the colonies' allegiance.

All these assumptions proved false. North and Germain vastly underestimated Americans' commitment to armed resistance. Battlefield defeats did not lead patriots to abandon their political aims and sue for peace. The ministers in London also failed to recognize the significance of the American population's dispersal over an area 1,500 miles long. Although Great Britain would control each of the most important American ports at one time or another during the war, less than 5 percent of the population lived in those cities. Furthermore, the coast offered so many excellent harbors that essential commerce was easily rerouted. In other words, the loss of cities did little to damage the American cause.

Most of all, British officials failed at first to understand that military triumph would not necessarily lead to political victory. Securing the colonies permanently would require hundreds of thousands of Americans to return to their original allegiance. The British thus needed to both overpower and convert the patriots. After 1778, the ministry adopted a strategy designed to achieve that goal through the expanded use of loyalist forces and the restoration of civilian authority in occupied areas. But the new policy came too late. Britain's leaders never fully realized that they were fighting not a conventional European war but rather an entirely new kind of conflict: the first modern war of national liberation.

Great Britain at least had a bureaucracy ready to supervise the war effort. The Americans had only the Second Continental Congress, originally planned as a brief gathering to consider the ministry's response to the Continental Association. Instead, the delegates who convened in Philadelphia on May 10, 1775, found that they had to assume the mantle of intercolonial government. As the summer passed, Congress authorized the printing of money with which to purchase necessary goods, established a committee to supervise relations with foreign countries, and took steps to strengthen the militia. Most important, it created the Continental Army and appointed its generals.

Second Continental Congress

Until Congress met, the Massachusetts provincial congress had taken responsibility for organizing the militiamen encamped at Boston. Because the cost of maintaining that army was a burden, Massachusetts asked the Continental Congress to assume the task of directing the army. As a first step, Congress had to choose a commander-in-chief. Since the war had thus far been a wholly northern affair, many delegates recognized the importance of naming someone who was not a New Englander. There seemed only one obvious candidate: they unanimously selected their fellow delegate, the Virginian George Washington.

Washington was no fiery radical, nor had he played a prominent role in the prerevolutionary agitation. But his devotion to the American cause was unquestioned. He was dignified, conservative, and respectable—a man of unimpeachable integrity. Though unmistakably an aristocrat, he was unswervingly committed to representative government. His stamina was remarkable, and he both looked and acted like a leader.

George Washington: A Portrait of Leadership

Washington needed all the coolness and caution he could muster when he took command of the army outside Boston in July 1775. It took him months to impose hierarchy and discipline on the unruly troops and to bring order to the supply system. But by March 1776, when the arrival of cannon from Ticonderoga finally enabled him to put direct pressure on the redcoats in the city, the army was prepared to act. As it happened, an assault on Boston proved unnecessary. Sir William Howe, who had replaced Gage, had for some time planned to transfer his troops to New York City. The patriots' new cannon decided the matter. On March 17, the British and more than a thousand of their loyalist allies abandoned Boston forever.

British Evacuate Boston

That spring of 1776, as the British fleet left Boston for the temporary haven of Halifax, Nova Scotia, the colonies were moving inexorably toward the unthinkable—a declaration of independence. Even months after fighting began, American leaders still denied seeking a break with

Thomas Paine, the English radical who wrote Common Sense. *James Watson prepared this 1783 engraving from a portrait by Charles Willson Peale, who depicted his subject accompanied by the tools of the writer's trade—several sheets of paper and a quill pen.*   National Portrait Gallery, Smithsonian Institution, Washington, D.C.

Great Britain. But in January 1776 there appeared a pamphlet by a man who both thought and advocated the unthinkable.

Thomas Paine's *Common Sense* exploded on the American scene like a bombshell. Within three months of publication, it sold 120,000 copies.

Thomas Paine's Common Sense

The author, a radical English printer who had lived in America only since 1774, called stridently and stirringly for independence. More than that: Paine rejected the notion that a balance of monarchy, aristocracy, and democracy was necessary to preserve freedom. Instead, he advocated the establishment of a *republic*, a government by the people with no king or nobility. Paine also denied the benefits of links to the mother country, insisting that Britain had exploited the colonies unmercifully. In place of the frequently heard assertion that an independent America would be weak and divided, he substituted an unlimited confidence in America's strength when freed from European control.

There is no way of knowing how many people were converted to the cause of independence by reading *Common Sense*. But by late spring in 1776 independence had become inevitable. On May 10, the Second Continental Congress formally recommended that individual colonies "adopt such governments as shall, in the opinion of the representatives of the people, best conduce to the happiness and safety of their constituents in particular, and America in general." From that source stemmed the first state constitutions.

June 7 brought confirmation of the movement toward independence. Richard Henry Lee of Virginia, seconded by John Adams of Massachusetts, introduced the crucial resolution: "that these United Colonies are, and of right ought to be, free and independent States, that they are absolved of all allegiance to the British Crown, and that all political connection between them and the State of Great Britain is, and ought to be, totally dissolved." Congress debated Lee's resolution and directed Thomas Jefferson, John Adams, and Benjamin Franklin to draft a declaration of independence. The committee assigned primary responsibility for writing the declaration to Jefferson.

Thomas Jefferson was at the time thirty-four years old, a Virginia lawyer educated at the College of William and Mary. A member of the House of Burgesses, he had read widely in history and political theory. His broad knowledge was evident not only in the declaration but also in his draft of the Virginia state constitution.

Thomas Jefferson and the Declaration of Independence

The draft of the declaration was laid before Congress on June 28, 1776. The delegates officially voted for independence four days later, then debated the wording of the declaration for two more days, adopting it with some changes on July 4. Since Americans had long ago ceased to see themselves as legitimate subjects of Parliament, the Declaration of Independence concentrated on George III (see the Appendix). That focus also provided an identifiable villain. The document accused the king of attempting to destroy representative government in the colonies and of oppressing Americans through the unjustified use of excessive force.

The declaration's chief long-term importance, however, lay not in its lengthy catalog of grievances against George III but in its ringing statements of principle that have served ever since as the ideal to which Americans aspire: "We hold these truths to be self-evident: That all men are created equal; that they are endowed by their Creator with certain unalienable rights; that among these are life, liberty and the pursuit of happiness; that, to secure these rights, governments are instituted among men, deriving their just powers from the consent of the governed; that whenever any form of government becomes destructive of these ends, it is the right of the people to alter or to abolish it, and to institute new government." These phrases have echoed down through American history like no others.

When the delegates in Philadelphia adopted the declaration, they risked their necks: they were committing treason. Thus when they concluded the declaration with the assertion that they "mutually pledge[d] to each other our lives, our fortunes, and our sacred honor," they spoke no less than the truth.

The Long Struggle in the North

In late June 1776, the first ships carrying Sir William Howe's troops from Halifax appeared off the coast of New York (see map). On July 2, the day Congress voted for independence, redcoats landed on Staten Island. Howe, though, waited until mid-August, after the arrival of more troops from England, to begin his attack on the city. The delay gave Washington sufficient time to march his army of seventeen thousand south to meet the threat. But both he and his men, still inexperienced in

Loss of New York City

The War in the North, 1775–1777 The early phase of the Revolutionary War, as shown in this map, was dominated by British troop movements in the Boston area, the redcoats' evacuation to Nova Scotia in the spring of 1776, and the subsequent British invasion of New York and New Jersey.

fighting and maneuvering, made major mistakes, losing battles at Brooklyn Heights and on Manhattan Island. The city fell to the British, who captured nearly three thousand American soldiers.

During the autumn months, Washington retreated across New Jersey, with Howe in leisurely pursuit. The British took control of most of the state, and hundreds of New Jerseyites and Pennsylvanians accepted pardons for their "treasonous" activities. Occupying troops met little opposition, and the revolutionary cause appeared to be in disarray.

Campaign in New Jersey

The British let their advantage slip away as redcoats stationed in New Jersey went on a rampage of rape and plunder. Because loyalists and patriots were indistinguishable to British and Hessian troops, families on both sides suffered nearly equally. The troops seized crops, looted houses, and desecrated churches and public buildings. Yet nothing was better calculated to rally doubtful

Americans to the cause than the murder of innocent civilians and the rape of women.

The soldiers' marauding alienated potentially loyal New Jerseyites and Pennsylvanians whose allegiance the British could ill afford to lose. It also spurred Washington's determination to strike back. Moving quickly, he attacked a Hessian encampment at Trenton early in the morning of December 26, while the redcoats were still reeling from their Christmas celebration. A few days later, Washington attacked again at Princeton. Having gained command of the field and buoyed American spirits with the two swift victories, Washington set up winter quarters at Morristown, New Jersey.

The 1776 campaign established patterns that persisted throughout much of the war, despite changes in British leadership and strategy. The British forces were usually more numerous and often better led than the Americans. But their ponderous style of maneuvering, lack of familiarity with the terrain, and inability to live off the land without antagonizing the populace partially offset those advantages. Furthermore, although Washington always seemed to lack regular troops—the Continental Army never numbered more than 18,500 men—he could usually count on the militia to join him at crucial times. American militiamen did not like to sign up for long terms of service or to fight far from home; but when their homes were threatened, they rallied to the cause.

As the war dragged on, the Continental Army and the militia took on decidedly different

At the Battle of Princeton in early 1777, American forces under George Washington cemented the victory they had won a few days earlier at Trenton. This view was painted in 1787 by James Peale, who fought in the battle. Princeton University Library.

characters. State governments, responsible for filling military quotas, discovered that most men willing to enlist for long periods in the regular army were young, single, and footloose. Farmers with families tended to prefer short-term militia duty. As the supply of men willing to sign up with the Continentals dwindled, recruiters in northern states turned increasingly to African-Americans, both slave and free. Perhaps as many as five thousand blacks eventually served in the army, and most of them won their freedom as a result. Also attached to the American forces were a number of wives and widows of poor soldiers. Such camp followers worked as cooks, nurses, and launderers in return for rations and low wages. The American army was unwieldy and difficult to manage, yet its shapelessness provided an almost unlimited reservoir of manpower and womanpower.

The American Army

In 1777, the chief British effort was planned by Howe's subordinate, "Gentleman Johnny" Burgoyne, a playboy general who had gained the ear of Lord George Germain. Burgoyne convinced Germain that he could lead an invading force of redcoats and Indians down the Hudson River from Canada, cutting off New England from the rest of the states. He proposed to rendezvous near Albany with a similar force that would move east along the Mohawk River valley. The combined forces would then presumably link up with Sir William Howe's troops in New York City.

Planning the 1777 Campaign

That Burgoyne's scheme would give "Gentleman Johnny" all the glory did not escape Sir William's notice. While Burgoyne was plotting in London, Howe was laying his own plans to take Philadelphia. Just as Burgoyne left Howe out of his plans, Howe left Burgoyne out of his. Thus the two major British armies in America would operate independently in 1777, and the result would be a disaster.

Howe captured Philadelphia, but he did so in inexplicable fashion, taking six weeks to transport his troops by sea instead of marching them overland. That maneuver cost him at least a month, debilitated his men, depleted his supplies, and placed him only 40 miles closer to Philadelphia than when he started. By the time Howe was ready to move on Philadelphia, Washington had had time to prepare its defenses. Twice, at Brandywine Creek and again at Germantown, the two armies clashed near the patriot capital. Although the British won both engagements, the Americans handled themselves well. The redcoats took Philadelphia in late September, but to little effect. The campaign season was nearly over, and far to the north, Burgoyne was going down to defeat.

Howe Takes Philadelphia

Burgoyne and his men set out from Montréal in mid-June 1777, floating down Lake Champlain into New York. They easily took Fort Ticonderoga, but they started having trouble when Burgoyne began an overland march. Because his clumsy artillery carriages and baggage wagons foundered in the heavy forests and ravines, Burgoyne's troops took twenty-four days to travel 23 miles. In August, the campaign suffered two sharp blows—first, when a force of redcoats and Indians turned back after a battle at Oriskany, New York; second, when in a clash near Bennington, Vermont, American militiamen nearly wiped out eight hundred of Burgoyne's German mercenaries. Yet the general continued to dawdle, giving the Americans more than enough time to prepare for his coming. After several skirmishes with an American army commanded by General Horatio Gates, Burgoyne was surrounded near Saratoga, New York. On October 17, 1777, he surrendered his entire force of more than six thousand men.

Burgoyne's Campaign in New York

The August 1777 battle at Oriskany was also important because it revealed a division in the Iroquois Confederacy (see page 55). In 1776 the Six Nations had formally pledged to remain neutral in the Anglo-American struggle. But two influential Mohawk leaders, Joseph and Mary Brant, worked tirelessly to persuade the Iroquois to join the British. Mary Brant, a pow-

Split of the Iroquois Confederacy

erful tribal matron, was also the widow of the Indian superintendent Sir William Johnson. Her younger brother Joseph, a renowned warrior, was convinced that the Six Nations should ally themselves with the British in order to prevent American encroachment on their lands. The Brants won over to the British the Senecas, Cayugas, and Mohawks. But the Oneidas preferred the American side and brought the Tuscaroras with them. The Onondagas split into three factions, one on each side and one supporting neutrality. At Oriskany, the three-hundred-year league of friendship was torn apart as confederation warriors fought on both sides.

The collapse of Iroquois unity and the confederacy's abandonment of neutrality had significant consequences. In 1778, Iroquois warriors allied with the British raided frontier villages in Pennsylvania and New York. Americans under General John Sullivan retaliated by so thoroughly destroying Iroquois crops and settlements that many bands had to abandon their ancestral homeland. A large number of Iroquois people never returned to New York but settled in British Canada.

Burgoyne's surrender at Saratoga so discouraged the British that Lord North authorized a peace commission to offer the Americans what they had requested in 1774—in effect, a return to the imperial system of 1763. It was, of course, far too late for that: the patriots rejected the overture.

Most important of all, the American victory at Saratoga drew France formally into the conflict. Ever since 1763, the French had sought to avenge their defeat in the Seven Years' War, and the American Revolution gave them that opportunity. Even before Benjamin Franklin arrived in Paris in late 1776, France was covertly supplying the revolutionaries with military necessities.

Franklin worked tirelessly to strengthen ties between the two nations. By presenting himself as a representative of American simplicity, he played on the French image of Americans as virtuous yeomen. Franklin's efforts culminated in 1778 when the countries signed two treaties. In the Treaty of Amity and Commerce, France recognized American independence and established trade ties

Franco-American Alliance of 1778

with the new nation. In the Treaty of Alliance, France and the United States promised—assuming that France would go to war with Britain, which it soon did—that neither would negotiate peace with the enemy without consulting the other. France also abandoned all its claims to Canada and to North American territory east of the Mississippi River.

The French alliance had two major benefits for the patriot cause. First, France began to aid the Americans openly, sending troops and naval vessels in addition to arms, ammunition, clothing, and blankets. Second, Great Britain could no longer focus solely on the American mainland, for it had to fight France in the Caribbean and elsewhere. Spain's entry into the war in 1779 as an ally of France (but not of the United States) further magnified Britain's problems, for the Revolution then became a global war.

The Long Struggle in the South

In the aftermath of the Saratoga disaster, the British reassessed their strategy and decided that they might attain success by shifting the field of battle southward. Howe's replacement, Sir Henry Clinton, became convinced that a southern strategy would succeed. In late 1779 he sailed down the coast from New York to attack Charleston, the most important city in the South (see map, page 115).

The Americans worked hard to bolster Charleston's defenses, but the city fell to the British on May 12, 1780. General Benjamin Lincoln surrendered the entire southern army—5,500 men—to the invaders. In the weeks that followed, the redcoats spread through South Carolina, established garrisons at key points in the interior, and organized loyalist regiments.

Fall of Charleston

Yet the British triumph was less complete than it appeared. The success of the southern campaign depended on British control of the seas, for only by sea could the widely dispersed British armies coordinate their efforts. For the moment, the Royal Navy safely dominated the American coastline, but

French naval power posed a threat to the entire southern enterprise. Moreover, patriot bands continued to operate freely in the state and thus denied loyalists the guaranteed protection they desired. Last but not least, the fall of Charleston did not dishearten the patriots; instead, it spurred them to greater exertions.

Nevertheless, the war in South Carolina went badly for the patriots throughout most of 1780. In August, a reorganized southern army under Horatio Gates was crushingly defeated at Camden by the forces of Lord Cornwallis, the new British commander in the South. The redcoats were joined wherever they went by enslaved African-Americans seeking freedom on the basis of Lord Dunmore's proclamation. They ran away from their patriot masters in such numbers that they seriously disrupted planting and harvesting in 1780 and 1781. More than fifty-five thousand slaves were lost to their owners as a result of the war. Not all of them joined the British or won their freedom if they did, but their flight had exactly the effect Dunmore wanted.

After the defeat at Camden, Washington appointed General Nathanael Greene of Rhode Island to command the southern campaign. Greene adopted a conciliatory policy toward loyalists and neutrals, persuading the governor of South Carolina to offer pardons to those who had fought for the British if they would join the patriot militia. He also ordered his troops to treat captives fairly and not to loot loyalist property. Greene recognized that the patriots could win only by convincing the populace that they could bring stability to the region.

Greene Rallies South Carolina

Greene also took a conciliatory approach to the southern Indians. With his desperate need for soldiers, he could not afford to have frontier militia companies occupied in defending their homes against Indian attacks. Greene's diplomatic efforts with the southern Indians worked and by war's end only the Creeks remained allied with Great Britain.

Even before Greene took command of the southern army in December 1780, the tide had begun to turn. In October, at King's Mountain, a force from the settlements west of the Appalachians defeated a large party of redcoats and loyalists. Then in January 1781 Greene's trusted aide Brigadier General Daniel Morgan brilliantly defeated the crack British regiment Tarleton's Legion at Cowpens. Greene himself confronted the main body of British troops under Lord Cornwallis at Guilford Court House, North Carolina, in March. Although Cornwallis controlled the field at the end of the day, most of his army had been destroyed. He had to retreat to the coast, to receive supplies and fresh troops from New York by sea.

Cornwallis had already ignored explicit orders not to leave South Carolina unless the state was safely in British hands. He headed north into Virginia, where he joined forces with a detachment of redcoats commanded by the American traitor Benedict Arnold. Instead of acting decisively with his new army of 7,200 men, Cornwallis withdrew to the peninsula between the York and James Rivers, where he fortified Yorktown and waited for supplies and reinforcements. Seizing the opportunity, Washington quickly moved more than 7,000 troops south from New York City. When a French fleet defeated the Royal Navy vessels sent to relieve Cornwallis, the British general was trapped (see map, page 115). On October 19, 1781, Cornwallis surrendered to the combined American and French forces.

Surrender at Yorktown

When news of the surrender reached London, Lord North's ministry fell. Parliament voted to cease offensive operations in America and authorized peace negotiations. But guerrilla warfare between patriots and loyalists continued to ravage the Carolinas and Georgia for more than a year, and in the North vicious raids by both sides kept the frontier aflame. The persistence of conflict among guerrillas, frontiersmen, and Indians after the Battle of Yorktown serves to underscore the significance of the internal conflict that accompanied the war's more famous battles.

The costs of winning independence were heavy. More than twenty-five thousand American men died in the war, only about one-quarter of them from wounds suffered in battle. The rest were declared missing in action or died of disease

The War in the South *The southern war—after the British invasion of Georgia in late 1778—was characterized by a series of British thrusts into the interior, leading to battles with American defenders in both North and South Carolina. Finally, after promising beginnings, Cornwallis's foray into Virginia ended with disaster at Yorktown in October 1781.*

or as prisoners of war. In the South, years of guerrilla warfare and the loss of thousands of runaway slaves shattered the economy. Indebtedness soared, and local governments were crippled for lack of funds, since few people could afford to pay their taxes.

Americans rejoiced when they learned of the signing of a preliminary peace treaty at Paris in November 1782. The American diplomats—Benjamin Franklin, John Jay, and John Adams—ignored their instructions from Congress to be guided by France and instead negotiated directly with Great Britain. Their instincts were sound: the

Treaty of Paris

French government was more an enemy to Britain than a friend to the United States. In fact, French ministers worked secretly behind the scenes to try to prevent the establishment of a strong and unified government in America. But the American delegates proved adept at playing the game of power politics, and the new British ministry, headed by Lord Shelburne was weary of war and made numerous concessions.

The treaty, signed formally on September 3, 1783, granted the Americans unconditional independence. The boundaries of the new nation were generous: to the north, approximately the present-day boundary with Canada; to the south, the 31st parallel (about the modern northern border of Florida); to the west, the Mississippi River. Florida, which Britain had acquired in 1763, was returned to Spain. The Americans also gained unlimited fishing rights off Newfoundland. In ceding so much land to the United States, Great Britain ignored the territorial rights of its Indian allies, sacrificing their interests to the demands of European politics. Loyalists and British merchants were also poorly served by British diplomats. The treaty's ambiguously worded clauses pertaining to the payment of prewar debts and the postwar treatment of loyalists caused trouble for years to come and proved impossible to enforce.

 ## Conclusion

The victorious Americans could look back on their achievement with satisfaction and awe. They had taken on the world's greatest military power and won. The Americans won few victories, but their army survived its defeats and ultimately wore down the enemy. In winning the war, the Americans abandoned the British identity that once was so important to them and began the process of creating loyalty to a new nation. They also established a claim to most of the territory east of the Mississippi River and south of the Great Lakes, thereby greatly expanding the land potentially open to their settlements.

In achieving independence, Americans surmounted formidable challenges. But in the future they would face perhaps even greater ones:

How do historians know that Americans had only incomplete knowledge of the boundaries of their new nation? They know from consulting written documents and from looking at early maps like this one, *"A New and Correct Map of the United States of North America,"* produced in 1784. New it certainly was, but correct it was not. A comparison with a standard map of the United States and Canada today shows many errors of scale, proportion, and placement of natural features. To point out just a few: the Ohio River is shown much too far south; the northern part of the Mississippi River is misplaced to the west; Lake Superior is too small, and its islands are too large; and the Nova Scotia peninsula is misshapen. What links all these features is that they were on the periphery of the new nation and thus on the margins of Americans' knowledge. But even so well known a waterway as Chesapeake Bay is inaccurately drawn, suggesting that residents of the United States still had much to learn about the geography of their country.   Photo: New Jersey Historical Society.

establishing stable republican governments at the state and national levels and ensuring their government's continued existence in a world of bitter rivalries among the major powers—Britain, France, and Spain. Those European rivalries soon posed significant threats to the survival of the new nation.

Suggestions for Further Reading

General

Colin Bonwick, *The American Revolution* (1991); Edward Countryman, *The American Revolution* (1985); Theodore Draper, *A Struggle for Power: The American Revolution* (1996); Robert Middlekauff, *The Glorious Cause: The American Revolution, 1763–1783* (1982); Harry M. Ward, *The American Revolution: Nationhood Achieved, 1763–1788* (1995); Alfred F. Young, ed., *Beyond the American Revolution* (1993).

Military Affairs

E. Wayne Carp, *To Starve the Army at Pleasure: Continental Army Administration and American Political Culture, 1775–1783* (1984); Stephen Conway, *The War of American Independence 1775–1783* (1995); John C. Dann, ed., *The Revolution Remembered: Eyewitness Accounts of the War for Independence* (1980); Don Higginbotham, *The War of American Independence: Military Attitudes, Policies, and Practice, 1763–1789* (1971); Piers Mackesy, *The War for America, 1775–1783* (1964); Charles Royster, *A Revolutionary People at War: The Continental Army and American Character, 1775–1783* (1980).

Local and Regional Studies

Richard Buel, *Dear Liberty: Connecticut's Mobilization for the Revolutionary War* (1980); Edward Countryman, *A People in Revolution: The American Revolution and Political Society in New York, 1760–1790* (1981); Jeffrey Crow and Larry Tise, eds., *The Southern Experience in the American Revolution* (1978); David Hackett Fischer, *Paul Revere's Ride* (1994); Robert A. Gross, *The Minutemen and Their World* (1976); Ronald Hoffman, *A Spirit of Dissension: Economics, Politics, and the Revolution in Maryland* (1973); Ronald Hoffman, Thad W. Tate, and Peter Albert, eds., *An Uncivil War: The Southern Backcountry During the American Revolution* (1985); Jean B. Lee, *The Price of*

Nationhood: The American Revolution in Charles County (1994); John Selby, *The Revolution in Virginia, 1775–1783* (1988).

Indians and African-Americans

Colin Calloway, *The American Revolution in Indian Country: Crisis and Diversity in Native American Communities* (1995); Sylvia Frey, *Water from the Rock: Black Resistance in a Revolutionary Age* (1991); Barbara Graymont, *The Iroquois in the American Revolution* (1972); James H. O'Donnell III, *Southern Indians in the American Revolution* (1973).

Loyalists

Bernard Bailyn, *The Ordeal of Thomas Hutchinson* (1974); Robert McCluer Calhoon, *The Loyalists in Revolutionary America, 1760–1781* (1973); Mary Beth Norton, *The British-Americans: The Loyalist Exiles in England, 1774–1789* (1972); James W. St. G. Walker, *The Black Loyalists: The Search for a Promised Land in Nova Scotia and Sierra Leone, 1783–1870* (1976).

Women

Richard Buel and Joy Buel, *The Way of Duty: A Woman and Her Family in Revolutionary America* (1984); Ronald Hoffman and Peter Albert, eds., *Women in the Age of the American Revolution* (1989); Linda K. Kerber, *Women of the Republic: Intellect and Ideology in Revolutionary America* (1980); Mary Beth Norton, *Liberty's Daughters: The Revolutionary Experience of American Women, 1750–1800* (1980).

Foreign Policy

Jonathan Dull, *A Diplomatic History of the American Revolution* (1985); Ronald Hoffman and Peter Albert, eds., *Peace and the Peacemakers: The Treaty of 1783* (1986); Ronald Hoffman and Peter Albert, eds., *Diplomacy and Revolution: The Franco-American Alliance of 1778* (1981); Jan Willem Schulte Nordholt, *The Dutch Republic and American Independence* (1982).

Patriot Leaders

Fawn M. Brodie, *Thomas Jefferson: An Intimate History* (1974); Richard Brookhiser, *Founding Father: Rediscovering George Washington* (1996); Eric Foner, *Tom Paine and Revolutionary America* (1976); Norman Risjord, *Thomas Jefferson* (1994); Charles Royster, *Light-Horse Harry Lee and the Legacy of the American Revolution* (1981); Sheila Skemp, *Benjamin and William Franklin: Father and Son, Patriot and Loyalist* (1994); Esmond Wright, *Franklin of Philadelphia* (1986).

CHAPTER

7

Forging a National Republic
1776–1789

On January 25, 1787, an army of fifteen hundred farmers from western Massachusetts advanced on the Springfield federal armory. Inside the arsenal, General William Shepard prepared his group of one thousand militiamen to resist the assault. First, though, he dispatched two aides to warn the farmers that they would soon draw the fire of men who had been their officers during the Revolutionary War. "That is all we want, by God!" replied one of the rebels. The farmers moved toward the armory, urged on by the commands of Daniel Shays, one of their leaders. Shepard fired two cannon over the heads of the farmers, and then—when that did not frighten them—ordered his men to shoot directly at the straggling ranks. Four men died, twenty were wounded, and the rebels withdrew.

What caused this violent clash between former comrades in arms? Massachusetts farmers were angered by high taxes and the scarcity of money. Since the preceding summer, they had organized committees and crowd actions—the tactics used so successfully in the 1760s and early 1770s—to halt state efforts to seize property for nonpayment of taxes. Many of the insurgents were respected war veterans. Clearly the episode could not be dismissed as the work of an unruly rabble. What did the uprising mean for the republic's future?

The protesters explained their position in an address to the Massachusetts government. They proclaimed their loyalty to the nation but objected to the state's fiscal policies, which, they said, prevented them from providing adequately for their families. Referring to their experience as revolutionary soldiers, they asserted that they "esteem[ed] one moment of Liberty to be worth an eternity of Bondage." The Massachusetts gov-

A woodcut of Daniel Shays and one of his chief officers, Job Shattuck, in 1787.   National Portrait Gallery, Smithsonian Institution, Washington, D.C.

ernment was "tyrannical," Shays asserted, and, like that of Great Britain, deserved to be overthrown.

To the state's elected leaders, the most ominous aspect of the uprising was the farmers' attempt to link their rebellion with the earlier struggle for independence. The state legislature insisted that "in a republican government the majority must govern. If the minor part governs it becomes aristocracy; if every one opposed at his pleasure, it is no government, it is anarchy and confusion." In short, the crowd actions that once had been a justifiable response to British tyranny were no longer legitimate. In a republic, reform had to come through the ballot box rather than by force.

The confrontation at the Springfield armory symbolized for many Americans the trials facing the new nation. To American political leaders, Shays's Rebellion suggested the first signs of disintegration of the republic.

Republicanism—the idea that governments should be based wholly on the consent of the people—originated with political theorists in ancient Greece and Rome. Republics, such writers declared, were desirable yet fragile forms of government. Unless their citizens were especially virtuous—that is, sober, moral, and industrious—and largely in agreement on key issues, republics were doomed to failure. When Americans left the British Empire, they committed themselves to republicanism. Now they faced the task of creating a stable republic based upon a popular consensus.

America's political and intellectual leaders worked hard to inculcate virtue in their fellow countrymen and countrywomen. After 1776, American literature, theater, art, architecture, and education all pursued explicitly moral goals. The education of women was considered particularly important, for as the mothers of the republic's children, they were primarily responsible for ensuring the nation's future. On such matters Americans could agree, but they disagreed on many other critical issues. Almost all white men concurred that women, Indians, and African-Americans should be excluded from formal participation in politics, but they found it difficult to reach a consensus on how many of their own number should be included, how often elections should be held, or how their new governments should be structured.

Republican citizens had to make many other decisions as well. Should a republic conduct its dealings with Indian nations and foreign countries any differently than other types of governments did? Were republics, in other words, obliged to negotiate fairly and honestly at all times? And how could republicans who proclaimed that "all men are created equal" justify holding African-Americans in perpetual bondage? Some answered that question by freeing their slaves or by voting for state laws that abolished slavery. Others denied blacks were "men" in the same sense as whites.

The most important task facing Americans in these years was the construction of a genuinely national government. Before 1765, the British mainland colonies had rarely cooperated on common endeavors, but fighting the Revolutionary War had fostered a new nationalistic spirit in which Americans began the process of replacing loyalties to state and region with loyalties to the nation.

Still, forging a national republic was neither easy nor simple. America's first such government, under the Articles of Confederation, proved to be inadequate. But some of the nation's political leaders learned from their experiences and tried another approach when they drafted the Constitution in 1787. Though some historians have argued that the Constitution represents an "aristocratic" counterrevolution against the "democratic" Articles, the two documents are more accurately viewed as successive attempts to solve the same problems.

 ## Creating a Virtuous Republic

When the colonies declared their independence from Great Britain, John Dickinson recalled many years later, "there was no question concerning forms of Government, no enquiry whether a Republic or a limited Monarchy was best. . . . We knew that the people of this country must unite themselves under some form of Government and that this could be no other than the republican form." But how should that goal be implemented?

Three different definitions of *republicanism* emerged in the new United States. The first, held chiefly by members of the educated elite, was based directly on ancient history and political theory. The histories of popular governments in Greece and Rome seemed to prove that republics could succeed only if they were small in size and homogeneous in population. Unless a republic's citizens were willing to sacrifice their own private interests for the good of the whole, the government would collapse. In return for sacrifices, though, a republic offered its citizens equality of opportunity. Under such a government, society would be governed by members of a "natural aristocracy" of men whose rank would be based on merit rather than inherited wealth and status.

Varieties of Republicanism

A second definition, advanced by other members of the elite but also by some skilled craftsmen, drew more on economic theory than on political thought. Instead of perceiving the nation as an organic whole composed of people nobly sacrificing for the common good, this version of republicanism followed the Scottish theorist Adam Smith in emphasizing individuals' pursuit of rational self-interest. When republican men sought to improve their own economic and social circumstances, the entire nation would benefit. Republican virtue would be achieved through the pursuit of private interests, rather than through subordination to some communal ideal.

The third notion of republicanism was more egalitarian than the other two. This view was less influential because many of its proponents were illiterate or barely literate and thus wrote little to promote their beliefs. Men who advanced the third version of republicanism called for widening men's participation in the political process. They also wanted government to respond directly to the needs of ordinary folk, rejecting any notion that the "lesser sort" should automatically defer to

1776	Second Continental Congress directs states to draft constitutions			Constitutional Convention drafts new form of government
1777	Articles of Confederation sent to states for ratification		**1788**	Hamilton, Jay, and Madison write *The Federalist* to urge ratification of the Constitution by New York
1781	Articles of Confederation ratified			Constitution ratified
1786	Annapolis Convention meets, discusses reforming government		**1794**	Defeat of Miami Confederacy at Fallen Timbers
1786–87	Shays's Rebellion in western Massachusetts raises questions about future of the republic		**1795**	Treaty of Greenville opens Ohio to white settlement
1787	Northwest Ordinance organizes territory north of Ohio River and east of Mississippi River		**1800**	Mason Locke Weems publishes his *Life of Washington*

their "betters." They were, indeed, democrats in more or less the modern sense.

Despite the differences, the three strands of republicanism shared many of the same assumptions. All three contrasted a virtuous, industrious America to the corruption of Britain and Europe. In the first version, that virtue manifested itself in frugality and self-sacrifice; in the second, it would prevent self-interest from becoming vice; in the third, it was the justification for including even propertyless free men in the ranks of voters.

As citizens of the United States set out to construct their republic, they believed they were embarking on an unprecedented enterprise. With

Virtue and the Arts

great pride in their new nation, they expected to replace the vices of monarchical Europe with the sober virtues of republican America. They wanted to embody republican principles not only in their governments but also in their society and culture. They looked to painting, literature, drama, and architecture to convey messages of nationalism and virtue to the public.

Americans faced a crucial contradiction at the very outset of their efforts. To some republicans, the fine arts themselves were manifestations of

vice. What need did a frugal yeoman have for a painting, a novel, or a play? The first American artists, playwrights, and authors thus confronted an impossible dilemma. They wanted to produce works embodying virtue, but those very works were viewed by many as corrupting.

Still, they tried. William Hill Brown's *The Power of Sympathy* (1789), the first novel written in the United States, was a lurid tale of seduction intended as a warning to young women, who made up a large proportion of America's fiction readers. In Royall Tyler's *The Contrast* (1787), the first successful American play, the virtuous conduct of Colonel Manly was contrasted (hence the title) with the reprehensible behavior of the fop Billy Dimple. The most popular book of the era, Mason Locke Weems's *Life of Washington*, published in 1800 shortly after George Washington's death, was intended by its author to "hold up his great Virtues . . . to the imitation of Our Youth."

Painting and architecture, too, were expected to embody high moral standards. Two of the most prominent artists of the period, Gilbert Stuart and Charles Willson Peale, painted innumerable portraits of upstanding republican citizens. John Trumbull's vast canvases depicted milestones of American history, such as the Battle of Bunker

Hill and Cornwallis's capitulation at Yorktown. Such works were intended to instill patriotic sentiments in their viewers.

Architects likewise hoped to convey in their buildings a sense of the young republic's ideals. When the Virginia government asked Thomas Jefferson for advice on the design of the state capitol in Richmond, Jefferson unhesitatingly recommended copying a Roman building. Jefferson set forth ideals that would guide American architecture for a generation to come: simplicity of line, harmonious proportions, a feeling of grandeur. Nowhere were these rational goals of republican art manifested more clearly than in Benjamin H. Latrobe's plans for the majestic domed United States Capitol in Washington, D.C., built in the early 1800s.

Despite the artists' efforts (or, some would have said, because of them), some Americans were beginning to detect signs of luxury and corruption by the mid-1780s. The resumption of European trade after the war brought a return to fashionable clothing and abandonment of the homespun garments patriots had once worn with pride. Elite families again attended balls and concerts. Parties no longer seemed complete without gambling and cardplaying. Especially alarming to fervent republicans was the establishment in 1783 of the Society of the Cincinnati, a hereditary organization of Revolutionary War officers and their descendants. Many feared that the group would become the nucleus of a native-born aristocracy. All these developments directly challenged the United States's self-image as a virtuous republic.

Americans' deep-seated concern for the future of the infant republic focused their attention on their children, the "rising generation." Throughout the history of the colonies, education had been seen chiefly as a private means to personal advancement, of concern only to individual families. Now, though, education would serve a public purpose. If young people were to resist the temptations of vice, they would have to learn the lessons of virtue at home and at school. In fact, the very survival of the nation depended on it. The early republican

Educational Reform

period was thus a time of major educational reform.

The 1780s and 1790s brought two significant changes in American educational practice. First, in contrast to the colonies, where nearly all education had been privately financed, some northern states began to use tax money to support public elementary schools. In 1789, Massachusetts became one of the first states to require towns to offer their citizens free public elementary education.

Second, schooling for girls was improved. Americans' recognition of the importance of the rising generation led to the realization that mothers would have to be properly educated if they were to instruct their children adequately. Therefore Massachusetts insisted in its 1789 law that town elementary schools be open to girls as well as boys. Throughout the United States, private academies were founded to give teenage girls from well-to-do families an opportunity for advanced schooling. No one yet proposed opening colleges to women, but a few fortunate girls could study history, geography, rhetoric, and mathematics.

The chief theorist of women's education in the early republic was Judith Sargent Murray of Gloucester, Massachusetts. In a series of essays published in the 1780s and 1790s, Murray argued that women and men had equal intellectual capacities, that boys and girls should have equivalent scholastic training, and that girls should be taught to support themselves by their own efforts.

Judith Sargent Murray and Women's Education

Murray's educational theories were part of a general rethinking of women's position that occurred as a result of the Revolution. Male patriots who enlisted in the army or served in Congress were away from home for long periods of time. In their absence their wives, who previously had handled only the "indoor affairs" of the household, shouldered the responsibility for "outdoor affairs" as well. The shift in responsibilities caused subtle but significant change. Like other women, for example, Abigail Adams (the wife of John Adams) stopped calling their farm "yours" in letters to her husband and began referring to it as "ours." Both men and women realized that female patriots had made vital and important contributions to winning the war and that notions of proper gender roles had to be rethought. Americans began to develop new ideas about the role women should play in a republican society.

The best-known example of those new ideas is a letter Abigail Adams addressed to her husband in March 1776. "In the new Code of Laws which I suppose it will be necessary for you to make I desire you would Remember the Ladies," she wrote. "If particuliar care and attention is not paid to the Laidies we are determined to foment a Rebelion, and will not hold ourselves bound by any Laws in which we have no voice, or Representation." With these words, Abigail Adams took a step that was soon to be duplicated by other disfranchised Americans. She deliberately applied the ideology developed to combat parliamentary supremacy to purposes revolutionary leaders had never intended.

Abigail Adams: "Remember the Ladies"

Abigail Adams did not ask that women be allowed to vote, but others claimed that right. The men who drafted the New Jersey state constitution in 1776 defined voters carelessly as "all free inhabitants" who met certain property qualifications. They thereby unintentionally gave the vote to property-holding white spinsters and widows, as well as to free blacks. Qualified women and African-Americans regularly voted in New Jersey's local and congressional elections until 1807, when they were disfranchised by the state legislature. Yet the fact that women voted at all was evidence of their altered perception of their place in political life of the country.

Such dramatic episodes were unusual. After the war, European-Americans still viewed women in traditional terms, continuing to believe that women's primary function was to be good wives, mothers, and mistresses of households. They perceived significant differences between male and female characters. That distinction eventually enabled Americans to resolve the conflict between

Women's Role in the Republic

the two most influential strands of republican thought. Because wives could not own property or participate directly in economic life, women in general came to be seen as the embodiment of self-sacrificing, disinterested republicanism. Through new female-run charitable associations founded after the war, better-off women assumed public responsibilities, in particular through caring for poor widows and orphaned children. Thus men were freed from the naggings of conscience as they pursued their economic self-interest (that other republican virtue), secure in the knowledge that their wives and daughters were fulfilling the family's obligation to the common good. The ideal republican man, therefore, was an individualist, seeking advancement for himself and his family. The ideal republican woman, by contrast, always put the well-being of others ahead of her own.

Together white men and women established the context for the creation of a virtuous republic. But nearly 20 percent of the American population was black. How did approximately 700,000 African-Americans fit into the developing national plan?

Emancipation and the Growth of Racism

Revolutionary ideology exposed one of the primary contradictions in American society. Both blacks and whites saw the irony in slaveholding Americans' claims that one of their aims in taking up arms was to prevent Britain from "enslaving" them. In 1773 Dr. Benjamin Rush called slavery "a vice which degrades human nature," and he warned that liberty "cannot thrive long in the neighborhood of slavery."

African-Americans did not need ideology to tell them that slavery was wrong, but they quickly took advantage of that revolutionary ideology. In 1779 a group of slaves from Portsmouth, New Hampshire, asked the state legislature "from what authority [our masters] assume to dispose of our lives, freedom and property." The same year several bondspeople in Fairfield, Connecticut, petitioned the legislature for their freedom, characterizing slavery as a "dreadful Evil" and "flagrant Injustice."

Both legislatures responded negatively, but the postwar years did witness the gradual abolition of slavery in the North. Vermont abolished slavery in its 1777 constitution. Mass-

Gradual Emancipation

achusetts courts decided in the 1780s that a clause in the state constitution prohibited slavery. Pennsylvania passed an abolition law in 1780; four years later Rhode Island and Connecticut provided for gradual emancipation, followed by New York (1799) and New Jersey (1804).

No southern state adopted similar general emancipation laws, but the legislatures of Virginia (1782), Delaware (1787), and Maryland (1790 and 1796) altered laws that previously had restricted slaveowners' ability to free their bondspeople. South Carolina and Georgia never considered adopting such acts, and North Carolina insisted that all manumissions (emancipations of individual slaves) be approved by county courts.

Revolutionary ideology thus had limited impact on the well-entrenched economic interests of large slaveholders. Only in the North, where slaves were relatively rare and where little money was invested in human capital, could state legislatures easily vote to abolish slavery. Even there, legislators' concern for property rights led them to favor gradual emancipation over immediate abolition. Most states provided only for the freeing of children born after passage of the law. And even those children were to remain slaves until reaching adulthood. Still, by 1840 in only one northern state—New Jersey—were African-Americans legally held in bondage.

Despite the slow progress of abolition, the number of free people of African descent in the United States grew dramatically in the first years

Growth of Free Black Population

after the Revolution. Before the war there had been few free blacks in America. But wartime disruptions radically changed the size of the freed population. Slaves who had escaped from plantations during the war, others who had served

in the American army, and still others who had been emancipated by their owners or by state laws were now free. By 1790 there were nearly 60,000 free people of color in the United States; ten years later they numbered more than 108,000, nearly 11 percent of the total African-American population.

In the 1780s and thereafter, freed people often made their way to northern port cities. Boston and Philadelphia, where slavery was abolished sooner than in New York City, were

Migration to Northern Cities

popular destinations. Women outnumbered men among the migrants by a margin of three to two. Black women found more opportunities for employment, particularly as domestic servants, in the cities than in the countryside. Some freedmen also worked in domestic service, but larger numbers were employed as unskilled laborers and seamen. A few of the women and a sizable proportion of men (nearly one-third of those in Philadelphia in 1795) were skilled workers or retailers. As soon as possible these freed people established independent two-parent nuclear families instead of continuing to live in their employers' households. They also began to occupy distinct neighborhoods, probably as the combined result of discrimination and a desire for racial solidarity.

Emancipation did not bring equality. Even whites who recognized African-Americans' right to freedom were unwilling to accept them as equals. Laws discriminated against emancipated blacks as they had against slaves. South Carolina, for example, did not permit free blacks to testify against whites in court. Public schools often refused to educate their children. Freedmen found it difficult to purchase property and find good jobs. And whites rarely allowed African-Americans an equal voice in church affairs.

Gradually, freed people developed their own institutions. In Charleston, they formed the Brown Fellowship Society, which provided insur-

Freed People's Churches and Associations

ance coverage for its members, financed a school, and helped to support orphans. In 1794, blacks in Philadelphia and Baltimore founded societies that

How do historians know that the 1780s and 1790s marked a key turning point in the history of slavery and racism in the United States? The emancipation and manumission laws adopted by state legislatures, coupled with debates in pamphlets and newspapers, are important indications of a shift in Americans' thinking. But a painting such as the one reproduced here, Liberty Displaying the Arts and Sciences, *offers a unique visual perspective on the same developments. In 1792, the Library Company of Philadelphia, a private lending library founded in the mid-eighteenth century, commissioned the artist Samuel Jennings to produce a depiction of slavery and abolitionism showing the "figure of Lib-* erty (with her Cap and proper Insignia) displaying the arts." *The library's directors reportedly were well pleased with the results. The painting, probably the first to celebrate emancipation, shows the blonde goddess presenting books (symbolizing knowledge and freedom) to several suppliant and grateful blacks, while in the background a group of former slaves dances joyfully around a liberty pole. Although the theme is abolition and the African-Americans in the foreground have realistic features, the portrayal of blacks in passive roles and diminutive sizes portends future stereotypical images. Thus the picture simultaneously linked emancipation and the growth of racism.* The Library Company of Philadelphia.

eventually became the African Methodist Episcopal (AME) denomination. AME churches later sponsored schools in a number of cities and, along with African Baptist, African Episcopal, and African Presbyterian churches, became cultural centers of the free black community.

Such endeavors were all the more necessary because the postrevolutionary years witnessed the development of a coherent racist theory in the United States. Whites had long regarded their slaves as inferior, but the most influential writers on race attributed that inferiority to environmental rather than hereditary factors. In the Revolution's aftermath, though, white southerners needed to defend their enslavement of other human beings against the notion that "all men are created equal." Consequently, they began to argue that blacks were less than fully human and that the principles of republican equality applied only to whites.

Development of Racist Theory

This racism had several intertwined elements. First was the assertion that, as Thomas Jefferson suggested in 1781, blacks were "inferior to the whites in the endowments both of body and mind." Then came the belief that blacks were congenitally lazy, dishonest, and uncivilized (or uncivilizable). Third, and of crucial importance, was the notion that all blacks were sexually promiscuous and that black men lusted after white women. The specter of sexual intercourse between black men and white women haunted early American racist thought. Significantly, the more common sexual exploitation of enslaved black women by their white masters aroused little comment.

African-Americans did not allow these developing racist notions to go unchallenged. Benjamin Banneker, a free black surveyor, astronomer, and mathematical genius, directly disputed Thomas Jefferson's belief in blacks' intellectual inferiority. In 1791 Banneker sent Jefferson a copy of his latest almanac (which included his astronomical calculations) as an example of blacks' mental powers. Jefferson's response admitted Banneker's capability but indicated that he regarded Banneker as an exception.

At its birth, then, the republic was defined by its leaders as an exclusively white enterprise. Indeed, some historians have argued that the subjugation of blacks was a necessary precondition for equality among whites. They have pointed out that identifying a common racial antagonist helped to create white solidarity and to lessen the threat to gentry power posed by the enfranchisement of poorer whites. Some have asserted that it was less dangerous to allow whites with little property to participate formally in politics than to open the possibility that they might join with former slaves to question the rule of the "better sort." That was perhaps one reason why after the Revolution the division of American society between slave and free was transformed into a division between blacks—some of whom were free—and whites. The wielders of power ensured their continued dominance in part by substituting race for enslavement as the primary determinant of African-Americans' status.

A Republic for Whites Only

Designing Republican Governments

In May 1776 the Second Continental Congress directed states to devise new republican governments to replace the provincial congresses and committees that had met since 1774. Thus Americans initially concentrated on drafting state constitutions and devoted little attention to their national government.

They first faced the problem of defining just what a constitution is. The British Constitution could not serve as a model because it was a mixture of law and custom; Americans wanted tangible documents specifying the fundamental structures of government. Several years passed before states concluded that their constitutions could not be drafted by regular legislative bodies. Following the lead established by Vermont in 1777 and Massachusetts in 1780, they began to call conventions for the sole purpose

Drafting of State Constitutions

of drafting constitutions. Thus states sought direct authorization from the people—the theoretical sovereigns in a republic—before establishing new governments. After preparing new constitutions, delegates submitted them to voters for ratification.

The framers of state constitutions concerned themselves primarily with outlining the distribution of and limitations on government power. Because of their experiences under British rule, Americans had learned to fear the power of the governor—usually, the appointed agent of king or proprietor—and to see the legislature as their defender. Accordingly, the first state constitutions typically provided for the governor to be elected annually (commonly by the legislature), limited the number of terms he could serve, and gave him little independent authority. Simultaneously, the constitutions expanded the legislature's powers. Every state except Pennsylvania and Vermont retained a two-house structure, with members of the upper house having longer terms and being required to meet higher property-holding standards than members of the lower house. But they also redrew electoral districts to reflect population patterns more accurately, and they increased the number of members in both houses. Finally, most states lowered property qualifications for voting. Thus the revolutionary era witnessed the first deliberate attempt to broaden the base of American government.

The constitutions also contained provisions, including explicit limitations on government power, to protect the people from those who would misuse power. Seven of the con-

Limits on State Governments

stitutions contained formal bills of rights, and the others had similar clauses. Most guaranteed citizens freedom of the press and of religion, the right to a fair trial, the right of consent to taxation, and protection against general search warrants. An independent judiciary was charged with upholding such rights.

In sum, the constitution makers put far greater emphasis on preventing state governments from becoming tyrannical than on making them effective wielders of political authority. Their approach to shaping governments was understand-

able, given the American experience with Great Britain. But establishing such weak political units, especially in wartime, practically ensured that the constitutions soon would need revision.

When Americans realized that legislative supremacy did not in itself guarantee good government, they attempted to achieve that goal by balancing the powers of the legislative, executive, and judicial branches against one another.

The constitutional theories that Americans applied at the state level did not at first influence their conception of national government. Since American political leaders had little time to devote to legitimizing their de facto government while organizing the military struggle against Britain, the powers and structure of the Continental Congress evolved by default early in the war. Not until late 1777 did Congress send the Articles of Confederation to the states for ratification.

The chief organ of national government was a unicameral (one-house) legislature in which each state had one vote. Its powers included conduct-

Articles of Confederation

ing foreign relations, settling disputes between states, controlling maritime affairs, regulating Indian trade, and valuing state and national coinage. The Articles did not give the national government the ability to raise revenue effectively or to enforce a uniform commercial policy. The United States of America was described as "a firm league of friendship" in which each state "retains its sovereignty, freedom and independence, and every Power, Jurisdiction and right, which is not by this confederation expressly delegated to the United States, in Congress assembled."

The Articles required the unanimous consent of the state legislatures for ratification or amendment, and a clause concerning western lands proved troublesome. The draft accepted by Congress allowed states to retain all land claims derived from their original colonial charters. Because Maryland feared being overpowered by states that would grow in size and power through western land claims, it refused to accept the Articles until 1781, when Virginia finally promised to surrender its western holdings to national jurisdiction. Other states followed suit, establishing the principle that unorganized lands would be held by the nation as a whole.

The capacity of a single state to delay ratification for three years was a portent of the fate of American government under the Articles of Confederation. The Articles' authors had not given adequate thought to the distribution of power within the national government or to the relationship between the Confederation and the states. The Congress they created was simultaneously a legislative body and a collective executive, but it had no independent income and no authority to compel the states to accept its rulings. What is surprising is not how poorly the Confederation functioned but rather how much the government was able to accomplish.

Trials of the Confederation

The most persistent problem faced by the American governments, state and national, was finance. Because of a reluctance to levy taxes, both Congress and the states tried to finance the war by printing currency. Even though the money was backed by nothing but good faith, it circulated freely and without excessive depreciation during 1775 and most of 1776. But in late 1776, as the American army suffered reverses in New York and New Jersey, prices began to rise and inflation set in. The currency's value rested on Americans' faith in their government, a faith that was sorely tested in the years that followed. By early 1780 it took forty paper dollars to purchase one silver dollar. Soon, Continental currency was worthless.

Financial Problems

In 1781, faced with total collapse of the monetary system, the congressmen undertook ambitious reforms. After establishing a department of finance under the wealthy Philadelphia merchant Robert Morris, they asked the states to amend the Articles of Confederation to allow Congress to levy a duty of 5 percent on imported goods. Morris put national finances on a solid footing, but the customs duty was never adopted. First Rhode Island and then New York refused to agree to the

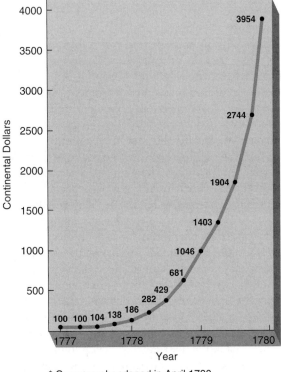

Depreciation of Continental Currency, 1777–1780

Depreciation of Continental Currency, 1777–1780 The depreciation of Continental currency accelerated in 1778, as is shown in this graph measuring its value against one hundred silver dollars. Thereafter, its value dropped almost daily. Source: Data from John J. McCusker, "How Much Is That in Real Money? A Historical Price Index for Use as a Deflator of Money Values in the Economy of the United States," *Proceedings of the American Antiquarian Society,* Vol. 101, Pt. 2 (1991), Table C-1.

tax. The states' resistance reflected fear of a too-powerful central government.

Congress also faced major diplomatic problems at the close of the war. Chief among them were issues involving the peace treaty itself. Article 4, which promised the repayment of prewar debts (most of them owed by Americans to British merchants), and Article 5, which recommended that states allow loyalists to recover

Weakness in Foreign Affairs and Commerce

their confiscated property, aroused considerable opposition. States passed laws denying British subjects the right to sue for recovery of debts or property in American courts. Since most purchasers of confiscated loyalist property had been prominent patriots, states had no desire to enforce Article 5.

The refusal of state and local governments to comply with Articles 4 and 5 gave Britain an excuse to maintain military posts on the Great Lakes long after its troops were supposed to have withdrawn. Furthermore, Congress's inability to convince states to implement the treaty pointed up its lack of power. Concerned nationalists argued publicly that enforcement of the treaty, however unpopular, was a crucial test for the republic. "Will foreign nations be willing to undertake anything with us or for us," asked Alexander Hamilton, "when they find that the nature of our governments will allow no dependence to be placed on our engagements?"

Congress's weakness was especially evident in the realm of trade because the Articles of Confederation denied it the power to establish a national commercial policy. Immediately after the war, Britain, France, and Spain all restricted American trade with their colonies. Americans watched helplessly as British manufactured goods flooded the United States while American produce could no longer be sold in the British West Indies. Although Americans reopened commerce with other European countries and started a profitable trade with China in 1784, neither substituted for access to closer and larger markets.

Congress also had difficulty dealing with the threat posed by Spain's presence on the nation's southern and western borders. Determined to prevent the republic's expansion, Spain in 1784 closed the Mississippi River to American navigation. It thus deprived the growing settlements west of the Appalachians of their major access route to the rest of the nation and the world. Congress opened negotiations with Spain in 1785, but even John Jay, one of the nation's most experienced diplomats, could not win the necessary concessions on navigation. The talks collapsed the fol-

Failed Negotiations with Spain

lowing year after Congress divided sharply on the question of whether agreement should be sought on other issues. Southerners, voting as a bloc, insisted on navigation rights on the Mississippi; northerners were willing to abandon that claim in order to win commercial concessions.

Diplomatic problems of another sort confronted congressmen when they considered the status of land beyond the Appalachians. Although tribal claims were not discussed by British and American diplomats, the United States assumed that the Treaty of Paris (1783) cleared its title to all land east of the Mississippi except the area still held by Spain. But recognizing that some sort of land cession should be obtained from the most powerful tribes, Congress initiated negotiations with both northern and southern Indians (see map, page 130). At Fort Stanwix, New York, in 1784, and at Hopewell, South Carolina, in late 1785 and early 1786, American diplomats signed separate treaties with chiefs purporting to represent the Iroquois and with emissaries from the Choctaw, Chickasaw, and Cherokee nations. Later, all four groups denied that the men who agreed to the treaties had been authorized to speak for them. But the United States still took the treaties as confirmation of its sovereignty over the territories in question. European-Americans soon poured over the southern Appalachians, provoking the Creeks—who had not agreed to the Hopewell treaties—to defend their territory by declaring war. Only in 1790 did they come to terms with the United States.

Encroachment on Indian Lands

In 1786 the Iroquois Confederacy repudiated the Fort Stanwix treaty and threatened new attacks on frontier settlements, but everyone knew the threat was empty. The flawed treaty stood by default. By 1790 the once-dominant confederacy was confined to a few scattered reservations.

Led by a remarkable prophet, Handsome Lake, the Iroquois sought to adapt to their new circumstances by embracing the traditional values of their culture and renouncing drinking alcohol, gambling, and other destructive European customs. Yet simultaneously,

Handsome Lake's Reforms

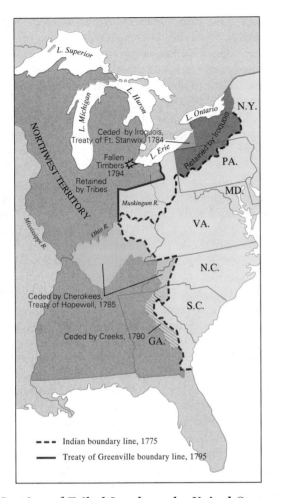

Cession of Tribal Lands to the United States, 1775–1790 *The land claims of the United States meant little as long as Indian nations still controlled vast territories within the new country's formal boundaries. A series of treaties in the 1780s and 1790s opened some lands to white settlement.*   Source: From Lester J. Cappon et al., eds., *Atlas of Early American History: The Revolutionary Era, 1760–1790.* Copyright ©1976 by Princeton University Press, Reprinted by permission of Princeton University Press.

with Handsome Lake's approval, Quaker missionaries taught the Iroquois Anglo-American styles of agricultural subsistence. Men were now to be cultivators rather than hunters—since their hunting territories were lost—and women to be housekeepers rather than cultivators. Paradoxically, only by adopting a sexual division of labor that had

originated in Europe could the Iroquois maintain a semblance of their culture.

Western nations such as the Shawnees, Chippewas, Ottawas, and Potawatomis formed a new confederacy, hoping to present a united front and avoid the piecemeal surrender of land by individual tribes. They demanded direct negotiations with the United States, but Congress ignored them. Congress then began to organize the Northwest Territory, bounded by the Mississippi River, the Great Lakes, and the Ohio River (see map). Ordinances passed in 1784, 1785, and 1787 outlined the process through which the land could be sold to settlers and formal governments could be organized.

Northwest Ordinances

To ensure orderly development, Congress in 1785 directed that the land be surveyed into townships 6 miles square, each divided into thirty-six sections of 640 acres (1 square mile). Revenue from the sale of the sixteenth section of each township was to be reserved for the support of public schools—the first instance of federal aid to education in American history. The minimum price per acre was set at one dollar, and the minimum sale was one section. The minimum outlay of $640 was beyond the reach of ordinary Americans. Proceeds from land sales were the first independent revenues available to the national government.

The most important ordinance was the third, passed in 1787. The Northwest Ordinance contained a bill of rights guaranteeing settlers freedom of religion and the right to a jury trial, forbidding cruel and unusual punishments, and nominally prohibiting slavery. The prohibition had little immediate effect. Some residents of the territory already held slaves, and Congress did not intend to deprive them of their property. Moreover, the ordinance also contained a provision allowing slaveowners to "lawfully reclaim" runaway bondspeople who took refuge in the territory— the first national fugitive slave law. Still, the ordinance prevented slavery from taking deep root by discouraging slaveholders from moving into the territory with their human chattel, but not until 1848 was enslavement abolished throughout the region, now known as the Old Northwest.

The ordinance also specified the process by which residents of the territory could organize state governments and seek admission to the Union "on an equal footing with the original States." Early in the nation's history, therefore, Congress laid down a policy of admitting new states on the same basis as the old and assuring residents of the territories the same rights held by citizens of the original states.

In a sense, the Northwest Ordinance was purely theoretical at the time it was passed. The Miamis, Shawnees, and Delawares refused to acknowledge American sovereignty. In 1788 the Ohio Company, to which Congress had sold a large tract of land at reduced rates, established the town of Marietta at the juncture of the Ohio and Muskingum Rivers. But Indians prevented the company from extending settlement very far into the interior. After General Arthur St. Clair, the Northwest Territory's first governor, failed to negotiate a meaningful treaty with the tribes in early 1789, it was apparent that the United States would clash with the Miami-led western confederacy.

Little Turtle, the able war chief of the Miami Confederacy, defeated first General Josiah Harmar (1790) and then St. Clair himself (1791) in

War in the Old Northwest

major battles near the present border between Indiana and Ohio. More than six hundred of St. Clair's men were killed and scores more wounded; it was the whites' worst defeat in the entire history of the American frontier. In 1793 the Miami Confederacy declared that peace could be achieved only if the United States recognized the Ohio River as its northwestern boundary. But the national government refused to relinquish its claim in the region. A new army under the command of General Anthony Wayne, a Revolutionary War hero, attacked and defeated the confederacy in August 1794 at the Battle of Fallen Timbers. Peace negotiations began after the victory.

The Treaty of Greenville (1795) gave each side a portion of what it wanted. The United States gained the right to settle much of what was to become the state of Ohio, the tribes retaining only the northwest corner of the region. Indians, though, received the acknowledgment they had long sought: American recognition of their rights to the soil. At Greenville, the United States formally accepted the principle of Indian sovereignty, by virtue of residence, over all lands the tribes had not ceded. Never again would the United States government claim that it had acquired Indian territory solely through negotiation with a European or North American country.

The problems the United States encountered in ensuring safe settlement of the Northwest Territory pointed up the basic weakness of the Confederation government. Not until after the Articles of Confederation were replaced with a new constitution could the United States muster sufficient force to implement the Northwest Ordinance.

 From Crisis to the Constitution

The most obvious inadequacies of the Articles of Confederation concerned finance, overseas trade, and foreign affairs. Congress could not levy taxes, nor could it impose its will on the states to establish a uniform commercial policy or to ensure the enforcement of treaties. The problems involving trade were particularly serious. Less than a year after the war's end, the American economy slid into a depression. The postwar restrictions that European powers imposed on American commerce hurt exporters of such staple crops as rice and tobacco. Although some of the restrictions were eased and recovery began by 1786, the war's effects proved impossible to erase entirely.

The war had permanently changed the American economy. The near total cessation of foreign commerce in nonmilitary items during the war years stimulated domestic man-

Economic Change

ufacturing. Consequently, despite the influx of European goods after 1783, the postwar period witnessed the stirrings of American industrial development. For example, the first American textile mill began production in Pawtucket, Rhode Island, in 1793. Moreover, foreign trade patterns shifted from Europe and toward the West Indies. Foodstuffs shipped to the

French and Dutch Caribbean islands became America's largest single export.

Recognizing the Confederation Congress's inability to deal with commercial matters, Virginia invited the other states to a convention at Annapolis, Maryland, to discuss trade policy. Although eight states named representatives to the meeting in September 1786, only five delegations attended.

Annapolis Convention

Those present realized that they were too few in number to have any real impact on the political system. They issued a call for another convention, to be held in Philadelphia nine months later, "to devise such further provisions as shall . . . appear necessary to render the constitution of the federal government adequate to the exigencies of the Union." The other states did not respond immediately, but then Shays's Rebellion occurred.

The reaction to the rebellion hastened the movement toward comprehensive revision of the Articles. After most of the states had already appointed delegates, the Confederation Congress belatedly endorsed the convention. In mid-May 1787, fifty-five men, representing all the states but Rhode Island, assembled in Philadelphia to begin their deliberations.

The vast majority of delegates to the Constitutional Convention were men of property and substance. Among their number were merchants, planters, physicians, generals, governors, and especially lawyers. Most had been born in America. In an era when only a tiny proportion of the population had any advanced education, more than half of the delegates had attended college. A few had been educated in Britain, but most were graduates of American institutions. The youngest delegate was twenty-six, the oldest—Benjamin Franklin—eighty-one. Like George Washington, whom they elected their presiding officer, most were in their vigorous middle years. A dozen men did the bulk of the convention's work. Of these, James Madison of Virginia was by far the most important; he truly deserves the title "Father of the Constitution."

Constitutional Convention in Philadelphia

Madison was unique among the delegates in his systematic preparation for the Philadelphia meeting. He bought more than two hundred books on history and government, carefully analyzing their accounts of past confederacies and republics. A month before the Constitutional Convention began, he summed up the results of his research in a lengthy paper entitled "Vices of the Political System of the United States." In this paper, Madison set forth the principle of checks and balances. The government, he believed, had to be constructed in such a way that it could not become tyrannical or fall wholly under the influence of a particular interest group. He regarded the large size of a potential national republic as an advantage in that respect. Rejecting the common assertion that republics had to be small, Madison argued that a large, diverse republic should be preferred. Because the nation would include many different interest groups, no one of them would be able to control the government. Political stability would result from compromises among the contending parties.

James Madison: Father of the Constitution

Madison's conception of national government was embodied in the so-called Virginia Plan, introduced on May 29 by his fellow Virginian Edmund Randolph. The plan provided for a two-house legislature, the lower house elected directly by the people and the upper house selected by the lower; proportional representation in both houses; an executive elected by Congress; a national judiciary; and congressional veto over state laws. The Virginia Plan gave Congress the broad power to legislate "in all cases to which the separate states are incompetent." Had it been adopted intact, it would have created a government in which national authority reigned unchallenged and state power was greatly diminished. Proportional representation in both houses would also have given large states a dominant voice in the national government.

Virginia and New Jersey Plans

The convention included many delegates who recognized the need for change but believed the

Virginians had gone too far in the direction of national consolidation. The disaffected delegates united under the leadership of William Paterson of New Jersey, who presented an alternative scheme—the New Jersey Plan, calling for modifying the Articles rather than completely overhauling the government. Paterson proposed retaining a unicameral congress but giving it new powers of taxation and trade regulation. Although the convention initially rejected Paterson's position, he and his allies won a number of victories in the months that followed.

The delegates began their work by discussing the structure and functions of Congress. They readily agreed that the new national government should have a two-house (bicameral) legislature. But they proposed different answers to three key questions: Should representation in both houses of Congress be proportional to population? How was representation in either or both houses to be apportioned among the states? And, finally, how were the members of the two houses to be elected?

The Debates: Houses of Congress

The last issue was the easiest to resolve. To quote John Dickinson, the delegates thought it "essential" that members of the lower branch of Congress be elected directly by the people and "expedient" that members of the upper house be chosen by state legislatures. Since legislatures had selected delegates to the Confederation Congress, they would expect a similar privilege in the new government.

Considerably more difficult was the matter of proportional representation in the Senate. The delegates accepted without much debate the principle of proportional representation in the lower house. But small states argued for equal representation in the Senate, while large states supported a proportional plan for the upper house. For weeks the convention deadlocked on the issue. A committee appointed to work out a compromise recommended equal representation in the Senate, coupled with a proviso that all appropriation bills originate in the lower house. But not until the convention accepted a suggestion that a state's two senators vote as individuals rather than as a unit was a breakdown averted.

One critical question remained: how was representation in the lower house to be apportioned among states? Delegates from states with large numbers of slaves wanted African and European inhabitants to be counted equally; delegates from states with few slaves wanted only free people to be counted. Delegates resolved the dispute by using a formula developed by the Confederation Congress in 1783 to allocate financial assessments among states: three-fifths of slaves would be included in population totals. (The formula reflected delegates' judgment that slaves were less efficient producers of wealth than free people, not that they were 60 percent human and 40 percent property.) The three-fifths compromise on representation won unanimous approval.

The Debates: Slavery and Representation

Although the words *slave* and *slavery* do not appear in the Constitution (the framers used euphemisms such as *other persons*), direct and indirect protections for slavery were deeply embedded in the document. The three-fifths clause, for example, assured white southern voters not only congressional representation out of proportion to their numbers but also a disproportionate influence on the selection of the president, since the number of each state's electoral votes was determined by the size of its congressional delegation. Congress was prevented from outlawing the slave trade for at least twenty years. By guaranteeing that the national government would aid any states threatened with "domestic violence," the Constitution promised aid in putting down future slave revolts.

Constitutional Protections for Slavery

Once agreement was reached on the problems of slavery and representation, the delegates readily achieved consensus on the other issues confronting them. All agreed that the national government needed the authority to tax and to regulate commerce. And while the delegates enumerated congressional powers, they then provided for flexibility by granting all authority "necessary and proper" to carry out those powers. Foreign policy was placed in the hands of the executive, who was also made commander-in-chief of the armed forces. Moreover, the Constitution plus national laws and treaties would constitute "the supreme law of the land; and the judges in every state shall be bound thereby." As another means of circumscribing state powers, the delegates drafted a long list of actions forbidden to the states—such as "impair[ing] the obligation of contracts." Finally, the delegates established the electoral college and a four-year term for the chief executive, who could seek reelection.

The key to the Constitution was the distribution of political authority—separation of powers among executive, legislative, and judicial branches of the national government, and division of powers between states and nation. The system of checks and balances would make it difficult for the government to become tyrannical. At the same time, though, the elaborate system would sometimes prevent the government from acting quickly and decisively. Furthermore, the line between state and national powers was ambiguously and vaguely drawn.

Separation of Powers

The convention held its last session on September 17, 1787. Of the forty-two delegates present, only three refused to sign the Constitution. (Two of the three declined in part because of the lack of a bill of rights.) Though the delegates had accepted the Constitution, another question remained: would the states ratify it?

Opposition and Ratification

The ratification clause provided for the new system to take effect once it was approved by special conventions in at least nine states, with delegates being elected by qualified voters. Thus the national Constitution, unlike the Articles of Confederation, would rest directly on popular authority.

As states began to elect delegates to the special conventions, discussion of the proposed government grew more heated. Federalists (sup-

THE FEDERAL ALMANACK.

FEDERAL HALL.

LET Trumpets found, and fwift wing'd Fame,
Thefe glorious tidings far proclaim ;
On Virtue's bafe, by Wifdom plann'd ;
And rear'd by Union's facred hand ;
The FEDERAL DOME, is rais'd fublime :
Its PILLARS folid, ftrong as time ;
Rife ! Commerce ! rife ! unfurl the fail,
Rich Golden harvefts blefs the vale :
Arts ! Science ! Genius ! fpring to light ;
And Freedom burft on realms of Night

The Federal Almanack for 1789 trumpeted the virtues of the new Constitution. Not all Americans were so certain that the national government, here symbolized as an edifice supported by thirteen pillars, was as "solid, strong as time" as the printer proclaimed. American Antiquarian Society.

porters of the Constitution) and Antifederalists (its opponents) published newspaper essays and pamphlets vigorously defending or attacking the convention's decisions. The extent of the debate was unprecedented, and it quickly became apparent that the disputes within the Constitutional

Convention had been mild compared with divisions of opinion within the populace as a whole.

Federalists claimed that the nation did not need to fear centralized authority when good men were in charge and that the carefully structured government would preclude the possibility of tyranny. A republic could be large, they declared, if the government was designed to prevent any one group from controlling it. The separation of powers among legislative, executive, and judicial branches, and the division of powers between states and nation, would accomplish that goal. Thus people did not need to be protected from the powers of the new government in a formal way.

Federalists

Antifederalists feared a too-powerful central government, although they recognized the need for a national source of revenue. They saw the states as the chief protectors of individual rights; consequently, their weakening could bring the onset of arbitrary power. Antifederalist arguments against the Constitution often consisted of lists of potential abuses of government authority.

Antifederalists

Heirs of the Real Whig ideology of the late 1760s and early 1770s, Antifederalists stressed the need for constant popular vigilance to avert oppression. Indeed, some of the Antifederalists were the very men who originally promulgated those ideas—Samuel Adams, Patrick Henry, and Richard Henry Lee were leaders of the opposition to the Constitution. The Antifederalist ranks were also peopled by small farmers, who were preoccupied with guarding their property against excessive taxation, and by ambitious, upwardly mobile men who would gain more from an economic and political system less tightly controlled than the one the Constitution promised to establish.

As public debate continued, Antifederalists focused on the Constitution's lack of a bill of rights. Even if states were weakened by the new system, they believed, people could still be protected from tyranny if their rights were specifically guaranteed. *Letters of a Federal Farmer*, perhaps the most

Importance of a Bill of Rights

widely read Antifederalist pamphlet, listed the rights that should be protected: freedom of the press and of religion, the right to trial by jury, and guarantees against unreasonable search warrants. America's minister to France, Thomas Jefferson, was also concerned over "the omission of a bill of rights."

As state conventions met to consider ratification, the lack of a bill of rights loomed ever larger as a flaw in the proposed government. Four of the first five states to ratify did so unanimously, but serious disagreements then surfaced. Massachusetts, in which Antifederalist forces had been bolstered by a backlash against the state government's heavy-handed treatment of the Shays rebels, ratified by a majority of only 19 votes out of 355 cast. In June 1788, when New Hampshire ratified, the requirement of nine states was satisfied. But New York and Virginia had not yet voted, and everyone realized the new Constitution could not succeed unless those key states accepted it.

Ratification of the Constitution

Despite a valiant effort by the Antifederalist Patrick Henry, pro-Constitution forces won by 10 votes in the Virginia convention. In New York, James Madison, John Jay, and Alexander Hamilton campaigned for ratification by publishing *The Federalist*, a political tract that explained the theory behind the Constitution and masterfully answered its critics. Their reasoned arguments, coupled with Federalists' promise to add a bill of rights to the Constitution, helped win the battle. On July 26, 1788, New York ratified the Constitution by the slim margin of 3 votes. Although the last state (Rhode Island) did not formally join the Union until 1790, the new government was a reality.

Conclusion

During the 1770s and 1780s the nation took shape as a political union. It began to develop an economy independent of the British Empire, and it designed a foreign policy that attempted to chart its own course in the world in order to protect the national interests. An integral part of the formation of the Union was the systematic formulation of American racist thought. Emphasizing race as a determinant of African-Americans' standing in the nation allowed white men to define republicanism to exclude all people but themselves and thus ensure their control of the country.

The experience of fighting a war and of struggling for survival as an independent nation altered the political context of American life in the 1780s. At the outset of the war, most politically aware Americans believed that "that government which governs best governs least," but by the late 1780s many had changed their minds. These were the drafters and supporters of the Constitution.

Suggestions for Further Reading

General

Richard Beeman et al., eds., *Beyond Confederation: Origins of the Constitution and American National Identity* (1987); Joseph M. Ellis, *After the Revolution: Profiles of Early American Culture* (1979); Ronald Hoffman et al., eds., *The Economy of Early America: The Revolutionary Period, 1763–1790* (1988); Cathy Matson and Peter S. Onuf, *A Union of Interests: Political and Economic Thought in Revolutionary America* (1990); Kenneth Silverman, *A Cultural History of the American Revolution* (1976); Gordon S. Wood, *The Radicalism of the American Revolution* (1992); Gordon S. Wood, *The Creation of the American Republic, 1776–1787* (1969); Alfred F. Young et al, eds., *We the People: Voices and Images of the New Nation* (1993).

Continental Congress and Articles of Confederation

E. James Ferguson, *The Power of the Purse: A History of American Public Finance, 1776–1790* (1961); H. James Henderson, *Party Politics in the Continental Congress* (1974); Merrill Jensen, *The New Nation: A History of the United States During the Confederation, 1781–1789* (1950); Richard B. Morris, *The Forging of the Union, 1781–1789* (1987); Peter S. Onuf, *Statehood and Union: A History of the Northwest Ordinance* (1987); Jack N. Rakove, *The Beginnings of National Politics: An Interpretive History of the Continental Congress* (1979).

State Politics

Willi Paul Adams, *The First American Constitutions: Republican Ideology and the Making of the State Constitutions in the Revolutionary Era* (1980); Robert Gross, ed., *In Debt to Shays* (1992); Ronald Hoffman and Peter Albert, eds., *Sovereign States*

in an Age of Uncertainty (1981); Jackson Turner Main, *The Sovereign States, 1775–1783* (1973); David P. Szatmary, *Shays' Rebellion: The Making of an Agrarian Insurrection* (1980).

The Constitution

Thornton Anderson, *Creating the Constitution: The Convention of 1787 and the First Congress* (1993); Lance Banning, *The Sacred Fire of Liberty: James Madison and the Founding of the Federal Republic* (1995); Roger H. Brown, *Redeeming the Republic: Federalists, Taxation, and the Origins of the Constitution* (1993); Christopher Duncan, *The Anti-Federalists and Early American Political Thought* (1995); Frederick W. Marks III, *Independence on Trial: Foreign Affairs and the Making of the Constitution* (1973); Jack N. Rakove, *Original Meanings: Politics and Ideas in the Making of the Constitution* (1996); Robert A. Rutland, *The Ordeal of the Constitution: The Antifederalists and the Ratification Struggle of 1787–88* (1966); Abraham Sofaer, *War, Foreign Affairs, and Constitutional Power*, vol. 1, *The Origins* (1976).

Women

Edith Gelles, *Portia: The World of Abigail Adams* (1992); Susan Juster, *Disorderly Women: Sexual Politics and Evangelicalism in Revolutionary New England* (1994); Linda K. Kerber, *Women of the Republic: Intellect and Ideology in Revolutionary America* (1980); Mary Beth Norton, *Liberty's Daughters: The Revolutionary Experience of American Women, 1750–1800* (1980); Rosemarie Zagarri, *A Woman's Dilemma: Mercy Otis Warren and the American Revolution* (1995).

African-Americans and Slavery

Ira Berlin and Ronald Hoffman, eds., *Slavery and Freedom in the Age of the American Revolution* (1983); David Brion Davis, *The Problem of Slavery in the Age of Revolution, 1770–1823* (1975); Paul Finkelman, *Slavery and the Founders: Race and Liberty in the Age of Jefferson* (1996); Duncan J. Macleod, *Slavery, Race, and the American Revolution* (1974); Gary Nash, *Forging Freedom: The Formation of Philadelphia's Black Community, 1720–1840* (1988); Donald L. Robinson, *Slavery in the Structure of American Politics, 1765–1820* (1971); Shane White, *Somewhat More Independent: The End of Slavery in New York City, 1770–1810* (1991); Arthur Zilversmit, *The First Emancipation: The Abolition of Slavery in the North* (1967).

Indians

Harvey L. Carter, *The Life and Times of Little Turtle* (1987); Gregory E. Dowd, *A Spirited Resistance: The North American Indian Struggle for Unity, 1745–1815* (1992); Francis Paul Prucha, *American Indian Policy in the Formative Years: The Indian Trade and Intercourse Acts, 1790–1834* (1962); Wiley Sword, *President Washington's Indian War: The Struggle for the Old Northwest, 1790–1795* (1985); Anthony F. C. Wallace, *The Death and Rebirth of the Seneca* (1969).

CHAPTER
8

Politics and Society
in the Early Republic
1789–1800

"Shall I commence my journal, my dear Elizabeth, with a description of the pain I felt at taking leave of all my friends, or shall I leave you to imagine?" wrote Margaret Dwight as she began a chronicle of her arduous journey from New Haven, Connecticut, to Warren, Ohio. An orphan at age twenty, Margaret was traveling west to live with relatives. She filled her pages with comments on poor roads, dirty taverns, profane wagoneers, troublesome fellow travelers, and brawling "dutchmen" (Germans), whose failure to observe the Sabbath disgusted her. Margaret also noticed differences in English usage: "The people here talk curiously, they all reckon instead of expect—Youns is a word I have heard used several times, but what it means I don't know."

Many people she encountered assumed that Margaret was moving west to find a husband. But Margaret resisted, writing that she was "determin'd not to oblige myself to spend my days there, by marrying should I even have an opport[unit]y." At the end of her trip Margaret found Warren "pleasanter than I expected." About a year later, she married William Bell, a local merchant who soon relocated to Pittsburgh. Eventually, she gave birth to eight children in the West she had disdained.

Margaret Dwight was just one of the many thousand people who moved west in the decades following the Revolution. Their mobility signaled the beginnings of a new age, as large numbers of European-Americans and African-Americans poured through the Appalachian

Mountains for the first time. North of the Ohio River (Margaret's destination), the strength of the Miami Confederacy blocked westward expansion until after the Treaty of Greenville in 1795. South of the river, western settlements appeared as early as the 1770s, but they were isolated from the Atlantic coast by the long chain of mountains.

The dispersal of the population was accompanied by political fragmentation and economic difficulties. The United States economy still depended on the export trade. When warfare between England and France resumed in 1793, Americans found their commerce disrupted yet again. And the fight over the Constitution presaged an even wider division over the major political, economic, and diplomatic questions confronting the young republic.

Believing that the Constitution would resolve the problems that had arisen during the Confederation period, Americans did not anticipate the political disagreements that would characterize the 1790s. Moreover, they could not understand or fully accept the division of America's political leaders into two factions—not yet political parties—known as Federalists and Republicans, because in republics factions were seen as signs of decay and corruption. As the decade closed with the first fully partisan presidential election, Americans still had not come to terms with the implications of partisan politics.

 ## Building a Workable Government

Americans in many cities celebrated the ratification of the Constitution with a series of parades on July 4, 1788. The processions were carefully planned to symbolize the unity of the new nation. Like pre-revolutionary protest meetings, the parades served as political lessons for literate and illiterate Americans alike. Men and women who could not read were thereby educated about the significance of the new Constitution for the nation.

Celebrating Ratification

They also were instructed about political leaders' hopes for industry and frugality on the part of a virtuous American public.

The nationalistic spirit expressed in the ratification processions carried over to the first session of Congress. Only a few Antifederalists ran for office in the congressional elections held late in 1788, and even fewer were elected. Thus the First Congress consisted chiefly of men who supported a strong national government. The drafters of the Constitution had deliberately left many key issues undecided, so the nationalists' domination of Congress meant that their views on those points quickly prevailed.

Nationalism in the First Congress

Congress faced four immediate tasks when it convened in April 1789: raising revenue to support the new government, responding to state ratification conventions' call for a bill of rights, setting up executive departments, and organizing the federal judiciary. The last task was especially important. The Constitution established a Supreme Court but left it to Congress to decide whether to have other federal courts as well.

James Madison, who had been elected to the House of Representatives, soon became as influential in Congress as he had been at the Constitutional Convention. A few months into the first session, he persuaded Congress to adopt the Revenue Act of 1789, imposing a 5 percent tariff on certain imports. Thus the First Congress quickly achieved what the Confederation Congress never had: an effective national tax law. The new government would have problems in its first years, but lack of revenue was not one of them.

Madison also took the lead on the issue of constitutional amendments. He placed nineteen proposed amendments before the House. Eventually, the states ratified ten, which officially became part of the Constitution on December 15, 1791 (see the Appendix for the Constitution and all amendments). Their adoption defused Antifederalist opposition and rallied support for the new government. The First Amendment specifically prohibited Congress

Bill of Rights

• *Important Events* •

1789	George Washington inaugurated as first president	**1795**	Jay Treaty with England
	Judiciary Act of 1789 organizes federal court system	**1796**	First contested presidential election: John Adams elected president, Thomas Jefferson vice president
	French Revolution begins	**1798**	XYZ affair arouses American opinion against France
1790	Alexander Hamilton's *Report on Public Credit* proposes assumption of state debts		Alien and Sedition Acts punish political dissenters
1791	First ten amendments (Bill of Rights) ratified		Virginia and Kentucky resolutions protest suppression of dissent
1793	France declares war on Britain, Spain, and Holland	**1798–99**	Quasi-War with France
	Washington's neutrality proclamation keeps the United States out of the war	**1800**	Franco-American Convention ends the Quasi-War
	Democratic-Republican societies founded, the first grassroots political organizations		Jefferson elected president, Aaron Burr vice president
			Gabriel's Rebellion threatens slaveholders
1794	Whiskey Rebellion in western Pennsylvania protests taxation	**1801**	Second Great Awakening sweeps through Kentucky

from passing any law restricting the right to freedom of religion, speech, press, peaceable assembly, or petition. The next two amendments arose directly from the former colonists' fear of standing armies as a threat to freedom. The Second Amendment guaranteed people's right "to keep and bear arms" because of the need for a "well-regulated Militia." Thus the constitutional right to bear arms was based on the expectation that most able-bodied men would serve the nation as citizen soldiers and there would be little need for a standing army. The Third Amendment defined the circumstances in which troops could be quartered in private homes.

The Fourth Amendment prohibited "unreasonable searches and seizures." The Fifth and Sixth established the rights of accused persons. The Seventh specified the conditions for jury trials in civil (as opposed to criminal) cases, and the Eighth forbade "cruel and unusual punishments."

The Ninth and Tenth Amendments reserved to the people and the states other unspecified rights and powers. In short, the amendments' authors made clear that, in listing some rights, they did not mean to preclude the exercise of others.

While debating proposed amendments, Congress also considered the organization of the executive branch. It readily agreed to continue

Executive Branch

the three administrative departments established under the Articles of Confederation: War, Foreign Affairs (renamed State), and Treasury. Congress instituted two lesser posts: the attorney general—the nation's official lawyer—and the postmaster general. Congress also established the principle that the heads of executive departments are responsible to the president when it agreed that the president alone could dismiss officials he had originally appointed with the consent of the Senate.

Aside from constitutional amendments, the most far-reaching piece of legislation enacted by the First Congress was the Judiciary Act of 1789, which defined the jurisdiction of the federal judiciary and established a six-member Supreme Court, thirteen district courts, and three circuit courts of appeal. Its most important provision, Section 25, allowed appeals from state courts to federal courts when cases raised certain types of constitutional issues. Section 25 thus implemented Article VI of the Constitution, which stated that federal laws and treaties were to be considered "the supreme Law of the Land."

Judiciary Act of 1789

During its first decade, the Supreme Court handled few cases of any importance. But in a significant 1796 decision, *Ware* v. *Hylton*, the Court for the first time declared a state law unconstitutional. The same year it also reviewed the constitutionality of an act of Congress, upholding its validity in the case of *Hylton* v. *U.S.* The most important case of the decade, *Chisholm* v. *Georgia* (1793), established that states could be sued in federal courts by citizens of other states. This decision, unpopular with state governments, was overruled five years later by the Eleventh Amendment to the Constitution.

The Early Supreme Court

John Trumbull, known primarily for his larger-than-life portraits of patriot leaders, painted this miniature of George Washington, who posed for it during his presidency (c. 1792–1794).   Division of Political History, Smithsonian Institution, Washington, D.C.

Domestic Policy Under Washington and Hamilton

In 1783 George Washington returned to Mount Vernon with thoughts of peaceful life as a planter. Within a few years, however, his countrymen would again seek his service. Once the Constitution was ratified, Americans concurred that only George Washington had sufficient stature to serve as the republic's first president. The unanimous vote of the electoral college was just a formality, and he was inaugurated in 1789.

Election of the First President

Washington acted cautiously during his first months in office, knowing that whatever he did would set precedents for the future. When the title by which he should be addressed aroused controversy (Vice President John Adams favored "His Highness, the President of the United States of America, and Protector of their Liberties"), Washington said nothing. The accepted title soon became a plain "Mr. President." By using the heads of the executive departments collectively as his chief advisers, he created the cabinet. Washington also concluded that he should exercise his veto power over congressional legislation very sparingly—only, indeed, if he was convinced a bill was unconstitutional.

Washington's First Steps

Washington's first major task as president was to choose the heads of the executive departments. For the War Department he selected an old comrade-in-arms, Henry Knox. His choice for the State Department was his fellow Virginian Thomas Jefferson, who had just returned to the United States from his post as minister to France. And for the crucial position of secretary of the treasury, the president chose the brilliant, intensely ambitious Alexander Hamilton.

Two traits distinguished Hamilton from most of his contemporaries. First, he displayed an undivided loyalty to the nation as a whole. As a West

Alexander Hamilton

Indian who had lived on the mainland only briefly before the war, Hamilton had no ties to a particular state. He showed little sympathy for, or understanding of, demands for local autonomy. Thus the aim of his fiscal policies was always to consolidate power at the national level. Further, he never feared the exercise of centralized executive authority, as did older counterparts who had clashed repeatedly with colonial governors, nor was he afraid of maintaining close political and economic ties with Britain.

Second, he regarded his fellow human beings with unvarnished cynicism. Perhaps because of his difficult early life (he was the illegitimate child of an aristocrat and had lived in poverty) and his own overriding ambition, Hamilton believed people to be motivated primarily by self-interest. Unlike some other Americans, he foresaw no rosy future in which public-spirited citizens would pursue the common good rather than their own private advantage.

In 1789, Congress ordered the new secretary of the treasury to assess the public debt and to submit recommendations for supporting the government's credit. Hamilton found

National and State Debts

that the country's remaining war debts fell into three categories: those owed by the nation to foreign governments and investors, mostly to France (about $11 million); those owed by the national government to merchants, former soldiers, holders of revolutionary bonds, and the like (about $27 million); and, finally, similar debts owed by state governments (roughly $25 million). With respect to the national debt, there was little disagreement: politi-

cally aware Americans recognized that if their new government was to succeed it would have to repay its indebtedness at full face value.

The state debts were another matter. Some states—notably Virginia, Maryland, North Carolina, and Georgia—already had paid off most of their war debts. They would oppose the national government's assumption of responsibility for other states' debts, since their citizens would be taxed to pay such obligations. Massachusetts, Connecticut, and South Carolina, by contrast, still had sizable unpaid debts and would welcome a system of national assumption. The possible assumption of state debts also had political implications. Consolidating the debt in the hands of the national government would help to concentrate economic and political power at the national level. A contrary policy would reserve greater independence of action for the states.

Hamilton's first *Report on Public Credit*, sent to Congress in January 1790, reflected both his national loyalty and his cynicism. He proposed

Hamilton's Financial Plan

that Congress assume outstanding state debts, combine them with national obligations, and issue new securities covering both the principal and the accumulated unpaid interest. Current holders of state or national debt certificates would have the option of taking a portion of their payment in western lands. Hamilton's aims were clear: he wanted to expand the financial reach of the United States government, simultaneously reducing the states' economic power. He also wanted to ensure that holders of public securities—many of them wealthy merchants and speculators—would have a significant financial stake in the survival of the national government.

Hamilton's plan stimulated lively debate in Congress. The opposition coalesced around his former ally James Madison. Well aware that speculators had purchased large quantities of debt certificates at a small fraction of their face value, Madison proposed that the original holders of the debt also be compensated by the government. Madison's plan, though fairer than Hamilton's, would have been difficult, if not impossible, to administer. The House of Representatives rejected it.

At first, the House also rejected the assumption of state debts. The Senate, however, adopted Hamilton's plan largely intact, and a series of compromises followed. Hamilton agreed to changes in the assumption plan that would benefit Virginia (Madison's home state) in particular. The assumption bill also became linked to the other controversial issue of that congressional session: the location of the permanent national capital. Both northerners and southerners wanted the capital in their region. The legend that Hamilton and Madison agreed over Jefferson's dinner table to exchange assumption of state debts for a southern site is not supported by the surviving evidence, but a political deal was undoubtedly struck. The Potomac River was designated as the site for the capital, and the first part of Hamilton's financial program became law in August 1790.

Four months later Hamilton submitted to Congress a second report on public credit, recommending the chartering of a national bank. The

First Bank of the United States

Bank of the United States was to be capitalized at $10 million, of which only $2 million would come from public funds. Private investors would supply the rest. The bank's charter would run for twenty years, and the government would name one-fifth of the directors. The bank's notes would circulate as the nation's currency. The bank would also act as collecting and disbursing agent for the Treasury and would lend money to the government. Most political leaders recognized that such an institution would be beneficial, especially because it would solve the problem of America's perpetual shortage of an acceptable medium of exchange. But another issue loomed large: did the Constitution give Congress the power to establish such a bank?

James Madison answered that question with a resounding no. He pointed out that Constitutional Convention delegates had specifically rejected a clause authorizing Congress to issue corporate charters. Consequently, he argued, that power could not be inferred from other parts of the Constitution.

Madison's contention disturbed Washington, who decided to request other opinions before signing the bill into law. Thomas Jefferson, the

Strict and Broad Constructions of the Constitution

secretary of state, agreed with Madison that the bank was unconstitutional. Jefferson referred to Article I, Section 8, of the Constitution, which gave Congress the power "to make all Laws which shall be necessary and proper for carrying into Execution the foregoing Powers." The key word, Jefferson argued, was *necessary*: Congress could do what was needed, but could not do what was merely desirable. Thus Jefferson formulated the strict-constructionist interpretation of the Constitution.

Washington asked Hamilton to reply to the negative assessments of his proposal. Hamilton's *Defense of the Constitutionality of the Bank*, presented to the president in February 1791, was a brilliant exposition of what has become known as the broad-constructionist view of the Constitution. Hamilton argued forcefully that Congress could choose any means not specifically prohibited by the Constitution to achieve a constitutional end. If the end was constitutional and the means was not unconstitutional, then the means was also constitutional. Washington was convinced and signed the bill.

In December 1791, Hamilton presented to Congress his *Report on Manufactures*, the last of his prescriptions for the American economy. In it he outlined an ambitious plan for encouraging and protecting the United States's infant industries, like shoemaking and textile manufacturing. Hamilton argued that the nation could never be truly independent as long as it relied heavily on Europe for manufactured goods. He thus urged Congress to promote the immigration of technicians and laborers and to support industrial development through a limited use of protective tariffs. Many of Hamilton's ideas were implemented in later decades, but in 1791 most congressmen believed that America's future lay in agriculture and that the mainstay of the republic was the virtuous yeoman farmer. They therefore rejected the report.

That same year Congress accepted another feature of Hamilton's financial program, an excise tax on whiskey. The tax was needed to pay the cost of funding the state debts. An excise tax on whiskey was attractive because it affected relatively few farmers—those in the West who sold their grain in the form of distilled spirits as a means of avoiding the high cost of transportation—and because it might reduce consumption of whiskey. Moreover, Hamilton knew that those western farmers were Jefferson's supporters, and he saw the benefits of taxing them rather than the merchants who supported his own policies.

Whiskey Rebellion

News of the excise law set off protests in frontier areas of Pennsylvania. For two years unrest persisted on the frontiers not only of Pennsylvania but also of Maryland and Virginia. President Washington responded with restraint until violence erupted in July 1794, when western Pennsylvania farmers resisted a federal marshal and a tax collector trying to enforce the law. Three rioters were killed and several militiamen wounded. About seven thousand rebels convened on August 1 to plot the destruction of Pittsburgh but decided not to face the heavy guns of the fort guarding the town. Washington then took decisive action to prevent a crisis reminiscent of Shays's Rebellion. On August 7, he called on the insurgents to disperse and summoned nearly thirteen thousand militia from Pennsylvania and neighboring states. By the time federal forces marched westward in October and November, the disturbances had ended.

The chief importance of the Whiskey Rebellion was the forceful message Washington's response conveyed to the American public: he had demonstrated that the national government would not allow violent resistance to its laws. In the republic, change would be effected peacefully, by legal means.

By 1794, a group of Americans was already beginning to seek change systematically through electoral politics, even though traditional political theory regarded organized opposition—especially in a republic—as illegitimate. The controversy grew out of the belief by opposition leaders Thomas Jefferson and James Madison that Hamil-

Republicans and Federalists

ton's policies of favoring wealthy commercial interests at the expense of agriculture would impose a corrupt, aristocratic government on the United States. They contended that they were the true heirs of the Revolution and that Hamilton was plotting to subvert republican principles. To dramatize their point, Jefferson, Madison, and their followers in Congress began calling themselves *Republicans*.

Hamilton in turn accused Jefferson and Madison of the same crime: attempting to destroy the republic. Hamilton and his supporters began calling themselves *Federalists*, to legitimize their claims and link themselves with the Constitution. In short, each group accused the other of being an illicit faction working to destroy the republican principles of the Revolution. (By traditional definition, a faction was a group opposed to the public good.)

At first, President Washington tried to remain aloof from the political dispute that divided Hamilton and Jefferson, his chief advisers. Even so, the controversy helped persuade him to seek a second term of office in 1792 in hopes of promoting political unity. But in 1793 and thereafter, developments in foreign affairs magnified the disagreements.

Partisan Politics and Foreign Policy

The initial years under the Constitution were blessed by international peace. Soon, however, the French Revolution, which began in 1789, brought about the resumption of hostilities between France, America's wartime ally, and Great Britain, America's most important trading partner.

At first Americans welcomed the news that France was turning toward republicanism, but by the early 1790s the reports from France were disquieting. Outbreaks of violence continued; ministries succeeded each other with bewildering rapidity; executions were commonplace.

The French Revolution

The king himself was beheaded in early 1793. Although many Americans, including Jefferson and Madison, retained their sympathy for the revolutionaries, others including Hamilton, began to view France as a prime example of the perversion of republicanism.

When France declared war on Britain, Spain, and Holland in 1793, the Americans faced a dilemma. The 1778 Treaty of Alliance with France bound them to that nation "forever," and a mutual commitment to republicanism created ideological bonds. Yet the United States was connected to Great Britain through a shared history and language, and through an economic partnership. Americans purchased most of their manufactured goods from Great Britain. Indeed, since the financial system of the United States depended heavily on import tariffs as a source of revenue, the nation's economic health in effect required uninterrupted trade with Britain.

The political and diplomatic climate was further complicated in April 1793, when Citizen Edmond Genêt, a representative of the French government, landed in Charleston.

Citizen Genêt

As Genêt made his way northward to New York City, he recruited Americans for expeditions against British and Spanish colonies in the Western Hemisphere, and he distributed privateering commissions with a generous hand. Genêt's arrival raised a series of troubling questions for President Washington. Should he receive Genêt, thus officially recognizing the French revolutionary government? Should he acknowledge an obligation to aid France under the terms of the 1778 Treaty of Alliance? Or should he proclaim American neutrality?

For once, Hamilton and Jefferson saw eye to eye. Both told Washington that the United States could not afford to ally itself with either side. Washington agreed. He received Genêt but also issued a proclamation informing the world that the United States would adopt "a conduct friendly and impartial toward the belligerent powers."

Genêt himself was removed from politics when his faction fell from power in Paris, but his disappearance from the diplomatic scene did not lessen the impact of the French Revolution in America. The domestic divisions Genêt helped to widen

were perpetuated by clubs called Democratic-Republican societies, formed by Americans sympathetic to the French Revolution and worried about the policies of the Washington administration.

More than forty Democratic-Republican societies were organized between 1793 and 1800. Their members saw themselves as heirs of the

Democratic-Republican Societies

Sons of Liberty, seeking the protection of people's liberties against encroachments by corrupt and self-serving rulers. They criticized the Washington administration's fiscal and foreign policies and repeatedly proclaimed their belief in the rights to free speech, free press, and assembly. Like the Sons of Liberty, the Democratic-Republican societies were composed chiefly of artisans and craftsmen, although professionals, farmers, and merchants also joined.

The rapid growth of such groups deeply disturbed Hamilton and eventually Washington himself. Some newspapers charged that the societies were subversive agents of a foreign power. The climax of the counterattack came in the fall of 1794, when Washington accused the societies of having fomented the Whiskey Rebellion.

In retrospect, Washington and Hamilton's reaction to the Democratic-Republican societies seems disproportionately hostile. But it must be recalled that factional disputes were believed to endanger the survival of republics. As the first organized political dissenters in the United States, the Democratic-Republican societies alarmed elected officials, who had not yet accepted the idea that one component of a free government was an organized loyal opposition.

Also in 1794 George Washington dispatched Chief Justice John Jay to London to negotiate four unresolved questions affecting Anglo-American

Jay Treaty

affairs. The first point at issue was recent British seizures of American merchant ships trading in the French West Indies. The United States wanted to establish the principle of freedom of the seas and to assert its right, as a neutral nation, to trade freely with both combatants. Second, in violation of the 1783 peace treaty, Great Britain had not yet evacuated its posts in the American Northwest. The Americans also hoped for a commercial treaty and sought compensation for the slaves who had left with the British army at the end of the war.

The negotiations in London proved difficult, since Jay had little to offer in exchange for the concessions he sought. Britain did agree to evacuate the western forts and ease restrictions on American trade to England and the West Indies. No compensation for slaves was agreed to, but the treaty established two arbitration commissions—one to deal with prewar debts Americans owed to British creditors and the other to hear claims for captured American merchant ships. Under the circumstances, Jay did remarkably well: the treaty averted war with England. Nevertheless, most Americans, including the president, were dissatisfied.

At first, potential opposition was blunted because the Senate debated and ratified the treaty in secret. Not until after it was approved by a vote of 20 to 10 in June 1795 was the public informed of its provisions. The Democratic-Republican societies led protests against the treaty. Once President Washington had signed the treaty, though, there seemed to be little the Republicans could do to prevent it from taking effect. Just one opportunity remained: Congress had to appropriate funds to carry out the treaty provisions.

When the House debated the issue in March 1796, members opposing the treaty tried to prevent approval of the appropriations. To that end, they asked Washington to submit to the House all documents pertinent to the negotiations. In successfully resisting the House's request, Washington established the doctrine of *executive privilege*—the power of the president to withhold information from Congress if he believes circumstances warrant doing so.

The treaty's opponents initially appeared to be in the majority. Frontier residents, however, were eager to have the British posts evacuated, and merchants wanted to reap benefits from expanded trade. Furthermore, Thomas Pinckney of South Carolina had negotiated a treaty with Spain giving the United States navigation privileges on the Mississippi, which would be an economic boost to the West and South. The popularity of Pinckney's Treaty helped to overcome opposition to the Jay Treaty. For all these reasons, the House voted the necessary funds by the narrow margin of 51 to 48.

Analysis of the vote reveals both the regional nature of the division and the growing cohesion of the Republican and Federalist factions in Congress. Voting for the appropriations were 44 Federalists and 7 Republicans; voting against were 45 Republicans and 3 Federalists. The final tally was also split by region. Southerners cast the vast majority of votes against the bill, and almost all proponents came from New England and the middle states.

Partisan Divisions in Congress

The small number of defectors on both sides reveals a new force at work in American politics: partisanship. Voting statistics from the first four Congresses show the ever-increasing tendency of members of the House of Representatives to vote as cohesive groups, rather than as individuals. The growing division cannot be accurately explained in the terms used by Jefferson and Madison (aristocrats versus the people) or by Hamilton and Washington (true patriots versus subversive rabble). Simple economic differences between agrarian and commercial interests do not provide the answer either.

Bases of Partisanship

Yet certain distinctions can be made. Republicans, who were especially prominent in the southern and middle states, tended to be self-assured, confident, and optimistic about both politics and the economy. Southern planters, firmly in control of their region, foresaw a prosperous future based partly on continued westward expansion, which they expected to dominate. Republicans employed democratic rhetoric to win the allegiance of small farmers south of New England. Members of non-English ethnic groups—especially Irish, Scots, and Germans—found Republicans' words attractive. Republicans of all descriptions emphasized developing America's own resources and were less concerned than the Federalists about the nation's position in the world. Republicans also remained sympathetic to France in international affairs.

By contrast, Federalists, concentrated in New England, came mostly from English stock. They

How do historians know that Americans were intensely patriotic in the early years of the republic? One piece of evidence is supplied by the many items incorporating patriotic motifs that decorated the homes of American citizens. The artisans of the new nation (and of England as well) quickly recognized that "patriotism sold," so they created a wide variety of objects to satisfy Americans' demand for furniture, wallpaper, curtains, and pottery goods displaying such themes. Only middling and well-to-do Amreicans could afford to buy such items, but a less-well-off American woman could produce some of these goods for herself. We do not know who made this eagle hooked rug, but a poor woman with just a few moments to spare each day could well have labored for months to display her allegiance to the new nation in this fashion. New York State Historical Association, Cooperstown.

drew considerable support from commercial interests and were insecure, uncertain of the future. They stressed the need for order, authority, and regularity in the political world. Federalists had no grassroots political organization and put little emphasis on involving ordinary people in government. Many were farmers who, prevented from expanding agricultural production because of New England's poor soil, gravitated toward the more conservative party. Federalists, like Republicans, assumed that southern interests would dominate the land west of the mountains, so they had little incentive to work actively to develop that potentially rich territory. In Federalist eyes, the nation was perpetually threatened by potential enemies, both internal and external, and was best protected by a continuing alliance with Great Britain.

The presence of the two organized groups—not yet parties in the modern sense—made the presidential election of 1796 the first that was seriously contested. Tired of the criticism to which he had been subjected, George Washington decided to retire from office. In September he published his Farewell Address. In it Washington outlined two principles that would guide American foreign policy at least until the late 1940s: to maintain commercial but not political ties to other nations and to enter no permanent al-

Washington's Farewell Address

liances. In doing so, Washington stressed the need for unilateralism (independent action in foreign affairs). He also lamented the existence of factional divisions among his countrymen, and he attacked the legitimacy of the Republican opposition.

To succeed Washington, the Federalists in Congress put forward Vice President John Adams, with the diplomat Thomas Pinckney as his running mate. Congressional Republicans caucused and chose Thomas Jefferson as their presidential candidate; the lawyer, Revolutionary War veteran, and active Republican politician Aaron Burr of New York agreed to run for vice president.

Election of 1796

That the election was contested did not mean that its outcome was decided by the people. Voters could cast their ballots only for electors, not for the candidates themselves. More than 40 percent of the members of the electoral college were chosen by state legislatures rather than by popular vote. Moreover, the method of voting in the electoral college did not take into account the possibility of party slates. The Constitution's drafters had not foreseen the development of competing national political organizations, so the Constitution provided no way to express support for one person for president and another for vice president. The electors simply voted for two people. The man with the highest total became president; the second highest, vice president. Thus Adams, the Federalist, with 71 votes became the president, and Jefferson, the Republican, with 68 votes became the vice president.

John Adams and Political Dissent

John Adams took over the presidency peculiarly blind to the partisan developments of the previous four years. As president he never abandoned an outdated notion that the president should be above politics, an independent and dignified figure who did not seek petty factional advantage. Thus Adams kept Washington's cabinet intact, despite its key members' allegiance to his chief rival, Alexander Hamilton. Adams often adopted a passive posture, letting others (usually Hamilton) take the lead when

he should have acted decisively. As a result, his administration gained a reputation for inconsistency. When Adams's term ended, the Federalists were severely divided, and the Republicans had won the presidency. But Adams's detachment from Hamilton's maneuverings did enable him to weather the greatest international crisis the republic had yet faced: the so-called Quasi-War with France.

The Jay Treaty improved America's relationship with Great Britain, but it provoked retaliation by France. Angry that the United States had reached agreement with its enemy, the French government ordered its vessels to seize American ships carrying British goods. In response, Adams appointed three commissioners to try to reach a settlement with France. Simultaneously, Congress increased military spending.

For months, the American commissioners sought negotiations with Talleyrand, the French foreign minister, but Talleyrand's agents demanded a bribe of $250,000 before talks could begin. The Americans retorted, "No, no; not a sixpence," and reported the incident in dispatches that President Adams received in early March 1798. Adams informed Congress of the impasse and recommended increased appropriations for defense.

XYZ Affair

Convinced that Adams had deliberately sabotaged the negotiations, congressional Republicans insisted that the dispatches be turned over to Congress. Adams complied, aware that releasing the reports would work to his advantage. He withheld only the names of the French agents, referring to them as *X*, *Y*, and *Z*. The revelation that the Americans had been treated with contempt stimulated a wave of anti-French sentiment in the United States. Cries for war filled the air. Congress formally abrogated the Treaty of Alliance and authorized American ships to seize French vessels.

Thus began an undeclared war with France. The so-called Quasi-War was fought in the West Indies, between warships of the United States Navy and French privateers seeking to capture American merchant vessels. Initial American losses of merchant shipping were heavy. By early

Quasi-War with France

This cartoon drawn during the XYZ affair depicts the United States as a maiden being victimized by the five leaders of the French government's directorate. In the background, John Bull (England) watches from on high, while other European nations discuss the situation. The Lilly Library, Indiana University, Bloomington, Indiana.

1799, however, the United States Navy had established its superiority in Caribbean waters, easing the threat to America's vital West Indian trade.

The Republicans, who opposed war and continued to sympathize with France, could do little to stem the tide of anti-French feelings. The Federalists saw this climate of opinion as an opportunity to deal a death blow to their Republican opponents. Now that the country seemed to see the truth of what they had been saying ever since the Whiskey Rebellion in 1794—that Republicans were subversive foreign agents—Federalists sought to codify that belief into law. In 1798, the Federalist-controlled Congress adopted a set of four laws known as the Alien and Sedition Acts, intended to suppress dissent and to prevent further growth of the Republican party.

Alien and Sedition Acts

Three of the acts were aimed at immigrants, whom Federalists accurately suspected of being Republican in their sympathies. The Naturalization Act lengthened the residency period required for citizenship and ordered all resident aliens to register with the federal government. The two Alien Acts provided for the detention of enemy aliens in time of war and gave the president authority to deport any alien he deemed dangerous to the nation's security. Neither act was implemented during the Adams administration, however.

The fourth act, the Sedition Act, sought to control both citizens and aliens. It outlawed conspiracies to prevent the enforcement of federal laws and set the maximum punishment for such offenses at five years in prison and a $5,000 fine. The act also tried to control speech. Writing, printing, or uttering "false, scandalous and malicious" statements against the government or the president "with intent to defame . . . or to bring them or either of them, into contempt or disrepute" became a crime punishable by as much as two years' imprisonment and a fine of $2,000.

The Sedition Act led to fifteen indictments and ten convictions. Most of the accused were outspoken Republican newspaper editors. But the first victim—whose story may serve as an example of the rest—was a hot-tempered Republican congressman from Vermont, Matthew Lyon. The Irish-born Lyon was convicted, fined $1,000, and sent to prison for four months for declaring in print that John Adams had displayed "a continual grasp for power" and "an unbounded thirst for ridiculous pomp, foolish adulation, and selfish avarice." While in jail, Lyon ran a successful reelection campaign.

Faced with prosecutions of their supporters, Jefferson and Madison sought an effective means of combating the acts. They turned to constitutional theory and the state legislatures. Carefully concealing their own role—it would not have been desirable for the vice president to be indicted for sedition—Jefferson and Madison each drafted a set of resolutions. Introduced into the Kentucky and Virginia legislatures, respectively, in the fall of 1798, the resolutions differed somewhat but had the same import. Since the Constitution was created by a compact among the states, they contended, people speaking through their states had a legitimate right to judge the constitutionality of actions taken by the federal government. Both sets of resolutions pronounced the Alien and Sedition Acts null and void and asked other states to join in the protest.

Virginia and Kentucky Resolutions

Although no other state endorsed them, the Virginia and Kentucky resolutions were nevertheless influential. First, they were superb political propaganda, rallying Republican opinion and placing the party squarely in the revolutionary tradition of resistance to tyrannical authority. Second, the theory of union they proposed inspired southern states' rights advocates in the 1830s and thereafter. Jefferson and Madison had identified a key constitutional issue: how far could states go in opposing the national government? How could a conflict between the two be resolved?

Meanwhile, the Federalists split over the course of action the United States should take toward France. Hamilton and his supporters still called for a declaration legitimizing the undeclared naval war. But Adams received a number of private signals that the French government regretted its treatment of the American commissioners. Acting on these assurances, he dispatched the envoy William Vans Murray to Paris. The United States asked for two things: compensation for ships the French had seized since 1793 and abrogation of the treaty of 1778. The Convention of 1800, which ended the Quasi-War, provided for the latter but not the former. The results of the negotiations were not known in the United States until after the presidential election of 1800. By then, the split in the Federalist camp had already cost Adams the election.

Convention of 1800

The Republicans entered the 1800 presidential race firmly united behind Jefferson and Burr. Although they would win the election, their lack of foresight almost cost them dearly. The problem was the system of voting in the electoral college. All Republican electors voted for both Jefferson and Burr, giving each 73 votes (Adams had 65). Because neither Republican had a plurality, the Constitution required that the contest be decided in the House of Representatives, with each state's representatives voting as a unit. Because the new House, dominated by Republicans, would not take office for some months, Federalist representatives decided the election by selecting Jefferson—to them, a lesser evil than Burr—on the thirty-fifth ballot. In response to the tangle, the Twelfth Amendment to the Constitution (1804) changed the method of voting in the electoral college to allow for a party ticket.

Election of 1800

Westward Expansion, Social Change, and Religious Ferment

The United States experienced a dramatic increase in internal migration in the postrevolutionary years. As much as 5 to 10 percent of the population moved each year, approximately half relocating to another state. The major population shifts were from east to west (see map): from New England to upstate New York and Ohio, from New Jersey to western Pennsylvania, from the Chesapeake to the new states of Kentucky and Tennessee. Very few people moved north or south.

The first permanent white settlements beyond the Appalachian Mountains were established in western North Carolina in 1771. But not until af-

Settlement in the West

ter the defeat of the Shawnees in 1774 and the Cherokees in 1776 was the way cleared for a more general migration. By 1790, more than 100,000 peo-

ple lived in the future states of Kentucky and Tennessee. Settlements grew more slowly north of the Ohio River because of the strength of the Miami Confederacy. But once the Treaty of Greenville was signed in 1795, the Ohio country also grew rapidly.

The transplanted New Englanders in particular did their best to re-create the societies they had left behind, laying out farms and towns in neat checkerboard patterns and founding libraries and Congregational churches. Early arrivals' enthusiastic letters describing Ohio's rich soil and potential for growth recruited others to join them, setting off a phenomenon known in New England as "Ohio Fever."

The westward migration of slaveholders, first to Kentucky and Tennessee and then later into the rich lands of western Georgia and eventually the Gulf Coast, had an adverse impact on African-Americans.

African-Americans in the West

The web of family connections built up over several generations of residence in the Chesapeake was torn apart by the population movement. Even those few large planters who moved their entire slave force west rarely owned all the members of every family on their plantations. Most commonly the migrants were either younger sons of eastern slaveholders, whose inheritance included only a portion of the family's slaves, or small farmers with just one or two bondspeople. In the early years of American settlement in the West, the population was widely

dispersed; accordingly, African-Americans raised among large numbers of kin in the Chesapeake had to adapt to lonely lives on isolated farms. Many of them also had to build new families to replace those unwillingly left behind in the East.

The mobility of the population created a volatile mix in southern frontier areas. Since most of the migrants were young, single men just starting to lead inde-

Second Great Awakening

pendent lives, western society was at first unstable. Like the seventeenth-century Chesa-peake, the late–eighteenth-

century American West was a society in which single women like Margaret Dwight married quickly. The few women among the migrants lamented their lack of congenial female friends. Isolated, far from familiar surroundings, women and men strove to create new communities to replace those left behind.

Among the migrants to Kentucky and Tennessee were clergymen and committed lay members of the evangelical sects that had arisen in America after the First Great Awakening: Baptists, Presbyterians, and Methodists. That First Awakening had flourished in the southern backcountry well into the 1760s, and the Second Great Awakening, which began around 1800 in the West and continued into the 1840s, was an extension of the earlier revival.

At protracted camp meetings, sometimes attended by thousands of people, clergymen exhorted their audiences to repent their sins. Many declared that salvation was open to all, rejecting the Calvinistic doctrine of predestination. Stressing the emotional nature of the conversion experience and downplaying the need for Bible study, such preachers were in effect democratizing American religion, making it available to all rather than to a preselected and educated elite.

The most famous camp meeting took place in August 1801 at Cane Ridge, Kentucky. At a time when the largest settlement in the state had no more than two thousand inhabitants, about ten thousand people came to Cane Ridge. One witness saw "sinners dropping down on every hand, shrieking, groaning, crying for mercy." Such scenes were to be repeated many times in the decades that fol-

Western Expansion, 1785–1805 *After the Revolutionary War, large numbers of white and black Americans ventured west of the Appalachian Mountains for the first time.*

lowed. Revivals swept across different regions of the country, leaving an indelible legacy of evangelism to many American Protestant churches.

The established churches of the colonial era—supported, like the Congregationalists in Massachusetts or the Anglicans in Virginia, by tax revenues—came under vigorous

Attacks on Established Churches

attack from dissenters who used revolutionary ideology to great advantage. Consequently, many states dissolved their ties to churches during or immediately after the war, and others vastly reduced state support for established denominations. Without state support, churches had to generate new sources of revenue. Revivals, which were genuine outpourings of religious sentiment, also proved a convenient means of increasing church membership and contributions.

An analysis of secular society can help to explain the conversion patterns of the Second Awakening. Unlike the First Great Awakening, when converts were evenly divided by sex, more women than men—particularly young women—answered the call of Christianity during the Second Awakening. The increase in female converts seems to have been directly related to fundamental changes in women's circumstances in the late eighteenth century. In some areas of the country, especially New England, women outnumbered men after 1790 (see map). Thus eastern girls could no longer count on finding marital partners. The uncertainty of their social and familial position seems to have led them to seek spiritual certainty in the church. In the churches, they created hundreds of associations to aid widows and orphans, collect money for foreign missions, and improve the quality of maternal care. Thus American women collectively assumed the role of keepers of the nation's conscience, taking the lead in charitable enterprises and freeing men from concern for such moral issues.

Women and the Second Awakening

The religious ferment in frontier regions of the Upper South contributed to racial ferment as well, for people of both races attended the

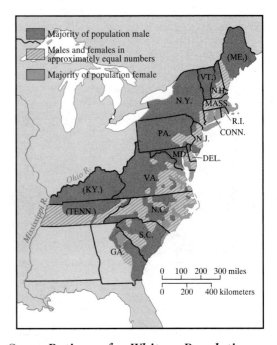

Sex Ratio of White Population, 1790 *The first census revealed that the sex ratio varied dramatically in different parts of the country. In many older, coastal areas, women predominated; on the frontier, men were in the majority. The variations had important implications for life in those regions, as the text points out.* Source: From Lester J. Cappon et al., eds., *Atlas of Early American History: The Revolutionary Era, 1760–1790.* Copyright ©1976 by Princeton University Press. Reprinted by permission of Princeton University Press.

Unrest Among African-Americans

camp meetings to hear black and white preachers. When revivals spread eastward into more heavily slave-holding areas, planters became fearful of the egalitarianism implied in the evangelical message of universal salvation and harmony. Their fear was heightened by events in the West Indies. In 1793, in the French colony of Saint Domingue (Haiti), mulattos and blacks under the leadership of Toussaint L'Ouverture overthrew European rule in a bloody revolt. News of the successful rebellion traveled rapidly among slaves and slaveowners in the South.

The West Indies revolt coincided with the single most massive inflow of Africans into North America since the beginnings of the slave trade. The two sources of the new demand for bondspeople were the expansion of cotton production after the invention of the cotton gin in 1793 and the beginnings of the large-scale westward migration of settlers. Before the legal trade was halted in 1808, more than ninety thousand new Africans had been imported into the United States. Their mere presence increased slaveholders' anxieties about the possibilities for revolt. Moreover, like their white compatriots, African-Americans (both slave and free) had become familiar with notions of liberty and equality. The circumstances were thus ripe for an explosion.

At this juncture in Virginia, Gabriel, an enslaved Richmond blacksmith who argued that African-Americans should fight for their freedom, planned a large-scale revolt.

Gabriel's Rebellion

Identifying his targets not as all whites but rather as those "merchants" who oppressed artisans of both races, Gabriel first recruited to his cause other skilled African-Americans who like himself lived in semifreedom under minimal supervision. Next he enlisted rural slaves. The conspirators planned to attack Richmond on the night of August 30, 1800, setting fire to the city, seizing the state capitol, and capturing the governor. At that point, Gabriel believed, other slaves and sympathetic poor whites would join in.

The plan showed considerable political sophistication, but heavy rain forced a postponement. Several planters then learned of the plan from their slaves and spread the alarm. Gabriel avoided capture for some weeks, but most of the other leaders of the rebellion were quickly arrested and interrogated. Twenty-six conspirators, including Gabriel himself, were hanged, but that outcome did not put an end to unrest among Virgina's slaves.

At his trial, one of Gabriel's followers had made explicit the links that so frightened Chesapeake slaveholders. He told his judges that, like George Washington, "I have adventured my life in endeavouring to obtain the liberty of my countrymen, and am a willing sacrifice in their cause."

Southern state legislature responded to such claims by increasing the severity of the laws regulating slavery. Before long, all talk of emancipation (gradual or otherwise) ceased, and slavery became even more firmly entrenched as an economic instituion and way of life.

Conclusion

As the nineteenth century began, inhabitants of the United States were moving toward an accommodation to their changed lives in the new republic. Native American peoples east of the Mississippi found that they had to give up some parts of their traditional culture to preserve others. African-Americans and European-Americans tried to create new lives for themselves in the West and to adjust to changed economic circumstances in the East. Building on successful negotiations with both Britain and France, the United States developed its diplomatic independence, striving to avoid entanglement with the European powers. The 1790s spawned vigorous debates over foreign and domestic policy and saw the beginnings of a system of political parties. Religious revivals swept portions of the countryside and contributed to social unrest.

At the end of the 1790s, after years of struggle, the Jeffersonian interpretation of republicanism finally prevailed over Hamilton's approach. In the years to come the country would be characterized by a decentralized economy, minimal government (especially at the national level), and maximum freedom of action and mobility for individual white men. Jeffersonian Republicans, like other white men before them, failed to extend to white women, Indian peoples, and African-Americans the freedom and individuality they recognized as essential for themselves.

Suggestions for Further Reading

National Government and Administration

Ralph Adams Brown, *The Presidency of John Adams* (1975); William R. Casto, *The Supreme Court in the Early Republic: The Chief Justiceships of John Jay and Oliver Ellsworth* (1995); Stanley

Elkins and Eric McKitrick, *The Age of Federalism, 1788–1800* (1993); Morton Frisch, *Alexander Hamilton and the Political Order* (1991); Forrest McDonald, *The Presidency of George Washington* (1974); John R. Nelson, Jr., *Liberty and Property: Political Economy and Policymaking in the New Nation, 1789–1812* (1987); James R. Sharp, *American Politics in the Early Republic: The New Nation in Crisis* (1993); Garry Wills, *Cincinnatus: George Washington and the Enlightenment* (1984).

Partisan Politics

Joyce Appleby, *Capitalism and a New Social Order: The Republican Vision of the 1790s* (1984); Lance Banning, *The Jeffersonian Persuasion: Evolution of a Party Ideology* (1978); Richard Buel, *Securing the Revolution: Ideology in American Politics, 1789–1815* (1972); Joseph Charles, *The Origins of the American Party System* (1956); Richard Hofstadter, *The Idea of a Party System: The Rise of Legitimate Opposition in the United States, 1780–1840* (1970); John Zvesper, *Political Philosophy and Rhetoric: A Study of the Origins of American Party Politics* (1977).

Foreign Policy

Harry Ammon, *The Genêt Mission* (1973); Jerald A. Combs, *The Jay Treaty* (1970); Alexander DeConde, *The Quasi-War: Politics and Diplomacy of the Undeclared War with France, 1797–1801* (1966); Felix Gilbert, *To the Farewell Address: Ideas of Early American Foreign Policy* (1961); Reginald Horsman, *The Diplomacy of the New Republic, 1776–1815* (1985); Bradford Perkins, *The First Rapprochement: England and the United States, 1795–1805* (1967); William Stinchcombe, *The XYZ Affair* (1981).

Civil Liberties

Leonard W. Levy, *Emergence of a Free Press* (1985); Leonard W. Levy, *Origins of the Fifth Amendment* (1968); Robert A. Rutland, *The Birth of the Bill of Rights, 1776–1791*, rev. ed. (1983); James Morton Smith, *Freedom's Fetters: The Alien and Sedition Laws and American Civil Liberties* (1956).

Social Change and Westward Expansion

Andrew Cayton, *The Frontier Republic: Ideology and Politics in the Ohio Country, 1789–1812* (1986); Douglas Egerton, *Gabriel's Rebellion: The Virginia Slave Conspiracies of 1800 and 1802* (1993); John Mack Faragher, *Daniel Boone: The Life and Legend of an American Pioneer* (1992); Allen Kulikoff, *The Agrarian Origins of American Capitalism* (1992); Malcolm Rohrbough, *The Trans-Appalachian Frontier: Peoples, Societies, and Institutions, 1775–1850* (1979); Thomas Slaughter, *The Whiskey Rebellion* (1986).

Religion

Catharine Albanese, *Sons of the Fathers: The Civil Religion of the American Revolution* (1976); Ruth Bloch, *Visionary Republic: Millennial Themes in American Thought* (1985); Paul Conkin, *Cane Ridge: America's Pentecost* (1990); Nathan O. Hatch, *The Democratization of American Christianity* (1990); Ronald Hoffman and Peter J. Albert, eds., *Religion in a Revolutionary Age* (1994).

9

The Empire of Liberty
1801–1824

Nez Perce villagers on the western slope of the Rockies were fearful of the group of bearded strangers who descended upon them in September 1805. The strangers, a scouting party headed by William Clark, were invited into the village by an old man who used signs to communicate. The Nez Perce fed Clark and his group pieces of buffalo, dried salmon, and camas bread. Clark's party then traveled to the next Nez Perce village, where the people also welcomed them. A Nez Perce chief mapped out the terrain for them, indicating that in another camp was an important leader, Twisted Hair. Clark then sent a message to his partner Meriwether Lewis and the majority of the exploring group, saying he and his companions would meet them at Twisted Hair's settlement.

According to the Nez Perce's oral tradition, their cautious but friendly welcome of Lewis and Clark was due in part to the efforts of Watkuweis, an elderly woman whose experience with white people had been positive, although she had once been a slave of a white trader. The Nez Perce also welcomed Lewis and Clark because they wanted guns and ammunition, which the expedition was carrying. In the spring of 1805 men from a Nez Perce band had traded with other Indians for six guns and had heard about the Lewis and Clark expedition. Lewis and Clark gave the chiefs the usual gifts—tobacco, clothing, flags, and medals—but Nez Perce self-interest, not trading goods, was responsible for the good relations.

Prior to crossing the Rockies, Shoshones had warned Lewis and Clark that the trail was treacherous and that little game was to be had. But they also told Lewis and Clark that the Nez Perce traversed it frequently, and the American explorers believed that if the Indians could make the climb, so could they. Only thirty members of the fifty-man party survived to reach the Nez Perce villages. From there they went on to the Pacific Ocean and then spent another year on the return journey.

President Thomas Jefferson had commissioned Lewis and Clark in 1803 to explore the newly purchased Lousiana Territory. Their mission had both scientific and political importance. They gathered information on the natural history of the areas they passed through, but they had political goals as well: to counter British advances to the Indians and to map the territory so that it could be opened to settlement and exploitation.

The Lewis and Clark expedition (1804–1806) proved successful. The explorers reached the Pacific, and their good relations with the Indians and the fame of their travels led to the opening of the territory to settlement and prevented British advances. Their collection of information about natural specimens and artifacts from the area was thorough. Along the way they had been aided by trappers and Native Americans.

The Lewis and Clark expedition was part of American expansion. Like the purchase of the Louisiana Territory from France in 1803 it extended, in Jefferson's phrase, the American "empire of liberty." Lewis and Clark were harbingers of the future, of the expansion and settlement of the United States.

Americans passed a political test at home when President Jefferson succeeded President Adams peacefully in 1800, despite the bitterness of the election and political intrigue. Presidential succession by ballot rather than arms helped secure constitutional government.

The transfer of power to the Republicans from the Federalists intensified political conflict. In the tradition of the Revolution, Republican presidents would seek to restrain the national government, believing that limited government would foster republican virtue. The Federalists would advocate a strong national government with centralized authority to promote economic development. As both factions competed for popular support, they laid the basis for the evolution of democratic politics. But factionalism, personal animosities, and partisanship within each group prevented the development of cohesive political parties, and the Federalists, unable to build a strong base of popular support, slowly faded away.

Events abroad and in the West encouraged and threatened Americans. Seizing one opportunity, the United States purchased the Louisiana Territory, pushing its border to the Pacific Ocean. But then from the high seas came war. Caught between the warring British and French, the United States found its ships seized and its sailors impressed, in violation of its rights as a neutral and independent nation. When the humiliation and threat to United States interests became too great, Americans took up arms in the War of 1812 both to defend their rights as a nation and to expand farther to the west and north.

The War of 1812 unleashed a wave of nationalism and self-confidence. War needs promoted domestic manufacturing and internal improvements. With peace, the federal government championed business and the construction of roads and canals. The new spirit encouraged economic growth and western expansion at home, trade abroad, and assertiveness throughout the Western Hemisphere. By the 1820s, the United States was no longer an experiment; a new nation had emerged.

Economic growth and territorial expansion, however, generated new problems. In 1819 a financial panic brought hardship and conflict that sowed the seeds for the Jacksonian movement in the 1820s and 1830s. More ominously, sectional differences and the presence of slavery created divisions that would widen in the wake of further westward expansion during the 1840s and 1850s.

 Jefferson in Power

Thomas Jefferson viewed the election of 1800 as a revolution that restored government to its limited role. He stressed republican virtues of independ-

• *Important Events* •

1801	John Marshall becomes Chief Justice of the United States Thomas Jefferson inaugurated as first Republican president
1801–05	United States defeats Barbary pirates in Tripoli War
1803	*Marbury* v. *Madison* establishes judicial review United States purchases Louisiana Territory from France
1804	Burr kills Hamilton in a duel Jefferson reelected
1804–06	Lewis and Clark explore Louisiana Territory
1805	Prophet emerges as Shawnee leader
1807	*Chesapeake* affair almost leads to war with Great Britain Embargo Act halts foreign trade
1808	Congress bans importation of slaves to the United States James Madison elected president
1808–13	Prophet and Tecumseh organize Native American tribal resistance
1812–15	United States and Great Britain fight the War of 1812
1813	Death of Tecumseh ends effective pan-Indian resistance

1814	Andrew Jackson's defeat of Creeks at Battle of Horseshoe Bend gives rise to process of Indian removal from the South Treaty of Ghent ends the War of 1812
1814–15	Hartford Convention undermines Federalists
1815	Battle of New Orleans makes Jackson a national hero
1816	Second Bank of the United States chartered James Monroe elected president
1817	Rush-Bagot Treaty limits British and American naval forces on Lake Champlain and the Great Lakes
1819	*McCulloch* v. *Maryland* establishes supremacy of federal over state law Adams-Onís Treaty with Spain gives Florida to United States and defines Louisiana territorial border
1819–23	Financial panic and depression: hard times for Americans
1820	Missouri Compromise creates a formula for admitting slave and free states Monroe reelected
1823	Monroe Doctrine closes Western Hemisphere to European intervention

ence, self-reliance, and equality. He believed in a limited and frugal government. He cut federal operations, and with his Republican successors (James Madison and James Monroe) invigorated the federal government. Jefferson did not hesitate to use federal power, even when questionable, as in the purchase of Louisiana. Although he stressed the importance of domestic issues, during his term of office foreign crises, in particular, strengthened federal institutions.

In his inaugural address Jefferson sought unity by declaring, "We are all Republicans, we are all Federalists." Still, the Federalists and Republicans continued to distrust each other. Republicans considered Federalists antidemocratic. Federalists accused Republicans of favoring egalitarianism, which they believed had recently led to anarchy in France. By doing away with Federalist social pomp and excessive government, Jefferson intended to restore the simplicity and civic virtue that had fueled the American Revolution.

Jefferson aggressively extended the Republicans' grasp on the national government. Virtually all officials appointed during the administrations

This portrait of President Thomas Jefferson was painted by Rembrandt Peale in 1805. Charles Willson Peale (Rembrandt's father) and his five sons helped establish the reputation of American art in the new nation. Rembrandt Peale was most famous for his presidential portraits; here he captured Jefferson in a noble pose without the usual symbols of office or power, befitting the Republican age. New-York Historical Society.

Republican Appointments

of Washington and Adams were loyal Federalists. To bring into his administration men who shared his vision of an agrarian republic and individual liberty, Jefferson refused to recognize appointments that Adams had made in the last days of his presidency, and he dismissed Federalist customs collectors from New England ports and awarded vacant treasury and judicial offices to Republicans. By July 1803 Federalists still held only 130 of 316 presidentially controlled offices. Jefferson adroitly used patronage to build a party organization.

The Republican Congress proceeded to affirm its belief in limited government. Albert Gallatin, secretary of the treasury, and Representative John Randolph of Virginia put the federal government on a diet. Congress repealed all internal taxes, including the whiskey tax. Gallatin cut the army budget in half and reduced the 1802 navy budget by two-thirds. Gallatin moved to reduce the national debt—which Alexander Hamilton viewed as the engine of economic growth—from $83 million to $57 million, as part of a plan to retire it altogether by 1817.

More than frugality, however, distinguished Republicans from Federalists. Opposition to the Alien and Sedition Acts of 1798 had helped unite Republicans. Jefferson now declined to use the acts against his opponents, and Congress let them expire in 1801 and 1802. Congress also repealed the Naturalization Act of 1798, which had required fourteen years of residency for citizenship. The 1802 act that replaced it required only five years of residency.

The Republicans turned next to the judiciary, the last stronghold of Federalist power. During the 1790s not a single Republican had occupied the federal bench. The Judiciary Act of 1801, passed in the final days of the Adams administration, created fifteen new judgeships, which Adams filled by signing midnight appointments until his term was just hours away from expiring. The act also reduced by attrition the number of justices on the Supreme Court from six to five. Since that reduction would have denied Jefferson a Supreme Court appointment until two vacancies had occurred, the new Republican-dominated Congress repealed the 1801 act.

The Republicans also targeted opposition judges for removal. Federalist judges had refused to review the Sedition Act under which Federalists had prosecuted critics of the Adams administration. At Jefferson's prompting, the House impeached (indicted) Federal District Judge John Pickering of New Hampshire, an emotionally disturbed alcoholic, and in 1804 the Senate removed him from office.

Attacks on the Judiciary

The day Pickering was convicted, the House impeached Supreme Court Justice Samuel Chase for judicial misconduct. Chase had repeatedly denounced Jefferson's administration from the bench. The Republicans, however, failed to muster the two-thirds majority of senators necessary to convict him. Their failure to remove Chase preserved the Court's independence and established the precedent that criminal actions, not political disagreements, were the only proper grounds for impeachment. Time soon cured the Republicans' grievances; in his tenure as president, Jefferson appointed three new Supreme Court justices. Nonetheless, the Court remained a Federalist stronghold under Chief Justice of the United States John Marshall.

John Marshall

Marshall, a Virginia Federalist, was an astute lawyer with keen political sense. Under his domination, the Supreme Court retained a Federalist outlook even after Republican justices achieved a majority in 1811. Throughout his tenure (from 1801 until 1835), the Court consistently upheld federal supremacy over the states and protected the interests of commerce and capital.

Marshall made the Court an equal branch of government in practice as well as theory. He unified the Court, influencing the justices to issue joint majority opinions rather than a host of individual concurring judgments. Marshall himself became the voice of the majority: from 1801 through 1810 he wrote 85 percent of the Court's opinions, including every important decision.

Marbury v. Madison

Marshall also increased the Court's power, notably in the landmark case *Marbury* v. *Madison* (1803). William Marbury, one of Adams's midnight appointees, had been named a justice of the peace in the District of Columbia. James Madison, Jefferson's new secretary of state, declined to certify Marbury's appointment so that the president could appoint a Republican. Marbury sued, requesting a writ of mandamus (a court order forcing the president to appoint him). The case presented a political dilemma. If the Supreme Court ruled in favor of Marbury and issued a writ of mandamus, the president probably would not comply with it, and the Supreme Court had no way to force him to do so. But if the Federalist-dominated Court refused to issue the writ, it would be handing the Republicans a victory.

Marshall avoided both pitfalls. Speaking for the Court, he ruled that Marbury had a right to his appointment but that the Court could not compel Madison to honor the appointment because the Constitution did not grant the Court power to issue a writ of mandamus. In the absence of any specific mention in the Constitution, Marshall ruled, the section of the Judiciary Act of 1789 that authorized the Court to issue such writs was unconstitutional. In *Marbury* v. *Madison*, the Supreme Court denied itself the power to issue writs of mandamus but established its great power to judge the constitutionality of laws passed by Congress.

In succeeding years Marshall fashioned the theory of *judicial review*, the power of the Court to decide the constitutionality of legislation. Since the Constitution was the supreme law, he reasoned, any federal or state act contrary to the Constitution must be null and void. The Supreme Court, whose duty it was to uphold the law, would decide whether or not a legislative act contradicted the Constitution. The power of judicial review established with *Marbury* v. *Madison* permanently enhanced the independence of the judiciary.

Louisiana Purchase

While Marshall was enlarging the power of the Court, President Jefferson had his eye on enlarging the borders of the nation. Jefferson shared with other Americans the belief that the United States was destined to expand its "empire of liberty." By 1800 hundreds of thousands of Americans in search of land had settled in the rich Mississippi and Ohio valleys. These settlers floated their farm goods down the Mississippi and Ohio Rivers to New Orleans for export. Whoever controlled the port of New Orleans thus had a hand on the throat of the American economy. Spain had owned Louisiana since 1763, but rumors of a transfer back to France persisted.

The rumors proved true. The United States learned of the transfer in 1802, when Napoleon threatened to rebuild a French empire in the New World. "Every eye in the United States is now focused on the affairs of Louisiana," Jefferson wrote to Robert R. Livingston, the American minister in Paris. Then, on the eve of ceding control to the

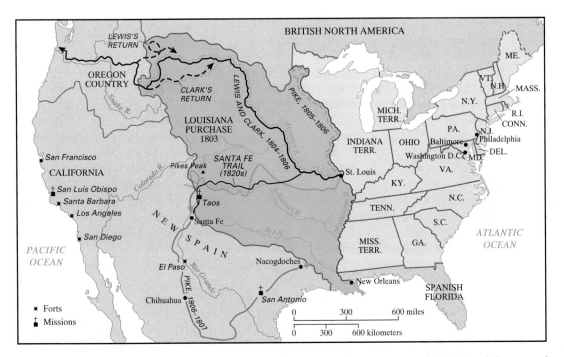

Louisiana Purchase   *The Louisiana Purchase (1803) doubled the area of the United States and opened the trans-Mississippi West for American settlement.*

French, Spain violated Pinckney's Treaty by denying Americans the privilege of storing their products at New Orleans prior to transshipment to foreign markets. Western farmers and eastern merchants thought a devious Napoleon had closed the port; they grumbled and talked war.

To relieve the pressure for war and to win western farm support, Jefferson prepared for war while sending James Monroe to join Robert Livingston in France to try to buy the port of New Orleans. Meanwhile, Congress authorized the call-up of eighty thousand militiamen in case war became necessary. Arriving in Paris in April, Monroe was astonished to learn that France already had offered to sell all 827,000 square miles of Louisiana to the United States for a mere $15 million. On April 30 Monroe and Livingston signed the Louisiana treaty to purchase the vast territory, whose borders were undefined and whose land was uncharted (see map).

The Louisiana Purchase doubled the size of the nation and promised fulfillment of Jefferson's dream of a continental nation reaching to the Pa-

cific. But was this most popular move of his presidency legal? The Constitution did not authorize the president to acquire new territory and incorporate it into the nation. Jefferson considered proposing a constitutional amendment to allow the purchase but decided not to. His justification for authorizing the purchase was that he was exercising the president's implied powers to protect the nation. The people signaled their approval of Jefferson's decision on election day in 1804.

Americans eager to expand the nation sought information and routes westward. Lieutenant Zebulon Pike followed Lewis and Clark in 1805 and 1806 in search of the source of the Mississippi and a navigable water route to the Far West. The vast lands were not uninhabited, as Lewis and Clark had demonstrated. When Pike and his men wandered into Spanish territory to the south, the Spanish held them captive for several months in Mexico. After his release, Pike wrote an account of his experiences that set commercial minds spin-

Exploration of the West

ning. Over the next few decades, as Americans avidly read accounts of western exploration, expansion seized their imagination. The vision of a road to the Southwest became a reality with the opening of the Santa Fe Trail in the 1820s.

Tejas—Texas—was a buffer province between Spain's Mexican colonies and the Louisiana Territory. Texas officials welcomed Americans, some of whom migrated and fought with Indians and Mexican rebels in a twelve-year war with Spain that ended in 1821 with Mexican independence. The establishment of an independent Mexico stirred dreams of an independent Texas nation. Many Americans, however, did not want to include Mexicans—a mix of European, Indian, and African peoples—in the "empire of liberty."

Republicans Versus Federalists

Prior to the Republican victory in 1800, most Federalists, unlike their Republican opponents, had disdained popular campaigning. They believed in government by the "best" people—those whose education, wealth, and experience qualified them to be leaders. For candidates to debate their own merits in front of their inferiors—the voters—seemed demeaning.

After the resounding Federalist defeat in 1800, however, a younger generation of Federalists began to imitate the Republicans. Led by men like Josiah Quincy, a Massachusetts congressman, the Younger Federalists campaigned for popular support. Quincy cleverly presented the Federalists as the people's party, attacking Republicans as autocratic planters. In attacking frugal government, the Younger Federalists played on fears of a weakened army and navy. Eastern merchants depended on a strong navy to protect ocean trade; westerners looked to the army for support as they encroached on the territory of Native Americans.

Political Campaigning

In states where both factions organized and ran candidates, people became more involved in politics. In some states about 90 percent of the eligible voters—nearly all of whom were white males—cast ballots between 1804 and 1816. As popular interest and participation in elections increased, states expanded suffrage. But the popular base remained restricted: property qualifications for voting and holding office persisted.

Yet political competition and a vigorous, partisan press prompted grassroots campaigning. Political barbecues symbolized the new style of campaign. At these barbecues, people ate, drank beer, and listened to candidates deliver lengthy speeches in which they often made wild accusations about their opponents. Given the slow speed of communications, the accusations might go unanswered until after the election.

Both factions held political barbecues, but the Federalists never fully mastered the art of wooing voters. Older Federalists still opposed blatant campaigning. And though strong in Connecticut, Delaware, and a few other states, the Federalists never offered the Republicans sustained competition. Moreover, the extremism of some Older Federalists discredited them all. A case in point was Timothy Pickering, a Massachusetts congressman and former secretary of state. Pickering opposed the Louisiana Purchase, feared Jefferson's reelection, and urged the secession of New England in 1803 and 1804. He won some support, but most Federalists opposed his plan for secession. Ever the opportunist, Vice President Aaron Burr flirted with Pickering, fantasizing about leading New York into secession, with other states following. But when Burr lost his bid to become governor of New York in 1804, his and Pickering's dream of a northern confederacy evaporated.

Both Republicans and Federalists suffered from divisiveness and personal animosities. Aaron Burr and Alexander Hamilton, for instance, had long despised each other. Hamilton always seemed to block Burr's path. He thwarted Burr's attempt to steal the election of 1800 from Jefferson, and in the 1804 New York gubernatorial race Burr lost to a rival Republican faction backed by the Federalist Hamilton. The embittered Burr challenged Hamilton to a duel, which Hamilton, though he found dueling repugnant, accepted.

Hamilton-Burr Duel

How do historians know that popular interest in elections was increasing early in the nineteenth century? Election data are not available, but paintings like John Lewis Krimmel's Election Day in Philadelphia *(1815) convey that interest. Only white males could vote at the time, and the crowd is composed mostly of white men, although at least one African-American and some women and children are present. The artist depicts a festive occasion. Citizens riding on a float in the background carry their own flag; they have created a parade. A holiday spirit seems to prevail as men cluster in groups talking, arguing, sharing jokes, and generally appearing to have a good time. Perhaps there is a hint of overindulgence as well. The man sitting in front of an overturned chair (left foreground), with his hat on* the ground behind him, seems to have fallen, perhaps from too much drink—a common affliction in the party atmosphere of election day. Among the spectators are two women (center foreground), one of whom is holding the hand of a little girl. They suggest a restraining force on the raucous scene. The woman dressed in white and her friend offer a common female image of the time: the woman as an emblem of republican virtue. The space between the female and male figures suggests that the women stand apart not only as nonvoters but also as symbols of virtue and seriousness absent in the male world. Overall, the painting depicts a popular event, mixing a party atmosphere with civic duty. From a sober exercise of democratic responsibility, voting had become a popular, festive occasion.   Photo: Winterthur Museum.

The duel took place in New Jersey. (New York had banned dueling.) Hamilton did not fire a shot and was killed; Burr was indicted for murder.

His political career in ruins, Burr plotted to create in the Southwest a new empire carved out of the Louisiana Territory. With the collusion of General James Wilkinson, the United States com-mander in the Mississippi valley, Burr planned to raise a private army to grab land from the United States or from Spain (his exact plans remain uncertain). Wilkinson switched sides and informed President Jefferson of Burr's intention. In 1807 Burr was acquitted on the charge of treason. He then fled to Europe to avoid further prosecution.

Campaigning for reelection in 1804, Jefferson claimed credit for western expansion and the restoration of republican values. Republicans bragged of ending the Federalist threat to liberty by repealing the Alien and Sedition and Judiciary Acts. They also had reduced the size of government by cutting spending. Despite his opponents' charges, Jefferson had demonstrated that Republicans supported commerce and promoted free trade. American trade with Europe was flourishing.

Jefferson's Reelection

Jefferson's opponent was Charles Cotesworth Pinckney, a wealthy South Carolina lawyer and former Revolutionary War aide to George Washington. As Adams's vice-presidential running mate in 1800, Pinckney had inherited the Federalist leadership. Jefferson easily won reelection. His victory was a personal and an organizational triumph. The political dissenters of the 1790s had fashioned the Democratic-Republican societies into successful political organizations. More than anything else, opposition to the Federalists had given them cohesion. Indeed, in areas where the Federalists were strongest—in commercial New York and Pennsylvania in the 1790s and in New England in the 1800s—the Republicans had organized most effectively.

Although this period is commonly called the era of the first party system, parties as such were not fully developed. Competition at the polls encouraged rudimentary party organization, but personal ambition, personality clashes, and local, state, and regional loyalties undermined it. Increasingly, too, external events overpowered party ties.

 ## Preserving American Neutrality in a World at War

"Peace, commerce, and honest friendship with all nations, entangling alliance with none," President Jefferson had proclaimed in his first inaugural address. Jefferson's efforts to stand aloof from European conflict were successful until 1805. Indeed, American commerce initially benefited from the May 1803 renewal of the Napoleonic wars. As the world's largest neutral carrier, the United States became the chief supplier of food to Europe. American merchants also gained control of most of the West Indian trade.

Meanwhile, the United States victory in the Tripoli War on the north coast of Africa (against the Barbary states) provided Jefferson with his one clear success in protecting American trading rights. In 1801 the sultan of Tripoli had demanded payment not to prey on American vessels and sailors in the Mediterranean. Jefferson refused to pay and instead sent a naval squadron to protect American merchant ships from the Barbary pirates. The United States signed a peace treaty with Tripoli in 1805 but continued to pay tribute to other Barbary states until 1815. That year the navy, again under the command of Stephen Decatur, forced Algiers and Tunis to renounce attacks against Americans. The Tripoli War and its aftermath made clear that the United States would protect its commerce anywhere.

American merchants grew increasingly concerned about Anglo-French interference with trade. In October 1805 Britain tightened its control of the high seas by defeating the French and Spanish fleets at the Battle of Trafalgar. Two months later Napoleon defeated the Russian and Austrian armies at Austerlitz. Stalemated, France and Britain launched a commercial war, blockading each other's trade. As a trading partner of both countries, the United States paid a high price.

Britain was suffering a severe shortage of sailors. Few men were enlisting, and those in service frequently deserted, demoralized by poor shipboard conditions. The Royal Navy resorted to stopping American ships and seizing British deserters, British-born naturalized American seamen, and other unlucky sailors suspected of being British. Perhaps six to eight thousand Americans were impressed (forcibly drafted) in this way between 1803 and 1812.

Impressment of American Sailors

In February 1806 the Senate denounced British impressment. In protest, Congress passed the Non-Importation Act, prohibiting importation from Great Britain of cloth and metal articles. In November Jefferson suspended the act temporarily while William Pinckney, a Baltimore lawyer, joined James Monroe in London to negotiate a settlement. But the treaty Monroe and Pinckney carried home violated their instructions—it did not mention impressment—and Jefferson never submitted it to the Senate for ratification.

Less than a year later, the *Chesapeake* affair exposed American military weakness. In June 1807 the forty-gun frigate U.S.S. *Chesapeake* left Norfolk, Virginia, and while still inside American territorial waters, it met the fifty-gun British frigate *Leopard*. When the *Chesapeake* refused to be searched for deserters, the *Leopard* repeatedly fired its guns broadside into the American ship. Three Americans were killed and eighteen wounded, including the ship's captain. The British seized four deserters from the Royal Navy—three of them American citizens.

Chesapeake Affair

Had the United States been better prepared militarily, the ensuing howl of public indignation might have brought about a declaration of war. But the United States was no match for the British navy. With Congress in recess, Jefferson was able to avoid hostilities. In July, the president closed American waters to British warships to prevent similar incidents, and soon thereafter he increased military and naval expenditures. In December Jefferson again invoked the Non-Importation Act, followed eight days later by a new restriction, the Embargo Act. Jefferson thought of the embargo as a short-term measure intended to avoid war. The embargo forbade virtually all exports from the United States to any country. Foreign ships delivering goods left American ports with empty holds. Smuggling blossomed overnight.

Embargo Act

Few American policies were as well intentioned or as unpopular and unsuccessful as Jefferson's embargo. Mercantile New England, the heart of Federalist opposition to Jefferson, felt the brunt of the resulting economic depression. Shipping collapsed as exports fell by 80 percent between 1807 and 1808. In the winter of 1808–1809, talk of secession spread through New England port cities. Great Britain, meanwhile, was only mildly affected by the embargo, and France used the policy as an excuse to set privateers against American ships that had escaped the embargo. The French cynically claimed that such vessels were British ships in disguise, because the embargo prevented American vessels from sailing.

In the election of 1808, the Republicans faced not only the Federalists but also dissatisfaction with the embargo and factional dissent. Jefferson followed Washington's lead in renouncing a third term. He supported James Madison, his secretary of state, as the Republican standard-bearer. Madison won the endorsement of the Republican congressional caucus, and with his running mate, Vice President George Clinton, defeated the Federalist ticket.

Election of 1808

Under the pressure of domestic opposition, the embargo eventually collapsed. In his last days in office Jefferson had tried to lighten the burden through the Non-Intercourse Act of 1809. This act reopened trade with all nations except Britain and France, and it authorized the president to resume trade with Britain or France if either of them ceased to violate neutral rights. But the new act solved only the problems created by the embargo; it did not prevent further British and French interference with American commerce.

Non-Intercourse Act

When the Non-Intercourse Act expired in 1810, Congress substituted a variant, Macon's Bill Number 2. The bill reopened trade with both Great Britain and France but provided that when either nation stopped violating American commercial rights, the president could suspend American commerce with the other. Madison, eager to avoid war, was tricked at his own game. When Napoleon accepted the offer, Madison declared nonintercourse with Great Britain in 1811. Napoleon, however, did not keep his word. The French continued to seize American ships, and nonintercourse failed a second time. But because the Royal Navy dominated the seas, Britain, not France, became the main target of American hostility.

Angry American leaders tended to blame problems in the West on British agitation, ignoring the Indians' legitimate protests against treaty violations. In the early 1800s two Shawnee brothers, Prophet and Tecumseh, attempted to build a pan-Indian federation. Prophet's early experiences typified the experiences of the Indians of the Old Northwest. Born in 1775, a few months after his father's death in battle, Prophet, called Lalawethika ("Noisemaker") as a young man, was expelled to Ohio along with other Shawnees under the 1795 Treaty of Greenville (see page 131), and he later moved to Indiana. Within the shrunken territory granted the Shawnees, game soon became scarce. Encroachment by whites and the periodic ravages of disease brought further misery to the Shawnees.

Shawnee Resistance

In 1804, Lalawethika became a tribal medicine man. The next year, after a bout with an illness, he assumed the name Tenskwatawa or "the Prophet." Claiming to have died and been resurrected, he traveled widely in the Ohio River valley as a religious leader, attacking the decline of moral values among Native Americans, warning of damnation for those who drank whiskey, condemning intertribal battles, and stressing harmony and respect for elders. He urged Indians to return to the old ways and abandon white customs. Prophet's message was well received by the Shawnees and other western groups. As the message spread, settlers and the federal government became alarmed.

By 1808, Prophet and his older brother Tecumseh were talking less about spiritual renewal and more about resisting American aggression. Their refusal to leave lands claimed by the government was encouraged by the British. In repudiating land cessions to the government under the Treaty of Fort Wayne (1809), Tecumseh told Indiana's governor William Henry Harrison at Vincennes in 1810 that "the only way to check and stop this evil is, for all the red men to unite in claiming a common and equal right in the land, as it was at first, and should be yet; for it . . . belongs to all, for the use of each. . . . No part has a right to sell, even to each other, much less to strangers." Tecumseh, who had overshadowed his brother as

The Prophet and Tecumseh

the Shawnee leader, then warned Harrison that they would resist white occupation of the 2.5 million acres on the Wabash River that they had ceded in the Treaty of Fort Wayne.

The War of 1812

Conflict over Native American loyalties in the West and over impressment on the seas strained relations between Britain and the United States. Having exhausted all efforts to alter British policy, the United States in 1811 and early 1812 drifted toward war with Great Britain until Republican "War Hawks" elected to Congress in 1810 led the charge to war. Meanwhile, in June 1812, Britain reopened the seas to American shipping. Hard times had hit the British Isles: the Anglo-French conflict had blocked much of British commerce with the European continent, and exports to the United States had fallen 80 percent. But two days after the change in British policy, before word of it had crossed the Atlantic, Congress declared war.

The War of 1812 was the logical outcome of United States policy after the renewal of warfare in Europe in 1803. The grievances President Madison enumerated in his message to Congress on June 1, 1812, were old ones: impressment, interference with neutral commerce, and British alliances with the western tribes. Not mentioned was the resolve to defend American independence and honor and American expansionists' thirst for British Canada.

The Vote for War

The war Congress was a partisan one. Much of the war fever came from the War Hawks, land-hungry southerners and westerners, all Republicans, led by John C. Calhoun of South Carolina and House Speaker Henry Clay of Kentucky. Most representatives from the coastal states opposed war, because armed conflict with the great naval power would interrupt American shipping. In June, when the votes were tallied in the House and the Senate, not a single Federalist voted for war.

Though unprepared for war in 1812, the nation could not avoid it. The United States had tried economic pressure, but had failed to protect

American ships and sailors. The United States Army and Navy and the state militias were not fully prepared to wage war against the British.

After six months of preparation, American forces were still not ready for war. The United States Navy had a corps of experienced officers, but compared with the Royal Navy the American navy was minuscule. And the United States Army had neither an able staff nor an adequate force of enlisted men. By 1812 the United States Military Academy at West Point, founded in 1802, had produced only eighty-nine regular officers. The American army thus turned to political leaders and the state militias to recruit volunteers, and not all states cooperated. The government courted enlistees with a sign-up bonus of $16, monthly pay of $5, a full set of clothes, and a promise of three months' pay and 160 acres of western land upon discharge.

Recruiting an Army

Canada offered the United States the only readily available battlefront on which to confront Great Britain and conquer land. The mighty Royal Navy could not reach the Great Lakes separating the United States and Canada, because there was no river access to them from the Atlantic.

Invasion of Canada

Begun with high hopes, the invasion of Canada ended in disaster. The American strategy concentrated on the West, aiming to split Canadian forces and isolate the Indians who were supporting the British. Tecumseh joined the British when the war began in return for the promise of an Indian nation in the Great Lakes region. United States General William Hull, governor of the Michigan Territory, marched his troops into Upper Canada, near Detroit. Despite superior numbers, Hull waged a timid campaign, retreating more than he attacked. His abandonment of Mackinac Island and Fort Dearborn in Chicago and his surrender of Fort Detroit left the entire Midwest exposed to the enemy. The only bright spot was the September 1812 defense of Fort Harrison in Indiana Territory by Captain Zachary Taylor, who provided the Americans with their first land victory. By the winter of 1812–1813, the British controlled about half of the Old Northwest.

The United States had no greater success on the Niagara front, where New York borders Canada. At the Battle of Queenstown, north of Niagara, the United States Army met defeat because the New York militia refused to leave New York. This scenario was repeated near Lake Champlain, where American plans to attack Montréal were foiled when the New York militia again declined to cross the border into Canada.

The navy provided the only bright ray in the first year of the war: the U.S.S. *Constitution*, the U.S.S. *Wasp*, and the U.S.S. *United States* all bested British warships on the Atlantic. In victory, the Americans lost 20 percent of their ships. In defeat, however, the British lost just 1 percent of their naval strength. The British admiralty simply shifted its fleet away from the American ships, and by 1813 the Royal Navy again commanded the seas.

The Royal Navy blockaded the Chesapeake and Delaware Bays in December 1812, and by 1814 the blockade covered nearly all American ports along the Atlantic and Gulf coasts. Since 1811, American trade overseas had declined nearly 90 percent, and the decline in revenues from customs duties threatened to bankrupt the federal government.

The contest for control of the Great Lakes, the key to the war in the Northwest, was largely a shipbuilding race. Under Master Commandant Oliver Hazard Perry and shipbuilder Noah Brown, the United States outbuilt the British on Lake Erie and defeated them at the bloody Battle of Put-in-Bay on September 10, 1813. With this costly victory, the Americans gained control of Lake Erie.

Great Lakes Campaign

General William Henry Harrison then began the march that proved to be among the United States's most successful moments in the war. Harrison's force of forty-five hundred men attacked and took Detroit and then entered Canada. They pursued the British, Shawnee, and Chippewa forces, defeating them on October 5 at the Battle of the Thames. This victory permitted the United

States to retain control of the Old Northwest. Tecumseh died in the battle, and with his death expired Native American unity. After the Battle of the Thames, the Americans razed York (now Toronto), the Canadian capital.

After defeating Napoleon in April 1814, the British stepped up the land campaign against the United States, concentrating on the Chesapeake Bay region. In retaliation for the burning of York—and to divert American troops from Lake Champlain, where the British planned a new offensive—royal troops occupied Washington, D.C., in August and set it ablaze. The attack on the capital, however, was only a diversion. The major battle occurred at Baltimore, where the Americans held firm. Francis Scott Key, witnessing the British fleet's bombardment of Fort McHenry in Baltimore harbor, was inspired to write the verses of "The Star-Spangled Banner" (which became the national anthem in 1931). Although the British inflicted heavy damage, they achieved little militarily. Equally unsuccessful was their offensive at Lake Champlain. That offensive was discontinued, and the war was essentially a stalemate.

The last campaigns of the war were waged in the South, along the Gulf of Mexico against the Creeks and against the British around New Orleans. The Creeks had responded to Tecumseh and Prophet's calls to resist United States expansion.In December 1812 General Andrew Jackson raised his Tennessee militia to fight the Creeks. By late 1813 his anti-Creek campaign was stalled by lack of supplies, and his men, who had signed up for a year, were talking about going home. Jackson refused to discharge them. In March 1814 Jackson executed John Woods, a militiaman, for disobedience and mutiny. This act broke the opposition within the ranks, and Jackson's men defeated the Creek nation at the Battle of Horseshoe Bend in Mississippi Territory in March 1814. As a result, the Creeks ceded two-thirds of their land and withdrew to southern and western Alabama. Jackson continued south toward the Gulf of Mexico. To forestall a British invasion at Pensacola Bay, which guarded an overland route

Campaign Against the Creeks

to New Orleans, Jackson seized Pensacola—in Spanish Florida—in November 1814. Then, after securing Mobile, he marched on to New Orleans.

The Battle of New Orleans was the last campaign of the war. Early in December the British fleet landed fifteen hundred men east of the city, hoping to control the Mississippi River and thus strangle the lifeline of the American West. They faced American regular army troops, Tennessee and Kentucky volunteers, and two companies of free African-Americans from New Orleans. For three weeks the British and the Americans played cat-and-mouse. Finally, on January 8, 1815, the two forces met head-on. In fortified positions, Jackson's poorly trained army held its ground against two frontal assaults from a British contingent of six thousand. At day's end, more than two thousand British soldiers lay dead or wounded; the Americans suffered only twenty-one casualties. Andrew Jackson emerged a national hero. Unknown to the participants, a peace treaty had been signed at Ghent, Belgium, two weeks before the battle.

Battle of New Orleans

The Ghent treaty made no mention of the issues that had led to war. The United States received no satisfaction on impressment, blockades, or other maritime rights for neutrals. British demands for an independent Indian nation in the Northwest and territorial cessions from Maine to Minnesota were not satisfied. Essentially, the Treaty of Ghent restored the prewar status quo. It provided for an end to hostilities with the British and with Native Americans, release of prisoners, restoration of conquered territory, and arbitration of boundary disputes.

Treaty of Ghent

Why did the negotiators settle for so little? Events in Europe had made these terms acceptable. Napoleon's fall from power and the subsequent peace in Europe made impressment and interference with American trade moot questions. And Britain—its treasury nearly depleted—stopped pressing for a military victory.

The War of 1812 affirmed the independence of the American republic. Although conflict with

Great Britain continued, it never again led to war.

<table>
<tr><td>

**Consequences
of the War
of 1812**

</td><td>

The experience strengthened America's resolve to steer clear of European politics, for it had been the British-French conflict that had drawn the United States into war. For the rest of

</td></tr>
</table>

the century, the United States would shun involvement in European political issues and wars. The war also convinced the government in Washington, D.C., to maintain a standing army of ten thousand men—triple the number from Jefferson's time.

The war had disastrous results for most Native Americans. Although they were not a party to the Treaty of Ghent, the ninth article of the treaty pledged the United States to end hostilities and to restore "all the possessions, rights, and privileges" that Indians had enjoyed before the war. More than a dozen treaties were signed with midwestern Indian leaders in 1815, but they had little meaning. With the death of Tecumseh in 1813, the Indians had lost their most powerful political and military leader; with the withdrawal of the British, they had lost their strongest ally. The Shawnees, Potawatomis, Chippewas, and others had lost the means to resist American expansion.

Perhaps most important of all, the war stimulated economic growth. The embargo, the Non-Importation and Non-Intercourse Acts, and the war itself spurred the production of manufactured goods: New England capitalists began to invest in home manufactures. The effects of these changes were to be far-reaching. Finally, the war sealed the fate of the Federalists.

That party's presidential candidate, DeWitt Clinton, lost to President Madison in 1812, despite increases in the number of Federalists in Congress and despite the vigorous campaign waged by

**Hartford
Convention**

the Younger Federalists. Once more, extremism had hurt the party. During the war Federalists had revived talk of secession. With the war stalemated, delegates from New England met in Hartford, Connecticut, for three weeks in the winter of 1814–1815 to discuss revising the national compact or pulling out of the republic.

Moderates prevented a resolution of secession, but convention members condemned the war and the embargo and endorsed radical changes in the Constitution. They wanted to restrict the presidency to one term and require a two-thirds congressional vote to admit new states to the Union. They proposed forbidding naturalized citizens from holding office. The proceedings were a fruitless attempt to preserve New England Federalist political power as electoral strength shifted to the South and West and immigrants became politically active.

The timing of the Hartford Convention proved lethal. The victory at New Orleans and news of the peace treaty made the convention look ridiculous if not treasonous. Rather than harassing a beleaguered wartime administration, the Federalists found themselves in retreat before a rising tide of nationalism. Though Federalism survived in a handful of states until the 1820s, the Federalist faction began to dissolve.

 **Postwar Nationalism
and Diplomacy**

With peace came a new surge of American nationalism. Self-confident, the nation asserted itself at home and abroad as Republicans borrowed a page from Federalists' agenda and encouraged commerce and economic development. In his message to Congress in December 1815, President Madison embraced Federalist doctrine by recommending military expansion and a program of economic growth. Wartime experiences, he said, had demonstrated the need for a national bank (the charter of the first Bank of the United States had expired) and the need for better transportation. To raise government revenues and perpetuate the wartime growth of manufacturing, Madison called for a protective tariff—a tax on imported goods designed to protect American manufactures. Though he strayed from Jeffersonian Republicanism, Madison did so within limits. Only a constitutional amendment, he argued, could give the federal government the authority to build roads and canals that were less than national in scope.

The congressional leadership pushed Madison's nationalist program energetically in the belief that it would unify the country. Republican Congressman John C. Calhoun of South Carolina and Speaker of the House Henry Clay of Kentucky believed the tariff would stimulate industry. The agricultural South and West would sell cotton to the new mills and sell food to the millworkers. New roads would make possible the flow of produce and goods, and tariff revenues would provide the money to build them. A national bank would facilitate all these transactions.

Nationalist Program

In 1816, Congress enacted much of the nationalistic program. The Second Bank of the United States was chartered. Like its predecessor, the bank was a blend of public and private ownership, and had one-fifth of its directors appointed by the government. To aid America's young industries, Congress also passed the nation's first substantial protective tariff—the Tariff of 1816. The act levied taxes on imported woolens and cottons (especially inexpensive ones) and on iron, leather, hats, paper, and sugar, in effect raising their cost. Some New England members of Congress viewed the tariff as interference in free trade, and southern members (except Calhoun and a few others) opposed it because it raised the cost of imported goods to southern families. But the western and Middle Atlantic states backed it.

Congress did not share Madison's scruples about the constitutionality of using federal funds to build local roads. "Let us, then, bind the republic together," Calhoun declared, "with a perfect system of roads and canals." Madison, insisting that internal improvements were the province of the states and private enterprise, vetoed Calhoun's internal improvements bill. He did, however, approve funds for the extension of the National Road, which began in western Maryland, to Ohio, on the grounds that the road was a military necessity.

James Monroe, Madison's successor as president, continued Madison's domestic program, supporting the national bank and tariffs and vetoing internal improvements on constitutional grounds. In 1816, after defeating the last Federalist candidate, Monroe declared that "discord does not belong to our system." The American people were, he said, "one great family with a common interest." A Boston newspaper dubbed the one-party period the "Era of Good Feelings."

Led by Federalist chief justice John Marshall, the Supreme Court became the bulwark of a nationalist point of view. In *McCulloch* v. *Maryland* (1819), the Court struck down a Maryland law taxing a branch of the federally chartered Second Bank of the United States. Maryland had imposed the tax in an effort to destroy the bank's Baltimore branch. The issue was thus one of state versus federal jurisdiction. Speaking for a unanimous Court, Marshall asserted the supremacy of the federal government over the states.

McCulloch v. Maryland

The Court went on to consider whether Congress could issue a bank charter. The Constitution did not spell out such power, but Marshall noted that Congress had the authority to pass "all laws which shall be necessary and proper for carrying into execution" the enumerated powers of the government. Echoing Alexander Hamilton's notion of implied powers, Marshall ruled that Congress could legally exercise "those great powers on which the welfare of the nation essentially depends." If the ends were legitimate and the means were not prohibited, Marshall ruled, a law was constitutional. The bank charter was declared legal.

McCulloch v. *Maryland* thus combined Federalist nationalism with Federalist economic views. By asserting federal supremacy, Marshall was protecting the commercial and industrial interests that favored a national bank. The decision was only one in a series. In *Fletcher* v. *Peck* (1810), the Court had voided a Georgia law that violated individuals' rights to make contracts. In *Dartmouth College* v. *Woodward* (1819), the Court nullified a New Hampshire act altering the charter of Dartmouth College. Marshall ruled that the charter was a contract, and in protecting such contracts he thwarted state interference in commerce and business.

Monroe's secretary of state, John Quincy Adams, matched the self-confident Marshall Court in assertiveness and nationalism. From 1817 to

1825 he brilliantly managed the nation's foreign policy, stubbornly pushing for expansion, fishing rights for Americans in Atlantic waters, political distance from the Old World, and peace. An ardent expansionist, he nonetheless placed conditions on expansion, believing that it must come about through negotiations, not war, and that newly acquired territories must bar slavery.

An Anglophobe, Adams nonetheless worked to strengthen the peace with Great Britain. In 1817 the two nations agreed in the Rush-Bagot Treaty to limit their naval forces to one ship each on Lake Champlain and Lake Ontario and to two ships each on the four other Great Lakes. This first disarmament treaty of modern times led to the demilitarization of the border between the United States and Canada. Adams then pushed for the Convention of 1818, which fixed the United States–Canadian border from Lake of the Woods in Minnesota westward to the Rockies along the 49th parallel (see map, page 173). When agreement could not be reached on the territory west of the Rockies, Britain and the United States settled on joint occupation of Oregon for ten years (renewed indefinitely in 1827).

Adams next moved to settle long-term disputes with Spain. During the War of 1812 the United States had seized Mobile and the remainder of West Florida. After the war Adams took advantage of Spain's preoccupation with domestic and colonial troubles to negotiate for the purchase of East Florida. During the talks, which took place in 1818, General Andrew Jackson took it on himself to occupy much of present-day Florida on the pretext of suppressing Seminole raids against American settlements across the border. Adams was furious with Jackson but defended his brazen act.

The following year, Don Luís de Onís, the Spanish minister to the United States, agreed to cede Florida to the United States without payment. The Adams-Onís, or Transcontinental, Treaty also defined the southwestern boundary of the Louisiana Purchase. In return, the United

States government assumed $5 million worth of claims by American citizens against Spain and gave up its dubious claim to northern Mexico (Texas). Expansion was thus achieved at little cost and without war.

When the Spanish flag was last raised over Florida, its residents differed in the welcome they gave to the United States. Some planter-slaveholders and traders were pleased to be living under the American flag, but Creeks and Seminoles, free blacks, runaway slaves who had escaped to Florida, smugglers who worked the coast, and Spanish-speaking town dwellers, were not pleased.

Conflict between the United States and European nations was temporarily resolved by the Rush-Bagot Treaty of 1817, the Convention of 1818, and the Adams-Onís Treaty, but events to the south still threatened American interests. John Quincy Adams's desire to insulate the United States and the Western Hemisphere from European conflict brought about his greatest achievement: the Monroe Doctrine.

The immediate issue was the recognition of new governments in Latin America. Between 1808 and 1822, the United Provinces of the Río de la Plata (present-day northern Argentina, Paraguay, and Uruguay), Chile, Peru, Colombia, and Mexico all broke free from Spain. Although many Americans favored recognizing their independence, Monroe and Adams moved cautiously. They sought to avoid conflict with Spain and to be assured of the stability of the new regimes. Then in 1822, shortly after the Adams-Onís Treaty was signed and ratified, the United States became the first nation outside Latin America to recognize the new states.

Soon events in Europe again threatened the stability of the New World. Spain suffered a domestic revolt, and France, in an attempt to bolster the weak Spanish monarchy against the rebels, occupied Spain. The United States feared that France would return the new Latin American states to colonial rule. Great Britain, similarly distrustful of France, proposed a joint United States–British declaration against European intervention in the Western Hemisphere and a joint disavowal of territorial ambitions in the region. Adams rejected the British overture. In accordance with George Washington's admonition to avoid foreign entanglements, he insisted that the United States act independently.

The result was the Monroe Doctrine, a unilateral declaration against European interference in the New World. President Monroe presented the

Monroe Doctrine

American position to Congress in December 1823. His message called for *noncolonization* of the Western Hemisphere by European nations, a principle that addressed American anxiety not only about Latin America but also about Russian expansion on the West Coast. (Russia held Alaska and had built settlements and forts as far south as California.) He also demanded *nonintervention* by Europe in the affairs of independent New World nations, and he pledged *noninterference* by the United States in European affairs, including those of Europe's existing New World colonies.

Monroe's words, however, carried no force. Indeed, the policy could not have succeeded without the support of the British, who already were committed to keeping other European nations out of the hemisphere to protect their dominance in the Atlantic trade. Europeans ignored the Monroe Doctrine; it was the Royal Navy they respected, not American policy.

The Panic of 1819 and Renewed Sectionalism

Monroe's domestic record did not match the diplomatic successes of his administration. In 1819, financial panic subverted postwar confidence and revived sectional loyalties. Neither panic nor the resurgence of sectionalism hurt Monroe politically; without a rival political party to rally opposition, he won a second term in 1820 unopposed.

But hard economic times spread. The postwar expansion has been built on easy credit; state banks had printed notes too freely, fueling speculative buying of western land.

Hard Times

When manufacturing fell in 1818, prices spiraled downward. The Second Bank of the United States cut back on loans, thus further contracting the economy. Distressed urban workers became politically involved by demonstrating for easy credit and internal improvements. Farmers clamored for lower tariffs on imported manufactured goods. Hurt by a sharp decline in the price of cotton, southern planters railed at the protective Tariff of 1816, which had raised prices on all imported goods. Manufacturers, by contrast, demanded greater tariff protection and eventually got it in the Tariff of 1824.

Western farmers suffered, too. Those who had purchased public land on credit could not repay their loans. To avoid mass bankruptcy, Congress delayed the deadlines for repayment, and western state legislatures passed "stay laws" restricting mortgage foreclosures. Many westerners blamed the panic on the Second Bank of the United States for tightening the money supply. As state banks folded, westerners bitterly accused the Second Bank of saving itself while the nation went to ruin.

Far more divisive was the question of slavery. Ever since the drafting of the Constitution, political leaders had tried to avoid the issue. The one

The Slavery Question

exception was an act ending the foreign slave trade after January 1, 1808, which passed without much opposition. In 1819, however, slavery crept onto the political agenda when Missouri residents petitioned Congress for admission to the Union as a slave state. For the next two-and-a-half years the issue dominated all congressional action.

The debate transcended slavery in Missouri. At stake were the compromises that had kept the issue under wraps since the Constitutional Convention. Five new states had joined the Union since 1812: Louisiana (1812), Indiana (1816), Mississippi (1817), Illinois (1818), and Alabama (1819). Of these, Louisiana, Mississippi, and Alabama permitted slavery. Because Missouri was on the same latitude as free Illinois, Indiana, and Ohio (a state since 1803), its admission as a slave state would thrust slavery farther northward. It would also tilt the uneasy political balance in the Senate toward the slave states. In 1819 the Union consisted of eleven slave and eleven free states. If

Missouri joined, slave states would have a two-vote edge in the Senate.

The moral issues made slavery an explosive question. The settlers of Missouri were mostly Kentuckians and Tennesseeans who had grown up with slavery. But many northerners had concluded that it was evil. When Representative James Tallmadge, Jr., of New York proposed gradual emancipation in Missouri, a passionate and sometimes violent debate ensued. The House, which had a northern majority, passed the Tallmadge amendment, but the Senate rejected it. The two sides were deadlocked.

A compromise emerged in 1820 under pressure from House Speaker Henry Clay: the admission of free Maine, carved out of Massachusetts,

Missouri Compromise

was linked with the admission of slave Missouri. In the rest of the Louisiana Territory north of latitude 36°30′ (Missouri's southern boundary), slavery was prohibited forever (see map). The compromise carried, but the agreement almost came apart in November when Missouri submitted a constitution that barred free blacks from entering the state. Congressional arguments over Missouri's constitution were resolved when Clay produced a second compromise: Missouri guaranteed that none of its laws would discriminate against citizens of other states.

Although political leaders succeeded in removing slavery from the congressional agenda, sectional issues undermined Republican unity. The Republican party came apart in 1824 as presidential candidates from different sections of the country scrambled for support. Sectionalism and the question of slavery ultimately would threaten the Union itself.

 ## Conclusion

The first decades of the nineteenth century were a time of self-definition and growth for the young republic. Political parties broadened white male involvement in politics and quieted factional divisions. A tradition of peaceful transition of power

through presidential elections was established. And the United States expanded continuously, from the acquisition of Louisiana to the purchase of Florida.

The Revolution still cast a shadow over the new nation. Federalists harked back to British precedents. Republicans sought to maintain the ideals and virtues associated with the Revolution and the founding of a republic in which citizens would place civic virtue above individual gain. A second war with Britain—the War of 1812—reaffirmed American independence and thwarted Indian opposition to United States expansion.

The War of 1812 and diplomatic assertiveness brought a sense of national identity and self-confidence. After the war, all branches of the government pursued a vigorous national policy. The Supreme Court promoted national unity by extending federal power over the states and encouraging commerce and economic growth. In spite of Jefferson's vision of an agrarian society, the country was gradually shifting to a market economy in which people produced goods to sell to others. Developments in transportation further stimulated the economy and expansion. Under the guidance of John Quincy Adams, the United States pursued its interests through diplomacy, not direct intervention. The Monroe Doctrine was among his finest achievements.

Sectionalism accompanied nationalism and geographic expansion. War, tariffs, economic hard times, and slavery brought out sectional discord. Politicians kept the question of slavery off the national agenda as long as possible and worked out the Missouri Compromise as a stopgap measure. But territorial acquisitions and further westward expansion in the 1840s and 1850s would collide with a rising tide of reform to make the question of slavery unavoidable.

Over the next two decades, the way Americans lived and worked changed at a quickening pace. When Americans celebrated the fiftieth anniversary of the signing of the Declaration of Independence in 1826, they recognized that their future would be very different from the world of the founders. Economic development, rising population, the spread of settlement, and the growth of

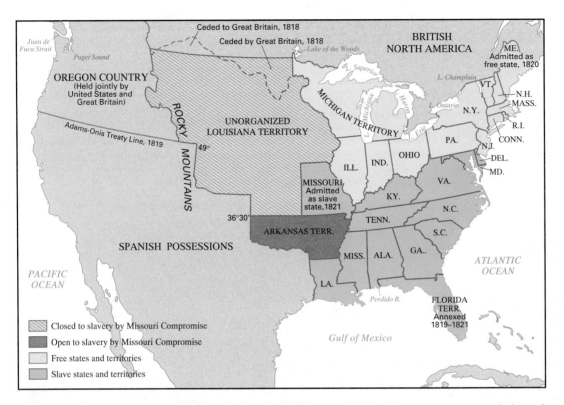

Legend:
- Closed to slavery by Missouri Compromise
- Open to slavery by Missouri Compromise
- Free states and territories
- Slave states and territories

Missouri Compromise and the State of the Union, 1820   *The compromise worked out by House Speaker Henry Clay established a formula that avoided debate over whether new states would allow or prohibit slavery. In the process, it divided the United States into northern and southern regions.*

cities were transforming people, their lives, and their communities.

Suggestions for Further Reading

General

Noble E. Cunningham, Jr., *The United States in 1800: Henry Adams Revisited* (1988); George Dangerfield, *The Awakening of American Nationalism, 1815–1828* (1965); George Dangerfield, *The Era of Good Feelings* (1952); Jean V. Matthews, *Toward a New Society: American Thought and Culture, 1800–1830* (1991); John Mayfield, *The New Nation, 1800–1845* (1981).

Party Politics

James M. Banner, *To the Hartford Convention: The Federalists and the Origins of Party Politics in the Early Republic, 1789–1815* (1967); Noble E. Cunningham, Jr., *The Jeffersonian Republicans in Power: Party Operations, 1801–1809* (1963); David Hackett Fischer, *The Revolution of American Conservatism: The Federalist*

Party in the Era of Jeffersonian Democracy (1965); Linda K. Kerber, *Federalists in Dissent* (1970); Milton Lomask, *Aaron Burr*, 2 vols. (1979, 1983); Richard P. McCormick, *The Presidential Game: The Origins of American Presidential Politics* (1982); Drew McCoy, *The Elusive Republic* (1980); James Sterling Young, *The Washington Community, 1800–1828* (1966).

The Virginia Presidents

Harry Ammon, *James Monroe: The Quest for National Identity* (1971); Noble E. Cunningham, Jr., *In Pursuit of Reason: The Life of Thomas Jefferson* (1987); Ralph Ketcham, *Presidents Above Party: The First American Presidency, 1789–1829* (1984); Drew R. McCoy, *The Last of the Fathers: James Madison and the Republican Legacy* (1989); Norman K. Risjord, *Thomas Jefferson* (1994); Robert W. Tucker and David C. Hendrickson, *Empire of Liberty: The Statecraft of Thomas Jefferson* (1990).

The Supreme Court and the Law

Leonard Baker, *John Marshall: A Life in Law* (1974); Robert Lowry Clinton, *Marbury v. Madison and Judicial Review* (1989); Richard E. Ellis, *The Jeffersonian Crisis: Courts and Politics in the*

Young Republic (1971); Morton J. Horowitz, *The Transformation of American Law, 1780–1860* (1977); R. Kent Newmyer, *The Supreme Court Under Marshall and Taney* (1968).

Expansionism, the War of 1812, and Diplomacy

Alexander De Conde, *This Affair of Louisiana* (1976); R. David Edmunds, *Tecumseh and the Quest for Indian Leadership* (1984); Clifford L. Egan, *Neither Peace nor War: Franco-American Relations, 1803–1812* (1983); Donald R. Hickey, *The War of 1812* (1989); Bradford Perkins, *The Creation of a Republican Empire, 1776–1865* (1993); James P. Ronda, *Lewis and Clark Among the Indians* (1984); J. C. A. Stagg, *Mr. Madison's War:*

Politics, Diplomacy, and Warfare in the Early Republic, 1783–1830 (1983); Anders Stephanson, *Manifest Destiny: American Expansionism and the Empire of Right* (1995); Steve Watts, *The Republic Reborn: War and the Making of a Liberal America, 1790–1820* (1987); David J. Weber, *The Spanish Frontier in North America* (1992).

The Monroe Doctrine

Samuel F. Bemis, *John Quincy Adams and the Foundations of American Foreign Policy* (1949); Walter LaFeber, ed., *John Quincy Adams and American Continental Empire* (1965); Ernest R. May, *The Making of the Monroe Doctrine* (1976).

10

Rails, Markets, and Mills:
The North and West
1800–1860

The Hutchinson family—Abby, Asa, Jesse, John, and Judson—also known as the Tribe of Jesse, was the most popular singing group in nineteenth-century America. They performed throughout the United States and across the Atlantic, singing the patriotic, religious, and sentimental songs that had dominated popular music since the Revolution. Unlike most groups that just sang, the Tribe of Jesse presented well-rehearsed and elaborately produced performances. They used traditional airs but wrote political lyrics advocating such reforms as abolitionism and temperance.

The Hutchinson Family was part of a new phenomenon: singers, songwriters, musicians, publishers, and managers who made a business of music and entertainment. Drawing their largest audiences in the growing cities, they entered the commercial world and made a living from writing and performing music. Each performance was planned and choreographed, and the group had an entourage of managers, agents, publishers, and concert-hall representatives. Hawkers sold sheet music, portraits, and songbooks at their concerts. A traditional rural pastime had become a big business.

The Hutchinsons were able to tour the nation in concert because of advances in transportation and communications that linked the growing national economy between 1800 and 1860. The canal boat, steamboat, locomotive, and telegraph made possible a Hutchinson Family concert tour. But more enduringly, these technological advances opened up the frontier and helped expand farm production for markets at home and abroad. Equally significant to improved transportation was increased specialization in agriculture, manufacturing, and finance, which fostered a nationwide, capitalist, market-oriented economy.

This dramatic transformation began early in the century and spread nearly everywhere. In 1800 most of the 5.3 million Americans earned their living working the land or serving those who did. Settlements clustered on the East Coast, along the Ohio and Mississippi river valleys, along the Gulf Coast, across present-day Texas, and on the West Coast. By 1860, 31.4 million Americans had spread across the continent. Meanwhile, the economy, though still primarily agricultural, was being transformed by enormous commercial and manufacturing expansion.

Promotion of economic growth became the hallmark of the federal government, which encouraged individual enterprise by promoting an environment in which farming and industry could flourish. New financial institutions amassed the capital for large-scale enterprises like factories and railroads. Mechanization took hold; factories and precision-made machinery competed successfully with home workshops and handmade goods, and reapers and sowers revolutionized farming.

Not everyone profited from economic growth. The experience of a journeyman tailor displaced by retailers and cheaper labor was far different from that of the new merchant princes. New England farm daughters who became wage workers found their world changing no less radically. Moreover, boom-and-bust cycles became part of the fabric of ordinary life. And canals, railroads, and urban and industrial growth brought with them destruction of the environment.

Transportation and Regionalization

The North, South, and West followed distinct economic paths between 1800 and 1860. Everywhere, agriculture remained the foundation of the American economy. Nevertheless, the North increasingly invested its resources in industry, commerce, and finance; the South in plantations and subsistence farms; and the West in commercialized family farms, agricultural processing, and implement manufacturing. This tendency toward regional specialization made the various sections of the country at once less alike and more interdependent.

The revolution in transportation and communications was probably the single overriding cause of these changes. Heavy investment in canals and railroads made the North the center of American commerce. The South, with most of its capital invested in slave labor, built fewer canals, railroads, and factories and remained mostly rural and undeveloped.

Before the 1820s and 1830s, it was by no means certain that New England and the Middle Atlantic states would dominate American finance and commerce. Indeed, the southward-flowing Mississippi and Ohio Rivers oriented the frontier of 1800—Tennessee, Kentucky, and Ohio—toward the South. Flatboats transported western grain and hogs southward for consumption or transfer to oceangoing vessels at New Orleans. Steamboats, successfully introduced in 1807 when Robert Fulton's *Clermont* paddled up the Hudson River from New York City, began in 1815 to carry cargo upstream on the Mississippi and Ohio Rivers, further reinforcing ties between the South and the West.

Change in Trade Routes

But this pattern changed in the 1820s when new arteries opened up east-west travel. The National Road—a stone-based, gravel-topped highway originating in Cumberland, Maryland—reached Wheeling, Virginia (now West Virginia), in 1818 and Columbus, Ohio, in 1833. More important, the Erie Canal, completed in 1825, linked the Great Lakes with New York City and the Atlantic Ocean. Railroads and later the telegraph would solidify these east-west links. By contrast, at only one place—Bowling Green, Kentucky—did northern and southern railroads connect with one another. Although trade still moved southward along the Ohio and Mississippi, the bulk of western trade flowed eastward by 1850. Thus by the

Important Events

1790	First American textile mill, using water-powered spinning machines, opens in Pawtucket, Rhode Island	**1825**	Erie Canal completed
1807	Robert Fulton's steamboat, *Clermont*, makes its debut	**1834**	Women workers strike at Lowell textile mills
		1836	Second Bank of the United States closes
1812–15	War of 1812 stimulates domestic manufactures War of 1812 is fought	**1837**	*Charles River Bridge* v. *Warren Bridge* encourages new enterprises
1813	New England capitalists found the Boston Manufacturing Company and build the first large-scale American factory	**1839–43**	Hard times strike again
		1844	A government grant develops telegraph line between Baltimore and Washington
1816	Congress charters the Second Bank of the United States	**1848**	Regularly scheduled steamship passage begins between Liverpool and New York City
1818	National Road reaches Wheeling, Virginia, opening the West	**1849**	California gold rush transforms the West Coast
1819–23	Hard times bring unemployment and business bankruptcies	**1853**	British study of American system of manufacturing
1820s	New England textile mills expand	**1857**	Hard times mark end of third boom-or-bust cycle
1824	*Gibbons* v. *Ogden* affirms federal over state authority in interstate commerce		

eve of the Civil War, the northern and Middle Atlantic states were closely linked to the former frontier of the Old Northwest.

Construction of the 363-mile-long Erie Canal (completed in 1825) was a visionary enterprise. When the state of New York authorized it in 1817,

Canals

the longest American canal was only 28 miles long. Vigorously promoted by Governor DeWitt Clinton, the Erie Canal shortened the journey between Buffalo and New York City from twenty to six days and reduced freight charges from $100 to $5 a ton. By 1835, traffic was so heavy that the canal had to be widened from forty to seventy feet and deepened from four to seven feet.

Sensing the advantage New York had gained, other states and cities rushed to follow suit. By 1840, canals crisscrossed the Northeast and Midwest, and total canal mileage reached 3,300—an increase of more than 2,000 miles in a single decade. Unfortunately for investors, none of these canals enjoyed the financial success achieved by the Erie. As the high cost of construction combined with an economic contraction, investment in canals began to slump in the 1830s. By 1850 more miles were being abandoned than built, and the canal era had unmistakably ended.

Meanwhile, railroad construction boomed. The railroad era in the United States began in 1830 when Peter Cooper's locomotive Tom

Railroads

Thumb first steamed along 13 miles of track constructed by the Baltimore and Ohio Railroad. In 1833 the nation's second railroad ran 136 miles from Charleston to

Hamburg in South Carolina. By 1850 the United States had nearly 9,000 miles of railroad; by 1860, roughly 31,000 (see figure). Canal fever stimulated this early railroad construction. Promoters of the Baltimore and Ohio believed that railroads would compete successfully with canals. Similarly, the line between Boston and Worcester in Massachusetts was intended as the first link in a rail line to Albany, at the eastern end of the Erie Canal.

The earliest railroads connected nearby cities; not until the 1850s did railroads offer long-distance service at reasonable rates. But in the 1850s technological improvements, competition, economic recovery, and a desire for national unity prompted development of regional and, eventually, national rail networks. By 1853 rail lines linked Chicago to eastern cities. By 1860 rails stretched as far west as St. Joseph, Missouri. Short lines merged to create two unified systems, the New York Central and the Pennsylvania Railroad. Most lines, however, were still independently run.

Railroad Mileage, 1830–1860

Railroad Mileage, 1830–1860 In the 1850s, railroads developed a natural rail network east of the Mississippi River.   Source: U.S. Bureau of the Census, *Historical Statistics of the United States, Colonial Times to 1970*, 2 parts (Washington, D.C., 1975), Part 2, p. 731.

Differences in gauge, scheduling, car design, and a commitment to serve their hometowns first and foremost prevented cooperation and mergers.

Railroads did not completely replace water transportation. The federal government assisted water transportation by improving ports and clearing rivers for navigation. Shipping routes linked newer areas, like Texas and California, to the rest of the United States. At midcentury, steamships still carried bulk cargo more cheaply than railroads did, except during freezing weather. The sealike Great Lakes accommodated giant ships with propellers in place of paddlewheels; these leviathans carried heavy bulk cargoes like lumber, grain, and ore. On the high seas, steamships gradually replaced sailing vessels, which were dependent on prevailing winds and thus usually could not meet regular schedules. The biggest breakthrough occurred in 1848, when Samuel Cunard introduced regularly scheduled steamships between Liverpool and New York, reducing travel time across the Atlantic from twenty-five days eastbound and forty-nine days westbound to between ten and fourteen days each way.

Steamboats

By far the fastest-spreading technological advance of the era was the magnetic telegraph. Invented by Samuel F. B. Morse, the telegraph made instantaneous communication, even over long distances, possible. By 1853, only nine years after construction of the first experimental telegraph line, 23,000 miles of telegraph wire had spread across the United States; by 1860, 50,000 miles were in use. In 1861 the telegraph bridged the continent, literally joining the nation together and ending the isolation of Texans and Californians. Rarely has an innovation had so great an impact so quickly: it revolutionized newsgathering, provided advance information for railroads, and altered patterns of business and finance.

Telegraph

Time was key to the revolutionary changes in transportation and communications that took place from 1800 to 1860. In 1800 it took four days to travel by coach from New York City to Baltimore and nearly four weeks to reach Detroit. By 1830 Baltimore was only a day-and-a-half away, and by 1857, Detroit was an overnight train ride from New York City. Reduced travel time not only saved money and facilitated commerce but also brought frontier areas under the control of Chicago and eastern businesses. During the first two decades of the century, wagon transportation cost 30 to 70 cents per ton per mile. By 1860, railroads moved wheat from Chicago to New York for 1.2 cents per ton-mile. In sum, the transportation revolution transformed the economy.

 ## The Market Economy

Before the transportation revolution, most farmers had geared production to family needs and to local and foreign markets. They lived in interdependent communities and kept detailed accounts of labor and goods exchanged with their neighbors. Farm families produced much of what they needed and traded for or purchased items they could not produce. By the Civil War, however, the United States was industrializing. Increasing numbers of men and women worked for wages, and most people outside the South—farmers and workers alike—purchased increasing amounts of store-bought goods produced in workshops and factories.

In the market economy, men and women grew crops and produced goods for sale at home or abroad. The money that individuals received from market transactions—from the sale of goods or from the sale of a person's labor—purchased items produced by other people. Such a system encouraged specialization. Farmers began to grow only one or two crops or to raise only livestock for market. Farm women gave up spinning and weaving and purchased fabric produced by wage-earning farm girls in Massachusetts textile mills.

Definition of a Market Economy

Improvements in transportation and technology, the division of labor, and new methods of financing all fueled the expansion of the economy. Goods and services multiplied. This growth, in turn, prompted new improvements and greater opportunities for wage labor. The effect was cumulative; by the 1840s the economy was growing at a faster rate than in the previous four decades. While per capita income doubled between 1800 and 1860, the price of manufactured goods and food fell.

The pace of economic growth, however, was uneven. Prosperity reigned during two long periods, from 1823 to 1835 and from 1843 to 1857. But there were long stretches of economic contraction as well. Between Jefferson's 1807 embargo and the end of the War of 1812, the growth rate was negative—that is, fewer goods and services were produced. Contraction and deflation (decline in the general price level) occurred again during the hard times of 1819–1823, 1839–1843, and 1857. During these periods banks collapsed, businesses went under, wages and prices declined, and jobs were hard to find or to keep.

Boom-and-Bust Cycles

Hard times were devastating for workers. In 1857, the Mercantile Agency—the forerunner of Dun and Bradstreet—recorded 5,123 bankruptcies, nearly double the number of the previous year. Contemporary reports estimated twenty to thirty thousand unemployed people in Philadelphia, and thirty to forty thousand in New York City. Female benevolent societies expanded their soup kitchens and distributed free firewood to the needy. In New York, the city hired the unemployed to repair streets and develop Central Park; in Fall River, Massachusetts, a citizens' committee disbursed public funds on a weekly basis to nine hundred families. The soup kitchen, the bread line, and public aid had become fixtures in urban America.

What caused the boom-and-bust cycles? Generally speaking, they were a direct result of the market economy. Prosperity stimulated demand for staples and for finished goods such as clothing and furniture. Increased demand in turn led not only to higher prices and still higher production but also, because of business confidence and expectation of higher prices, to speculation in land and to the flow of foreign currency into the country. Eventually production surpassed demand, causing prices and wages to

Cause of Boom-and-Bust Cycles

fall; in response, inflated land and stock values collapsed. The inflow of foreign money led first to easy credit and then to collapse when unhappy investors withdrew their funds.

Some contemporary economists considered this process beneficial—a self-adjusting cycle in which unprofitable economic ventures were eliminated. In theory, people concentrated on the activities they did best, and the economy as a whole became more efficient. Advocates of the system also argued that it enhanced individual freedom, since theoretically each seller, whether of goods or labor, was free to determine the conditions of the sale. But in fact the system tied workers to a perpetual roller coaster; they became dependent on wages—and on the availability of jobs—for their very existence.

The market economy also ushered in another type of boom-and-bust cycle: harvest and destruction. Canals and railroads stimulated demand for distant resources, then accelerated the destruction of forests, natural waterways, and any landscape features that represented obstacles. Railroads made possible large-scale lumbering of pinewood forests in northern Michigan, Wisconsin, and Minnesota. During the 1850s, 40 million acres were cleared of lumber, leaving most of that land unfit even for agriculture. Similarly, the extension of railroads to Kansas and Nebraska brought hunters who slaughtered the great herds of bison for sport. The process of harvest and destruction eventually would change the ecology of the United States.

 ## Government Promotes Economic Growth

The eighteenth-century political ideas that had captured the imagination of the Revolutionary War generation and found expression in the ideal of republican virtue had economic counterparts in the writings of Adam Smith, a Scottish political economist. Smith's *The Wealth of Nations* first appeared in 1776, the year of the Declaration of Independence. Both works emphasized individual liberty, and both were reactions against active government: Thomas Jefferson denounced monarchy and distant government; Smith rejected mercan-

tilism, or government regulation of the economy to benefit the state. Both declared that virtue resided in individual freedom and that the community would benefit most from individuals' pursuit of their own self-interest.

Jefferson believed that freedom thrived where individuals were unfettered by government, monopoly, or economic dependence. Limited government was not an end, according to Jefferson, but a means to greater freedom. Committed to the idea that republican democracy would flourish best in a nation of independent farmers and artisans and in an atmosphere of widespread political participation, Jefferson recognized that government was needed to promote individual freedom. Beginning with the purchase of Louisiana in 1803, Republican policy, no less than that of the Federalists, endorsed using the federal government to promote economic growth.

After acquiring Louisiana, the federal government facilitated economic growth and geographic expansion by encouraging westward exploration and settlement, by promoting agriculture, and by developing transportation. The Lewis and Clark expedition (see page 160) began ongoing federal interest in geographic and geologic surveying and opened western lands to exploitation and settlement. In subsequent decades, Henry Rowe Schoolcraft explored the Missouri and Arkansas region (1817–1818), Major Stephen Long the Great Plains (1819–1820), and John C. Frémont the areas along the Oregon Trail and then south to California (1843–1844). Frémont dispelled a long-standing myth that the center of the continent was a desert.

To encourage settlement and cultivation of western lands, the federal government evicted Indians from their traditional lands and offered the land at reasonable prices. The government also first financed roads and canals and later subsidized railroad construction by means of land grants. Even the State Department aided agriculture: its consular offices overseas collected horticultural information, seeds, and cuttings, and it published technical reports in an effort to improve American farming.

The federal government also played an active role in technological and industrial growth. Federal arsenals pioneered new manufacturing techniques and helped to develop the machine-tool industry. The United States Post Office provided a communications link that stimulated interregional trade and briefly played a crucial role in the development of the telegraph. The federal government financed the first telegraph line, from Washington to Baltimore, in 1844; it was briefly managed by the Post Office. To create an atmosphere conducive to economic growth and individual creativity, the government protected inventions and domestic industries. Patent laws gave inventors a seventeen-year monopoly on their inventions, and tariffs protected American industry from foreign competition.

The federal judiciary validated government promotion of the economy and encouraged business enterprise. In *Gibbons* v. *Ogden* (1824), the

Legal Foundations of Commerce

Supreme Court overturned the New York State law that had given Robert Fulton and Robert Livingston a monopoly on the New York–New Jersey steamboat trade. Aaron Ogden, their successor, lost the monopoly when Chief Justice of the United States John Marshall ruled that the congressional prerogative of licensing new enterprises took precedence over New York's grant of monopoly rights to Fulton and Livingston. Marshall declared that Congress's power under the commerce clause of the Constitution extended to "every species of commercial intercourse," including transportation systems. In defining interstate commerce broadly, the Marshall Court expanded federal powers over the economy while restricting the ability of states to control economic activity within their borders.

Federal and state courts, in conjunction with state legislatures, also encouraged the proliferation of corporations—organizations entitled to hold property and transact business as if they were a person. Corporation owners, called shareholders, were granted *limited liability*, or freedom from responsibility for the company's debts. In 1800 the United States had about three hundred incorporated firms; in 1817 there were about two thousand. By 1830 the New England states alone had issued nineteen hundred charters. At first each firm needed a special legislative act to incorporate,

but after the 1830s, applications became so numerous that states established routine procedures allowing firms to incorporate.

Another encouragement to corporate development and free enterprise was the Supreme Court's ruling in *Charles River Bridge* v. *Warren Bridge* (1837) that new enterprises could not be restrained by implied privileges under old charters. The case involved issues of great importance: should a new interest be allowed to compete against existing enterprises, and should the state protect existing privilege or encourage innovation and the growth of commerce through competition?

The Massachusetts legislature had chartered the Charles River Bridge Company in 1785 and six years later extended its charter for seventy years. In return for assuming the risk of building a bridge between Charlestown and Boston, the owners were granted the privilege of collecting tolls. In 1828 the legislature chartered another company to build the Warren Bridge across the Charles nearby; the owner would have the right to collect tolls for six years, after which the bridge would be turned over to the state and be free of tolls. The Charles River Bridge Company sued in 1829, claiming that the new bridge breached the earlier charter.

Speaking for the Court majority, Marshall's successor Roger Taney declared that the original charter did not confer the privilege of monopoly and that exclusivity could not therefore be implied. Taney further ruled that charter grants should be interpreted narrowly and that ambiguities would be decided in favor of the public interest. New enterprises should not be restricted by old charters.

In promoting the economy, state governments far surpassed the federal government. From 1815 through 1860, for example, 73 percent of the $135 million invested in canals was government money, most of it from the states. In the 1830s the states started to invest in rail construction. Though the federal government played a larger role in constructing railroads than in building canals, state and local governments provided more than half the capital for southern rail lines.

State Promotion of the Economy

State governments also invested in corporate and bank stocks, providing corporations and banks with much-needed capital.

Largely as a result of government efforts, the United States experienced uneven but sustained economic growth from the end of the War of 1812 until 1860. Political controversy raged over questions of state versus federal activity, but all parties agreed on the general goal of economic expansion. Indeed, during these years the major restraint on government action was not philosophical but financial: the public purse was small.

The Rise of Manufacturing and Commerce

In 1851, hundreds of American products made their international debut at the 1851 London Crystal Palace Exhibition, the first modern world's fair. There the design and quality of American machines and wares astonished observers, and American manufacturers returned home with dozens of medals. Most impressive to the Europeans were three simple machines: Alfred C. Hobb's unpickable padlocks, Samuel Colt's revolvers, and Robbins and Lawrence's rifles with completely interchangeable parts. All were machine-tooled rather than handmade, products of what the British called the American system of manufacturing. So impressed were the British—whose nation was the leading industrial power of the time—that in 1853 they sent a parliamentary commission to study the American system. Other nations quickly followed Great Britain's lead, sending delegations across the Atlantic to bring back American machines.

The American system of manufacturing used precision machinery to produce interchangeable parts that did not require individual adjustment to fit. Eli Whitney had promoted the idea of interchangeable **American System of Manufacturing** parts in 1798 when he contracted with the federal government to make ten thousand rifles in twenty-eight months. By the 1820s the United States Ordnance Department had contracted with private firms to introduce machine-made interchangeable parts for

firearms. The American system quickly spread beyond the arsenals, giving birth to the machine-tool industry—the manufacture of machines for the purposes of mass production. One outcome was an explosion in consumer goods of uniformly high quality.

Interchangeable parts and the machine-tool industry were uniquely American contributions to the industrial revolution. Both paved the way for the swift industrialization the nation experienced after the Civil War. In 1800, however, manufacturing was a relatively unimportant component of the American economy. Most took place in small workshops and homes, where master craftsmen supervised journeymen and taught apprentices, and women worked alone spinning thread and weaving cloth. Tailors, shoemakers, and blacksmiths made articles by hand, to order for specific customers.

The rise of textile mills illustrates the changes in manufacturing wrought by the market economy. Although some farm families continued to make their own cloth, the nineteenth-century machine **Production of Cloth** tool industry made textile and clothing production a function of mills and factories rather than kitchens and home workshops. The first American textile mill—Almy and Brown's 1790 Pawtucket, Rhode Island, factory—used water-powered spinning machines constructed from British models by the English immigrant Samuel Slater. Soon other mills sprang up, stimulated by the embargo on British imports from 1807 through 1815.

These early mills, dependent on waterpower, were located in rural areas. By erecting dams and watercourses, mill owners diverted water from farmers and destroyed fishing, an important source of income and protein in rural and village America. To protect their customary rights, fishermen and farmers fought the manufacturers in New England state legislatures, but petitions from hopeful job seekers in the mill environs supported the manufacturers. The ensuing compromises promoted mill development.

Construction of the first American power loom and the chartering of the Boston Manufacturing Company in 1813 radically transformed textile manufacturing. The

Waltham (Lowell) System

corporation was capitalized at $400,000—ten times the amount behind the Rhode Island mills—by Francis Cabot Lowell and other Boston merchants. Its goal was to eliminate the problems of coordination, quality control, and shipping inherent in the subcontracting of work in the putting-out system. The owners erected their factories in Waltham, Massachusetts, bringing all the manufacturing processes to a single location. They employed a resident manager to run the mill, thus separating ownership from management. Workers were paid by the piece or by the hour, and the cloth was sold throughout the United States.

When managers could not find enough hands in rural Waltham to staff the mill, they recruited New England farm daughters, accepting responsibility for their living conditions. As inducements, they offered cash wages, company-run boarding houses, and cultural events such as evening lectures—none of which was available on the farm. This paternalistic approach, called the Waltham (or Lowell) system, was adopted in other mills erected alongside New England rivers.

By 1860 a cotton mill resembled a modern factory. The work force consisted mainly of immigrant Irish women who lived at home, not in mill-subsidized housing.

Textile Mills

New England farm women continued to live in the few remaining boarding houses. Technological improvements in the looms and other machinery had made the work less skilled and more routine. The mills could thus pay lower wages, drawing from a reservoir of unskilled labor.

Textiles became the most important industry in the nation before the Civil War, employing 115,000 workers in 1860, more than half of them women and immigrants. The key to the success of the textile industry was that the machines, not the women, spun the yarn and wove the cloth. Workers watched the machines and intervened to maintain smooth operation. When a thread broke, the machine stopped automatically; a worker found the break, pieced the ends together, and restarted the machine. New England textile mills used increasingly specialized machines, relying heavily on advances in the machine-tool industry. Their application of the American system of manufacturing enabled American firms to compete successfully with British cotton mills.

The appearance of ready-made clothing was a major change in the textile industry. Before the 1820s, most clothing was sewn at home by women.

Ready-made Clothing

Tailors and seamstresses made wealthy men's and women's clothing to order. By the 1820s and 1830s, ready-made clothing became common. Manufacturers produced it by one of two methods: production within a factory, or by the putting-out system. This time, however, a journeyman tailor typically cut the fabric panels in the factory, and the sewing was put out at piece rates to unskilled or semiskilled labor, often women working at home.

Most of the first mass-produced clothes, crudely made and limited to a few loose-fitting sizes, were produced for men, and they were purchased by men who lived in city boarding houses and rooming houses. Improvements in fit and changes in men's fashion eventually made ready-to-wear apparel more acceptable to white-collar and professional men. By the 1850s many were wearing the short sack coat. A forerunner of the modern suit jacket, it fit loosely and needed little custom tailoring. Now even upper-class men were willing to consider ready-made apparel. In 1818 Henry Sands Brooks (later Brooks Brothers), offered tailoring services and ready-made apparel to the carriage trade.

Retail clothing stores well stocked with ready-made clothes appeared in the 1820s. Their owners often bought goods wholesale, though many manufactured garments in their own factories. Lewis and Hanford of New York City boasted of cutting more than one hundred thousand garments in the winter of 1848–1849. The New York firm sold most of its clothing in the South and owned its own retail outlet in New Orleans. In the West, Cincinnati became the center of the new men's clothing industry. By midcentury, Cincinnati's ready-to-wear apparel industry employed fifteen hundred men and ten thousand women.

Though cotton-textile mills and factories were in the vanguard, large-scale manufacturing also transformed woolen textiles, farm implements, machine tools, iron, steel, glass, and finished consumer goods. "White coal"—waterpower—was widely used to run the machines. By 1860, manufacturing accounted for one-third of the nation's total production, an increase of 200 percent in twenty years.

To a striking extent, large-scale manufacturing in this period was an outcome rather than an agent of change in American life. For example, in the early republic, greater profits could be made by transporting British products to the United States than by producing them at home. Surplus capital thus flowed into the merchant marine, but the embargo and the War of 1812 reversed this situation and merchants began to shift their capital from shipping to manufacturing. Industry was also stimulated by population growth, government policy (protective tariffs, for example), the rise of commercial agriculture, and the transportation revolution.

Stimulants to Industry

Commerce expanded hand in hand with manufacturing. Cotton, for instance, had once been traded by plantation agents, who sold the raw cotton and bought manufactured goods that they then sold to plantation owners, extending them credit when necessary. As cotton became a great staple export after the invention of the cotton gin in 1793, cotton exports rose from half a million pounds in that year to 83 million pounds in 1815. Gradually, some agents came to specialize in finance alone: they were cotton brokers, who for a commission brought together buyers and sellers. Similarly, wheat and hog brokers sprang up in the West—in Cincinnati, Louisville, and St. Louis. The distribution of finished goods also became more specialized as wholesalers bought large quantities of particular items from manufacturers, and jobbers broke down the wholesale lots for retail stores and country merchants.

Specialization of Commerce

Commercial specialization transformed some traders in big cities, especially New York, into virtual merchant princes. After the Erie Canal opened, New York City became a standard stop on every major trade route from Europe, the southern ports, and the West. New York traders were the middlemen for southern cotton and western grain trading. Merchants in other cities played a similar role within their own regions. Newly rich traders in turn invested their profits in processing enterprises and then in manufacturing. Some cities specialized: Rochester became a milling center, and Cincinnati—"Porkopolis"—became the first meatpacking center.

Banks and other financial institutions, which played a significant role in the expansion of commerce and manufacturing, also became a leading industry themselves. Financial institutions (banks, insurance companies, and corporations) linked savers—those who deposited money in banks—with producers and speculators who wished to borrow money. The expiration of the first Bank of the United States in 1811 acted as a stimulus to state-chartered banks, and over the next five years, the number of such banks more than doubled. When state banks proved inadequate to spur national growth, Congress chartered the Second Bank of the United States in 1816.

Banking and Credit Systems

The closing of the Second Bank in 1836 (see Chapter 13) caused a nationwide credit shortage, which, in conjunction with the Panic of 1837, stimulated fundamental reforms in banking. Michigan and New York introduced charter laws promoting what was called *free banking*. Previously, every new bank needed a special legislative charter before it could open for business; thus each bank incorporation was in effect a political decision. Under the new laws, any proposed bank that met certain minimum conditions—amount of capital invested, number of notes issued, and types of loans to be made—would receive a state charter automatically. Banks in Michigan, New York, and soon, other states were thus freer to incorporate, although the legislatures placed some restrictions on their operation to reduce the risk of bank failure.

Free banking proved to be a significant stimulus to the economy in the late 1840s and 1850s.

New banks sprang up everywhere, providing merchants and manufacturers with the credit they needed. The free-banking laws also served as a precedent for general incorporation statutes that allowed manufacturing firms to receive state charters without special acts of the state legislature.

In the 1850s, with both credit and capital easily obtainable, manufacturing spread. In the North, industry began to rival agriculture and commerce in dollar volume. Meanwhile, commercial farming, financed by the credit boom, was integrating the early frontier into the northern economy. By 1860 Massachusetts, New York, Pennsylvania, Connecticut, Rhode Island, and Ohio were highly industrialized. Their clothing, textile, and shoe industries employed more than one hundred thousand workers each; lumber, seventy-five thousand; iron, sixty-five thousand; and woolens and leather, fifty thousand. Although agriculture still predominated even in these states, industrial employment would soon surpass it.

 ## Workers and the Workplace

Oh, sing me the song of the Factory Girl!
So merry and glad and free!
The bloom in her cheeks, of health how it speaks,
Oh! a happy creature is she!
She tends the loom, she watches the spindle,
And cheerfully toileth away,
Amid the din of wheels, how her bright eyes kindle,
And her bosom is ever gay.

This idyllic portrait of factory work appeared in the Chicopee, Massachusetts, *Telegraph* in 1850. It was a fitting anthem for the teenage single women who first left the villages and farms of New England to work in the mills. New England mill owners, convinced that the degradation of English factory workers arose from their living conditions and not from the work itself, designed boarding-house communities offering airy courtyards and river views, prepared meals, and cultural activities.

The promise of steady work, good pay, and kinship ties at first lured eager rural young women to the mills. Many pairs of sisters and cousins worked in the same mill and helped each other adjust; their letters home drew other kin to the mills.

Young women then had few opportunities for work outside their own homes, and the commercial production of yarn and cloth had reduced their workload in New England farm households. Averaging sixteen and one-half years of age when they entered the mills, the girls usually stayed only about five years. Most left the mills to marry and were replaced by other women interested in earning a wage.

Between 1837 and 1842, most mills ran only part-time because of a decline in demand for cloth. Subsequently managers applied still greater pressures on workers by means of the speed-up, the stretch-out, and the premium system. The speed-up increased the speed of the machines; the stretch-out increased the number of machines each worker had to operate; and premiums paid to the overseers whose departments produced the most cloth encouraged them to pressure workers for greater output. Thus the concern for workers' living conditions gave way to the corporate quest to maximize profits by cutting wages, lengthening the workday, and tightening discipline.

New England millworkers responded to their deteriorating working conditions by organizing and striking. In 1834, in reaction to a 25 percent wage cut, they unsuccessfully "turned out" (struck) against the Lowell mills. Two years later, when boarding-house rates increased, they turned out again. In the 1840s, Massachusetts mill women adopted another method of resistance: they joined forces with other workers to press for state legislation mandating a ten-hour day.

Protests by Mill Women

The women's labor organizations were weakened by the short tenure of most workers. Few of the militant native-born millworkers stayed on to fight the managers and owners, and gradually there were fewer New England daughters to enter the mills. By the end of the 1850s the women who constituted the majority of millworkers were mostly Irish immigrants, driven to the mills by the need to support their families and unable to afford to complain about their working conditions.

A growing gender division in the workplace, especially in the textile, clothing, and shoemaking industries, was one important outcome of large-scale manufacturing. Although women and men in traditional agricultural and artisan households tended to perform different tasks, they worked as a family unit. As wage work spread, however, men's and women's work cultures became increasingly separate. The women and girls who left home to work in textile mills worked and lived in a mostly female world. In the clothing and shoemaking industries, whose male artisans had once worked at home assisted by unpaid family labor, men began working outside the home while women continued to work at home through the putting-out system. Tasks and wages, too, became rigidly differentiated: women sewed, whereas men shaped materials and finished products, receiving higher wages in shops employing men only.

Gender Divisions in Work

The market system, wage labor, and the specialization of labor had an impact on unpaid household labor as well. As home and workplace became separate and labor came to be defined in terms of wages (what could be sold in the marketplace) rather than production, the unpaid labor of women was devalued. But the family depended on women's work within the household, and as the family became more dependent on wage labor, more family members sought outside employment and had less time to do their share of household labor. Thus gender defined household labor and placed a low value on it.

The new textile mills, shoe factories, iron mills, wholesale stores, and railroads were the antithesis of traditional workshop and household production. Factories created a workplace in which authority was hierarchically organized. Factory workers lost their sense of autonomy as impersonal market forces seemed to dominate their lives. Competition among mills in the growing textile industry of the 1820s and 1830s led to layoffs and the replacement of operatives with cheaper, less-skilled workers or children. The formal rules of the factory contrasted sharply with the more relaxed pace and atmos-

Changes in the Workplace

phere of artisan shops and farm households. Supervisors represented owners whom workers never saw. The division of labor and the use of machines narrowed the skills required of workers. And the flow of work was governed by the bell, the steam whistle, or the clock. The factory bell controlled when the workers awoke, ate, began and ended work, and went to sleep. The central problem, of course, was the quickening pace of the work between the bells. Moreover, mill-workers had to tolerate the roar of the looms, and all workers on power machines risked accidents that could kill or maim. Perhaps most demoralizing, opportunities for advancement in the new system were virtually nil.

Changes in the workplace in turn transformed the workers. Initially, mill women drew on kinship, village, and gender ties to build supportive networks in factories. In the 1840s and after, as recently arrived Irish immigrant women came to predominate, more workers were strangers to each other before they entered the mills. Once employed, their only bases for friendship and mutual support were their work experiences. As a sense of distance from their employers took hold, so did deep-seated differences among workers.

Nationality, religion, education, and future prospects separated Irish and Yankee millworkers. Many New England women resented the immigrants, and management set one group against the other through selective hiring and promotions. Mill work was not a stage in the life of most Irish women; it was permanent employment. Unlike their Yankee sisters, they could not risk striking and losing their jobs; they and their families were dependent on their earnings.

While some female textile workers and shoemakers organized and protested, many male workers became active in reform politics. Organized labor's greatest achievement during this period was to gain relief from the threat of conspiracy laws. When journeyman shoemakers organized during the first decade of the century, their employers turned to the courts, charging criminal conspiracy. The cordwainers' (shoemakers') cases, which resulted in six trials be-

Emergence of a Labor Movement

How do historians know what *working conditions New England millworkers experienced? This 1853 timetable from the Lowell Mills is among the rich sources historians consult to reconstruct workers' experiences in the mills. Textile factories were the first corporations to impose rigid work rules. The size of the labor force, the management structure, and the organization of the work made it necessary to publish work rules. Exact times were established for beginning and ending work and for meals. Few workers carried their own timepieces, so a system of bells regulated the lives of the factory community. From March 20 to September 19, when work began at 6:30 A.M., bells alerted the workers at 4:30 and 5:50 A.M. and again at 6:20 A.M., ten minutes before they had to be at the factory. For their main meal at midday, they had forty-five minutes away from work; the 12:35 P.M. bell warned that they had ten minutes to return. For young mill women from the New England countryside, and later for Irish women, such regimentation must have seemed a world apart from the rhythms of rural life.*   Photo: Museum of American Textile History.

TIME TABLE OF THE LOWELL MILLS,

Arranged to make the working time throughout the year average 11 hours per day.

TO TAKE EFFECT SEPTEMBER 21st., 1853,

The Standard time being that of the meridian of Lowell, as shown by the Regulator Clock of AMOS SANBORN, Post Office Corner, Central Street.

From March 20th to September 19th, inclusive.

COMMENCE WORK, at 6.30 A. M. LEAVE OFF WORK, at 6.30 P. M., except on Saturday Evenings. BREAKFAST at 6 A. M. DINNER, at 12 M. Commence Work, after dinner, 12.45 P. M.

From September 20th to March 19th, inclusive.

COMMENCE WORK at 7.00 A. M. LEAVE OFF WORK, at 7.00 P. M., except on Saturday Evenings. BREAKFAST at 6.30 A. M. DINNER, at 12.30 P. M. Commence Work, after dinner, 1.15 P. M.

BELLS.

From March 20th to September 19th, inclusive.

Morning Bells.	Dinner Bells.	Evening Bells.
First bell,............4.30 A. M.	Ring out,...............12.00 M.	Ring out,............6.30 P. M.
Second, 5.30 A. M.; Third, 6.20.	Ring in,............12 35 P. M.	Except on Saturday Evenings.

From September 20th to March 19th, inclusive.

Morning Bells.	Dinner Bells.	Evening Bells.
First bell,............5.00 A. M.	Ring out,............12.30 P. M.	Ring out at............7.00 P. M.
Second, 6.00 A. M.; Third, 6.50.	Ring in,............1.05 P. M.	Except on Saturday Evenings.

SATURDAY EVENING BELLS.

During APRIL, MAY, JUNE, JULY, and AUGUST, Ring Out, at 6.00 P. M.
The remaining Saturday Evenings in the year, ring out as follows :

SEPTEMBER.	NOVEMBER.	JANUARY.
First Saturday, ring out 6.00 P. M.	Third Saturday ring out 4.00 P. M.	Third Saturday, ring out 4.25 P. M.
Second " " 5.45 "	Fourth " " 3.55 "	Fourth " " 4.35 "
Third " " 5.30 "		
Fourth " " 5.20 "	**DECEMBER.**	**FEBRUARY.**
	First Saturday, ring out 3.50 P. M.	First Saturday, ring out 4.45 P. M.
OCTOBER.	Second " " 3.55 "	Second " " 4.55 "
First Saturday, ring out 5.05 P. M.	Third " " 3.55 "	Third " " 5.00 "
Second " " 4.55 "	Fourth " " 4.00 "	Fourth " " 5.10 "
Third " " 4.45 "	Fifth " " 4.00 "	
Fourth " " 4.35 "		**MARCH.**
Fifth " " 4.25 "		First Saturday, ring out 5.25 P. M.
	JANUARY.	Second " " 5.30 "
NOVEMBER.	First Saturday, ring out 4.10 P. M.	Third " " 5.35 "
First Saturday, ring out 4.15 P. M.	Second " " 4.15 "	Fourth " " 5.45 "
Second "· " 4.05 "		

YARD GATES will be opened at the first stroke of the bells for entering or leaving the Mills.

SPEED GATES commence hoisting three minutes before commencing work.

Penhallow, Printer, Wyman's Exchange, 28 Merrimack St.

tween 1806 and 1815, left labor organizations in a tenuous position. Although the journeymen's right to organize was acknowledged, the courts ruled unlawful any coercive action by them that would harm other businesses or the public. In other words, strikes were ruled illegal. Eventually a Massachusetts case, *Commonwealth* v. *Hunt* (1842),

effectively reversed this decision when Chief Justice Lemuel Shaw ruled that Boston journeyman bootmakers could strike "in such manner as best to subserve their own interests." Conspiracy laws no longer thwarted unionization.

Yet permanent labor organizations were difficult to maintain. Most workers outside the crafts were unskilled or semiskilled at best. Moreover, religion, race, ethnicity, and gender divided workers. The first unions arose among urban journeymen in printing, woodworking, shoemaking, and tailoring. These early labor unions tended to be local; the strongest resembled medieval guilds in that members sought to protect themselves against the competition of inferior workmen by regulating apprenticeship and establishing minimum wages. They also excluded women and African-Americans.

Umbrella organizations composed of individual craft unions, like the National Trades Union (1834), arose in several cities in the 1820s and 1830s. But the movement fell apart amid wage reductions and unemployment in the hard times of 1839–1843. In the 1850s the deterioration of working conditions strengthened the labor movement again, and affiliated craft unions began to organize into national unions. Workers won a reduction in hours, and the ten-hour day became standard. Though the Panic of 1857 wiped out the umbrella organizations, some of the new national unions in specific trades survived.

Economic and technological change inevitably affected individual workers more heavily than it affected their organizations. As a group, workers' share of the national wealth declined after the 1830s. Individual producers—craftsmen, factory workers, and farmers—had less economic power than they had had a generation or two earlier. And workers were increasingly losing control over their own work.

 ## Commercial Farming

Although manufacturing increased steadily, agriculture remained the backbone of the economy. In 1800 New England and Middle Atlantic farmers worked as their fathers and mothers had. Life centered around a household economy in which the needs of the family and the labor at its disposal determined what was produced and in what amounts. Most implements—wooden plows, rakes, shovels, and yokes—were homemade, with iron parts obtained from the local blacksmith.

When canals and railroads began transporting grain, especially wheat, eastward from the fertile Old Northwest, northeastern agriculture could not compete. Eastern farmers had already cultivated all the land available to them; expansion was impossible. Moreover, small New England farms with their uneven terrain did not lend themselves to the new labor-saving farm implements introduced in the 1830s—mechanical sowers, reapers, threshers, and balers.

Northeastern Agriculture

In response to these problems and to competition from the West, many northern farmers either moved west or gave up farming for jobs in the merchant houses and factories. Between 1820 and 1860 the percentage of the population of the North living on farms declined from 71 to 40 percent. The farmers who remained proved as adaptable on the farm as were their children working at copy desks and waterpowered looms. By the 1850s many New England and Middle Atlantic farm families had abandoned the commercial production of wheat and corn and stopped tilling poor land. Instead, they were improving their livestock, especially cattle, and specializing in vegetable and fruit production and dairy farming, financing these initiatives through land sales and borrowing. In fact, their greatest potential profit was from increasing land values, not from farming itself.

Farm families everywhere gradually adjusted to market conditions. In 1820 about one-third of all food produced was intended for market. By 1860 the amount had increased to about two-thirds. Middlemen specializing in the grain and food trades replaced the country storekeepers who had handled all transactions for local farmers, acting both as retailers and as marketing and purchasing agents.

Women's earning power from wages or market sales was an important factor in the market economy. With increasing commercialization and dependency on cash, women's earnings became essential to the survival of the family farm. The put-out work that women did in New England had its parallel in the Middle Atlantic states and in Ohio—especially near towns and cities—in women's dairy production, which was crucial to

Women's Paid Labor

family income. Butter and cheese making for local and regional markets replaced spinning and weaving as farm women's major activity. The work was physically demanding and did not replace regular home and farm chores but was added to them. Yet women took pride in their work; it gave many a sense of independence.

Most farm families seemed to welcome the opportunities offered by the market economy. While continuing to take pride in self-sufficiency and to value rural culture, they shifted toward specialization and market-oriented production. The rewards for such flexibility were great. Produce sold at market financed land and equipment purchases and made credit arrangements possible. Many farm families flourished.

Others—hired hands and farm tenants—were less fortunate. The rising cost of land and farming meant that by the 1850s it took from ten to twenty years for a rural laborer to save enough money to farm for himself. Thus the number of tenant farmers increased.

Individually and collectively, Americans still valued agrarian life. State governments energetically promoted commercial agriculture to spur economic growth and sustain the values of an agrarian-based republic. Massachusetts in 1817 and New York in 1819 subsidized agricultural prizes and county fairs. New York required contestants to submit written descriptions of how they grew their prize crops; the state then published the best essays to encourage the use of new methods and promote specialization. Farm journals also helped familiarize farmers with developments in agriculture.

Even so, the Old Northwest gradually and inevitably replaced the northeastern states as the center of American family agriculture. Farms in the Old Northwest were much larger and better suited to

Mechanization of Agriculture

the new mechanized farming implements than were their northeastern counterparts. The farmers of the region bought machines such as the McCormick reaper on credit and paid for them with the profits from their high yields. By 1847 Cyrus McCormick was selling a thousand reapers a year. By introducing interchangeable parts, he

expanded production to five thousand a year, but demand still outstripped supply. Similarly, John Deere's steel plow, invented in 1837, replaced the inadequate iron plow; steel blades kept the soil from sticking and were tough enough to break the roots of prairie grass. By 1856, Deere's sixty-five employees were making 13,500 plows a year.

Mechanized farming was the basis of expanded production. In the 1850s alone wheat production surged 70 percent. By that time the area that had been the western wilderness in 1800 had become one of the world's leading agricultural regions. Midwestern farm families fed an entire nation and still had enough food to export.

Settling and Conquering the West

Integral to the development of the market economy was the steady expansion of the United States. In 1800 the edge of settlement extended in an arc from western New York State through the new states of Kentucky and Tennessee and south to Georgia. By 1820, it had shifted westward to Ohio, Indiana, and Illinois in the North, and Louisiana, Alabama, and Mississippi in the South. By 1860, Texas and California were states, and settlement had reached its twentieth-century continental limits. Unsettled and sporadically settled land remained—mostly the plains and mountain territory between the Mississippi River and the Sierra Nevada—but elsewhere the land and its Indian inhabitants had given way to white settlement (see maps).

Most Americans saw western settlers as civilizers; a minority, including Indians, viewed them as conquerors. In myth, literature, and song Americans glorified the explorers, fur trappers and scouts, and pioneers. James Fenimore Cooper's Leatherstocking tales, a series of novels that began appearing in 1823, introduced Hawkeye (Natty Bumppo), America's first popular fictional hero. At heart a romantic, Hawkeye preferred the freedom of the virgin forest to domesticated society. Yet

Conquerors and Civilizers

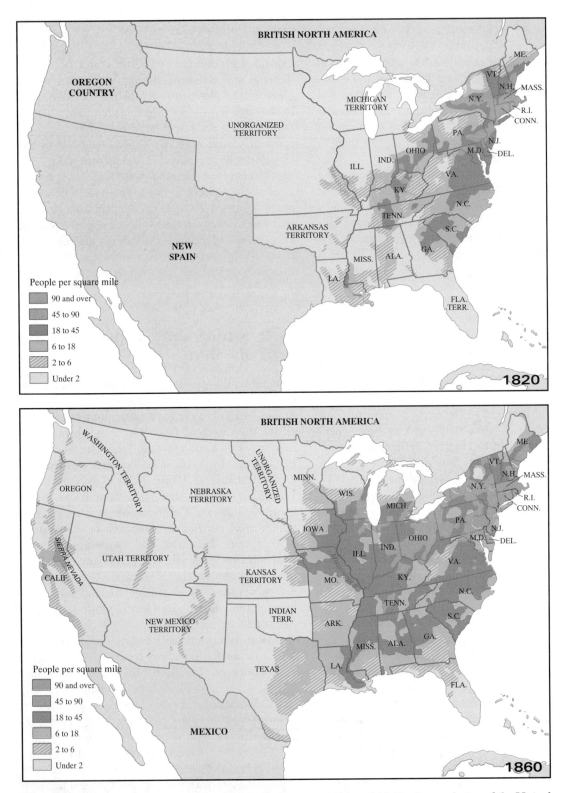

United States Population, 1820 and 1860 *Between 1820 and 1860, the population of the United States grew from 9.6 million to 31.4 million, and the density increased significantly in the North, the Old Northwest, and California. Settlement, too, spread farther away from the eastern seaboard.*

SIR JOS JEBB.

The fur trade was part of a market system that extended from the Far West through St. Louis, Montréal, and New York to the hat merchants of Europe. These Ottawa fur traders, painted at Fort Michilimackinac in Upper Michigan, most likely traded with fur merchants based in Montréal.   National Archives of Canada.

whatever noble Eden the wilderness offered, it inevitably gave way, as Cooper described in *The Last of the Mohicans* (1826), to civilization.

The frontier represented not only the peaceful settlement of the West and the extension of farming and republican virtue but also the conquering of the native inhabitants and the environment. The history of the West was often violent and intolerant. The Mormons who sought a new Jerusalem near the Great Salt Lake were fleeing the gehenna (hell) imposed on them by frontier folk farther east (see page 216). Those who sought to farm the land, dig the gold, trap the furs, and cut the lumber destroyed the natural landscape

and ecological balance in the name of progress and development.

The market economy provided a great impetus for expansion. Early on, the fur trapper system brought the Far West—way beyond settlement—into a market system that extended through St. Louis, Montréal, and New York to the hat merchants of Europe. Then, in the late 1840s, settlement jumped over the trapping areas to the West Coast of the American continent, when the promise of instant wealth in the form of gold sparked a gold rush.

Gold stimulated a mass migration to the West Coast. The United States had acquired Alta

California from Mexico in the Treaty of Guadalupe Hidalgo (see page 259),

California Gold Rush

and the province was inhabited mostly by native peoples, some Mexicans living on large estates, and a chain of small settlements around military forts (presidios) and missions. That changed almost overnight after James Marshall, a carpenter, spotted gold particles in the millrace at Sutter's Mill (now Coloma, California, northwest of Sacramento) in January 1848. Word of the discovery spread, and other Californians rushed to scrabble for instant fortunes.

By 1849 the news had spread around the world, and hundreds of thousands of fortune seekers streamed into California. The newcomers came for one reason: instant wealth. Success in the market economy required capital, hard labor, and time; by contrast, gold mining seemed to promise instant riches. Most "forty-niners," however, never found enough gold to pay their expenses. "The stories you hear frequently in the States," one gold seeker wrote home, "are the most extravagant lies imaginable—the mines are a humbug. . . . The almost universal feeling is to get home." But many stayed, either unable to afford the passage home or tempted by the growing labor shortage in California's cities and agricultural districts.

The forty-niners had their eyes on gold nuggets, but they had to be fed. Thus began the great California agricultural boom. Wheat was the preferred staple; it required minimal investment, was easily planted, and offered a quick return at the end of a relatively short growing season. By the mid-1850s, California was exporting wheat. Meanwhile, enterprising merchants rushed to supply, feed, and clothe the new settlers. One such merchant was Levi Strauss, a German Jewish immigrant, whose tough mining pants found an enduring and eventually worldwide market as blue jeans.

In the Midwest, family farms were the basic unit of production. In California, by contrast, mining, grazing, and large-scale wheat farming

Women Settlers

were overwhelmingly male occupations. The experiences of women, who constituted about one-seventh of the travelers on the overland trails, differed from those of men moving westward. Most men came alone. Women who accompanied their husbands found their lives uprooted. Moving was a traumatic experience for many; they left behind networks of friends and kin to journey, often with children, along an unknown path to a strange environment. Yet in the West their domestic skills were in great demand. They received high fees for cooking, laundering, and sewing, and they ran boarding houses and hotels (men shunned domestic work). Not all women, however, were entrepreneurs. Some wives, at their spouses' behest, cooked for and served their husbands' friends, enabling their husbands to build reputations as hosts.

Gold altered the pattern of settlement along the entire Pacific coast. Before 1848 most overland traffic flowed north over the Oregon Trail; few pioneers turned south to California. By 1849 a pioneer observed that the Oregon Trail "bore no evidence of having been much traveled this year." Traffic was flowing south instead, and California was becoming the new population center of the Pacific Slope. One measure of this shift was the overland mail routes. In the 1840s the Oregon Trail had been the main communications link between the Midwest and the Pacific. But the post office officials who organized mail routes in the 1850s terminated them in California, not Oregon; there was no route north of Sacramento.

By 1860 farmers in California, as in the Great Plains and prairies farther east, had become firmly linked to the market economy. They cleared the

Western Farming

land of trees or prairie grass, hoed corn and wheat, fenced in animals, and constructed cabins of logs or sod. Success often depended on their access to water, and they sought to divert the streams and rivers of the West to irrigate their land. As settled areas expanded, farmers built roads to carry their stock and produce to market and bring back supplies they could not produce for themselves. Growth brought specialization; as western farmers shifted from self-sufficiency to commercial farming, they too tended to concentrate on one crop.

What made farm settlements possible was the availability of land and credit. Some public lands were granted as a reward for military service: veterans of the War of 1812 received 160 acres; veterans of the Mexican War could purchase land at reduced prices. And until 1820, civilians could buy government land at $2 an acre (a relatively high price) on a liberal four-year payment plan. From 1800 to 1817 the government successively reduced the minimum purchase from 640 to 80 acres, bringing the land within the reach of more Americans. But when the availability of land prompted the flurry of land speculation that ended in the Panic of 1819, the government discontinued credit sales. Instead, it reduced the price further, to $1.25 an acre.

Land Grants and Sales

Some eager pioneers settled land before it had been surveyed and offered for sale. Such illegal settlers, or squatters, then had to buy the land at auction and faced the risk of being unable to purchase it. In 1841, to facilitate settlement and end property disputes, Congress passed the Pre-emption Act, which legalized settlement prior to surveying.

Since most settlers needed to borrow money, private credit systems arose: banks, private investors, country storekeepers, and speculators all extended credit to farmers. Railroads also sold land on credit—land they had received from the government as construction subsidies. (The Illinois Central, for example, received 2.6 million acres in 1850.) Indeed, nearly all economic activity in the West involved credit, from land sales to the shipping of produce to railroad construction.

From the start, the agricultural West was dependent on its links with towns and cities. Cities along the Ohio River—Louisville and Cincinnati—and the old French settlements—Detroit on the Great Lakes, St. Louis on the Mississippi River—predated and promoted the earliest settlement of much of the West. New population centers, however, bypassed such old French towns as Vincennes and Kaskaskia. Chicago spearheaded settlement farther west. Steamboats connected the

Frontier Cities

river cities with eastern markets and ports, carrying grain east and returning with finished goods. As the center of a rail network, Chicago exercised sway over the settling and development of most of the middle United States. As in the Northeast, western cities eventually developed into manufacturing centers as merchants shifted their investments from commerce to industry.

Urban growth in the West was so spectacular that by 1860 Cincinnati, St. Louis, and Chicago each had populations exceeding one hundred thousand, and Buffalo, Louisville, San Francisco, Pittsburgh, Detroit, and Milwaukee had surpassed forty thousand. Thus commerce, urban growth, and industrialization overtook the farmers' frontier, wedding the West to the Northeast.

Conclusion

For the North and the West the period from 1800 through 1860 was one of explosive growth. Population increased sixfold. The United States now extended from sea to sea, incorporating new peoples—Indians, Mexicans, Californians—sending out settlers to plow the land and inhabit the cities, and recruiting immigrants from around the world. Agriculture, which had completely dominated the nation at the turn of the century, was by midcentury being challenged by a booming manufacturing sector. And agriculture itself was becoming market-oriented and mechanized.

Economic development changed the way people lived. Canals, railroads, steamboats, and telegraph lines linked economic activities hundreds and even thousands of miles apart. The market economy brought sustained growth; it also ushered in cycles of boom and bust. Hard times and unemployment became frequent occurrences. The growing economy meant larger-scale destruction of the environment.

Large-scale manufacturing also altered traditional patterns of production and consumption. Farmers began to purchase goods formerly made by their wives and daughters, and farm families geared production to faraway markets. Farm women increasingly contributed income from market sales to the family farm. In New England many young women left the family farm to become the first factory workers in the new textile industry. As the master-journeyman-apprentice system faded away, workplace relations became more impersonal and working conditions harsher, and men's and women's work became increasingly dissimilar. Industrial jobs began to attract large numbers of immigrants, and some workers organized labor unions.

The American people, too, were changing. Immigration and western expansion were making the population more diverse. Urbanization, commerce, and industry were creating significant divisions among Americans, reaching deeply into the home as well as the workshop. The South was not totally insulated from these changes, but its dependence on slave rather than free labor set it apart. Above all else, slavery defined the South.

Suggestions for Further Reading

General

David Klingaman and Richard Vedder, eds., *Essays in Nineteenth-Century History* (1975); Jack Larkin, *The Reshaping of Everyday Life, 1790–1840* (1988); Otto Mayr and Robert C. Post, eds., *Yankee Enterprise: The Rise of the American System of Manufactures* (1981); Douglass C. North, *Economic Growth of the United States, 1790–1860* (1966); Nathan Rosenberg, *Technology and American Economic Growth* (1972); Melvyn Stokes and Stephen Conway (eds.), *The Market Revolution in America: Social, Political, and Religious Expressions, 1800–1860* (1996).

Transportation

Carter Goodrich, *Government Promotion of American Canals and Railroads, 1800–1890* (1960); Louis C. Hunter, *Steamboats on the Western Rivers* (1949); Ronald E. Shaw, *Canals for a Nation: The Canal Era in the United States, 1790–1860* (1990); George R. Taylor, *The Transportation Revolution, 1815–1860* (1951); James A. Ward, *Railroads and the Character of America, 1820–1887* (1986).

Commerce and Manufacturing

Alfred D. Chandler, Jr., *The Visible Hand: Managerial Revolution in American Business* (1977); Robert F. Dalzell, Jr., *Enterprising Elite: The Boston Associates and the World They Made* (1987); Louis Hartz, *Economic Policy and Democratic Thought: Pennsylvania, 1776–1860* (1954); Stanley I. Kutler, *Privilege and Creative Destruction: The Charles River Bridge Case* (1971); Walter Licht, *Industrializing America: The Nineteenth Century* (1995); Merritt Roe Smith, *Harpers Ferry Armory and the New Technology* (1977); Theodore Steinberg, *Nature Incorporated: Industrialization and the Waters of New England* (1991); Anthony F. C. Wallace, *Rockdale: The Growth of an American Village in the Early Industrial Revolution* (1978).

Agriculture

Jeremy Atack and Fred Bateman, *To Their Own Soil: Agriculture in the Antebellum North* (1987); Allen G. Bogue, *From Prairie to Corn Belt: Farming on the Illinois and Iowa Prairies in the Nineteenth Century* (1963); Christopher Clark, *The Roots of Rural Capitalism: Western Massachusetts, 1780–1860* (1990); John Mack Faragher, *Sugar Creek: Life on the Illinois Prairie* (1986); Paul W. Gates, *The Farmer's Age: Agriculture, 1815–1860* (1962); Joan M. Jensen, *Loosening the Bonds: Mid-Atlantic Farm Women, 1750–1850* (1986); Robert Leslie Jones, *History of Agriculture in Ohio to 1880* (1983); Sally McMurry, *Transforming Rural Life: Dairying Families and Agricultural Change, 1820–1885* (1995).

Conquerors and Civilizers

William Cronon, *Nature's Metropolis: Chicago and the Great West* (1991); John Mack Faragher, *Women and Men on the Overland Trail* (1979); William H. Goetzmann, *Exploration and Empire: The Explorer and the Scientist in the Winning of the American West* (1966); Theodore J. Karamanski, *Fur Trade and Exploration: Opening the Far Northwest, 1821–1852* (1983); Lillian Schlissel, *Women's Diaries of the Westward Journey* (1982); David J. Weber, *The Spanish Frontier in North America* (1992).

Workers

Jeanne Boydston, *Home and Work: Housework, Wages, and the Ideology of Labor in the Early Republic* (1990); Alan Dawley, *Class and Community: The Industrial Revolution in Lynn* (1977); Thomas Dublin, *Transforming Women's Work: New England Lives in the Industrial Revolution* (1994); Thomas Dublin, *Women at Work: The Transformation of Work and Community in Lowell, Massachusetts, 1826–1860* (1979); Bruce Laurie, *Artisans into Workers: Labor in Nineteenth-Century America* (1989); Howard B. Rock, Paul A. Gilje, and Robert Asher, eds., *American Artisans: Crafting Social Identity, 1750–1850* (1995); Sean Wilentz, *Chants Democratic: New York City and the Rise of the American Working Class, 1788–1850* (1984).

CHAPTER

11

Slavery and the Growth of the South

1800 – 1860

Dressed in silk and adorned in jewelry, Eliza seemed bewildered as she clung to the hands of her children, a little boy and a girl. That morning in 1841 Eliza had been told that she was going into Washington, D.C., to receive her long-promised freedom. Now she found herself in "a slave pen within the very shadow of the Capitol."

Eliza had been her owner's concubine, but a division of his property had placed her under the control of his resentful daughter. The daughter, deciding to remove all evidence of her father's illicit relationship, arranged for a slave trader to move Eliza and her children by ship to New Orleans. At the New Orleans slave market a man offered to purchase her son. To no avail, Eliza pleaded with him to buy the family group. Later, when her daughter was sold away, Eliza had to be physically torn apart from the last person she loved.

Sent to work in the fields of a plantation on Bayou Boeuf, Eliza grew "feeble and emaciated." Within two years she was dead. Eliza's fate was one of many human tragedies accompanying the vast expansion of plantation slavery that took place between 1800 and 1860. Tens of thousands of African-Americans suffered as slavery spread westward; across the Mississippi River and into Texas.

Many northerners remained undisturbed by slavery, but a growing number came to see it as shocking and backward. In the years after the Revolution, northerners—possessing few slaves and influenced by the revolutionary concept of natural rights—had adopted gradual emancipation laws. At the same time, the North's emerging industrial society rendered forced labor obsolete.

Meanwhile, the South witnessed a different kind of growth and prosperity. New lands were settled and new states peopled, but growth in the South only reinforced existing economic patterns. Steadily the South emerged as the world's most extensive and vigorous slave economy. Its people were slaves, slaveholders, and nonslaveholders rather than farmers, merchants, mechanics, mill girls, and manufacturers. Southern wealth came from export crops; its population thus remained almost wholly rural rather than both rural and urban.

Migration, Growth, and the Cotton Boom

Between 1800 and 1860, a vastly larger slaveholding society emerged. Attracted by rich new lands, thousands of southerners moved across the Appalachian Mountains. Small farmers and ambitious slaveowners poured across the mountains, pushing the Indians off their lands in the Gulf region. The floodtide of westward migration reached Alabama and Mississippi in the 1830s, then spilled into Texas in the 1850s.

The earliest settlers in the swelling stream of migration were often yeomen—small farmers, most of whom owned no slaves. Yeomen pioneered the southern wilderness, moving into undeveloped regions and building log cabins. After the War of 1812, they moved in successive waves down the southern Appalachians into new Gulf lands, first as herders of livestock and then as farmers.

Yeoman Farmers

Migration became almost a way of life for some yeoman families. Lured by stories of good land beyond the horizon, many men uprooted their wives and children repeatedly. Their wives, often dreading the loneliness of the frontier, seldom shared the men's excitement about moving. Once in the new environment, women labored in the household economy and patiently re-created the social ties—to relatives, neighbors, fellow churchgoers—that enriched everyone's experience.

Some yeomen acquired large tracts of level land, purchased slaves, and became wealthy. Others clung to the beautiful mountainous areas they loved or kept moving as independent subsistence farmers. Those who moved tended to stick to the climate and soils they knew best. Yeomen could not afford the richest bottomlands, which were swampy and required expensive draining, but they acquired land almost everywhere else.

For slaveholding southerners another powerful motive impelled westward movement: the chance to profit from a spectacular cotton boom. Southern planters were not sentimentalists, holding onto slavery while northerners grew rich from commerce and manufacturing. Like other Americans, slaveholding southerners were profit oriented, and the cotton boom caused nonmechanized, slave-based agriculture to remain highly profitable in the South.

Rise of the Cotton South

This outcome had not always seemed likely. At the time of the Revolution, slave-based agriculture was not very profitable in the Upper South, where most southerners then lived. Persistent debt plagued Virginia's extravagant and aristocratic tobacco growers. Farther south, along the coast of the Carolinas and Georgia, slaves grew rice and some indigo. Cotton was a profitable crop only for the Sea-Island planters of South Carolina and Georgia, who grew the luxurious long-staple variety. Short-staple cotton, which grew readily in the interior, was unmarketable because its sticky seeds lay tangled in the fibers.

Then England's burgeoning textile industry demanded more and more cotton. Sea Island cotton became so profitable between 1785 and 1795 that thousands of farmers in the interior tried growing the short-staple variety, most with the hope that some innovation would make the crop salable to the English. Eli Whitney, an inventor from Connecticut, responded in 1793 with a simple machine that removed the seeds from the fibers. By 1800 cotton was spreading rapidly westward from the seaboard states.

The voracious appetite of English mills caused a meteoric rise in cotton production (see maps). Despite occasional periods of low prices, the demand for cotton surged ahead every decade. Southerners with capital bought more land and more slaves and planted ever more cotton. By 1825 the South was the world's dominant supplier of cotton; by the 1850s the South was the source of over 70 percent of all the cotton that Britain imported.

Thus the antebellum South—the Old South before the Civil War—became primarily a cotton South. Large amounts of tobacco and hemp continued to be grown in the Upper South, and rice and sugar were important crops in certain coastal areas. But cotton was the largest and most widespread cash crop, and the wealth it generated shaped the society.

Small slaveowners and wealthier planters (those who owned twenty or more slaves) sought out alluvial bottomland and other fertile soils, eager to grasp the opportunity for wealth the cotton boom offered. The desire to plant more cotton and buy more slaves often caused men with new wealth to postpone the enjoyment of luxuries. Yet the planters' wealth put ease and refinement within their grasp, and riches and high social status arrived quickly for some.

Slavery's expansion across the Appalachians meant another kind of migration—involuntary—for black southerners. Since Congress had closed the international slave trade in 1808, slaves for new cotton regions had to come from the Upper South, where the slave population was growing through natural increase while tobacco prices fell. Worried by soil exhaustion and low prices, planters in Virginia and North Carolina were shifting toward less labor-intensive crops and were glad to sell excess slaves to fertile regions in the cotton South.

Between 1810 and 1820 alone, 137,000 slaves were forced to move from North Carolina and the

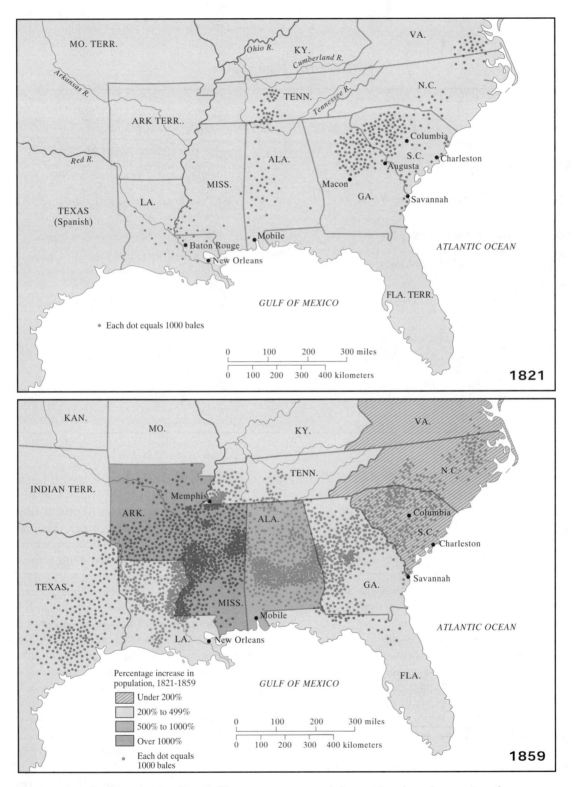

Cotton Production in the South *These two maps reveal the rapid westward expansion of cotton production and its importance to antebellum South.*

Chesapeake states to Alabama, Mississippi, and other western regions. Interregional sales and transfers continued thereafter: an estimated 2 million people were sold between 1820 and 1860 to satisfy the need for slave labor. Thousands of black families like Eliza's were disrupted every year to serve the needs of the cotton economy.

To white southerners the period from 1800 to 1860 was a time of great change and progress. The South was growing and expanding, but its growth was different from the North's: its distinguishing features were those of an agricultural and a slave society.

An Agrarian Society

The South did exhibit some of the diversity of the North. There were merchants, artisans, and craftsmen in the larger cities, as well as men who promoted railways and transportation improvements. Immigrants from Ireland and other parts of Europe arrived in southern ports in increasing numbers during the 1840s and 1850s. But these developments were only faint shadows of their northern counterparts and had little impact. Southern development was dominated by agriculture and slavery and by the prominence of rural slaves, slaveholders, and yeoman farmers in the population.

Population distribution remained thin. Cotton growers spread out over as large an area as possible to maximize production and income. Farms were set far apart, rather than clustered around villages, and southern society remained predominantly rural. Because most immigrants to the United States sought urban locations, population growth fell behind the North's. Population density was low in the older plantation states and extremely low in the frontier areas. In 1860 there were only 2.3 people per square mile in largely unsettled Texas and 15.6 in Louisiana. By contrast, population density in the nonslaveholding states east of the Mississippi River was almost three times higher. The Northeast had an average of 65.4 people per square mile.

Population Distribution

Even in the 1850s, much of the South seemed a virtual wilderness. Frederick Law Olmsted, a northerner later renowned as a landscape architect, made several trips through the South in the 1850s as a journalist. Olmsted found that the few trains and stagecoaches available to travelers offered crude accommodations and kept their schedules poorly. Indeed, he had to do most of his traveling on horseback along primitive trails. Between Columbus, Georgia, and Montgomery, Alabama, Olmsted found "a hilly wilderness, with a few dreary villages, and many isolated cotton farms."

Society in such rural areas was characterized by relatively weak institutions, for it takes a concentration of people to create and support organized activity. Where people were scarce, it was difficult to finance and operate schools, churches, libraries, or even inns. Southerners were strongly committed to their churches, and some believed in the importance of universities, but all such institutions were far less developed than those in the North.

The South's cities were likewise smaller and less developed. Confined to the region's perimeter, the largest urban areas functioned as ports rather than centers of a vigorous internal commerce. They exported mainly staple crops, such as cotton or tobacco, and imported only a few necessary manufactured goods and luxuries. Factories were rare because planters invested most of their capital in slaves. A few southerners did invest in iron or textiles on a small scale. But the largest southern "industry" was lumbering, and the largest factories used slave labor to make cigars.

Weak Urban Sector

More decisively, the South was slower than the North to develop a unified market economy and a regional transportation network. Because planters could use waterways for transportation, far less money was spent on canals, turnpikes, or railroads. The South had only 26 percent of the nation's railroad mileage in 1850. As a result, urban growth after 1820 was far less vigorous than in the North, and metropolitan centers were almost nonexistent. In 1860 less than 3 percent of Mississippi's population and 7 percent of South Carolina's lived in towns with at least 2,500 residents. In the same year, the population of Richmond, Virginia, was only 38,000. New Orleans, by far the largest southern city, had only 169,000 residents and was being left behind because it was not linked to the national railroad network.

Thus although the South sold huge amounts of cotton on the international market, its economy at home was semideveloped relative to other sections of the country. Its white people were prospering, but not as rapidly as most residents of the North. There, changes in commerce and industry brought unprecedented advances in productivity, raising the average person's standard of living. In the South, change was quantitative rather than qualitative: the region grew but remained rural and its internal market undeveloped.

Free Southerners: Farmers, Planters, and Free Blacks

A large majority of white southern families (three-quarters in 1860) owned no slaves. Some lived in towns, but most were yeoman farmers who owned their own land and grew their own food. They were the typical whites, but the social distance between different groups of whites was great. Still greater was the distance between whites and blacks.

The yeomen were independent, individualistic, and given to hard work. Though they were a numerical majority, their status did not mean that they set the direction of the slave society. Absorbed in the work of their farms, they normally occupied a relatively autonomous position within the slavery-based staple-crop economy expanding around them. By slowly improving their acreage or settling new and better land, yeoman families improved their lot and made steady progress.

Because few railroads penetrated the southern interior, yeomen generally had little contact with the market or the type of progress it could introduce. Families might raise a small surplus to sell for cash or to trade for needed items, but they were remote from large market networks and therefore not particularly concerned about increasing their cash income. Yeomen constituted an important, though often silent, part of southern society. If their rights were threatened, however, they could react strongly.

The yeomen were mostly from Scottish and Irish backgrounds, and they enjoyed a folk culture based on family, church, and neighborhood.

Folk Culture of the Yeomen

Once a year they flocked to religious revivals called protracted meetings or camp meetings, and in between they enjoyed house-raisings, log-rollings, quilting bees, and corn-shuckings. Such occasions combined work with fun, offered food in abundance, and provided fellowship that was especially welcome to isolated rural dwellers.

Social conventions imposed uniform roles on yeoman women. At harvest they frequently helped in the fields, and throughout the year the drying, preserving, and preparing of food consumed much of their time. Household tasks continued during frequent pregnancies and the care of small children. Primary nursing and medical care also fell to the mother, who might have a book of remedies but often relied on family and folk wisdom. In some evangelical churches women played respected roles on certain committees, but overwhelmingly the busy life of the yeoman woman was tied to the home.

Among the men there were many who aspired to wealth, eager to join the race for slaves, land, and profits from cotton. Others were content with their independence, recreation, family life, and religion. But whether they strove to become rich or were satisfied with their status, they worked hard.

Ferdinand L. Steel, a North Carolinian who moved to Tennessee and later to Mississippi, was a typical yeoman. He rose every day at five and worked until sundown. With the help of his family he raised corn, wheat, pork, and vegetables for the family table. Cotton was his cash crop: he sold five or six bales (about 2,000 pounds) a year to obtain money for sugar, coffee, salt, calico, gunpowder, and a few other store-bought goods.

Steel's life in Mississippi in the 1840s retained much of the flavor of the frontier. He made all the family's shoes; his wife and sister sewed dresses, shirts, and "pantiloons." The Steel women also rendered their own soap and spun and wove cotton into cloth; the men hunted game. For Steel, God and family—not work and entertainment—were the focal points of life. Eventually he became

How do historians know about the values and ways of life of nonslaveholders in the South? Letters, diaries, and family papers of these people, who generally were not rich or famous, have not been preserved as frequently as the records of the slaveholding elite. Thus historians have turned to various other sources—including travelers' accounts, folklore, and United States census records—to learn more about them. This page from the manuscript "Population Schedules" of the census of 1860 supplies information on family structure and a variety of personal characteristics. The "Census of Agriculture" contains much additional information about the size of each family's farm and the crops grown there.   Photo: North Carolina Division of Archives and History.

a traveling Methodist minister. "My life is one of toil," he reflected, "but blessed be God that it is as well with me as it is."

Toil was also the lot of two other groups of free southerners: landless whites and free blacks. A sizable minority of white southern workers—from 25 to 40 percent—were unskilled laborers who owned no land and worked for others in the countryside and towns.

Landless Whites

Their property consisted of a few household items and some animals—usually pigs—that could feed themselves on the open range. The landless included some immigrants, especially Irish, who did heavy and dangerous work such as building railroads and digging ditches.

In the countryside, white farm laborers struggled to become yeomen in the face of low wages or, if they rented, unpredictable market prices for their crops. Thus when James and Nancy Bennitt of North Carolina succeeded in their ten-year struggle to buy land, they decided to avoid the unstable market in cotton; thereafter they raised extra corn and wheat as sources of cash.

For the nearly quarter-million free blacks in the South in 1860, conditions were often little better than the slave's. The free blacks of the Upper South were usually descendants of men and women emancipated by their owners in the 1780s and 1790s. They usually did not own land and had to labor in someone else's fields, often beside slaves. By law free blacks could not own a gun, buy liquor, violate curfew, assemble (except in church), testify in court, or (throughout the South after 1835) vote. Still, a minority bought land, and others found jobs as artisans, draymen, boatmen, and fishermen. A few prospered and bought slave laborers, but most who owned slaves had purchased their own wives and children (whom they could not free, since laws required newly emancipated blacks to leave their state).

Free Blacks

Farther south, in the cotton and Gulf regions, a large proportion of free blacks were mulattos, the offspring of wealthy planters. Not all planters freed their mixed-race offspring, but those who did often recognized a moral obligation and gave their children good educations and financial backing. In a few cities like New Orleans and Mobile, extensive interracial sex had produced a mulatto population that was recognized as a distinct class. These people formed a society of their own and sought a status above slaves and other freedmen, if not equal to that of planters. But outside New Orleans, Mobile, and Charleston, such groups were rare.

At the opposite end of the social spectrum from free blacks were slaveholders. As a group they lived well, on incomes that enabled them to enjoy superior housing, food, clothing, and luxuries. But most lived in comfortable farmhouses, not on the opulent scale that legend suggests. A few statistics tell the story: 50 percent of southern slaveholders had fewer than five slaves; 72 percent had fewer than ten; 88 percent had fewer than twenty. Thus the average slaveholder was not a wealthy aristocrat but an aspiring farmer, usually a person of humble origins, with little formal education and many rough edges to his manner.

Planters

Slaveholding men dominated society and, especially among the wealthiest and oldest families, justified their dominance through a paternalistic ideology. Instead of stressing the profitable aspects of commercial agriculture, they focused on noblesse oblige, seeing themselves as custodians of the welfare of society as a whole and of the black families who depended on them in particular. The paternalistic planter viewed himself not as an oppressor but as the benevolent guardian of an inferior race. He developed affectionate feelings toward his slaves (as long as they knew their place) and was genuinely shocked at criticism of his behavior.

Southern Paternalism

The letters of Paul Carrington Cameron, North Carolina's largest slaveholder, illustrate this mentality. After a period of sickness among his one thousand North Carolina slaves, Cameron wrote, "I fear the Negroes have suffered much from the want of proper attention and kindness under this

Most slaveowners lived in comfortable country homes rather than in stately mansions. This rare daguerreotype, dating from about 1853, shows a family in front of their home. Notice the presence of a male slave in the left background.   The J. Paul Getty Museum, Los Angeles, California.

late distemper . . . no love of lucre shall ever induce me to be cruel, or even to make or permit to be made any great exposure of their persons at inclement seasons."

It was comforting to the richest southern planters to see themselves in this way, and slaves—accommodating to the realities of power—encouraged their masters to think their benevolence was appreciated. Paternalism also served as a defense against abolitionist criticism. Still, paternalism affected the manner and not the substance of most planters' behavior. Its softness and warmth were a matter of style, covering harsher assumptions: blacks were inferior, and planters should make money.

Relations between men and women in the planter class were similarly paternalistic. The life of an upper-class southern woman was bound by the household, and she was raised and educated to be a wife, mother, and subordinate companion to men. South Carolina's Mary Boykin Chesnut wrote of her husband, "He is master of the house. To hear is to obey. . . . All the comfort of my life depends upon his being in a good humor." In a social system based on the coercion of an entire race, women were not allowed to challenge society's rules on sexual or racial relations.

Elite Women's Role

After spending her early years within the family circle, a planter's daughter usually attended one of the South's rapidly multiplying academies or boarding schools. There she received an education that emphasized grammar, composition, penmanship, geography, literature, and languages, but little science and mathematics. Typically the young woman maintained dutiful and affectionate ties with her parents and entertained suitors whom they approved.

Upon marriage, she ceded to her husband most of her legal rights, became part of his family, and was expected to get along with numerous in-laws during extended visits. Most of the year she was isolated on a large plantation, where she had to oversee the cooking and preserving of food, manage the house, supervise care of the children, and attend sick slaves. It is not surprising that an intelligent and perceptive young woman sometimes approached marriage with anxiety, for her future depended on the man she chose.

Childbearing brought grief and sickness, as well as joy, to southern women. In 1840 the birth rate for white southern women in their childbearing years was almost 30 percent higher than the national average. The average southern white woman could expect to bear eight children in 1800; by 1860 the figure had decreased only to six, with one or more miscarriages likely. For those women who wanted to plan their families, methods of contraception were uncertain. Complications of childbirth were a major cause of death, occurring twice as often in the hot, moist South as in the Northeast. Moreover, a mother had to endure the loss of many of the children she bore. In the South in 1860 almost five out of ten children died before age five.

Slavery was another source of problems that white women had to endure but were not supposed to notice. "Violations of the moral law . . . made mulattoes as common as blackberries," protested a woman in Georgia, but wives had to play "the ostrich game."

In the early 1800s, some southern women, especially Quakers, had spoken out against slavery. Although most white women did not criticize the "peculiar institution," they often viewed it less as a system and more as a series of relationships among individuals. Perhaps sensing this, southern men tolerated no discussion by women of the slavery issue. In the 1840s and 1850s, as northern and international criticism of slavery increased, southern

men published a barrage of articles stressing that women should restrict their concerns to the home.

But some southern women were beginning to seek a larger role. A study of women in Petersburg, Virginia, has revealed behavior that valued financial autonomy. Over several decades before 1860, the proportion of women who never married, or did not remarry after the death of a spouse, grew to exceed 33 percent. Likewise the number of women who worked for wages, controlled their own property, and ran businesses increased. In managing property, women benefited from legal changes—beginning with Mississippi's Married Women's Property Act of 1839—that had been intended to protect families from the husband's indebtedness during business panics and recessions. The legal reforms gave married women some property rights.

For a large category of southern men and women, rights were nil, freedom was wholly denied, and education in any form was not allowed. Male and female slaves were expected to accept bondage and ignorance as their condition.

 ## Slaves and Their Status in Bondage

For African-Americans, slavery was a curse that brought no blessings other than the strengths they developed to survive it. Slaves knew a life of poverty, coercion, toil, heartbreak, and resentment. They had to bear separation from their loved ones and were despised as an inferior race. That they endured and found loyalty and strength among themselves is a tribute to their courage.

Southern slaves enjoyed few material comforts beyond the bare necessities. Although they generally had enough to eat, their diet was plain and monotonous. The basic ration was cornmeal, fat pork, molasses, and occasionally coffee. Many masters allowed slaves to tend gardens, which provided the variety and extra nutrition of greens and sweet potatoes, and some could fish and hunt. Slaves' diets were often nutri-

Slaves' Diet, Clothing, and Housing

tionally deficient, with the result that many slaves suffered from such diseases as beriberi and pellagra.

Clothing too was plain, coarse, and inexpensive. Few slaves received more than one or two changes of clothing for hot and cold seasons and one blanket each winter. When big enough to go to the fields, boys received a work shirt and a pair of breeches, and girls a simple dress. On many plantations slave women made their own clothing of osnaburg, a coarse cotton fabric. Many slaves had to go without shoes until December. The shoes they received were uncomfortable brass-toed brogans or stiff wraparounds made from leather tanned on the plantation.

Slaves typically lived in small one-room cabins. Logs chinked with mud formed the walls; dirt was the only floor; and a wattle-and-daub or stone chimney vented the fireplace, which provided both heat and light. Bedding consisted of heaps of straw, straw mattresses, or wooden bedframes lashed to the walls with rope. A few crude pieces of furniture and cooking utensils completed the furnishings. The gravest drawback of slave cabins was their unhealthfulness. Each small cabin housed one or two entire families. Crowding and lack of sanitation fostered the spread of infection and contagious diseases.

Hard work was the central fact of slaves' existence. The long hours and large work gangs that characterized Gulf Coast cotton districts seemed

Slaves' Work Routines

like factories in the field compared to the small clusters of slaves who had worked in the eighteenth-century Chesapeake. Overseers rang the morning bell before dawn, thus ensuring that slaves would be in the fields by first light. Except in urban settings and on some rice plantations, where slaves were assigned daily tasks to complete at their own pace, working "from sun to sun" became universal in the South. Long hours and hard work were at the heart of the advantage that slave labor gave slaveowners.

Profit also took precedence over paternalistic "protection" of women: slave women did heavy fieldwork, often as much as the men and even during pregnancy. Old people—of whom there were few—were kept busy caring for young children,

doing light chores, or carding, ginning, and spinning cotton. Children had to gather kindling, carry water to the fields, or sweep the yard. But slaves had a variety of ways to keep from being worked to death. It was impossible to supervise every slave every minute, and slaves slacked off when they were not being watched.

Slaves could not slow their pace too much, of course, because the owner enjoyed a monopoly on force and violence. Whites throughout the

Physical and Mental Abuse of Slaves

South believed that slaves "can't be governed except with the whip." Evidence suggests that whippings were less frequent on small farms than on large plantations, but even most small farmers plied the lash. These beatings symbolized authority to the master and tyranny to the slaves, who made them a benchmark for evaluating a master. In the words of former slaves, a good owner was one who did not "whip too much," whereas a bad owner "whipped till he's bloodied you and blistered you."*

As these reports suggest, terrible abuses could and did occur. The master wielded virtually absolute authority on his plantation, and courts did not recognize the word of chattel. Pregnant women were whipped, and there were burnings, mutilations, tortures, and murders. Yet physical cruelty may have been less prevalent in the United States than in other slaveholding parts of the New World. In sugar-growing and mining regions of the Western Hemisphere in the 1800s, slaves were regarded as an expendable resource to be replaced after seven years. Treatment was so poor that death rates were high and the heavily male slave population rapidly shrank in size. In the United States, by contrast, the slave population experienced a steady natural increase as births exceeded deaths and each generation grew larger.

---

*Accounts by ex-slaves are quoted from *The American Slave: A Composite Autobiography*, edited by George P. Rawick (Westport, Conn.: Greenwood Press, First Reprint Edition 1972, Second Reprint Edition 1974), from materials gathered by the Federal Writers' Project and originally published in 1941. The spelling in these accounts has been standardized.

The worst evil of American slavery was not its physical cruelty but the nature of slavery itself: coercion, lack of freedom, belonging to another person, virtually no hope for change. A woman named Delia Garlic made the essential point when she said, "It's bad to belong to folks that own you soul an' body." American slaves hated their oppression and, contrary to whites' stereotype of slaves as docile Sambos, were not grateful to their oppressors. They had to be subservient and speak honeyed words to their masters, but they talked quite differently among themselves. The evidence of their resistant attitudes comes from their actions and their own life stories.

Former slaves reported some warm feelings between masters and slaves, but the prevailing picture was one of antagonism and resistance.

Slaves' Attitudes Toward Whites

Slaves mistrusted kindness from whites and saw the self-interest in it. A man recalled that his owners took good care of their slaves, "and Grandma Maria say, 'Why shouldn't they—it was their money.'" Christmas presents of clothing from the master did not mean anything, observed another, "'cause he was going to [buy] that anyhow."

Slaves were alert to the signs of their degraded status. One man recalled his master eyeing the slave children and saying, "'That one will be worth a thousand dollars.' . . . You see, it was just like raisin' young mules." Another recollected, "Us catch lots of 'possums," but "the white folks ate 'em. Our mouths would water for some of that 'possum, but it wasn't often they let us have none." If the owner took his slaves' garden produce to town and sold it for them, the slaves suspected him of pocketing part of the profits.

Suspicion and resentment often grew into hatred. According to a former slave from Virginia, white people treated blacks "so mean that all the slaves prayed God to punish their cruel masters." As late as the 1930s an elderly ex-slave named Minnie Fulkes cherished the conviction that God was going to punish white people for their cruelty to blacks. She described the whippings that her mother had had to endure, and then she exclaimed, "Lord, Lord, I hate white people and the flood waters goin' to drown some more."

 ## Slave Culture and Everyday Life

The resource that enabled slaves to maintain such defiance was their culture: a body of beliefs and values born of their past and their present and of fellowship in their own community. It was not possible for slaves to change their world, but by drawing strength from their culture they could resist their condition and struggle on against it.

Slave culture changed significantly after the turn of the century. For a few years South Carolina reopened the international slave trade. After 1808, however, when Congress banned further importations, the proportion of native-born blacks rose steadily, reaching 96 percent in 1840 and almost 100 percent in 1860. Meanwhile, more and more slaves adopted Christianity as African culture gave way to a maturing African-American culture.

African influences remained strong, for African practices and beliefs reminded slaves that they were and ought to be different from their oppressors.

Influence of African Culture

The most visible features of African culture were slaves' appearance and forms of recreation. Some slave men plaited their hair into rows and fancy designs; slave women often wore their hair "in string"—tied in small bunches secured by a string or piece of cloth. A few men and many women wrapped their heads in kerchiefs of the styles and colors of West Africa.

For entertainment slaves made musical instruments with carved motifs that resembled African stringed instruments. Their drumming and dancing clearly followed African patterns; whites marveled at them. One visitor to Georgia in the 1860s described a ritual dance of African origin: "A ring of singers is formed. . . . They then utter a kind of melodious chant, which gradually increases in strength, and in noise, until it fairly shakes the house."

Many slaves continued to believe in spirits. Their belief resembled the African concept of the living dead—the idea that deceased relatives visit the earth for many years until the process of dying is complete. Slaves also practiced conjuration, voodoo, and quasi-magical root medicine. By 1860 the most notable conjurers and root doctors were reputed to live in South Carolina, Georgia, Louisiana, and other isolated coastal areas of heavy slave importation.

These cultural survivals provided slaves with a sense of their separate past. Conjuration and folk-lore also directly fed resistance; slaves could cast a spell or direct the power of a hand (a bag of arti-cles belonging to the person to be conjured) against the master. Not all masters felt confident enough to dismiss such a threat.

Slaves fashioned Christianity into an instru-ment of support and resistance. Theirs was a relig-ion of justice, quite unlike the religious propa-ganda their masters pushed at them. "You ought to have heard that preachin'," said one man. "'Obey your master and mistress, don't steal chickens and eggs and meat,' but nary a word about havin' a soul to save." Slaves believed that Jesus cared about their souls and their plight and that slave-holders would be "broilin' in hell for their sin" when God's justice came.

Slaves' Religion

For slaves, Christianity was a religion of personal and group salvation. Beyond seeking personal guidance, slaves prayed for deliverance. Many nurtured an unshakable belief that God would end their bondage. This faith—and the joy and emotional release that accompanied wor-ship—sustained blacks.

Enslaved African-Americans also developed a sense of racial identity. They naturally drew to-gether, helping each other in danger, need, and re-sistance. "We never told on each other," one woman declared. Although some slaves did betray others, former slaves were virtually unanimous in denounc-ing those who were disloyal to the group or sought personal gain through allegiance to whites.

Of course, different jobs, talents, and circum-stances created variations in status among slaves. But most slaves did not encounter a class system within the black community. Only one-quarter of all slaves lived on plantations of fifty or more blacks, so few sensed a wide chasm separating house servants and lowly field hands.

The main source of support for individuals was the family. Slave families faced severe dangers. At any moment the master could sell a husband or wife, give a slave child away as a wedding present, or die in debt, forcing a division of his property. Many families were broken up in such ways. Oth-ers were separated in the trans-Appalachian ex-pansion of the South. When the Union Army reg-istered thousands of black marriages in Mississippi and Louisiana in 1864 and 1865, fully 25 percent of the men over forty reported that they had been forcibly separated from a previous wife.

Slaves' Family Life

But this did not mean that slave families could not exist. American slaves clung tenaciously to the personal relationships that gave meaning to life. Although American law did not protect slave fami-lies, masters permitted them; in fact, slaveowners expected slaves to form families and have children. As a result, there was a normal ratio of men to women, young to old, even on the frontier.

Following African kinship taboos, African-Americans avoided marriage between cousins. Adapting the West African custom of polygyny to American circumstances, they did not condemn unwed mothers but did expect a young woman to enter a monogamous relationship after one preg-nancy, if not before. By naming their children after relatives of past generations, African-Americans emphasized their family histories. If they chose to bear the surname of a slaveowner, it was often the name of the owner under whom their family had begun in America.

Slaves abhorred interference in their family lives. Some of their strongest protests sought to prevent the breakup of a family. Rape was a horror for both men and women. Some husbands faced death rather than permit their wives to be sexually abused, and the women sometimes fought back. In other cases slaves seethed with anger at the injus-tice but could do nothing except soothe each other and condemn the guilty party.

Slave men and women followed gender roles similar to West African customs. After work in the fields was done, men's activities focused on

This photograph of five generations of a slave family, taken in Beaufort, South Carolina, in 1862, is silent but powerful testimony to the importance that enslaved African-Americans placed on their ever-threatened family ties.   Library of Congress.

Gender Roles in Slavery

"outdoor" tasks and women did "indoor" work. Men hunted and fished, made furniture, and repaired implements; women cooked, mended, and cleaned house. Slave families resembled white families in that African-American men held a respected place in their homes. The men did not dominate their wives in a manner similar to that of free husbands, but it would be misleading to say that slave women enjoyed equality in gender roles and family life. Under the pressures of bondage men and women had to share parental and household responsibilities. At any time, each might have to stand in for the other and assume extra duties. Similarly, uncles, aunts, and grandparents sometimes raised the children of those who had been sold away.

Work routines frequently promoted among slave women close associations that heightened their sense of sisterhood. On plantations young girls worked together as house servants. Nursing mothers got together to feed and care for their children, and adults worked together at tasks like soap making and stitching quilts. Female slaves thus spent significant portions of their lives as participants in a group of women, an experience that strengthened their ties to each other.

American slavery produced some fearless and implacable revolutionaries. Gabriel's conspiracy apparently was known to more than a thousand slaves when it was discovered in 1800, just before it was put into action (see page 153). A similar conspiracy in Charleston in 1822, led by a

Resistance to Slavery

free black named Denmark Vesey, involved many of the prominent whites' most trusted slaves. And the most famous rebel of all, Nat Turner, rose in violence in Southampton County, Virginia, in 1831.

The son of an African woman who passionately hated her enslavement, Nat Turner was a precocious child who learned to read when he was very young. Encouraged by his first owner to study the Bible, he enjoyed certain privileges but also endured hard work and changes of masters. Eventually young Nat became a preacher; he also developed a tendency toward mysticism and became increasingly withdrawn. After nurturing his plan for several years, Turner led a band of rebels from farm to farm in the predawn darkness of August 22, 1831. The group severed limbs and crushed skulls with axes or killed their victims with guns. Before they were stopped, Turner and his followers had slaughtered sixty whites of both sexes and all ages. The rebellion was crushed, Turner was hanged, and an estimated two hundred African-Americans, including many innocent individuals, were killed by retaliating whites.

Nat Turner Rebellion

Most slave resistance, however, was not violent, for the odds against revolution were especially poor in North America. Consequently slaves directed their energies toward creating the means of survival and resistance within slavery. Many individual slaves attempted to run away to the North, and some received assistance from a loose network of sympathetic citizens, known collectively as the Underground Railroad. But it was more common for slaves to run off temporarily to hide in the woods. Every day that a slave "lay out" in this way, the master lost a day's labor. Most owners chose not to mount an exhaustive search and instead sent word through other slaves that the grievances would be redressed. The runaway would then return to bargain with the master, who often was glad to have his property back.

Other modes of resistance had the same object: to resist but survive under bondage. Appropriating food (stealing, in the master's eyes) was common. Blacks also learned to ingratiate themselves and play off one white person against another. Field hands frequently tested a new overseer to intimidate him or win more favorable working conditions.

Harmony and Tension in a Slave Society

As the 1800s advanced, slavery impinged on laws and customs, individual values, and—increasingly—every aspect of southern politics. Legal restrictions on slaves, in effect since the seventeenth century, steadily increased. In all things, slaves fell under the supervision of whites. State courts held that a slave "has no civil right" and could not even hold property "except at the will and pleasure of his master." In response to revolts, legislators tightened the legal straitjacket: after the Nat Turner insurrection of 1831, for example, they prohibited owners from teaching their slaves to read. As political conflicts between North and South deepened, fears of slave revolt grew, and restrictions on slaves increased accordingly.

State and federal laws aided the capture of fugitive slaves and required nonslaveholders to support the slave system. All white male citizens had a legal duty to ride in patrols to discourage slave movements at night. Ship captains and harbor masters were required to scrutinize the papers of African-Americans who might be attempting to escape bondage. Urban residents who did not supervise their domestic slaves as closely as planters did were subject to criticism for endangering the community. And the South's few manufacturers often felt pressure to substitute slave labor for free labor.

Slavery had a deep effect on southern values precisely because it was the main determinant of wealth in the South. Ownership of slaves guaranteed the labor to produce cotton and other crops on a large scale. Slaves were therefore vital to the acquisition of a fortune. In fact, throughout southern society, slaveholding indicated overall wealth with

Slavery as the Basis of Wealth and Social Standing

remarkable precision. Variations in wealth from county to county corresponded very closely to variations in slaveholding; important economic enterprises not based on slavery were too rare to affect this pattern.

Wealth in slaves also translated into political power: a solid majority of political officeholders were slaveholders, and the most powerful were usually large-scale slaveholders. Lawyers and newspaper editors were sometimes influential, but they did not hold independent positions in the economy or society. Dependent on planters for business and support, they served planters' interests and reflected their outlook.

Slavery also left its imprint on the values of nonslaveholders. Its existence tended to debase free labor; thus nonslaveholders often refused jobs they considered demeaning. Such thinking engendered an aristocratic value system ill-suited to a newly established democracy.

The values of the aristocrat—lineage, privilege, pride, and refinement of person and manner—gained considerable respect among the masses.

Aristocratic Values and Frontier Individualism

Many of those qualities were in short supply, however, in the recently settled portions of the cotton kingdom, where frontier values of courage and self-reliance modified the aristocratic ideal. Independence and defense of one's honor became highly valued traits for planter and frontier farmer alike. Thus, instead of gradually disappearing as it did in the North, the *code duello*, which required men to defend their honor through violence, hung on in the South and gained acceptance throughout the society.

Other aristocratic values of the planter class were less acceptable to the average voter. Planters believed they were better than other people. In their pride, planters expected not only to wield power but to receive special treatment. By the 1850s, some openly rejected the democratic creed, vilifying Thomas Jefferson for his statement that all men were equal.

Such beliefs were never acceptable to the individualistic members of the yeoman class. Independent and proud, yeomen resisted any infringement

of their rights. They believed they were as good as anyone, and many belonged to evangelical faiths that exalted values of simplicity and other-worldliness that were alien to the planters' love of wealth. They were conscious, too, that they lived in a nation in which democratic ideals were gaining strength. Thus occasional conflicts erupted between aristocratic pretensions and democratic zeal.

Yeoman farmers and other citizens resented their underrepresentation in state legislatures, the corruption in government, and the undemocratic control over local government.

Movements for Electoral Reform

In the 1820s and 1830s, the reformers won most of their battles. Voters in more recently settled areas—Alabama, Mississippi, Tennessee, Arkansas, and Texas—adopted white manhood suffrage and other electoral reforms, including popular election of governors, legislative apportionment based on white population only, and locally chosen county government. Only South Carolina and Virginia effectively defended property qualifications for office, legislative malapportionment, appointment of county officials, and selection of the governor by lawmakers. The formal structure of government thus became more democratic than many planters wished.

Slaveowners knew that a more open government structure could permit troubling issues to arise. In Virginia, nonslaveholding westerners raised a basic challenge to the slave system in 1832, a year after the Nat Turner Rebellion. Advocates of gradual abolition forced a two-week legislative debate on slavery, arguing that it was injurious to the state and inherently dangerous. When the House of Delegates finally voted, the motion favoring abolition lost by just 73 to 58. This was the last public debate on slavery in the antebellum South.

Given such tensions, it was perhaps remarkable that slaveholders and nonslaveholders did not experience more overt conflict. Why were class confrontations among whites so infrequent? One of the most important factors was race. The South's racial ideology stressed the superiority of all whites to blacks. Moreover,

Relations Between the Classes

family ties linked some nonslaveholders to wealthy planters. The experience of frontier living, in which all were starting out together, also created a relatively informal, egalitarian atmosphere. And the cotton boom itself relieved tension by bringing opportunity to thousands of whites. The "Old South" was a new and mobile society in which many people rose in status by acquiring land or slaves and far more moved about geographically.

Most important, in their daily lives yeomen and slaveholders were seldom in conflict. Before the Civil War most yeomen were able to pursue unhindered their independent lifestyle. Marginally involved in the market economy, they worked their farms, avoided debt, and lived their lives with little reference to, or interference from, slaveholders. Likewise, slaveholders pursued their goals quite independently of yeomen.

Suppression of dissent also played a significant and increasing role. After 1830 white southerners who criticized the slave system were intimidated, attacked, or legally prosecuted. Intellectuals developed elaborate justifications for slavery, and by the 1850s, the defense of the South's "peculiar institution" had become the top priority of southern politicians.

Still, there were disquieting signs between slaveholders and nonslaveholders. As cotton lands filled up, nonslaveholders saw their opportunities beginning to narrow. The risks of entering cotton production were becoming too great and the cost of slaves too high for many yeomen to rise in society. From 1830 to 1860 the percentage of white southern families holding slaves declined steadily from 36 to 25 percent. At the same time, the monetary gap between the classes was widening. By 1860, the average slaveholder was almost fourteen times as rich as the average nonslaveholder.

Hardening of Class Lines

Urban artisans and mechanics felt the pinch acutely. Their numbers were few and their place in society was hardly recognized. Moreover, they faced stiff competition from urban slaves, whose masters wanted to hire them out to practice trades. White workers demanded that economic competition from slaves be forbidden, but slaveowners would not tolerate interference with their property and their income. The angry protests of white workers, however, resulted in harsh restrictions on *free* African-American workers and craftsmen.

Pre–Civil War politics reflected these tensions. Anticipating the prospect of a war to defend slavery, slaveowners expressed growing fear about the loyalty of nonslaveholders. Schemes to widen the ownership of slaves were discussed, including reopening the African slave trade. In North Carolina, a prolonged and increasingly bitter controversy erupted over the combination of high taxes on land and low taxes on slaves, and a class-conscious nonslaveholder named Hinton R. Helper denounced the slave system in *The Impending Crisis*, published in New York in 1857. Discerning planters knew that such fiery controversies could easily erupt in every southern state.

But for the moment slaveowners stood secure. They occupied from 50 to 85 percent of the seats in state legislatures and a similarly high percentage of the South's congressional seats. They had established their point of view in all the other major social institutions, too. Professors who criticized slavery had been dismissed from colleges and universities; schoolbooks that contained "unsound" ideas had been replaced. And almost all the Methodist and Baptist clergy had given up preaching against slavery. In fact, except for a few obscure persons of conscience, southern clergy had become slavery's most vocal defenders.

 ## Conclusion

The South of the early to mid-1800s was a diverse society that embraced a variety of elements and differing viewpoints, but the coercive influence of slavery was increasingly pressing the region into a single mold. Powerful groups dependent on slavery worked tirelessly to promote unity and eradicate dissent. The potential for conflict persisted, but few southerners saw it. Instead, they saw a system that seemed to be stable, with threats to the status quo under control. The static appearance of the slave South contrasted sharply with the dynamic market forces in the North, where industrialism was rapidly changing society.

Suggestions for Further Reading

Southern Society

Bradley G. Bond, *Political Culture in the Nineteenth-Century South* (1995); William J. Cooper, *The South and the Politics of Slavery, 1828–1856* (1978); Clement Eaton, *Freedom of Thought in the Old South* (1940); William W. Freehling, *Prelude to Civil War* (1965); Eugene D. Genovese, *The Political Economy of Slavery* (1965); Peter Kolchin, *Unfree Labor: American Slavery and Russian Serfdom* (1987); Donald G. Mathews, *Religion in the Old South* (1977); James Hebron Moore, *The Emergence of the Cotton Kingdom in the Old Southwest: Mississippi, 1770–1860* (1987); Frederick Law Olmsted, *The Slave States*, ed. Harvey Wish (1959); Charles S. Sydnor, *The Development of Southern Sectionalism, 1819–1848* (1948); Larry E. Tise, *Proslavery* (1987); Ralph A. Wooster, *The People in Power* (1969); Gavin Wright, *The Political Economy of the Cotton South* (1978); Bertram Wyatt-Brown, *Southern Honor* (1982).

Slaveholders and Nonslaveholders

Bennet H. Barrow, *Plantation Life in the Florida Parishes of Louisiana, as Reflected in the Diary of Bennet H. Barrow*, ed. Edwin Adams Davis (1943); Ira Berlin, *Slaves Without Masters* (1974); Joan E. Cashin, *A Family Venture* (1991); Bill Cecil-Fronsman, *The Common Whites* (1992); Everett Dick, *The Dixie Frontier* (1948); Paul D. Escott, ed., *North Carolina Yeoman* (1996); Drew Faust, *James Henry Hammond and the Old South* (1982); John Inscoe, *Mountain Masters* (1989); Michael P. Johnson and James L. Roark, *Black Masters* (1984); Robert E. May, *John A. Quitman* (1985); Stephanie McCurry, *Masters of Small Worlds* (1995); Robert Manson Myers, ed., *The Children of Pride* (1972); James Oakes, *The Ruling Race* (1982); Frank L. Owsley, *Plain Folk of the Old South* (1949); Loren

Schweninger, *Black Property Owners in the South, 1790–1915* (1990).

Southern Women

Carol Bleser, ed., *Tokens of Affection* (1995); Victoria Bynum, *Unruly Women* (1992); Jane Turner Censer, *North Carolina Planters and Their Children, 1800–1860* (1984); Elizabeth Fox-Genovese, *Within the Plantation Household* (1988); Jean E. Friedman, *The Enclosed Garden* (1985); Harriet Jacobs, *Incidents in the Life of a Slave Girl*, ed. Jean Fagan Yellin (1987); Frances Anne Kemble, *Journal of a Residence on a Georgia Plantation in 1838–1839* (1863); Suzanne Lebsock, *Free Women of Petersburg* (1984); Sally McMillen, *Motherhood in the Old South* (1990); Patricia Morton, ed., *Discovering the Women in Slavery* (1995); Mary D. Robertson, ed., *Lucy Breckinridge of Grove Hill* (1979); Deborah G. White, *Ar'n't I a Woman?* (1985).

Conditions of Slavery

Kenneth F. Kiple and Virginia H. Kiple, "Black Tongue and Black Men," *Journal of Southern History* 43 (August 1977): 411–428; Peter Kolcin, *American Slavery, 1619–1877* (1993); Richard G. Lowe and Randolph B. Campbell, "The Slave Breeding Hypothesis," *Journal of Southern History* 42 (August 1976): 400–412; Todd L. Savitt, *Medicine and Slavery* (1978); Kenneth M. Stampp, *The Peculiar Institution* (1956); Robert S. Starobin, *Industrial Slavery in the Old South* (1970).

Slave Culture and Resistance

John W. Blassingame, *The Slave Community* (1979); Judith Wragg Chase, *Afro-American Art and Craft* (1971); Douglas Egerton, *Gabriel's Rebellion* (1993); Dena J. Epstein, *Sinful Tunes and Spirituals* (1977); Paul D. Escott, *Slavery Remembered: A Record of Twentieth-Century Slave Narratives* (1979); Eric Foner, ed., *Nat Turner* (1971); Eugene D. Genovese, *Roll, Jordan, Roll* (1974); Herbert G. Gutman, *The Black Family in Slavery and Freedom, 1750–1925* (1976); Lawrence W. Levine, *Black Culture and Black Consciousness* (1977); Robert S. Starobin, *Denmark Vesey* (1970); Sterling Stuckey, *Slave Culture* (1987).

12

The American Social
Landscape
1800–1860

"I hope that things will get better," Anna Maria Klinger wrote from New York to her family in Germany in March 1849. "For it's always like that, no one really likes it at first, and especially if you are so lonely and forlorn in a foreign land like I am, no friends or relatives around." Twenty-eight-year-old Anna Maria had crossed the Atlantic among strangers. Her religious faith kept her going. "The dear Lord is my shield and refuge," she wrote home.

Anna Maria was the first in her immediate family to emigrate. Soon after arriving in New York, she found work as a domestic servant at $4 a month, and she also met her future husband, Franz Schano, a deserter from the Bavarian army. Over the next decade she and Schano brought five of her siblings to New York: Babett, Gottlieb, Katharina, Daniel, and Rosina.

Finding work could be difficult—Franz, a stonecutter, was unemployed for a time—but teenagers like Babett and Katharina could always get jobs as servants. Babett, who now called herself Barbara, found work and repaid her sister for her fare to America. But within a year of Barbara's arrival, she became pregnant. She gave birth to a son, but the father refused to marry her. He did, however, provide a cash settlement of $80.

Anna Maria, assisted by Franz, guided the family, keeping them together by sheer force of will. But the siblings' lives eventually diverged. In 1855 Anna Maria and Franz moved to Albany, New York, where Franz died of consumption five years later. Within thirteen months, Anna Maria married Adam Plantz, a Prussian-born blacksmith; he too died of consumption, only five weeks after the wedding. Anna Maria now had a son and a stepson to support. She feared losing her home, but she had been left enough money to prosper. As Anna Maria became more preoccupied with providing for her son and stepson, her brother Gottlieb took over the role of head of the family.

Through Gottlieb, the Klinger siblings stayed in touch for most of their lives. Gottlieb and his brother, Daniel, settled in Albany near Anna Maria and rode the roller coaster of the economy, prospering in good times, unemployed in hard times. Barbara moved to Indiana where she married, became a widow, remarried, and raised seven "Christian children" on her farm. Eventually, the family lost touch with two of their sisters. After Katharina, a widow, married a prosperous New York grocer, they no longer heard from her. They also lost contact with Rosina, who had moved to Canada. Years later they heard she was living again in New York and had "a whole brood of children" with her tinsmith husband.

The Klingers represented both the old values of traditional culture and the new values of the market system. Anna Maria worked hard, saved money, and found success in Albany. Barbara lived a hard-scrabble life and was an unwed mother before eventually finding peace in a German-American rural community 700 miles from New York. Katharina worked hard but spent most of her income on herself; her siblings complained of her selfishness. Even after years in the United States, the Klinger siblings were only partially Americanized. They always lived in German neighborhoods, and they socialized almost exclusively with family and fellow immigrants.

The Klinger family's experiences were similar to those of millions of other Americans. From the 1830s through the 1850s, millions of immigrants arrived on America's shores, and hundreds of thousands of native-born Americans moved from farm to town and from town to city. The populations of the largest cities numbered in the hundreds of thousands and were highly diverse ethnically, religiously, and racially. Within large cities and in the countryside, whole districts became enclaves of ethnic groups.

What it meant to be an American had changed. European immigrants, slaves, free people of color, and Native Americans had cultural traditions different from those of the American colonial past. New cultural patterns flourished. Economic opportunity, the market economy, and expansionism energized Americans. In the nation's cities, both wealth and poverty reached extremes unknown in agrarian America. As in the past, Americans sought community in their neighborhoods, not in the nation, but ethnic, racial, and religious differences were greater than ever before. Farm families attempted to maintain cohesive, rural villages while utopians and groups like the Mormons sought to create self-governing communal havens.

Family life was changing too. With the growth of commerce and industry, the home began to lose its function as a workplace and center of leisure. Cities took over some of the traditional family's educational role, and consumer items and leisure became commodities to be purchased. Families shrank in size, and more people lived outside family units.

Many Americans were uncomfortable with the new direction of American life. Antipathy toward immigrants was common among native-born Americans, who feared competition for jobs. Riots and violence became commonplace in cities. Free African-Americans fought their second-class status, and Indians tried unsuccessfully to prevent their forced removal to lands west of the Mississippi River. In a society growing ever more diverse and complex, conflict became common.

The United States remained a predominantly agricultural country, but economic and social traditions were yielding to the influence of the market economy, urban growth, and immigration. Clearly, an industrializing, urbanizing, and pluralist society was emerging before the Civil War.

 ## Country Life

Rural life changed significantly in the first half of the nineteenth century. Within a generation many western settlements became sources rather than

• *Important Events* •

1821	Horseracing legalized in New York State
1823	Catharine and Mary Beecher establish Hartford Female Seminary
1824	President Monroe proposes removal of Indians west of the Mississippi
1830	Joseph Smith founds Mormon Church Congress passes Indian Removal Act
1830s–50s	Urban riots commonplace
1831	Cherokees turn to courts to defend treaty rights in *Cherokee Nation* v. *Georgia*
1831–32	Alexis de Tocqueville travels across America: his observations form the basis for *Democracy in America*
1831–38	Indian tribes resettled in the West
1832	Chief Justice Marshall declares the Cherokee nation to be a distinct political community in *Worcester* v. *Georgia*, but the ruling is never enforced

1835	Arkansas passes first women's property law
1835–42	Seminoles resist removal in Second Seminole War
1837	Boston employs paid policemen
1837–48	Horace Mann heads the Massachusetts Board of Education
1841–47	Brook Farm combines spirituality, work, and play in a utopian rural community
1842	Knickerbocker baseball club formed
1845	Start of the Irish potato famine
1846–47	Mormon trek to the Great Salt Lake
1847–57	Peak period of immigration before the Civil War
1848	Abortive revolutions in German states
1868	Louisa May Alcott publishes *Little Women*

destinations of migrants. The villages of western New York State had lured the sons and daughters of New England in the first two decades of the century; after the mid-1820s, New York sent its young people to new lands in the Midwest. Later, Ohio and Michigan towns and farms would watch their young people move farther west. Their counterparts in the Upper South went to Illinois and Ohio, and those farther south settled the Gulf states.

Government policy fostered farm life. The acquisition of Louisiana in 1803 and later annexations of Florida, Texas, and Oregon all increased available agricultural land. The internal improvements—harbors, roads, canals, and railroads—following the War of 1812 were a boost to agriculture. Indian removal opened additional land for farmers, and the inexpensive sale of public lands facilitated new farm settlements. State govern-

ments promoted agricultural education through schools and county and state fairs.

The farm village, with its churches, post office, general store, and tavern, was the center of rural life. But rural social life was not limited to trips to

Farm Communities

the village; families gathered on one another's farms to accomplish as a community what they could not manage individually. Barn-raisings regularly brought people together. A farmer and an itinerant carpenter prepared the site before the neighbors arrived to help on the appointed day. After the walls were put together and raised into position, they attached a roof. Then everyone celebrated with a communal meal and sang, danced, and played games. Similar gatherings took place at harvest time and on special occasions.

People had active social lives. Men met frequently at general stores, weekly markets, and taverns, and they hunted and fished together. Some women also attended market. More typically, they met at after-church dinners, prayer and Bible-study groups, sewing and corn-husking bees, and quilting parties. These were occasions to exchange experiences, thoughts, and spiritual support, and to swap letters, books, and news.

Traditional country bees had their town counterparts. Fredrika Bremer, a Swedish visitor to the United States, described a sewing bee in Cambridge, Massachusetts, in 1849, at which neighborhood women made clothes for "a family who had lost all their clothing by fire." Yet town bees were not the all-day family affairs of the countryside, and those who moved from farm to town often missed the country gatherings.

Americans were increasingly conscious of such changes. Some turned to rural utopian experiments in an effort to find an antidote to the market economy and the untamed growth of large urban communities and an opportunity to restore tradition and social cohesion. In the religious ferment of the Second Great Awakening (see pages 150, 152), many people reacted favorably to new religious communities, whatever their philosophy. Virtually all of the utopian experiments offered a cooperative rather than a competitive environment; communal living; and nontraditional work, family, and gender roles.

The Shakers, named for the way they danced at worship services, undertook one of the earliest utopian experiments. Founder Ann Lee imported
Shakers
this offshoot of the Quakers to America in 1774. While living in England, she had experienced a vision foretelling Jesus's second coming in America and urging her to go there. The Shakers believed that the end of the world was near and that sin entered the world through sexual intercourse. They considered existing churches too worldly and viewed the Shaker community as the instrument of salvation.

In 1787 the Shakers "gathered in" at New Lebanon, New York, to live and work communally. At its peak, between 1820 and 1860, the sect had about six thousand members in twenty settlements in eight states; it was the largest and most permanent of the utopian experiments. Though economically conservative, the Shakers were social radicals. They abolished individual families, practiced celibacy, and gave women new prospects for spiritual leadership. During its period of greatest growth, the Shaker ministry was headed by a woman, Lucy Wright. The sect's practice of celibacy, however, led inevitably to its demise.

The most successful communitarian group was the Church of Jesus Christ of Latter-day Saints, known as the Mormons. Joseph Smith, a young farmer in western New York, reported in 1827 that he had been visited by the angel Moroni, who gave
Mormon Community of Saints
him a set of gold plates engraved with divine revelation. Smith published his revelations as the *Book of Mormon* and organized a church in western New York in 1830. Violence stalked the Mormons; angry mobs drove them from Ohio, Illinois, and Missouri. People objected most to the Mormon belief in continuous revelation and the practice of allowing men to have several wives at once. Finally in 1846 and 1847 the Mormons found a home in the Great Salt Lake valley. There, under Brigham Young, they established a patriarchal community of Saints based on communal republicanism. They achieved not only religious freedom but political self-government.

In Utah the Mormons distributed agricultural land according to family size. An extensive irrigation system, constructed by men who contributed their labor in proportion to the quantity of land they received and the amount of water they expected to use, transformed the arid valley into a rich oasis. As the colony developed, the church elders gained control of water, trade, industry, and even the territorial government of Utah.

Not all utopian communities were founded by religious sects. In 1825 Robert Owen, a wealthy Scottish industrialist, attempted to establish a socialist utopia in New Harmony, Indiana. According to his plan, its nine hundred members were to exchange their labor for goods at a communal store. Handicrafts (hat and boot making) flourished at New Harmony, but a textile mill—which was to have been the economic base of the community—failed after Owen gave it to the community to run. By 1827 Owen's experiment had ended.

The impact of the Brook Farm cooperative in West Roxbury, Massachusetts, was longer lasting. Inspired by transcendentalism—the belief that the physical world is secondary to the spiritual realm—Brook Farm's members rejected materialism in favor of rural communalism, combining spirituality, manual labor, intellectual life, and play.

Brook Farm

Though short-lived (1841–1847), Brook Farm played a significant role in the flowering of a national literature. During these years Nathaniel Hawthorne, Ralph Waldo Emerson, and Margaret Fuller, editor of the *Dial* (the leading transcendentalist journal), joined Henry David Thoreau, James Fenimore Cooper, Herman Melville, and others in creating what is known today as the American Renaissance. In its philosophical intensity and moral idealism, their work was both distinctively American and an outgrowth of the European romantic movement. Their themes were universal, their settings and character American.

The essayist Ralph Waldo Emerson was the prime mover of the American Renaissance and a pillar of the transcendental movement. "We live in succession, in division, in parts, in particles," Emerson wrote. "We see the world piece by piece, as the sun, the moon, the animal, the tree; but the whole, of which these are the shining parts, is the soul." Intuitive experience of God is attainable, insisted Emerson, because "the Highest dwells" within every individual in the form of the "Over-soul."

Utopian communities can be seen as attempts to recapture the cohesiveness of traditional agricultural and artisan life in reaction to the competitive pressures of the market economy and urbanization. Utopians, like the Separatists of seventeenth-century New England (see page 37), sought to begin anew in their own colonies.

 ## City Life

The transportation revolution and the expansion of commerce and manufacturing enabled the urban population to grow geometrically between 1800 and 1860, especially in the North. The nation's population increased during this period from 5 million to 31 million. Meanwhile, settlement spread westward, and small rural settlements became towns. In 1800 the nation had only 33 towns with 2,500 or more people and only 3 with more than 25,000. By 1860, 392 towns exceeded 2,500 residents, 35 had more than 25,000, and 9 exceeded 100,000 (see maps, page 218).

New York City became the nation's foremost metropolis, growing from 60,500 in 1800 to over 800,000 in 1860. Although contemporary depictions of New York appear almost pastoral, the city's energy and aromas of sweat, horse dung, and garbage would make twentieth-century cities seem sanitized in comparison. An immigrant port city, mostly Irish and German by the 1850s, New York City teemed with people.

New York City

New York City literally had burst its boundaries in the 1820s. Up to that time New Yorkers regarded the city as a village because they could walk from one end to the other in an hour. Until the 1820s nearly all New Yorkers lived within two miles of City Hall. Mass transit, however, made it possible for cities to expand. Horse-drawn buses appeared in New York in 1827, and the Harlem Railroad, completed in 1832, ran the length of Manhattan. By the 1850s all big cities had horse-drawn streetcars.

By modern standards early-nineteenth-century cities were disorderly, unsafe, and unhealthy. Expansion occurred so rapidly that few cities could handle the problems it brought. For example, migrants from rural areas were accustomed to relieving themselves outside and throwing refuse in any vacant area. In the city, such waste smelled, spread disease, and polluted water. New York City partially solved the problem in the 1840s by abandoning wells in favor of reservoir water piped into

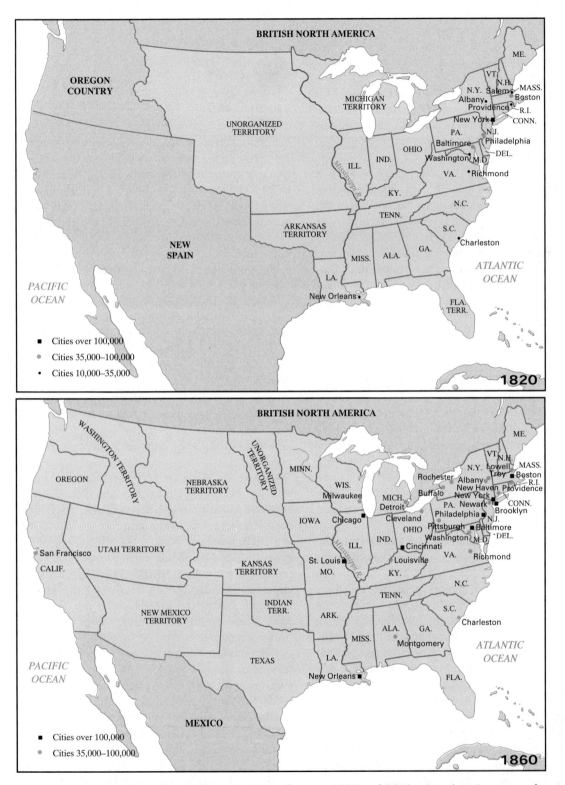

Major American Cities in 1820 and 1860 *Between 1820 and 1860 many Americans moved to cities with the result that the number of communities with populations exceeding 100,000 increased from one to nine.*

buildings and outdoor fountains. In some districts, scavengers and refuse collectors carted away garbage and human waste, but in much of the city it just rotted on the ground. Only one-quarter of New York City's streets had sewers by 1857.

New York and other cities lacked adequate taxing power to provide services for all. The best the city could do was to assess the adjoining property for the cost of sewers, street paving, and water mains. Thus the spread of new services and basic sanitation depended on residents' ability to pay. As a result, those most in need of services typically got them last. Another solution was to charter private companies to sell basic services. This plan worked well with gas service. Baltimore first chartered a private gas company in 1816. By mid-century every major city was lit by a private gas supplier. The private sector, however, failed to supply the water the cities needed. Private firms lacked the capital to build adequate systems, and they laid pipe only in commercial and well-to-do residential areas, ignoring the poor. As population grew, city governments had to take over.

A singular urban innovation was the creation of public education. In 1800 there were no public schools outside New England; by 1860 every state offered some public education.

Horace Mann and Public Schools

Massachusetts led in expansion of schooling under Horace Mann, secretary of the state board of education from 1837 to 1848. Massachusetts established a minimum school term of six months, formalized the training of teachers, and emphasized secular subjects and applied skills rather than religious training. In the process, schoolteaching became a woman's profession.

Mann's preaching on behalf of free, state-sponsored education changed schooling throughout the nation. "If we do not prepare children to become good citizens," he argued, "if we do not develop their capacities, . . . then our republic must go down to destruction." The abolition of ignorance, according to Mann, would end misery, crime, and suffering. He advocated educating all children. Mann and others were responding to the changes wrought by the market economy, urbanization, and immigration. The typical city dweller was a newcomer, whether from abroad or from the country. Public schools would take the children of strangers and give them shared values.

Free public schools altered the scope of education. Schooling previously had focused on literacy, religious training, and discipline. Under Mann's leadership, the school curriculum became more secular and appropriate for the future clerks, farmers, and workers of America. Students studied geography, American history, arithmetic, and science. Moral education was retained, but direct religious indoctrination was dropped.

The basic texts—*McGuffey's Eclectic Readers*—used Protestant Scripture to teach children to accept their position in society. A good child, McGuffey taught, does not envy the rich: "It is God who makes some poor and others rich." Although Catholics, immigrants, blacks, and working-class people sought to have local control over their own schools, the state legislatures established secular statewide standards under Protestant educators. Catholics in New York responded by building their own educational system over the next half-century.

Urban population concentration, growth in commerce, and shifts in work altered patterns of leisure. In rural society, both leisure and work activities often took place at home. But in cities, new dedicated spaces—streets, theaters, sports fields—constituted a social sphere where people could come together away from home. Through the sale of admission tickets or membership in various types of associations, leisure became a commodity to be purchased. Even in cities, some traditional activities continued as they had since colonial times. Fishing remained popular, men played games of skill and strength in taverns, and churches continued to serve as centers for leisure.

Leisure

But Americans also read more. Thanks to the expansion of public education, the vast majority of native-born white Americans were literate by the 1850s. For the reading public, fiction and autobiographies competed with religious tracts as popular literature. Susanna Rowson's 1794 novel *Charlotte Temple*, which offered a critique of women's dependence on men, and the powerful attack on slavery in the *Narrative of the Life of Frederick Douglass*, *an American Slave, Written by Himself* (1845) were widely read. Many popular novels, written by women, often for women, were set in the home and upheld Christian values. Some might also be read as a challenge to prevailing values. Rowson's *Charlotte Temple*, for instance, never depicts the heroine performing domestic chores. And, although Susan Warners' *The Wide, Wide, Wide World* (1850), Nathaniel Hawthorne's *The House of the Seven Gables* (1851), and Fanny Fern's *Ruth Hall* (1855) did not challenge women's traditional domestic roles, they gave women a special moral bearing. In describing in positive terms community and republican virtue, they implicitly criticized the growing market economy.

Theater was a central institution in American life. A theater was often the second public building constructed in a town—after a church. Large cities boasted two or more theaters catering to different classes. Some plays, however, cut across class lines. Shakespeare was performed so often and appreciated so widely that even illiterate theatergoers knew passages of his blank verse well. In the 1840s, musical and dramatic presentations took on a more professional tone; newly popular minstrel shows and traveling circuses offered carefully rehearsed routines.

Sports, like theater, increasingly involved city dwellers as spectators. Horseracing, boxing, walking races, and, in the 1850s, baseball began to attract large urban male crowds.

Sports

After New York State legalized horseracing in 1821, a track opened in Queens County across the East River from New York City. Two years later a single race drew fifty thousand people. By 1849 boxing was so popular that a round-by-round account of a Maryland boxing match was telegraphed throughout the East.

Increasingly, urban sports and recreation became more formal and a commodity to be purchased. A group of Wall Street office workers formed the Knickerbocker Club in 1842, and in 1845 they drew up rules for the game of baseball. Their rules continue to serve as the basis for the game. Entertainment became a commodity: one had to buy a ticket to go to the theater, the circus, the racetrack, or the ballpark.

Ironically, public leisure soon developed a private dimension. Exclusive private associations arose to provide space and occasions for leisure. Some represented class divisions, as the growing middle and upper classes distanced themselves from the crowds and rowdiness of public events. Others were created by ethnic, racial, or religious groups seeking to socialize and share and preserve similar traditions. Thus the Irish had their Hibernian Society; African-Americans, their chapters of the Prince Hall Masons; and Jewish men, B'nai B'rith. Women, too, organized their own associations, ranging from social organizations to benevolent societies.

As cities grew, their populations seemed increasingly fragmented. Finding people similar to oneself required more of a conscious effort. The new associations served as a bulwark against the cultures of other groups—immigrants, migrants, blacks, and artisans. Middle- and upper-class New Yorkers who felt alienated in the city of their birth founded exclusive clubs. Some joined the Masonic order, which offered everything the bustling city did not: an elaborate hierarchy, an orderly code of deference between ranks, harmony, and shared values. Members knew each other. Americans of all sorts—native- and foreign-born, black and white—also formed churches and church-associated clubs. Associations brought together like people, but they also formalized divisions between different groups.

City Culture

Cities offered not only diversity but also anonymity. People interested in same-sex liaisons, though often publicly ostracized, could find each other in the city and live together in urban boarding houses.

Even a youth culture developed on the Bowery in the 1840s. Older New Yorkers feared the "Bowery boys and gals," whose ostentatious dress and behavior seemed threatening to them. A Bowery Boy's swaggering gait, especially when he had a girlfriend on his arm, frightened many in the middle class. Equally disturbing to old New Yorkers were the young working women who promenaded on the Bowery. Unlike more genteel ladies who wore modest veils or bonnets, Bowery "gals" drew attention to themselves with bright, outlandish clothes and ornate hats.

Most working people spent much of their lives outdoors; they worked in the streets as laborers, shopped in open markets, and paraded on special occasions. Young people courted, neighbors argued, and ethnic groups defended their turf on the streets. Increasingly, urban streets served as a political arena as crowds formed to listen to speakers, to parade, and sometimes to form mobs.

In the 1830s, riots became commonplace as professionals and merchants, craftsmen and laborers vented their rage against political and economic rivals. "Gentlemen of

Urban Riots

property and standing," unnerved by antislavery proponents, sacked abolitionist and antislavery organizations, even murdering newspaper editor Elijah Lovejoy in Alton, Illinois, in 1837. In the 1840s, "respectable" citizens drove the Mormons out of Illinois and Missouri. In Philadelphia native-born workers attacked Irish weavers in 1828, and whites and blacks fought on the docks in 1834 and 1835. Philadelphia's riots came to a head in 1844 when mostly Protestant skilled workers attacked Irish Catholics. Smaller cities, too, became battlegrounds as nativist riots peaked in the 1850s. By 1840 more than 125 people had died in urban riots, and by 1860 fatalities exceeded 1,000.

As public disorder spread, Boston hired uniformed policemen in 1837 to supplement its part-time watchmen and constables, and New York in 1845 established an entirely uniformed force. Nonetheless, middle-class men and women did not venture out alone at night, and even during the day they avoided certain districts. Ironically, in the midst of so much noise, crime, and conflict, the rich built lavish residences.

 ## Extremes of Wealth

The French nobleman Alexis de Tocqueville (in 1831 and 1832) and other observers characterized the United States before the Civil War as primarily a place of equality and opportunity. Tocqueville attributed American equality—the relative fluidity

of the social order—to Americans' mobility and restlessness. Geographic mobility offered people a chance to start anew, regardless of where they came from or who they were. Wealth and family mattered little; a person could be known by deeds alone. According to the conventional wisdom, anyone could advance by working hard and saving money.

Others disagreed with this egalitarian view of American life. Among those who traced the rise of a new aristocracy based on wealth and power was

"If Not an Aristocracy"

New York Sun publisher Moses Yale Beach. Author of twelve editions of *Wealth and Biography of the Wealthy Citizens of New York City*, Beach listed 750 New Yorkers with assets of $100,000 or more in 1845. John Jacob Astor led the list of nineteen millionaires with a fortune of $25 million. Ten years later, Beach reported more than a thousand New Yorkers worth $100,000, among them twenty-eight millionaires. Tocqueville himself, sensitive to conflicting trends in American life, had described the new industrial wealth. The rich and well educated "come forward to exploit industries," Tocqueville wrote, and become "more and more like the administrators of a huge empire. . . . What is this if not an aristocracy?"

Wealth throughout the United States was becoming concentrated in the hands of a relatively small number of people. In New York City between 1828 and 1845, the richest 4 percent of the city's population increased their holdings from an estimated 63 percent to 80 percent of all individual wealth. By 1860 the top 5 percent of American families owned more than half of the nation's wealth.

Meanwhile, a cloud of uncertainty hovered over working men and women. Many feared hard times and resented the competition of immigrant and slave labor. They dreaded

Urban Poverty

the insecurities and indignities of poverty, chronic illness, disability, old age, widowhood, and desertion. Women feared having to raise a family without a spouse. And they had good reason: few women could find a job that paid sufficient money to support a family.

Poverty dogged the urban working class. Newly arrived immigrants, indigent free blacks, the working poor, and thieves, beggars, and prostitutes eked out a living in urban slums. New York City's Five Points exemplified the worst of urban life. The predominantly Irish and black neighborhood lacked running water and sewers. More than a thousand people crowded into the Old Brewery there, which had been converted to housing. Throughout the city, houses built for two families often held four; tenements built for six families held twelve.

In a world apart from Five Points lived the upper-class elite society of Philip Hone, one-time mayor of New York. Hone's diary, meticulously kept from 1826 until his death in 1851, records the activities of an American aristocrat. On February 28, 1840, for instance, Hone attended a masked ball at the Fifth Avenue mansion of Henry Breevoort, Jr., and Laura Carson Breevoort. The ball began at the fashionable hour of 10 P.M., and the five hundred ladies and gentlemen who filled the mansion wore costumes adorned with ermine and gold. At one time or another similar parties were held in Boston, Philadelphia, Baltimore, and Charleston.

The Urban Elite

Much of this new wealth was inherited. For every John Jacob Astor who made millions in the western fur trade, ten others used money they had inherited or married as a steppingstone to additional wealth. Many of the wealthiest New Yorkers bore the names of the colonial commercial elite: Beekman, Breevoort, Roosevelt, Van Rensselaer, and Whitney. These rich New Yorkers were not idle; they worked at increasing their fortunes and power by investing in the transportation, commercial, and manufacturing revolutions. Wealth begat wealth, and marriage cemented family ties.

Meanwhile, a distinct middle class became part of the urban scene, and the growth and specialization of trade rapidly increased its numbers. Middle-class families enjoyed the new consumer items: wool carpeting, fine wallpaper, rooms full of furniture, and indoor toilets. They filled the family pews in

The Middle Class

church on Sunday, and their children pursued the available educational opportunities. They were as distant from Philip Hone's world as they were from the working class and the poor.

Women, Families, and the Domestic Ideal

Marriage and family life were the central adult experiences of most women. Families were dominated by husbands and fathers who by English common law had control over the family. Men owned their wives' personal property and all wealth produced by family members. They also were the legal guardians of the children. Married women, however, began to make modest gains in property and spousal rights from the 1830s on. Arkansas in 1835 passed the first women's property law, and by 1860 sixteen more states had followed suit. In those states, women, including wives, could own and convey property: when a wife inherited, earned, or acquired property, it was hers, not her husband's; and she could write a will. In the 1830s states began to liberalize divorce, adding cruelty and desertion as grounds for divorce. Women who had the financial means could leave unhappy marriages.

As the urban workplace and home became separate, men worked for wages outside the home. Rural sons worked on their family farms, worked for hire on other people's farms, or sought wage work in towns. New England daughters left farms to work in textile mills. In the 1840s the new urban department stores hired young women as clerks and cash runners. Many women worked for a time as teachers. Paid employment typically represented a brief stage in women's lives before they left their parental households and entered their marital households.

Supporting Families

Working-class women—the poor, widows, and free blacks—worked to support themselves and their families. Leaving their parental homes as early as age twelve, they earned wages most of their lives, with only short respites for bearing and rearing children. But unlike men and New England farm daughters, most of these women did not work in the new shops and factories. Instead, they worked as domestic servants and as laundresses, seamstresses, and cooks. Few of these occupations enabled them to support themselves or a family at a respectable level.

Most women's work continued to be unpaid labor in the home. As the urban family lost its role in the production of goods, household upkeep and child rearing claimed women's full-time attention. Religion, morality, domestic arts, and music and literature filled the void left by the decline in the economic functions of the family; these realms came to be known as woman's sphere. A woman who achieved mastery in these areas lived up to the middle-class ideal of the cult of domesticity.

Middle-class Americans idealized the family as a moral institution characterized by selflessness and cooperation. Women were idealized in turn as the embodiment of self-sacrificing republicanism. The role of the mother was to strengthen the nation by rearing her children in a spiritual and virtuous environment unlike the world outside the home. The world of work—the market economy—was seen as an arena of conflict increasingly identified with men and dominated by base self-interest. In a rapidly changing world, the family represented stability and traditional values.

The domestic ideal restricted the range of paying jobs available to middle-class women. Most paid work was viewed with disapproval, but one occupation was considered consonant with the genteel female role: teaching. In 1823 the Beecher sisters, Catharine and Mary, established the Hartford Female Seminary and offered history and science in addition to the traditional women's curriculum of domestic arts and religion. A decade later Catharine Beecher successfully campaigned for teacher-training schools for women. By the 1850s teaching was regarded as a woman's vocation, and most urban teachers were unmarried women who were paid about half the salary of male teachers.

Meanwhile, family size was shrinking. In 1800 American women bore an average of six to seven children; by 1860 the figure had dropped to five.

Decline in Family Size

A number of factors reduced family size. Small families were viewed as increasingly desirable in an economy in which the family was a unit of consumption rather than production. Children in smaller families would have greater opportunities: parents could give them more attention, better education, and more financial help. Also, contemporary marriage manuals stressed that too many births had a harmful effect on a woman's health. Thus, evidence suggests, many wives and husbands made deliberate decisions to limit the size of families.

Limiting Families

How did men and women limit their families in the early nineteenth century? Average age at marriage rose, thus shortening the period of potential childbearing. Women also bore their last child at a younger age, suggesting that family planning was becoming more common. Many couples used traditional forms of birth control, such as coitus interruptus (withdrawal of the male before completion of the sexual act) and breastfeeding, which makes some women temporarily infertile. Some couples used the rhythm method—attempting to confine intercourse to a woman's infertile periods—but awareness of the "safe period" was uncertain. Others used cheap rubber condoms, which became available in the 1850s. For those desiring to terminate a pregnancy, surgical abortions became common after 1830. By 1860, however, twenty states restricted or outlawed abortions.

Significantly, the birth-control methods that women themselves controlled—the rhythm method, abstinence, and abortion—became increasingly common. The new emphasis on domesticity encouraged women's autonomy in the home and by extension gave them greater control over their own bodies. Women ruled the household, including the bedroom, with refinement and purity.

Urban life and the market economy offered independence and new roles for women. Single women departed from the centuries-old pattern in

Single Men and Women

which a woman moved from her father's household to the household of her husband. Louisa May Alcott (1832–1888), the author of *Little Women* (1868), sought independence and financial security for herself. Alcott worked as a seamstress, governess, teacher, and housemaid before her writing brought her success. "I think I shall come out right, and prove that . . . I *can* support myself," she wrote her father in 1856. "I like the independent feeling; and though not an easy life, it is a free one, and I enjoy it."

Louisa May Alcott foreswore marriage. She and other single women pursued careers and a life defined by female relationships. Given the difficulty women had finding work that would allow them to be self-supporting, they undertook independence at great risk. Nonetheless, the proportion of single women in the population increased significantly in the first three quarters of the nineteenth century. Independent white women, in sum, were taking advantage of new opportunities offered by the market economy and urban expansion.

Immigrant Lives in America

The 5 million immigrants who came to the United States between 1820 and 1860 outnumbered the entire population of the country recorded in the first census in 1790. They came from every continent, though the vast majority were European (see figure). During the peak period of pre–Civil War immigration, from 1847 through 1857, 3.3 million immigrants entered the United States; 1.3 million were from Ireland and 1.1 million from the German states. By 1860, 15 percent of the white population was foreign-born.

This massive migration had been set in motion decades earlier. At the turn of the nineteenth century, the Napoleonic wars had given rise to one of the greatest population shifts in history; it was ultimately to last more than a century. War, revolution, famine, religious persecution, and the lure of industrialization led many Europeans to leave home. Most Asian immigrants came from southern China to work in heavy construction. The United States beckoned, offering economic opportunity and religious freedom.

Both private firms and governments recruited European immigrants. Midwestern and western states lured potential settlers to promote economic growth. In the 1850s, for instance, Wisconsin appointed a commissioner of emigration, who advertised the state's advantages in European newspapers. Wisconsin also opened an office in New York and hired European agents to compete with other states and with firms like the Illinois Central Railroad in recruiting immigrants.

Promotion of Immigration

Large construction projects and mines needed strong young laborers. Textile mills and cities attracted young women workers. Europeans' awareness of the United States grew as employers, states, and shipping companies advertised opportunities across the Atlantic. The price of a ticket on the regularly scheduled sailing ships crossing the ocean after 1848 was within easy reach of millions of Europeans.

So they came, enduring the hardships of travel and of living in a strange land. The average transatlantic crossing took six weeks; in bad weather it could take three months. Disease spread unchecked among people packed together like cattle in steerage. More than seventeen thousand immigrants, mostly Irish, died from "ship fever" in 1847. On arrival, immigrants became fair game for the con artists and swindlers who worked the docks. Boarding-house and employment agents tried to lure them from their chosen destinations. In response, New York State established Castle Garden as an immigrant center in 1855. There, at the tip of Manhattan Island, the major port for European entry, immigrants were somewhat sheltered from fraud. Authorized transportation companies maintained offices in the large rotunda and assisted new arrivals with their travel plans.

Most immigrants gravitated toward cities. Many stayed in New York City itself; of its 623,000 inhabitants, 52 percent were immigrants in 1855. Boston also took on a European tone; throughout

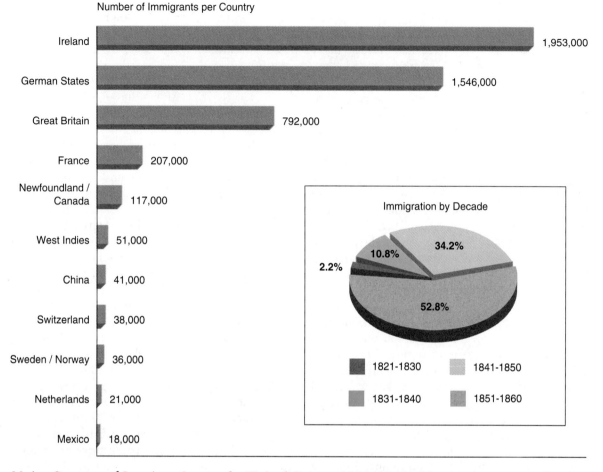

Major Sources of Immigration to the United States, 1821–1860

Number of Immigrants per Country

Country	Number
Ireland	1,953,000
German States	1,546,000
Great Britain	792,000
France	207,000
Newfoundland / Canada	117,000
West Indies	51,000
China	41,000
Switzerland	38,000
Sweden / Norway	36,000
Netherlands	21,000
Mexico	18,000

Immigration by Decade

2.2% — 1821-1830
10.8% — 1831-1840
52.8% — 1841-1850
34.2% — 1851-1860

Major Sources of Immigration to the United States, 1821–1860 *Most immigrants came from two areas: Great Britain, of which Ireland was a part, and the German states. These two areas sent more immigrants between 1820 and 1860 than the inhabitants of the United States enumerated at the first census in 1790. By 1860, 15 percent of the white population was of foreign birth.*   Source: U.S. Bureau of the Census, *Historical Statistics of the United States, Colonial Times to 1970,* 2 parts (Washington, D.C., 1975), Part 1, pp. 206, 208.

the 1850s the city was about 35 percent foreign-born, of whom more than two-thirds were Irish. Southern cities also had sizable immigrant populations. In 1860 New Orleans was 44 percent foreign-born, Savannah 33 percent, and the western city of St. Louis 61 percent. On the West Coast, San Francisco had a foreign-born majority.

Some immigrants settled in rural areas. German, Dutch, and Scandinavian farmers, in particular, gravitated toward the Midwest. Greater percentages of Scandinavians and Netherlanders took up farming than did other nationalities; both groups came mostly as religious dissenters and migrated in family units. The Dutch who founded colonies in Michigan and Wisconsin, for instance, had seceded from the official Reformed Church of the Netherlands, fleeing persecution in their native land to establish new and more pious communities such as Holland and Zeeland in Michigan.

Not all immigrants found success in the United States; hundreds of thousands returned to their homelands disappointed. Before the potato blight hit Ireland, American recruiters had lured many Irish to swing picks and shovels on American canals and railroads and to work in construction. Among them was Michael Gaugin, who for thirteen years had been an assistant engineer in the construction of a Dublin canal. Gaugin was attracted to the United States by the promise that "he should soon become a wealthy man." The Dublin agent for a New York firm convinced him to quit his job, which included a house and an acre of ground, and emigrate. Gaugin had the misfortune to land in New York City during the financial panic of 1837, and within two months of arriving he was a pauper.

Immigrant Disenchantment

Such experiences did not deter other Irish men and women from coming to the United States. Ireland was the most densely populated place in Europe and among the most impoverished. From 1815 on, small harvests prompted a steady stream of Irish to emigrate to America. Then in 1845 and 1846 potatoes—Ireland's staple food—rotted in the fields. From 1845 to 1849, death from starvation, malnutrition, and typhus spread. In all, 1 million died and about 1.5 million fled, two-thirds of them to the United States. Ireland's major export was its people. Indeed, with only two exceptions, the Irish constituted the largest group of immigrants annually between 1820 and 1854.

Irish Immigrants

The new Irish immigrants differed greatly from those who had left Ireland to settle in the American colonies. The Protestant Scots-Irish who predominated in the eighteenth century (see page 68) had journeyed from one part of the British Empire to another. The nineteenth-century Irish immigrants to America, however, were mostly Roman Catholic, and they moved from a British colony to an independent republic. Moreover, most of the new immigrants from Ireland were young, female, and from rural counties.

In American cities Irish immigrants met anti-Catholic sentiment. "No Irish Need Apply" signs were common. During the colonial period, white Protestants had feared "popery" as a system of tyranny and had discriminated against the few Catholics in America. After the Revolution anti-Catholicism receded, but in the 1830s it reappeared wherever the Irish did.

Anti-Catholicism

The native-born who embraced anti-Catholicism were motivated largely by anxiety. They feared the Roman Catholic Church, unskilled Irish workers, and the urban slums inhabited by the Irish (among others). They blamed every social problem—from immorality and alcoholism to poverty and economic upheaval—on immigrant Irish Catholics. And the new public schools, with their Protestant bias, represented another form of attack on Irish Catholics. Friction increased as Irish-American men fought back by entering politics.

In 1854, Germans replaced the Irish as the largest group of new arrivals. Potato blight also had prompted emigration from the German states in the 1840s; other hardships added to the steady stream. Many people came from regions where small landholdings made it hard to eke out a living. Others were craftsmen displaced by the industrial revolution. These refugees were joined by middle-class Germans—a whole generation of liberals and freethinkers who emigrated to the United States after the abortive revolutions of 1848.

German Immigrants

It is not easy to characterize German-Americans. Germans settled everywhere in the United States. In the South they were peddlers and merchants; in the North and West they worked as farmers, urban laborers, and businessmen. Their tendency to migrate as families and groups helped them maintain German culture and institutions. Many settled in small towns and rural areas where they could preserve their local and regional identities. In larger cities immigrants from the same German states tended to cluster together. Their presence transformed the tone and culture of cities like Cincinnati and Milwaukee.

Native-born Americans accepted German immigrants more readily than they accepted the Irish, stereotyping Germans as hard working, self-reliant, and intelligent. Many believed that Germans would "harmonize" better with American culture. Nevertheless, Germans, too, encountered hostility. A significant number of German immigrants were Jewish, and they experienced anti-Semitism. Many German immigrants were Catholic, and their Sabbath traditions differed from those of Protestants. On Sundays urban German families customarily gathered at beer gardens to eat and drink beer, to dance, sing, and listen to band music, and sometimes to play cards. Protestants were outraged by this behavior, which they believed to be a violation of the Lord's day.

Some Hispanic groups became "immigrants" to the United States without actually moving. Mexican inhabitants of northern Mexico—present-day New Mexico and California—

Hispanics were unhappy because under the Mexican constitution of 1824 they lived in Mexican territory, not states. Similarly Texas was part of the Mexican state of Coahuila. Lack of political autonomy made Mexicans in these areas unhappy, and many welcomed the events that brought them into the United States: the independence and later annexation of Texas, the Mexican War, and the Gadsden Purchase (see pages 254, 258).

In Texas, Anglos and European immigrants seized economic and political power. For instance, in Nueces County, Texas, at the time of the Texas Revolution (1836), Mexicans held all the land; twenty years later, they had lost it all. Moreover, although many Tejanos had fought for Texas's independence, arriving Anglo settlers tended to treat them as inferiors. They became second-class citizens on land where they had lived for generations.

Nonetheless, Tejanos retained their culture. They held fast to Roman Catholic and Hispanic traditions. San Antonio illustrates the persistence of Hispanic culture. The church, free public schools (established in 1827), life-cycle events from baptism to marriage to funerals, and public holidays and celebrations all supported Hispanic Roman Catholic traditions. Thus during the period of Texas independence, from 1836 to 1845, and after Texas statehood in 1845, Hispanic identity continued even in the face of a loss of political power.

In California—unlike Texas, New Mexico, and Arizona—Hispanic culture quickly gave way to American and European culture. Californios, the Mexican population, numbered 10,000 in 1848, or two-thirds of the non-Indian population. By the end of the century the Hispanic population was 15,000 out of 1.5 million, and Hispanic culture was only a remnant, though it would be reestablished by Mexican immigrants in the twentieth century.

For immigrants, becoming part of American society involved conflict, but once in the United States they claimed their right to a fair economic and political share. Native Americans, however, like the Hispanics in the Southwest, had to defend what they regarded as prior rights. Their lands, their religions, and their ways of life came under constant attack.

 Indian Resistance and Removal

The Constitution gave the United States government responsibility for dealing with Indians. For better or worse, there had to be a federal Indian policy. From the Indians' point of view, it usually was for the worse. United States territorial expansion took place at the Indians' expense. The result was removal of the great Native American nations to lands west of the Mississippi. While the population of other groups was increasing by leaps and bounds, the Indian population was shrinking. In the 1830s alone, more than half of the Pawnees, Omahas, Otoes, Missouris, and Kansas died.

Like the colonial powers in North America, the United States government treated Native American groups as sovereign nations, until Congress ended the practice in 1871. Agreements between a given Indian nation and the United States were signed, sealed, and ratified like any other international pact. In practice, however, Native American sovereignty was a fiction. Treaty making was essentially a tactic that the American government used to acquire Indian land. Instead of bargains struck by two equal nations, treaties often were agreements imposed by the victor on the vanquished. Old treaties gave way to new ones requiring Native Americans to cede their traditional holdings in return for different lands in the West.

The War of 1812 snuffed out whatever realistic hopes eastern Indian leaders had of resisting American expansion by warfare. After the war, Indian armed resistance persisted, but it only delayed the inevitable. The Shawnee chiefs Prophet and Tecumseh led the most significant movement against the United States (see page 165), but Prophet failed to sustain the movement after Tecumseh's death.

The experiences of Prophet and other Shawnees were typical of the wanderings of an uprooted people. After giving up 17 million acres in Ohio in the 1795 Treaty of Greenville (see page 131), the

Shawnees

Shawnees scattered to Indiana and eastern Missouri. After the War of 1812, Prophet's Indiana group withdrew to Canada. In 1822 other Shawnees sought Mexican protection and moved from Missouri to present-day eastern Texas. As the United States government began promoting removal to Kansas, Prophet returned from Canada to lead a group to the new Shawnee lands in eastern Kansas in 1825. When Missouri achieved statehood in 1821, Shawnees living there were also forced to move to Kansas, where they were joined in the 1830s by Shawnees removed from Ohio and others expelled from Texas. By 1854 Kansas was open to white settlement, and the Shawnees had to cede back seven-eighths of their land there—1.4 million acres.

Removal had a profound impact on all Shawnees. The men had to give up their traditional role as providers; their methods of hunting and their knowledge of woodland animals were useless on the prairies of Kansas. As grain became the tribe's dietary staple, Shawnee women played a greater role as providers, supplemented by government aid under treaty provisions. Remarkably, the Shawnees preserved their language and culture in the face of these drastic changes.

In the 1820s Indians in Ohio, southern Indiana and Illinois, southwestern Michigan, most of Missouri, central Alabama, and southern Mississippi were pressured to cede their lands. They gave up nearly 200 million acres for pennies an acre. The federal Indian agency system, which monopolized trade with Indians and paid out the rations, supplies, and annuities they received in exchange for abandoning their land, made Indians dependent on government payments. Dependency made them pliant in treaty negotiations and furthered assimilation by bringing them into the market system.

Federal Indian Policy

Ever since the early days of European colonization, the assimilation of Native Americans through education and Christianity had been an explicit goal of whites. It took on renewed urgency as the United States expanded westward. In 1819, in response to missionary lobbying, Congress appropriated $10,000 annually for "civilization of the tribes adjoining the frontier settlements." Protestant missionaries administered the "civilizing fund" and established mission schools. These new boarding schools substituted English for native languages and taught agriculture alongside the Christian Gospel. To settlers eyeing Indian land, assimilation through education seemed too slow a process. At any given time there were never more than fifteen hundred students in all the schools; at that rate it would take centuries to assimilate all the Indians. Thus wherever Indians lived, illegal settlers disrupted their lives. Though obligated to protect the integrity of treaty lands, the federal government did so only halfheartedly. With government supporting westward expansion, legitimate Indian claims had to give way to the advance of white civilization.

In the 1820s it became apparent that not economic dependency, education, or Christianity could persuade Indians to cede more land to meet the demands of expansionists. Attention focused on southeastern tribes—Cherokees, Creeks, Choctaws, Chickasaws, and Seminoles—because much of their land remained intact after the War of 1812 and because they aggressively resisted white encroachment.

In his last annual message to Congress in late 1824, President James Monroe suggested that all

Indians be moved beyond the Mississippi River. Three days later he sent a special message to Congress proposing removal. The proposal was aimed at the Cherokees, Creeks, Choctaws, and Chickasaws, and they unanimously rejected it.

Indian Removal to the West

Pressure from Georgia had prompted Monroe's policy. Cherokees and Creeks lived in northwestern Georgia, and in the 1820s the state accused the federal government of not fulfilling its 1802 promise to remove the Indians in return for the state's renunciation of its claim to western lands. Georgia was satisfied neither by Monroe's removal messages nor by further cessions by the Creeks. In 1826, under federal pressure, the Creek nation ceded all but a small strip of its Georgia acreage. But Georgia still was not satisfied. Only the removal of the Georgia Creeks to the West could resolve the conflict between Georgia and the federal government.

If civilizing Indians was the American goal, no tribe met that test better than the Cherokees. Between 1819 and 1829 the tribe became economically self-sufficient and politically self-governing: during this Cherokee renaissance the twelve to fifteen thousand adult Cherokees came to think of themselves as a nation, not a collection of villages. Between 1820 and 1823 the Cherokees created a formal government with a bicameral legislature, a court system, and a salaried bureaucracy. In 1827 they adopted a written constitution, modeled after that of the United States. Cherokee land laws, however, differed from United States law. The tribe as a whole owned all Cherokee land, and complex provisions covered land sales (forbidden to outsiders). Nonetheless, the Cherokees assimilated American cultural patterns. By 1833 they held fifteen hundred black slaves whose legal status was the same as that of slaves held by southern whites. Moreover, missionaries had been so successful that the Cherokees could be considered a Christian community.

Cherokees

Although the Cherokees developed a political system similar to that of an American state, they failed to win respect or acceptance from southerners. Georgia pressed them to sell the 7,200 square miles of land they held in the state. Most Cherokees, however, preferred to stay where they were. Impatient with their refusals to negotiate cession, Georgia annulled the Cherokee's constitution, extended the state's sovereignty over them, and ordered their lands seized.

Backed by sympathetic whites but not by the new president, Andrew Jackson, the Cherokees under Chief John Ross turned to the federal courts to defend their treaty with the United States and prevent Georgia's seizure of their land. In *Cherokee Nation* v. *Georgia* (1831), Chief Justice John Marshall ruled that under the federal Constitution an Indian tribe was neither a foreign nation nor a state and therefore had no standing in federal courts. Nonetheless, said Marshall, the Indians had an unquestionable right to their lands; they could lose title only by voluntarily giving it up. A year later, in *Worcester* v. *Georgia*, Marshall defined the Cherokee position more clearly. The Indian nation was, he declared, a distinct political community in which "the laws of Georgia can have no force" and into which Georgians could not enter without permission or treaty privilege. Georgia refused to comply.

Cherokee Nation v. Georgia

President Andrew Jackson refused to interfere because the case involved a state action. Keen to open up new lands for settlement, Jackson was determined to remove the Cherokees. In the Removal Act of 1830 Congress provided Jackson with the funds he needed to negotiate new treaties and resettle the resistant tribes west of the Mississippi (see map).

The Choctaws were the first to go; they made the forced journey from Mississippi and Alabama to the West in the winter of 1831 and 1832. Other tribes soon joined the forced march. The Creeks in Alabama resisted removal until 1836, when the army pushed them westward. A year later the Chickasaws followed.

Trail of Tears

Having fought removal in the courts, the Cherokees were divided. Some believed that further resistance was hopeless and accepted removal as the only chance to preserve their civilization. The leaders of this minority agreed in 1835 to

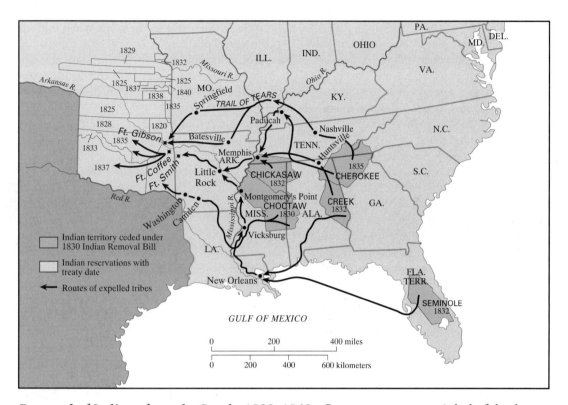

Removal of Indians from the South, 1820–1840   *Over a twenty-year period, the federal government and southern states forced Indians to exchange their traditional homes for western land. Some tribal groups remained in the South, but most settled in the alien western environment.*   Source: Acknowledgment is due to Martin Gilbert and George Weidenfeld and Nicholson Limited for permission to reproduce this map taken from *American History Atlas.*

exchange their southern home for western land. But when the time for evacuation came in 1838, most Cherokees refused to move. President Martin Van Buren sent federal troops to round them up. About twenty thousand Cherokees were evicted, held in detention camps, and marched to Indian Territory in present-day Oklahoma under military escort. Nearly one-quarter of them died of disease and exhaustion on what came to be known as the Trail of Tears.

When the forced march to the West ended, the Indians had traded about 100 million acres east of the Mississippi for 32 million acres west of the river plus $68 million. Only a few scattered remnants, among them the Seminoles in Florida and the Cherokees in the southern Appalachian Mountains, remained in the East and South.

The impact of the forced removal on Indian life was disastrous. In the West they encountered an alien environment, and, lacking traditional ties with the new land, few felt at peace with it. The animals and plants they found were unfamiliar. No longer able to live off the land, many Native Americans became dependent on government payments for survival. Removal also brought new internal conflicts. The Cherokees in particular struggled over their tribal government. Moreover, conflicts arose among migrating Indian groups from the South and East and Indians already living in the West, as they were forced to share land and scarce resources.

Some waged war to avoid removal. In the Southeast a small band of Seminoles successfully resisted and remained in Florida. Some Seminole

The Trail of Tears *by contemporary Cherokee artist Brummet Echohawk. About twenty thousand Cherokees were evicted in 1838–1839, and about one quarter of them died on the forced march to present-day Oklahoma.*   Thomas G. Krease Institute

Second Seminole War

leaders agreed in the 1832 Treaty of Payne's Landing to relocate to the West within three years. A minority under Osceola, a charismatic leader, refused to vacate their homes and fought the pro-treaty group. When federal troops were sent to impose removal in 1835, Osceola waged a fierce guerrilla war against them. Though Osceola—who was captured under a white flag of truce—died in an army prison in 1838, the Seminoles continued the war. Finally, in 1842 the United States abandoned the removal effort. Most of Osceola's followers agreed to move west to Indian Territory in 1858, but many Seminoles remained in the Florida Everglades, proud of having resisted conquest.

A complex set of attitudes drove whites to remove Indians forcibly. Most wanted land and had little or no respect for the Indians' rights or culture. Others were aware of the injustice but believed that Indians inevitably had to give way to white settlement. Some, like John Quincy Adams, believed the only way to preserve Indian civilization was to separate Indians and white settlers physically. Others hoped to "civilize" Indians and assimilate them gradually into American culture. Whatever the source of white attitudes, it resulted in the devastation of Native American cultures.

 Free People of Color

Free people of color also struggled for recognition and legal rights. Like Indians, they were involuntary participants in American society. Unlike Indians, however, they wished to partake fully in American life.

On the surface, the Bill of Rights seemed to protect free African-Americans. The Fifth Amendment specified that "no person shall . . . be deprived of life, liberty, or property, without due process of law." But eighteenth-century political theory had defined the republic as being for whites only (see page 126), and early federal legislation reflected this exclusionist thinking: naturalization, for example, was limited to white aliens in 1790. After the admission of Missouri in 1821, every new state admitted until the Civil War banned blacks from voting. When the Oregon and New Mexico Territories were organized, public land grants were reserved for whites.

African-Americans in the North were second-class citizens. Newly admitted states barred free blacks or required them to post bonds ranging from $500 to $1,000 to guarantee their good conduct. Only in Massachusetts, New Hampshire, Vermont, and Maine could blacks vote on an equal basis with whites throughout the pre–Civil War period. In 1842 African-Americans gained the right to vote in Rhode Island, but they had lost it earlier in Pennsylvania and Connecticut. Only Massachusetts permitted blacks to serve on juries. Four midwestern states and California did not allow African-Americans to testify against whites. In Oregon, blacks could not own real estate, make contracts, or sue in court. Throughout the North white social custom excluded or segregated free people of color. Hotels and restaurants barred them, as did most theaters and white churches. Discrimination in hiring existed everywhere. Countinghouses, retail stores, and factories refused to hire black men except as janitors and handymen. New England mills hired only whites.

Exclusion and Segregation of African-Americans

Free people of color faced severe legal and social barriers in the southern slave states. Whites viewed their presence as subversive. Fearing free African-Americans, southern states restricted their presence. After the Nat Turner Rebellion in 1831, the position of free blacks deteriorated throughout the South. Within five years nearly every southern state prohibited the freeing of slaves without legislative or court approval, and by the 1850s Texas, Mississippi, and Georgia had banned manumission altogether.

Southern Free Blacks

In essence, the legal status of southern free people of color was somewhere between slave and free. Southern states adopted elaborate "black codes" to curtail the activities and opportunities of African-Americans, who provided most of the South's skilled labor. Virginia and Georgia denied work to black riverboat captains and pilots. Some states forbade blacks to assemble without a license. Some prohibited them from learning to read and write. In the late 1830s, the codes were tightened,

and free people of color moved northward even though northern states discouraged the migration.

In spite of these obstacles, the free African-American population rose from 108,000 in 1800 to almost 500,000 in 1860. Nearly half lived in the North, some in rural settlements but far more in cities like Philadelphia, New York, and Cincinnati. Baltimore had the largest community, but sizable free black populations formed in New Orleans, Charleston, and Mobile.

The ranks of free people of color were constantly increased by ex-slaves. Some, like Frederick Douglass and Harriet Tubman, were fugitives. Tubman, a slave in Maryland, escaped to Philadelphia in 1849 when it was rumored that she would be sold out of the state. Within the next two years she returned twice to free her two children, her sister, her mother, and her brother and his family. Some slaves received freedom in owners' wills when masters sought, at death, to rid themselves of the stain of owning slaves. Other owners freed elderly slaves after a lifetime of service rather than support them in old age.

Free people of color forged cohesive communities and created autonomous institutions within them. Churches became the center of community life, and pastors became political leaders. Church buildings functioned as town halls, and they housed schools, political forums and conventions, protest meetings, and benevolent and self-help associations.

African-American Communities

Like European immigrants, free people of color sought to assist members of their own community. But they had a greater burden. Although their taxes supported white schools, for instance, they had to raise additional funds to establish African-American schools because their children were excluded from the new public schools. A network of voluntary associations—self-help societies, female benevolent societies, and literary and social clubs—became the hallmark of their communities. Most of these organizations were political as well as social.

In the majority of states where free blacks were excluded from the ballot, they formed

How do historians know about African-American political thought and activity in the early nineteenth century? One important source is the published minutes of black conventions, first held in 1830. Free people of color held at least eleven national conventions and about forty state conventions prior to the Civil War. The first national convention, a special meeting in Philadelphia in September 1830, was presided over by Bishop Richard Allen, founder of the African Methodist Episcopal Church. The delegates agreed to explore a settlement in Canada as a haven for free people of color and fugitive slaves. They also called for pursuing "all legal means for the speedy elevation of ourselves and brethren to the scale and standing of men." Less than a year later, delegates to the "First Annual Meeting of the People of Colour" condemned the persecution of African-Americans, appealed for funds to support their work, called for the establishment of a college for poor blacks, and stressed the importance of education. They also were consciously building a movement of annual conventions. The report of this convention, and subsequent convention minutes and addresses, demonstrate the involvement of African-Americans in the reforms of the times and the importance they placed on education and equality of opportunity. At conventions held in the 1850s nationalism took hold among African-Americans.

The convention movement was democratic. Most communities elected their delegates to the national conventions at public meetings or at local and state conventions. Although the minutes reveal a wide range of opinion within black communities, there was agreement about the abolition of slavery, immediate emancipation, and equal rights for free people of color. Minutes of the Proceedings of the Natural Negro Convention, 1831.

CONSTITUTION

OF THE

AMERICAN SOCIETY

OF

FREE PERSONS OF COLOUR,

FOR IMPROVING THEIR CONDITION IN THE UNITED STATES;
FOR PURCHASING LANDS; AND FOR THE ESTABLISH-
MENT OF A SETTLEMENT IN UPPER CANADA.

ALSO

THE PROCEEDINGS OF THE CONVENTION,

WITH THEIR

ADDRESS

TO

THE FREE PERSONS OF COLOUR

IN THE

UNITED STATES.

PHILADELPHIA:
PRINTED BY J. W. ALLEN, NO 26, STRAWBERRY-ST.
1831.

protest organizations to fight for equal rights. Among the early efforts to organize for self-defense was the Negro Convention movement. From 1830 to 1835, and irregularly thereafter, free blacks held national conventions with delegates drawn from city and state organizations. Under the leadership of the small black middle class, which included the Philadelphia sail manufacturer James Forten and the orator Reverend Henry Highland Garnet, the convention movement served as a forum to attack slavery and agitate for equal rights. Militant new black newspapers joined the struggle.

The mood of free blacks began to shift in the late 1840s and 1850s. Many were frustrated by the failure of the abolitionist movement and angered by the passage of the Fugitive Slave Act of 1850 (see page 263). Some were swept up in a wave of black nationalism that stressed racial solidarity, self-help, and a growing interest in Africa. Before this time, efforts to send African-Americans "back to Africa" had originated with whites seeking to rid the United States of blacks. But in the 1850s blacks held emigrationist conventions of their own under the leadership of abolitionists Henry Bibb and Martin Delany. With the coming of the Civil War, the status of blacks would move onto the national political agenda, and African-Americans would focus on their position at home.

Black Nationalism

Conclusion

The American people and communities were far more diverse and turbulent in 1860 than they had been in 1800. The market economy, immigration, and the growth of cities had altered the way people lived and worked. Inequality increased everywhere, and competition and insecurity produced resentment and conflict. Cities housed both ostentatious wealth and abject poverty, and disorder became commonplace. Many Americans felt as if they were strangers to each other.

In the midst of these changes, middle-class families sought to insulate their homes from the competition of the market economy. Many women found fulfillment in the domestic ideal: others found it confining. Middle-class urban women became associated with nurturing roles, first in homes and schools, then in churches and reform societies. Working-class women had more modest goals: escaping poverty and winning respect. Most Americans found some comfort in religion.

Famine and religious and political oppression in Europe propelled millions of people across the Atlantic. They were drawn to the United States by the promise of jobs and tolerance. Most found the going rough. In the process of adapting, immigrants changed the profile of the American people. Competition and diversity in turn bred intolerance. Native Americans, free African-Americans, and Hispanics were made to feel like aliens in their own land.

Conflict became increasingly commonplace in the public arena. The manifestations of division in America were many: utopian communities, conflicts over public space, backlash against immigrants, urban riots, black protest, and Indian resistance. Conflict also took the form of reform movements, which came to characterize American life from the 1820s through the 1850s. Through reform and political action, many Americans sought to harness and control the forces of change. Spurred on by religious revival and individualism, they turned to politics as a collective means of restoring harmony and order. In the process, divisions became even sharper.

Suggestions For Further Reading

Rural and Utopian Communities

Priscilla J. Brewer, *Shaker Communities, Shaker Lives* (1986); David B. Danbom, *Born in the Country: A History of Rural America* (1995); John Mack Faragher, *Sugar Creek: Life on the Illinois Prairie* (1986); Steven Hahn and Jonathan Prude, eds., *The Countryside in the Age of Capitalist Transformation* (1985); Joan M. Jensen, *Loosening the Bonds: Mid-Atlantic Farm Women, 1750–1850* (1986); Sally McMurry, *Families and Farmhouses in Nineteenth Century America: Vernacular Design and Social Change* (1988); Anthony F. C. Wallace, *Rockdale: The Growth of an American Village in the Early Industrial Revolution* (1978); Kenneth H. Winn, *Exiles in a Land of Liberty: Mormons in America, 1830–1846* (1989).

Urban Communities

Stuart M. Blumin, *The Emergence of the Middle Class: Social Experience in the American City, 1760–1900* (1989); Susan G. Davis, *Parades and Power: Street Theater in Nineteenth-Century Philadelphia* (1986); Timothy J. Gilfoyle, *City of Eros: New York City, Prostitution, and the Commercialization of Sex, 1790–1920* (1992); Karen V. Hansen, *A Very Social Time: Crafting Community in Antebellum New England* (1994); Jack Larkin, *The Reshaping of Everyday Life, 1790–1840* (1988); Edward Pessen, *Riches, Class and Power Before the Civil War* (1973); Christine Stansell, *City of Women: Sex and Class in New York, 1789–1860* (1986); Richard B. Stott, *Workers in the Metropolis: Class, Ethnicity, and Youth in Antebellum New York City* (1990); Alexis de Tocqueville, *Democracy in America*, 2 vols. (1835, 1840).

American Families

Virginia K. Bartlett, *Keeping House: Women's Lives in Western Pennsylvania, 1790–1850* (1994); Janet Farrell Brodie, *Contraception and Abortion in Nineteenth-Century America* (1994); Lee Virginia Chambers-Schiller, *Liberty, A Better Husband: Single Women in America: The Generations of 1780–1840* (1984); Nancy F. Cott, *The Bonds of Womanhood: "Woman's Sphere" in New England, 1780–1835* (1977); Joan Hoff, *Law, Gender and Injustice: A Legal History of U.S. Women* (1991); Suzanne Lebsock, *The Free Women of Petersburg: Status and Culture in a Southern Town, 1784–1860* (1984); Mary P. Ryan, *Women in Public: Between Banners and Ballots, 1825–1880* (1990); Mary P. Ryan, *Cradle of the Middle Class: The Family in Oneida County, New York, 1790–1865* (1981); Kathryn Kish Sklar, *Catharine Beecher: A Study in American Domesticity* (1973); Robert V. Wells, *Revolutions in Americans' Lives* (1982); Barbara Welter, "The Cult of True Womanhood, 1820–1860," *American Quarterly* 18 (Summer 1966): 151–174.

Immigrants and Hispanics

Gunther Barth, *Bitter Strength: A History of Chinese in the United States, 1850–1870* (1964); Kathleen Neils Conzen, *Immigrant Milwaukee: 1836–1860* (1976); Hasia R. Diner, *Erin's Daughters in America: Irish Immigrant Women in the Nineteenth Century* (1983); Jay P. Dolan, *The Immigrant Church: New York's Irish and German Catholics, 1815–1865* (1975); David A. Gerber, *The Making of an American Pluralism: Buffalo, New York, 1825–60* (1989); Walter D. Kamphoefner, *The Westfalians: From Germany to Missouri* (1987); Walter D. Kamphoefner et al., eds., *News from the Land of Freedom: German Immigrants Write Home* (1991); Timothy M. Matovina, *Tejano Religion and Ethnicity: San Antonio, 1821–1860* (1995); Kerby A. Miller, *Emigrants and Exiles: Ireland and the Irish Exodus to North America* (1985); Philip Taylor, *The Distant Magnet: European Emigration to the United States of America* (1971).

Native Americans

Robert F. Berkhofer, Jr., *The White Man's Indian* (1978); James W. Covington, *The Seminoles of Florida* (1993); Michael D. Green, *The Politics of Indian Removal: Creek Government and Society in Crisis* (1982); William G. McLoughlin, *Cherokee Renascence in the New Republic* (1986); Francis P. Prucha, *American Indian Policy in the Formative Years* (1967); Ronald N. Satz, *American Indian Policy in the Jacksonian Era* (1975); Anthony F. C. Wallace, *The Long, Bitter Trail: Andrew Jackson and the Indians* (1993); Richard White, *The Roots of Dependency: Subsistence, Environment, and Social Change Among the Choctaws, Pawnees, and Navajos* (1983).

Free People of Color

Ira Berlin, *Slaves Without Masters: The Free Negro in the Antebellum South* (1974); James O. Horton and Lois E. Horton, *In Hope of Liberty: Culture, Community and Protest Among Northern Free Blacks, 1700–1860* (1996); Luther Porter Jackson, *Free Negro Labor and Property Holding in Virginia, 1830–1860* (1942); David M. Katzman, *Before the Ghetto: Black Detroit in the Nineteenth Century* (1973); Rudolph M. Lapp, *Blacks in Gold Rush California* (1977); Leon Litwack, *North of Slavery: The Negro in the Free States, 1790–1860* (1961); Floyd J. Miller, *The Search for a Black Nationality: Black Colonization and Emigration, 1787–1863* (1975).

CHAPTER

13

Reform, Politics, and Expansion
1824–1844

"I proceed, Gentlemen, briefly to call your attention to the *present* state of Insane persons confined within this Commonwealth," Dorothea Dix petitioned the Massachusetts legislature in 1843, "in *cages, closets, stalls, pens! Chained, naked, beaten with rods and lashed into obedience.*"

A year earlier, in a surprise visit to a Newburyport almshouse, Dix had discovered one man residing in a shed whose door opened to the local "dead room" or morgue; the man's only companions were corpses. Shocked, she heard from an attendant about another insane inmate whom no one spoke of: "a woman in a *cellar.*"

She asked to see the woman. The superintendent tried to dissuade her, but Dix pressed on: "If you will not go with me," she said, "give me the keys and I will go alone." They unlocked the doors and entered an underground cell. In the shadows Dix saw "a female apparently wasted to a skeleton, partially wrapped in blankets." When the inmate saw the visitors, she wailed with despair: "Why am I consigned to hell? I have done no crime in my heart; I had friends, why have all forsaken me!—my God! my God! why hast *those* forsaken me?"

What drove Dix in her obsession to explore the ill treatment of the insane was not only her sense of outrage but also a belief in human perfectibility and in the corollary idea that the insane could be treated and cured. Proper humane treatment, Dix argued, could bring them back to the community; they could be healed if they were treated as ill rather than as criminal.

Dix epitomized so much of early- to mid-nineteenth-century reform. She started with a belief in individual self-improvement that led her to advocate collective responsibility, especially on behalf of those dependent on the kindness of others. She was single-minded, expressing little concern for abolition or women's rights. Unlike Susan B. Anthony, Lucretia Mott, or Elizabeth Cady Stanton, Dix never joined the early feminists in agitating for women's political equality. Nonetheless, her obsession with reform took her into politics. In investigating asylums, in petitioning the Massachusetts General Court in 1843, and in lobbying other state legislatures and Congress, she joined other women in moving from reform to politics, and she helped create a new public role for women.

The reform fervor of the 1820s to the 1850s arose in part as a response to the enormous transformation that the United States experienced after the War of 1812. Immigration, internal migration, urbanization, the spread of a market economy, growing inequality, loosening family and community ties, the westward advance of settlement, and territorial expansion all contributed to the remaking of the United States. Many Americans felt they were no longer masters of their own fate and that the changes in society were undermining traditional values.

Religious reformers sought to reimpose order on a society in which economic change and discord had reached a crescendo. Prompted by the evangelical spirit of the Second Great Awakening and convinced of their moral rectitude, they crusaded for individual self-improvement. Many renounced alcohol and gambling. Gradually the personal impulse to reform oneself led to the creation of benevolent and reform societies. Religious ardor drew men and women to reform, in time broadening the political base. Reform soon eclipsed benevolent work and became an instrument for restoring discipline and order in a changing society. Women became prominent in reform, first to improve life for others, then to secure rights and freedom for themselves.

Members of reform organizations eventually turned to politics, viewing it as an instrument of change. The line between social reform and politics was not always clear, however. Temperance, institutional reform, and, most notably, Antimasonry and abolition lured new voters into politics. But opponents of reform were just as concerned with social problems and just as interested in political solutions. What distinguished them from reformers was their skepticism about human perfectibility and their distrust of institutions and the exercise of power, both public and private. To them, government coercion was the greater evil. They sought to reverse, not shape, change.

Two issues in particular served as bridges between reform and politics: the short-lived Antimasonry frenzy and the intense, uncompromising crusade for immediate emancipation. Though Antimasons organized the first third-party movement, abolition eventually overrode all other concerns. No single issue evoked the passion that slavery did. Moreover, territorial expansion in the 1840s and 1850s made slavery politically explosive.

Opponents of religious reform found a champion in Andrew Jackson and a home in the Democratic Party in the late 1820s. Yet the Jacksonians, too, saw themselves as reformers; they sought to foster individualism and restore restraint in the federal government. They opposed special privileges and the Second Bank of the United States. President Jackson believed that a strong federal government restricted individual freedom by favoring one group over another. In response, social reformers rallied around the new Whig Party, which became the vehicle of humanitarian reform. Democrats and Whigs constituted a new party system, characterized by strong organizations, intensely loyal followings, and energetic religious and ethnic competition.

Both parties eagerly promoted expansionism during the prosperous 1840s. Democrats saw the agrarian West as an antidote to urbanization and industrialization; Whigs focused on the new commercial opportunities it offered. Expansion from coast to coast seemed to Americans to be the manifest destiny of the United States.

From Revival to Reform

Religion was probably the prime motivating force behind organized benevolence and reform. Religious revival stimulated by the Second Great Awakening galvanized Protestants, especially women, from the late 1790s to the 1840s. Under its influence, the role of churches and ministers in community life began to change, and Christians in all parts of the country tried to right the wrongs of the world.

Revivals—the lifeblood of evangelical Christianity—won converts to a religion of the heart rather than the head. In 1821 New York lawyer Charles G. Finney, the father of modern revivalism, experienced a soul-shaking conversion that he interpreted as "a retainer from the Lord Jesus Christ to plead his cause." Finney then began taking revival services and three- to four-day camp meetings to towns in western New York. Using everyday language, he preached that "God has made man a moral free agent." In other words, evil was avoidable: Christians were not doomed by original sin, and anyone could achieve salvation.

Second Great Awakening

The Second Great Awakening raised people's hopes for the Second Coming of the Christian messiah and establishment of the Kingdom of God on earth. Revivalists resolved to speed the Second Coming by creating a heaven on earth, marshaling the forces of good and light—reform—to combat the forces of evil and darkness.

Regardless of theology, all revivalists shared a belief in individual self-improvement. Thus the Second Great Awakening bred reform. Evangelical Protestants became missionaries for both religious and secular salvation and helped organize associations to address pressing issues: temperance, education, Sabbath observance, dueling, and (later) antislavery. Collectively these groups constituted a national web of benevolent and moral-reform societies.

Women were the earliest converts to evangelism, and they tended to sustain the Second Great Awakening. Pious middle-class women in Rochester, New York, for instance, responded to Finney's prayer meetings by spreading the word to other women during the day while their husbands were at work. Gradually they brought their families and husbands into church and reform. Women more than men tended to feel personally responsible for counteracting the increasingly secular orientation of the expanding market economy. Many felt guilty for neglecting their religious duties, and the emotionally charged conversion experience returned them to what they believed was the right path.

Role of Women

Beyond conversion, the great influence of the Second Great Awakening was the spread of women's participation in benevolent societies to ameliorate social ills. In cities women responded to the growing inequality, turbulence, and wretched conditions around them. The poverty and vice that accompanied urbanization touched the hearts of women. By 1800 most cities had women's benevolent societies to help needy women and orphans.

Religion and Reform

Both female and male reformers sometimes opposed traditional political leaders. An exposé of prostitution in New York City illustrates the gulf between reform-minded men and women and the political establishment. In response to an 1830 report documenting the prevalence of prostitution in New York City, New York businessmen and politicians united to defend the city's good name against "those base slanders." Reform-minded women, however, moved by the plight of "fallen women" organized to fight prostitution. While male reformers made the prostitutes the target of their zeal, the newly organized Female Moral Reform Society focused on the men who victimized young women, publicizing the names of men who entered brothels in New York City.

The New York–based Female Moral Reform Society led the crusade against prostitution. During the 1830s, the organization expanded its activities, calling itself the American Female Moral Reform Society. By 1840 it had 555 affiliated female societies across the nation. They combated prostitution by focusing on men and by assisting poor women whose economic desperation might lead them to

Important Events

1790s–1840s	Second Great Awakening spreads religious fervor	**1836**	Republic of Texas established after breaking from Mexico
1820s	Reformers in New York and Pennsylvania establish model penitentiaries		Specie Circular ends credit purchase of public lands
			Martin Van Buren elected president
1824	No presidential candidate wins a majority in the electoral college	**1837**	Financial panic ends boom of the 1830s
1825	House of Representatives elects John Quincy Adams president	**1838–39**	United States and Canada mobilize their militias over Maine–New Brunswick border dispute
1826	American Society for the Promotion of Temperance founded	**1839–43**	Hard times spread unemployment and deflation
	Morgan affair is catalyst for Antimasonry movement	**1840**	Whigs win presidency under William Henry Harrison
1828	Protectionist Tariff stirs nullification	**1841**	John Tyler assumes the presidency after Harrison's death
	Andrew Jackson elected president		"Oregon fever" attracts settlers to the Northwest and intensifies expansionism
1830	Webster-Hayne debate explores the nature of the Union		
1830s–40s	Democratic-Whig competition gels in second party system	**1843**	Dorothea Dix petitions Massachusetts legislature regarding deplorable condition of insane asylums
1831	Abolitionist newspaper *The Liberator* begins publication		
	First national Antimason convention	**1844**	James K. Polk elected president
1832	Jackson vetoes rechartering of the Second Bank of the United States	**1848**	Woman's Rights Convention at Seneca Falls, New York, calls for women's suffrage
	Jackson reelected president		
1832–33	South Carolina nullifies the Tariff of 1832, prompting nullification crisis		

turn to prostitution. They also entered the political sphere. In New York State in the 1840s the movement successfully crusaded for criminal sanctions against the men who seduced women into prostitution and against the prostitutes themselves.

As the pace of social change quickened in the 1830s and 1840s, so did religious fervor and reform. In western New York and Ohio, Finney's preaching acted as a catalyst to reform. Western New York experienced such continuous and heated waves of revivalism that it became known as "the burned-over district." The westward movement of people carried the religious ferment into Ohio where revivalist institutions—notably Ohio's Lane Seminary and Oberlin College—sent committed graduates out into the world to spread the gospel of reform. The efforts of those early reformers stirred nonevangelical Protestants, Catholics, and Jews, as well as evangelical Christians, and they became involved in new grassroots political movements. In the late 1830s and 1840s they rallied around the Whig Party in hopes of using government as an instrument of reform.

One of the most successful reform efforts was the campaign against alcohol. American men gathered in public houses, saloons, and rural inns to gossip, talk politics, play cards, escape work and home, and drink. Respectable women did not drink in public, but many regularly tippled alcohol-based patent medicines promoted as cure-alls. Why then did temperance become such a vital issue? And why were women especially active in the movement? Like all nineteenth-century reform, temperance had a strong religious foundation.

Temperance

Evangelicals considered drinking a sin, and forsaking alcohol was part of conversion. The sale of whiskey often involved a Sabbath violation, for workers commonly labored six days a week and spent Sunday at the public house drinking and socializing. Equally important, alcoholism destroyed families. In the early 1840s thousands of ordinary women formed Martha Washington societies to protect families by reforming alcoholics, raising children as teetotalers, and spreading temperance.

As the temperance movement gained momentum, its goal shifted from moderate use of alcohol to voluntary abstinence and finally to prohibition. The American Society for the Promotion of Temperance, organized in 1826 to sign drinkers to a pledge of abstinence, became a pressure group for state prohibition legislation. By the mid-1830s there were five thousand state and local temperance societies, and more than a million people had taken the pledge. As the movement spread, the per capita consumption of alcohol fell from five gallons to less than two gallons in the 1840s. Moreover, a number of northern states followed Maine's lead and outlawed the sale of alcohol except for medicinal purposes.

Temperance Societies

Another aspect of the temperance movement was opposition to gambling. People gambled in taverns, and reformers believed that both drinking and gambling undermined independence and self-reliance. Of special concern in the nineteenth century was the spread of lotteries.

Lotteries were common in colonial times. The Continental Congress tried to raise $1.5 million from a lottery to wage revolutionary war against England. In the early nineteenth century, state and local governments seeking to ease the tax burden used lotteries to raise money for capital improvements. Lotteries, however, became a target of reform, and between 1830 and 1860 every state banned them.

Lotteries

Reformers compared lotteries to slavery and alcohol. Others objected to the abuses inherent in the states' practice of delegating their lottery powers to private sponsors. An 1831 Pennsylvania investigation, for instance, revealed that a state-authorized lottery to raise $27,000 a year for internal improvements had generated enormous profits for the lottery company. From annual sales of $5 million, the state received its $27,000, and the sponsors received $800,000.

The age of reform also brought about the construction of asylums and other institutions to house prisoners, the mentally ill, orphans, delinquent children, and the poor. Such institutions were needed, reformers believed, to shelter victims of society's instability and turbulence. In an environment of order, stability, and discipline, inmates would have an opportunity to become self-reliant and responsible.

Penitentiaries and Asylums

The penitentiary movement exemplified this outlook. In the 1820s New York and Pennsylvania rejected incarceration simply to punish criminals or remove them from society. Believing instead that rehabilitation was possible, the two systems sought to separate criminals from evil societal and individual influences and to expose them to a regimen of order and discipline. Because idleness was believed to be both a symptom and a cause of individual corruption and crime, the clock governed a prisoner's day, and idleness was banished.

Similar approaches were employed in insane asylums, hospitals, and orphanages. By exposing the inhumane treatment of the mentally ill, Dorothea Dix built a national movement. Through her efforts and those of reform societies, twenty-eight of the thirty-three states had public institutions for the mentally ill by 1860.

Antimasonry

More intense though of shorter duration than the asylum movement was the crusade against Freemasonry, a secret middle- and upper-class fraternity that had come to the United States from England in the eighteenth century. Sons of the Enlightenment such as Benjamin Franklin and George Washington were attracted to Masonry, with its emphasis on individual belief in a deity (as opposed to organized religion) and on brotherhood (as opposed to one church). In the early nineteenth century Freemasonry attracted men prominent in commerce and civic affairs.

Opponents of Masonry charged that the order's secrecy was antidemocratic and antirepublican. Evangelicals labeled the order satanic. Antimasons argued that Masonry threatened the family because it excluded women and encouraged men to neglect their families for alcohol and ribald entertainments at Masonic lodges.

The Antimasonry movement arose overnight in the burned-over district of western New York in 1826 and virtually disappeared in the 1830s. Foreshadowing abolitionism, it quickly became a political movement. Antimasonry created the first third-party movement and drew new white voters into politics at a time when male suffrage was being extended. Antimasons sought to liberate society from the grip of what they considered a powerful and antirepublican secret fraternity. The political arena quickly absorbed Antimasonry, and its short life illustrates the close association of politics and reform between the 1820s and the 1840s.

The catalyst for Antimasonry as an organized movement was the Morgan affair. In 1826 William Morgan, a disillusioned Mason, published an exposé of Masonry to which his printer, David Miller, added a scathing attack on the order. Just prior to the book's appearance, a group of Masons abducted Morgan in

Morgan Affair

Canandaigua, New York. It was widely believed that they murdered him.

Events seemed to confirm the Antimasonry crusade's depiction of Masonry as a secret conspiracy. Many officeholders in western New York, especially prosecutors, were Masons, and they appeared to obstruct the investigation of Morgan's abduction. The public pressed for justice, and the series of notorious trials that ensued from 1827 through 1831 led many to suspect a conspiracy. The cover-up became as much of an issue as distrust of Masonry itself, and the

Antimasonic publications, such as this 1831 almanac, made much of the allegedly sinister initiation rites that bound a new member "to keep all Masonic secrets, under the penalty of having his throat cut, his tongue torn out, and his body buried in the ocean." Print collection, Miriam and Ira D. Wallach Division of Art, Prints, and Photographs, New York Public Library.

movement spread from the burned-over district to other states.

As a moral crusade, Antimasonry spilled over into the political arena almost immediately. The issue itself was political, because of the perceived obstruction of justice. Furthermore, Antimasonry attracted the lower and middle classes, pitting them against higher-status Masons and exploiting the general public's distrust and envy of local political leaders.

Unwittingly, the Masons stoked the fires of Antimasonry. By their silence they seemed to condone the murder of Morgan, and by their construction of monumental lodges in Boston and elsewhere they called attention to their affluence and prominence. The conflict aroused a high level of public interest in politics. Wherever religious fervor flared and wherever families were entering the market economy for the first time, Antimasonry flourished.

As Antimasonry won a popular following, it introduced the convention system in place of caucuses for choosing political candidates. In-

Convention System

voking public morality and republican principles, the Antimasons held conventions in 1827 to select candidates to oppose Masons. The next year the conventions supported the National Republican candidate, John Quincy Adams, and opposed Andrew Jackson because he was a Mason. The Antimasons held the first national political convention in Baltimore in 1831, and a year later nominated William Wirt as their presidential candidate. Thus the Antimasons became a rallying point for those opposed to President Andrew Jackson.

By the mid-1830s, Antimasonry had lost momentum as a moral and political movement. A single-issue party, the Antimasons declined along with Freemasonry. Yet the movement left its mark on the politics of the era. As a moral crusade focused on public officeholders, it inspired broad participation in the political process. The Antimasons also changed party organization by pioneering the convention system and stimulating grassroots involvement.

Abolitionism and the Women's Movement

The issue of slavery eventually became so compelling that it consumed all other reforms. Passions became so heated that they threatened the nation itself. Those who advocated immediate emancipation saw slavery as, above all, a moral issue—evidence of the sinfulness of the American nation.

Before the 1830s few whites advocated the abolition of slavery. Some, most notably the Quakers, hoped that moral suasion would convince slaveholders to free their chattels. Others favored gradual abolition coupled with the resettling of former slaves in Africa. In 1816 the American Colonization Society had been founded with this in mind.

African-Americans rejected this gradual approach and demanded an immediate end to slavery. By 1830 more than fifty black abolition-

Black Abolitionists

ist societies assisted fugitive slaves, lobbied for emancipation, exposed the evils of slavery, and reminded the nation that its mission as defined in the Declaration of Independence remained unfulfilled. A free black press helped to spread the word. Black abolitionists Frederick Douglass, Sojourner Truth, and Harriet Tubman joined forces in the 1840s with white reformers in the American Anti-Slavery Society.

In the 1830s a small minority of white reformers, driven by moral urgency, also crusaded for immediate emancipation. The most prominent and uncompromising immedia-

William Lloyd Garrison

tist was William Lloyd Garrison, who demanded "immediate and complete emancipation."

In 1831 Garrison broke with moderate abolitionists and began publishing *The Liberator*, which was to be his major weapon against slavery for thirty-five years. As he declared in the first issue, "I am in earnest—I will not equivocate—I will not excuse—I will not retreat a single inch—*and I will be heard.*" Garrison's staunch refusal to work with anyone who tolerated the delay of emancipation isolated him from other opponents of slavery.

Still, through sheer rhetorical power, Garrison helped to make antislavery a national issue.

It is difficult to differentiate between those who became immediatists and those who did not. Immediatists were often young evangelicals active in benevolent societies in the 1820s; many became ordained ministers or flirted with the ministry as a career; and they had personal contact with free blacks and were sympathetic to African-American rights. They were convinced that slaveholding was a sin. They also shared great moral intensity and were unwilling to compromise their beliefs.

Immediatists

Most benevolent workers and reformers kept their distance from the immediatists. Many regarded the intensity of the immediatist approach as unchristian. They shared with immediatists the view that slavery was a sin but believed in gradual emancipation.

Immediatists' greatest recruitment successes resulted from their defense of their own constitutional and natural rights, not the rights of slaves. Wherever they went, immediatists found their civil rights, especially free speech at risk. Hostile crowds threatened abolitionist speakers and presses. Abolitionist conventions provoked hostility by welcoming blacks and women. Fear and hatred moved proslavery proponents to take to the streets. In 1837 a mob in Alton, Illinois, murdered abolitionist editor Elijah P. Lovejoy. Public outrage at Lovejoy's murder broadened the base of antislavery support in the North. Southern mobs blocked the distribution of abolitionist literature, much of which was printed by the immediatists and their main organizational vehicle, the American Anti-Slavery Society (1831). South Carolina seized such materials from the United States mails and burned it.

Opposition to Abolitionists

The opposition saw danger in abolitionism. At a rally in Boston's Faneuil Hall in 1835 former Federalist Harrison Gray Otis portrayed abolitionists as subversives. The abolitionists, he predicted, would soon turn to politics, causing unforeseeable calamity. "What will become of the union?" Otis asked. Others believed that the immediatists' opposition to sending black people back to Africa undermined the best solution.

Another confrontation focused on the House of Representatives. Abolitionists, exercising their constitutional right to petition Congress, campaigned to abolish slavery and the slave trade in the District of Columbia. The House responded in 1836 by adopting the "gag rule," which automatically tabled abolitionist petitions, effectively preventing debate on them. In a dramatic defense of the right of petition, former president John Quincy Adams, a Massachusetts representative, took to the floor repeatedly to defy the gag rule and in 1844 succeeded in getting it repealed.

Gag Rule

Frustration with the federal government also fed northern support for antislavery. Generally speaking, politicians and government officials sought to avoid the question of slavery. The Missouri Compromise of 1820 had been an effort to make debate on the slave or free status of new states unnecessary (see map, page 253). Censorship of the mails and the gag rule also represented attempts to keep the issue out of the political arena. Yet the more intensely the national leaders, especially Democrats, worked to avoid the matter, the more they hardened the resolve of the antislavery forces.

The unlawful and violent tactics used by opponents of abolition unified the movement by forcing the various factions to work together for mutual defense. Antislavery was not at the outset a unified movement. Its adherents divided over Garrison's emphasis on "moral suasion" versus the more practical political approach of James G. Birney, the Liberty Party's candidate for president in 1844. They also split over support for other reforms, especially the rights of women. And they disagreed about the place of free people of color in American society.

Many women joined local female antislavery societies through churches as part of the network of reform societies. Though some opposed extending benevolent work into the political arena, issues related to abolition and women's rights had that result. Moreover, in abolitionists' circles

Women Abolitionists

How do historians know how the abolitionists, especially women and African-Americans, built their movement? Abolitionists lived open lives. They used newspapers, pamphlets, speeches, and sermons to expose the evils of slavery, to mount a crusade for emancipation, and to build a network of like-minded people. Much of their correspondence and most of their speeches were printed in abolitionist newspapers, such as The Liberator, *published by William Lloyd Garrison.*

Here, twentieth-century African-American artist Jacob Lawrence depicts abolitionist Frederick Douglass lecturing in eastern Massachusetts, describing his life as a slave and telling of the cruelty of the system. In 1841

Douglass became a supporter of Garrison and a contributor to The Liberator, *which appeared from 1831 to 1866. The newspaper printed passionate attacks on slavery, reported on meetings of antislavery societies, and published letters, especially from women and African-American abolitionists. Under the banners "No Union with Slaveholders" and "The United States Constitution is a 'convenant with death, and an agreement with hell,'"* The Liberator *circulated to abolitionists advocating immediate emancipation. The subscription lists that have survived indicate that a majority of its subscribers probably were African-Americans.* Hampton University Museum, Hampton Virginia.

women took an equal role with men. Lydia Maria Child, Maria Chapman, and Lucretia Mott all joined the American Anti-Slavery Society's executive committee. Child edited its official organ, the *National Anti-Slavery Standard*, from 1841 to 1843, and Chapman coedited it from 1844 until 1848. Garrison's *moral* suasion attracted many women be-

cause it gave them a platform from which to oppose slavery. Where *political* power was stressed, women were often excluded because they could not vote.

Opposition to women's prominent public roles in reform movements led some women to reexamine their position in society. In the 1830s Angelina and Sarah Grimké challenged slavery and women's right to speak out. Born into a slaveholding family in South Carolina, both sisters experienced conversion and became Quakers. Concerned about slavery, they found in Garrison's immediatism a home. Yet they were soon attacked for speaking before mixed groups of men and women. This reaction turned the Grimkés' attention from slavery to the women's condition. The two attacked the concept of "subordination to man," insisting that men and women had the "same rights and same duties." Sarah Grimké's *Letters on the Condition of Women and the Equality of the Sexes* (1838) and her sister's *Letters to Catharine E. Beecher* (1838) were the opening volleys in the long war over the legal and social inequality of women.

In July 1848 three hundred women and men reformers gathered at the Woman's Rights Convention at Seneca Falls, New York, to demand po-

Women's Rights

litical, social, and economic equality for women. Led by Elizabeth Cady Stanton, Lucretia Mott, and Lucy Stone, they protested women's legal disabilities—inability to vote, limited property rights—and their social restrictions—exclusion from advanced schooling and from most occupations. Their Declaration of Sentiments was an indictment of the injustices suffered by women, and it launched the women's rights movement. "All men and women are created equal," the declaration proclaimed. If women had the vote, participants argued, they could protect themselves and realize their full potential as moral and spiritual leaders.

Advocates of women's rights were slow to garner support, especially from men. Even within the antislavery movement, a majority declared themselves opposed to women's rights. Still, some men joined the ranks, notably Garrison and Frederick Douglass.

Jacksonianism and Party Politics

In the 1820s the distinction between reform and politics began to erode as reform pushed its way into politics. No less than reformers, politicians sought to control the direction of change in the expanding nation. After a brief flirtation with single-party politics after the War of 1812, the United States entered a period of intense political competition.

The election of 1824, in which John Quincy Adams and Andrew Jackson faced off for the first time, heralded a new, more open political system.

End of the Caucus System

From 1800 through 1820 the system in which a congressional caucus chose Jefferson, Madison, and Monroe as the Republican nominees had worked well. Such a system limited voter involvement in choosing candidates but at first was not an anomaly because in 1800 only five of the sixteen states selected presidential electors by popular vote. (In most cases, state legislatures selected the electors who voted for president.) By 1824, however, eighteen of the twenty-four states chose electors by popular vote.

The Republican caucus in 1824 chose William H. Crawford, secretary of the treasury, as its presidential candidate. But other Republicans, emboldened by the chance to appeal directly to voters, put themselves forward as sectional candidates. Secretary of State John Quincy Adams drew support from New England, and westerners backed Speaker of the House Henry Clay of Kentucky. Secretary of War John C. Calhoun looked to the South for support and hoped to win Pennsylvania as well. The Tennessee legislature nominated Andrew Jackson, a popular military hero whose political views were unknown. Jackson had the most widespread support. By boycotting the caucus and by attacking it as undemocratic, these men and their supporters ended the role of Congress in nominating presidential candidates.

In the four-way presidential election of 1824, Andrew Jackson led in both electoral and popular votes, but no candidate received a majority in the

Election of 1824

electoral college. Adams finished second, and Crawford and Clay trailed far behind. (Calhoun had dropped out of the race before the election.) As required by the Constitution, the House of Representatives, voting by state delegation, one vote to a state, in 1825 selected the next president from among the leaders in electoral votes. Clay, who had received the fewest votes, was dropped. Crawford, a stroke victim, never received serious consideration. The influential Clay—Speaker of the House and leader of the Ohio valley states—backed Adams, who received the votes of thirteen of twenty-four state delegations. Clay then became secretary of state in the Adams administration, the traditional steppingstone to the presidency. With angry Jacksonians denouncing the election's outcome as a "corrupt bargain" that had stolen the office from the front-runner, the Republican Party split. The Adams wing emerged as the National Republicans, and the Jacksonians became the Democratic-Republicans (shortened to Democrats). The Jacksonians immediately began planning for 1828.

After taking the oath of office, Adams proposed a strong nationalist policy incorporating Henry Clay's program of protective tariffs, a national bank, and internal improvements. Adams believed the federal government should take an activist role not only in the economy but also in education, science, and the arts. Brilliant as a secretary of state, Adams was an inept president. He underestimated the lingering effects of the Panic of 1819 and the resulting bitter opposition to a national bank and protective tariffs. Meanwhile, supporters of Andrew Jackson sabotaged Adams's administration at every opportunity.

The 1828 campaign pitted Adams against Jackson in an intensely personal conflict. Principles gave way to mudslinging by both sides. When

Election of 1828

Rachel Jackson died a month after the election, the president-elect attributed his wife's death to the abuse heaped on him in the campaign. Jackson had swamped Adams at the polls, with 56 percent of the popular vote, and he won in the electoral college by 178 to 83 votes. He and his supporters believed that the will of the people had finally been served. Through a lavishly financed coalition of state parties, political leaders, and newspaper editors, a popular movement had elected the president, and an era had ended. The Democratic Party became the first well-organized national political party in the United States. Tightly organized parties would become the hallmark of nineteenth-century American politics.

Nicknamed "Old Hickory" after the toughest of the American hardwoods, Andrew Jackson was a rough-and-tumble, ambitious man. He rose from

Andrew Jackson

humble beginnings to become a wealthy planter and slaveholder and the first American president from the West.

Though given to violent displays of temper, he could charm away the suspicions of those opposed to him. He had an instinct for politics and picked both issues and supporters shrewdly.

Jackson and his Democratic supporters offered a distinct alternative to the strong federal government advocated by John Quincy Adams. The Democrats represented a wide range of views but shared a fundamental commitment to the Jeffersonian concept of an agrarian society. They harkened back to the belief that a strong central government is the enemy of individual liberty, a tyranny to be feared.

Jacksonians feared the concentration of economic and political power. They believed that government intervention in the economy benefited special-interest groups and favored the rich. They sought to restore the independence of the individual—the artisan and the yeoman farmer—by ending federal support of banks and corporations and restricting the use of paper currency, which they distrusted.

Jackson and his supporters also opposed reform as a movement. Reformers eager to turn their programs into legislation were calling for a more activist and interventionist government. But Democrats tended to oppose programs like educational reform and the establishment of public education. They believed, for instance, that public schools restricted individual liberty by interfering with parental responsibility and undermined freedom of religion by replacing church schools. Nor did Jackson share reformers' humanitarian concerns.

Jackson and the Jacksonians considered themselves reformers in a different way. By restraining government and emphasizing individualism, they

President Andrew Jackson is portrayed here on a snuff box, an example of the campaign paraphernalia that were widely sold to partisan Jackson supporters.   David R. and Janice L. Frent.

Jacksonians as Reformers

sought to restore old republican virtues, such as prudence and economy. Jackson sought to encourage self-reliance and to restore the harmony and unity that he saw disrupted by economic and social change.

Like Jefferson, Jackson strengthened the executive branch of government even as he weakened the federal role. Given his popularity and the strength of his personality, this concentration of power in the presidency was perhaps inevitable, but in combining the roles of party leader and chief of state, he increased the centralization of power in the White House. Invoking the principle that rotating officeholders would make government more responsive to the public will, Jackson used the spoils system to appoint loyal Democrats to office. Patronage thus became a means to strengthen party organization and loyalty.

Jackson stressed rejection of elitism and special favors, rotation of officeholders, and belief in popular government. Time and again he declared that sovereignty resided with the people, not with the states or the courts. In this respect Jackson was

a reformer; he returned government to majority rule. Yet it is hard to distinguish between Jackson's belief in himself as the instrument of the people and demagogic arrogance.

Animosity grew year by year among President Jackson's supporters and opponents. Massachusetts senator Daniel Webster feared the men around Jackson; Henry Clay most feared Jackson himself. Rotation in office, they contended, corrupted government. Opponents mocked Jackson as "King Andrew I," charging him with abusing his presidential powers by ignoring the Supreme Court's ruling on Cherokee rights, by his use of the spoils system, and by his dependence on the "Kitchen Cabinet"—political friends—for advice. Critics rejected his claim of restoring republican virtue. They charged him with recklessly and impulsively destroying the economy.

Jackson injected new vigor into the philosophy of limited government. In 1830 he vetoed the Maysville Road bill—which would have funded construction of a 60-mile turnpike from Maysville to Lexington, Kentucky. A federally subsidized internal improvement confined to one state was unconstitutional, he charged; such projects were properly a state responsibility. The veto undermined Henry Clay's nationalist program and personally embarrassed Clay because the project was in his home district.

 ## Federalism at Issue: The Nullification and Bank Controversies

Soon Jackson had to face more directly the question of the proper division of sovereignty between state and central government. The slave South feared federal power, no state more so than South Carolina, where the planter class was strongest.

To protect their interests, South Carolinian political leaders articulated the doctrine of *nullification*, according to which a state had the right to overrule, or nullify, federal legislation. Nullification was based on the idea expressed in the Virginia and Kentucky Resolutions of 1798 (see page 149)—that the states, representing the people, have a right to judge the constitutionality of federal actions. Jackson's vice president, John C. Calhoun of South Carolina, argued in his unsigned *Exposition and Protest* that, in any disagreement between the federal government and a state, a special state convention—like the conventions called to ratify the Constitution—should decide the conflict by either nullifying or affirming the federal law. Only the power of nullification, Calhoun asserted, could protect the minority against the tyranny of the majority.

In public, Calhoun let others take the lead in advancing nullification. He hoped to avoid embarrassing the Democratic ticket and to gain Jackson's support as the Democratic presidential heir-apparent. Thus Calhoun presided silently over the Senate and its packed galleries when Senator Daniel Webster of Massachusetts and Senator Robert Y. Hayne of South Carolina debated nullification in early 1830. The debate explored North-South frictions and the nature of the Union. At the climax of the debate, Webster, whose remarks were aimed at Calhoun, invoked two powerful images. One was the outcome of nullification: "States dissevered, discordant, belligerent; on a land rent with civil feuds, or drenched . . . in fraternal blood!" The other was a patriotic vision of a great nation flourishing under the motto "Liberty *and* Union, now and forever, one and inseparable."

Webster-Hayne Debate

Though sympathetic to states' rights and distrustful of the federal government, Jackson rejected the idea of state sovereignty. He strongly believed that sovereignty rested with the people, and he shared Webster's dread of nullification. Soon after the Webster-Hayne debate, the president made his position clear at a Jefferson Day dinner with the toast "Our Federal Union, it *must* and *shall be* preserved." Vice President Calhoun, when his turn came, toasted: "The Federal Union—next to our liberty the most dear." Calhoun had revealed his preference for states' rights.

South Carolina invoked the theory of nullification against the Tariff of 1832, which reduced some duties but retained high taxes on imported iron, cottons, and woolens. Though a majority of southern representatives supported the new tariff, South Carolinians refused to go along. In their eyes, the constitutional right to control their own destiny had been sacrificed to the demands of northern industrialists. More than the tariff, they feared the consequences of accepting such an act, because it could set a precedent for congressional legislation on slavery. In November 1832 a South Carolina state convention nullified the tariff, making it unlawful for Federal officials to collect duties in the state.

Nullification Crisis

Old Hickory responded with toughness. In December he issued a presidential proclamation nullifying nullification. He moved troops to federal forts in South Carolina and prepared United States marshals to collect the required duties. At Jackson's request, Congress passed the Force Act, which gave the president renewed authority to call up troops but also offered a way to avoid using force by collecting duties before foreign ships reached South Carolina. At the same time, Jackson extended an olive branch by recommending tariff reductions.

Calhoun, disturbed by South Carolina's drift toward separatism, resigned as vice president and soon won election to represent South Carolina in the United States Senate. There he worked with Henry Clay to draw up the compromise Tariff of 1833. Quickly passed by Congress and signed by the president, the new tariff lengthened the list of duty-free items and reduced duties over nine years. Satisfied, South Carolina's convention repealed its nullification law. In a final salvo, it also nullified Jackson's Force Act. Jackson ignored the gesture.

Nullification offered a genuine debate on the nature and principles of the republic. Each side believed it was upholding the Constitution. Neither side won a clear victory, though both claimed to have done so. It took another crisis, over a central bank, to define the powers of the federal government more clearly.

At stake was survival of the Second Bank of the United States, whose twenty-year charter was scheduled to expire in 1836. One of the bank's func-

Second Bank of the United States

tions was to act as a clearing-house for state banks, keeping them honest by refusing to accept in transactions state bank notes from any state bank that had insufficient gold in reserve. Most state banks resented the central bank's police role: by presenting a state bank's notes for redemption all at once, the Second Bank could easily ruin a state bank. Moreover, with less money in reserve, state banks found themselves unable to compete on an equal footing with the Second Bank.

Many state governments also regarded the national bank, with its headquarters in Philadelphia, as unresponsive to local needs. Westerners and urban workers remembered with bitterness the bank's conservative credit policies during the Panic of 1819. As a private, profit-making institution, the bank's policies reflected the interest of its owners. Its president, Nicholas Biddle, was an eastern patrician who symbolized all that westerners found wrong with the bank.

Rechartering was a volatile issue in the 1832 presidential campaign. The bank's charter was valid until 1836, but Henry Clay, the National Republican presidential candidate, persuaded Biddle to ask Congress to approve an early rechartering. This strategy was designed to marshal public pressure to force Jackson to sign the rechartering bill or to override his veto of it. The plan backfired when the Senate failed to override the president's veto. Jackson's veto message was an emotional attack on the undemocratic nature of the bank. The bank thus became the prime issue in the presidential campaign of 1832, and Jackson used it to denounce special privilege and economic power.

After his sweeping victory and second inauguration, Jackson moved in 1833 to permanently destroy the Second Bank of the United States.

Jackson's Second Term

He deposited federal funds in state-chartered banks (critics called them his "pet banks"). Without federal money, the Second Bank shriveled. When its federal charter expired in 1836, it became just another Pennsylvania-chartered private bank. Five years later it closed its doors.

In conjunction with this coup de grâce to the Bank of the United States, Congress passed the Deposit Act of 1836. The act authorized the secretary of the treasury to designate one bank in each state and territory to provide the services formerly performed by the Bank of the United States. The act provided that the federal surplus in excess of $5 million be distributed to the states as interest-free loans beginning in 1837.

The surplus had derived from wholesale speculation in public lands: speculators bought public land on credit, used the land as collateral to borrow more money to buy additional acreage, and repeated

Specie Circular

the cycle. The state banks providing the loans issued bank notes. Jackson, an opponent of paper money, feared that the speculative craze threatened the stability of state banks and undermined the interests of settlers, who could not compete with speculators in bidding for the best land.

In keeping with his hard-money instincts and opposition to paper currency, the president ordered Treasury Secretary Levi Woodbury to issue the Specie Circular. It provided that after August 1836 only specie—gold or silver—or Virginia scrip would be accepted as payment for federal lands. By ending credit sales, the circular significantly reduced purchases of public land and the federal budget surplus. As a result the government suspended its loan payments to the states soon after they began.

The policy was a disaster. Although federal land sales were sharply reduced, speculation continued as available land for sale became scarce. The ensuing increased demand for specie squeezed banks, and many suspended the redemption of bank notes for specie. Credit contracted further as banks issued fewer notes and gave less credit. In the waning days of Jackson's administration, Congress voted to repeal the circular, but the president pocket-vetoed the bill. Finally in mid-1838, a joint resolution of Congress overturned the circular. Restrictions on land sales ended, but the speculative fervor was over. The federal government did not revive loans to states.

From George Washington to John Quincy Adams, presidents had vetoed nine bills; Jackson vetoed twelve. Previous presidents believed that vetoes were justified only on constitutional grounds, but Jackson considered policy disagreement legitimate grounds as well. He made the veto an effective weapon for controlling Congress, since representatives and senators had to consider the possibility of a presidential veto in their deliberations on any bill. In effect, Jackson made the executive for the first time a rival branch of government, equal in power to Congress.

Use of the Veto

The Whig Challenge and the Second Party System

Most modern historians view the 1830s and 1840s as an age of reform and popularly based political parties. Only when the passionate concerns of reformers and abolitionists spilled over into politics did party differences become paramount and party loyalties solidify. For the first time in American history, grassroots political groups, organized from the bottom up, set the tone of political life.

Opponents of the Democrats found shelter under a common umbrella, the Whig Party, in the 1830s. Resentful of Jackson's domination of Congress, the Whigs borrowed the name of the British party that had opposed the tyranny of Hanoverian monarchs in the eighteenth century. From 1834 through the 1840s, the Whigs and the Democrats competed on a nearly equal footing. They fought at the city, county, state, and national levels and achieved a stability previously unknown in American politics. The political competition of this period—known as the second party system—was more intense and well organized than that of the first party system of Republicans and Federalists.

The two parties adopted different approaches to the basic issues of the 1830s and the 1840s. Whigs favored economic expansion through an activist government; Democrats, through limited central government. Whigs supported corporate charters, a national bank, and paper currency; Democrats were opposed. Whigs also favored more humanitarian reforms than did Democrats, including public schools, abolition of capital punishment, prison and asylum reform, and temperance.

Whigs

Whigs were more optimistic than Democrats, generally speaking, and more enterprising. They did not object to helping a specific group if doing so would promote the general welfare. The chartering of corporations, they argued, expanded economic opportunity for everyone, including laborers and farmers. Democrats, distrustful of concentrated economic power and of moral and economic coercion, held fast to the Jeffersonian principle of limited government.

Religion and ethnicity rather than economics and class most influenced party membership. The Whigs won the favor of evangelical Protestants in the North, as well as the small number of free black voters. Democrats, by contrast, tended to be foreign-born Catholics and nonevangelical Protestants, both of whom preferred to keep religious and secular affairs separate.

The Whig Party was the vehicle of revivalist Protestantism. The membership rolls of reform societies overlapped those of the party. Indeed, Whigs practiced a kind of political revivalism. Their rallies resembled camp meetings; their speeches employed evangelical rhetoric; their programs embodied the perfectionist beliefs of reformers.

Whigs and Reformers

In their appeal to evangelicals, Whigs alienated members of other faiths. The evangelicals' ideal Christian state had no room for Catholics, Mormons, Unitarians, Universalists, or religious freethinkers. Those groups opposed Sabbath laws and temperance legislation in particular and state interference in moral and religious questions in general. As a result, more than 95 percent of Irish Catholics, 90 percent of Reformed Dutch, and 80 percent of German Catholics voted Democratic.

Vice President Martin Van Buren, handpicked by Jackson, headed the Democratic ticket in the presidential election of 1836. The Whigs, who in 1836 had not yet coalesced into a national party, entered three sectional candidates: Daniel Webster of New England, Hugh White of the

Election of 1836

South, and William Henry Harrison of the West. By splintering the vote, they hoped to throw the election into the House. Van Buren, however, comfortably captured the electoral college even though he had only a 25,000-vote edge out of a total of 1.5 million votes cast.

Van Buren took office just weeks before the American credit system collapsed. In response to the impact of the Specie Circular, New York banks stopped redeeming paper currency with gold in mid-1837. Soon all banks suspended payments in hard coin. Thus began a cycle that led to curtailment of bank loans and reduced business confidence. Hard times persisted until 1843.

President Martin Van Buren and Hard Times

Ill advisedly, Van Buren followed Jackson's hard-money policies. He cut federal spending, which caused prices to drop further, and he opposed a national bank, which would have expanded credit. Even worse, the president proposed a new regional treasury system for government deposits. The proposed treasury branches would accept and pay out only gold and silver coin; they would not accept paper currency or checks drawn on state banks. Van Buren's independent treasury bill became law in 1840. By creating a constant demand for hard coin, it deprived banks of gold and further accelerated the deflation of prices.

With the nation in the grip of hard times, the Whigs prepared confidently for the election of 1840. The Democrats renominated President Van

Using techniques that look familiar to twentieth-century politicians, General William Henry Harrison in 1840 ran a "log cabin and hard cider" campaign against Jackson's heir, President Martin Van Buren. The campaign handkerchief shows Harrison welcoming two of his comrades to his log cabin, with a barrel of cider outside. The Log Cabin, *a newspaper edited by Horace Greeley, was the voice of the Harrison campaign, and it reached eighty thousand partisans.* Handkerchief: New-York Historical Society. Newspaper: Division of Political History, Smithsonian Institution, Washington, D.C.

William Henry Harrison Wins Election of 1840

Buren at a somber convention. The Whigs rallied behind a military hero, General William Henry Harrison, conqueror of the Shawnees at Tippecanoe Creek in 1811. Harrison, or "Old Tippecanoe," and his running mate, John Tyler of Virginia, ran a people's crusade against the aristocratic incumbent in "the palace." In a huge turnout, 80 percent of eligible voters cast ballots. Harrison won the popular vote by a narrow margin but swept the electoral college by 234 to 60.

Unfortunately for the Whigs, the sixty-eight-year-old Harrison died within a month of his inauguration. His successor, John Tyler, was a former Democrat who had left the party to protest Jackson's nullification proclamation. In office, Tyler turned out to be more of a Democrat than a Whig. He consistently opposed the Whig congressional program. He repeatedly vetoed Henry Clay's protective tariffs, internal improvements, and bills aimed at reviving the Bank of the United States. The only important measures that became law during his term were repeal of the independent treasury system and passage of a higher tariff. Two days after Tyler's second veto of a bank bill, the entire cabinet except Secretary of State Daniel Webster resigned; Webster, busy negotiating a new treaty with Great Britain, left shortly thereafter. Tyler thus became a president without a party, and the Whigs lost the presidency without losing an election.

Hard times in the late 1830s and early 1840s deflected attention from a renewal of Anglo-American tensions that had multiple sources:

Anglo-American Tensions

northern commercial rivalry with Britain, the default of state governments and corporations on British-held debts during the Panic of 1837, rebellion in Canada, boundary disputes, southern alarm over West Indian emancipation, and American expansionism.

A major crisis with Great Britain erupted over an unresolved border dispute between Maine and New Brunswick. The area was wooded, and in the winter of 1838–1839 Canadian lumbermen moved into the region to cut trees. Maine residents then attempted to expel them. The lumbermen captured the Maine land agent and posse, both sides mobilized their militias, and Congress authorized a call-up of fifty thousand men. Ultimately, no blood was spilled. General Winfield Scott was dispatched to Aroostook, Maine, where he arranged a truce. The two sides compromised on their conflicting claims in the Webster-Ashburton Treaty (1842).

The border dispute with Great Britain prefigured the conflicts that were to erupt in the 1840s over the expansion of the United States. With Tyler's succession to power in 1841 and a Democratic victory in the presidential election of 1844, federal activism in the domestic sphere ended for the rest of the decade, and attention turned to the debate over territorial expansion.

 ## Manifest Destiny and Expansionism

The belief that American expansion westward and southward was inevitable, just, and divinely ordained was first labeled *manifest destiny* by John L. O'Sullivan, editor of the *United States Magazine and Domestic Review*. The annexation of Texas, O'Sullivan wrote in 1845, was "the fulfillment of our manifest destiny to overspread the continent allotted by Providence for the free development of our yearly multiplying millions." In the 1840s expansionism reached a new fervor.

Since colonial days Americans had hungered for more land. As the proportion of Americans living west of the Appalachians grew (see map), both national parties joined the popular clamor for expansion. Agrarian Democrats saw the West as an antidote to urbanization and industrialization. Enterprising Whigs looked to the new commercial opportunities the West offered. Southerners envisioned the extension of slavery and more slave states.

Fierce national pride spurred the quest for land. Americans were convinced that theirs was the greatest country on earth, with a special role to play in the world. The acquisition of new territory, many Americans reasoned, would extend the ben-

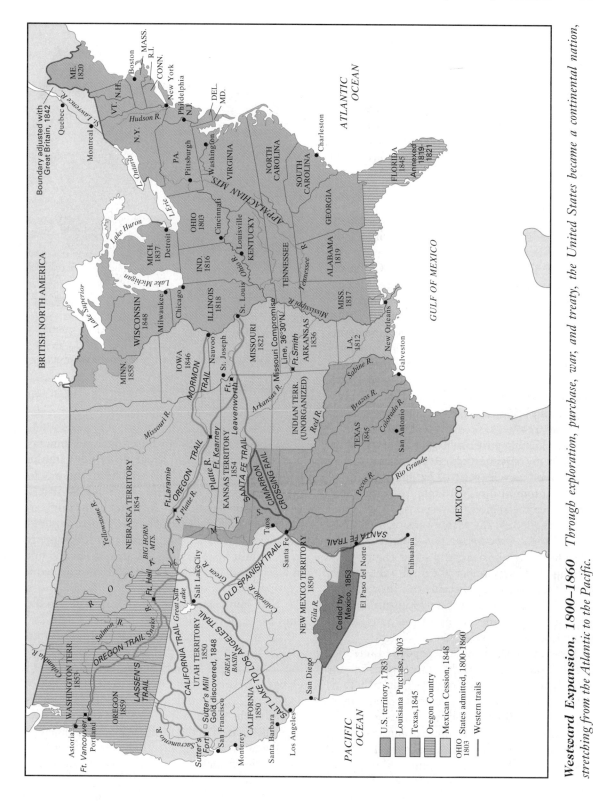

Westward Expansion, 1800–1860 *Through exploration, purchase, war, and treaty, the United States became a continental nation, stretching from the Atlantic to the Pacific.*

efits of America's republican system of government to the less fortunate and the inferior.

In part, racism drove the belief in manifest destiny. Native Americans were perceived as savages best confined to small areas in the West. Hispanics were seen as inferior peoples, best controlled or conquered. Thus the same racism that justified slavery in the South and discrimination in the North supported expansion in the West. But racism also could limit expansion, for Americans did not look on Mexicans—whether Indian, European, African, or mestizo—with favor.

Among the long-standing objectives of expansionists was the Republic of Texas, which in addition to Texas included parts of present-day Oklahoma, Kansas, Colorado, Wyoming, and New Mexico.

Republic of Texas

After winning its independence from Spain in 1821, Mexico encouraged the development of its rich but remote northern province, offering large tracts of land virtually free to settlers called *empresarios*. The settlers in turn agreed to become Mexican citizens, adopt the Catholic religion, and bring two hundred or more families into the area.

By 1835, thirty-five thousand Americans, including many slaveholders, lived in Texas. The new settlers' power grew. The dictatorship of General Antonio López de Santa Anna tightened control over the region. In response, Anglos and Tejanos rebelled. At the Alamo mission in San Antonio in 1836, fewer than two hundred Texans made a heroic but unsuccessful stand against three thousand Mexicans under General Santa Anna. "Remember the Alamo" became the Texans' rallying cry. A few months later, Sam Houston's victory over Santa Anna in the Battle of San Jacinto gained Texas its independence.

Texas established the independent Lone Star Republic but soon sought annexation to the United States. The issue, however, quickly became politically explosive. Southerners favored annexing proslavery Texas; abolitionists, many northerners, and most Whigs opposed annexation. In recognition of the political dangers, President Jackson reneged on his promise to recognize

Texans believed that their war for independence paralleled the Revolutionary War. The lady of liberty on this banner, carried by Texans in 1836, brings to mind similar images that stirred patriots during the American Revolution. Archives Division, Texas State Library.

Texas, and President Van Buren ignored annexation. Texans then talked about closer ties with the British and extending their republic all the way to the Pacific coast. President Tyler feared that a Texas alliance with the British might threaten American independence. He was also committed to expansion and hoped to build political support in the South by extending the area of slavery. But in a sectional vote, the Senate in 1844 rejected a treaty of annexation.

Like southerners who sought expansion to the Southwest, northerners looked to the Northwest. "Oregon fever" struck thousands in 1841. Lured

Oregon Fever

by the glowing reports, migrants in wagon trains took to the Oregon Trail. The 2,000-mile journey took six months or more, but within a few years five thousand settlers had arrived in the fertile Willamette valley.

Britain and the United States had jointly occupied the disputed Oregon Territory since the

Anglo-American Convention of 1818 (see page 170). Beginning with the administration of President John Quincy Adams, the United States had tried to fix the boundary at the 49th parallel, but Britain refused. Time only increased the American appetite. In 1843 a Cincinnati convention of expansionists demanded the entire Oregon Country for the United States, up to its northernmost border at latitude 54°40'. Soon "Fifty-four Forty or Fight" became the rallying cry of American expansionists.

Expansion into Oregon and rejection of the annexation of Texas, both favored by antislavery forces, worried southern leaders. Anxious about their diminishing ability to control the debate over slavery, they persuaded the 1844 Democratic convention to adopt a rule requiring the presidential nominee to receive two-thirds of the convention votes. In effect, the southern states acquired a veto, and they blocked Van Buren as the nominee; most southerners objected to his antislavery stance and opposition to Texas annexation. Instead, the party chose House Speaker James K. Polk, a hard-money Jacksonian, avid expansionist, and slaveholding cotton planter from Tennessee. Henry Clay, the Whig nominee, who believed that the Democrats' belligerent nationalism would lead to war with Great Britain, Mexico, or both, favored expansion through negotiations.

James K. Polk Wins Election of 1844

With a well-organized campaign, Polk and the Democrats won the election by 170 electoral votes to 105. (They won the popular vote by just 38,000 out of 2.7 million votes cast.) Polk won New York's 36 electoral votes by just 6,000 popular votes. Abolitionist James G. Birney, the Liberty party candidate, had drawn almost 16,000 votes away from Clay, handing New York and the election to Polk.

Interpreting Polk's victory as a mandate for annexation, President Tyler proposed in his final days in office that Texas be admitted by joint resolution of Congress. Congress approved the resolution, Tyler signed it, and Mexico immediately broke relations with the United States. War was inevitable.

 ## Conclusion

Religion, reform, and expansionism colored politics in the 1830s and 1840s. As the Second Great Awakening spread through villages and towns, the converts, especially women, changed American religion and organized to reform a rapidly changing society. Religion imbued men and women with zeal to right the wrongs of American society and the world. Reformers pursued perfectionism and republican virtue by doing battle with the evils of the growing cities, seeking to ban alcohol and gambling, and expanding education.

Once reform forced itself into politics, it generated a broader-based interest in politics that would remake the political system. The ensuing conflicts, and the highly organized parties that arose during the era, stimulated even greater interest in campaigns and political issues. The Democrats, who rallied around Andrew Jackson, and Jackson's opponents, who found shelter under the Whig tent, competed almost equally for the loyalty of voters.

Territorial expansion would provide the kindling for the firestorm that would overtake the United States in 1861. Manifest destiny, the admission of Texas, and debates over territorial expansion awaited a spark. Ultimately, one issue would rivet the attention of nearly all Americans and ignite the fire that would threaten to sever the Union: slavery.

Suggestions for Further Reading

Religion, Revivalism, and Reform

Robert H. Abzug, *Cosmos Crumbling: American Reform and the Religious Imagination* (1994); Michael Barkun, *Crucible of the Millennium: The Burned-over District of New York in the 1840s* (1986); Terry Bilhartz, *Urban Religion and the Second Great Awakening: Church and Society in Early National Baltimore* (1986); Clifford S. Griffen, *Their Brother's Keepers: Moral Stewardship in the United States, 1800–1865* (1960); Keith J. Hardman, *Charles Grandison Finney, 1792–1875: Revivalist and Reformer* (1987); Nathan O. Hatch, *The Democratization of American Christianity* (1989); Curtis D. Johnson, *Islands of Holiness: Rural Religion in Upstate New York, 1790–1860* (1989); Paul E. Johnson, *A Shopkeeper's Millennium: Society and Revivals* in Rochester, New York, 1815–1837 (1978); Steven Mintz, *Moralists and Modernizers: America's Pre–Civil War Reformers* (1995); Richard D. Shiels, "The Scope of the Second Great Awakening: Andover, Massachusetts, as a Case Study," *Journal of the Early Republic* 5 (Summer 1985): 223–246; Timothy L. Smith, *Revivalism and Social Reform in Mid–Nineteenth Century America* (1957); Alice Felt Tyler, *Freedom's Ferment* (1944); Ronald G. Walters, *American Reformers, 1815–1860* (1978).

Temperance, Asylums, and Antimasonry

David Gollaher, *Voice for the Mad: The Life of Dorothea Dix* (1995); Paul Goodman, *Towards a Christian Republic: Antimasonry and the Great Transition in New England, 1826–1836* (1988); Gerald N. Grob, *Mental Institutions in America: Social Policy to 1875* (1973); Kathleen Smith Kutolowski, "Antimasonry Reexamined: Social Bases of the Grass-Roots Party," *Journal of American History* 71 (September 1984): 269–293; W. J. Rorabaugh, *The Alcoholic Republic: An American Tradition* (1979); David J. Rothman, *The Discovery of the Asylum: Social Order and Disorder in the New Republic* (1971); Ian R. Tyrrell, *Sobering Up: From Temperance to Prohibition in Antebellum America, 1800–1860* (1979); William Preston Vaughn, *The Antimasonic Party in the United States, 1826–1843* (1983).

Women and Reform

Barbara J. Berg, *The Remembered Gate: Origins of American Feminism: The Woman and the City, 1800–1860* (1977); Ellen C. Du Bois, *Feminism and Suffrage: The Emergence of an Independent Woman's Movement in America, 1848–1869* (1978); Barbara Leslie Epstein, *The Politics of Domesticity: Women, Evangelism, and Temperance in Nineteenth-Century America* (1981); Lori D. Ginzberg, *Women and the Work of Benevolence: Morality, Politics, and Class in the Nineteenth-Century United States* (1990); Debra Gold Hansen, *Strained Sisterhood: Gender and Class in the Boston Female Anti-Slavery Society* (1993); Nancy A. Hewitt, *Women's Activism and Social Change: Rochester, New York, 1822–1872* (1984); Sylvia D. Hoffert, *When Hens Crow: The Woman's Rights Movement in Antebellum America* (1995); Gerda Lerner, *The Grimké Sisters of South Carolina* (1967); Mary P. Ryan, *Cradle of the Middle Class: The Family in Oneida County, New York, 1790–1865* (1981); Shirley J. Yee, *Black Women Abolitionists: A Study in Activism, 1828–1860* (1992); Jean Fagan Yellin, *Women & Sisters: The Antislavery Feminists in American Culture* (1989).

Antislavery and Abolitionism

David Brion Davis, *Slavery and Human Progress* (1984); Frederick Douglass, *Life and Times of Frederick Douglass* (1881);

George M. Fredrickson, *The Black Image in the White Mind: The Debate on Afro-American Character and Destiny, 1817–1914* (1971); Lawrence J. Friedman, *Gregarious Saints: Self and Community in American Abolitionism, 1830–1870* (1982); Aileen S. Kraditor, *Means and Ends in American Abolitionism: Garrison and His Critics on Strategy and Tactics* (1967); William Lee Miller, *Arguing About Slavery: The Great Battle in the United States Congress* (1995); William H. Pease and Jane H. Pease, *They Who Would Be Free: Blacks' Search for Freedom, 1830–1861* (1974); Benjamin Quarles, *Black Abolitionists* (1969); John L. Thomas, *The Liberator: William Lloyd Garrison* (1963); Ronald G. Walters, *The Antislavery Appeal: American Abolitionism After 1830* (1976).

Andrew Jackson and the Jacksonians

Donald B. Cole, *Martin Van Buren and the American Political System* (1984); Daniel Feller, *The Jacksonian Promise: America, 1815–1840* (1995); Marvin Meyers, *The Jacksonian Persuasion* (1960); John Niven, *Martin Van Buren* (1983); Edward Pessen, *Jacksonian America: Society, Personality, and Politics*, rev. ed. (1979); Robert V. Remini, *The Legacy of Andrew Jackson: Essays on Democracy, Indian Removal, and Slavery* (1988); Robert V. Remini, *The Life of Andrew Jackson* (1988); Charles Sellers, *The Market Revolution: Jacksonian America, 1815–1846* (1991); Harry L. Watson, *Liberty and Power: The Politics of Jacksonian America* (1990).

Democrats and Whigs

William J. Cooper, *The South and the Politics of Slavery, 1828–1856* (1978); Ronald P. Formisano, *The Transformation of Political Culture: Massachusetts Parties, 1790s–1840s* (1983); William W. Freehling, *Prelude to Civil War: The Nullification Controversy in South Carolina* (1966); Daniel Walker Howe, *The Political Culture of the American Whigs* (1979); Richard P. McCormick, *The Second American Party System: Party Formation in the Jacksonian Era* (1966); Robert V. Remini, *Henry Clay: Statesman for the Union* (1991); James Roger Sharp, *The Jacksonians Versus the Banks: Politics in the States After the Panic of 1837* (1970).

Manifest Destiny and Foreign Policy

John M. Belohlavek, *"Let the Eagle Soar!" The Foreign Policy of Andrew Jackson* (1985); Thomas R. Hietala, *Manifest Destiny: Anxious Aggrandizement in Late Jacksonian America* (1985); Reginald Horsman, *Race and Manifest Destiny* (1981); Michael Hunt, *Ideology and U.S. Foreign Policy* (1987); Bradford Perkins, *The Creation of a Republican Empire, 1776–1865* (1993); Charles G. Sellers, Jr., *James K. Polk: Continentalist, 1843–1846* (1966); Anders Stephanson, *Manifest Destiny: American Expansionism and the Empire of Right* (1995).

14

Slavery and America's Future:
The Road to War

1845–1861

Almost sixty and a widower, Robert Newsom lived with his two adult daughters and four of his grandchildren. In Missouri in 1850 he purchased Celia, a fourteen-year-old slave. She probably assumed that Newsom wanted her to cook and clean for the family, but he had more in mind for Celia. Almost immediately he raped her and made it clear that he would continue to demand her sexual services. Newsom's adult daughters and his neighbors knew what he was doing to Celia but said nothing. They respected him and knew that slavery spawned such arrangements.

In 1855, Celia began a relationship with George, another of the Newsom slaves, and resolved to end the relationship with her master. Neither pleas to Newsom's daughters nor appeals to him stopped the assaults, however. One night after Newsom brushed aside her objections to sex, Celia grabbed a club and struck him on the skull. As he sank to the floor, she struck him again. He never arose. Panicked at having killed her master, Celia proceeded to burn his body all through the night in her large fireplace.

Physical evidence of Newsom's murder soon came to light, and Celia was arrested. Celia's attorneys sympathized with her plight enough to argue, unsuccessfully, that laws against rape entitled her to defend herself. After a jury of twelve white men convicted her, Celia went to the gallows four days before Christmas.

By the time Celia was hanged, her drama had been overshadowed by a larger drama of violence in the territory of Kansas. Open warfare had broken out there between advocates and foes of slavery. Proslavery men, intent on spreading the peculiar institution and preserving a balance of free and slave states in the United States Senate, rode across the border from Missouri, stole elections by voting illegally, and physically attacked those who wanted Kansas to be free soil. Antislavery activists organized the New England Emigrant Aid Company to send opponents of slavery to Kansas. As new territories were opened, the passions over slavery intensified. Thus in the 1850s, slavery pulled Americans deeper and deeper into a maelstrom of conflict and violence.

Between 1845 and 1853 the United States added Texas, the West Coast, and the Southwest to its domain and launched the settlement of the Great Plains. Each time the nation expanded, it confronted a thorny issue: should new territories and states be slave or free? This question stirred disagreements too extreme for compromise. A host of political leaders, including Henry Clay, Lewis Cass, Stephen A. Douglas, and Presidents Jackson and Van Buren, tried to postpone or resolve disagreements about slavery in the territories. Repeatedly, though, these disputes injected into national politics the bitterness surrounding slavery.

The United States had always been a diverse society. Now, however, diverse interests that used to balance each other became linked to a divisive issue. The second party system disintegrated, and a realigned system with sectional parties that emphasized conflict emerged. The new Republican Party charged that southerners were taking over the federal government and planning to make slavery legal throughout the Union. Republicans believed that America's future depended on the free labor of free men, whose rights were protected by a government devoted to liberty. Southern leaders defended slavery and charged the North with lawless behavior in violation of the Constitution. To these southerners enslavement of blacks was the foundation of equality and republicanism among whites, and a government that failed to protect slavery was un-American.

Not all citizens were obsessed with these conflicts. In fact, the results of the 1860 presidential election indicated that most voters wanted neither disunion nor civil war. Within six months, however, they had both.

Conflict Begins: The Mexican War

Territorial expansion surged forward under the leadership of President James K. Polk. The annexation of Texas just before his inauguration did not weaken Polk's determination to acquire California and the Southwest, and he desired Oregon as well. Polk achieved his goals but was unaware of the price in domestic harmony that expansion would exact. Territorial conquest divided the Whig Party, drove southern Whigs into a full embrace of slavery, and brought into the open an aggressive new southern theory about slavery's position in the territories. Expansion also sparked protests and proposals from the North that angered southerners.

During the 1844 campaign, Polk's supporters had threatened war with Great Britain to gain all of Oregon. As president, however, Polk turned first to diplomacy. Not wanting to fight Mexico and Great Britain at the same time, he tried to avoid bloodshed in the Northwest, where America and Britain had jointly occupied disputed territory since 1818. Dropping the demand for a boundary at latitude 54°40', he pressured the British to accept the 49th parallel. In 1846 Great Britain agreed. The Oregon Treaty gave the United States all of present-day Oregon, Washington, and Idaho and parts of Wyoming and Montana.

Toward Mexico, Polk was more aggressive. He ordered American troops to defend the border claimed by Texas but contested by Mexico (see map, page 260), and he attempted to buy from the angry Mexicans a huge tract of land in the Southwest. When that effort failed, Polk resolved to ask Congress for a declaration of war. As he was drawing up a list of grievances, word arrived that Mexican forces had engaged American troops on disputed territory and American blood had been shed. Eagerly, Polk declared that "war exists by the act of Mexico itself."

Important Events

1846	War with Mexico begins
	Oregon Treaty negotiated
	Wilmot Proviso inflames sectional
	  divisions
		1856	"Bleeding Kansas" troubles nation
			Preston Brooks attacks Charles Sumner in
			  Senate chamber
			James Buchanan elected president

1847	Lewis Cass proposes idea of popular
	  sovereignty
		1857	*Dred Scott* v. *Sanford* endorses southern views
			  on race and territories
			Lecompton Constitution proposed;
			  President Buchanan supports it

1848	Treaty of Guadalupe Hidalgo gives
	  United States new territory in the
	  Southwest
	Free-Soil Party formed
	Zachary Taylor elected president
		1858	Kansas voters reject Lecompton Constitution
			Lincoln-Douglas debates attract attention
			Stephan A. Douglas proposes Freeport
			  Doctrine

1849	California applies for admission to Union as free state	**1859**	John Brown raids Harpers Ferry
1850	Compromise of 1850 passed in separate bills	**1860**	Democratic party splits in two Abraham Lincoln elected president Crittenden Compromise fails South Carolina secedes from Union

1852	Publication of *Uncle Tom's Cabin*, by Harriet
	  Beecher Stowe
	Franklin Pierce elected president
		1861	Six more Deep South states secede
			Confederacy established at Montgomery,
			  Alabama
			Attack on Fort Sumter begins Civil War
			Four states in the Upper South join the
			  Confederacy

1854	Kansas-Nebraska Act wins approval and
	  ignites controversy
	Republican Party formed
	Democrats lose ground in congressional
	  elections		

Congress recognized a state of war between Mexico and the United States in May 1846, and soon American forces made significant gains. Despite the quarreling of politically ambitious officers, progress was steady. General Zachary Taylor's forces attacked and occupied Monterrey, securing northeastern Mexico (see map, page 260). Polk then ordered Colonel Stephen Kearny and a small detachment to invade the remote and thinly populated provinces of New Mexico and California. Taking Santa Fe without opposition, Kearny pushed into California, where he joined forces with rebellious American settlers led by Captain John C. Frémont and with a couple of United States naval units. A quick victory was followed by reverses, but American soldiers soon reestablished their dominance in distant California.

Because losses on the periphery had not broken Mexican resistance, General Winfield Scott carried the war to the enemy's heartland. From Veracruz on the Gulf of Mexico, he led fourteen thousand men toward Mexico City. After a series of hard-fought battles, United States troops captured the Mexican capital and brought the war to an end.

Representatives of both countries signed the Treaty of Guadalupe Hidalgo in February 1848. The United States gained California and New Mexico (including present-day Nevada, Utah, and Arizona) and recognition of the Rio Grande as the southern boundary of Texas. In return, the American government agreed to settle the claims of its citizens against Mexico and to pay Mexico a mere $15 million.

Treaty of Guadalupe Hidalgo

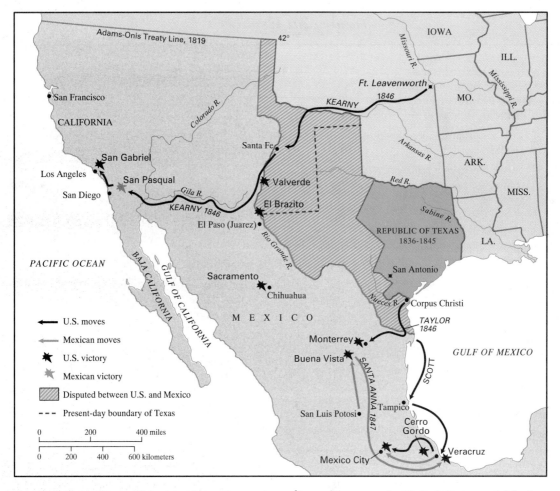

The Mexican War *This map shows the territory disputed between the United States and Mexico. After United States gains in northeastern Mexico and in New Mexico and California, General Winfield Scott captured Mexico City in the decisive campaign of the war.*

The war led to the deaths of thirteen thousand Americans and fifty thousand Mexicans. It also sharply divided public opinion in the United States. Southwesterners were enthusiastic about the war; New Englanders strenuously opposed it. Whigs in Congress charged that Polk, a Democrat, had "literally provoked" an unnecessary war (which they called "Mr. Polk's war") and "usurped the power of Congress." The aged John Quincy Adams denounced the war; and a tall, young, Illinois Whig named Abraham Lincoln questioned its justification. Abolitionists and a small minority of antislavery Whigs charged that the war was no less than a plot to extend slavery.

These charges fed northern fear of the so-called Slave Power. Abolitionists had long warned of a Slave Power—a slaveholding oligarchy that controlled the South and intended to dominate the nation. The Slave Power's assault on northern liberties, abolitionists argued, had begun in 1836, when Congress passed the gag rule (see page 243). Many white northerners, even those who saw

Idea of a Slave Power

nothing wrong with slavery, had opposed restrictions on free speech and the right of petition. It was the battle over free speech that first made the idea of a Slave Power credible. The Mexican War deepened fears about this sinister power. Why, asked antislavery northerners, had claims to part of Oregon been abandoned and a questionable war begun for slave territory?

Northern opinion began to shift, but the impact of events on southern opinion and southern leaders was even more dramatic. At first many southern leaders criticized the war with Mexico. Southern Whigs attacked the Democratic president for causing the war. Once slavery became the central issue, however, no Southern Whig could oppose it. That happened in August 1846, when David Wilmot, a Pennsylvania Democrat, proposed an amendment, or proviso, to a military appropriations bill: that "neither slavery nor involuntary servitude shall ever exist" in any territory gained from Mexico. His proviso did not pass both houses of Congress, but it immediately transformed the debate.

John C. Calhoun responded to the proviso with a radical new southern position. The territories, Calhoun insisted, belonged to all the states, and the federal government could do nothing to limit the

Wilmot Proviso

spread of slavery there. Southern slaveholders had a constitutional *right*, Calhoun claimed, to take their slaves anywhere in the territories. This position was a radical reversal of history. In 1787 the Confederation Congress had excluded slavery from the Northwest Territory (see pages 130–131); Article IV of the federal Constitution had authorized Congress to make "all needful rules and regulations" for the territories; and the Missouri Compromise had barred slavery from most of the Louisiana Purchase. Now, however, southern leaders demanded protection for slavery.

In the North, the Wilmot Proviso became a rallying cry for abolitionists. Eventually the legislatures of fourteen northern states endorsed it—and not because all its supporters were abolitionists. David Wilmot, like most white northerners, was neither an abolitionist nor an antislavery Whig. His

goal, for instance, was to defend "the rights of white freemen" and to obtain California "for free white labor."

Fear of the Slave Power, however, was building a potent antislavery movement that united abolitionists *and* antiblack voters. The latter's concern was to protect themselves, not southern blacks, from the Slave Power.

The slavery question divided northerners and southerners in both parties and could not be kept out of national politics. After Polk renounced

Election of 1848 and Popular Sovereignty

a second term as president, the Democrats nominated Senator Lewis Cass of Michigan for president. In 1847 Cass had devised the idea of "popular sovereignty" for the territories—letting residents in the territories decide the question of slavery for themselves. His party's platform declared that Congress lacked the power to interfere with slavery and criticized those who pressed the question. The Whigs nominated General Zachary Taylor, a southern slaveholder and the conqueror of Monterrey; Congressman Millard Fillmore of New York was his running mate. The Whig convention similarly refused to assert that Congress had power over slavery in the territories.

Among northerners, concern over slavery led to the formation of a new party. New York Democrats committed to the Wilmot Proviso rebelled against Cass and nominated former president Van Buren. Antislavery Whigs and former supporters of the Liberty Party then joined them to organize the Free-Soil Party, with Van Buren as its candidate (see table). This party, whose slogan was "Free Soil, Free Speech, Free Labor, and Free Men," won almost 300,000 northern votes. Taylor polled 1.4 million votes to Cass's 1.2 million and won the White House, but the results were more ominous than decisive. In both public opinion and the political parties, a North-South division was deepening.

The conflicts of 1848 would dominate politics throughout the 1850s, as slavery in the territories colored every other national issue. Debate over slavery pushed other issues aside, raised questions

New Political Parties

Party	Period of Influence	Area of Influence	Outcome
Liberty Party	1839–1848	North	Merged with other antislavery groups to form Free-Soil Party
Free-Soil Party	1848–1854	North	Merged with Republican Party
Know-Nothings (American Party)	1853–1856	Nationwide	Disappeared, freeing some northern voters to join Republican Party
Republican Party	1854–present	North (later nationwide)	Became rival of Democratic Party in third party system

about the nature of the Union, and led to the demise of the second party system.

Territorial Problems Are Compromised but Reemerge

The first sectional battle of the decade involved California. More than eighty thousand Americans flooded into California during the gold rush of 1849. With Congress unable to agree on a formula to govern the territories, President Taylor urged these settlers to apply directly for admission to the Union. They promptly did so, proposing a state constitution that prohibited slavery. Southern politicians, who at a minimum wanted to extend the Missouri Compromise line west to the Pacific, objected.

Henry Clay sensed that the Union was in peril. Twice before—in 1820 and 1833—Clay, the "Great Pacificator," had taken the lead in shaping sectional compromise; now he struggled one last time to preserve the nation. In a problem-laded compromise package, Clay sought to resolve several basic questions. Should all or part of California be free? How should the lands gained from Mexico be governed? What was the solution to Texas's land claims? Could the slave trade be abolished in the nation's capital? What should be done about fugitive slaves who escaped to free areas and were neither arrested nor returned to their owners? Of all the questions, the most troublesome dealt with the status of slavery in the territories.

Clay and Senator Stephen A. Douglas of Illinois, his partner in steering the compromise through debate, hoped to avoid a specific formula, for Lewis Cass's idea of popular sovereignty possessed a vagueness that appealed to practical politicians. Like many others, Cass wanted Congress to stay out of the territorial wrangle. Ultimately Congress would have to approve statehood for a territory, but "in the meantime," he said, it should allow the people living there "to regulate their own concerns in their own way."

Those simple words proved highly ambiguous. When could settlers prohibit slavery? To avoid dissension within their party, northern and southern Democrats explained Cass's statement to their constituents in two incompatible ways. Southerners claimed that neither Congress nor a territorial legislature could bar slavery. Only when settlers assumed sovereignty under a state constitution could they take that step. Northerners insisted that Americans living in a territory could outlaw slavery at any time.

The cause of compromise gained a powerful supporter when Senator Daniel Webster committed his prestige and eloquence to Clay's bill. Yet even Webster's influence was not enough. After months of labor, Clay and Douglas finally brought their legislative package to a vote, and lost. Then, with Clay sick and absent from Washington, Douglas reintroduced the compromise measures one at a time. He shrewdly realized that different majorities might be created for the separate measures. The strategy worked, and the Compromise of 1850 became law.

Under its various measures, California became a free state, and the Texas boundary was set at its present limits. The United States paid Texas $10 million in consideration of the boundary agreement.

Compromise of 1850

The territories of New Mexico and Utah were organized with power to legislate on "all rightful subjects . . . consistent with the Constitution." A stronger fugitive slave law and an act to suppress the slave trade in the District of Columbia completed the compromise.

Jubilation greeted passage of the compromise; crowds in Washington celebrated the happy news, but there was less cause for celebration than people hoped. Fundamentally, the Compromise of 1850 was not a settlement of sectional disputes. At best, it was an artful evasion that bought time for the nation without setting guidelines for solving future territorial questions. Furthermore, the compromise had two basic flaws. The first concerned the ambiguity of territorial legislation: what were "rightful subjects of legislation, consistent with the Constitution"? During debate, southerners said these words meant that there would be no prohibition of slavery during the territorial stage, and northerners declared that settlers could bar slavery whenever they wished.

The second flaw lay in the Fugitive Slave Act, which empowered slaveowners to go into court in their own states to present evidence that a slave who owed them service had escaped. The resulting transcript and a description of the fugitive would then serve as legal proof of a person's slave status, even in free states and territories. Court officials would decide only whether the person brought before them was the person described, not whether he or she was indeed a slave. Penalties discouraged citizens from harboring fugitives, and the fees paid to United States marshals seemed to favor slaveholders. (Authorities were paid $10 if the alleged fugitive was turned over to the slave-

Fugitive Slave Act

owner, $5 if not.) Because of the law's provisions, especially the denial of an alleged fugitive's right to a jury trial, northerners staged protests in several states.

At this point a novel portrayed the humanity and suffering of slaves in a way that touched millions of northerners. Harriet Beecher Stowe, whose New England family had produced many prominent ministers, wrote *Uncle Tom's Cabin* out of deep moral conviction. Her story, serialized in 1851 and published as a book in 1852, conveyed the agonies faced by slave families. Stowe also portrayed slavery's evil effects on slaveholders, indicting the institution itself more harshly than she indicted the southerners caught in its web. By mid-1853 the book had sold over a million copies and led many who had ignored slavery to now see its evil.

Uncle Tom's Cabin

The popularity of *Uncle Tom's Cabin* alarmed southern whites. In the territorial controversies and now in popular literature they saw threats to their way of life. Behind the South's aggressive claims about territorial rights lay the fear that nearby free soil areas would be used as bases from which to spread abolitionism into the slave states. To defend slavery against political threats, southern leaders relied on Calhoun's territorial theories and the dogmas of states' rights and strict construction.

To protect slavery in the arena of ideas, southerners needed to counter indictments of the institution as a moral wrong. Accordingly, proslavery theorists elaborated numerous arguments based on partially scientific or pseudoscientific data. They discussed anthropological evidence suggesting separate origins of the races and physicians' views on the physical infirmities of blacks. Other proslavery spokesmen expounded the new "science" of phrenology, citing measurements of skulls to "prove" that blacks were an inferior race. Yet in private and in their hearts, most southern leaders fell back on two rationales for slavery: their belief that blacks were inferior and biblical accounts of slaveholding. Some, like Jefferson Davis, reverted to the eighteenth-century argument that southerners

Proslavery Theories

were doing the best they could with a situation they had inherited.

The 1852 election gave Davis and other southerners hope that slavery would be secure under the administration of a new president. Franklin Pierce, a Democrat from New Hampshire, won an easy victory over the Whig presidential nominee, General Winfield Scott. Pierce believed that the defense of each section's rights was essential to the nation's unity. And the victory of a proponent of the Compromise of 1850 suggested its popular support.

Election of 1852

That interpretation of the election, however, was erroneous. Pierce's victory derived less from his strengths than from the Whig Party's weakness. The Whigs were a congressional and state-based party that never had achieved much success in presidential politics. Sectional discord was splitting the party in two, and the deaths of President Taylor, Daniel Webster, and Henry Clay had deprived Whigs of the few dominant personalities they had. In 1852 the Whig Party ran on little but its past reputation.

In 1854, upon learning that a runaway slave named Anthony Burns was in custody in Boston, President Pierce moved decisively to enforce the Fugitive Slave Act. He telegraphed local officials to "incur any expense to insure the execution of the law" and sent marines, cavalry, and artillery to Boston. When Burns's owner seemed willing to sell his property, the United States attorney blocked the sale and won a decision that Anthony Burns must return to slavery. United States troops marched Burns to Boston harbor through streets draped in black and hung with American flags at half mast. At a cost of $100,000, equivalent to roughly $2 million today, a single black man was returned to slavery through the power of federal law.

This demonstration of federal support for slavery radicalized opinion. Textile manufacturer Amos A. Lawrence observed that "we went to bed one night old fashioned, conservative, Compromise Union Whigs & waked up stark mad Abolitionists." In New England, states passed personal-liberty laws designed to impede or block federal enforcement. But where northerners saw evidence that the Slave Power was dominating American government, outraged slaveholders saw northern "faithlessness" to the law.

Pierce seemed unable to avoid sectional conflict in other arenas as well. His proposal for a transcontinental railroad derailed when congressmen fought over its location, North or South. His attempts to acquire foreign territory stirred more trouble. An annexation treaty with Hawai'i failed because southern senators would not vote for another free state, and efforts to acquire slaveholding Cuba angered antislavery northerners. Then another territorial bill threw Congress and the nation into a bitter conflict that was to have significant results.

Territorial Problems Shatter the Party System

In 1854, Stephen A. Douglas introduced a bill to establish the Kansas and Nebraska Territories. As a senator from Illinois, Douglas hoped for a midwestern transcontinental railroad to boost Chicago's economy and encourage settlement of the Great Plains. No company, however, would build such a railroad before Congress organized the territories it would cross. Thus it was probably for the sake of promoting the construction of a railroad that Douglas introduced a bill that inflamed sectional passions, finished off the Whig Party, damaged the northern Democrats, and gave birth to a new Republican Party.

The Kansas-Nebraska bill exposed the first flaw of the Compromise of 1850—the conflicting interpretations of popular sovereignty. Douglas's bill left "all questions pertaining to slavery in the Territories . . . to the people residing therein." Northerners and southerners, however, still disagreed violently over what territorial settlers could constitutionally do. Moreover, the Kansas and Nebraska Territories lay within the Louisiana Purchase, and the Missouri Compromise prohibited slavery in all that land from latitude 36°30' north to the Canadian border. If popular sovereignty were to mean anything in Kansas and Nebraska, it had to mean that the Missouri Com-

Kansas-Nebraska Bill

promise was no longer in effect and that settlers could establish slavery there.

After a titanic struggle in Congress, lasting more than three months, the bill became law in May 1854 (see map below). Northern reaction to the bill was immediate, widespread, and enduring. Abolitionists charged sinister aggression by the Slave Power, and northern fears of slavery's influence deepened. Opposition to the Fugitive Slave Act grew dramatically; between 1855 and 1859 Connecticut, Rhode Island, Massachusetts, Michigan, Maine, Ohio, and Wisconsin passed personal-liberty laws. These laws interfered with the Fugitive Slave Act—and enraged southern leaders—by providing counsel for alleged fugitives and requiring trial by jury. More important was the devastating impact of the Kansas-Nebraska Act on political parties. The weakened Whig Party broke apart into northern and south-

ern wings that could no longer cooperate nationally. One of the two foundations of the second party system was now gone. The Democrats survived, but their support in the North fell drastically in the 1854 elections.

The beneficiary of northern voters' wrath was a new political party. During the summer and fall of 1854, antislavery Whigs and Democrats, Free-Soilers, and other reformers throughout the Old Northwest met to form the new Republican Party, dedicated to keeping slavery out of the territories. The influence of the Republicans rapidly spread to the East, and they won a stunning victory in the 1854 elections by capturing a majority of northern House seats.

For the first time, too, a sectional party had gained significant power in the political system.

The New Republican Party

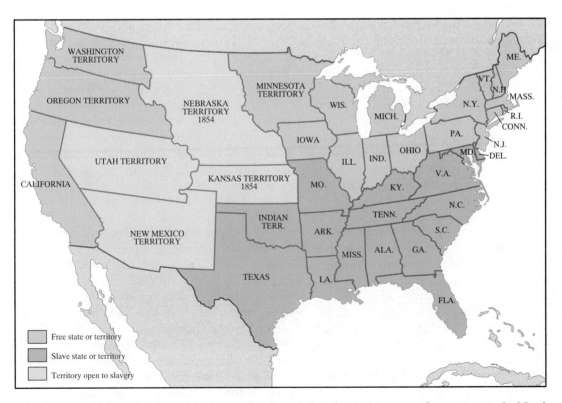

The Kansas-Nebraska Act, 1854 *Stephen Douglas's bill raised a storm of opposition in the North because it repealed the Missouri Compromise's limitation on slavery. In Kansas and Nebraska, land was opened to slavery where it had been prohibited before.*

Previously, every major party was a national organization whose leaders patched up sectional differences to achieve partisan goals. Now the Whigs were gone, and only the Democrats struggled to maintain a national following. The sectional Republican Party, which absorbed the Free-Soil Party, grew rapidly in the North by raising moral issues that angered many southerners.

Nor were Republicans the only new party. For a brief period, an anti-immigrant organization, the American Party, seemed likely to replace the

Know-Nothings

Whigs. This party, popularly known as the Know-Nothings (because its first members kept their purposes secret, answering "I know nothing" to all questions), exploited nativist fear of foreigners. Between 1848 and 1860, nearly 3.5 million immigrants entered the United States—proportionally the heaviest inflow of foreigners ever in American history (see pages 224–227). In 1854 anti-immigrant fears gave the Know-Nothings more supporters in some northern states than either the Republicans or the Free-Soilers. But like the Whigs, the Know-Nothings could not keep their northern and southern wings together, and they melted away after 1856. That left the field to the Republicans (see table, page 262).

Republicans, Know-Nothings, and Democrats were all scrambling to attract former Whig voters. The demise of that party ensured a major

Realignment of the Political System

realignment of the political system, with nearly half of the old electorate up for grabs. To woo these homeless Whigs, the remaining parties made appeals to various segments of the electorate. Immigration, temperance, homestead bills, the tariff, internal improvements—all played important roles in attracting voters during the 1850s.

The Republicans appealed strongly to those interested in the economic development of the West. Commercial agriculture was booming in

Republican Appeals

the Ohio–Mississippi–Great Lakes area, but residents of that region desired more canals, roads, and river and harbor improvements to reap

the full benefit of their labors. There was also widespread interest in a program that would provide homesteaders with western public land at no cost. Whigs had favored and Democrats opposed all these things. Seizing their opportunity, the Republicans added internal improvements and land-grant planks to their platform. They also backed higher tariffs as an enticement to industrialists and businessmen.

Partisan ideological appeals, which had a significant impact on the sectional crisis, were another major feature of the realigned political system. In the North, Republicans attracted many voters through effective use of ideology. When they preached "Free Soil, Free Labor, Free Men," they captured an image that northerners had of themselves and their future. These phrases resonated with traditional ideals of equality, liberty, and opportunity.

"Free Soil, Free Labor, Free Men" seemed an appropriate motto for a northern economy that was energetic, expanding, and prosperous. The

Republican Ideology

key to progress appeared, to many people, to be free labor. Any hard-working and virtuous man, it was thought, could improve his condition and achieve economic independence by seizing opportunities that the country had to offer. Republicans argued that the South, which relied on slave labor and had little industry, was backward and retrograde by comparison, and their arguments captured much of the spirit of the age in the North.

The Republican Party thus attracted support from a variety of sources. Opposition to the extension of slavery had brought the party into being, but party members carefully broadened their appeal by adopting the causes of other groups. They were wise to do so. As the New York newspaper editor Horace Greeley wrote in 1860, "an Anti-Slavery man *per se* cannot be elected." But, he added, "a Tariff, River-and-Harbor, Pacific Railroad, Free Homestead man, *may* succeed *although* he is Anti-Slavery." As these elements joined the Republican Party, they also learned more about the dangers of slavery. Thus the process of party building deepened the sectional conflict.

A similar process was under way in the South. In the increasingly tense atmosphere of sectional crisis, homeless southern Whigs were highly susceptible to strong states' rights positions and defense of slavery. Democratic leaders emphasized such appeals and managed to convert most of the formerly Whig slaveholders, who responded to their class interests. South of the Mason-Dixon line, however, yeomen—not planters—constituted the Democratic Party's heart. Thus Democratic politicians, though often slaveowners themselves, lauded the common man and argued that their policies advanced his interests. According to the southern version of republicanism, white citizens in a slave society enjoyed liberty and social equality *because* black people were enslaved. As Jefferson Davis put it in 1851, slavery elevated every white person's status and allowed the nonslaveholder to *"stand upon the broad level of equality with the rich man."* Slave-holding Democrats warned that the issue was "shall negroes govern white men, or white men govern negroes?" Southern leaders also portrayed the well-ordered South as the true defender of constitutional principles.

Southern Democrats

The arguments had their effect. Racial fears and traditional political loyalties helped keep the political alliance between yeoman farmers and planters intact through the 1850s. No viable party emerged to replace the Whigs. The result was a one-party system that emphasized sectional issues. In the South as in the North, political realignment sharpened sectional divisions.

Political leaders of both sections argued that racial change threatened opportunity. The *Montgomery* (Alabama) *Mail* warned southern whites in 1860 that the Republicans intended "to free the negroes and force amalgamation between them and the children of the poor men of the South." Republicans warned northern workers that if slavery entered the territories, the great reservoir of opportunity for ordinary citizens would be poisoned. Such charges aroused fear and anxiety, but events in the territory of Kansas did more to deepen the conflict. When implemented, the Kansas-Nebraska Act spawned hatred and violence. Abolitionists and religious groups sent in armed Free-Soil settlers; southerners sent in their reinforcements to establish slavery and prevent "northern hordes" from stealing Kansas away. Soon the whole nation was talking about "Bleeding Kansas."

Politics in the territory resembled war more than democracy. During elections for a territorial legislature in 1855, thousands of proslavery Missourians invaded the polls and ran up a large but fraudulent majority for slavery candidates. The resulting legislature legalized slavery, and in response Free-Soilers held an unauthorized convention at which they created their own government and constitution. A proslavery posse sent to arrest the Free-Soil leaders sacked the town of Lawrence. In revenge John Brown, an antislavery zealot who saw himself as God's instrument to destroy slavery, murdered five proslavery settlers. Soon, armed bands of guerrillas roamed the state.

Bleeding Kansas

These passions brought violence to the United States Senate in May 1856, when Charles Sumner of Massachusetts denounced "the Crime against Kansas." Radical in his antislavery views, Sumner bitterly assailed the president, the South, and Senator Andrew P. Butler of South Carolina. Soon thereafter Butler's cousin, Representative Preston Brooks, approached Sumner at the latter's Senate desk, raised his cane, and began to beat Sumner on the head. Shocked northerners recoiled from what they saw as another southern assault on free speech and the South's readiness to use violence to have its way. South Carolina voters reelected Brooks and sent him dozens of new canes. The country was becoming polarized.

The election of 1856 showed how extreme that polarization had become. The Democrats bypassed prominent figures and nominated James Buchanan of Pennsylvania, whose chief virtue was that for the past four years he had been ambassador to Britain and thus uninvolved in territorial controversies. This anonymity and superior party organization helped Buchanan win the election, but he owed his victory to southern support. The Republican candidate, John C. Frémont, won eleven of the sixteen free states; Republicans had become the dominant party in the North. The

Know-Nothing candidate won almost 1 million votes, but this election was to be his party's last hurrah. Only a sectional Republican Party and divided Democratic Party remained.

 ## Slavery and the Nation's Future

For years the issue of slavery in the territories had convulsed Congress, and for years Congress had tried to settle the issue with vague formulas. In 1857 the Supreme Court took up this emotionally charged subject and attempted to silence controversy with a definitive verdict.

A Missouri slave named Dred Scott had sued his owner for his freedom. Scott based his claim on the fact that his former owner, an army surgeon, had taken him for several years into Illinois, a free state, and into the Wisconsin Territory, from which slavery had been barred by the Missouri Compromise. Scott first won and then lost his case as it moved on appeal through the state courts, into the federal system, and finally to the Supreme Court.

***Dred Scott* Case**

Was a black person like Dred Scott a citizen of the United States and thus eligible to sue in federal court? Had residence in a free state or free territory made him free? Did Congress have the power to prohibit slavery in a territory or to delegate that power to a territorial legislature?

In March 1857, Chief Justice Roger B. Taney of Maryland answered each of the questions when he delivered the majority opinion of a divided Court in *Dred Scott* v. *Sanford*. Taney declared that Scott was not a citizen of either the United States or Missouri; that residence in free territory did not make Scott free; and that Congress had no power to bar slavery from a territory, as it had done in the Missouri Compromise. The decision not only overturned a sectional compromise that had been honored for years; it also invalidated the basic ideas of the Wilmot Proviso and probably popular sovereignty as well.

The Slave Power seemed to have won a major constitutional victory. African-Americans were especially dismayed, for Taney's decision asserted that the founders had never intended for black people to be citizens. Taney was mistaken, however. African-Americans had been citizens in several of the original states. Nevertheless, the *Dred Scott* decision seemed to shut the door permanently on their hopes for justice and equal rights.

A storm of angry reaction broke in the North. The decision alarmed a wide variety of northerners and seemed to confirm every charge against the aggressive Slave Power.

Abraham Lincoln on the Slave Power

"There is such a thing as the slave power," warned the *Cincinnati Daily Commercial.* "It has marched over and annihilated the boundaries of the states. We are now one great homogenous slaveholding community." "Where will it end?" asked the *Atlantic Monthly.* To Abraham Lincoln, the territorial question affected every citizen. "The whole nation," he declared as early as 1854, "is interested that the best use shall be made of these Territories. We want them for homes of free white people. This they cannot be, to any considerable extent, if slavery shall be planted within them." After the *Dred Scott* decision, he charged, it was clear that slavery's advocates, including highly placed government officials, were trying to "push it forward, till it shall become lawful in *all* the states . . . *North* as well as *South.*" The next step in the unfolding Slave Power conspiracy, Lincoln alleged, would be a Supreme Court decision "declaring that the Constitution does not permit a State to exclude slavery from its limits. . . ." This charge was not pure hyperbole, for lawsuits soon challenged state laws that freed slaves brought within their borders.

Lincoln's most eloquent statement against the Slave Power was his famous "House Divided" speech, in which he declared:

> I do not expect the Union to be dissolved—I do not expect the House to fall—but I do expect it to cease to be divided. It will become all one thing or all the other. Either the opponents of slavery will arrest the further spread of it, and place it where the public mind shall rest in the belief that it is in the course of ultimate extinction; or its advocates will push it forward, till it shall become alike lawful in all the States, old as well as new, North as well as South.

How do historians know what motivated Abraham Lincoln to oppose the extension of slavery? Lincoln, of course, was a public man who made many addresses and public statements. His words as a politician and leader of the Republican Party show his reverence for the Declaration of Independence and America's heritage of freedom. But Lincoln also produced many private writings. The page reproduced below comes from a notebook in which he recorded his reactions to a proslavery book, *Slavery Ordained of God,* by *Rev. Fred A. Ross.* Criticizing Ross, Lincoln revealed his dislike of privilege and exposed the self-interest of those who would exploit others: "Dr. Ross sits in the shade, with gloves on his hands, and subsists on the bread that Sambo is earning in the burning sun" rather than "delv[ing] for his own bread."   Illinois State Historical Society and Library.

Events convinced countless northerners that slave-holders were nearing their goal of making slavery a national institution.

Politically, these forceful Republican arguments offset the difficulties that the *Dred Scott* decision posed. By endorsing Calhoun's theories, the Court had in effect declared that the central position of the Republican Party—no extension of slavery—was unconstitutional. Republicans could only repudiate the decision, appealing to a "higher law," or hope to change the personnel of the Court. They did both.

Stephen A. Douglas, however, as a northern Democrat with presidential aspirations, faced an awful dilemma. He could not afford to offend the southern wing of the party; yet he had to ease the fears of the northern wing. Douglas chose to stand by his principle of popular sovereignty. In 1857 Kansans voted on a proslavery constitution that had been drafted at Lecompton. It was defeated by more than ten thousand votes. The evidence was overwhelming that Kansans did not want slavery, but President Buchanan tried to force the Lecompton Constitution through Congress. Breaking with the administration, Douglas threw his weight against the Lecompton Constitution. He gauged opinion in Kansas correctly; in 1858, voters there rejected the constitution again. But his action infuriated southern Democrats.

Douglas further alienated the South in his debates with Abraham Lincoln, who challenged him for the Illinois Senate seat in 1858. Speaking at Freeport, Illinois, Douglas attempted to revive the concept of popular sovereignty with some tortured arguments. Asserting that the Supreme Court had ruled only on the powers of Congress, not on the powers of a *territorial* legislature, Douglas claimed that the latter could bar slavery either by passing a law against it or by doing nothing. Without the patrol laws and police regulations that supported slavery, he reasoned, the institution could not exist. This argument, called the Freeport Doctrine, temporarily shored up Douglas's crumbling position in the North. But it gave southern Democrats further evidence that

Stephen Douglas Proposes the Freeport Doctrine

Douglas was unreliable. Some, like Representative William L. Yancey of Alabama, concluded that southern rights and slavery would be safe only in a separate nation.

The immediate consequence for politics, however, was the likelihood of a split in the Democratic Party. Northern Democrats could not support the territorial protection for slavery that southern Democrats insisted was theirs as a constitutional right. Thus the issue of slavery in the territories continued to generate wider conflict, even though it had little immediate, practical significance. In territories outside Kansas the number of settlers was small, and in all territories the number of African-Americans was negligible—less than 1 percent of the populations of Kansas and New Mexico. Nevertheless, the situation had become explosive.

 ## Breakup of the Union

One year before the 1860 presidential election, John Brown led a small band in an attack on the federal arsenal at Harpers Ferry, Virginia. Hoping to trigger a slave rebellion, Brown failed miserably and was quickly captured, tried, and executed. Yet his attempted insurrection struck fear into the South. Then it became known that Brown had received financial backing from several prominent abolitionists. When northern intellectuals such as Emerson and Thoreau praised Brown as a hero and a martyr, white southerners' fears and anger multiplied many times over.

Many believed that the election of 1860 would decide the fate of the Union. Only the Democratic Party remained as an organization that was truly national in scope. Even religious denominations had split into northern and southern wings during the 1840s and 1850s. "One after another," wrote a Mississippi newspaper editor, "the links which have bound the North and South together, have been severed . . . [but] the Democratic party looms gradually up, its nationality intact, and waves the olive branch over the troubled waters of politics." At its 1860 convention, however, the Democratic Party broke in two.

Stephen A. Douglas wanted his party's presidential nomination, but he could not afford to alienate northern voters by accepting the southern position on the territories.

Splintering of the Democratic Party

Southern Democrats, however, insisted on recognition of their rights and they moved to block Douglas's nomination. When Douglas obtained a majority for his version of the platform, delegates from eight slave states walked out of the party convention in Charleston. After efforts at compromise failed, the Democrats presented two nominees: Douglas for the northern wing, and Vice President John C. Breckinridge of Kentucky for the southern. The Republicans nominated Abraham Lincoln. A Constitutional Union Party, formed to preserve the nation but strong only in the Upper South, nominated John Bell of Tennessee.

The results of the balloting were sectional in character. Lincoln won, but Douglas, Breckinridge, and Bell together received most of the votes. Douglas had broad-based support but won few states.

Election of 1860

Breckinridge carried nine southern states. Bell won pluralities in Virginia, Kentucky, and Tennessee. Lincoln prevailed in the North, but in the states that ultimately remained loyal to the Union he gained only a plurality, not a majority. Lincoln's victory was won in the electoral college.

Given the heterogeneous nature of Republican voters, it is likely that many of them did not view the issue of slavery in the territories as paramount. But opposition to slavery's extension was the core issue of the Republican Party, and abolitionists and supporters of free soil in the North worked to keep the Republicans from compromising on their territorial stand. Meanwhile in the South, proslavery advocates and secessionists demanded that state conventions assemble to consider secession.

Lincoln made the crucial decision not to soften his party's position on the territories. His refusal to compromise probably derived both from conviction and from concern for the unity of the Republican Party. Although many conservative Republicans—eastern businessmen and former Whigs who did not feel strongly about slavery—hoped for a compromise, the original and most committed Republicans—antislavery voters and "conscience Whigs"—were adamant for free soil. Lincoln chose to preserve party unity by standing firm against slavery's extension.

Southern leaders in the Senate were willing, conditionally, to accept a compromise drawn up by Senator John J. Crittenden of Kentucky. Crittenden proposed that the two sections divide the territories between them at latitude 36°30'. But the southerners would agree to this *only* if the Republicans did, too. When Lincoln ruled out concessions on the territorial issue, Crittenden's peacemaking effort collapsed. Virginians called for a special convention in Washington, but this gathering, too, failed to find a solution.

Misjudgment also played a role in the coming of war. Lincoln and other prominent Republicans believed that southerners were bluffing when they threatened secession; Republicans expected a pro-Union majority in the South to assert itself. On their side, southern leaders had become convinced that northern leaders were not taking them seriously and that a posture of strength was necessary to win respect for their demands. Confrontation was more likely than compromise.

Meanwhile, the Union was being destroyed. On December 20, 1860, South Carolina passed an ordinance of secession. This step marked the inauguration of the strategy of separate-state secession.

Secession of South Carolina

Recognizing the difficulty of persuading all the southern states to challenge the federal government simultaneously, secessionists concentrated their efforts on the most extreme proslavery state. They hoped South Carolina's secession would induce other states to follow, with each decision building momentum for disunion.

Southern extremists soon got their way in the Deep South. They called separate state conventions and passed secession ordinances in

Confederate States of America

Mississippi, Florida, Alabama, Georgia, Louisiana, and Texas. By February 1861 these states had joined South Carolina to form a new government in Montgomery, Alabama: the Confederate States of America. The delegates at Montgomery chose Jefferson Davis as their president.

This apparent unanimity of action was deceiving. Many southerners who in 1860 had voted in the United States presidential election stayed home a few months later rather than vote for delegates who would decide upon secession. Even so, in some state conventions the vote to secede was close, with secession decided by overrepresentation of plantation districts. Furthermore, the conventions were noticeably unwilling to let voters ratify their acts. Four states in the Upper South—Virginia, North Carolina, Tennessee, and Arkansas—flatly rejected secession and did not join the Confederacy until after fighting had begun. In the border states, popular sentiment was deeply divided; minorities in Kentucky and Missouri tried to secede, but these slave states ultimately came under Union control, along with Maryland and Delaware (see map, page 273).

Such misgivings were not surprising. Secession posed the possibility of war and the question of who would die. Analysis of election returns from 1860 and 1861 indicates that heavily slaveholding counties strongly supported secession and that most counties with few slaves took an antisecession position or were staunchly Unionist (see figure, page 274). Thus, with war on the horizon, nonslaveholders were beginning to consider their class interests and to ask how far they would go to support slavery and slaveowners.

The dilemma facing President Lincoln on inauguration day in March 1861 was how to maintain the authority of the federal government without provoking war. Proceeding cautiously, he sought only to hold on to forts in the states that had left the Union, reasoning that in this way he

Attack on Fort Sumter

On February 18, 1861, in Montgomery, Alabama, Jefferson Davis took an oath as president of the Confederate States of America. Davis later recalled that he foresaw "troubles innumerable" but was committed to seek independence as his paramount goal. Boston Athenaeum.

could assert federal sovereignty while waiting for a restoration of relations. But Jefferson Davis, who could not claim to lead a sovereign nation if the Confederate forts were under foreign (that is, United States) control, was unwilling to be so patient. A collision was inevitable.

It arrived in the early morning hours of April 12, 1861, at Fort Sumter in Charleston harbor. A federal garrison there ran low on food, and Lincoln notified the South Carolinians that he was sending a ship to resupply the fort. For the Montgomery government, the alternatives were to attack the fort or to acquiesce to Lincoln's authority. After the Confederate cabinet met, the Secretary of War ordered local commanders to obtain a sur-

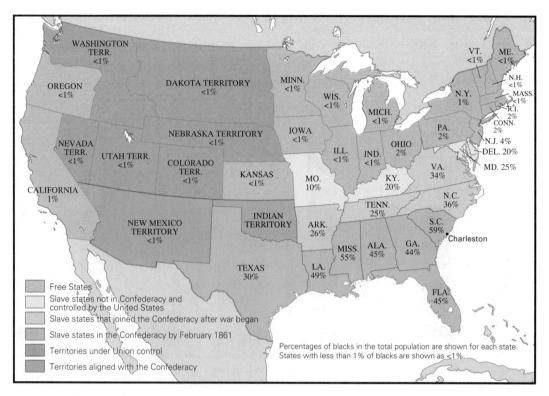

The Divided Nation—Slave and Free Areas, 1861 *After fighting began, the Upper South joined the Deep South in the Confederacy.*

render or attack the fort. After two days of heavy bombardment, the federal garrison finally surrendered. Confederates permitted the United States troops to sail away on unarmed vessels while Charlestonians celebrated wildly. Thus began the bloodiest war in America's history.

 ## Conclusion

Throughout the 1840s and 1850s many able leaders had worked diligently to avert this outcome. Most people, North and South, had hoped to keep the nation together. As late as 1858 even Jefferson Davis had declared, "This great country will continue united," saying that "to the innermost fibers of my heart I love it all, and every part." Why, then, had war broken out?

Slavery was an issue on which compromise was impossible. The emotions bound up in attacking and defending it were too powerful, and the motives it affected too vital, for compromise. Because it was deeply entwined with major policy questions of the present and the foreseeable future, each section ultimately regarded slavery as too important to be put aside.

North and South had fundamentally different attitudes toward the institution. The logic of Republican ideology tended in the direction of abolishing slavery, even though Republicans denied any such intention. The logic of southern leaders' arguments led toward establishing slavery everywhere, though southern leaders denied that they sought to do any such thing. Lincoln put these facts succinctly. In a postelection letter to his old friend Alexander Stephens of Georgia, Lincoln wrote, "You think slavery is *right* and ought to be

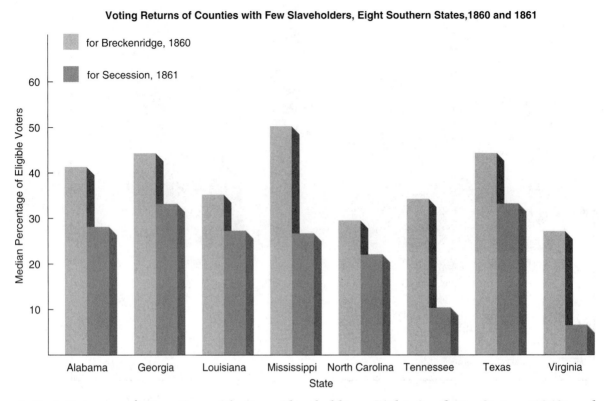

Voting Returns of Counties with Few Slaveholders, Eight Southern States, 1860 and 1861

Voting Returns of Counties with Few Slaveholders, Eight Southern States, 1860 and 1861 *This graph depicts voting in counties whose percentage of slaveholders ranked them among the lower half of the counties in their state. How does voters' support for secession in 1861 compare with support for John Breckenridge, the southern Democratic candidate in 1860? Why was their support for secession so weak? At this time counties with many slaveholders were giving increased support to secession.*

expanded; while we think it is *wrong* and ought to be restricted. That I suppose is the rub."

The issue of slavery in the territories made conflict impossible to avoid. Territorial expansion generated disputes so frequently that the nation never enjoyed a breathing space. As the conflict recurred, its influence on policy and effect on the government deepened. Every southern victory increased fear of the Slave Power, and each new expression of Free-Soil sentiment made alarmed slaveholders more insistent in their demands. Concern over slavery had driven all the other conflicts. But as the fighting began, this, the war's central issue, was shrouded in confusion. How would the Civil War affect slavery, its place in the law, and African-Americans' place in society?

Suggestions for Further Reading

Politics: General

Thomas B. Alexander, *Sectional Stress and Party Strength* (1967); Tyler Anbinder, *Nativism and Slavery* (1992); Paul Bergeron, *The Presidency of James K. Polk* (1987); Frederick J. Blue, *The Free Soilers: Third Party Politics, 1848–1854* (1973); Stanley W. Campbell, *The Slave Catchers* (1968); Don E. Fehrenbacher, *The Dred Scott Case* (1978); George M. Fredrickson, *The Black Image in the White Mind* (1971); Holman Hamilton, *Prologue to Conflict: The Crisis and Compromise of 1850* (1964); Michael F. Holt, *The Political Crisis of the 1850s* (1978); William Lee Miller, *Arguing About Slavery* (1996); Russell B. Nye, *Fettered Freedom* (1949); Merrill D. Peterson, *The Great Triumvirate: Webster, Clay, and Calhoun* (1987); David M. Potter, *The Impending Crisis, 1848–1861* (1976); Joel H. Silbey, *The Transformation of American Politics, 1840–1960* (1967); Kenneth M. Stampp,

America in 1857 (1991); Gerald W. Wolff, *The Kansas-Nebraska Bill* (1977).

The South and Slavery

William L. Barney, *The Secessionist Impulse* (1974); Steven A. Channing, *A Crisis of Fear: Secession in South Carolina* (1970); William J. Cooper, Jr., *The South and the Politics of Slavery, 1828–1856* (1978); Daniel W. Crofts, *Reluctant Confederates: Upper South Unionists in the Secession Crisis* (1989); Lacy K. Ford, Jr., *Origins of Southern Radicalism* (1988); William W. Freehling, *The Road to Disunion* (1990); Eugene D. Genovese, *The Political Economy of Slavery* (1967); Michael P. Johnson, *Toward a Patriarchal Republic: The Secession of Georgia* (1977); John Niven, *John C. Calhoun and the Price of Union* (1988); Thomas E. Schott, *Alexander H. Stephens of Georgia* (1988); William R. Stanton, *The Leopard's Spots* (1960); J. Mills Thornton III, *Politics and Power in a Slave Society* (1978); Ralph Wooster, *The Secession Conventions of the South* (1962).

The North and Antislavery

Dale Baum, *The Civil War Party System* (1984); Eugene H. Berwanger, *The Frontier Against Slavery* (1967); David Donald, *Charles Sumner and the Coming of the Civil War* (1960); Louis Filler, *The Crusade Against Slavery, 1830–1860* (1960); Eric Foner, *Free Soil, Free Labor, Free Men* (1970); Louis S. Gerteis, *Morality and Utility in American Antislavery Reform* (1987); William E. Gienapp, *The Origins of the Republican Party, 1852–1856* (1986); Robert W. Johannsen, *Stephen A. Douglas* (1973); Aileen S. Kraditor, *Means and Ends in American Abolitionism* (1969); Lewis Perry and Michael Fellman, eds., *Antislavery Reconsidered* (1979).

The Mexican War and Foreign Policy

K. Jack Bauer, *Zachary Taylor* (1985); Gene M. Brack, *Mexico Views Manifest Destiny, 1821–1846* (1976); Richard Griswold del Castillo, *The Treaty of Guadalupe Hidalgo* (1990); Neal Harlow, *California Conquered* (1982); Reginald Horsman, *Race and Manifest Destiny* (1981); Robert W. Johannsen, *To the Halls of the Montezumas: The Mexican War and the American Imagination* (1985); Ernest M. Lander, Jr., *Reluctant Imperialists: Calhoun, the South Carolinians, and the Mexican War* (1980); Robert E. May, *The Southern Dream of a Caribbean Empire, 1854–1861* (1973); Frederick Merk, *Manifest Destiny and Mission in American History* (1963); David M. Pletcher, *The Diplomacy of Annexation: Texas, Oregon, and the Mexican War* (1973); Dirk Raat, *Mexico and the United States* (1992); Anders Stephanson, *Manifest Destiny* (1995); David J. Weber, *The Mexican Frontier, 1821–1846* (1982).

15

Transforming Fire:
The Civil War
1861–1865

He was a living legend—a frontiersman who had a distinguished career as lawyer, congressman, and governor of Tennessee. But in 1829 he abruptly resigned his governorship and spent the next three years living among the Cherokees. In 1836 he reemerged as commander-in-chief of the armies winning Texan independence. He then served two terms as president of the Republic of Texas and later was a United States senator. After being elected governor of Texas in 1859, Sam Houston was deposed in March 1861. Why? Houston opposed secession, refused to take an oath of allegiance to the Confederacy, and challenged the authority of the secession convention. Its members ended his career by declaring his office vacant.

The Civil war brought astonishing, unexpected changes everywhere in the nation. For some, wealth changed to poverty and hope to despair; for others, the suffering of war spelled opportunity. Contrasts abounded between noble and crass motives. Even slaves, who hoped they were witnessing God's "Holy War for liberation," encountered unsympathetic liberators. When a Yankee soldier ransacked a slave woman's cabin, she denounced him for betraying his cause of freedom. Angrily the soldier contradicted her, saying, "I'm fightin' for $14 a month and the Union."

Northern troops were not the only ones to feel anger over their sacrifice. Impoverished by the war, one southern farmer had endured inflation, taxes, and shortages to support the Confederacy. Then an impressment agent arrived to take still more from him—grain and meat, horses and mules, and wagons. In return, the agent offered only a certificate promising repayment sometime in the future. Bitter and disgusted, the farmer declared, "The sooner this damned Government falls to pieces, the better it will be for us."

For these people and millions of others, the Civil War was a life-changing event. It obliterated the normal patterns and circumstances of life. Millions of men were swept away into training camps and battle units. Families struggled to survive without their men; businesses tried to cope with the loss of workers. Women in both North and South took on extra responsibilities in the home and moved into new jobs in the work force. No sphere of life was untouched.

Change was most drastic in the South, where the leaders of the secession movement had launched a revolution for the purpose of keeping things unchanged. Their actions, however, led to a war that turned southern life upside down, imperiled the very existence of slavery, and resulted in policies more objectionable to the elite than any proposed by President-elect Lincoln. Life in the Confederacy proved to be a shockingly unsouthern experience.

War altered the North as well, but less deeply. Because most of the fighting took place on southern soil, northern farms and factories remained virtually unscathed. The drafting of workers and the changing need for products slowed the pace of industrialization somewhat, but factories and businesses remained busy. Workers lost ground to inflation, but the economy hummed. A new probusiness atmosphere dominated Congress. To the alarm of many, the powers of the federal government and of the president increased during the war.

Ultimately, the Civil War forced on the nation new social and racial arrangements. Its greatest effect was to compel leaders and citizens to deal directly with the issue they had debated and argued over but had been unable to resolve: slavery.

"Fighting Means Killing": The War in 1861 and 1862

Few Americans understood what they were getting into when the war began. The onset of hostilities sparked patriotic sentiments and joyous ceremonies in both North and South. Northern communities raised companies of volunteers eager to save the Union. In the South, confident recruits boasted of whipping the Yankees and returning home in time for dinner.

Through the spring of 1861 both sides scrambled to organize and train their armies. On July 21, 1861, the first battle took place outside Manassas Junction, Virginia, near a stream called Bull Run. General Irvin McDowell and 30,000 Union troops attacked General P. G. T. Beauregard's 22,000 southerners (see map, page 278). As raw recruits struggled amid the confusion of their first battle, federal forces began to gain ground. Then they ran into a line of Virginia troops under General Thomas Jackson. "There is Jackson standing like a stone wall," shouted one Confederate. "Stonewall" Jackson's line held, and the arrival of 9,000 Confederate reinforcements won the day for the South. Union troops fled back to Washington and shocked northerners, who feared their capital would be taken.

Battle of Bull Run

The unexpected rout at Bull Run gave northerners their first hint of the nature of the war to come. Victory would not be easy, even though the United States enjoyed an enormous advantage in resources. Pro-Union feeling was growing in western Virginia, and loyalties were divided in the four border slave states—Missouri, Kentucky, Maryland, and Delaware. But the rest of the Upper South had joined the Confederacy. Moved by an outpouring of regional loyalty, half a million southerners volunteered to fight.

Lincoln gave command of the army to General George B. McClellan, an officer who proved to be better at organization and training than at fighting. McClellan devoted the fall and winter of 1861 to readying a formidable force of a quarter-million men. The Union also began to implement other parts of its overall strategy, which called for a blockade of southern ports and eventual capture of the Mississippi River. Like a constricting snake, this "Anaconda plan" would strangle the Confederacy (see map, page 280). At first the Union Navy had too few ships to patrol 3,550 miles of coastline. Gradually, however, the navy increased the

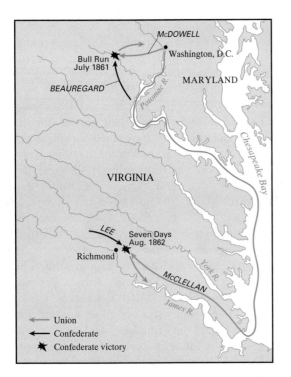

McClellan's Campaign   *The water route chosen by McClellan to threaten Richmond during the peninsular campaign.*

blockade's effectiveness, though it never bottled up southern commerce completely.

Confederate strategy was essentially defensive. A defensive posture not only was consistent with the South's claim that it merely wanted to be left alone, but also took into account the North's advantage in resources (see figure, page 281). Jefferson Davis, however, rejected a wholly defensive strategy. The South would pursue an "offensive defensive," taking advantage of opportunities to attack and using its interior lines of transportation to concentrate troops at crucial points.

Strategic thinking on both sides slighted the importance of "the West," that vast expanse of territory between Virginia and the Mississippi River. When the war began, both sides were unprepared for large-scale and sustained operations in the West, but before the end of the war it would prove to be a crucial theater.

The last half of 1861 brought no major land battles, but the North made gains by sea. Late in the summer Union naval forces captured Cape Hatteras and then seized Hilton Head, one of the Sea Islands off Port Royal, South Carolina (see map, page 280).

Union Naval Campaign

A few months later, similar operations secured vital coastal points in North Carolina, as well as Fort Pulaski, which defended Savannah. The coastal victories off South Carolina frightened planters, who abandoned their lands and fled. Their slaves greeted what they hoped to be freedom with rejoicing and broke the hated cotton gins. The Lincoln administration, however, was initially unwilling to wage a war against slavery and did not recognize their freedom.

The coastal incursions worried southerners, but the spring of 1862 brought even stronger evidence of the war's seriousness. In April Union ships commanded by Admiral David Farragut smashed through log booms blocking the Mississippi River and fought their way upstream to capture New Orleans. Farther west a Union victory at Elkhorn Tavern, Arkansas, shattered Confederate control of Indian Territory.

In February 1862 Union land and river forces in northern Tennessee won significant victories. There, General Ulysses S. Grant secured two prime routes to the Confederacy's heartland by capturing Forts Henry and Donelson. A path into Tennessee, Alabama, and Mississippi now lay open before the Union Army.

Grant's Campaign in Tennessee

Grant moved on into southern Tennessee and the first of the war's shockingly bloody encounters, the Battle of Shiloh. On April 6, Confederate General Albert Sidney Johnston caught Grant's troops with their backs to the Tennessee River. The Union forces took heavy casualties, but Johnson was killed. The next day federal reinforcements arrived and the Confederates withdrew. Neither side won a victory, yet the losses were staggering. Northern troops lost 13,000 men (killed, wounded, or cap-

Battle of Shiloh

• *Important Events* •

1861	Battle of Bull Run takes place		Battle of Chancellorsville ends in Confederate victory but General "Stonewall" Jackson's death

1861   Battle of Bull Run takes place
General George McClellan organizes Union Army
Union blockade begins
United States Congress passes first confiscation act
Trent affair

1862   Union captures Fort Henry and Fort Donelson
United States Navy captures New Orleans
Battle of Shiloh shows the war's destructiveness
Confederacy enacts conscription
General Robert E. Lee thwarts McClellan's offensive on Richmond
United States Congress passes second confiscation act
Confederacy mounts offensive in Maryland and Kentucky
Battle of Antietam ends Lee's drive into Maryland

1863   Emancipation Proclamation takes effect
United States Congress passes National Banking Act
Union enacts conscription
African-American soldiers join Union Army
Food riots occur in southern cities

Battle of Chancellorsville ends in Confederate victory but General "Stonewall" Jackson's death
Union wins key victories at Gettysburg and Vicksburg
Draft riots take place in New York City
Battle of Chattanooga leaves South vulnerable to General William T. Sherman's march

1864   Battles of the Wilderness and Spotsylvania produce heavy casualties on both sides in the effort to capture and defend Richmond
Battle of Cold Harbor continues carnage in Virginia
Abraham Lincoln requests Republican Party plank abolishing slavery
General Sherman captures Atlanta
Lincoln wins reelection
Jefferson Davis proposes emancipation within the Confederacy
Sherman marches through Georgia

1865   United States Congress approves Thirteenth Amendment
Hampton Roads Conference
Lee abandons Richmond and Petersburg
Lee surrenders at Appomattox Courthouse
Lincoln assassinated

---

tured) out of 63,000; southerners sacrificed 11,000 out of 40,000.

Meanwhile, on the Virginia front, President Lincoln had a different problem. Conquest was impossible without battles, but General McClellan seemed unwilling to fight. Habitually overestimating the size of enemy forces, McClellan called repeatedly for reinforcements and ignored Lincoln's directions to advance. Finally McClellan chose to move by a roundabout water route, sailing his troops around the York peninsula and advancing on Richmond from the east (see map, page 278). By June the sheer size of the federal armies outside the Confederacy's capital was highly threatening. But southern leaders foiled McClellan's legions. First, Stonewall Jackson moved north into the Shenandoah valley behind Union forces and threatened Washington, D.C., drawing some of the federal troops away from Richmond to protect their own capital. Then, in a series of engagements known as the Seven Days Battles, General Robert E. Lee struck at McClellan's army and on August 3 McClellan withdrew to the Potomac. Richmond remained safe for almost two more years.

Buoyed by these results, Jefferson Davis conceived an ambitious plan to turn the tide of the war and gain recognition of the Confederacy by

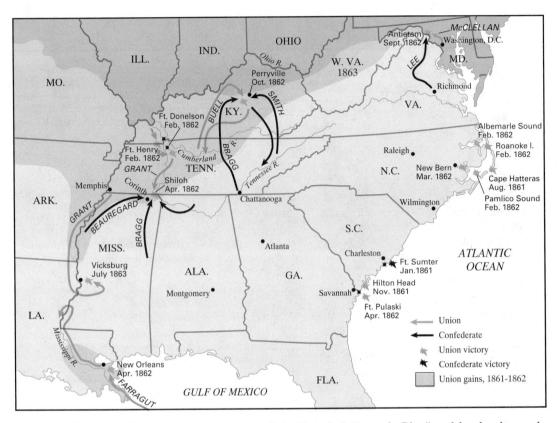

The Civil War, 1861–1863 *An overview of the Union's "Anaconda Plan" and key battles on the coast and in the West, 1861–1863.*

Confederate Offensive in Maryland and Kentucky

European nations. He ordered a general offensive, sending Lee north into Maryland and Generals Kirby Smith and Braxton Bragg into Kentucky, calling on residents of Maryland and Kentucky to make a separate peace with his government.

The plan was promising, but every part of the offensive failed. In the bloodiest day of the entire war, September 17, 1862, McClellan turned Lee back in the Battle of Antietam near Sharpsburg, Maryland. In Kentucky Generals Smith and Bragg were also forced to withdraw. Outnumbered and disadvantaged in resources (see figure, page 281) and having failed in its general offensive, the South's only long-range hope seemed to be a tenacious defense and stoic endurance.

But 1862 also brought painful lessons to the North. Confederate General James E. B. (Jeb) Stuart executed a daring cavalry raid into Pennsylvania in October. Then on December 13 Union general Ambrose Burnside unwisely ordered his soldiers to attack Lee's army, which held fortified positions on high ground at Fredericksburg, Virginia. Lee's men controlled the engagement so thoroughly that Lee was moved to say, "It is well that war is so terrible. We should grow too fond of it."

War Transforms the South

Even more than the fighting itself, disruptions in civilian life robbed southerners of their gaiety and nonchalance. The war altered southern society

Comparative Resources, Union and Confederate States, 1861

Union States   Confederate States

Total Population, 2.5 to 1

Free Men 18–60 Yrs., 4.4 to 1

Free Men in Military Service, 1864   44%   90%

Wealth Production, 3 to 1

Railroad Mileage, 2.4 to 1

Merchant Ship Tonnage, 9 to 1

Naval Ship Tonnage, 25 to 1

Factory Production Value, 10 to 1

Textile Goods Production, 14 to 1

Iron Production, 15 to 1

Coal Production, 38 to 1

Firearms Production, 32 to 1

Farm Acreage, 3 to 1

Draft Animals, 1.8 to 1

Livestock, 1.5 to 1

Wheat Production, 4.2 to 1

Corn Production, 2 to 1

Cotton Production, 1 to 24

Comparative Resources, Union and Confederate States, 1861 *The North had vastly superior resources. Although the North's advantages in manpower and industrial capacity proved very important, the South could not really be conquered until it chose to give up the fight.* Source: From *The Times Atlas of World History.* Time Books, London, 1978. Used with permission.

beyond all expectations. One of the first traditions to fall was the southern preference for local government. The South had been characterized by limited government. States' rights had been its motto, but by modern standards even the state governments were weak. To withstand the massive power of the North, the South needed to centralize, and no one saw the necessity of centralization more clearly than Jefferson Davis.

Although Davis moved promptly to bring all arms, supplies, and troops under his control, by early 1862 the scope and duration of the conflict required something more. When the states failed to provide sufficient numbers of troops, Davis secured passage in April 1862 of the first national conscription (draft) law in American history. He also adopted a firm leadership role toward the Confederate congress, which raised taxes and later passed a tax-in-kind—a tax paid in farm products. Where opposition arose, the government suspended the writ of habeas corpus (which prevented individuals from being held without trial) and imposed martial law. In the face of political opposition that cherished states' rights, Davis proved unyielding.

Soon the Confederate administration in Richmond was exercising virtually complete control over the southern economy. Because it controlled the supply of labor through conscription, the administration could compel industry to work on government contracts and supply the military's needs. The Confederate Congress also gave the central

Centralization of Power

In October 1862 in New York City, photographer Matthew Brady opened an exhibition of photographs from the Battle of Antietam. The camera, whose modern form had been invented only in 1826, made war's carnage hideously real. Although few knew it, Brady's vision was very poor, and this photograph of Confederate dead was actually made by his assistants, Alexander Gardner and James F. Gibson.   Confederate dead: Library of Congress; camera: George Eastman House Collection.

government almost complete control of the railroads; in 1864 shipping, too, came under extensive regulation. New statutes even limited corporate profits and dividends. A large bureaucracy sprang up to administer these operations. By the war's end, the southern bureaucracy was larger in proportion to population than its northern counterpart.

Clerks and subordinate officials crowded the towns and cities where Confederate departments had their offices. The sudden population booms

Effects of War on Southern Cities and Industry

that resulted overwhelmed the housing supply and stimulated new construction. The pressure was especially great in Richmond, whose population increased 250 percent. But there was another prime cause of urban growth in the South: industrialization. The Union blockade caused the traditionally agricultural South to become interested in industry. Davis exulted that manufacturing was making the

South "more and more independent of the rest of the world." Indeed, beginning almost from scratch, the Confederacy achieved tremendous feats of industrial development.

Southerners adopted new ways in response to these changes. Women, restricted to narrow roles in antebellum society, gained substantial new responsibilities. The wives and mothers of soldiers now headed households and performed men's work, adding to their traditional chores the tasks of raising crops and tending animals. Women in non-slaveowning families cultivated fields themselves, while wealthier women suddenly had to manage field hands. In cities, white women—who had been virtually excluded from the labor force—found a limited number of respectable new paying jobs. "Government girls" staffed the Confederate bureaucracy, and female schoolteachers became commonplace in the South for the first time. Some women gained confidence from their new responsibilities. Others, especially some wealthy women, found their changed situation and new tasks both difficult and distasteful.

Change in the Role of Southern Women

For millions of ordinary southerners the war brought privation and suffering. Mass poverty descended for the first time on a large minority of the white population. Many yeoman families had lost their breadwinners to the army. As a South Carolina newspaper put it, "The duties of war have called away from home the sole supports of many, many families. . . . Help must be given, or the poor will suffer." The poor sought help from relatives, neighbors, friends, anyone. Sometimes they pleaded their cases to the Confederate government.

Human Suffering

Other factors aggravated the effect of the labor shortage. The South was in many places so sparsely populated that the conscription of one skilled craftsman could work a hardship on the people of an entire county. Often they begged in unison for the exemption or discharge of a local miller, a neighborhood tanner, or—especially—a blacksmith needed to repair farm implements.

Inflation raged out of control, fueled by the Confederate government's heavy borrowing and inadequate taxes, until prices had increased almost 7,000 percent. Inflation particularly imperiled urban dwellers and the many who could no longer provide for themselves. As early as 1861 and 1862, newspapers reported that "want and starvation are staring thousands in the face." Some concerned citizens tried to help. "Free markets," which disbursed goods as charity, sprang up in various cities, and some families came to the aid of their neighbors. But other people were less generous. The need was so vast that it overwhelmed private charity. A rudimentary relief program organized by the Confederacy offered hope but was soon curtailed to supply the armies. Thus southern yeomen sank into poverty and suffering.

As their fortunes declined, people of once-modest means looked around and found abundant evidence that all classes were not sacrificing equally. They saw that the wealthy gave up only their luxuries, while many poor families went without necessities. And they noted that the Confederate government contributed to these inequities through policies that favored the upper class. Until the last year of the war, for example, prosperous southerners could avoid military service by hiring substitutes. Anger at such discrimination exploded in October 1862 when the Confederate Congress exempted from military duty anyone who was supervising at least twenty slaves. Protests poured in from every corner of the Confederacy, and North Carolina's legislators formally condemned the law. Its defenders argued, however, that the exemption preserved order and aided food production, and the statute remained on the books.

Inequities of the Confederate Draft

Dissension spread as growing numbers of citizens concluded that the struggle was "a rich man's war and a poor man's fight." Alert politicians and newspaper editors warned that class resentment was building to a dangerous level. The bitterness of letters to Confederate officials during this period suggests the depth of the people's anger. "If I and my little children suffer [and] die while there Father is in service," threatened one woman, "I invoke God Almighty that our blood rest upon the South." War was magnifying social tensions in the Confederacy.

The Northern Economy Copes with War

With the onset of war, a tidal wave of change rolled over the North as well. Factories and citizens' associations geared up to support the war, and the federal government and its executive branch gained new powers. The energies of an industrializing, capitalist society were harnessed to serve the cause of the Union. Idealism and greed flourished together, and the northern economy proved its awesome productivity.

At first the war was a shock to business. Northern firms lost their southern markets, and many companies had to change their products and find new customers in order to remain open. Southern debts became uncollectible, jeopardizing not only northern merchants but also many western banks. In farming regions, families struggled with an aggravated shortage of labor.

Initial Slump in Northern Business

Overall the war slowed the pace of industrialization in the North, but its economic impact was not all negative. Certain entrepreneurs, such as wool producers, benefited from shortages of competing products. As demand for war-related goods soared, the federal government pumped unprecedented sums into the economy to feed the hungry war machine. Companies producing weapons, munitions, uniforms, boots, saddles, ships, and other war necessities soon prospered.

War production promoted the development of heavy industry in the North. Coal output rose substantially. Iron makers improved the quality of their product while boosting the production of pig iron. Foundries developed new and less expensive ways to make steel. Although new railroad construction slowed, repairs helped the manufacture of

Effects of War on Northern Industry and Agriculture

rails to increase. Of considerable significance for the future was the railroad industry's adoption of a standard gauge (width) for track, which eliminated the unloading and reloading of boxcars and created a unified transportation system.

Another strength of the northern economy was the complementary relationship between agriculture and industry. Mechanization of agriculture had begun before the war. Wartime recruitment and conscription, however, gave western farmers an added incentive to purchase labor-saving machinery. The shift from human labor to machines created new markets for industry and expanded the food supply for the urban industrial work force. Mechanization also meant that northern farm families whose breadwinners went to war did not suffer as their counterparts did in the South. "We have seen," one magazine observed, "a stout matron whose sons are in the army, cutting hay with her team . . . and she cut seven acres with ease in a day, riding leisurely upon her cutter."

Compared with farmers, northern industrial and urban workers did not fare so well. After the initial slump, jobs became plentiful, but inflation ate up much of a worker's paycheck. Between 1860 and 1864 consumer prices rose at least 76 percent, while daily wages rose only 42 percent. Workers' families consequently suffered a substantial decline in their standard of living.

As their real wages shrank, industrial workers lost job security. To increase production, some employers were replacing workers with labor-saving machines. Other employers urged the government to promote immigration so they could import cheap labor. Workers responded by forming unions and sometimes by striking. Skilled craftsmen organized to combat the loss of their jobs and status to machines; women and unskilled workers, excluded by the craftsmen, formed their own unions. In recognition of the increasingly national scope of business activity, thirteen occupational groups—including tailors, coal miners, and railway engineers—formed national unions during the Civil War.

New Militancy Among Northern Workers

Employers reacted with hostility to this new spirit among workers. Manufacturers viewed labor activism as a threat to their property rights and freedom of action, and accordingly formed statewide or craft-based associations to cooperate and pool information. These employers shared blacklists of union members and required new workers to sign "yellow dog" contracts (promises not to join a union). To put down strikes, they hired strikebreakers from the ranks of the poor and desperate—blacks, immigrants, and women— and sometimes received additional help from federal troops.

Troublesome as unions were, they did not prevent many employers from making a profit. The highest profits were made from profiteering on government contracts. Unscrupulous businessmen took advantage of the suddenly immense demand for army supplies by selling clothing and blankets made of "shoddy"—wool fibers reclaimed from rags or worn cloth. Shoddy goods often came apart in the rain; most of the shoes purchased in the early months of the war were worthless, too. Contractors sold inferior guns for double the usual price and passed off tainted meat as good.

Legitimate enterprises also made healthy profits. The output of woolen mills increased so dramatically that dividends in the industry nearly tripled. Some cotton mills made record profits on what they sold, even though they reduced their output. Railroads carried immense quantities of freight and passengers, increasing their business to the point that railroad stocks doubled or even tripled in value.

Wartime Benefits to Northern Business

Railroads also were a leading beneficiary of government largesse. Congress had failed in the 1850s to resolve the question of a northern versus a southern route for the first transcontinental railroad. With the South absent from Congress, the northern route quickly prevailed. In 1862 and 1864 Congress chartered two corporations, the Union Pacific Railroad and the Central Pacific Railroad, and assisted them financially in connecting Omaha, Nebraska, with Sacramento, California. Overall, the two corporations gained approximately 20 million acres of public land and nearly $60 million in loans.

Other businessmen benefited handsomely from the Morrill Land Grant Act (1862). To promote public education in agriculture, engineering, and military science, Congress granted each state 30,000 acres of federal land for each of its congressional districts.

Morrill Land Grant Act

Hard-pressed to meet wartime expenses, some states sold their land cheaply to wealthy entrepreneurs. Still, the intent of the land grant act was fulfilled in that the law eventually fostered sixty-nine colleges and universities.

Higher tariffs also pleased many businessmen. Northern businesses did not uniformly favor high import duties; some manufacturers desired cheap imported raw materials more than they feared foreign competition. But northeastern congressmen traditionally supported higher tariffs, and after southern lawmakers left Washington, they had their way: the Tariff Act of 1864 raised tariffs generously. Some healthy industries earned artificially high profits by raising their prices to a level just below that of the foreign competition. By 1865, tariff rates were more than double those of 1857.

Wartime Society in the North

The outbreak of war stimulated patriotism in the North just as it initially had done in the South. Northern society, which had suffered the stresses associated with industrialization, immigration, and widespread social change, found a unifying cause in the preservation of the nation. In thousands of self-governing towns and communities, northern citizens felt a personal connection to representative government. Secession threatened to destroy their system, and northerners rallied to its defense.

Such enthusiasm proved useful as northerners encountered a multitude of wartime changes. The powers of the federal government and the

Expanded Powers of the United States President

president grew steadily during the crisis. At the beginning of the conflict, President Lincoln launched a major shipbuilding program without waiting for Congress to assemble. The lawmakers later approved his decision, and Lincoln continued to act in advance of Congress when he deemed such action necessary. In one striking exercise of executive power, Lincoln, acting to ensure the loyalty of Maryland, suspended the writ of habeas corpus for everyone living between Washington, D.C. and Philadelphia. On occasion Lincoln used his wartime authority to bolster his own political fortunes. He and his generals proved adept at furloughing soldiers so they could vote in close elections; those whom Lincoln furloughed, of course, usually voted Republican.

Among the clearest examples of the wartime expansion of federal authority were the National Banking Acts of 1863, 1864, and 1865. Before the Civil War, the nation lacked a uniform currency. Banks operating under state charters issued no fewer than seven thousand different kinds of notes, which were difficult to distinguish from a variety of forgeries. On the recommendation of Secretary of the Treasury Salmon Chase, Congress established a national banking system empowered to issue national bank notes. At the close of the war in 1865, Congress imposed a prohibitive tax on state bank notes and forced most state institutions to join the national system.

War also bred changes in social attitudes on the home front, and some of the lavish displays would have shocked the soldiers in the field. In

Extravagance Amid War

the largest cities, an eagerness to display one's wealth flourished. *Harper's Monthly* reported that "the suddenly enriched contractors, speculators, and stock-jobbers ... are spending money with a profusion never before witnessed in our country. ... The men button their waistcoats with diamonds ... and the women powder their hair with gold and silver dust." And a writer for the *New York Herald* observed that the "individual who makes the most money—no matter how—and

spends the most—no matter for what—is considered the greatest man."

Yet idealism coexisted with ostentation. Abolitionists, after initial uncertainty over whether to let the South go, campaigned to turn the war into a crusade against slavery. Free black communities and churches both black and white responded to the needs of slaves who flocked to the Union lines, sending clothing, ministers, and teachers to aid the runaways.

Northern women, like their southern counterparts, took on new roles. Those who stayed home organized over ten thousand soldiers' aid societies, rolled innumerable bandages, and raised $3 million to aid injured troops. Thousands served as nurses in front-line hospitals, where they pressed for better care of the wounded. Women, however, had to fight for a chance to serve at all. The professionalization of medicine since the Revolution had created a medical system dominated by men, and many male physicians did not want women's aid. Female nurses proved their worth, but only the wounded welcomed them. Even Clara Barton, the most famous female nurse, was ousted from her post in 1863.

Thus northern society embraced strangely contradictory tendencies. Materialism and greed flourished alongside idealism, religious conviction, and self-sacrifice. While some risked their lives willingly out of a desire to preserve the Union or extend freedom, others avoided military service by providing a substitute or paying a $300 commutation fee. In all, 118,000 substitutes were provided and 87,000 commutations paid before Congress ended the commutation system in 1864.

 ## The Strange Advent of Emancipation

At the highest levels of government in the United States and in the Confederacy there was a similar lack of clarity about the purpose of the war. Both Davis and Lincoln studiously avoided references to slavery. Davis, realizing that emphasis on the issue could increase class conflict in the South, told southerners they were fighting for constitutional liberty. Lincoln avoided the issue because he did not want to anger the border slave states. He also hoped that a pro-Union majority would assert itself in the South. It might be possible, he thought, to coax the South back into the Union and stop the fighting. Moreover, not all Republicans burned with moral outrage over slavery. A forthright stand by Lincoln on the subject of slavery could split the party, gratifying some groups and alienating others.

Lincoln first broached the subject of slavery in a substantive way in March 1862, when he proposed that the states consider emancipation on

Lincoln's Plan for Gradual Emancipation

their own. He asked Congress to promise aid to any state that decided to emancipate, and he appealed to border-state representatives to consider this course seriously. What Lincoln proposed was gradual emancipation, with compensation for slaveholders and colonization of the freed slaves outside the United States, in some region like Central America. To a delegation of free blacks he explained that "it is better for us both . . . to be separated." Thus his was a conservative scheme, and since the states would make the decision voluntarily, no responsibility for it would attach to Lincoln.

Others wanted to go much further. A group of Republicans in Congress, known as the Radicals, had from the early days of the war concerned themselves with slavery. In

Confiscation Acts

August 1861, at the Radicals' instigation, Congress passed its first confiscation act. Designed to punish the Confederate rebels, the law confiscated all property used for "insurrectionary purposes." Thus if the South used slaves in a hostile action, those slaves were declared seized and liberated. A second confiscation act (July 1862) was much more drastic: it confiscated the property of all those who supported the rebellion, even those who merely resided in the South and paid Confederate taxes. Their slaves were declared "forever free of their servitude, and not again [to be] held as slaves." Let the government use its full powers, free the slaves, and crush the revolution, urged the Radicals.

Lincoln refused to adopt that view. He stood by his proposal of voluntary gradual emancipation by the states and made no effort to enforce the second confiscation act. His stance provoked a public protest from Horace Greeley, editor of the powerful *New York Tribune*. In an open letter to the president, Greeley pleaded with Lincoln to "execute the laws" and declared, "On the face of this wide earth, Mr. President, there is not one disinterested, determined, intelligent champion of the Union cause who does not feel that all attempts to put down the Rebellion and at the same time uphold its inciting cause are preposterous and futile."

Lincoln's reply was an explicit statement of his complex and calculated approach to the question: "I would save the Union. If I could save the Union without freeing *any* slave I would do it, and if I could save it by freeing *all* the slaves I would do it; and if I could save it by freeing some and leaving others alone I would also do that. What I do about slavery, and the colored race, I do because I believe it helps to save the Union."

When he wrote those words, Lincoln had already decided on a new step: issuance of the Emancipation Proclamation. On the advice of the

Emancipation Proclamations

cabinet, however, he was waiting for a Union victory before announcing the proclamation. On September 22, 1862, shortly after the Battle of Antietam, Lincoln issued the first part of his two-part proclamation. Invoking his powers as commander-in-chief of the armed forces, he announced that on January 1, 1863, he would emancipate the slaves in states whose people "shall then be in rebellion against the United States." Thus his September proclamation was less a declaration of the right of slaves to be free than a threat to southerners to end the war. Lincoln may not actually have expected southerners to give up their effort, but he was careful to offer them the option, thus putting the onus of emancipation on them.

When Lincoln designated the areas in rebellion on January 1, his proclamation excepted every Confederate county or city that had fallen under Union control. Those areas, he declared, "are, for the present, left precisely as if this proclamation were not issued." Nor did Lincoln liberate slaves in the border slave states that remained in the Union. "The President has purposely made the proclamation inoperative in all places where . . . the slaves [are] accessible," charged the anti-administration *New York World.* "He has proclaimed emancipation only where he has notoriously no power to execute it."

As a moral and legal document, the Emancipation Proclamation, which in reality freed no slaves, was inadequate. As a political document it was nearly flawless. Because the proclamation defined the war as a war against slavery, radicals could applaud it, even if the president had not gone as far as Congress. Yet at the same time it protected Lincoln's position with conservatives, leaving him room to retreat if he chose and forcing no immediate changes on the border slave states.

The need for men soon convinced the administration to recruit northern and southern blacks for the Union Army. By the spring of 1863, African-American troops were proving their value. Lincoln came to see them as "the great *available* and yet *unavailed of* force for restoring the Union." African-American leaders hoped that military service would secure equal rights for their people. Once the black soldier had fought for the Union, wrote Frederick Douglass, "there is no power on earth which can deny that he has earned the right of citizenship in the United States."

In June 1864, Lincoln gave his support to a constitutional ban on slavery. On the eve of the Republican national convention, Lincoln called the party's chairman to the White House and instructed him to have the party "put into the platform as the keystone, the amendment of the Constitution abolishing and prohibiting slavery forever." The party promptly called for a new amendment, the Thirteenth. Lincoln demonstrated his commitment by lobbying Congress for quick approval of the measure. The proposed amendment passed in 1865 and was sent to the states for ratification or rejection. Lincoln's strong support for the Thirteenth Amendment—an unequivocal prohibition of slavery—constitutes his best claim to the title "Great Emancipator."

Yet Lincoln soon clouded that clear stand, for in 1865 the newly reelected president considered allowing the defeated southern states to reenter the Union and delay or defeat the amendment. In February he and Secretary of State Seward met with three Confederate commissioners at Hampton Roads, Virginia. With the end of the war in sight, Lincoln was apparently contemplating the creation of a new national party based on a postwar alliance with southern Whigs and moderate and conservative Republicans. The cement for the coalition would be concessions to planter interests.

Hampton Roads Conference

Pointing out that the Emancipation Proclamation was only a war measure, Lincoln predicted that the courts would decide whether it had granted all, some, or none of the slaves their freedom. Seward observed that the Thirteenth Amendment, which would be definitive, was not yet ratified and that reentry into the Union would allow the southern states to defeat it. Lincoln did not contradict Seward but spoke in favor of "prospective" ratification: approval with the effective date postponed for five years. He also promised to seek $400 million in compensation for slaveholders. The financial aid would provide an economic incentive for planters to rejoin the Union and capital to cushion the economic blow of emancipation. Most northerners opposed such proposals. In the South, Jefferson Davis, who rejected anything short of independence, prevented them from being discussed.

Before the war was over, the Confederacy, too, addressed the issue of emancipation. Jefferson Davis offered a strong proposal in favor of liberation. He was dedicated to independence, and he was willing to sacrifice slavery to achieve that goal. After considering the alternatives for some time, Davis concluded late in 1864 that the military status of the Confederacy was desperate and that independence with emancipation was preferable to defeat with emancipation. He proposed that the Confederate government purchase forty thousand

Davis's Plan for Emancipation

slaves to work for the army as laborers, with a promise of freedom at the end of their service. Soon Davis upgraded his proposal, calling for the recruitment and arming of slaves as soldiers, who likewise would gain their freedom at the end of the war. The wives and children of these soldiers, he made plain, must also receive freedom from the states.

Confederate emancipation began too late to revive southern armies or win diplomatic advantages with antislavery Europeans. By contrast, Lincoln's Emancipation Proclamation stimulated a vital infusion of forces into the Union armies. Beginning in 1863, slaves shouldered arms for the North. Before the war was over, 134,000 slaves (and 52,000 free African-Americans) had fought for freedom and the Union. Their participation aided northern victory while it discouraged recognition of the Confederacy by foreign governments.

 ## The Soldier's War

The intricacies of policymaking were far from the minds of ordinary soldiers. Military service completely altered their lives. Army life meant tedium, physical hardship, and separation from loved ones even in the best of times. Soldiers in battle confronted fear and danger, and the risk of death from wounds or disease was very high. For many soldiers, however, wartime experiences led to bonds with their comrades and a connection to a noble purpose that they cherished for years afterward.

Soldiers benefited from certain new products, such as canned condensed milk, but blankets, clothing, and arms were often of poor quality. Vermin abounded. Hospitals were badly managed at first. Rules of hygiene in large camps were badly written or unenforced; latrines were poorly made or carelessly used. Water supplies were unsafe and typhoid epidemics common. About 57,000 army men died from dysentery and diarrhea. Overall, the Union death toll of 224,000 from disease or accidents vastly exceeded the 140,000 who died as a result of battle.

On both sides troops quickly learned that soldiering was far from glorious. Beyond sleeping on the ground in all types of weather, being unable to wash one's clothes, and dealing with body lice, there was carnage. "Any one who goes over a battlefield after a battle," wrote one Confederate, "never cares to go over another. . . . It is a sad sight to see the dead and if possible more sad to see the wounded—shot in every possible way you can imagine."

Realities of a Soldier's Life

Advances in technology made the Civil War particularly deadly. By far the most important were the rifle and the "minie ball." Bullets fired from a smooth-bore musket tumbled and wobbled as they flew through the air and thus were not accurate at distances over eighty yards. Cutting spiraled grooves inside the barrel gave the projectile a spin and much greater accuracy, but rifles remained difficult to load and use until the Frenchman Claude Minie and the American James Burton developed a new kind of bullet. Civil War bullets were sizable lead slugs with a cavity at the bottom that expanded upon firing so that the bullet "took" the rifling and flew accurately. With these bullets, rifles were accurate at four hundred yards and useful up to one thousand yards.

This meant, of course, that soldiers assaulting a position defended by riflemen were in greater peril than ever before, and the toll from Civil War battles was very high. Never before in Europe or America had such massive forces pummeled each other with weapons of such destructive power. Yet even in the bloodiest engagements, in which thousands of men died, the losing army was never destroyed.

Impact of the Rifle

Civil War soldiers nonetheless developed deep commitments to each other and to their task. The bonding may have been most dramatic among officers and men in the northern black regiments, for there white and black troops took their first steps toward bridging a deep racial divide. Racism in the Union Army was strong. Most white soldiers wanted nothing to do

Black Soldiers Fight for Acceptance

How do historians know what the average soldier thought and felt? *A vast number of diaries and letters written by soldiers have been preserved in archives and libraries and reveal a wide range of experiences. Many soldiers acted on noble ideals, but others did not. Papers at the University of Michigan document one Union soldier's worry that "If this experiment in self-government by the people shall fail, where are the oppressed and the downtrodden millions of the earth to look for hope of better days?" They also contain letters from Private Robert* Sherry *of New York, shown here. Sherry cared little for the Republican Party. The enlisted men and officers in his regiment rarely got along, and after twenty soldiers were sent to Dry Tortugas, in the Gulf of Mexico, as punishment for a mutiny, Sherry wrote bitterly that he hoped "to see the day when we will get into some battle that will be the means of getting a great portion of our Officers killed or wounded." A rough man in a rough regiment, Sherry enjoyed looting and fighting.* William I. Clements Library University of Michigan.

with black people and regarded them as inferior. "I never came out here for to free the black devils," wrote one soldier. For many, acceptance of black troops grew only because they could do heavy labor and "stop Bullets as well as white people."

But some changed their initial views. White officers who volunteered for black units only to gain promotion found that experience altered their opinions. One general reported that his "colored regiments" possessed "remarkable aptitude for military training," and another observer said, "They fight like fiends." Black troops created this change through their dedication. They had a mission to destroy slavery and demonstrate their equality. Corporal James Henry Gooding of Massachusetts's black 54th Regiment explained that his unit intended "to live down all prejudice against its color, by a determination to do well in any position it is put." After an engagement he was proud that "a regiment of white men gave us three cheers as we were passing them," because "it shows that we did our duty as men should."

African-Americans demonstrated valor in battle despite blatant discrimination. The Union government, for instance, paid white privates $13 per month plus a $3.50 clothing allowance. Black privates received $10 a month, less $3 for clothing.

The Tide of Battle Begins to Turn

The fighting in the spring and summer of 1863 did not settle the war, but it began to place clear limits on the outcome. The campaigns began in a deceptively positive way for Confederates, as their Army of Northern Virginia performed brilliantly in the Battle of Chancellorsville. On May 2 and 3, some 130,000 members of the Union Army of the Potomac bore down on fewer than 60,000 Confederates. Boldly, as if they enjoyed being outnumbered, Lee and Stonewall Jackson divided their forces, ordering 30,000 men under Jackson on a day-long march westward to gain position for a flank attack. Jackson's seasoned "foot cavalry"

Battle of Chancellorsville

found unprepared Union troops laughing, smoking, and playing cards. The Confederate attack drove the entire right side of the Union Army back in confusion. The next day Union forces left in defeat. Chancellorsville was a remarkable southern victory but costly because Jackson's own men had inadvertently killed him.

July brought crushing defeats for the Confederacy in two critical battles—Vicksburg and Gettysburg—that effectively circumscribed Confederate hopes for independence. Vicksburg was the last major fortification on the Mississippi River in southern hands. With the intent of cutting the Confederacy in half and securing a path to its interior, General Grant laid siege to the city in May. Meanwhile, General Robert E. Lee proposed a Confederate invasion of the North.

Battle of Vicksburg

Lee's troops streamed through western Maryland and into Pennsylvania, threatening both Washington and Baltimore. The possibility of a major victory near the Union capital became more and more likely. Confederate prospects along the Mississippi, however, darkened. Davis repeatedly wired General Joseph E. Johnston, urging him to concentrate his forces and attack Grant's army. Johnston, however, did nothing effective. Grant's men, meanwhile, were supplying themselves from the abundant crops of the Mississippi River valley and could continue their siege indefinitely.

In such circumstances the fall of Vicksburg was inevitable, and on July 4, 1863, its commander surrendered. The same day a battle that had been raging for three days concluded at Gettysburg, Pennsylvania. On July 1 Confederate forces collided with part of the Union Army. Heavy fighting on the second day left federal forces in possession of high ground along Cemetery Ridge. There they enjoyed the protection of a stone wall and a clear view of their foe across almost a mile of open field. Undaunted, Lee believed his splendid troops could break the Union line, and on July 3 he ordered a direct assault. Brave troops under General George E. Pickett marched up the slope

Battle of Gettysburg

in a doomed assault later known as Pickett's Charge. For a moment a hundred Confederates breached the enemy's line, but most fell in heavy slaughter. On July 4 Lee withdrew, having suffered almost 4,000 dead and about 24,000 missing and wounded.

Southern troops displayed unforgettable courage and dedication at Gettysburg, but the results there and at Vicksburg were disastrous. The Confederacy was split in two, with its heartland exposed to invasion. Moreover, Lee's defeat spelled the end of major southern offensive actions. Too weak to prevail in attack, the Confederacy henceforth would have to conserve its limited resources and rely on a prolonged defense.

 ## The Disintegration of Confederate Unity

Both northern and southern governments waged the final two years of the war in the face of increasing opposition at home. Dissatisfactions that had surfaced earlier grew more intense and sometimes violent. The gigantic costs of a war that neither side seemed able to win fed the unrest. But protest also arose from fundamental stresses in the social structures of North and South.

One ominous development was the planters' increasing opposition to their own government, whose actions often had a negative effect on them. Not only did the Richmond government impose new taxes and the tax-in-kind, but Confederate military authorities also impressed slaves to build fortifications. And when Union forces advanced on plantation areas, Confederate commanders burned stores of cotton that lay in the enemy's path. Such interference with plantation routines and financial interests was not what planters had expected of their government, and they complained bitterly.

Nor were the centralizing policies and the increasing size and power of the Richmond administration popular. In fact, the Confederate constitution had granted substantial powers to the central government. But many planters assumed with R. B. Rhett, editor of the *Charleston Mercury*, that the Confederate constitution "leaves the

States untouched in their Sovereignty, and commits to the Confederate Government only a few simple objects, and a few simple powers to enforce them."

Years of opposition to the federal government within the Union had frozen southerners in a defensive posture. Now they erected the barrier of states' rights as a defense against change. Planters sought, above all, a guarantee that their plantations and their lives would remain untouched; they were not deeply committed either to building a southern nation or to winning independence. If the Confederacy had been allowed to depart from the Union in peace and continue as a semideveloped cotton-growing region, they would have been content. When secession revolutionized their world, they could not or would not adjust.

Meanwhile, for ordinary southerners, the dire predictions of hunger and suffering were becoming a reality. Food riots occurred in the spring of 1863 in Atlanta, Macon, Columbus, and Augusta, Georgia, and in Salisbury and High Point, North Carolina. On April 2, a crowd assembled in Richmond, the Confederate capital, to demand relief. A passerby, noticing the excitement, asked a young girl, "Is there some celebration?" "We celebrate our right to live," replied the girl. "We are starving. As soon as enough of us get together we are going to the bakeries and each of us will take a loaf of bread." Soon they did just that, sparking a riot that Davis himself had to quell at gunpoint.

Food Riots in Southern Cities

Throughout the rural South, ordinary people resisted more quietly—by refusing to cooperate with conscription, tax collection, and impressments of food. "In all the States impressments are evaded by every means which ingenuity can suggest, and in some openly resisted," wrote a high-ranking commissary officer. Farmers who did provide food for the army refused to accept payment in certificates of credit or government bonds, as required by law. Conscription officers increasingly found no one to draft—men of draft age were hiding out in the forests.

Such discontent was certain to affect the Confederate armies. Worried about their loved ones and resentful of what they saw as a rich man's war,

Desertions from the Confederate Army

large numbers of men did indeed leave the armies. The problem of desertion became so acute by late 1863 that Secretary of War James Seddon admitted that one-third of the army could not be accounted for. The situation was to worsen.

The defeats at Gettysburg and Vicksburg dealt a body blow to Confederate morale. In desperation President Davis and several state governors resorted to threats and racial scare tactics to drive southern whites to further sacrifice. Instead of greater sacrifices, the pace of internal disintegration quickened. Support from the common people waned, and a few newspapers began openly to call for peace.

Southern Peace Movements

In North Carolina a peace movement grew under the leadership of William W. Holden, a popular Democratic politician and editor. Over one hundred public meetings took place there in the summer of 1863 in support of peace negotiations. Early in 1864, Governor Joseph E. Brown and Alexander H. Stephens, vice president of the Confederacy, led a similar effort in Georgia. Although these movements ultimately came to naught, the fact that they existed at all demonstrates deep disaffection.

By 1864 much of the opposition to the war had moved entirely outside the political sphere. Southerners were simply giving up the struggle and withdrawing their cooperation from the government. Deserters dominated whole towns and counties. Secret societies favoring reunion sprang up. Active dissent spread everywhere and was particularly common in upland and mountain regions. The government was losing the support of its citizens.

Antiwar Sentiment in the North

In the North opposition to the war was similar but less severe. Alarm intensified over the growing centralization of government, and war-weariness was widespread. Resentment of the draft sparked protest, especially among poor citizens, and the Union Army struggled with a desertion rate as high as the Confederates'. But the Union was so much richer than the South in human resources that fresh recruits were always available and its people never faced food shortages.

Also, Lincoln possessed a talent Davis lacked: he knew how to stay in touch with the ordinary citizen. Through letters to newspapers and to soldiers' families, he reached the common people and demonstrated that he had not forgotten them. The daily carnage, the tortuous political problems, and the ceaseless criticism weighed heavily on him. But this self-educated man of humble origins was able to communicate his suffering with words that helped to contain northern discontent.

Peace Democrats

Much of the wartime protest in the North was political in origin. The Democratic Party fought to regain power by blaming Lincoln for the war's carnage, the expansion of federal powers, inflation and the high tariff, and the emancipation of blacks. Appealing to tradition, its leaders called for an end to the war and reunion on the basis of "the Constitution as it is and the Union as it was." The Democrats denounced conscription and martial law and defended states' rights and the interests of agriculture. In the 1862 congressional elections, the Democrats made a strong comeback, and peace Democrats had influence in New York State and majorities in the legislatures of Illinois and Indiana.

Led by outspoken men like Representative Clement L. Vallandigham of Ohio, the peace Democrats made themselves highly visible. Vallandigham criticized Lincoln as a dictator who had suspended the writ of habeas corpus without congressional authority and had arrested thousands of innocent citizens. Like other Democrats, Vallandigham condemned both conscription and emancipation. He stayed carefully within legal bounds, but his attacks seemed so damaging to the war effort that military authorities arrested him for treason after Lincoln suspended habeas corpus. Lincoln wisely decided against punishment—and martyr's status—for the senator and exiled him to the Confederacy.

Lincoln believed that antiwar Democrats were linked to secret organizations that harbored traitorous ideas. Likening such groups to a poisonous snake, Republicans sometimes branded them—and by extension the peace Democrats—as Copperheads. Though Democrats were connected with these organizations, most engaged in politics rather than treason.

More violent opposition to the government arose from ordinary citizens facing the draft enacted in 1863. The urban poor and immigrants in strongly Democratic areas were especially hostile to conscription. Many men managed to avoid the army by hiring a substitute or paying commutation, but the poor viewed the commutation fee as discriminatory. Many immigrants suspected (wrongly, on the whole) that they were called in disproportionate numbers.

As a result, enrolling officers received rough treatment in many parts of the North, and riots occurred in New Jersey, Ohio, Indiana, Pennsylvania, Illinois, and Wisconsin.

New York City Draft Riot

By far the most serious outbreak of violence occurred in New York City in July 1863, where three days of rioting left seventy-four people dead. The riots had racist and class overtones. Working-class New Yorkers feared an inflow of black labor from the South, and Irish immigrants resented being forced to serve in the place of others who could afford to avoid the draft.

Discouragement and war-weariness reached a peak in the summer of 1864, when the Democratic Party nominated the popular General George B. McClellan for president and inserted a peace plank into its platform. Lincoln, running with Tennessee's Andrew Johnson on a "National Union" ticket, concluded that it was "exceedingly probable that this Administration will not be reelected." The fortunes of war, however, soon changed the electoral situation.

Northern Pressure and Southern Will

The North's long-term diplomatic goal was to prevent recognition of the Confederacy by European nations and the financial and military

Northern Diplomatic Strategy

aid it would bring. The British elite, however, felt considerable sympathy for southern planters, whose aristocratic values were similar to their own. And both England and France stood to benefit from a divided and weakened America. Thus to achieve their goal, Lincoln and Secretary of State Seward needed to avoid both serious military defeats and unnecessary controversies with the European powers.

Aware that the textile industry employed one-fifth of the British population directly or indirectly, southerners assumed that British leaders would have to recognize the Confederacy. But at the beginning of the war, British mills had a 50 percent surplus of cotton on hand; later, new sources of supply helped to meet Britain's needs. Refusing to be stampeded into recognition of the Confederacy, the British government kept its eye on the battlefield. France, though sympathetic to the South, was unwilling to act independently of Britain.

More than once the Union strategy nearly broke down. In one crisis in 1861, the commander of an American frigate stopped the British steamer *Trent* and removed two Confederate ambassadors. The British protested this violation of freedom of the seas and demanded the prisoners' release. Lincoln and Seward waited until northern public opinion cooled and then released the two southerners. Another incident that sparked vigorous protest from the North was the sale to the Confederacy of warships constructed in England. A few English-built ships, notably the *Alabama*, reached open water to serve the South. Over a period of twenty-two months, the *Alabama* destroyed or captured more than sixty northern ships. But the British government, as a neutral power, soon barred delivery of warships such as the Laird rams, formidable vessels whose pointed prows were designed to end the blockade by battering the Union ships.

Despite such diplomatic victories, the northern victory on the battlefield was far from won in 1864. Military authorities had long agreed that deep invasion is extremely risky: the farther an army penetrates enemy territory, the more vulnerable its own communications and support become. General Grant, by now in command of all the federal armies, decided to test these conditions—and southern will—with a strategic innovation of his own: raids on a massive scale. Grant proposed to use whole armies, not just cavalry, to destroy Confederate railroads, thus ruining the enemy's transportation and damaging the South's economy. Abandoning their lines of support, Union troops would live off the land while laying to waste all resources useful to the military and to the civilian population of the Confederacy. After General George H. Thomas's troops won the Battle of Chattanooga in November 1863 by ignoring orders and charging up Missionary Ridge, the heartland of the South lay open. Moving to Virginia, Grant entrusted General Sherman with 100,000 men for a raid deep into the South, toward Atlanta.

Jefferson Davis countered by positioning the army of General Joseph E. Johnston in Sherman's path. Davis's entire political strategy for 1864 was based on demonstrating Confederate military strength and successfully defending Atlanta. The United States presidential election of 1864 was approaching, and Davis hoped that southern resolve would lead to the defeat of Lincoln and the election of a president who would sue for peace. When General Johnston slowly but steadily fell back toward Atlanta, Davis grew anxious and sought assurances that Atlanta would be held. From a purely military point of view, Johnston maneuvered skillfully, but Davis replaced him with the one-legged General John Hood, who knew his job was to fight. Hood attacked but was beaten, and Sherman's army occupied Atlanta on September 2, 1864. The victory buoyed northern spirits, ensured Lincoln's reelection, and cleared the way for Sherman's march from Atlanta to the sea (see map below).

Sherman's army was an unusually formidable force, composed almost entirely of battle-tested

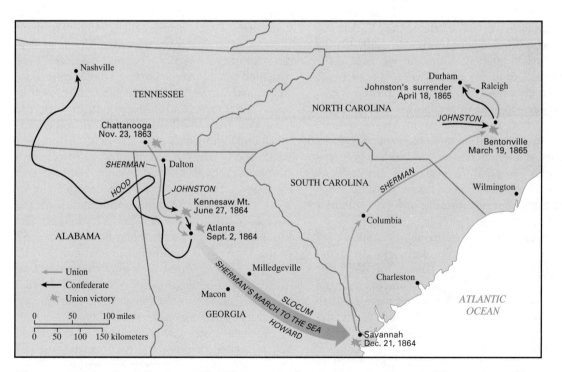

Sherman's March to the Sea   *The West proved a decisive theater at the end of the war. From Chattanooga, Union forces drove into Georgia, capturing Atlanta. Then General Sherman embarked on his march of destruction through Georgia to the coast and then northward through the Carolinas.*

veterans and officers who had risen through the ranks. Tanned, bearded, tough, and unkempt, they were determined, as one put it, "to Conquer this Rebelien or Die." As the army marched across Georgia, it cut a path 50 to 60 miles wide and more than 200 miles long. The totality of the destruction they caused was awesome. A Georgia woman described the "Burnt Country" this way: "The fields were trampled down and the road was lined with carcasses of horses, hogs, and cattle that the invaders, unable either to consume or to carry with them, had wantonly shot down to starve our people and prevent them from making their crops. The stench in some places was unbearable." Such devastation diminished the South's material resources and sapped its will to resist.

The March to the Sea

In Virginia the preliminaries to victory proved protracted and ghastly. Throughout the spring and summer of 1864, intent on capturing Richmond, Grant hurled his troops at Lee's army in Virginia and suffered appalling losses: almost 18,000 casualties in the Battle of the Wilderness; more than 8,000 at Spotsylvania; and 12,000 in the space of a few hours at Cold Harbor. Before the last battle, Union troops pinned scraps of paper bearing their names and addresses to their backs, certain they would be mowed down as they rushed Lee's trenches. In four weeks in May and June, Grant lost as many men as were enrolled in Lee's entire army. Though costly, these battles prepared the way for eventual victory: Lee's army shrank until offensive action was no longer possible, while Grant's army kept replenishing its forces with new recruits.

The end finally came in the spring of 1865. Grant kept battering Lee, who tried but failed to break through the Union line. With the numerical superiority of Grant's army now greater than two to one, Confederate defeat was inevitable. On April 2 Lee abandoned Richmond and Petersburg. On April 9, hemmed in by Union troops, short of rations, and having fewer than thirty thousand men left, Lee surrendered at Appomattox Courthouse. Grant

Heavy Losses Force Lee's Surrender

treated his rival with respect and paroled the defeated troops. Within weeks, Davis was captured in Georgia, and the remaining Confederate forces laid down their arms and surrendered. The war was over at last.

Lincoln did not live to see the war's end. On the evening of Good Friday, April 14, he went to Ford's Theater in Washington, D.C., where the assassin John Wilkes Booth shot him in the head at point-blank range. The Union had lost its wartime leader, and millions publicly mourned the martyred chief. Relief at the war's end mingled uncomfortably with a renewed sense of loss and uncertainty about the future.

Costs and Effects

The human costs of the Civil War were enormous. The total number of military casualties on both sides exceeded 1 million—a frightful toll for a nation of 31 million people. Approximately 364,000 Union soldiers died, 140,000 of them from wounds suffered in battle. Another 275,175 Union soldiers were wounded but survived. On the Confederate side, an estimated 258,000 lost their lives, and almost as many suffered wounds. More men died in the Civil War than in all other American wars combined until Vietnam.

Casualties

Property damage and financial costs were also enormous, though difficult to tally. United States loans and taxes during the conflict totaled almost $3 billion, and interest on the war debt was $2.8 billion. The Confederacy borrowed over $2 billion but lost far more in the destruction of homes, crops, livestock, and other property. Scholars have noted that small farmers lost just as much, proportionally, as planters whose slaves were emancipated.

Financial Cost of the War

Estimates of the total cost of the war exceed $20 billion—five times the total expenditures of the federal government from its creation to 1861. The northern government increased its spending by 700 percent in the first full year of the war; by the last year its spending had soared to twenty times the prewar level. By 1865 the federal government accounted for over 26 percent of the gross national product.

Many of these changes were more or less permanent. In the 1880s, interest on the war debt still accounted for approximately 40 percent of the federal budget and Union soldiers' pensions for as much as 20 percent. Thus although many southerners had hoped to remove government from the economy, the war made such separation an impossibility. After the war, federal expenditures shrank but stabilized at twice the prewar level, or at 4 percent of the gross national product.

 ## Conclusion

The Civil War altered American society in many ways. During the war, in both North and South, women had taken on new roles, which could grow or stagnate. Industrialization and large economic enterprises played a larger role than ever before. Politically, the defense of national unity brought far-reaching changes in government and policy. Under Republican leadership, the federal government had expanded its power. Extreme forms of states' rights dogma clearly were dead, but would Americans continue to favor a state-centered federalism? How would white southerners respond to efforts to reconstruct the nation?

Closely related to these issues was a question of central importance: what would be the place of black men and women in American life? The Union victory provided a partial answer: slavery as it had existed before the war could not persist. But whether full citizenship and equal rights would take slavery's place remained unclear.

Suggestions for Further Reading

The War and the South

Thomas B. Alexander and Richard E. Beringer, *The Anatomy of the Confederate Congress* (1972); Stephen Ash, *When the Yankees Came* (1995); Richard E. Beringer et al., *Why the South Lost the Civil War* (1986); Richard N. Current, *Lincoln's Loyalists* (1992) Robert F. Durden, *The Gray and the Black: The Confederate Debate on Emancipation* (1972); Paul D. Escott, *After Secession: Jefferson Davis and the Failure of Confederate Nationalism* (1978);

Ella Lonn, *Desertion During the Civil War* (1928); Mary Elizabeth Massey, *Refugee Life in the Confederacy* (1964); Harry P. Owens and James J. Cooke, eds., *The Old South in the Crucible of War* (1983); James L. Roark, *Masters Without Slaves* (1977); Georgia Lee Tatum, *Disloyalty in the Confederacy* (1934); Emory M. Thomas, *The Confederate Nation* (1979); William A. Tidwell, *April '65* (1995); Bell Irvin Wiley, *The Plain People of the Confederacy* (1943); W. Buck Yearns, ed., *The Confederate Governors* (1985).

The War and the North

Ralph Andreano, ed., *The Economic Impact of the American Civil War* (1962); David Donald, ed., *Why the North Won the Civil War* (1960); James W. Geary, *We Need Men* (1991); Wood Gray, *The Hidden Civil War* (1942); Frank L. Klement, *The Copperheads in the Middle West* (1960); James M. McPherson, *Battle Cry of Freedom* (1988); Phillip S. Paludan, *"A People's Contest": The Union and the Civil War, 1861–1865* (1989); George Winston Smith and Charles Burnet Judah, *Life in the North During the Civil War* (1966); George Templeton Strong, *Diary*, 4 vols., ed. Allan Nevins and Milton Hasley Thomas (1952); Paul Studenski, *Financial History of the United States* (1952).

Women

John R. Brumgardt, ed., *Civil War Nurse: The Diary and Letters of Hannah Ropes* (1980); Beth Gilbert Crabtree and James W. Patton, eds., *"Journal of a Secesh Lady": The Diary of Catherine Ann Devereux Edmondston, 1860–1866* (1979); George C. Rable, *Civil Wars: Women and the Crisis of Southern Nationalism* (1989); C. Vann Woodward and Elisabeth Muhlenfeld, eds., *Mary Chesnut's Civil War* (1981); Agatha Young, *Women and the Crisis* (1959).

African-Americans

Virginia M. Adams, ed., *On the Altar of Freedom: A Black Soldier's Civil War Letters from the Front* (1991); Ira Berlin, ed., *Freedom: A Documentary History of Emancipation, 1861–1867*, Series I, *The Destruction of Slavery* (1979), and Series II, *The Black Military Experience* (1982); Dudley Cornish, *The Sable Arm* (1956); Joseph T. Glatthaar, *Forged in Battle* (1990); Leon Litwack, *Been in the Storm So Long* (1979); James M. McPherson, *The Negro's Civil War* (1965); James M. McPherson, *The Struggle for Equality* (1964); Clarence L. Mohr, *On the Threshold of Freedom* (1986).

Military History

Albert Castel, *Decision in the West* (1992); Benjamin Franklin Cooling, *Forts Henry and Donelson* (1988); Peter Cozzens, *This Terrible Sound* (1992); Michael Fellman, *Citizen Sherman* (1995); Shelby Foote, *The Civil War, a Narrative*, 3 vols. (1958–1974); Douglas Southall Freeman, *R. E. Lee*, 4 vols. (1934–1935); Joseph T. Glatthaar, *The March to the Sea and Beyond* (1985); Herman Hattaway and Archer Jones, *How the North Won* (1983); Laurence M. Hauptman, *Between Two Fires:*

American Indians in the Civil War (1995); Archer Jones, *Civil War Command and Strategy* (1992); Alvin M. Josephy, Jr., *The Civil War in the American West* (1991); Thomas L. Livermore, *Numbers and Losses in the Civil War in America* (1957); Grady McWhiney and Perry D. Jamieson, *Attack and Die* (1982); J. B. Mitchell, *Decisive Battles of the Civil War* (1955); Reid Mitchell, *Civil War Soldiers* (1988); Roy Morris, Jr., *Sheridan* (1992); Stephen W. Sears, *To the Gates of Richmond* (1992); Emory M. Thomas, *Robert E. Lee* (1995); Steven E. Woodworth, *Jefferson Davis and His Generals* (1990).

Foreign Relations

Kinley J. Brauer, "The Slavery Problem in the Diplomacy of the American Civil War," *Pacific Historical Review* 46, no. 3 (1977): 439–469; David P. Crook, *The North, the South, and the Powers, 1861–1865* (1974); Howard Jones, *Union in Peril* (1992); Frank J. Merli, *Great Britain and the Confederate Navy* (1970); Frank L. Owsley and Harriet Owsley, *King Cotton Diplomacy* (1959); Gordon H. Warren, *Fountain of Discontent: The Trent Affair and Freedom of the Seas* (1981).

Abraham Lincoln and the Union Government

Allan G. Bogue, *The Earnest Men: Republicans of the Civil War Senate* (1981); Richard N. Current, *The Lincoln Nobody Knows* (1958); Leonard P. Curry, *Blueprint for Modern America: Non-Military Legislation of the First Civil War Congress* (1968); Christopher Dell, *Lincoln and the War Democrats* (1975); David Donald, *Charles Sumner and the Rights of Man* (1970); Ludwell H. Johnson, "Lincoln's Solution to the Problem of Peace Terms, 1864–1865," *Journal of Southern History* 34 (November 1968): 441–447; Peyton McCrary, *Abraham Lincoln and Reconstruction: The Louisiana Experiment* (1978); James M. McPherson, *Abraham Lincoln and the Second American Revolution* (1990); Mark Neely, *The Fate of Liberty* (1991); Joel Silbey, *A Respectable Minority: The Democratic Party in the Civil War Era* (1977).

CHAPTER

16

Reconstruction:
A Partial Revolution
1865–1877

For both men, war and Reconstruction brought stunning changes and swift reversals of fortune. In 1861 Robert Smalls was a slave in South Carolina, while Wade Hampton was a South Carolina legislator and one of the richest planters in the South. The events of the next fifteen years turned each man's world upside down more than once.

Robert Smalls became a Union hero when he stole a Confederate ship from Charleston harbor and piloted it to the blockading federal fleet. Thereafter, he guided Union gunboats and toured the North recruiting black troops. After the war, Smalls entered politics and served in both the state legislature and Congress. There he worked for educational and economic opportunity for African-Americans.

Wade Hampton joined the Confederate Army in 1861 and soon became a lieutenant-general. The South's defeat profoundly shocked him. The postwar years brought further painful and unexpected changes, including forced bankruptcy. By 1876 Hampton's fortunes were again on the rise: Democrats nominated him for governor, promising that he would "redeem" South Carolina from Republican misrule. While Hampton spoke misleadingly of respect for blacks' rights, each member of the paramilitary Red Shirts who supported him pledged to "control the vote of at least one Negro, by intimidation, purchase," or other means. Hampton won the governor's chair and then a seat in the United States Senate.

As the careers of Smalls and Hampton suggest, Reconstruction's change was extensive but not lasting. Smalls rose from bondage to experience glory, emancipation, political power, and, ultimately, disappointment. Hampton fell from privilege to endure failure, bankruptcy, powerlessness, and, eventually, a return to power. Similarly, American society experienced both extraordinary change and fundamental continuity. Unprecedented social, political, and constitutional changes took place, but the underlying realities of economic power, racial prejudice, and judicial conservatism limited Reconstruction's revolutionary potential.

Nowhere was the turmoil of Reconstruction more evident than in national politics. Lincoln's successor, Andrew Johnson, and Congress fought bitterly over the shaping of a plan for Reconstruction. Though a southerner, Johnson had always been a foe of the South's wealthy planters, and his first acts as president suggested that he would be tough on traitors. Before the end of 1865, however, Johnson's policies changed direction. Although Jefferson Davis stayed in prison for two years, Johnson pardoned other rebel leaders and allowed them to occupy high offices. He also ordered tax officials to return plantations to their original owners, including abandoned coastal lands on which forty thousand freed men and women had settled by order of General William Tecumseh Sherman early in 1865.

This turn of events alarmed northern voters. Republican congressmen began to discuss plans to keep rebels from regaining control of the South or of Congress. Northern legislators produced a new Reconstruction program, embodied in the Fourteenth Amendment. But southern intransigence blocked that plan and forced a more radical step, the Reconstruction Act of 1867. When Congress put the act into effect, Johnson tried to subvert it, and by 1868 the president and Congress were bitterly antagonistic.

Before these struggles were over, Congress had impeached the president, enfranchised the freed men, and given them a role in reconstructing the South. The nation also adopted the Fourteenth and Fifteenth Amendments. Yet little was done to open the doors of economic opportunity to black southerners. Moreover, by 1869 the Ku Klux Klan was employing extensive violence to thwart Reconstruction and undermine black freedom.

As the 1870s advanced, northerners grew weary of Reconstruction and began to focus on other issues. Industrial growth accelerated, interest in territorial expansion revived, and political corruption became a nationwide scandal. Eventually these other forces triumphed. As politics moved on to new concerns, the courts turned their attention away from civil rights, and even northern Republicans abandoned racial reforms in 1877.

Only limited change emerged from this period of tremendous upheaval. Congress asserted the principle of equality before the law for African-Americans and gave black men the right to vote. But few whites saw equal rights for African-Americans as the central aim of Reconstruction, and thus more far-reaching measures to advance black freedom never had much support in Congress. And Supreme Court interpretations soon crippled the Fourteenth and Fifteenth Amendments. Reconstruction proclaimed anew the American principle of human equality but failed to secure it in reality.

Equal Rights: The Unresolved Issue

For America's former slaves, Reconstruction had one paramount meaning: a chance to explore freedom. A southern white woman admitted in her diary that the black people "showed a natural and exultant joy at being free." Former slaves remembered singing far into the night after federal troops reached their plantations. The slaves on a Texas plantation jumped up and down and clapped their hands as one man shouted, "We is free—no more whippings and beatings." Another man recalled that he and others "started on the move," either to search for family members or just to exercise their new-found freedom of movement.

• *Important Events* •

1865	President Andrew Johnson begins Reconstruction	**1871**	Congress passes second Enforcement Act and Ku Klux Klan Act
	Confederate leaders regain power	**1872**	Amnesty Act frees almost all remaining Confederates from restrictions on holding office
	White southern governments pass restrictive black codes		Liberal Republicans organize
	Congress refuses to seat southern representatives		Debtors urge government to keep greenbacks in circulation
	Thirteenth Amendment ratified		Grant reelected
1866	Congress passes Civil Rights Act and renewal of Freedmen's Bureau over Johnson's veto	**1873**	*Slaughter-House* cases limit power of Fourteenth Amendment
	Congress approves Fourteenth Amendment		Panic of 1873 damages economy
	Most southern states reject Fourteenth Amendment	**1874**	Grant vetoes increase in supply of paper money
	In *Ex parte Milligan* the Supreme Court reasserts its influence		Democrats win majority in House of Representatives
1867	Congress passes Reconstruction Act and Tenure of Office Act	**1875**	Several Grant appointees indicted for corruption
	Constitutional conventions called in southern states		Congress passes weak Civil Rights Act
1868	House impeaches Johnson; Senate acquits him		Congress requires that after 1878 greenbacks be convertible into gold
	Most southern states gain readmission to the Union	**1876**	*U.S.* v. *Cruikshank* and *U.S.* v. *Reese* further weaken Fourteenth Amendment
	Fourteenth Amendment ratified		Presidential election disputed
	Ulysses S. Grant elected president	**1877**	Congress elects Rutherford B. Hayes president
1869	Congress approves Fifteenth Amendment (ratified in 1870)		Exodusters migrate to Kansas
1870	Congress passes first Enforcement Act		

Most freed men and women reacted cautiously and shrewdly, taking care to test the boundaries of their new condition. As slaves they had learned to expect hostility from white people, and they did not presume it would instantly disappear. Life in freedom might still be a matter of what was allowed, not what was right. One sign of this shrewd caution was the way freed people evaluated potential employers. If a white person had been relatively considerate to blacks in bondage, they stayed on the plantation, reasoning that he might prove a desirable employer in freedom. Others left their plantations all at once, for, as one

put it, "that master am sure mean and if we doesn't have to stay we shouldn't, not with that master."

In addition to a fair employer, freed men and women wanted opportunity through education and, especially, through landownership. Land ownership represented their chance to enjoy the independence that generations of American farmers valued. A northern observer noted that slaves freed in the Sea Islands of South Carolina and Georgia made "plain, straight-forward" inquiries as they settled the land

African-Americans' Desire for Land

set aside for them by Sherman. They wanted to be sure the land "would be theirs after they had improved it."

But how much of a chance would whites give to blacks? There were some victories for civil rights. In 1864 the federal courts accepted black testimony, and the next year the Thirteenth Amendment became law. One state, Massachusetts, enacted a comprehensive public accommodations law. But there were defeats, too. The Democratic Party fought hard against equality, charging that Republicans favored race-mixing and were undermining the status of white workers. Voters in three states—Connecticut, Minnesota, and Wisconsin—rejected black suffrage in 1865.

Even northern reformers showed little sympathy for black aspirations. In the Sea Islands, for instance, the former slaves wanted to establish small, self-sufficient farms. Northern officials and missionaries, however, emphasized profit and insisted that the freedmen grow more cotton. And when tax officials sold Sea Island land that had been seized for nonpayment of taxes, 90 percent of it went to wealthy northern investors. The tracts, as one African-American complained, were made "too big, and cut we out." Thus, with only partial support from their strongest advocates, former slaves awaited the answer to one vital question. How much opportunity would freedom bring?

 ## Johnson's Reconstruction Plan

When Reconstruction began under President Andrew Johnson, many expected his policies to be harsh. Throughout his career in Tennessee he had criticized the wealthy planters and championed the small farmers. Southern aristocrats and northern Radicals thus had reason to believe that Johnson would deal sternly with the South.

Through 1865 Johnson alone controlled Reconstruction policy, for Congress recessed shortly before he became president and did not reconvene until December. In the following eight months,

Johnson devised and put into operation his own plan, forming new state governments in the South by using his power to grant pardons.

Wartime proposals for Reconstruction had produced much controversy but no consensus. In December 1863 Lincoln had proposed a "10 percent" plan for a government being organized in captured parts of Louisiana. Under this plan, a state government could be established as soon as 10 percent of those who had voted in 1860 took an oath of future loyalty to the Union. Only high-ranking Confederate officials would be denied a chance to take the oath, and Lincoln urged that at least a few well-qualified blacks be given the ballot. Radicals bristled, however, at such a mild plan, and Congress backed the much stiffer Wade-Davis bill, which required 50 percent of the voters to swear an "iron-clad" oath that they had never voluntarily supported the rebellion. Lincoln pocket-vetoed this measure. At the time of his death, he had given tentative approval to a plan, drafted by Secretary of War Edwin Stanton, to impose military authority and appoint provisional governors as steps toward the creation of new state governments.

Lincoln's Reconstruction Plan

Johnson began with Stanton's plan, but his advisers split evenly on the question of giving voting rights to black men in the South. Johnson claimed that he favored black suffrage, but *only* if the southern states adopted it voluntarily. A champion of states' rights and no friend of African-Americans, he regarded this decision as too important to be taken out of the hands of the states.

This racial conservatism had an enduring effect on Johnson's policies. Where whites were concerned, however, Johnson seemed to be pursuing radical changes in class relations. He proposed rules that would keep the wealthy planter class out of power. Southerners were required to swear an oath of loyalty as a condition of gaining amnesty or pardon, but Johnson barred several categories of people from taking the oath. Former federal

Oaths of Amnesty and New State Governments

Combative and inflexible, President Andrew Johnson contributed greatly to the failure of his own reconstruction program.   Library of Congress.

moved from power and replaced by deserving yeomen.

Johnson appointed provisional governors who began the Reconstruction process by calling constitutional conventions. The delegates chosen had to draft new constitutions that eliminated slavery and invalidated secession. After ratification of these constitutions, new governments could be elected, and the states would be restored to the Union with full congressional representation. Only southerners who had taken the oath of amnesty and been eligible to vote on the day the state seceded could participate in this process. Thus unpardoned whites and former slaves were not eligible.

If Johnson intended to strip the old elite of its power, his plan did not work as he hoped. Surprisingly, Johnson helped to subvert his own plan by pardoning aristocrats and leading rebels. These pardons, plus the return of planters' abandoned lands, restored the old elite to power. After the states drafted new constitutions, Johnson endorsed their governments and proclaimed Reconstruction complete. In the elections held under these constitutions, many former Confederate leaders, including the vice president of the Confederacy, were elected to serve in Congress.

The election of such prominent rebels troubled many northerners. So did other results of Johnson's program. Some of the state conventions were slow to repudiate secession; others admitted only grudgingly that slavery was dead. Furthermore, to define the status of freed men and women and control their labor, some legislatures merely revised large sections of the slave codes by substituting the word *freedmen* for *slave*. The new black codes compelled the former slaves, now supposedly free, to carry passes, observe a curfew, live in housing provided by a landowner, and give up hope of entering many desirable occupations. Stiff vagrancy laws and restrictive labor contracts bound supposedly free laborers to plantations. State-supported institutions in the South, such as schools and orphanages, excluded blacks entirely.

It seemed to northerners that the South was intent on returning African-Americans to a position

Black Codes

officials who had violated their oaths to support the United States and had aided the Confederacy could not take the oath. Nor could high-ranking Confederate officers and political leaders or graduates of West Point or Annapolis who had resigned their commissions to fight for the South. To this list Johnson added another important group: all southerners who aided the rebellion and whose taxable property was worth more than $20,000. All such individuals had to apply personally to the president for pardon and restoration of their political rights; otherwise, they risked legal penalties, which included confiscation of their land. Thus it appeared that the leadership class of the Old South would be re-of servility. Thus the Republican majority in Congress decided to take a closer look at the results of Johnson's plan. On reconvening, the House and Senate considered the credentials of the newly elected southern representatives and decided not to admit them. Instead, they established a joint committee to study Reconstruction and consider new policies. Reconstruction thus entered a second phase, one in which Congress would play the decisive role.

 ## The Congressional Reconstruction Plan

Northern congressmen disagreed about what to do, but they did not doubt their right to shape Reconstruction policy. The Constitution mentioned neither secession nor reunion, but it declared that the United States shall guarantee to each state a republican government. This provision, legislators believed, gave them the right to devise policies for Reconstruction.

They soon found that other constitutional questions affected their policies. What, for example, had rebellion done to the relationship between southern states and the Union? Lincoln had always insisted that states could not secede and that the Union remained intact. In contrast, congressmen who favored vigorous Reconstruction measures argued that the war *had* broken the Union. They maintained that the southern states had committed legal suicide and reverted to the status of territories, or that the South was a conquered nation subject to the victor's will. Moderate congressmen held that the states had forfeited their rights through rebellion and thus had come under congressional supervision.

These diverse theories mirrored the diversity of Congress itself. Northern Democrats denounced any idea of racial equality and supported Johnson's policies. Conservative Republicans, despite their party loyalty, favored a limited federal role in Reconstruction. The Radical Republicans wanted to transform the South. Although a minority within their

The Radicals

party, they had the advantage of a clearly defined goal. They believed it was essential to democratize the South, establish public education, and ensure the rights of freed people. They favored black suffrage, often supported land confiscation and redistribution, and were willing to exclude the South from the Union for several years if necessary to achieve their goals. A large group of moderate Republicans did not want to go as far as the Radicals but believed some change in Johnson's policies was necessary.

Ironically, Johnson and the Democrats forced the diverse Republican factions to coalesce by refusing to cooperate with moderate and conservative Republicans and insisting that Reconstruction was over and that southern representatives should be seated in Congress. Moreover, Johnson rejected an apparent compromise on Reconstruction. Under its terms Johnson would agree to two modifications of his program: extension of the life of the Freedmen's Bureau—which Congress had established in 1865 to feed the hungry, negotiate labor contracts, and start schools—and passage of a civil rights bill to counteract the black codes. This bill would force southern courts to practice equality before the law by allowing federal judges to remove from state courts cases in which blacks were treated unfairly. Its provisions applied to discrimination by private individuals as well as by government officials. This was the first major bill to enforce the Thirteenth Amendment's abolition of slavery.

Congress Struggles for a Compromise

Johnson destroyed the compromise by vetoing both bills. (They later became law when Congress overrode the president's veto.) Denouncing any change in his program, the president condemned Congress's action and questioned its right to make policy. All hope of working with the president was now dead. Instead of a compromise program, the various Republican factions drew up a new plan. It took the form of a proposed amendment to the Constitution, and it represented a compromise between radical and conservative elements of the party. The Fourteenth Amendment was Congress's alternative to Johnson's program of Reconstruction.

Of the four points in the amendment, there was near-universal agreement on one: the Confederate debt was declared null and void, and the war debt of the United States was guaranteed. There was also general support for prohibiting prominent Confederates from holding political office. The amendment therefore barred Confederate leaders from state and federal office. Only Congress, by a two-thirds vote of each house, could remove the penalty.

Fourteenth Amendment

The first section of the Fourteenth Amendment, which would have the greatest legal significance in later years, conferred citizenship on freedmen and prohibited states from abridging their constitutional "privileges and immunities." It also barred any state from taking a person's life, liberty, or property "without due process of law" and from denying "equal protection of the laws." These broad phrases became powerful guarantees of African-Americans' civil rights—indeed, of the rights of all citizens—in the twentieth century.

The second section of the amendment dealt with representation. Under the Constitution, each slave had counted as three-fifths of a person. Emancipation made every former slave five-fifths of a person, a fact that would increase southern representation. Thus the postwar South stood to *gain* power in Congress, and if white southerners did not allow blacks to vote, former secessionists would derive all the political benefit from emancipation. To prevent this result, the Fourteenth Amendment stipulated that states denying black men the vote would have their representation reduced accordingly. States enfranchising black men would have their representation increased proportionally—but, of course, Republicans could seek the support of the new black voters.

The Fourteenth Amendment raised the possibility of suffrage for black men but ignored female citizens, black and white. When legislators defined women as nonvoting citizens, prominent leaders such as Elizabeth Cady Stanton and Susan B. Anthony decided that it was time to end their alliance with abolitionists and fight more determinedly for themselves. Thus the amendment infused new determination into the independent women's rights movement.

In 1866, however, the major question in Reconstruction politics was how the public would respond to the amendment. Johnson did his best to block the Fourteenth Amendment in both North and South.

Southern Rejection of the Fourteenth Amendment

Condemning Congress for its refusal to seat southern representatives, the president urged state legislatures in the South to vote against ratification. Every southern legislature except Tennessee's rejected the amendment by a wide margin.

To present his case to northerners, Johnson organized a National Union Convention and took to the stump himself. He boarded a special train for a "swing around the circle" that carried his message deep into the Midwest and then back to Washington, D.C. Increasingly, however, audiences rejected his views and hooted and jeered at him.

The elections of 1866 were a resounding victory for Republicans in Congress. Radical and moderate Republicans whom Johnson had denounced won reelection by large margins, and the Republican majority grew. The North had spoken clearly: Johnson's policies were giving the advantage to rebels and traitors. Thus Republican congressional leaders won a mandate to pursue their Reconstruction plan.

Recognizing that nothing could be accomplished under the existing southern governments and with blacks excluded from the electorate, Congress passed the Reconstruction Act of 1867. The act incorporated only a small part of the Radical program. Until new state governments could be set up, Union generals assumed control in five military districts in the South. Confederate leaders designated in the Fourteenth Amendment were barred from voting until new state constitutions were ratified. The law guaranteed freedmen the right to vote in elections for state constitutional conventions and in subsequent elections under the

Reconstruction Act of 1867

Plans for Reconstruction Compared

	Johnson's Plan	Radicals' Plan	Fourteenth Amendment	Reconstruction Act of 1867
Voting	Whites only; Confederate leaders must seek pardons	Give vote to black males	Southern whites may decide but can lose representation	Black men gain vote; whites barred from office by Fourteenth Amendment cannot vote while new state governments are being formed
Officeholding	Many prominent Confederates regain power	Only loyal white and black males eligible	Confederate leaders barred until Congress votes amnesty	Fourteenth Amendment in effect
Time out of Union	Brief	Years; until South is thoroughly democratized	Brief	Brief
Other change in southern society	Little; gain of power by yeomen not realized	Expand public education; confiscate land and provide farms for freedmen	Probably slight	Depends on action of new state governments

new constitutions. In addition, each southern state was required to ratify the Fourteenth Amendment and to ratify its new constitution and submit it to Congress for approval. Thus African-Americans gained an opportunity to fight for a better life through the political process.

Congress's role as the architect of Reconstruction was not quite over. To restrict Johnson's influence and safeguard its plan, Congress passed a number of controversial laws. First, it set the date for its own reconvening—an unprecedented act, for the president traditionally summoned legislators to Washington. Then it limited Johnson's power over the army by requiring the president to issue military orders through the General of the Army, Ulysses S. Grant, who could not be sent from Washington without the Senate's consent. Finally, Congress passed the Tenure of Office Act, which gave the Senate power to interfere with changes in the president's cabinet. Designed to protect Secretary of War Stanton, who sympa-

thized with the Radicals, this law violated the tradition that a president controlled his own cabinet.

Johnson took several belligerent steps of his own. He issued orders to military commanders in the South limiting their powers and increasing the powers of the civil governments he had created in 1865. Then he removed officers who were conscientiously enforcing Congress's new law. Finally, he tried to remove Secretary of War Stanton. With that attempt the confrontation reached its climax.

In 1868, the House Judiciary Committee initiated impeachment proceedings against the president. The indictment concentrated on his violation of the Tenure of Office Act, though modern scholars regard his efforts to impede enforcement of the Reconstruction Act of 1867 as a far more serious offense. Johnson's trial in the Senate began promptly and lasted more than three months. The prosecution at-

Impeachment of President Johnson

tempted to prove that Johnson was guilty of "high crimes and misdemeanors." But they also argued that the trial was a means to judge Johnson's performance, not a judicial determination of guilt or innocence. The Senate ultimately rejected such reasoning, which could have made removal from office a political weapon against any chief executive who disagreed with Congress. Although a majority of senators voted to convict Johnson, the prosecution fell one vote short of the necessary two-thirds majority. Johnson remained in office, politically weakened and with only a few months left in his term. His acquittal established a precedent that only serious misdeeds merited removal from office.

In 1869, in an effort to write democratic principles and colorblindness into the Constitution, the Radicals succeeded in presenting the Fifteenth

Fifteenth Amendment

Amendment for ratification. This measure forbade states to deny the right to vote "on account of race, color, or previous condition of servitude." Such wording did not guarantee the right to vote. It deliberately left states free to restrict suffrage on other grounds so that northern states could continue to deny suffrage to women and certain groups of men. Ironically, the votes of four uncooperative southern states—compelled by Congress to approve the amendment as an added condition to rejoining the Union—proved necessary to impose even this language on parts of the North. Although several states outside the South refused to ratify, the Fifteenth Amendment became law in 1870.

Reconstruction Politics in the South

From the start, Reconstruction encountered the resistance of white southerners. In the black codes and in private attitudes, many whites stubbornly opposed emancipation, and the

White Resistance

former planter class proved especially unbending. In 1866 a Georgia newspaper frankly observed that "most of the white citizens believe that the institution of slavery was right, and . . . they will believe that the condition, which comes nearest to slavery, that can now be established will be the best."

Fearing loss of control over their slaves, some planters attempted to postpone freedom by denying or misrepresenting events. Former slaves reported that their owners "didn't tell them it was freedom" or "wouldn't let [them] go." To hold onto their workers, some landowners claimed control over black children and used guardianship and apprentice laws to bind black families to the plantation. Whites also blocked blacks from acquiring land and used force to keep them submissive.

After President Johnson encouraged the South to resist congressional Reconstruction, white conservatives worked hard to capture the new state governments. Many whites also boycotted the polls in an attempt to defeat Congress's plans; by sitting out the elections, whites might block the new constitutions, which had to be approved by a majority of registered voters. This tactic was tried in North Carolina and succeeded in Alabama, forcing Congress to base ratification on a majority of those voting.

Very few black men stayed away from the polls. Enthusiastically and hopefully, they voted Republican. Illiteracy did not prohibit blacks from making intelligent choices. One Mississippi black testified that he and his friends had no difficulty selecting the Republican ballot. "We stood around and watched," he explained. "We saw D. Sledge vote; he owned half the county. We knowed he voted Democratic so we voted the other ticket so it would be Republican."

Thanks to a large black turnout and the restrictions on prominent Confederates, a new southern Republican Party came to power in the constitutional conventions. Republican delegates consisted of a sizable contingent of blacks (265 out of the total of just over 1,000 delegates throughout the South), some northerners who had moved to the South, and native southern whites who favored change. Together these Republicans brought the South into line with progressive reforms that had been adopted in the rest of the nation. The new constitutions were more democratic. They eliminated property qualifications for voting and holding office, and they

How do historians know about the relationships between former slaves and former slaveholders during Reconstruction? The records of the Federal Bureau of Refugees, Freedmen, and Abandoned Lands contain a wealth of information on daily conflicts and confrontations. They reveal that one strategy used by planters to retain the labor of their former slaves was to control the slaves'

children. The entry shown here, from a Bureau record book in Texas, recounts the complaint of Amanda Hayes. In 1866, her former owner, Captain William Hayes, took her son "to help him drive his cattle." In July 1867, "Mr. Hayes has not returned the boy yet," and Amanda Hayes "wishes the Bureau to compel" his return, with pay. National Archives.

turned many appointed offices into elective posts. They provided for public schools and institutions to care for the mentally ill, the blind, the deaf, the destitute, and the orphaned. They also put an end to imprisonment for debt and to punishments such as branding.

The conventions broadened women's rights in property holding and divorce. Usually, the goal was not to make women equal with men but to provide relief to thousands of suffering debtors. In families left poverty-stricken by the war and weighed down by debt, it was usually the husband who had contracted the debts. Thus giving women legal control over their own property provided some protection to their families. The goal of some delegates, however, was to elevate women. Blacks in particular called for laws to provide for women's suffrage, but they were ignored by their white colleagues.

Under these new constitutions the southern states elected new governments. Again the Republican Party triumphed, putting new men in positions of power. For the first

Triumph of Republican Governments

time, the ranks of state legislators in 1868 included some black southerners. Congress's second plan for Reconstruction was well under way. It remained to be seen what these new governments would do and how much social change they would bring about.

One way to achieve radical change would have been to disfranchise substantial numbers of Confederate leaders. Barring many whites from politics as punishment for rebellion would have given the Republicans a solid electoral majority based on black voters and their white allies. Land reform and the assurance of racial equality would have been possible. No Republican government ever seriously considered this course of action, for two reasons.

First, they appreciated the realities of power and the depth of racial enmity. In most states, whites were in the majority and former slaveowners controlled the best land and other sources of economic power. James Lynch, a leading black politician from Mississippi, explained why African-Americans shunned the "folly" of disfranchisement. Unlike northerners who "can leave when it becomes too

uncomfortable," landless former slaves "must be in friendly relations with the great body of the whites in the state." Second, blacks believed in the principle of universal suffrage and the Christian goal of reconciliation. Far from being vindictive, they treated leading rebels with generosity.

The South's Republican Party therefore committed itself to a strategy of winning white support. To put the matter another way, the Republican Party condemned itself to defeat if white voters would not cooperate. But for a time both Republicans and their opponents, who called themselves Conservatives or Democrats, moved to the center and appealed for a broad range of support. Some propertied whites accepted congressional Reconstruction as a reality and declared themselves willing to compete under the new rules. While these Democrats angled for some black votes, Republicans sought to attract more white voters. Both parties found an area of agreement in economic policies.

The Reconstruction governments enthusiastically promoted industry. This policy reflected northern ideals, but it also sprang from a growling southern eagerness to

Industrialization

build up the region. Accordingly, Reconstruction legislatures encouraged investment with loans, subsidies, and exemptions from taxation for periods up to ten years. The southern railroad system was rebuilt and expanded, and coal and iron mining made possible Birmingham's steel plants. Between 1860 and 1880, the number of manufacturing establishments in the South nearly doubled. This emphasis on big business, however, produced higher state debts and taxes, drew money away from schools and other programs, and multiplied possibilities for corruption.

Policies appealing to African-American voters never went beyond equality before the law. In fact, the whites who controlled the southern Repub-

Other Republican Policies

lican Party were reluctant to allow blacks a share of offices proportionate to their electoral strength. Aware of their weakness, black leaders did not push for revolutionary economic or social change. Though land was important to African-Americans, few promoted confiscation. Instead, they led efforts to establish public schools but usually did not press for integrated facilities. Having a school to attend was the most important thing at the time. As a result, virtually every public school organized during Reconstruction was racially segregated, and these separate schools established a precedent for segregated theaters, trains, and other public accommodations in the South.

Within a few years, as centrists in both parties met with failure, white hostility to congressional Reconstruction began to dominate. Some conservatives had always desired to fight Reconstruction through pressure and racist propaganda. Charging that the South had been turned over to ignorant blacks, conservatives deplored "black domination" and "Negro rule."

Such attacks were inflammatory but inaccurate. African-Americans participated in politics but did not dominate or control events. They were a majority in only two out of ten state conventions (transplanted northerners were a majority in one). In the state legislatures, only in the lower house in South Carolina did blacks ever constitute a majority; among officeholders, their numbers generally were far inferior to their proportion in the population. Sixteen blacks won seats in Congress before Reconstruction was over, but none was ever elected governor. Only eighteen served in a high state office such as lieutenant governor, treasurer, superintendent of education, or secretary of state.

Conservatives also assailed the allies of black Republicans. Their propaganda denounced whites from the North as "carpetbaggers," greedy crooks

Carpetbaggers and Scalawags planning to pour stolen tax revenues into their sturdy luggage made of carpet material. In fact, most northerners who settled in the South had come seeking business opportunities or a warmer climate and never entered politics. Those who did enter politics generally wanted to democratize the South and to introduce northern ways, such as industry, public education, and the spirit of enterprise.

Conservatives invented the term *scalawag* to discredit any native white southerner who cooperated with the Republicans. A substantial number of southerners did so. Most scalawags were yeoman farmers, men from mountain areas and nonslaveholding districts who saw that they could benefit from the education and opportunities promoted by Republicans. Banding together with freedmen, they pursued common class interests and hoped to make headway against the power of long-dominant planters. Most scalawags, however, shied away from support for racial equality.

Taxation was a major problem for the Reconstruction governments. Republicans wanted to maintain prewar services, repair the war's destruction, stimulate industry, and support important new ventures such as public schools. But the Civil War had destroyed much of the South's tax base. Thus an increase in taxes was necessary even to maintain traditional services, and new ventures required still higher taxes.

Corruption was another serious charge levied against the Republicans. Unfortunately, it often was true. Many carpetbaggers and black politicians engaged in fraudulent schemes, sold their votes, or padded expenses. Many white Democrats shared in corruption, and some Republicans fought it, but the Democrats successfully pinned the blame on unqualified blacks and greedy carpetbaggers.

All these problems hurt the Republicans, but in many southern states the deathblow came through violence. The Ku Klux Klan, a secret

Ku Klux Klan veterans' club that began in Tennessee, spread through the South and rapidly evolved into a terrorist organization. Violence against African-Americans occurred from the first days of Reconstruction but became far more organized and purposeful after 1867. Klansmen rode to frustrate Reconstruction and keep the freedmen in subjection. Nighttime harassment, whippings, beatings, and murder became common, and terrorism dominated some areas.

The Klan's main purpose was political. Lawless nightriders made active Republicans the target of their attacks. Leading white and black Republi-

Members of the Ku Klux Klan devised ghoulish costumes to heighten the terror inspired by their acts. This photograph shows the costume of a Mississippi Klansman from 1871. Courtesy, Herbert Peck, Jr.

cans were killed in several states. After freedmen who worked for a South Carolina scalawag started voting, terrorists visited the plantation and, in the words of one victim, "whipped every nigger man they could lay their hands on." Klansmen also attacked Union League Clubs—Republican organizations that mobilized the black vote—and schoolteachers who were aiding the freedmen.

Klan violence was not a spontaneous outburst of racism; very specific social forces shaped and di-

rected it. In North Carolina, for example, Alamance and Caswell Counties were the sites of the worst Klan violence. Slim Republican majorities there rested on cooperation between black voters and white yeomen. Together, these black and white Republicans had ousted officials long entrenched in power. In a successful effort to restore Democratic control, wealthy and powerful men served as Klan leaders. Through a campaign of terror, the Ku Klux Klan weakened the Republican coalition and restored a Democratic majority.

Klan violence injured Republicans across the South. No fewer than one-tenth of the black leaders who had been delegates to the 1867–1868 state constitutional conventions were attacked, seven fatally. In Eutaw, Alabama, a single Klan attack left four blacks dead and fifty-four wounded. In South Carolina five hundred masked Klansmen lynched eight black prisoners at the Union County jail. According to historian Eric Foner, the Klan "made it virtually impossible for Republicans to campaign or vote in large parts of Georgia."

Thus a combination of difficult fiscal problems, Republican mistakes, racial hostility, and terror brought down the Republican regimes. In most southern states so-called Radical Reconstruction lasted only a few years. The most enduring failure of Reconstruction, however, was not political; it was social and economic. Reconstruction failed to alter the South's social structure or its distribution of wealth and power. Without land of their own, blacks were dependent on white landowners who could and did use their economic power to compromise blacks' political freedom. Armed only with the ballot, freed men in the South had little chance to effect major changes.

Failure of Reconstruction

 The Social and Economic Meaning of Freedom

Black southerners entered into life after slavery hopefully but not naively. They had had too much experience with white people to assume that all would be easy. Expecting hostility, freed men and women tried to gain as much as they could from their new circumstances. Often the changes they valued the most were personal.

One of the first decisions was whether to leave the old plantation. This choice meant making a judgment about where opportunities for liberty and progress were likely to be greatest. Many cruel slaveholders saw their former property walk off en masse, as former slaves used their experience in bondage to assess the whites with whom they had to deal.

After choosing an employer, ex-slaves reached out for valuable things in life that had been denied them. One of these was education. They started schools and filled class-rooms both day and night. On log seats and dirt floors, freed men and women of all ages studied their letters in old almanacs, discarded dictionaries, or whatever was available. Young children brought infants to school with them, and adults attended at night or after "the crops were laid by." The federal government and northern reformers of both races assisted this pursuit of education. In its brief life the Freedmen's Bureau founded over four thousand schools, and idealistic northerners established and staffed others.

Education for African-Americans

Blacks and their white allies also saw the need for colleges and universities to train teachers, ministers, and professionals for leadership. The American Missionary Association founded seven colleges, including Fisk and Atlanta Universities, between 1866 and 1869. The Freedmen's Bureau helped to establish Howard University in Washington, D.C., and northern religious groups supported dozens of seminaries, colleges, and teachers' colleges. By the late 1870s black churches had joined in the effort, founding numerous colleges despite limited resources.

Even during Reconstruction, African-American leaders often were highly educated individuals; many of them came from the prewar elite of free people of color. This group had benefited from its association with wealthy whites, many of whom were blood relatives; some planters had given their mulatto children outstanding educations. The two

black senators from Mississippi, Blanche K. Bruce and Hiram Revels, for instance, had had privileged educations. Bruce was the son of a planter who had provided tutoring at home; Revels was the son of free North Carolina mulattos who had sent him to Knox College in Illinois. These men and many self-educated former slaves brought to political office their experience as artisans, businessmen, lawyers, teachers, and preachers.

Meanwhile, millions of former slaves concentrated on improving life on their farms and in their neighborhoods. Surrounded by an unfriendly white population, black men and women sought to insulate themselves from white interference and to strengthen the bonds of their own community. Throughout the South they devoted themselves to reuniting their families, moving away from the slave quarters, and founding black churches. Given the eventual failure of Reconstruction, the gains African-Americans made in their daily lives often proved the most enduring.

The search for family members who had been sold away during slavery was awe inspiring. With only shreds of information to guide them, thousands of freed people embarked on odysseys in search of a husband, wife, child, or parent. By relying on the black community for help and information, many succeeded. Others walked through several states and never found loved ones.

Reunification of African-American Families

Husbands and wives who had belonged to different masters established homes together for the first time, and parents asserted the right to raise their own children. A mother bristled when her old master claimed a right to whip her children. She informed him that "he warn't goin' to brush none of her chilluns no more." The freed men and women were too much at risk to act recklessly, but, as one man put it, they were tired of punishment and "sure didn't take no more foolishness off of white folks."

Many black people wanted to minimize contact with whites. To avoid overbearing whites who were used to supervising and controlling them, blacks abandoned the slave quarters and fanned out to distant corners of the land they worked. Others established small all-black settlements that still exist today.

The other side of movement away from whites was closer communion within the black community. Freed from slavery, blacks could build their own institutions as they saw fit, and the secret churches of slavery came out into the open. Within a few years independent branches of the Methodist and Baptist denominations had attracted the great majority of black Christians in the South.

Founding of Black Churches

The desire to gain as much independence as possible also shaped the former slaves' economic arrangements. Since most of them lacked money to buy land, they preferred the next best thing: renting the land they worked. But few whites would consider renting land to blacks, and most blacks had no means to get cash before the harvest. Thus other alternatives had to be tried.

Northerners and officials of the Freedmen's Bureau favored contracts between owners and laborers. To northerners who believed in "Free Soil, Free Labor, Free Men," contracts and wages seemed the key to progress. For a few years the Freedmen's Bureau helped draw up and enforce such contracts, but they proved unpopular with both races. Owners often filled the contracts with detailed requirements that led to close supervision and reminded blacks of their circumscribed lives under slavery. Besides, cash for wages was not readily available in the early years of Reconstruction. Times were hard, and the failure of Confederate banks had left the South with a shortage of credit facilities.

Black farmers and white landowners therefore turned to sharecropping, a system in which farmers kept part of their crop and gave the rest to the landowner while living on his property. The landlord or a merchant "furnished" food and supplies needed before the harvest, and he received payment from the crop.

Rise of the Sharecropping System

Although landowners tried to set the laborers' share at a low level, black farmers had some bargaining power.

The sharecropping system originated as a desirable compromise. It eased landowners' problems with cash and credit; blacks accepted it because it gave them more freedom from daily supervision. Instead of working under a white overseer, as in slavery, they farmed a plot of land on their own in family groups. But sharecropping later proved to be a disaster for all concerned. Because African-Americans lived in a discriminatory society, the system placed them at the mercy of unscrupulous white landowners and merchants. The South suffered because the region became increasingly dependent upon cotton at the very time the growth rate in world demand for that crop began to drop, compared with the prewar years.

 ## Reconstruction's Decline and Fall

Northerners had always been far more interested in suppressing rebellion than in aiding southern blacks, and by the early 1870s the North's partial commitment to bringing about change in the South was weakening. Criticism of the southern governments grew, new issues captured people's attention, and soon voters began to look favorably on reconciliation with southern whites. In one southern state after another, Democrats regained control, and soon the situation had returned to "normal" in the eyes of southern whites.

Antagonism between Unionists and rebels was still very strong in 1868. That year Ulysses S. Grant, running as a Republican, defeated Horatio Seymour, a New York Democrat, for president. Grant was not a Radical, but his platform supported congressional Reconstruction and endorsed black suffrage in the South. (Significantly, Republicans stopped short of endorsing it in the North.)

Election of 1868

In office Grant acted as an administrator of Reconstruction but not as its enthusiastic advocate. He vacillated in his dealings with the southern states, sometimes defending Republican regimes and sometimes currying favor with Democrats. On occasion Grant called out federal troops to stop violence or enforce acts of Congress, but neither he nor Andrew Johnson imposed anything approaching a military occupation on the South.

In 1870 and 1871 the violent campaigns of the Ku Klux Klan forced Congress to pass two Enforcement Acts and an anti-Klan law. These laws made actions by *individuals* against the civil and political rights of others a federal criminal offense for the first time. They also provided for election supervisors and permitted martial law and suspension of the writ of habeas corpus to combat murders, beatings, and threats by the Klan. Federal prosecutors used the laws rather selectively. In 1872 and 1873 Mississippi and the Carolinas saw many prosecutions; but in other states where violence flourished, the laws were virtually ignored. Southern juries sometimes refused to convict Klansmen.

Some conservative but influential Republicans opposed the anti-Klan laws. Rejecting other Republicans' arguments that the Thirteenth, Fourteenth, and Fifteenth Amendments had made the federal government the protector of the rights of citizens, these dissenters echoed an old Democratic charge that Congress was infringing on states' rights. This opposition foreshadowed a more general revolt within Republican ranks in 1872.

Disenchanted with Reconstruction, a group calling itself the Liberal Republicans bolted the party in 1872 and nominated Horace Greeley, the well-known editor of the *New York Tribune*, for president. The Liberal Republicans were a varied group, including civil service reformers, foes of corruption, and advocates of a lower tariff. They were united by two popular attitudes: distaste for federal intervention in the South and a desire to let market forces and the "best men" determine events there. The Dem-

Liberal Republicans Revolt

ocrats also gave their nomination to Greeley in 1872. The combination was not enough to defeat Grant, who won reelection, but it reinforced Grant's desire to avoid confrontation with white southerners.

Dissatisfaction with Grant's administration grew during his second term. Corruption within the administration had become widespread, and Grant defended some of the culprits. In 1874, as Grant's popularity and his party's prestige declined, the Democrats recaptured the House of Representatives.

The effect of Democratic gains in Congress was to weaken the legislature's resolve on southern issues. Congress had already lifted the political disabilities of the Fourteenth Amendment from many former Confederates. In 1872 it had adopted a sweeping Amnesty Act, which pardoned most of the remaining rebels and left only five hundred barred from political officeholding. In 1875 Congress passed a Civil Rights Act purporting to guarantee black people equal accommodations in public places, but the bill was watered down and contained no effective provisions for enforcement. Moreover, by 1876 the Democrats had regained control in all but three southern states.

Amnesty Act

Meanwhile, new concerns were capturing the public's attention. Industrialization and immigration were surging, hastening the pace of change in national life. Within only eight years, postwar industrial production increased by an impressive 75 percent. For the first time, nonagricultural workers outnumbered farmers, and only Britain's industrial output was greater than that of the United States.

Then the Panic of 1873 ushered in over five years of economic contraction. Three million people lost their jobs, and the clash between labor and capital became the major issue of the day. Class attitudes diverged, especially in large cities. Debtors and the unemployed sought easy money policies to spur economic expansion. Businessmen, disturbed by the strikes and industrial violence that accompanied the panic, became increasingly concerned about the defense of property.

Class conflict fueled a monetary issue: whether paper money—the Civil War greenbacks—should be kept in circulation. In 1872, Democratic farmers and debtors urged this policy to expand the money supply and raise prices, but businessmen, bankers, and creditors overruled them. Now hard times swelled the ranks of the "greenbackers"—voters who favored greenbacks and easy money. Congress voted in 1874 to increase the number of greenbacks in circulation, but Grant vetoed the bill in deference to the opinions of financial leaders. The next year, "sound money" interests prevailed in Congress, winning passage of a law requiring that greenbacks be convertible into gold after 1878. This law limited the inflationary impact of the greenbacks and aided creditors rather than debtors (such as the hard-pressed and angry farmers).

Greenbacks Versus Sound Money

The Supreme Court also participated in the northern retreat from Reconstruction. During the Civil War, the Court, had been cautious and reluctant to assert itself. Reaction to the *Dred Scott* decision (1857) had been so violent, and the Union's wartime emergency so great, that the Court avoided interference with government actions. In 1866, however, a case, *Ex parte Milligan*, reached the Court. Lambdin P. Milligan of Indiana had plotted to free Confederate prisoners of war and overthrow state governments. For these acts a military court sentenced Milligan, a civilian, to death. Milligan challenged the authority of the military tribunal, claiming that he had a right to a civil trial. The Supreme Court declared that military trials were illegal when civil courts were open and functioning, and its language indicated that the Court intended to reassert itself as a major force in national affairs.

In the 1870s the Court successfully renewed its challenge to Congress's actions when it narrowed the meaning and effectiveness of the Fourteenth Amendment. The *Slaughter-House* cases (1873) began in 1869, when the Louisiana legislature granted one company a monopoly on the slaughtering of livestock in

Supreme Court Decisions on Reconstruction

New Orleans. Rival butchers in the city promptly sued. Their attorney, former Supreme Court justice John A. Campbell, argued that the Fourteenth Amendment had revolutionized the constitutional system by bringing individual rights under federal protection.

The Court rejected Campbell's argument and thereby dealt a stunning blow to the scope and vitality of the Fourteenth Amendment. Indeed, it interpreted the "privileges and immunities" of citizens so narrowly that it reduced them almost to trivialities. State citizenship and national citizenship were separate, the Court declared. National citizenship involved only matters such as the right to travel freely from state to state and to use the navigable waters of the nation, and only these narrow rights were protected by the Fourteenth Amendment. With this interpretation, the words "No state shall make or enforce any law which shall abridge the privileges or immunities of citizens of the United States" disappeared, from that day until now, as a meaningful and effective part of the Constitution.

The Supreme Court also concluded that the butchers who sued had not been deprived of their rights or property in violation of the due-process clause of the amendment. The Court's majority declared that the framers of the recent amendments had not intended to "destroy" the federal system, in which the states exercised "powers for domestic and local government, including the regulation of civil rights." Thus the justices severely limited the amendment's potential for securing and protecting the rights of black citizens.

The next day the Court decided *Bradwell* v. *Illinois*, a case in which Myra Bradwell, a female attorney, had been denied the right to practice law in Illinois on account of her gender. Pointing to the Fourteenth Amendment, Bradwell's attorneys contended that the state had unconstitutionally abridged her "privileges and immunities" as a citizen. The Supreme Court rejected her claim, alluding to women's traditional role in the home.

In 1876 the Court weakened the Reconstruction-era amendments even further by emasculating the enforcement clause of the Fourteenth Amendment and revealing deficiencies inherent in the Fifteenth Amendment. In *U.S. v. Cruikshank* the Court overruled the conviction under the 1870 Enforcement Act of Louisiana of whites who had attacked a meeting of blacks and conspired to deprive them of their rights. The justices ruled that the Fourteenth Amendment did not give the federal government power to act against these whites. The duty of protecting citizens' equal rights "was originally assumed by the States; and it still remains there." As for the protection of "unalienable rights," the Court said that "Sovereignty, for this purpose, rests alone with the States." In *U.S. v. Reese* the Court noted that the Fifteenth Amendment did not guarantee a citizen's right to vote but merely listed certain impermissible grounds for denying suffrage. Thus a path lay open for southern states to disfranchise blacks for supposedly nonracial reasons—lack of education or property or descent from a grandfather qualified to vote before the Reconstruction Act of 1867. These "grandfather clauses" became a means to give the vote to illiterate whites while excluding blacks.

As the 1876 elections approached, most political observers saw that the North was no longer willing to pursue the goals of Reconstruction. The results of a disputed presidential election confirmed this fact. Samuel J. Tilden, the Democratic governor of New York, ran strongly in the South and needed only one more electoral vote to triumph over Rutherford B. Hayes, the Republican nominee. Nineteen votes from Louisiana, South Carolina, and Florida were disputed; both Democrats and Republicans claimed to have won in those states despite fraud committed by their opponents. One vote from Oregon was undecided because of a technicality.

To resolve this unprecedented situation, Congress established a fifteen-member electoral commission. In the interest of impartiality, membership on the commission was to be balanced between Democrats and Republicans. But one independent Republican, Supreme Court Justice

Election of 1876

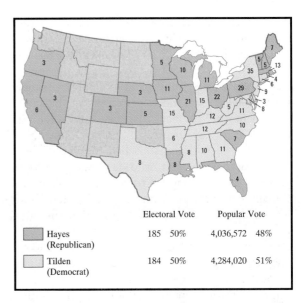

	Electoral Vote		Popular Vote	
Hayes (Republican)	185	50%	4,036,572	48%
Tilden (Democrat)	184	50%	4,284,020	51%

Presidential Election, 1876 In 1876 a combination of solid southern support and Democratic gains in the North gave Samuel Tilden the majority of popular votes, but Rutherford B. Hayes won the disputed election in the electoral college.

David Davis, refused appointment in order to accept his election as a senator. A regular Republican took his place, and the Republican Party prevailed 8 to 7 on every decision, along strict party lines. Hayes would become president if Congress accepted the commission's findings.

Congressional acceptance was not certain, and many citizens worried that the nation had entered a major constitutional crisis and would slip once again into civil war. The crisis was resolved when Democrats acquiesced in the election of Hayes (see map above). Scholars have found evidence of negotiations between Hayes's supporters and southerners who wanted federal aid to railroads, internal improvements, federal patronage, and removal of troops from southern states. But studies of Congress conclude that these negotiations did not have a deciding effect on the outcome: neither party was well enough organized to implement and enforce a bargain between the sections. Northern and southern

Democrats simply decided they could not win and did not contest the election. Thus Hayes became president, and Reconstruction was unmistakably over.

Southern Democrats rejoiced, but African-Americans grieved over the betrayal of their hopes for equality. For many African-Americans, the only hope was to leave the South, where real freedom was no longer a possibility. In South Carolina, Louisiana, Mississippi, and other southern states, thousands gathered up their possessions and migrated to Kansas. They were known as Exodusters, disappointed people still searching for their share in the American dream.

Exodusters Move West

 Conclusion

The nation ended over fifteen years of bloody Civil War and controversial Reconstruction without establishing full freedom for African-Americans. This contradictory record typified the results of Reconstruction in many other ways. A tumultuous period brought tremendous change, yet many things remained the same. Because extraordinary situations required revolutionary changes, the North had acted. The Union victory brought about an increase in federal power, stronger nationalism, unprecedented federal intervention in the southern states, and landmark amendments to the Constitution. But there was no commitment to make these changes endure, so the revolution remained partial. The nation turned away from the needs of its African-American citizens and began to focus on issues related to industrialism and an increasingly interrelated national economy.

Suggestions for Further Reading

National Policy, Politics, and Constitutional Law

Richard H. Abbott, *The Republican Party and the South, 1855–1877* (1986); Herman Belz, *Emancipation and Equal Rights* (1978); Michael Les Benedict, *A Compromise of Principle:* *Congressional Republicans and Reconstruction, 1863–1869* (1974); Michael Les Benedict, *The Impeachment and Trial of Andrew Johnson* (1973); Michael Kent Curtis, *No State Shall Abridge* (1987); Harold M. Hyman, *A More Perfect Union* (1973); Ronald J. Jensen, *The Alaska Purchase and Russian-American Relations* (1975); William S. McFeely, *Grant* (1981); Brooks D. Simpson, *Let Us Have Peace* (1991); Kenneth M. Stampp, *The Era of Reconstruction* (1965); Hans L. Trefousse, *Andrew Johnson* (1989).

The Freed Slaves

Ira Berlin, ed., *Freedom: A Documentary History of Emancipation, 1861–1867* (1984); Orville Vernon Burton, *In My Father's House Are Many Mansions* (1985); Edmund L. Drago, *Black Politicians and Reconstruction in Georgia* (1982); Gerald Jaynes, *Branches Without Roots: The Genesis of the Black Working Class in the American South, 1862–1882* (1986); Leon Litwack, *Been in the Storm So Long* (1979); Edward Magdol, *A Right to the Land* (1977); Robert Morris, *Reading, 'Riting and Reconstruction* (1981); Howard Rabinowitz, ed., *Southern Black Leaders in Reconstruction* (1982); Clarence Walker, *A Rock in a Weary Land* (1982).

Politics and Reconstruction in the South

Richard N. Current, *Those Terrible Carpetbaggers* (1988); Jonathan Daniels, *Prince of Carpetbaggers* (1958); W. E. B. Du Bois, *Black Reconstruction* (1935); Paul D. Escott, *Many Excellent People: Power and Privilege in North Carolina, 1850–1900* (1985); W. McKee Evans, *Ballots and Fence Rails: Reconstruction on the Lower Cape Fear* (1966); Michael W. Fitzgerald, *The Union League Movement in the Deep South* (1989); Eric Foner, *Reconstruction: America's Unfinished Revolution, 1863–1877* (1988); William C. Harris, *The Day of the Carpetbagger* (1979); Thomas Holt, *Black over White: Negro Political Leadership in South Carolina During Reconstruction* (1977); Michael Perman, *The Road to Redemption* (1984); Michael Perman, *Reunion Without Compromise* (1973); Lawrence N. Powell, *New Masters* (1980); George C. Rable, *But There Was No Peace* (1984); James Roark, *Masters Without Slaves* (1977); James Sefton, *The United States Army and Reconstruction, 1865–1877* (1967); Mark W. Summers, *Railroads, Reconstruction, and the Gospel of Prosperity* (1984); Allen Trelease, *White Terror* (1967); Michael Wayne, *The Reshaping of Plantation Society* (1983); Sarah Woolfolk Wiggins, *The Scalawag in Alabama Politics, 1865–1881* (1977).

Women, Family, and Social History

Ellen Carol Dubois, *Feminism and Suffrage* (1978); Herbert G. Gutman, *The Black Family in Slavery and Freedom, 1750–1925* (1976); Elizabeth Jacoway, *Yankee Missionaries in the South* (1979); Jacqueline Jones, *Labor of Love, Labor of Sorrow* (1985); Jacqueline Jones, *Soldiers of Light and Love* (1980); Mary P. Ryan, *Women in Public* (1990).

The End of Reconstruction

William Gillette, *Retreat from Reconstruction, 1869–1879* (1980); William Gillette, *The Right to Vote* (1969); Keith Ian Polakoff, *The Politics of Inertia* (1973); C. Vann Woodward, *Reunion and Reaction* (1951).

Reconstruction's Legacy for the South

Robert G. Athearn, *In Search of Canaan* (1978); Jay R. Mandle, *The Roots of Black Poverty* (1978); Nell Irvin Painter, *Exodusters* (1976); Howard Rabinowitz, *Race Relations in the Urban South, 1865–1890* (1978); Roger L. Ransom and Richard Sutch, *One Kind of Freedom* (1977); Jonathan M. Wiener, *Social Origins of the New South* (1978); C. Vann Woodward, *Origins of the New South* (1951).

CHAPTER
17

The Development of the West and South
1877–1892

I n August 1867, Roaming Leader, a member of the Skidi band of the Pawnee nation, led a scouting party to look for buffalo. The whole band—several dozen men, women, and children—had left its village of mud lodges in northwestern Nebraska two months earlier for the annual buffalo hunt. Eventually, the Skidi party shot three buffalo. The animals were butchered and their carcasses were carried back to camp. There women deftly cut up and dried the meat, made mats out of the intestines, robes and blankets out of the hides, and implements out of the bones.

In September, Roaming Leader's band returned to its village to harvest the corn the Skidi had planted that spring. At the harvest, the women again controlled the food preparation, roasting and drying vegetables in a deep pit and grinding grain into flour. Meanwhile, men collected firewood. Finally, after nearly two weeks of strenuous work, the Skidi celebrated the harvest with elaborate rituals of song, dance, and food offerings.

Indians had managed land and resources in this way for centuries. The Pawnees planted crops in the spring, then left to hunt buffalo. Their technology was simple, and they survived by developing and using natural resources respectfully. Moreover, concepts of private property, commercial exchange, and profit had little meaning for them.

For white Americans, however, natural resources were to be utilized for economic gain. As they settled the West and redeveloped the South in the late nineteenth century, they dug into the earth to remove valuable minerals, cut down forests for lumber, built railroads, dammed the rivers, and plowed the soil. Their goal was buying and selling goods and services and achieving a more comfortable life. As they transformed the landscape, the triumph of their market economies transformed the entire nation.

In American history, the meaning of the expression "the West" has changed over time. By the years following the Civil War, "the West" was most of the area between the Mississippi River and the Pacific Ocean. Between 1870 and 1890, the population living between the Mississippi River and the Pacific Ocean swelled from 7 million to nearly 17 million. Growth characterized the South as well. Shortly after Reconstruction ended, cotton production reached pre–Civil War levels, and southerners found new ways to profit from the region's natural resources.

The abundance of land, food, and raw materials in the West and South filled white Americans with faith that anyone eager and persistent enough could succeed. But their self-confidence rested on an arrogant belief that white people were somehow special, and individualism often asserted itself at the expense of racial minorities and the poor. Americans rarely thought about conserving resources because there always seemed to be more territory to exploit.

By 1890, farms, ranches, mines, towns, and cities could be found in almost every corner of the present-day continental United States. The frontier, so long a part of American history, apparently had disappeared. Indeed, in 1890 the superintendent of the United States census declared that the American frontier no longer existed. Though the fading of the frontier had great symbolic importance, vast stretches of unsettled land remained.

 ## The Transformation of Native American Cultures

Historians once defined the American frontier as "the edge of the unused," implying that the frontier faded when white men and women began to use supposedly open land for farming or for building cities. Scholars now acknowledge that American Indians had settled the West long before other Americans migrated there. Nevertheless, almost all native economic systems weakened in the late nineteenth century.

Western Indian cultures varied, but all based their economies on four activities: crop raising; livestock raising; hunting, fishing, and gathering; and raiding. Corn was the most common crop; sheep and horses, acquired from Spanish colonizers, were the livestock; and buffalo were the primary prey of hunts. Indians raided each other for food, hides, and livestock. The goal of all these activities was *subsistence*, the maintenance of life at its most basic level. To achieve subsistence, Indians tried to balance their economic systems. When a buffalo hunt failed, they could still subsist on crops. When their crops failed, they could still hunt buffalo and steal food in a raid. Indians also traded with each other and with whites.

Subsistence Cultures

For Indians on the Great Plains, everyday life focused on the buffalo. They cooked and preserved buffalo meat; fashioned hides into clothing, shoes, and blankets; used sinew for thread and bowstrings; and carved tools from bones and horns. They also depended on horses. To provide food for their herds, Plains Indians practiced environmental management by periodically setting fire to tall-grass prairies. This facilitated the growth of grass in the spring so horses could feed all summer.

This world of subsistence began to dissolve after 1850 when whites, perceiving the buffalo and the Indians as hindrances to their ambitions on the Great Plains, endeavored to eliminate both. As one United States army officer put it, "Kill every buffalo you can. Every buffalo dead is an Indian gone." Railroads sponsored hunts in which eastern sportsmen shot at the bulky targets from slow-moving trains. Some hunters collected from $1 to $3 from tanneries for hides; others did not even stop to pick up their kill. By the 1880s only a few hundred remained of the estimated 13 million buffalo that had existed in 1850. The scarcity of buffalo disturbed the subsistence system, leaving the Indians with less food to supplement their diets if crops failed or were stolen.

Slaughter of Buffalo

• *Important Events* •

1862	Homestead Act grants free land to citizens who live on and cultivate the land for five years
	Morrill Land Grant Act gives states public lands to finance agricultural and industrial colleges
1876	Custer's Last Stand (Battle of Little Big Horn): Sioux annihilate federal troops led by Colonel George A. Custer
1878	Timber and Stone Act allows citizens to buy timber land cheaply but also enables large companies to acquire huge tracts of forest land
1880–81	George Manypenny's *Our Indian Wards* and Helen Hunt Jackson's *A Century of Dishonor* influence public conscience about poor government treatment of Indians
1883	Supreme Court, in *Civil Rights* cases, strikes down 1875 Civil Rights Act and reinforces claim that the federal government cannot regulate behavior of private individuals in matters of race relations
	National time zones standardized

1887	Dawes Severalty Act ends communal ownership of Indian lands and grants land allotments to individual Native American families
	Hatch Act provides for agricultural experiment stations in every state
1889	Statehood granted to North Dakota, South Dakota, Washington, and Montana
1890	Census Bureau announces closing of the frontier
	Statehood granted to Wyoming and Idaho
	Yosemite National Park established
1896	*Plessy* v. *Ferguson* upholds doctrine of "separate but equal" among blacks and whites in public facilities
	Rural Free Delivery made available
	Statehood granted to Utah
1899	*Cummins* v. *County Board of Education* applies separate-but-equal doctrine to public schools
1902	Newlands Reclamation Act passed

Government policy reinforced private efforts to remove Indians from the path of white ambitions. North American natives were organized not so much into tribes, as whites believed, but rather into hundreds of bands and confederacies, with more than two hundred distinct languages and dialects. In its quest to fashion a policy toward Indians, the federal government gave more meaning to tribal organization than was warranted. After the Treaty of Greenville in 1795, American officials considered Indian "tribes" to be separate nations with which they could make treaties. But a chief or chiefs who agreed to a treaty could not guarantee that all bands within the group would abide by it. Moreover, whites seldom accepted treaties as guarantees of the Indians' future land

Territorial Treaties

rights; whites assumed that they could settle wherever they wished. Some bands acquiesced; others took revenge by attacking settlements, herds, and troops. The army responded with murders and massacres of entire villages.

By the 1870s, federal officials and reformers were promoting more peaceful means of dealing with western Indians. Instead of being considered foreign nations, they would be "civilized" and "uplifted" through education. White missionaries and teachers would attempt to force on Native Americans the values of the American work ethic: ambition, thrift, and materialism. To achieve this transformation, however, Indians would have to abandon their traditional cultures.

From the 1860s to the 1880s, the federal government tried to force Indians onto reservations, where, it was thought, they could be "civilized."

Reservation Policy

Reservations usually consisted of those areas of a group's previous territory that were least desirable to whites (see map, page 328). When assigning Indians to restricted territories, the government promised protection from white encroachment and agreed to provide food, clothing, and other necessities.

Reservation policy had disturbing consequences. First, Indians had no say over their own affairs on reservations. Supreme Court decisions in 1884 and 1886 denied them the ability to become United States citizens, leaving them unprotected by the Fourteenth and Fifteenth Amendments. Second, it was impossible to protect reservations from whites, who continually sought Indian lands for their own purposes. Third, the government ignored native history, even combining on the same reservation Indian bands that habitually had waged war with each other. Rather than serving as civilizing communities, reservations made Indians more vulnerable than they had been.

Native Resistance

Not all Indians succumbed to market forces and reservation restrictions. Some tried to preserve their traditional cultures even as they became dependent on whites. Pawnees, for instance, agreed to leave their Nebraska homelands for a reservation in the hope that they could hunt buffalo and grow corn as they once had done.

Indians also actively defended their homelands from intrusion in a series of bloody conflicts and revolts. These battles climaxed in June 1876 when 2,500 Lakotas led by Chiefs Rain-in-the-Face, Sitting Bull, and Crazy Horse surrounded and annihilated 256 government troops led by the rash Colonel George A. Custer near the Little Big Horn River in southern Montana. Though Indians consistently demonstrated military skill, shortages of supplies and relentless pursuit by white troops eventually overwhelmed armed Indian resistance.

These conditions, the publication of George Manypenny's *Our Indian Wards* (1880), Helen Hunt Jackson's *A Century of Dishonor* (1881), and unfavorable comparisons with Canada's management of Indian affairs aroused the American con-science. Canada had granted native peoples the rights of British subjects, and the Royal Mounted Police defended them against whites. A high inter-marriage rate between Indians and Canadian whites also promoted smoother relations.

Reform of Indian Policy

In the United States, most reformers believed Indians were culturally inferior to whites and assumed Indians could succeed economically only if they adopted middle-class values of diligence, monogamy, and education. Reformers particularly deplored Indians' sexual division of labor. Women seemed to do all the work—tending crops, raising children, cooking, curing hides, making tools and clothes—and to be servile to men, who hunted but were otherwise idle. White-dominated reform groups thus wanted Indian men to bear more responsibilities, to treat Indian women more respectfully, and to resemble the male heads of white middle-class households.

Dawes Severalty Act

In 1887 Congress reversed its reservation policy and passed the Dawes Severalty Act. The act ended communal ownership of Indian lands and granted land allotments to individual Native American families, awarding citizenship (after a twenty-five-year waiting period) to all who accepted allotments. It also authorized the government to sell surplus—unallocated—land to whites. These provisions applied to western groups except the Pueblo peoples, who retained land rights that were granted to them by the Spanish.

Indian policy, as carried out by the Interior Department, now took on three main features. First, land was distributed to individual families in the belief that they would acquire white people's wants and values by learning how to manage their own property. Second, officials believed that Indians would abandon their "barbaric" habits more quickly if their children were educated in boarding schools away from the reservations. Third, officials tried to suppress what they believed were dangerous religious ceremonies by funding white church groups to teach Indians to become good Christians.

How do historians know the In-
dians' side of conflicts between whites and Native
Americans? The Plains Indians often expressed themselves through art, painting on buffalo hides or, in the
nineteenth century, in notebooks that they acquired
from whites. These painted scenes are known as ledger
drawings. The ledger drawing shown here, by an
unknown Cheyenne artist, depicts a skirmish in the
Sioux battles leading up to the Battle of Little Big
Horn ("Custer's Last Stand") in 1876. Warriors advance bravely in defense of their village as they are led
by a comrade wearing a war bonnet and carrying a
long bow-spear, which were symbols of power. The
image of invincibility is emphasized by the multitude
of bullets surrounding the Indians, who remain unscathed.   Newberry Library.

Cheyenne Camp attacked at Powder River
by Soldiers. (Mackenzie.)
Fall of 1876

The Losing of the West

The Dawes Act reduced native control over land. Eager speculators induced Indians to sell their newly acquired property, in spite of some federal safeguards against such practices. Between 1887 and the 1930s, Indian landholdings dwindled from 138 million acres to 52 million. Land-grabbing whites were particularly cruel to the Ojibwas of the northern plains. A 1906 law contained a rider declaring that mixed-blood adults on the White Earth reservation were "competent" enough to sell their land without having to observe the twenty-five-year waiting period stipulated in the Dawes Act. Speculators then duped many Ojibwas, whom white "experts" had declared "mixed-bloods," into signing away their land in return for counterfeit money and worthless merchandise.

The government's policy had other harmful effects on Indians' ways of life. The boarding-school program educated thousands of children, but most returned to their families demoralized and confused. After four years spent at the Sherman Institute in Riverside, California, Polingaysi

Reformers established boarding schools to take Indian children off the reservations and teach them a new and allegedly better culture. As one white leader remarked, "They should be educated, not as Indians, but as Americans." Upon their arrival at the Carlisle School in Pennsylvania, one of twenty-four such schools, Sioux youths (on the left) received new attire to make them look (on the right) as their teachers wanted them to look.   Smithsonian Institute, Washington, D.C.

Qoyawayma recalled, "As a Hopi, I was misunderstood by the white man; as a convert of the missionaries, I was looked upon with suspicion by the Hopi people."

Ultimately, the western Indians were overcome by political and ecological crises. Buffalo extinction and disease, in addition to military force, combined to hobble subsistence culture to the point that Indians had no alternative but to yield their lands to market-oriented whites. Although they tried to retain their culture by both adapting and yielding to the various demands they faced, by the end of the century they had lost control of the land and were under increasing pressure to shed their group identity. To this day they remain casualties of an aggressive age.

 ## The Exploitation of Natural Resources

In sharp contrast to the Indians, who used land and water to meet subsistence needs, whites were driven by the desire to get rich quick. To their eyes, the vast stretches of territory were untapped reservoirs of resources and wealth. Extraction of these resources advanced settlement and created new markets; it also fueled the revolutions in transportation, agriculture, and industry that swept the United States in the late nineteenth century. At the same time, the exploitation of nature's wealth gave rise to careless interaction with the environment and fed habits of racial and sexual oppression.

In the years just before the Civil War, eager prospectors began to comb remote forests and mountains for gold, silver, timber, oil, and copper.

Mining and Lumbering

The mining frontier advanced rapidly, drawing thousands of people to California, Nevada, Idaho, Montana, and Colorado. Prospectors tended to be restless optimists whose ultimate goal was to find and sell a large quantity of minerals. Digging for and transporting minerals, however, was extremely expensive, so prospectors who did discover veins of metal usually sold their claims to mining syndicates that had the resources to bring in engineers, heavy machinery, railroad lines, and work crews. Although discoveries of gold and silver first drew attention to the West and its resources, mining companies usually exploited less romantic but equally lucrative metals.

Lumber production, another large-scale extractive industry, required vast amounts of forest land. Lumber companies moving into the Northwest grabbed millions of acres by exploiting the Timber and Stone Act, passed by Congress in 1878 to stimulate settlement in California, Nevada, Oregon, and Washington. It allowed private citizens to buy, at a low price, 160-acre plots "unfit for cultivation" and "valuable chiefly for timber." Lumber companies hired seamen from waterfront boarding houses to register private claims to timberland and then transfer those claims to the companies. By 1900, private citizens had bought over 3.5 million acres, but most of that land belonged to corporations.

While lumber companies were acquiring timberlands in the Northwest, oil companies were beginning to drill for oil in the Southwest. In 1900 most of the nation's petroleum still came from the Appalachians and Midwest, but rich oil reserves had been discovered in southern California and eastern Texas. Although oil and kerosene were still used mostly for lubrication and lighting, oil later became a vital new source of fuel.

The natural-resource frontier was largely a man's world. Still, many western communities did have substantial populations of women who had

Frontier Society

come for the same reason as men: to find a fortune. But on the mining frontier as elsewhere, their independence was limited; they usually accompanied a husband or father. Few women prospected, but many earned money by cooking and laundering. Some women also provided sexual services for the miners, but many others helped bolster family and community life by campaigning against drinking, gambling, and prostitution. They also exercised moral authority by building homes to rescue women—unmarried mothers, Mormons, Indians, and Chinese immigrants—who they believed had fallen prey to men or who had not yet accepted the conventions of Christian virtue.

The West was a multiracial society, including not only Native Americans and Anglo (native-born white) migrants but also Hispanics, African-Americans, and Asians. Indians

A Complex Population

could be found throughout the West, and Anglo miners and farmers became an increasing presence after 1850. A crescent of territory, stretching from western Texas through New Mexico and Arizona to northern California, supported Hispanic ranchers and sheepherders, descendants of the Spanish who originally had claimed the land. In New Mexico, Hispanics had mixed with Indians to form a mestizo population of small farmers and ranchers. And, before federal law excluded them in 1881 and 1882, some 200,000 Chinese immigrants came to the United States; because almost all were young males, they constituted a sizable proportion of the work force in California and other West Coast states.

Racial minorities in western communities occupied the bottom half of a two-tiered labor system. Whites dominated the top tier of managerial and skilled labor positions. Unskilled laborers, often Chinese and Mexicans, worked in the mines, on railroad construction, and as agricultural laborers. Blacks also worked in railroad and mining camps, doing cooking and cleaning, while Indians barely participated in the white-controlled labor system at all. All of these nonwhite groups encountered prejudice.

As whites were wresting control of the land from the Indians, new questions arose over control of the nation's oil, mineral, and timber resources.

Use of Western Lands

Much of the undeveloped land west of the Mississippi was in the public domain, and some people believed that the federal government, as its owner, should control its exploitation. Others, however, believed in unlimited use of the land.

Developers of natural resources were seldom interested in landowning. They wanted trees, not forest land that would become useless once they had cut the trees. They wanted oil, not the scrubby plain that would be worthless if—as often happened—they dug wells but found no oil. To avoid purchase costs, oilmen and iron miners often leased property from private owners or from the government and paid royalties on the minerals extracted. Some lumbermen simply cut trees on public lands without paying a cent and used trickery to buy land cheaply under the Timber and Stone Act.

Questions about natural resources caught Americans between a desire for progress and a fear of spoiling the land. By the late 1870s, people eager to protect the natural landscape began to organize a conservation movement. Prominent among them was western naturalist John Muir, who helped establish Yosemite National Park in 1890. The next year, pressured by Muir and others, Congress authorized President Benjamin Harrison to create forest reserves—public land protected from cutting by private interests. Such policies met with strong objections from those wanting to exploit western resources. As a rule, conservation's supporters were easterners and its opponents were westerners.

Admission of New States

Development of the mining and forest frontiers, and of the farms and cities that followed, brought western territories to the threshold of statehood. In 1889, Congress passed an omnibus bill granting statehood to North Dakota, South Dakota, Washington, and Montana. Wyoming and Idaho were admitted the following year. Congress denied

statehood to Utah until 1896, when the Mormon majority agreed to abandon polygamy. Those states' mining towns and lumber camps spiced American folk culture and fostered a go-getter optimism that distinguished the American spirit. The lawlessness and hedonism of places like Deadwood, in Dakota Territory, and Tombstone, in Arizona Territory, gave the West notoriety and romance. But violence and eccentricity were far from common. Most men and women worked long hours. Few had the time, energy, or money for excesses. There were sharpshooters and dance-hall queens, but for most, western life was a matter of adapting and surviving.

 Water and Western Agriculture

Glittering gold, tall trees, and gushing oil shaped the popular image of the West, but water gave it life. If the western territories and states promised wealth from mining, cutting, and drilling, their agricultural potential promised more—but only if settlers could find a way to bring water to the arid land. The economic development of the West is the story of how public and private interests used technology and organization to develop the region's river basins and make the land agriculturally productive.

For centuries, Indians had irrigated southwestern lands to sustain their subsistence farming. When the Spanish arrived, they began tapping the Rio Grande to irrigate their farms in southwest Texas and New Mexico. The first Americans of northern European ancestry to practice extensive irrigation were the Mormons. Arriving in Utah in 1847, they quickly diverted streams and rivers into a network of canals, whose water enabled them to farm the hard-baked soil.

Who Owns the Water?

Efforts at land reclamation through irrigation in Colorado and California raised controversies over rights to the precious streams that flowed through the West. Americans had inherited the English common-law principle of *riparian rights*, which held that only people who owned land along the banks of a river could appropriate from the water's flow. The stream itself, according to riparianism, belonged only to God; those who lived on its banks could take water for normal needs but were not to diminish the river by damming or diverting water at the expense of others who lived along the banks.

Americans rejected riparianism in favor of the doctrine of *prior appropriation*, which awarded a river's water to the first person who claimed it. Western farmers wanted to be allowed, as nonriparian property owners, to dam rivers and transport water as far as they wished. Moreover, they believed that anyone intending a beneficial or "reasonable" (economically productive) use of river water should have the right to appropriation.

Without appropriated water, agriculture could not have flourished in the arid West. Allowing water-drawing rights only to farmers who lived along riverbanks would give them a monopoly and effectively prevent development of most of the land. The unspoken premise, however, was that *all* land existed for potential human development and that *all* natural resources should be used—even used up—to maximize economic gain. Most white people assumed that the doctrine of appropriation made sense.

Under appropriation, those who dammed and diverted water often reduced the flow of water available to potential users downstream. One way people disadvantaged by such action could protect their interests was by establishing a public authority to regulate water usage. Thus in 1879 Colorado created a number of water divisions, each with a commissioner to determine and regulate water rights. In 1890 Wyoming adopted a constitutional provision declaring the state's rivers public property, subject to state supervision of their use.

California was the scene of the most dramatic water-related developments. Unlike other western states that had opted for appropriation rights over riparian rights, California maintained a mixed legal system that upheld riparianism while allowing for some appropriation. This system put irrigators at a disadvantage and prompted them to seek a change in state law. In 1887 the state legislature passed a law permitting farmers to organize into irrigation districts that would sponsor the construction and operation of irrigation projects. An irrigation district could use its public author-

California's Solution

ity to purchase water rights, seize private property to build irrigation canals, and finance its projects through taxation or by issuing bonds. As a result of this legislation, California became the nation's leader in irrigated acreage and boasted the most profitable agriculture in the country.

Though state irrigation provisions stimulated development, the federal government still owned most of the West in the 1890s. Prodded by land-hungry developers, the states wanted the federal government to transfer to them all, or at least part, of the public domain lands. States claimed they could make these lands profitable through *reclamation*—providing them with irrigated water. For the most part, Congress refused such transfers. If federal lands were transferred to state control for the purpose of water development, who would regulate waterways that flowed through more than one state or that potentially could provide water to a nearby state? If, for example, California received control of the Truckee River, which flowed westward out of Lake Tahoe, how would Nevadans be assured that California would give them any water? Only the federal government, it seemed, had the power to regulate water development.

Newlands Reclamation Act

In 1902, Congress passed the Newlands Reclamation Act, which allowed the federal government to sell western public lands to individuals in parcels not to exceed 160 acres, and to use the proceeds from such sales to finance irrigation projects. The Newlands Act provided for control but not conservation of water—some three-fourths of the water used in open-ditch irrigation, the most common form, was lost to evaporation. Thus the legislation fell squarely within the tradition of exploitation of nature for human profit. It also represented a direct decision by the federal government to aid the agricultural and general economic development of the West.

The Age of Railroad Expansion

The discovery and development of natural riches provided the base on which the nation's economy expanded. But raw wealth would have been of

The American West, 1860–1890 *This map shows the dispersed nature of economic activity in the trans–Mississippi West and the importance of railroads in linking those activities.*

limited value without the means to carry it to factories and marketplaces. Railroads filled this need.

Railroad construction after the Civil War was extensive and complex. Between 1865 and 1890, total track in the United States grew from 35,000 to 200,000 miles (see map, page 328). By 1910 the nation had one-third of all the railroad track in the world. After 1880, when durable steel rails began to replace iron rails, railroads helped to boost the nation's steel industry to international leadership. Railroad expansion also spawned a number of related industries, including coal production, passenger- and freight-car manufacture, and depot construction.

Effects of Railroad Construction

Railroads altered conceptions of time and space. First, by overcoming physical barriers to travel, railroads transformed space into time. Instead of expressing the distance between places in miles, people began to refer to the amount of time it took to travel from one place to another. Second, railroad scheduling required the nationwide standardization of time. Before railroads, local church bells and clocks struck noon when the sun was directly overhead, and people set their clocks and watches accordingly. But because the sun was not overhead at exactly the same moment everywhere, time varied from place to place. To impose some regularity, railroads created their own time zones. By 1880 there were nearly fifty different standards, but in 1883 the railroads finally agreed—without consulting anyone in government—to establish four standard time zones for the whole country. Railroad time thus became national time.

Railroad construction brought about technological and organizational reforms as well. By the late 1880s, almost all lines had adopted standard-gauge rails so their tracks could connect with one another. Air brakes, automatic car couplers, standardized handholds on freight cars, and other devices made rail transportation safer and more efficient. Organizational advances included systems for coordinating complex passenger and freight schedules, and the adoption of uniform freight-classification systems.

Railroads accomplished these feats with the help of some of the largest government subsidies in American history. Executives argued that because railroads benefited the public, the government should aid them by giving them land from the public domain. Sympathetic officials at the federal, state, and local levels responded with massive subsidies. The federal government granted railroad companies in excess of 180 million acres, and state grants totaled 50 million acres. Local governments assisted by offering loans or by purchasing railroad bonds or stocks.

Government Subsidy of Railroads

Government subsidies had mixed effects. Although capitalists argued against government interference, they nevertheless accepted government aid and pressured governments into meeting their needs. The Southern Pacific, for example, threatened to bypass Los Angeles unless the city came up with a bonus and built a depot. Without public help, few railroads could have prospered sufficiently to attract private investment, yet public aid was not always salutary. During the 1880s, the policy of assistance haunted communities whose zeal had prompted them to commit too much to railroads that were never built or that defaulted on loans. Some laborers and farmers fought subsidies, arguing that companies like the Southern Pacific would become too powerful. Many communities boomed, however, because they had linked their fortunes to the iron horse. Moreover, railroads drew farmers into the market economy.

 Farming the Plains

Settlement of the Great Plains and the West involved the greatest migration in American history. During the 1870s and 1880s, hundreds of thousands of people streamed into states like Kansas, Nebraska, Texas, and California. More acres were put under cultivation during these two decades than in the previous 250 years. In taming the windswept prairies, settlers transformed agriculture into big business and made America the world's breadbasket.

Settlement of the Farm Frontier

Most, though not all, migrants came from the eastern states or Europe. Several western states opened offices in the East and in European ports to lure settlers westward. Land-rich railroads were especially aggressive, advertising cheap land, arranging credit terms, offering reduced fares, and promising instant success. In California, fruit and vegetable growers imported laborers from Japan and Mexico to work in the fields and canneries.

Most migrants went west because opportunities there seemed to promise a better life. Life on the farm, however, was much harder than the advertisements and railroad agents suggested. The open prairies contained little lumber for housing and fuel. Pioneer families were thus forced to build houses of sod and to burn manure for heat. Water was sometimes as scarce as timber.

Hardship of Life on the Plains

Even more formidable than the terrain was the climate. The expanse between the Missouri River and the Rocky Mountains divides climatologically along a line running from Minnesota southwest through Oklahoma, then south, bisecting Texas. West of this line, annual rainfall averages less than 28 inches, not enough for most crops.

Weather seldom followed predictable cycles. In summer, weeks of torrid heat and parching winds suddenly gave way to violent storms that washed away crops and property. In the winter, blizzards piled up mountainous snowdrifts that halted all outdoor movement. In the spring, melting snow swelled streams, and floods threatened millions of acres. And in the fall, a week without rain could turn dry grasslands into tinder; the slightest spark could then ignite a raging prairie fire.

Nature could be cruel even under good conditions. Weather that was favorable for crops was also good for breeding insects. In the 1870s and 1880s swarms of grasshoppers virtually ate up entire farms. As one farmer lamented, the "hoppers left behind nothing but the mortgage."

Settlers of the Plains also had to contend with social isolation, a factor accentuated by the pattern of settlement. Under the Homestead Act of 1862 and other measures adopted to encourage western settlement, most plots of land were rectangular-shaped 160-acre tracts. The rectangular shape meant that at most four families could live near each other, and then only if they congregated around the shared four-corner boundary intersection. In practice, farm families usually lived back from their boundary lines, and at least a half-mile separated farmhouses.

Social Isolation

Farm families survived by sheer resolve and by organizing churches and clubs where they could socialize a few times a month. By 1900, two developments had brought most rural settlers into closer contact with modern consumer society. First, mail-order companies—Montgomery Ward and Sears, Roebuck—made new consumer products available to almost everyone by the 1870s and 1880s. Emphasizing personal attention to customers, Ward's and Sears were outlets for sociability as well as material goods. Letters from customers to Mr. Ward often reported family news and sought advice on everything from gifts to childcare.

Mail-Order Companies and Rural Free Delivery

Second, in 1896 the government postal service made Rural Free Delivery (RFD) widely available. Farmers would no longer lack news and information; they could receive letters, newspapers, and catalogs at home nearly every day. In 1913 the postal service inaugurated parcel post, which enabled people to receive packages, such as orders from Ward's and Sears, more cheaply.

The agricultural revolution that followed the Civil War would not have been possible without the expanded use of machinery. When the Civil War drew men away from farms in the upper Mississippi River valley, the women and men who remained behind began using reapers and other mechanical implements to satisfy demand for food and take advantage of high grain prices. After the war, continued demand and high prices encouraged farmers to depend more on machines, and inventors developed new implements for farm use.

Mechanization of Agriculture

Machines increased productivity, cut costs, and dramatically reduced the number of hours needed to harvest a crop.

Meanwhile, Congress and scientists worked to improve existing crops and develop new ones. The 1862 Morrill Land Grant Act had given each state federal lands to sell in order to finance the establishment of educational institutions that aided agricultural development. A second Morrill Act in 1890 aided more schools, including a number of black colleges. The Hatch Act of 1887 provided for agricultural experiment stations in every state, further encouraging the advancement of farming technology.

Legislative and Scientific Aid to Farmers

Scientific advances enabled farmers to use the soil more efficiently. Researchers developed the technique of dry farming, a system of plowing and harrowing that minimized the evaporation of precious moisture. Botanists perfected varieties of "hard" wheat whose seeds could withstand northern winters. In California, Luther Burbank developed a multitude of new plants by crossbreeding, and chemist George Washington Carver of Alabama's Tuskegee Institute created hundreds of new products from peanuts, soybeans, sweet potatoes, and cotton wastes. These and other scientific and technological developments helped make America what one journalist called "the garden of the world."

 ## The Ranching Frontier

While commercial farming was spreading, cattle ranching—one of the West's most romantic industries—was evolving. Early in the nineteenth century herds of cattle, introduced by the Spanish and expanded by Mexican ranchers, roamed southern Texas and bred with cattle brought by Anglo settlers. The resulting longhorn breed multiplied and became valuable by the 1860s, when population growth increased demand for beef and railroads facilitated the transportation of food. By 1870, drovers (as many as 25 percent of whom were African-American) were herding thousands

of Texas cattle northward to Kansas, Missouri, and Wyoming (see map, page 328).

The long drive gave rise to romantic lore but was not very efficient. Trekking 1,500 miles made cattle sinewy and tough. Herds traveling through Indian lands and farmers' fields were sometimes shot at and later prohibited from such trespass by state laws. Ranchers adjusted by eliminating long drives and raising herds nearer to railroad routes. When ranchers discovered that crossing Texas longhorns with heavier Hereford and Angus breeds produced animals better able to survive northern winters, cattle raising spread across the Great Plains.

Cattle raisers needed vast pastures to graze their herds, and they wanted to incur as little expense as possible from using such land. Thus they often bought a few acres bordering a stream and turned their herds loose on adjacent public domain that no one wanted because it lacked water access. By this method, called open-range ranching, a cattle raiser could control thousands of acres by owning only a hundred or so.

Open-Range Ranching

Cowboy crews rounded up the cattle twice each year to brand new calves in the spring and to drive mature animals to market in the fall. Roundups delighted easterners with colorful images of western life: bellowing cattle, mounted rope-swinging cowboys, and smoky campfires. But roundups and open-range ranching proved short-lived because they lured too many people into the business with the result that cattle began to overrun the range.

Meanwhile, the farming frontier was advancing and generating new demands for land. Fearing loss of control over grazing fields, ranchers began to fence in pastures with barbed wire, even though they had no legal title to such land. Fences eliminated the open range and often provoked disputes between competing ranchers, between cattle raisers and sheep raisers, and between ranchers and farmers who claimed use of the same territory. In 1885, President Grover Cleveland ordered the removal of illegal fences on public lands and Indian reservations. Enforcement was slow, but the order signaled that free use of public domain was ending. By 1890, big businesses were taking over the cattle industry and applying scientific methods of breeding and feeding. Most ranchers now owned or leased the land they used, though some illegal fencing persisted.

 ## The South After Reconstruction

While the Great Plains and West were being transformed, the South was developing its own forms of resource exploitation, market economies, and land control. Ravaged by the Civil War, southern agriculture recovered slowly. Rather than diversify, farmers concentrated on growing cotton even more single-mindedly than before the war. High prices for seed and implements, declining prices for crops, taxes, and, most of all, debt trapped many families in poverty.

To achieve sectional independence, some southerners tried to promote industrialization. Their efforts partially succeeded, but by the 1900s many southern industries remained mere subsidiaries of northern firms. Moreover, southern planters, shippers, and manufacturers depended heavily on northern banks to finance their operations. Equally important, low wages and stunted opportunities discouraged potential migrants and immigrants who might have brought needed labor and capital. Thus although in some ways the South grew economically, it remained a dependent region locked into a subordinate position in the national economy.

During and after Reconstruction, a significant shift in the nature of agriculture swept the South. Between 1860 and 1880, the total number of farms in southern states more than doubled, but the size of the average farm decreased from 347 to 156 acres. Moreover, the number of landowners did not increase, because a growing proportion of southern farmers rented, rather than owned, their farms. Southern agriculture became dominated by landlords, and the system was characterized by sharecropping and tenant farming. More than one-third of the farmers counted in the 1880 census were sharecroppers and tenants, and the proportion increased to two-thirds by 1920.

Sharecropping and tenant farming entangled millions of southerners in a web of debt and humiliation, at whose center stood the crop lien.

Crop-Lien System

Most farmers, too poor to have cash on hand, borrowed to buy necessities. They could offer as collateral only what they could grow. A farmer in need of supplies dealt with a nearby "furnishing merchant," who would exchange supplies for a *lien*, or legal claim, on the farmer's forthcoming crop. After the crop was harvested and brought to market, the merchant collected his debt. Because the debt often exceeded the crop's value, the farmer—still in need of food and supplies—had no choice other than to give the merchant a lien on his next crop.

Merchants frequently took advantage of farmers' powerlessness by inflating prices and charging credit customers interest ranging from 33 to 200 percent on the advances they received. Suppose, for example, that a cash-poor farmer needed a 20-cent bag of seed. The furnishing merchant would sell him the goods on credit but would boost the price to 28 cents. At year's end that 28-cent loan would have accumulated interest, raising the farmer's debt to 42 cents—more than double the item's original cost.

The crop-lien system caused hardship in former plantation areas where tenants and sharecroppers—black and white—grew cotton for the same markets that had existed before the Civil War. In the southern backcountry, which in the antebellum era had been characterized by small farms, relatively few slaves, and diversified agriculture, the crop-lien problem was compounded by other economic changes.

New spending habits of backcountry farmers illustrate these changes. In 1884, Jephta Dickson of Jackson County in the northern Georgia hills bought $53.37 worth of flour, peas, meat, corn, and syrup from one merchant and $2.53 worth of potatoes, peas, and sugar from another. Such expenditures would have been rare in the upcountry before the Civil War, when farmers grew almost all the food they needed. But after the war, yeomen like Dickson shifted from semisubsistence agriculture to commercial farming; in the South that meant raising cotton. This change came about for two reasons: debts incurred during the war and Reconstruction forced farmers to grow a crop that would bring in cash, and railroad expansion enabled them to transport cotton to markets more easily than before. As backcountry yeomen devoted more acres to cotton, they raised less of what they needed on a daily basis and found themselves more frequently at the mercy of merchants.

At the same time, backcountry farmers suffered from laws that essentially closed the southern range (lands owned by the federal government but used freely by southern herders). This change, too, resulted from the commercialization of agriculture. Before the 1870s, southern farmers had let their livestock roam freely in search of food and water. By custom, farmers who wished to protect their crops from foraging animals were supposed to build fences around those crops. But as commercial agriculture reached the backcountry, large landowners and merchants induced county and state governments to require the fencing-in of animals rather than crops. These laws hurt poor farmers who had little land, requiring them to use more of their precious acreage for pasture.

Closing the Southern Range

Poor whites in the rural South, facing economic losses, also feared that newly enfranchised blacks would challenge whatever political and social superiority (real and imagined) they enjoyed. Wealthy white landowners and merchants fanned these fears, using racism to divide whites and blacks and to distract poor whites from protesting their economic subjugation.

The majority of the nation's African-Americans lived in the South, worked in agriculture, and found that slavery's abolition had not improved their opportunities relative to those of whites. In 1880, 90 percent of all southern blacks depended for a living on farming or personal and domestic service—the same occupations they had held as slaves.

Condition of African-Americans

The New South, moreover, proved to be as violent for African-Americans as the Old South had been. Between 1889 and 1909, for instance, more than seventeen hundred African-Americans

In the years after Reconstruction, lynchings of African-American men occurred with increasing frequency, chiefly in sparsely populated areas where whites looked on strangers, especially black strangers, with fear and suspicion. © R. P. Kingston Collection/The Picture Cube.

were lynched in the South. Most lynchings occurred in sparsely populated rural districts where whites felt threatened by an inflow of blacks. Most victims of lynchings were vagrants usually accused of an assault—rarely proved—on a white woman.

Threatened by violence, pushed into sharecropping, and burdened with crop liens, African-Americans also contended with new forms of social and political oppression. With slavery dead, white supremacists fashioned new ways to keep blacks in a position of inferiority. As part of this effort, southern leaders instituted measures to discourage blacks from voting and to segregate them legally from whites.

Despite intimidation, however, the end of Reconstruction did not stop blacks from voting. They still formed the backbone of the southern Republican Party and some still won elective offices. As white politicians sought to discourage the "Negro vote," southern states, beginning with Georgia in 1877, levied taxes of $1 to $2 on all citizens wishing to vote. These *poll taxes* proved prohibitive to most black voters. Other schemes disfranchised black voters who could not read. Voters might be required, for instance, to deposit ballots for different candidates in different ballot boxes. To do so correctly, voters had to be able to read the instructions.

Disfranchisement of African-American Voters

Disfranchisement devices were effective. In South Carolina, 70 percent of eligible blacks voted in the 1880 presidential election; by 1896, the rate had dropped to 11 percent. By the 1900s, African-Americans had effectively lost their political rights in all southern states except Tennessee.

Racial discrimination also stiffened in social affairs. In a series of cases during the 1870s, the Supreme Court opened the door to discrimination by ruling that the Fourteenth Amendment protected citizens' rights only against infringement by state governments. The federal government, according to the Court, had no authority over what individuals or organizations might do. If blacks wanted legal protection, the Court said, they must seek it from the states.

Jim Crow Laws

These rulings climaxed in 1883 when in the *Civil Rights* cases the Court struck down the 1875 Civil Rights Act, which had prohibited segregation in public facilities such as streetcars, hotels, theaters, and parks. Subsequent lower-court rulings established the principle that blacks could be restricted to "separate-but-equal" facilities. The Supreme Court upheld the separate-but-equal doctrine in *Plessy* v. *Ferguson* (1896) and officially applied it to schools in *Cummins* v. *County Board of Education* (1899).

Thereafter, segregation laws—popularly known as Jim Crow laws—multiplied throughout the South, confronting African-Americans with daily reminders of their inferior status. Laws restricted them to the rear of streetcars, to separate drinking fountains and toilets, and to separate sections of hospitals and cemeteries. Atlanta mandated separate Bibles for the swearing-in of black witnesses in court.

In industry, new initiatives brought breezes of change, though not for African-Americans. Two of the South's leading industries in the late 1800s relied on traditional staple crops—cotton and tobacco. In the 1870s, textile mills began to appear in the Cotton Belt. Powered by the region's abundant rivers, manned cheaply by poor whites, and aided by low taxes, such factories multiplied. By 1900 the South had four hundred mills, and twenty years later the region was eclipsing New England in textile-manufacturing supremacy. Proximity to raw materials and cheap labor also aided the tobacco industry.

Industrialization of the South

Cigarette factories, located in cities, employed both black and white workers (though in segregated sections of the factories). Textile mills, concentrated in small towns, developed their own exploitative labor system. Financed mostly by local investors, mills employed women and children from poor white families and paid 50 cents a day for twelve or more hours of work. Many companies built villages around their mills, where they controlled the housing, stores, schools, and churches, and they also squelched attempts at union organization.

Other industries were launched under the sponsorship of northern or European capitalists. In the Gulf states, the lumber industry became significant, and iron and steel production made Birmingham, Alabama, a boom city. Yet in 1900, the South remained as rural as it had been in 1860. A New South eventually would emerge, but not until after a world war and a massive black exodus had shaken up old attitudes.

 Conclusion

Americans of all races developed the West with courage and creativity. The extraction of raw minerals, the use of irrigation and mechanization to bring forth agricultural abundance, and the construction of railroads to tie the nation together transformed half of the continent within a few decades. The optimistic conquerors, however, employed power, violence, and greed that overwhelmed the culture of the land's original inhabitants, left many farmers feeling cheated and betrayed, kindled contests over use of water, and sacrificed environmental balance for market profits. In the South, recovery and growth kindled new optimism, but careless exploitation exhausted the soil and left poor farmers as downtrodden as ever. In an age of expansion, African-Americans saw their rights and opportunities narrowing. Industrialization failed to reduce the dominance of southern staple-crop agriculture, and by 1900 the South was more dependent economically on the North than it had been before the Civil War.

Suggestions for Further Reading

The Western Frontier

Ray A. Billington and Martin Ridge, *Westward Expansion*, 5th ed. (1982); Sara Deutsch, *No Separate Refuge: Culture, Class, and Gender on an Anglo-Hispanic Frontier in the American Southwest* (1987); Robert V. Hine, *The American West*, 2d ed. (1984); Julie Roy Jeffrey, *Frontier Women* (1979); Patricia Limerick, *The Legacy of Conquest: The Unbroken Past of the American West* (1987); Timothy R. Mahoney, *River Towns in the Great West* (1990); Ruth Moynihan, *Rebel for Rights: Abigail Scott Duniway* (1983); Peggy Pascoe, *Relations of Rescue: The Search for Female Moral Authority in the American West* (1990); Rodman W. Paul, *The Far West and the Great Plains in Transition, 1859–1900* (1988); Robert J. Rosenbaum, *Mexican Resistance in the Southwest* (1981); Lillian Schlissel, *Women's Diaries of the Westward Journey* (1982); Kent Ladd Steckmesser, *The Western Hero in History and Legend* (1965); Richard White, *"It's Your Misfortune and None of My Own": A New History of the American West* (1991).

Water and the Environment

Roderick Nash, *American Environmentalism*, 3d ed. (1990); Joseph M. Petulla, *American Environmental History* (1977); Thurman Wilkins, *John Muir: Apostle of Nature* (1995); Donald Worster, *Rivers of Empire: Water, Aridity, and the Growth of the American West* (1985).

Railroads

Alfred D. Chandler, ed., *Railroads* (1965); Robert W. Fogel, *Railroads and Economic Growth* (1964); Edward C. Kirkland, *Men, Cities, and Transportation* (1948); George R. Taylor and Irene Neu, *The American Railroad Network* (1956); Alan Trachtenberg, *The Incorporation of America* (1982); O. O. Winther, *The Transportation Frontier* (1964).

Native Americans

Ralph K. Andrist, *The Long Death: The Last Days of the Plains Indians* (1964); Leonard A. Carlson, *Indians, Bureaucrats, and Land: The Dawes Act and the Decline of Indian Farming* (1981); Frederick E. Hoxie, *A Final Promise: The Campaign to Assimilate the Indians, 1880–1920* (1984); Janet A. McDonnell, *The Dispossession of the American Indian* (1991); Francis Paul Prucha, *The Great Father: The United States Government and the American Indians* (1984); Robert M. Utley, *The Lance and the Shield: The Life and Times of Sitting Bull* (1993); Robert M. Utley, *The Indian Frontier of the American West, 1846–1890* (1984); Philip Weeks, *Farewell, My Nation: The American Indian and the United States* (1990); Richard White, *The Roots of Dependency* (1983).

Ranching and Settlement of the Plains

Lewis Atherton, *The Cattle Kings* (1961); William Cronon, *Nature's Metropolis: Chicago and the Great West* (1991); Gilbert C. Fite, *The Farmer's Frontier* (1963); Robert V. Hine, *Community on the American Frontier* (1980); Richard W. Slatta, *Cowboys of the Americas* (1990); Walter Prescott Webb, *The Great Plains* (1931).

The New South

Edward L. Ayers, *The Promise of the New South* (1992); Orville Vernon Burton and Robert C. McMath, Jr., eds., *Toward a New South?: Post–Civil War Southern Communities* (1982); Paul Gaston, *The New South Creed* (1970); Steven Hahn, *The Roots of Southern Populism: Yeoman Farmers and the Transformation of the Georgia Upcountry, 1850–1890* (1983); Stanley P. Hirshson, *Farewell to the Bloody Shirt: Northern Republicans and the Southern Negro* (1962); J. Morgan Kousser, *The Shaping of Southern Politics* (1974); Melton A. McLaurin, *Paternalism and Protest: Southern Cotton Mill Workers and Organized Labor* (1971); Howard N. Rabinowitz, *Race Relations in the Urban South, 1865–1890* (1978); Theodore Saloutos, *Farmer Movements in the South, 1865–1933* (1960); C. Vann Woodward, *The Strange Career of Jim Crow*, 3d rev. ed. (1974); C. Vann Woodward, *Origins of the New South*, rev. ed. (1951); Gavin Wright, *Old South, New South* (1986).

CHAPTER

18

The Machine Age
1877–1920

The shoemaker known only as "S" was a beaten and bitter man. Interviewed by the Massachusetts Bureau of the Statistics of Labor in 1871, "S" reported that he and his three children each worked in a shoe factory ten hours a day, five days a week, and nine hours on Saturdays. His wife worked in another factory from 5:30 A.M. to 10 A.M. every day.

"S" complained to the interviewer that ever since his factory had introduced machinery, he had lost control of his craft. He could no longer teach his sons the skill of shoemaking because they had been moved to another room to carry out just one task instead of having responsibility for assembling the whole product. "S" hoped his sons would not be factory workers all their lives, but he also realized they had little other choice. The cost of living had risen, making it difficult if not impossible for his family to sustain itself in any other way.

"S" felt embittered by the homage being paid to supply and demand: "We have it constantly dinned in our ears that supply and demand govern prices, but we have found out to a certainty that this is not so. . . . [W]ithout the aid of machinery, six men will make a case of 60 pairs [of shoes] in a day, . . . which would give each man about $1.70 . . . a day; . . . with the machinery, three men will do the same amount of work in the same time, and get about the same pay [$1.70] each, as the men on hand work. . . . Who gets the difference in money saved by machinery? and how far does supply and demand govern in these things?"

The new industrial order about which "S" testified was both exciting and ominous. The factory and the machine divided manufacturing into minute, routinized tasks and organized work according to the dictates of the clock. Workers who had long thought of themselves as valued producers found themselves struggling to avoid becoming slaves to machines. Meanwhile, in the quest for productivity, profits, and growth, corporations merged and amassed awesome power.

Industrialization is a complex process whose chief feature is the production of goods by machine rather than by hand. By using machines, manufacturers lower production costs and significantly raise workers' output. In the United States, the results of industrialization have included the concentration of production and laborers in large, organized factories; technological innovation; expanded markets, no longer merely local and regional in scope; a rapid increase in population; and growth of a nationwide transportation network.

In 1860 only about one-fourth of the American labor force worked in manufacturing and transportation; by 1900 over half did so. As the twentieth century dawned, the United States was the world's largest producer of raw materials and food but also the most productive industrial nation (see map, page 338). Accelerated migration from farms and mass immigration from abroad swelled the industrial work force, but more than people, machines boosted American productivity. Moreover, innovations in business organization and marketing, as well as in technology, fueled the drive for profits.

These developments had momentous effects on standards of living and everyday life. During the years between the end of Reconstruction and the end of the First World War, a new consumer society took shape. Farms and factories produced so much that Americans could afford to satisfy their material wants. What had once been accessible only to a few was becoming available to many. Yet the accomplishments of industrial expansion involved waste and greed.

 ## Technology and the Triumph of Industrialism

In 1876 Thomas A. Edison and his associates moved into a long wooden shed in Menlo Park, New Jersey, where they intended to turn out "a minor invention every ten days and a big thing every six months or so." Edison envisioned his laboratory as an invention factory, where creative people would pool their ideas and skills to fashion marketable products. Here was the brash American spirit adapting itself to a systematic work ethic. If Americans wanted new products, they had to organize and work purposefully to bring about progress. Such efforts reflected a forward-looking spirit that enlivened American industrialization at the end of the nineteenth century.

In the years between 1865 and 1920, the machine fired American optimism. Between 1790 and 1860 the United States Patent Office had granted a total of 36,000 patents; between 1860 and 1930 it registered 1.5 million. As innovative as the inventions themselves was the marriage between technology and business organization.

Perhaps the biggest of Edison's "big thing" projects began in 1878 when he formed the Edison Electric Light Company and embarked on a search for a cheap, efficient means of indoor lighting.

Birth of the Electrical Industry

After tedious trial-and-error experiments, Edison perfected an incandescent bulb that used a filament in a vacuum. At the same time he worked out a *system* of power production and distribution—an improved dynamo and a parallel circuit of wires—to provide convenient power to a large number of customers. To market his ideas, Edison acted as his own publicist. During the 1880 Christmas season he illuminated Menlo Park with forty incandescent bulbs, and in 1882 he built a power plant that would light eighty-five buildings in New York's Wall Street financial district.

Edison's system could send electric power only a mile or two. George Westinghouse, an inventor from Schenectady, New York, solved that problem. Westinghouse purchased patent rights to generators that used alternating current and transformers that reduced high-voltage power to lower voltage levels, thus making transmission over long distances cheaper.

Other entrepreneurs utilized new business practices to market and refine Edison's and Westinghouse's technological breakthroughs. Samuel

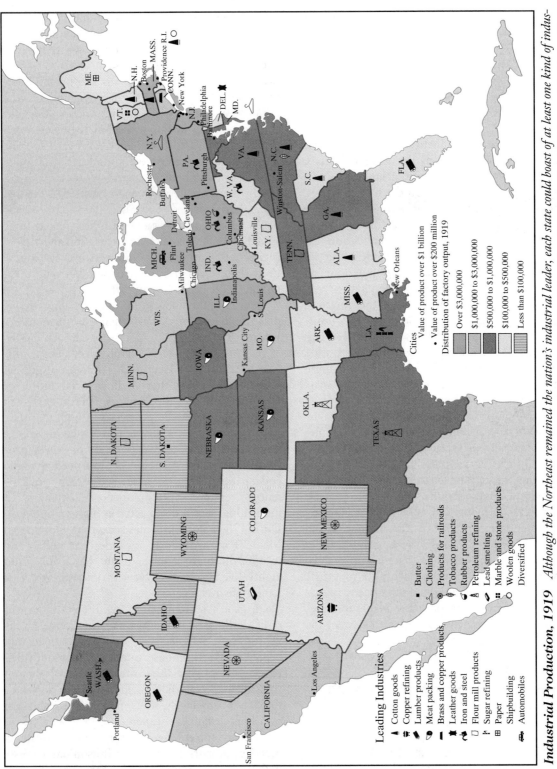

Industrial Production, 1919   *Although the Northeast remained the nation's industrial leader, each state could boast of at least one kind of industrial production.*   Source: © American Heritage Publishing Co., Inc., *American Heritage Pictorial Atlas of United States History;* data from U.S. Bureau of the Census, *Fourteenth Census of the United States, 1920.*

• *Important Events* •

1860	Knights of Labor founded		**1893–97**	Economic depression causes high unemployment and business failures
1873–78	Economic decline results from overly rapid expansion		**1894**	Workers at Pullman Palace Car Company strike against exploitative policies
1877	Widespread railroad strikes protest wage cuts		**1895**	*U.S.* v. *E. C. Knight Co.* limits Congress's power to regulate manufacturing
1878	Edison Electric Light Company founded, leading to development of incandescent bulb		**1896**	*Holden* v. *Hardy* upholds law regulating miners' work hours
1880s	Chain-pull toilets spread across the United States		**1898**	Frederick W. Taylor promotes scientific management as efficiency measure in industry
	Doctors accept germ theory of disease			
	Mass production of tin cans begins		**1901–03**	U.S. Steel Corporation founded
1882	Standard Oil Trust formed		**1903**	Women's Trade Union League founded
1884–85	Economic decline results from numerous causes		**1905**	*Lochner* v. *New York* overturns law limiting bakery workers' work hours and limits labor protection laws
1886	Haymarket riot in Chicago protests police brutality against labor demonstrators			Industrial Workers of the World founded
	American Federation of Labor (AFL) founded		**1908**	*Muller* v. *Oregon* upholds law limiting women to ten-hour workday
1888	Edward Bellamy's *Looking Backward* depicts utopian world free of monopoly, politicians, and class divisions			First Ford Model T built
			1913	First moving assembly line begins operation at Ford Motor Company
1890	Sherman Anti-Trust Act outlaws "combinations in restraint of trade"		**1914**	Ford offers Five-Dollar-a-Day plan to workers
1892	Homestead (Pennsylvania) steelworkers strike against Carnegie Steel Company		**1919**	Telephone operator unions strike in New England

Insull, Edison's private secretary, attracted investments and organized Edison power plants across the country, turning energy into big business. In the late 1880s and early 1890s financiers Henry Villard and J. P. Morgan consolidated patents in electric lighting and merged small equipment-manufacturing companies into the General Electric Company. Equally important, General Electric and Westinghouse Electric established research laboratories that paid scientists to create new electrical products for everyday use.

Some inventors continued to work independently and tried to sell their handiwork to manufacturing companies. One such inventor was Granville T. Woods, an African-American engineer from Columbus, Ohio. Working in machine shops in Cincinnati and in New York City, Woods patented thirty-five devices vital to electronics and communications, including an automatic circuit breaker, an electromagnetic brake, and various instruments to aid communications between railroad trains.

Henry Ford was the era's most visionary manufacturer. In the 1890s, he experimented in his spare time with a gasoline-burning internal-combustion engine to power a vehicle. Like Edison, Ford had a scheme as well as a product. In 1909 he declared, "I am going to democratize the automobile. When I'm through everybody will be able to afford one." Ford proposed to reach this goal through *mass production*—producing thousands of identical cars in exactly the same way.

Mass Production of the Automobile

The key to mass production was flow. Ford's engineers set up assembly lines where each worker was given responsibility for only one task, performed repeatedly, using the same specialized machine. By means of a continuous flow of these tasks, the work force fashioned each component part and progressively assembled the entire car. In 1908, the first year it built the Model T, Ford sold 10,000 cars. In 1913, the company's first full assembly line began producing cars, and the next year 248,000 Fords were sold. Rising automobile production created more jobs, higher earnings, and higher profits in related industries such as oil, paint, rubber, and glass.

By 1914, many Ford cars cost $490, only about one-fourth of their cost a decade earlier. Yet even $490 was too much for many workers, who earned at best $2 a day. That year, however, Ford tried to spur productivity, prevent high labor turnover, head off unionization, and better enable his workers to buy the cars they produced. He offered them the Five-Dollar-Day plan—combined wages and profit sharing equal to $5 a day.

The timing of technological innovation varied from one industry to another, but machines altered the economy and everyday life between 1865 and 1900. Telephones and typewriters revolutionized communications. Sewing machines made mass-produced clothing available to almost everyone. Refrigeration changed dietary habits. Cash registers and adding machines revamped accounting and created new clerical jobs.

Profits from these products resulted from higher production at lower costs. As technological innovations made large-scale production more economical, some owners used their profits to replace small factories with larger ones. Only large companies could afford to buy new machines and operate them at full capacity. And large companies could best take advantage of discounts for shipping products in bulk and for buying raw materials in quantity. Economists call such advantages *economies of scale*.

Profitability depended as much on how production was arranged as on the machines in use. By the 1890s engineers and managers with specialized knowledge planned every task to increase output. Their efforts standardized mass production, which then required less skill and independent judgment from workers. The most influential advocate of efficient production was Frederick W. Taylor. In 1898 Taylor took his stopwatch to the Bethlehem Steel Company to illustrate how his principles of scientific management worked. His experiments, he explained, involved studying workers and devising "a series of motions which can be made quickest and best." Applying this technique to the shoveling of ore, Taylor designed fifteen kinds of shovels and prescribed the proper motions for using each one. He succeeded in reducing a crew of 600 men to 140, who received higher wages, though their new jobs were more stressful.

New Emphasis on Efficiency

As a result of Taylor's writings and experiments, time, as much as quality, became the measure of acceptable work, and science rather than tradition determined the "best" ways of doing things. As integral features of the assembly line, where work was divided into specific time-determined tasks, employees had become another kind of interchangeable part.

 ## Mechanization and the Changing Status of Labor

By 1880, the status of labor had undergone a dramatic shift. Technological innovation and assembly-line production subordinated workers to rigid schedules and repetitive routines that transformed the nature of work. Most workers could no longer accurately be termed *producers*, as craftsmen like shoemaker "S" had traditionally thought of themselves. The enlarged working class consisted mainly of *employees*—people who worked only when someone hired them. Producers were paid by consumers in accordance with the quality of what they produced; employees received wages for time they spent on the job.

As mass production subdivided manufacturing into small tasks, workers continually repeated the same specialized operation, coordinated with the running of machinery. This production process also deprived employees of their independence. Workers could no longer decide when to begin and end the workday, when to rest, and what tools and techniques to use.

Those affected by these changes did not accept them passively. Workers struggled to retain independence and self-respect in the face of employers' ever-increasing power. Artisans such as cigar makers and coopers (barrel makers) fought to preserve the pace and quality of their jobs and to retain customs such as appointing a fellow worker to read aloud while they worked. Conversely, employers sought to impose standards of behavior and work incentives that they thought would enhance productivity.

As machines and assembly-line production reduced the need for skilled workers, employers cut labor costs by hiring women and children. Between 1880 and 1900, the numbers of employed women soared

Employment of Women

from 2.6 million to 8.6 million. At the same time their occupational patterns underwent striking changes. The proportion of women in domestic-service jobs (maids, cooks, laundresses)—traditionally the most common and lowest-paid form of female employment—dropped dramatically as jobs opened in other sectors. In manufacturing, jobs for women were usually menial positions in textile mills and food-processing plants that paid as little as $1.56 a week for seventy hours of labor.

Enormous expansion in the industrial and retail sectors, however, caused the numbers and percentages of women in clerical jobs—typists, bookkeepers, sales clerks—to skyrocket. By 1920 nearly half of all clerical workers were women; in 1880 only 4 percent had been women. Previously, when sales

and office positions had demanded accounting and letter-writing skills, men had dominated such jobs. Then, new inventions such as the typewriter, cash register, and adding machine simplified these tasks. Companies eagerly hired women who had taken courses in typing and shorthand in school and were streaming into the labor market, looking for the better pay and conditions that clerical jobs offered relative to factory and domestic work. Even so, sex discrimination pervaded the clerical sector. The new jobs offered women some opportunities for advancement to supervisory positions, but women posed no threat to male managers.

Although most working children toiled on their parents' farms, the number in nonagricultural occupations tripled between 1870 and 1900.

Employment of Children

In 1890, over 18 percent of all children between ages ten and fifteen were gainfully employed. Conditions were especially hard for child laborers in the South, where burgeoning textile mills needed unskilled hands.

Several states, especially in the Northeast, passed laws specifying the minimum age and maximum workday hours for child labor. But most large companies could avoid regulations because state statutes did not apply to firms engaged in interstate commerce. Furthermore, it was difficult to enforce age requirements, and to supplement the family income many parents lied about children's ages. By 1900, state laws and automation had reduced the number of children working in manufacturing, but many more worked at street trades—shining shoes and peddling newspapers and other merchandise—and as helpers in stores.

Although working conditions were often dangerous and unhealthy, low wages were usually the immediate catalyst of worker unrest. Many employers believed in the "iron law of wages," which dictated that employees be paid according to conditions of supply and demand. As practiced, the "iron law" meant that employers did not have to raise wages—and could even cut them—as long as there were workers who would accept whatever pay was offered. Employers justified the system by invoking individual freedom: a worker who did not like the wages being offered was free to quit and find a job elsewhere. Courts reinforced this principle, denying workers the right to organize and bargain collectively on the grounds that an employee's wages should be the result of an individual negotiation between employee and employer.

Even steady employment was insecure. Repetitive tasks using high-speed machinery dulled concentration, and the slightest mistake could cause serious injury. Industrial accidents rose steadily before 1920, killing or maiming hundreds of thousands of people each year. As late as 1913, after factory owners had installed safety devices, some 25,000 people died in industrial mishaps, and close to 1 million were injured.

Industrial Accidents

Because disability insurance and pensions were almost nonexistent, families stricken by such accidents suffered acutely. Prevailing free-market views stifled protective legislation for workers, and employers denied responsibility for employees' well-being. The only recourse for a stricken family was to sue and prove in court that the killed or injured worker had not realized the risks involved and had not caused the accident.

Reformers and union leaders in several states lobbied Congress successfully for laws to improve working conditions, but the Supreme Court limited the scope of such legislation by narrowly defining what jobs were dangerous and which workers needed protection. Initially, in *Holden* v. *Hardy* (1896),

Courts Restrict Labor Reform

Factories employed children from the early nineteenth century well into the twentieth. In textile mills like the one pictured here, girls operated machines, and boys ran messages and carried materials back and forth. Mill girls had to tie up their hair to keep it from getting caught in the machines. The girl posing here with a shawl over her head would not have worn that garment while she was working. National Archives.

the Court upheld a law regulating the working hours of miners because overly long hours would increase the threat of injury. In *Lochner* v. *New York* (1905), however, the Court struck down a law limiting bakery workers to a sixty-hour week and a ten-hour day. In response to the argument that states had the authority to protect workers' health and safety, the Court ruled that baking was not a dangerous enough occupation to justify restricting the right of workers to sell their labor freely.

In *Muller* v. *Oregon* (1908), the Court used a different rationale to uphold a law limiting women to a ten-hour workday. In this case, the Court asserted that women's health and reproductive functions required protection. According to the Court, a woman's health "becomes an object of public interest and care in order to preserve the strength and vigor of the race." As a result, women were barred from occupations such as printing and transportation, which required long hours or night work.

Throughout the nineteenth century, tensions rose and fell as workers confronted mechanization. Some people bent to the demands of the factory, machine, and time clock. Some tried to blend old ways of working into the new system. Others, however, turned to organized resistance.

The year 1877 in many ways marked a watershed. In July a series of strikes broke out among unionized railroad workers who were protesting

Strikes of 1877

wage cuts. Violence spread from Pennsylvania to the Midwest, Texas, and California. Venting pent-up anger, rioters attacked railroad property, derailing trains and burning railroad yards. State militia companies, organized and commanded by employers, broke up picket lines and fired into threatening crowds.

The worst violence occurred in Pittsburgh, where on July 21 militiamen from Philadelphia bayoneted and fired on a crowd of rock-throwing demonstrators, killing ten and wounding many more. Infuriated, the mob drove the soldiers into a railroad roundhouse and set fires that destroyed 39 buildings, 104 engines, and 1,245 freight and passenger cars. The next day, the troops shot their way out of the roundhouse and killed twenty more citizens before fleeing the city. After more than a month of unprecedented carnage, President

Rutherford B. Hayes sent federal troops to end the strikes—the first significant use of troops to quell labor unrest.

 ## The Union Movement

The union movement had precedents but few successes. Craft unions dated from the early nineteenth century, but the narrowness of their membership left them without broad power. The National Labor Union, founded in 1866, claimed 640,000 members in 1868 but died when members' loyalty seeped away during the hard times of the 1870s. The only broad-based labor organization to survive that depression was the Knights of Labor.

Founded in 1860 by Philadelphia garment cutters, the Knights opened their doors to other workers in the 1870s. In 1879, Terence V. Powderly, a machinist and former

Knights of Labor

mayor of Scranton, Pennsylvania, was elected grand master. Under his forceful guidance, Knights membership mushroomed, peaking at 730,000 in 1886. At a time when most labor organizations were trade unions—which excluded everyone except skilled workers in particular crafts—the Knights welcomed women, African-Americans, immigrants, and all unskilled and semiskilled workers.

Powderly's goal was to help create a cooperative society in which laborers worked for themselves and not for those who possessed capital. He, as well as other Knights leaders, opposed strikes because they diverted attention from the goal of a cooperative society. Moreover, he believed workers lost more strikes than they won. But some Knight leaders and the rank and file did support militant action. Thus when Powderly began to denounce radicalism and violence during an 1886 railroad strike, the more militant craft unions broke away from the Knights. As Knight membership dwindled, broad-based but often vague dreams of labor unity also faded.

During the early 1880s, labor groups, including the Knights, had begun to campaign for an eight-hour workday. This effort by laborers to regain control of their work gathered momentum

Haymarket Riot

in Chicago, where radical anarchists—who believed that voluntary cooperation should replace all government—as well as various craft unions agitated for the cause. On May 3, 1886, Chicago police stormed an area near the McCormick reaper factory, where striking unionists were battling nonunion strikebreakers. In the ensuing confrontation police killed two unionists and wounded several others.

The next evening, labor groups rallied at Haymarket Square, near downtown Chicago, to protest police brutality. As a company of police officers approached, a bomb exploded near their front ranks, killing seven and injuring sixty-seven. Mass arrests of anarchists and unionists followed. Eventually eight anarchists were tried and convicted of the bombing, though the evidence of their guilt was questionable. Four were executed and one committed suicide in prison. (The remaining three were pardoned in 1893 by Illinois governor John P. Altgeld, who believed they had been victims of the "malicious ferocity" of the courts.)

The Haymarket bombing drew attention to the growing discontent of labor and revived middle-class fear of radicalism. Some cities strengthened their police forces and armories. Employer associations—coalitions of manufacturers in the same industry—worked to counter labor militancy by agreeing to resist strikes and by purchasing strike insurance.

The American Federation of Labor (AFL) emerged from the 1886 upheavals as the major workers' organization. An alliance of national craft unions, the AFL had about 140,000 members, most of them skilled native-born workers. Led by Samuel Gompers, a pragmatic and opportunistic immigrant who headed the Cigar Makers' Union, the AFL avoided the idealistic rhetoric of worker solidarity to press for concrete goals—higher wages, shorter hours, and the right to bargain collectively. The national organization required constituent unions to hire organizers to expand membership, and it collected dues for a fund to aid members on strike. The AFL

American Federation of Labor

avoided party politics, adhering instead to Gompers's dictum to support labor's friends and oppose its enemies, regardless of party. By 1917, the AFL would grow to 2.5 million members under Gompers's leadership.

The AFL and the labor movement suffered a series of setbacks in the early 1890s, however, when once again labor violence stirred public fears. In July 1892, the AFL-affiliated Amalgamated Association of Iron and Steelworkers refused to accept pay cuts and went on strike in Homestead, Pennsylvania. Henry C. Frick, the president of Carnegie Steel Company, closed the plant. Shortly thereafter, angry workers attacked and routed three hundred Pinkerton guards hired to protect the plant. State militiamen were summoned, and after five months the strikers gave in.

Workers at the Pullman Palace Car Company also suffered defeat when they walked out in protest in 1894 over exploitative policies at the company town near Chicago. The paternalistic George Pullman provided everything for the twelve thousand residents of his so-called model town. As one laborer grumbled, "We are born in a Pullman house, fed from the Pullman shop, taught in the Pullman school, catechized in the Pullman church, and when we die, we shall be buried in the Pullman cemetery and go to the Pullman hell."

Pullman Strike

When the hard times that began in 1893 threatened his business, Pullman maintained profits and stock dividends by cutting wages 25 to 40 percent while holding firm on rents and prices in the town. Enraged workers, most of whom had joined the American Railway Union, called a strike; Pullman retaliated by closing the plant. The union, led by the charismatic young organizer Eugene V. Debs, voted to aid the strikers by refusing to handle all Pullman cars. The railroad owners' association then enlisted the aid of United States Attorney General Richard Olney, who obtained a court injunction to prevent the union from "obstructing the railways and holding up the mails." President Grover Cleveland sent troops to Chicago, ostensibly to protect the mails but in reality to crush the strike. Within a month strikers gave in, and Debs was jailed for defying the court injunction.

In the West, radical labor activity arose among Colorado miners, who participated in a series of bitter struggles and violent strikes. In 1905 many of these workers helped form a new labor organization, the Industrial Workers of the World (IWW). The IWW's goal was to unify all laborers and to organize them into "One Big Union." But the "Wobblies," as IWW members were known, espoused socialism and tactics of violence and sabotage. Using the rhetoric of class conflict—"The final aim is revolution," according to an IWW organizer—Wobblies believed workers should seize and run the nation's industries. Though the Wobblies' anticapitalist goals and aggressive tactics attracted considerable publicity, IWW membership probably never exceeded 150,000. The organization faded during the First World War when federal prosecution—and persecution—sent many of its leaders to jail.

Many unions, notably those of the AFL, were openly hostile to women. Of the 6.3 million employed women in 1910, fewer than 2 percent belonged to unions. Fear of competition was the crucial reason for the exclusion. Because women were paid less than men, males worried that their own wages would be lowered or that they would lose their jobs altogether if women invaded the workplace. Moreover, male workers who were accustomed to sex segregation in employment could not imagine working side by side with women.

Women and the Labor Movement

Yet female employees could organize and fight employers as strenuously as men could. Since the early years of industrialization, women had formed their own unions. Some, such as the Collar Laundry Union of Troy, New York, organized in the 1860s, had successfully struck for higher wages. The "Uprising of the 20,000" in New York City, a 1909 strike by immigrant members of the International Ladies Garment Workers Union (ILGWU), was one of the largest strikes in the country to that time. Women were also prominent in the 1912 Lawrence (Massachusetts) textile workers' strike. Female trade-union membership swelled during the 1910s, but national trade unions were still led by men, even in industries with large female work forces.

Women did dominate, however—as both members and leaders—in one union, the Telephone Operators' Department of the International Brotherhood of Electrical Workers. Organized early in the twentieth century, the union spread throughout the Bell system, the nation's major telephone company and single largest employer of women. While sponsoring social and educational programs, the union focused on workplace issues. It opposed scientific management techniques and the tightening of worker supervision. In 1919 several particularly militant unions paralyzed the phone service of five New England states. The union collapsed after a failed strike in 1923, but not before women had proven that they could advance their own cause.

The first women's labor federation to parallel the AFL was the Women's Trade Union League (WTUL), founded in 1903. The WTUL worked for protective legislation for female workers, sponsored educational activities, and campaigned for women's suffrage. Initially the union's highest offices were held by middle-class women who sympathized with female wage laborers, but control shifted in the 1910s to forceful working-class leaders, notably Agnes Nestor, a glove maker, Rose Schneiderman, a cap maker, and Mary Anderson, a shoe worker. The WTUL advocated changes such as opening apprenticeship programs to women so they could enter skilled trades, and providing leadership training for female workers. It served as a vital link between the labor and women's movements into the 1920s.

Organized labor excluded not only women but also most immigrant and African-American workers. Some trade unions welcomed skilled immigrants, but only the Knights of Labor and the IWW had firm policies of accepting immigrants and blacks. Blacks were prominent in the coal miners' union, and they were partially unionized in trades such as construction, barbering, and dock work. But they could belong only to segregated local unions in the South, and the majority of northern AFL unions also had exclusion policies. Long-held prejudices were reinforced when blacks and immigrants worked as strikebreakers.

Immigrants, African-Americans, and the Labor Movement

The dramatic labor struggles in the half-century following the Civil War make it easy to forget that only a small fraction of American workers belonged to unions. In 1900, about 1 million out of a total of 27.6 million workers were unionized. By 1920, total union membership had grown to 5 million—still only 13 percent of the work force. For many workers, issues of wages and hours were meaningless; getting and holding a job was the real priority.

The machine age had mixed results for most workers. Industrial wages rose between 1877 and 1914, boosting purchasing power and creating a mass market for standardized goods. Yet in 1900 most employees worked sixty hours a week at wages that averaged 20 cents an hour for skilled work and 10 cents an hour for unskilled. Moreover, as wages rose, living costs increased even faster.

 ## Standards of Living

Some Americans distrusted machines, but few could resist the changes that mechanization brought to everyday life. Mass production and mass marketing made available myriad goods that previously had not existed or had been the exclusive property of the wealthy. The new material well-being, heralded by products such as ready-made clothes, canned foods, and home appliances, had a dual effect. It blended Americans of differing status into communities of consumers—communities defined not by place or class but by possessions—and it accentuated differences between those who could afford such goods and services and those who could not.

If a society's affluence can be measured by how it converts luxuries into commonplace articles, the United States was indeed becoming affluent in the years between 1880 and 1920. In 1880, for example, only wealthy women could afford silk stockings and only residents of Florida, Texas, and California could enjoy fresh oranges. By 1921, Americans ate 248 crates of oranges per 1,000 people and bought 217 million pairs of silk stockings.

How did people afford to make these changes in their standard of living? Data for the period are incomplete, but there is no doubt that many

Rising Personal Income Americans' incomes rose. The expanding economy spawned massive fortunes and created a new industrial elite. By 1920, the richest 5 percent of the population received almost one-fourth of all earned income and 85 percent of all stock and bond dividends. Incomes also rose among the expanding middle class (see table, page 347). After the turn of the century, employees of the federal executive branch averaged $1,072 a year, and college professors $1,100. With such incomes, the middle class could afford comfortable housing. A six- or seven-room house cost around $3,000 to buy or build and from $15 to $20 per month to rent.

Though wages for industrial workers increased, their income figures were deceptive because jobs were not always stable and workers had to expend a disproportionate amount of their income on necessities. On average, annual wages of factory workers rose from $486 in 1890 to $630 in 1910. In industries with large female work forces, such as shoe and paper manufacturing, hourly rates remained lower than in male-dominated industries. Regional variations were also wide. Nevertheless, most wages moved upward.

Wage increases mean little, however, if living costs rise as fast or faster. That is what happened. According to one economic index, the weekly cost of living for a typical wage earner's family of four rose **Cost of Living** over 47 percent between 1889 and 1913. In very few working-class occupations did income rise as fast as the cost of living.

How then could working-class Americans afford the new goods and services that the machine age offered? Some could not. Others raised their income and participated modestly in the consumer society **Supplements to Family Income** by sending children and women into the labor market. In a household where the father made $600 a year, the wages of other family members might lift total income to $800 or $900. Many families also rented rooms to boarders and lodgers, a practice that could yield up to $200 a year. These

American Living Standards, 1890–1910

	1890	1910
Income and earnings		
Annual income		
Clerical worker	$848	$1,156
Public school teacher	$256	$492
Industrial worker	$486	$630
Farm laborer	$233	$336
Hourly wage		
Soft-coal miner	$0.18[a]	$0.21
Iron worker	$0.17[a]	$0.23
Shoe worker	$0.14[a]	$0.19
Paper worker	$0.12[a]	$0.17
Labor statistics		
Number of people in labor force	28.5 million	41.7 million[b]
Average workweek in manufacturing	60 hours	51 hours

[a]1892.

[b]1920.

means of increasing family income enabled people to spend more and save more.

Science and technology eased some of life's struggles. Advances in medical care, better diets, and improved housing sharply reduced death rates and extended the life span. Between 1900 and 1920, life expectancy rose by fully six years. During this period there were notable declines in death from typhoid, diphtheria, influenza (except for a harsh pandemic in 1918 and 1919), tuberculosis, and intestinal ailments. There were, however, significantly more deaths from cancer, diabetes, and heart disease, afflictions of an aging population and of new environmental factors.

Higher Life Expectancy

Not only were amenities and luxuries more available in the early 1900s than they had been a half-century earlier, but the means to upward mobility seemed more accessible as well. Education increasingly became the key to success. Public education—aided by construction of new schools, particularly high schools, and passage of laws that required children to stay in school to age fourteen—equipped young people to achieve a standard of living higher than their parents'. Yet the inequities that had pervaded earlier eras remained in place. Race, gender, religion, and ethnicity still determined access to opportunity.

 The Quest for Convenience

One of the most representative agents of the revolution in American lifestyles at the end of the nineteenth century was the toilet. The chain-pull washdown water closet, invented in England around 1870, was adopted in the United States in the 1880s. Shortly after 1900 the flush toilet appeared; thanks to the mass production of enamel-coated fixtures, it became standard in American homes and buildings.

The indoor toilet brought about a shift in habits and attitudes. Before 1880, only luxury hotels and estates had private bathrooms. By the 1890s, the germ theory of disease had raised fears about carelessly disposed human waste. Much more rapidly than Europeans, Americans combined a desire for cleanliness with an urge for convenience, and water closets became common, especially in middle-class urban houses. Bodily functions took on an unpleasant image, and the home bathroom became a place of utmost privacy. At the same time, the toilet and the private bathtub gave Americans new ways to use—and waste—water. These advances in plumbing belonged to a broader democratization of convenience that accompanied mass production and consumerism.

The tin can also altered lifestyles. When combined with knowledge about the cooking-and-sealing process and the condensing and preserving of milk, the tin can made a variety of foods available to the public. By 1880 even people remote from markets, like sailors and cowboys, could readily consume tomatoes, milk, oysters, and other alternatives to previously monotonous diets. Moreover, refrigerated railroad cars enabled growers and meatpackers to ship perishables greater distances and to hold them for longer periods, and iceboxes preserved them once they reached consumers' homes.

Processed and Preserved Foods

Even the working class enjoyed a more diversified diet. As in the past, the poorest people still ate cheap foods, heavy in starches and carbohydrates. Now, however, many could purchase previously unavailable fruits, vegetables, and dairy products. Workers had to spend a high percentage of their income on food—almost half of the breadwinner's wages—but they never suffered the severe malnutrition that plagued other developing nations.

Just as tin cans and iceboxes made many foods widely available, the sewing machine brought about a revolution in clothing. Before 1850, nearly all Americans wore clothes made at home or by seamstresses and tailors. Then in the 1850s the sewing machine, invented in Europe but refined by Americans Elias Howe, Jr., and Isaac M. Singer, came into use in clothing and shoe manufacture. Mass production enabled manufacturers to turn out good-quality apparel at relatively low cost and to standardize sizes to fit different body shapes. By 1900, all but the poorest families could afford "ready-to-wear" clothes.

Ready-made Clothing

With mass-produced clothing came a concern for style. Restrictive Victorian fashions still dominated women's clothing, but as women's participation in work and leisure activities became more active, dress styles began to place greater emphasis on comfort. In the 1890s, long sleeves and skirt hemlines receded, and high-boned collars disappeared.

Men's clothes, too, became more lightweight and stylish. Before 1900, a man in the middle and affluent working classes would have owned no more than two suits, one for Sundays and special occasions and one for everyday wear. After 1900, however, manufacturers began to produce garments from fabrics of different weights and for different seasons. Even for those of modest means, clothing was becoming something to be bought instead of made and remade at home.

Department stores and chain stores helped to create and serve this new consumerism. Between 1865 and 1900, companies such as Macy's, Wanamaker's, Jordan Marsh, and Marshall Field became fixtures of metropolitan America. Previously, the working classes had bought their goods in stores with limited inventories, and wealthier people had patronized fancy shops. Now department stores, with their open displays of clothing, housewares, and furniture, as well as home deliveries, exchange policies,

Department and Chain Stores

and charge accounts, created a merchandising revolution.

The Transformation of Mass Communications

As in the past, most people made up their own minds about what they wanted. But with so much to do and buy, consumers needed fuller information about what was available. Thus new types of communication—modern advertising and popular journalism—arose to influence tastes and opinions.

A society of scarcity does not need advertising: when demand exceeds supply, producers have no trouble selling what they market. But in a society of abundance, supply frequently outstrips demand, necessitating a means to increase or even create demand.

Advertising

The aim of advertising is to *invent* a need by convincing *entire groups* that everyone in that group should buy a specific product. In the late nineteenth century, advertisers began creating "consumption communities"—bodies of consumers loyal to a particular brand name. The prime vehicle for advertising was the newspaper. In the mid-nineteenth century, publishers began to pursue higher revenues by selling more ad space, especially to urban department stores. Wanamaker's placed the first full-page ad in 1879, and at about the same time newspapers began to allow advertisers to print pictures of products. Such attention-getting techniques transformed advertising into news. More than ever before, people read newspapers to find out what was for sale as well as what was happening.

Manufacturers used new marketing techniques to advance their products. James B. Duke, whose American Tobacco Company made cigarettes a big business, saturated communities with billboards and free samples and offered premium gifts to retailers for selling more cigarettes. Companies like International Harvester and Singer Sewing Machine set up systems for servicing their products and introduced financ-

ing schemes to permit customers to buy the machines more easily.

The Corporate Consolidation Movement

Neither the industrial wonders nor the new marketing techniques masked unsettling factors in the American economy. In the final third of the nineteenth century, financial panics afflicted the economy during every decade, ruining businesses and destroying workers' jobs. Economic declines that began in 1873, 1884, and 1893 each lingered for several years. Business leaders disagreed on what caused them. Some blamed overproduction; others pointed to underconsumption; still others blamed lax credit and investment practices. Whatever the explanation, businesspeople began seeking ways to combat the uncertainty of boom-and-bust business cycles. Many adopted centralized forms of business organization, notably corporations, pools, trusts, and holding companies.

The corporation proved to be the best instrument for businesspeople to raise capital for industrial expansion. Under existing state laws, almost anyone could start a company and raise money by selling stock to investors. Stockholders could share in profits without high risk, because the laws limited their liability for company debts to the amount of their own investment. Nor did they need to concern themselves with the day-to-day operation of the firms; full responsibility for company administration was left in the hands of managers. Moreover, corporations won broad judicial protection in the 1880s and 1890s when the Supreme Court ruled that they, like individuals, are protected by the Fourteenth Amendment. In other words, states could not deny corporations equal protection under the law and could not deprive them of rights or property without due process of law. Such rulings insulated corporations against vigorous government interference in their operations.

But as economic disorder and the urge for profits mounted, corporation managers sought

Role of Corporations

greater stability in new and larger forms of economic concentration. At first such efforts were tentative and informal, consisting mainly of cooperative agreements among firms that manufactured the same product or offered the same service. Through these arrangements, called *pools*, competing companies tried to control the market by agreeing how much each should produce and sharing profits. Such "gentlemen's agreements" worked during good times, but during slow periods, the desire for profits often tempted pool members to evade their commitments by secretly reducing prices or by selling more than the agreed quota.

Pools, Trusts, and Holding Companies

John D. Rockefeller disliked pools, calling them "ropes of sand"—weak and undependable. In 1879 one of his lawyers, Samuel Dodd, devised a more stable means of dominating the market. Since state laws prohibited one corporation from holding stock in another corporation, Dodd adapted an old device called a *trust*, which in law existed as an arrangement whereby responsible individuals would manage the financial affairs of a person unwilling or unable to handle them alone. Dodd reasoned that one company could control an industry by luring or forcing the stockholders of smaller companies in that industry to yield control of their stock "in trust" to the larger company's board of trustees. This device allowed Rockefeller to achieve *horizontal integration* of the highly profitable petroleum industry in 1882 by combining his Standard Oil Company of Ohio with other refineries he bought up.

In 1888 New Jersey adopted new laws allowing corporations chartered there to own (not merely control) property in other states and stock in other corporations. These laws led to the creation of the *holding company*, which owned a partial or complete interest in other companies. Holding companies could in turn merge their companies' assets as well as their management. Under this arrangement, Rockefeller's holding company, Standard Oil of New Jersey, merged forty refining companies. Holding companies also encouraged *vertical integration*, enabling companies to control all aspects of their operation from raw materials to production to distribution.

Another form of economic concentration, mergers, became the answer to industry's search for order. Between 1889 and 1903, some three hundred combinations were formed, most of them trusts and holding companies. The most spectacular was the U.S. Steel Corporation, financed by J. P. Morgan in 1901. Other mammoth combinations included the Amalgamated Copper Company, American Sugar Refining Company, American Tobacco Company, and U.S. Rubber Company.

The merger movement created a new species of businessman, whose vocation was financial organizing rather than producing a particular good or service. Shrewd operators sought opportunities for combination, formed corporations, and then persuaded producers to sell their firms to the new company. These financiers usually raised money by selling stock and borrowing from banks. Investment bankers like J. P. Morgan and Jacob Schiff piloted the merger movement, inspiring awe with their financial power and organizational skills.

Role of Financiers

The Gospel of Wealth and Its Critics

Business leaders turned to corporate consolidation not to promote competition but to minimize it. At the same time, defenders of business sought a philosophical theory that would enable them to justify the size and power of the huge companies that resulted from corporate mergers and explain their tactics to a public accustomed to a belief in open competition.

The doctrine of Social Darwinism furnished the needed answers. Social Darwinism loosely grafted Charles Darwin's theory of the evolutionary survival of the fittest onto laissez faire, the doctrine that government should not interfere in private economic affairs. Social Darwinists reasoned that in an unconstrained economy power would flow

Social Darwinism

naturally to the most capable people. Acquisition and possession of property were thus sacred rights, and wealth was a mark of well-deserved power and responsibility. By this reasoning, monopolies resulted from the natural accumulation of economic power by those best suited for wielding it.

Social Darwinists reasoned, too, that wealth carried moral responsibilities. Steel baron Andrew Carnegie asserted what he called "the Gospel of Wealth"—that he and other industrialists were trustees for society's wealth and that they had a duty to fulfill that trust in humane ways. Such philanthropy, however, also implied a right for men like Rockefeller and Carnegie to define what they believed was good and necessary for society as a whole.

Paradoxically, the same business executives who extolled individual initiative and denounced measures to aid unions or regulate factory conditions as interference with natural economic laws now lobbied for subsidies, loans, and tax relief to encourage business growth. By far the most extensive form of government assistance to American industry was tariffs, which raised the prices of foreign products by placing an import tax on them. When Congress imposed high tariffs on foreign goods, American producers could sell their goods at relatively high prices. Industrialists argued that tariff protection encouraged the development of new products and the founding of new enterprises. But tariffs also forced consumers to pay artificially high prices for many goods.

Government Assistance to Business

Critics of trusts and other new forms of business organization argued within the same framework of values as did the corporate leaders they opposed. While defenders insisted that trusts were a natural and efficient outcome of economic development, critics charged that trusts were unnatural because they were created by greed and stifled opportunity. Such charges gave voice to an ardent fear of *monopoly*, the domination of an economic activity by one powerful company.

Dissenting Voices

Many believed in a better path to progress. By the mid-1880s, a number of young professors began to challenge Social Darwinism and laissez-faire economics. Brown University sociologist Lester Ward attacked the application of evolutionary theory to social and economic relations. In *Dynamic Sociology* (1883), Ward argued that human control of nature, not natural law, accounted for the advance of civilization. According to Ward, a system that guaranteed survival only to the fittest was wasteful and brutal; instead, he reasoned, cooperative activity fostered by planning and government intervention was more moral. Economists Richard Ely, John R. Commons, and Edward Bemis denounced the laissez-faire system for its "unsound morals" and praised the positive assistance that government could offer.

While academics endorsed intervention in the natural economic order, others more directly questioned why the United States had to have so many poor people while a few became fabulously wealthy. Henry George, the author of *Progress and Poverty* (1879), argued that economic inequality stemmed from the ability of a few to profit from rising land values. Such profits, George said, made speculators rich simply because of increased demand for living and working space, especially in cities. To prevent profiteering, he proposed to replace all taxes with a "single tax" on the "unearned increment"—the rise in property values caused by increased market demand rather than by owners' improvements.

Utopian Economic Schemes

Novelist Edward Bellamy offered another solution. Believing that capitalism and competition promoted waste, he proposed the establishment of a state in which government owned the means of production. Bellamy outlined his dream in *Looking Backward, 2000–1887* (1888). The novel, which sold over a million copies, depicted Boston in the year 2000 as a peaceful community where everyone had a job and a technological elite managed the economy according to scientific principles. Though in this utopia a council of elders ruled and ordinary people could not vote, Bellamy tried to convince readers that a "principle of fraternal

How do historians know what turn-of-the-century Americans thought about big business? Political cartoons and the symbols that cartoonists often used indicate prevailing attitudes and can serve as a kind of shorthand representation of how the same historical circumstance can arouse differing opinions. These two cartoons illustrate quite different points of view. The top one depicts the Standard Oil Trust as a greedy octopus with sprawling tentacles that are snaring Congress, state legislatures, and the taxpayer and are reaching for the White House. The cartoonist obviously believed that the economic giant was exercising dangerous power. The second cartoon portrays a more benevolent view. The cartoonist depicts John D. Rockefeller of Standard Oil and Andrew Carnegie of U.S. Steel at work, using their profits to nurture a garden of colleges and libraries.   Octopus: Library of Congress. Garden: Baker Library, Harvard Business School.

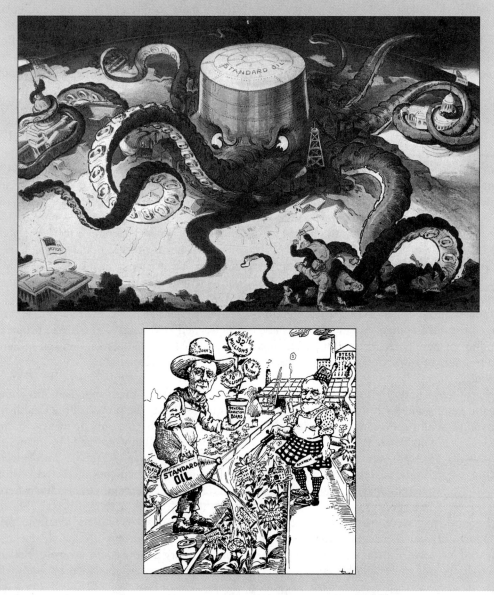

cooperation" could replace vicious competition and wasteful monopoly.

Before 1900 few people supported the government ownership envisioned by Bellamy, but several states did take steps to prohibit monopolies and regulate business. By the end of the nineteenth century, fifteen states had constitutional provisions outlawing trusts, and twenty-seven had laws forbidding pools. Most were agricultural states in the South and West that were responding to antimonopolistic pressure from various farm organizations. But state attorneys general lacked the staff and judicial support for an effective attack on big business. Only national legislation, it seemed, could work.

Antitrust Legislation

Congress moved hesitantly toward such legislation and in 1890 finally passed the Sherman Anti-Trust Act. The law made illegal "every contract, combination in the form of trust or otherwise, or conspiracy in the restraint of trade." However, the law was left purposely vague so as to attract broad support. It did not clearly define restraint of trade and consigned interpretation of its provisions to the courts, which at the time were strong allies of business.

Judges used the law's vagueness to blur distinctions between reasonable and unreasonable restraints of trade. When in 1895 the federal government prosecuted the so-called Sugar Trust for owning 98 percent of the nation's sugar-refining capacity, eight of the nine Supreme Court justices ruled that control of manufacturing did not necessarily mean control of trade (*U.S.* v. *E. C. Knight Co.*). According to the Court, the Constitution empowered Congress to regulate interstate *commerce*, but not *manufacturing*. Ironically, courts that did not consider monopolistic production a restraint on trade willingly applied antitrust provisions to strikes.

 Conclusion

Mechanization and new inventions thrust the United States into the vanguard of industrial nations and immeasurably altered daily life between 1877 and 1920. But in industry, as in farming and mining, bigness and consolidation engulfed the individual, changing the nature of work from individual activity undertaken by producers to mass production undertaken by employees. Workers fought to regain control of their efforts but failed to develop well-organized unions that could meet their needs. The outpouring of products created a new mass society based on consumerism, but not even the "democratization of consumption" could benefit all social groups.

The problems of enforcing the Sherman Anti-Trust Act reflected the uneven distribution of power among interest groups. Corporate enterprises had effectively consolidated, and they controlled great resources of economic and political power. Other groups—farmers, laborers, and reformers—had numbers and ideas but lacked influence. Members of these groups desired the material gains that technology and mass production were providing, but they feared that business was acquiring too much influence.

Suggestions for Further Reading

General

Daniel J. Boorstin, *The Americans: The Democratic Experience* (1973); Alan Dawley, *Struggle for Justice: Social Responsibility and the Liberal State* (1991); Carl N. Degler, *The Age of the Economic Revolution* (1977); Ray Ginger, *The Age of Excess* (1965); Samuel P. Hays, *The Response to Industrialism* (1975); Thomas J. Schlereth, *Victorian America: Transformations in Everyday Life* (1991).

Technology and Invention

Robert W. Bruce, *Bell: Alexander Graham Bell and the Conquest of Solitude* (1973); David Hounshell, *From the American System to Mass Production* (1984); Thomas Parke Hughes, *American Genesis: A Century of Technological Enthusiasm* (1989); John P. Kasson, *Civilizing the Machine: Technology and Republican Values in America* (1976); Leo Marx, *The Machine in the Garden: Technology and the Pastoral Ideal* (1964); Andre Millard, *Edison and the Business of Innovation* (1990); David E. Nye, *Electrifying America* (1990); Peter Temin, *Steel in Nineteenth-Century America* (1964).

Industrialism, Industrialists, and Corporate Growth

W. Eliot Brownlee, *Dynamics of Ascent: A History of the American Economy*, 2d ed. (1979); Stuart Bruchey, *Growth of the Modern Economy* (1973); Vincent P. Carosso, *The Morgans* (1987); Alfred

D. Chandler, *The Visible Hand: The Managerial Revolution in American Business* (1977); Thomas C. Cochran, *Business in American Life* (1972); Francis L. Eames, *The New York Stock Exchange* (1968); David F. Hawkes, *John D.: The Founding Father of the Rockefellers* (1980); Robert Higgs, *The Transformation of the American Economy, 1865–1914* (1971); Harold C. Livesay, *Andrew Carnegie and the Rise of Big Business* (1975); Glen Porter, *The Rise of Big Business* (1973); Martin J. Sklar, *The Corporate Reconstruction of American Capitalism* (1988); Richard Tedlow, *The Rise of the American Business Corporation* (1991); Joseph Wall, *Alfred I. du Pont: The Man and His Family* (1990).

Work and Labor Organization

Alan Derickson, *Workers' Health, Workers' Democracy: The Western Miners' Struggle, 1891–1925* (1988); Melvin Dubofsky, *We Shall Be All: A History of the Industrial Workers of the World* (1969); Sarah Eisenstein, *Give Us Bread, Give Us Roses: Working Women's Consciousness in the United States* (1983); Leon Fink, *Workingmen's Democracy: The Knights of Labor and American Politics* (1982); Philip S. Foner, *The Great Labor Uprising of 1877* (1977); Herbert G. Gutman, *Work, Culture and Society in Industrializing America* (1976); Tamara K. Hareven, *Family Time and Industrial Time* (1982); Alice Kessler-Harris, *Out to Work: A History of Wage Earning Women in the United States* (1982); Susan Lehrer, *Origins of Protective Labor Legislation for Women* (1987); Harold Livesay, *Samuel Gompers and Organized Labor in America* (1978); Milton Meltzer, *Bread and Roses: The Struggle of American Labor, 1865–1915* (1967); Stephen Meyer III, *The Five Dollar Day: Labor Management and Social Control in the Ford Motor Company, 1908–1921* (1981); Ruth Milkman, ed., *Women, Work, and Protest* (1985); David Montgomery, *The Fall of the House of Labor: The Workplace, the State, and American Labor Activism, 1865–1925* (1987); Stephen H. Norwood, *Labor's Flaming Youth: Telephone Operators and Worker Militancy* (1990); Elizabeth Ann Payne, *Reform, Labor, and Feminism: Margaret Dreier Robins and the Women's Trade Union League* (1988); Daniel J. Walkowitz, *Worker City, Company Town* (1978); Leon J. Wolff, *Lockout: The Story of the Homestead Strike of 1892* (1965).

Living Standards and New Conveniences

Susan Porter Benson, *Counter Cultures: Saleswomen, Managers, and Customers in American Department Stores, 1890–1940* (1986); Stephen Fox, *The Mirror Makers: A History of American Advertising and Its Creators* (1984); T. J. Jackson Lears and Richard W. Fox, eds., *The Culture of Consumption* (1983); Godfrey M. Lebhar, *Chain Stores in America* (1962); Harvey A. Levenstein, *Revolution at the Table: The Transformation of the American Diet* (1988); Daniel Pope, *The Making of Modern Advertising* (1983); Peter R. Shergold, *Working Class Life* (1982); Susan Strasser, *Satisfaction Guaranteed: The Making of the American Mass Market* (1989); Gwendolyn Wright, *Building the Dream: A Social History of Housing in America* (1983).

Attitudes Toward Industrialism

Sidney Fine, *Laissez Faire and the General Welfare State* (1956); Louis Galambos and Barbara Barron Spence, *The Public Image of Big Business in America* (1975); Richard Hofstadter, *Social Darwinism in American Thought*, rev. ed. (1955); T. J. Jackson Lears, *No Place of Grace: Antimodernism and the Transformation of American Culture* (1981); Robert McCloskey, *American Conservatism in the Age of Enterprise* (1951); John L. Thomas, *Alternative America: Henry George, Edward Bellamy, Henry Demarest Lloyd, and the Adversary Tradition* (1983).

CHAPTER

19

The Vitality and Turmoil
of Urban Life

1877 – 1920

I n a few short weeks, Antanas Kaztauskis learned just about everything he needed to know about living in Chicago. An immigrant
from Lithuania, Antanas first lived in a boarding house near his job
in the stockyards. One morning some friends took him to a store and
bought him some American clothes. Then they went for a walk "down
town." There, Antanas discovered the wonders of the city.

> We stood by one theater and watched for half an hour. Then we walked all around a
> store that filled one whole block and had walls of glass. . . . I saw men with dress
> suits, I saw women with such clothes that I could not think at all. . . . [My friends
> said,] "See what money can do?" Then we walked home and I felt poor and my shoes
> got very bad.

Antanas lost his job after a few weeks; out of desperation, he sought help
from a politician—and learned how the city really worked:

> The Republican boss in our district, Jonidas, was a saloon keeper. A friend took
> me there. Jonidas shook hands and treated me fine. He taught me to sign my
> name, and the next week I went with him to an office and signed some paper, and
> then I could vote. I voted as I was told, and then they got me back into the
> [stock]yards to work.

As he saved money, Antanas was able to bring his wife from
Lithuania and rent an apartment in a respectable part of town. He
joined some Lithuanian clubs and on Sundays took trolley rides into
the countryside.

The experiences of Antanas Kaztauskis illustrate many themes characterizing urban life in America as the nineteenth century merged into the twentieth. Where to live, where to work, the awesomeness of the consumer economy, the functions of personal and machine politics, the expression of ethnic consciousness, and the rise from rags to respectability—all these things and more made cities places of hope, frustration, satisfaction, and conflict.

The nation's urban population started to grow much faster than its rural population in the 1830s. But not until the 1880s did the United States begin to become a truly urban nation. By 1920 a symbolic milestone of urbanization was passed: that year's census showed that, for the first time, a majority of Americans (51.4 percent) lived in cities (settlements with more than 2,500 people). This new fact of national life was as symbolically significant as the disappearance of the frontier in 1890.

Cities served as marketplaces and forums, bringing together the people, resources, and ideas responsible for many of the changes American society was experiencing. By 1900 a network of small, medium, and large cities spanned every section of the country. Some people relished the opportunities and excitement cities offered. Others found the crudeness of American cities disquieting. But whatever people's personal impressions, the city had become central to American life.

Transportation and Industrial Growth in the Modern City

By 1900, the compact American city of the early nineteenth century, where residences were mingled among shops, factories, and warehouses, had burst open. From Boston to Los Angeles, the built environment sprawled several miles beyond the original central core. No longer did walking distance determine a city's size. No longer did different social groups live close together. Instead, cities subdivided into distinct districts: working-class and ethnic neighborhoods, African-American ghettos, downtown, a ring of suburbs. Two forces, mass transportation and economic change, were responsible for the new neighborhood patterns.

During the 1850s and 1860s, steam-powered commuter railroads serviced a few cities, such as New York and Boston, but not until the late 1870s did mechanized mass transit appear. The first power-driven devices were cable cars, carriages that moved by clamping onto a moving underground wire. Cheaper than horse cars, cable cars also were more efficient at hauling passengers up and down hills. By the 1880s, cable-car lines operated in Chicago, San Francisco, and many other cities.

Mechanization of Mass Transportation

In the 1890s, electric-powered streetcars began replacing early forms of mass transit. Trolley companies in a few cities raised track onto stilts, enabling vehicles to travel without interference above jammed downtown districts. In Boston, New York, and Philadelphia, transit firms dug underground passages for their cars, also to avoid delays. Because elevated railroads and subways were extremely expensive to construct, they appeared in only a few cities.

Another form of mass transit, the electric interurban railway, helped link nearby cities. Interurbans operated between cities in areas with growing suburban populations and furthered urban development by making outer regions attractive for settlers and businesses. The extensive network of the Pacific Electric Railway in southern California, for example, facilitated both travel and economic development in that region.

Mass-transit lines launched millions of urban dwellers into outlying neighborhoods and created a commuting public. Those who could afford the fare—usually a nickel a ride—could live beyond the crowded central city and commute there for work, shopping, and entertainment. Working-class families, whose incomes rarely topped a dollar a day, found streetcar fares unaffordable. But the growing middle class could escape to quiet neighborhoods on the urban outskirts and live in bungalows with their own yards. Real-estate development boomed

Beginnings of Urban Sprawl

• *Important Events* •

1867	First law regulating tenements passes, in New York State	**1898**	Race riot erupts in Wilmington, North Carolina
1870	One-fourth of Americans live in cities	**1900–10**	Immigration reaches peak Vaudeville rises in popularity
1876	National League of Professional Baseball Clubs founded	**1903**	Boston plays Pittsburgh in first baseball World Series
1880s	"New" immigrants from eastern and southern Europe begin to arrive in large numbers Thomas A. Edison invents the motion picture and viewing device	**1905**	Intercollegiate Athletic Association, forerunner of National College Athletic Association (NCAA), is formed and restructures rules of football
1883	Joseph Pulitzer buys *New York World* and creates a major vehicle for yellow journalism	**1906**	Race riot erupts in Atlanta, Georgia
1886	First settlement house opens, in New York City	**1915**	D. W. Griffith directs *Birth of a Nation*, one of the first major technically sophisticated movies
1890s	Electric trolleys replace horse-drawn mass transit	**1920**	Majority (51.4 percent) of Americans live in cities

around the borders of cities. Between 1890 and 1920, for example, developers in the Chicago area opened 800,000 new lots.

Urban sprawl was essentially unplanned, but certain patterns did emerge. Investors who bought land in anticipation of settlement paid little attention to the need for parks, traffic control, and public services. Construction of mass transit was guided by the profit motive and thus benefited the urban public unevenly. Streetcar lines serviced mainly those districts that promised the most riders—whose fares, in other words, would increase company profits.

Streetcars, elevateds, and subways altered commercial as well as residential patterns. When consumers moved outward, businesses followed. Branches of department stores and banks joined groceries, theaters, taverns, and specialty shops to create neighborhood shopping centers. Meanwhile, the urban core became the work zone, where offices and stores loomed over streets clogged with traffic.

Cities also became the main arenas for industrial growth. As centers of labor, transportation, and communications, cities provided everything factories needed. Once mass production became possible, capital accumulated by the cities' mercantile enterprises fed industrial investment. Urban populations also furnished consumers for new products. Thus urban growth and industrialization wound together in a mutually advantageous spiral. The further industrialization advanced, the more opportunities it created for work and investment. Increased opportunity in turn drew more people to cities; as workers and as consumers, they fueled further industrialization.

Urban-Industrial Development

The influence of urban and industrial growth was felt at the national level, too, where it transformed the economy and freed the United States from dependence on European capital and manufactured goods. Imports and foreign investments still flowed into the United States. But by the early

1900s, cities and their factories, stores, and banks were converting America from a debtor agricultural nation into an industrial, financial, and exporting power.

Peopling the Cities: Migrants and Immigrants

Between 1870 and 1920, the number of Americans living in cities exploded almost 550 percent, from 10 million to 54 million. During the same period, the number of cities with more than 100,000 people grew from fifteen to sixty-eight, and the number with more than 500,000 swelled from two to twelve (see maps, page 359). These figures, dramatic in themselves, represent millions of stories of dreams and frustration, adjustment and confusion, success and failure.

A city can increase its population in three ways: by extending its borders to annex land and people; by natural increase (an excess of births over deaths); and by net migration (an excess of in-migrants over out-migrants). Between the 1860s and early 1900s, many cities annexed nearby territory, thereby instantly increasing their populations. The most notable consolidation occurred in 1898 when New York City, which previously consisted only of Manhattan and the Bronx, merged with Brooklyn, Staten Island, and part of Queens and grew overnight from 1.5 million to over 3 million people. Although annexation increased urban populations, its major effect was to enlarge the physical size of cities.

How Cities Grew

Natural increase did not account for much of any city's population growth. In the late nineteenth century, death rates declined in most regions of the country, but birth rates fell as well. In most cities, the number of people who were born in a given year was roughly equal to the number who died that year. Migration and immigration made by far the greatest contribution to urban population growth. Urban newcomers arrived from two major sources: the American countryside and Europe. Asia, Canada, and Latin America also supplied immigrants, though in smaller numbers.

In general, rural populations declined as urban populations burgeoned. A variety of factors such as low crop prices and high debts dashed farmers' hopes and drove them off the land toward the opportunities that cities seemed to offer. Many more of the newcomers were immigrants who had fled foreign villages and cities for American shores. The dream of a large number was not to stay but to make enough money to return home and live in greater comfort and security. For every hundred foreigners who entered the country, around thirty left. Still, most of the 26 million immigrants who arrived between 1870 and 1920 remained, and the great majority settled in cities, where they helped reshape American culture.

Major Waves of Migration and Immigration

The United States had been the main destination of northern and western European immigrants since the 1840s, but after 1880 economic and demographic changes propelled a second wave of immigrants from other regions. Northern and western Europeans continued to arrive, but the new wave brought more people from eastern and southern Europe, plus smaller contingents from Canada, Mexico, and Japan (see figure page 360). Two-thirds of the newcomers who arrived in the 1880s came from Germany, England, Ireland, and Scandinavia; between 1900 and 1909, two-thirds came from Italy, Austria-Hungary, and Russia.[1] By 1910, arrivals from Mexico were beginning to outnumber arrivals from Ireland, and large numbers of Japanese had moved to the West Coast and Hawai'i. Foreign-born blacks, chiefly from the West Indies, also increased in number.

The New Immigration

The immigrants varied widely in age, marital status, and other characteristics, but certain traits stood out. Approximately two-thirds of the newcomers were males, especially after 1900, and about two-thirds were between the ages of fifteen

---

[1]Immigrants from Austria-Hungary and Russia included Poles, Czechs, Slovaks, Serbs, Croats, and Romanians, all of whom could have been Jewish, Catholic, or Greek Orthodox.

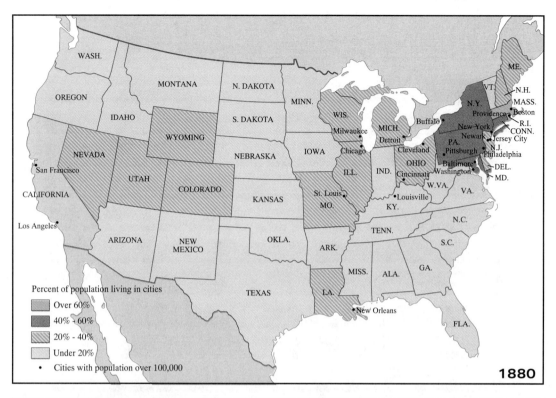

1880

Percent of population living in cities
- Over 60%
- 40% - 60%
- 20% - 40%
- Under 20%
- • Cities with population over 100,000

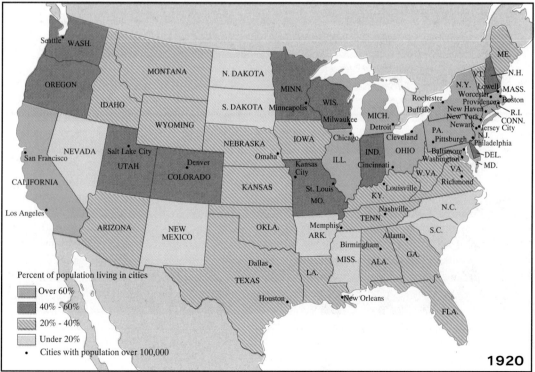

1920

Percent of population living in cities
- Over 60%
- 40% - 60%
- 20% - 40%
- Under 20%
- • Cities with population over 100,000

Urbanization, 1880; Urbanization, 1920 *In 1880 the vast majority of states still were heavily rural. By 1920 only a few had less than 20 percent of their population living in cities.*

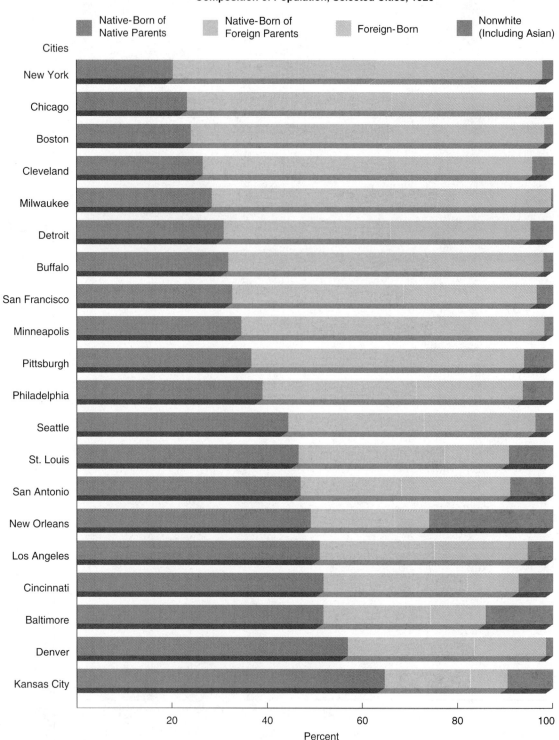

Composition of Population, Selected Cities, 1920

Legend: Native-Born of Native Parents · Native-Born of Foreign Parents · Foreign-Born · Nonwhite (Including Asian)

Cities (top to bottom): New York, Chicago, Boston, Cleveland, Milwaukee, Detroit, Buffalo, San Francisco, Minneapolis, Pittsburgh, Philadelphia, Seattle, St. Louis, San Antonio, New Orleans, Los Angeles, Cincinnati, Baltimore, Denver, Kansas City

Percent axis: 20, 40, 60, 80, 100

Composition of Population, Selected Cities, 1920 *Immigration and migration made native-born whites of native-born parents minorities in almost every major city by the early twentieth century. Moreover, foreign-born residents and native-born whites of foreign parents constituted absolute majorities in numerous places.*

and thirty-nine. Not all groups were equally educated, but almost three-fourths of the immigrants could read and write, at least in their native languages. Among those reporting occupations at the time of entry, half identified themselves as unskilled laborers or domestic workers (maids, cooks, cleaners).

In the West, Hispanics, who once had been a predominantly rural population, lived increasingly in cities. They took over ditch-digging and street-grading jobs once held by Chinese laborers. In some Texas cities native Mexicans (called Tejanos) held the majority of all unskilled jobs.

Many Americans feared the customs, Catholic and Jewish faiths, illiteracy, and poverty of "new" immigrants, considering them less desirable and assimilable than "old" immigrants, whose languages and beliefs seemed less alien. In reality, however, old and new immigrants closely resembled each other. The majority of both groups came from societies that made the family the focus of all undertakings. Whether and when to emigrate was decided in light of the family's needs, and family bonds continued to prevail after immigrants reached the New World. New arrivals often received aid from relatives who had already immigrated. In many instances, workers helped kin obtain jobs, and family members pooled their resources to maintain, if not improve, their standard of living.

All immigrants adjusted to American life guided by the light of memories they brought from their homelands. In their strange new surroundings, immigrants anchored their lives to the rock they knew best: their culture. Old World customs persisted in immigrant enclaves of Italians from the same province, Japanese from the same island district, or Russian Jews from the same *shtetl* (village). People practiced religion as they always had, held traditional feasts and pageants, married within their group, and pursued old feuds with people from rival villages.

Immigrant Cultures

Yet, as Antanas Katzauskis discovered, the very diversity of American cities forced immigrants to modify their attitudes and habits. Few newcomers could avoid contact with people different from

Those who wished to "Americanize" the immigrants believed the public schools could provide the best setting for assimilation. This 1917 poster from the Cleveland Board of Education and the Cleveland Americanization Committee used the languages most common to the new immigrants—Slovene, Italian, Polish, Hungarian, and Yiddish—as well as English to invite newcomers to free classes where they could learn "the language of America" and "citizenship." National Park Service Collection, Ellis Island Immigration Museum.

themselves, and few could prevent such contacts from altering their traditional ways of life. Everywhere, Old World culture mingled with New World realities. Immigrants struggled to maintain their native languages and to pass them down to younger generations. But English was taught in the schools and needed on the job. Foreigners cooked ethnic meals using American foods and fashioned

European clothes from American fabrics. Music especially revealed adaptations. Polka bands entertained at Polish social gatherings, but their repertoires expanded to blend American and Polish folk music. Mexican ballads acquired new themes that described the adventures of border crossing and the hardship of labor in the United States.

The inflow of so many immigrants between 1870 and 1920 transformed the United States from a basically Protestant nation into one com-

Influence on Religion

posed of Protestants, Catholics, and Jews. Newcomers from Italy, Hungary, Poland, and Slovakia joined Irish and Germans to boost the proportion of Catholics in many cities. Catholic Mexicans constituted over half of the population of El Paso, and German and Russian immigrants gave New York one of the largest Jewish populations in the world.

In the 1880s, another group of migrants began to enter American cities. Thousands of rural African-Americans moved northward and westward, seeking

African-American Migration to the Cities

better employment and fleeing crop liens, the ravages of the boll weevil on cotton crops, racial violence, and political oppression. Though black urban dwellers grew more numerous after 1915, thirty-two cities al-

ready had more than ten thousand black residents by 1900, and 79 percent of all blacks outside the South lived in cities. These migrants resembled foreign immigrants in their rural backgrounds and economic motivations, but they differed in several important ways. Because few factories would employ African-Americans, most found jobs in the service sector—cleaning, cooking, and driving—rather than in the industrial trades. Also, because most service openings were traditionally female jobs, black women outnumbered black men in cities such as New York, Baltimore, and New Orleans.

Each of the three major migrant groups that peopled American cities—native-born whites, foreigners of various races, and native-born blacks—helped create modern American culture. The cities nurtured rich cultural variety: American folk music and literature, Italian and Mexican cuisine, Irish comedy, Yiddish theater, African-American jazz and dance, and much more. Like their predecessors, newcomers in the late nineteenth century changed their environment as much as they were changed by it.

Living Conditions in the Inner City

Urban population growth created intense pressures on the public and private sectors. The masses of people who jammed inner-city districts were recognized more for the problems they bred than for their cultural contributions. American cities seemed to harbor all the afflictions that plague modern society: poverty, disease, crime, and other unpleasant conditions that occur when large numbers of people live close together. City dwellers adjusted as best they could. Although technology, science, private enterprise, and public authority could not solve every problem, city officials and engineers achieved some remarkable successes. In the late nineteenth and early twentieth centuries, construction of buildings, homes, streets, sewers, and schools proceeded at a furious pace. American cities set world standards for fire protection and water purification. But many problems still await solution.

One of the most persistent shortcomings—the failure to provide adequate housing for all who need it—has its roots in nineteenth century

Housing Problems

urban development. In spite of massive construction in the 1880s and early 1900s, population growth outpaced housing supplies. The scarcity of inexpensive housing especially afflicted working-class families who, because of low wages, had to rent their living quarters. As cities grew, landlords took advantage of shortages in low-cost rental housing by splitting up existing buildings to house more people, constructing multiple-unit tenements, and hiking rents. Low-income families adapted to high costs and short supply by sharing space and expenses. Thus it became common in many big cities for a "one-family" apartment to be occupied by two or three families or by a single family plus several boarders. The result was unprecedented crowding. In 1890, New York City's immigrant-packed Lower East Side averaged 702 people per acre.

Inside many buildings, living conditions were harsh. The largest rooms were barely ten feet wide, and interior rooms either lacked windows or opened onto narrow shafts that bred vermin and rotten odors. Few buildings had indoor plumbing, and the only source of heat was dangerous, polluting coal-burning stoves.

Housing problems aroused reform campaigns in several places. New York State took the lead by legislating light, ventilation, and safety codes

Housing Reform

for new tenement buildings in 1867, 1879, and 1901. A few reformers, such as journalist Jacob Riis and humanitarian Lawrence Veiller, advocated housing low-income families in "model tenements," with more spacious rooms and better facilities. Model tenements, however, required landlords to accept lower profits—a sacrifice few were willing to make. Neither reformers nor public officials would consider government financing of better housing, fearing that such a step would undermine private enterprise.

While housing reforms had only limited success, scientific and technological advances eventually enabled city dwellers and the entire nation to live in greater comfort and safety. By the 1880s, most doctors had accepted the theory that microorganisms (germs) cause disease. In response, cities established more efficient systems of water purification and sewage disposal. Public health regulations helped to control dread diseases such as cholera, typhoid fever, and diphtheria. Moreover, electric street lighting and modernized firefighting equipment made American cities safer places in which to live. They did not, however, ease the burden of poverty.

Since colonial days, Americans have disagreed about how much responsibility the public should assume for poor relief. According to traditional beliefs, still widespread in the late nineteenth and early twentieth centuries, anyone could escape poverty through hard

Urban Poverty

work and clean living; poverty existed only because some people were morally weaker than others. Such reasoning bred fear that aid to poor people would encourage paupers to rely on public relief rather than their own efforts. As poverty increased, this attitude hardened, and city governments discontinued direct grants of food, fuel, and clothing to needy families. Instead, cities provided relief in return for work on public projects and sent special cases to state-run almshouses; orphanages; and homes for the blind, deaf, and mentally ill.

Close observation of the poor, however, prompted some humanitarians to conclude that people's environments, not their personal shortcomings, caused poverty. In turn, they came to believe that poverty could be prevented and eliminated by improving housing, education, sanitation, and job opportunities rather than admonishing the poor to be more moral. This attitude, which had been gaining ground since the mid-nineteenth century, supported drives for building codes, factory regulations, and public health measures. Still, most middle- and upper-class Americans continued to endorse the creed that in a society of abundance only the unfit were poor and that poverty relief should be tolerated but never encouraged.

More than crowding and pauperism, crime and disorder nurtured fears that urban growth, especially the slums, threatened the nation. The

Crime and Violence

more cities grew, it seemed, the more they shook with violence. While homicide rates declined in industrialized nations such as England and Germany, those in America rose alarmingly: 25 murders per million people in 1881; 107 per million in 1898. Pickpockets, swindlers, and burglars roamed every city.

Despite fears of increasing robberies and violence, urban crime may simply have become more conspicuous and sensational, rather than more prevalent. To be sure, concentrations of wealth and the mingling of different peoples provided new opportunities for larceny, vice, and violence. Though natives were quick to blame Irish bank robbers, German pickpockets, and Italian Black Hand murderers for urban disorder, there is little evidence

How do historians know the biases of reformers? Jacob Riis was a journalist who wrote How the Other Half Lives (1890), a landmark investigation of slum life in New York City. He was one of the first to use the camera as a reform tool, supplementing his accounts of poverty and crowding with moving photographs of poor people (mostly immigrants) and their surroundings. For many readers, these photographs provided what one reformer called "added realism" and "an inherent attraction not found in other forms of illustration." But is a photograph always completely "real"? This one taken by Riis shows three "street arabs," homeless boys living and sleeping outdoors away from adult care. What emotions does it raise? The picture looks unposed, but how can the viewer be sure? The nature of photography in 1890 was such that a photographer had to induce his subjects to remain motionless for thirty seconds or more in order for their image to be fixed on film. Do the boys in this photo seem to be posing? Did Riis exaggerate their plight by perhaps asking them to huddle together and remove their shoes? As is the case with other kinds of evidence, historians must use "realistic" photography carefully and look beyond the image to find out what biases it might represent.   Museum of the City of New York, the Jacob Riis Collection.

that more immigrant than native-born Americans populated the rogues' gallery.

Whatever the extent of criminality, city life in this period supports the thesis that the United States has a tradition of violence. Cities served as arenas for many of the era's worst riots. In addition to violent confrontations between labor and management, a series of race riots spread across the nation: Wilmington, North Carolina, 1898; Atlanta, Georgia, 1906; Springfield, Illinois, 1908. In cities of the Southwest and Pacific coast, Chinese and Mexican immigrants often felt the sting of intolerance.

Since the mid-nineteenth century, city dwellers had gradually overcome their resistance to professional law enforcement and increasingly depended on the police to protect life and property. By the early 1900s, however, law enforcement had become complicated and controversial because various groups differed in their views of the law and how it should be enforced. For instance, while some Americans favored crackdowns on drinking, gambling, and prostitution, others wanted loose enforcement of the so-called customer crimes. And disadvantaged groups—notably ethnic and racial minorities—could not escape arrest as easily as those with economic or political influence.

Role of the Police

The mounting problems of city life seemed to demand greater government action. Thus city governments passed more ordinances that regulated housing, provided poverty relief, and expanded police power to protect health and safety. Yet public responsibility mostly ended at the boundaries of private property. Eventually advances in housing construction, sanitation, and medical care reached slum dwellers. But for most people, the only hope was that their children would do better or that better opportunities would open somewhere else.

Family Life

Although the overwhelming majority of Americans continued to live within families, this most basic of social institutions suffered strain during the era of urbanization and industrialization. New institutions—schools, social clubs, political organizations, and others—increasingly competed with the family to provide nurture, education, and security. Observers warned that rising divorce rates, the growing separation between home and work, the entrance of numerous women into the work force, and loss of parental control over children spelled peril for home and family. Yet the family retained its fundamental role as a cushion in a hard, uncertain world.

Throughout modern Western history, most people have lived in two overlapping social units: household and family. A *household* is a group of people, related or unrelated, who share the same residence. A *family* is a group related by kinship, some members of which typically live together. The vast majority of households (75 to 80 percent) consisted of *nuclear families*—usually a married couple, with or without children. About 15 to 20 percent of households consisted of *extended families*—usually a married couple, with or without children, plus one or more relatives such as parents, adult siblings, grandchildren, aunts, and uncles. About 5 percent of households consisted of people living alone.

Family and Household Structures

The average size of nuclear families changed over time. In 1880 the birth rate was 40 live births per 1,000 people; by 1900 it had dropped to 32; by 1920 to 28. There were three main reasons for this decline. First, the United States was becoming an urban nation, and birth rates are generally lower in cities than in rural areas. On farms, where children worked at home or in the fields at an early age, each child born represented a new set of hands for the family work force. In the wage-based urban economy, children could not contribute significantly to the family income for many years, and a new child simply represented another mouth to feed. Second, infant mortality fell as diet and medical care improved, and families did not have to bear many children just to ensure that some would survive. Third, awareness that smaller families meant an improved quality of life seems to have stimulated decisions to limit family size. Although fertility was consistently higher among blacks, immigrants, and rural people than among white native-born city dwellers, birth rates of all groups fell. As a result, families with six or eight children became rare; three or four became more usual. Thus the nuclear family tended to reach its maximum size and then shrink faster than in earlier eras.

Declining Birth Rates

The household tended to expand and contract over the lifetime of a given family. Family size grew as children were born, and it shrank as

Boarding

children left home. The process of leaving home also changed households; huge numbers of young people—and some older people—lived as boarders and lodgers, especially in cities. Middle- and working-class families commonly took in boarders to occupy rooms vacated by grown children and to help pay expenses. Housing reformers charged that boarding caused overcrowding and loss of privacy. Yet for people on the move, boarding was a beneficial transitional stage, providing them with a quasi-family environment until they set up their own households.

For immigrants and migrants, the family served as a refuge in a strange new place. At a time when welfare agencies were rare, the family was the institution to which people could turn in times of need. Even when relatives did not live together, they often lived nearby and aided each other with childcare, meals, shopping, advice, and consolation. They also obtained jobs for each other.

Importance of Kinship

But obligations of kinship were not always welcome. Immigrant families often put pressure on last-born children to stay at home to care for aging parents, a practice that stifled opportunities for education, marriage, and economic independence. Tensions also developed when one relative felt that another was not helping out enough. Nevertheless, for better or worse, kinship provided people a means of coping with the stresses caused by an urban-industrial society. Social and economic change did not burst family ties.

Large numbers of city dwellers lived beyond the haven of traditional family relationships, however. In 1890, almost 42 percent of all American men and 37 percent of women aged fifteen and older were single. Some of these unmarried people also numbered among the homosexual population that thrived especially in large cities like New York and Boston. Though their numbers are difficult to estimate, gay men and women had their own subculture complete with clubs, restaurants, coffeehouses, theaters, and support networks. A number of gay couples formed lasting marriage-type relationships (sometimes called "Boston marriages" when they involved middle-class women); others "cruised" in the sexual underground of the streets and bars.

By the early 1900s, family life and functions were both changing and holding firm. New institutions were assuming tasks formerly performed by the family. Schools were making education a community responsibility. Employment agencies, personnel offices, labor unions, and legislatures were taking responsibility for employee recruitment and job security. In addition, migration and a soaring divorce rate seemed to be splitting families apart: 19,633 divorces were granted nationwide in 1880; by 1920, that number had reached 167,105. Yet in the face of these pressures, the family adjusted by expanding and contracting to meet temporary needs, and kinship remained a dependable though not always appreciated institution.

The New Leisure and Mass Culture

On December 2, 1889, as hundreds of workers paraded through Worcester, Massachusetts, in support of shorter working hours, a group of carpenters hoisted a banner proclaiming "Eight Hours for Work, Eight Hours for Rest, Eight Hours for What We Will." The phrase "for What We Will" was significant, for it laid claim to a special segment of daily life that belonged to the individual. Increasingly, among all social classes, leisure activities filled this time segment.

American inventors had long tried to create labor-saving devices, but not until the late 1800s did technological development become truly time-saving. Mechanization and assembly-line production not only replaced skilled work but also helped to cut the average workweek in manufacturing from sixty-six hours in 1860 to forty-seven in 1920. This reduction meant shorter workdays and freer weekends. To be sure, thousands still spent twelve- or fourteen-hour shifts in steel mills and sweatshops and had no time or energy for leisure. But more Americans began to partake of a variety of diversions, and a substantial segment of the economy began providing for—and profiting

Increase in Leisure Time

from—leisure. By the early 1900s, many Americans were enmeshed in the business of play.

The vanguard of new leisure pursuits was sports, and baseball was the most popular organized sport. An outgrowth of older bat, ball, and base-circling games, baseball was formalized in 1845 by a group of wealthy New Yorkers—the Knickerbocker Club—who codified the rules of play. By the 1880s, professional baseball was a big business. In 1903, the National League (founded in 1876) and competing American League (formed in 1901) began a World Series between their championship teams, entrenching baseball as the national pastime. The Boston Red Sox beat the Pittsburgh Pirates in that first series.

Baseball and Football

American football began as a sport for people of high social rank. As an intercollegiate sport, football attracted players and spectators wealthy enough to have access to higher education. By the end of the nineteenth century, however, the game was appealing to a broader audience. The 1893 Princeton-Yale game drew fifty thousand spectators.

College football became a national scandal because of its violence and use of "tramp athletes," nonstudents whom colleges hired to help their teams win. The scandals climaxed in 1905, when 18 players died from game-related injuries and over 150 were seriously injured. President Theodore Roosevelt, a strong advocate of athletics, convened a White House conference to discuss ways to eliminate brutality and foul play. The conference founded the Intercollegiate Athletic Association (renamed the National College Athletic Association in 1910) to police college sports. In 1906 the association altered the games to make football less violent and more open.

Baseball and football appealed mostly to men. But croquet, which also swept the nation, attracted both sexes. Middle- and upper-class people held croquet parties and even outfitted wickets with candles for night games. In an era when the departure of paid work from the home had separated men's from women's spheres, croquet in-

Croquet and Cycling

creased opportunities for social contact between the sexes.

Meanwhile, bicycling achieved popularity rivaling that of baseball. Like croquet, cycling brought men and women together, combining opportunities for courtship and exercise. Moreover, the bicycle played an influential role in freeing women from the constraints of Victorian fashions. In order to ride the dropped-frame female models, women had to wear divided skirts and simple undergarments. Gradually, freer styles of cycling costumes began to influence everyday fashions. As the 1900 census declared, "Few articles . . . have created so great a revolution in social conditions as the bicycle."

As more women enrolled in college, they began to pursue physical activities besides croquet, horseback riding, and cycling. Believing that to succeed intellectually they needed to be active and healthy, college women participated in sports such as rowing, track, and swimming. Eventually basketball became the most popular sport among college women. Invented in 1891 as a winter sport for men, basketball was given women's rules (which limited dribbling and running and encouraged passing) by Senda Berenson of Smith College in the 1890s, and intercollegiate games became common.

Paralleling the rise of sports, American show business also became a mode of leisure created by and for common people. Circuses—traveling shows of acrobats and animals—had existed since the 1820s. But after the Civil War, railroads enabled them to reach more of the country. Circuses offered two main attractions: so-called freaks of nature, both human and animal, and the temptation and conquest of death. At the heart of their appeal was the sheer astonishment that trapeze artists, lion tamers, acrobats, and clowns aroused.

Circuses

Three branches of American show business matured with the growth of cities. Popular drama, musical comedy, and vaudeville offered audiences a chance to escape the harshness of urban-industrial life into melodrama, adventure, and comedy. The plots were simple, the heroes and villains recognizable. For

Popular Drama and Musical Comedy

urbanized people increasingly distant from the frontier, popular plays brought to life the mythical Wild West and Old South. Virtue, honor, and justice always triumphed in melodramas, reinforcing popular faith that even in an uncertain and disillusioning world, goodness would prevail.

Musical comedies raised audiences' spirits with song, humor, and dance. American musical comedy grew out of the lavishly costumed operettas common in Europe. By introducing American themes (often involving ethnic groups), folksy humor, and catchy tunes, these shows launched the nation's most popular songs and entertainers. George M. Cohan, a spirited singer, dancer, and songwriter born into an Irish family of entertainers, became the master of American musical comedy after the turn of the century. Drawing on urbanism, patriotism, and traditional values in songs like "Yankee Doodle Boy" and "You're a Grand Old Flag," Cohan helped bolster national morale during the First World War. Comic opera, too, became popular, and the talented, beautiful Lillian Russell was its most admired performer. The first American comic operas imitated European musicals, but by the early 1900s composers like Victor Herbert were writing for American audiences. Shortly thereafter Jerome Kern began to write more sophisticated musicals, and American musical comedy came into its own.

Vaudeville was probably the most popular entertainment in early-twentieth-century America. Shows included, in rapid succession, acts such as jugglers, dancing bears, pantomimists, storytellers, magicians, puppeteers, acrobats, comedians, and, of course, singers and dancers. Around 1900, the number of vaudeville theaters and troupes skyrocketed. Its most famous promoter, Florenz Ziegfeld, brilliantly packaged shows in a stylish format—the Ziegfeld Follies—and gave the nation a new model of femininity, the Ziegfeld Girl, whose graceful dancing and alluring costumes suggested a haunting sensuality.

Vaudeville

Show business provided new economic opportunities for women, African-Americans, and immigrants, but it also encouraged stereotyping and exploitation. Lillian Russell, vaudeville singer and comedienne Fanny Brice, and burlesque queen Eva Tanguay attracted intensely loyal fans, commanded handsome fees, and won respect for their genuine talents. But lesser female performers were often exploited by male promoters and theater owners, many of whom wanted only to titillate the public with the sight of scantily clad women.

Before the 1890s, the chief form of commercial entertainment open to African-American performers was the minstrel show. By century's end, however, minstrel shows had given way to more sophisticated musicals, and blacks had begun to break into vaudeville. As stage settings shifted from the plantation to the city, music shifted from folk tunes to ragtime. Pandering to the prejudices of white audiences, composers and performers of both races ridiculed blacks. Even Burt Williams, a talented and highly paid black comedian and dancer, achieved success by playing the stereotypical roles of darky and dandy.

African-Americans and Immigrants in Vaudeville

Much of the uniqueness of American mass entertainment arose from its ethnic flavor. Indeed, immigrants occupied the core of American show business. Vaudeville in particular utilized ethnic humor, exaggerating dialects and other national traits. Skits and songs reinforced ethnic stereotypes and made fun of ethnic groups, but such distortions were more self-conscious and sympathetic than those directed at blacks.

Shortly after 1900, live entertainment began to yield to a more accessible form of amusement: moving pictures. Perfected by Thomas Edison in the 1880s, movies began as slot-machine peepshows in penny arcades and billiard parlors. Eventually images were projected onto a screen so that large audiences could view them, and a new medium was born.

Movies

Producers soon discovered that a film could tell a story in exciting ways. Thanks to creative directors like D. W. Griffith, motion pictures became a distinct art form. Griffith's *Birth of a Nation* (1915), an epic film about the Civil War and Reconstruction, fanned racial prejudice by depicting African-Americans as a threat to white moral values. The infant National Association for the Advancement of Colored People (NAACP) led an organized protest against it. But the film's innovative techniques—close-ups, fade-outs, and battle scenes—gave viewers heightened drama and excitement.

The still camera, modernized by inventor George Eastman, enabled ordinary people to make their own photographic images, especially useful for preserving family memories. The phonograph, another Edison invention, brought musical performances into the home. The spread of movies, photography, and phonograph records meant that access to live performances no longer limited people's exposure to art and entertainment. By making it possible to mass-produce sound and images, technology made entertainment a highly desirable consumer good.

News also became a consumer product. Canny publishers made people crave news just as they craved amusements. Joseph Pulitzer, a Hungarian immigrant who bought the *New York World* in 1883, pioneered journalism as a branch of mass culture. Pulitzer filled the *World* with stories of disasters, crimes, and scandals. Sensational headlines, set in large bold type like that used for advertisements, screamed from every page. His journalists not only reported news but sought it out and even created it. Pulitzer also popularized the comics, and the yellow ink they were printed in gave rise to the term *yellow journalism* as a synonym for sensationalism. The success enjoyed by Pulitzer (in a single year, circulation rose from 20,000 to 100,000) prompted others—most notably William Randolph Hearst—to adopt his techniques.

Yellow Journalism

Pulitzer and his rivals boosted circulation even further by emphasizing sports and women's news. Newspapers had always reported on sporting events, but yellow-journalism papers gave such stories far greater prominence by printing separate, expanded sports sections. While expanding sports news, mostly for male readers, newspapers also added special sections devoted to household tips, fashion, decorum, and club news to capture female readers. Like crime and disaster stories, sports and women's sections helped to make news a mass commodity.

By the early twentieth century, mass-circulation magazines were overshadowing the expensive elitist journals of earlier eras. Publications such as *McClure's*, *Saturday Evening Post*, and *Ladies' Home Journal* offered human-interest stories, muckraking exposés, titillating fiction, photographs, and eye-catching ads to a growing mass market. Meanwhile, the total number of books published more than quadrupled between 1880 and 1917. This rising popular consumption of news and books reflected growing literacy (94 percent in 1920).

Magazines for the Mass Market

Other forms of communication also expanded. In 1891 there was less than one telephone for every 100 people in the United States; by 1921 the number had swelled to 12.6. In 1900 Americans used 4 billion postage stamps; in 1922 they used 14.3 billion. The term *community* took on new dimensions, as people used the media, mail, and telephone to extend their horizons far beyond their immediate localities. More than ever before, people in different parts of the country knew about and discussed the same news event. America was becoming a mass society.

To some extent, new amusements and pastimes had a homogenizing influence, bringing together ethnic and social groups to share a common experience. Yet different groups of consumers often used new leisure activities to reinforce their own cultural habits. In some communities, for example, working-class immigrants occupied parks and amusement areas as sites for family and ethnic gatherings. To the dismay of reformers who hoped that recreation would assimilate newcomers and teach them habits of restraint, immigrants used picnics and Fourth of July celebrations as occasions for boisterous drinking and sometimes violent behavior.

 ## Promises of Mobility

Baptist minister Russell Conwell delivered the same sermon more than six thousand times across the United States between the Civil War and the First World War. Titled "Acres of Diamonds,"

this popular lecture affirmed the faith that any American could achieve success. People did not have to look far for riches, Conwell preached; acres of diamonds lay at their feet. Night after night he would insist to his audience that it was one's "Christian and Godly duty" to attain riches. Basically, there were three ways a person could get ahead: occupational advancement; acquisition of property; and migration to an area that offered better conditions and greater opportunity. These options were open chiefly to white men.

Many women held paying jobs, owned property, and migrated, but their economic standing was usually defined by the men in their lives—husbands, fathers, or other male kin. Women could improve their status by marrying men with wealth or potential, but other avenues were mostly closed. Men and women who were African-American, American Indian, Mexican-American, or Asian-American had even fewer opportunities. Pinned to the bottom of society by prejudice, they were forced to accept their imposed station.

For large numbers of people, however, occupational mobility was a reality, thanks to urban and industrial expansion. Thousands of new businesses were needed to supply goods and services to burgeoning urban populations. As corporations grew and centralized their operations, they required new managerial personnel. If few Americans were able to go from rags to riches, a considerable number were able to go from rags to moderate success.

Occupational Mobility

Rates of occupational mobility in American communities were slow but steady between 1870 and 1920. Some men slipped from a higher to a lower rung on the occupational ladder, but rates of upward movement usually doubled those of downward movement. Though patterns were not consistent, immigrants generally experienced less upward and more downward mobility than the native-born did. Still, regardless of birthplace, the chances for a white male to rise occupationally over the course of his career or to have a higher-status job than his father had were relatively good.

In addition to, or instead of, advancing occupationally, a person could achieve social mobility by acquiring property. But property was not easy to acquire. Banks and savings-and-loan institutions had far stricter lending practices than they did after the 1930s, when the federal government began to insure real-estate financing. Before then, mortgage loans carried high interest rates and short repayment periods. Thus renting, even of single-family houses, was common, especially in big cities. A general rise in wage rates nevertheless enabled many families to amass savings, which they could use as down payments on property. Ownership rates varied regionally—higher in western cities, lower in eastern cities—but 36 percent of all urban American families owned their homes in 1900, the highest homeownership rate of any Western nation except for Denmark, Norway, and Sweden.

Acquisition of Property

Following the maxim that movement means improvement, millions of families each year packed up and moved elsewhere. The urge to move affected every region, every city. From Boston to San Francisco, from Minneapolis to San Antonio, no more than half the families residing in a city at any one time were still there ten years later.

Residential Mobility

In addition to movement between cities, extraordinary numbers of people moved within the same city. In American communities today, one in every five families changes residence in a given year. A hundred years ago, the proportion was closer to one in four or one in three. Population turnover affected almost every neighborhood, every ethnic and occupational group.

Rapid residential flux undermined the stability of even the most homogeneous neighborhoods. Because immigrants rapidly dispersed from their original places of settlement, it was rare for a single nationality to make up a clear majority in any large area, even when that area was known as Little Italy, Jewtown, Polonia, or Greektown. Ethnically homogeneous districts did exist in New York, Boston, and other eastern ports, and people tended to change residences within those districts rather than leave altogether. Elsewhere, however, most white immigrant fam-

Ethnic Neighborhoods and Ghettos

ilies lived in ethnically mixed neighborhoods rather than in ghettos.

In most cities an area's institutions and enterprises, more than the people who actually lived there, identified a district as an ethnic neighborhood. A Bohemian Town, for example, received its nickname because it was the location of Swoboda's Bakery, Cermak's Drug Store, Cecha's Jewelry, Knezacek's Meats, St. Wenceslaus Church, and the Bohemian Benevolent Association. Such institutions gave the district an ethnic identity even though the surrounding neighborhood was mixed and unstable.

The West provides an arena for studying concepts of race in the late nineteenth century. Anglos (native-born whites) tended to identify four non-

Race and Discrimination

white races but in doing so created racial identities for people who, except for blacks, previously had not thought of themselves as a single race. Hispanics, born in the United States and in Mexico, were

Though Chinese immigrants struggled, like other immigrants, to succeed in American society, they often faced severe discrimination because of their different lifestyles. As this photo of a San Francisco grocery shows, Chinese looked, dressed, and ate differently than did white Americans. Occasionally, they suffered from racist violence that caused them to fear not only for their personal safety but also for the safety of establishments like this one that might suffer damage from resentful mobs.   The Bancroft Library, University of California.

mixtures of Spanish, Indian, and African ancestry and had their own racial distinctions. Asians, often called "Mongolians" by whites, also had internal divisions, not only between Chinese and Japanese but within those two nationalities. And whites imposed on Indians a racial unity that never existed.

Whites used racial distinctions to characterize nonwhites with derogatory stereotypes and to make them victims of discrimination, thereby stifling their mobility. Wherever Asians and Mexicans settled, they encountered discrimination in housing, employment, and other facets of public life. Although these groups often preferred to remain separate in Chinatowns and *barrios*, Anglos also made every effort to keep them confined.

The same discrimination trapped African-Americans at the bottom of the occupational ladder and limited their housing opportunities. Whites organized protective associations that pledged not to sell homes to blacks and occasionally used violence to scare them away from white neighborhoods. In almost every city, blacks concentrated into homogeneous residential districts. By 1920 in Chicago, Detroit, Cleveland, and other cities outside the South, two-thirds or more of the total African-American population lived in only 10 percent of the residential area. Within these districts, they nurtured cultural institutions that helped them adjust to urban life. But the ghettos also bred frustration, the result of stunted opportunity and racial bigotry.

All groups, however, including people of color, could and did move—if not from one neighborhood to another, then from one city to another. Americans were always seeking greener pastures, and hope for better conditions elsewhere acted as a safety valve, relieving some of the tensions and frustrations that simmered inside the city. If migration, occupational mobility, and property acquisition offered little hope of improvement or relief, there was still one sphere to which city dwellers could turn: politics.

 ## The Politics of Bossism and Civic Reform

City governments faced daunting challenges in the late nineteenth century. Burgeoning populations, business expansion, and technological change created urgent needs for sewers, police and fire protection, schools, parks, and other services. Such needs strained municipal resources beyond their capacities. Furthermore, city governments approached these needs in a disorganized fashion.

Power thrives on confusion, and out of governmental chaos arose political machines, organizations whose main goals were the rewards—money, influence, and prestige—of getting and keeping political power. Machine politicians routinely used bribery and graft to further their ends. But machines needed popular support, and they could not have succeeded if they had not provided relief, security, and services to large numbers of people. By meeting those needs machine politicians accomplished things that other agencies had been unable or unwilling to attempt.

Political Machines

Machines bred political bosses, leaders who could smooth the way so that special-interest groups could attain their goals and who could simultaneously meet the needs of urban working classes. Bosses and machines established power bases among new immigrant voters and used politics to solve important urban problems. Most bosses had immigrant backgrounds and had grown up in the inner city, so they knew their constituents' needs firsthand. Machines made politics a full-time profession. And while fraud, bribery, and thievery tainted the system, bosses and machines were rarely as evil as critics charged.

The system rested on a popular base and was held together by loyalty and service. Machines were coalitions of smaller organizations that derived power directly from inner-city neighborhoods inhabited by native and immigrant working classes. In return for votes, bosses provided jobs, built parks and bathhouses, distributed food and clothing to the needy, and helped when someone ran afoul of the law. Such personalized service cultivated mass attachment to the boss; never before had public leaders assumed such responsibility for people in need.

Techniques of Bossism

To finance their activities and campaigns, bosses exchanged favors for votes or money. Power over local government enabled machines to control the letting of public contracts, the granting of utility or streetcar franchises, and the distribution of city jobs. Recipients of city business and jobs were expected to repay the machine with a portion of their profits or salaries and to cast supporting votes on election day. Critics called this process graft; bosses called it gratitude. Machines constructed public buildings, sewer systems, and mass-transit lines that otherwise might not have been built; but bribes and kickbacks made such projects costly to taxpayers. In addition, machines dispersed favors to legal and illegal businesses. Payoffs from gambling, prostitution, and illegal liquor traffic became important sources of machine revenue.

While bosses were consolidating their power, others were attempting to destroy them. Many middle- and upper-class Americans feared that immigrant-based political machines menaced the republic and that unsavory alliances between bosses and businesses wastefully depleted municipal finances. Anxious over the poverty, crowding, and disorder that accompanied population expansion, and convinced that urban services were making taxes too high, civic reformers organized to install more responsible leaders at the helm of urban administrations.

Urban reform arose in part from the industrial system's emphasis on eliminating inefficiency. Government could be made more competent, business-minded reformers were convinced, if it were run like a business. The only way to achieve this goal, they believed, was to elect officials who would hold down expenses and prevent corruption. Thus they decided that they must reduce city budgets, make public employees work more efficiently, and cut taxes.

To impose sound business principles on government, civic reformers supported structural changes such as the city-manager and commission

Structural Reforms in Government

forms of government and nonpartisan citywide election of officials. These reforms were meant to put decision making in the hands of experienced experts. Armed with such strategies, reformers believed they could cleanse party politics and undermine bosses' power bases in

the neighborhoods. They rarely realized, however, that bosses succeeded because they used government to meet people's needs. Reformers only noticed the waste and corruption that machines bred.

A few reform mayors moved beyond structural changes to address social problems. Hazen S. Pingree of Detroit, Samuel "Golden Rule" Jones of Toledo, and Tom Johnson of Cleveland worked to provide jobs for poor people, reduce charges by transit and utility companies, and promote governmental responsibility for the welfare of all citizens. They also supported public ownership of gas, electric, and telephone companies, a quasi-socialist reform that alienated their business allies. But few civic reformers could match the bosses' political savvy; most soon found themselves out of power.

Urban Professionals: Engineers and Social Workers

A different type of reform arose outside politics. Driven by an urge to improve society, social reformers—mostly young and middle class—embarked on campaigns to identify and solve urban problems.

Social Reform

Housing reformers pressed local governments for building codes to ensure safety in tenements. Protestant activists influenced by the Social Gospel reformers, who believed that service to fellow humans was the way to salvation, built churches in slum neighborhoods and urged businesses to be socially responsible. Educational reformers saw public schools as a means of preparing immigrant children for citizenship by teaching them American values as well as the English language.

Perhaps the most ambitious and inspiring feature of urban reform movements was the settlement house. Located in slum neighborhoods and run mostly by women, settlements were buildings where middle-class young people went to live and work in order to bridge the gulf between social classes. The first American settlement house, patterned after London's Toynbee Hall, opened in New York City in 1886, and others quickly appeared in Chicago, Boston, and elsewhere. Early settlement leaders such as Jane Addams and Florence Kelley wanted to improve the lives of slum dwellers by helping them obtain education, appreciation of the arts, better jobs, and better housing. Although working-class and immigrant neighborhood residents sometimes mistrusted them as outsiders, settlement workers attracted support with activities ranging from vocational classes to child-care and ethnic pageants.

As they broadened their scope to fight for school nurses, building safety codes, public playgrounds, and better working conditions, settlement workers became reform leaders in cities and in the nation. Their efforts to involve national and local governments in the solution of social problems later made them the vanguard of the Progressive era, when a reform spirit swept the nation. Moreover, the activities of settlement houses helped create new professional opportunities for women in social work, public health, and child welfare. These professions enabled female reformers to build a dominion of influence over social policy independent of male-dominated professions and to make valuable contributions to national as well as inner-city life.

A contrast developed between white female reformers and black female reformers. Middle-class white women lobbied for government programs to aid needy people and focused on helping mostly white immigrant and native-born working classes. Black women, barred by their race from white political institutions, raised funds from private institutions and focused on helping members of their own race. African-American women were especially active in financing schools, old-age homes, and hospitals, but they also worked for advancement of the race and protection of black women from sexual exploitation. Their ranks included women such as Jane Hunter, who founded a home for unmarried black working women in Cleveland in 1911, and Modjeska Simkins, who organized a program to address health problems among blacks in South Carolina.

Urban reformers wanted to save cities, not abandon them. They believed they could improve urban life by restoring cooperation among all citizens. They often failed to realize, however, that cities were places of great diversity and that differ-

ent people held very different views about what reform actually meant. To civic reformers, distributing city jobs on the basis of civil service exams rather than party loyalty meant progress, but to working-class men, civil service signified reduced employment opportunities. Moral reformers believed that prohibiting the sale of alcoholic beverages would prevent working-class breadwinners from wasting their wages and ruining their health, but immigrants saw such crusades as interference in their private drinking customs. Thus urban reform merged idealism with naiveté and insensitivity.

At the same time, efforts of still a different sort were making cities more livable. Technical and professional creativity, not political or humanitarian action, was required to address sanitation, street lighting, bridge and street construction, and other such needs. In addressing these issues, American urban dwellers, and the engineering profession in particular, developed new systems and standards of worldwide significance.

Engineering Reforms

To solve their problems, cities increasingly depended on engineers. By 1900, engineers were applying technical expertise to devise systems for incinerating refuse, for dumping trash while safeguarding water supplies, for constructing efficient sewers, and for providing for regular street cleaning and snow removal. Engineers also advised officials on budgets and contracts. They had similar influence in matters of street lighting, parks, fire protection, and more.

Engineers and their technology also brought about unheralded but momentous changes in home life. New "systems" of central heating (furnaces), artificial lighting, and modern indoor plumbing created a new kind of consumption first for middle-class households and later for most other households. Whereas formerly families had chopped wood for their cooking and heating, made candles for light, and hauled water for bathing, they now were connected to outside utilities for gas, electricity, and water. Moreover, these utilities erased the inconveniences of nature. Central heat and artificial

Engineers and the Home

light made it possible to enjoy a steady, comfortable temperature and turn night into day.

 ## Conclusion

Much of what American society is today originated in the urbanization of the late nineteenth century. When old-fashioned native inventiveness met the traditions of European, African, and Asian cultures, a new kind of society emerged. It was not so much a melting pot as a salad bowl. As one immigrant priest told a social worker, "There is no such thing as an American." He meant the same thing that literary critic Randolph Bourne meant when he dubbed the United States "a cosmopolitan federation of national colonies." This kind of reasoning produced hyphenated identifications: people considered themselves Irish-American, Italian-American, Polish-American, and the like.

Pluralism and interest-group loyalties enhanced the importance of politics. If America was not a melting pot, then different groups were competing for power, wealth, and status. Some people carried polarization to extremes and tried to suppress everything allegedly un-American. Efforts to enforce homogeneity generally failed. By 1920, immigrants and their offspring outnumbered the native-born in many cities, and the national economy depended on these new workers and consumers. Migrants and immigrants transformed the United States into an urban nation. They gave American culture its rich and varied texture, and they laid the foundations for the liberalism that characterized American politics in the twentieth century.

Suggestions for Further Reading

Urban Growth

Howard P. Chudacoff and Judith E. Smith, *The Evolution of American Urban Society*, 4th ed. (1993); David Goldfield and Blaine Brownell, *Urban America*, 2d ed. (1990); Kenneth T. Jackson, *The Crabgrass Frontier: The Suburbanization of the United States* (1985); Raymond A. Mohl, *The New City* (1985); Jon Teaford, *The Unheralded Triumph: City Government in America, 1870–1900* (1984); Sam Bass Warner, Jr., *The Urban Wilderness* (1982).

Immigration, Ethnicity, and Religion

Aaron I. Abell, *American Catholicism and Social Action* (1960); John Bodnar, *The Transplanted* (1985); John Bodnar, Roger Simon, and Michael P. Weber, *Lives of Their Own: Blacks, Italians, and Poles in Pittsburgh, 1900–1960* (1982); Sucheng Chan, ed., *Entry Denied: Exclusion and the Chinese Community in America, 1882–1943* (1990); Elizabeth Ewen, *Immigrant Women in the Land of Dollars* (1985); Mario T. Garcia, *Desert Immigrants: The Mexicans of El Paso, 1880–1920* (1981); Milton Gordon, *Assimilation in American Life* (1964); Victor Greene, *For God and Country: The Rise of Polish and Lithuanian Ethnic Consciousness in America* (1975); Oscar Handlin, *The Uprooted*, 2d ed. (1973); John Higham, *Strangers in the Land: Patterns of American Nativism* (1955); Yusi Ichioka, *The Issei: The World of the First Japanese Immigrants, 1885–1924* (1988); Matt S. Maier and Felciano Rivera, *The Chicanos* (1972); Henry F. May, *Protestant Churches and Industrial America* (1949); Werner Sollors, *Beyond Ethnicity* (1986); Ron Takaki, *Iron Cages: Race and Culture in Nineteenth-Century America* (1979); Stephan Thernstrom, ed., *Harvard Encyclopedia of American Ethnic Groups* (1980).

Urban Services

Charles W. Cheape, *Moving the Masses* (1980); Lawrence A. Cremin, *American Education: The Metropolitan Experience* (1988); David R. Johnson, *American Law Enforcement* (1981); Martin V. Melosi, *Garbage in the Cities* (1981); Eric Monkkonen, *America Becomes Urban* (1988); Barbara Gutmann Rosencrantz, *Public Health and the State* (1972); Stanley K. Schultz, *Constructing Urban Culture: American Cities and City Planning* (1989); Mel Scott, *American City Planning Since 1890* (1969).

Family and Individual Life Cycles

W. Andrew Achenbaum, *Old Age in the New Land* (1979); George Chauncey, *Gay New York* (1995); Howard P. Chudacoff, *How Old Are You? Age in American Culture* (1989); Carl N. Degler, *At Odds: Women and the Family in America* (1980); John D'Emilio and Estelle B. Freedman, *Intimate Matters: A History of Sexuality in America* (1988); Michael Gordon, ed., *The American Family in Social-Historical Perspective*, 3d ed. (1983); Carole Haber, *Beyond Sixty-five: Dilemmas of Old Age in America's Past* (1983); Tamara K. Hareven, *Family Time and Industrial Time* (1981); Joseph Kett, *Rites of Passage: Adolescence in America* (1979); E. Anthony Rotundo, *American Manhood* (1994).

Mass Entertainment and Leisure

Gunther Barth, *City People* (1980); Jessica H. Foy and Thomas J. Schlereth, eds., *American Home Life, 1880–1930* (1992); Allen Guttmann, *A Whole New Ball Game: An Interpretation of American Sports* (1988); George Juergens, *Joseph Pulitzer and the New York World* (1966); John F. Kasson, *Amusing the Millions: Coney Island at the Turn of the Century* (1978); Frank L. Mott, *American Journalism*, 3d ed. (1962); David Nasaw, *Going Out: The Rise and Fall of Popular Amusements* (1993); Kathy Peiss, *Cheap Amusements: Working Women and Leisure in Turn-of-the-Century New York* (1986); Benjamin G. Rader, *American Sports*

(1983); Steven A. Riess, *City Games* (1989); Roy Rosenzweig, *Eight Hours for What We Will! Workers and Leisure in an Industrial City, 1870–1920* (1983); Robert Sklar, *Movie-Made America* (1976); Ronald A. Smith, *Sports and Freedom: The Rise of Big-Time College Athletics* (1988); Robert V. Snyder, *The Voice of the City: Vaudeville and Popular Culture in New York City, 1880–1920* (1990); Robert C. Toll, *On with the Show: The First Century of Show Business in America* (1976).

Mobility and Race Relations

James Borchert, *Alley Life in Washington* (1980); Howard P. Chudacoff, *Mobile Americans* (1972); Clyde Griffen and Sally Griffen, *Natives and Newcomers* (1977); Jacqueline Jones, *Labor of Love, Labor of Sorrow: Black Women, Work and the Family from Slavery to the Present* (1985); David M. Katzman, *Before the Ghetto* (1973); Kenneth L. Kusmer, *A Ghetto Takes Shape* (1976); Gilbert Osofsky, *Harlem: The Making of a Ghetto* (1966); Elizabeth H. Pleck, *Black Migration and Poverty: Boston, 1865–1900* (1979); Howard N. Rabinowitz, *Race Relations in the Urban South* (1978); Allan H. Spear, *Black Chicago* (1967); Stephan Thernstrom, *The Other Bostonians: Poverty and Progress in the American Metropolis* (1973); Olivier Zunz, *The Changing Face of Inequality* (1982).

Boss Politics

John M. Allswang, *Bosses, Machines and Urban Voters* (1977); Alexander B. Callow, Jr., ed., *The City Boss in America* (1976); Lyle Dorsett, *The Pendergast Machine* (1968); Leo Hershkowitz, *Tweed's New York: Another Look* (1977); Terrence J. McDonald, *The Parameters of Urban Fiscal Policy* (1986); Zane L. Miller, *Boss Cox's Cincinnati* (1968); Bruce M. Stave and Sondra Stave, eds., *Urban Bosses, Machines, and Progressive Reformers* (1984).

Urban Reform

John D. Buenker, *Urban Liberalism and Progressive Reform* (1973); James B. Crooks, *Politics and Progress* (1968); Doris Groshen Daniels, *Always a Sister: The Feminism of Lillian D. Wald* (1989); Allen F. Davis, *Spearheads for Reform* (1967); Lori Ginzberg, *Women and the Work of Benevolence* (1991); Melvin Holli, *Reform in Detroit* (1969); Roy M. Lubove, *The Progressives and the Slums* (1962); Clay McShane, *Technology and Reform* (1974); Robyn Muncy, *Creating a Female Dominion in American Reform* (1991); Martin J. Schiesl, *The Politics of Efficiency* (1977); Kathryn Kish Sklar, *Florence Kelley and the Nation's Work* (1995).

20

Gilded Age Politics
1877 – 1900

Early one winter evening in 1899, E. L. Godkin, one of the nation's most respected editors, spotted two policemen casually conversing. Convinced that the officers were shirking their duty, Godkin filed an indignant complaint with the Police Commissioner. "I [saw] them gossiping . . . and there [was] an air of swagger about them."

What could have made this dignified newspaperman become so irate over an incident so seemingly minor? Godkin believed his society was surrounded by corruption and hypocrisy. The possibility for quick wealth in business and politics, coupled with the resulting bribery and irresponsibility, frightened him. In his view, democracy in the age of industrialism had failed.

To be sure, there was much in American society to disturb Godkin. So-called robber barons were exercising monumental greed in expanding large corporations across the continent. Public servants, from state legislators to congressmen, were swayed and bribed to do the bidding of moneyed men. And vote fraud poisoned elections. The era's venality seemed so widespread that when, twenty years earlier, novelists Mark Twain and Charles Dudley Warner published their novel, *The Gilded Age*, satirizing America as a land of shallow money grubbers, the name stuck: historians have used the expression "Gilded Age" to characterize the late nineteenth century ever since.

To Godkin, then, those two cops, talking to each other instead of walking their beats as their duty prescribed, were part of the evil undermining American society. Godkin and people like him thought that everyone should conform to their ideals of duty and nobility, and their personal assessment of their era colored the ways in which Americans have thought about the period. But like any historical period, the Gilded Age was one of great complexity.

Between 1877 and 1900, industrialization, urbanization, and the commercialization of agriculture altered politics and government as much as they shaped everyday life. Congress grappled with railroad regulation, tariffs, currency, civil service, and other important issues and had major accomplishments. Meanwhile, the judiciary supported big business by consistently defending property rights against state and federal regulation. The presidency was occupied by honest, respectable men.

Three phenomena shaped Gilded Age politics: powerful special interests, achievement amid limitations, and exclusion. The influence of powerful private interests—manufacturers, railroad managers, creditors, and wealthy men in general—and the conflict between them and the public interest was the most prominent of the three. Second, despite flaws and corruption and the public's preference for limited government power, governments at the federal and state levels achieved more than historians have credited them with accomplishing. Even so, exclusion—the third phenomenon—prevented the majority of Americans—including women, southern blacks, Indians, uneducated whites, and unnaturalized immigrants—from voting.

Until the 1890s, those phenomena operated within a delicate equilibrium characterized by a stable party system and a balance of power among the country's geographical sections. Then in the 1890s rural discontent erupted in the West and South, and a deep economic depression bared flaws in the industrial system. Amid these crises, a presidential campaign in 1896 stirred Americans as they had not been stirred for a generation.

 ## The Nature of Party Politics

At no other time in the nation's history was public interest in elections more avid than it was between 1870 and 1896. Consistently, 80 to 90 percent of eligible voters cast ballots in local and national elections. (About 50 percent typically do so today.) Politics was more popular than baseball, vaudeville, or circuses. Actual voting was only the final stage in a process that included parades, picnics, and speeches, all of which were as much public amusement as civic responsibility.

Party loyalties in part reflected the pluralism of American society. With the exception of some southerners, groups who opposed interference by government in matters of personal liberty identified with the Democratic Party, and those who believed government could be an agent of moral reform identified with the Republican Party. Democrats included immigrant Catholics and Jews. Republicans consisted mostly of native and immigrant Protestants. Democrats took a restricted view of government power. Republicans believed in direct government action.

Cultural-Political Alignments

At the state and local levels, adherents of these two cultural traditions battled over how much control government should exercise over people's lives. The most contentious issues were use of leisure time and celebration of Sunday, the Lord's day. To prevent desecration of the Christian Sabbath, Protestant Republicans favored "blue laws" that prohibited baseball games or the opening of stores on Sunday. Immigrant Democrats, accustomed to feasting and playing after church, fought saloon closings and other restrictions on the only day they had free for fun and relaxation. Similar splits developed over public versus parochial schools and prohibition versus the free availability of liquor.

Allegiances to national parties and candidates were so evenly divided that no faction or party gained control for any sustained period of time. Between 1877 and 1897, Republicans held the presidency for three terms, Democrats for two, and only rarely did the same party control the presidency and both houses of Congress simultaneously.

• *Important Events* •

1873	Congress ends coinage of silver dollars	**1890**	McKinley Tariff raises tariff rates
1873–78	Economic hard times hit		Sherman Silver Purchase Act commits Treasury to buying 4.5 million ounces of silver each month
1876	Rutherford B. Hayes elected president		
1877	*Munn* v. *Illinois* upholds state regulation of railroad rates		"Billion-Dollar Congress" passes first federal budget surpassing $1 billion
1878	Bland-Allison Act requires Treasury to buy between $2 million and $4 million worth of silver each month	**1892**	Populist convention in Omaha draws up reform platform
			Cleveland elected president
	Susan B. Anthony–backed bill for women's suffrage amendment is defeated in Congress	**1893–97**	Major economic depression hits United States
		1893	Sherman Silver Purchase Act repealed
1880	James Garfield elected president	**1894**	Wilson-Gorman Tariff attempts to reduce tariff rates; Senate Republicans restore cuts made by House
1881	Garfield assassinated; Chester Arthur assumes the presidency		
1883	Pendleton Civil Service Act creates Civil Service Commission to oversee competitive examinations for government positions		Pullman strike; Eugene V. Debs arrested and turns to socialism
			Coxey's army marches on Washington, D.C.
1884	Grover Cleveland elected president	**1895**	President Cleveland deals with bankers to save the gold reserve
1886	*Wabash* case declares that only Congress can limit interstate commerce rates		
		1896	William McKinley elected president
		1897	Dingley Tariff raises duties
1887	Interstate Commerce Act creates commission to regulate rates and practices of interstate shippers		*Maximum Freight Rate* decision rules that the Interstate Commerce Commission has no power to set rates
1888	Benjamin Harrison elected president	**1900**	Gold Standard Act requires all paper money to be backed by gold
1880s–1890s	Farm prices collapse		McKinley reelected president

Republicans and Democrats competed against each other, but internal quarrels split both parties. Among Republicans, one faction was known as the "Stalwarts," led by New York's pompous Senator Roscoe Conkling. Conkling worked the spoils system to win government jobs for his supporters. The Stalwarts' rivals were the "Half Breeds," led by James G. Blaine

Party Factions

of Maine, who pursued influence as blatantly as Conkling did. On the sidelines were the more idealistic Republicans, or "Mugwumps." Mugwumps such as Senator Carl Schurz of Missouri believed that only righteous, educated men like themselves should govern. Meanwhile, the Democrats tended to subdivide into white-supremacy southerners, immigrant-stock and working-class urban political machines, and business-oriented advocates of low tariffs. Like Republicans, Democrats eagerly pursued the spoils of office.

 ## National Issues

In Congress, political and economic issues such as sectional controversies, patronage abuses, railroad regulation, tariffs, and currency provoked heated debates. Well into the 1880s, bitter hostilities left from the Civil War continued to divide Americans. Republicans capitalized on war memories by "waving the bloody shirt" at Democrats. In the South, Democratic candidates also waved the bloody shirt, calling Republicans traitors to white supremacy and states' rights.

Sectional Conflict

Other Americans also sought advantages by invoking memories of the war. The Grand Army of the Republic, an organization of more than 400,000 Union army veterans, allied with the Republican Party and cajoled Congress into providing generous pensions for former Union soldiers and their widows. Many pensions were deserved, but for many veterans, the war's emotional wake provided an opportunity to profit at public expense.

Few politicians could dare to oppose Civil War pensions, but some attempted to dismantle the spoils system. The practice of awarding government jobs to party workers, regardless of their qualifications, had taken root before the Civil War and flourished after it. As the postal service and other government activities expanded, so did the public payroll. Between 1865 and 1891 the number of federal jobs tripled, from 53,000 to 166,000. Elected officials scrambled to control these jobs as a means of cementing support for themselves and their parties. In return for comparatively short hours and high pay, appointees to federal jobs pledged their votes and a portion of their earnings to their patrons.

Civil Service Reform

Shocked by such corruption, some reformers began advocating appointments and promotions based on merit rather than political connections. Civil service became a fervent reform crusade in 1881 with the formation of the National Civil Service Reform League. The same year, the assassination of President James Garfield by a frustrated and demented job seeker hastened the drive for reform.

The Pendleton Civil Service Act, passed by Congress in 1882 and signed by President Chester Arthur in 1883, outlawed political contributions by officeholders and created the Civil Service Commission to oversee competitive examinations for government positions. The act gave the commission jurisdiction over only about 10 percent of federal jobs, though the president could expand the list.

Civil War pensions and civil service reform were not representative issues of the Gilded Age, however. Rather, economic policymaking occupied congressional business more than ever before in the nation's history. Railroad expansion had become a particularly controversial issue. As the rail network spread, so did competition. In their quest for customers, railroad lines reduced rates to outmaneuver rivals, but rate wars soon cut into profits and wildly fluctuating rates angered shippers and farmers. On noncompetitive routes, railroads often boosted rates as high as possible to compensate for low rates on competitive routes. Thus charges on short-distance shipments served by only one line could be far higher than those on long-distance shipments served by competing lines. Railroads also reduced rates to large shippers and offered free passenger passes to preferred customers and politicians.

Such favoritism stirred farmers, small merchants, and reform politicians to demand public regulation of railroad rates. Attempts at regulation occurred first at the state level. By 1880, fourteen states had established commissions to limit the freight and storage charges of state-chartered lines. Railroads fought these measures, arguing that the Constitution guaranteed them freedom to acquire and use property without government restraint. But in 1877, in *Munn* v. *Illinois*, the Supreme Court upheld the principle of rate regulation by the states.

Railroad Regulation

State legislatures, however, could not regulate large interstate lines, a limitation affirmed by the Supreme Court in the *Wabash* case of 1886, in which the Court declared that only Congress could limit rates involving interstate commerce. Congress responded in 1887 by passing the Interstate Commerce Act. The act prohibited pools, rebates, and long-haul/short-haul rate discrimination. It also created the Interstate Commerce Commission (ICC) to investigate railroad rate-making methods, issue cease-and-desist orders against illegal practices, and seek court aid to enforce compliance. The legislation's lack of provisions for enforcement left the railroads ample room for evasion, and federal judges chipped away at ICC powers. In the *Maximum Freight Rate* case (1897), the Supreme Court ruled that the ICC did not have power to set rates; and in the *Alabama Midlands* case (1897), the Court overturned prohibitions against long-haul/short-haul discrimination. Even so, the principle of government regulation, though weakened, remained in force.

The economic issue of tariffs carried strong political implications. Congress initially had created tariffs to protect American manufactured goods and some agricultural products from European competition. But tariffs quickly became a tool by which special interests could protect and enhance their profits. By the 1880s separate tariffs applied to more than four thousand items. A few economists and farmers argued for free trade, but most politicians still insisted that tariffs were a necessary form of government assistance to support industry and preserve jobs.

Tariff Policy

The Republican Party, claiming credit for economic growth, put protective tariffs at the core of its political agenda. Democrats complained that tariffs made prices artificially high by keeping out less expensive foreign goods, thereby benefiting manufacturers while hurting farmers whose crops were not protected and consumers who had to buy manufactured goods. Thus Democrats, while acknowledging a need for tariff protection of some manufactured goods and raw materials, favored lower rates to encourage foreign trade and to reduce an embarrassing Treasury surplus.

Manufacturers and their congressional allies maintained control over tariff policy. The McKinley Tariff of 1890 boosted already-high rates by another 4 percent. When House Democrats supported by President Grover Cleveland passed a bill to reduce

tariff rates in 1894, Senate Republicans, aided by southern Democrats eager to protect their region's infant industries, added six hundred amendments restoring most of the cuts (Wilson-Gorman Tariff). In 1897 the Dingley Tariff raised rates further.

Monetary policy aroused even stronger emotions than did the tariff. When increased industrial and agricultural production caused prices to fall after the Civil War, debtors and creditors had opposing reactions. Farmers suffered because the prices they received for their crops were dropping, but they had to pay high interest rates on money they borrowed to pay off their mortgages and other debts. They favored schemes like the coinage of silver to increase the amount of currency in circulation. An expanded money supply, they reasoned, would make their debts less burdensome because interest rates would be lower, and thus their costs would be lower relative to the prices they received for their crops. Creditors believed that overproduction had caused prices to decline. They favored a more stable, limited money supply backed by gold as the best means to maintain investors' confidence in the United States economy.

Monetary Policy

Underlying the money issue were other conflicts, both social and regional. Creditor-debtor conflict translated into class divisions between haves and have-nots. The debate also represented sectional cleavages: western silver-mining areas and agricultural regions of the South and West against the more conservative industrial Northeast.

By the early 1870s, the currency controversy had boiled down to gold versus silver. Previously, the government had coined both gold and silver dollars. A silver dollar weighed sixteen times more than a gold dollar, meaning that gold was officially worth sixteen times more than silver. Gold discoveries after 1848, however, increased the supply of gold and lowered its market price relative to the price of silver. When silver came to be worth more than one-sixteenth the value of gold, silver producers preferred to sell their metal on the open market rather than to the government. Silver dollars disappeared from circulation—because of their inflated value, owners hoarded them—and in 1873 Congress officially stopped coining silver dollars, an act that silver partisans later called the "Crime of '73." Europeans also stopped buying silver, and the United States and many of its trading partners unofficially adopted the gold standard, meaning that their currency was backed chiefly by gold.

Within a few years, new mines in the American West began to flood the market with silver, and its price dropped. Gold then became worth *more* than sixteen times the value of silver. It would have been worthwhile to sell silver to the government in return for gold, but the government was no longer buying silver. Debtors, hurt by falling prices and the economic hard times of 1873–1878, saw silver as a means of expanding the currency supply. They joined with silver producers to denounce the "Crime of '73" and press for the resumption of silver coinage at the old sixteen-to-one ratio.

Split into silver and gold factions, Congress at first tried to compromise. The Bland-Allison Act of 1878 required the Treasury to buy between $2 million and $4 million worth of silver each month, and the Sherman Silver Purchase Act of 1890 increased the government's monthly purchase of silver by specifying weight (4.5 million ounces) rather than dollars. Neither act satisfied the different interest groups. The minting of silver dollars, which these laws allowed, failed to expand the money supply as substantially as debtors had hoped, and it failed to erase the impression that the government favored creditors' interests.

Amid debates over tariffs and money, Congress and the state legislatures heard fervent arguments from supporters of women's suffrage. In 1878 Susan B. Anthony persuaded Senator A. A. Sargent of California to introduce a constitutional amendment stating that "the right of citizens of the United States to vote shall not be denied or abridged by the United States or by any state on account of sex." A Senate committee killed the bill, but the National Woman Suffrage Association (NWSA) had it reintroduced repeatedly over the next eighteen years. On the few occasions when the bill reached the Senate floor, it was voted down by

Women's Suffrage

senators who claimed that suffrage would interfere with women's family obligations and ruin female virtue.

While the NWSA fought for suffrage on the national level, the American Woman Suffrage Association worked for amendments to state constitutions. (The two groups merged in 1890 to form the National American Woman Suffrage Association.) Between 1870 and 1910, eleven states (eight of them in the West) legalized women's suffrage. By 1890 nineteen states allowed women to vote on school issues, and three granted suffrage on tax and bond issues.

During the Gilded Age, some members of Congress were tools of special interests, but most had to satisfy conflicting interests. The close and intense two-party rivalry often resulted in stalemate, but what is surprising is how much legislation was passed, not how little. Both the tariff and currency issues signaled that Congress believed the federal government should play a large part in determining economic policy and prosperity. The legislation creating the Interstate Commerce Commission and Civil Service Commission represented new directions toward government regulation.

Legislative Accomplishments

The Presidency Restrengthened

Operating under the cloud of Andrew Johnson's impeachment, Grant's scandals, and doubts about the legitimacy of the election of 1876, American presidents between 1877 and 1900 moved gingerly to restore the authority of their office. Proper and honest, Presidents Rutherford Hayes (1877–1881), James Garfield (1881), Chester Arthur (1881–1885), Grover Cleveland (1885–1889 and 1893–1897), Benjamin Harrison (1889–1893), and William McKinley (1897–1901) tried to act as legislative as well as administrative leaders. Moreover, each initiated legislation and used the veto to combat Congress and guide national policy.

Rutherford B. Hayes emphasized national unity over sectional rivalry and opposed violence of all kinds. When Hayes ordered out troops to

**Hayes,
Garfield,
and Arthur**

disperse railroad strikers in 1877, he acted not to suppress them but because he believed the rioting and looting that the strikes engendered threatened social harmony. He tried to overhaul the spoils system by appointing civil service reformer Carl Schurz to his cabinet and by battling New York's patronage king, Senator Conkling. Hayes believed society was obligated to help the oppressed, including American Chinese and Indians, and after retiring from the presidency, he worked diligently to aid former slaves.

When Hayes declined to run for reelection in 1880, Republicans nominated another Ohio Congress member and Civil War hero, James A. Garfield. A solemn and cautious man, Garfield defeated Democrat Winfield Scott Hancock, also a Civil War hero, by just 40,000 votes out of 9 million cast. Garfield spent most of his brief presidency trying to secure an independent position among party potentates. He hoped to reduce the tariff and develop United States economic interests in Latin America. His chance to make lasting contributions ended in July 1881 when he was shot by a disappointed patronage seeker.

Garfield's vice president and successor was New York's Chester A. Arthur, a spoilsman Hayes had fired in 1878. Though his elevation to the presidency made reformers shudder, Arthur became a dignified and temperate executive. He signed the Pendleton Civil Service Act, urged Congress to modify outdated tariff rates, and supported federal regulation of railroads. He wielded the veto aggressively, killing several bills that excessively benefited privileged interests. But congressional partisans frustrated his hopes for reducing the tariff and building up the navy. Arthur wanted to run for reelection in 1884, but lost the nomination to James G. Blaine.

To oppose Blaine, Democrats named New York governor Grover Cleveland, a bachelor who had tainted his respectable reputation when he fathered an illegitimate son—a fact he admitted during the campaign. On election day Cleveland beat Blaine by only 23,000 popular votes; his tiny margin of 1,149 votes in New York gave him that state's 36 electoral votes and victory in the electoral college. Cleveland may have won New York thanks to last-minute efforts of a local Protestant minister, who publicly equated Democrats with "rum, Romanism, and rebellion." Democrats used the slur to get New York's Irish Catholics to turn out and vote for Cleveland.

Cleveland, the first Democratic president since James Buchanan (1857–1861), tried to exert vigorous leadership. He vetoed excessive pension bills and expanded the merit-based civil service. He acted most forcefully for tariff reform. Worried about the growing Treasury surplus, Cleveland urged Congress to cut duties on raw materials and manufactured goods. When advisers warned that his stand might weaken his chances for reelection, the president retorted, "What is the use of being elected or reelected, unless you stand for something?" But the Mills tariff bill of 1888, passed by the House in response to Cleveland's wishes, died in the Senate.

**Cleveland and
Harrison**

In 1888 the Republicans nominated Benjamin Harrison, a former senator from Indiana and grandson of President William Henry Harrison, to oppose Cleveland. The campaign was less savage than that of 1884 but far from clean. Bribery and multiple voting helped Harrison to win Indiana and New York. (Democrats also indulged in bribery and vote fraud, but this time Republicans proved more successful at it.) Those states assured Harrison's victory.

Harrison was the first president since 1875 whose party had majorities in both houses of Congress. Using a variety of methods, ranging from threats of vetoes to informal dinners and consultations, Harrison helped guide the course of legislation. He also showed his support for civil service by appointing the energetic reformer Theodore Roosevelt a civil service commissioner. Yielding to pressure, Congress enacted and Harrison signed the Dependents' Pension Act. The law increased the number of welfare recipients from 490,000 to 966,000 by providing disability pensions for Union veterans and aid to their widows and minor children.

The Pension Act and other grants and appropriations pushed the federal budget past $1 billion in 1890 for the first time in the nation's history. Democrats blamed the "Billion-Dollar Congress" on spendthrift Republicans. Seeking to capitalize on voters' irritation with incumbents, Democrats nominated Cleveland to run against Harrison again in 1892. This time Cleveland attracted large contributions from business and beat Harrison.

In office once more, Cleveland moved boldly to address problems of currency, tariffs, and labor unrest. But his actions reflected a narrow orientation toward the interests of business and bespoke political weakness. During his campaign Cleveland had promised sweeping tariff reform, but he made little effort to line up support in the Senate. And during the bitter Pullman strike of 1894, Cleveland bowed to requests from railroad managers and Attorney General Richard Olney to send in troops. Throughout Cleveland's second term, events at home—particularly economic downturn and agrarian ferment—seemed too much for the president.

 ## Agrarian Unrest and Populism

While the federal government labored to sustain prosperity, inequities in the new agricultural and industrial order were arousing a mass movement that was to shake American society. An agrarian revolt began in Grange organizations in the early 1870s. The revolt accelerated when Farmers' Alliances formed in Texas in the late 1870s and the Alliance movement spread across the Cotton Belt and Great Plains in the 1880s. The movement caught on chiefly in areas where farm tenancy, crop liens, merchants, railroads, banks, weather, and insects threatened the well-being of hopeful farmers. Once under way, the agrarian rebellion inspired visions of a truly cooperative and democratic society.

Agricultural expansion in the West, Great Plains, and South exposed millions of people to the hardships of rural life. Uncertainties might have been more bearable if rewards had been more promising, but such was not the case. As growers cultivated more land, as mechanization boosted productivity, and as foreign competition increased, supplies exceeded national and worldwide demand for agricultural products. Consequently, prices for staple crops dropped steadily. Meanwhile, transportation, storage, and sales fees remained high relative to other prices. Expenses for seed, fertilizer, manufactured goods, taxes, and mortgage interest trapped many farm families in troubling and sometimes desperate circumstances. In order to buy necessities and pay bills, farmers had to produce more, but the more they produced, the more crop prices fell.

Even before the full impact of these developments was felt, small farmers began to organize. With aid from Oliver H. Kelley, a clerk in the Department of Agriculture, farmers in almost every state during the 1860s and 1870s founded local organizations called Granges. By 1875 the Grange had twenty thousand branches and more than a million men and women members. Strongest in the Midwest and South, Granges at first served a chiefly social function, sponsoring meetings and educational events to help relieve the loneliness of farm life.

Grange Movement

As membership flourished, Granges turned to economic and political action. Local branches formed cooperative associations to buy equipment and supplies and to market crops and livestock. In a few instances, Grangers operated farm-implement factories and insurance companies. Most of these enterprises failed, however, because farmers lacked capital for cooperative buying and because competition from large manufacturers and dealers undercut them.

Grangers used their numbers to some political advantage, especially in convincing states to adopt so-called Granger laws to regulate transportation and storage rates. But these efforts faltered when corporations won court support to overturn Granger laws. Granges disavowed party politics, but could not withstand the power of business interests within the two major parties. Thus after a brief assertion of influence, the Granges again became farmers' social clubs.

Rural activism shifted to the Farmers' Alliances. The first Farmers' Alliances arose in Texas, where hard-pressed small farmers rallied against crop liens, merchants, and railroads in particular, and against "money power" in general. Using traveling lecturers to recruit members, Alliance leaders extended the movement to other southern states. By 1889 the southern Alliance boasted 3 million members, including the powerful Colored Farmers' National Alliance, which claimed over 1 million black members. A similar movement flourished in the Great Plains, where by the late 1880s 2 million members were organized in Kansas, Nebraska, and the Dakotas.

Farmers' Alliances

Like Granges, Farmers' Alliances advocated cooperative buying and selling and had women members, but they also proposed a scheme to relieve the most serious rural problems: lack of cash and lack of credit. Called the subtreasury plan, it had two parts. The first called for the federal government to construct warehouses where farmers could store nonperishable crops while awaiting higher prices; the government would then loan farmers Treasury notes amounting to 80 percent of the market price that the stored grain or cotton would bring. Farmers could use these notes as legal tender to pay debts and make purchases. Once the stored crops were sold, farmers would repay the loans plus a small amount of interest and storage fees. The second part called for the government to provide low-interest loans to farmers who wanted to buy land.

Subtreasury Plan

Growing membership and rising confidence drew the Alliances more deeply into politics. By 1890, farmers had elected several officeholders sympathetic to their programs, especially in the South. In the Midwest, Alliance candidates often ran on third-party tickets and achieved some success in Kansas, Nebraska, and the Dakotas.

Rise of Populism

During the summer of 1890, the Kansas Alliance held a "convention of the people" and nominated candidates who swept the state's fall elections. Formation of this People's Party, whose members were called Populists (from *populus*, the Latin word for "people"), gave a name to Alliance political activism. Two years later, after overcoming regional differences, the People's Party held a national convention in Omaha, where they drafted a platform and nominated a presidential candidate.

The new party's Omaha platform was one of the most comprehensive reform documents in American history. It addressed the three central sources of rural unrest: transportation, land, and money. Frustrated with weak state and federal regulation, Populists demanded government ownership of railroad and telegraph lines. They urged the federal government to reclaim all land owned for speculative purposes by railroads and foreigners. The monetary plank called for the government to inflate the currency system by printing money to be made available for farm loans and by basing the money on the free and unlimited coinage of silver. Other planks advocated a graduated income tax, postal savings banks, direct election of United States senators, and a shorter workday. As its presidential candidate, the People's Party nominated James B. Weaver of Iowa, a former Union general.

Weaver garnered 8 percent of the total popular vote in 1892, majorities in four states, and twenty-two electoral votes. Not since 1856 had a third party won so many votes in its first national effort. Nevertheless, disturbing factors had emerged. The party's central dilemma was whether to stand by its principles at all costs or compromise in order to gain power. The election had been successful for Populists only in the West. The vote-rich Northeast had ignored Weaver; and Alabama was the only southern state that gave the Populists as much as one-third of its votes.

Although Populists were flawed democrats—their mistrust of blacks and foreigners gave them a reactionary streak—they sought change to fulfill their version of American ideals. Amid hardship and desperation, millions of people began to believe that a cooperative democracy in which government would ensure equal opportunity could overcome corporate power.

How do historians know that President Harrison's support for big ranchers provoked small stock raisers to support the People's Party in the West? In April 1892, large cattle ranchers in Johnson County, Wyoming, hired twenty-five Texas gunmen to suppress a group of small stock raisers with whom they were competing for grazing land. The ranchers claimed that the gunmen were necessary to put an end to cattle rustling, but their real intent was intimidation. After the gunmen had killed two alleged rustlers, an angry band of stockmen besieged the mercenaries and threatened armed revolt in what subsequently was called the Johnson County War. Wyoming's governor and senators then petitioned President Harrison for help, and the president responded with the telegram reproduced below. Federal troops rescued the gunmen and sent them home, but the readiness of the Republican-controlled state and federal government to aid large ranchers and their hired army, as the telegram reveals, caused many small stock raisers to oppose what they believed were monopolistic practices and to join the Populist movement.

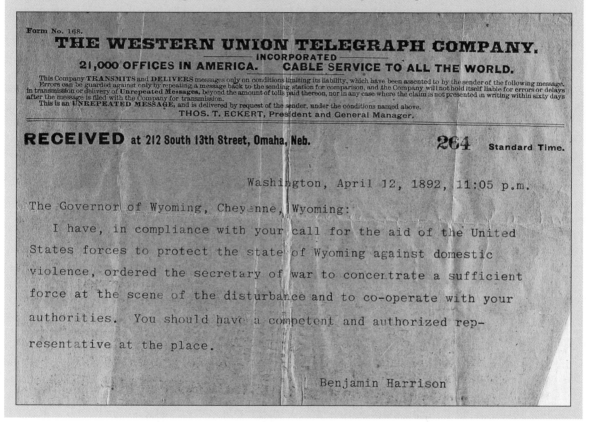

Form No. 168.

THE WESTERN UNION TELEGRAPH COMPANY.

INCORPORATED

21,000 OFFICES IN AMERICA.   CABLE SERVICE TO ALL THE WORLD.

This Company TRANSMITS and DELIVERS messages only on conditions limiting its liability, which have been assented to by the sender of the following message. Errors can be guarded against only by repeating a message back to the sending station for comparison, and the Company will not hold itself liable for errors or delays in transmission or delivery of Unrepeated Messages, beyond the amount of tolls paid thereon, nor in any case where the claim is not presented in writing within sixty days after the message is filed with the Company for transmission.
This is an UNREPEATED MESSAGE, and is delivered by request of the sender, under the conditions named above.
THOS. T. ECKERT, President and General Manager.

RECEIVED at 212 South 13th Street, Omaha, Neb.   **264** Standard Time.

Washington, April 12, 1892, 11:05 p.m.

The Governor of Wyoming, Cheyenne, Wyoming:

I have, in compliance with your call for the aid of the United States forces to protect the state of Wyoming against domestic violence, ordered the secretary of war to concentrate a sufficient force at the scene of the disturbance and to co-operate with your authorities. You should have a competent and authorized representative at the place.

Benjamin Harrison

The Depression of the 1890s

In 1893, shortly before Grover Cleveland's inauguration, the Philadelphia and Reading Railroad, once a thriving and profitable line, went bankrupt. Like other railroads, the Philadelphia and Reading had borrowed heavily to lay track and build stations and bridges. But overexpansion cut into profits, and ultimately the company was unable to pay its debts.

The same problem beset manufacturers. For example, output at McCormick farm machinery factories was nine times greater in 1893 than it had been in 1879, but revenues had only tripled. To compensate, the company bought more machines and squeezed more work out of fewer laborers. This strategy, however, only enlarged debt and increased unemployment. Jobless workers found themselves in the same plight as their employers: they could not pay their creditors. Banks suffered, too, when their customers defaulted. The failure of the National Cordage Company in May 1893 accelerated a chain reaction of business and bank closings. Business and banking failures in early 1893 signaled the onset of a devastating economic depression.

As the depression deepened, the currency problem reached a crisis. The Sherman Silver Purchase Act of 1890 had committed the government to buy 4.5 million ounces of silver each month. Payment was to be in gold, at the ratio of one ounce of gold for every sixteen ounces of silver. But a western mining boom made silver more plentiful, causing its value relative to gold to fall. Thus every month the government exchanged gold, whose worth remained fairly constant, for cheaper silver. Fearing a decrease in the value of the dollar, which was based on Treasury holdings in silver and gold, merchants at home and abroad began to cash in paper money and securities for gold. The nation's gold reserve soon dwindled, falling below the psychologically significant level of $100 million in early 1893.

Currency Problems

Vowing to protect the gold reserve, President Cleveland called a special session of Congress to repeal the Sherman Silver Purchase Act. Repeal passed in late 1893, but the run on the Treasury continued. In early 1895 gold reserves fell to $41 million. In desperation, Cleveland accepted an offer of 3.5 million ounces of gold in return for $62 million worth of federal bonds from a banking syndicate led by financier J. P. Morgan. When the bankers resold the bonds to the public, they profited handsomely at the nation's expense. Cleveland claimed that he had saved the gold reserves, but many saw only humiliation in the president's deal with big businessmen.

Like previous hard times, the depression ultimately ran its course, but the downturn of the 1890s hastened the crumbling of the old economic system and the emergence of a new one. The central features of the new business system—consolidation and a trend toward bigness—had just begun to solidify when the depression hit. The economy of the United States become national rather than sectional; the fortunes of a large business in one part of the country had repercussions elsewhere. By the 1890s many companies had expanded too rapidly. When contraction occurred, their reckless debts dragged them down, and they pulled other industries down with them. In 1893 more than sixteen thousand businesses and five hundred banks filed for bankruptcy. European economies also slumped, and more than ever before, the fortunes of one country affected the fortunes of other countries. The downward spiral ended late in 1897, but the depression exposed problems that demanded reform and set an agenda for the years to come.

Emergence of a New Economic System

 Depression-Era Protests

The depression exposed fundamental tensions in the industrial system. The gap between employees and employers had been widening steadily for half a century. By the 1890s workers' protests against exploitation were threatening to spark a full-fledged economic and political explosion. In 1894 there were over thirteen hundred strikes and countless riots. Contrary to the fears of business leaders, only a few protesters were anarchists or communists who had come from Europe to sabotage American democracy. The disaffected included hundreds of thousands of men and women who believed that in a democracy their voices should be heard.

Small numbers of socialists did participate in the era's strikes and riots, and many workers who never became socialists came to agree with Karl Marx (1818–1883), the German philosopher and father of communism, that whoever controls the means of production holds the power to determine how well people live. Marx had predicted that workers throughout the world would become so discontented that they

Socialism

would revolt and seize factories, farms, banks, and transportation lines. The societies resulting from this revolution would establish a socialist order of justice and equality.

American socialism suffered from a lack of strong leadership. It splintered into small groups, such as the Socialist Labor Party, led by Daniel DeLeon, a fiery West Indian–born lawyer. DeLeon and other socialist leaders failed to attract the mass of unskilled laborers, in part because American socialists often focused on fine points of doctrine while ignoring workers' everyday needs. Social mobility and the philosophy of individualism also undermined socialist aims. Workers hoped that they or their children would improve their lives through education and acquisition of property or by becoming their own boss; thus most workers sought individual advancement rather than the betterment of all.

Events in 1894 triggered changes within the socialist movement. That year an inspiring new socialist leader arose in response to the government's quashing of the Pullman strike and of the newly formed American Railway Union. Eugene V. Debs, the president of the railway union, had become a socialist while serving a six-month prison term for defying an injunction against the strike. Once released, he became the leading spokesman for American socialism. Though never good at organizing, Debs captivated audiences with passionate eloquence and indignant attacks on the free-enterprise system.

Eugene V. Debs

In 1894 Debs shared public attention with Jacob S. Coxey, a quiet businessman from Massillon, Ohio. Like Debs, Coxey had a vision. He was convinced that, to aid debtors, the government should issue $500 million of "legal tender" paper money, make low-interest loans to local governments, and use the loans and money to pay the unemployed to build roads and other public works. He planned to publicize his scheme by leading a march from Massillon to Washington, D.C., gathering a "petition in boots" of unemployed workers along the way.

Coxey's Army

Coxey's army, about two hundred strong, left Massillon in March 1894 and entered Washington on April 30. The next day, the citizen army of five hundred, armed with "war clubs of peace," marched to the Capitol. When Coxey and a few others vaulted the wall surrounding the Capitol grounds, mounted police moved in and routed the crowd. Coxey tried to speak from the Capitol steps, but police dragged him away. As arrests and clubbings continued, Coxey's dream of a demonstration of 400,000 jobless workers dissolved. Like the strikes, the first people's march on Washington had yielded to police muscle.

Coxey's troops merely wanted more jobs and better living standards. Today, their goals do not appear radical. The brutal reactions of officials, however, reveal how threatening dissenters such as Coxey and Debs seemed to the defenders of the existing social order.

 ## Populists, the Silver Crusade, and the Election of 1896

The Populists encountered roadblocks just when their political goals seemed attainable. As late as 1894, Populist candidates made good showings in elections in the West and South. Like earlier third parties, though, Populists were underfinanced and underorganized. They had strong and colorful candidates but not enough of them to effectively challenge the major parties.

Issues of race also stymied voters. The possibility of biracial political action posed by the Farmers' Alliances in the early 1890s failed to materialize for two reasons. First, southern white Democrats had succeeded in preventing African-Americans from becoming a political force by establishing various restrictions on voting rights. Second, raw racism impeded the acceptance of blacks by white Populists. To be sure, some Populists sought to unite distressed black and white farmers, but most poor white farmers were unable to put aside their racism. Thus few Populists addressed the needs of black farmers, and many used white-supremacist rhetoric to evade charges that they encouraged race-mixing.

Stifling of Biracial Political Dissent

African-Americans had their own views about the political process. This drawing, by African-American cartoonist Henry Jackson Lewis, shows three major parties—Democratic, Temperance, and Republican—courting a black voter in 1888. The size differential emphasized Lewis's view of the importance of black voters. DuSable Museum of African American History.

In the national arena, the Populist crusade against "money power" settled on the issue of silver. Many people saw silver as a simple solution to the nation's complex ills. To them, free coinage of silver meant the end of special privileges for the rich and the return of government to the people. Populists made free coinage of silver their political battle cry. But as the election of 1896 approached, they had to decide how to translate their few previous electoral victories into larger success. Should they join with sympathetic factions of the major parties, thus risking a loss of identity, or should they re-

Free Silver

main an independent third party and settle for minor successes at best?

The presidential election of 1896 brought the political turbulence to a climax. Each party was divided. Republicans, directed by Marcus A. Hanna, a prosperous Ohio industrialist, had only minor problems. For over a year, Hanna had been maneuvering to win the nomination for Ohio's governor, William McKinley. By the time the party convened in St. Louis, Hanna had corralled enough delegates to succeed. The Republicans' only distress occurred when the party

Republican Nomination of McKinley

adopted a moderate platform supporting gold, rejecting a prosilver stance proposed by Senator Henry M. Teller of Colorado. Teller, who had been among the party's founders forty years earlier, walked out of the convention in tears, taking a small group of silver Republicans with him.

At the Democratic convention, prosilver delegates paraded through the Chicago Amphitheatre. All they need "is a Moses" quipped a reporter.

William Jennings Bryan

They soon found one in William Jennings Bryan. A former congressman and silverite, the thirty-six year old Nebraskan was highly distressed by the depression's impact on midwestern farmers. As a member of the party's resolutions committee, Bryan helped write a platform calling for free coinage of silver. When the committee presented the platform to the full convention, Bryan rose to speak on its behalf. His now-famous closing words ignited the delegates:

> Having behind us the producing masses of this nation and the world, supported by the commercial interests, the laboring interests, and the toilers everywhere, we will answer their [the wealthy classes'] demand for a gold standard by saying to them: You shall not press down upon the brow of labor this crown of thorns, you shall not crucify mankind upon a cross of gold.

The speech could not have been timed better. Friends who had been pushing Bryan for the presidential nomination now had no trouble enlisting support. Bryan, the "Boy Orator" won the nomination, but some gold Democrats bolted the party and nominated their own candidate.

Bryan's nomination presented the Populist Party (as it was now called) with a dilemma. Should Populists join Democrats in support of Bryan, or should they nominate their own candidate? Tom Watson of Georgia, expressing opposition to fusion with Democrats, warned that "the Democratic idea of fusion [is] that we play Jonah while they play whale." Others reasoned that supporting a different candidate would split the anti-McKinley vote and guarantee a Republican victory. In the end the convention compromised,

first naming Watson as its vice-presidential nominee to preserve party identity and then nominating Bryan for president.

The election results revealed that the political standoff had finally ended. McKinley, symbol of Republican pragmatism and corporate ascendancy,

Election Results

beat Bryan in the most lopsided presidential election since 1872 (see map). Bryan had worked hard to rally the nation, but obsession with silver undermined his effort and prevented Populists from building the urban-rural coalition that would have broadened their political appeal. Moreover, urban workers, most labor leaders, and socialists perceived their interests and needs as being different from those of the nation's farmers. Thus the Populist crusade collapsed.

As president, McKinley signed the Gold Standard Act (1900), which required that all paper money be backed by gold. He also supported the

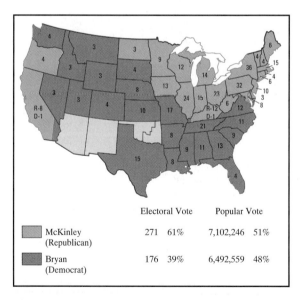

	Electoral Vote		Popular Vote	
McKinley (Republican)	271	61%	7,102,246	51%
Bryan (Democrat)	176	39%	6,492,559	48%

Presidential Election, 1896 *William Jennings Bryan had strong voter support in the South and West, but the numerically superior industrial states, plus California, created majorities for William McKinley.*

The McKinley Presidency

Dingley Tariff of 1897, which raised duties even higher. Domestic tensions subsided during McKinley's presidency; an upward swing of the business cycle and a money supply enlarged by gold discoveries in Alaska, Australia, and South Africa helped restore prosperity.

 ## Conclusion

Government during the Gilded Age was in the hands of many well-meaning people who succeeded in making modest, and some major, accomplishments. Much of what occurred in government prepared the nation for the twentieth century. Laws encouraging economic growth with some principles of regulation, measures expanding government agencies while reducing crass patronage, federal intervention in trade and currency issues, and the emergence of an energetic presidency all evolved during the 1870s and 1880s. Because the division of power between the major parties was so even, politicians had to avoid extreme stands on issues, and the system could not tolerate radical views such as those expressed by socialists, Coxey, or Populists.

The 1896 election realigned national politics. The Republican Party had become the majority party by emphasizing active government aid to business expansion, broadening its social base to include urban workers, and playing down its moralism. The Democratic Party miscalculated on the silver issue and held its traditional support only in the South. After 1896, however, party loyalties weakened and a new kind of politics was brewing, one in which technical experts and scientific organization would attempt to supplant the back-room deals and favoritism that had characterized the previous age.

In retrospect, it is easy to see that the Populists never had a chance. Yet by 1920 many Populist goals would be achieved, including regulation of railroads, banks, and utilities; shorter workdays; a variant of the subtreasury plan; a graduated income tax; direct election of senators; and the secret ballot. The Populist vision of democratic capitalism sustained hope for only a brief historical moment; by the late twentieth century the Populist call for a renunciation of "special privilege" would be transformed into a rejection of the welfare state.

Suggestions for Further Reading

General

Charles W. Calhoun, ed., *The Gilded Age: Essays on the Origins of Modern America* (1995); Sean Denis Cashman, *America in the Gilded Age* (1984); Ray Ginger, *The Age of Excess*, 2d ed. (1975); H. Wayne Morgan, ed., *The Gilded Age* (1970); Nell Irvin Painter, *Standing at Armageddon* (1987); Alan Trachtenberg, *The Incorporation of America: Culture and Society in the Gilded Age* (1982).

Parties and Political Issues

Paula Baker, *The Moral Framework of Public Life* (1991); Beverly Beeton, *Women Vote in the West: The Suffrage Movement, 1869–1896* (1986); Christine Bolt, *American Indian Policy and American Reform* (1987); Elisabeth Griffith, *In Her Own Right: The Life of Elizabeth Cady Stanton* (1984); J. Rogers Hollingsworth, *The Whirligig of Politics: The Democracy of Cleveland and Bryan* (1963); Ari A. Hoogenboom, *Outlawing the Spoils: The Civil Service Movement* (1961); Richard J. Jensen, *The Winning of the Midwest* (1971); Morton Keller, *Affairs of State* (1977); Paul Kleppner, *The Third Electoral System, 1853–1892* (1979); Paul Kleppner, *The Cross of Culture* (1970); Michael E. McGerr, *The Decline of Popular Politics* (1986); Walter T. K. Nugent, *Money and American Society* (1968); A. M. Paul, *Conservative Crisis and the Rule of Law: Attitudes of Bar and Bench, 1887–1895* (1969); John G. Sproat, *The Best Men: Liberal Reformers in the Gilded Age* (1968); Hal R. Williams, *Years of Decision: American Politics in the 1890s* (1978).

The Presidency

Kenneth E. Davison, *The Presidency of Rutherford B. Hayes* (1972); Justus D. Doenecke, *The Presidencies of James A. Garfield and Chester A. Arthur* (1981); Lewis L. Gould, *The Presidency of William McKinley* (1981); Homer E. Socolotsky and Allen B. Spetter, *The Presidency of Benjamin Harrison* (1987); Richard G. Welch, *The Presidency of Grover Cleveland* (1988).

Protest and Socialism

William M. Dick, *Labor and Socialism in America* (1972); Ray Ginger, *Bending Cross: A Biography of Eugene Victor Debs* (1969); Nick Salvatore, *Eugene V. Debs: Citizen and Socialist* (1982);

Carlos A. Schwantes, *Coxey's Army* (1985); David Shannon, *The Socialist Party of America* (1955).

Populism and the Election of 1896

Donna A. Barnes, *Farmers in Rebellion: The Rise and Fall of the Southern Farmers Alliance and People's Party in Texas* (1984); Paolo Coletta, *William Jennings Bryan: Political Evangelist* (1964); Paul W. Glad, *McKinley, Bryan, and the People* (1964); Lawrence Goodwyn, *Democratic Promise: The Populist Movement in America* (1976); Steven Hahn, *The Roots of Southern Populism* (1983); Richard Hofstadter, *The Age of Reform: From Bryan to FDR* (1955); J. Morgan Kousser, *The Shaping of Southern Politics* (1974); Robert C. McMath, Jr., *American Populism* (1993); Walter T. K. Nugent, *The Tolerant Populists* (1963); Jeffrey Ostler, *Prairie Populism* (1993); Norman Pollack, *The Populist Response to Industrial America* (1962); Barton C. Shaw, *The Wool-Hat Boys: Georgia's Populist Party* (1984); Allan Weinstein, *Prelude to Populism: Origins of the Silver Issue* (1970).

CHAPTER

21

The Progressive Era
1895 – 1920

O nce described as a "guerrilla warrior" in the "wilderness of industrial wrongs," Florence Kelley accomplished as much as anyone in
guiding the United States out of the tangled swamp of unregulated industrial capitalism into the uncharted seas of the twentieth-century
welfare state.

The daughter of a Republican congressman, Kelley hoped to prepare
for the study of law, but the University of Pennsylvania denied her admission to its graduate school because of her gender. Instead, she went
to Europe, where socialist friends alerted her to the plight of the poor.
She married a Russian socialist and returned to New York City in 1886.
After five years of an abusive marriage, Kelley took her three children to
Chicago. Later that year she moved into Hull House, a residence in the
slums where middle-class reformers went to live in order to help and
learn from working-class immigrants.

Over the next decade, Kelley became one of the nation's most ardent
advocates of improved conditions for working-class women and children. She investigated and publicized abuses of the sweatshop system in
Chicago's garment industry, lobbied for laws to prohibit child labor and
regulate women's working hours, and served as Illinois's first chief factory inspector. Her work helped create new professions for women in
social service, and her strategy of investigating, publicizing, and crusading for action became a model for Progressive reform. Perhaps most
significant, she helped involve government in the solution of pressing
social problems.

During the 1890s a severe economic depression, labor violence, political upheaval, and foreign entanglements shook the nation. By 1900, however, the political tumult of the previous decade had died down, and the economic depression seemed to be over. The nation had just emerged victorious from a war, and a new political era of dynamic leaders such as Theodore Roosevelt and Woodrow Wilson was dawning. A sense of renewal served both to intensify anxiety over continuing social and political problems and to raise hopes that somehow such problems could be fixed.

By the 1910s many reformers were calling themselves "Progressives." Historians have since used the term *Progressivism* to refer to the era's reformist spirit. The era—1895 to 1920—was characterized by a series of movements, each aiming in one way or another to renovate or restore American society, values, and institutions.

The reform impulse had many sources. Industrialization and corporate capitalism had created awesome technology, unprecedented productivity, and a cornucopia of consumer goods. But they also brought overproduction, competition that squashed small companies, labor strife, and the spoiling of natural resources. Burgeoning cities facilitated the amassing and distribution of goods, services, and cultural amenities; they also bred poverty, disease, and crime. The social order was reconstructed by massive inflows of immigrants and the rise of a new class of managers and professionals. And the depression of the 1890s forced many leading citizens to realize what working people had known for some time: the central promise of American life was not being kept, equality of opportunity was a myth.

Progressives organized their ideas and actions around three goals. First, they sought to end abuses of power. Trustbusting, consumers' rights, and good government became compelling political issues. Second, Progressives aimed to supplant corrupt power with reformed versions of institutions such as schools, charities, medical clinics, and the family. Third, they wanted to apply scientific principles and efficient management to economic, social, and political institutions.

 ## The Variety of the Progressive Impulse

At the time Progressives began to address many of the nation's problems, party loyalty was eroding and voter turnout declining. Parties and elections, it seemed, were losing their influence over government policies. At the same time, the political system was opening up to multiple and shifting interest groups, each of which championed its own causes.

These organizations included professional associations such as the American Bar Association; women's organizations such as the National American Woman Suffrage Association; issue-oriented groups such as the National Consumers League; civic clubs such as the National Municipal League; and associations oriented toward minority groups, such as the National Negro Business League and the Society of American Indians. Because they were not usually tied to either of the established political parties, such groups made politics much more fragmented and issue focused than in earlier eras.

Although goals of the rural-based Populist movement lingered—moral regeneration, political democracy, and antimonopolism—the Progressive quest for social justice, educational and legal reform, and streamlining of government had a largely urban bent. Those interested in working to achieve the three Progressive goals—ending the abuse of power, reforming social institutions, and promoting bureaucratic and scientific efficiency—existed in almost all levels of society. But the new middle class—men and women in professions of law, medicine, engineering, social work, religion, teaching, and business—formed the vanguard of reform. Offended by inefficiency and immorality, they set out to apply the scientific techniques they had learned in their professions to problems of the larger society.

Urban Middle-Class Reformers and Muckrakers

• *Important Events* •

1893	Anti-Saloon League founded
1895	Booker T. Washington gives Atlanta Compromise speech
	National Association of Colored Women founded
1898	*Holden* v. *Hardy* upholds limits on miners' work hours
1900	William McKinley reelected
1901	McKinley assassinated; Theodore Roosevelt assumes the presidency
1904	Theodore Roosevelt elected president
	Northern Securities case dissolves railroad trust
1905–06	Niagara Falls Convention promotes more militant pursuit of African-American rights
	Lochner v. *New York* removes limits on bakers' work hours
	Hepburn Act tightens control over railroads
1906	Upton Sinclair's novel *The Jungle* raises public awareness of poor working conditions in meatpacking factories
	Meat Inspection Act passed
	Pure Food and Drug Act passed
1907	Reckless speculation causes economic panic
1908	William H. Taft elected president
	Supreme Court upholds limits on women's work hours
1909	NAACP founded
	Payne-Aldrich Tariff passed
1910	Mann-Elkins Act reinforces ICC powers
	White Slave Traffic Act prohibits transportation of women for "immoral purposes"
	Ballinger-Pinchot controversy angers conservationists
1911	Society of American Indians founded
1912	Theodore Roosevelt runs for president on the Progressive (Bull Moose) ticket
	Woodrow Wilson elected president

1913	Sixteenth Amendment ratified; legalizes federal income tax
	Seventeenth Amendment ratified; provides for direct election of United States senators
	Underwood Tariff institutes income tax
	Federal Reserve Act establishes central banking system
1914	Federal Trade Commission created to investigate unfair trade practices
	Clayton Anti-Trust Act outlaws monopolistic business practices
	Margaret Sanger indicted for sending articles on contraception through the mail
1916	Wilson reelected
	Federal Farm Loan Act provides credit to farmers
	Adamson Act mandates an eight-hour workday for railroad workers
1919	Eighteenth Amendment ratified; prohibits manufacture, sale, and transportation of alcoholic beverages
1920	Nineteenth Amendment ratified; gives women the vote in federal elections
1921	Margaret Sanger founds American Birth Control League

Motivated by personal indignation at corruption and injustice, many middle-class Progressive reformers sought to end abuses of power. Their views were voiced by journalists whom Theodore Roosevelt dubbed *muckrakers* (after a character in the Puritan allegory *Pilgrim's Progress* who rejected a crown for a muckrake). Muckrakers fed the public's taste for scandal and sensation by exposing social, economic, and political wrongs. Their investigative articles and books attacked adulterated foods, fraudulent insurance, prostitution, and other offenses. Lincoln Steffens's articles in *McClure's*, later published as *The Shame of the Cities* (1904), epitomized the muckraking style. Steffens hoped his exposés of bosses' misrule would inspire mass outrage and, ultimately, reform. Other well-known muckraking efforts included Upton Sinclair's *The Jungle* (1906), a novel that disclosed crimes of the meatpacking industry, and Ida M. Tarbell's critical history of Standard Oil (1904).

Middle-class reformers also deplored the self-serving that they believed infected boss-ridden parties. To improve the political process, Progressives advocated nominating candidates through direct primaries instead of party caucuses and holding nonpartisan elections to prevent the fraud and bribery bred by party loyalties.

To make officeholders more responsible, Progressives advocated three reforms: the *initiative*, which permitted voters to propose new laws; the *referendum*, which enabled voters to accept or reject a law; and the *recall*, which allowed voters to remove offending officials and judges from office before their terms were up. Their goal was efficiency: they would reclaim government by replacing the boss system with accountable managers chosen by a responsible electorate.

Middle-class Progressives recoiled from party politics but not from government itself. Rather, they turned to government for aid in achieving their goals, for they were convinced that only government offered the leverage they needed. Science and scientific method—planning, control, and predictability—were their central values. Just as corporations applied scientific management to achieve economic efficiency, Progressives favored using expertise and planning to achieve social and political efficiency.

The Progressive spirit also stirred some elite business leaders. Some executives supported government regulation and political reforms to protect their interests from more radical political elements.

Upper-Class Reformers

Others were humanitarians who worked unselfishly for social justice. Business-dominated organizations like the Municipal Voters League and U.S. Chamber of Commerce supported limited political and economic reform. They aimed to stabilize society by running schools, hospitals, and local government like efficient businesses. Elite women often led organizations like the Young Women's Christian Association, which aided growing numbers of unmarried working women, and the Women's Christian Temperance Union, which supported numerous causes besides abstinence from drinking.

Not all Progressive reformers were middle- or upper-class. Vital elements of what soon became modern American liberalism derived from working-class urban experience. By 1900, many urban workers were pressing for government intervention to ensure safe factories, a shorter workday, workers' compensation, better housing, and health safeguards. Often these were the same people who supported political bosses, supposedly the enemies of reform. In fact, bossism was not necessarily at odds with humanitarianism.

Working-Class Reformers

After 1900, voters from urban working-class districts elected several Progressive legislators who had trained in the trenches of machine politics. Their goal was to have government take responsibility for alleviating hardships that resulted from urban-industrial growth. They opposed reforms such as prohibition, Sunday closing laws, civil service, and nonpartisan elections, which conflicted with their constituents' interests.

Some disillusioned people wanted more than reform; they wanted a different society. These people turned to the socialist movement. The majority of socialists united behind Eugene V. Debs. As the Socialist Party's presidential candidate, Debs won 400,000

Socialists

Though their objectives sometimes differed from those of middle-class Progressive reformers, socialists also became a more active force in the early twentieth century. Socialist parades on May Day, such as this one in 1910, were meant to express the solidarity of all working people.   Library of Congress.

votes in 1904, and in 1912, at the pinnacle of his and his party's career, he polled over 900,000.

With stinging rebukes of exploitation and unfair privilege, socialist leaders made compelling overtures to reform-minded people. Some, such as Florence Kelley, joined the Socialist Party. But most Progressives had too much at stake in the capitalist system to want to overthrow it. Municipal ownership of public utilities was as far as they would go toward radical change.

It would be a mistake to assume that a Progressive spirit captured all of American society. Large numbers of people, heavily represented in Congress, disliked government interference in economic affairs and found no fault with existing power structures. Government interference, they contended, contradicted the natural law of survival of the fittest. Tycoons like J. P. Morgan and John D. Rockefeller, for instance, insisted that progress would result only from maintaining the profit incentive.

Opponents of Progressivism

Progressive reformers operated from the center of the ideological spectrum. They believed on the one hand that the laissez-faire system was obsolete and on the other that a radical shift away from free enterprise was dangerous. Like Jeffersonians, they believed in the conscience and will of the people; like Hamiltonians, they opted for a strong central government to act in the interests of conscience.

Progressive Contradictions

Governmental and Legislative Reform

By 1900, professionals and intellectuals were rejecting the traditional American belief that government should be small and unobtrusive. They were instead concluding that government should exert more power to ensure justice and well-being. Increasingly aware that a simple, inflexible government was inadequate in a complex industrial age, they reasoned that public authority needed to counteract inefficiency, corruption, and exploitation. But before reformers could effectively use such power, they would have to capture government from politicians whose greed had soiled the democratic system.

Reformers first attacked corruption in cities. Between 1870 and 1900, opponents of the boss system tried to restructure government through reforms such as civil service hiring, nonpartisan elections, and tighter scrutiny of public expenditures. After 1900 reform momentum brought into being the city-manager and commission forms of government (in which urban officials were chosen for professional expertise, rather than political connections) and public ownership of utilities (to prevent monopolistic gas, electric, and streetcar companies from profiting at the public's expense).

Reformers found, however, that the city was too small an arena for the changes they sought. State and federal governments offered better opportunities for enacting needed legislation. Because of their faith in strong, fair-minded executives, Progressives supported a number of skillful and charismatic governors who used executive power to achieve change. Their ranks included Braxton Bragg Comer of Alabama and Hoke Smith of Georgia, who introduced business regulation and other reforms in the South; Albert Cummins of Iowa and Hiram Johnson of California, who battled the railroads that dominated their states; and Woodrow Wilson of New Jersey, whose administrative reforms were imitated by other governors. Such men, however, were not saints. Bowing to prevailing racist sentiments, Smith supported disfranchisement of African-Americans, and Johnson promoted discrimination against Japanese-Americans.

Progressive Governors

The most forceful Progressive governor was Wisconsin's Robert M. La Follette. After taking office in 1900, La Follette initiated a reform program distinguished by direct primaries, more equitable taxes, and regulation of railroad rates. He also appointed commissions staffed by experts, who sup-

Robert M. La Follette

plied him with the facts and figures he used in fiery speeches to arouse public support for his policies. After three terms as governor, La Follette was elected to the United States Senate and carried his ideals into national politics.

The crusade against corrupt politics brought about some permanent changes. By 1916 all but three states had direct primaries, and many had adopted the initiative, referendum, and recall. Political reformers achieved a major goal in 1913 with adoption of the Seventeenth Amendment, which provided for direct election of United States senators (they had been elected by state legislatures). But political reforms did not always help. Party bosses were still able to control elections, and courts often aided rather than reined in entrenched power.

The Seventeenth Amendment

State laws to improve labor conditions had greater impact than did political reforms. Many states broadly interpreted their constitutional powers to protect public health and safety (police power) and enacted factory inspection laws, and by 1916 nearly two-thirds of the states required compensation for victims of industrial accidents. Under pressure from the National Child Labor Committee, nearly every state set a minimum age for employment (varying from twelve to sixteen) and prohibited employers from working children more than eight or ten hours a day. Child labor laws, however, were hard to enforce and often violated.

Reform of Labor Conditions

Several groups joined forces to restrict working hours for women. After the Supreme Court upheld Oregon's ten-hour limit in 1908, more states passed laws protecting female workers. Meanwhile, in 1914 efforts of the American Association for Old Age Security showed signs of success when Arizona established old-age pensions. The courts struck down the law, but demand for pensions continued, and in the 1920s many states enacted laws to provide for needy elderly people.

Reformers themselves were not always certain about what was Progressive, especially in human behavior. The main question was whether it was

Moral Reform

possible to create a desirable moral climate through legislation. Some reformers, notably adherents of the Social Gospel movement, believed that only church-based inspiration and humanitarian work, rather than legislation, could transform society. Others argued that state intervention was necessary to enforce purity.

The Anti-Saloon League, formed in 1893, intensified the long-standing campaign against drunkenness and its costs to society. This organi-

The War on Alcohol

zation allied with the Woman's Christian Temperance Union (founded in 1873) to publicize the role of alcoholism in liver disease and other health prob-

lems. The League was especially successful in shifting attention from the individual's responsibility for temperance to the alleged link between the drinking that saloons encouraged and the accidents, poverty, and inefficient productivity that were consequences of drinking.

By 1900 almost one-fourth of the nation's population lived in "dry" communities (which prohibited the sale of liquor). Finally, in 1918 Congress passed the Eighteenth Amendment (ratified in 1919 and implemented in 1920) outlawing the manufacture, sale, and transportation of intoxicating liquors.

Public outrage erupted in another area when muckraking journalists charged that international rings were kidnapping young women and forcing

Prostitution and White Slavery

them into prostitution, a practice called white slavery. Already alarmed by a perceived link between immigration and prostitution and fearful that prostitutes were producing ge-

netically inferior children, middle-class moralists prodded governments to investigate the problem and pass corrective legislation. In 1910 Congress passed the White Slave Traffic Act, known as the Mann Act, prohibiting interstate and international transportation of a woman for immoral purposes. By 1915 nearly every state had outlawed brothels and solicitation of sex. Prohibition and the Mann Act reflected reformers' belief that social environments created evil and that evil could thus be eradicated through human—government—action.

New Ideas in Education, Law, and Social Sciences

While the reform impulse traveled on legislative paths, new vistas opened in education, law, and social service. The preoccupation with efficiency and scientific management challenged teachers, judges, and social scientists to come to grips with modern society. Darwin's theory of evolution had undermined traditional beliefs in a God-created world; immigration had replaced social uniformity with diversity; and technology had made old habits of production and consumption obsolete. Thoughtful people in a number of professions grappled with how to respond to the new era yet preserve what was best from the past.

In education, the early nineteenth-century school curricula had consisted chiefly of moralistic pieties. Late in the century, however, psy-

John Dewey and Progressive Education

chologist G. Stanley Hall and educational philosopher John Dewey insisted that personal development, not subject matter, should be the focus of the curriculum. Education, ar-

gued Dewey, must relate directly to experience; children should be encouraged to discover knowledge for themselves. Learning relevant to students' lives should replace rote memorization and outdated subjects.

Personal growth became the driving principle behind higher education as well. Previously, the purpose of American colleges and universities had

Growth of Colleges and Universities

been to train a select few for the professions of law, medicine, teaching, and religion. But in the late 1800s, institutions of higher education mul-

tiplied, aided by land grants and by an increase in the number of people who could afford tuition. Curricula expanded as educators sought to make learning more appealing and to keep up with technological and social changes. Harvard University, under President Charles W.

Eliot, pioneered in substituting electives for required courses and experimenting with new teaching methods.

As colleges and universities expanded, so did female enrollments. Between 1890 and 1920 the number of women in these institutions swelled from 56,000 to 283,000, accounting for 47 percent of total enrollment. These numbers disproved contentions that women were unfit for higher learning because they were mentally and physically inferior to men, but discrimination lingered in admissions and curriculum policies. Women were encouraged (indeed, they usually sought) to take home economics and education courses rather than science and mathematics, and most medical schools refused to admit women.

The new emphasis on experience and scientific principle also influenced the legal profession. Oliver Wendell Holmes, Jr., associate justice of the Supreme Court between 1902 and 1932, led the attack on the traditional view of law as universal and unchanging. His opinion that law should reflect society's needs challenged the practice of invoking inflexible legal precedents that often obstructed social legislation. Louis D. Brandeis, a lawyer who later joined Holmes on the Supreme Court, carried legal reform one step further by insisting that judges' opinions be based on factual, scientifically gathered information about social realities.

Progressive Legal Thought

The new legal thinking met with some resistance. Judges raised on laissez-faire economics and strict construction of the Constitution continued to overturn laws progressives thought necessary for effective reform. Thus despite Holmes's forceful dissent, in 1905 the Supreme Court, in *Lochner* v. *New York*, revoked a New York law limiting bakers' working hours. As in similar cases, the Court's majority argued that the Fourteenth Amendment protected an individual's right to make contracts without government interference and that this protection superseded police power.

Courts did uphold some regulatory measures, particularly those protecting public safety. A string of decisions beginning with *Holden* v. *Hardy* (1898), in which the Supreme Court upheld Utah's mining

regulations, supported the use of state police powers to protect health, safety, and morals. Judges also affirmed federal police powers and Congress's authority over interstate commerce by sustaining federal legislation such as the Pure Food and Drug Act, the Meat Inspection Law (see pages 405–406), and the Mann Act (see page 399).

But the concept of general welfare posed thorny legal problems. The United States was a mixed nation; gender, race, religion, and ethnicity deeply influenced law. In many localities a native-born white Protestant majority imposed Bible reading in public schools (offending Catholics and Jews), required business establishments to close on Sundays, restricted the religious practices of Mormons and other groups, prohibited interracial marriage, and enforced racial segregation. Justice Holmes asserted that laws should be made for "people of fundamentally differing views," but even today debate continues over whether such laws are possible in a nation of so many different interest groups.

In public health, organizations like the National Consumers League (NCL) joined with physicians and social scientists to bring about some of the most far-reaching Progressive reforms. Founded by Josephine Shaw, a socially prominent Massachusetts widow, the NCL initially focused on improving the wages and working conditions of young women. After Florence Kelley became the NCL's general secretary, the organization expanded its activities to encompass women's suffrage, protection of child laborers, and elimination of potential health hazards. Local branches were joined by women's clubs in supporting consumer protection measures such as the licensing of food vendors and inspection of dairies. They also urged city governments to fund neighborhood clinics that provided health education and medical care to the poor.

National Consumers League and Public Health Reform

These and other men and women were among the new breed pressing for institutional change as well as political reform in the two decades before the First World War. Largely middle class, trained by new professional standards, confident that new ways of thinking could bring about progress, these people helped to broaden government's role to meet the needs of a mature industrial society. But their questioning of prevailing assumptions also unsettled conventional attitudes toward race and gender.

Challenges to Racial and Sexual Discrimination

W. E. B. Du Bois, a forceful black scholar and writer, ended an essay in *The Souls of Black Folk* (1903) with a blunt prediction for American society. "The problem of the Twentieth Century," he wrote, "is the problem of the color line." Du Bois's assertion rang true; people of color continued to endure violent treatment and degradation. But at the same time, women of all races also suffered from an underprivileged status.

For both African-Americans and women, the Progressive challenge to entrenched ideas and customs gave impetus to their struggles for equal rights, but it also posed a dilemma. Should women and people of color strive to become just like white men, with white men's values as well as their rights? Or was there something unique about racial and sexual cultures that should be preserved at the risk of sacrificing some gains?

African-American leaders differed sharply over how—and whether—to pursue assimilation. In the wake of emancipation, ex-slave Frederick Douglass urged "ultimate assimilation through self-assertion, and on no other terms." Those who favored separation from white society supported migration to Africa or the establishment of all-black communities in Oklahoma Territory and Kansas. Others advocated violence.

Most blacks, however, could neither escape nor conquer white society. They had to find other routes to economic and social improvement. Self-help, a strategy articulated by educator Booker T. Washington, was one popular alternative. Born to slave parents in 1856, Washington worked his way through school and in 1881 founded Tuskegee Institute in Alabama, a vocational school for blacks. There he developed

Booker T. Washington and Self-Help

the philosophy that blacks' best hopes for assimilation lay in at least temporarily accommodating to whites. Rather than fighting for political rights, Washington said, blacks should work hard, acquire property, and prove they were worthy of rights.

Washington voiced his views in a widely acclaimed speech at the Atlanta Exposition in 1895. In this speech, which became known as the Atlanta Compromise, Washington observed that "in all things that are purely social we can be as separate as the fingers, yet one as the hand in all matters essential to mutual progress." Whites welcomed Washington's accommodation policy because it urged patience and reminded black people to stay in their place.

Some blacks thought that Booker T. Washington seemed to favor a degrading second-class citizenship. In 1905 a group of "anti-Bookerites" convened near Niagara Falls and pledged a militant pursuit of rights such as unrestricted voting, economic opportunity, integration, and equality before the law. Spokesperson for the Niagara movement was W. E. B. Du Bois, an outspoken critic of the Atlanta Compromise.

A New Englander with a Ph.D. from Harvard, Du Bois was both a Progressive and a member of the black elite. He held an undergraduate degree from all-black Fisk University and had studied in Germany, where he learned about scientific investigation. Du Bois had compiled fact-filled sociological studies of black ghetto dwellers and had written poetically in support of civil rights. He treated Washington politely but could not accept white domination.

W. E. B. Du Bois and the "Talented Tenth"

Du Bois demonstrated that accommodation was an unrealistic strategy, but his solution had its own drawbacks. A blunt elitist, Du Bois believed that an intellectual vanguard of cultured, highly trained blacks, the "Talented Tenth," would save the race by setting an example to whites and uplifting other blacks. Such sentiment had more appeal for middle-class white liberals than for African-American sharecroppers. Thus in 1909 when Du Bois and his allies formed the National Association for the Advancement of Colored People (NAACP), which aimed to end racial discrimination by pursuing legal redress in the courts, the leadership consisted chiefly of white Progressives.

Whatever their views, African-Americans faced continued oppression. Those who managed to acquire property and education encountered bitter resentment, especially when they fought for civil rights. The federal government only aggravated biases. During Woodrow Wilson's presidency, discrimination within the federal government expanded: southern cabinet members supported racial separation in restrooms, restaurants, and government office buildings and balked at hiring black workers.

Disfranchisement, instituted by southern states in the late nineteenth century (see page 334), still prevented blacks from becoming full American citizens. Washington seemed to accept disfranchisement; Du Bois believed suffrage was essential to protect social and economic rights.

African-Americans still sought to fulfill the American dream, but many wondered whether their goals should include membership in a corrupt white society. Du Bois voiced these doubts poignantly, observing that "one ever feels his twoness—an American, a Negro, two souls, two thoughts, two unreconciled strivings, two warring ideals in one dark body."

The dilemma of identity haunted Native Americans as well, but it had an added tribal dimension. Since the 1880s, Native American reformers had joined white-led Indian organizations. In 1911 educated, middle-class Indian men and women formed their own association, the Society of American Indians (SAI), which worked for better education, civil rights, and healthcare. It also sponsored "American Indian Days" to cultivate pride.

Society of American Indians

The SAI's emphasis on racial pride, however, was squeezed between pressures for assimilation from one side and tribal allegiance on the other. Its small membership did not genuinely represent the diverse and unconnected Indian nations, and its attempt to establish a governing body faltered. At the same time, the goal of achieving acceptance in white society proved elusive, and attempts to redress grievances through legal action bogged down for lack of funds. Ultimately, the SAI had to rely on rhetoric and moral exhortation, which had little effect on poor and powerless Indians. Torn by internal disputes, the association folded in the early 1920s.

What tactics should women use to achieve equality? What should be their role in society? Could women achieve equality with men and at the same time change male-dominated society? The answers that women found involved a subtle but important shift in women's politics. Before about 1910, those engaged in the quest for women's rights referred to themselves as "the woman movement." This label was given to middle-class women striving to move beyond the home into social welfare activities, higher education, and paid labor. They argued that legal and voting rights were indispensable to such moves. These women's rights advocates based their claims on the theory that women's special, even superior, traits as guardians of family and morality would humanize all of society.

"The Woman Movement"

The women's club movement represented a unique dimension of Progressive era reform. Originating as middle-class literary and educational organizations, women's clubs began taking stands on public affairs in the late nineteenth century. Because female activists were excluded from holding office, they were drawn less to government reform than to drives for social betterment. Women reformers tended to work for factory inspection, regulation of children's and women's labor, housing improvement, upgrading of education, and consumer protection. Such efforts were not confined to white women. The National Association of Colored Women, founded in 1895, was the nation's first African-American social service organization; it concentrated on establishing nurseries, kindergartens, and retirement homes.

Women's Clubs

Around 1910 some people concerned with women's place in society began using a new term, *feminism*. Whereas members of the woman movement spoke generally of duty and moral purity, feminists—more explicitly conscious of their identity as

Feminism

How do historians know that female Progressive organizations combined gender-based notions of service with bureaucratic organization? Visiting nurses, represented in this photograph of a professional nurse entering a tenement, was one of the most effective social welfare programs established during the Progressive era. The photograph was published in The House on Henry Street *(1915), a book by Lillian Wald about the early years of the Henry Street Visiting Nurses Service.*

Wald, a nurse and one of the movement's leading figures, saw that many people were not sick enough to require hospitalization but needed medical care that could be provided during a house call by a medical professional. Responding to this need, she formed an organization that sent nurses out on home visits. By 1913, home nurses were making 200,000 visits annually in New York, and other cities had copied Wald's model.

She wrote, "[W]e planned to create a service on terms most considerate of the dignity and independence of the patients. . . . The new basis of the visiting nurse service which we thus inaugurated reacted almost immediately upon the relationship of the nurse to the patient, reversing the position the nurse had formerly had. Chagrin at having the neighbors see in her an agent whose presence proclaimed the family's poverty or its failure to give adequate care to its sick member was changed to the gratifying consciousness that her presence . . . proclaimed the family's liberality and anxiety to do everything possible for the sufferer." Those words, with their emphasis on both compassion and organized service, and the sympathetic yet professional appearance of the nurse in the photograph, illustrate one way in which women contributed to Progressive reform. The House of Henry Street by Lillian D. Wald, Henry Holt and Company, New York, 1915.

women—emphasized rights and self-development. Feminism focused primarily on economic and sexual independence. Charlotte Perkins Gilman articulated feminist goals in *Women and Economics* (1898), declaring that domesticity and female innocence were obsolete and attacked the male monopoly on economic opportunity.

Feminists also supported "sex rights"—a single standard of behavior for men and women—and a number of feminists joined the birth-control movement led by Margaret Sanger. As a visiting nurse in New York's immigrant neighborhoods, Sanger distributed information about contraception, in hopes of helping poor women prevent unwanted pregnancies. Her crusade won support from middle-class women who wanted both to limit their own families and to control the growth of the immigrant masses. It also aroused opposition from those who saw birth control as a threat to family and morality.

Margaret Sanger's Crusade

In 1914, Sanger's opponents caused her to be indicted for defying an 1873 law that prohibited the sending of obscene literature (articles on contraception) through the mails, and she fled the country for a year. Sanger persevered and in 1921 formed the American Birth Control League, which enlisted physicians and social workers to convince judges to allow distribution of birth-control information.

Feminists achieved an important victory in 1920 when enough states ratified the Nineteenth Amendment to give women the vote in federal elections. Until the 1890s, the suffrage crusade was led by elite women who believed that the political system needed more participation by refined and educated people like themselves, and that working-class women would defer to better-educated women on political matters.

Woman Suffrage

The younger generation of feminists ardently opposed this logic. To them, achievement rather than wealth and refinement was the best criterion for public influence. Thus women should exercise the vote not to enhance the power of elites in public life but to promote and protect women's economic roles.

Despite internal differences, suffragists achieved some successes. Nine states, all in the West, allowed women to vote in state and local elections by 1912, and women continued to press for national suffrage. Their tactics ranged from the moderate but persistent propaganda campaigns of the National American Woman Suffrage Association, led by Carrie Chapman Catt, to rousing meetings and marches of the National Woman's Party, led by feminist Alice Paul. All these activities heightened public awareness. The First World War contributions of women as factory workers, medical volunteers, and municipal workers served as the final impetus to secure political support for the suffrage amendment.

The activities of women's clubs, suffragists, and feminists failed to create an interest group united or powerful enough to dent the political, economic, and social power of men. Like blacks, women knew that voting rights would mean little until society's attitudes changed. The Progressive era helped women to clarify the issues that concerned them, but major reforms were not achieved until a later era.

Theodore Roosevelt and the Revival of the Presidency

The Progressive era's theme of reform—in politics, institutions, and social relations—drew attention to government, especially the federal government, as the foremost agent of change. At first, the federal government seemed incapable of assuming such responsibility. For many years the federal government had acted mainly on behalf of special interests when it acted at all. Then, in September 1901, the political climate suddenly changed. The assassination of President William McKinley vaulted Theodore Roosevelt, the vigorous young vice president, into the White House.

Political manager Mark Hanna had warned fellow Republicans against running Roosevelt for the vice presidency in 1900. "Don't any of you realize," Hanna asked after the nominating convention, "that there's only one life between that madman and the presidency?" As governor of New

Theodore Roosevelt

Theodore Roosevelt (1858–1919) liked to think of himself as a great outdoorsman, one who loved the most rugged country-side and one who believed that he and his country should serve as examples of "manliness." California Museum of Photography, University of California.

York, Roosevelt had angered Republican bosses by showing sympathy for regulatory legislation, so they rid themselves of their pariah by pushing him into national politics.

As president, Roosevelt concurred with Progressives that the economic developments of the industrial era made necessary a powerful Hamiltonian system of government. Especially in economic affairs, he wanted the government to act as an umpire, deciding when big business was good and when it was bad. But his brash patriotism and dislike of anything he considered effeminate also recalled the previous era of unbridled expansion when raw power prevailed in social and economic affairs.

The federal regulation of the economy that has characterized twentieth-century American history began with Roosevelt's presidency. Roosevelt

Regulation of Trusts

turned his attention first to big business, where consolidation had created giant trusts that exerted powerful control. Although Roosevelt was labeled a "trustbuster," he actually considered consolidation the most efficient means to achieve material progress. He believed in distinguishing between good and bad trusts and preventing bad ones from manipulating markets. Thus he instructed the Justice Department to use antitrust laws to prosecute the railroad, meatpacking, and oil trusts, which he believed were unscrupulously exploiting the public. Roosevelt's policy triumphed in 1904 in the *Northern Securities* case. The Supreme Court, convinced by the government's arguments, ordered the breakup of the Northern Securities Company, the huge railroad combination created by J. P. Morgan and his business allies.

As a rule, Roosevelt favored cooperation between government and business and the use of pressure on business to regulate itself. But he also supported regulatory legislation, especially after his resounding electoral victory in 1904. After a year of wrangling, Roosevelt persuaded Congress to pass the Hepburn Act (1906), which gave the Interstate Commerce Commission (ICC) more authority to set the freight and storage rates that railroads charged, though it did allow the courts to overturn rate decisions.

As he had done in securing passage of the Hepburn Act, Roosevelt showed a willingness to compromise on legislation to ensure the purity of food and drugs. For decades reformers had been urging government regulation of processed meat and patent medicines. Public outrage at fraud and adulteration heightened in 1906 when Upton Sinclair published *The Jungle*, a fictionalized exposé of Chicago meatpacking plants. After reading the novel, Roosevelt ordered an investigation. Finding Sinclair's descriptions accurate, the president supported the Meat Inspection Act, which passed in 1906. Like the Hepburn Act, this law reinforced the principle of government regulation. But as part of the compromise to pass the bill, the government, rather than the meatpackers,

Pure Food and Drug Laws

had to pay for inspections, and meatpackers could appeal adverse decisions in court.

The Pure Food and Drug Act (1906) addressed abuses in the patent medicine industry. Producers of various tonics and pills were not only making undue claims about their products' effects but also liberally using alcohol and narcotics as ingredients. Ads in popular publications, such as one for a "Brain Stimulator and Nerve Tonic" in the Sears, Roebuck catalogue, had wildly exaggerated claims. Although the new law did not ban such products, it did require labels listing the ingredients—a goal consistent with Progressive confidence that if people knew the truth, they would make wiser purchases.

Roosevelt's approach to labor resembled his stance toward business. When the United Mine Workers struck against Pennsylvania coal-mine owners in 1902 over an eight-hour workday and higher pay, the president employed the Progressive tactics of investigation and arbitration. Owners stubbornly refused to recognize the union or arbitrate grievances. As winter approached and fuel shortages threatened, Roosevelt roused public opinion. He would use federal troops to reopen the mines, he warned, thus forcing management to accept arbitration of the dispute by a special commission. The commission decided in favor of higher wages and reduced hours and required management to deal with grievance committees elected by the miners, but it did not require recognition of the union. The decision, according to Roosevelt, provided a "square deal" for all. The settlement also embodied Roosevelt's belief that the president or his representatives should have a say in which labor demands were legitimate and which were not.

In matters of resource conservation, Roosevelt combined the Progressive impulse for efficiency with his love for the great outdoors. Before Roosevelt, the government's policy had been to transfer ownership and control of natural resources on federal land to the states and to private interests. Roosevelt, however, believed the most efficient way to use and conserve these resources would be for the government to retain public ownership. Owner-

Conservation

ship did not necessarily mean that no one could have access; rather, it meant that the federal government would manage and control use of those lands that remained in the public domain. Under Roosevelt the number of national forests and the acreage within them tripled, and it was during his administration that the Newlands Reclamation Act of 1902 was enacted to control the sale of irrigated land in the West. Roosevelt also supported conservationist Gifford Pinchot in creating the United States Forest Service. Pinchot advocated scientific management of the nation's forests to protect the land and water from overuse by timber cutters, farmers, and herders.

During his last year in office, Roosevelt retreated from the Republican Party's traditional friendliness to big business. He lashed out at the irresponsibility of "malefactors of great wealth." Having promised that he would not seek reelection, Roosevelt backed his friend Secretary of War William Howard Taft for the Republican nomination in 1908, hoping that Taft would continue his initiatives. Democrats nominated William Jennings Bryan for the third time, but the "Great Commoner" lost again.

Early in 1909 Roosevelt went to Africa to shoot game, leaving Taft to face political problems that his predecessor had managed to postpone. Foremost among them was the tariff controversy. Honoring Taft's pledge to cut rates, the House passed a bill sponsored by Representative Sereno E. Payne that provided for numerous reductions. Protectionists in the Senate prepared to amend the House bill and revise rates upward. But Senate Progressives, led by La Follette, organized a stinging attack on the tariff for benefiting vested interests. Taft was caught between reformers who claimed to be preserving Roosevelt's antitrust campaign and protectionists who still controlled the Republican Party. In the end, Senator Nelson Aldrich and other protectionists restored many of the tariff cuts the Payne bill had made, and Taft signed what became known as the Payne-Aldrich Tariff (1909). In the eyes of Progressives, Taft had failed the test of filling Roosevelt's shoes.

Taft Administration

Progressive and conservative wings of the Republican Party were rapidly drifting apart. Soon after the tariff controversy, a group of insurgents in the House mounted a challenge to Speaker "Uncle Joe" Cannon of Illinois, whose power over committee assignments and the scheduling of debates could make or break a piece of legislation. Taft first supported and then abandoned the insurgents, who nevertheless managed to liberalize procedures by enlarging the influential Rules Committee and removing selection of its members from Cannon's control. In 1910 Taft also angered conservationists by firing Gifford Pinchot when he protested Secretary of the Interior Richard A. Ballinger's questionable sale of coal lands in Alaska.

In reality Taft was as sympathetic to reform as Roosevelt was. He prosecuted more trusts than Roosevelt; expanded national forest reserves; signed the Mann-Elkins Act (1910), which bolstered the regulatory powers of the ICC; and supported labor reforms such as the eight-hour workday and mine safety legislation. The Sixteenth Amendment, which legalized the federal income tax, and the Seventeenth Amendment, which provided for direct election of United States senators, were initiated during Taft's presidency (and ratified in 1913).

In 1910, when Roosevelt returned from Africa, he found his party torn and tormented. Reformers, angered by Taft's apparent insensitivity to their cause, formed the National Progressive Republican League and rallied behind Robert La Follette for president in 1912. Another wing of the party remained loyal to Taft. Disappointed by Taft's performance (particularly his firing of Pinchot), Roosevelt began to speak out. When La Follette became ill early in 1912, Roosevelt, proclaiming himself fit as a "bull moose," threw his hat into the ring for the Republican presidential nomination.

Taft's supporters controlled the convention and nominated Taft for a second term, but Roosevelt's supporters bolted and reconvened in August to form a third party—the Progressive, or Bull Moose, Party—and nominated the fifty-three-year-old former president. Meanwhile, Democrats took forty-six ballots to select their candidate, New Jersey's Progressive governor Woodrow Wilson.

Socialists, by now an organized and growing party, again nominated Eugene V. Debs.

Woodrow Wilson and the Extension of Reform

Wilson won the 1912 election with 42 percent of the popular vote. He was a minority president, though he did capture 435 out of 531 electoral votes. Roosevelt received 27 percent of the popular vote. Taft finished third, polling 23 percent of the popular vote and only 8 electoral votes. Debs won 902,000 votes, or 6 percent of the total, but no electoral votes. Fully three-quarters of the electorate thus supported a more active government than the restrained one Taft represented.

Sharp debate over the fundamentals of Progressive government had characterized the campaign. Roosevelt offered voters the "New Nationalism." Roosevelt foresaw an era of national unity in which government would coordinate and regulate economic activity. He would not destroy big business, which he saw as an efficient organizer of production. Instead, he would establish regulatory commissions of experts who would protect citizens' interests and ensure wise use of concentrated economic power.

New Nationalism and New Freedom

Wilson offered a more idealistic scheme, the "New Freedom." He believed that concentrated economic power threatened individual liberty and that monopolies had to be broken up so the marketplace could become genuinely open. Like Roosevelt, Wilson wanted to enhance government authority to protect and regulate, but he stopped short of the cooperation between business and government inherent in the New Nationalism.

Both Roosevelt and Wilson strongly supported equality of opportunity (though chiefly for white males), conservation of natural resources, fair wages, and social betterment for all classes. And neither would hesitate to expand government activity through strong personal leadership and bureaucratic reform.

As president, Wilson found it necessary to blend New Freedom competition with New Nationalism regulation, and in so doing he set the direction of future federal economic policy. The corporate merger movement had proceeded so far that restoration of free competition proved impossible. Wilson could only try to prevent corporate abuses by expanding government's regulatory powers. His administration moved toward that end with passage in 1914 of the Clayton Anti-Trust Act and a bill creating the Federal Trade Commission (FTC).

Wilson's Policy on Business Regulation

The Clayton Act extended the Sherman Anti-Trust Act of 1890 by outlawing monopolistic practices such as *price discrimination* (efforts to destroy competition by lowering prices in some regions but not in others) and *interlocking directorates* (management of two or more competing companies by the same executives). The FTC was to investigate companies and issue cease-and-desist orders against unfair trade practices. As in ICC rulings, accused companies could appeal FTC orders in court. Nevertheless, the FTC represented another step in consumer protection.

Wilson broadened regulation of finance with the Federal Reserve Act of 1913, which established the nation's first central banking system since Andrew Jackson's destruction of the Second Bank of the United States in 1832. The act created twelve district banks to hold the reserves of member banks throughout the nation. The district banks would lend money to member banks at a low interest rate called the *discount rate*. By adjusting this rate, district banks could increase or decrease the amount of money in circulation. In other words, in response to the nation's needs, the Federal Reserve Board could loosen or tighten credit. Monetary affairs no longer would depend on the gold supply, and interest rates would be fairer, especially for small borrowers.

The only act of Wilson's first administration that promoted free competition was the Under-wood Tariff, passed in 1913. By the 1910s, prices for some consumer goods were unnaturally high because tariffs had discouraged the importation of cheaper foreign materials and manufactured products. By drastically reducing or eliminating tariff rates, the Underwood Tariff encouraged imports. To replace revenues lost because of tariff reductions, the act levied a graduated income tax on United States residents—an option made possible when the Sixteenth Amendment was ratified earlier that year. The income tax was tame by today's standards. Incomes under $4,000 were exempt; thus almost all factory workers and farmers escaped taxation. Individuals and corporations earning between $4,000 and $20,000 had to pay a 1 percent tax, and rates for higher incomes rose gradually to a maximum of 6 percent on earnings over $500,000.

Tariff and Tax Reform

The outbreak of the First World War and the approaching presidential election campaign prompted Wilson to support stronger reforms in 1916. Concerned that farmers needed a better system of long-term mortgage credit, the president backed the Federal Farm Loan Act. This measure created twelve federally supported banks that would lend money at moderate interest to farmers who belonged to credit institutions. To stave off railroad strikes that might disrupt transportation at a time of national emergency, Wilson pushed passage of the Adamson Act, which mandated an eight-hour workday and time-and-a-half overtime pay for railroad laborers. Finally, Wilson courted support from social reformers: he backed laws against child labor and he supported workers' compensation for federal employees who suffered work-related injuries or illness.

In selecting a candidate to oppose Wilson in 1916, Republicans snubbed Theodore Roosevelt in favor of Charles Evans Hughes, a Supreme Court justice and former reform governor of New York. Acutely aware of the First World War's impact on national affairs, Wilson ran for reelection on a platform of peace, Progressivism, and preparedness; his supporters used the cam-

Election of 1916

paign slogan "He Kept Us Out of War." Roosevelt's bellicose speeches hurt Hughes, and Wilson won a narrow victory (277 to 254) in the electoral college.

 Conclusion

By 1920, government, economy, and society as they had existed in the nineteenth century were gone forever. The Progressives had established the principle of public intervention to ensure fairness, health, and safety. Concern over poverty and injustice reached new heights. But in the face of a growing affluence, reform could not be sustained indefinitely. To be sure, Progressive values lingered after the First World War, but a mass consumer society began to refocus people's attention from reform to materialism.

The Progressive era was characterized by multiple and sometimes contradictory goals. By no means was there a single Progressive movement. Reform programs on the national level ranged from Roosevelt's New Nationalism, with its faith in big government as a coordinator of big business, to Wilson's New Freedom, with its promise to dissolve economic concentrations and legislate open competition. At the state and local levels, reformers pursued causes as varied as government reorganization, public ownership of utilities, betterment of working conditions, and moral revival.

The failure of many Progressive initiatives indicates the strength of the opposition, as well as weaknesses within the reform movements themselves. Courts asserted constitutional and liberty-of-contract doctrines in striking down key Progressive legislation, notably the federal law prohibiting child labor. In states and cities, adoption of the initiative, referendum, and recall did not encourage greater participation in government as had been hoped; those mechanisms either were seldom used or became tools of those in power. On the federal level, regulatory agencies rarely had enough resources for thorough investigations; they had to obtain information from the very companies they policed. Progres-

sives thus failed in many respects to redistribute power. In 1920 as in 1900, government remained under the influence of business and industry.

Yet the reform movements that characterized the Progressive era did shape the nation's future. Trustbusting, however faulty, forced industrialists to become more sensitive to public opinion, and insurgents in Congress partially diluted the power of dictatorial politicians. Progressive legislation equipped government with tools to protect consumers against price fixing and dangerous products. The income tax, created to redistribute wealth, also became a source of government revenue. And perhaps most important, Progressives challenged old ways of thinking and made the nation acutely aware of its principles and promises.

Suggestions for Further Reading

General

Paul M. Boyer, *Urban Masses and Moral Order in America, 1820–1920* (1978); John M. Cooper, Jr., *The Pivotal Decades: The United States, 1900–1920* (1990); Louis Filler, *The Muckrakers,* rev. ed. (1980); Richard Hofstadter, *The Age of Reform* (1955); William R. Hutchinson, *The Modernist Impulse in American Protestantism* (1976); Morton Keller, *Regulating a New Economy* (1990); Gabriel Kolko, *The Triumph of Conservatism* (1963); Arthur Link and Robert L. McCormick, *Progressivism* (1983); David W. Noble, *The Progressive Mind,* rev. ed. (1981); Robert Wiebe, *The Search for Order* (1968).

Regional Studies

Dewey Grantham, *Southern Progressivism* (1983); Richard L. McCormick, *From Realignment to Reform: Political Change in New York State, 1893–1910* (1981); David P. Thelen, *Robert La Follette and the Insurgent Spirit* (1976); Richard White, *"It's Your Misfortune and None of My Own": A History of the American West* (1991); C. Vann Woodward, *Origins of the New South* (1951).

Legislative Issues and Reform Groups

Allen F. Davis, *Spearheads for Reform: The Social Settlements and the Progressive Movement, 1890–1914* (1967); Ruth Rosen, *The Lost Sisterhood: Prostitution in America, 1900–1918* (1982); James H. Timberlake, *Prohibition and the Progressive Crusade* (1963); Walter I. Trattner, *Crusade for the Children* (1970); Irwin Yellowitz, *Labor and the Progressive Movement in New York State* (1965); James Harvey Young, *Pure Food* (1989). (For works on socialism, see the listings under "Protest and Socialism" at the end of Chapter 20.)

Education, Law, and the Social Sciences

Jerold S. Auerback, *Unequal Justice: Lawyers and Social Change in Modern America* (1976); Lawrence Cremin, *The Transformation of the School: Progressivism in American Education* (1961); Paula S. Fass, *Outside In: Minorities and the Transformation of American Education* (1989); Ellen Fitzpatrick, *Endless Crusade: Women Social Scientists and Progressive Reform* (1990); Lynn D. Gordon, *Gender and Higher Education in the Progressive Era* (1990); Thomas L. Haskell, *The Emergence of Professional Social Science* (1977); Helen Horowitz, *Alma Mater: Design and Experience in Women's Colleges* (1984); David W. Marcell, *Progress and Pragmatism: James, Dewey, Beard, and the American Idea of Progress* (1974); Lawrence Veysey, *The Emergence of the American University* (1970).

Women

Ruth Borden, *Women and Temperance* (1980); Ellen Chesler, *Woman of Valor: The Life of Margaret Sanger* (1992); Nancy F. Cott, *The Grounding of American Feminism* (1987); Carl N. Degler, *At Odds: Women and the Family in America* (1980); Linda Gordon, *Woman's Body, Woman's Right: A Social History of Birth Control in America* (1976); Evelyn Higginbotham, *Righteous Discontent: The Women's Movement in the Black Baptist Church, 1880–1920* (1993); Alice Kessler-Harris, *Out to Work: A History of Wage-Earning Women in the United States* (1982); Robyn Muncy, *Creating a Female Dominion in American Reform* (1991); William L. O'Neill, *Everyone Was Brave: The Rise and Fall of Feminism in America* (1969); Rosalind Rosenberg, *Beyond Separate Spheres: Intellectual Roots of Modern Feminism* (1982); Sheila M. Rothman, *Woman's Proper Place* (1978).

African-Americans

John Dittmer, *Black Georgia in the Progressive Era, 1900–1920* (1977); George Frederickson, *The Black Image in the White Mind* (1971); Louis R. Harlan, *Booker T. Washington* 2 vols. (1972 and 1983); Jacqueline Jones, *Labor of Love, Labor of Sorrow: Black Women, Work and the Family from Slavery to the Present* (1985); August Meier, *Negro Thought in America, 1880–1915* (1963); Elliot M. Rudwick, *W. E. B. Du Bois* (1969).

Roosevelt, Taft, and Wilson

Francis L. Broderick, *Progressivism at Risk: Electing a President in 1912* (1989); Paolo E. Coletta, *The Presidency of William Howard Taft* (1973); John Milton Cooper, Jr., *The Warrior and the Priest: Woodrow Wilson and Theodore Roosevelt* (1983); Lewis Gould, *The Presidency of Theodore Roosevelt* (1991); August Hecksher, *Woodrow Wilson* (1991); Edmund Morris, *The Rise of Theodore Roosevelt* (1979); James Pednick, Jr., *Progressive Politics and Conservation: The Ballinger-Pinchot Affair* (1968).

CHAPTER

22

The Quest for Empire
1865–1914

American lawyers, businessmen, and sugar planters, many of them the sons of Protestant missionaries, decided to become revolutionaries in Hawai'i. These *haole* (foreigners) sought a new order that favored their interests. So, in January 1893, members of this white American elite brought to a climax their treasonous plot to overthrow the native government of Queen Liliuokalani.

By the 1890s, Americans owned about three-quarters of the islands' wealth, though they represented a mere 2.1 percent of the population. Because diseases brought by foreigners had diminished the native population, causing a labor shortage, the American oligarchy imported Chinese and Japanese workers for the expanding sugar industry. By 1890, 17 percent of Hawai'i's population was Chinese-born, 14 percent was Japanese-born, and native Hawaiians accounted for only 53.5 percent. Hawai'i became a multiracial society dominated by white Americans whose sugar exports entered the American marketplace duty-free.

Earlier, in 1887, the American conspirators forced King Kalakaua to accept a constitution that granted foreigners the right to vote and shifted decision-making authority from the monarchy to the legislature. The same year, Hawai'i granted the United States naval rights to Pearl Harbor.

The McKinley Tariff of 1890 created an economic crisis for Hawai'i that further undermined the native government. The tariff eliminated

411

Hawaiian sugar's favored status by admitting *all foreign* sugar into the United States duty-free. The measure also provided a bounty of 2 cents a pound to domestic United States growers, making it possible for them to sell their sugar at a price lower than the price charged for foreign sugar. For United States producers and planters in Hawai'i, the tariff led to declining profits. Prominent Americans in Hawai'i soon pressed for annexation of the islands by the United States so that their sugar would be classified as domestic rather than foreign.

When Kalakaua's sister Princess Liliuokalani assumed the throne upon his death in 1891, "they were lying in wait," she remembered. In collusion with John L. Stevens, the chief United States diplomat in Hawai'i, the conspirators struck in January 1893—but only after American troops from the ship U.S.S. *Boston* occupied Honolulu. The queen was forced to surrender to the new regime, headed by Sanford B. Dole, son of missionaries and a prominent attorney. Up went the American flag.

Against the queen's protests and those of Japan, President Benjamin Harrison hurriedly sent a treaty of annexation to the Senate. Sensing foul play, incoming President Grover Cleveland withdrew the treaty and ordered an investigation. His investigator's report confirmed a conspiracy by the white economic elite in league with John Stevens and noted that a majority of Hawaiians opposed annexation. Down came the American flag. Nevertheless, annexation came in 1898.

Seizing foreign opportunities was common practice for those who governed in Washington, D.C. In the early nineteenth century, Americans had purchased Louisiana; annexed Florida, Oregon, and Texas; pushed Indians out of the path of white migration westward; seized California and other western areas from Mexico; and acquired the Gadsden Purchase. Moreover, the United States had developed a lucrative foreign trade with most of the world.

From the Civil War to the First World War the United States became one of the world's premier expansionist nations, building, managing, and protecting an overseas empire. In that imperialistic age, the international system was becoming multipolar. Germany challenged an overextended Great Britain, and Japan expanded in Asia at the expense of both China and Russia. As for the United States, it emerged as a great power with particular clout in Latin America.

The United States imperialist surge, however, sparked considerable opposition. Abroad, native nationalists, commercial competitors, and other imperial nations tried to block the spread of United States influence, while anti-imperialists at home stimulated a momentous debate over the fundamental course of American foreign policy. Most Americans applauded *expansionism*— the outward movement of goods, ships, dollars, people, and ideas—as a traditional feature of their nation's history. But many became uneasy whenever expansionism gave way to *imperialism*—the imposition of control over other peoples, undermining their sovereignty so that they lose the freedom to make their own decisions. Imperial control could be imposed either formally (by annexation, colonialism, or military occupation) or informally (by economic domination, political manipulation, or the threat of intervention). As the informal methods indicate, imperialism meant more than the taking of territory.

Critics disparaged territorial imperialism as unbefitting the United States. Would not an overseas territorial empire, incorporating people of color living far from the United States, undermine institutions at home, threaten American culture, invite perpetual war, and violate honored principles? Most Americans endorsed economic expansion as essential to the nation's prosperity and security, but anti-imperialists drew the line between expansionism and imperialism: profitable and fair trade relationships, yes; exploitation, no.

In the late nineteenth century the federal government sometimes failed to fund adequately the vehicles of expansion, such as the navy, and most businessmen ignored foreign commerce in favor of the domestic marketplace. Still, the direction of United States foreign policy became unmistak-

1861–69	Secretary of State Seward sets expansionist course
1866	Transatlantic cable completed
1867	Alaska and Midway acquired by United States
1868	Burlingame Treaty with China regulates immigration
1871	Anglo-American treaty sends *Alabama* claims issue to tribunal
1874	United States foreign trade shifts to favorable balance
1876	Porfirio Díaz, friendly to United States investment, begins long rule in Mexico
1880	Treaty with China limits Chinese immigration to the United States
1883	Advent of the New Navy
1885	Josiah Strong's book *Our Country* celebrates Anglo-Saxons
1887	United States gains naval rights to Pearl Harbor, Hawai'i
1889	First Pan-American Conference
1890	Alfred T. Mahan's *The Influence of Sea Power upon History* is published McKinley Tariff hurts Hawaiian sugar exports
1893	Severe economic depression begins Frederick Jackson Turner sets forth his frontier thesis Americans in Hawai'i overthrow Queen Liliuokalani
1894	Wilson-Gorman Tariff imposes tariff on Cuban sugar
1895	Venezuelan crisis with Britain Cuban Revolution against Spain begins Japan defeats China to become a major Asian power
1896	McKinley elected president
1898	De Lôme letter is published Sinking of the *Maine* heightens chances of war Spanish-American-Cuban-Filipino War Hawai'i annexed by the United States

1899	Senate approves Treaty of Paris after debate over empire First Open Door note calls for equal trade opportunity in China Philippine Insurrection against the United States breaks out
1900	Second Open Door note issued during Boxer Rebellion in China United States exports total $1.5 billion McKinley reelected
1901	Theodore Roosevelt becomes president Emilio Aguinaldo captured in Philippines Hay-Pauncefote Treaty allows United States development of ship canal
1903	Panama breaks from Colombia and grants canal rights to United States Platt Amendment subjugates Cuba
1904	Roosevelt Corollary declares United States a "police power"
1904–05	Russo-Japanese War
1905	Taft-Katsura Agreement gains Japanese pledge to respect Philippines Portsmouth Conference ends Russo-Japanese War
1906	San Francisco School Board segregates Asian schoolchildren United States invades Cuba to put down rebellion
1907	"Great White Fleet" of the United States Navy makes world tour "Gentleman's agreement" with Japan restricts immigration
1908	Root-Takahira Agreement with Japan reaffirms Open Door in China
1910	Mexican Revolution begins against Díaz and United States interests
1912	United States troops invade Cuba again United States troops occupy Nicaragua
1914	United States troops invade Mexico First World War begins Panama Canal opens

able: Americans intended to exert their influence beyond the continental United States.

Imperial Promoters: The Foreign Policy Elite and Economic Expansion

Foreign policy has always sprung from the domestic setting of a nation—its needs, wants, moods, ideology, and culture. The leaders who

guided America's expansionist foreign relations were the same people who guided the economic development of the machine age, forged the transcontinental railroad, built America's bustling cities and giant corporations, espoused ideas of American exceptionalism, and shaped a mass culture.

Unlike domestic policy, foreign policy is seldom shaped by "the people." Most Americans simply do not follow international relations or express themselves on foreign issues. In the post–Civil War era, as in others, foreign policy

U.S. Trade Expansion, 1865–1914

United States Trade Expansion, 1865–1914 This figure illustrates two key characteristics of U.S. foreign trade: first, that the United States began in the 1870s to enjoy a favorable balance of trade (exporting more than it imported); second, that U.S. exports expanded tremendously, making the United States one of the world's economic giants. Source: From Thomas G. Paterson, J. Garry Clifford, and Kenneth J. Hagan, *American Foreign Relations: A History.* 4th edition. Copyright 1995.

was dominated by the so-called foreign policy elite: opinion leaders in politics, business, labor, agriculture, religion, journalism, education, and the military. This small group—better read and better traveled than most Americans, more cosmopolitan in outlook, and politically active—believed that United States prosperity and security depended on the exertion of United States influence abroad. Among them were two future secretaries of state (John Hay and Elihu Root), a member of the Senate Foreign Relations Committee (Henry Cabot Lodge), and Theodore Roosevelt, who would become president in 1901. Increasingly in the late nineteenth century, and especially in the 1890s, the foreign policy elite urged not only expansionism but both formal and informal imperialism.

These American leaders believed that selling, buying, and investing in foreign marketplaces were important to the United States. Why? One reason was profits from foreign sales. Fear helped make the case for foreign trade as well, because the nation's farms and factories produced more than Americans could consume. Foreign commerce might serve as a safety valve to relieve overproduction, unemployment, economic depression, and the social tensions that arise from them.

Foreign trade figured prominently in the tremendous economic growth of the United States after the Civil War. In 1865 United States exports totaled $234 million; by 1914 American exports had reached $2.5 billion. In 1874 the United States reversed its historically unfavorable balance of trade (importing more than it exported) and began to enjoy a long-term favorable balance (exporting more than it imported).

Growth of Foreign Trade

Agricultural goods accounted for about three-fourths of total exports in 1870 and about two-thirds in 1900. In 1913, however, manufactured goods led United States foreign sales for the first time. Meanwhile, direct American investments abroad had reached $3.5 billion by 1914. Thus, on the eve of the First World War, the United States had a favorable balance of trade, was among the top four investor nations, and was producing a greater percentage of the world's manufactured goods than Great Britain and Germany combined.

Ideology, Culture, and Empire

In the American march toward empire, ideology and culture figured prominently. An intertwined set of ideas conditioned United States foreign relations. Nationalism, exceptionalism, capitalism, Social Darwinism, paternalism, and the categorization of foreigners in derogatory race-, age-, and gender-based terms—all influenced American leaders. Prejudice and fear—of social disorder stirred by revolution, of economic depression, of racial and ethnic mixing, of women's rights, of a closed frontier, of losing international stature—infused many American ideas about the world. Leaders exported American culture and sought to remake other societies in the image of the United States. The intersection of American and foreign cultures, however, bred not only adoption but rejection, not only imitation but clash.

After the Civil War, leaders again put the United States on an expansionist course and championed a nationalism based on notions of American supremacy. In their idea of a racial hierarchy, Americans ranked "uncivilized" people of black color and Indians at the bottom and "civilized" white Americans of Anglo-Saxon heritage at the top. Near the top but beneath Anglo-Saxons, Americans placed European peoples—"aggressive" Germans, followed by "peasant" Slavs, "sentimental" French and Italians, and "Shylock" Jews. In the middle rank came Latinos, the Spanish-speaking people of Latin America, and East Asian peoples, the "Orientals" or "Mongolians."

Race Thinking

Reverend Josiah Strong's popular and influential *Our Country* (1885) celebrated an Anglo-Saxon race destined to lead others. Strong believed that "to be a Christian and an Anglo-Saxon and an American . . . is to stand at the very mountaintop of privilege." Social Darwinists saw Americans as a superior people certain to overcome all competition.

The magazine *National Geographic*, which chronicled with photographs America's new overseas possessions, chose pictures that reflected prevailing

How do historians know that Americans in the imperial age of the late nineteenth century disparaged people of other societies as "uncivilized" and in need of "civilization" from a superior United States? Historians interpret speeches, diaries, letters, tourist-industry advertisements, cartoons, fair exhibits, and more to identify the derogatory racist, age-based, and gendered language that Americans often used to describe foreigners. Especially revealing are the images on picture postcards of the era, because they capture expressions of supremacy in their depictions of the "civilized" (modern) and the "wild" (premodern). As photographs, postcards provide historians with a detailed documentary record, a testimony of feelings, and a visual representation of the values and attitudes of the time.

Government-made postcards were first issued in Austria in 1869 as a way to reduce the expense of corresponding by mail (they cost just a penny). Privately or commercially printed picture postcards appeared elsewhere in Europe in the 1880s and in the United States in the 1890s. Collecting postcards immediately became popular as a hobby; the collection and study of postcards today is called deltiology. At the turn of the century, card subjects included humor, anniversaries, patriotic events, advertisements, street scenes, historic sites, romantic messages, famous leaders, art, and costumes. The images of foreign peoples on American postcards often communicated a message that denigrated indigenous life through contrast with "Western" ways. The Singer Manufacturing Company handed out the promotional postcard reproduced here as a souvenir from the firm's exhibit at the 1893 Columbian Exposition in Chicago. About three-quarters of all sewing machines sold in the world were Singers. The machine shown in this postcard was marketed in South Africa, where, the company advised, the "Zulus are a fine warlike people" who were moving toward "civilization" with Singer's help.   State Historical Society of Wisconsin.

American ethnocentric attitudes toward foreigners. The image portrayed was that of strange, exotic, premodern people who had not become "Western." Emphasizing this point, *National Geographic* regularly pictured women with naked breasts.

A male ethos also characterized American views of foreigners. The language of American leaders was weighted with words such as *manliness*

Images of Foreign Peoples

and *weakling*. Some leaders, in-

Male Ethos

cluding Theodore Roosevelt, often described other nations as effeminate—unable to cope with the demands of world politics. The gendered imagery prevalent in United States foreign relations joined race thinking to place women, people of color, and nations weaker than the United States in the low ranks of the hierarchy of power and, hence, in a necessarily dependent status justifying United States hegemony.

Issues of race and gender also marked the experiences of religious missionaries, many of whom were women. Missionaries dispatched to China,

Missionaries

Korea, and Africa helped spur the transfer of American culture and power abroad. Like Grace Roberts in China, missionaries taught the Bible, hoping to convert "natives" and "savages" to Christianity. When American missionary women criticized non-Christian foreign societies as more exploitative of women than the United States, they perpetuated cultural stereotypes of Anglo-Saxon superiority that undergirded imperialism.

Expansionists believed that empire benefited both Americans and those who came under their control. When the United States intervened in

Remaking Societies and Gaining Markets

other lands, Americans claimed that in remaking foreign societies they were extending liberty and prosperity to less fortunate people. To critics, however, American paternalism appeared hypocritical. To impose on Filipinos an American-style political system, for example, United States officials censored the press, jailed critics, and picked candidates for public office.

 Eyes Abroad, 1860s–1880s

The American empire grew gradually, sometimes haltingly. One of its chief architects was William H. Seward. As a senator from New York (1849–1861) and as secretary of state (1861–1869), Seward envisioned a large, coordinated United States empire encompassing Canada, the Caribbean, Cuba, Central

America, Mexico, Hawai'i, Iceland, Greenland, and Pacific islands. This empire would be built not by war but by a natural gravitation toward the United States. Commerce would hurry the process, as would a canal across Central America, a transcontinental American railroad to link up with Asian markets, and a telegraph system to speed communications.

Most of Seward's grandiose plans did not reach fruition in his own day. Both political foes and anti-imperialists such as Senator Carl Schurz and E. L. Godkin, editor of the

William H. Seward's Quest for Empire

magazine *The Nation*, blocked some of Seward's territorial schemes. They argued that the country already had enough unsettled land and that the creation of a showcase of democracy and prosperity at home would best persuade other peoples to adopt American institutions and principles.

But Seward did enjoy some successes. In 1867 Seward paid Russia $7.2 million for the 591,000 square miles of Alaska—land twice the size of Texas. Some critics lampooned "Seward's Icebox," but the Senate voted overwhelmingly for the treaty. That same year, Seward laid claim to the Midway Islands in the Pacific Ocean.

Seward realized his dream of a world knit together into a giant communications system. In 1866, an underwater transatlantic cable linked European and American telegraph networks. In 1903 a submarine

International Communications

cable reached across the Pacific to the Philippines; three years later it reached to Japan and China. More than a decade earlier, American-strung telegraph lines had reached Chile. Information about markets, crises, and war flowed steadily and quickly.

Alongside Seward's dreams, however, were some knotty problems, and his successor, Hamilton Fish (1869–1877), inherited one in the form of

Disputes with Britain and Canada

the *Alabama* claims. The *Alabama* and other vessels built in Great Britain for the Confederacy during the Civil War had preyed on Union shipping. Senator Charles Sumner demanded that Britain pay $2 billion in damages or cede Canada to the United States, but Fish favored negotiations. In 1871 Britain and America signed the Washington Treaty, whereby the British apologized and agreed to the creation of a tribunal, which later awarded the United States $15.5 million. Disputes over fishing rights along the North Atlantic coast, however, continued to dog Anglo-Canadian-American relations, as did sealing near Alaska.

In China the United States experienced both opportunity and trouble. American missionaries became targets of Chinese nationalist anger, while American oil and textile companies sent their wares into

Sino-American Relations

a China market they dreamed was boundless. Although the Burlingame Treaty (1868), which allowed free immigration between China and the United States, pledged Sino-American friendship, frequent riots against Chinese immigrants erupted in the American West. Sinophobia was also reflected in an 1880 treaty that allowed Congress to suspend Chinese immigration to the United States.

The convening in 1889 of the first Pan-American Conference in Washington, D.C., bore witness to growing United States influence in the Western Hemisphere, too.

Pan-American Conference

Conferees from Latin America toured United States factories and then pledged support for reciprocity treaties to improve hemispheric trade. To encourage inter-American cooperation, they founded the Pan American Union.

In contrast to Latin America, Africa generated little interest in the United States. American tobacco, kerosene, and rum claimed a good share of African markets and the United States Navy patrolled the African coast to protect American lives and property, but through tariff barriers the European colonizers reduced the continent's commerce with the United States.

As the United States acquired new markets and territories, expansionists argued that a bigger, modernized United States Navy had become imperative. Captain Alfred T.

Alfred T. Mahan and the New Navy

Mahan became a major popularizer for a "New Navy." Because foreign trade was vital to the United States, he argued, the nation required an efficient navy to protect its shipping; in turn, a navy required colonies for bases. Mahan's *The Influence of Sea Power upon History* (1890) was a widely read book that sat on every serious expansionist's shelf. Theodore Roosevelt and Henry Cabot Lodge eagerly consulted Mahan, sharing his belief in the links among trade, navy, and colonies.

Moving toward naval modernization, Congress in 1883 authorized construction of the first steel-hulled warships. American factories went to work to produce steam engines, high-velocity shells, powerful guns, and precision instruments. The navy shifted from sail power to steam and from wood construction to steel. Often named for states and cities to kindle patriotism and local support for naval expansion, New Navy ships such as the *Maine*, the *Oregon*, and the *Boston* thrust the United States into naval prominence.

Crises in the 1890s: Hawai'i, Venezuela, and Cuba

In the depression-plagued 1890s, crises in Hawai'i, Venezuela, and Cuba gave expansionist Americans opportunities to act on their zealous arguments for what Senator Lodge called a "large policy."

Belief that the frontier at home had closed accentuated the expansionist case. In 1893 the historian Frederick Jackson Turner postulated the

Turner's Frontier Thesis

thesis that an ever-expanding continental frontier had shaped the American character. That "frontier has gone," Turner wrote. He did not explicitly say that a new frontier had to be found overseas, but he did write that "American energy will continually demand a wider field for its exercise."

Hawai'i emerged as a new frontier for Americans. The Hawaiian Islands had long commanded American attention—commercial, missionary, naval,

Annexation of Hawai'i

and diplomatic. Secretary of State James Blaine had warned other nations away from the archipelago in 1881, declaring the Hawaiian Islands "essentially a part of the American system." President Cleveland thwarted the attempt to annex Hawai'i in 1893, although American expansionists did conspire to overthrow Queen Liliuokalani that year. In 1898, Congress voted for annexation by a majority vote.

Venezuelan Crisis

The Venezuelan crisis of 1895 also saw the United States in an expansive mood. For decades Venezuela and Great Britain had squabbled over the border between Venezuela and British Guiana. The disputed territory contained rich gold deposits and the mouth of the Orinoco River, a commercial gateway to northern South America. Venezuela asked for United States help. Following the tone set by President Cleveland, the secretary of state lectured the British that the Monroe Doctrine prohibited European intervention in the Western Hemisphere. The British, seeking international friends to counter intensifying competition from Germany, quietly retreated from the crisis. In 1896 an Anglo-American arbitration board divided the disputed territory between Britain and Venezuela. The Venezuelans were barely consulted. Thus the United States displayed a trait common to imperialists: disregard for the rights and sensibilities of small nations.

Cuba in the United States Vortex

In 1895 came yet another crisis, this one in Cuba. From 1868 to 1878, the Cubans had battled Spain. Slavery was abolished but independence denied. While the Cuban economy suffered depression, Spanish rule continued to be repressive. Insurgents committed to *Cuba Libre* waited for another chance. José Martí, one of the heroes of Cuban history, collected arms and men in the United States. This was but one of the many ways the lives of Americans and Cubans were linked, a popular attraction to baseball being another. Their economies also became integrated. U.S. investments of $50 million, mostly in sugar

Queen Liliuokalani (1838–1917), ousted from her throne in 1893 by wealthy revolutionaries, vigorously protested in her autobiography and diary, as well as in interviews, the United States's annexation of Hawai'i in 1898. For years she defended Hawaiian nationalism and emphasized that United States officials in 1893 had conspired with Sanford B. Dole and others to overthrow the native monarchy. Courtesy of the Liliuokalani Trust.

plantations, dominated the Caribbean island. More than 90 percent of Cuba's sugar was exported to the United States, and most island imports came from the United States.

A change in American tariff policy hastened the Cuban Revolution against Spain and that island's further incorporation into "the American system." The Wilson-Gorman Tariff (1894) imposed a duty on Cuban sugar, which had been entering the United States duty-free. The Cuban economy, highly dependent on exports, plunged into deep crisis.

From American soil, Martí launched a revolution in 1895 that mounted in human and material costs. The rebels destroyed property and used guerrilla tactics to avoid head-on clashes with Spanish soldiers. The Spanish retaliated under the command of General Valeriano Weyler, who instituted a policy of "reconcentration" to separate the insurgents from their supporters among the Cuban people. Some 300,000 Cubans were herded into fortified towns and camps, where hunger, starvation, and disease led to tens of thousands of deaths.

The Cuban Revolution

All across Cuba, United States investments went up in smoke and Cuban-American trade dwindled. As reports of atrocity and destruction became headline news in the American yellow press, Americans sympathized increasingly with the insurrectionists. In late 1897, a new government in Madrid modified reconcentration and promised some autonomy for Cuba.

Events in early 1898, however, caused President William McKinley to lose faith in Madrid's ability to bring peace to Cuba. In January, when antireform pro-Spanish loyalists and army personnel rioted in Havana, Washington ordered the battleship *Maine* to Havana harbor to demonstrate United States concern and to protect American citizens. On February 15 an explosion ripped the *Maine*, killing 266 of 354 American officers and crew. Just a week earlier, William Randolph Hearst's inflammatory *New York Journal* had published a stolen private letter written by the Spanish minister in Washington, Enrique Dupuy de Lôme, who belittled McKinley's leadership and suggested that Spain would fight on. Congress soon complied unanimously with McKinley's request for $50 million in defense funds. The naval board created to investigate the sinking of the *Maine* then reported that a mine had caused the explosion.

Sinking of the *Maine*

The impact of these events narrowed McKinley's diplomatic options. He decided to send Spain an ultimatum. In late March the United States insisted that Spain accept an armistice, end reconcentration altogether, and designate McKinley as arbiter. Implicit was the demand that Spain grant Cuba its independence. No Spanish government could have given up Cuba and remained in office, but Madrid nonetheless made concessions. It abolished reconcentration and accepted an armistice on the condition that the insurgents agree first. Wanting more, McKinley drafted a war message. Then he received news that Spain had gone a step further and declared a unilateral armistice. McKinley hesitated, but he would no longer tolerate chronic disorder just 90 miles off the American coast. On April 11, the president asked Congress for authorization to use United States force against Spain.

On April 19 Congress declared Cuba free and independent and directed the president to use force to remove Spanish authority from the island. The legislators also passed the Teller Amendment, which disclaimed any United States intention to annex Cuba. McKinley beat back a congressional amendment to recognize the rebel government. Believing that the Cubans were not ready for self-government, he argued that they needed a period of American tutoring.

The Spanish-American-Cuban-Filipino War

The motives of Americans who favored war were mixed and complex. McKinley's April message expressed a humanitarian impulse to stop the bloodletting, a concern for commerce and property, and the psychological need to end the nightmarish anxiety once and for all. Republican politicians advised McKinley that their party would lose the upcoming congressional elections unless the Cuban question was solved. Many businesspeople, who had been hesitant before the crisis of early 1898, joined many farmers in the belief that ejecting Spain from Cuba would open new markets for surplus production.

Motives for War

Inveterate imperialists saw war as an opportunity to fulfill expansionist dreams. Naval enthusiasts could prove the worth of the New Navy.

Conservatives, alarmed by Populism and violent labor strikes, welcomed war as a national unifier. Sensationalism also figured in the march to war, with the yellow press in particular exaggerating stories of Spanish misdeeds. Some too young to remember the bloody Civil War looked on war as adventure and used inflated rhetoric to trumpet the call to arms. Overarching all explanations for the 1898 war were expansionism and imperialism.

More than 263,000 regulars and volunteers served in the army and another 25,000 in the navy during the war. Most never left the United States, and 5,462 of them died—but only 379 of them in combat. The rest fell to malaria and yellow fever spread by mosquitoes. About 10,000 African-American troops, assigned to segregated regiments, found no relief from racism and Jim Crow. For all, food was bad and medical care was unsophisticated.

**United States
Military Forces**

To the surprise of most Americans, the first war news actually came from faraway Asia, from the Spanish colony of the Philippines. On May 1, 1898, Commodore George Dewey's New Navy ship the *Olympia*, leading an American squadron, steamed into Manila Bay and wrecked the Spanish fleet. Dewey's sailors had to be handed volumes of the *Encyclopaedia Britannica* to acquaint them with this strange land, but officials in Washington knew better. Manila ranked with Pearl Harbor as a choice harbor and the Philippines sat significantly on the way to China and its potentially huge market.

**Dewey in
the Philippines**

American troops saw their first ground-war action on June 22, the day they landed near Santiago de Cuba and laid siege to the city. On July 3, United States warships sank the Spanish Caribbean squadron in Santiago harbor. American forces then assaulted the Spanish colony of Puerto Rico. Losing on all fronts and facing rebels as well as the Americans in both Cuba and the Philippines, Madrid sued for peace.

On August 12, Spain and the United States signed an armistice to end the Spanish-American-Cuban-Filipino War. In Paris in December 1898,

Treaty of Paris

American and Spanish negotiators agreed on the peace terms: independence for Cuba; cession of the Philippines, Puerto Rico, and Guam (an island in the Pacific) to the United States; and American payment of $20 million to Spain for the territories. The American empire now stretched deep into Asia; and the annexation of Wake Island (1898), Hawai'i (1898), and Samoa (1899) gave American traders, missionaries, and naval promoters other steppingstones to China.

The Taste of Empire: Imperialists Versus Anti-Imperialists

During the war, the *Washington Post* detected "a new appetite, a yearning to show our strength. . . . The taste of empire is in the mouth of the people." But as the nation debated the Treaty of Paris, it became evident that many Americans found the taste bitter. Anti-imperialists such as Mark Twain, William Jennings Bryan, Jane Addams, Andrew Carnegie, and Senator George Hoar of Massachusetts argued vigorously against annexation of the Philippines. They were disturbed that a war to free Cuba had led to empire.

Some critics appealed to principle, citing the Declaration of Independence and the Constitution: the conquest of people against their will violated the concept of self-determination. Other anti-imperialists argued that the United States could acquire markets without having to subjugate foreign peoples. Still others claimed that to maintain empire, the president repeatedly would have to dispatch troops overseas. Because he could do so as commander-in-chief, he would not have to seek congressional approval, thus subverting the constitutional checks-and-balances system. Reform-minded critics of the treaty insisted that domestic issues—including race

**The Anti-
Imperialist
Case**

relations—deserved first priority on the national agenda.

The anti-imperialists entered the debate with many handicaps and never launched an effective campaign. Their differences over domestic issues made it difficult for them to speak with one voice on a foreign question. They also appeared inconsistent: Carnegie would accept colonies if they were not acquired by force; Hoar voted for annexation of Hawai'i but not of the Philippines. Finally, possession of the Philippines was an established fact, very hard to undo.

The imperialists answered their critics with appeals to patriotism, destiny, and commerce. They sketched a scenario of American greatness:

Advocates of Empire

merchant ships plying the waters to boundless Asian markets; naval vessels cruising the Pacific to protect American interests; missionaries uplifting inferior peoples. And with Japan and Germany apparently ready to seize the Philippines if the United States did not, national honor dictated that Americans keep what they had shed blood to take.

In February 1899, the Senate passed the Treaty of Paris by a 57-to-27 vote, with most Republicans voting "yes" and most Democrats voting "no." An amendment promising independence as soon as the Filipinos formed a stable government lost only by the tie-breaking ballot of the vice president. The Democratic presidential candidate William J. Bryan carried the anti-imperialist case into the election of 1900. But the victorious McKinley refused to apologize for American imperialism.

 ## Asian Encounters: Open Door in China, Philippine Insurrection, and Japan

In 1895, the same year as the Venezuelan crisis and the advent of the Cuban Revolution, Japan claimed victory over China in a short war. Outsiders had been pecking away at China since the 1840s, but the Japanese onslaught intensified the international scramble. The Germans carved out a sphere of interest in Shandong; the Russians

moved into Manchuria and the Liaodong Peninsula; the French took Guangzhou Bay; the British, already holding Hong Kong, drove in new stakes in Shandong; Japan controlled Formosa and Korea as well as parts of China proper (see map, page 423). Within their spheres, the imperial powers built fortified bases and claimed exclusive economic privileges.

Secretary Hay knew that the United States could not force the imperial powers out of China, but he was determined to protect American commerce.

Open Door Policy

In September 1899 Hay sent the imperial nations a note asking them to respect the principle of equal trade opportunity—an Open Door. The recipients sent evasive replies, privately complaining that the United States was seeking for free in China the trade rights that they had gained at considerable cost. The next year, a Chinese secret society called the Boxers laid siege to the foreign legations in Beijing. The United States joined the imperial powers in sending troops to lift the siege and sent a second Open Door note in July that instructed other nations to preserve China's territorial integrity and to honor "equal and impartial trade."

Though Hay's foray into Asian politics settled little, the Open Door policy became a cornerstone of United States diplomacy. The "open door" had actually been a long-standing American principle, for as a trading nation the United States opposed barriers to international commerce. After 1900, however, when the United States began to emerge as the premier world trader, the Open Door policy became an instrument first to pry open markets and then to dominate them, not just in China but throughout the world. The Open Door also developed as an ideology with several tenets: first, that America's domestic well-being required exports; second, that foreign trade would suffer interruption unless the United States intervened abroad to implant American principles and keep foreign markets open; and, third, that the closing of any area to American products, citizens, or ideas threatened the survival of the United States itself.

In the Philippines, meanwhile, United States occupation authorities soon antagonized their new

Imperialism in Asia: Turn of the Century *The United States participated in the race for influence in the Pacific region by annexing the Philippines, Wake, Guam, and Hawai'i, announcing the Open Door policy, and expanding trade in the area. As the "spheres" in China demonstrate, that besieged nation succumbed to imperial outsiders despite the Open Door policy.*

"wards," as McKinley labeled them. Emilio Aguinaldo, the Philippine nationalist leader who had been battling the Spanish for years, believed that American officials had promised independence for his country. But after the victory, Aguinaldo was ordered out of Manila and isolated from decisions affecting his nation. Racial slurs infuriated nationalistic Filipinos, who also felt betrayed by the Treaty of Paris.

In January 1899, Aguinaldo proclaimed an independent Philippine Republic and took up arms. Before the Philippine Insurrection was suppressed in 1902, more than 200,000 Filipinos and 5,000 Americans lay dead in a war fought viciously by both sides. After capturing Aguinaldo in 1901, stern United States military rule imposed a policy of "attraction." American teachers were imported, English was declared the official language, and the University of the Philippines was founded (1908) to train an American-oriented elite. The Philippine economy grew as a United States satellite, and a sedition act silenced critics of United States authority by sending them to prison. In 1916 the Jones Act promised independence to the Philippines, but it did not become a reality until thirty years later.

Philippine Insurrection

As the United States disciplined the Filipinos, Japan was becoming the dominant power in Asia. Gradually the United States had to make concessions to Japan to protect the vulnerable Philippines and to sustain the Open Door policy. Japan smashed the Russians in the Russo-Japanese War (1904–1905). President Theodore Roosevelt mediated the crisis at the Portsmouth Conference in New Hampshire and won the Nobel Peace Prize for this ultimately vain effort to preserve peace and a balance of power in Asia.

Japan's Expansionism

In 1905, in the Taft-Katsura Agreement, the United States conceded Japanese hegemony over Korea in return for Japan's pledge not to undermine the United States's position in the Philippines. Three years later, in the Root-Takahira Agreement, the United States recognized Japan's interests in Manchuria, whereas Japan again pledged the security of the United States's Pacific possessions and endorsed the Open Door in China. In 1907, Roosevelt sent on a world tour the navy's "Great White Fleet" (so named because the ships were painted white for the voyage). Duly impressed, the Japanese began to build a bigger navy of their own.

President William Howard Taft thought he might counter Japanese advances in Asia through *dollar diplomacy*—the use of private funds to serve American diplomatic goals and at the same time to garner profits for American financiers. In this case, Taft induced American bankers to join an international consortium to build a railway in China. Taft's venture seemed only to embolden Japan.

Japanese-American relations also became tense over the treatment of Japanese citizens in the United States. In 1906 the San Francisco School Board ordered the segregation of all Chinese, Koreans, and Japanese in a special school. Tokyo protested the discrimination against its citizens. The following year, President Roosevelt quieted the crisis by striking a "gentleman's agreement" with Tokyo restricting the inflow of Japanese immigrants; San Francisco then rescinded its segregation order.

Anti-Japanese Bias in California

In 1914, when the First World War broke out in Europe, Japan seized Shandong and some Pacific islands from the Germans. In 1915 Japan issued its Twenty-One Demands, virtually insisting on hegemony over all of China. The Chinese door was being slammed shut, but the United States lacked the power in Asia to thwart Japan.

 ## Latin America, Europe, and International Rivalry

Intense international rivalry also troubled Latin America, where United States economic and strategic interests and usable power towered (see map, page 425). In Europe, repeated political and military disputes persuaded Americans to develop friendlier relations with Great Britain while avoiding entrapment in the Continent's troubles.

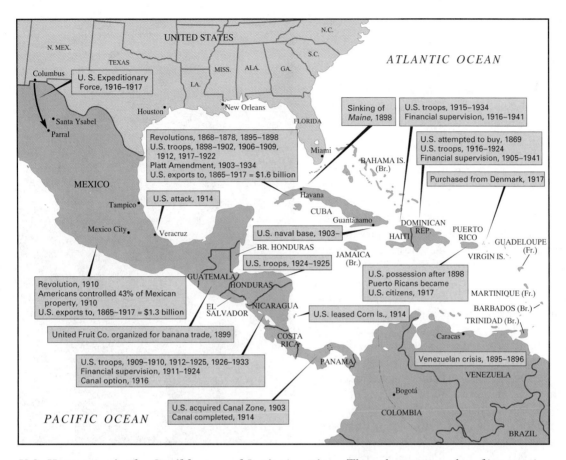

U.S. Hegemony in the Caribbean and Latin America   *Through a great number of interventions and persistent economic expansion, the United States became the predominant power in Latin America in the early twentieth century. The United States often backed up the Roosevelt Corollary and its declaration of a "police power" by dispatching troops to Caribbean nations, where they met nationalist opposition.*

As United States economic interests expanded in Latin America, so did United States political influence. United States exports to Latin America, which had exceeded $50 million in the 1870s, reached $300 million in 1914. Investments by United States citizens in Latin America climbed to a commanding $1.26 billion in 1914.

Economic Penetration of Latin America

With the destructive war in Cuba ended, United States citizens and corporations soon acquired title to more than 60 percent of Cuba's rural lands and came to dominate the island's sugar, mining, tobacco, and utilities industries. North American troops remained there until 1902 and United States officials forced the Cubans to append to their constitution the Platt Amendment. The amendment prohibited Cuba from making a treaty with another nation that might impair its independence; in practice, this meant that all treaties had to have United States approval. Most important, another Platt Amendment provision granted the United States

Platt Amendment for Cuba

"the right to intervene" to preserve the island's independence and to maintain domestic order. Cuba was also required to lease to the United States a naval base (at Guantánamo Bay). Formalized in a 1903 treaty, the amendment governed Cuban-American relations until 1934. Because of Cuban resistance, the United States found it necessary to maintain troops in Cuba from 1906 to 1909, in 1912, and from 1917 to 1922.

Soon after the turn of the century, Panama became the site of a much bolder United States expansionist venture. Before a waterway could be

Panama Canal

cut across the narrow isthmus of Panama, a province of Colombia, obstacles had to be overcome. The Clayton-Bulwer Treaty with Britain (1850) provided for joint control of a canal. The British, recognizing their diminishing influence in the region and cultivating friendship with the United States as a counterweight to Germany, stepped aside in the Hay-Pauncefote Treaty (1901) to permit a solely United States canal. But Colombia hesitated to meet the United States's terms. Impatient with Bogotá, Roosevelt encouraged Panamanian rebels to declare independence from Colombia and ordered American warships to the isthmus to back them. In 1903 the new Panama awarded the United States a canal zone and long-term rights to its control. The completion of the Panama Canal in 1914 marked a major technological achievement.

As for the rest of the Caribbean, Roosevelt—worried that Latin American nations' defaults on huge debts owed to European banks were provoking European intervention—issued the Roosevelt Corollary

Roosevelt Corollary

to the Monroe Doctrine in 1904. He warned Latin Americans to stabilize their politics and finances. "Chronic wrongdoing," the corollary lectured, might require "intervention by some civilized nation," and "in flagrant cases of such wrongdoing or impotence," the United States would have to assume the role of "an international police power."

Roosevelt and his successors were not bluffing. From 1900 to 1917, United States troops

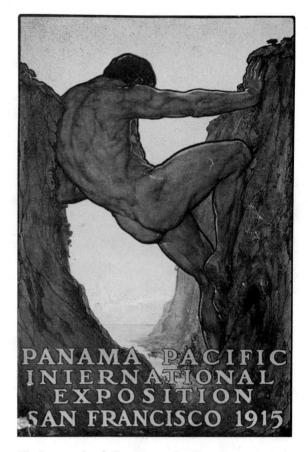

The Panama-Pacific Exposition in San Francisco in 1915 celebrated the opening of the Panama Canal with this official poster by Perham Nahl, "The Thirteenth Labor of Hercules." The artist commemorates the ten-year construction feat using symbols that reflect the imperialism and male hegemony of that time: a gigantic, muscular Hercules (the powerful United States) forcibly opens the land (a yielding Panama) to make space for the canal. When President Theodore Roosevelt asked Secretary of War Elihu Root whether he had adequately defended himself against charges that the United States had acted imperialistically in helping to sever Panama from Colombia in 1903, Root replied: "You have shown that you were accused of seduction and you have conclusively proved that you were guilty of rape." The Oakland Museum, Oakland, California.

intervened in Cuba, Panama, Nicaragua, the Dominican Republic, Mexico, and Haiti. United States authorities ran elections, trained national guards that became politically powerful, renegotiated foreign debts, and took over customs houses to control tariff revenues and government budgets.

In neighboring Mexico, the long-time (1876–1910) dictator Porfirio Díaz recruited foreign investors through tax incentives and land grants.

Economic Links with Mexico

American capitalists came to own Mexico's railroads and mines and invested heavily in petroleum and banking. By 1910, Americans controlled 43 percent of Mexican property and produced more than half of the country's oil. The Mexican revolutionaries who ousted Díaz in 1910 set out to reclaim their nation's sovereignty by ending their economic dependency on the United States.

As the United States reaffirmed the Monroe Doctrine and demonstrated the power to enforce it, European nations reluctantly honored United States hegemony in Latin America. In turn, the United States held to its tradition of standing outside European embroilments. A special feature of European-American relations was growing cooperation with Great Britain. One outcome of the German-British rivalry and the rise of the United States to world power was London's quest for friendship with the United States. British overtures paid off in 1917 when the United States threw its weapons and soldiers into the First World War on the British side.

Relations with Europe

 ## Conclusion

In the years from the Civil War to the First World War, expansionism and imperialism elevated the United States to world-power status. By 1914 Americans held extensive economic, strategic, and political interests in a world made smaller by modern technology. The outward reach of United States foreign policy sparked opposition from domestic critics, other imperial nations, and foreign nationalists, but the trend toward empire endured.

From Asia to Latin America, economic and strategic needs and ideology motivated and justified expansion and empire. The belief that the United States needed foreign markets to absorb surplus production to save the domestic economy joined missionary zeal to reform other societies through the promotion of American culture and products. Notions of racial and male supremacy and appeals to national greatness also fed the appetite for foreign adventure and commitments.

In August 1914, having become a *world power*, the United States had to face a tough test of its self-proclaimed greatness and reconsider its political isolation from Europe, when a *world war* broke out.

Suggestions for Further Reading

General

Robert L. Beisner, *From the Old Diplomacy to the New, 1865–1900*, 2d ed. (1986); Daniel R. Headrick, *The Invisible Weapon* (1991) (on communications); David Healy, *United States Expansionism* (1970); Ronald J. Jensen, *The Alaska Purchase and Russian-American Relations* (1975); Paul Kennedy, *The Rise and Fall of the Great Powers* (1987); Walter LaFeber, *The American Search for Opportunity, 1865–1913* (1993); Walter LaFeber, *The New Empire* (1963); Ernest R. May, *American Imperialism* (1968); Thomas G. Paterson and Stephen G. Rabe, eds., *Imperial Surge* (1992); David M. Pletcher, *The Awkward Years* (1962); Emily Rosenberg, *Spreading the American Dream* (1982); William Appleman Williams, *The Tragedy of American Diplomacy*, new ed. (1988).

Imperial Promoters

Howard K. Beale, *Theodore Roosevelt and the Rise of America to World Power* (1956); H. W. Brands, *TR* (1998); John M. Cooper, Jr., *The Warrior and the Priest: Woodrow Wilson and Theodore Roosevelt* (1983); Louis L. Gould, *The Presidency of Theodore Roosevelt* (1991); Lewis L. Gould, *The Presidency of William McKinley* (1981); William H. Harbaugh, *The Life and Times of Theodore Roosevelt* (1975); Frederick Marks III, *Velvet on Iron* (1979) (on Roosevelt); Edmund Morris, *The Rise of Theodore Roosevelt* (1979); William C. Widenor, *Henry Cabot Lodge and the Search for an American Foreign Policy* (1980).

Economic Expansion

William H. Becker, *The Dynamics of Business-Government Relations* (1982); Robert B. Davies, *Peacefully Working to Conquer the World: Singer Sewing Machines in Foreign Markets, 1854–1920* (1976); David Pletcher, *The Diplomacy of Trade and Investment* (1998); Tom Terrill, *The Tariff, Politics, and American Foreign Policy, 1874–1901* (1973); Mira Wilkins, *The Emergence of the Multinational Enterprise* (1970); William Appleman Williams, *The Roots of the Modern American Empire* (1969).

Ideology and Culture

Gail Bederman, *Manliness and Civilization* (1995); Alexander DeConde, *Ethnicity, Race, and American Foreign Policy* (1992); Thomas G. Dyer, *Theodore Roosevelt and the Idea of Race* (1980); Willard B. Gatewood, Jr., *Black Americans and the White Man's Burden* (1975); Michael H. Hunt, *Ideology and U.S. Foreign Policy* (1987); Robert D. Johnson, ed., *On Cultural Ground* (1994); Amy Kaplan and Donald E. Pease, eds., *Cultures of United States Imperialism* (1993); Catherine A. Lutz and Jane L. Collins, *Reading National Geographic* (1993); Robert Rydell, *All the World's a Fair* (1985); David Spurr, *The Rhetoric of Empire* (1993).

The United States Navy

Benjamin F. Cooling, *Gray Steel and Blue Water Navy* (1979); Frederick C. Drake, *The Empire of the Seas* (1984) (on Shufeldt); Kenneth J. Hagan, *This People's Navy* (1991); Walter R. Herrick, *The American Naval Revolution* (1966); Peter Karsten, *The Naval Aristocracy* (1972); Robert Seager II, *Alfred Thayer Mahan* (1977); Ronald Spector, *Admiral of the New Empire* (1974) (on Dewey).

The Spanish-American-Cuban-Filipino War

Graham A. Cosmas, *An Army for Empire* (1971); Gerald F. Linderman, *The Mirror of War* (1974); Ernest R. May, *Imperial Democracy* (1961); Joyce Milton, *The Yellow Kids* (1989); John Offner, *An Unwanted War* (1992); Julius Pratt, *Expansionists of 1898* (1936); David F. Trask, *The War with Spain in 1898* (1981).

Anti-Imperialism and the Peace Movement

Robert L. Beisner, *Twelve Against Empire* (1968); Kendrick A. Clements, *William Jennings Bryan* (1983); Charles DeBenedetti, *Peace Reform in American History* (1980); C. Roland Marchand, *The American Peace Movement and Social Reform, 1898–1918* (1973); Thomas J. Osborne, *"Empire Can Wait": American Opposition to Hawaiian Annexation, 1893–1898* (1981); David S. Patterson, *Toward a Warless World* (1976); E. Berkeley Tompkins, *Anti-Imperialism in the United States* (1970).

Cuba, Mexico, Panama, and Latin America

Arturo M. Carrión, *Puerto Rico* (1983); Richard H. Collin, *Theodore Roosevelt's Caribbean* (1990); David Healy, *Drive to Hegemony* (1989) (on the Caribbean); Walter LaFeber, *Inevitable Revolutions*, 2d ed. rev. (1993) (on Central America); Walter LaFeber, *The Panama Canal*, rev. ed. (1990); Lester D. Langley, *Struggle for the American Mediterranean* (1980); Lester D. Langley, *The United States and the Caribbean, 1900–1970* (1980); John Major, *Prize Possession* (1993) (on the Panama Canal); David McCullough, *The Path Between the Seas* (1977) (on the Panama Canal); Louis A. Pérez, Jr., *Cuba and the United States* (1998); Louis A. Pérez, Jr., *Cuba Under the Platt Amendment, 1902–1934* (1986); Dexter Perkins, *The Monroe Doctrine, 1867–1907* (1937); Brenda G. Plummer, *Haiti and the Great Powers, 1902–1915* (1988); Stephen J. Randall, *Colombia and the United States* (1998); Ramón E. Ruíz, *The People of Sonora and Yankee Capitalists* (1988); Josefina Vázquez and Lorenzo Meyer, *The United States and Mexico* (1985).

Hawai'i, China, Japan, and the Pacific

Charles S. Campbell, *Special Business Interests and the Open Door Policy* (1951); Warren I. Cohen, *America's Response to China*, 3d ed. (1989); Michael H. Hunt, *The Making of a Special Relationship* (1983) (on China); Jane Hunter, *The Gospel of Gentility* (1984) (on women missionaries in China); Akira Iriye, *Across the Pacific* (1967); Jerry Israel, *Progressivism and the Open Door* (1971); Paul M. Kennedy, *The Samoan Tangle* (1974); Ralph S. Kuykendall, *The Hawaiian Kingdom* (1967); Charles J. McClain, *In Search of Equality* (1994) (on discrimination against Chinese); Thomas J. McCormick, *China Market* (1967); Charles E. Neu, *The Troubled Encounter* (1975) (on Japan); Craig Storti, *Incident at Bitter Creek* (1991) (on Rock Springs massacre); Merze Tate, *Hawaii* (1968); Merze Tate, *The United States and the Hawaiian Kingdom* (1965); Marilyn Blatt Young, *The Rhetoric of Empire* (1968).

The Philippines

John M. Gates, *Schoolbooks and Krags* (1973) (on the United States Army); Stanley Karnow, *In Our Image* (1989); Brian M. Linn, *The U.S. Army and Counterinsurgency in the Philippine War, 1898–1902* (1989); Glenn A. May, *Battle for Batangas* (1991); Glenn A. May, *Social Engineering in the Philippines* (1980); Stuart C. Miller, *"Benevolent Assimilation"* (1982); Peter Stanley, *A Nation in the Making* (1974); Richard E. Welch, *Response to Imperialism: American Resistance to the Philippine War* (1972); Walter L. Williams, "United States Indian Policy and the Debate over Philippine Annexation," *Journal of American History* 66 (1980): 810–831.

Great Britain and Canada

Robert Bothwell, *Canada and the United States* (1992); Kenneth Bourne, *Britain and the Balance of Power in North America, 1815–1908* (1967); Robert C. Brown, *Canada's National Policy, 1883–1900* (1964); Charles S. Campbell, *From Revolution to Rapprochement: The United States and Great Britain, 1783–1900* (1974); Adrian Cook, *The Alabama Claims* (1975); James T. Gay, *American Fur Seal Diplomacy* (1987); Bradford Perkins, *The Great Rapprochement* (1968).

CHAPTER

23

Americans at War
1914–1920

The medical case files listed him as "A.P." In June 1918, eighteen-year-old A.P. and his Marine Corps company trudged forward to the battle lines, past the bodies of French soldiers dismembered by the big guns. His commanding officer detailed A.P. to bury the mangled corpses. For several nights thereafter the young man could not sleep. Artillery fire frightened him. During a bombardment on June 14, he began to tremble uncontrollably. A.P. was evacuated to a hospital, where noise easily startled him and horrifying dreams haunted him.

Doctors were seeing tens of thousands of such patients, whom they diagnosed as suffering from a mental illness they called war neurosis or war psychosis—shell shock, for short. The symptoms became all too familiar: a fixed empty stare, violent tremors, paralyzed limbs, listlessness, jabbering, screaming, and terrifying dreams. Treatment enabled some shell-shock victims to resume their military duties, but the very ill went home to the United States. Even cured shell-shocked soldiers had lingering mental problems—flashbacks, nightmares, and a persistent disorientation that made it difficult for them to make decisions or organize their lives. Thousands of the most severely afflicted remained in veterans' hospitals.

Many Progressive era professionals and reformers found rewards and opportunities in the wrenching national emergency of World War I. The psychiatrists who treated the shell-shock victims, for example, hoped to use their wartime medical experience later, at home, to improve care for the mentally ill. For them, the cataclysm of foreign crisis and the opportunity for domestic social betterment went hand in hand.

The outbreak of the Great War in Europe in 1914 had at first stunned Americans. For years their nation had participated in the international competition for colonies, markets, and weapons supremacy. But full-scale war seemed unthinkable. "Civilization is all gone, and barbarism come," moaned one social reformer.

For almost three years President Woodrow Wilson kept America out of the war. Eventually, however, American neutrality, lives, and property fell victim to British and German naval warfare. In early 1917, when the president finally asked Congress for a declaration of war, he did so with his characteristic crusading zeal. America entered the battle not just to win the war but to reform the postwar world.

Even after more than a decade of Progressive reform, Americans remained a heterogeneous and fractious people at the start of the Great War. Headlines still trumpeted labor-capital confrontations. Racial antagonisms were evident in Wilson's decision to segregate federal buildings in Washington and in continued lynchings of African-Americans (fifty-one in 1914). Ethnic groups eyed one another suspiciously. Many women argued for equality between the sexes and for the suffrage, but many men wanted to sustain traditional practices. To these conditions the war added new divisions. War hawks harassed pacifists, the federal government trampled on civil liberties to silence critics, and race riots revealed the depth of racial prejudice.

America's participation in the war wrought massive changes and accelerated ongoing trends. Wars are emergencies, and during such times normal ways of doing things surrender to the extraordinary and exaggerated. The United States government, more than ever before, became a manager— of people, prices, production, and minds. The presidency assumed greater powers. Unprecedented centralization and integration of the economy, increased standardization of products, and unusual cooperation between government and business also characterized the times. The war experience also helped splinter and thus undermine the Progressive movement.

The United States emerged from the war a major power in an economically hobbled world. Yet Americans who had marched to battle as if on a crusade grew disillusioned. They recoiled from the spectacle of the victors squabbling over the spoils, and they chided Wilson for failing to deliver the "peace without victory" he promised. When the president appealed for United States membership in the new League of Nations, which he touted as a vehicle for reforming world politics, the Senate rejected his call. They were fearful that the League might further entangle Americans in Europe, impede the growth of the United States's empire, and compromise the country's traditional unilateralism. On many fronts, then, Americans during the era of the First World War were at war with themselves.

 ## Precarious Neutrality

The war that erupted in August 1914 grew from years of European competition over trade, colonies, allies, and armaments. Two powerful alliance systems had formed: the Triple Alliance of Germany, Austria-Hungary, and Italy; and the Triple Entente of Britain, France, and Russia. All had imperial holdings and ambitions for more, but Germany seemed particularly bold as it rivaled Britain for world leadership.

Strategists said that Europe enjoyed a balance of power, but a series of crises in the Balkan countries of southeastern Europe started a chain of events that shattered the "balance." Slavic nationalists in the Balkans sought to enlarge Serbia, an independent Slavic nation, by annexing regions such as Bosnia, then a province of the Austro-Hungarian Empire. On June 28, 1914, at Sarajevo, a Slavic terrorist group assassinated the heir to the Austro-Hungarian throne. Long worried about the prospect of a large Slavic state on its border, Austria-Hungary consulted its Triple Alliance partner Germany, which urged toughness. Serbia called on its Slavic friend Russia for help; Russia in turn looked to its ally France. When

Outbreak of the First World War

• *Important Events* •

1914	United States troops invade Mexico during its revolution
	First World War begins in Europe
1915	Wilson denounces German sinking of the *Lusitania*
	Secretary of State Bryan resigns
1916	Congress votes down the Gore-McLemore resolution limiting travel on belligerent ships
	United States troops invade Mexico again
	After torpedoing the *Sussex*, Germany pledges not to attack merchant ships without warning
	National Defense Act provides for larger military
	Wilson reelected on platform of peace, Progressivism, and preparedness
1917	Germany declares unrestricted submarine warfare
	Zimmermann telegram aggravates Mexican-United States troubles
	Russian Revolution ousts the czar
	United States enters First World War
	Selective Service Act sets up compulsory military service (the draft)
	Espionage Act limits First Amendment rights
	Race riot in East St. Louis, Illinois
	War Industries Board created to manage the economy
	War Revenue Act raises taxes to control war profiteering
1918	Wilson announces Fourteen Points for new world order
	Sedition Act further limits free speech
	Eugene V. Debs imprisoned for speaking against the war
	American troops at Château-Thierry help turn back German offensive
	American troops intervene in Russian civil war against Bolsheviks
	Flu pandemic
	Republicans hand Wilson a setback by winning congressional elections
	Armistice ends the First World War
1919	Paris Peace Conference punishes Germany and launches League of Nations
	May Day bombings help stimulate Red Scare
	Chicago race riot
	Steelworkers strike
	Communist Party of the United States of America founded
	Wilson suffers stroke after speaking tour
	Senate rejects Treaty of Versailles and United States membership in League of Nations
	Schenck v. *U.S.* upholds Espionage Act
1920	Palmer Raids round up suspected radicals

Austria-Hungary declared war against Serbia, Russia began to mobilize its armies.

Germany—certain that war was next coming Berlin's way—struck first, declaring war against Russia on August 1 and against France two days later. The British hesitated, but when Germany slashed into Belgium to get at France, Britain declared war against Germany on August 4. Eventually Turkey joined Germany and Austria-Hungary (the Central Powers), and Japan and Italy teamed up with Britain, France, and Russia (the Allies). The world was aflame.

President Wilson at first sought to distance America from the conflagration by issuing a proclamation of neutrality. He also asked Americans to refrain from taking sides. Wilson's lofty appeal for American neutrality and unity at home, however, collided with several realities. First, ethnic groups in

Taking Sides

the United States took sides. Many German-Americans and anti-British Irish-Americans (Ireland was then trying to break free from British rule) cheered for the Central Powers. Americans of British and French ancestry and others with roots in Allied nations championed the Allied cause. Germany's attack on neutral Belgium at the start of the war confirmed in many people's minds that Germany had become the archetype of unbridled militarism and autocracy.

The pro-Allied sympathies of Wilson's administration also weakened the United States's proclamation of neutrality. Wilson and his advisers shared the conviction with British leaders that a German victory would destroy free enterprise and government by law. If Germany won the war, Wilson prophesied, "it would change the course of our civilization and make the United States a military nation."

United States economic links with the Allies also rendered neutrality difficult. England had long been one of the nation's best customers. Now the British flooded the United States with new orders for products, including arms. Between 1914 and 1916, American exports to England and France grew 365 percent. In the same period, however, largely because of Britain's naval blockade, exports to Germany dropped by more than 90 percent. Much of the United States trade with the Allies was financed through loans from private American banks. These loans totaled $2.3 billion during the period of neutrality; Germany received only $27 million in the same period. The Wilson administration, which at first frowned on these transactions, came to see them as necessary to the economic health of the United States.

Trade and Loans

From Germany's perspective, the linkage between the American economy and the Allies meant that the United States had become the Allied arsenal and bank. Under international law, Britain—which controlled the seas—could buy both contraband (war-related goods) and noncontraband from neutrals. It was Germany's responsibility, not America's, to stop such trade in ways that international law prescribed—that is, by an effective blockade of the enemy's territory, by the seizure of contraband from neutral (American)

ships, or by the confiscation of any goods from belligerent (British) ships.

The president and his aides believed, finally, that Wilsonian principles stood a better chance of international acceptance if Britain, rather than the Central Powers, sat astride the postwar world. "Wilsonianism," the cluster of ideas Wilson espoused, consisted of traditional American principles and an ideology of internationalism and exceptionalism. The central tenet was that only the United States could lead the world into a new, peaceful era of unobstructed commerce, free-market nonexploitative capitalism, democratic politics, and open diplomacy. Empires had to be dismantled to honor the principle of self-determination. Armaments had to be reduced. Critics charged that Wilson often violated his own tenets in his eagerness to force them on others. All agreed, though, that such ideals served the American national interest; in this way idealism and realism were married.

Wilsonianism

To say that American neutrality was never a real possibility given ethnic loyalties, economic ties, and Wilsonian preferences is not to say that Wilson sought to enter the war. He emphatically wanted to keep the United States out. But go in the United States finally did. Why?

Americans got caught in the Allied–Central Power crossfire. The British, "ruling the waves and waiving the rules," declared a blockade of water entrances to Germany and mined the North Sea. They also harassed neutral shipping by seizing cargoes and defined a broad list of contraband (including foodstuffs) that they prohibited neutrals from shipping to Germany; American vessels bearing goods for Germany seldom reached their destination. Furthermore, to counter German submarines (U-boats), the British flouted international law by arming their merchant ships and flying neutral (sometimes American) flags. Wilson frequently protested British violations of neutral rights, but London deftly defused American criticism by paying for confiscated cargoes. German provocations, moreover, made British behavior appear less offensive by comparison.

British Naval Policy

Unable to win the war on land and determined to lift the blockade and halt American-Allied commerce, Germany looked for victory at sea by using submarines. In February 1915 Berlin announced that it was creating a war zone around the British Isles; all enemy ships in the area would be sunk. Neutral vessels were warned to stay out so as not to be attacked by mistake, and passengers from neutral nations were advised to stay off Allied ships. President Wilson stiffly informed Germany that the United States was holding it to "strict accountability" for any losses of American life and property.

The Submarine and International Law

Wilson was interpreting international law in the strictest possible sense. The law that an attacker had to warn a passenger or merchant ship before attacking, so that passengers and crew could disembark safely into lifeboats, predated the emergence of the submarine as a major weapon. When Wilson refused to make adjustments, the Germans thought him unfair. As they saw the issue, the slender, frail, and sluggish *unterseebooten* (U-boats) should not be expected to surface to warn ships of their imminent destruction. Berlin frequently complained to Wilson that he was denying the Germans the one weapon they could use to break the British economic stranglehold, disrupt the Allies' substantial connection with American producers and bankers, and win the war.

Submarine Warfare and Wilson's Decision for War

Over the next few months the U-boats sank ship after ship. In May 1915 the luxurious British passenger liner *Lusitania* left New York City carrying more than twelve hundred passengers and a cargo of food and contraband, including 4.2 million rounds of ammunition. Before "Lucy's" departure, newspapers printed an unusual announcement from the German embassy: travelers on British vessels should know that Allied ships in war-zone waters "are liable

Sinking of the *Lusitania*

to destruction." The warning was generally ignored, and on May 7, submarine U-20 torpedoed the *Lusitania*, killing 1,198 people, 128 of them Americans.

Even if the ship was carrying armaments, argued Wilson, the sinking was a brutal assault on innocent people. But he ruled out a military response. Secretary of State William Jennings Bryan advised that Americans be prohibited from travel on belligerent ships and that passenger vessels be prohibited from carrying war goods. The president rejected Bryan's counsel, insisting on the right of Americans to sail on belligerent ships and demanding that Germany cease its inhumane submarine warfare. When Wilson refused to ban American travelers from belligerent ships, Bryan resigned in protest. The pro-Allied Robert Lansing took Bryan's place. When criticized for pursuing a double standard in favor of the Allies, Wilson responded that the British were taking cargoes and violating property rights but the Germans were taking lives and violating human rights.

Seeking to avoid war with America, Germany ordered its U-boat commanders to halt attacks on passenger liners. But in mid-August another British vessel, the *Arabic*, was sunk and two American lives were lost. The Germans hastened to pledge that an unarmed passenger ship would never again be attacked without warning. Meanwhile, Wilson's critics asked why Americans were not required to sail on American ships.

In early 1916 Congress began to debate the Gore-McLemore resolution to prohibit Americans from traveling on armed merchant vessels or on ships carrying contraband. The resolution, it was hoped, would prevent incidents such as the sinking of the *Lusitania* from hurtling the United States into war. But Wilson would tolerate no interference in the presidential making of foreign policy and no restrictions on American travel. After heavy politicking, Congress soundly defeated the resolution.

Gore-McLemore Resolution

In March 1916 a U-boat attack on the *Sussex*, a French vessel crossing the English Channel, took the United States a step closer to war. Four Americans were injured on that ship. Stop the marauding submarines, Wilson lectured Berlin, or the United States will sever diplomatic relations. Again the Germans backed off, pledging not to attack merchant vessels without warning.

As the United States became more entangled in the Great War, many Americans urged Wilson to keep the nation out. The various messages of these antiwar advocates were that war drained a nation of its youth, resources, and impulse for reform; that it fostered a repressive spirit at home; that it violated Christian morality; and that wartime business barons reaped huge profits at the expense of the people. The peace movement carried political and intellectual weight that Wilson could not ignore, and it articulated several ideas that he shared. In fact, he campaigned on a peace platform in the 1916 presidential election. After his triumph, Wilson futilely labored to bring the belligerents to the conference table. In early 1917 he advised them to temper their acquisitive war aims, appealing for "peace without victory."

Peace Movement

In early February 1917, Germany launched unrestricted submarine warfare. All vessels—belligerent or neutral, warship or merchant—would be attacked if sighted in the declared war zone. This bold decision represented a calculated risk that submarines could impede American munitions shipments to England and thus defeat the Allies before American troops could be ferried across the Atlantic. Wilson quickly broke diplomatic relations with Berlin.

Unrestricted Submarine Warfare

This German challenge to American neutral rights and economic interests was soon followed by a German threat to American security. In late February, British intelligence intercepted, decoded, and passed to officials in Washington a telegram addressed to the German minister in Mexico from German Foreign Secretary Arthur Zimmermann. If the Mexican government joined a military alliance against the United States, the German minister was instructed to tell Mexican leaders, Germany would help Mexico recover the territories it had lost to its northern neighbor in 1848.

United States officials took the message seriously, because Mexican-American relations had deteriorated recently. The Mexican Revolution, which began in 1910, had descended into a bloody civil war with strong anti-Yankee overtones, and the Mexican government had begun to take steps toward the nationalization of extensive American-owned properties. Wilson had twice ordered United States troops onto Mexican soil: in 1914, at Veracruz, to avenge a slight to the American uniform and flag and to destabilize the nationalistic government of President Venustiano Carranza; and again in 1916, in northern Mexico, where General John J. "Black Jack" Pershing spent months futilely pursuing Pancho Villa after the Mexican rebel had raided an American border town.

Mexican Revolution and Zimmermann Telegram

Soon after learning of Zimmermann's ploy, Wilson asked Congress for "armed neutrality" to defend American lives and commerce. He requested authority to arm American merchant ships. In the midst of the debate, Wilson released Zimmermann's telegram to the press. Americans expressed outrage. Still, antiwar senators saw the armed-ship bill as a blank check for the president to move the country to war, and they filibustered it to death. Wilson proceeded to arm America's commercial vessels anyway. The action came too late to prevent the sinking of several American ships. War cries echoed across the nation.

On April 2, 1917, the president stepped before a hushed Congress. Passionately and eloquently, Wilson explained American grievances: Germany's violation of freedom of the seas, disruption of commerce, fomenting of trouble in Mexico, and breach of human rights by killing innocent Americans. The "Prussian autocracy" had to be punished by "the democracies." Congress declared war against Germany on April 6 by a vote of 373 to 50 in the House and 82 to 6 in the Senate. The first woman ever to sit in Congress, Montana's Jeannette Rankin, cast a ringing "no" vote that won her high ranking in the pantheon of American pacifism. "Peace is a woman's job," she declared.

Wilson's War Message

For principle, for morality, for honor, for commerce, for security, for reform, Wilson took the United States into World War I. The submarine was certainly the culprit that drew a reluctant president and nation into the maelstrom. Yet critics did not attribute the United States's descent into war to the U-boat alone. They emphasized Wilson's rigid definition of international law, which did not take account of the submarine's tactics. They faulted his contention that Americans should be entitled to travel anywhere, even on a belligerent ship loaded with contraband. They criticized his policies as unneutral. But they lost the debate.

America went to war to reform world politics. By early 1917 Wilson had come to believe that America would not be able to claim a seat at the postwar peace conference unless it had become a combatant. At the peace conference, Wilson intended to promote the principles he thought essential to a stable world order, to advance democracy and the Open Door, and to outlaw revolution and aggression.

Taking Up Arms and Winning the War

Even before the United States's declaration of war, the Wilson administration had been beefing up the military. The National Defense Act of 1916 provided for increases in the army and National Guard and for summer training camps modeled on the one in Plattsburg, New York, where a slice of America's social and economic elite had trained in 1915 as "citizen soldiers." The Navy Act, providing for a three-year naval expansion program, soon followed. To pay part of the huge cost of these undertakings, Congress passed the Revenue Act in 1916. The act raised the surtax on high incomes and corporate profits, imposed a federal tax on large estates, and significantly increased the tax on the gross receipts of munitions manufacturers.

To raise an army after the declaration of war, Congress in May 1917 passed the Selective Service Act, requiring all males between the ages of

The Draft

twenty and thirty (later changed to eighteen and forty-five) to register. National service, proponents believed, would not only prepare the nation for battle but instill patriotism and respect for order, democracy, and personal sacrifice. Critics feared that "Prussianism," not democratization, would be the likely outcome. By war's end, 24 million men had been registered by local draft boards and 4.8 million had served in the armed forces, 2 million of them in France. Approximately 3 million men evaded draft registration and another 338,000 men who had registered failed to show up for induction.

The typical American soldier in the First World War was a draftee between twenty-one and twenty-three years old, white, single, and poorly educated (most had not attended high school). Perhaps as many as 18 percent were foreign-born, and 400,000 were African-American. Though women were excluded from military service, some women became navy clerks; others served as telephone operators in the Army Signal Corps or as nurses and physical therapists.

American leaders worried that the young soldiers, once away from home, would be tempted by vice—especially by the saloons and houses of prostitution surrounding training camps. To protect the supposed novices with "invisible armor," the government created the Commission on Training Camp Activities to coordinate the work of the Young Men's Christian Association (YMCA) and other groups that dispensed food, showed movies, held athletic contests, and distributed books. Men in uniform were not permitted to drink. Alarmed by the spread of venereal disease, commission officials declared "sin-free" zones around military bases and exhorted soldiers to abstain from sex.

Commission on Training Camp Activities

Jim Crow was in the army, too. Although some southern politicians feared arming African-Americans, the army drafted men of color, put them in segregated units, and assigned them to menial labor. Racist slang became common in the camps. In August 1917 in Houston, Texas, angry African-American soldiers retaliated against whites who had been harassing them, killing sixteen. Nineteen of the black soldiers were ultimately executed; others were court-martialed and given long prison terms.

Seeking to ameliorate such white racism, W. E. B. Du Bois, in July 1918, endorsed the NAACP's support for the war. He urged blacks to join the fight for "world liberty," in the hope that a war to make the world safe for democracy might also blur the color line at home. A year earlier he had backed creation of a segregated, all-black officers' training camp. Black colleges encouraged students

W. E. B. Du Bois Urges Support for the War

to join the camp. Eventually fourteen hundred black officers served in the war.

In Europe, American soldiers soon learned about the devastation wrought by technological innovations: poison gas, machine guns, artillery. Many suffered shell shock, and by today's standards army medicine and psychiatry were primitive. Away from the front lines, Red Cross canteens staffed by women volunteers served the soldiers as way stations in a strange land, offering haircuts, food, and recreation. Some ten thousand Red Cross nurses also cared for the young warriors. United States troops might even have met some American literary figures. Early in the war Ernest Hemingway, John Dos Passos, and other writers

A United States soldier of Company K, 110th Infantry Regiment, receives aid during fighting at Verennes, France.   National Archives.

had volunteered for ambulance service in Allied countries.

General John J. Pershing, head of the American Expeditionary Forces (AEF), insisted that his troops remain an independent army. He was not

Trench Warfare

about to put his troops under the leadership of Allied commanders, who had become wedded to unimaginative and deadly trench warfare, producing a military stalemate and ghastly casualties on the western front. Zigzag trenches fronted by barbed wire and mines stretched across France. Beyond the muddy and stinking trenches lay "no man's land," denuded by artillery fire. When ordered out, soldiers would charge the German lines, also a maze of trenches. Machine guns mowed them down; chlorine gas, first used by Germany in 1915, poisoned them. Little was gained.

The influx of American men and materiel decided the outcome of the First World War. With both sides virtually exhausted, the Americans

AEF Battles in France

tipped the balance toward the Allies. American forces did not actually engage in much combat until after the severe winter of 1917–1918. The Germans launched a major offensive in March 1918, after they had knocked Russia out of the war and shifted troops from the eastern front to France. By May, Kaiser Wilhelm's forces had stormed to within 50 miles of Paris. Late that month, troops of the United States First Division helped blunt the German advance at Cantigny. In June the Second Division attacked the Germans west of Château-Thierry in the Belleau Wood. American soldiers won the battle after three weeks of fighting, but 5,183 of 8,000 marines died or were wounded after they made almost sacrificial frontal assaults against German machine guns. From this costly victory, the AEF learned to adopt more flexible attack methods.

Allied victory in the Second Battle of the Marne in July 1918 seemed to turn the tide against the Germans. In September the Allies began their massive Meuse-Argonne offensive. More than 26,000 Americans died before the Allies claimed the Argonne Forest on October 10. For Germany—its ground war a shambles, its submarine warfare a dismal fail-

ure, its troops and cities mutinous, and its allies Turkey and Austria dropping out—peace became imperative. The Germans accepted an armistice on November 11, 1918.

The belligerents counted 8 million soldiers and 6.6 million civilians dead and 21.3 million people wounded. Fifty thousand American soldiers died in battle, and another 62,000 died from disease—many from the influenza pandemic. More than 200,000 Americans were wounded.

Mobilizing and Managing the Home Front

"It is not an army that we must shape and train for war," declared President Wilson, "it is a nation." The United States was a belligerent for only nineteen months, but the war had a tremendous impact at home. The federal government quickly created a command economy to meet war needs and intervened in American life as never before. The vastly enlarged Washington bureaucracy managed the economy, labor force, military, public opinion, and more. Federal expenditures increased tremendously, and the federal debt rose from $1 billion in 1914 to $25 billion in 1919. War expenses climbed to $33.5 billion. The total cost of the war was probably triple that figure, since future generations would have to pay veterans' benefits and interest on loans.

The federal government and private business became partners during the war. Dollar-a-year executives flocked to the nation's capital from major

Business-Government Cooperation

companies; they retained their corporate salaries while serving in official administrative and consulting capacities. Early in the war, the government relied on several industrial committees for advice on purchases and prices, but evidence of self-interested businesspeople cashing in on the national interest aroused public protest. The committees were disbanded in July 1917 and replaced later that year by the War Industries Board. But the government continued to work closely with business through trade associations. The federal government suspended antitrust laws and signed cost-plus contracts, which guaranteed companies a healthy profit and a means to pay higher wages to head off labor strikes. Competitive bidding was virtually abandoned. Under these wartime practices, big business got bigger.

Hundreds of new government agencies, staffed largely by businesspeople, placed controls on the economy in order to shift the nation's resources to the war effort. The Food Administration launched voluntary programs to increase production and conserve food; it also set prices and regulated distribution. The Railroad Administration took over the snarled railway industry. The Fuel Administration controlled coal supplies and rationed gasoline.

The largest of the superagencies was the War Industries Board (WIB), headed by the financier Bernard Baruch. Designed as a clearing-house to coordinate the national economy, the WIB made **War Industries Board** purchases, allocated supplies, and fixed prices. Although the WIB seemed all powerful, in reality it had to conciliate competing interest groups and compromise with the businesspeople whose advice it so valued.

The performance of the mobilized economy was mixed, but it delivered enough men and materiel to France to ensure the defeat of the Central Powers. About a quarter of all American production was diverted to war needs. Farmers enjoyed boom years as they put more acreage into production and received higher prices. Some industries also realized substantial growth because of wartime demand. From a problem perspective, weapons deliveries fell short of demand and the War Shipping Board failed to build enough ships. Moreover, wartime demand and the government's liberal credit policies led to inflation.

In 1918, the consumer price index was 98 percent higher than it had been in 1913. And, despite tax increases that were designed to pull into the treasury some of the profits reaped from high prices, the government financed only one-third of the war through taxes. The other two-thirds came from loans, including Liberty Bonds sold to the American people through aggressive campaigns. The War Revenue Act of 1917 provided for a more steeply graduated personal income tax, a corporate income tax, and an excess-profits tax. Although these taxes did curb excessive corporate profiteering, they had several loopholes. Sometimes companies inflated costs to conceal profits or paid high salaries and bonuses to their executives.

For unions, the war seemed to offer opportunities for recognition and better pay through partnership with government. Without consulting rank-and-file members, Samuel Gompers threw the AFL's loyalty to the Wilson administration, promising to deter strikes. **Workers and the War** Gompers and other moderate labor leaders received appointments to federal agencies. The National War Labor Board, created to mediate labor disputes, forbade strikes and lockouts and required management to negotiate with existing unions. Union membership climbed from roughly 2.5 million in 1916 to more than 4 million in 1919. The AFL, however, could not curb strikes by the radical Industrial Workers of the World (IWW) or rebellious AFL locals. In the nineteen war months, more than six thousand strikes expressed workers' discontent with their wages and working conditions. Wartime inflation, which diminished the increased incomes workers derived from full employment and time-and-a-half pay for overtime, also fueled worker unrest.

When 16 percent of the male work force trooped off to battle and when immigration dropped off, businesses recruited women to fill the vacancies. Although the total number of women in the work **Women in the Work Force** force increased only slightly, the real story was that many changed jobs, sometimes moving into formerly male domains. Some white women left domestic service for factories or departed textile mills for employment in firearms plants. At least 20 percent of all workers in the wartime electrical-machinery, airplane, and food industries were women. As white women took advantage of these new opportunities, black women took some of their places in domestic service and in textile factories. Overall, most working women remained concentrated in sex-segregated occupations.

Some male workers, unaccustomed to working beside women, complained that women destabilized the work environment with their higher productivity. Some men protested that women undermined the wage system by working for lower pay. Women pointed out that male-dominated companies discriminated against them and unions denied them membership. Male employees also resented the spirit of independence evident among women.

After the war, women lost many of the gains they had made. The attitude that women's proper sphere was the home had changed very little. Married working women found their family relationships growing tense; their husbands and children resented the disruption of home life. Critics charged that working mothers neglected their children and their housework. Day nurseries were scarce and beyond the means of most working-class families, and few employers provided childcare facilities. Whether married or single—the great majority of working women were unmarried—women lost their jobs to the returning veterans.

War mobilization wrought significant change for the African-American community as southern blacks undertook a great migration to north-

African-American Migration to the North

ern cities to work in railroad yards, packing houses, steel mills, and shipyards. Between 1910 and 1920, about a half-million African-Americans uprooted themselves to move to the North. Most of the migrants were males—young (in their early twenties), unmarried, and skilled or semiskilled. Wartime jobs in the North provided an escape from low wages, sharecropping, tenancy, crop liens, debt peonage, lynchings, and political disfranchisement.

But African-Americans continued to experience discrimination in both North and South. When the United States entered the First World War, there was not one black judge in the entire country. Segregation remained social custom. The Ku Klux Klan was reviving, and racist films such as

D. W. Griffith's *The Birth of a Nation* (1915) fed prejudice. Lynching remained a national disgrace: between 1914 and 1920, 382 blacks were lynched, some of them in military uniform.

Northern whites who resented "the Negro invasion" vented their anger in riots. In East St. Louis, Illinois, in July 1917, whites opposed to

Race Riots

black employment in a defense plant rampaged through the streets; forty blacks and nine whites lost their lives. During the bloody "Red Summer" of 1919, race riots rocked two dozen cities and towns. The worst violence occurred in Chicago, where thirty-eight people (twenty-three of them black) died in riots after an African-American youth swimming at a segregated white beach was hit by a rock and drowned.

Another home-front crisis cut across race, gender, and class lines: the influenza pandemic that engulfed the world in 1918–1919. The conta-

Influenza Pandemic

gious flu virus first unleashed an epidemic in the United States in the spring of 1918 and then spread to Europe. In many cases, severe pneumonia set in, and victims' lungs filled with fluid. Seven hundred thousand people died from the killer disease in the United States; 40 million people died worldwide.

Emergence of the Civil Liberties Issue

"Woe be to the man that seeks to stand in our way in this day of high resolution," warned President Wilson. An official and unofficial campaign soon began to silence dissenters who questioned Wilson's decision for war or who protested the draft. The targets of governmental and quasi-vigilante repression were the hundreds of thousands of Americans and aliens who refused to support the war.

Shortly after the declaration of war in 1917, the president appointed George Creel, a Progressive journalist, to head the Committee on Public

Committee on Public Information

Information (CPI). The CPI used propaganda to shape and mobilize public opinion. Pamphlets and films demonized the Germans, and CPI "four-minute men" spoke at schools and churches to pump up a patriotic mood. The Committee also urged the press to practice "self-censorship" and encouraged people to spy on their neighbors. Exaggeration, fear-mongering, distortion, half-truths—such were the stuff of the CPI's "mind mobilization."

The Wilson administration also guided through Congress the Espionage Act (1917) and the Sedition Act (1918). The first statute forbade

Espionage and Sedition Acts

"false statements" designed to impede the draft or promote military insubordination, and it banned from the mails materials considered treasonous. The Sedition Act made it unlawful to obstruct the sale of war bonds and to use "disloyal, profane, scurrilous, or abusive" language to describe the government, the Constitution, the flag, and the military uniform. Under these laws, the government prosecuted more than two thousand people and intimidated many others.

The war emergency gave Progressives and conservatives alike an opportunity to throttle the IWW and the Socialist Party. Government agents raided IWW meetings, and the army marched into western mining and lumber regions to put down IWW strikes. By the end of the war most of the union's leaders were in jail. The Socialist Party fared little better. In the summer of 1918, after Eugene V. Debs delivered a spirited oration, he was arrested, convicted, and sentenced to ten years in prison.

Intolerance knew few boundaries. Local school boards dismissed teachers who questioned the war. At Wellesley College, economics professor Emily Greene Balch was fired because of her pacifist views (she won the Nobel Peace Prize in 1946). In Illinois, a German-American miner was wrapped in a flag and lynched. In Hilger, Montana, citizens burned history texts that mentioned Germany. By the end of the war, sixteen states had banned the teaching of the German language.

Roger Baldwin and the Issue of Free Speech

Prior to World War I, American citizens could freely express mainstream political views, whereas those expressing radical opinions sometimes met with harsh treatment. In 1914, few questioned restrictions on political dissent. Yet the Wilson administration's vigorous suppression of dissidents led some Americans, most notably a conscientious objector named Roger Baldwin, to reformulate the traditional definition of allowable speech. Baldwin founded the Civil Liberties Bureau (forerunner of the American Civil Liberties Union) to defend the rights of those people accused under the Espionage and Sedition Acts. For the first time, Baldwin advanced the idea that a patriotic American could—indeed should—defend the right of someone to express political beliefs abhorrent to his or her own.

Supreme Court Decisions

In unanimously upholding the Espionage Act in *Schenck* v. *U.S.* (1919), the Supreme Court adhered to the traditional view rather than to Baldwin's view. In time of war, Justice Oliver Wendell Holmes wrote, the First Amendment could be restricted: "Free speech would not protect a man falsely shouting fire in a theater and causing panic." If, according to Holmes, words "are of such a nature as to create a clear and present danger that they will bring about the substantial evils that Congress has a right to prevent," free speech could be limited. A few months later, the Court upheld the Sedition Act, in *Abrams* v. *U.S.* (1919).

The Bolshevik Revolution, Labor Strikes, and the Red Scare

In the last few months of the war, guardians of Americanism began to label dissenters not only pro-German but pro-Bolshevik. After the Bolshevik Revolution in the fall of 1917, American hatred for the Kaiser's Germany was readily transferred to communist Russia. When the new Russian government under V. I. Lenin made peace with Germany in early 1918, Americans grew angry. Many lashed out at American radicals, casually applying the term "Red" (derived from the red flag used by Communists) to discredit them.

The Wilson administration's ardent anti-Bolshevism became clear in mid-1918 when the president ordered American troops to northern Russia and Siberia, where they joined other Allied contingents. Wil-

Intervention in Russia Against Bolsheviks

son announced that the military expeditions were intended to guard Allied supplies and Russian railroads from German seizure and to rescue a group of Czechs who wished to return home to fight the Germans. Worried that the Japanese were building influence in Siberia and closing the Open Door, Wilson also hoped to deter Japan from further advances in Asia. Mostly he wanted to smash the infant Bolshevik government. Wilson also backed an economic blockade of Russia, sent arms to anti-Bolshevik forces, and refused to recognize the radical Bolshevik government. These interventions in civil war–torn Russia immediately embittered Washington-Moscow relations.

By the war's close, Americans had become edgy. The war had exacerbated racial tensions. It had disrupted the workplace and the family. Americans had suffered an increase in the cost of living, and postwar unemployment loomed. To add to Americans' worries, Russian communists in 1919 established the Comintern to promote world revolution. Already hardened by wartime violations of civil liberties, Americans found it easy to blame their postwar troubles on new scapegoats.

A rash of labor strikes in 1919 sparked the Red Scare. All told, more than thirty-three hundred strikes jolted the nation that year, including the Seattle general strike in January and a Boston police strike

Labor Strikes in 1919

in September. On May 1, traditionally a day of celebration for workers around the world, bombs were sent through the mails to prominent Americans. Although most of the devices were intercepted and dismantled, police never captured the conspirators.

Unrest in the steel industry in September stirred more ominous fears. Many steelworkers worked twelve hours a day seven days a week and lived in squalid housing. When 350,000 steel workers struck, management hired strikebreakers and depicted strike leaders as Bolsheviks. In early 1920 the strike collapsed.

One of the leaders of the steel strike was William Z. Foster, an IWW member and militant labor organizer who later joined the Communist Party of the United States of America (founded in 1919). His presence in a labor movement seeking bread-and-butter goals permitted political and business leaders to dismiss the steel strike as a foreign threat orchestrated by American radicals. There was in fact no conspiracy. The American left was badly splintered and posed virtually no threat to the established order.

Wilson's attorney general, A. Mitchell Palmer, however, claimed that "revolution" was "eating its way into the homes of the American workmen." Palmer created a new Bureau of Investigation and appointed J. Edgar Hoover to run it. During 1919, Hoover's agents jailed IWW members; Palmer also saw to it that 249 alien radicals were deported to Russia. Again, state and local governments took their cue from Washington. States passed peacetime sedition acts under which hundreds of people were arrested. Vigilante groups and mobs flourished, and the New York State legislature expelled five duly elected socialist members.

The Red Scare reached a climax in January 1920 in the Palmer Raids, in which government agents in thirty-three cities broke into meeting halls and homes without search

Palmer Raids

warrants. More than four thousand people were jailed and denied counsel; nearly six hundred of them were deported. Palmer's disregard for elementary civil liberties drew criticism. Civil libertarians and lawyers charged that his tactics violated the Constitution. Many of the arrested "Communists" had committed no crimes. When Palmer called for a peacetime sedition act, he alarmed both liberal and conservative leaders. His dire prediction that serious violence would mar May Day 1920 proved mistaken, and Palmer soon lost his credibility.

The campaigns against free speech from 1917 through 1920 left casualties. Debate, so essential to democracy, was wounded. Reform suffered as reformers either joined in the antiradicalism or became victims of it. Radical groups were badly weakened: the IWW became virtually extinct, and the Socialist Party became paralyzed. Wilson's intolerance of those who disagreed with him seemed to bespeak a fundamental distrust of democracy.

The Peace Conference, League Fight, and Postwar World

While Woodrow Wilson trampled civil liberties at home, he envisioned a brighter future in international relations. In January 1918 he announced his Fourteen Points, a framework for world order. The first five points called for diplomacy "in the public view," freedom of the seas, lower tariffs, reductions in armaments, and the decolonization of empires. The next eight points specified the evacuation of foreign troops from Russia, Belgium, and France and appealed for self-determination for nationalities in Europe. For Wilson, the fourteenth point was the most important—the mechanism for achieving all the others: "a general association of nations" or League of Nations.

The Fourteen Points

When the president departed for the Paris Peace Conference in December 1918, he faced obstacles erected by his political enemies, by the Allies, and by himself. During the 1918 congressional elections, Wilson had urged a vote for Democrats as a sign of support for his peace goals. But the American people did just the opposite. The Republicans gained control of both houses, signaling trouble for Wilson in two ways. First, a peace treaty would have to be submitted for approval to a potentially hostile Senate. Second, the election results at home diminished Wilson's stature in the eyes of foreign leaders. Wilson aggravated his political problems by not naming a senator to his advisory American Peace Commission. He also refused to take any prominent Republicans with him

to Paris or to consult with the Senate Foreign Relations Committee before the conference.

Another obstacle in Wilson's way was the Allies' determination to impose a harsh, vengeful peace on the Germans. Georges Clemenceau of France, David Lloyd George of Britain, and Vittorio Orlando of Italy—with Wilson, the Big Four—became formidable adversaries. They had signed secret treaties during the war to grab German-controlled territories, and they scoffed at the pious, headstrong, self-impressed president who wanted to deny them the spoils of war. The victors met in the palace of Versailles in 1919, where they demanded that Germany pay a huge reparations bill. Wilson instead called for a small indemnity, fearing that a resentful and economically hobbled Germany might turn to Bolshevism or disrupt the postwar community. But the president reluctantly gave way, agreeing to a clause blaming the war on the Germans and to the creation of a commission to determine the amount of reparations (later set at $33 billion).

Paris Peace Conference

As for the breaking up of empires and the principle of self-determination, Wilson could deliver on only some of his goals. Creating a League-administered "mandate" system, the conferees placed former German and Turkish colonies under the control of other imperial nations. France and Britain, for example, obtained parts of the Middle East, and Japan gained authority over Germany's colonies in the Pacific. In other arrangements, Japan replaced Germany as the imperial overlord of China's Shandong Peninsula, and France was permitted occupation rights in Germany's Rhineland. Elsewhere in Europe, Wilson's prescriptions fared better. Out of Austria-Hungary and Russia came the newly independent states of Austria, Hungary, Yugoslavia, Czechoslovakia, and Poland. Wilson and his colleagues also built a *cordon sanitaire* (buffer zone) of new westward-looking nations (Finland, Estonia, Latvia, and Lithuania) around Russia to quarantine the Bolshevik contagion (see map, page 443).

Wilson worked hardest on the charter for the League of Nations. In the long run, he believed, such an organization would moderate the

Boundaries of German, Russian, and
Austro-Hungarian Empires in 1914
Areas lost by Austro-Hungarian Empire
Areas lost by Russian Empire
Areas lost by German Empire
Areas lost by Bulgaria
Demilitarized Zone
Boundaries of 1926

Europe Transformed by War and Peace   *After President Wilson and the other conferees at Versailles nego-tiated the Treaty of Paris, empires were broken up. In Eastern Europe, in particular, new nations were established.*

How do historians know that President Woodrow Wilson (pictured here on the right) suffered a disabling illness that seriously impaired his ability to conduct government business during the great debate over American membership in the League of Nations and that the severity of his incapacity was deliberately hidden from the public? Historians had long suspected the worst, but not until the diary and medical records kept by Wilson's private physician, Dr. Cary T. Grayson, were published in 1990 and 1991 as part of editor Arthur S. Link's The Papers of Woodrow Wilson did they have a detailed account of the bed-ridden president's precarious condition.

A portion of Dr. Grayson's diary for September 26, 1919, is reproduced here. During the fall of 1919, after a massive stroke had incapacitated the president on October 2, Edith Bolling Wilson insisted that Grayson (pictured on the left) issue only general statements about her husband's status. No mention was ever made publicly that Wilson had suffered a debilitating stroke; he was said to be down with "nervous exhaustion." When Grayson published a memoir in 1960, he still did not reveal the truth.

Long before the major stroke, Wilson had been ill. His medical history included hypertension, arteriosclerosis (hardening of the arteries), and several small strokes (the first in 1896) that caused dementia (impaired reasoning and memory loss). Wilson and his doctors had conspired to keep this information from the American people. During the Paris Peace Conference and the League fight, Wilson's health had deteriorated further. He suffered severe headaches and insomnia. After a speech in Colorado on September 25, 1919, he collapsed.

The stroke of October 2 left Wilson partially paralyzed and haggard. He could not lead because he seldom could concentrate on any subject for very long and he secluded himself from cabinet members. This

League of Nations and Article 10

harshness of the Allied peace terms and temper imperial ambitions. The League reflected the power of large nations such as the United States: it consisted of an influential council of five permanent members and elected delegates from smaller states, an assembly of all members, and a World Court. Wilson identified Article 10 as the "backbone" of the League covenant: "The Members of the League undertake to respect and preserve as against external aggression the territorial integrity and existing political independence of all Members of the League." This collective-security provision, along with the entire League charter, became part of the peace treaty.

In March 1919, thirty-nine senators (enough to deny the treaty the necessary two-thirds vote) had signed a petition stating that the League's structure did not adequately protect United States interests.

Critique of the Treaty

Wilson denounced his critics, but he persuaded the peace conference to exempt the Monroe Doctrine and domestic matters from League jurisdiction. Having made these concessions to senatorial advice, Wilson would budge no more. Still, criticism of the treaty mounted: Wilson had bastardized his own principles. He had conceded Shandong to Japan. He personally had killed a provision affirming the racial equality of all peoples. The treaty did not mention freedom of the seas, and tar-

irascible, stubborn, very sick man refused to compromise with senators who said that they would vote for United States membership in the League of Nations if he would accept changes in, or "reservations" to, the League charter. Given the serious issues raised by the collective security provision of the covenant, some historians wonder whether even a healthy Wilson could have changed the negative Senate vote. But other scholars argue that Wilson's illness so impaired his rationality and the cover-up so distorted truth that the Senate's defeat of the treaty can be understood only in the context of the stricken president's medical history as documented in Dr. Grayson's records. Grayson and Wilson: National Archives. Diary entry: From the Grayson papers transcript at Princeton University Library.

Friday, September 26, 1919

This morning at two o'clock I was awakened from my sleep and told that the President was suffering very much. I went at once to the private car and found him unable to sleep and in a highly nervous condition, the muscles of his face were twitching, and he was extremely nauseated. The strain of the trip had at last taken its toll from him and he was very seriously ill. He had a very bad asthmatic attack—the worst that he had had on the trip. For a few minutes it looked as if he could hardly get his breath. I was obliged to give him every possible care and attention. His condition was such that I did not feel that he ought to continue the trip. Although I was reluctant to do so, I felt that it was my duty to suggest to him that he call the trip off and that we return to Washington. He begged me not to make any such suggestion. . . .

As soon as I had secured the President's consent to call the trip off I went out and got Secretary Tumulty and brought him back, telling him definitely that the President had agreed that there should be no further meetings. The President said to Secretary Tumulty: "I don't seem to realize it, but I seem to have gone to pieces. The Doctor is right. I am not in condition to go on. I have never been in a condition like this, and I just feel as if I am going to pieces." The President looked out of the window and he was almost overcome by his emotions. He choked and big tears fell from his eyes as he turned away.

---

iffs were not reduced. Reparations promised to be punishing, and empires still existed. And Article 10 raised serious questions: Would the United States be obligated to use armed force to ensure collective security?

Senator Henry Cabot Lodge of Massachusetts boldly disputed Wilson. Lodge packed the Foreign Relations Committee with critics. He introduced several reservations to the treaty: one stated that Congress had to approve any obligation under Article 10.

In September 1919, Wilson embarked on a speaking tour of the United States. In Colorado the president awoke to nausea and uncontrollable facial twitching. A few days later, back in Washington, he suffered a massive stroke and became increasingly unable to conduct the heavy business of the presidency. Advised to placate senatorial critics so the treaty would have a chance of passing, Wilson rejected "dishonorable compromise." From Senate Democrats he demanded utter loyalty—a vote against all reservations.

Twice in November the Senate rejected the Treaty of Versailles. In the first vote, Democrats joined a group of sixteen "Irreconcilables," mostly Republicans who opposed any treaty whatsoever, to defeat the treaty *with* reservations. In the second vote, Republicans and Irreconcilables turned down the treaty *without* reservations. Had Wilson permitted Democrats to compromise—to

Senate Rejection of the Treaty

accept reservations—he could have achieved his fervent goal of United States membership in the League of Nations.

At the core of the debate lay a basic issue in American foreign policy: whether the United States would endorse collective security or con-

Collective Security Versus Unilateralism

tinue to travel the path of unilateralism. In a world dominated by imperialist states unwilling to subordinate their selfish ambitions to an international organization, Americans preferred their traditional nonalignment and freedom of choice over binding commitments to collective action. That is why so many of Wilson's critics targeted Article 10 and why the president was so adamant against its revision.

In the end, Woodrow Wilson failed to create a new world order through reform. Still, the United States emerged from the First World War an even greater world power. It had also become the world's leading economic power.

The international system born in these years was unstable and fragmented. Taking to heart the Wilsonian principle of self-determination, nation-

Unstable International System

alist leaders such as Ho Chi Minh of Indochina and Mohandas K. Gandhi of India vowed to achieve independence for their peoples. Communism became a disruptive force in world politics, and the Russians bore a grudge against those invaders who had tried to thwart their revolution. The new states in central and eastern Europe proved weak. Germans bitterly resented the harsh peace settlement, and the war debts and reparations problems dogged international order for years.

 Conclusion

America emerged from the war years an unsettled mix of the old and the new. The war exposed deep divisions among Americans: white versus black, nativist versus immigrant, capital versus labor, "dry" versus "wet," men versus women, radical versus Progressive and conservative, pacifist versus interventionist, nationalist versus internationalist.

During the war the federal government intervened in the economy and influenced people's everyday lives as never before. Centralization of control in Washington, D.C., and mobilization of the home front served as a model for the future. The partnership of government and business in managing the wartime economy contributed to the further development of a mass society through the standardization of products and the promotion of efficiency. Wilsonian wartime policies also nourished the continued growth of oligopoly through the suspension of antitrust laws. Business power dominated the next decade. American labor, by contrast, entered lean years.

The war also changed the nation's mood. American soldiers, tired of Wilson's idealism, craved the latest baseball scores and their regular jobs. Those Progressives who had believed that entry into the war would deliver the millennium, later marveled at their naiveté. Many lost their enthusiasm for crusades.

Woodrow Wilson himself had remarked, soon after taking office in 1913 before the Great War, that "there's no chance of progress and reform in an administration in which war plays the principal part." Wilson was right, progress and reform had taken a beating.

Suggestions for Further Reading

General

John W. Chambers, *The Tyranny of Change*, 2d ed. (1992); Stanley Cooperman, *World War I and the American Mind* (1970); Paul Fussell, *The Great War and Modern Memory* (1975); Otis L. Graham, Jr., *The Great Campaigns* (1971); Ellis W. Hawley, *The Great War and the Search for a Modern Order*, 2d ed. (1992); D. Clayton James and Anne Sharp Wells, *America and the Great War* (1997); Henry F. May, *The End of American Innocence* (1964); Stuart I. Rochester, *American Liberal Disillusionment in the Wake of World War I* (1977); Ronald Steel, *Walter Lippmann and the American Century* (1980); David P. Thelan, *Robert M. La Follette and the Insurgent Spirit* (1976); John A. Thompson, *Reformers and War* (1987).

Wilson, Wilsonianism, and World War I

Lloyd E. Ambrosius, *Wilsonian Statecraft* (1991); Thomas A. Bailey and Paul B. Ryan, *The Lusitania Disaster* (1975); Frederick S. Calhoun, *Power and Principle* (1986); Kendrick A. Clements, *The Presidency of Woodrow Wilson* (1992); John W.

Coogan, *The End of Neutrality* (1981); John M. Cooper, Jr., *The Warrior and the Priest* (1983); Robert H. Ferrell, *Woodrow Wilson and World War I* (1985); Manfred Jonas, *The United States and Germany* (1984); Thomas J. Knock, *To End All Wars* (1992); N. Gordon Levin, Jr., *Woodrow Wilson and World Politics* (1968); Arthur S. Link, ed., *Woodrow Wilson and a Revolutionary World, 1913–1921* (1982); Arthur S. Link, *Woodrow Wilson: Revolution, War and Peace* (1979); Arthur S. Link, *Wilson*, 5 vols. (1947–1965); Bert E. Park, *Ailing, Aging, Addicted* (1993) (on Wilson's health); J. W. Schulte Nordholt, *Woodrow Wilson* (1991); Tony Smith, *America's Mission* (1994); David Stevenson, *The First World War and International Politics* (1988); Edwin A. Weinstein, *Woodrow Wilson: A Medical and Psychological Biography* (1981).

The Military and the Great War in Europe

Allan M. Brandt, *No Magic Bullet* (1985) (on venereal disease); John W. Chambers, *To Raise an Army* (1987); J. Garry Clifford, *The Citizen Soldiers* (1972); Edward M. Coffman, *The War to End All Wars* (1968); Harvey A. DeWeerd, *President Wilson Fights His War* (1968); Thomas C. Leonard, *Above the Battle* (1978); Dorothy Schneider and Carl J. Schneider, *Into the Breach: American Women Overseas in World War I* (1991); Donald Smythe, *Pershing* (1986); Stephen R. Ward, ed., *The War Generation: Veterans of the First World War* (1975); Russell F. Weigley, *The American Way of War* (1973).

The Home Front

William J. Breen, *Uncle Sam at Home* (1984); Valerie Jean Conner, *The National War Labor Board* (1983); Alfred W. Crosby, *America's Forgotten Pandemic* (1989) (on influenza); Robert D. Cuff, *The War Industries Board* (1973); Maurine W. Greenwald, *Women, War, and Work* (1980); Frank L. Grubbs, Jr., *The Struggle for Labor Loyalty* (1968); David M. Kennedy, *Over Here* (1980); Seward W. Livermore, *Politics Is Adjourned* (1966); Joseph A. McCartin, *Labor's Great War* (1998); John F. McClymer, *War and Welfare: Social Engineering in America, 1890–1925* (1980); George H. Nash, *The Life of Herbert Hoover* (1996); Ronald Schaffer, *America in the Great War: The Rise of the War Welfare State* (1991); Barbara J. Steinson, *American Women's Activism in World War I* (1982); Stephen L. Vaughn, *Holding Fast the Inner Lines* (1979) (on the CPI); Neil A. Wynn, *From Progressivism to Prosperity* (1986).

Race Relations and the Great Migration

Arthur E. Barbeau and Florette Henri, *The Unknown Soldiers* (1974) (on black troops); Marvin E. Fletcher, *The Black Soldier and Officer in the United States Army, 1891–1917* (1974); James B. Grossman, *Land of Hope: Chicago, Black Southerners, and the Great Migration* (1989); Robert V. Haynes, *A Night of Violence:*
The Houston Riot of 1917 (1976); Carole Marks, *Farewell—We're Good and Gone* (1989) (on migration); Elliot M. Rudwick, *Race Riot at East St. Louis, July 2, 1917* (1964); Joe William Trotter, Jr., ed., *The Great Migration in Historical Perspective* (1991); William M. Tuttle, Jr., *Race Riot: Chicago in the Red Summer of 1919* (1970).

Dissenters, Wartime Civil Liberties, and the Red Scare

David Brody, *Labor in Crisis* (1965) (on steel strike); Charles Chatfield, *The American Peace Movement* (1992); Stanley Coben, *A. Mitchell Palmer* (1963); Charles DeBenedetti, *Origins of the Modern Peace Movement* (1978); Sondra Herman, *Eleven Against War* (1969); Donald Johnson, *The Challenge to American Freedoms* (1963); C. Roland Marchand, *The American Peace Movement and Social Reform, 1898–1918* (1973); Elizabeth McKillen, *Chicago Labor and the Quest for a Democratic Diplomacy, 1914–1924* (1995); Paul L. Murphy, *World War 1 and the Origin of Civil Liberties* (1979); Robert K. Murray, *Red Scare* (1955); William Pencak, *For God and Country* (1989) (on the American Legion); H. C. Peterson and Gilbert C. Fite, *Opponents of War, 1917–1918* (1968); Richard Polenberg, *Fighting Faiths* (1987) (on the *Abrams* case); William Preston, *Aliens and Dissenters*, 2d ed. (1995); Francis Russell, *A City in Terror* (1975) (on the Boston police strike); James Weinstein, *The Decline of Socialism in America, 1912–1923* (1967).

The United States and the Bolshevik Revolution

Peter G. Filene, *Americans and the Soviet Experiment, 1917–1933* (1967); David S. Foglesong, *America's Secret War Against Bolshevism* (1995); John L. Gaddis, *Russia, the Soviet Union, and the United States*, 2d ed. (1990); George F. Kennan, *The Decision to Intervene* (1958); George F. Kennan, *Russia Leaves the War* (1956); Christopher Lasch, *The American Liberals and the Russian Revolution* (1962); David McFadden, *Alternative Paths* (1993); Betty M. Unterberger, *The United States, Revolutionary Russia, and the Rise of Czechoslovakia* (1989); Betty M. Unterberger, *America's Siberian Expedition, 1918–1920* (1956).

Paris Peace Conference and League Fight

Lloyd Ambrosius, *Woodrow Wilson and the American Diplomatic Tradition* (1987); Inga Floto, *Colonel House in Paris* (1973); Herbert Hoover, *The Ordeal of Woodrow Wilson* (1958); Warren F. Kuehl, *Seeking World Order* (1969); Arno Mayer, *Politics and Diplomacy of Peacemaking* (1967); Keith Nelson, *Victors Divided* (1973); Ralph A. Stone, *The Irreconcilables* (1970); Arthur Walworth, *Wilson and the Peacemakers* (1986); William C. Widenor, *Henry Cabot Lodge and the Search for an American Foreign Policy* (1980).

CHAPTER

24

The New Era of the 1920s

On the afternoon of June 26, 1926, a crowd of over fifty thousand jammed the Los Angeles railroad station and waited anxiously for Aimee Semple McPherson. The evangelist preacher was returning after disappearing and being presumed dead six weeks earlier. McPherson claimed she had been kidnapped, taken to Mexico, and then escaped. Her story was suspect, but few people cared.

McPherson was a remarkable character. She traveled the country preaching the "old-time religion"; in 1923 she opened a huge church, Angelus Temple in Los Angeles. Sister Aimee's antics included riding a motorcycle down the church aisle. Critics called her a fraud, but Sister Aimee was remarkably effective because she gave people what they wanted and needed: a combination of the "tried and true" of Christian spiritual fervor with modern technological apparatus. She provided moral counseling over the telephone, published a monthly magazine promoting God's mercy, and broadcast her theatrical services over her own radio station.

In many ways, Aimee Semple McPherson symbolizes the clash of values that characterized the 1920s. On the one hand was the search to safeguard the "tried and true," whether it was religious certainty, business capitalism, or patriotic commitment. On the other hand, there existed the increasing appeal of the "modern": new technology, consumer goods, and mass entertainment.

During the 1920s the flower of consumerism reached full bloom. Although poverty beset small farmers, workers in declining industries, and nonwhites in inner cities, most other people enjoyed a high standard of living. Spurred by advertising and new forms of credit, Americans eagerly bought radios, automobiles, real estate, and stocks. As in the

Gilded Age, government policies supported the interests of business. Yet important reforms were undertaken at state and local levels of government.

Complexity characterized the 1920s. Its fads and frivolities were accompanied by creativity in the arts and by advances in science and technology. Changes in work habits, family responsibilities, and healthcare fostered new uses of time and new attitudes about behavior. While material bounty and leisure time enticed Americans into new amusements, winds of change also stirred up waves of reaction. New liberal values repelled various groups and individuals who reacted by trying to create a society in which traditional beliefs prevailed.

Threatening clouds were gathering as well. The consumer culture that dominated everyday life blinded Americans to rising debts and other negative economic signs. Just before the decade closed, a stormy depression swept through the economy, bringing the era to a brutal close.

Private Power Triumphant

The 1920s began with a jolting economic decline. Shortly after the First World War ended, industrial output dropped as wartime orders dried up and farm income plunged because of falling exports. In 1921, unemployment exceeded 12 percent.

Aided by electric energy, a recovery began in 1922 and continued unevenly until 1929. By the decade's end, electric motors powered 70 percent of American industry. Electrically driven assembly lines added radios, refrigerators, and other new products to the market. New metal alloys, chemicals, synthetic materials such as rayon, and preserved foods became commonplace. This new consumerism was fueled by the installment or time-payment plan.

Beneath the economic expansion, the consolidation movement that had created trusts and holding companies in the late nineteenth century reached a new stage. Although trustbusting had partially harnessed big business, it had not eliminated oligopoly—control of an entire industry by a few large firms. By the 1920s oligopolies dominated not only production but also marketing, distribution, and even finance.

Business and professional organizations that had come into being around 1900 also matured in the 1920s. Retailers and manufacturers formed trade associations to swap information and coordinate planning. Farm bureaus promoted scientific agriculture and tried to stabilize markets. These and other special-interest groups participated in what has been called the "new lobbying." In a complex society in which government was playing an increasingly influential role, hundreds of organizations sought the support of federal and state legislators.

Business thrived because of government assistance. Congress reduced taxes on corporations and wealthy individuals in 1921 and the next year raised tariff rates. Presidents Warren G. Harding, Calvin Coolidge, and Herbert Hoover appointed cabinet officers who pursued policies favorable to business. Regulatory agencies such as the Federal Trade Commission and Interstate Commerce Commission cooperated with corporations more than they regulated them.

The Supreme Court protected business and private property as aggressively as it had done in the Gilded Age. In *Coronado Coal Company* v. *United Mine Workers* (1922), the Court ruled that a striking union, like a trust, could be prosecuted for illegal restraint of trade. Restrictions on child labor were voided (*Bailey* v. *Drexel Furniture Company*, 1922) and a minimum-wage law affecting women was overturned (*Adkins* v. *Children's Hospital*, 1923).

Organized labor suffered other setbacks during the 1920s. Influenced by a fear of communism, public opinion turned against workers who disrupted everyday life with strikes. Perpetuating tactics used during the Red Scare, the Harding administration obtained a sweeping court injunction to quash a strike by 400,000 railroad shop workers. Meanwhile, large corporations countered the appeal of unions by offering pensions, profit sharing, and company-sponsored picnics and sporting events—a policy known as *welfare capitalism*. State legislators aided employers by prohibiting *closed shops* (workplaces where union membership was mandatory). In this atmosphere, union membership fell from 5.1 million in 1920 to 3.6 million in 1929.

A Business-Minded Presidency

A symbol of government's good will toward business was President Warren G. Harding, elected in 1920 when the populace no longer desired national or international crusades. He selected some capable assis-

Harding Administration

tants, notably Secretary of State Charles Evans Hughes, Secretary of Commerce Herbert Hoover, and Secretary of the Treasury Andrew Mellon. Harding also backed some reforms. He helped streamline federal spending with the Budget and Accounting Act of 1921, supported antilynching legislation, approved bills assisting farm cooperatives and liberalizing farm credit, and, unlike his predecessor Wilson, was generally tolerant on civil liberties issues.

Harding's problem was that he had some predatory friends. Charles Forbes of the Veterans Bureau went to federal prison after being convicted of fraud and bribery in connection with government contracts. Attorney General Harry Daugherty was implicated in bribery and other fraudulent schemes. Most notoriously, a congressional inquiry in 1923 and 1924 revealed that Secretary of the Interior Albert Fall had accepted bribes to lease government property to private oil companies. For his role in the affair—called the Teapot Dome scandal after a Wyoming oil reserve that had been turned over to Mammoth Oil Company—Fall was fined $100,000 and spent a year in jail, the first cabinet officer ever to be so disgraced.

By mid-1923, Harding had become disillusioned. Amid rumors of mismanagement and crime, he told a journalist, "My God, this is a hell of a job. I have no trouble with my enemies. . . . But my friends, my God-damned friends. . . ." On a speaking tour that summer, Harding became ill, and he died in San Francisco on August 2.

Vice President Calvin Coolidge succeeded Harding. This somber former governor of Mass-

achusetts had attracted national attention in 1919 with his active stand against striking Boston policemen.

Coolidge Prosperity

Coolidge's presidency coincided with unusual business prosperity. Respectful of private enterprise and aided by Andrew Mellon, whom he retained as secretary of the treasury, Coolidge's administration balanced the budget, reduced government debt, lowered income-tax rates (especially for the rich), and began construction of a national highway system. His only major disputes with Congress arose over farm policy. Responding to farmers' complaints of falling prices, Congress twice passed bills to establish government-backed price supports for staple crops (the McNary-Haugen bills of 1927 and 1928). Coolidge, however, vetoed the measure both times.

"Coolidge prosperity" was the decisive issue in the presidential election of 1924. Both major parties ran candidates who favored private initiative. Republicans nominated Coolidge with little dissent. At their national convention, Democrats first debated whether to condemn the newly aroused Ku Klux Klan, voting 542 to 541 against condemnation. They then endured 103 ballots before nominating John W. Davis, a New York corporation lawyer. Remnants of the Progressive movement, along with various farm, labor, and socialist groups, formed a new Progressive Party and nominated Robert M. La Follette, the aging reformer from Wisconsin. Coolidge easily beat Davis, with La Follette in third place.

Extensions of Reform

Struck by the triumph of business influence, political analysts claimed that Progressivism had died. They were partly right. The reform spirit waned in the 1920s, yet many of the Progressive era's achievements were sustained and extended in these years. Trustbusting declined, but regulatory commissions and other government agencies still monitored company activities and

Extension of Progressive Reforms

Important Events

1920	Nineteenth Amendment ratified, legalizing the vote for women in federal elections
	Warren G. Harding elected president
	KDKA transmits first commercial radio broadcast
1920–21	Postwar deflation and depression occurs
1921	Federal Highway Act funds national highway system
	Johnson Act establishes immigration quotas
	Sacco and Vanzetti convicted
	Sheppard-Towner Act allots funds to states to set up maternity and pediatric clinics
1922	Economic recovery raises standard of living
	Coronado Coal Company v. *United Mine Workers* rules that strikes may be illegal actions in restraint of trade
	Bailey v. *Drexel Furniture Company* voids restrictions on child labor
	Federal government ends strikes by railroad shop workers
1923	Harding dies; Calvin Coolidge assumes the presidency
	Adkins v. *Children's Hospital* overturns a minimum-wage law affecting women
	Ku Klux Klan activity peaks
	Aimee Semple McPherson opens Angelus Temple in Los Angeles
1923–24	Government scandals (Teapot Dome) exposed
1924	Johnson-Reid Act revises immigration quotas
	Coolidge elected president
1925	Scopes trial highlights battle between religious fundamentalists and religious liberals
1927	Lindbergh pilots solo transatlantic flight
	Babe Ruth hits sixty home runs
	The Jazz Singer, the first movie with sound, is released
1928	Stock market soars
	Herbert Hoover elected president
1929	Stock market crashes; Great Depression begins

worked to reduce wasteful business practices. A corps of congressional reformers kept Progressive causes alive by supporting labor legislation, aid to farmers, and a government-owned hydroelectric dam at Muscle Shoals, Alabama.

Most reform, however, occurred at state and local levels. Following initiatives begun before the First World War, thirty-four states instituted or expanded workers' compensation laws in the 1920s. Many states established employee-funded old-age pensions and welfare programs for the indigent. In cities, social workers strived for better housing and poverty relief, and planning and zoning commissions worked to harness physical growth to the common good. During the 1920s the nation's statehouses, city halls, and universities trained a new generation of reformers who later influenced national affairs.

The federal government's generally apathetic Indian policy disturbed some reformers. Organizations such as the Indian Rights Association and the General Federation of Women's Clubs worked to obtain racial justice and social services, including better education and return of tribal lands. But Native Americans, no longer a threat to whites' ambitions, were treated by the general population like other minorities: as objects of discrimination who were expected to assimilate. Severalty, the policy

Indian Affairs

of allotting land to individuals rather than to tribes, had failed. Indian farmers had to contend with poor soil, lack of irrigation, scarce medical care, and cattle thieves. Deeply attached to their land, they showed little inclination to move to cities. Whites remained insensitive to indigenous cultures.

Meanwhile, the federal government struggled to clarify Indians' citizenship status. The Dawes Severalty Act had conferred citizenship on all Indians who accepted individual allotments of land but not on those who remained on reservations. After several court challenges, Congress finally passed a law in 1924 granting full citizenship to all Indians who previously had not received it. President Herbert Hoover's administration later reorganized the Bureau of Indian Affairs and increased expenditures for health, education, and welfare. Much of the money, however, went to enlarge the bureaucracy rather than into Indian hands.

Even after achieving suffrage in 1920 with final ratification of the Nineteenth Amendment, politically active women still were excluded from

Women and Politics

party power structures, but they remained active in voluntary organizations whose techniques contributed to modern pressure-group politics. Whether the issue was birth control, peace, education, Indian affairs, or opposition to lynching, women in these associations publicized their cause and lobbied legislators rather than trying to elect their own candidates. Action by women's groups persuaded Congress to pass the Sheppard-Towner (Maternity and Infancy) Act (1921), which allotted funds to states to set up maternity and pediatric clinics. (The measure ended in 1929 when Congress, under pressure from private physicians, canceled funding.) At the state level, women achieved additional rights, such as the ability to serve on juries.

As new voters, however, women accomplished relatively little. The National Woman's Party remained the champion of feminism. To ensure women's equality with men in all facets of society, it pressed for the adoption of an equal rights amendment. The proposal met with little support from women's groups that supported sex-based

legislation designed to protect working women. And like men, women of all types seemed preoccupied by the new era's materialism.

Materialism Unbound

Poor Richard's Almanac would have sold poorly in the 1920s. Americans rejected such homilies as "Waste not, want not" and succumbed to the advice of an advertising executive: "Make the public want what you have to sell. Make 'em pant for it."

Between 1919 and 1929 the gross national product—the total value of all goods and services produced in the United States—swelled by 40 per-

Expansion of the Consumer Society

cent. Wages and salaries also grew, while the cost of living remained relatively stable. People had more purchasing power, and they spent as Americans had never spent. By 1929 two-thirds of all Americans lived in dwellings that had electricity, compared with one-sixth in 1912. In 1929 one-fourth of all families owned vacuum cleaners. Many could afford goods such as radios, washing machines, and movie tickets only because more than one family member worked or because the breadwinner took a second job.

The automobile stood as vanguard of all the era's material wonders. During the 1920s automobile registrations soared from 8 million to 23

Effects of the Automobile

million. Mass production and competition brought down prices, making cars affordable even to some working-class families. A Ford Model T cost less than $300 and a Chevrolet sold for $700 by 1926—when workers in manufacturing earned about $1,300 a year and clerical workers about $2,300.

The car altered American life as much as the railroad had seventy-five years earlier. Women who learned to drive achieved new-found independence. By 1927, most autos were enclosed (they had had open tops in 1919), enabling youths to escape watchful eyes and creating a privacy that bred fears of "houses of prostitution on wheels." And most important, the car was the ultimate symbol of social equality.

Americans' new passion for driving necessitated extensive construction of roads and abundant supplies of fuel. In 1921 Congress passed the Federal Highway Act, providing money for state roads, and in 1923 the Bureau of Public Roads planned a national highway system. The automobile also forced public officials to pay more serious attention to safety regulations and traffic control.

Demand for automobiles and other goods and services was whetted by advertising. By 1929 more

money was spent on advertising than on all types of formal education. Advertising became a new gospel for business-minded Americans. In his best-selling *The Man Nobody Knows* (1925), advertising executive Bruce Barton called Jesus "the founder of modern business" because he "picked up twelve men from the bottom ranks of business and forged them into an organization that conquered the world."

As newspaper circulation declined in the 1920s, radio assumed a vital role for advertisers. By 1929

Advertising

This advertisement indicates two major themes of the 1920s: the need for electricity to power a wonderful variety of home appliances and the use of advertising to promote the purchase of consumer goods. Notice the way in which the ad directs its appeal to women. Private Collection, New York, © 1993.

over 10 million families owned radios. Station KDKA in Pittsburgh pioneered commercial broadcasting in 1920; within two years there were 508 such stations. By 1929 the National Broadcasting Company, which had begun to assemble a network of radio stations three years earlier, was charging advertisers $10,000 to sponsor an hour-long show. Highway billboards and commercials projected during intermissions at movie houses also reminded viewers to buy.

Cities, Migrants, and Suburbs

Consumerism signified not merely an economically mature nation but an urbanized one. The 1920 federal census revealed that for the first time

Continuing Urbanization

a majority of Americans lived in urban areas (defined as places with 2,500 or more people); the city had become the focus of national experience. Indeed, growth in industry and services was closely tied to urbanization. And promises of comfort and profit stimulated rapid growth in warm-climate cities.

During the 1920s, 6 million Americans left their farms for nearby or distant cities. African-Americans constituted a sizable portion of the migrants. Pushed from cotton farming by a boll weevil plague and lured by industrial jobs, 1.5 million blacks moved cityward during the 1920s, doubling the African-American populations of cities such as New York, Chicago, Detroit, and Houston. Forced by low wages and discrimination to seek the cheapest housing, newcomers squeezed into low-rent districts from which escape was difficult at best.

In response to discrimination, threats, and violence, thousands of urban blacks joined movements that glorified racial independence. The

Marcus Garvey

most influential of these nationalist groups was the Universal Negro Improvement Association (UNIA), headed by Marcus Garvey, a Jamaican immigrant who believed blacks should separate themselves from

corrupt white society. Proclaiming "I am the equal of any white man," Garvey cultivated racial pride with mass meetings and parades. He also promoted black-owned businesses. *Negro World*, his newspaper, refused to publish ads for hair straighteners and skin-lightening cosmetics, and he set up the Black Star shipping line to help blacks emigrate to Africa.

The UNIA declined in the mid-1920s when the Black Star line went bankrupt. Unscrupulous dealers had deceived Black Star managers into buying dilapidated ships, and antiradical fears had prompted persecution by the government. (Ten UNIA leaders were arrested on charges of anarchism, and Garvey was deported for mail fraud.) Although middle-class black leaders like W. E. B. Du Bois opposed the UNIA, the organization attracted a large following and it served notice that African-Americans had aspirations that they could and would translate into action.

The newest immigrants to American cities came from Mexico and Puerto Rico. In the 1920s, most Mexicans migrated to work as agricul-

Mexican and Puerto Rican Immigrants

tural laborers in the Southwest, but many also were drawn to growing cities like Denver, San Antonio, Los Angeles, and Tucson. They generally lacked resources and skills, and they crowded into low-rent districts plagued by poor sanitation, poor police protection, and poor schools.

The inflow of Puerto Ricans began when a shift in the island's economy from sugar to coffee production created a surplus of workers. Attracted by contracts from employers seeking cheap labor, most Puerto Rican migrants moved to New York City, where they created *barrios* (communities).

Within their communities, both Puerto Ricans and Mexicans maintained traditional customs and values and developed businesses and social organizations to help themselves adapt to American society. Educated elites—doctors, lawyers, business owners—tended to become community leaders.

As urban growth peaked, suburban growth accelerated. Although towns had clustered around city edges since the nation's earliest years, pros-

Growth of the Suburbs

perity and automobile transportation made the urban fringe more accessible to those wishing to flee crowded cities in the 1920s. Between 1920 and 1930, suburbs of Chicago, Cleveland, and Los Angeles grew five to ten times faster than did the central cities. Most suburbs were middle- and upper-class bedroom communities whose residents wanted to escape big-city taxes, dirt, and crime. They opposed annexation and fought to preserve control over their own police, fire protection, and water and gas services.

Cities and suburbs fostered the mass culture that gave the decade its character. Most of the consumers who jammed shops, movie houses, and sporting arenas and embraced fads like crossword puzzles, miniature golf, and marathon dancing were city and suburban dwellers. Cities and suburbs were the places where people defied law and morality by patronizing speakeasies (illegal saloons), wearing outlandish clothes, and listening to jazz. Yet the ideal of small-town society survived, and Americans reminisced about the innocence and simplicity of a world gone by. This was the dilemma the modern nation faced: how does one anchor oneself in a world of rampant materialism and social change?

 ## New Rhythms of Everyday Life

Amid all the changes to modern society, Americans developed new ways of using time. People increasingly split their daily lives into distinct compartments: work, family, and leisure. Each type of time was altered in the 1920s. For many people, time on the job shrank. The workweek for many industrial laborers shortened from six days to five and a half. Many white-collar employees worked a forty-hour week and enjoyed a full weekend off. Annual vacations were becoming a standard job benefit for white-collar workers.

Family time is harder to measure, but certain trends are clear. Family size decreased between 1920 and 1930. Meanwhile, the divorce rate rose. In 1920 there was 1 divorce for every 7.5 mar-

riages; by 1929 the national ratio was 1 in 6. In conjunction with longer life expectancy, lower birth rates and more divorce meant that adults were devoting a smaller portion of their lives to raising children.

The availability of ready-to-wear clothes, canned foods, and mass-produced furniture allowed family members to spend less time producing household necessities.

Household Management

Wives still worked long hours cleaning, cooking, and raising children, but machines—especially electric irons and washing machines—lightened some tasks. And while no longer a producer of food and clothing as her predecessors had been, a wife now became the chief consumer, responsible for making sure the family spent its money wisely.

Prudent expenditure of family money related to a shift in American eating habits. With the discovery of vitamins between 1915 and 1930, nutritionists began advocating the consumption of certain foods to prevent illness. Giant food companies scrambled to advertise their products as filled with vitamins and minerals beneficial to growth and health. This emphasis on nutrition added a scientific dimension to housewives' responsibilities.

Better diets and shorter workdays made Americans generally healthier. Life expectancy at birth increased from fifty-four to sixty years between 1920 and 1930. During that decade, the population over age sixty-five grew 35 percent; the growth for the rest of the population was 15 percent. Longer life spans and the worsening economic status of the elderly stirred interest in old-age pensions and other forms of assistance. Recognizing the needs of aging citizens, most European countries had established state-supported pension systems in the early 1900s. Many Americans, however, believed that individuals should prepare for old age by saving in their youth; pensions, they felt, smacked of socialism.

Older Americans and Retirement

Yet conditions were alarming. Most inmates in state poorhouses were older people, and almost one-third of Americans age sixty-five and older

How do historians know about individual and family life in the 1920s? The manuscript census schedules (the pages on which census takers actually recorded information) from the 1920 federal census contain extraordinarily rich information. By sampling, tabulating, and analyzing large numbers of census entries—after trying to decipher often illegible handwriting—historians raise and attempt to answer questions about everyday life and the environments in which ordinary people lived. The excerpt on this page reproduces the records from a few families living on Stamford Street in Boston and yields numerous insights into how these households were organized.

The Bradley household at 16 Stamford consisted of a middle-aged husband, who was born in Massachusetts and worked as a railroad baggage master; his wife, born in New Brunswick (Nova Scotia) and of British descent, and a middle-aged boarder, who worked as a painter. Why was the boarder living there? Did the Bradleys have extra space because their children had grown up and moved away?

The Milkowski household at 10 Stamford was larger and more complex. It contained ten people, including three young children and five lodgers. Mr. and Mrs. Milkowski were from Russia, but their lodgers came from a variety of places. What kinds of social and economic relationships might have existed in this household?

A lone Chinese man lived at 8 Stamford. He worked in a laundry, and the census notes that he was married. Where was his wife?

Census data often must be combined with other sources in order to answer such questions. Nevertheless, manuscript censuses have helped to provide an important place in the historical record for people previously excluded because they did not leave diaries or letters and were not famous enough to be the subject of newspaper stories. Photo: National Archives Records and Census Bureau.

DEPARTMENT OF COMMERCE-BUREAU OF THE CENSUS
FOURTEENTH CENSUS OF THE UNITED STATES: 1920-POPULATION

STATE Massachusetts   ENUMERATOR Harry Hoffman
COUNTY Suffolk   ENUMERATED BY ME AN THE 7 DAY OF Jan 1920

TOWNSHIP OR OTHER DIVISION OF COUNTY Tract 33 14.13   NAME OF INCORPORATED PLACE Boston

STREET	HOUSE NUMBER	NAME	RELATION	SEX	COLOR OR RACE	AGE	SINGLE, MARRIED, WIDOWED OR DIVORCED	YEAR OF IMMIGRATION	CITIZENSHIP	PERSON PLACE OF BIRTH	FATHER PLACE OF BIRTH	MOTHER PLACE OF BIRTH	ENGLISH SPEAKING	OCCUPATION
	22	Garrigan, James	step-son	M	W	20	S			Mass.	New York	Ireland	yes	Chauffeur
		— Ellen	step-dghtr	F	W	16	S			Mass.	New York	Ireland	yes	Laundry
	16	Bradley, George	Head	M	W	53	M			Mass.	Mass.	Mass.	yes	Railroad
		— Carla A.	wife	F	W	52	M	1880		New Brunswick	New Brunswick	New Brunswick	yes	none
		Hart, Dennis	Lodger	M	W	49	wd.			Mass.	Ireland	Ireland	yes	Painter
Stamford Street	12	Sidlinger, Albert	Head	M	W	65	M			Maine	Maine	Maine	yes	none
		— Catherine	wife	F	W	49	M	1886		Nova Scotia	Ireland	Nova Scotia	yes	none
		— Albert K.	son	M	W	29	S			Mass.	Maine	Nova Scotia	yes	Insurance Broker
	10	Milkowski, Sam	Head	M	W	34	M	1906		Russia	Russia	Russia	yes	cook
		— Mary	wife	F	W	27	M	1908		Russia	Russia	Russia	yes	none
		— Helen	dghtr	F	W	6½	S			Mass.	Russia	Russia		none
		— Jennie	dghtr	F	W	5½	S			Mass.	Russia	Russia		none
		— Peter	son	M	W	1½	S			Mass.	Russia	Russia		none
		McQuard, Francis	Lodger	M	W	33	M			Mass.	Ireland	Ireland	yes	Reporter
		— Frieda	wife	F	W	22	M	1899		Switzerland	Italy	Germany	yes	none
		White, Irwin	Lodger	M	W	37	M	1897		England	England	England	yes	Hospital Handyman
		Blake, John	Lodger	M	W	38	M	1894		Ireland	Ireland	Ireland	yes	Laborer
		Miller, Harry	Lodger	M	W	44	S	1910		Norway	Norway	Norway	yes	Waiter's ship
	8	Ling, Chintung	Head	M	ch	60	M	1890		China	China	China	no	Laundry
	6	Ross, Frank	Head	M	W	45	M	1889		Italy	Italy	Italy	yes	Marble Polisher
		—, Effie	wife	F	W	43	M			New Hampshire	New Hampshire	Maine	yes	none

depended financially on someone else. Only a few employers offered pension plans. Resistance to pension plans finally broke at the state level in the 1920s, when reformers persuaded voluntary associations, labor unions, and legislators to endorse the principle of old-age assistance through pensions, insurance, and retirement homes. By 1933 almost every state provided at least minimal assistance to needy elderly people.

As people spent more time away from work and family, new habits and values were inevitable. Clothes became a means of self-expression and personal freedom. Both men and women wore more casual and gaily colored styles than their parents would have considered. The line between acceptable and inappropriate behavior blurred as smoking, swearing, and frankness about sex became fashionable. Birth-control advocate Margaret Sanger, who a decade earlier had been accused of promoting race suicide, gained a large following in respectable circles. Newspapers, magazines, motion pictures, and popular songs (such as "Hot Lips" and "Burning Kisses") made certain that Americans did not suffer from "sex starvation."

Social Values

Other trends helped to weaken tried-and-true systems. Because child-labor laws and compulsory-attendance laws kept children in school longer than ever before, peer groups played a more influential role in socializing children. In earlier eras, different age groups had shared the same activities: children had worked with older people in fields and kitchens, and young apprentices had toiled in workshops beside older journeymen and craftsmen. Now, school, sports, and clubs constantly brought together children of the same age, separating them from the company and influence of adults. Meanwhile, parents tended to rely less on family tradition and more on childcare manuals in raising children.

After the First World War, women continued to stream into the labor force. By 1930, 10.8 million women held paying jobs, an increase of over 2 million since the war's end. The sex segregation that had long characterized workplaces persisted; most women took jobs that men seldom held.

Jobs for Women

Wherever women were employed, their wages seldom exceeded half of the wages paid to men.

For many women, employment outside the home represented an extension of their family roles. Women worked for a variety of reasons, but their families' economic needs were paramount. The consumerism of the 1920s tempted working-class and middle-class families to satisfy their wants by living beyond their means or by sending women and children into the labor force. Though the vast majority of married women remained outside the work force (only 12 percent were employed in 1930), the number of employed married women swelled from 1.9 million to 3.1 million.

Women of racial minorities were the exception; the proportions of these women who worked for pay were double that of white women. Often they entered the labor force because their husbands were unemployed or underemployed. The vast majority of African-American women worked in domestic jobs doing cooking, cleaning, and laundry. Though specific data are hard to find, it is certain that many Mexican women worked as pickers in western farm fields and as domestic servants in urban households. Next to black women, Japanese women were the most likely to hold paying jobs. They, too, worked as field hands and domestics. And, like Mexican and African-American women, Japanese women encountered racial bias, low pay, and little chance for advancement.

Employment of Minority Women

Employed or not, women confronted alternative images of femininity. Short skirts and bobbed hair of the 1920s "flapper" signified independent-mindedness and sexual freedom. The flapper look became fashionable among office workers and store clerks as well as college coeds. As models of female behavior, chaste, modest heroines were eclipsed by movie vamps like Clara Bow, known as the "It Girl," and Gloria Swanson, known for her torrid love affairs on and off the screen. Many women, not just flappers, were asserting a new social equality with men.

Alternative Images of Femininity

The era's openness regarding sexuality also enabled the underground homosexual culture to emerge a little more than in previous eras. In nontraditional city neighborhoods, an apparent tolerance of alternate lifestyles attracted gay men and lesbians. Commercial amusement establishments that catered to a gay clientele remained targets for police raids, however, demonstrating that homosexual men and women could not expect respect from the rest of society.

 ## Lines of Defense

Early in 1920 the leader of a newly formed organization hired two public relations experts to recruit members. The experts used modern advertising techniques to canvass communities in the South, Southwest, and Midwest, where they found thousands of men eager to pay a $10 membership fee and another $6 for a white uniform. By 1923 the organization, a revived version of the Ku Klux Klan, claimed 5 million members.

Reconstituted in 1915 by William J. Simmons, an Atlanta evangelist and insurance salesman, the Klan was the most sinister reactionary movement of the 1920s. The new Klan had broader membership and objectives than the old. It fanned outward from the Deep South and for a time wielded frightening power in every region of the country, its activity peaking in 1923. Unlike the original Klan, which directed its terrorist tactics at emancipated blacks, the new Klan targeted a variety of racial and religious groups. One phrase summed up the Klan's goals: "Native, white, Protestant supremacy."

Ku Klux Klan

Assuming the role of moral protector, the Klan meted out vigilante justice to suspected bootleggers, wife beaters, and adulterers; forced schools to adopt Bible reading and to stop teaching the theory of evolution; campaigned against Catholic and Jewish political candidates; and fueled racial tensions against Mexicans in border cities. By 1925, however, the Invisible Empire was on the wane, outnumbered by immigrants and their offspring and rocked by scandal.

The Ku Klux Klan had no monopoly on bigotry in the 1920s; intolerance pervaded American society. Nativists had been urging an end to free immigration since the 1880s. They charged that Catholic and Jewish immigrants clogged city slums, flouted community norms, and stubbornly held to alien religious and political beliefs.

Fear of radicalism fueled antiforeign flames. The most notorious debate occurred in 1921, when a court convicted and sentenced to death Nicola Sacco and Bartolomeo Vanzetti, two immigrant anarchists, for murdering a guard and paymaster during a robbery in South Braintree, Massachusetts. Sacco and Vanzetti's main offenses seem to have been their political beliefs and Italian origins. Though the evidence failed to prove their involvement in the robbery, Judge Webster Thayer openly sided with the prosecution and privately called the defendants "anarchist bastards."

Sacco and Vanzetti Case

Meanwhile, Congress yielded to nativist sentiment and enacted immigration-resisting legislation that set yearly immigration quotas for each nationality. The quotas favored northern and western Europeans, in keeping with nativist prejudices against immigrants from southern and eastern Europe. By stipulating that annual immigration of a given nationality could not exceed 3 percent of the number of immigrants from that nation residing in the United States in 1910, the Quota (Johnson) Act of 1921 mainly limited immigrants from southern and eastern Europe, whose numbers were small in 1910 relative to those from northern Europe.

Immigration Quotas

The Johnson Act did not satisfy restrictionists, so Congress replaced it with the Immigration Act (Johnson-Reid Act) of 1924. This law set quotas at 2 percent of each nationality residing in the United States in 1890. It thus further restricted southern and eastern Europeans. The act also established a "national-origins" system, to become effective in 1927. Instead of basing quotas on the 1890 census, national-origins policy set an annual limit of 150,000 immigrants, and each country received a fraction of that number equal to the percentage of people in the United States population in 1920 who derived from that country by *birth or descent*. This system set a quota of roughly 66,000 for Great Britain and only 6,000 for Italy. It also excluded almost all Asians, but set no quotas for peoples from the Western Hemisphere. Soon Canadians, Mexicans, and Puerto Ricans became the largest groups of newcomers (see figure).

While various groups lobbied for racial purity, the pursuit of moral purity stirred religious fun-

damentalists. In 1925 Christian fundamentalism clashed with scientific theory in a celebrated case in Dayton, Tennessee. Early that year the state legislature passed a law forbidding public school instructors to teach the theory that humans had evolved from lower forms of life rather than from Adam and Eve. Shortly thereafter, high school teacher John Thomas Scopes was arrested for violating the law; he had volunteered to

Scopes Trial

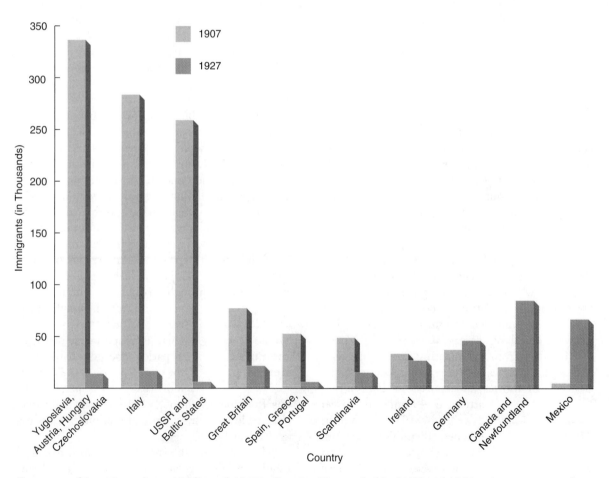

Sources of Immigration, 1907 and 1927   *Immigration peaked in 1907 and 1908, when newcomers from southern and eastern Europe poured into the United States. After immigration restriction laws were passed in the 1920s, the greatest number of immigrants came from the Western Hemisphere (Canada and Mexico), which was exempted from the quotas, and the number coming from eastern and southern Europe shrank.*

serve in a test case. Scopes's trial that summer became a headline event. William Jennings Bryan, the former secretary of state and three-time presidential candidate, argued for the prosecution, and a team of civil liberties lawyers headed by Clarence Darrow argued for the defense. News correspondents crowded into town, and radio stations broadcast the trial. Although Scopes was convicted—clearly he had broken the law—modernists claimed victory. The testimony, they believed, had shown fundamentalism to be illogical.

The defensive and emotional responses of many Americans in the 1920s represented an attempt to sustain old-fashioned ways and values in a fast-moving and materialistic world. Yet, even as they worried about a lost past, most Americans tried to adjust to the modern order in one way or another.

 The Age of Play

An insatiable thirst for recreation gripped Americans in the 1920s, and entrepreneurs responded to the nation's appetite for fads, fun, and "ballyhoo"—a blitz of publicity that lent exaggerated importance to some person or event. Games and fancies particularly attracted newly affluent middle-class families. Mahjong, a Chinese tile game, was the rage in the early 1920s. By the mid-1920s people were popularizing crossword puzzles. A few years later fun seekers adopted miniature golf as their new fad. Dance crazes like the Charleston riveted public attention throughout the country, aided by live and recorded music on radio and the growing popularity of jazz.

In addition to participating actively in leisure activities, Americans were avid spectators, particularly of movies and sports. In 1922 movies attracted 40 million viewers a week; by 1930 the number

Movies reached 100 million—at a time when the nation's population was 120 million and total weekly church attendance was 60 million. The introduction of sound in *The Jazz Singer* in 1927, and of color a few years later, made movies even more exciting and realistic.

Spectator sports also boomed. Each year millions packed stadiums and parks to watch athletic events. In an age when technology and mass production had robbed experiences and objects of their uniqueness, sports provided the unpredictability and drama that people craved. Baseball's drawn-out suspense, variety of plays, and potential for keeping statistics attracted a huge following. Newspapers and radios magnified the drama of sports, feeding news to an eager public and glorifying events with unrestrained narrative.

Sports, movies, and the news created a galaxy of heroes. As technology and mass society made the individual less significant, people clung to heroic personalities as a means of identifying with the unique.

Sports Heroes Names such as Gertrude Ederle in swimming (in 1926 she became the first woman to swim across the English Channel), and Bobby Jones in golf became household words. But boxing, football, and baseball produced the most popular sports heroes. Heavyweight champion Jack Dempsey, a brawler from Manassa, Colorado; Harold "Red" Grange, running back for the University of Illinois football team; and baseball's George Herman "Babe" Ruth thrilled fans. Ruth's exaggerated gestures on the field, defiant lifestyle, and boyish grin endeared him to millions.

While admiring the physical exploits of sports stars, Americans fulfilled a yearning for romance and adventure through movie stars. The films and personal lives of Douglas Fairbanks, Gloria Swanson, and

Movie Stars and Public Heroes Charlie Chaplin were discussed in parlors and pool halls across the country. One of the decade's most ballyhooed personalities was Rudolph Valentino, whose smooth seductiveness made women swoon and men imitate his pomaded hairdo.

The most notable news hero was Charles A. Lindbergh, the airplane pilot who made a daring nonstop solo flight across the Atlantic in 1927. A modest, independent midwesterner whom writers dubbed the Lone Eagle, Lindbergh accepted fame but did not try to profit from it. The stark contrast between his personality and the ballyhoo that surrounded him made Americans admire him even more fervently.

Some people may have idolized Lindbergh because they felt guilty at having abandoned virtues of restraint and moderation. In their quest for fun and self-expression, Americans became lawbreakers and supporters of crime. The Eighteenth Amendment (1919) and the federal law (1920) that prohibited the manufacture, sale, and transportation of alcoholic beverages worked well at first. Per capita consumption of liquor dropped. But after about 1925 the so-called noble experiment broke down in cities, where desire for personal freedom overwhelmed weak enforcement.

Prohibition

Drinking, like gambling and prostitution, was a business with willing customers, and criminal organizations quickly capitalized on public demand. The most notorious of such mobs belonged to Al Capone, a burly tough who seized control of illegal liquor and vice in Chicago and maintained his grip through intimidation, bribery, and violence. Neither prohibition nor its weak enforcement created organized crime, however. Gangs like Capone's had provided illegal goods and services long before the 1920s.

Al Capone

Thus the expansion of leisure activities during the 1920s caught Americans between two value systems. A tradition of hard work, sobriety, and restraint still prevailed, especially in rural areas. Elsewhere modern, liberating opportunities to play beckoned.

Cultural Currents

The tension between conflicting value systems pulled artists and intellectuals in new directions. In literature, art, and music, rejection of old beliefs prompted experimentation. Concern over modern materialism and conformity gave the era's artistic output a bitterly critical tinge. Artists wanted not so much to reject modern society as to fend off the era's rampant vulgarity.

The disillusioned writers who found crass materialism at odds with art became known as the Lost Generation. A number of them, including novelist Ernest Hemingway and poets Ezra Pound and T. S. Eliot, moved to Europe. Others, such as novelists William Faulkner and Sinclair Lewis, remained in America but assailed the racism and irrationality that swirled around them. Indictments of modern society's materialism and impersonality dominated literature. F. Scott Fitzgerald's novels and Eugene O'Neill's plays exposed Americans' preoccupation with money. Edith Wharton explored the clash of old and new moralities in *The Age of Innocence* (1921). John Dos Passos's *Three Soldiers* (1921) and Hemingway's *A Farewell to Arms* (1929) interwove antiwar sentiment with critiques of the emptiness in modern relationships.

Literature of Alienation

Spiritual discontent quite different from that of white writers inspired a new generation of African-American artists. Middle class, well educated, and proud of their African heritage, these writers rejected white culture and exalted the militantly assertive "New Negro." Most of them lived in Harlem, in upper Manhattan; in this "Negro Mecca" black intellectuals and artists celebrated black culture during what became known as the Harlem Renaissance.

Harlem Renaissance

Harlem in the 1920s fostered a number of gifted writers, among them Langston Hughes, whose poems captured the mood and rhythms of blues and jazz; Countee Cullen, a poet of moving lyrical skill; and Claude McKay, whose militant verses urged rebellion against bigotry. Jean Toomer's poems and his novel *Cane* (1923) portrayed black life with passionate realism, and Alain Locke's essays defined the spirit of the artistic renaissance. The movement also included visual artists such as James A. Porter, whose paintings received wide acclaim; and Augusta Savage, who sculpted busts of famous black personalities.

Issues of identity troubled the Harlem Renaissance. Although intellectuals and artists cherished their African heritage, they realized that blacks had to come to terms with themselves as Americans. Thus Alain Locke urged that the New Negro should "lay aside the status of beneficiary and ward for that of a collaborator and participant in American civilization."

The Jazz Age, as the 1920s is sometimes called, owed its name to music that derived from black culture. Evolving from African and black American folk music, early jazz communicated an exuberance, humor, and authority that African-Americans seldom expressed in their public and political lives. With its emotional rhythms and emphasis on improvisation, jazz blurred the distinction between composer and performer and created intimacy between performer and audience. Jazz also endowed America with its most distinctive art form.

Jazz

In many ways the 1920s were the most creative years the nation had yet experienced. Painters such as Georgia O'Keeffe and John Marin tried to forge a unique American style of painting. European composers and performers still dominated classical music, but Americans such as Henry Cowell, who pioneered electronic music, and Aaron Copland, who built orchestral works around native folk motifs, began careers that later won wide acclaim. George Gershwin blended jazz rhythms, classical forms, and folk melodies in his serious compositions, musical dramas and hit tunes. In architecture the skyscraper boom drew worldwide attention, and Frank Lloyd Wright's "prairie-style" houses, churches, and schools celebrated the magnificence of the American landscape.

The Election of 1928 and the End of the New Era

Intellectuals' uneasiness about 1920s materialism seldom affected the confident rhetoric of politics. Herbert Hoover voiced that confidence in his speech accepting the Republican nomination for president in 1928. "We in America today," Hoover boasted, "are nearer to the final triumph over poverty than ever before in the history of any land."

As Hoover's opponent, Democrats chose Governor Alfred E. Smith of New York, whose background contrasted sharply with Hoover's. Hoover had rural, native, Protestant, business roots and had never run for public office. Smith was an urbane, gregarious politician of immigrant stock with a career rooted in New York City's Tammany Hall. Smith was the first Roman Catholic to run for president on a major party ticket. His religion contributed to his considerable appeal among urban ethnics, who were voting in increasing numbers, but intense anti-Catholic sentiments lost him southern and rural votes.

Al Smith

Smith waged a spirited campaign, but Hoover, who stressed the nation's prosperity under Republican administrations, won the popular vote by 21 million to 15 million, the electoral vote by 444 to 87. Smith's candidacy nevertheless had beneficial effects on the Democratic Party. He carried the nation's twelve largest cities, which formerly had given majorities to Republican candidates, and he lured millions of foreign-stock voters to the polls for the first time. From 1928 onward, the Democratic Party solidified this urban base, which in conjunction with its traditional strength in the South would make the party a formidable force in national elections.

At his inaugural, Hoover proclaimed a New Day, "bright with hope." His cabinet, composed mostly of businessmen committed to the existing order, included six millionaires. To the lower ranks of government Hoover appointed young professionals who agreed with him that scientific methods could be applied to solve national problems. If Hoover was optimistic, so were most Americans. Reverence for what Hoover called "the American system" ran high. The belief was widespread that individuals were responsible for their own situations and that unemployment or poverty suggested personal failing. Prevailing opinion also held that the ups and downs of the business cycle were natural and therefore not to be tampered with by government.

Hoover's Administration

This confidence was jolted in the fall of 1929 when stock prices suddenly plunged. Analysts explained the drop as a temporary condition caused

Stock Market Crash

by a "lunatic fringe." But on October 24, "Black Thursday," panic selling set in. The prices of many stocks hit record lows; some sellers could find no buyers. At noon, leading bankers met at the headquarters of J. P. Morgan and Company. To restore faith, they put up $20 million and ceremoniously began buying stocks. The mood changed and some stocks rallied.

But as news of Black Thursday spread, fearful investors decided to sell their stocks rather than risk further losses. On "Black Tuesday," October 29, stock prices plummeted again. The market settled into a grim pattern of declines and weak rallies. Hoover, who never had approved of what he called "the fever of speculation," assured Americans that the economy was sound. He shared the popular assumptions that the stock market's ills could be quarantined and that the economy was strong enough to endure until the market righted itself.

But instead, the crash ultimately helped to unleash a devastating depression. The economic downturn did not arrive suddenly (see Chapter 25); it was more like a slow leak than a blowout. Had conditions been as sound as businesspeople maintained, the nation might have weathered the Wall Street crash. In fact, however, some historians suggest that the stock market collapse merely moved an ongoing recession into depression.

The economic weakness that underlay the Great Depression had several interrelated causes. The first was declining demand. Coal, railroads,

Declining Demand

textiles, and some other industries were in distress long before 1929, but the major growth industries—automobiles, construction, and mechanized agriculture—had been able to expand as long as consumers bought their products. Frenzied expansion, however, could not continue unabated. When demand leveled off, unsold inventories stacked up in warehouses, and laborers were laid off. The more wages and purchasing power lagged behind industrial production, the greater was the number of workers who produced consumer products but could not afford to buy them in sufficient quantities to sustain the economy's momentum.

Farmers, too, had to trim their purchases. Thus by 1929 a sizable population of underconsumers was causing serious repercussions.

Underconsumption also resulted from maldistribution of income. Between 1920 and 1929, per capita disposable income rose about 9 percent, but the income of the wealthiest 1 percent rose 75 percent, accounting for most of the increase. Much of this increase was put into stock market investments instead of being spent on consumer goods.

Furthermore, American businesses were overloaded with debt. In 1929 the top two hundred nonfinancial corporations controlled 49 percent of corporate wealth. Many corporations built pyramid-like empires supported by shady,

Corporate Debt

though legal, manipulation of assets and weakly supported liabilities. When one part of the edifice collapsed, the entire structure crumbled.

The depression also derived from largely unregulated speculation on the stock market. Corporations and banks invested huge sums in stocks. Individual buyers borrowed heavily to purchase

Speculation on the Stock Market

stocks, putting up little or no cash, and then used the stocks they had bought but not fully paid for as collateral for more loans. When stock prices collapsed, brokers demanded that buyers repay their loans. Buyers tried to do so by withdrawing their savings from banks or selling their stocks at a loss for whatever they could get. Bankers in turn needed cash and put pressure on brokers to pay back their loans, tightening the vise further. The more obligations went unmet, the more the system tottered; inevitably, banks and investment companies collapsed.

International economic troubles also contributed to the crash and depression. As the world's leading creditor and trader, the United States was tightly tied to the world economy. Billions of dollars in loans had flowed to Europe during the First World War and during postwar reconstruction. By the late 1920s, however,

International Economic Troubles

American investors were keeping their money at home, to invest it in the more lucrative United States stock market. Europeans, unable to borrow more funds and unable to sell their goods easily in the American market because of high tariffs, began to buy less from the United States and to default on their debts. Pinched at home, they raised their own tariffs, further disabling international commerce, and withdrew their investments from America.

Government policies also contributed to the crash and depression. The federal government failed to regulate wild speculation, contenting itself with occasionally scolding bankers and businesspeople. The Fed-

Failure of Federal Policies eral Reserve Board pursued easy credit policies before the crash, even though easy money was financing the speculative mania.

Partly because of optimism and partly because of the relatively undeveloped state of economic analysis, neither the experts nor people on the street realized in 1929 what factors had brought on the depression. Conventional wisdom, based on the experience of previous depressions, held that little could be done to correct economic problems—they simply had to run their course.

 ## Conclusion

The onset of the Great Depression revealed with brutal clarity how many of the characteristics of the 1920s had been consequences of prosperity. The decade's consumerism, preoccupation with leisure and entertainment, tendency toward free-wheeling behavior, celebration of the automobile, and suburbanization all resulted from higher incomes and shorter workdays. And when the bubble of prosperity broke, these new habits were all the more difficult to modify.

Suggestions for Further Reading

Overviews of the 1920s

William E. Akin, *Technocracy and the American Dream* (1977); Frederick Lewis Allen, *Only Yesterday* (1931); Paul A. Carter, *Another Part of the Twenties* (1977); Lynn Dumenil, *Modern*

Temper (1995); William E. Leuchtenburg, *The Perils of Prosperity* (1958); Robert Lynd and Helen Lynd, *Middletown* (1929); Donald R. McCoy, *Coming of Age* (1973).

Business and the Economy

William W. Barber, *Herbert Hoover, the Economists, and American Economic Policy, 1921–1933* (1986); Irving L. Bernstein, *The Lean Years: A History of the American Worker, 1920–1933* (1960); Morton Keller, *Regulating a New Economy* (1990); David Montgomery, *The Fall of the House of Labor* (1987); Allan Nevins, *Ford*, 2 vols. (1954–1957); Emily Rosenberg, *Spreading the American Dream* (1982).

Politics and Law

Christine Bolt, *American Indian Policy and American Reform* (1987); Paula Eldot, *Governor Alfred E. Smith: The Politician as Reformer* (1983); Allan J. Lichtman, *Prejudice and the Old Politics: The Presidential Election of 1928* (1979); Alpheus Mason, *The Supreme Court from Taft to Warren* (1958); Donald R. McCoy, *Calvin Coolidge* (1967); Robert K. Murray, *The Politics of Normalcy* (1973); George Tindall, *The Emergence of the New South* (1967); James Weinstein, *The Decline of Socialism in America, 1912–1925* (1967); Joan Hoff Wilson, *Herbert Hoover: The Forgotten Progressive* (1975).

African-Americans, Asians, and Hispanics

Rodolfo Acuna, *Occupied America: A History of Chicanos* (1980); Roger Daniels, *Asian America* (1988); James R. Grossman, *Land of Hope* (1989); Jacquelyn Jones, *Labor of Love, Labor of Sorrow* (1985); Kenneth Kusmer, *A Ghetto Takes Shape* (1976); Gilbert Osofsky, *Harlem: The Making of a Ghetto* (1965); Ricardo Romo, *East Los Angeles: History of a Barrio* (1983); Judith Stein, *The World of Marcus Garvey* (1986); Ronald Takaki, *Strangers from a Different Shore* (1989).

Women, Family, and Lifestyles

W. Andrew Achenbaum, *Shades of Gray: Old Age, American Values, and Federal Policies Since 1920* (1983); Dorothy M. Brown, *Setting a Course: American Women in the 1920s* (1987); George Chauncey, *Gay New York* (1995); Howard P. Chudacoff, *How Old Are You? Age in American Culture* (1989); Nancy F. Cott, *The Grounding of Modern Feminism* (1987); John D'Emilio and Estelle B. Freedman, *Intimate Matters: A History of Sexuality in America* (1988); Elizabeth Ewen, *Immigrant Women in the Land of Dollars* (1985); Lillian Faderman, *Odd Girls and Twilight Lovers* (1991); Linda Gordon, *Woman's Body, Woman's Right: A Social History of Birth Control in America* (1976); J. Stanley Lemons, *The Woman Citizen: Social Feminism in the 1920s* (1973); Lois Scharf, *To Work and to Wed* (1980); Susan Strasser, *Never Done: A History of American Housework* (1982); Winifred D. Wandersee, *Women's Work and Family Values, 1920–1940* (1981).

Lines of Defense

Paul Avrich, *Sacco and Vanzetti* (1991); Edith L. Blumhofer, *Aimee Semple MacPherson* (1993); Joseph R. Gusfeld, *Symbolic Crusade* (1963); John Higham, *Strangers in the Land: Patterns of American Nativism* (1955); Kenneth T. Jackson, *The Ku Klux Klan and the City* (1967); George M. Marsden, *Fundamentalism and American Culture* (1980); Leonard J. Moore, *Citizen Klansmen* (1991).

Mass Culture

Stanley Coben, *Rebellion Against Victorianism* (1991); Robert Creamer, *Babe* (1974); Kenneth S. Davis, *The Hero, Charles A. Lindbergh* (1959); Susan J. Douglas, *Inventing American Broadcasting* (1987); Paula Fass, *The Damned and the Beautiful: American Youth in the 1920s* (1977); James J. Flink, *The Car Culture* (1975); Richard Wightman Fox and T. Jackson Lears, eds., *The Culture of Consumption* (1983); William R. Leach, *Land of Desire* (1993); Harvey J. Levenstein, *Revolution at the Table: The Transformation of the American Diet* (1988); Roland Marchand, *Advertising the American Dream* (1985); Randy Roberts, *Jack Dempsey, the Manassa Mauler* (1979); Robert Sklar, *Movie-made America* (1976); Ronald A. Smith, *Sports and Freedom: The Rise of Big-Time College Athletics* (1988); Susan Smulyan, *Selling Radio* (1994).

Literature and Thought

Mary Campbell, *Harlem Renaissance: Art of Black America* (1987); Robert Crunden, *From Self to Society: Transition in American Thought, 1919–1941* (1972); George H. Douglas, *H. L. Mencken* (1978); Nathan I. Huggins, *Harlem Renaissance* (1971); Gloria T. Hull, *Color, Sex and Poetry: Three Woman Writers of the Harlem Renaissance* (1987); David L. Lewis, *When Harlem Was in Vogue* (1981); Roderick Nash, *The Nervous Generation: American Thought, 1917–1930* (1969); Kenneth M. Wheller and Virginia L. Lussier, eds., *Women and the Arts and the 1920s in Paris and New York* (1982).

Boom and Bust: The Crash

Peter Fearon, *War, Prosperity, and Depression* (1987); John Kenneth Galbraith, *The Great Crash: 1929* (1989); and Robert T. Patterson, *The Great Boom and Panic, 1921–1929* (1965).

CHAPTER

25

The Great Depression
and the New Deal
1929–1941

In late 1937 on a farm near Stigler, Oklahoma, Marvin Montgomery counted up his assets: $53 and a car—a 1929 Hudson that he had just bought to take himself, his wife, and four children to California. Times in Oklahoma had been tough for Montgomery's family. Across the plains, farm families were being dislodged from their homes by the combined disasters of soil exhaustion, drought, and dust storms. In addition, tractors were replacing the labor of men, women, and children in the cotton fields; and farm policies under the New Deal of President Franklin D. Roosevelt often benefited landowners at the expense of tenant farmers and sharecroppers.

Marvin Montgomery believed that he could have held out, but he wanted more than that. Above all, he wanted work and circulars held out the promise of jobs aplenty in the fields of California. Montgomery and his family thus became part of the approximately 400,000 dispossessed Americans who made the trek west.

There was never any doubt that the Montgomery family's destination would be California, where their married daughter and oldest son had already moved. "Yes, sir. I knew right where I was coming to," Marvin Montgomery told a congressional committee, which in 1940 held hearings in a migratory labor camp in California's San Joaquin valley. But for the Montgomerys the trip was not easy. The car broke down twice, and while they were crossing Arizona, their money ran out, and the family had to stop to work in the cotton fields for five weeks before they could afford to resume the trip. And once in California, Marvin said, there was little work.

The Montgomerys were relieved to be able to live in the housing for farm workers provided by the federal government through the Farm Security Administration (FSA). The FSA camp at Shafter in Kern County had 240 tents and forty two-room houses. For nine months the Montgomery family of six lived in a tent 14 by 16 feet.

Statistics suggest the magnitude of the Great Depression's human tragedy. Between 1929 and 1933, a hundred thousand businesses failed, corporate profits fell from $10 billion to $1 billion, and the gross national product was cut in half. Banks failed by the thousands, and the savings of Americans disappeared with the banks. People also lost their jobs. Thousands of men and women received severance slips every day. At the beginning of 1930 the number of jobless reached at least 4 million; in 1933, about one-fourth of the labor force was idle—13 million workers—and millions more were underemployed. Unemployment strained relations within the family. African-Americans and other minorities sank deeper into destitution. Overall, the economic catastrophe aggravated old tensions: labor versus capital, white versus black, male versus female.

Elected in 1928 amid prosperity and optimism, Herbert Hoover spent most of his term presiding over a gloomy and sometimes angry nation. Although he activated more of the federal government's resources than had any of his predecessors in an economic crisis, he opposed direct relief payments for the unemployed. When Hoover refused to take measures strong enough to relieve people's hardships, voters turned him out of office in 1932. His successor in the White House was Franklin D. Roosevelt, the governor of New York.

From the first days of his presidency, Roosevelt displayed a willingness to experiment. He acted not only to reform the banks and securities exchanges but also to provide central planning for industry and agriculture and direct government relief for the jobless. This sweeping emergency legislation was based on the concept of "pump priming," or deficit financing—pouring billions of federal dollars into the economy to stimulate consumer buying power, business and industrial activity, and employment. Roosevelt's New Deal vastly expanded the scope of the federal government, established America's welfare system, and increased the popularity of the Democratic Party.

During these years several million workers seized the chance to organize for better wages and working conditions. The new Congress of Industrial Organizations (CIO) established unions in the automobile, steel, meatpacking, and other major industries. Blacks registered political and economic gains, too, though they benefited less from the New Deal than did whites. Two-and-a-half million additional women workers joined the labor force during the 1930s. But female workers were segregated in low-income jobs, and New Deal legislation excluded many women from Social Security coverage and minimum-wage protection.

The New Deal was not a revolution, but it transformed the United States. The elderly and disabled still collect Social Security payments. The Federal Deposit Insurance Corporation still insures bank deposits. The Securities and Exchange Commission still monitors the stock exchanges. But the New Deal did not accomplish one of its goals—putting back to work all the people who wanted jobs. That would await the nation's entry into the Second World War in 1941.

Hoover and Hard Times: America's Worsening Depression, 1929–1933

As the Great Depression deepened in the early 1930s, its underlying causes—principally overproduction and underconsumption—grew in severity. So too did instability in the banking industry. What happened to America's banks illustrates the cascading nature of the depression. Banks tied into the stock market or foreign

Causes of the Deepening Depression

investments were badly weakened. When nervous Americans made runs on banks to salvage their threatened savings, a powerful momentum—panic—set in. In 1929, 659 banks folded; in 1930 the number of failures more than doubled to 1,350. The Federal Reserve Board blundered after the crash, drastically raising interest rates and thus tightening the money market when just the opposite was needed: loosening to spur borrowing and spending. In 1931, 2,293 banks shut their doors, and another 1,453 ceased to do business in 1932.

During these years people's diets deteriorated, malnutrition became common, and the undernourished frequently fell victim to disease.

Deterioration of Health

Some people quietly lined up at soup kitchens or in breadlines. Others ate only potatoes, crackers, or dandelions or scratched through garbage cans for bits of food. Millions of Americans were also cold. Unable to afford fuel, they huddled in unheated tenements and shacks. Families doubled up in crowded apartments, and those unable to pay the rent were evicted. The homeless created shantytowns, where they lived in shacks made of everything from egg crates to discarded boards and bricks.

In the countryside, hobbled long before the depression struck, economic hardship deepened. Between 1929 and 1933 farm prices dropped 60 percent. At the same time, production decreased only 6 percent as individual farmers tried to make up for lower prices by producing more, thus adding to the surplus and depressing prices even further. Drought, foreclosure, clouds of hungry grasshoppers, and bank failures also plagued American farmers.

Plight of the Farmers

Economic woe also affected marriage patterns and family life. People postponed marriage, and married couples postponed having children. Divorces declined, but desertions rose as husbands unable to provide for their families simply took off.

Most Americans met the crisis with resignation rather than with protest or violence. Some, though, were angry, and scattered protests raised the specter of popular revolt. Farmers in the Midwest prevented evictions and slowed foreclosures on farm properties by harassing sheriffs, judges, and lawyers. In Nebraska, Iowa, and Minnesota, farmers protesting low prices stopped trucks, smashed headlights, and dumped milk and vegetables in roadside ditches. Some of these demonstrations were organized by the Farmers' Holiday Association, which encouraged farmers to take a holiday—a farm strike that would keep their products off the market until they commanded a better price.

Farmers' Holiday Association

Isolated protests also sounded in cities and in mining regions. In Chicago, Los Angeles, and Philadelphia, the unemployed marched on city halls. In Harlan County, Kentucky, when miners struck against wage reductions, mine owners responded with strikebreakers, bombs, the National Guard, the closing of relief kitchens, and evictions from company-owned housing.

The most spectacular confrontation shook Washington, D.C., in the summer of 1932. Congress was considering a bill to authorize immediate issuance of $2.4 billion in bonuses already allotted to First World War veterans but not due for payment until 1945. To lobby for the bill, fifteen thousand unemployed veterans and their families converged on the tense nation's capital, calling themselves the Bonus Expeditionary Force (BEF), or "Bonus Army," and camping on vacant lots and in empty government buildings. President Hoover threw his weight against the bonus bill, and the Senate voted it down. Much of the BEF left Washington, but several thousand stayed on during the summer. In July, General Douglas MacArthur, assisted by Major Dwight D. Eisenhower and Major George S. Patton, confronted the veterans and their families with cavalry, tanks, and bayonet-bearing soldiers. What followed shocked the nation. Men and women were chased down by horsemen; children were teargassed; shacks were set afire. When presidential hopeful Franklin D. Roosevelt heard about the attack on the Bonus Army, he turned to his friend

Bonus Expeditionary Force

• *Important Events* •

1929	Stock market crash (Oct.); Great Depression begins
	Agricultural Marketing Act establishes Federal Farm Board to support crop prices
1930	Hawley-Smoot Tariff raises rates on imports
1931	Nine African-American men arrested in Scottsboro affair
	President Herbert Hoover declares moratorium on First World War debts and reparations
1932	Reconstruction Finance Corporation established to make loans to banks, insurance companies, and railroads
	Bonus Expeditionary Force marches on Washington
	Franklin D. Roosevelt elected president
	Revenue Act raises corporate, excise, and personal income taxes
1933	13 million Americans unemployed
	National bank holiday suspends banking activities
	Agricultural Adjustment Act encourages decreased farm production
	Civilian Conservation Corps provides jobs to young men
	Tennessee Valley Authority established
	Banking Act creates Federal Deposit Insurance Corporation
	National Industrial Recovery Act attempts to spur industrial growth
	Twenty-first Amendment repeals Eighteenth (Prohibition) Amendment
1934	Francis E. Townsend devises Old Age Revolving Pensions plan
	Huey Long starts Share Our Wealth Society
	Indian Reorganization (Wheeler-Howard) Act restores lands to tribal ownership
1935	Emergency Relief Appropriation Act authorizes establishment of public works programs
	Works Progress Administration creates jobs in public works projects
	Schechter v. *U.S.* invalidates NIRA
	National Labor Relations (Wagner) Act grants workers the right to unionize
	Social Security Act establishes insurance for the aged, the unemployed, and needy children
	Committee for Industrial Organization (CIO) established
	Revenue (Wealth Tax) Act raises taxes on business and the wealthy
1936	9 million Americans unemployed
	U.S. v. *Butler* invalidates AAA
	Roosevelt defeats Alf Landon
	United Auto Workers hold sit-down strike against General Motors
1937	Roosevelt's court-packing plan fails
	NLRB v. *Jones & Laughlin* upholds Wagner Act
	Memorial Day Massacre of striking steelworkers
	Farm Security Administration established to aid farm workers
	National Housing Act establishes United States Housing Authority
1937–39	Business recession
1938	10.4 million Americans unemployed
	AFL expels CIO unions
	Fair Labor Standards Act establishes minimum wage
1940	Roosevelt defeats Wendell Willkie
1941	African-Americans threaten to march on Washington to protest unequal access to defense jobs
	Fair Employment Practices Committee prohibits discrimination in war industries and government

Felix Frankfurter and remarked: "Well, Felix, this will elect me."

With capitalism on its knees, American Communists in various parts of the nation organized "unemployment councils" to raise class consciousness and agitate for jobs and food. In 1930 they led urban demonstrations, some of which ended in violent clashes with local police, and in 1931 they led a hunger march on Washington, D.C. The Communists' tangles with authority publicized the human tragedy of the depression. Still, total party membership in 1932 remained small at twelve thousand. The Socialist Party, which took issue with both capitalists and Communists, fared better. Most Americans rejected both left-wing doctrines and violence. They turned instead to their local, state, and federal governments.

Communist Party

But when urgent daily appeals for government relief for the jobless reached the White House, Hoover at first became defensive, if not hostile, rejecting direct relief in the belief that it would undermine character and individualism. To a growing number of Americans, Hoover seemed heartless and inflexible. True to his beliefs, the president urged people to help themselves and their neighbors. He applauded private voluntary relief through charitable agencies. Yet when the need was greatest, donations declined. State and urban officials found their treasuries drying up, too.

As the depression intensified, Hoover's opposition to federal action gradually diminished. He hesitantly began energizing the White House and federal agencies to take action—more action than the government had taken before. He won pledges from business and labor leaders to maintain wages and production and to avoid strikes. He urged state governors to increase their expenditures on public works. And he created the President's Organization on Unemployment Relief (POUR) to generate private contributions for relief of the destitute.

Hoover's Antidepression Remedies

Though POUR proved ineffective, Hoover's spurring of federal public works projects (including Hoover and Grand Coulee Dams) did provide some jobs. Help also came from the Federal Farm Board, created under the Agricultural Marketing Act of 1929, which supported crop prices by lending money to cooperatives to buy products and keep them off the market. To retard the collapse of the international monetary system, Hoover in 1931 announced a moratorium on the payment of First World War debts and reparations.

The president also asked Congress to charter the Reconstruction Finance Corporation (RFC). Created in 1932, the RFC made loans to banks, insurance companies, and railroads and later to state and local governments. In theory, the RFC would lend money to large entities at the top of the economic system, and benefits would filter down to people at the bottom. It did not work.

Reconstruction Finance Corporation

Despite warnings from prominent economists, Hoover also signed into law the Hawley-Smoot Tariff (1930). The tariff raised duties by about one-third, and further weakened the economy by making it even more difficult for foreign nations to sell their products and thus to earn dollars to buy American products.

Hawley-Smoot Tariff

Like most of his contemporaries, Hoover believed that a balanced budget was sacred and deficit spending sinful. In 1931 he therefore appealed for a decrease in federal expenditures and an increase in taxes. The Revenue Act of 1932 raised corporate, excise, and personal income taxes. Hoover seemed tangled in a contradiction: he urged people to spend to spur recovery, but his tax policies deprived them of spending money. Nor did he ever balance the budget.

Although Hoover expanded public works projects and approved loans to some institutions, he vetoed a variety of relief bills. In rejecting a public power project for the Tennessee River, he argued that its inexpensive electricity would compete with power from private companies. Hoover's traditionalism also was well demonstrated by his handling of prohibition. Although the law could

Hoover's Traditionalism

not be enforced, Hoover resisted mounting public pressure for repeal. Opponents of prohibition argued not only that it encouraged crime but also that its repeal would stimulate economic recovery by reviving the nation's breweries and distilleries. But the president declared that the liquor industry was best left depressed. After Hoover left office in 1933, prohibition was repealed through ratification of the Twenty-first Amendment.

Still, President Hoover stretched governmental activism as far as he thought he could without violating his cherished principles. He also inadvertently prepared the way for massive federal activity by giving private enterprise the opportunity to solve the depression—and to fail in the attempt.

Franklin D. Roosevelt and the Election of 1932

Herbert Hoover and the Republican Party faced dreary prospects in 1932. What soured public opinion most was that Hoover did not offer leadership when the times required it. So unpopular had he become by 1932 that Republicans who did not want to be associated with a loser ran independent campaigns.

Franklin D. Roosevelt enjoyed quite a different reputation. Though born into the upper class of old money and privilege, he appealed to people of all classes, races, and regions, and he shared the American penchant for optimism.

Franklin D. Roosevelt

After serving as assistant secretary of the navy under Woodrow Wilson and running as the Democratic Party's vice-presidential candidate in 1920, Roosevelt was stricken with polio and left totally paralyzed in both legs. What should Roosevelt do next? Should he retire from public life, a rich invalid? His answer and his wife Eleanor's was "no." Throughout the 1920s the Roosevelts worked to rebuild his body. Friends commented that his fight against polio had given him new moral and physical strength.

For her part, Eleanor Roosevelt—who had grown up shy and sheltered—launched her own career in public life. She worked hard to become

In November 1930 Franklin D. Roosevelt (1882–1945) read the good news. Reelected governor of New York by 735,000 votes, he immediately became a leading contender for the Democratic presidential nomination. Note Roosevelt's leg braces, rarely shown in photographs because of an unwritten agreement by photographers to shoot him from the waist up. UPI/Corbis-Bettmann.

Eleanor Roosevelt

an effective public speaker and participated in the activities of the League of Women Voters, the Women's Trade Union League, and the Democratic Party. In a short time, she became the leading figure in a network of feminist activists. She became deeply committed to equal opportunity for women and for African-Americans and wanted to alleviate the suffering of the poor. On these issues, she served as her husband's conscience.

To prepare a national political platform, Roosevelt surrounded himself with a "Brain Trust" of lawyers and university professors. These experts

Roosevelt's "Brain Trust"

reasoned that bigness was unavoidable in the modern American economy. It thus followed that the cure for the nation's ills was not to go on a rampage of trustbusting but to place large corporations, monopolies, and oligopolies under effective government regulation.

Roosevelt and his Brain Trust also agreed that it was essential to restore purchasing power to farmers, blue-collar workers, and the middle classes, and that the way to do so was to cut production. If demand for a product remained constant and the supply were cut, they reasoned, the price would rise. Producers would make higher profits, and workers would earn more. This method of combating a depression has been called "the economics of scarcity," which the Brain Trust at the time saw as the preferred alternative to deficit spending, or pump priming, in which the government borrowed money to prime the economic pump and thereby revive purchasing power.

Roosevelt and Hoover both campaigned as fiscal conservatives committed to a balanced budget. But Roosevelt, unlike Hoover, also advocated immediate and direct relief to the unemployed. And Roosevelt demanded that the federal government engage in centralized economic planning and experimentation to bring about recovery.

Upon accepting the Democratic nomination, Roosevelt called for a "new deal for the American people." The two party platforms differed little,

1932 Election Results

but the Democrats were willing to abandon prohibition and to launch federal relief. The presidential election of 1932 was never much of a contest: Roosevelt's 22.8 million popular votes far outdistanced Hoover's 15.8 million (see map). Democrats also won overwhelming control of the Senate and the House.

On March 2, 1933, Roosevelt boarded a train for Washington, D.C., and the inauguration ceremony. He was carrying with him rough drafts of two presidential proclamations, one summoning a special session of Congress, the other declaring a national bank holiday, suspending banking transactions throughout the nation.

Launching the New Deal and Restoring Confidence

"First of all," declared the newly inaugurated president, "let me assert my firm belief that the only thing we have to fear is fear itself." In his in-

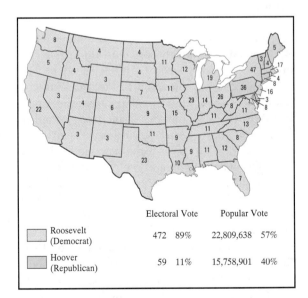

	Electoral Vote		Popular Vote	
Roosevelt (Democrat)	472	89%	22,809,638	57%
Hoover (Republican)	59	11%	15,758,901	40%

Presidential Election, 1932 *One factor above all decided the 1932 presidential election: the Great Depression. Roosevelt won forty-two states, Hoover six.*

augural address Roosevelt scored his first triumph as president, instilling hope and courage in the rank and file. He invoked "the analogue of war," asserting that, if need be, "I shall ask the Congress for . . . broad Executive power to wage a war against the emergency, as great as the power that would be given to me if we were in fact invaded by a foreign foe."

The next day, Roosevelt declared a four-day national bank holiday and summoned Congress to an emergency session. Congress convened on March 9 to launch what observers later called the First Hundred Days. This marked the beginning of the vast legislative output of 1933 and 1934, which historians call the First New Deal. Roosevelt's first measure, the Emergency Banking Relief Bill, was introduced on March 9, passed sight unseen by unanimous House vote, approved 73 to 7 in the Senate, and signed into law by the president that evening. The new law provided for the reopening, under Treasury Department license, of banks that were solvent and for the reorganization and management of those that were not. It also prohibited the hoarding and export of gold.

Launching the First New Deal

On March 12, a Sunday evening, the president broadcast the first of his "fireside chats," and 60 million people heard his comforting voice on their radios. His message: banks were once again safe places for depositors' savings. On Monday morning the banks opened their doors, and people were waiting outside to deposit their money. The bank runs were over; Roosevelt had reestablished people's confidence in their political leadership, their banks, even their economic system.

First Fireside Chat

Roosevelt next pursued a measure, the Beer-Wine Revenue Bill, that was deflationary because it would actually take money out of people's pockets. The bill would generate revenues by legalizing the sale of low-alcohol wines and beers and levying a tax on them. (Congress had proposed repeal of Prohibition in February 1933 in the Twenty-first Amendment, and the states ratified it by December 1933.)

In mid-March Roosevelt sent to Congress the Agricultural Adjustment Bill to restore farmers' purchasing power. If overproduction was the cause of farmers' problems, then the government had to encourage farmers to grow less food. Under the domestic allotment plan, the government would pay farmers to reduce their acreage or plow under crops already in the fields. Farmers would receive payments based on *parity*, a system of regulated prices for corn, cotton, wheat, rice, hogs, and dairy products that would provide them the same purchasing power they had had during the prosperous period of 1909 to 1914. The subsidies would be funded by taxes levied on the processors of agricultural commodities. After overcoming vehement opposition, Roosevelt's supporters passed the Agricultural Adjustment Act (AAA), on May 12. A month later the Farm Credit Act was passed, providing short- and medium-term loans that enabled many farmers to refinance their mortgages and hang onto their homes and land.

Agricultural Adjustment Act

Still other relief measures also became law. On March 21 the president requested three kinds of massive relief: a job corps called the Civilian Conservation Corps (CCC), direct cash grants to the states for relief payments to needy citizens, and public works projects. Ten days later Congress approved the CCC, which ultimately put 2.5 million young men aged eighteen to twenty-five to work planting trees; clearing camping areas and beaches; and building bridges, dams, reservoirs, fish ponds, and fire towers. Then on May 12, Congress passed the Federal Emergency Relief Act, which authorized $500 million in aid to state and local governments.

Civilian Conservation Corps

Roosevelt's proposed plan for public works became Title II of the National Industrial Recovery Act. Passed on June 16, the act established the Public Works Administration (PWA) and appropriated $3.3 billion for hiring the unemployed to build roads, sewage and water systems, public buildings, ships, naval aircraft, and a host of other projects. The key purpose of the PWA was to prime the economic pump to spur recovery.

If the AAA was the agricultural cornerstone of the New Deal, the National Industrial Recovery Act was the industrial cornerstone. The act, which established the National Recovery Administration (NRA), was a testimony to the New Deal belief in national planning as opposed to a laissez-faire economy. It was essential, planners argued, for businesses to end cutthroat competition and raise prices by limiting production. Under NRA auspices, competing businesses met with representatives of workers and consumers to draft codes of fair competition, which limited production and established prices. Section 7(a) of the National Industrial Recovery Act guaranteed workers the right to unionize and to bargain collectively.

National Recovery Administration

The New Deal also strengthened public confidence in the stock exchanges and banks. Roosevelt signed the Federal Securities Act, which compelled brokers to tell the truth about new securities issues, and the Banking Act of 1933, which set up the Federal Deposit Insurance Corporation (FDIC) for insuring bank deposits. During the First Hundred Days, Roosevelt also took the United States off the gold standard, no longer guaranteeing the gold value of the dollar abroad. Freed from the gold standard, the Federal Reserve Board could expand the supply of currency in circulation, thus enabling monetary policy to become another weapon for economic recovery.

One of the boldest programs enacted by Congress addressed the badly depressed Tennessee River valley, which runs through Tennessee, North Carolina, Kentucky, Virginia, Mississippi, Georgia, and Alabama. An expansion of a Progressive proposal, Roosevelt's Tennessee Valley Authority (TVA) built dams both to control floods and to generate hydroelectric power. The TVA also would produce and sell nitrogen fertilizers to private citizens and nitrate explosives to the government; dig a 650-mile navigation channel from Knoxville, Tennessee, to Paducah, Kentucky; and construct public power facilities as a yardstick for determining fair rates for privately produced electric power. The goal of the TVA was nothing less than enhancement of the economic well-being of the entire Tennessee River valley.

TVA

The TVA achieved its goals but became a major polluter. TVA strip mining caused soil erosion. Its coal-burning generators released sulfur oxides, which combined with water vapor to produce acid rain. The TVA also dumped toxic chemicals, raw sewage, and metal pollutants into streams and rivers. It proved to be a disaster in America's environmental history.

TVA's Environmental Legacy

Congress finally adjourned on June 16, 1933. During the First Hundred Days, Roosevelt had delivered fifteen messages to Congress, and fifteen significant laws had been enacted (see table, page 475). Within a few months of Roosevelt's succession to office, the United States had rebounded from hysteria and near collapse.

End of the First Hundred Days

Throughout the remainder of 1933 and the spring and summer of 1934, more New Deal bills became law, benefiting farmers, the unemployed, investors, homeowners, workers, and the environment. In 1934 additional hundreds of millions of federal dollars were appropriated for unemployment relief and public works. Legislation that year also established the Securities and Exchange Commission, the National Labor Relations Board, the Federal Housing Administration, and the Grazing Service (later to become the Bureau of Land Management).

New Deal legislation seemed to promise something for every group. This was interest-group democracy at work. In the midst of this coalition of special interests was President Roosevelt, the artful broker, who pointed to the economy as proof that this approach was working. After the passage of New Deal legislation, unemployment fell steadily from 13 million in 1933 to 9 million in 1936. Net farm income rose from just over $3 billion in 1933 to $5.85 billion in 1935. Manufacturing salaries and

Interest-Group Democracy

New Deal Achievements

Year	Labor	Agriculture	Business and Industrial Recovery	Relief	Reform
1933	Section 7(a) of NIRA	Agricultural Adjustment Act Farm Credit Act	Emergency Banking Relief Act Economy Act Beer-Wine Revenue Act Banking Act of 1933 (guaranteed deposits) National Industrial Recovery Act	Civilian Conservation Corps Federal Emergency Relief Act Home Owners Refinancing Act Public Works Administration Civil Works Administration	TVA Federal Securities Act
1934	National Labor Relations Board				Securities Exchange Act
1935	National Labor Relations (Wagner) Act	Resettlement Administration Rural Electrification Administration		Works Progress Administration National Youth Administration	Social Security Act Public Utility Holding Company Act Revenue Act (wealth tax)
1937		Farm Security Administration		National Housing Act	
1938	Fair Labor Standards Act	Agricultural Adjustment Act of 1938			

Source: Adapted from Charles Sellers, Henry May, and Neil R. McMillen, *A Synopsis of American History*, 6th ed. Copyright © 1985 by Houghton Mifflin Company. Reprinted by permission.

wages also increased, from $6.25 billion in 1933 to almost $13 billion in 1937.

Opposition to the First New Deal

With the arrival of partial economic recovery, many businesspeople and conservatives became vocal critics of the New Deal. Some charged that

Conservative Critics of the New Deal

there was too much taxation and government regulation. Others criticized the deficit financing of relief and public works. In 1934, the leaders of several major corporations joined with Al Smith, John W. Davis, and disaffected conservative Democrats to establish the American Liberty League. Members of the Liberty League contended that the New Deal was subverting individual initiative and self-reliance by providing welfare payments.

While businesspeople considered the government their enemy, others thought the government favored business too much. Critics argued that NRA codes favored industry's needs over those of workers and consumers. Farmers, labor unions, and individual entrepreneurs complained that the NRA set prices too high and favored large producers over small businesses.

The Agricultural Adjustment Act (AAA) also came under attack for its encouragement of cutbacks in production. Farmers had plowed under 10.4 million acres of cotton and slaughtered 6 million pigs in 1933—a time when people were ill clothed and ill fed. Although for landowning farmers the program was successful, the average person found such waste shocking. And very few of the tenant farmers and sharecroppers who were supposed to receive government payments for taking crops out of cultivation got what they were entitled to, especially if they were African-American. Furthermore, the AAA's hopes that landlords would keep their tenants on the land even while cutting production were not fulfilled. The result was a homeless population, dispossessed Americans heading to cities and towns in all parts of the country.

Joining the migration to the West Coast were "Okies," such as Oklahoman Marvin Montgomery, and "Arkies"; many of them had been evicted from their tenant farms during the depression. They

The Dust Bowl also took to the road to escape the drought that plagued the southern plains states of Kansas, Colorado, New Mexico, Oklahoma, Arkansas, and Texas. This region, known in the mid-1930s as the Dust Bowl, was an ecological disaster. In the 1920s farmers on the southern plains had bought tens of thousands of tractors and plowed millions of acres. In the 1930s, the rain stopped, and the strong winds that prevail on the plains swept up the loose soil and created enormous dust storms. Farmers shuttered their homes against the dust as tightly as possible, but, as a woman in western Kansas recounted in 1935, "those tiny particles seemed to seep through the very walls."

Some farmers blamed the government for their woes; others blamed themselves. As dissatisfaction mounted, so too did the appeal of various demagogues, who presented an analysis of American society

Demagogic Attacks on the New Deal that people understood: the wealthy and powerful were ruling people's lives. Two of the better-known critics were Father Charles Coughlin and Dr. Francis Townsend. Coughlin, an anti-Semitic Catholic priest, had a weekly radio program in which he criticized the New Deal and attempted to blame the nation's woes on an international conspiracy of Jewish bankers. Townsend, a public health officer from California, proposed to cure the depression through the Old Age Revolving Pensions plan, under which the government would pay monthly pensions of $200 to all citizens older than sixty on condition that they spend the money in the same month they received it. The plan was fiscally impossible but recognized the real needs of elderly Americans.

Then there was Huey Long, perhaps the most successful demagogue in American history. Long was elected governor of Louisiana in 1928 with the slogan "Every Man a King, but No One Wears a Crown." As a United States senator, Long at first supported the New Deal but began to believe that Roosevelt had fallen captive to big business. Long countered in 1934 with the Share Our Wealth Society, which advocated the seizure by taxation of all incomes greater than $1 million and all inheritances of more than $5 million. With the resulting funds, the government would furnish each family a homestead allowance of $5,000 and an annual income of $2,000. By mid-1935 Long's movement claimed 7 million members, and few doubted that Long aspired to the presidency. An assassin's bullet extinguished his ambition in September 1935.

Some politicians, like Governor Floyd Olson of Minnesota, declared themselves socialists in the 1930s. In Wisconsin the left-wing Progressive Party reelected Robert La Follette, Jr. (son of "Bat-

Left-Wing Critics of the New Deal tling Bob"), to the Senate in 1934, sent seven of the state's ten representatives to Washington, and placed La Follette's brother Philip in the governorship. But perhaps the most controversial alternative to the New Deal was the Communist Party of the United States of America. In 1935 the party disclaimed any intention of overthrowing the United States government and began to cooperate with left-wing labor unions, student groups, and writers' organizations in opposition to racism and fascism. In 1938, at its high point for the decade, the party had only fifty-five thousand members.

In addition to challenges from the right and the left, the New Deal was also subject to challenge by the Supreme Court. A majority of

Supreme Court Decisions Against the New Deal

the justices feared that some hastily drafted New Deal legislation had vested too much power in the presidency. In 1935, the Court unanimously struck down the NIRA (*Schechter* v. *U.S.*), asserting that it granted the White House excessive legislative power and that the commerce clause of the Constitution did not give the federal government authority to regulate intrastate businesses. Roosevelt's industrial recovery program was dead. In early 1936, his farm program met a similar fate when the Court invalidated the AAA (*U.S.* v. *Butler*).

As Roosevelt looked ahead to the presidential election of 1936, he foresaw the danger of losing his capacity to lead and to govern. His coalition of all interests was breaking up, radicals and demagogues were offering Americans alternative programs, and the Supreme Court was dismantling the New Deal. In early 1935, Roosevelt took the initiative once more. So impressive was the spate of new legislation that historians call it the Second New Deal.

The Second New Deal and the Election of 1936

The Second New Deal differed in important ways from the First New Deal. When the chief legislative goal had been economic recovery, Roosevelt

Emergency Relief Appropriation Act

had cooperated with business. Beginning in 1935, however, he denounced business leaders for placing their own selfish interests above the national welfare. The first triumph of the Second New Deal was the Emergency Relief Appropriation Act, which authorized the president to establish massive public works programs for the jobless. The first such program was the Works Progress Administration (WPA), later renamed the Work Projects Administration. The WPA ultimately employed more than 8.5 million people and built more than 650,000 miles of highways and roads, 125,000 public buildings, and 8,000 parks. But the WPA did more than lay bricks. Its Federal Theater Project brought plays, vaudeville, and circuses to cities and towns across the country, and its Federal Writers' Project hired talent like John Steinbeck and Richard Wright to write local guidebooks and regional and folk histories. The Emergency Relief Appropriation Act also funded the Rural Electrification Administration, which brought electricity to isolated rural areas; and the National Youth Administration, which sponsored work-relief programs for young adults and part-time jobs for students.

Roosevelt also wanted new legislation aimed at controlling the activities of big business. Businesspeople had become increasingly critical of the New Deal. The president thus decided that if business would not cooperate with government, then government should "cut the giants down to size" through antitrust suits and heavy corporate taxes. In 1935 he asked Congress to enact a labor bill, a Social Security bill, and a "soak-the-rich" tax bill.

When the summer of 1935, which constituted the Second Hundred Days, was over, the president had everything he had requested. The National

National Labor Relations Act

Labor Relations (Wagner) Act granted workers the right to unionize and bargain collectively with management. The act also empowered the National Labor Relations Board to guarantee democratic union elections and to penalize unfair labor practices by employers, such as firing workers for union membership.

The Social Security Act established several welfare programs, including a cooperative federal-state system of unemployment compensation and

Social Security Act

Aid to Dependent Children (later renamed Aid to Families with Dependent Children, AFDC). The act also established old-age insurance for workers who paid Social Security taxes out of their wages.

Social Security was a conservative measure: the government did not pay for old-age benefits; workers and their bosses did. The tax was regressive in that the more workers earned, the less they were taxed proportionally. It was deflationary, because it took out of people's pockets money that it did not repay for years. And the law excluded from coverage farm workers, domestic servants, and many hospital and restaurant workers. Nevertheless, the Social Security Act was a milestone. With its passage, the federal government acknowledged its responsibility for the aged, the temporarily jobless, dependent children, and disabled people.

Congress next enacted Roosevelt's Wealth Tax Act, which some critics saw as the president's attempt to "steal Huey Long's thunder." The tax act helped achieve a slight redistribution of income by raising the income taxes of the wealthy. It also imposed a new tax on excess business profits and increased taxes on inheritances, large gifts, and profits from the sale of property.

The Second Hundred Days made it unmistakably clear that the president was once again in charge and preparing to run for reelection. Roo-

Election of 1936 and the New Deal Coalition

sevelt won by a landslide, easily defeating the Republican nominee, Governor Alf Landon of Kansas, by a margin of 27.8 million votes to 16.7 million. By 1936, Roosevelt and the Democrats had forged what observers have called the "New Deal coalition." The coalition consisted of the urban masses—especially immigrants from southern and eastern Europe and their sons and daughters—organized labor, the eleven states of the Confederacy (the "Solid South"), and northern blacks. With the New

Deal coalition, the Democratic Party had become the dominant half of the two-party system.

Roosevelt's Second Term: Court Packing and Other Failures

Roosevelt faced a darkening horizon during his second term. The economy faltered again between 1937 and 1939. And Europe drew closer to war, threatening to drag the United States into the conflict (see Chapter 26). To gain support for his foreign and military policies, Roosevelt began to court conservative opponents of his domestic reforms. The eventual result was the demise of the New Deal.

In several instances Roosevelt's own actions helped bring about the end of the New Deal. Concerned that the Supreme Court would invalidate

Roosevelt's Court-packing Plan

much of the Second Hundred Days, as it had done to the First Hundred Days, Roosevelt concluded that what the federal judiciary needed was a more progressive world-view. His Judiciary Reorganization Bill of 1937 requested the authority to add a federal judge whenever an incumbent failed to retire within six months of reaching age seventy; he also wanted the power to name up to fifty additional federal judges, including six to the Supreme Court. Roosevelt frankly envisioned using the reorganization to create a Supreme Court sympathetic to the New Deal. Liberals joined Republicans and conservative Democrats in resisting the bill. The bill Roosevelt signed provided pensions to retiring judges but denied him the power to increase the number of judges.

The episode had a final, ironic twist. During the public debate over court packing, the two swing-vote justices on the Supreme Court began to vote in favor of liberal, pro–New Deal rulings. In short order the Court upheld both the Wagner Act (*NLRB* v. *Jones & Laughlin Steel Corp.*) and the Social Security Act. Moreover, the new pensions encouraged judges older than seventy to retire, and the president was able to appoint seven new associate justices in the next four years.

Another New Deal setback was the renewed economic recession of 1937–1939. Roosevelt had never abandoned his commitment to a balanced budget. In 1937, confident that the depression had largely been cured, he began to order drastic cutbacks in government spending. At the same time the Federal Reserve Board, concerned about a 3.6 percent inflation rate, tightened credit. The two actions sent the economy into a tailspin: unemployment climbed from 7.7 million in 1937 to 10.4 million in 1938. Soon Roosevelt resumed deficit financing.

Recession of 1937–1939

In the spring of 1938, with conflict over events in Europe commanding more and more of the nation's attention, the New Deal came to an end. Roosevelt sacrificed further domestic reforms in return for conservative support for his programs of military rearmament and preparedness. The last significant New Deal laws enacted were the National Housing Act (1937), which established the United States Housing Authority and built housing projects for low-income families; a new Agricultural Adjustment Act (1938); and the Fair Labor Standards Act (1938), which forbade labor by children younger than sixteen and established a minimum wage and forty-hour workweek for many, but by no means all, workers.

Industrial Workers and the Rise of the CIO

New Deal legislation that gave workers the right to organize unions and to bargain collectively invigorated the labor movement. Union membership in 1929 stood at 3.6 million; in mid-1938 it surpassed 7 million. The gains, however, did not always come easily. Management resisted vigorously in the 1930s, relying on the police or hiring armed thugs to intimidate workers and break up strikes.

Labor confronted yet another obstacle in the American Federation of Labor (AFL) craft unions' traditional hostility toward industrial unions. Craft unions typically consisted of skilled workers in a particular trade. Industrial unions represented all the workers in a given industry. The organizational gains of the 1930s were far more impressive in industrial unions than in craft unions, as hundreds of thousands of workers organized in industries such as autos, garments, rubber, and steel. Attempts to reconcile the craft and industrial union movements failed, and in 1935 John L. Lewis of the United Mine Workers resigned as vice president of the AFL. He and other industrial unionists then formed the Committee for Industrial Organization (CIO). The AFL expelled the CIO unions in 1938, and the CIO reorganized as the Congress of Industrial Organizations. By that time CIO membership had reached 3.7 million, more than the AFL's 3.4 million.

Rivalry Between Craft and Industrial Unions

The CIO evolved during the 1930s into a pragmatic, bread-and-butter labor organization that organized millions of workers, including women and African-Americans, who never before had had an opportunity to join a union. One union, the United Auto Workers (UAW), scored a major victory in late 1936. The UAW demanded recognition from General Motors (GM), Chrysler, and Ford. When GM refused, workers at the Fisher Body plant in Flint, Michigan, launched a sit-down strike and refused to leave the building. The strike lasted for weeks. General Motors obtained a court order to evacuate the plant, but the strikers stood firm. With the support of their families and neighborhoods, and a women's "emergency brigade" that delivered food and supplies to the strikers, the UAW prevailed. GM agreed to recognize the union. Chrysler signed a similar agreement, but Ford held out for four more years. As a tactic, the sit-down strike spread dramatically; it was used by workers in the textile, glass, and rubber industries.

Sit-down Strikes

Some confrontations turned violent. In 1937, the Steel Workers Organizing Committee signed a contract with the nation's largest steelmaker,

Memorial Day Massacre

U.S. Steel, that guaranteed an eight-hour workday and a forty-hour workweek. Other steel companies, including Republic Steel in Chicago, refused to go along. On Memorial Day, strikers and their families joined with sympathizers in a picket line in front of the Republic Steel plant. Violence erupted, ten strikers were killed, and forty suffered gunshot wounds. Police claimed the marchers attacked them with clubs and bricks and they responded with reasonable force to defend themselves and disperse the mob. Strikers argued that the police, without provocation, had brutally attacked citizens peacefully asserting their constitutional rights.

Though senseless, the Memorial Day Massacre was not surprising. During the 1930s industries had hired private police agents and accumulated large stores of arms and ammunition for use in deterring workers from organizing and joining unions. Meanwhile, the CIO continued to enroll new members. By the end of the decade the CIO had succeeded in organizing most of the nation's mass-production industries.

Mixed Progress for People of Color

The Great Depression plunged the vast majority of African-Americans deeper into fear, political disfranchisement, Jim Crow segregation, and privation. In 1930 about three-fourths of all blacks lived in the South, where segregation continued to exist from the cradle to the grave. Whether in town or on the tenant farm, southern African-Americans were caught in a cycle of poverty. They had a shorter life expectancy than whites and the specter of the lynch mob remained. Racism also plagued African-Americans living in the North, and unemployment rates ran high. In Pittsburgh 48 percent of black workers were jobless in 1933, compared with 31 percent of white laborers.

African-Americans in the Great Depression

As African-Americans were aware, President Herbert Hoover shared prevailing white racial attitudes. In 1930, the president demonstrated his racial insensitivity by nominating Judge John J. Parker of North Carolina to the Supreme Court. Ten years earlier Parker had endorsed the disfranchisement of blacks. Pressure from the NAACP and the AFL helped to defeat Parker's nomination in the Senate.

Shortly thereafter, a celebrated civil rights case revealed the ugliness of race relations. In March 1931, nine African-Americans who were riding a freight train near Scottsboro, Alabama, were arrested and charged with roughing up some white hoboes and throwing them off the train. Two white women removed from the same train claimed the nine men had raped them. Medical evidence later showed that the women were lying. But within two weeks, eight of the so-called Scottsboro boys were convicted of rape by all-white juries and sentenced to death.

Scottsboro Trials

After several trials, the first defendant, Haywood Patterson, was condemned to die. A Supreme Court ruling intervened, however, on the ground that African-Americans were systematically excluded from juries in Alabama. Patterson was found guilty again in 1936 and was given a seventy-five-year jail sentence. Four of the other youths were sentenced to life imprisonment. Not until 1950 were all five out of jail—four by parole and Patterson by escaping from a work gang.

African-Americans coped with their white-circumscribed environment and fought racism in a variety of ways. The NAACP lobbied quietly against a long list of injustices, and the Brotherhood of Sleeping Car Porters, under the astute leadership of A. Philip Randolph, fought for the rights of black workers. In Harlem the militant Harlem Tenants League fought rent increases and evictions, and African-American consumers began to boycott white merchants who refused to hire blacks as clerks.

With the election of Franklin D. Roosevelt, blacks' attitudes toward government changed, as did their political affiliation. For African-Americans, Franklin D. Roosevelt would become the most appealing president since Abraham Lincoln.

How do historians know that police officers were largely responsible for the 1937 Memorial Day Massacre in Chicago? There is both photographic and medical evidence of police culpability. Covering the story at the Republic Steel plant were a cameraman from Paramount News and photographers from Life magazine and Wide World Photos (see photograph). Paramount News suppressed its film footage, claiming that releasing it "might very well incite local riots," but an enterprising reporter alerted a congressional committee to its existence, and a private viewing was arranged. Spectators at this showing, the reporter noted, "were shocked and amazed by scenes showing scores of uniformed policemen firing their revolvers pointblank into a dense crowd of men, women, and children, and then pursuing the survivors unmercifully as they made frantic efforts to escape." Medical evidence also substantiated the picketers' version: none of the ten people killed by police were shot from the front. Clearly, the picketers were trying to flee the police when they were shot or clubbed to the ground.   Photo: World Wide Photos.

They were heartened by photographs of African-American visitors at the White House and by news stories about Roosevelt's black advisers. Most important, New Deal programs aided black people in their struggle for economic survival.

The "Black Cabinet," or black brain trust, was unique in United States history. Never before had there been so many African-American advisers at the White House. There were black lawyers, journalists, and Ph.D.s and black experts on housing, labor, and social welfare. William H. Hastie and Robert C. Weaver, holders of advanced degrees from Harvard, served

Black Cabinet

in the Department of the Interior. Mary Mc-Leod Bethune, educator and president of the National Council of Negro Women, was director of the Division of Negro Affairs of the National Youth Administration. Also among the New Dealers were some whites who had committed themselves to first-class citizenship for African-Americans. Foremost among these people was Eleanor Roosevelt.

The president himself, however, remained uncommitted to African-American civil rights. Fearful of alienating southern whites, he never endorsed two key civil rights goals: a federal law against lynching and abolition of the poll tax. And some New Deal programs were definitely damaging to African-Americans. Rather than benefiting black tenant farmers and sharecroppers, the Agricultural Adjustment Act (AAA) had the effect of forcing many of them off the land. The Federal Housing Administration refused to guarantee

The New Deal's Racism

mortgages on houses purchased by blacks in white neighborhoods, and the Civilian Conservation Corps was racially segregated. Also, Social Security coverage and the minimum-wage provisions of the Fair Labor Standards Act of 1938 excluded waiters, cooks, hospital orderlies, janitors, farm workers, and domestics, many of whom were African-Americans.

In short, though African-Americans benefited from the New Deal, they did not get their fair share. Even so, the large majorities they gave Roosevelt at election time demonstrated their appreciation of the benefits they did receive. Not all African-Americans, however, trusted the mixed message of the New Deal. Some concluded that they could depend only on themselves and organized self-help and direct-action movements.

Black Protest

Nowhere was the trend toward direct action more evident than in the March on Washington movement in 1941. That year, billions of federal

Mary McLeod Bethune, pictured here with her friend and supporter Eleanor Roosevelt, became the first African-American woman to head a federal agency as director of the Division of Negro Affairs of the National Youth Administration. UPI/Corbis-Bettmann.

March on Washington Movement

dollars flowed into American industry as the nation prepared for the possibility of another world war. Thousands of new jobs were created, but discrimination deprived blacks of their fair share. Randolph, leader of the porters' union, proposed that blacks march on the nation's capital to demand equal access to jobs in defense industries. Fearing that the march might provoke riots and that Communists might infiltrate the movement, Roosevelt announced that he would issue an executive order prohibiting discrimination in war industries and in the government if the march was canceled. The result was Executive Order No. 8802, which established the Fair Employment Practices Committee (FEPC).

A New Deal for American Indians

The New Deal approach to Native Americans differed greatly from that of earlier administrations; as a result, Indians benefited more directly than blacks from the New Deal. Indians had been sinking further into malnutrition and disease during the early 1930s. In Oklahoma, where the Choctaws, Cherokees, and Seminoles lived, three-fourths of all Native American children were undernourished. Tuberculosis swept through the reservations. At the heart of the problem was a 1929 ruling by the United States comptroller general that landless tribes were ineligible for federal aid. Not until 1931 did the Bureau of Indian Affairs take steps to relieve the suffering.

Early in his first term, Roosevelt appointed John Collier, founder of the American Indian Defense Association, as commissioner of Indian affairs. Collier had crusaded for tribal landownership and an end to the allotment policy established by the Dawes Severalty Act of 1887. After 1887, Indian landholdings had dropped from 138 million acres to 52 million acres, 20 million of which were arid or semiarid. To reverse this process, the Indian Reorganization (Wheeler-Howard) Act (1934) restored lands to tribal ownership and prohibited future division of Indian lands into individual parcels. Other provisions of the act enabled tribes to obtain loans for economic development and to establish self-government. Under Collier, the Bu-

reau of Indian Affairs also encouraged the perpetuation of Indian religions and cultures.

Depression Hardships of Mexican-Americans

Mexican-Americans also suffered extreme hardship during the Great Depression, but no government programs benefited them. During these years many Mexicans and Mexican-Americans packed up their belongings and moved south of the border, sometimes willingly and sometimes deported by immigration officials or forced out by California officials eager to purge them from the relief rolls. In addition, many employers had changed their minds about the desirability of hiring Mexican-American farm workers. Before the 1930s farmers had boasted that Mexican-Americans were an inexpensive, docile labor supply and that they would not join unions. But in the 1930s Mexican-Americans overturned the stereotype by engaging in prolonged and sometimes bloody strikes.

The New Deal offered Mexican-Americans little help. The AAA was created to assist property-owning farmers, not migratory farm workers. The Wagner Act did not cover farm workers' unions, nor did the Social Security Act or the Fair Labor Standards Act cover farm laborers. One New Deal agency, the Farm Security Administration (FSA), was established in 1937 to help farm workers, in part by setting up migratory labor camps. But the FSA came too late to help Mexican-Americans, most of whom by then had been replaced in the fields by dispossessed white farmers from the Dust Bowl states.

Women, Work, and the Great Depression

Mothers and Households Face Hard Times

In *It's Up to the Women* (1933), Eleanor Roosevelt wrote that "women know that life must go on and that the needs of life must be met." Wives and mothers followed the maxim "Use it up, wear it out, make it do, or do without." Women bought day-old bread and cheap cuts of meat; they relined old coats with blankets. Many families were able to maintain their standard of living only because of astute spending and because women substituted their own labor for goods and services they once purchased.

While cutting corners to make ends meet, women were also seeking paid work outside the home. In 1930 approximately 10.5 million women were paid workers; ten years later, the female labor force exceeded 13 million. Many women were their families' sole providers. Despite that reality, most Americans believed that women should not take jobs outside the home, that they should strive instead to be good wives and mothers, and that women who worked were doing so for "pin money" to buy frivolous things.

These attitudes resulted in severe job discrimination. Most insurance companies, banks, railroads, and public utilities had policies against hiring married women. And from 1932 to 1937, federal law prohibited more than one family member from working for the civil service. Because wives usually earned less than their husbands, they were the ones who quit their government jobs.

Job Discrimination Against Married Women

The generalizations that women took jobs from men and that they worked for "pin money" were inaccurate. First, women were heavily concentrated in "women's jobs," including clerical positions, teaching, and nursing. Men rarely sought these jobs and probably would not have been hired to fill them had they applied. Second, most women workers (71 percent in 1930) were single and thus self-supporting. This was, however, changing. By 1940, married women constituted 35 percent of the female work force, up from 29 percent in 1930 and 15 percent in 1900. They worked to keep their families from slipping into poverty, but their assistance with family expenses did not improve their status. Their husbands, including those without jobs, still expected to rule the roost and to remain exempt from childcare and housework.

The New Deal did take women's needs into account, but only when forcefully reminded to do so by the activist women who advised the adminis-tration. These women, mainly government and Democratic Party officials, formed a network united by their commitment to social reform, to protective laws for women's health and safety on the job, and to the participation of women in politics and government. The network's most prominent member was Eleanor Roosevelt, who was her husband's valued adviser. Secretary of Labor Frances Perkins was the nation's first woman cabinet officer. Other historic New Deal appointments included the first woman federal appeals judge and the first women ambassadors.

Women in the New Deal

Even with increased participation by women, however, New Deal provisions for women were mixed. The maximum-hour and minimum-wage provisions mandated by the NRA helped women workers in the lowest paying jobs, but some NRA codes mandated pay differentials based on gender, making women's minimum wages lower than men's. Moreover, federal relief agencies hired only one woman for every eight to ten men placed in relief jobs, the Civilian Conservation Corps was limited to young men, and women in agriculture and domestic service were not protected by the 1938 Fair Labor Standards Act. Most important, the 1935 Social Security Act failed to provide coverage for large numbers of women workers, including not only farm women and domestic servants but also many women teachers, nurses, librarians, and social workers.

The Election of 1940 and the Legacy of the New Deal

No president had ever served more than two terms, and as the presidential election of 1940 approached, many Americans speculated about whether Roosevelt would run for a third term. Roosevelt seemed undecided until May 1940, when Adolf Hitler's military advances in Europe apparently convinced him to stay on.

The Republican candidate was Wendell Willkie, an Indiana lawyer and utilities executive who was once a Democrat but had become a promi-

The 1940 Election

nent business opponent of the New Deal. Willkie campaigned against the New Deal, and he also criticized the government's lack of military preparedness. When Roosevelt preempted the defense issue by beefing up military and naval contracts, Willkie reversed his approach and accused Roosevelt of warmongering. The president then promised, "Your boys are not going to be sent into any foreign wars." On election day Roosevelt received 27 million popular votes to Willkie's 22 million. The election clearly indicated that although the New Deal was over at home, Roosevelt was still riding a wave of public approval.

Any analysis of the New Deal must begin with Franklin Delano Roosevelt himself. Most historians consider him a truly great president,

Roosevelt and the New Deal Assessed

citing his courage and buoyant self-confidence, his willingness to experiment, and his capacity to inspire the nation during the most somber days of the depression. Those who criticize him charge that he lacked vision and failed to formulate a bold and coherent strategy of economic recovery and political and economic reform. Some also charge that he initiated the "imperial presidency."

But even his critics agree that he transformed the presidency. "Only Washington, who made the office, and Jackson, who remade it, did more than Roosevelt to raise it to its present condition of strength, dignity, and independence," wrote political scientist Clinton Rossiter. Roosevelt personified the presidency, and with his fireside chats he

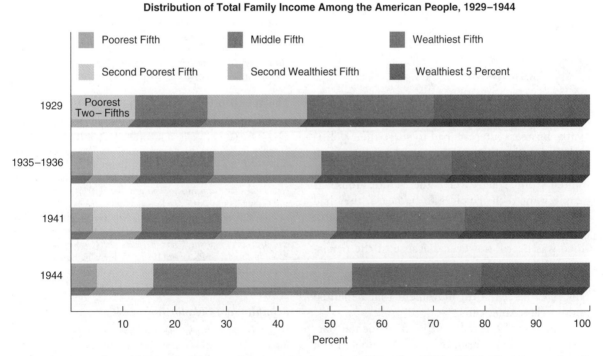

Distribution of Total Family Income Among the American People, 1929–1944 (Percentage) *Although the New Deal provided economic relief to the American people, it did not, as its critics so often charged, significantly redistribute income downward from the rich to the poor.* Source: Adapted from U.S. Bureau of the Census, *Historical Statistics of the United States, Colonial Times to 1970,* 2 parts (Washington, D.C., 1975), Part 1, p. 301.

became the first president to use the radio to appeal directly for the people's support. Whether for good or ill, Roosevelt strengthened not only the presidency but the whole federal government. Under him the federal government became *the* government.

The New Deal laid the foundation of the welfare system on which subsequent presidential administrations would build. For the first time the

**Origins of
America's
Welfare System**

federal government acknowledged a responsibility to offer relief to the jobless and the needy, and for the first time it resorted to deficit spending to stimulate the economy. But the economy itself remained basically capitalistic. The profit motive and private property remained fundamental to the system. Some redistribution of wealth did result, but the wealthy survived as a class. Most of the income lost by the wealthy ended up in the pockets of the middle and upper-middle classes, not those of the poor (see figure, page 485).

Conclusion

The New Deal brought about limited change in the nation's power structure. Beginning in the 1930s, business interests had to share their political clout with others. Labor gained influence in Washington, and farmers got more of what they wanted from Congress and the White House. If people wanted their voices to be heard, they had to organize into labor unions, trade associations, or other special-interest lobbies. Not everybody's voice was heard, however. Because of the persistence of racism, there was no real increase in the power of minorities. Historians generally view the New Deal as a reform movement that benefited middle-class Americans.

The New Deal failed in its fundamental purpose: to put people back to work. As late as 1939, more than 10 million men and women were still jobless. That year, unemployment was 19 percent. In the end it was not the New Deal but massive government spending during the Second World War that put people back to work. In 1941, as a result

of mobilization for war, unemployment declined to 10 percent, and in 1944, at the height of the war, only 1 percent of the labor force was jobless.

The New Deal's most lasting accomplishments were its programs to ameliorate the suffering of unemployed people. During several economic recessions since 1945, even Republican presidents have primed the pump. Before the New Deal, the United States had experienced a major depression every fifteen or twenty years. The Great Depression was the last of its kind. Since the New Deal, thanks to unemployment compensation, Social Security, and other measures, the United States has not reexperienced this national nightmare.

Suggestions for Further Reading

Hoover and the Worsening Depression

William J. Barber, *Herbert Hoover, the Economists, and American Economic Policy, 1921–1933* (1986); Michael A. Bernstein, *The Great Depression: Delayed Recovery and Economic Change in America, 1929–1939* (1988); David Burner, *Herbert Hoover* (1979); Martin L. Fausold, *The Presidency of Herbert C. Hoover* (1985); John A. Garraty, *The Great Depression* (1986); James S. Olson, *Herbert Hoover and the Reconstruction Finance Corporation, 1931–1933* (1977); Jordan A. Schwarz, *Interregnum of Despair* (1970).

The New Deal

Anthony J. Badger, *The New Deal: The Depression Years, 1933–1940* (1989); William J. Barber, *Designs Within Disorder: Franklin D. Roosevelt, the Economists, and the Shaping of American Economic Policy, 1933–1945* (1996); Roger Biles, *A New Deal for the American People* (1991); Alan Brinkley, *The End of Reform: New Deal Liberalism in Recession and War* (1995); Steve Fraser and Gary Gerstle, eds., *The Rise and Fall of the New Deal Order, 1930–1980* (1989); Colin Gordon, *New Deals: Business, Labor, and Politics in America, 1920–1935* (1994); William E. Leuchtenburg, *The Supreme Court Reborn: The Constitutional Revolution in the Age of Roosevelt* (1995); William E. Leuchtenburg, *Franklin D. Roosevelt and the New Deal* (1963); Albert U. Romasco, *The Politics of Recovery: Roosevelt's New Deal* (1983).

Franklin and Eleanor Roosevelt

James MacGregor Burns, *Roosevelt: The Lion and the Fox* (1956); Blanche Wiesen Cook, *Eleanor Roosevelt: Volume One, 1884–1933* (1992); Kenneth S. Davis, *FDR: Into the Storm, 1937–1940* (1993); Kenneth S. Davis, *FDR: The New Deal Years, 1933–1937* (1986); Frank Freidel, *Franklin D. Roosevelt: A Rendezvous with Destiny* (1990); Joseph P. Lash, *Eleanor and Franklin* (1971); Arthur M. Schlesinger, Jr., *The Age of Roosevelt*, 3 vols. (1957–1960).

Voices from the Depression

James Agee, *Let Us Now Praise Famous Men* (1941); Federal Writers' Project, *These Are Our Lives* (1939); Robert S. McElvaine, ed., *Down and Out in the Great Depression* (1983); Studs Terkel, *Hard Times: An Oral History of the Great Depression* (1970); Tom E. Terrill and Jerrold Hirsch, eds., *Such as Us: Southern Voices of the Thirties* (1978).

Alternatives to the New Deal

Alan Brinkley, *Voices of Protest: Huey Long, Father Coughlin, and the Great Depression* (1982); William Ivy Hair, *The Kingfish and His Realm: The Life and Times of Huey P. Long* (1992); Robin D. G. Kelley, *Hammer and Hoe: Alabama Communists During the Great Depression* (1991); Fraser M. Ottanelli, *The Communist Party of the United States from the Depression to World War II* (1991); Leo Ribuffo, *The Old Christian Right: The Protestant Far Right from the Great Depression to the Cold War* (1983); Donald Warren, *Radio Priest: Charles Coughlin, the Father of Hate Radio* (1996); Frank A. Warren, *An Alternative Vision: The Socialist Party in the 1930s* (1976); Clyde P. Weed, *The Nemesis of Reform: The Republican Party During the New Deal* (1994).

Workers and Organized Labor

Irving Bernstein, *A Caring Society: The New Deal, the Worker, and the Great Depression* (1985); Irving Bernstein, *Turbulent Years: A History of the American Worker, 1933–1941* (1969); Lizabeth Cohen, *Making a New Deal: Industrial Workers in Chicago, 1919–1939* (1991); Melvin Dubofsky and Warren Van Tine, *John L. Lewis* (1977); Sidney Fine, *Sit-Down: The General Motors Strike of 1936–1937* (1969); Gary Gerstle, *Working-Class Americanism: The Politics of Labor in a Textile City, 1914–1960* (1989); Nelson Lichtenstein, *The Most Dangerous Man in Detroit: Walter Reuther and the Fate of American Labor* (1995); Robert H. Zieger, *The CIO, 1935–1955* (1995).

Agriculture and the Environment

William U. Chandler, *The Myth of TVA: Conservation and Development in the Tennessee Valley, 1933–1983* (1984); David E. Conrad, *The Forgotten Farmers: The Story of Sharecroppers in the New Deal* (1965); James N. Gregory, *American Exodus: The Dust Bowl Migration and Okie Culture in California* (1989); David E. Hamilton, *From New Day to New Deal: American Farm Policy from Hoover to Roosevelt, 1928–1933* (1991); Theodore M. Saloutos, *The American Farmer and the New Deal* (1982); John L. Shover, *Cornbelt Rebellion: The Farmers' Holiday Association* (1965); Donald Worster, *Dust Bowl: The Southern Plains in the 1930s* (1979).

People of Color

Dan T. Carter, *Scottsboro*, rev. ed. (1979); James Goodman, *Stories of Scottsboro* (1994); Camille Guerin-Gonzales, *Mexican Workers and American Dreams: Immigration, Repatriation, and California Farm Labor, 1900–1939* (1994); Laurence M. Hauptman, *The Iroquois and the New Deal* (1981); Laurence C. Kelly, *The Assault on Assimilation: John Collier and the Origins of Indian Policy Reform* (1983); John B. Kirby, *Black Americans in the Roosevelt Era* (1980); Donald J. Lisio, *Hoover, Blacks, and Lily-Whites* (1985); Donald L. Parman, *The Navajos and the New Deal* (1975); George J. Sanchez, *Becoming Mexican American: Ethnicity, Culture and Identity in Chicano Los Angeles, 1900–1945* (1993); Harvard Sitkoff, *A New Deal for Blacks* (1978); Patricia Sullivan, *Days of Hope: Race and Democracy in the New Deal Era* (1996); Nancy J. Weiss, *Farewell to the Party of Lincoln: Black Politics in the Age of FDR* (1983).

Women

Glen H. Elder, Jr., *Children of the Great Depression: Social Change in Life Experience* (1974); Linda Gordon, *Pitied but Not Entitled: Single Mothers and the History of Welfare, 1890–1935* (1994); Alice Kessler-Harris, "Designing Women and Old Fools: The Construction of the Social Security Amendments of 1939," in Linda K. Kerber et al., eds., *U.S. History as Women's History* (1995): 87–106; Lois Scharf, *To Work and to Wed: Female Employment, Feminism, and the Great Depression* (1980); Winifred Wandersee, *Women's Work and Family Values, 1920–1940* (1981); Susan Ware, *Holding Their Own: American Women in the 1930s* (1982); Susan Ware, *Beyond Suffrage: Women in the New Deal* (1981).

Cultural and Intellectual History

Daniel Aaron, *Writers on the Left: Episodes in American Literary Communism* (1961); Andrew Bergman, *We're in the Money: Depression America and Its Films* (1971); Jerre Mangione, *The Dream and the Deal: The Federal Writers' Project, 1935–1943* (1972); David P. Peeler, *Hope Among Us Yet: Social Criticism and Social Solace in Depression America* (1987); Richard H. Pells, *Radical Visions and American Dreams: Culture and Social Thought in the Depression Years* (1973); Warren I. Susman, "The Culture of the Thirties," in Warren I. Susman, ed., *Culture as History* (1984): 150–183.

26

Peaceseekers and Warmakers: United States Foreign Relations, 1920–1941

I n 1921 the Rockefeller Foundation declared war on the mosquito in Latin America. As the carrier of yellow fever, the biting insect transmitted a deadly virus that threatened public health, political and economic order, and United States hegemony in the region. With clearance from the United States Department of State, the foundation funded dedicated scientists who, learning from the pioneering work of Carlos Juan Finlay of Cuba, Oswaldo Cruz of Brazil, and United States army surgeon Walter Reed, sought to destroy the mosquito in its larval stage, before it became an egg-laying adult.

Besides killing people, yellow fever disrupted international trade and immigration because ports had to be quarantined. And insufficient official attention to outbreaks of the fever stirred public discontent against regimes the United States supported. The opening of the Panama Canal to ships in 1914, moreover, had raised urgent fears that the death-dealing disease would spread.

The foundation's antimosquito campaign in Latin America proved very successful in maritime and urban areas. It also strengthened central governments by providing a national public health infrastructure. And much-welcomed foundation activities diminished anti–United States sentiment in a region known for virulent anti-Yankeeism.

In the years between the First and Second World War, the Rockefeller Foundation became one of many instruments that Americans utilized in their effort to build a stable world order. Despite the tag "isolationist" that is sometimes still applied to United States foreign relations after World War I, Americans did not cut themselves off from international affairs. They wished to avoid entanglements in Europe, but they remained very active in the world in the 1920s and 1930s.

The most apt description of interwar United States foreign policy is *independent internationalism.* The United States was active on a global scale but retained its independence of action, its traditional unilateralism. Nevertheless, many Americans did think of themselves as *isolationists,* by which they meant that they wanted to isolate themselves from Europe's squabbles, from military alliances and interventions, and from the League of Nations. Americans, then, were isolationists in their desire to avoid war but independent internationalists in their behavior.

In the aftermath of the First World War, Americans had grown disenchanted with military methods of achieving order and protecting American prosperity and security. American diplomats thus increasingly sought to exercise the power of the United States through conferences, humanitarian programs, moral lectures and calls for peace, nonrecognition of disapproved regimes, arms control, and economic and financial ties in accord with the principle of the Open Door. Downgrading military interventions, for example, United States leaders fashioned a Good Neighbor policy for Latin America.

The United States, however, failed to create a stable world order. Some nations schemed to disrupt it, and severe economic problems undercut it. The debts and reparations bills left over from the First World War bedeviled the 1920s, and the Great Depression of the 1930s shattered world trade and finance. The depression spawned revolutions in Latin America and political extremism, militarism, and war in Europe and Asia. As Nazi Germany marched toward world war, the United States tried to protect itself from the conflict by adopting a policy of neutrality. At the same time, the United States sought to defend its interests in

Asia against Japanese aggression by invoking the venerable Open Door policy.

After the outbreak of war in Europe in September 1939, many came to agree with President Franklin D. Roosevelt that Germany and Japan had become menaces to the national interest. Roosevelt first pushed for American military preparedness and then for the abandonment of neutrality in favor of aiding Britain and France. To deter Japanese expansion in the Pacific, the United States ultimately cut off supplies of vital American products such as oil. But economic warfare only intensified antagonism. Japan's surprise attack on Pearl Harbor, Hawai'i, in December 1941 finally brought the United States into the Second World War.

 ## Searching for Peace and Order in the 1920s

Europe lay in shambles at the end of the First World War. Between 1914 and 1921, Europe suffered 60 million casualties from world war, civil war, massacre, epidemic, and famine. Crops, livestock, factories, trains, forests, bridges—little was spared. The American Relief Administration and private charities delivered food to needy Europeans, including Russians wracked by famine in 1921 and 1922.

The League of Nations, envisioned as a peacemaker, actually proved feeble, its members usually unwilling to use the new organization to settle disputes. Starting in the mid-1920s, American officials participated discreetly in League meetings on public health, prostitution, drug trafficking, and other questions. American jurists served on the Permanent Court of International Justice (World Court) at The Hague, though the United States also refused to join that body.

American peace societies, such as the National Committee for the Prevention of War, worked for international stability. Most highlighted the carnage of the First World War and the futility of war as a solution to international problems, but they differed over strategies to ensure world order. Some urged cooperation with

**American
Peace
Movement**

the League of Nations and the World Court. Others championed the arbitration of disputes, disarmament and arms reduction, the outlawing of war, and strict neutrality during wars.

The Washington Conference (November 1921 to February 1922) seemed to mark a substantial step toward peace through arms control. The United

Washington Conference Treaties

States and eight other nations (Britain, Japan, France, Italy, China, Portugal, Belgium, and the Netherlands) met to discuss limits on naval armaments. Britain, the United States, and Japan—the three major powers—were facing a costly naval arms race, and, as Secretary of State Charles Evans Hughes argued, huge military spending endangered economic rehabilitation.

The conference produced three treaties. The Five-Power Treaty set a ten-year moratorium on the construction of capital ships (battleships and aircraft carriers) and established total tonnage limits of 500,000 for Britain and the United States, 300,000 for Japan, and 175,000 for France and Italy. The first three nations actually agreed to dismantle some existing vessels to satisfy the ratio. They also pledged not to build new fortifications in their Pacific possessions. In the Nine-Power Treaty, the conferees reaffirmed the Open Door in China, recognizing Chinese sovereignty. In the Four-Power Treaty, the United States, Britain, Japan, and France agreed to respect each other's Pacific possessions. The three treaties did not limit submarines, destroyers, or cruisers; nor did they provide enforcement powers for the Open Door declaration. By the 1930s, to the great disappointment of peace groups, rearmament was supplanting disarmament.

Peace advocates welcomed the Kellogg-Briand Pact of 1928. In this document, sixty-two nations agreed to "condemn recourse to war for

Kellogg-Briand Pact

the solution of international controversies, and renounce it as an instrument of national policy." Although weak, the Kellogg-Briand Pact reflected popular opinion that war was barbaric and wasteful and should be outlawed.

The World Economy and Great Depression

While Europe struggled to recover from the ravages of the First World War, the international economy wobbled and then, in the early 1930s, collapsed. The Great Depression set off a political chain reaction that carried the world to war. Cordell Hull, secretary of state under President Franklin D. Roosevelt from 1933 to 1944, often pointed out that political extremism and militarism sprang from maimed economies.

Leaders such as Hughes and Hull believed that American economic expansion and the nation's prominent position in the international economy

Economic and Cultural Expansion

would stabilize world politics. By the late 1920s the United States produced nearly half of the world's industrial goods, ranked first among exporters, and served as the world's financial capital. Hollywood movies dominated the global market and stimulated interest in American ways and products. Although some foreigners warned against "Americanization," others aped American mass-production methods and emphasis on efficiency and modernization. Coca-Cola opened a bottling plant in Essen, Germany, and Ford built an automobile assembly plant in Cologne.

The United States government facilitated this cultural expansion by assisting business activities abroad. The Webb-Pomerene Act (1918) excluded from antitrust prosecution those combinations set up for export trade; the Edge Act (1919) permitted American banks to open foreign branch banks; and the overseas offices of the Department of Commerce gathered valuable market information.

Europeans watched American economic expansion with wariness and branded the United States stingy for its handling of First World War debts

War Debts

and reparations. Twenty-eight nations became entangled in the web of inter-Allied government debts, which totaled $26.5 billion ($9.6 billion of it owed to the United States government). Europeans owed private American creditors another $3 billion.

Important Events

1921	Washington Conference opens and limits naval arms in 1922
	Rockefeller Foundation begins battle against yellow fever in Latin America
1922	Mussolini comes to power in Italy
	Fordney-McCumber Tariff raises duties
1924	Dawes Plan eases German reparations payments
	United States troops leave the Dominican Republic
1926	United States troops occupy Nicaragua
1927	Jiang Jieshi breaks with Communists to begin civil war in China
1928	Kellogg-Briand Pact outlaws war
1929	Great Depression begins
	Young Plan reduces German reparations
1930	Hawley-Smoot Tariff raises duties
1931	Japan seizes Manchuria
1932	Stimson Doctrine protests Japanese control of Manchuria
	Franklin Delano Roosevelt elected president
1933	Hitler establishes Nazi government in Germany
	United States recognizes Soviet Union
	Good Neighbor policy announced for Latin America
1934	Fulgencio Batista comes to power in Cuba
	Reciprocal Trade Agreements Act passed to lower tariffs
	United States troops withdraw from Haiti
	Export-Import Bank founded to expand foreign trade
1935	Italy invades Ethiopia
	Neutrality Act prohibits United States arms shipments
1936	United States votes for nonintervention at Pan-American Conference
	Germany reoccupies the Rhineland
	Spanish Civil War breaks out between Loyalists and Franco's fascists
	Neutrality Act forbids United States loans to belligerents
	Agreement between Germany and Italy creates the Rome-Berlin Axis
	Germany and Japan unite against Soviet Union in the Anti-Comintern Pact
	Roosevelt reelected
1937	Neutrality Act creates cash-and-carry trade with warring nations
	Sino-Japanese war breaks out ("China incident")
	Roosevelt's quarantine speech against aggressors
1938	Mexico nationalizes American-owned oil companies
	Munich Conference grants part of Czechoslovakia to Germany
1939	Nazi-Soviet Pact carves up eastern Europe
	Germany invades Poland
	Second World War begins
	United States repeals arms embargo to help Allies
1940	Soviet Union invades Finland
	Germany invades Denmark, Belgium, the Netherlands, and France
	Committee to Defend America by Aiding the Allies formed
	Germany, Italy, and Japan join in Tripartite Pact
	The United States and Great Britain swap destroyers for military bases
	Roosevelt reelected again
	Isolationists form America First Committee
	Selective Training and Service Act starts first peacetime draft
1941	Lend-Lease Act gives aid to Allies
	Germany attacks Soviet Union
	United States freezes Japanese assets
	Atlantic Charter produced at Roosevelt-Churchill meeting
	Roosevelt exploits *Greer* incident in order to convoy British ships
	Japanese flotilla attacks Pearl Harbor, Hawai'i
	United States enters Second World War

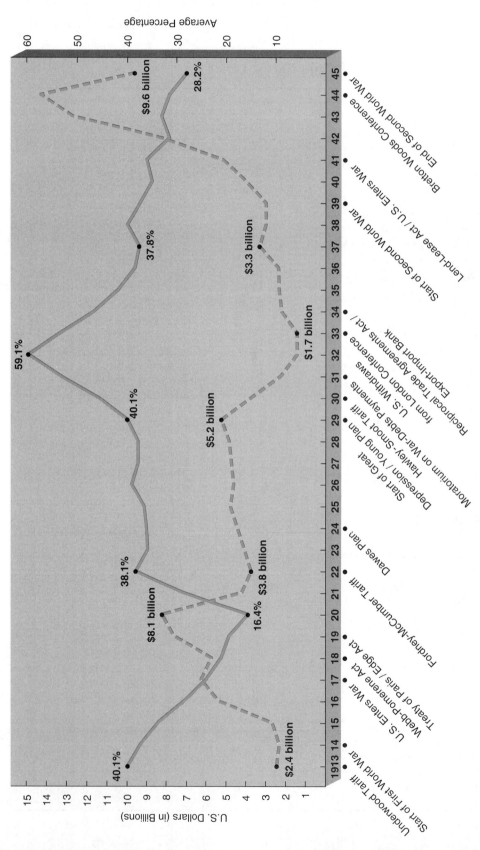

The United States in the World Economy   In the 1920s and 1930s, global depression and war scuttled the United State's hope for a stable economic order. This graph suggests, moreover, that high American tariffs meant lower exports, further impeding world trade. The Reciprocal Trade Agreements program initiated in the early 1930s was designed to ease tariff wars with other nations.   Source: U.S. Bureau of the Census, Historical Statistics of the United States, Colonial Times to 1970 (Washington, D.C., 1975).

The debts question became linked to Germany's $33 billion reparations bill. Hobbled by inflation and economic disorder, Germany began to default on its payments.

German Reparations

To keep the nation afloat and to forestall the radicalism that might thrive on economic troubles, American bankers loaned millions of dollars. A triangular relationship developed: American investors' money flowed to Germany; Germany paid reparations to the Allies, and the Allies then paid some of their debts to the United States. The American-crafted Dawes Plan of 1924 greased the financial tracks by reducing Germany's annual payments, extending the repayment period, and providing still more loans. The United States also gradually scaled down Allied obligations, cutting the debt by half during the 1920s.

But the triangular arrangement depended on continued German borrowing in the United States, and in 1928 and 1929 American lending abroad dropped sharply in the face of more lucrative opportunities in the stock market at home. The United States–negotiated Young Plan of 1929, which reduced Germany's reparations, salvaged little as the world economy sputtered and collapsed. By 1931, when Hoover declared a moratorium on payments, the Allies had paid back only $2.6 billion. Staggered by the Great Depression, they defaulted on the rest.

As the depression accelerated, tariff wars revealed a reinvigorated economic nationalism. By 1932 some twenty-five nations had retaliated against rising American tariffs (created in the Fordney-McCumber Act of 1922 and the Hawley-Smoot Act of 1930) by imposing higher rates on foreign imports. From 1929 to 1933, world trade declined in value by some 40 percent. Exports of American merchandise slumped from $5.2 billion to $1.7 billion.

Tariffs and Economic Nationalism

Many nations contributed to the worldwide economic cataclysm. The United States might have lowered its tariffs so that Europeans could sell their goods in the American market and thus earn dollars to pay off their debts. Vengeful Europeans might have trimmed Germany's huge indemnity. The Germans might have borrowed less and taxed themselves more. The Soviets might have paid rather than repudiate Soviet Russia's debt.

Calling the protective tariff the "king of evils," Secretary Hull successfully pressed Congress to pass the Reciprocal Trade Agreements Act in 1934 (see graph). This important legislation empowered the president to reduce United States tariffs by as much as 50 percent through special agreements with foreign countries.

Reciprocal Trade Agreements Act

The central feature of the act was the *most-favored-nation principle*, whereby the United States was entitled to the lowest tariff rate set by any nation with which it had an agreement.

In 1934 Hull also helped create the Export-Import Bank, a government agency that provided loans to foreigners for the purchase of American goods. The bank stimulated trade and became a diplomatic weapon, allowing the United States to exact concessions through the approval or denial of loans. But in the short term, Hull's ambitious programs—examples of America's independent internationalism—brought only mixed results.

 ## United States Hegemony in Latin America

Before the First World War the United States had thrown an imperial net over much of Latin America. United States soldiers occupied Cuba, the Dominican Republic, Haiti, Panama, and Nicaragua. Schools, roads, telephones, and irrigation systems built by North Americans dotted Caribbean and Central American nations. North American advisers or "money doctors" in Colombia and Peru helped reform tariff and tax laws and invite North American companies to build public works projects. United States authorities maintained Puerto Rico as a colony (see map, page 495).

Criticism of United States imperialism in the region mounted in the interwar years. Business-people feared that Latin American nationalists

Criticism of United States Interventionism

would vent their anti-Yankee feelings against American-owned property. And in 1932 Hoover's secretary of state, Henry L. Stimson, worried about a dual standard. How could he object to Japan's incursions in China if the United States used troops in Latin America?

Renouncing unpopular military intervention, the United States tried other methods to maintain its influence in Latin America: Pan-Americanism, support for strong local leaders, the training of national guards, economic penetration, Export-Import Bank loans, and political subversion. Franklin D. Roosevelt gave the new approach a name in 1933: the Good Neighbor policy. It meant that the United States would be less blatant in its domination—less willing to defend exploitative business practices, less eager to launch military expeditions, and less reluctant to consult with Latin Americans.

Good Neighbor Policy

To secure its interests, the United States trained national guards and supported dictators. For example, before the United States withdrew its troops from the Dominican Republic in 1924, United States personnel created a guard. One of its first officers was Rafael Leonidas Trujillo, who became head of the national army in 1928 and president two years later. Trujillo ruled with an iron fist until his assassination in 1961. "He may be an S.O.B.," Roosevelt supposedly remarked, "but he is our S.O.B."

National Guard in the Dominican Republic

Nicaraguans endured a similar experience. United States troops occupied Nicaragua from 1912 to 1925 and returned in late 1926 during a civil war. Nationalistic Nicaraguan opposition, led by César Augusto Sandino, who denounced the Monroe Doctrine as meaning "America for the Yankees," helped persuade Washington to end the occupation. In 1933 the marines departed, but they left behind a powerful national

Somoza and Sandino in Nicaragua

guard headed by General Anastasio Somoza, who "always played the game fairly with us," recalled a top United States officer. With backing from the United States, the Somoza family ruled Nicaragua from 1936 to 1979 through corruption, political suppression, and torture.

The marine occupation of black, French-speaking Haiti from 1915 to 1934 also left a negative legacy. United States officials censored the Haitian press, manipulated elections, wrote the constitution, jailed or killed protesters, managed government finances, and created a national guard. The National City Bank of New York became the owner of the Haitian Banque Nationale, and the United States became Haiti's largest trading partner. Haiti nonetheless remained one of the poorest, most unstable nations in Latin America.

Occupation of Haiti

The Cubans, too, grew restless under North American domination. By 1929 North American investments in the Caribbean nation totaled $1.5 billion, including two-thirds ownership of the sugar industry. The United States military uniform remained conspicuous at the Guantánamo naval base. In 1933, Cubans rebelled against the dictator and United States ally Gerardo Machado. In open defiance of United States warships cruising offshore, Professor Ramón Grau San Martín became president and declared the Platt Amendment null and void. His government also seized some North American–owned mills, refused to repay North American bank loans, and debated land reform. Unsettled by this nationalistic "social revolution," United States officials plotted with army sergeant Fulgencio Batista to overthrow Grau in 1934.

Cuban Revolution of 1933

During the Batista era, which lasted until Fidel Castro overthrew Batista in 1959, Cuba attracted and protected United States investments while it aligned itself with United States foreign policy goals. The United States provided military aid and Export-Import Bank loans, abrogated the Platt Amendment, and gave Cuban sugar a favored position in the United States market. American tourists flocked to Havana and nationalistic

The United States and Latin America Between the Wars *The United States often intervened in other nations to maintain its hegemonic power in Latin America, where nationalists resented outside meddling in their sovereign affairs.*

Cubans grumbled that their nation had become a mere extension of the United States.

In Puerto Rico throughout the 1920s and 1930s, United States officials on the Caribbean island disparaged Puerto Ricans as people of

Puerto Rico

color unfit to govern themselves. The Jones Act of 1917 had granted Puerto Ricans United States citizenship, but the United States rejected calls for the colony's independence or statehood. Under United States paternalism, schools and roads were improved, but 80 percent of the island's rural folk were landless and others crowded into urban slums.

Students, professors, and graduates of the Universidad de Puerto Rico formed the nucleus of islanders critical of United States tutelage. Some founded the Nationalist Party under the leadership of Harvard-trained lawyer Pedro Albizo Campos, who eventually advocated the violent overthrow of United States rule. Other Puerto Ricans followed the socialist Luis Muñoz Marín, whose Popular Democratic Party ultimately settled for the compromise of commonwealth status (officially conferred in 1952). To this day, Puerto Ricans remain divided into statehood, commonwealth, and independence factions.

Mexico stood as a unique case in inter-American relations. In 1917 the Mexicans openly threatened American-owned landholdings and oil interests by adopting a new

United States Clash with Mexican Nationalism

constitution specifying that all "land and waters" and all subsoil raw materials (such as petroleum) belonged to the Mexican nation. United States officials worried that if Mexico succeeded in restricting the ownership of private property, other Latin Americans might also defy United States hegemony.

In 1938 Mexico boldly expropriated the property of all foreign-owned petroleum companies. The United States countered by encouraging a business boycott against the nation. But President Roosevelt decided to compromise because he feared that the Mexicans would sell their oil to Germany and Japan. In a 1942 agreement the United States conceded that Mexico owned its raw materials and could treat them as it saw fit, and Mexico compensated the companies for their lost property.

The Good Neighbor policy paid off for the United States, especially after the Roosevelt administration endorsed nonintervention at the 1936 Pan American Conference. Pan Americanism was also expressed in the Declaration of Panama (1939), in which Latin American governments drew a security line around the hemisphere and warned aggressors away. In exchange for more United States trade and foreign aid, Latin Americans also reduced their sales of raw materials to Germany, Japan, and Italy and increased shipments to the United States. On the eve of the Second World War, then, the United States's sphere of influence in the hemisphere seemed intact, and most Latin American regimes backed United States diplomatic objectives.

Nazi Germany and Appeasement in Europe

In depression-wracked Germany, Adolf Hitler came to power in 1933. Like Benito Mussolini, who had gained control of Italy in 1922, Hitler was a fascist. Fascism (called Nazism, or National Socialism, in Germany) was a collection of ideas and prejudices that celebrated supremacy of the state over the individual; of dictatorship over democracy; of authoritarianism over freedom of speech; of a regulated, state-oriented economy over a free-market economy; and of militarism and war over peace. The Nazis vowed not only to revive German economic and military strength but also to cripple communism and "purify" the German "race" by destroying Jews and other people, such as homosexuals and Gypsies, whom Hitler disparaged as inferiors.

Resentful of the punitive terms of the 1919 Treaty of Versailles, Hitler immediately withdrew Germany from the League of Nations, ended reparations payments, and began to

Hitler's Aggression

rearm. He watched admiringly as Mussolini's troops invaded the African nation of Ethiopia in 1935. The next year Hitler ordered German troops into the demilitarized Rhineland, and France did nothing.

Soon the aggressors joined hands. In 1936 Italy and Germany formed an alliance called the Rome-Berlin Axis. Shortly thereafter Germany and Japan united against the Soviet Union in the Anti-Comintern Pact. Britain and France naively responded with a policy of appeasement, hoping to curb Hitler's expansionist appetite by permitting him a few nibbles.

In those hair-trigger times, a civil war in Spain soon turned into an international struggle. From 1936 to 1939, the Loyalists defended Spain's elected republican government against Francisco Franco's fascist movement. About three thousand American volunteers, known as the Abraham Lincoln Battalion of the "International Brigades," joined the fight on the side of the Loyalist republicans, which also had the backing of the Soviet Union. Hitler and Mussolini sent military aid to Franco. France and Britain stayed out. Franco won in 1939, tightening the grip of fascism on the European continent.

Czechoslovakia and Munich

Early in 1938 Hitler sent soldiers into Austria to annex the nation of his birth. Then in September he seized the Sudeten region of Czechoslovakia. Appeasement reached its apex that month when France and Britain, without consulting the helpless Czechs, agreed at the Munich Conference to allow Hitler another territorial bite. In March 1939 Hitler swallowed the rest of Czechoslovakia.

Poland and the Onset of World War II

Poland was next on the German leader's list. Scuttling appeasement, London and Paris announced that they would stand by their ally Poland. Undaunted, Berlin signed the Nazi-Soviet Pact with Moscow in August. On September 1, Hitler attacked Poland; Britain and France declared war on Germany two days later. The Second World War had begun.

As the world hurtled toward war, Soviet-American relations remained embittered. During the 1920s the United States refused to open diplomatic relations with the Soviet government, which had failed to pay $600 million for confiscated American-owned property. American businesses nonetheless entered the Soviet marketplace, and by 1930 the Soviet Union had become the largest buyer of American farm and industrial equipment.

United States Recognition of the Soviet Union

In the early 1930s, when trade began to slump, some American business leaders lobbied for diplomatic recognition of the Soviet Union. President Roosevelt himself concluded that nonrecognition had failed to alter the Soviet system, and he speculated that closer Soviet-American relations might deter Japanese expansion. In 1933 Roosevelt granted United States diplomatic recognition of the Soviet Union in return for Soviet agreement to discuss the debts question, to forgo subversive activities in the United States, and to grant Americans in the Soviet Union religious freedom and legal rights. Nevertheless, relations soon deteriorated, especially after the Nazi-Soviet Pact was signed.

Isolationism, Neutrality, and Roosevelt's Foreign Policy

As conditions deteriorated in Europe, Americans endorsed isolationism to distance themselves from Europe's wars. Conservative isolationists feared higher taxes and increased executive power if the nation went to war again. Liberal isolationists worried that domestic problems might go unresolved as the nation spent more on the military. The vast majority of isolationists opposed fascism and condemned aggression, but they did not think the United States should have to do what Europeans themselves refused to do: block Hitler.

Nye Committee Hearings

Isolationism was a nationwide phenomenon that cut across socioeconomic, ethnic, party, and sectional lines. Some isolationists charged that corporate "merchants of death" had promoted war and were assisting the aggressors. As a result of such allegations, a committee chaired by Senator Russell P. Nye of North Dakota held hearings from 1934 to 1936 on the role of business in the nation's decision to enter the First World War. The evidence failed to prove that munitions makers had dragged the United States into war, but it did demonstrate that corporations had bribed foreign officials to bolster arms sales, signed contracts with Nazi Germany and fascist Italy, and lobbied against arms control.

Reflecting the popular desire to avoid European squabbles, President Roosevelt signed a series of neutrality acts. Congress sought to protect the nation by outlawing the kinds of contacts that had compromised United States neutrality during World War I. The Neutrality Act of 1935 prohibited arms shipments to either side in a war once the president had declared the existence of belligerency, and the

Neutrality Acts

Neutrality Act of 1936 forbade loans to belligerents. After a joint resolution in 1937 declared the United States neutral in the Spanish Civil War, Roosevelt embargoed arms shipments to both sides. The Neutrality Act of 1937 introduced the cash-and-carry principle: warring nations wishing to trade with the United States would have to pay cash for their nonmilitary purchases and carry the goods away in their own ships. The act also forbade Americans from traveling on the ships of belligerent nations.

President Roosevelt shared some isolationist views in the early 1930s. In a passionate speech in August 1936 at Chautauqua, New York, Roose-

The German Advance, 1939–1942 *Hitler's drive to dominate Europe carried German troops deep into France and the Soviet Union. Great Britain took a beating but held on with the help of American economic and military aid before the United States itself entered the Second World War.*

velt said: "I have seen war. . . . I have seen blood running from the wounded. I have seen men coughing out their gassed lungs. . . . I have seen the agony of mothers and wives. I hate war." The United States, he promised, would remain distant from European conflict.

Roosevelt's Changing Views

All the while, Roosevelt was becoming increasingly troubled by the arrogant behavior of Germany, Italy, and Japan—the aggressors he tagged the "three bandit nations." Because he worried that the United States was ill prepared to confront the aggressors, his New Deal public works programs included millions for the construction of new warships. In 1935 the president requested the largest peacetime defense budget in American history. Three years later, in the wake of Munich, he asked Congress for funds to build up the air force. In January 1939 the president secretly decided to sell bombers to France.

Early in 1939 the president lashed out at the international lawbreakers. He also tried but failed to persuade Congress to repeal the arms embargo and permit the sale of munitions to belligerents on a cash-and-carry basis. When Germany's September 1939 invasion of Poland plunged Europe into war (see map), Roosevelt declared neutrality. With Roosevelt's prodding and after much debate, Congress in November lifted the embargo on contraband and approved cash-and-carry exports of arms. Using "methods short of war," Roosevelt was ready to aid the Allies.

Repeal of the Arms Embargo

Japan, China, and a New Order in Asia

In Asia, where Japan was on the march, the United States had interests: the Philippines and Pacific islands, religious missions, trade and investments, and the Open Door in China. In traditional missionary fashion, Americans also believed that they were China's special friend. In contrast, Japan seemed bent on subjugating China and unhinging the Open Door doctrine of equal trade and investment opportunity.

In the late 1920s, civil war broke out in China when Jiang Jieshi (Chiang Kai-shek) ousted Mao Zedong and his Communist followers from the ruling Guomindang Party. Americans applauded this display of anti-Bolshevism and Jiang's conversion to Christianity in 1930. Warming to Jiang, American officials abandoned one imperial vestige by signing a treaty in 1928 restoring control of tariffs to the Chinese.

Rise of Jiang Jieshi in China

The Japanese grew increasingly suspicious of United States–Chinese ties. In the early twentieth century, Japanese-American relations were seldom cordial as Japan gained influence in Manchuria, Shandong, and Korea. The Japanese sought not only to oust Western imperialists from Asia but also to dominate Asian territories that produced the raw materials that their import-dependent island nation required. The Japanese also resented the discriminatory immigration law of 1924, which excluded them from entry into the United States.

Relations deteriorated further in 1931 after the Japanese military seized Manchuria in China. Although the seizure of Manchuria violated the Nine-Power Treaty and the Kellogg-Briand Pact, the United States did not have the power to compel Japanese withdrawal. The American response therefore went no further than a moral lecture known as the Stimson Doctrine, which declared that the United States would not recognize any impairment of China's sovereignty or of the Open Door policy.

Japanese Seizure of Manchuria

Hardly cowed by protests from Western capitals, Japan continued to harry China. In mid-1937 the Sino-Japanese War erupted. In an effort to help China by permitting it to buy American arms, Roosevelt refused to declare the existence of war, thus avoiding activation of the Neutrality Acts. And in a speech denouncing the aggressors on October 5, 1937, the president called for a "quarantine" to curb the "epidemic of

Roosevelt's Quarantine Speech

H. S. Wong's widely circulated photograph of a child after the Japanese bombing of Shanghai, in 1937, helped galvanize world opinion against Tokyo's brutal subjugation of China.   National Archives.

world lawlessness." People who thought Washington had been too gentle with Japan cheered. Isolationists warned that the president was edging toward war.

Japan's declaration of a "New Order" in Asia, in the words of one American official, "banged, barred, and bolted" the Open Door. Alarmed, the Roosevelt administration during the late 1930s gave loans and sold military equipment to the Chinese. Secretary Hull declared a moral embargo on the shipment of airplanes to Japan. In mid-1939 the United States abrogated the 1911 Japanese-American trade treaty; yet America continued to ship oil, cotton, and machinery to Japan. The administration hesitated to initiate economic sanctions because such pressure might spark a Japanese-American war.

 ## Collision Course, 1939–1941

Polls showed that Americans strongly favored the Allies and that most supported aid to Britain and France—but the great majority emphatically

wanted the United States to remain at peace. Troubled by this conflicting advice—oppose Hitler, aid the Allies, but stay out of the war—the president gradually moved the nation from neutrality to undeclared war against Germany and then to full-scale war itself.

Because the stakes were so high, unprecedented numbers of Americans spoke out on foreign affairs. The American Legion, the League of Women Voters, labor unions, and local chapters of the Committee to Defend America by Aiding the Allies and the isolationist America First Committee (both organized in 1940) provided outlets for citizen participation in the national debate.

National Debate

In April 1940 Germany invaded Denmark and Norway (see map, page 498). In March the Soviet Union had invaded Finland. Then, on May 10, 1940, several German divisions attacked Belgium, the Netherlands, and France, pushing French and British forces back to the English Channel. At Dunkirk, France, be-

Fall of France

tween May 26 and June 6, more than 300,000 Allied soldiers frantically escaped to Britain on a flotilla of small boats. The Germans occupied Paris a week later. With France knocked out of the war, the Germans launched massive bombing raids against Great Britain. Stunned Americans asked, is the United States next?

As Americans became increasingly alarmed, isolationist sentiment waned. Roosevelt began to aid the beleaguered Allies to prevent the fall of Britain. In May 1940 he ordered the sale of old surplus military equipment to Britain and France. In July he cultivated bipartisan support by naming Republicans Henry L. Stimson and Frank Knox as secretaries of war and the navy, respectively. In September, by executive agreement, the president traded fifty old American destroyers for leases to eight British military bases, including Newfoundland, Bermuda, and Jamaica. Two weeks later he signed into law the nar-

rowly passed Selective Training and Service Act, the first peacetime military draft in American history.

Roosevelt claimed that the United States could stay out of the war by enabling the beleaguered British to win. The United States, he said, must become the "great arsenal of democracy." In January 1941 Congress debated the president's lend-lease bill. Because Britain was broke, the president explained, the United States should lend rather than sell weapons, much as a neighbor lends a garden hose to fight a fire. Congress passed the Lend-Lease Act with an initial appropriation of $7 billion. By the end of the war the amount had reached $50 billion, more than $31 billion of it for England.

Lend-Lease Act

To ensure the safe delivery of lend-lease goods, Roosevelt ordered the United States Navy to patrol halfway across the Atlantic, and he dispatched

President Franklin D. Roosevelt (left) and British Prime Minister Winston Churchill (1874–1965) confer on board a ship near Newfoundland during their summit meeting of August 1941. During the conference, they signed the Atlantic Charter. Upon his return to Great Britain, Churchill told his advisers that Roosevelt had promised to "wage war" against Germany and do "everything" to "force an incident." Franklin D. Roosevelt Library, Hyde Park, New York.

American troops to Greenland. After Germany invaded the Soviet Union in June 1941, Roosevelt sent lend-lease aid to the Soviet Union.

In August 1941 British prime minister Winston Churchill and Roosevelt met for four days on a British battleship off the coast of Newfoundland. The two leaders issued the Atlantic Charter, a set of war aims reminiscent of Wilsonianism: collective security, disarmament, self-determination, economic cooperation, and freedom of the seas. On January 1, 1942, twenty-six nations signed the Declaration of the United Nations, pledging allegiance to the Atlantic Charter.

Atlantic Charter Conference

In September 1941 came an incident that Roosevelt could exploit: a German submarine fired on (but did not hit) the American destroyer *Greer*. The president protested German "piracy" and announced a policy he already had promised Churchill in private: American naval vessels would convoy British merchant ships all the way to Iceland and would shoot German submarines on sight. Roosevelt did not mention that the *Greer* had been tailing a German U-boat for hours, signaling the submarine's location to British airplanes hunting the ship with depth charges.

***Greer* Incident**

Thus the United States entered into an undeclared war with Germany. In October, after a submarine sank the destroyer *Reuben James* with the loss of more than one hundred American lives, Congress scrapped the cash-and-carry policy and further revised the Neutrality Acts to permit transport of munitions to England on armed American merchant ships.

Why War Came: Pearl Harbor and the Interwar Era

The Second World War came to the United States by way of Asia, which in retrospect, seems ironic. Roosevelt had wanted to avoid war with Japan in order to concentrate American resources on the defeat of Germany. In September 1940, after Germany, Italy, and Japan had signed the Tripartite Pact, Roosevelt slapped an embargo on shipments of aviation fuel and scrap metal to Japan. Because the president believed the petroleum-thirsty Japanese would consider a cutoff of oil a life-or-death matter, he did not embargo that vital commodity. But after Japanese troops occupied French Indochina in July 1941, Washington froze Japanese assets in the United States, virtually ending trade (including oil) with Japan.

Tokyo recommended a summit meeting between President Roosevelt and Prime Minister Prince Konoye, but the United States rejected the idea. American officials insisted that the Japanese first agree to respect China's sovereignty and territorial integrity and to honor the Open Door policy— in short, to get out of China. Roosevelt told his advisers to string out ongoing Japanese-American talks to gain time—time to fortify the Philippines and check the fascists in Europe. And though Europe remained Roosevelt's first priority, he supported Secretary Hull's hard-line policy against Japan's pursuit of the Greater East Asia Co-Prosperity Sphere—the name Tokyo gave to the vast Asian region it intended to dominate.

United States Demands on Japan

By breaking the Japanese diplomatic code and deciphering intercepted messages through Operation MAGIC, American officials learned that Tokyo's patience with diplomacy was fast dissipating. An intercepted message decoded on December 3 instructed the Japanese embassy in Washington to burn codes and destroy cipher machines—a sure sign that war was coming. The Japanese were plotting a daring raid on Pearl Harbor in Hawai'i. An armada, with a core of 6 carriers, crossed 3,000 miles of the Pacific Ocean. In the early morning of December 7, Japan's carrier-based planes swept down on the unsuspecting American naval base and nearby airfields, killing 2,403 people, sinking or damaging 8 battleships, and destroying 160 aircraft on the ground. By chance, three aircraft carriers were at sea and escaped the disaster.

Surprise Attack on Pearl Harbor

How do historians know that American leaders knew in December 1941, before the attack on Pearl Harbor, that Japan intended to go to war with the United States? In September 1940, United States cryptanalysts—codebreakers—of the Signal Intelligence Service cracked the most secret diplomatic cipher used by the Japanese government, a machine they called PURPLE. The codebreakers discovered patterns in the incoherent letters of telegraphed messages, produced texts, and even duplicated the complicated PURPLE machine (shown here). Thereafter, under Operation MAGIC, they decoded thousands of intercepted messages sent by Japanese officials around the world. Important intercepts such as the one shown here were delivered to a handful of top American leaders, including the president. These dispatches made increasingly clear through 1941 that Tokyo expected all-out war with the United States. An intercept on December 3, just a few days before the attack on Pearl Harbor, revealed that Tokyo had ordered the Japanese embassy in Washington to destroy all codes and cipher machines, a sure sign that war was imminent.

After the attack against Pearl Harbor, and after it became public knowledge that the United States had broken the Japanese diplomatic code, the cry sounded that President Roosevelt must have known what was coming yet failed to prepare the naval base for the assault. The many messages intercepted in the fall and winter of 1941, however, never revealed Japan's military plans. Not one intercepted message mentioned an attack on Pearl Harbor; indeed, Japanese diplomats in Washington were never told that Pearl Harbor would be hit. National Archives.

```
From:  Tokyo
To:    Washington
7 December 1941
(Purple-Eng)

#902        Part 14 of 14

           (Note: In the forwarding instructions to the
           radio station handling this part, appeared the
           plain English phrase "VERY IMPORTANT")

           7. Obviously it is the intention of the American
           Government to conspire with Great Britain and other countries
           to obstruct Japan's efforts toward the establishment of
           peace through the creation of a New Order in East Asia,
           and especially to preserve Anglo-American rights and interests
           by keeping Japan and China at war. This intention has
           been revealed clearly during the course of the present
           negotiations. Thus, the earnest hope of the Japanese
           Government to adjust Japanese-American relations and to
           preserve and promote the peace of the Pacific through
           cooperation with the American Government has finally been
           lost.

           The Japanese Government regrets to have to notify
           hereby the American Government that in view of the attitude
           of the American Government it cannot but consider that it is
           impossible to reach an agreement through further negotiations.

JD-1:7143     SECRET     (M) Navy trans. 7 Dec. 1941 (S-TT)
```

How could the stunning attack on Pearl Harbor have happened? After all, American cryptanalysts had broken the Japanese diplomatic code. Although the intercepted Japanese messages told policymakers that war lay ahead, the intercepts never revealed naval or military plans and never specifically mentioned Pearl Harbor. Roosevelt did not, as some

**Explaining
Pearl Harbor**

critics charged, conspire to leave the fleet vulnerable to attack so that the United States could enter the Second World War through the "back door" of Asia. The base at Pearl Harbor was not ready—not on red alert—because a message sent from Washington warning of the imminence of war had been too casually transmitted by a slow method and had arrived too late. Base commanders were too relaxed, believing Hawai'i too far from Japan to be a target for all-out attack. The Pearl Harbor calamity stemmed from mistakes and insufficient information, not from conspiracy.

On December 8, referring to the previous day as "a date which will live in infamy," Roosevelt asked Congress for a declaration of war against Japan. A unanimous vote in the Senate and a 388-to-1 vote in the House thrust America into war. Again, Representative Jeannette Rankin of Montana voted "no," matching her vote against entry into the First World War. Three days later, Germany and Italy, honoring the Tripartite Pact they had signed with Japan in September 1940, declared war against the United States.

Remembering the bitter experience of the First World War, Americans had tried to stay out of the Second. But diplomacy and economic sanctions had not stopped the aggressors, who kept pushing on, threatening United States interests. A fundamental clash of systems explains why diplomacy failed and war came. Germany and Japan preferred a world divided into closed spheres of influence. The United States sought a liberal capitalist world order in which all nations enjoyed freedom of trade and investment. American principles manifested respect for human rights; fascists in Europe and militarists in Asia defiantly trampled such rights. The United States prided itself on its democratic system; Germany and Japan embraced authoritarian regimes backed by the military.

Clash of Systems

 Conclusion

Looking back with sadness, Americans had to admit that in the 1920s and 1930s they had failed to create a peaceful and prosperous world order. The Washington Conference treaties failed to curb a naval arms race or to protect China; the Dawes Plan collapsed; the Kellogg-Briand Pact proved ineffective; philanthropic activities fell short of need; the process of "Americanization" provided no panacea; Germany and the aggressors ignored repeated United States protests, from the Stimson Doctrine onward; recognition of the Soviet Union barely improved relations; trade policies did not liberate commerce from protectionism; and the Neutrality Acts failed to prevent United States entanglements in Europe. Even where American power and policies seemed to work to satisfy United States goals—in Latin America—nationalist resentments simmered, and Mexico challenged United States hegemony.

The Second World War offered yet another opportunity for Americans to set things right in the world. As the publisher Henry Luce wrote in *American Century* (1941), the United States must "exert upon the world the full impact of our influence, for such purposes as we see fit and by such means as we see fit." As they had so many times before, Americans flocked to the colors.

Suggestions for Further Reading

General

Thomas H. Buckley, *The United States and the Washington Conference, 1921–1922* (1970); Warren I. Cohen, *Empire Without Tears* (1987); Justus D. Doenecke and John E. Wilz, *From Isolation to War, 1931–1941*, 2d ed. (1991); Akira Iriye, *The Globalizing of America, 1914–1945* (1993); Melvyn P. Leffler, *The Elusive Quest* (1979); Elting E. Morison, *Turmoil and Tradition* (1964) (on Stimson); Emily S. Rosenberg, *Spreading the American Dream* (1982); Michael S. Sherry, *The Rise of American Airpower* (1987); Raymond Sontag, *A Broken World, 1919–1939* (1971); Mark A. Stoler, *George Marshall* (1989); Joan Hoff Wilson, *Herbert Hoover* (1975).

Peace Movement

Harriet H. Alonso, *The Women's Peace Union and the Outlawry of War* (1989); Charles Chatfield, *For Peace and Justice: Pacifism in America, 1914–1941* (1971); Charles DeBenedetti, *The Peace Reform in American History* (1980); Charles DeBenedetti, *Origins of the Modern American Peace Movement, 1915–1929* (1978); Carrie A. Foster, *The Women and the Warriors* (1995); Robert D. Johnson, *The Peace Progressives and American Foreign Relations* (1995); Sybil Oldfield, *Women Against the Iron Fist* (1990); Lawrence Wittner, *Rebels Against War* (1984).

The United States in the World Economy

Frederick Adams, *Economic Diplomacy* (1976); Derek H. Aldcroft, *From Versailles to Wall Street, 1919–1929* (1977); Michael J. Hogan, *Informal Entente* (1977) (on Anglo-American relations); Charles Kindleberger, *The World in Depression* (1973);

Stephen J. Randall, *United States Foreign Oil Policy, 1919–1948* (1986); Mira Wilkins, *The Maturing of Multinational Enterprise* (1974); Joan Hoff Wilson, *American Business and Foreign Policy, 1920–1933* (1971).

Cultural Expansion and Philanthropy

Frank Costigliola, *Awkward Dominion* (1984); Marcos Cueto, ed., *Missionaries of Science: The Rockefeller Foundation and Latin America* (1994); Mary Nolan, *Visions of Modernity: American Business and the Modernization of Germany* (1994); Thomas J. Saunders, *Hollywood in Berlin* (1994).

Latin America and the Good Neighbor Policy

John A. Britton, *Revolution and Ideology* (1995) (on Mexico); Bruce J. Calder, *The Impact of Intervention* (1984) (on the Dominican Republic); Arturo Morales Carrión, *Puerto Rico* (1983); Paul W. Drake, *The Money Doctors in the Andes* (1989); Alton Frye, *Nazi Germany and the American Hemisphere, 1933–1941* (1967); Irwin F. Gellman, *Good Neighbor Diplomacy* (1979); Walter LaFeber, *Inevitable Revolutions*, 2d ed. rev. (1993) (on Central America); Lester D. Langley, *The United States and the Caribbean, 1900–1970* (1980); Abraham F. Lowenthal, ed., *Exporting Democracy* (1991); Thomas F. O'Brien, *The Revolutionary Mission: American Enterprise in Latin America, 1900–1945* (1996); Louis A. Pérez, *Cuba and the United States* (1990); Louis A. Pérez, *Cuba Under the Platt Amendment* (1986); Frederick B. Pike, *FDR's Good Neighbor Policy* (1995); Brenda G. Plummer, *Haiti and the United States* (1992); W. Dirk Raat, *Mexico and the United States* (1992); Stephen G. Rabe, *The Road to OPEC* (1982) (on Venezuela); Bryce Wood, *The Making of the Good Neighbor Policy* (1961).

Isolationists and Isolationism

Wayne S. Cole, *Roosevelt and the Isolationists, 1932–1945* (1983); Wayne S. Cole, *America First* (1953); Manfred Jonas, *Isolationism in America, 1935–1941* (1966); Thomas C. Kennedy, *Charles A. Beard and American Foreign Policy* (1975); Richard C. Lower, *A Bloc of One* (1993) (on Hiram Johnson); Richard Lowitt, *George W. Norris*, 3 vols. (1963–1978); John Wiltz, *In Search of Peace: The Senate Munitions Inquiry, 1934–1936* (1963).

Europe, Roosevelt, and the Coming of World War II

Edward Bennett, *Franklin D. Roosevelt and the Search for Security* (1985) (on the Soviet Union); J. Garry Clifford and Samuel R. Spencer, Jr., *The First Peacetime Draft* (1986); David H. Culbert, *News for Everyman* (1976) (on radio); Robert Dallek, *Franklin D. Roosevelt and American Foreign Policy, 1932–1945*, new ed. (1995); Robert A. Divine, *Roosevelt and World War II* (1969); Frank Freidel, *Franklin D. Roosevelt* (1990); Manfred Jonas, *The United States and Germany* (1984); Warren F. Kimball, *The Juggler* (1991); Warren F. Kimball, *The Most Unsordid Act* (1969) (on lend-lease); Douglas Little, *Malevolent Neutrality* (1985) (on the Spanish Civil War); Thomas R. Maddux, *Years of Estrangement* (1980) (on United States–Soviet relations); Arnold A. Offner, *American Appeasement* (1969); David Reynolds, *The Creation of the Anglo-American Alliance, 1937–1941* (1982); David F. Schmitz, *The United States and Fascist Italy, 1922–1944* (1988); James C. Schneider, *Should America Go to War?* (1989); Richard Steele, *Propaganda in an Open Society* (1985); Donald C. Watt, *How War Came* (1989); Theodore A. Wilson, *The First Summit*, rev. ed. (1991).

China, Japan, and the Coming of War in Asia

Charles A. Beard, *President Roosevelt and the Coming of the War, 1941* (1948); Dorothy Borg and Shumpei Okomoto, eds., *Pearl Harbor as History* (1973); R. J. C. Butow, *Tojo and the Coming of War* (1961); Warren I. Cohen, *America's Response to China*, 3d ed. (1989); Hilary Conroy and Harry Wray, eds., *Pearl Harbor Reexamined* (1990); Herbert Feis, *The Road to Pearl Harbor* (1950); Waldo H. Heinrichs, Jr., *Threshold of War* (1988); Akira Iriye, *The Origins of the Second World War in Asia and the Pacific* (1987); Akira Iriye, *Across the Pacific* (1967); Akira Iriye, *After Imperialism* (1965); Jonathan Utley, *Going to War with Japan* (1985).

Attack on Pearl Harbor

David Kahn, *The Codebreakers* (1967); Robert W. Love, Jr., ed., *Pearl Harbor Revisited* (1995); Martin V. Melosi, *The Shadow of Pearl Harbor* (1977); Gordon W. Prange, *Pearl Harbor* (1986); Gordon W. Prange, *At Dawn We Slept* (1981); John Toland, *Infamy* (1982); Roberta Wohlstetter, *Pearl Harbor* (1962).

27

The Second World War at Home and Abroad, 1941–1945

In the spring of 1942, when recruiters from the United States Marine Corps came to the Navajo reservation in Shiprock, New Mexico, William Dean Wilson was only sixteen years old and a student at the Shiprock Boarding School. The marines were seeking young men who spoke both English and Navajo, a language understood by fewer than thirty non-Navajos—none of whom were Japanese. The Navajo recruits of 1942 would become not only marines but also "code talkers" in the war against the Japanese.

William Dean Wilson volunteered. "I said I was eighteen," he recalled. His parents were opposed, but he had removed a note from his file that read "parents will not consent" and was inducted. Wilson was among an initial group of thirty Navajos chosen for a project with an important goal: to prevent the Japanese from deciphering radio messages sent by American troops landing on the shores of Pacific islands.

By the time William Dean Johnson's seventeenth birthday arrived, he was in the Pacific. Beginning with the Battle of Guadalcanal, he and 420 other Navajo code talkers took part in every assault the marines conducted in the Pacific from 1942 to 1945. Usually, two code talkers were assigned to a batallion, one going ashore and the other remaining aboard ship. Those who went ashore quickly set up their radio equipment and began transmitting, reporting sightings of enemy forces and directing shelling by American detachments.

While in the marines and even under battle conditions, the code talkers maintained traditional beliefs and practices. To prepare the young men to fight the enemy, Navajo families had special "Blessingway" ceremonies performed for them. Many of the men went to battle carrying bags of sacred corn pollen, and they held traditional beliefs about the evil ghosts of unburied bodies. When Navaho veterans returned home, they participated in purification ceremonies to dispel the ghosts of the battlefield and invoke blessings for the future.

The Second World War was a turning point in the lives of millions of Americans, as well as in the history of the United States. Most deeply affected were those who fought the war. For forty-five months Americans fought abroad to subdue the German, Italian, and Japanese aggressors. After military engagements against fascists in North Africa and Italy, American troops joined the dramatic crossing of the English Channel on D-Day in June 1944. The Nazis finally capitulated in May 1945. In the Pacific, Americans drove the Japanese from one island to another before turning to the just-tested atomic bombs, which demolished Hiroshima and Nagasaki in August and helped spur a Japanese surrender.

Throughout the war the Allies—Britain, the Soviet Union, and the United States—were held together by their common goal of defeating Germany. But they squabbled over many issues: when to open a second front; how to structure a new international organization; how eastern Europe, liberated from the Germans, would be reconstructed; how Germany would be governed after defeat. At the end of the war, Allied leaders seemed more intent on retaining and expanding their own nations' spheres of influence than on building a community of mutual interest. The prospects for postwar international cooperation seemed bleak, and the advent of the atomic age frightened everyone.

The war transformed America's soldiers and sailors. Horizons expanded for the more than 16 million Americans, including 350,000 women, who served in the armed forces, seeing new parts of the world and acquiring new skills. But at war's end many felt they had sacrificed the best years of their lives.

Millions of noncombatant Americans were on the move during the Second World War. Some 12 million Americans moved permanently to another state during the war. Among the migrants were African-Americans, Mexican-Americans, whites, and women of all races who moved to war-production centers in the North and the West. The war offered new economic and political opportunities for numerous African-Americans. And as employers' negative attitudes toward women workers eased, millions of married middle-class women took jobs in war industries.

The American people united behind the war effort, but more than national unity and enthusiasm were required to win the war. Essential to victory was the successful mobilization of all sectors of the economy—industry, finance, agriculture, and labor. The federal government had the monumental task of coordinating activity in these spheres, as well as in a couple of new ones: higher education and science. For the Second World War was a scientific and technological war, supported by the development of new weapons like radar and the atomic bomb. For all these reasons the Second World War was a watershed in American history.

Winning the Second World War in Europe

"We are now in the midst of a war . . . for a world in which this Nation, and all that this Nation represents, will be safe for our children." President Franklin D. Roosevelt was speaking just two days after the surprise attack on Pearl Harbor. Americans agreed with Roosevelt that they were defending their homes and families against aggressive, even satanic, Japanese and Nazis.

America's men and women responded eagerly to Roosevelt's call to arms. In 1941, only 1.8 million people were serving on active duty. In 1945 the number of women and men serving in the army, navy, and marines peaked at 12.1 million.

Despite nearly unanimous support for the war effort, government leaders worried that public morale might lag during a long war. To elicit the

Selling the War at Home

people's support, in 1942 President Roosevelt established the Office of War Information (OWI), which took charge of domestic propaganda and hired Hollywood filmmakers and New York copywriters to sell the war at home.

Wartime propaganda depicted Allied unity, but in reality relations among the United States, Great Britain, and the Soviet Union ran hot and cold. Although winning the war was the top priority, Allied leaders knew that military decisions had political consequences. Moreover, the positions of troops at the end of the war might determine the politics of the regions they occupied. Thus an undercurrent of mutual suspicion ran just beneath the surface of Allied cooperation.

Roosevelt, British prime minister Winston Churchill, and Soviet premier Joseph Stalin differed vigorously over the opening of a second, or western, front in Europe. After Germany conquered France in 1940 and invaded Russia in 1941, the Russians bore the brunt of the war until mid-1944, suffering millions of casualties. Stalin pressed for a British-American landing on the northern coast of Europe to draw German troops away from the eastern front, but Churchill would not agree. The Russians therefore did most of the fighting and dying on land, while the British and Americans concentrated on getting lend-lease supplies across the Atlantic and harassing the Germans from the air with attacks on factories and civilians alike.

Second-Front Controversy

Roosevelt was both sensitive to the Soviets' burden and fearful that the Soviet Union might be knocked out of the war, leaving Hitler free to invade England. In 1942 he told the Soviets that they could expect the Allies to cross the English Channel and invade France later that year. But Churchill balked. Rather than risk heavy losses in a premature cross-Channel invasion, Churchill favored a series of small jabs at the enemy's Mediterranean forces.

Churchill won the debate. Instead of attacking France, the British and Americans invaded North Africa in November 1942 (see map, page 510). The invasion and news from the Soviet Union buoyed Roosevelt. In the battle for Stalingrad (September 1942–January 1943)—probably the turning point of the European war—the Red Army defeated the Germans. But shortly thereafter, the president once again angered the Soviets by declaring another delay in launching the second front. Stalin was not mollified by the Allied invasion of Italy in the summer of 1943. Italy surrendered in September to American and British officers; Soviet officials were not invited to participate. Stalin grumbled that the arrangement smacked of a separate peace.

With the alliance badly strained, Roosevelt sought reconciliation through personal diplomacy. The three Allied leaders met in Teheran, Iran, in December 1943. Stalin dismissed Churchill's repetitious justifications for further delaying the second front. Roosevelt agreed with Stalin. The three finally decided to launch Operation Overlord—the cross-Channel invasion of France—in early 1944.

Teheran Conference

On June 6, 1944—D-Day—the second front opened with the largest amphibious invasion in history. Once ashore at Normandy, France, the soldiers immediately encountered the enemy. Meanwhile, Allied airborne troops dropped behind German lines. Although heavy aerial and naval bombardment and the clandestine work of saboteurs had softened the German defenses, the fighting was ferocious. Allied troops soon spread across the countryside, liberating France and Belgium and entering Germany itself in September. In December, German armored divisions counterattacked in Belgium's Ardennes Forest, hoping to push on to Antwerp to halt the flow of Allied supplies through that Belgian port. After weeks of heavy fighting in what has come to be called the Battle of the Bulge, the Allies pushed the enemy back once again. Meanwhile, battle-hardened Soviet troops marched through Poland and cut a path to Berlin. American forces crossed the Rhine River in March 1945 and captured the heavily industrial Ruhr valley. Several units peeled off to enter Austria and Czechoslovakia, where they met up with Soviet soldiers.

D-Day and After

• *Important Events* •

1941	Germany invades Russia Japan attacks Pearl Harbor United States enters Second World War
1942	National War Labor Board created to deal with labor-management conflict War Production Board begins to oversee conversion to military production West Coast Japanese-Americans interned in prison camps Office of Price Administration created to control inflation United States defeats Japanese forces at Battles of the Coral Sea and Midway Office of War Information created to maintain support for the war at home Manhattan Project set up to produce atomic bomb Synthetic-rubber program begins Allies invade North Africa Republicans gain in Congress
1943	Red Army defeats German troops at Stalingrad Soft-coal and anthracite miners strike Congress passes War Labor Disputes (Smith-Connally) Act Race riots break out in Detroit, Harlem, and forty-five other cities Allies invade Italy

	Hirabayashi v. *U.S.* upholds restrictions on personal liberties of Japanese-Americans because of their ethnicity Roosevelt, Churchill, and Stalin meet at Teheran Conference
1944	Roosevelt requests Economic Bill of Rights War Refugee Board established to set up refugee camps in Europe GI Bill of Rights provides educational benefits for veterans Allied troops land at Normandy on D-Day Dumbarton Oaks Conference approves charter for United Nations Roosevelt reelected United States retakes the Philippines *Korematsu* v. *U.S.* upholds removal of Japanese-Americans from the West Coast
1945	Roosevelt, Stalin, and Churchill meet at Yalta Conference Battles of Iwo Jima and Okinawa result in heavy American and Japanese losses Roosevelt dies; Harry S Truman becomes president United Nations founded Germany surrenders Atomic bombs devastate Hiroshima and Nagasaki Japan surrenders

As the Americans marched east, a new president took office in Washington: Franklin D. Roosevelt died on April 12, and Harry S Truman became president and commander-in-chief. Eighteen days later, in bomb-ravaged Berlin, Adolf Hitler killed himself. On May 8 Germany surrendered.

Winning the Second World War in the Pacific

Allied strategists had devised a "Europe first" formula: knock out Germany and then concentrate on an isolated Japan. Nevertheless, the Pacific theater of operations claimed headlines throughout the war. By mid-1942 Japan had seized the Philippines, Guam, Wake, Hong Kong, Singapore, Malaya, and the Netherlands East Indies. In the Philippines in 1942, Japanese soldiers forced American and Filipino prisoners weakened by insufficient rations to walk 65 miles, clubbing, shooting, or starving to death about ten thousand of them. This so-called Bataan Death March intensified American hatred of the Japanese.

In April 1942, Americans began to hit back, initially by bombing Tokyo. In May, in the momentous Battle of the Coral Sea, carrier-based

The Allies on the Offensive in Europe, 1942–1945 *The United States pursued a "Europe first" policy: first defeat Germany, then focus on Japan. American military efforts began in North Africa in late 1942 and ended in Germany in 1945 on May 8 (V-E Day).*

Battle of Midway

American planes halted a Japanese advance toward Australia (see map below). The next month American forces defeated the Japanese at Midway, sinking four of the enemy's aircraft carriers. The Battle of Midway was a turning point in the Pacific war, breaking the Japanese momentum and relieving the threat to Hawai'i.

American strategy was to "island-hop" toward Japan, skipping the most strongly fortified islands whenever possible and taking the weaker ones. The first United States offensive—at Guadalcanal in the Solomon Islands in mid-1942—gave American troops their first taste of jungle warfare. In 1943 and 1944 American troops attacked the enemy in the Gilberts, Marshalls, and Marianas. And in October 1944, General Douglas MacArthur landed at Leyte to retake the Philippines for the United States. Early the next year, both sides took heavy casualties at Iwo Jima and Okinawa. In the battle for Okinawa, the Japanese launched *kamikaze* (suicide) attacks in which pilots crashed their planes directly into American ships.

Still, Japanese leaders refused to admit defeat. Hoping to avoid a humiliating unconditional surrender (and to preserve the emperor's sovereignty),

The Pacific War *The strategy of the United States was to "island-hop"—from Hawai'i in 1942 to Iwo Jima and Okinawa in 1945. Naval battles were also decisive, notably the Battles of the Coral Sea and Midway in 1942. The war in the Pacific ended with Japan's surrender on August 15, 1945 (V-J Day).* Source: From Paterson et al., *American Foreign Policy: A History*, vol. 2, 3d ed. rev., copyright 1991, page 494. Reprinted by permission of Houghton Mifflin Company.

they hung on even while American bombers leveled their cities. In one staggering attack on Tokyo on May 23, 1945, American planes dropped napalm-filled bombs, killing 83,000 people.

Impatient for victory, American leaders began to plan a fall invasion of Japan's home islands, an expedition that was sure to incur high casualties. The invasion never occurred because American scientists working on the secret Manhattan Project developed the atomic bomb. On August 6, 1945, approximately 130,000 people were killed when an American B-29 plane, the *Enola Gay*, dropped an atomic bomb that destroyed the city of Hiroshima. On August 9 another atomic attack flattened Nagasaki, killing at least 60,000 people. Five days later the Japanese, who had been sending out peace feelers since June, surrendered. The victors promised that the Japanese emperor could remain as the nation's titular head. Formal surrender ceremonies were held September 2 aboard the battleship *Missouri*. The Second World War was over.

The Atomic Bomb

Most Americans agreed with President Truman that the atomic bombing of Hiroshima and Nagasaki was necessary to end the war as quickly as possible and to save American lives. At the highest government levels and among atomic scientists, alternatives had been discussed: detonating the bomb on an unpopulated Pacific island, with international observers as witnesses; blockading and bombing Japan conventionally; following up on Tokyo's peace feelers. Truman, however, had rejected these options because he believed they would take too long and would not convince the tenacious Japanese that they had been beaten.

Why the Atomic Bomb Was Used

Diplomatic considerations also influenced the decision to use the bomb. American leaders wanted to take advantage of the real and psychological power the bomb would bestow on the United States. It might serve as a deterrent against aggression; it might intimidate the Soviet Union into making concessions in eastern Europe; it might end the war in the Pacific before the Soviet Union could claim a role in the postwar management of Asia.

Economic Effects of the War at Home

The Second World War was won at great cost, not only abroad but also on the American home front. While the guns boomed in Europe and Asia, the war was changing American lives and institutions. One month after Pearl Harbor, President Roosevelt established the War Production Board (WPB) and assigned to it the task of converting the economy from civilian to military production. Factories had to be expanded and new ones built. The wartime emergency also spurred the establishment of totally new industries, most notably synthetic rubber. The Japanese had captured 90 percent of the world's supply of crude rubber.

War Production Board

New pollutants, as well as increased levels of old ones, accompanied wartime productivity. Some industries spewed forth dangerous gases; others fouled the water and the soil with both solid and petrochemical wastes. The dumping of radioactive waste began at Hanford, Washington, where plutonium was produced for the atomic bomb. Air pollution—smog—was first detected in Los Angeles in 1943.

War Production and the Environment

To gain the cooperation of business, the government guaranteed profits in the form of cost-plus-fixed-fee contracts, generous tax writeoffs, and exemptions from antitrust prosecution. Such concessions made sense for a nation that wanted vast quantities of war goods manufactured in the shortest possible time. From mid-1940 through September 1944 the government awarded

Government Incentives to Business

How do historians know what motivated President Harry Truman to order the dropping of the atomic bomb? Truman explained that he did it for only one reason: to end the war as soon as possible and thus prevent the loss of a million American lives in an invasion of Japan. An earlier generation of historians, writing in the aftermath of the war, echoed the president's explanation. But more recently historians have revised this interpretation: they argue that Japan might have surrendered even if the atomic bombs had not been dropped, and they dispute Truman's estimate of a million casualties as being many times the actual figure. These revisionists have studied the Potsdam Conference of July 1945 attended by Truman, Joseph Stalin, and Winston Churchill; and they have consulted the diaries kept by certain participants, notably Secretary of War Henry Stimson and Truman himself.

Scholars cite Stimson's diary (excerpted here) as an indication that Truman's chief motivation was the desire to impress the Soviet Union, as well as to minimize Russia's military participation in the final defeat of Japan. On July 21, Stimson reported to Truman that the army had successfully tested an atomic device in New Mexico. Clearly emboldened by the news, Truman said that possession of the bomb "gave him an entirely new feeling of confidence." The next day, Stimson discussed the news with Britain's Prime Minister Winston Churchill. "Now I know what happened to Truman," Churchill responded. "When he got to the meeting after having read this report he was a changed man. He told the Russians just where they got off and generally bossed the whole meeting." A few historians contend that the decision to drop the atomic bomb was at least partly racist. As evidence, they point to Truman's handwritten diary entry in which he discussed using the bomb against "the Japs," whom he denounced as "savages, ruthless, merciless and fanatic."

The deeply emotional and political question about the necessity for dropping the atomic bomb has stirred debates not only among historians but also within the general public. In 1995, for example, the Smithsonian Institution provoked a public furor with its plans for an exhibit prompted by the fiftieth anniversary of the decision to drop the bomb. Rather than incur the wrath of politicians, veterans' groups, and many other Americans outraged by its interpretation of events, the Smithsonian shelved most of the exhibit.   Diary entry: Henry L. Stimson Papers. Yale University Library

TOP SECRET

I also discussed with him Harrison's two messages. He was intensely pleased by the accelerated timetable. As to the matter of the special target which I had refused to permit, he strongly confirmed my view, and said he felt the same way.

At ten forty Bundy and I again went to the British headquarters and talked to the Prime Minister and Lord Cherwell for over an hour. Churchill read Groves' report in full. He told me that he had noticed at the meeting of the three yesterday, Truman was evidently much fortified by something that had happened, and that he stood up to the Russians in a most emphatic and decisive manner, telling them as to certain demands that they absolutely could not have, and that the United States was entirely against them. Churchill said he now understood how this popping up had taken place and that he felt the same way. His own attitude confirmed this admission. He now not only was not worried about giving the Russians information of the matter, but was rather inclined to use it as an argument in our favor in the negotiations. The sentiment of the four of us was unanimous in thinking that it was advisable to tell the Russians at least that we were working
      if and when it was successfully
on that subject, and intended to use it until finished.

At twelve fifteen I called General Arnold over, showed him Harrison's two cables, showed him my answer to them and showed him Groves' report, which he read in its entirety. He told me that he agreed with me about the target which I had struck off the program. He said that it would take considerable hard work to organize the operations now that it was to move forward.

TOP SECRET

contracts totaling $175 billion, no less than two-thirds of which went to the top one hundred corporations. Big awards went to automobile, aircraft, steel, electrical, and chemical companies. Although the expression "military-industrial complex" had not yet been coined, the web of military-business interdependence had begun to be woven.

In science and higher education, too, the big got bigger. Massachusetts Institute of Technology was a major recipient for its development of radar.

Universities and War Research

MIT received $117 million, followed by the California Institute of Technology, Harvard, and Columbia. The most spectacular result of government contracts with universities was the atomic bomb. The Manhattan Project, run by the army, financed research at the University of Chicago, which in 1942 was the site of the world's first sustained nuclear chain reaction. The University of California at Berkeley had a contract to operate the Los Alamos Scientific Laboratory in New Mexico, where the atomic bomb was tested.

Organized labor also grew during the war. Membership in unions ballooned from 8.5 million in 1940 to 14.75 million in 1945. Less than a week after Pearl Harbor, a White House labor-management conference agreed to a no-strike/no-lockout pledge to guarantee uninterrupted war production.

Unions and Wartime Labor Strikes

To minimize labor-management conflict, in 1942 President Roosevelt created the National War Labor Board (NWLB). Unions were permitted to enroll as many new members as possible, but workers were not required to join a union.

When the NWLB attempted in 1943 to limit wage increases to cost-of-living pay increases, workers responded with strikes that tripled the amount of lost production time over that of the previous year. The worst labor disruptions of 1943 occurred in the coal fields. To discourage further work stoppages, Congress passed the War Labor Disputes (Smith-Connally) Act in June 1943. The act conferred on the president the authority to

seize and operate any strike-bound plant deemed necessary to the national security, and it established a mandatory thirty-day cooling-off period before any new strike could be called. The Smith-Connally Act also gave the NWLB the legal authority to settle labor disputes for the duration of the war.

Agriculture, especially through increased mechanization, made impressive contributions to the war effort. Mechanization, however, was expensive, and the prewar trend away from family-owned farms to large-scale agribusinesses dominated by banks, insurance companies, and farm co-ops accelerated. Thus from 1940 to 1945, the farm population fell from 30.5 million to 24.4 million people.

Wartime Changes in Agriculture

At the apex of the burgeoning national economy stood the federal government, the size and importance of which was mushrooming. The executive branch grew most dramatically. Besides raising the armed forces, mobilizing industrial production, and pacifying labor and management, the executive branch also had to manage the labor supply and control inflation. The Office of Price Administration (OPA), established in 1942, imposed maximum prices on commodities to control inflation. It also introduced rationing programs. Consumers became skilled at handling ration stamps. Most Americans abided by the rules, but some hoarded sugar and coffee or bought beef on the "black market."

Growth in the Federal Government

 The Military Life

To American servicepeople in Asia and in Europe, the Second World War was a grimy job, and millions of GIs were simply eager to get it over with. The largest of the services was the army, in which a total of 11.3 million Americans served; 4.2 million were on active duty in the navy, and 670,000 in the Marine Corps. Total deaths exceeded 405,000.

Some combat veterans returned home with an illness that remained unnamed until 1980, when the American Psychiatric Association (APA) identified it as post-traumatic stress disorder. Although the APA identification applied to Vietnam War veterans, it is clear in retrospect that veterans of earlier wars also suffered from the illness. The symptoms included nightmares and flashbacks to the battlefield, depression and anger, and widespread alcoholism.

Large numbers of women also served in America's armed forces. The WACs (Women's Army Corps) enlisted 140,000 women, while 100,000 served in the navy's WAVES (Women Accepted for Volunteer Emergency Service) and 39,000 in the Marine Corps and Coast Guard. Another 75,000 women served in the army and navy's Nursing Corps. Women also served as pilots in the WASP (Women Air Service Pilots), teaching basic flying, towing aerial targets for gunnery practice, ferrying planes across the country, and serving as test pilots. WASP flying duty was often hazardous; thirty-eight women lost their lives.

Women in the Armed Forces

Among the millions of Americans who left home to join the armed forces were men and women who had experienced homosexual attraction in peacetime. Freed of their familial environments, many acted on their feelings. The military court-martialed homosexuals, but gay relationships usually went unnoticed by the heterosexual world. For lesbians in the armed forces, the military environment offered friendships and a positive identity. "For many gay Americans," the historian John D'Emilio has written, "World War II created something of a nationwide coming out situation."

Wartime service broadened horizons. Many GIs returned to civilian life with new skills they had learned in the military's technical schools. Still others took advantage of the educational benefits provided by the GI Bill of Rights (1944) to study for a college degree. Still, after two or three years abroad, men and women in the

The GIs' Postwar Ambitions

service returned to the United States not knowing what to expect from civilian life.

Enemy Aliens, Conscientious Objectors, and the Internment of Japanese-Americans

After the United States entered the war, American leaders had to consider whether enemy agents were operating within the nation's borders. It was clear that not all Americans were enthusiastic supporters of the nation's participation in the war. After Pearl Harbor, several thousand "enemy aliens" were arrested and taken into custody, including some Nazi agents. Some Americans had conscientious objections to war. During the Second World War conscientious objectors (COs) had to have a religious (as opposed to a moral or an ethical) reason for refusing military service. About 12,000 COs worked on conservation projects or as orderlies in hospitals. Approximately 5,500, three-fourths of whom were Jehovah's Witnesses, refused to participate in any way; they were imprisoned.

Compared with the First World War, the nation's wartime civil liberties record was generally creditable. But there was one enormous exception: the internment in "relocation centers" of, ultimately, 120,000 Japanese-Americans. Of these people, 77,000 were Nisei—native-born citizens of the United States. Their imprisonment was based not on suspicion or evidence of treason; their crime was solely their race—the fact that they were of Japanese descent.

"An Enemy Race"

During the war, no Japanese-American was ever indicted or tried for espionage, treason, or sedition. Nevertheless in 1942, all the 112,000 Japanese-Americans living in California, Oregon, and the state of Washington were rounded up and imprisoned. "It was really cruel and harsh," recalled Joseph Y. Kurihara, a citizen and a veteran of the First World War. "To pack and evacuate in forty-eight hours was an impossibility. Seeing mothers

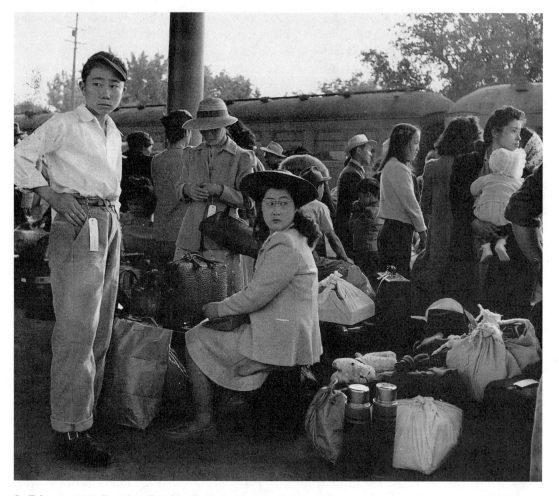

In February 1942 President Franklin D. Roosevelt ordered that all Japanese-Americans living on the West Coast be rounded up and placed in prison camps. These families were awaiting a train to take them to an assembly center in Merced, California; from there, they would be sent to relocation camps in remote inland areas.   National Archives.

completely bewildered with children crying . . . and peddlers . . . offering prices next to robbery made me feel like murdering those responsible."

The internees were sent to flood-damaged lands at Relocation, Arkansas; to the intermountain terrain of Wyoming and the desert of western Arizona; and to other arid and desolate spots in the West. The camps were bleak and demoralizing. Behind barbed wire stood tarpapered wooden barracks where entire families

Life in the Internment Camps

lived in a single room furnished only with cots, blankets, and a bare light bulb. Toilets and dining and bathing facilities were communal; privacy was almost nonexistent. Japanese-Americans also lost their positions in the truck-garden, floral, and fishing industries. Indeed, their economic competitors were among the most vocal proponents of their relocation.

The Supreme Court upheld the government's policy of internment. In wartime, the Court ruled in *Hirabayashi* v. *U.S.* (1943), "residents having ethnic affiliations with an invading enemy may be a greater source of danger than those of different ancestry." In *Korematsu* v. *U.S.* (1944), the Court approved the removal of the Nisei from the West Coast.

In 1983, forty-one years after he had been sent to a government camp, Fred Korematsu had the satisfaction of hearing a federal judge rule that he—and by implication all detainees—had been the victim of "unsubstantiated facts, distortions and misrepresentations of at least one military commander whose views were affected by racism." A year earlier, the government's special Commission on Wartime Relocation and Internment of Civilians had recommended compensating the victims of this policy. Finally, in 1988, Congress voted to award $20,000 and a public apology to each of the surviving sixty thousand Japanese-American internees.

 ## Jobs and Racism on the Home Front

At peak enrollment the army had more than 700,000 African-American troops. An additional 187,000 black men and women enlisted in the navy, the Coast Guard, and the once all-white Marine Corps. In response to the March on Washington movement of 1941, the Selective Service System and the War Department agreed to draft black Americans in proportion to their presence in the population: about 10 percent.

Although they served in segregated units, African-Americans made real advances toward racial equality during these years. For the first time the War Department sanctioned the training of blacks as pilots.

African-American Troops

After instruction at Tuskegee Institute in Alabama, pilots saw heroic service in all-black units such as the Ninety-ninth Pursuit Squadron, winner of eighty Distinguished Flying Crosses. In 1940 Colonel Benjamin O. Davis was the first African-American to be promoted to brigadier general.

Serious failures in race relations, however, undercut these accomplishments. Race riots instigated by whites broke out on military bases,

and white civilians assaulted black soldiers and sailors throughout the South. When the War Department issued an order in mid-1944 forbidding racial segregation in military recreation and transportation, the *Montgomery Advertiser* replied, "Army orders, even armies, even bayonets, cannot force impossible and unnatural social relations upon us." African-Americans in the military rankled at such comments and were angered by the Red Cross practice of separating blood according to the donor's race. Many African-Americans wondered what they were fighting for, and some saw the conflict as a white man's war in which there was little difference between American and German racism.

But there were persuasive reasons for African-Americans to participate in the war effort. Perhaps, as the NAACP believed, this was an opportunity "to persuade, embarrass, compel and shame our government and our nation . . . into a more enlightened attitude toward a tenth of its people." Proclaiming that in the Second World War they were waging a "Double V" campaign (for victory at home and abroad), blacks were more militant than before and readier than ever to protest. Membership in civil rights organizations soared.

The war also created opportunities in industry. To secure defense jobs, 1.5 million black Americans migrated from the South to the industrial cities of the North and West in the 1940s. More than half a million became active members of CIO unions like the United Auto Workers and United Steel Workers. African-American voters in northern cities were beginning to constitute a vital swing vote, not only in local and state elections but also in presidential contests.

African-American War Workers

But the benefits of urban life came with a high price tag. The migrants had to make enormous emotional and cultural adjustments, and white hostility and ignorance made their task difficult. Southern whites who had migrated north brought with them the racial prejudices of the Deep South. Also hostile were the northern

Race Riots of 1943

whites. In 1942 more than half of them believed that blacks should be segregated in separate schools and neighborhoods. Such attitudes, and the competition between blacks and whites for jobs and housing, caused many people to fear that the summer of 1943 would be like 1919—another "Red Summer." Indeed, in 1943 almost 250 racial conflicts exploded in forty-seven cities. Outright racial warfare bloodied the streets of Detroit in June. At the end of thirty hours of rioting, twenty-five blacks and nine whites lay dead.

The federal government did practically nothing to prevent further racial violence. But this time, government neglect could not discourage African-Americans and the century-old civil rights movement. By war's end they were ready—politically, economically, and emotionally—to wage a struggle for voting rights and for equal access to public accommodations and institutions.

Racial violence was also directed against people of Mexican origin. In 1942, American farms and war industries needed workers, and the United States and Mexico had agreed

Bracero Program

to the *bracero* program, whereby Mexicans were admitted to the United States on short-term work contracts. Although the newcomers suffered racial discrimination and segregation, they seized the economic opportunities that had become available. In Los Angeles, seventeen thousand people of Mexican descent found shipyard jobs where before the war none had been available to them.

Ethnic and racial animosities intensified during the war. In 1943 Los Angeles witnessed the "zoot-suit riot," in which whites, most of them sailors and soldiers, wantonly attacked Mexican-Americans. White racist anger focused on Mexican-American street gangs (*pachucos*), who had adopted ducktail haircuts and zoot suits: long coats with wide padded shoulders, pegged pants, wide-brimmed hats, and long watch chains. For four days in June, mobs invaded Mexican-American neighborhoods. Not only did white police officers look the other way during these assaults, but the city of Los Angeles passed an ordinance that made wearing a zoot suit within city limits a crime.

Women and Children in the War Effort

During the Great Depression, public opinion had been hostile to the hiring of women. The war, however, created millions of defense industry jobs. Filling these new jobs were African-Americans, southern whites, Mexican-Americans, and, above all, women.

No matter how impressive, statistics tell only part of the story. Changes in people's attitudes were also important. Until early in the war, em-

Women in War Production

ployers had insisted that women were not suited for industrial jobs. As labor shortages began to threaten the war effort, employers did an about-face. "Almost overnight," said Mary Anderson, head of the Women's Bureau of the Department of Labor, "women were reclassified by industrialists from a marginal to a basic labor supply for munitions making." Women became riveters, welders, crane operators, tool makers, shell loaders, lumberjacks and cowgirls.

During the war years, the number of working women increased by 57 percent. The economist Claudia Goldin has observed that labor-force participation rates increased most for women over age forty-five, and that "married, rather than single women, were the primary means of bolstering the nation's labor force." By 1945 more working women were married than single.

New employment opportunities also increased women's occupational mobility. Especially noteworthy were the gains made by African-American women; over 400,000 quit work as domestic servants to enjoy the better working conditions, higher pay, and union benefits of industrial employment. To take advantage of the new employment opportunities, over 7 million black and white women moved to war-production areas.

Although newspapers, magazines, radio, and the movies proclaimed Rosie the Riveter a war hero, few asserted that women's war work should bring about a permanent shift in sex roles. The societal assumption was that after the war women should go back to nurturing their husbands and children, leaving their jobs to returning GIs. Wartime surveys, however, showed that many of the women wanted to remain in their jobs—80 percent of New York's women workers felt that way.

Although women's wages rose when they acquired better jobs, they still received lower pay than men. In 1945, women in manufacturing earned only 65 percent of what men were paid. Working mothers suffered in other ways as well. Even as they were being encouraged to work in the national defense, there was still opposition to their doing so. One form this campaign took was a series of exaggerated articles in mass-circulation magazines about the suffering of "eight-hour orphans" or "latchkey children," left alone or deposited in all-night movie theaters while their mothers worked eight-hour shifts in war plants. Childcare centers were in short supply in some war-boom areas; communal or neighborhood kitchens were almost nonexistent.

Discrimination Against Women

By and large, however, the home-front children of working women were not neglected or abused during the war. Families made their own childcare arrangements, which often involved leaving children in the care of their grandmothers. Some families benefited from the Lanham Act of 1940, which provided federal aid, including funds for childcare centers, to communities that had to absorb large war-related populations.

Childcare in Wartime

While millions of women were entering the work force, hundreds of thousands of women were also getting married. The number of marriages rose from 73 per 1,000 unmarried women in 1939 to 93 in 1942. Some couples scrambled to get married so they could live together before the man was sent overseas; others doubtless married and had children to qualify for military deferments. Many of these hasty marriages did not survive long military separations, and divorces soared, too—from 25,000 in 1939 to 485,000 in 1945. As might be expected, the birth rate also climbed: total births rose from about 2.4 million in 1939 to 3.1 million in 1943. Many births were "goodbye babies," conceived as a guarantee that the family would be perpetuated if the father died in battle overseas.

Increase in Marriage, Divorce, and Birth Rates

Ironically, women's efforts to hold their families together during the war posed problems for returning fathers. Women war workers had brought home the wages; they had taken over the budgeting of expenses and the writing of checks. In countless ways they had proved they could hold the reins in their husbands' absence. Many husbands returned home to find that the lives of their wives and children seemed complete without them.

What of the women who wanted to remain in the labor market? In 1945 many such women were pushed out of the factories and shipyards to make way for returning veterans. Others chose to leave their jobs for a year or two before returning to work. But those who tried later to return to high-paying industrial work were discouraged, and many were forced into low-paying jobs in restaurants and laundries.

The Decline of Liberalism and the Election of 1944

Even before Pearl Harbor, political liberals had suffered major defeats. Some Democrats hoped to revive the reform movement during the war, but Republicans and conservative Democrats were on guard against such a move. In the 1942 elections, the Republicans, aided by a small voter turnout, scored impressive gains. Part of the Democrats' problem was that once people acquired jobs and gained some economic security, they began to be more critical of New Deal policies. The New Deal coalition had always been a fragile

Republican Gains in 1942

alliance: southern white farmers had little in common with northern blacks or white factory workers. In northern cities, blacks and whites who had voted for Roosevelt in 1940 were competing for jobs and housing and soon would collide in race riots.

But though New Deal liberalism was enfeebled, it was far from dead. At its head still stood Franklin D. Roosevelt, and it had a program to present to the American people. The liberal agenda began with a pledge to secure full employment. Roosevelt emphasized the concept in his Economic Bill of Rights, delivered as part of his 1944 State of the Union address. Every American, the president declared, had a right to a decent job, to sufficient food, shelter, and clothing, and to financial security in unemployment, illness, and old age. To accomplish these things, Roosevelt first had to be reelected.

Wartime Liberalism

By 1944 Roosevelt looked tired, and rumors of his ill health persisted. Nonetheless, he selected Harry S Truman, a loyal New Deal senator from Missouri, as his running mate. Truman was inexperienced in international affairs, and there was little evidence that he possessed the capacities for national and world leadership that he would need as president. Nor did Roosevelt take Truman into his confidence, failing even to inform his running mate about the atomic bomb project.

Roosevelt and Truman

Republicans were optimistic about their prospects for regaining the presidency. New York's Governor Thomas E. Dewey, who won the nomination on the first ballot, was moderate in his criticism of Roosevelt's foreign policy and did not advocate repeal of the essentials of the New Deal—Social Security, unemployment relief, collective bargaining, and price supports for farmers. Dewey had one great liability—his public image. He was stiff in manner and bland in personality.

Roosevelt won a fourth term. It was the urban vote that returned Roosevelt to the White House. Wartime population shifts had enhanced the Dem-

Roosevelt's Fourth-Term Victory

ocrats' political clout: southern whites who had been lifelong Democrats, along with southern blacks who had never voted before, had migrated to the urban industrial centers. Added to the Democrats' urban vote was a less obvious factor. Many voters seemed to be exhibiting what has been called "depression psychosis." Fearful that hard times would return once war contracts were terminated, they remembered New Deal relief programs and voted for Roosevelt. With victory within grasp, many Americans wanted Roosevelt's experienced hand to guide both the nation and the world to a lasting international peace. Roosevelt's death in April 1945, however, meant that Harry Truman would deal with the postwar world.

 ## Wartime Diplomacy

Throughout the war, American leaders vowed to make a peace that would ensure a postwar world free from economic depression, totalitarianism, and war. American goals included the Open Door and lower tariffs; self-determination for liberated peoples; avoidance of the debts-reparations tangle that had plagued Europe after the First World War; expansion of the United States's sphere of influence; and management of world affairs by what Roosevelt once called the Four Policemen: the Soviet Union, China, Great Britain, and the United States.

Although the Allies concentrated on defeating the aggressors, their suspicions of one another undermined cooperation. Questions about eastern Europe proved the most difficult. The Soviet Union sought to fix its boundaries where they had stood before Hitler attacked in 1941. This meant that the part of Poland that the Soviets had invaded and captured in 1939 would become Soviet territory. The British and Americans hesitated, preferring to deal with eastern Europe at the end of the war. Yet in an October 1944 agreement, Churchill and Stalin

Allied Disagreement over Eastern Europe

struck a bargain: the Soviet Union would gain Romania and Bulgaria as a sphere of influence; Britain would have the upper hand in Greece; and the two countries would share authority in Yugoslavia and Hungary.

Poland was a special case. In 1943, Moscow had broken off diplomatic relations with the conservative Polish government-in-exile in London. The Poles had angered Moscow by asking the International Red Cross to investigate German charges that the Soviets had massacred thousands of Polish army officers in the Katyn Forest in 1940. Then an uprising in Warsaw in 1944 complicated matters still further. Encouraged by approaching Soviet troops to expect assistance, the Warsaw underground rose against the occupying Germans. To the dismay of the world community, Soviet armies stood by as German troops slaughtered 166,000 people and devastated the city. The Soviets then set up a pro-Communist government in Lublin. Thus Poland had two competing governments, one in London, recognized by America and Britain, and another in Lublin.

Early in the war the Allies had begun talking about a new international peacekeeping organization. At Teheran in 1943 Roosevelt called for an institution controlled by the Four Policemen. The next year, at a Washington, D.C., mansion called Dumbarton Oaks, American, British, Russian, and Chinese representatives approved a preliminary charter for a United Nations Organization, providing for a supreme Security Council dominated by the great powers and a weak General Assembly. The Security Council would have five permanent members, each with veto power. Britain had insisted that France be one of the permanent members. Meanwhile, the Soviet Union, hoping to counter pro-American and pro-British blocs in the General Assembly, asked for separate membership in the General Assembly for each of the sixteen Soviet republics. This issue was not resolved at Dumbarton Oaks, but the meeting proved a success nevertheless.

Creation of the United Nations Organization

Diplomatic action on behalf of the European Jews, however, proved to be a tragic failure. By war's end, about 6 million Jews had been forced into Nazi concentration camps and systematically murdered, most by firing squads and in gas chambers. The Nazis also exterminated as many as 250,000 Gypsies and about 60,000 gay men. During the depression, the United States and other nations had refused to relax their immigration restrictions to save Jews fleeing persecution. Because of anti-Semitism and concern over competition for scarce jobs, American immigration officials applied the rules so strictly—requiring legal documents that fleeing Jews could not possibly provide—that otherwise-qualified refugees were kept out of the country.

Jewish Refugees from the Holocaust

Even the tragic voyage of the *St. Louis* did not change government policy. The vessel left Hamburg in mid-1939 carrying 930 desperate Jewish refugees who lacked proper immigration documents. Denied entry to Havana, the *St. Louis* headed for Miami, where Coast Guard cutters prevented it from docking. The ship was forced to return to Europe.

As evidence mounted that Hitler intended to exterminate the Jews, British and American representatives met in Bermuda in 1943 but came up with no plans. Secretary of State Hull submitted a report to the president that emphasized "the unknown cost of moving an undetermined number of persons from an undisclosed place to an unknown destination." Appalled, Secretary of the Treasury Henry Morgenthau, Jr., charged that the State Department's foot-dragging made the United States an accessory to murder. Early in 1944, stirred by Morgenthau's well-documented plea, Roosevelt created the War Refugee Board, which set up refugee camps in Europe and played a crucial role in saving 200,000 Jews from death.

America's Response to the Holocaust

American officials, however, had waited too long to act, and they also missed a chance to destroy the gas chambers and ovens at the extermination camp at Auschwitz in occupied Poland. They possessed aerial photographs of the camp, but they argued that bombing it would detract from the war effort or prompt the Germans to step up the anti-Jewish terror. In 1944, American planes bombed factories in the industrial sector of Auschwitz but left untouched the gas chambers and crematoria.

 ### The Yalta Conference and a Flawed Peace

With the war in Europe nearing an end, Roosevelt called for another summit meeting. The three Allied leaders met at Yalta, in the Russian Crimea, in early February 1945. Controversy has surrounded the conference ever since. Roosevelt was obviously ill, and critics of the Yalta agreements later charged that he was too weak to resist Stalin's cunning and that he struck a poor bargain. The evidence suggests, however, that Roosevelt was mentally alert and managed to sustain his strength during negotiations.

Each of the Allies arrived at Yalta with definite goals. Britain sought to make France a partner in the postwar occupation of Germany, to curb Soviet influence in Poland, and to ensure protection for the vulnerable British Empire. The Soviet Union wanted reparations from Germany to assist in the massive task of rebuilding at home, possessions in Asia, continued influence in Poland, and a permanently weakened Germany. The United States lobbied for the United Nations Organization, in which it believed it could exercise influence; for a Soviet declaration of war against Japan; for recognition of China as a major power; and for compromise between rival factions in Poland.

Allied Goals at Yalta

Military positions at the time of the conference helped to shape the final agreements. Soviet troops had occupied much of eastern Europe, including Poland, and Stalin insisted on a government friendly to Moscow—the Lublin regime. He also demanded boundaries that would give Poland part of Germany in the west and the Soviet Union part of Poland in the east. Churchill boiled over in protest;

Compromise on Poland

he wanted the London government-in-exile to return to Poland.

With Roosevelt's help, a compromise was reached: a boundary favorable to the Soviet Union in the east; postponement of the western boundary issue; the creation of a "more broadly based" coalition government that would include members of the London regime; and free elections to be held sometime in the future. The agreement was vague but, given Soviet occupation of Poland, Roosevelt considered it "the best I can do."

As for Germany, the Big Three agreed that it would be divided into four zones, the fourth zone to be administered by France. Berlin, within the Soviet zone, also would be divided among the four victors. On the question of reparations, Stalin wanted a precise figure, but Churchill and Roosevelt insisted on determining Germany's ability to pay. With Britain abstaining, the Americans and Russians agreed that an Allied committee would consider the sum of $20 billion as a basis for discussion in the future.

Other issues led to tradeoffs. Stalin promised to declare war on Japan two or three months after Hitler's defeat. The Soviet premier also agreed to sign a treaty of friendship and alliance with Jiang Jieshi (Chiang Kai-shek), America's ally in China, rather than with the Communist Mao Zedong. In return, the United States agreed that the Soviets could take the southern part of Sakhalin Island and the Kurile Islands. Regarding the new world organization, Roosevelt and Churchill granted the Soviets three votes in the General Assembly. (Fifty nations officially launched the United Nations Organization three months later.) Finally, the conferees issued the Declaration of Liberated Europe, a pledge to establish order and to rebuild economies by democratic methods.

Yalta marked the high point of the Grand Alliance. Each of the Allies came away with something it wanted. But as the great powers jockeyed for influence at the close of the war, neither the spirit nor the letter of Yalta held firm. The crumbling of the alliance became evident almost immediately, at the Potsdam Conference, which began

Potsdam Conference

in mid-July. Roosevelt had died in April, and Truman—a novice at international diplomacy—was less patient with the Soviets. Truman also was emboldened by learning during the conference that the atomic test in New Mexico had been successful.

Despite major differences at Potsdam, the Big Three did agree on general policies toward Germany: complete disarmament, dismantling of industry used for military production, and dissolution of Nazi institutions and laws. In a compromise over reparations, they decided that each occupying nation should extract reparations from its own zone; but they could not agree on a total figure.

Potsdam left much undone. As the war drew to a close, little bound the Allies together. Roosevelt's cooperative style was gone; the spirit of Yalta was evaporating; the common enemy, Hitler, was defeated. And the United States, with the awesome atomic bomb, no longer needed or wanted Russia in the Pacific war. Moreover, each of the victors was seeking to preserve and enlarge its sphere of influence. Britain claimed authority in Greece and parts of the Middle East; the Soviet Union already dominated much of eastern Europe; and the United States retained its hegemony in Latin America. The United States also seized several Pacific islands as strategic outposts and laid plans to dominate a defeated Japan.

Hitler once said, "We may be destroyed, but if we are, we shall drag a world with us—a world in flames." Indeed, *rubble* was the word most often invoked to describe the European landscape at the end of

The War's Death Toll

the war. Hamburg, Stuttgart, and Dresden had been laid to waste; three-quarters of Berlin was in ruins. In England, Coventry and parts of London were bombed out. In Asia as well as in Europe, ghostlike people wandered about, searching desperately for food and mourning those who would never come home. The Soviet Union had suffered by far the greatest losses: more than 21 million military and civilian war dead. The Chinese calculated their war losses at 10 million, the Germans and Austrians at 6 million, and the Japanese at 2.5 million. And 6 million Jews had

been killed during the Holocaust. In all, the Second World War caused the deaths of 55 million people.

Only one major combatant escaped such grisly statistics: the United States. Its cities were not burned. American deaths from the war—405,399—

Postwar Strength of the United States

were few compared with the losses of other nations. In fact, the United States emerged from the Second World War more powerful than it had ever been. It alone had the atomic bomb. The United States Air Force and Navy were the largest anywhere. What is more, only the United States had the capital and economic resources to spur international recovery. America, gloated Truman, was "a giant."

 ## Conclusion

For many Americans life was fundamentally different in 1945 from what it had been before Pearl Harbor. The Academy Award for 1946 went to *The Best Years of Our Lives*, a painful film about the postwar readjustments of three veterans and their families and friends. Many men returned home suffering flashbacks, nightmares, and deep emotional distress. "Dad came home a different man," recalled one girl; "he didn't laugh as much and he drank a lot."

On another front, the Second World War stimulated the trend toward bigness, not only in business and labor but also in government, agriculture, higher education, and science. The seeds of the military-industrial complex were also sown during these years. Moreover, with the advent of the Cold War, millions of young men would be inducted into the armed forces during the next thirty years. War and the expectation of war would become part of American life.

At the same time, the Second World War was a powerful engine of social change in the United States. The gains made during the war by African-Americans and women were overdue. And by blending New Deal ideology and wartime urgency, the government assumed the responsibility of ensuring prosperity and stepping in when capitalism faltered. Americans emerged from the war fully confident that theirs was the greatest country in the world. Clearly, the Second World War was a turning point in the nation's history.

Suggestions for Further Reading

Fighting the War

Robert H. Abzug, *Inside the Vicious Heart: Americans and the Liberation of Nazi Concentration Camps* (1985); Stephen E. Ambrose, *D-Day, June 6, 1944* (1994); Stephen E. Ambrose, *Eisenhower: Soldier, General of the Army, President-Elect* (1983); Allan Berube, *Coming Out Under Fire: The History of Gay Men and Women in World War II* (1990); John W. Dower, *War Without Mercy: Race and Power in the Pacific War* (1986); Richard B. Frank, *Guadalcanal* (1991); Paul Fussell, *Wartime* (1989); John Keegan, *The Second World War* (1989); Eric Larabee, *Commander in Chief* (1987); Samuel Eliot Morison, *The Two-Ocean War* (1963); David Reynolds, *Rich Relations: The American Occupation of Britain, 1942–1945* (1995); Ronald Schaffer, *Wings of Judgment: American Bombing in World War II* (1985); Ronald H. Spector, *Eagle Against the Sun: The American War with Japan* (1984); Gerhard L. Weinberg, *A World at Arms: A Global History of World War II* (1994); Daniel Yergin, *The Prize: The Epic Quest for Oil, Money, and Power* (1991).

Wartime Diplomacy

Russell Buhite, *Decisions at Yalta* (1986); Diane Clemens, *Yalta* (1970); Robert Dallek, *Franklin D. Roosevelt and American Foreign Policy, 1932–1945* (1979); Henry L. Feingold, *Bearing Witness: How America and Its Jews Responded to the Holocaust* (1995); George C. Herring, *Aid to Russia, 1941–1946* (1973); Gary R. Hess, *The United States at War, 1941–1945* (1986); Robert C. Hilderbrand, *Dumbarton Oaks* (1990); Akira Iriye, *Power and Culture: The Japanese-American War, 1941–1945* (1981); Warren Kimball, *The Juggler: Franklin Roosevelt as Wartime Statesman* (1991); Verne W. Newton, ed., *FDR and the Holocaust* (1996); Keith Sainsbury, *Churchill and Roosevelt at War* (1994); Michael Stoff, *Oil, War, and American Security* (1980); Mark Stoler, *The Politics of the Second Front* (1977); David S. Wyman, *The Abandonment of the Jews* (1984).

Mobilizing for War

John Chambers, *To Raise an Army* (1980); George Q. Flynn, *The Draft, 1940–1973* (1993); Gregory Hooks, *Forging the Military-Industrial Complex: World War II's Battle of the Potomac* (1991); Nelson Lichtenstein, *Labor's War at Home: The CIO in World War II* (1983); Bartholomew H. Sparrow, *From the Outside In: World War II and the American State* (1996); Harold G. Vatter, *The U.S. Economy in World War II* (1985); Gerald T. White, *Billions for Defense* (1980); Allen M. Winkler, *The Politics of Propaganda: The Office of War Information, 1942–1945* (1978).

The Home Front

John Morton Blum, *V Was for Victory: Politics and American Culture During World War II* (1976); Alan Brinkley, *The End of Reform: New Deal Liberalism in Recession and War* (1995); John D'Emilio, *Sexual Politics, Sexual Communities: The Making of a Homosexual Minority in the United States, 1940–1970* (1983); Doris Kearns Goodwin, *No Ordinary Time: Franklin and Eleanor Roosevelt: The Home Front in World War II* (1994); Maurice Isserman, *Which Side Were You On? The American Communist Party During the Second World War* (1982); Clayton R. Koppes and Gregory D. Black, *Hollywood Goes to War* (1987); Gerald D. Nash, *The American West Transformed* (1985); William L. O'Neill, *A Democracy at War: America's Fight at Home and Abroad in World War II* (1993); Richard Polenberg, *War and Society: The United States, 1941–1945* (1972); George H. Roeder, Jr., *The Censored War: American Visual Experience During World War II* (1993); Studs Terkel, ed., *"The Good War": An Oral History of World War Two* (1984); William M. Tuttle, Jr., *"Daddy's Gone to War": The Second World War in the Lives of America's Children* (1993).

Japanese-American Internment

Roger Daniels, *Prisoners Without Trial* (1993); Stephen Fox, *The Unknown Internment: An Oral History of the Relocation of Italian Americans During World War II* (1990); Peter Irons, *Justice at War* (1983); Gary Okihiro, *Cane Fires: The Anti-Japanese Movement in Hawai'i, 1865–1945* (1991); Page Smith, *Democracy on Trial: The Japanese American Evacuation and Relocation in World War II* (1995); John Tateishi, ed., *And Justice for All: An Oral History of the Japanese-American Detention Camps* (1984).

African-Americans and Wartime Violence

A. Russell Buchanan, *Black Americans in World War II* (1977); Dominic J. Capeci, Jr., *The Harlem Riot of 1943* (1977); Dominic J. Capeci, Jr., and Martha Wilkerson, *Layered Violence: The Detroit Rioters of 1943* (1991); Mauricio Mazon, *The Zoot-Suit Riots* (1984); Patrick S. Washburn, *A Question of Sedition: The Federal Government's Investigation of the Black Press During World War II* (1986); Neil A. Wynn, *The Afro-American and the Second World War,* rev. ed. (1993).

Women at War

Karen T. Anderson, *Wartime Women* (1981); D'Ann Campbell, *Women at War with America* (1984); Sherna Berger Gluck, *Rosie the Riveter Revisited* (1987); Claudia Goldin, *Understanding the Gender Gap: An Economic History of American Women* (1990); Susan M. Hartmann, *The Home Front and Beyond* (1982); Judy Barrett Litoff and David C. Smith, eds., *We're in This War, Too: World War II Letters from American Women in Uniform* (1994); Ruth Milkman, *Gender at Work: The Dynamics of Job Discrimination by Sex During World War II* (1987); Leila J. Rupp,

Mobilizing Women for War: German and American Propaganda, 1939–1945 (1978); Peter A. Soderbergh, *Women Marines: The World War II Era* (1992).

The Atomic Bomb and Japan's Surrender

Gar Alperovitz, *The Decision to Use the Atomic Bomb and the Architecture of an American Myth* (1995); Gregg Herken, *The Winning Weapon* (1980); Michael Hogan, ed., *Hiroshima in History and Memory* (1995); Daniel J. Kevles, *The Physicists* (1977); Robert Jay Lifton and Greg Mitchell, *Hiroshima in America: Fifty Years of Denial* (1995); Richard Rhodes, *The Making of the Atomic Bomb* (1987); Martin J. Sherwin, *A World Destroyed: The Atomic Bomb and the Grand Alliance* (1975); Leon V. Sigal, *Fighting to a Finish* (1994); Ronald Takaki, *Hiroshima: Why America Dropped the Atomic Bomb* (1995).

28

Postwar America: Cold War Politics, Civil Rights, and the Baby Boom
1945–1961

We couldn't wait to be men," recalled Ron Kovic, who as a boy in the 1950s enjoyed nothing more than playing war games with his pals. Ronnie, a baby boomer, was a fervent patriot; most baby boomers were. "For me," Kovic recalled, "it began in 1946 when I was born on the Fourth of July." It was to him "a proud day to be born on." Kovic was one of the first of the baby boomers, but millions more followed. From 1946 through 1961, 64 million babies were born, compared with only 44 million from 1929 through 1945.

Ron Kovic grew up in the afterglow of the Second World War. Every Saturday afternoon, he and his friends went to a nearby movie theater to see war films. His all-time favorite was *To Hell and Back* (1955) starring Audie Murphy, who at the end of the film "jumps on top of a flaming tank that's about to explode and grabs the machine gun blasting it into the German lines. He was so brave," Kovic remembered. Afterward, Ronnie and his buddies fought war games in woods near their homes, turning the terrain into a battlefield. When their war games ended, they would then "walk out of the woods like the heroes we knew we would become when we were men." Boys of Kovic's generation also learned of America's new enemies—the Communists. They imagined themselves stopping the Communists, just as their fathers had defeated the Nazis.

As teenagers in the late 1950s and early 1960s, Ron Kovic and his best friend, Richie Castiglia, "made a solemn promise . . . that the day we turned seventeen we were both going down to the marine recruiter . . . and sign up for the United States Marine Corps." In the summer of 1964, Ron Kovic kept his promise and enlisted. A year later, he was in Vietnam, where he was severely wounded, losing the use of both legs. Ron Kovic was like millions of other American children growing up in Cold War America. What separated him from others sacrificed in Vietnam is that he wrote a magnificent autobiography, *Born on the Fourth of July*, about how the fierce anticommunism and superpatriotism of his childhood had led him to the battlefields of Indochina.

Postwar America was proud and boastful. From 1945 to the 1960s, the American people were in the grip of "victory culture"—that is, the belief that unending triumph was the nation's birthright and destiny. Americans believed that their nation was the greatest in the world, not only the most powerful but the most righteous. And, Americans agreed, it was getting better all the time.

As evidence of the nation's perfectibility, Americans pointed to the postwar economic boom, which began in 1945 and lasted twenty-five years. The cornerstones of the boom were the automobile, construction, and defense industries. As the gross national product (GNP) grew, income levels rose and property ownership spread. New houses and schools sprang up throughout the country, especially in the suburbs.

Most important, Americans began to have babies. The postwar baby boom was larger and in other ways different from increases in the birth rate that earlier generations had experienced. Parents who had grown up during the Great Depression were determined that their children's lives would be better than theirs had been. Often both parents worked to pay for a new home and a second car. And family togetherness—including evenings watching television as a family, family vacations, and family church attendance—took on an almost religious significance.

Although the postwar years comprised an age of consensus, Cold War politics were often volatile. When Harry S Truman became president in 1945, his initial response to the challenge was a deep feeling of inadequacy. As vice president, Truman had been kept ignorant by Franklin D. Roosevelt about crucial foreign and military initiatives. In domestic matters, the nation's reconversion from war to peace was not smooth, and Truman managed to anger liberals, conservatives, farmers, consumers, and union members early in his presidency. In 1946, voters reacted to inflation and a wave of strikes by electing a Republican majority to Congress. Truman's actions also heightened fears of a Communist conspiracy operating within the federal government. In 1947, he issued an executive order establishing a federal employee loyalty program.

In 1948, Truman was thought to be extremely vulnerable, but he confounded political experts by winning the presidency in his own right. His victory demonstrated the volatility of postwar politics. The key domestic issues of the period—civil rights for African-Americans and the anti-Communist witchhunt called McCarthyism—were both highly charged. Later, the outbreak of the Korean War in 1950 intensified discontent. The war, inflation, and corruption in the White House caused Truman's popularity to plummet. After twenty years of Democratic presidents, Americans in 1952 elected the Republican nominee, General Dwight D. Eisenhower.

Eisenhower's major goal was to promote economic growth, and he pursued staunchly Republican goals: a balanced budget, reduced taxes and government spending, low inflation, and a return of power to the states. Still, Eisenhower did not attempt to roll back the New Deal. In fact, however reluctantly, his administration expanded the welfare state.

It was the infant civil rights movement that challenged the national consensus. Most African-Americans were at the bottom of the economic ladder and were being denied their constitutional rights. How would blacks be incorporated into the consensus? The president, Congress, southern whites, and black civil rights activists all gave different answers as they debated *Brown* v. *Board of*

Education of Topeka, the Supreme Court's momentous decision of 1954 invalidating racial segregation in public schools.

Still, however fragile, the age of consensus remained basically intact. President Eisenhower was succeeded in 1961 by a much younger man, Democratic Senator John F. Kennedy of Massachusetts. During his administration, the nation began to deal with problems it had postponed for too long.

 ## Cold War Politics: The Truman Presidency

After the initial joyous reaction to the Second World War's end, Americans faced a number of important questions. What would be the effect of reconversion—the cancellation of war contracts, termination of wage and price controls, and expiration of wartime labor agreements? Would depression recur as the artificial stimulus of the war was withdrawn? Or would Americans spend the money they had saved during the war years and go on a buying spree?

Even before the war's end, cutbacks in production had caused layoffs. At Ford Motor Company's massive Willow Run plant outside Detroit, where nine thousand Liberator bombers had been produced, most workers were let go in the spring of 1945. Ten days after the victory over Japan, 1.8 million people nationwide received pink slips, and 640,000 filed for unemployment compensation. The employment picture was made more complex by the return of millions of discharged GIs in 1945 and 1946.

Postwar Job Layoffs

Despite high unemployment immediately after the war, the United States was not teetering on the brink of depression. In fact, after a brief period of readjustment, the economy soon blasted off into a quarter-century of unprecedented boom. People had plenty of savings to spend in 1945 and 1946, and suddenly there were new houses and cars for them to buy. Easy credit also promoted the buying spree.

Beginnings of the Postwar Economic Boom

As a result, despite the winding-down of war production, the gross national product continued to rise in 1945. The nation's most immediate postwar economic problem was not depression; it was inflation. Throughout 1945 and 1946 prices skyrocketed; inflation exceeded 18 percent in 1946.

As prices spiraled upward, many people were earning less in real income (actual purchasing power) than they had earned during the war. Industrial workers protested that the end of war production had eliminated much of their overtime work. A primary reason for workers' discontent was that as their wages and salaries declined slightly in 1946, net profits reached all-time highs. Indignant that they were not sharing in the prosperity, workers forced nationwide shutdowns in the coal, automobile, steel, and electric industries and halted railroad and maritime transportation.

Upsurges in Labor Strikes

By 1946 there was no doubt about the growing unpopularity of labor unions and their leadership. Many Americans blamed the unions for strikes, which restricted the output of consumer goods and inflated prices. In May, when a nationwide railroad strike was threatened, Truman hopped aboard the anti-union bandwagon and made a dramatic appearance before a joint session of Congress. If strikers in an industry deemed vital to the national security refused to honor a presidential order to return to work, he would "request the Congress immediately to authorize the President to draft into the Armed Forces of the United States all workers who are on strike against their government." Truman's speech alienated union members in general. Many vowed to defeat him in the upcoming 1948 presidential election.

Truman fared little better in his direction of the Office of Price Administration (OPA). Now that the war was over, powerful interests wanted price controls lifted. Consumers grew impatient with shortages and black-market prices, and manufacturers and farmers wanted to jack up prices legally. Yet when most controls expired in mid-1946 and inflation rose further, consumers grumbled. Republicans made the most of public

Consumer Discontent

• *Important Events* •

1945   Roosevelt dies; Harry S Truman becomes president
Millions of GIs demobilized

1946   Baby boom begins
Dr. Benjamin Spock's *Baby and Child Care* changes child-rearing practices
Over 1 million GIs enroll in colleges
Workers strike in coal, automobile, steel, and electric industries
Inflation exceeds 18 percent
Republicans win both houses of Congress

1947   Truman institutes employee loyalty program
Taft-Hartley Act limits power of unions
To Secure These Rights issued by the President's Committee on Civil Rights

1948   Truman issues executive orders ending racial discrimination in federal government and racial segregation in the armed forces
Truman elected president
Dr. Alfred Kinsey's *Sexual Behavior in the Human Male* sparks controversy

1950   Klaus Fuchs arrested as an atomic spy
Alger Hiss convicted of perjury
Senator Joseph McCarthy alleges Communists in government
Korean War begins
Julius and Ethel Rosenberg charged with conspiracy to commit treason
Internal Security (McCarran) Act requires members of "Communist front" organizations to register with the government

1951   *Dennis et al.* v. *U.S.* upholds the Alien Registration (Smith) Act, which outlawed membership in any organization that advocated violent overthrow of the United States government

1952   Ralph Ellison's *Invisible Man* shows African-Americans' exclusion from the American Dream
Dwight D. Eisenhower elected president
Republicans win both houses of Congress

1953   Korean War ends
Rosenbergs executed

Congress adopts termination policy for Native Americans
Kinsey causes a public uproar with *Sexual Behavior in the Human Female*

1954   *Brown* decision rules "separate but equal" is illegal
Communist Control Act makes Communist Party membership illegal
Senate condemns Senator McCarthy

1955   AFL and CIO merge
Rebel Without a Cause idealizes youth subculture
Montgomery bus boycott begins

1956   Highway Act launches interstate highway project
Eisenhower reelected
Allen Ginsberg's poem *Howl*, the anthem of the Beat generation, is published

1957   Martin Luther King, Jr., is elected first president of the Southern Christian Leadership Conference
Little Rock, Arkansas, has desegregation crisis
Congress passes Civil Rights Act
Soviet Union launches *Sputnik*
Jack Kerouac criticizes white middle-class conformity in *On the Road*

1958   Congress passes National Defense Education Act to improve education in mathematics, foreign languages, and science
Sherman Adams resigns over scandal

1960   Sit-in in Greensboro, North Carolina
Student Nonviolent Coordinating Committee formed
John F. Kennedy elected president

1961   Eisenhower warns against "military-industrial complex"

1962   Michael Harrington's *The Other America* creates awareness of America's poor
Rachel Carson's *Silent Spring* warns of dangers of DDT

discent. "Got enough meat?" asked Republican Congressman John M. Vorys of Ohio. "Got enough houses? Got enough OPA? . . . Got enough inflation? . . . Got enough debt? . . . Got enough strikes?" In 1946 the Republicans won a majority in both houses of the Eightieth Congress. The White House in 1948 seemed within their grasp.

The politicians who dominated the Eightieth Congress were committed conservatives. They perceived the Republican landslide as a mandate to reverse the New Deal—that is, to curb the power of government and of labor. Ironically, the Eightieth Congress ultimately would help Truman win the presidency in 1948. For if he had alienated labor and consumers, the Eightieth Congress made them livid.

The Eightieth Congress

Particularly unpopular with workers was the Taft-Hartley Act, which Congress approved over Truman's veto in 1947. The bill prohibited the closed shop, a workplace where membership in a particular union was a prerequisite for being hired. It also permitted the states to enact right-to-work laws banning union-shop agreements, which required all workers to join if a majority voted in favor of a union shop. In addition, the law forbade union contributions to political candidates in federal elections, required union leaders to sign non-Communist affidavits, and mandated an eighty-day cooling-off period before carrying out strikes that imperiled the national security. Taft-Hartley became labor's litmus test for political candidates. Thus Truman's veto vindicated him in the eyes of labor.

Taft-Hartley Act

Not since 1928 had Republicans been so confident of capturing the presidency, and most political experts agreed. At their national convention, Republicans strengthened their position by nominating the governors of two of the nation's most populous states: Thomas E. Dewey of New York for president and Earl Warren of California for vice president.

Presidential Campaign of 1948

Democrats were up against more than Republicans in 1948. Two years before, Henry A. Wallace, the only remaining New Dealer in the cabinet, had been fired by Truman for publicly criticizing United States foreign policy. In 1948 Wallace ran for president on the Progressive Party ticket, which advocated friendship with the Soviet Union, racial desegregation, and nationalization of basic industries. A fourth party, the Dixiecrats (States' Rights Democratic Party), was organized by southerners who walked out of the 1948 Democratic convention when it adopted a pro–civil rights plank; they nominated Governor Strom Thurmond of South Carolina. If Wallace's candidacy did not destroy Truman's chances, experts said, the Dixiecrats certainly would.

But Truman had a few ideas of his own. He called the conservative Eightieth Congress into special session and challenged it to enact all the planks in the Republican platform. If Republicans really wanted to transform their convictions into law, said Truman, this was the time to do it. After Congress had debated for two weeks and accomplished nothing of significance, Truman took to the road, denouncing the "do-nothing" Eightieth Congress. Still, no amount of furious campaigning by Truman seemed likely to change the predicted outcome.

Truman's Upset Victory

As the votes were counted, however, it was clear that Truman had confounded the experts. The final tally was 24 million popular votes and 303 electoral votes for Truman; 22 million popular votes and 189 electoral votes for Dewey. How and why did the upset occur? First, the United States was prosperous, at peace, and essentially united on foreign policy. Second, Roosevelt's legacy—the New Deal coalition—had endured.

Truman began his new term brimming with confidence. It was time, he believed, for government to fulfill its responsibility to provide economic security for the poor and the elderly. In his 1949 State of the Union address, Truman proposed a fair deal for all Americans. Little of Truman's Fair Deal came to fruition, however, and he would leave office a highly unpopular president. One reason for the president's unpopularity was the Korean War, which broke out in 1950.

In June 1950, President Truman ordered American troops to fight in Korea. There was much grumbling among Americans as the nation again mobilized for war. People remembered the shortages of the last war and flocked to their grocery stores for sugar, coffee, and canned goods. Fueled by panic buying and large defense expenditures, inflation (which had not been a problem since 1948) began to eat away at the economy again. Moreover, people disliked the draft, and many reservists and national guardsmen resented being called to active duty. Between an unpopular war and influence peddling by some of Truman's cronies, the president's public approval rating slumped to an all-time low of 23 percent.

Korean War Discontent on the Home Front

Although Truman was highly unpopular when he left office in 1953, historians now rate him among the nation's ten best presidents. Truman was president at the beginning of the Cold War, and in eight years he strengthened the powers of the presidency. He was a New Dealer who fought for programs to benefit workers, African-Americans, farmers, homeowners, retired persons, and people in need of healthcare. Although little of Truman's Fair Deal was enacted during his presidency, much of it became law as part of the Great Society in the 1960s.

Truman's Presidential Legacy

Consensus and Conflict: The Eisenhower Presidency

What sealed the fate of the Democratic Party in 1952 was the Republican candidacy of General Dwight D. Eisenhower. A bona fide war hero, "Ike" seemed to embody the virtues Americans most admired: integrity, decency, lack of pretense, and native ability. Eisenhower's unlucky Democratic opponent was Adlai Stevenson, the thoughtful and witty governor of Illinois. It was never much of a contest, especially after Eisenhower promised to end the Korean War. The result was a landslide: Eisenhower and his running mate,

Senator Richard M. Nixon of California, won almost 34 million popular votes to the Democrats' 27 million. Eisenhower even carried four states in the once-solid Democratic South. Moreover, Eisenhower's coattails were long enough to carry other Republicans to victory; the party gained control of both houses of Congress.

Smiling Ike, with his folksy style, garbled syntax, and frequent escapes to the golf course, provoked Democrats to charge that he failed to lead. But Eisenhower was not that simple. His low-key style was a way of playing down his role as politician and highlighting his role as chief of state. Eisenhower relied heavily on staff work, delegating authority to cabinet members. Sometimes he was not well informed on details and gave the impression that he was out of touch with his own government. In fact, he was not, and he remained a very popular president.

During Eisenhower's presidency most Americans clung to the status quo. It was an era of both self-congratulation and constant anxiety, especially over communism. Demand for reform at such a time seemed to most Americans not only unnecessary but downright unpatriotic. Though a weak minority on the American left advocated checks on the political power of corporations and a noisy minority on the right accused the government of a wishy-washy campaign against communism, the vast majority of Americans accepted the nation without question. Thus both liberal Democrats and moderate Republicans avoided extremism, satisfied to be occupying what the historian Arthur M. Schlesinger, Jr., called "the vital center."

The "Consensus Mood"

In this age of consensus, President Eisenhower approached his duties with a philosophy he called "dynamic conservatism." He meant being "conservative when it comes to money and liberal when it comes to human beings." Eisenhower's was unabashedly "an Administration representing business and industry," as Interior Secretary Douglas McKay acknowledged. The president and his appointees gave priority to reducing the federal budget, but

"Dynamic Conservatism"

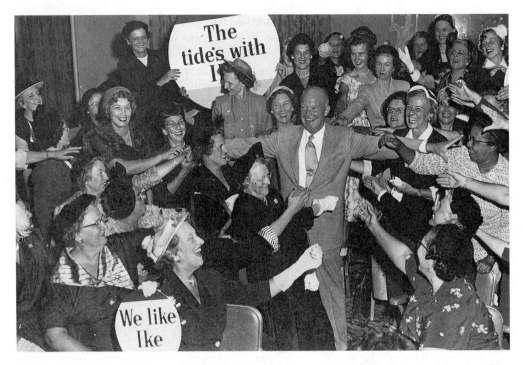

During the 1952 presidential campaign, Dwight D. Eisenhower (1890–1969) received a delegation of Republican national committeewomen at his New York City headquarters. As the women chanted "I Like Ike," the Republican candidate opened his arms to welcome them. UPI/Corbis-Bettmann.

they did not always succeed; and they recognized that dismantling New Deal and Fair Deal programs was politically impossible. The administration did try to remove the federal government from agriculture, but the effort failed.

Eisenhower made headway in other spheres. In 1954 Congress passed legislation to construct a canal, the St. Lawrence Seaway, between Montréal and Lake Erie. This inland waterway was intended to spur the economic development of the Midwest by linking the Great Lakes to the Atlantic Ocean. Also in 1954 Eisenhower signed into law amendments to the Social Security Act that raised benefits and added 7.5 million workers, mostly self-employed farmers, to the program's coverage. Congress also obliged the president with tax reform that raised business depreciation allowances and with the Atomic Energy Act of 1954, which granted private companies the right to own reactors and nuclear materials for the production of electricity.

Eisenhower also presided over a dramatic change in the lives of Native Americans. In 1953, Congress adopted a policy of *termination:* the liquidation of Indian reservations and an end to federal services. Another act of the same year made Indians subject to state laws. Under termination, the federal government withdrew its benefits from sixty-one tribes between 1954 and 1960. About one in eight Indians abandoned the reservations; many joined the ranks of the urban poor in low-paying jobs. The policy of termination and relocation was motivated largely by land greed. The Klamaths of Oregon, for example, lived on a reservation rich in ponderosa pine, which lumber interests coveted. Enticed by cash payments, almost four-fifths of the Klamaths accepted termination and voted to sell their shares of the forest land. With termination, their way of life collapsed.

In the 1954 congressional elections, most Americans revealed that, though they still liked

Eisenhower, they remained loyal to the Democratic Party. Voters gave the Democrats control of both houses of Congress. Lyndon B. Johnson of Texas became the Senate's new majority leader. An energetic, pragmatic politician, Johnson worked with the Republican White House to pass legislation. A notable accomplishment was the Highway Act of 1956, which launched the largest public works program in American history. This law authorized the spending of $31 billion over the next thirteen years to build a 41,000-mile interstate highway system, intended to facilitate commerce and enable the military to move around the nation more easily. The interstate highways invigorated the tourist industry, further weakened the railroads, and spurred the growth of suburbs farther and farther from the central cities.

Interstate Highway System

Eisenhower suffered a heart attack in 1955 but regained his strength and declared his intention to run again. The Democrats nominated Adlai E. Stevenson once more. Eisenhower won a landslide victory in 1956: 36 million votes and 457 electoral votes to Stevenson's 26 million and 73. Still, the Democrats continued to dominate Congress.

Election of 1956

Eisenhower faced rising federal expenditures in his second term, in part because of the tremendous expense of America's global activities. In 1959 federal expenditures climbed to $92 billion, about half of which went to the military. In fact, Eisenhower balanced only three of his eight budgets. The administration's resort to deficit spending also was fueled by the need to cushion the impact of three recessions—in 1953–1954, 1957–1958, and 1960–1961.

A lingering recession and other setbacks in 1958 made that year the low point for the administration. Scandal unsettled the White House when the president's chief aide, Sherman Adams, resigned under suspicion of influence peddling. Then came large Republican losses in the 1958 congressional elections.

Assessments of the Eisenhower administration used to emphasize its conservatism, passive style, limited achievements, and reluctance to

Eisenhower Presidency Assessed

confront difficult issues. In recent years, interpretations have been changing. Many now stress Eisenhower's command of policymaking, sensibly moderate approach to most problems, political savvy, and great popularity. Many historians now argue that Eisenhower was a competent, pragmatic leader.

The record of Eisenhower's presidency is nonetheless mixed. At home he failed to deal with poverty, urban decay, and blatant denials of civil rights—problems that would wrack the country in the next decade. But Eisenhower kept military budgets under control and managed crises adroitly so that the United States avoided major military ventures abroad. At home he curbed inflation, strengthened the infrastructure by building an interstate highway system, and expanded Social Security coverage. Eisenhower brought dignity to the presidency, and the American people respected him.

Just before leaving office in early 1961, Eisenhower delivered his farewell address to the nation. Because of the Cold War, he observed, the United States had been "compelled to create a permanent industry of vast proportions," as well as a standing army of 3.5 million. "This conjunction of an immense military establishment and a large arms industry is new in the American experience," Eisenhower noted. "The total influence—economic, political, even spiritual—is felt in every city, every statehouse, every office of the federal government." Then Eisenhower issued a direct warning, urging Americans to "guard against . . . the military-industrial complex." They did not.

The "Military-Industrial Complex"

 ## McCarthyism

The two most volatile political issues in postwar America were the anti-Communist hysteria known as McCarthyism and the growing protest movement for African-American equality. Both Truman and Eisenhower overreacted to the alleged threat of Communist subversion in government.

It is a misconception that McCarthyism began in 1950 with the furious speeches of Senator Joseph R. McCarthy of Wisconsin. Actually, anti-communism had been a prominent strand in the American political fabric ever since the First World War and the Red Scare of 1919 and 1920. The Cold War heightened anti-Communist fears, and McCarthy manipulated the fears to his own advantage; he became the most successful and frightening redbaiter the country had ever seen.

To a significant extent President Truman initiated the postwar anti-Communist crusade. He was bothered by the revelation in 1945 that classified government documents had been found in a raid on the offices of *Amerasia*, a little-known magazine whose editors sympathized with the Communist revolution in China. Who had supplied the documents to the magazine, and why? Similar concerns greeted the release of a Canadian royal commission report in 1946, which claimed that Soviet spies were operating in Canada; among them, the report said, was a scientist who had transmitted atomic secrets to a Soviet agent.

Spurred by these revelations, Truman in 1947 ordered investigations into the loyalty of the more than 3 million employees of the United States government. In 1950 the government began discharging people deemed "security risks," among them alcoholics, homosexuals, and debtors thought to be susceptible to blackmail. Others became victims of guilt by association. Their loyalty was considered questionable because they knew people thought to be subversive or disloyal.

Truman's Loyalty Probe

Truman was not alone in peddling fear; conservatives and liberal Democrats joined him. Republicans used the same methods to attack the Democratic candidates for president in 1948 and 1952; liberal Democrats used them to discredit the far-left, pro-Wallace wing of their party. The anti-Communist hysteria of the late 1940s, created by professional politicians, was embraced and promoted by labor union officials, religious leaders, media moguls, and other influential figures.

People began to point accusing fingers at each other. Hollywood film personalities who had been ardent left-wingers such as Will Geer and Zero Mostel were black-listed. Schoolteachers and college professors were fired for expressing dissenting viewpoints. Anti-Communists also exploited the hysteria to attack homosexuals. "Sexual perverts" were "perhaps as dangerous as the actual Communists" warned the Republican national chairman in 1950.

Victims of Anti-Communist Hysteria

Despite the rampant false accusations, there was cause for alarm. In 1949, a former State Department official, Alger Hiss, went on trial for perjury for swearing to a grand jury that he had never passed classified documents to his accuser, former American Communist spy Whittaker Chambers, and that he in fact had not seen Chambers since 1936. When Truman and Secretary of State Dean Acheson came to Hiss's defense, some people began to suspect that the Democrats had something to hide. Hiss was convicted of perjury in 1950. At the same time, a British court sentenced Klaus Fuchs, a nuclear scientist and Nazi refugee, to prison for turning over to Soviet agents secrets from the atomic-bomb project at Los Alamos, New Mexico.

Hiss Case

It was in this atmosphere that Senator Joseph McCarthy mounted a rostrum in Wheeling, West Virginia, in February 1950 and gave a name to the hysteria: McCarthyism. "The State Department," he asserted, was "thoroughly infested with Communists," and the most dangerous person in the department was Dean Acheson. The senator claimed to have a list of 205 Communists working in the department; McCarthy later lowered the figure to "57 card-carrying members," then raised it to 81. But the number did not matter. What McCarthy needed was a winning campaign issue, and he had found it. Republicans, distraught over losing what had appeared to be a sure victory in the 1948 presidential election, were eager to support his attack.

McCarthy's Attack on the State Department

McCarthy and McCarthyism gained momentum throughout 1950. Nothing seemed to slow

How do historians know that public anxiety about communism was heightened by the media? This comic book, published in 1947 by the Catechetical Guild Educational Society, enjoyed several reprintings; 4 million copies were distributed free to church groups. Claiming that Communists already had "wormed their way into . . . government offices, trade unions, and other positions of trust," it warned Americans that, unless they were vigilant, they might be "living in Communist slavery." Films such as Invasion U.S.A. *(1952) and* Red Nightmare *(1962) featured Communist-takeover scenarios, as did newspaper and magazine articles. The Hearst media empire, with nine maga-* zines and eighteen daily newspapers, including the Daily Mirror *in New York and the* Los Angeles Examiner, *was vociferous in demanding governmental investigations of alleged left-wing subversives. Right-wing publications also demanded that liberal publications be banned from public libraries. And some libraries responded;* The Nation *was removed from school libraries in New York City and Newark, New Jersey. But some librarians refused. In 1950 Ruth Brown lost her job in Bartlesville, Oklahoma, after a citizens committee objected to her placing copies of* The Nation *and* The New Republic *on the library shelves.*   Photo: The Michael Barson Collection/ Past Perfection.

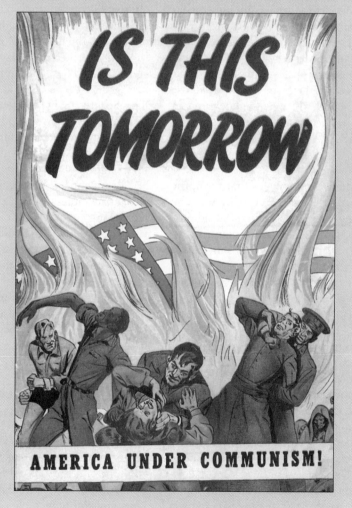

the senator down, not even attacks by other Republicans. Seven Republican senators broke with their colleagues in 1950 and publicly condemned McCarthy for his "selfish political exploitation of fear, bigotry, ignorance, and intolerance"; a Senate committee reported that his charges against the State Department were "a fraud and a hoax." But McCarthy had much to sustain him, including Julius and Ethel Rosenberg's 1950 arrest for conspiracy to commit espionage. During the war, they allegedly had recruited and supervised a spy who worked at the Los Alamos atomic laboratory. Perhaps even more helpful to McCarthy than the Rosenberg case was the outbreak of the Korean War in June 1950.

Widespread support for anti-Communist measures was also apparent in the adoption, over Truman's veto, of the Internal Security (McCarran) Act of 1950, which required members of "Communist-front" organizations to register with the government and prohibited them from holding defense jobs or traveling abroad. In a telling decision in 1951 (*Dennis et al.* v. *U.S.*), the Supreme Court upheld the Smith Act of 1940, under which eleven Communist Party leaders had been convicted and imprisoned.

During President Eisenhower's first term, the conduct of Senator Joseph R. McCarthy was one of the most vexing problems facing the administration. The Wisconsin senator's search for subversives in government turned up none and was an affront to political fair play, decency, and civil liberties. Eisenhower, fearing that a showdown would splinter the Republican party, avoided confronting McCarthy. Instead, he hoped the media and Congress would bring McCarthy down.

Eisenhower's Reluctance to Confront McCarthy

While Eisenhower pursued this indirect strategy to undermine the senator, his administration practiced its own brand of anticommunism. A new executive order in 1953 expanded the criteria under which federal workers could be dismissed as "security risks." One of Eisenhower's most controversial decisions was his denial of clemency to Julius and Ethel Rosenberg. The two, having been sentenced to death, were executed in 1953. The

next year congressional liberals and conservatives enacted, with only two dissenting votes, the Communist Control Act, a measure that in effect made membership in the Communist party illegal.

As for Senator McCarthy, he finally transgressed the limits of what the Senate and the public would tolerate. In front of millions of television viewers, McCarthy accused the United States Army of shielding and promoting Communists. The so-called Army-McCarthy hearings, held by a Senate subcommittee in 1954, became a showcase for the senator's abusive treatment of witnesses. McCarthy, apparently drunk, alternately ranted and slurred his words. Finally, after he maligned a young lawyer who was not even involved in the hearings, Joseph Welch, counsel for the army, protested, "Have you no sense of decency, sir?" The gallery erupted in applause, and McCarthy's career as a witch-hunter plummeted. The Senate finally condemned McCarthy in December 1954 for sullying the dignity of the Senate. He remained a senator, but exhaustion and alcohol took their toll. McCarthy died in 1957 at the age of forty-eight.

Army-McCarthy Hearings

President Eisenhower's reluctance to discredit McCarthy publicly had given the senator, other right-wing members of Congress, and some private and public institutions enough rein to divide the nation and destroy the careers of many innocent people. The anti-Communist campaigns of the 1950s also discouraged people from freely expressing themselves and hence from debating critical issues. Fear and a contempt for the Bill of Rights, in short, helped sustain the Cold War consensus.

The Civil Rights Movement in Postwar America

Ironically, Cold War pressures benefited the civil rights movement. As the Soviet Union was quick to point out, the United States could hardly condemn the denial of human rights in Eastern Europe and the Soviet Union if it condoned racism at home. Nor could the United States convince new African and Asian nations of its dedication to human rights if African-Americans were subjected to segregation, disfranchisement, and racial violence. To win the support of nonaligned nations, the United States would have to live up to its own ideals.

African-Americans had made sacrifices to defeat Nazi racism and were determined to improve their own lives in the postwar era. Moreover, the

Politicians Compete for African-American Votes

continued migration of southern blacks to the North and West gave them political clout. Harry Truman and other politicians, including some Republicans, knew they would have to compete for the growing African-American vote in California, New York, Illinois, Michigan, Pennsylvania, and other large states. But President Truman also felt a moral obligation to do something, for he genuinely believed it was only fair that every American, regardless of race, should enjoy the full rights of citizenship. Truman was also disturbed at the resurgence of a revived Ku Klux Klan and horrified by a report that police in Aiken, South Carolina, had gouged out the eyes of a black sergeant just three hours after he had been discharged from the army. Several weeks later, in December 1946, Truman signed an executive order establishing the President's Committee on Civil Rights.

The committee's report, *To Secure These Rights* (1947), would become the agenda for the civil rights movement for the next twenty years. Among

President Truman's Committee on Civil Rights

its recommendations were the enactment of federal antilynching and antisegregation legislation. *To Secure These Rights* also called for laws guaranteeing voting rights and equal employment opportunity and for the establishment of a permanent commission on civil rights. Although Congress failed to act and some evidence suggests that Truman's real goal was the African-American vote in 1948, his action was significant. For the first time since Reconstruction, a president had acknowledged the federal government's responsibility to protect blacks and strive for racial equality.

Truman took this responsibility seriously, and in 1948 he issued two executive orders declaring an end to racial discrimination in the federal government. One proclaimed a policy of "fair employment throughout the federal establishment" and created the Employment Board of the Civil Service Commission to hear charges of discrimination. The other ordered the racial desegregation of the armed forces.

African-Americans also benefited from a series of Supreme Court decisions. The trend toward judicial support of civil rights had begun in the

Supreme Court Decisions on Civil Rights

late 1930s, when the NAACP established its Legal Defense Fund. At the time, the NAACP was trying to destroy the separate-but-equal doctrine established in *Plessy* v. *Ferguson* (1896) by insisting on its literal interpretation. In higher education, the NAACP calculated, the cost of true equality in racially separate schools would be prohibitive. "You can't build a cyclotron for one student," as the president of the University of Oklahoma acknowledged. As a result of NAACP lawsuits in the 1930s and 1940s, African-American students won admission to professional and graduate schools at a number of state universities. In *Smith* v. *Allwright* (1944), the Supreme Court also outlawed the whites-only primaries held by the Democratic Party in some southern states, branding them a violation of the Fifteenth Amendment's guarantee of the right to vote. Two years later the Court struck down segregation in interstate bus transportation (*Morgan* v. *Virginia*). And in *Shelley* v. *Kraemer* (1948), the Court held that a racially restrictive covenant (private agreements among white homeowners not to sell to blacks) violated the equal protection clause of the Fourteenth Amendment.

A change in social attitudes accompanied these gains in black political and legal power. Books like Gunnar Myrdal's social science study *An American Dilemma* (1944) and Richard Wright's novels *Native Son* (1940) and *Black Boy* (1945) were increasing white awareness of the social injustice that plagued African-Americans. A new black middle class was emerging, composed of college-educated activists, war veterans, and union workers. Blacks and whites also worked together in CIO unions and service organizations such as the National Council of Churches. In 1947 a black baseball player, Jackie Robinson, broke the major-league color barrier.

In May 1954 the NAACP won a historic victory that stunned the white South and energized African-Americans to challenge segregation on several fronts. *Brown* v. *Board of Education of Topeka* incorporated cases

Brown v. Board of Education of Topeka

from several states, all involving segregated schools. Written by Chief Justice Earl Warren, the Court's unanimous decision concluded that "in the field of public education the doctrine of 'separate but equal' has no place. Separate educational facilities are inherently unequal." Such facilities, Warren wrote, produced in black children "a feeling of inferiority" and deprived them of "the equal protection of the laws guaranteed by the Fourteenth Amendment." But the ruling did not demand immediate compliance. A year later the Court finally ordered school desegregation, but only "with all deliberate speed." This vague timetable encouraged the southern states to resist.

Some border states quietly implemented the order, and many southern moderates advocated a gradual rollback of segregation. But the forces of white resistance soon came to dominate, urging southern communities to defy the

White Resistance to Civil Rights

Court. The Klan experienced another resurgence, and business and professional people created White Citizens' Councils for the express purpose of resisting the order. Known familiarly as "uptown Ku Klux Klans," the councils brought their economic power to bear against black civil rights activists. One of the most effective resistance tactics was enactment of state laws that paid the private-school tuition of white children who had left public schools to avoid integration. In some cases, desegregated public schools were ordered closed.

While personally disapproving of segregation, President Eisenhower objected to "compulsory federal law" in the belief that race relations would improve "only if it starts locally." He also feared that the ugly public confrontations likely to follow rapid desegregation would jeopardize Republican

inroads in the South. Eisenhower did not state forthrightly that the federal government would enforce the Court's decision, and thereby tacitly encouraged massive resistance.

Events in Little Rock, Arkansas, forced the president to stop sidestepping the issue. In September 1957 Governor Orval E. Faubus intervened to halt a local plan for the gradual desegregation of Little Rock's

Crisis in Little Rock, Arkansas

Central High School. Faubus mobilized the Arkansas National Guard to block the entry of black students. Eisenhower made no effort to impede Faubus's actions. Later that month, bowing to a federal judge's order, Faubus withdrew the guardsmen. As hundreds of jeering whites threatened to storm the school, eight black children entered Central High. The next day, fearing violence, Eisenhower federalized the Arkansas National Guard and dispatched paratroopers to Little Rock to ensure the children's safety. Troops patrolled the school for the rest of the year; in response, Little Rock officials closed all public high schools in 1958 and 1959 rather than desegregate them.

Elsewhere, African-Americans did not wait for Supreme Court or White House decisions to claim equal rights. In 1955 Rosa Parks, a department store seamstress and active member of the NAACP,

Montgomery Bus Boycott

was arrested for refusing to give up her seat to a white man on a public bus in Montgomery, Alabama. Local black groups decided to boycott the city's bus system, and they elected Martin Luther King, Jr., a minister, as their leader.

Martin Luther King, Jr., was a twenty-six-year-old Baptist minister who recently had earned a Ph.D. at Boston University. Disciplined and analytical, he was committed to nonviolent, peaceful protest in

Martin Luther King, Jr.

the spirit of India's leader Mohandas K. Gandhi. In 1957, King became the first president of the Southern Christian Leadership Conference, organized to coordinate civil rights activities.

During the bus boycott, King urged perseverance, and, bolstered by a Supreme Court decision that declared Alabama's Jim Crow laws unconsti-

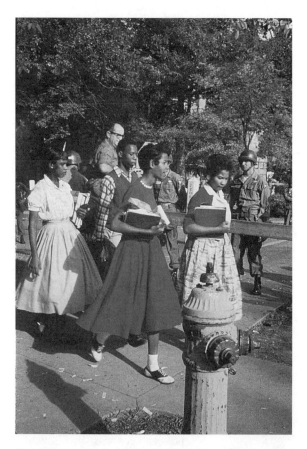

In 1957, paratroopers of the 101st Airborne Division stand ready as African-American students enter Central High School in Little Rock, Arkansas, thus desegregating public education in the state.   Ed Clarke, *Life* magazine © 1957 Time Inc.

tutional, Montgomery blacks triumphed in 1956. They and others across the nation were further heartened when Congress passed the Civil Rights Act of 1957, which created the United States Commission on Civil Rights to investigate systematic discrimination, such as voting discrimination. But this measure, like a voting-rights act passed three years later, proved ineffective.

Meanwhile, African-Americans adopted more aggressive tactics. In February 1960, four black students from North Carolina Agricultural and

Sit-Ins

Technical College in Greensboro ordered coffee at a department-store lunch counter. Told they would not be served,

the students refused to budge. Thus began the sit-in movement. Inspired by the sit-ins, southern black college and high-school students met on Easter weekend in 1960 and organized the Student Nonviolent Coordinating Committee (SNCC). In the face of angry white mobs, SNCC members challenged the status quo.

King personally joined the sit-in movement, and in October 1960 he was arrested in a sit-in to desegregate an Atlanta snack bar. Sent to a cold,

Civil Rights and the 1960 Election

cockroach-infested state penitentiary where he faced four months at hard labor, he became ill. As an apathetic Eisenhower White House looked on, Senator John F. Kennedy, the

Democratic presidential candidate, called King's wife to express support; his brother, Robert F. Kennedy, persuaded the sentencing judge to release King on bond.

 The Postwar Booms: Business and Babies

As the war neared its end in 1945, most Americans feared a return of economic hard times. After all, the war had created jobs; surely the war's end would bring a slump. This expectation proved false. Instead, the nation entered one of its longest, steadiest periods of growth and prosperity, the keys to which were increasing output and increasing demand.

When the economy produced more, Americans generally brought home bigger paychecks and had more money to spend. Between the end of the

Increased Purchasing Power

war and 1950, per capita real income (based on actual purchasing power) rose 6 percent—and that was only the beginning. In the 1950s it jumped another 15 percent; in the 1960s the in-

crease was even greater—32 percent. The result was a noticeable increase in the standard of living. To the vast majority of Americans, such prosperity was a vindication of the American system of free enterprise.

The baby boom, which began in 1946, was both a cause and an effect of prosperity. It was natural for the birth rate to soar immediately after a war; what was unusual was that the birth rate continued to do so throughout the 1950s. During the 1950s, the number of births exceeded 4 million per year, reversing the downward trend in birth rates that had prevailed for 150 years. Births began to decline after 1961 but continued to exceed 4 million per year through 1964. The baby-boom generation was the largest by far in the nation's history.

Baby Boom

The baby boom meant business for builders, manufacturers, and school systems. "Take the 3,548,000 babies born in 1950," wrote Sylvia F. Porter in her syndicated newspaper column. "Bundle them into a batch, bounce them all over the bountiful land that is America. What do you get?" Porter's answer: "Boom. The biggest, boomiest boom ever known in history."

Of the three cornerstones of the postwar economic boom—construction, automobiles, and defense—two were directly related to the upsurge in births. Demand for housing and schools for all these children generated a building boom, furthered by construction of shopping centers, office buildings, and airports. Much of this construction took place in the suburbs. The postwar suburbanization of America in turn would have been impossible without automobile manufacturing, for in the sprawling new communities a car was a necessity.

Housing and Auto Sales

The third cornerstone of the postwar economic boom was military spending. When the Defense Department was established in 1947, the nation was spending just over $10 billion a year on defense. In 1961, the total was $98 billion. Many defense contracts went to industries and universities to develop weapons, and the government supported space research. Defense spending also helped stimulate rapid advances in the electronics industry. The ENIAC computer, completed at the University of Pennsylvania in 1946, weighed fifty tons and required 18,000 vacuum tubes. The introduction of the transistor in the 1950s accelerated

Military Spending

the computer revolution; the silicon microchip in the 1960s inaugurated even more stunning advances in electronics. The microchip facilitated the shift from heavy manufacturing to high-technology industries in fiber optics, lasers, video equipment, robotics, and genetic engineering.

The evolution of electronics meant a large-scale tradeoff for the American people. As industries automated, computerized processes replaced slower mechanical ones, generating a rapid rise in productivity. But in doing so, they brought about technological unemployment. Electronic technology also promoted concentration of ownership in industry. Sophisticated technology was expensive. Typically, only large corporations could afford it; small corporations were shut out of the market. Indeed, large coporations with capital and experience in high-tech fields expanded into related industries.

Another kind of corporate expansion also marked the early 1950s. The third great wave of mergers swept across American business. The first two such movements, in the 1890s and 1920s, had tended toward vertical and horizontal integration respectively. The postwar era was distinguished by conglomerate mergers. A *conglomerate* brings together companies in unrelated industries as a hedge against instability in a particular market. International Telephone and Telegraph (IT&T), for instance, bought up companies in several fields, including suburban development, insurance, and hotels.

Conglomerate Mergers

The labor movement also experienced a postwar merger. In 1955 the American Federation of Labor and the Congress of Industrial Organizations finally put aside their differences and formed the AFL-CIO. Union membership grew slowly during the postwar years, increasing from just around 14.8 million in 1945 to 17.3 million in 1961. The main reason for the slow growth of union membership was a shift in employment patterns. Most new jobs were being created not in the heavy industries that hired blue-collar work-

Postwar Labor Movement

ers but in the union-resistant white-collar service trades.

The postwar economic boom was good for unionized blue-collar workers, many of whom won real increases in wages sufficient to enjoy a middle-class lifestyle that previously had been the exclusive province of white-collar workers and professionals. And they were more protected against inflation: in 1948 General Motors and the United Auto Workers agreed on automatic cost-of-living adjustments (COLAs) in workers' wages, a practice that spread to other industries.

The trend toward economic consolidation also changed agriculture. New machines, such as mechanical cotton-, tobacco-, and grape-pickers and crop-dusting planes revolutionized farming methods, and the increased use of fertilizers and pesticides raised the total value of farm output from $24.6 billion in 1945 to $38.4 billion in 1961. At the same time, farm labor productivity tripled. The resulting improvement in profitability drew large investors into agriculture.

Growth of Agribusiness

By the 1960s it took money—sometimes big money—to become a farmer. In many regions only banks, insurance companies, and large businesses could afford the necessary land, machinery, and fertilizer. The growth of agribusiness threatened the family farm and led to a decline in the nation's farm population from 24.4 million in 1945 to 14.8 million in 1961.

Environmental Costs of Economic Growth

Rapid economic growth also exacted environmental costs. Air, water, soil, and wildlife suffered degradation. Steel mills, coal-powered generators, and car engines burning lead-based gasoline polluted the air and imperiled people's health. America's water supplies suffered as well. Human and industrial waste befouled many rivers and lakes. Moreover, such practices as strip mining and clear cutting scarred the landscape, and toxic waste from chemical plants seeped deep into the soil.

Defense contractors and farmers were among the country's worst polluters. Refuse from nuclear weapons facilities at Hanford, Washington, and at Colorado's Rocky Flats arsenal polluted soil and water resources for years. Agriculture began employing massive amounts of pesticides and other chemicals. A chemical called DDT, for example, which had been used on Pacific islands during the war to kill mosquitoes and lice, was released for public use in 1945. During the next fifteen years, farmers eliminated chronic pests with DDT. In 1962, however, *Silent Spring* by Rachel Carson, a wildlife biologist, specifically indicted DDT for the deaths of mammals, birds, and fish. Because of Carson's book, many Americans finally realized that there were costs to human conquest of the environment. The federal government banned the sale of DDT in 1972.

DDT

America's Consumption of the World's Resources

Much of America's continued economic growth was based on encouraging habits that would make the country a throwaway society. The auto industry intentionally made cars less durable ("planned obsolescence") and through advertising urged consumers to buy a new car every year or two. And increasing numbers of disposable products such as plastic cups and paper diapers were marketed as conveniences. Moreover, as Americans consumed goods and services, they were using up the world's resources. By the 1960s the United States, with only 5 percent of the world's population, produced and consumed over one-third of the world's goods and services.

 ## The Affluent Society, the Sunbelt, and the Suburbs

As United States productivity increased in the postwar years, so did Americans' appetite for goods and services. During the depression and the Second World War, many Americans had dreamed of buying a home or a car. In the affluent postwar years they finally could satisfy those deferred desires. Easy credit was the economic basis of the consumer culture; when people lacked cash to buy what they wanted, they borrowed money. Consumer credit to support the nation's shopping spree grew from $5.7 billion in 1945 to $58 billion in 1961.

Millions of Americans began their search for affluence by migrating to the Sunbelt—roughly, the southern third of the United States. The mass

Growth of the Sunbelt

migration to the Sunbelt had started during the war, when GIs and their families were ordered to new duty stations and war workers moved to defense plants in the West and South. The economic bases of the Sunbelt's spectacular growth were agribusiness, the aerospace industry, the oil industry, real-estate development, recreation, and defense spending. Government policies—generous tax breaks for oil companies, siting of military bases, and awarding of defense and aerospace contracts—were crucial to the Sunbelt's development. Industry was also drawn to the southern rim by right-to-work laws, which outlawed closed shops, and by low taxes and low heating bills.

Another mass movement in postwar America was from the cities to the suburbs. A combination of motives drew people to the suburbs. Some

Growth of the Suburbs

wanted to leave behind the noise and smells of the city. Some white families moved out of urban neighborhoods because African-American families were moving in. Many were looking for a place where they could have a measure of political influence, particularly on the education their children received. Perhaps most important, for this generation of adults—who had suffered economic deprivation during the depression and separation from loved ones during the war—the home became a refuge, and family togetherness fulfilled a psychological need.

Government funding helped new families to settle in the suburbs. Low-interest GI mortgages and Federal Housing Administration (FHA) mort-

Housing Boom

gage insurance made the difference for people who otherwise would have been unable to afford a home. This easy credit,

combined with postwar prosperity, produced a construction boom. From 1945 to 1946, housing starts climbed from 326,000 to more than 1 million; they approached 2 million in 1950 and remained above 1.3 million in 1961. Never before had new starts exceeded 1 million.

As suburbia spread, pastures became neighborhoods with astounding rapidity. Highway construction was a central element in the transformation of rural land into suburbia. In

Highway Construction

1947 Congress authorized construction of a 37,000-mile chain of highways, and in 1956 President Eisenhower signed the Highway Act. Federal expenditures on highways swelled from $79 million in 1946 to $2.6 billion in 1961. State and local spending on highways also mushroomed. Highways both hastened suburbanization and homogenized the landscape. The high-speed trucking that highways made possible also accelerated the integration of the South into the national economy.

Highway construction in combination with the growth of suburbia produced a new phenomenon, the *megalopolis*, a term coined by urban experts in the early 1960s to refer to the almost uninterrupted metropolitan complex stretching along the northeastern seaboard from Boston 600 miles south through New York, Philadelphia, and Baltimore all the way to Washington, D.C. "Boswash" encompassed parts of eleven states and a population of 49 million people, all linked by interstate highways. Another megalopolis that took shape was "Milipitts," a band of heavy industry and dense population stretching from Milwaukee to Pittsburgh.

Sociologists and other critics denounced the suburbs for breeding conformity and status seeking. William H. Whyte's *The Organization Man*

Critics of Suburban Life

(1956), a study of Park Forest, Illinois, pronounced these suburbanites mindless conservatives and extreme conformists. And C. Wright Mills castigated white-collar suburbanites who "sell not only their time and energy but their personalities as well." Nonetheless, most residents of suburbia preferred their lifestyle to any other of which they were aware.

Women's Conflicting Roles and Dilemmas

In 1946, the anthropologist Margaret Mead noted that American society had contradictory expectations for women. On the one hand, the home was premised on a full-time housewife who, with little regard for her own needs, provided her husband and children with a cozy haven from the outside world. On the other hand, women continued to enter the labor force for a variety of reasons. Many worked because they were their family's sole source of income; they had to work. Others took jobs to supplement the family income. Indeed, the female labor force rose from 19.3 million in 1945 to 31.6 million in 1970. Despite the cult of motherhood, most new entrants to the job market were married mothers.

Women's responsibilities also increased at home after the war. Some of the change was due to the publication in 1946 of Dr. Benjamin Spock's *Baby and Child Care*. Unlike earlier manuals, *Baby and Child Care* urged mothers always to think of their children first (Spock assigned fathers little formal role in child rearing). Following Spock's advice, millions of women tried to be mother, teacher, psychologist, and playmate to their children. If they "failed" in any of these roles, guilt was the inevitable outcome.

Dr. Spock on Child Rearing

Social critic Philip Wylie denounced such selfless behavior as "Momism." In the guise of sacrificing for her children, Wylie wrote in *Generation of Vipers*, Mom was pursuing "love of herself." She smothered her children with affection to make them emotionally dependent on her and reluctant to leave home. Women were caught in a double bind, for if they pursued a life outside the home, they were accused of being "imitation men" or "neurotic" feminists. Echoing psychoanalyst Sigmund Freud,

"Momism"

critics of working mothers contended that a woman could be happy and fulfilled only through domesticity.

In an era in which wives tended to subordinate their career goals to those of their husbands, the percentage of women with college degrees dropped from 41 percent in 1940 to 24 percent in 1950. At the postgraduate level, only 10 percent of doctorates earned in the United States went to women, compared with 13 percent in 1940 and 18 percent in 1930. The 1960s would reverse this trend, but it would take another ten years to return to earlier levels.

In postwar America, there was a wide gap between sexual behavior and public discourse on the subject. When Dr. Alfred Kinsey, director of the Institute for Sex Research at Indiana University, published his pioneering study *Sexual Behavior in the Human Male* (1948), the American public was shocked. But five years later Kinsey caused an uproar with *Sexual Behavior in the Human Female*, which revealed that 62 percent of women masturbated and 50 percent had had intercourse before marriage.

Fear of Women's Sexuality

Family, church, state, and media alike warned Americans that sex was wrong outside marriage and that premarital, extramarital, and homosexual behavior would bring "familial chaos and weaken the country's moral fiber." Women often were blamed for the impending disaster; despite any evidence of significant increases in women's sexual activity from the 1920s to the 1960s, female lust was perceived to pose the greatest sexual threat to the future of the family. Thus from Momism to promiscuity, American women were the victims of male-inspired stereotypes.

Education, Religion, and the Consumer Culture

Education at all levels was a pressing concern for families in postwar America. Immediately after the Second World War, for example, many former GIs enrolled in college. The legislation that made this possible was the Servicemen's Readjustment Act of 1944, popularly known as the GI Bill of Rights, which provided living allowances and tuition payments to college-bound veterans. Over 1 million veterans enrolled in 1946—accounting for one of every two students. A downside of the ex-GI education story is that colleges turned away qualified women to make room for the veterans.

As the baby boom became a grade-school boom, American families became preoccupied with the education of their children. Convinced that

Education of the Baby-Boom Generation

success in school was a prerequisite for success in adult life, parents joined parent-teacher associations so they would have a voice in the educational process. Then in 1957 education became a matter of national security. In that year the Soviet Union launched *Sputnik*, the first earth-orbiting satellite. A concerned Congress responded in 1958 with the National Defense Education Act (NDEA), which funded enrichment of elementary and high-school programs in mathematics, foreign languages, and the sciences and offered fellowships and loans to college students.

As education became intertwined with national security, so religion became a matter of patriotism. As President Eisenhower put it, "Recognition of

Growth of Religion

the Supreme Being is the first, the most basic expression of Americanism." And in 1954, Eisenhower signed a law inserting the words "under God" after "one nation" in the Pledge of Allegiance to the flag. In America's Cold War with an atheistic enemy, religious leaders emphasized traditional values like family togetherness. The Bible topped the bestseller list, and church membership increased from 71.7 million in 1945 to 116 million in 1961.

The postwar religious revival was also spurred by the introduction of a revolutionary influence in American life: television. The evangelist Billy Graham, who preached in stadiums

TV Enters the American Home

throughout the country, could reach mass audiences on television. Television's most important impact, however, was not on religion but on its trans-

formation of family. "More than a year passed before we again visited a movie theater. . . . Social evenings with friends became fewer and fewer still because we discovered we did not share the same television program interests," recalled a man whose parents bought their first television set in 1950.

Television was a crucial force in the evolution of the consumer culture. TV told people what to buy; and as families strove to acquire the latest luxuries and conveniences, shopping became a form of recreation. TV's number-one product was entertainment, and situation comedies and action series were among the most popular shows. But as average TV-viewing time reached five hours a day in 1956 and continued to rise, critics worried that TV's distorted presentation of the world would significantly define people's sense of reality.

An obvious casualty of the stay-at-home suburban culture was the motion picture. From 1946 to 1948 Americans had attended movies at the rate

Rise of the Youth Subculture

of nearly 90 million a week. By 1950 that figure had dropped to 60 million a week; by 1960, to 40 million. The postwar years saw the steady closing of movie theaters—with the notable exception of the drive-in, which appealed to car-oriented suburban families and teenagers. In fact, teenagers were the one exception to the downturn in moviegoing. By the late 1950s the first wave of the postwar baby boom had reached adolescence, and they were flocking to the theaters. Hollywood catered to this new audience with films portraying young people as sensitive and insightful, adults as boorish and hostile. *Rebel Without a Cause* (1955), starring James Dean, was one such movie. The cult of youth had been born.

Soon the music industry began catering to teens with inexpensive 45-rpm records. Bored with the era's syrupy music, young Americans were electrified by the driving energy and hard beat of Bill Haley and the Comets, Chuck Berry, Little Richard, and Buddy Holly. Although few white musicians acknowledged the debt, the roots of rock 'n' roll lay in African-American rhythm and blues.

Consumerism was strikingly evident in Americans' postwar play and in the era's fads. Slinky, selling for a dollar, began loping down people's stairs in 1947; Silly Putty was introduced in 1950. The era also had 3-D movies and Hula-Hoops. Another postwar fad was the family vacation. With more money and leisure time and a much-improved highway system, middle-class families took vacations that formerly had been restricted to the rich.

The consumer society was unreceptive to social criticism. The filmgoing public preferred noncontroversial movies. Even serious artists tended to ignore the country's social problems. But there were exceptions. Ralph Ellison's *Invisible Man* (1952) gave white Americans a glimpse of the psychic costs to black Americans of exclusion from the American Dream. And one group of writers noisily repudiated the materialistic and self-congratulatory world of the middle class and the suburbs. Beat (for "beatific") writers rejected both social niceties and literary conventions and flaunted their freewheeling sexuality and consumption of drugs. The Beats produced some memorable prose and poetry, including Allen Ginsberg's angry incantational poem *Howl* (1956) and Jack Kerouac's novel *On the Road* (1957). Although the Beats were largely ignored during the 1950s, millions of young Americans discovered their writings and imitated their lifestyle in the 1960s.

Beat Generation

The Other America

In an age of abundance, most Americans dismissed poverty, if they noticed it at all, as the fault of poor people themselves. But in 1961 about 42.5 million Americans (nearly one of every four) were poor. Age, race, gender, education, and marital status were all factors in their poverty. One-fourth of the poor were over age sixty-five. One-fifth were people of color. Two-thirds lived in households headed by a person with an eighth-grade education or less, one-fourth in households headed by a single woman. More than one-third were under age eighteen. Few of these people had much reason for hope.

While millions of Americans (most of them white) were settling in the suburbs, the poor were congregating in the inner cities. Almost 4.5 million African-Americans migrated to the cities from the South between the war years and the end of the 1960s. Joining African-Americans in the exodus to the cities were poor whites from the southern Appalachians. Meanwhile, Latin Americans were arriving in growing numbers from Mexico, the Dominican Republic, Colombia, Ecuador, and Cuba. And New York City's Puerto Rican population exploded.

Poverty in the Inner Cities

Second only to African-Americans in numbers of urban newcomers were Mexican-Americans. Millions came as farm workers during and after the Second World War, and increasing numbers remained to make their lives in the United States. Despite the initiation in 1953 of Operation Wetback, a federal program to find and deport illegal aliens, Mexicans continued to enter the country in large numbers, many of them illegally. Most settled in cities. According to the 1960 census, over 500,000 Mexican-Americans had migrated to the *barrios* of the Los Angeles–Long Beach area since 1940. Estimates of uncounted illegal aliens suggest that the actual total was far higher. The same was true in the *barrios* in southwestern and northern cities.

Mexican-Americans

Native Americans, whose average annual income was barely half of the poverty level, were the country's poorest people. Many Native Americans moved to the cities in the 1950s and 1960s. Accustomed to semicommunal rural life on the reservation, many had difficulty adjusting to the urban environment. Like other migrant groups, they found cities to be not places of hope but dumping grounds for the poor.

American Indians

Not all of the poor, however, lived in cities. In 1960, 30 percent still lived in small towns, 15 percent on farms. Tenant farmers and sharecroppers, both black and white, continued to suffer severe economic hardship. Migratory farm workers lived in abject poverty. In postwar America, elderly people tended to be poor regardless of where they lived.

A disproportionate share of the poor were women. Occupational segregation was pervasive, thus many women were forced to take low-paying jobs as laundresses, short-order cooks, and janitors. Median annual earnings for full-time women workers stood at 60 percent of men's earnings in 1960. Moreover, many women's jobs were not covered by either the minimum wage or Social Security. And when families broke up, the woman was usually left with responsibility for the children. Many divorced fathers did not keep up their regular child-support payments. Single mothers and their children, dependent on welfare or low wages, more often than not slipped into poverty.

Women in Poverty

With the publication of Michael Harrington's *The Other America* in 1962, people became aware of the contradiction of poverty in their midst. America's poor, wrote Harrington, were "the strangest poor in the history of mankind." For they "exist within the most powerful and rich society the world has ever known."

The Election of 1960 and the Dawning of a New Decade

The election of 1960 was one of the closest and most hard fought in the twentieth century. The forty-three-year-old Democratic candidate, Senator John F. Kennedy, injected new vigor and glamour into presidential politics. The Republican candidate was Richard M. Nixon, the forty-seven-year-old vice president from California.

Kennedy, exploiting the media to great advantage, ran a risky but ultimately brilliant race. Aware that his major liability with voters was his Roman Catholicism, he addressed the issue head-on: he went to the Bible Belt to tell a group of Houston ministers that he respected the separation of church and state and would take his orders from the American people, not the pope. Seeing opportunity in the African-American vote and calculating that his running mate, Senator Lyndon B. Johnson of Texas, could keep the white South loyal to the Democrats, Kennedy courted black voters. Kennedy also ben-

How and Why Kennedy Beat Nixon

efited both from Eisenhower's lukewarm endorsement of Nixon and from the unsavory image Nixon projected in the nation's first televised presidential debates.

Foreign policy was another major issue. Nixon claimed that he alone knew how to deal with Communists, but Kennedy countered that Eisenhower and Nixon had let American prestige and power erode, and he promised victory instead of stalemate in the Cold War. Kennedy subscribed to the two fundamental tenets of the postwar consensus—economic growth and anticommunism—and asserted that he could expand the benefits of economic progress and win foreign disputes through more vigorous leadership.

In an election characterized by the highest voter participation (63 percent) in a half-century, Kennedy defeated Nixon by the razor-slim margin

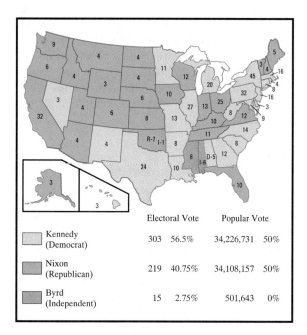

	Electoral Vote		Popular Vote	
Kennedy (Democrat)	303	56.5%	34,226,731	50%
Nixon (Republican)	219	40.75%	34,108,157	50%
Byrd (Independent)	15	2.75%	501,643	0%

Presidential Election, 1960 *In 1960, John F. Kennedy won the closest presidential election in twentieth-century American history. In fact, Richard M. Nixon won the popular votes of 26 states to Kennedy's 24. In the electoral college, 15 southerners voted for neither Kennedy nor Nixon but cast protest votes for Harry F. Byrd, a conservative senator from Virginia.*

of 118,000 votes. Kennedy's electoral college margin, 303 to 219, was much closer than the numbers suggest (see map, page 546). Slight shifts in the popular vote in Illinois and Texas—two states where electoral fraud helped produce narrow Democratic majorities—would have made Nixon president. Kennedy's victory made him the nation's first Roman Catholic president.

 ## Conclusion

Politically and culturally, the 1960s were to prove vastly different from the postwar years that immediately preceded them. During the Cold War presidencies of Truman and Eisenhower, the country was engaged in a moral struggle with communism; and during such a crusade, people believed, one should support, not criticize, the government. Most white Americans believed that the United States was the greatest nation in the world and that its potential was boundless. For middle-class Americans, the American dream seemed a reality.

Only a few years later, however, comfortable middle-class Americans discovered that millions of poor people were living in their midst and that most of them had been deprived of the civil rights the rest of the nation took for granted. Ironically, it would be the privileged children of suburbia—the generation of the baby boom—who would join the movement to eradicate not only racism and poverty but the whole value system of the postwar American middle class.

Suggestions for Further Reading

An Age of Consensus

Paul A. Carter, *Another Part of the Fifties* (1983); John Patrick Diggins, *The Proud Decades: America in War and Peace, 1941–1960* (1988); David Halberstam, *The Fifties* (1993); Marty Jezer, *The Dark Ages: Life in the United States, 1945–1960* (1982); Douglas T. Miller and Marion Novak, *The Fifties* (1977); William L. O'Neill, *American High: The Years of Confidence, 1945–1960* (1986); James T. Patterson, *Grand Expectations: The United States, 1945–1974* (1996); Richard H. Pells, *The Liberal Mind in a Conservative Age* (1985); Stephen J. Whitfield, *The Culture of the Cold War*, rev. ed. (1996).

The Presidency of Harry S Truman

Robert J. Donovan, *Tumultuous Years: The Presidency of Harry S Truman, 1949–1953* (1982), and *Conflict and Crisis: The Presidency of Harry S Truman, 1945–1948* (1977); Robert H. Ferrell, *Harry S Truman* (1994); Alonzo L. Hamby, *Man of the People: The Life of Harry S Truman* (1995); Donald R. McCoy, *The Presidency of Harry S Truman* (1984); David McCullough, *Truman* (1992).

Eisenhower and the Politics of the 1950s

Charles C. Alexander, *Holding the Line* (1975); Stephen E. Ambrose, *Eisenhower: The President* (1984); Robert F. Burk, *Dwight D. Eisenhower* (1986); Donald L. Fixico, *Termination and Relocation: Federal Indian Policy, 1945–1960* (1986); Fred I. Greenstein, *The Hidden-Hand Presidency* (1982); Chester J. Pach, Jr., and Elmo Richardson, *The Presidency of Dwight D. Eisenhower*, rev. ed. (1991); Mark H. Rose, *Interstate: Express Highway Politics, 1941–1956* (1979).

McCarthyism

Richard M. Fried, *Nightmare in Red* (1990); Robert Griffith, *The Politics of Fear: Joseph R. McCarthy and the Senate*, rev. ed. (1987); Maurice Isserman, *If I Had a Hammer . . . : The Death of the Old Left and the Birth of the New Left* (1987); Harvey Klehr and Ronald Radosh, *The Amerasia Spy Case* (1996); Stanley I. Kutler, *The American Inquisition* (1982); David M. Oshinsky, *A Conspiracy So Immense: The World of Joe McCarthy* (1983); Richard Gid Powers, *Not Without Honor: The History of American Anticommunism* (1995); Thomas C. Reeves, *The Life and Times of Joe McCarthy* (1982); Ellen W. Schrecker, *No Ivory Tower: McCarthyism in the Universities* (1986).

The Civil Rights Movement

Taylor Branch, *Parting the Waters: America in the King Years, 1954–1963* (1988); Robert F. Burk, *The Eisenhower Administration and Black Civil Rights* (1984); William H. Chafe, *Civilities and Civil Rights: Greensboro, North Carolina, and the Black Struggle for Freedom* (1980); Richard M. Dalfiume, *Desegregation of the U.S. Armed Forces* (1969); David J. Garrow, *Bearing the Cross: Martin Luther King, Jr., and the Southern Christian Leadership Conference* (1986); Richard Kluger, *Simple Justice: The History of Brown v. Board of Education and Black America's Struggle for Equality* (1975); Robyn D. Ladino, *Desegregating Texas Schools: Eisenhower, Shivers, and the Crisis at Mansfield High* (1996); Stephen B. Oates, *Let the Trumpet Sound: The Life of Martin Luther King, Jr.* (1982); Mark V. Tushnet, *The NAACP's Legal Strategy Against Segregated Education* (1987); Jules Tygiel, *Baseball's Great Experiment: Jackie Robinson and His Legacy* (1983); Stephen J. Whitfield, *A Death in the Delta: The Story of Emmett Till* (1991).

The Baby Boom and Cold War Families

Landon Y. Jones, *Great Expectations: America and the Baby Boom Generation* (1980); Donald Katz, *Home Fires: An Intimate Portrait of One Middle-Class Family in Postwar America* (1992); Paul

Leinberger and Bruce Tucker, *The New Individualists: The Generation After the Organization Man* (1991); Elaine Tyler May, *Homeward Bound: American Families in the Cold War Era* (1988); John Modell, *Into One's Own: From Youth to Adulthood in the United States, 1920–1975* (1989); Grace Palladino, *Teenagers* (1996).

Suburbia and the Spread of Education

Robert Fishman, *Bourgeois Utopias* (1987); Herbert J. Gans, *The Levittowners* (1967); Mark I. Gelfand, *A Nation of Cities* (1975); Dolores Hayden, *Redesigning the American Dream* (1984); Kenneth T. Jackson, *Crabgrass Frontier: The Suburbanization of the United States* (1985); Zane L. Miller, *Suburb* (1982); Diane Ravitch, *The Troubled Crusade: American Education, 1945–1980* (1983); Joel Spring, *The Sorting Machine: National Educational Policy Since 1945* (1976).

Women, Work, and Family Togetherness

Wini Breines, *Young, White, and Miserable: Growing Up Female in the Fifties* (1992); Ruth Schwartz Cowan, *More Work for Mother* (1983); Myra Dinnerstein, *Women Between Two Worlds* (1992); Barbara Ehrenreich, *The Hearts of Men: American Dreams and the Flight from Commitment* (1983); Cynthia Harrison, *On Account of Sex: The Politics of Women's Issues, 1945–1968* (1988); Eugenia Kaledin, *Mothers and More: American Women in the 1950s* (1984); Susan Lynn, *Progressive Women in Conservative Times* (1992); Glenna Matthews, *"Just a Housewife"* (1987); Joanne J. Meyerowitz, ed., *Not June Cleaver: Women and Gender in Postwar America, 1945–1960* (1994); Leila J. Rupp and Verta Taylor, *Survival in the Doldrums: The American Women's Rights Movement, 1945 to the 1960s* (1987); Susan Strasser, *Never Done: A History of American Housework* (1982).

The Affluent Society

Loren Baritz, *The Good Life: The Meaning of Success for the American Middle Class* (1982); Martin Campbell-Kelly and William Aspray, *Computer: A History of the Information Machine* (1996); John Kenneth Galbraith, *The Affluent Society* (1958); Ann Markusen et al., *Rise of the Gunbelt: The Military Remapping of Industrial America* (1991); Kirkpatrick Sale, *Power Shift: The Rise of the Southern Rim and Its Challenge to the Eastern Establishment* (1975).

Farmers and Laborers

Gilbert C. Fite, *American Farmers* (1981); James R. Green, *The World of the Worker* (1980); Nelson Lichtenstein, *The Most Dangerous Man in Detroit: Walter Reuther and the Fate of American Labor* (1995); George Lipsitz, *Rainbow at Midnight: Labor and Culture in the 1940s* (1994); John L. Shover, *First Majority—Last Minority: The Transforming of Rural Life in America* (1976).

The Other America

Richard B. Craig, *The Bracero Program* (1971); J. Wayne Flint, *Dixie's Forgotten People: The South's Poor Whites* (1979); Mario T. Garcia, *Mexican Americans: Leadership, Ideology, and Identity, 1930–1960* (1990); Michael Harrington, *The Other America*, rev. ed. (1981); Dorothy K. Newman et al., *Politics and Prosperity: Black Americans and White Institutions, 1940–75* (1978); James T. Patterson, *America's Struggle Against Poverty, 1900–1994*, rev. ed. (1994).

Postwar Culture

Peter Biskind, *Seeing Is Believing: How Hollywood Taught Us to Stop Worrying and Love the Fifties* (1983); Paul Boyer, *By the Bomb's Early Light: American Thought and Culture at the Dawn of the Atomic Age* (1985); Thomas Doherty, *Projections of War: Hollywood, American Culture, and World War II* (1993); James Gilbert, *A Cycle of Outrage: America's Reaction to the Juvenile Delinquent* (1986); Charlie Gillett, *The Sound of the City: The Rise of Rock and Roll*, rev. ed. (1983); Todd Gitlin, *Inside Prime Time* (1983); William S. Graebner, *The Age of Doubt: American Thought and Culture in the 1940s* (1991); Karal Ann Marling, *As Seen on TV: The Visual Culture of Everyday Life in the 1950s* (1994); Lary May, ed., *Recasting America: Culture and Politics in the Age of Cold War* (1989); Nora Sayre, *Running Time: Films of the Cold War* (1982); Ella Taylor, *Prime-Time Families: Television Culture in Postwar America* (1989); Allan M. Winkler, *Life Under a Cloud: American Anxiety About the Bomb* (1993).

29

Foreign Relations Glacier: The Cold War and Its Aftermath

1945–Present

Presidential Harry S Truman's advisers anxiously ranked his March 12, 1947, speech to Congress as important as any presidential address since Pearl Harbor. But they knew that Truman had a selling job to do if he wanted this Congress to endorse his request for $400 million in aid to Greece and Turkey. The Republican 80th Congress wanted less, not more, spending. Republican Senator Arthur Vandenberg of Michigan bluntly told the president that he would have to "scare hell out of the American people" to gain congressional approval.

The president delivered a speech laced with alarmist language intended to stake out the United States's role in the postwar world. Truman claimed that communism, feeding on economic dislocations, imperiled the world. "If Greece should fall under the control of an armed minority," he gravely concluded in an early version of the domino theory, "the effect upon its neighbor, Turkey, would be immediate and serious. Confusion and disorder might well spread throughout the entire Middle East." At the time, civil war in which communists played a prominent role rocked Greece. At issue, Truman insisted, was the very security of the United States.

Especially momentous in the dramatic speech were the words, later known as the *Truman Doctrine*, that would guide American policymakers

• Important Events •

1945 Roosevelt dies; Truman becomes president

1946 Winston Churchill gives "iron curtain" speech

Baruch Plan to control atomic weapons fails

1947 Truman Doctrine launches containment doctrine

Walter Lippmann's critique of containment, *The Cold War*, is published

Communists take power in Hungary

Kennan ("Mr. X") articulates containment doctrine

Marshall Plan for European recovery announced

National Security Act creates Defense Department and CIA

1948 Organization of American States founded

Fulbright Program of academic exchanges begins

Communists take power in Czechoslovakia

Truman recognizes Israel

United States organizes Berlin airlift

1949 North Atlantic Treaty Organization founded

USSR explodes atomic bomb

Communist victory brings Mao Zedong to power in China

1950 NSC-68 calls for a huge United States military buildup

Korean War breaks out in June; China enters in fall

1951 Truman fires General Douglas MacArthur

Armistice talks begin in Korea

United States occupation of Japan ended; Japanese-American security treaty is signed

1952 United States explodes first H-bomb

1953 Dwight D. Eisenhower becomes president

Soviet premier Joseph Stalin dies

Korean War ends

1954 Sino-American crisis over Jinmen (Quemoy) and Mazu (Matsu)

1955 Soviets organize Warsaw Pact

1956 Soviets crush uprising in Hungary

1957 Soviets fire first intercontinental ballistic missile and launch *Sputnik*

1958 United States and USSR sign cultural exchange agreement

National Aeronautics and Space Administration created

Jinmen-Mazu crisis recurs

Berlin crisis erupts

1959 Fidel Castro ousts Fulgencio Batista in Cuba

1960 United States imposes economic embargo on Cuba

Soviets shoot down U-2 spy plane

1961 John F. Kennedy becomes president

Bay of Pigs invasion fails in Cuba

Berlin Wall is built

1962 Cuban missile crisis brings world to brink of nuclear war

1963 Limited Test-Ban Treaty prohibits atmospheric testing of nuclear weapons

Kennedy is assassinated; Lyndon B. Johnson becomes president

1967 Summit meeting in Glassboro, New Jersey

1968 Nuclear nonproliferation treaty signed

Soviets invade Czechoslovakia

1969 Richard M. Nixon becomes president and, with Henry Kissinger, launches détente

1972 Nixon visits China and ends years of Sino-American isolation

SALT-I Treaty limits ABMs and strategic nuclear weapons

1977 Jimmy Carter becomes president and presses human-rights policy

1979 SALT-II Treaty acknowledges Soviet-American nuclear parity

Soviets invade Afghanistan

1980 Carter Doctrine declares United States will defend Persian Gulf area

United States imposes grain embargo and boycott of Olympic Games against Soviets

• *Important Events* •

1981	Ronald Reagan becomes president Soviet crackdown in Poland prompts United States trade restrictions on USSR Nuclear freeze movement grows worldwide	**1991**	START-I Treaty reduces nuclear warheads in USSR and the United States USSR dissolves into independent states Yeltsin replaces Gorbachev Agreement bans oil exploration and mining in Antarctica Ethnic wars break out in former Yugoslavia
1982	START negotiations, to reduce strategic nuclear forces, begin	**1992**	United States in the minority at Rio Earth Summit Canada, Mexico, and United States sign North American Free Trade Agreement START-II agreement reduces warheads and ICBMs
1983	United States announces Strategic Defense Initiative ("Star Wars") Soviets shoot down Korean airliner		
1985	Reagan Doctrine promises United States aid to anti-Soviet "freedom fighters" Premier Mikhail Gorbachev initiates *glasnost* and *perestroika* reforms in USSR United States and USSR disagree over "Star Wars" at Geneva summit	**1993**	Bill Clinton becomes president
		1994	NAFTA becomes operative, creating the world's largest free-trade bloc
1987	INF Treaty bans land-based intermediate-range nuclear missiles in Europe	**1995**	United States brokers peace agreement for Bosnia American troops join NATO peacekeeping force in Bosnia World Conference on Women calls for "human rights and fundmental freedoms"
1989	George Bush becomes president United States and other nations agree to phaseout of ozone-destroying chemicals Berlin Wall opens Chinese armed forces kill prodemocracy demonstrators in Tiananmen Square		
		1996	Clinton criticizes isolationism
		1997	Madeleine Albright is first woman to become secretary of state
1990	Communist regimes in eastern Europe collapse Iraq invades Kuwait to spark Persian Gulf War Reunification of Germany	**1998**	Clinton extends Bosnian mission Terrorists bomb United States embassy in Africa and United States retaliates

for almost a half-century: "I believe that it must be the policy of the United States to support free peoples who are resisting attempted subjugation by armed minorities or by outside pressures." Two new and young members of the House of Representatives, John F. Kennedy and Richard M. Nixon, applauded Truman's message that day. When they assumed the presidency in the 1960s, the Truman Doctrine still guided their policies.

The Truman Doctrine helped launch the *containment doctrine:* the idea that the United States had to draw the line against communism everywhere. American presidents from Truman to George Bush believed that a ruthless Soviet Union was directing a worldwide communist conspiracy against peace, free-market capitalism, and political democracy. Soviet leaders from Joseph Stalin to Mikhail Gorbachev protested that a militarized, economically aggressive United States sought nothing less than world domination. This contest between the United States and the Soviet Union soon acquired the name *Cold War.*

The Cold War was fundamentally a bipolar contest between the United States and the

Soviet Union over spheres of influence, over world power. The two nations never fought one another directly on the battlefield. Instead, they waged the Cold War through competing alliances (the capitalist "West" versus the communist "East"), regional wars between client states, rival ideologies, foreign aid and economic sanctions, covert operations and propaganda, and an arms race that included nuclear weapons. Like a glacier, the Cold War began in the 1940s to cut across the global terrain, changing the topography of international relations. The contest took the lives of millions, emptied the treasuries of the combatants, spawned fears of doomsday, and destabilized politics in one nation after another, dragging localized conflicts into its path. Sometimes the two superpowers signed agreements to temper the arms race; at other times they went to the brink of war and armed allies to fight vicious wars in the Third World (see Chapter 30).

Throughout the Cold War era, critics in the United States challenged the architects of the Cold War. In the atmosphere of the time, however, dissenters were suspect and discredited. The critics' searching questions about the necessity and consequences of a global, interventionist foreign policy and a nuclear strategy based on the doctrine of "mutual assured destruction" (MAD) were drowned out by redbaiting charges that they were "soft on communism," if not un-American.

Ultimately the two great powers, weakened by the huge costs of their competition and challenged by other nations and blocs, took steps in the late 1980s to halt the Cold War. Its end finally came in 1991 with the disintegration of the Soviet Union, the collapse of other communist regimes in Eastern Europe, and the reunification of Germany.

Like a retreating glacier, the Cold War left behind a scarred landscape and debris that complicated the shaping of a new world order. For years after the Cold War ended, American leaders found it difficult to define new doctrines and to clarify United States interests, responsibilities, and capabilities in a new era that lacked a Soviet threat. Americans expected a "peace dividend" redirecting Cold War spending to domestic needs, but it failed to materialize.

 ## Sources of the Cold War

After the Second World War, the international system was so unsettled that conflict became virtually inevitable. With much of Europe and Asia reduced to rubble, economic chaos rocked the two continents. The Americans and the Soviets offered very different models for piecing together the devastated economic world. The collapse of Germany and Japan, moreover, had created power vacuums that drew the two major powers into collision as they sought influence in countries where the Axis once had held sway. And the political turmoil that many nations experienced after the war also spurred Soviet-American competition.

Unsettled International System

The international system also became unstable because empires were disintegrating. Financial constraints and nationalist rebellions forced the European imperial states to set their colonies free. As new nations gained independence in the Middle East and Asia, America and the Soviet Union vied to win these Third World states as allies that might provide military bases, resources, and markets. The shrinkage of the globe also ensured conflict. With the advent of the airplane, the world had become more compact. Faster travel brought nations closer at the same time that it made them more vulnerable to surprise attack from the air. The Americans and the Soviets collided as they strove to establish defensive positions, sometimes far from home.

Driven by different ideologies and different economic and strategic needs, the United States and the Soviet Union downgraded diplomacy to build what Secretary of State Dean Acheson (1949–1953) called "situations of strength." Both nations marched into the Cold War with convictions of righteousness, and each saw the other as the world's bully. While Americans feared "communist aggression," Soviets feared "capitalist encirclement."

American officials vowed never to repeat the experience of the 1930s; they would accept no more Munichs, no more appeasement, and no more depressions that might spawn political extremism and war. To many Americans, it seemed that Soviet Russia had simply replaced Nazi Germany, that communism was simply the flip side of the totalitarian coin.

American officials also knew that the nation's economic well-being depended on an activist foreign policy. In the postwar years the United States stood as the largest supplier of goods to world markets, but that trade was jeopardized by the postwar economic paralysis of Europe and by discriminatory trade practices that violated the Open Door doctrine. To prevent another depression, America's factories and farms needed access to foreign markets. And the United States also had to import essential minerals such as zinc, tin, and manganese. Thus economic expansionism, so much a part of pre–Cold War history, remained a central feature of postwar foreign relations.

United States Economic and Strategic Needs

New strategic theory also propelled the United States toward an expansionist, globalist diplomacy. To be ready for a military challenge in the postwar "air age," American strategists believed, the nation's defenses had to extend far beyond its own borders. Thus the United States sought overseas bases to guard the approaches to the Western Hemisphere. These bases also would permit the United States to launch offensive attacks with might and speed.

President Truman, who shared those assumptions, had a personality ill suited for diplomacy. Whereas Franklin D. Roosevelt—whom Truman succeeded in 1945—had been ingratiating, patient, and evasive, Truman was brash, impatient, and direct. He often glossed over nuances, ambiguities, and counterevidence, preferring instead the simple answer stated in either-or terms. When Truman met the Soviet commissar for foreign affairs in 1945, the president sharply demanded that the Soviet Union honor the Yalta agreement on Poland. Though the commissar stormed out, the president bragged that "I gave it to him straight 'one-two to the

Truman's Get-Tough Style

jaw.'" Truman's display of toughness became a trademark of American Cold War diplomacy.

Fearful of a revived Germany and a resurgent Japan, anticipating that capitalist nations once again would attempt to extinguish the communist flame, and facing a monumental task of economic reconstruction, the Soviets made territorial gains. These included eastern Poland; the Baltic states of Lithuania, Latvia, and Estonia; and parts of Finland and Romania. In Eastern Europe Soviet officials began to suppress noncommunists and install communist clients. The Americans, Premier Joseph Stalin protested, were surrounding the USSR with hostile bases and practicing atomic and dollar diplomacy.

The Soviet Perspective

Throughout the Cold War era, Americans debated Soviet intentions and capabilities. Some believed that the Soviet Union—well armed, opportunistic, and aggressive—could never be trusted. Others charged that American officials exaggerated the Soviet/communist threat.

In fact, the Soviet Union of the immediate postwar period suffered a hobbled economy and was a regional power in Eastern Europe, not a global menace. American leaders feared that the ravaging postwar economic and social unrest abroad would leave American strategic and economic interests vulnerable to political disorders that the Soviets might exploit, perhaps through subversion. In other words, Americans feared Soviet seizure of opportunities to challenge United States's interests more than they feared a direct Soviet attack on Western Europe.

The United States took advantage of the postwar power vacuum to expand its overseas interests and shape a peace on American terms. The United States's pursuit of nuclear superiority, outlying bases, raw materials and markets, supremacy in Latin America, and control of the Atlantic and Pacific Oceans aroused many opponents, in particular the Soviet Union. To Americans, Soviet opposition simply confirmed Moscow's wicked obstructionism. George F. Kennan, one of the chief architects of Cold War policy, later came to believe that a distorted view of the Soviet Union as an "inhuman and malevolent adversary" had contributed to American abandonment of diplomacy during the early Cold War.

Europe, Containment, and Global Polarization

One of the first Soviet-American clashes came in Poland in 1945, when the Soviets refused to allow conservative Poles from London to join the communist government in Lublin.

Soviet Sphere in Eastern Europe

Truman officials argued that the refusal violated the Yalta Agreement. The Soviets also snuffed out civil liberties in the former Nazi satellite of Romania. They initially allowed free elections in Hungary and Czechoslovakia, but as the Cold War accelerated and United States influence in Europe expanded, the Soviets encouraged communist coups: first Hungary (1947) and then Czechoslovakia (1948) succumbed to Soviet subversion. Yugoslavia was a unique case: its independent Communist government, led by Josip Broz Tito, successfully broke with Stalin in 1948.

To justify their actions, the Soviets pointed out that the United States was reviving their traditional enemy, Germany. The Soviets also protested that the United States was pursuing a double standard—intervening in the affairs of Eastern Europe but demanding that the Soviet Union stay out of Latin America and Asia.

The atomic bomb also divided the two major powers. The Soviets believed that the United States was practicing "atomic diplomacy"—maintaining a nuclear monopoly to scare the Soviets into diplomatic concessions.

Atomic Diplomacy

Whereas Secretary of State James F. Byrnes (1945–1947) actively practiced atomic diplomacy, Secretary of War Henry L. Stimson in 1945 warned Truman that carrying the weapon "ostentatiously on our hip" would increase Soviet "suspicions and . . . distrust of our purposes and motives."

In this atmosphere of suspicion and distrust, Truman refused to turn over the weapon to an international control authority. In 1946 he backed the Baruch Plan, which provided for the United States's abandonment of its monopoly only after the world's fissionable materials were brought under the authority of an international agency.

The Soviets retorted that this plan would require them to shut down their atomic-bomb development project while the United States continued its own. Washington and Moscow soon became locked into an expensive and frightening nuclear arms race.

Soviets and Americans clashed on every front in 1946. When the United States turned down a Soviet request for a reconstruction loan, Moscow denounced Washington for using its dollars to manipulate foreign governments. The two Cold War powers also backed different groups in Iran, where the United States helped bring the pro-West shah to the throne. Unable to agree on the unification of Germany, they built up their zones independently. The new World Bank and International Monetary Fund, created at the 1944 Bretton Woods Conference to stabilize trade and finance, also became tangled in the Cold War struggle. The Soviets refused to join because the United States so dominated both institutions.

After Stalin gave a speech in February 1946 that depicted the world as threatened by capitalist acquisitiveness, the American chargé d'affaires in Moscow, George F. Kennan

Kennan and Churchill on Soviet Expansion

asserted that Soviet fanaticism made even a temporary understanding impossible. Kennan's remarks fed a growing belief among American officials that only toughness would work with the Soviets. The following month, Winston Churchill delivered a stirring speech in Fulton, Missouri, in which he warned that a Soviet-erected "iron curtain" had cut off Eastern European countries from the West.

The Cold War escalated further in early 1947, when the British requested American help in Greece to defend their conservative client government against a leftist insurgency.

Greek Civil War and Truman Doctrine

The president asked Congress for aid to Greece and Turkey and enunciated the Truman Doctrine. Critics correctly pointed out that the Soviet Union was hardly involved in the Greek civil war and that the resistance movement had noncommunist as well as communist members. Nor was the Soviet Union threatening Turkey at the time. After much debate, the Senate approved Truman's request. Using United States dollars and military advisers, the Greek government defeated the insurgents in 1949, and Turkey became a staunch United States ally on the Soviets' border.

Four months after Truman's speech, State Department official George F. Kennan published an influential statement of the containment doctrine. Writing as "Mr. X" in the magazine *Foreign Affairs*, Kennan advocated a "policy of firm containment, designed to confront the Russians with unalterable counterforce at every point where they show signs of encroaching upon the interests of a peaceful and stable world." With the Truman Doctrine, Kennan's "X" article became a key manifesto of Cold War policy. The veteran journalist Walter Lippmann took issue with the containment doctrine in *The Cold War* (1947), calling it a "strategic monstrosity" that failed to distinguish between areas vital and peripheral to United States security.

George F. Kennan's "X" Article

Despite such debate, the United States invoked the containment doctrine in 1947 and 1948 and began to build an international economic and defensive network to protect American prosperity and security and to advance United States hegemony. In Western Europe, the region of primary concern, American diplomats pursued several objectives: economic reconstruction; ouster of communists from governments, as occurred in 1947 in France and Italy; blockage of "third force" or neutralist tendencies; a gradual decolonization of European empires; creation of a military alliance; and unification of the western zones of Germany.

The first instrument designed to achieve United States goals in western Europe was the Marshall Plan. The plan was unveiled in June 1947 when Secretary of State George C. Marshall (1947–1949) announced that the United States would finance a massive European recovery program. Launched in 1948, the Marshall Plan sent $12.4 billion to Western Europe before the program ended in

Marshall Plan

1951 (see map, page 556). To stimulate business at home, the legislation provided that the foreign aid dollars must be spent in the United States on American-made products. The Marshall Plan proved a mixed success. The program caused inflation, failed to solve a balance-of-payments problem, and further divided Europe between "East" and "West." But the program spurred impressive Western European industrial production and investment and started the region toward self-sustaining economic growth.

To streamline the administration of United States defense, the National Security Act (July 1947) created the Department of Defense (replacing the Department of War), the National Security Council (NSC) to advise the president, and the Central Intelligence Agency (CIA) to conduct spying and information gathering. By the early 1950s the CIA had expanded its functions to include covert (secret) operations aimed at overthrowing unfriendly foreign leaders.

In 1948 the United States implemented the Fulbright Program. The brainchild two years earlier of Democratic senator J. William Fulbright of Arkansas, this example of "public diplomacy" attempted to overcome cultural barriers to reach foreign peoples with a positive message about the United States. The Fulbright Program sponsored educational exchanges: professors and students from the United States went abroad to teach and study, and their counterparts from foreign countries came to the United States.

"Public Diplomacy" and Fulbright Program

American officials also made military linkages around the world. The United States granted the Philippines independence in 1946 while retaining military and economic hegemony there. The following year, American diplomats created the Rio Pact in Latin America. To enforce this military alliance, the United States helped found the Organization of American States (OAS) in 1948. Under this and other agreements the Truman administration sent several military missions to Latin America and to Greece, Turkey, Iran, China, and Saudi Arabia to improve the armed forces of those nations.

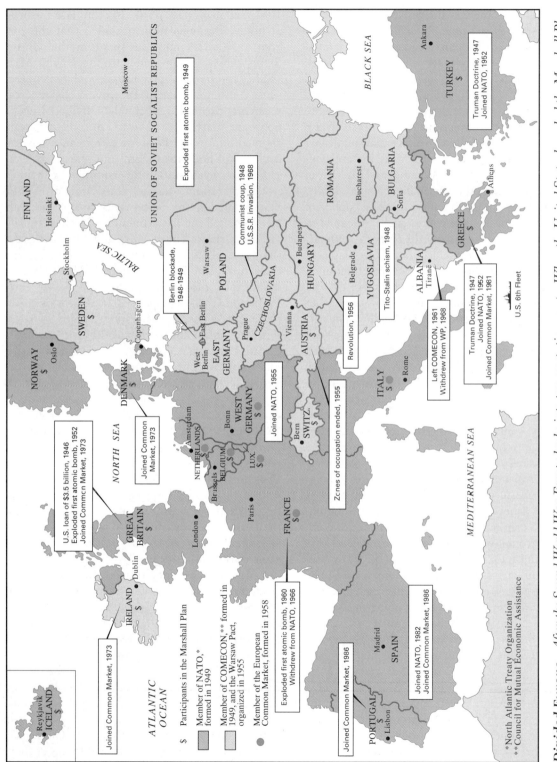

Divided Europe   *After the Second World War, Europe broke into two competing camps. When the United States launched the Marshall Plan in 1948, the Soviet Union countered with its own economic plan the following year. When the United States created NATO in 1949, the Soviet Union answered with the Warsaw Pact in 1955. On the whole, these two camps held firm until the late 1980s.*

In May 1948, Truman recognized the newly proclaimed state of Israel, which had been carved out of British-held Palestine. Despite State Department objection that recognition would alienate oil-rich Arab nations, Truman made the decision for three reasons: he believed that, after the Holocaust, Jews deserved a homeland; he desired Jewish-American votes in the upcoming election; and he sought another international ally.

Recognition of Israel

One of the most electric moments in the Cold War came in June 1948 after the Americans, French, and British had agreed to fuse their German zones, including their three sectors of Berlin. They sought to integrate West Germany (the Federal Republic of Germany) into the Western European economy, complete with a reformed German currency. Fearing a resurgent Germany tied to the American Cold War camp, the Soviets cut off Western access to the jointly occupied city of Berlin, located well inside the Soviet zone. In response to this bold move, President Truman ordered a massive airlift of food, fuel, and other supplies to Berlin. Their spoiling effort blunted, the Soviets finally lifted the blockade in May 1949 and founded the German Democratic Republic, or East Germany.

Berlin Blockade and Airlift

The Berlin crisis accelerated movement toward a Western security pact. The United States, Canada, and many western European nations founded the North Atlantic Treaty Organization (NATO) in April 1949 (see map, page 556). The treaty aroused considerable domestic debate, for not since 1778 had the United States entered a formal European military alliance. Administration officials defended the treaty by arguing that should the Soviets ever probe westward, NATO would function as a "tripwire," bringing the full force of the United States to bear on the Soviet Union. Truman officials also hoped that NATO would keep Western Europeans from embracing communism or neutralism. The Senate ratified the treaty, and the United States soon began to spend billions of dollars under the Mutual Defense Assistance Act.

Founding of NATO

In September 1949 the Soviets exploded an atomic bomb, ending the American nuclear monopoly. At the same time, communists led by Mao Zedong won the civil war in China. In early 1950, Truman ordered development of the hydrogen bomb. In April of that year, the National Security Council (NSC) delivered to the president a significant top-secret document tagged NSC-68. Predicting continued tension with expansionistic communists, the report appealed for a much enlarged military budget. Officials worried about how to sell this prescription to voters and budget-conscious members of Congress. "We were sweating over it, and then—with regard to NSC-68—thank God Korea came along," recalled one of Acheson's aides.

NSC-68

Confrontations in Asia: Japan, China, and the Korean War

Asia, like Europe, became ensnared in the Cold War. The victors in the Second World War dismantled Japan's empire. The United States and the Soviet Union divided Korea into competing spheres of influence. The Pacific islands (the Marshalls, Marianas, and Carolines) came under American control, and Formosa (Taiwan) was returned to China. As for Japan itself, the United States monopolized its reconstruction through a military occupation directed by General Douglas MacArthur. He wrote a democratic constitution for Japan, revitalized its economy, and destroyed the nation's weapons. In 1951, against Soviet protests, the United States and Japan signed a separate peace that restored Japan's sovereignty and ended the occupation. A Mutual Security Treaty that year provided for the stationing of United States forces on Japanese soil, including a base on Okinawa.

Reconstruction of Japan

Meanwhile, America's Chinese ally was faltering. The United States had long backed the Nationalists of Jiang Jieshi (Chiang Kai-shek)

Communist Victory in the Chinese Civil War

against Mao Zedong's communists. But Jiang had become an unreliable partner; his government had grown corrupt, inefficient, and out of touch with rebellious peasants, whom the communists enlisted with promises of land reform. Seeing Jiang as the only alternative to Mao, however, Truman backed him to the end.

American officials divided on the question of whether Mao was a puppet of the Soviet Union. Some considered him an Asian Tito—communist but independent—but most believed him to be part of an international communist movement that might give the Soviets a springboard into Asia. Thus when the Chinese communists made secret overtures to the United States to begin diplomatic talks in 1945 and again in 1949, American officials rebuffed them. Mao then "leaned" to the Soviet side in the Cold War, but China maintained a fierce independence that rankled the Soviets.

In the fall of 1949, Jiang fled to the island of Formosa, and Mao proclaimed the People's Republic of China (PRC). Truman hesitated to extend diplomatic recognition to the new government. He and other American officials became alarmed by the 1950 Sino-Soviet treaty of friendship and by the harassment of Americans and their property. Truman also chose nonrecognition because a vocal group of Republican critics, the so-called China lobby, was winning headlines by charging that the United States had "lost" China. Subsequent presidents also refused to recognize China, and not until 1979 did official Sino-American relations resume.

Nonrecognition of the People's Republic of China

In the early morning hours of June 25, 1950, a large military force of the Democratic People's Republic of Korea (North Korea) moved across the 38th parallel into the Republic of Korea (South Korea). Since 1945, when the great powers divided Korea, the two parts had been skirmishing along their supposedly temporary border. Both the

Outbreak of the Korean War

North's communist leader Kim Il Sung and the South's president Syngman Rhee sought to reunify their nation. Displaying the Cold War mentality of the time, however, President Truman refused to see the invasion as the outbreak of a civil war. Instead, he claimed that the Soviets had masterminded the North Korean attack.

Kim actually had to press a doubting Joseph Stalin, who only reluctantly approved the attack after Kim predicted an easy victory and after Mao Zedong backed Kim. The three communist leaders might have calculated that the United States would not come to South Korea's defense. In a public speech in early 1950, Secretary of State Dean Acheson had drawn the American defense line in Asia through the Aleutians, Japan, and Okinawa to the Philippines. Formosa and Korea clearly lay beyond that line. Acheson did say, however, that those areas could expect United Nations (and hence United States) assistance if attacked. Kim, Stalin, and Mao must have missed that point. Two other thoughts probably shifted Stalin to support Kim: first, if he did not support North Korea, Mao's China might gain influence over Kim; second, if the United States rearmed Japan, South Korea might once again become a beachhead for Japanese (and American) expansion.

Whatever Stalin's reasoning, his support for Kim's bold venture remained lukewarm. When the United Nations Security Council voted to defend South Korea, the Soviet representative was not even present to veto the resolution. And during the war, China grew angry at Stalin for reneging on promised Soviet airpower.

The president first ordered General Douglas MacArthur to send arms and troops to South Korea. Worried that Mao might attempt to take Formosa, Truman also directed the Seventh Fleet to patrol the waters between the Chinese mainland and Jiang's sanctuary on Formosa. After the Security Council voted to assist South Korea, MacArthur became commander of United Nations forces in Korea (90 percent of them American). Within weeks of the initial invasion, the North Koreans had pushed the South

Truman Commits United States Forces

Korean and American forces into the tiny Pusan perimeter at the base of South Korea.

General MacArthur planned a daring operation: an amphibious landing at heavily fortified Inchon, several hundred miles behind North Korean lines. After United States guns and bombs pounded Inchon, marines sprinted ashore on September 15, 1950. They soon liberated the South Korean capital of Seoul and pushed the North Koreans back to the 38th parallel.

In September Truman, with the intent of unifying the peninsula by force, authorized United Nations forces to cross the 38th parallel. These troops drove deep into North Korea, and American aircraft

Chinese Entry into the Korean War

began strikes against bridges on the Yalu River, the border between North Korea and China. Mao publicly warned that China could not permit the bombing of its transportation links with Korea and would not accept the annihilation of North Korea itself. Both MacArthur and officials in Washington shrugged off the warnings.

On October 25 Chinese soldiers entered the war near the Yalu. Perhaps to signal a willingness to begin negotiations, they pulled back after a brief offensive against South Korean troops. Then, after MacArthur sent the United States Eighth Army northward, tens of thousands of Chinese troops counterattacked on November 26, surprising United States forces and driving them pell-mell southward. MacArthur called for a massive air attack on China. Truman, reflecting on the costs and consequences of a wider war, rejected MacArthur's advice.

By early 1951 the front had stabilized around the 38th parallel. Both Washington and Moscow welcomed negotiations, but MacArthur recklessly called for an attack on China and for Jiang's return to the mainland. The general

Truman Fires MacArthur

also hinted that the president was practicing appeasement. In April, fed up with MacArthur's insubordination and backed by the Joint Chiefs of Staff, Truman fired him. Truman's popularity sagged, but he weathered demands for his impeachment.

Armistice talks began in July 1951, but the fighting and dying went on for two more years. The most contentious point in the negotiations was the fate of prisoners of war (POWs). Defying the Geneva

The POW Question

Prisoners of War Convention (1949), United States officials announced that only those North Korean and Chinese POWs who wished to go home would be returned. Responding to the American statement that there would be no forced repatriation, the North Koreans denounced forced retention.

Not until July 1953 was an armistice signed. The combatants agreed to hand over the POW question to a special panel of neutral nations, which later gave prisoners

War's End and Casualties

their choice of staying or leaving. (In the end, 70,000 of about 100,000 North Korean and 5,600 of 20,700 Chinese POWs elected to return home; 21 American and 325 South Korean POWs of some 11,000 decided to stay in North Korea.) The North Korean–South Korean borderline was set near the 38th parallel, the prewar boundary, and a demilitarized zone was created between the two Koreas. American casualties totaled 54,246 dead and 103,284 wounded. More than 4 million people died in the war, 2 million of them North Korean civilians.

The Korean War carried major political consequences. The failure to achieve victory and the public's impatience with a limited war undoubtedly helped to elect Eisenhower. The powers of the presidency grew as Congress repeatedly deferred to Truman. The president had never asked Congress for a declaration of war, believing that as commander-in-chief he had the authority to send troops wherever he wished.

The implementation of military containment worldwide became entrenched as United States policy. Increased American aid flowed to the French for their die-hard stand in Indochina against nationalist insurgents (see Chapter 30). Because of heightened Sino-American hostility, South Korea and Formosa became major recipients of American foreign aid. The United States's alliance with Japan strengthened. Australia and New Zealand joined the United

States in a mutual defense agreement, the ANZUS Treaty (1951). The United States Army sent six divisions to Europe, and the military budget shot up from $14 billion in 1949 to $44 billion in 1953. In sum, Truman's legacy was a highly militarized United States foreign policy active on a global scale.

 ## Eisenhower and the Nuclear Arms Race

President Dwight D. Eisenhower largely sustained Truman's Cold War policies after assuming the presidency in 1953. Eisenhower brought considerable experience in foreign affairs. As a general during the Second World War, he had negotiated with world leaders. After the war, he served as army chief of staff and NATO supreme commander. Eisenhower accepted the Cold War consensus about the threat of communism and the need for global vigilance. At the same time, however, he tamed the hawkish proposals of Vice President Richard Nixon and Secretary of State John Foster Dulles.

Eisenhower questioned Dulles's "practice of becoming a sort of international prosecuting attorney," but the president relied heavily on the stern, strong-willed secretary of state. Like the president, Dulles conceded much to the anticommunist McCarthyites, who claimed that the State Department was infested with communists. Dulles appointed one of Senator McCarthy's followers, Scott McLeod, chief security officer of the State Department. Targeting homosexuals and other "incompatibles," and making few distinctions between New Dealers and communists, McLeod and Dulles forced many talented officers out of the Foreign Service with unsubstantiated charges that they were disloyal. Among them were Asia specialists whose expertise was thus denied to the American leaders who later plunged the United States into war in Vietnam. "The wrong done," journalist Theodore A. White wrote, "was to poke out the eyes and ears of the State Department on Asian affairs, to blind American foreign policy."

Purge of the State Department

Dulles considered containment too defensive a stance toward communism. He called instead for *liberation*, although he never explained precisely how the countries of Eastern Europe could be freed from Soviet control. *Massive retaliation* was the administration's phrase for the nuclear obliteration of the Soviet state or its assumed client, the People's Republic of China, if either one took aggressive actions. The ability of the United States to make such a threat was thought to provide *deterrence*, the prevention of hostile Soviet behavior.

In their "New Look" for the American military, Eisenhower and Dulles emphasized airpower and nuclear weaponry. The president's preference for heavy weapons stemmed in part from his desire to trim the federal budget. The United States in the 1950s practiced *brinkmanship:* not backing down in a crisis, even if it meant taking the nation to the brink of war. Eisenhower also popularized the *domino theory:* the belief that small, weak, neighboring nations would fall to communism like a row of dominoes if they were not propped up by the United States.

Eisenhower increasingly utilized the Central Intelligence Agency as an instrument of foreign policy. The CIA put foreign leaders on its payroll, subsidized foreign labor unions and political parties, and planted false stories in newspapers through its "disinformation" projects. The CIA also launched covert operations (including assassination schemes) to subvert or destroy Third World governments that threatened United States economic interests and created unstable conditions communists could exploit.

CIA Covert Actions

The Eisenhower administration also sought to infiltrate American culture into the Soviet Union and its Eastern European allies as a means to popularize democratic principles and to stimulate public discontent with communist regimes. The primary propaganda tool was the United States Information Agency (USIA), founded in 1953. One of the USIA's agencies, Voice of America, broadcast news, editorials, and music worldwide. The CIA secretly funded Radio Free Europe,

Propaganda and Cultural Infiltration

operated since 1950 by anticommunist Eastern European émigrés.

The United States and the Soviet Union attempted to regularize cultural relations in January 1958 through an agreement that provided for reciprocal exchange of radio and television broadcasts, films, students, professors, and athletes.

Such expanded cultural relations did not calm the Cold War or tame the nuclear arms race. In November 1952 the United States detonated the

Nuclear Arms Race

first hydrogen bomb. The Soviets tested their first H-bomb in 1953. Four years later they shocked Americans by firing the world's first intercontinental ballistic missile (ICBM) and then propelling *Sputnik* into outer space. The United States soon tested its own ICBMs. It also enlarged its fleet of long-range bombers (B-52s) and deployed intermediate-range missiles in Europe, targeted against the Soviet Union. In 1960 the United States added Polaris missile–bearing submarines. To foster future technological advancement, it had created the National Aeronautics and Space Administration (NASA) in 1958.

The CIA's U-2 spy planes collected information demonstrating that the Soviets had deployed very few ICBMs. Yet politically partisan critics charged that Eisenhower had allowed the United States to fall behind in the missile race. The much-publicized "missile gap" was actually not in the Soviets' favor but rather America's. As the 1950s closed, the United States enjoyed overwhelming strategic dominance because of its air-sea-land "triad" of long-range bombers, submarine-launched ballistic missiles (SLBMs), and ICBMs.

President Eisenhower grew uneasy about the arms race. He feared nuclear war, and the cost of the new weapons made it difficult to balance the

Eisenhower's Critique of Nuclear Arms

budget. He also doubted the need for more and bigger nuclear weapons. Because of personal beliefs and neutralist and Soviet appeals, Eisenhower cautiously initiated arms control proposals. Even global concern over radioactive fallout, however, could not get the two powers to ban atmospheric testing. Neither the disarma-

Precariously balanced on the nuclear warhead of a menacing missile are Soviet premier Nikita Khrushchev (1894–1971) and United States president Dwight D. Eisenhower (1890–1969). In September 1959, Eisenhower hosted Khrushchev in the United States to "melt the ice" of the Cold War. Although the list of outstanding Soviet-American issues was lengthy—including the nuclear arms race and Berlin—their summit meeting did little to ease superpower tensions. © 1959 Newsweek Inc. All rights reserved. Reprinted by permission.

ment talks at Geneva, Switzerland, nor the 1955 summit meeting there between Eisenhower and Stalin's successor, Nikita Khrushchev, produced results. The best the Soviets and Americans could do was to suspend unilaterally atmospheric testing from 1958 to 1961.

In 1956 Soviet premier Nikita Khrushchev called for "peaceful coexistence" between capitalists and communists, denounced Stalin (who had

Hungarian Uprising

died in 1953), and suggested that Moscow would tolerate different brands of communism. Revolts against Soviet power erupted in Poland and Hungary, testing Khrushchev's new permissiveness. After a new Hungarian government in 1956 announced its withdrawal from the Warsaw Pact (the Soviet military alliance formed in 1955 with communist countries of Eastern Europe), Soviet troops and tanks battled students and workers in the streets of Budapest and crushed the rebellion. Although the Eisenhower administration had been encouraging "liberation" efforts, it was unable to aid the rebels without igniting a world war.

Hardly had the turmoil subsided in Eastern Europe when the divided city of Berlin once again became a Cold War flash point. The Soviets railed against the placement in West Germany of American bombers capable of carrying nuclear warheads, and they complained that West Berlin had become an escape route for disaffected East Germans. In 1958, Khrushchev announced that the Soviet Union would recognize East German control of all of Berlin unless the United States and its allies began talks on German reunification and rearmament. The United States refused to give up its hold on West Berlin or to break West German ties with NATO. Khrushchev backed away from his ultimatum but promised to raise the issue at future conferences.

Berlin and Germany were on the agenda of a summit meeting planned for Paris in mid-1960. On May 1, two weeks before the conference, a U-2 spy plane carrying high-powered cameras crashed 1,200 miles

U-2 Incident

inside the Soviet Union. Moscow claimed credit for shooting down the plane, which it put on display along with Francis Gary Powers, the captured CIA pilot. Moscow also demanded an apology. When Washington refused, the Soviets walked out of the Paris summit.

While sparring over Europe, both sides kept a wary eye on the People's Republic of China. Despite evidence of a widening Sino-Soviet split, most American officials still treated communism as a uni-

Jinmen (Quemoy) and Mazu (Matsu)

fied world movement. The isolation between Beijing and Washington stymied communication and made continued conflict between China and the United States likely. In a dispute over Jinmen (Quemoy) and Mazu (Matsu), two tiny islands off the Chinese coast, the United States and the People's Republic of China lurched toward the brink. Jiang used these islands as bases from which to raid the mainland. Communist China's guns bombarded

the islands in 1954. Eisenhower decided to defend the outposts; he even hinted that he might use nuclear weapons. Why massive retaliation over such an insignificant issue? "Let's keep the Reds guessing," advised John Foster Dulles. But what if they guessed wrong? critics replied.

Congress passed the Formosa Resolution (1955), authorizing the president to deploy American forces to defend Formosa and adjoining islands, and two years later the United States installed tactical nuclear weapons on Taiwan. War loomed again in 1958 over Jinmen and Mazu, but this time Washington pressed Jiang to back off. Eisenhower's nuclear threats, however, persuaded the Chinese that they, too, needed nuclear arms. In 1964 China exploded its first nuclear bomb.

As the United States went to the brink with China, it went to the market with Japan, rebuilding Japan with foreign aid as an anticommunist military partner and trader, all the while worrying China, the

"Japanese Miracle"

Soviet Union, and other past victims of Japanese aggression. Huge United States military purchases in Japan during the Korean War and American assistance in developing an export-oriented economy in the 1950s produced what many called the "Japanese miracle"—double-digit economic growth. Japan copied American technology (Motorola, for example, helped start the electronics industry), practiced trade protectionism, and gained a reputation for industrial efficiency and quality control. Before long, Japan became a major economic competitor with the United States.

In eight years of nurturing allies and applying the containment doctrine worldwide, Eisenhower held the line—against the Soviet Union, communist China, neutralism, communism, nationalism, and revolution everywhere. Eisenhower found no way to relax Cold War tensions, and ultimately he accelerated the nuclear arms race he so disliked.

 ## Kennedy, Johnson, and the Crises of the 1960s

John F. Kennedy's diplomacy owed much to the past. He disparaged the appeasement of the 1930s, praised the containment of the 1940s, and he vowed to rout communism in the 1960s. Indeed, his inaugural address suggested no halfway measures: "Let every nation know that we shall pay any price, bear any burden, meet any hardship, support any friend, oppose any foe to assure the survival and the success of liberty."

Kennedy's Views

Khrushchev took up the challenge by endorsing "wars of national liberation" in the Third World. He also bragged about Soviet ICBMs, raising American anxiety over Soviet capabilities. Intelligence data soon demonstrated that there was no "missile gap"—except the one in America's favor. Kennedy nonetheless sought to fulfill his campaign commitment to a military buildup based on the principle of *flexible response*: the capability to make any kind of war, from guerrilla combat to nuclear showdown. With this capability the United States would be able to contain both the Soviet Union and revolutionary movements in the Third World.

In 1961 Kennedy's first year in the presidency, the military budget shot up 15 percent; by mid-1964, United States nuclear weapons had increased by 150 percent. Although Kennedy inaugurated the Arms Control and Disarmament Agency and signed the Limited Test Ban Treaty with the Soviet Union (1963), which banned nuclear testing in the atmosphere, in outer space, and under water, his legacy would be an accelerated arms race.

In 1961, the Soviets again demanded negotiations to end Western occupation of West Berlin. Calling the city "the great testing place of Western courage and will," Kennedy rejected negotiations and asked Congress for an additional $3.2 billion for defense and the authority to call up reservists. In August 1961 the Soviets, on the urging of the East German regime, erected a barricade to halt the exodus of East Germans to West Berlin. The Berlin Wall inspired protests throughout the noncommunist world, but Kennedy privately sighed that "a wall is a hell of a lot better than a war."

Berlin Wall

United States hostilities with Cuba provoked Kennedy's most serious confrontation with the Soviet Union. Cold War and Third World issues dramatically intersected in Cuba. In early 1959 Fidel Castro's rebels, driven by profound anti-American nationalism, had ousted the dictator Fulgencio Batista, a long-time United States ally. From the start Castro sought to roll back the influence of American business, which had invested some $1 billion on the island, and to end United States domination of Cuban trade. His increasing authoritarianism and anti-Yankee declarations alarmed Washington. In early 1960, after Cuba signed a trade treaty with the Soviet Union, Eisenhower ordered the CIA to organize an invasion force of Cuban exiles to overthrow Castro. The president also drastically cut United States purchases of Cuban sugar. Castro responded by seizing all North American–owned companies. Threatened by United States decisions designed to bring his revolution down, Castro appealed to the Soviet Union, which offered loans and expanded trade.

The Cuban Revolution

Just before leaving office, Eisenhower broke diplomatic relations with Cuba and advised Kennedy to advance plans for the invasion. The scenario sketched by the CIA appealed to Kennedy: Cuban exiles would land and secure a beachhead; the Cuban people would rise up against Castro and welcome a new government brought in from the United States. Because he felt uneasy over such a blatant attempt to topple a sovereign government, Kennedy ordered that the United States's hand be kept hidden. The president never attempted to negotiate Cuban-American troubles with Castro.

When the Bay of Pigs attack began in April 1961, however, the United States's role became widely publicized, and the Cuban people did not rise up against Castro. Within two days most of the invaders had been captured by troops loyal to Castro. Although Kennedy refused to order an air strike to aid the invaders when the landing was failing, the operation never had much chance of success. The Cuban leader, concluding that the United States would not take defeat well and might launch another invasion, looked even more toward the Soviet Union for a lifeline.

Bay of Pigs Invasion

Kennedy vowed to bring Castro down. The CIA then hatched a project called Operation Mongoose to disrupt the island's trade, support raids on Cuba from Miami, and plot with organized-crime bosses to assassinate Castro. The United States also tightened its economic blockade, engineered Cuba's eviction from the Organization of American States, and undertook military maneuvers that Castro read as threatening.

Had there been no Bay of Pigs invasion, no Operation Mongoose, no assassination plots, and no program of diplomatic and economic isolation, there probably would have been no Cuban missile crisis.

Cuban Missile Crisis

For Castro, the relentless hostility of the United States represented a real threat to Cuba's independence. For the Soviets, the United States's actions challenged the only procommunist regime in Latin America. Premier Khrushchev also saw an opportunity to improve the Soviet position in the nuclear arms race. Castro and Khrushchev devised a risky plan to deter any new United States intervention: In mid-1962 they agreed to install in Cuba nuclear-armed missiles capable of hitting the United States. The world soon faced frightening brinkmanship.

In mid-October 1962 a U-2 plane flying over Cuba photographed sites for medium-range missiles. The president immediately organized a special Executive Committee to find a way to force the missiles and their nuclear warheads out of Cuba. Some members advised a surprise air strike. The Joint Chiefs of Staff recommended a full-scale military invasion, an option that risked a prolonged war with Cuba, a Soviet attack against West Berlin, or even nuclear holocaust. The Soviet expert Charles Bohlen unsuccessfully urged quiet, direct negotiations with Soviet officials. Secretary of Defense Robert S. McNamara proposed the formula that the president found most acceptable: a naval quarantine of Cuba. The proposal left the administration free to attack or negotiate, depending on the Soviet response.

Kennedy addressed the nation on television on October 22 to demand that the Soviets retreat. United States warships began crisscrossing the Caribbean, while B-52s loaded with nuclear bombs took to the skies. Khrushchev replied that the missiles would be withdrawn if Washington pledged never to attack Cuba. And he added that American Jupiter missiles aimed at the Soviet Union must be removed from Turkey. On October 27 a Soviet commander shot down a U-2 plane over Cuba. Edgy advisers predicted war, but on October 28 came a Soviet-American compromise. The United States promised to respect Cuban sovereignty and to withdraw the Jupiters from Turkey in exchange for the withdrawal of Soviet offensive forces from Cuba. Technicians soon dismantled the missiles for shipment back to the Soviet Union. Forcing the Soviets to back down, many said, was John F. Kennedy's finest hour.

Critics—then and later—questioned Kennedy's actions, however. Would the crisis have occurred at all if he had not been hell-bent on overthrowing the Castro regime and expunging the Cuban Revolution from the Western Hemisphere?

Questions About Kennedy's Crisis Management

Should not the president at the start have initiated quiet negotiations rather than practiced dangerous brinkmanship? And—since the strategic balance of power was not seriously altered by the missiles in Cuba (the United States still enjoyed a tremendous advantage over the Soviets in the nuclear arms race)—did Kennedy risk doomsday unnecessarily?

The Cuban missile crisis did produce some relaxation in Soviet-American relations. In August 1963, the adversaries signed a treaty banning nuclear tests in the atmosphere, and they installed a Teletype "hot line." They also refrained from further confrontation in Berlin. In June 1963 Kennedy had spoken at American University in conciliatory terms, urging cautious Soviet-American steps toward disarmament. Some analysts predicted a thaw in the Cold War, but the assassination of President Kennedy in November left unresolved the question of whether he was shedding his strong Cold War views.

Kennedy's successor, Lyndon B. Johnson, held firmly to ideas about United States superiority, the menace of communism, and the necessity of global

How do historians know that, at the outset of the Cuban missile crisis, President John F. Kennedy seemed to downgrade diplomacy in favor of military action to force the Soviet missiles from Cuba? Months before that dangerous October 1962 crisis, Kennedy had ordered the Secret Service to install an audiotape system to record meetings in the Oval Office and the Cabinet Room. The system recorded its first meeting on July 30, 1962. A Dictabelt system for recording telephone conversations was installed later, in early September. Secretary of State Dean Rusk (with the window behind him to Kennedy's right) and Secretary of Defense Robert McNamara (with the flag behind him to Kennedy's left) did not know that their remarks were being taped. Only a few members of the presidential staff knew about the secret system. Whether Kennedy wanted the recordings because he sought an accurate record for the memoirs he intended to write or because he hoped to protect himself against public misrepresentations of what he said to others in private, he left historians a rich source on high-level decision making in the White House: 127 audiotapes (248 hours) and 73 Dictabelts (12 hours) on wide-ranging foreign and domestic topics.

During the missile crisis of October 1962, President Kennedy regularly convened and taped meetings of an advisory Executive Committee, shown gathered here. Also shown here is a page from the transcript of the very first Executive Committee meeting, 11:50 A.M. to 12:57 P.M., October 16, 1962. The John F. Kennedy presidential library in Boston has declassified many of the recordings and has made them available to researchers. Because of such tapes (some of Kennedy's predecessors and successors also made recordings), historians can study the minute-by-minute, hour-by-hour handling of significant issues, in this case a crisis that brought the Soviet Union and the United States to the nuclear brink. John F. Kennedy Library.

	...at... be h..., if we could maybe take some, uh, general war preparation type of action that would show them that we're ready if they want to start anything, without what you might, with starting anything.
Bundy:	One. . . .
Dillon:	You just don't know.
Bundy:	On this track, one obvious element on the political side is do we say something simultaneously or, uh, to the Cubans, to the Soviets, or do we let the action speak for itself?
Rusk:	This point whether we say something to the Cubans and the Soviets before any, before . . .
JFK:	I think we ought to, what we ought to do is, is, uh, after this meeting this afternoon, we ought to meet tonight again at six, consider these various, uh, proposals. In the meanwhile, we'll go ahead with this maximum, whatever is needed from the flights, and, in addition, we will. . . . I don't think we got much time on these missiles. They may be. . . . So it may be that we just have to, we can't wait two weeks while we're getting ready to, to roll. Maybe just have to just take them out, and continue our other preparations if we decide to do that. That may be where we end up. I think we ought to, beginning right now, be preparing to. . . . Because that's what we're going to do anyway. We're certainly going to do number one; we're going to take out these, uh, missiles. Uh, the questions will be whether, which, what I would describe as number two, which would be a general air strike. That we're not ready to say, but we should be in preparation for it. The third is the, is the, uh, the general invasion. At least we're going to do number one, so it seems to me that we don't have to wait very long. We, we ought to be making those preparations.
Bundy:	You want to be clear, Mr. President, whether we have definitely...

Johnson and the Cold War

intervention. He saw the world in simple terms—them against us. Often exaggerating and sometimes lying, he created what became known as a credibility gap. Although Johnson improved Soviet-American relations somewhat by meeting with Soviet Premier Alexei Kosygin at Glassboro State College in New Jersey in 1967 and by pushing for the nonproliferation treaty to curb the spread of nuclear weapons in 1968, the Cold War hardly relented. The Soviets—having vowed to catch up with the United States after the Cuban missile crisis—reached nuclear parity with the United States by the end of the decade. Their invasion of Czechoslovakia in 1968 to stymie a nationalist movement caused Johnson to shelve further arms control talks. Such events and United States involvement in the Vietnam War diminished hopes of a relaxation of Cold War tensions.

 ## Nixon, Kissinger, and Détente

Richard M. Nixon had been an ardent Cold Warrior as a member of Congress, senator, and vice president, and few observers expected him to produce a thaw in the Cold War during his presidency (1969–1974). Yet he did so dramatically with the assistance of Henry A. Kissinger, a German-born political scientist from Harvard University. Kissinger served as Nixon's national security adviser until 1973, when he became secretary of state.

Nixon and Kissinger pursued a grand strategy designed to promote a global balance of power. The first part of the strategy was *détente:* measured cooperation with the Soviets through negotiations within a general environment of rivalry.

The Pursuit of Détente

Détente's primary purpose, like that of the containment doctrine it resembled, was to check Soviet expansion and limit the Soviet arms buildup. The second part of the strategy sought to curb revolution and radicalism in the Third World so as to quash threats to American interests.

Nixon and Kissinger pursued détente with extraordinary energy and fanfare. They expanded trade relations with the Soviet Union; a 1972 deal sent $1 billion worth of American grain to the Soviets at bargain prices. To slow the costly arms race, they initiated the Strategic Arms Limitations Talks (SALT). In 1972 Soviet and American negotiators produced the SALT-I Treaty, which limited antiballistic missile (ABM) systems. (By making offensive missiles less vulnerable to attack, these defensive systems had accelerated the arms race because both sides built more missiles to overcome the ABM protection.) A second agreement imposed a five-year freeze on the number of offensive nuclear missiles each side could possess. At the time of the agreement the Soviets held an advantage in total strategic forces (ICBMs, SLBMs, and long-range bombers). But the United States had more warheads per missile because it could outfit each missile with MIRVs (multiple independently targeted reentry vehicles) that could send warheads to several different targets. In short, the United States had a two-to-one advantage in deliverable warheads (5,700 to 2,500). Because SALT did not restrict MIRVs, the nuclear arms buildup actually continued.

SALT

While cultivating détente with the Soviet Union, the United States also sought to end almost three decades of Sino-American hostility.

Opening to China

The Chinese welcomed the change because they wanted to improve trade and hoped that friendlier Sino-American relations would make their enemy, the Soviet Union, more cautious. In early 1972 Nixon made a historic trip to "Red China," where he and the venerable Chinese leaders Mao Zedong and Zhou Enlai agreed to disagree on a number of issues, except one: the Soviet Union should not be permitted to make gains in Asia. Official diplomatic recognition and the exchange of ambassadors followed in 1979.

Global economic instability bedeviled the Nixon-Kissinger grand design. The worldwide recession early in the 1970s was the worst since the 1930s. Inflation and high oil prices pinched rich and poor nations alike. Protectionist tendencies raised tariffs and impeded world trade. And the debt-ridden developing nations of the Third World—sometimes called the "South"—insisted that the wealthier, industrial "North" share economic resources. The United States could not escape these problems. It began to suffer a trade deficit—importing more goods than it exported (see figure below).

Americans nonetheless remained the richest people in the world. The United States produced about one-third of the world's goods and services. Many American companies earned more than half of their profits abroad, and one-fourth of agri-

cultural sales came from exports; one out of every nine manufacturing jobs depended on exports. The economy of the United States also depended on imports of strategic raw materials. Such ties, as well as American investments abroad totaling more than $133 billion in the mid-1970s, explain in part why the United States welcomed détente as a means to calm international relations and protect the American stake in the world economy.

Carter and a Reinvigorated Cold War

President Jimmy Carter promised fresh initiatives and diplomatic activism when he took office in 1977. He asked Americans to put their "inordinate

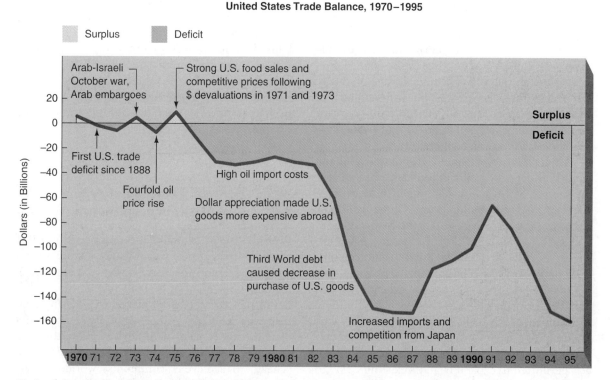

United States Trade Balance, 1970–1995 *Importing more than it exports, the United States has suffered trade deficits for years. Foreign political and economic crises and growing competition from Japanese products in the American marketplace have weakened the United States's position in the world economy. Trade deficits must be financed by borrowing. One result has been a mounting United States external debt.* Source: U.S. Department of State.

Jimmy Carter's Goals

fear of Communism" behind them so that they could attend to North-South issues. With reformist zeal, Carter vowed to reduce the American military presence overseas, to cut back arms sales, and to slow the nuclear arms race. He also promised preventive diplomacy: advancing the peace process in the Middle East, mediating conflict in the Third World, and creating worldwide economic stability through agreements on the law of the sea, energy, and clean air and water. A deeply religious man, Carter said he intended to infuse international relations with moral force. "The soul of our foreign policy," he declared, would be the championing of individual human rights abroad.

Carter spoke and acted inconsistently, in part because in the post-Vietnam years no consensus existed in foreign policy and in part because his advisers squabbled among themselves. One source of the problem was the stern-faced Zbigniew Brzezinski, a Polish-born political scientist who became Carter's national security adviser. An old-fashioned Cold Warrior, Brzezinski blamed foreign crises on the Soviet Union. Carter gradually listened more to Brzezinski than to Secretary of State Cyrus Vance, an experienced public servant who advocated quiet diplomacy to find avenues toward Soviet-American cooperation.

Under Carter, détente deteriorated and the Cold War deepened. Soviet leaders protested that the United States was playing its "China card"—building up China in order to threaten the Soviet Union.

SALT-II

Still, a new treaty, SALT-II, codified Soviet-American nuclear parity in 1979. The agreement placed a ceiling of 2,250 delivery vehicles on each side, capped MIRVed launchers at 1,200 for each, and limited the number of warheads per delivery vehicle. The Soviet Union had to dismantle more than 250 existing delivery vehicles, whereas the United States was permitted to expand from its existing 2,060 to the new ceiling. The treaty did not affect nuclear warheads, which stood at 9,200 for the United States and 5,000 for the Soviet Union. To win votes for the treaty from skeptical conservatives, Carter announced an expensive military expansion program and deployment of Pershing II missiles and cruise missiles in NATO countries.

As Senate ratification of SALT-II stalled and Moscow fumed over the Pershings, events in Afghanistan led to Soviet-American confrontation. In late 1979 the Red Army bludgeoned its way into Afghanistan to shore up a faltering communist government under siege by Muslim rebels. Carter shelved SALT-II (the two powers nonetheless unilaterally honored its terms later), suspended shipments of grain and high-technology equipment to the Soviet Union, and initiated an international boycott of the 1980 Summer Olympics in Moscow. The president also announced the *Carter Doctrine*: the United States would intervene, unilaterally and militarily if necessary, should Soviet aggression threaten the petroleum-rich Persian Gulf. The Soviets still refused to withdraw their forces from Afghanistan.

Carter lost the 1980 election to Ronald Reagan amid charges that the president had contradicted many of his own goals and had diminished United States power in the world. Carter had earned some diplomatic successes in the Middle East, Africa, and Latin America, but the revived Cold War and the prolonged Iranian hostage crisis had politically hurt the administration (see Chapter 30).

Reagan, Devil Theory, and Military Expansion

Ronald Reagan assumed the presidency in 1981 with no firm grasp of world issues, history, or geography. He and the conservatives he appointed, including Secretary of State George P. Shultz, believed that enlarged free-market capitalism could help win the Cold War. Reagan also embraced a devil theory: A malevolent Soviet Union, the "evil empire," would "commit any crime," "lie," and "cheat" to achieve a communist world. He attributed Third World disorders to Soviet intrigue as well, rejecting arguments that the civil wars in Central America and elsewhere derived from deep-seated economic instability, poverty, and class oppression.

Reagan asserted that a substantial military buildup would thwart the Soviet threat and intimidate Moscow. He thus launched the largest peacetime arms buildup in American history. In 1983

Reagan's Military Expansion

Reagan announced development of an antimissile defense system in space; he called it the Strategic Defense Initiative (SDI) or "Star Wars."

In 1985 the president declared the *Reagan Doctrine*: the United States will openly support anticommunist movements—"freedom fighters"—

Reagan Doctrine

wherever they are battling the Soviets or Soviet-backed governments. Under this doctrine, the CIA funneled aid to insurgents in Afghanistan, Nicaragua, Angola, and Ethiopia. In open defiance of the sovereignty of those nations, Reagan worked to overthrow governments he deemed hostile to the interests of the United States.

Reagan's first decision affecting the Soviets was actually friendly. Fulfilling a campaign pledge to help American farmers, in 1981 he lifted the grain embargo that Carter had imposed after the Soviet invasion of Afghanistan, and he sold the Soviet Union grain worth $3 billion. But bitter hostility soon followed when the Soviets cracked down on the Solidarity labor movement in Poland. In response, Washington placed restrictions on Soviet-American trade and hurled angry words at Moscow. In 1983, Reagan restricted commercial flights to the Soviet Union after a Soviet fighter pilot mistakenly shot down a South Korean commercial jet that had strayed some 300 miles off-course into Soviet airspace. The world was shocked by the death of 269 passengers, and Reagan exploited the tragedy to score Cold War points.

Reagan's expansion of the military, his careless utterances about winning a limited nuclear war, and his quest for nuclear supremacy stimulated worldwide debate. In 1981 hundreds of thousands of marchers

Debate over Nuclear Weapons

in Western Europe demanded Soviet-American negotiations to prevent a nuclear holocaust. The next year, a million peo-

ple marched through New York City to support a freeze, and in 1983 Roman Catholic bishops in the United States issued a pastoral letter condemning nuclear weapons as "immoral" and urging an end to the arms race.

In 1982 Reagan substituted the Strategic Arms Reduction Talks (START) for the inactive SALT talks. At the 1985 Geneva summit meeting, Reagan and the new Soviet leader Mikhail S. Gorbachev agreed in principle that strategic weapons should be substantially reduced, and at the 1986 Reykjavik, Iceland, meeting they came very close to a major reduction agreement. SDI, however, continued to block an accord: Gorbachev insisted that the "Star Wars" project be shelved, and Reagan refused to part with it despite widespread scientific opinion that it would cost billions of dollars and never work.

Near the end of Reagan's presidency, Soviet-American relations markedly improved, mainly because in 1985 a younger generation of Soviet leaders had come to power with Gorbachev. They began

Mikhail S. Gorbachev's Reforms

to restructure and modernize the highly bureaucratized, decaying economy (a reform program called *perestroika*) and to liberalize the authoritarian political system (a reform program called *glasnost*). For these reforms to work, Soviet military expenditures had to be reduced and foreign aid decreased.

In 1987 Gorbachev and Reagan signed a treaty banning all land-based intermediate-range nuclear missiles in Europe (the INF Treaty). Soon began the destruction of 2,800 missiles. Gorbachev also unilaterally reduced his nation's armed forces and helped settle regional conflicts. In 1989 Soviet troops departed Afghanistan.

 ## Bush, Clinton, and the End of the Cold War

George Bush entered the White House in 1989 and seemed to have few long-range foreign policy goals. He and Secretary of State James Baker, finding it difficult to imagine a world without communism, became, in the words of one analyst, "orphans of containment" when the Soviet Union collapsed and communism lost favor around the world.

Gorbachev had set loose cascading changes in his own country, but he also had encouraged the people of East Germany and Eastern Europe to

Communist Regimes Collapse in Eastern Europe

go their own ways. No longer would Moscow prop up unpopular communist regimes. In 1989 East Germans startled the world by repudiating their communist government, and in November joyful Germans tore down the Berlin Wall. The next year the two Germanys reunited and veteran communist oligarchs fell—in Poland, Hungary, Czechoslovakia, and Romania. Bulgaria and Albania soon held elections.

Meanwhile, the Union of Soviet Socialist Republics itself was unraveling (see map, page 571). In 1990 the Baltic states of Lithuania, Latvia, and Estonia declared independence. The following year, after Gorbachev himself denounced communism, the Soviet Union disintegrated into independent successor states—Russia, Ukraine, Tajikistan, and many others. Gorbachev himself soon lost power and was replaced by Boris Yeltsin in 1991.

The breakup of the Soviet empire, the dismantling of the Warsaw Pact, the repudiation of communism by its own leaders, the shattering of

Why the Cold War Ended

the myth of monolithic communism, the reunification of Germany on October 2, 1990, and the significant reduction in the risk of nuclear war signaled the end of the Cold War. It ended because of the relative decline of the United States and the Soviet Union in the international system from the 1950s through the 1980s. Because the contest had undermined the power of its two major protagonists, they moved gradually toward a cautious cooperation whose urgent goals were the restoration of their economic well-being and the preservation of their diminishing global positions.

Four influential trends explain this gradual decline and the resulting attractions of détente. First was the burgeoning economic cost of the Cold War—trillions of dollars spent on weapons and interventions rather than on improvements in the domestic infrastructure. Foreign ventures starved domestic programs and strained budgets. Second, challenges to the two major powers from within their own spheres of influence also help explain why the United States and the Soviet Union welcomed détente. Cuba's revolution and France's withdrawal from NATO in the 1960s are but two pieces of evidence that the United States was losing power. The uprisings in Hungary and Czechoslovakia and the Sino-Soviet rift undercut the Soviet Union's hegemony within its network of allies. Détente seemed to offer a means to restore great-power management of unruly states.

Third, the Cold War ended because of the emergence of the Third World, which introduced new players into the international game, further diffused power, and eroded bipolarism (see Chapter 30). Soviet-American détente represented a means to deal with the volatile Third World, a fulcrum by which to apply leverage to Third World nations. Finally, the worldwide antinuclear movement of the 1980s pressed leaders, especially in western Europe, to seek détente in order to stop the arms race.

These four elements combined to weaken the standing of the two adversaries and ultimately to persuade them to halt their nations' decline by ending the Cold War. Though Americans crowed that they had won, the contest had no winners. Both sides—and all the peoples of the world—paid an enormous price for the waging of the Cold War.

Critics known as declinists spotlighted a fundamental characteristic of the Cold War: large military spending came at the expense of domes-

Declinists

tic development. According to historian Paul Kennedy's *The Rise and Fall of the Great Powers* (1987), the United States suffered from "imperial overstretch." Kennedy argued that American power would continue to erode unless the nation restored its productive vitality and international marketplace competitiveness, reduced its huge federal debt, and improved its educational system. One way to stem economic decline, argued declinists, was to curb America's global interventionism. President Bush dismissed the declinists and envisioned the United States as the supreme power in a unipolar world.

ARCTIC OCEAN

Former states in the Union of Soviet Socialist Republics, which dissolved in 1991

PACIFIC OCEAN

Sea of Okhotsk

Sea of Japan

JAPAN

N. KOREA

S. KOREA

Barents Sea

RUSSIA

Largest and most influencial of the former Soviet republics after 1991

Lake Baikal

MONGOLIA

CHINA

800 Mi.

800 Km.

400

400

0

0

VIETNAM

MYANMAR

BHUT.

BANG.

NEPAL

Gorbachev in power, 1985–1991

Moscow

Broke into Czech Republic and Slovakia in 1993

Alma Alta

Frunze

KYRGYZSTAN

Dushambe

TAJIKISTAN

KAZAKHSTAN

Tashkent

UZBEKISTAN

Aral Sea

Caspian Sea

AFGHANISTAN

PAKISTAN

German reunification, 1990

Wall opened, Nov. 1989

Elections, 1989

SWEDEN

NORWAY

FINLAND

Tallinn

ESTONIA

Riga

LATVIA

LITHUANIA

Vilnus

Minsk

BELARUS

Communist regimes collapse, 1989

Kiev

UKRAINE

Warsaw

POLAND

Kishinev

MOLDOVA

TURKMENISTAN

Ashkhabad

Baku

AZERBAIJAN

ARMENIA

Yerevan

GEORGIA

Tbilisi

IRAN

Arabian Sea

IRE.

U.K.

FRANCE

BELG.

NETH.

DEN.

GERMANY

Berlin

Prague

CZECH. REP.

Bratislava

SLOVAKIA

AUS.

SWITZ.

ITALY

SLOVENIA

CROATIA

BOSNIA HERZE.

YUGOSLAVIA

MACED.

HUNGARY

Budapest

Dissolved into warring states

ROMANIA

Bucharest

Sofia

BULGARIA

GR.

ALB.

TURKEY

SYRIA

LEB.

ISR.

JORDAN

IRAQ

KUWAIT

SAUDI ARABIA

YEMEN

OMAN

U.A.E.

The End of the Cold War in Europe *Mikhail Gorbachev initiated reforms that ultimately undermined the communist regimes in Eastern Europe and East Germany and led to the breakup of the Soviet Union itself.*

When the Cold War ended, Bush struggled futilely to explain the dimensions or shape the agenda of a new world order. His administration sustained a large defense budget and continued to use military force abroad (especially in the Persian Gulf War of 1990–1991)—signaling that United States interventionist policies toward the Third World had hardly changed with the end of the Cold War. But in mid-1991 the Soviet Union and the United States signed the START-I Treaty to reduce each's nuclear warheads to 6,000 and each's strategic delivery systems to 1,600. In late 1992, Bush signed a START-II agreement, which provided for the reduction of warheads to about 3,000 each by the year 2003 and the elimination of land-based intercontinental ballistic missiles (ICBMs) with more than one warhead, leaving each side with about 500 ICBMs.

START Treaties

The Bush administration negotiated the North American Free Trade Agreement (NAFTA) with Canada and Mexico. Signed in late 1992, the pact defined tariff-free trade among the three nations. Critics claimed that the agreement would cost many United States workers their jobs because corporations would move south to exploit less expensive Mexican labor and minimal environmental controls. The Clinton administration nonetheless lobbied NAFTA through Congress in 1993; the agreement became operative the following year. In 1994, moreover, Congress approved United States membership in the new World Trade Organization, which replaced the General Agreement on Tariffs and Trade as the main body overseeing international trade and settling disputes.

NAFTA and Trade Issues

Trade issues lay at the center of tense United States–Japanese relations in the 1980s and 1990s. Most nettlesome was the huge trade deficit in Japan's favor (about $50 billion in 1989). Japanese products flooded American stores and won customers who appreciated their price and quality. The bestselling car in the United States in 1989 was the

Tense Japanese-American Relations

Honda Accord (many of which were assembled by American workers in the United States). In 1990 the world's ten largest banks were all in Japan, as were seven of the world's largest public companies (ranked by market value).

American manufacturers complained that Japan's tariffs, cartels, and government subsidies made it difficult for American goods to penetrate Japanese markets. The Japanese countered that obsolete equipment, poor education, and inadequate spending on research and development undercut United States competitiveness. Trade talks with Japan proved acrimonious and produced small gains, but both nations knew that their economies were too interdependent for one to punish or isolate the other.

Elsewhere in Asia, Sino-American relations became rocky in June 1989, when Chinese armed forces stormed into Beijing's Tiananmen Square. They slaughtered hundreds—perhaps thousands—of unarmed students and other citizens who for weeks had been holding peaceful prodemocracy rallies. Bush officials initially expressed revulsion, but they believed that America's global security and trade needs required friendly Sino-American ties. In 1994, when granting China most-favored-nation trading status, President Bill Clinton stated that the United States henceforth would decouple trade and human-rights issues.

Tiananmen Square Massacre

Clinton had emphasized domestic issues and said little about foreign affairs during his successful 1992 campaign against Bush. Once in office, Clinton and his secretary of state, the veteran diplomat Warren Christopher (replaced by Madeleine Albright in 1997), soon had to deal with the highly volatile, multipolar world of the post–Cold War era. They oversaw a changing CIA, which increasingly practiced economic espionage on the business activities and weapons contracts of other nations and on the destabilizing political effects of rapid population growth, soil erosion, and famine. The promotion of free-market trade and democracy abroad became Clinton goals. The ad-

Clinton Administration

ministration patiently moved adversaries toward significant agreements in the Middle East peace process (see Chapter 30).

One consequence of the end of the Cold War in Europe proved savage: ethnic wars in the former Yugoslavia, where, beginning in 1991, Bosnian Muslims, Bosnian Serbs, and Croats killed one another, taking 250,000 lives. Clinton talked tough against Serbian aggression and atrocities in Bosnia-Herzegovina, especially the Serbs' cruel "ethnic cleansing" of Muslims through massacres and rape camps. On occasion he ordered United States airpower to strike Serb positions that threatened vulnerable civilian populations, as in historic Sarajevo. United Nations peacekeeping troops failed to halt the bloodshed. In late 1995, after American diplomats brokered an agreement in Dayton, Ohio, among the belligerents for a new multiethnic state in Bosnia, Clinton offered some twenty thousand ground troops to a NATO Implementation Force.

Bosnia

In early 1998 the president announced plans to extend the mission. Clinton believed that American ideals were being tested in Bosnia. In 1996, he had denounced an "isolationist backlash" and appealed for United States leadership as the world's "best peacemaker."

While Clinton struggled with Bosnia, the global agenda remained crowded with long-term issues. Arms sales, including surface-to-surface missiles, accelerated across the post–Cold War world. In 1993 the United States accounted for 73 percent of the world's total arms-export trade. Nuclear proliferation continued to worry leaders, especially after India's 1998 testing of nuclear devices. Terrorists with access to deadly explosives also threatened danger, as in their attack on United States' Embassies in Africa in August 1998.

Weapons Proliferation

Environmental issues remained high on the international agenda, threatening world order because they caused political instability. Acid rain,

When President Bill Clinton (b.1946) decided in 1995 to send United States troops into the former Yugoslav republic of Bosnia to enforce a peace accord among warring parties, critics reminded him that he had earlier opposed America's participation in the Vietnam War and that he should be vigilant against another long-term American military commitment. Walt Handelsman. *The Times-Picayune.*

International Environmental Issues

toxic waste, deterioration of the protective ozone layer (it blocks the sun's ultraviolet rays, which can cause cancer), soil erosion, water pollution, and destruction of tropical forests spoiled the natural environment, killed wildlife, and poisoned land. Warming of the earth's climate due to the greenhouse effect—the buildup of carbon dioxide and other gases in the atmosphere—threatened a rise in ocean levels, flooding farmland and dislocating millions of people.

The Bush administration achieved some advances: in 1989 eighty-six nations, including the United States, agreed to phase out use of ozone-destroying chemicals by the year 2000, and Bush signed a tough Clean Air Act in 1990. The following year the United States and twenty-five other nations agreed to protect the fragile environment of Antarctica by banning oil exploration and mining there for fifty years. But Bush rejected key international control agreements at the 1992 Earth Summit held in Rio de Janeiro, Brazil, charging that they would cost jobs in the United States. The Clinton administration, advised especially by Vice President Al Gore, worked for more international environmental accords.

In the mid-1990s the State Department and the United Nations studied the treatment of women as a worldwide human-rights issue. The

Human Rights and Women

grim findings included not only job and political discrimination but also forced sterilization and abortion, coerced prostitution, and genital mutilation. The 1995 Fourth World Conference on Women, held in Beijing, called for the "empowerment of women" through "human rights and fundamental freedoms."

Conclusion

The Cold War dominated world affairs for almost a half-century. In the United States in those years, long-neglected domestic needs begged for attention and resources. A large arms industry secured a firm hold on the American economy, and hundreds of thousands of workers owed their jobs to defense contracts. The nation seemed better equipped to fight wars than to improve their troubled educational system or to make their cities inhabitable and safe.

During the Cold War era, the power of the presidency expanded greatly at the expense of the checks-and-balances system; presidents launched covert operations, dispatched troops, and ordered invasions while barely consulting Congress. The Cold War also bequeathed a record of political extremism, cover-ups, lies, and scandals that made many Americans feel cynical about their government.

Throughout the world, the two great powers intervened in civil wars, transforming local conflicts into Cold War contests. Given these conflicts, millions probably would have died whether or not there was a Cold War, but millions more surely died because of it. The superpowers, moreover, paid scant attention to environmental crises or the injustice of gender inequality.

The central questions of post–Cold War American foreign policy continued in the late 1990s to fuel national debate: should or could the United States play the expensive role of global policeman and nation builder while at the same time undertaking the expensive task of economic renewal at home? What mix of retrenchment and international activism, of unilateralism and multilateralism, lay ahead? Under what circumstances should the United States apply its predominant military power? Which foreign disturbances threatened vital American interests and which did not? These questions revealed how unsettled Americans were in their foreign policy views as they approached the twenty-first century.

Suggestions for Further Reading

For United States relations with the nations of the Third World since 1945, see Chapter 30.

The Cold War: Overviews

Stephen Ambrose and Alan Brinkley, *Rise to Globalism*, 8th ed. (1998); H. W. Brands, *The Devil We Knew* (1993); Warren Cohen, *America in the Age of Soviet Power, 1945–1991* (1993);

Gordon A. Craig and Francis L. Loewenheim, eds., *The Diplomats, 1939–1979* (1994); John L. Gaddis, *Russia, the Soviet Union, and the United States*, 2d ed. (1990); John L. Gaddis, *The Long Peace* (1987); John L. Gaddis, *Strategies of Containment* (1982); Walter Isaacson and Evan Thomas, *The Wise Men* (1986); Robert H. Johnson, *Improbable Dangers: U.S. Perceptions of Threat in the Cold War and After* (1994); Charles W. Kegley, ed., *The Long Post War Peace* (1991); Paul Kennedy, *The Rise and Fall of the Great Powers* (1987); Walter LaFeber, *America, Russia, and the Cold War, 1945–1992*, 8th ed. (1997); Ralph Levering, *The Cold War* (1994); Thomas McCormick, *America's Half-Century*, 2d ed. (1994); Thomas G. Paterson, *On Every Front: The Making and Unmaking of the Cold War* (1992); Thomas G. Paterson, *Meeting the Communist Threat* (1988).

Cold War Origins and the Containment Doctrine

Michael Cohen, *Truman and Israel* (1990); Carolyn W. Eisenberg, *Drawing the Line* (1996) (on the United States and Germany); Frazer Harbutt, *The Iron Curtain* (1986); Walter Hixson, *George F. Kennan* (1990); Michael Hogan, *The Marshall Plan* (1987); Lawrence S. Kaplan, *The United States and NATO* (1984); Gabriel Kolko and Joyce Kolko, *The Limits of Power* (1972); Bruce R. Kuniholm, *The Origins of the Cold War in the Near East* (1980); Melvyn Leffler, *The Specter of Communism* (1994); Melvyn Leffler, *A Preponderance of Power* (1992); Alan Milward, *The Reconstruction of Western Europe* (1984); Wilson D. Miscamble, *George F. Kennan and the Making of American Foreign Policy, 1947–1950* (1992); Thomas A. Schwartz, *America's Germany* (1991); Mark A. Stoler, *George C. Marshall* (1989); Lawrence S. Wittner, *American Intervention in Greece, 1943–1949* (1982); Vladislav Zubok and Constantine Pleshakov, *Inside the Kremlin's Cold War* (1996).

Atomic Diplomacy and Nuclear Arms Race

Howard Ball, *Justice Downwind* (1986) (on testing); Paul Boyer, *By the Bomb's Early Light* (1986); McGeorge Bundy, *Danger and Survival* (1988); Robert A. Divine, *The Sputnik Challenge* (1993); Robert A. Divine, *Blowing in the Wind* (1978) (on the test-ban debate); Gregg Herken, *Counsels of War* (1985); Gregg Herken, *The Winning Weapon* (1981); James G. Hershberg, *James B. Conant* (1993); Richard G. Hewlett and Jack M. Hall, *Atoms for Peace and War, 1953–1961* (1989); David Holloway, *Stalin and the Bomb* (1994); Robert Jervis, *The Meaning of the Nuclear Revolution* (1989); Fred Kaplan, *The Wizards of Armageddon* (1983); Milton Katz, *Ban the Bomb* (1986); Charles Morris, *Iron Destinies, Lost Opportunities* (1988); National Academy of Sciences, *Nuclear Arms Control* (1985); John Newhouse, *War and Peace in the Nuclear Age* (1989); John Newhouse, *Cold Dawn* (1973) (on SALT); Richard Rhodes, *Dark Sun* (1995) (on the H-bomb); David N. Schwartz, *NATO's Nuclear Dilemmas* (1983); Martin Sherwin, *A World Destroyed* (1975); Strobe Talbott, *The Master of the Game* (1988) (on Nitze); Strobe Talbott, *Deadly Gambit* (1984) (on Reagan); Strobe Talbott, *Endgame* (1979) (on SALT-II); Spencer Weart, *Nuclear Fear* (1988); Allan M. Winkler, *Life Under a Cloud* (1993); Lawrence S. Wittner, *One World or None* (1993).

Occupation and Rebuilding of Japan

Richard B. Finn, *Winners in Peace* (1995); Kyoko Hirano, *Mr. Smith Goes to Tokyo: Japanese Cinema Under the American Occupation, 1945–1952* (1992); Michael Schaller, *Douglas MacArthur* (1989); Michael Schaller, *The American Occupation of Japan* (1985).

China and United States Nonrecognition Policy

Dorothy Borg and Waldo Heinrichs, eds., *Uncertain Years* (1980); Gordon Chang, *Friends and Enemies* (1990); Warren I. Cohen, *America's Response to China*, 3d ed. (1989); Akira Iriye, *The Cold War in Asia* (1974); Paul G. Lauren, ed., *The "China Hands" Legacy* (1987); Robert P. Newman, *Owen Lattimore and the "Loss" of China* (1992); Robert S. Ross, *Negotiating Cooperation* (1995) (on 1969–1989); William W. Stueck, Jr., *The Road to Confrontation* (1981); Nancy B. Tucker, *Patterns in the Dust* (1983).

The Korean War

Roy E. Appleman, *Disaster in Korea* (1992); Roy E. Appleman, *Escaping the Trap* (1990); Roy E. Appleman, *Ridgeway Duels for Korea* (1990); Chen Jian, *China's Road to the Korean War* (1995); Bruce Cumings, *The Origins of the Korean War*, 2 vols. (1980, 1991); Rosemary Foot, *A Substitute for Victory* (1990); Rosemary Foot, *The Wrong War* (1985); Sergei Goncharov et al., *Uncertain Partners: Stalin, Mao, and the Korean War* (1993); John Halliday and Bruce Cumings, *Korea* (1989); Burton I. Kaufman, *The Korean War* (1997); Callum A. MacDonald, *Korea* (1987); John W. Spanier, *The Truman-MacArthur Controversy and the Korean War* (1959); William Stueck, *The Korean War* (1995); Richard Whelan, *Drawing the Line* (1990); Allen Whiting, *China Crosses the Yalu* (1960).

Eisenhower-Dulles Foreign Policy

Stephen E. Ambrose, *Eisenhower*, 2 vols. (1982, 1984); Stephen E. Ambrose, *Ike's Spies* (1981); Michael Beschloss, *MAYDAY* (1986) (on the U-2 crisis); Jeff Broadwater, *Eisenhower and the Anti-Communist Crusade* (1992); Robert A. Divine, *Eisenhower and the Cold War* (1981); Fred Greenstein, *The Hidden-Hand Presidency* (1982); Townsend Hoopes, *The Devil and John Foster Dulles* (1973); Richard Immerman, ed., *John Foster Dulles* (1990); Burton I. Kaufman, *Trade and Aid* (1982); Frederick W. Marks, *Power and Peace* (1993) (on Dulles); Richard A. Melanson and David A. Mayers, eds., *Reevaluating Eisenhower* (1986); Jack M. Schick, *The Berlin Crisis* (1971).

Kennedy, Johnson, and Globalism

Michael Beschloss, *The Crisis Years* (1991); Warren I. Cohen, *Dean Rusk* (1980); Warren I. Cohen and Nancy B. Tucker, eds., *Lyndon Johnson Confronts the World* (1995); James N. Giglio, *The Presidency of John F. Kennedy* (1991); David Halberstam, *The Best and the Brightest* (1972); Doris Kearns, *Lyndon Johnson and the American Dream* (1976); Diane Kunz, ed., *The Diplomacy of the Crucial Decade* (1994); Herbert S. Parmet, *JFK* (1983); Thomas

G. Paterson, ed., *Kennedy's Quest for Victory* (1989); Arthur M. Schlesinger, Jr., *Robert Kennedy and His Times* (1978); Thomas J. Schoenbaum, *Waging Peace and War* (1988); Randall Woods, *Fulbright* (1995). For the Vietnam War, see Chapter 30.

Cuba and the Missile Crisis

Graham Allison, *Essence of Decision* (1971); James G. Blight, *The Shattered Crystal Ball* (1990); James G. Blight et al., *Cuba on the Brink* (1993); James G. Blight and David A. Welch, *On the Brink* (1989); Raymond Garthoff, *Reflections on the Cuban Missile Crisis*, rev. ed. (1989); Trumbull Higgins, *The Perfect Failure* (1987) (on the Bay of Pigs); Richard Ned Lebow and Janice Gross Stein, *We All Lost the Cold War* (1993); Morris Morley, *Imperial State and Revolution* (1987); James Nathan, ed., *The Cuban Missile Crisis Revisited* (1992); Louis A. Pérez, Jr., *Cuba and the United States* (1990); Scott D. Sagan, *The Limits of Safety* (1993); Mark J. White, *The Cuban Missile Crisis* (1996).

Nixon, Kissinger, and Détente

Stephen Ambrose, *Nixon*, 3 vols. (1987–1991); Michael B. Froman, *The Development of the Idea of Détente* (1992); Raymond L. Garthoff, *Détente and Confrontation* (1985); John R. Greene, *The Limits of Power* (1992); Seymour Hersh, *The Price of Power* (1983); Joan Hoff, *Nixon Reconsidered* (1994); Walter Isaacson, *Kissinger* (1992); Keith L. Nelson, *The Making of Détente* (1995); Herbert S. Parmet, *Richard Nixon and His America* (1990); Andrew J. Pierre, *The Global Politics of Arms Sales* (1982); Robert D. Schulzinger, *Henry Kissinger* (1989).

The World Economy and Natural Environment

Richard J. Barnet, *The Lean Years* (1980); Richard J. Barnet and John Cavanaugh, *Global Dreams* (1994); Richard J. Barnet and Ronald Müller, *Global Reach* (1974); Richard E. Benedick, *Ozone Diplomacy* (1991); David P. Calleo, *The Imperious Economy* (1982); Alfred E. Eckes, *The United States and the Global Struggle for Minerals* (1979); David E. Fisher, *Fire & Ice* (1990) (on ozone depletion); Edward M. Graham and Paul R. Krugman, *Foreign Direct Investment in the United States* (1989); Stephen D. Krasner, *Defending the National Interest* (1978); John McCormick, *Reclaiming Paradise*, (1989); Robert A. Pastor, *Congress and the Politics of U.S. Foreign Economic Policy, 1929–1976* (1980); Joan E. Spero, *The Politics of International Economic Relations*, 4th ed. (1990); Herman Van Der Wee, *The Search for Prosperity*, (1986).

Carter Foreign Policy and Human Rights

Erwin C. Hargrove, *Jimmy Carter as President* (1988); Ole R. Holsti and James N. Rosenau, *American Leadership in World Affairs: Vietnam and the Breakdown of Consensus* (1984); Charles O. Jones, *The Trusteeship Presidency* (1988); Burton I. Kaufman, *The Presidency of James Earl Carter, Jr.* (1993); David S. McLellan, *Cyrus Vance* (1985); Richard A. Melanson, *Reconstructing Consensus* (1990); A. Glenn Mower, Jr., *Human Rights and American Foreign Policy* (1987); Kenneth A. Oye et al., *Eagle Entangled* (1979); Herbert D. Rosenbaum and Alezej Ugrinsky, eds., *Jimmy Carter* (1994); Gaddis Smith, *Morality, Reason, and Power* (1986); Sandy Vogelgesang, *American Dream, Global Nightmare* (1980).

Reagan, Bush, Clinton, and the End and Aftermath of the Cold War

Dana H. Allin, *Cold War Illusions* (1995); Michael R. Beschloss and Strobe Talbott, *At the Highest Levels* (1993); Archie Brown, *The Gorbachev Factor* (1996); Lou Cannon, *President Reagan* (1991); Michael Cox, *U.S. Foreign Policy After the Cold War* (1995); Elizabeth Drew, *On the Edge* (on Clinton); John Ehrman, *The Rise of Neoconservatism* (1995); John L. Gaddis, *The United States and the End of the Cold War* (1992); Raymond L. Garthoff, *The Great Transition* (1994); Seymour Hersh, *"The Target Is Destroyed"* (1987) (on the Korean airliner); Michael Hogan, ed., *The End of the Cold War* (1992); Haynes Johnson, *Sleepwalking Through History* (1991); Robert G. Kaiser, *Why Gorbachev Happened* (1991); Sean Lynn-Jones, ed., *The Cold War and After* (1991); Michael McGwire, *Perestroika and Soviet National Security* (1991); Joseph S. Nye, Jr., *Bound to Lead* (1990); Don Oberdorfer, *The Turn* (1991); Kenneth A. Oye et al., eds., *Eagle in a New World* (1992); Kenneth A. Oye et al., eds., *Eagle Resurgent?* (1987); John G. Ruggie, *Winning the Peace* (1996); Michael Schaller, *Reckoning with Reagan* (1992); Robert W. Tucker and David C. Hendrickson, *The Imperial Temptation* (1992); Daniel Wirls, *Buildup* (1992) (on Reagan military); Susan Woodward, *Balkan Tragedy* (1995).

30

Foreign Relations Storm: Contesting Revolution and Nationalism in the Third World

1945–Present

The "Deer" Team leader slammed into a banyan tree on July 16, 1945, when he parachuted into northern Vietnam. Colonel Allison Thomas and the other five members of his Office of Strategic Services (OSS) unit had been ordered to work with the Vietminh, a nationalist Vietnamese organization, and to sabotage Japanese forces that in March had seized Vietnam from France. Ho Chi Minh, head of the Vietminh, cordially greeted the OSS team and offered supper. The next day Ho denounced the French but remarked that "we welcome 10 *million* Americans."

A communist who had worked for decades to win his nation's independence, Ho helped supply information on Japanese military forces and rescue downed American pilots during the Second World War. He also met in March 1945 with United States officials in Kunming, China. He was receiving no aid from his ideological allies in the Soviet Union and hoped that the United States, on record in the Atlantic Charter as supporting self-determination for all peoples, would favor his nation's long quest for liberation from colonialism.

• *Important Events* •

1945	OSS teams cooperate with Vietminh Ho Chi Minh declares independence for Democratic Republic of Vietnam
1946	United States grants independence to Philippines War against France begins in Vietnam
1948	State of Israel created amid Arab-Jewish hostilities
1949	Truman announces Point Four technical assistance for developing nations Communists come to power in China
1950	United States recognizes Bao Dai in Vietnam and provides military aid to the French
1954	Siege of Dienbienphu spells end of French rule in Vietnam CIA overthrows government in Guatemala Geneva accords partition Vietnam Southeast Asia Treaty Organization founded
1955	United States backs Diem government in South Vietnam Bandung Conference organizes Non-aligned Movement
1956	Suez crisis pits Nasser's Egypt against Israel, France, and Britain
1957	Eisenhower Doctrine promises containment of communism in Middle East
1958	United States troops land in Lebanon
1959	North Vietnam begins sending aid to communists in the South
1960	Eighteen African colonies become independent nations National Liberation Front (Vietcong) organized in South Vietnam
1961	Peace Corps is founded Kennedy initiates Alliance for Progress to spur Latin American economies Kennedy begins to increase aid to Vietnam
1963	Strategic Hamlet Program established in South Vietnam United States cooperates in removal of Diem Lyndon B. Johnson becomes president

1964	Tonkin Gulf Resolution authorizes Johnson to handle the Vietnam War his way
1965	Operation Rolling Thunder bombs North Vietnam Johnson Americanizes Vietnam War
1965–66	Teach-ins at American universities oppose United States intervention in Vietnam
1967	Peace rallies held across the United States Six-Day War in the Middle East
1968	Secretary of Defense McNamara resigns Tet offensive in Vietnam Dollar/gold crisis threatens United States economy Massacre in My Lai leaves hundreds dead Vietnam peace talks open in Paris
1969	Under "Vietnamization" Nixon begins withdrawal of American troops Nixon Doctrine declares United States will help nations that help themselves
1970	Invasion of Cambodia sets off demonstrations on American college campuses Senate repeals Tonkin Gulf Resolution
1971	*Pentagon Papers* indicate that American leaders lied about Vietnam
1972	American warplanes pound North Vietnam in "Christmas bombing"
1973	Vietnam cease-fire agreement reached CIA helps oust Allende government in Chile Outbreak of Arab-Israeli war and imposition of Arab oil embargo War Powers Act restricts presidential war-making authority
1974	United Nations proposes "New International Economic Order"
1975	Egyptian-Israeli accord authorizes United Nations peacekeeping force in Sinai Vietnam War ends
1977	President Carter announces United States human-rights policy
1978	Congress approves Panama Canal treaties Carter negotiates Egyptian-Israeli peace accord at Camp David

● *Important Events* ●

1979	Shah of Iran overthrown; American hostages seized
1981	American hostages in Iran released United States steps up role in El Salvador's civil war CIA begins to train contras for attacks against Nicaragua
1982	President Reagan sends American troops to Lebanon for peacekeeping
1983	Terrorist bombing kills United States marines in Lebanon Reagan orders invasion of Grenada to remove leftist government
1984	Reagan administration aids contras, despite congressional ban
1985	Reagan Doctrine promises United States aid to anti-Soviet "freedom fighters"
1986	Iran-contra scandal breaks United States imposes economic sanctions against South Africa
1987	Palestinian uprising in West Bank
1989	Third World debt reaches $1.2 trillion United States troops invade Panama
1990	Sandinistas lose Nicaraguan elections After Iraq invades Kuwait, United States forces ordered to Persian gulf South Africa begins to dismantle apartheid
1991	Persian Gulf War Haitian political and refugee crisis Israelis and Arabs negotiate Mideast peace
1992	United Nations mediation ends Salvadoran civil war United States sends troops to Somalia to ensure delivery of relief supplies
1993	Israel-PLO agreement for Palestinian self-rule
1994	Mandela elected president in South Africa World's governments react too late to stop genocide in Rwanda United States troops land in Haiti
1995	International Conference on Women
1996	Helms-Burton Act tightens United States economic embargo against Cuba United States establishes diplomatic relations with Vietnam
1997	Israeli-Palestinian peace process stalls
1998	Crisis with Iraq over inspections of weapons sites

Note: For events in the history of the Cold War, see Chapter 29.

As a sign of friendship, the Americans in Vietnam named Ho OSS Agent 19. Everywhere the Americans went, impoverished villagers thanked them with gifts of food and clothing—interpreting the foreigners' presence as a sign of United States anticolonial and anti-Japanese sentiments. In early August, the "Deer" Team began to give Vietminh soldiers weapons training. Ho had many conversations with OSS members. Citing history, he remarked that "your statesmen make eloquent speeches about . . . self-determination. We are self-determined. Why not help us?"

Another OSS unit, the "Mercy" Team headed by Captain Archimedes Patti, arrived in the city of Hanoi on August 22. When Patti met Ho, the Vietminh leader applauded America's assistance and called for future "collaboration." But, unbeknownst to these OSS members, who believed that President Franklin D. Roosevelt's general sympathy for eventual Vietnamese independence remained United States policy, the new Truman administration had decided to let France, Vietnam's long-time colonial master, decide the fate of Vietnam.

On September 2, 1945, amid great fanfare in Hanoi, with OSS personnel present, an emaciated but emotional Ho Chi Minh read his declaration of independence for the Democratic Republic of Vietnam: "All men are created equal; they are endowed by their Creator with certain unalienable Rights; among these are Life, Liberty, and the pursuit of Happiness." Having borrowed from the internationally renowned 1776 American document, Ho then itemized Vietnamese grievances against France.

By late September both OSS teams had departed from Vietnam. In a last meeting with Patti, Ho expressed his sadness that the United States had not opposed France's return to Vietnam. Sure, Ho said, United States officials in Washington judged him a "Moscow puppet" because he was a communist. But Ho claimed that he was foremost "a free agent," a nationalist. If necessary, he insisted, the Vietnamese would go it alone, with or without American or Soviet help. And they did— first against the French and eventually against more than half a million United States troops in what became America's longest war.

Vietnam was part of the *Third World*, a general term for those nations that during the Cold War era belonged neither to the capitalist "West" (the United States and its allies) nor to the communist "East" (the Soviet Union and its allies). Sometimes called developing countries, Third World nations on the whole were nonwhite, nonindustrialized, and located in the southern half of the globe—in Asia, Africa, the Middle East, and Latin America. Many of them at one point were colonies of European nations or Japan. After the Second World War, when the United States and the Soviet Union coveted allies, the Third World became entangled in the Cold War. Even though the highly diverse Third World peoples had their own histories, cultures, and aspirations, they often found that they could not escape the pervasive effects of the great-power rivalry.

Americans often interpreted Third World anticolonialism, political instability, and restrictions on foreign-owned property as Soviet or communist inspired, rather than as expressions of profound nationalism or as consequences of indigenous developments. The Soviets did support guerrilla wars and revolution, and some Third World nations did work to forge links with the Soviet Union to fend off counterrevolutionary efforts by the United States. But had there been no Soviet Union or Cold War, the Third World would still have challenged the United States and its allies. These anticolonialist developing nations sought to end the economic, military, and cultural hegemony of the "West." As Assistant Secretary of State Thomas Mann told his colleagues in early 1959, when revolutionaries came to power in Cuba: "You fellows better batten down the hatches, because there's going to be some real stormy weather."

Interventions—military and otherwise—in the Third World, United States leaders believed, would impress Moscow with American might and resolve. They would ensure supplies of strategic raw materials. They would build cultural ties with the United States. They would also counter nationalism and radical anticapitalist social change that threatened American strategic and economic interests. To thwart nationalist, radical, and communist challenges, the United States directed its massive resources toward the Third World. Washington also allied with undemocratic but anticommunist regimes, meddled in civil wars, and unleashed CIA covert operations. Bitter resentments built up in the Third World, where millions of lives were lost in conflicts aggravated by United States intervention.

The emergence of the Third World in the 1950s began to undermine the bipolar Cold War international system the United States and the Soviet Union had constructed at the end of the Second World War. By the 1980s, power had become more diffused: great-power management of world affairs had diminished, and international relations had become more fluid and less predictable as more and more nations demanded a voice and a vote. Even when the Cold War ended in the early 1990s, the Third World remained to bedevil the United States, which continued its tradition of intervention—in Iraq, Somalia, Haiti, and elsewhere.

 ## Stormy Weather: The Third World Challenge

The process of decolonization accelerated after the end of the Second World War, when the economically wracked imperial countries proved incapable of resisting their colonies' demands for freedom. A cavalcade of new nations earned independence. The United States granted independence to the Philippines in 1946.

Decolonization

India and Pakistan (and present-day Bangladesh) won their freedom from Britain in 1947, as did Burma (Myanmar) and Ceylon (Sri Lanka) in 1948. The Dutch reluctantly let go of Indonesia in 1949. The French fought on in Indochina (Vietnam, Cambodia, and Laos) but finally gave up in 1954. In 1960 alone, eighteen new African nations became independent. From 1943 to 1989 a total of ninety-six countries cast off their colonial bonds. At the same time, the long-independent Third World nations of Latin America unsettled the world order by repeatedly challenging the hegemony of the United States.

By the late 1940s, when Cold War lines were drawn fairly tightly in Europe, Soviet-American rivalry shifted increasingly to the Third World. Much was at stake. Third World nations possessed strategic raw materials. They also attracted foreign investment and became markets for American manufactured products and technology. The great powers looked to these new states for votes in the United Nations and sought sites within their borders for military and intelligence bases.

Many Third World states—notably India, Ghana, Egypt, and Indonesia—did not wish to take sides in the Cold War. To the dismay of both Washington and Moscow, they declared themselves nonaligned, or neutral. Non-alignment became an organized movement in 1955 when twenty-nine Asian and African nations met at the Bandung Conference in Indonesia. Secretary of State John Foster Dulles, alarmed that neutralist tendencies would deprive the United States of potential allies, denounced neutralism as a step on the road to communism. Both he and President Eisenhower insisted that every nation should take a side in the life-and-death Cold War struggle.

The Nonaligned Movement

American leaders argued that Third World peoples needed Western-induced capitalist development and modernization in order to enjoy economic growth, social harmony, and political moderation. American leaders ascribed stereotyped race, age-based, and gendered characteristics to Third World peoples, seeing them as de-

American Images of the Third World

pendent, emotional, and irrational. American officials also used gendered language, suggesting that Third World countries were weak women—passive and servile, unable to resist the menacing appeals of communists and neutralists. For example, such thinking conditioned United States relations with India, a neutralist nation that Americans deemed effeminate and submissive—a place where, said President Eisenhower, "emotion rather than reason seems to dictate policy." And American leaders insisted that the peoples of the Third World were technologically "backward." Overall, American policymakers placed these peoples low in the hierarchy of power and claimed that they needed fatherly tutelage by the United States.

Racism and segregation in the United States especially influenced relations. In 1955, G. L. Mehta, the Indian ambassador to the United States, was refused service in the whites-only section of a restaurant at Houston International Airport. Fearing damaged relations with India, a large, neutralist nation whose allegiance the United States sought in the Cold War, Secretary of State John Foster Dulles apologized to Mehta. Dulles knew that racial segregation in the United States was spoiling American efforts to win friends in Third World countries. Thus when the United States attorney general appealed to the Supreme Court to strike down segregation in public schools, he underlined that the humiliation of dark-skinned diplomats "furnished grist for the Communist propaganda mills."

Racism

The hostility of the United States toward revolution also obstructed the American quest for influence in the Third World. In the twentieth century, the United States openly opposed revolutions in other nations. Americans celebrated the Spirit of '76 but grew intolerant of revolutionary disorder because many Third World revolutions arose against America's Cold War allies and threatened American investments, markets, and military bases. During revolutionary crises, therefore, the United States usually supported its European allies or the conservative, propertied classes in the Third World.

American Intolerance of Revolution

How do historians know that the Central Intelligence Agency tried to assassinate foreign leaders? During the 1970s, Senator Frank Church, Democrat of Idaho, chaired a special investigating committee that looked into the activities of the CIA and other intelligence agencies. Although there had long been speculation that Washington headquarters ordered CIA agents to kill certain foreign leaders, incontrovertible evidence did not come to public light until Church's probe forced the CIA to declassify secret documents. Here, on November 20, 1975, Church holds a copy of his committee's report on assassination plots. Among other findings in this report, the committee detailed several bungled attempts on the life of Fidel Castro, the revolutionary leader of Cuba. In this case, the CIA actually hired Mafia crime bosses to help with the unsuc-

cessful schemes. In other cases, the Church committee discovered that the CIA tried to kill Patrice Lumumba of the Congo and either promoted or was associated with plots against Rafael Trujillo of the Dominican Republic and Ngo Dinh Diem of South Vietnam. Most of the assassination plots failed. The committee could not confirm whether Presidents Eisenhower, Kennedy, and others personally ordered assassinations, although the report hinted that they gave orders that underlings could only have interpreted as licenses to kill. Because of such revelations, the CIA was later prohibited from conducting assassinations. But until another committee such as Church's opens classified documents, the secrecy that enshrouds CIA operations will make it difficult for historians to know whether the ban has been observed.   UPI/Corbis-Bettmann.

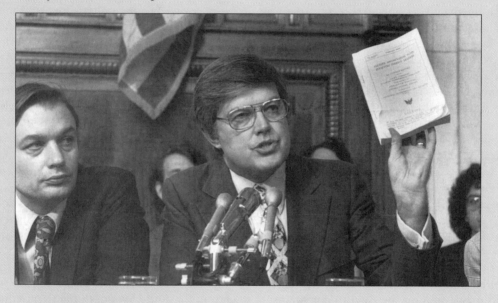

Development and Modernization

Believing that Third World peoples craved modernization and that the American economic model was best for them, American policymakers launched "development" projects. Such projects held out the promise of sustained economic growth, prosperity, and stability, which the benefactors hoped would undermine radicalism. President Truman announced in 1949 the Point Four program of sending American know-how to developing nations. In the 1950s the Carnegie, Ford, and Rockefeller Foundations worked with the United States Agency for International Development (AID) to sponsor a "Green Revolution"—a dramatic increase in agricultural production by, for example, the use of hybrid seeds.

Propaganda was also used to combat radical doctrines and neutralism in the Third World. The United States Information Agency used films, radio broadcasts, the magazine *Free World*, book displays, exhibitions, exchange programs, and libraries to trumpet the theme of "People's Capitalism." Citing America's economic success, the message showcased well-paid American workers, political democracy, and religious freedom.

USIA Propaganda Campaigns

Some Third World peoples yearned to be like Americans—to enjoy their consumer goods, their music, their clothes, their educational opportunities. Conversely, they also resented Americans for having so much and wasting so much while poorer peoples went without. The popular American novel *The Ugly American* (1958) spotlighted the "golden ghettoes" where American diplomats lived in compounds separated from their poorer surroundings by high walls. The people of many countries, moreover, resented the ample profits that American corporations extracted from them. Third World peoples also rejected unsavory aspects of American life, including racial segregation, political corruption, and drug abuse.

Third World Views of the United States

The Central Intelligence Agency became a major instrument of United States policy in the Third World. Through its covert operations, the CIA bribed foreign politicians, subsidized foreign newspapers, hired mercenaries, conducted sabotage, sponsored labor unions, dispensed "disinformation" (false information), plotted the assassination of foreign leaders, and staged coups. It helped overthrow the governments of Iran (1953) and Guatemala (1954) but failed in attempts to topple regimes in Indonesia (1958) and Cuba (1961).

CIA Covert Activities

The CIA and other components of the American intelligence community followed the principle of *plausible deniability*: covert operations should be conducted in such a way, and the decisions that launched them concealed so well, that the president could deny any knowledge of them. Thus President Eisenhower and his successor Kennedy denied that they had instructed the CIA to assassinate Cuba's Fidel Castro.

The Eisenhower Interventions

Anti-Yankee feelings grew in Latin America, where poverty, class warfare, overpopulation, illiteracy, economic sluggishness, and foreign exploitation fed discontent. In 1951 the leftist Jacobo Arbenz Guzmán was elected president of Guatemala, a poor country whose largest landowner was the American-owned United Fruit Company. To fulfill his promise of land reform, Arbenz expropriated United Fruit's uncultivated land and offered compensation. United Fruit dismissed the offer.

Claiming that Arbenz employed too many communists in his government and that they were taking control of Guatemala, the CIA began a secret plot to overthrow him. When Arbenz learned that the CIA was working against him, he turned to Moscow for military aid, thus reinforcing American suspicions. The CIA airlifted arms into Guatemala, dropping them at United Fruit facilities, and in mid-1954 CIA-supported Guatemalans struck from Honduras. American planes bombed the capital city, and the invaders drove Arbenz from power. The new pro-American regime returned United Fruit's land. Latin Americans wondered what had happened to the Good Neighbor policy.

CIA in Guatemala

In the Middle East the Eisenhower administration confronted challenges to United States influence from Arab nationalists. American interests were conspicuous: survival of the Jewish state of Israel and extensive oil holdings. Oil-rich Iran had become a special friend. Its ruling shah had granted American oil companies a 40 percent interest in a new petroleum consortium in return for CIA help in the successful overthrow, in 1953, of his rival, Mohammed Mossadegh, who had attempted to nationalize foreign oil interests.

United States Interests in the Middle East

Egypt's Gamal Abdul Nasser became a towering figure in a pan-Arabic movement to reduce Western interests in the Middle East. Nasser vowed to expel the British from the Suez Canal Zone and the Israelis from Palestine. When Nasser declared neutrality in the Cold War, Dulles lost patience. In 1956 the United States abruptly reneged on its offer to Egypt to help finance the Aswan Dam, a project to provide inexpensive electricity and water for thirsty farmland. Nasser responded by nationalizing the British-owned Suez Canal, intending to use its profits to build the dam.

Fully 75 percent of western Europe's oil came from the Middle East, and most of it was transported through the Suez Canal. Fearing an interruption in this vital trade, the British and French conspired with Israel to bring down Nasser. On October 29, 1956, the Israelis invaded the Suez, joined two days later by Britain and France. Eisenhower fumed that the United States's allies had not consulted him. The president also speculated that the invasion would cause Nasser to seek help from the Soviets, inviting them into the Middle East. Eisenhower sternly demanded that London, Paris, and Tel Aviv pull their troops out, and they did. Egypt took possession of the canal, and the Soviets built the Aswan Dam. Nasser became a hero to Third World peoples. To counter Nasser's "evil influence," as Eisenhower called it, the United States pursued alignment with the conservative King Saud of Saudi Arabia.

Suez Crisis

In an effort to improve the deteriorating Western position in the Middle East and to protect American interests there, the president proclaimed the *Eisenhower Doctrine* in 1957. The United States would intervene in the Middle East, he declared, if any government threatened by a communist takeover asked for help. In 1958 fourteen thousand American troops scrambled ashore in Lebanon to quell an internal political dispute that Washington feared might be exploited by pro-Nasser groups or communists. By 1961, most analysts agreed, the Eisenhower administration had deepened Third World hostility toward the United States.

Eisenhower Doctrine

Kennedy's Quest for Victory

During the 1960 presidential campaign, John F. Kennedy vowed to win the race for influence in the Third World. After Khrushchev endorsed "wars of national liberation" such as the one in Vietnam, Kennedy called for "peaceful revolution" based on the concept of *nation building*. The president set out to help developing nations through the infant stages of nationhood with aid programs aimed at improving agriculture, transportation, and communications. Kennedy thus initiated the Alliance for Progress (1961) to spur economic development in Latin America. And in 1961 he created the Peace Corps to serve nation building. This agency sent American teachers, agricultural specialists, and health workers into developing nations.

Kennedy also relied on *counterinsurgency*—an organized effort to defeat revolutionaries who challenged Third World governments friendly with the United States. American military and technical advisers trained native troops and police forces to quell unrest. American soldiers provided a protective shield against insurgents while American civilian personnel worked on economic projects.

Nation building and counterinsurgency seldom worked. Americans assumed that the United States model of capitalism and government could be transferred successfully to foreign cultures. But as much as many foreign peoples craved United States economic assistance and praised America's wealth, they resented meddling by outsiders. And because aid was usually funneled through a self-interested elite, it often failed to reach the very poor. To people who preferred the relatively quick solutions of a managed economy, moreover, the American emphasis on private enterprise seemed inappropriate.

Descent into the Longest War: Vietnam

In Southeast Asia the belief that the United States could influence the internal affairs of Third World countries led to outright disaster. How Vietnam became the site of America's longest war, and how the world's most powerful nation failed to subdue a peasant people is one of the most remarkable and tragic stories of modern history.

For decades after the French takeover of Indochina (Vietnam, Cambodia, and Laos) in the late nineteenth century, France exploited Vietnam for its rice, rubber, tin, and tungsten. Although the French beat back recurrent rebellions, Vietnamese nationalists dedicated to independence grew in strength. Their leader Ho Chi Minh, born in 1890, joined the French Communist Party to use it as a vehicle for Vietnamese independence. During the Second World War, Ho and his Vietminh warriors harassed both French and Japanese forces—near the end of the war with OSS help.

French Imperialism in Vietnam

The Truman administration rejected Vietnam's independence in favor of the restoration of French rule for several reasons. First, Americans wanted France's cooperation in the Cold War. Second, Southeast Asia was an economic asset; its rice could feed America's soon-to-be ally Japan, and it was the world's largest producer of natural rubber and a rich source of other commodities. Third, the area seemed strategically vital to the defense of Japan and the Philippines. Finally, Ho Chi Minh was a communist, who, it was assumed, would assist Soviet expansionism. Overlooking the native roots of the nationalist rebellion against France, six American presidents took a globalist view of Vietnam, interpreting events through a Cold War lens.

United States Rejection of Vietnamese Independence

In the 1940s Vietnam was a French problem that few Americans followed. But when Jiang Jieshi (Chiang Kai-shek) went down to defeat in China in 1949, the Truman administration made two crucial decisions—both in early 1950, before the Korean War. First, it recognized the French puppet government of Bao Dai, a former emperor who had collaborated with the French and Japanese. In Vietnamese eyes, the United States thus became in essence a colonial

United States Support for the French

power, an ally of the hated French. Second, the administration agreed to send weapons, and ultimately military advisers, to the French. By 1954 the United States was bearing three-fourths of the cost of the war.

Despite American aid, the French lost steadily to the Vietminh. Finally, in early 1954, Ho's forces surrounded the French fortress at Dienbienphu in northwest Vietnam (see map, page 586). The United States had thus far not committed its own forces to the war, but now some of Eisenhower's advisers suggested a massive air strike against Vietminh positions. If the air strike failed, critics asked, would American ground forces be next?

Dienbienphu Crisis

Worrying aloud about a communist victory, Eisenhower compared the weak nations of the world to a row of dominoes, all of which would topple if just one fell. He decided to press the British to help form a coalition to address the Indochinese crisis, but they refused. At home, influential members of Congress warned the president to avoid any American military commitment, especially in the absence of cooperation from the United States allies. The issue became moot on May 7, when the weary French defenders at Dienbienphu surrendered.

The French wanted out of the war. In April they had entered into peace talks at Geneva with the United States, the Soviet Union, Britain, the People's Republic of China, Laos, Cambodia, and the competing Vietnamese regimes of Bao Dai and Ho Chi Minh. The 1954 Geneva accords, signed by France and Ho's Democratic Republic of Vietnam, temporarily divided Vietnam at the 17th parallel; Ho's government was confined to the North, Bao Dai's to the South. The 17th parallel was meant to serve as a military truce line, not a national boundary; the country was scheduled to be unified after national elections in 1956. In the meantime, neither North nor South was to join a military alliance or permit foreign military bases on its soil.

Geneva Accords

Certain that the Geneva agreements ultimately would mean communist victory, the United States and Bao Dai refused to accept the accords and set

Southeast Asia and the Vietnam War *America's lengthy effort to prevent the spread of communism in Southeast Asia failed, and in 1975, communist forces gained control of South Vietnam, Cambodia, and Laos.*

about to sabotage them. A CIA team soon entered Vietnam and undertook secret operations against the North. In fall 1954, the United States also joined Britain, France, Australia, New Zealand, the Philippines, Thailand, and Pakistan in the anticommunist Southeast Asia Treaty Organization (SEATO), one purpose of which was to protect the southern part of Vietnam.

In the South, the United States helped Ngo Dinh Diem push Bao Dai aside. A Catholic in a Buddhist nation, Diem had many enemies and no mass support, but he was a nationalist and an anticommunist. With American aid he staged a fraudulent election that gave him 98 percent of the vote. When Ho called for national elections in keeping with the Geneva agreements, Diem and Eisenhower refused, fearing that the popular Vietminh leader would win. From 1955 to 1961 the Diem government received more than $1 billion in American aid, most of it military. Diem's Saigon regime became dependent on the United States for its very existence, and the culture of southern Vietnam became increasingly Americanized.

Backing the Diem Regime

Diem proved a difficult ally. He acted dictatorially, abolishing village elections and throwing dissenters in jail. Noncommunists and communists alike began to strike back at Diem's corrupt and repressive government. In 1959 Ho's regime began to send aid to southern insurgents who embarked on a program of terror, assassinating hundreds of Diem's village officials. Then in late 1960, southern communists organized the National Liberation Front, known as the Vietcong. The Vietcong in turn attracted other anti-Diem groups in the South. The war against imperialism had become a two-part civil war: Ho's North versus Diem's South, and Vietcong guerrillas versus the Diem government.

Though fearing entrapment in an Asian war, President Kennedy decided to stand firm in Vietnam. In 1961 he ordered more United States military personnel to South Vietnam. By late 1963, Project Beef-up had sent more than 16,000 American "advisers." That year, 489 Americans were killed in Vietnam. Meanwhile, the

Kennedy's Escalation

United States Strategic Hamlet Program, which aimed to isolate peasants from the Vietcong by uprooting them into barbed-wire compounds, alienated villagers and actually strengthened resistance to Diem. Buddhist priests charged Diem with religious persecution. In the streets of Saigon, protesting monks poured gasoline over their robes and ignited themselves.

American officials divided over what to do. Some encouraged a group of ambitious South Vietnamese generals to remove Diem. Kennedy grew impatient with his squabbling advisers, but in the end he let plans go forward for a coup against Diem. With American cooperation, the generals struck on November 1, 1963, capturing and murdering Diem just a few weeks before Kennedy himself met death by an assassin's bullet.

Johnson and Americanization of the War

With new governments in Saigon and in Washington, some world leaders called for a coalition government in South Vietnam. But the new United States president, Lyndon Johnson, was an ardent anticommunist wedded to the global containment doctrine. Johnson would draw the line not only in Southeast Asia but also in Latin America. In 1965 he dispatched twenty thousand United States troops to the Dominican Republic to prevent a leftist government from coming to power. In the *Johnson Doctrine*, he declared that the United States would prevent "another Cuba" by stopping communists from coming to power in the Western Hemisphere.

On August 2, 1964, the U.S.S. *Maddox*—in the Gulf of Tonkin off the coast of North Vietnam on an intelligence-gathering patrol in an area where South Vietnamese commando raids recently had hit North Vietnam—came under attack from northern patrol boats (see map, page 586). The unharmed *Maddox* sailed away. Two days later, the *Maddox* and another destroyer moved toward the North Vietnamese shore. In bad weather on a moonless night, sonar technicians reported torpedo attacks; the two destroyers began firing ferociously.

Tonkin Gulf Incident

As Washington officials met to decide how to retaliate, the *Maddox* sent a flash message: "Review of action makes many reported contacts and torpedoes fired appear doubtful."

President Johnson, aware of the questionable evidence, nonetheless announced on television that the United States would retaliate against the "unprovoked" attack in the Tonkin Gulf by bombing North Vietnam. After brief debates Congress promptly passed the Tonkin Gulf Resolution, by 466 votes to 0 in the House and by 88 votes to 2 in the Senate. The resolution authorized the president to "take all necessary measures to repel any armed attack against the forces of the United States and to prevent further aggression." By passing the Tonkin Gulf Resolution, Congress essentially surrendered its powers in the foreign policy process by giving the president wide latitude to conduct the war as he saw fit.

In neighboring Laos, meanwhile, American bombers hit the "Ho Chi Minh Trail"—supply routes connecting the Vietcong with the North Vietnamese. The bombings

Laos

were kept secret from the American Congress and public. After winning the presidency in his own right in the fall of 1964, Johnson directed the military to plan stepped-up bombing of both Laos and North Vietnam.

In February 1965 the Vietcong, who controlled nearly half of South Vietnam, attacked the American airfield at Pleiku, killing nine Americans. In response, Johnson ordered reprisal strikes on the North. He then authorized Operation Rolling Thunder, a sustained bombing campaign above the 17th parallel.

In late July 1965, Johnson's advisers debated a request from the Joint Chiefs of Staff to add some 100,000 to the 80,000 American troops already in Vietnam. Only Undersecretary of State George Ball dissented, urging that the United States "take our losses, let their government fall apart, negotiate, discuss, knowing full well there will be a probable takeover by the Communists." Worried about the credibility of the United States, Johnson asked: "But George, wouldn't all these countries

George Ball's Dissent

say that Uncle Sam was a paper tiger?" "No sir," Ball retorted. "The worse blow would be that the mightiest power on earth is unable to defeat a handful of guerrillas."

President Johnson nonetheless decided in July to give the Joint Chiefs more troops. A turning point in the Vietnam War, this decision meant that the United States for the first time was assuming primary responsibility for fighting the war.

By the end of 1965, American combat forces in Vietnam totaled 184,300; in early 1969 troops peaked at 543,400. United States warplanes in 1967 alone dropped 226,000 tons of bombs on North Vietnam. And in that year the secret CIA-run Phoenix Program began to kill Vietcong leaders; probably 60,000 were assassinated. Undeterred, Ho increased the flow of arms and men to the rebels in the South. In this seemingly endless war of attrition, each American escalation begot a new Vietnamese escalation.

Americanization of the War

The Americanization of the war under Johnson troubled growing numbers of Americans, especially as television coverage brought the war into their homes. The pictures and stories were not pretty. Innocent civilians died; refugees straggled into "pacification" camps; villages went up in flames; crops were destroyed to starve the Vietcong. To expose and destroy Vietcong hiding places, pilots sprayed chemical defoliants such as Agent Orange over the landscape to denude it. The Vietcong and North Vietnamese contributed to the carnage and destruction, but American guns, bombs, and chemicals took by far the greatest toll, and the Vietnamese people knew it.

Stories of atrocities made their way home. Most gruesome was the My Lai massacre. On March, 16, 1968, a United States Army unit led by Lieutenant William Calley entered the hamlet of My Lai and for four hours mutilated, raped, sodomized, and killed more than three hundred unarmed Vietnamese civilians, most of them women and children.

Calley and the other rapists and killers had lost their moral bearings. But the aftermath reveals that United States officials had lost theirs too. The army covered up the massacre for twenty months. And though Calley was court-martialed in 1971, President Richard Nixon, exploiting the sentiment of many Americans that Calley should be cheered as a hero serving his nation, ordered him released from jail; three years later the mass murderer was paroled. Army juries acquitted and army officials dismissed murder and cover-up charges against all other personnel connected with the massacre.

Most American soldiers were not committing atrocities like those at My Lai. Most were doing their duty and trying to survive a seemingly endless war. Insects, leeches, and skin rotting inside wet boots all took their toll, as did the uncertainty of not knowing who or where the enemy was, and which Vietnamese might be Vietcong terrorists. As morale sagged, disobedience, desertions, and absent-without-official-leave (AWOL) cases steadily increased. Racial tensions between whites and blacks intensified. Drug abuse became serious. Many soldiers smoked plentiful, cheap marijuana, and 10 percent of the troops took heroin. "Fragging"—the mur-

der of officers by enlisted men, usually using hand grenades—took at least a thousand lives between 1969 and 1972.

At home, some young men were expressing their opposition to the war by fleeing the draft. By the end of 1972 more than thirty thousand draft resisters were living in Canada; thousands more had gone into exile in Sweden or Mexico or were living under false identities in the United States. Some 250,000 men refused to register for the draft; thousands more burned their draft cards.

As American military engagements in Vietnam escalated, so did protest at home. Teach-ins at universities began in 1965, and in October of that year the National Committee to End the War in Vietnam mobilized more than 80,000 in nationwide demonstrations. The next year, Senator J. William Fulbright held public hearings on whether the national interest was being served by pursuing the

Antiwar Protest

Wounded American soldiers after a battle in Vietnam.   Larry Burrows, *Life* magazine, ©1971, Time Warner, Inc.

war in Asia. What exactly was the threat? senators asked. In October 1967, 100,000 people marched on Washington to protest the war.

Disenchantment also rose in the administration itself. Secretary of Defense Robert McNamara, once a vigorous advocate of prosecuting the

Robert McNamara Questions Bombing

war, came to believe that continued bombing would not win the war. Publicly, McNamara endorsed Johnson's course and remained loyal to the beleaguered president until early 1968, when McNamara left office. Later, in his 1995 autobiography, the former defense secretary lamented that the decisions of the Kennedy and Johnson administrations on Vietnam "were wrong, terribly wrong."

Cheered by opinion polls that showed Americans favored escalation over withdrawal, Johnson dug in. Though on occasion he halted the bombing to encourage Ho Chi Minh to negotiate, such pauses often were accompanied by increases in American troop strength. The United States also sometimes resumed or accelerated the bombing just when a diplomatic breakthrough seemed imminent. The North demanded a complete suspension of bombing raids before sitting down at the conference table. And Ho could not accept American terms: nonrecognition of the Vietcong as a legitimate political organization, withdrawal of Northern soldiers from the South, and an end to North Vietnamese military aid to the Vietcong—in short, abandonment of his lifelong dream of an independent, unified Vietnam.

In January 1968, a shocking event forced Johnson to reappraise his position. During Tet, the Vietnamese holiday of the lunar new year, Vietcong

Tet Offensive

and North Vietnamese forces struck all across South Vietnam, capturing provincial capitals. United States and South Vietnamese units eventually regained much of the ground they lost, including the cities, and inflicted heavy casualties on the enemy. The Tet offensive, however, jolted Americans. If all of America's airpower and dollars and half a million troops could not defeat the Vietcong once and for all, could anything do so?

Though the Tet offensive led to an American military victory, it counted as a psychological defeat whose impact on public opinion hit the White House like a thunderclap. The new secretary of defense, Clark Clifford, told Johnson that the war could not be won, even if the 206,000 more soldiers requested by the army were sent to Vietnam. The ultimate Cold Warrior, Dean Acheson—one of the "wise men" Johnson brought in to advise him—bluntly told the surprised president that the military brass did not know what they were talking about.

The wise men were aware that the nation was suffering a financial crisis prompted by rampant deficit spending, largely due to heavy United States

Dollar/Gold Crisis

expenditures abroad to sustain the war and other global commitments. Nervous foreigners were exchanging their United States dollars for gold at an alarming rate. A post-Tet effort to take the initiative in Vietnam would surely cost billions more and thus further derail the budget, panic foreign owners of dollars, and wreck the economy.

Strained by exhausting sessions with skeptical advisers, troubled by the economic implications of escalation, sensing that more soldiers and firepower would not bring victory, and faced with serious opposition within his own party, Johnson changed course. On March 31 he announced on television that he had stopped the bombing of most of North Vietnam, and he asked Hanoi to begin negotiations. Then he stunned the nation by dropping out of the presidential race. Peace talks began in May 1968.

 ## The Nixon War and the Legacy of Vietnam

In July 1969, the new president, Richard Nixon, announced the *Nixon Doctrine*: the United States would help those nations that help themselves.

Nixon Doctrine

Washington knew that it no longer could afford to sustain its many overseas commitments and that the United States would have to rely more on regional allies to maintain an anticommunist world order. In Southeast Asia this doctrine translated into "Vietnami-zation"—building up South Vietnamese forces to replace American forces. Nixon began to withdraw United States troops from Vietnam, decreasing their number to 156,800 by the end of 1971. But he also intensified the bombing of the North, hoping to pound Hanoi into concessions.

In April 1970, South Vietnamese and American forces invaded Cambodia in search of arms depots and enemy forces that used the neutral nation as a

Cambodia and Antiwar Protest

sanctuary. This escalation of the war provoked angry demon-strations on college campuses. At Kent State University in Ohio, national guardsmen or-dered to suppress protest killed four people. Across the nation, students went "on strike" to protest the killing in Indochina and Amer-ica. In June the Senate joined the protest against Nixon's broadening of the war by terminating the Tonkin Gulf Resolution of 1964.

Nixon's troubles at home mounted in June 1971 when the *New York Times* began to publish the *Pentagon Papers*, a top-secret official study of United States decisions in the Vietnam War. Daniel Ells-berg, a former Defense Department official working at the RAND Corporation (a think tank for analyz-ing defense policy), leaked the report to the *Times*. The *Pentagon Papers* revealed that American leaders frequently had lied to the American people.

Nixon and Kissinger continued to expand the war, ordering "protective reaction strikes" against the North and the bombing of Cambodia. In De-cember 1972, they launched a massive air strike on the north—the "Christmas bombing." One of Kissinger's aides characterized it as "calculated bar-barism." The air terror of 20,000 tons of bombs punished the Vietnamese. At the same time, the United States lost twenty-six planes, including fif-teen B-52 bombers.

In Paris, meanwhile, the peace talks begun in 1968 seemed to be going nowhere. But Kissin-ger was also meeting privately with Le Duc Tho,

Cease-Fire Agreement

the chief delegate from North Vietnam. On January 27, 1973, Kissinger and Le Duc Tho signed a cease-fire agreement. President Nguyen Van Thieu

of South Vietnam objected to the agreement, but Nixon compelled him to accept it by threatening to cut off United States aid while at the same time promising to defend the South if the North vio-lated the agreement. In the accord, the United States promised to withdraw all of its troops within sixty days. Vietnamese troops would stay in place, and a coalition government that included the Viet-cong eventually would be formed in the South.

The United States pulled its troops out of Viet-nam, leaving behind some advisers, and reduced its aid program. Both North and South soon violated the cease-fire, and full-scale war erupted once more. As many had predicted, the feeble South Viet-namese government could not hold out. On April 29, 1975, the South Vietnamese government col-lapsed. Shortly thereafter Saigon was renamed Ho Chi Minh City for the persevering patriot, who had died in 1969.

The overall costs of the war were immense. More than 58,000 Americans and about 1.5 million Vietnamese had died. The war cost the United

Costs of the Vietnam War

States at least $170 billion, and billions more would be paid out in veterans' benefits. The vast sums spent on the war became unavailable for invest-ment at home to improve the infrastructure. In-stead, the nation suffered inflation and retreat from reform programs. The war also delayed détente with the Soviet Union and the People's Republic of China, fueled friction with allies, and alienated Third World nations.

In 1975 communists assumed control and instituted repressive governments in South Viet-nam, Cambodia, and Laos, but the domino effect once predicted by prowar United States officials never occurred. Acute hunger afflicted the people of those devastated lands. Soon refugees were crowding aboard unsafe vessels in an attempt to escape their battered homelands. Many of these "boat people" eventually emigrated to the United States, where they were received with mixed feel-ings by Americans reluctant to be reminded of de-feat in Asia.

Americans seemed both angry and confused about the nation's war experience. For the first time in their history, historian William Appleman

Lessons of Vietnam

Williams observed, Americans were suffering from a serious case of "empire shock"—that is, shock over having had their overseas sphere of influence violently pushed back. Hawkish leaders claimed that America's failure in Vietnam undermined the nation's credibility and tempted enemies to exploit opportunities at the expense of United States interests. They pointed to a "Vietnam syndrome"—a suspicion of foreign entanglements—that they feared would inhibit the United States from exercising its power. Next time, they said, the military should be permitted to do its job, free from the constraints of whimsical public opinion, stab-in-the-back journalists, and meddlesome politicians. America lost in Vietnam, they asserted, because Americans lost their guts and will at home.

Dovish leaders drew different lessons. Some blamed the war on an imperial presidency that had permitted strong-willed men to act without restraint. Make the president adhere to the checks-and-balances system—make him go to Congress for a declaration of war—these critics counseled, and America would become less interventionist. This view found expression in the War Powers Act of 1973, which sought to limit the president's war-making freedom.

Other critics claimed that as long as the United States remained a major power with compelling ideological, strategic, economic, and political needs that could be satisfied only through activism abroad, the nation would continue to be interventionist. The United States was destined to intervene abroad, they argued, to sustain its role as the world's policeman, teacher, social worker, banker, and merchant.

Some critics blamed the containment doctrine for failing to make distinctions between areas vital and peripheral to the national security and for relying too heavily on military means. Containment could not work, they believed, if there were no political stability and no effective popular government in the country where it was being applied.

Public discussion of the lessons of the Vietnam War also was stimulated by veterans' calls for help in dealing with post-traumatic stress dis-

Post-traumatic Stress Disorder

order. Thousands of Vietnam veterans suffered nightmares and extreme nervousness. Doctors reported that the disorder stemmed primarily from the soldiers' having seen so many children, women, and elderly people killed. Some GIs inadvertently killed these people; some killed them vengefully and later felt guilt. Many vets committed suicide.

Wars and Interventions in the 1970s

Besides struggling with Vietnam, the Nixon and Ford administrations repeatedly exerted United States power in the Third World. They calculated that revolutions and radicalism in the Third World still had to be contained and that the Third World challenge to American influence in international organizations such as the United Nations had to be thwarted.

Events in the Middle East revealed the fragility of the Nixon-Kissinger grand strategy. Israel, using American weapons, had scored victories against Egypt and Syria in the Six-Day War (1967), seizing the West Bank and the ancient city of Jerusalem from Jordan, the Golan Heights from Syria, and the Sinai Peninsula from Egypt—creating the enduring problem of the "occupied territories." To further complicate matters, Palestinians, many of them expelled from their homes in 1948 when the nation of Israel was created, had organized the Palestine Liberation Organization (PLO) and pledged to destroy Israel.

In October 1973, Egypt and Syria attacked Israel. In spite of détente, Moscow (backing Egypt) and Washington (backing Israel) put their armed forces—including their nuclear forces—on alert. In an attempt to push Americans into a pro-Arab stance, the Organization of Petroleum Exporting Countries (OPEC) embargoed shipments of oil to the United States. An energy crisis and dramatically higher oil prices rocked the nation. Soon Kissinger arranged a cease-fire and undertook "shuttle diplomacy," flying repeatedly between Middle Eastern

1973 War in the Middle East

capitals in search of a settlement. In March 1974, OPEC lifted the oil embargo. The next year Kissinger persuaded Egypt and Israel to accept a United Nations peacekeeping force in the Sinai. But peace did not come to the region because Palestinian and other Arabs still vowed to destroy Israel, and Israelis insisted on building Jewish settlements in occupied lands.

In 1970, Nixon spotted a communist threat in Chile, when the citizens of that South American nation elected a Marxist president, Salvador Allende.

Intervention in Chile

The CIA began secret operations to disrupt Chile ("make the economy scream") and encouraged military officers to stage a coup. In 1973 a military junta ousted Allende and installed an authoritarian regime in his place. Nixon and Kissinger privately pronounced their policy of "destabilization" successful, while publicly denying any role in the affair.

In Africa, Nixon backed the white-minority regime in Rhodesia (now Zimbabwe); activated the CIA in a failed effort to defeat a Soviet- and Cuban-backed faction in Angola's civil war; and tolerated the white rulers in South Africa who imposed the racist policy of apartheid on blacks.

Containing Radicalism in Africa

After the leftist government came to power in Angola, however, Washington took a keener interest in the rest of Africa, building economic ties and sending arms to friendly black nations such as Kenya and Zaire. The administration also began to distance the United States from the white governments of Rhodesia and South Africa. America had to "prevent the radicalization of Africa," said Kissinger.

The United States was interventionist in the Third World in part because the American economy depended on imports of strategic raw materials such as tin, zinc, and manganese. Furthermore,

United States Economic Interests Challenged

American investments abroad totaled more than $133 billion by the mid-1970s. American leaders thus read threats to markets, investments, and raw materials as deadly stabs at the high American

standard of living. In 1974, they were particularly alarmed by a call from the United Nations for a "New International Economic Order" for the Third World: low-interest loans, lower prices for technology, and higher prices for raw materials.

 ## Carter's Diplomatic Intervention

When President Jimmy Carter took office in 1977, he promised no more Vietnams. Instead he vowed to emphasize human rights and advance the dialogue with Third World nations. Carter promised to be an interventionist, too, but through diplomacy instead of armed force. Like his predecessors, however, he frowned on radicalism and nationalism because they threatened America's prominent global position.

In the Middle East, Carter markedly improved the peace process. Through tenacious personal diplomacy at a Camp David meeting in 1978 with Egyptian and Israeli leaders,

Camp David Agreements

the president gained Israel's promise to withdraw from the Sinai. The agreement was finalized the following year. Other Arab states denounced the agreement for not requiring Israel to relinquish additional occupied territories—namely, the West Bank and Golan Heights—and for not guaranteeing a Palestinian homeland. But the treaty at least ended warfare along one frontier in that troubled area of the world.

In Latin America, Carter sought compromise with nationalists (see map, page 596), even seeking to reduce tensions with Castro's Cuba by establishing limited diplomatic links. But a crisis in 1980, during which the island regime allowed 100,000 Cubans to sail to Florida from the port of Mariel soured relations once again.

In Panama, citizens longed for control over the Canal Zone, which they believed had been wrongfully taken from their nation in 1903. Carter

Panama Canal Treaties

advanced negotiations that had begun after anti-American riots in Panama in 1964. The United States signed two treaties with Panama in 1977. One provided for the return of the Canal Zone to Panama in 2000,

On March 26, 1979, Egypt's president Anwar el-Sadat (1918–1981) on the right, Israel's prime minister Menachem Begin (1913–1992) on the left, and United States president Jimmy Carter (b. 1924) signed a peace treaty known as the Camp David Accords. Studiously negotiated by Carter, the Egyptian-Israeli peace has held to this day—despite conflict in much of the rest of the Middle East. Jimmy Carter Presidential Library.

and the other guaranteed the United States the right to defend the canal after that time. The Senate narrowly endorsed both agreements in 1978.

Carter met his toughest foreign policy test in Iran, where in 1979 the United States–backed shah was overthrown by revolutionaries led by the Ayatollah Ruhollah Khomeini, a bitterly anti-American Muslim cleric. Much of his anti-Americanism stemmed from the CIA's training of the shah's ruthless secret police and the huge infusion of United States arms into Iran. When the ousted shah was then admitted to the United States for

Iranian Hostage Crisis

medical treatment, mobs stormed the American embassy in Teheran. They took American personnel as hostages, demanding the return of the shah to stand trial. Fifty-two of the hostages languished more than a year under Iranian guard.

President Carter would not return the shah to Iran or apologize for past United States aid to his regime. Unable to gain the hostages' freedom through diplomatic intermediaries, Carter took steps to isolate Iran economically, freezing Iranian assets in the United States. In April 1980, frustrated and at low ebb in public opinion polls, Carter broke diplomatic relations with Iran and ordered a daring rescue mission. But the rescue effort miscarried after equipment failure in the sandy Iranian desert. The hostages were not freed until January 1981, after the United States unfroze Iranian assets and promised not to intervene again in Iran's internal affairs.

Carter's diplomatic record failed to meet his aspirations. More American military personnel were stationed overseas in 1980 than in 1976. The defense budget climbed, and sales of arms abroad grew. Carter's human-rights policy also proved inconsistent: he followed a double standard by applying the human-rights test to some nations (the Soviet Union, Argentina, and Chile) but not to allies of the United States (South Korea, the shah's Iran, and the Philippines).

Carter's Mixed Record

Carter's performance did not satisfy Americans who wanted a post-Vietnam reinstatement of the economic hegemony and military edge the United States once enjoyed. During the 1980 presidential election, this nostalgia for old-fashioned American militancy and supremacy found a ringing voice in Ronald Reagan.

 ## Reagan's Confrontations with the Third World

Reagan blamed most Third World troubles on the Soviet Union and thought revolutionary movements took their orders from communists. Invoking the Reagan Doctrine (see page 569), the United States intervened both covertly and openly in civil wars in several Third World countries. The Reagan administration also preferred military solutions over negotiations. In 1983, for example, United States forces invaded the tiny Caribbean nation of Grenada to oust a leftist government with ties to Castro's Cuba.

Under the banner of private enterprise, Reagan pressed Third World nations to open their economies to competition and reduce the role of the state in managing economic affairs. The United Nations Convention on the Law of the Sea, patiently composed during the years 1973 to 1980 through extended negotiations and compromise, became a test case. Developing nations argued that rich seabed resources of petroleum and minerals should be shared under international supervision among all nations as a "common heritage of mankind." The industrial states preferred private exploitation with minimal international management. The treaty represented a compromise. The Reagan administration rejected the convention on the grounds that it did not adequately protect private American companies. In 1994 the Clinton administration sent the treaty to the Senate, where in early 1998 it remained in committee.

Reagan officials believed that the Soviets and their Cuban allies were fomenting disorder in Central America (see map, page 596). In small, very poor El Salvador, revolutionaries challenged the government, which was dominated by the military and a small landed

El Salvador

elite. The regime used (or could not control) right-wing death squads, which killed thousands of dissidents and other citizens as well as some American missionaries who had been working with landless peasants. Reagan eschewed negotiations and instead in 1981 increased military assistance to the Salvadoran regime.

The United States's intervention in the Salvadoran civil war sparked a debate much like the one that had erupted over Vietnam. Those who urged negotiations thought Reagan wrong to interpret the conflict as a Cold War contest. Oppression and poverty, not communist plots, caused people to pick up guns to fight the regime, they argued. Reagan retorted that the "communists" would soon be at the Mexican-American border if they were not stopped in El Salvador. He also made a strategic argument: Central America hugs the Caribbean Sea, "our lifeline to the outside world." After intense debate, Congress repeatedly gave Reagan the funds he wanted for El Salvador. The civil war continued, more bloody than before.

In 1979 leftist insurgents in Nicaragua overthrew Anastasio Somoza, a long-time ally of the United States. The revolutionaries, called Sandinistas, denounced the tradition of United States imperialism in their country. When the Sandinistas aided rebels in El Salvador, bought Soviet weapons, and invited Cubans to work in Nicaragua's hospitals and schools and to help reorganize their army, Reagan officials charged that Nicaragua was becoming a Soviet client. In 1981 the CIA began to train, arm, and direct more than ten thousand counterrevolutionaries, called contras, for the purpose of overthrowing the Nicaraguan government. From CIA bases in Honduras and Costa Rica, the contras crossed into Nicaragua to kill officials and destroy oil refineries, transportation facilities, medical clinics, and daycare centers.

Contra War Against Nicaragua

It became known in 1984 that the CIA had mined the harbors of Nicaragua, blowing up merchant ships. The World Court ruled that Nicaragua had the right to sue the United States for damages. At the same time Congress voted to stop United States military aid to the contras ("humanitarian" aid was soon sent in its place). Secretly, the Reagan administration lined up other countries, including Saudi Arabia, Panama, and Korea, to funnel money and weapons to the contras, and in 1985 Reagan imposed an economic embargo against Nicaragua. The next year, Congress once again voted military aid for the contras. During the undeclared United States war against Nicaragua, Reagan administration officials rejected opportunities for diplomacy.

Scandal tainted the North American crusade against the Sandinistas. It became known in 1986 that the president's national security affairs adviser, John M. Poindexter, and an aide, Colonel Oliver North, in collusion with CIA director William J. Casey, had covertly sold weapons to Iran and then

Iran-Contra Scandal

The United States in the Caribbean and Central America   *Geographical proximity, economic stakes, political disputes, security links, trade in illicit drugs, and Cuba's alliance with the Soviet Union have kept North American eyes fixed on events to the south.*

diverted the profits to the contras so that they could purchase arms. The diversion occurred after Congress had prohibited military assistance to the contras. Reagan claimed that he knew nothing of these activities. In late 1992, outgoing president George Bush pardoned several former government officials who had been convicted of lying to Congress. Critics smelled a cover-up, for Bush himself, as vice president, had participated in high-level meetings on Iran-contra deals.

In the 1980s, as before, the deeply divided Middle East continued to defy American solutions. An Iraqi-Iranian war, in which the United States aided Iraq, threatened the shipment of Middle East oil that fueled Western economies. And the Middle East was also a major source of the world's terrorism against United States citizens and property.

Even Israel gave the United States trouble. In retaliation for PLO shelling of Israel from Lebanon, the Israelis repeatedly bombed suspected PLO camps inside Lebanon, killing hundreds of civilians.

Crisis in Lebanon

And in 1981, without warning, Israel annexed the Syrian territory of the Golan Heights. The following year, Israeli troops invaded civil war–torn Lebanon, inflicting massive damage. The beleaguered PLO and various Lebanese factions called on Syria to contain the Israelis. Thousands of civilians died in the multifaceted conflict. Reagan sent United States marines to Lebanon to join a peacekeeping force. American troops soon became embroiled in a war between Lebanese factions. In October 1983, terrorist bombs demolished a barracks, killing 241 American servicemen. Four months later, Reagan pulled the remaining marines out.

Washington, which openly sided with Israel, continued to propose peace plans designed to persuade the Israelis to give back occupied territories and the Arabs to give up attempts to push the Jews out of the Middle East (the "land-for-peace" formula). As the peace process stalled in 1987, Palestinians living in the West Bank began an uprising called *intifada* against Israeli forces. Israel refused to negotiate, but the United States decided to reverse its policy and talk with PLO leaders after PLO chief Yasir Arafat renounced terrorism and accepted Israel's right to live in peace and security.

In South Africa, the Reagan administration at first followed a policy called "constructive engagement"—asking the white government to reform its repressive system. But many Americans demanded economic sanctions: cutting off imports from South Africa and pressing some 350 American companies to cease operations there. By 1985 eleven American cities and five states had passed divestment laws, withdrawing dollars (such as pension funds used to buy stock) from American companies active in South Africa. Public protest and congressional legislation forced the Reagan administration in 1986 to impose economic restrictions against South Africa.

South Africa

Meanwhile, the Third World continued to suffer economic setbacks that endangered American prosperity. Third World nations had sunk into staggering debt. Having borrowed heavily in the 1970s, they were unable to repay the loans when world prices for sugar, coffee, and other commodities slumped. By 1989 they owed creditors, including American banks, more than $1.2 trillion. Many Third World nations burdened with such debt had to cut back on imports of United States goods. Hundreds of thousands of jobs in the United States were lost as a result, while economic instability spawned political unrest throughout the Third World.

Bush and Clinton in the Storm

When the Cold War ended in the late 1980s and early 1990s, America's stormy relations with the Third World did not improve. In Central America, however, the Bush administration cooled the zeal with which Reagan had intervened, for the interventions had largely failed. The costly United States–financed contra war had not forced the Sandinistas from power in Nicaragua. In 1989 the Central American presidents devised a workable plan for free elections in Nicaragua and the disbanding of the contras. Yet when the Sandinista Front lost

Ending Civil Wars in Central America

the 1990 elections, Washington claimed victory. Bush's efforts to dampen crises in Central America came to fruition in early 1992 when United Nations mediation led to an agreement between Salvadoran rebels and the government to end their costly civil war.

The profitable trade in illicit drugs also troubled inter-American relations. By 1990 the United States drug market was probably worth $100 billion. As the "drug war" accelerated, Washington used the United States military to quash drug producers and traffickers in Colombia, Bolivia, and Peru, sources of cocaine and crack. North American officials concentrated in interrupting *supply* more than trying to halt *demand* inside the United States itself.

"Drug War"

The drug issue became conspicuous as relations between Panama and the United States deteriorated. Soon after General Manuel Antonio Noriega took power in Panama in 1983, he cut deals with Colombia's cocaine barons. By the late 1980s his dictatorial rule and drug running had angered North Americans eager to blame the swaggering Panamanian for the United States's drug problems. The American people were unaware—though President Bush knew—that Noriega had long been on the CIA payroll and that he had helped the United States aid the contras. Appreciative, Washington had long turned a blind eye to his drug trafficking. When exposés of Noriega's sordid record provoked protests in Panama, however, the United States decided to dump the dictator.

On December 20, 1989, the United States launched Operation Just Cause with an invasion force of 22,500 troops. More than 300 Panamanians died; 23 American soldiers perished. Noriega was captured and taken to Miami, where, in 1992, he was convicted of drug trafficking and imprisoned. Devastated Panama, meanwhile, like war-torn Nicaragua, became all the more dependent on the United States, which offered scant reconstruction aid.

Invasion of Panama

While the United States was managing its sphere of influence in Latin America, it was also helping to end apartheid in South Africa. In part because of the pressure created by American economic sanctions, South Africa's president F. W. de Klerk in 1990 lifted restrictions on dissent and legalized the militantly anti-apartheid African National Congress (ANC). De Klerk also released from prison his nation's most celebrated critic, ANC leader Nelson Mandela. In 1994, Mandela became his nation's first black president.

End of Apartheid in South Africa

Meanwhile, Iraq's dictator Saddam Hussein—resentful that Kuwait would not reduce the huge debt Iraq owed to it and eager to acquire Kuwait's oil—ordered his troops to invade his peaceful neighbor in August 1990. Oil-rich Saudi Arabia, long a United States ally, felt threatened. In Operation Desert Shield, Bush dispatched more than 500,000 United States forces to the region. Likening Saddam to Hitler and declaring the moment the first post–Cold War "test of our mettle," Bush rallied to war a deeply divided Congress. The United Nations also endorsed war and helped organize a coalition of forces. Many Americans believed that economic sanctions imposed on Iraq should be given more time to force Saddam's retreat. Bush would not wait. "This will not be another Vietnam," the president said.

Persian Gulf War

When Operation Desert Storm began on January 16, 1991, the greatest air armada in history began pummeling Iraqi targets. American missiles joined round-the-clock bombing raids on Baghdad, Iraq's capital. In late February, coalition forces launched a ground war that routed the Iraqis from Kuwait in just one hundred hours. The war's toll: at least 35,000 Iraqis dead, and 240 coalition soldiers dead, including 148 Americans.

After achieving the mission of driving Iraq from Kuwait, American leaders decided against sending ground forces into Baghdad. Instead, the CIA began to aid Kurds and other anti-Saddam Iraqis who claimed that they could overthrow the dictator. From 1991 through 1996, they received $100 million from the United States. Saddam, however, remained in power. In late 1997 and early 1998 a major crisis erupted over his refusal to open all sites to United Nations inspection teams looking for weapons of mass destruction. President Clinton readied American forces for missile and air strikes against Iraq. The crisis was defused when the United Nations' secretary general convinced Saddam to allow the inspections.

After the Persian Gulf War, the chances for peace in the Middle East improved for several reasons: Saudi Arabia, the Gulf states, and the recently collapsed Soviet Union trimmed their financial assistance to the PLO, which had backed Iraq; the war exposed divisions among the Arab nations; and the *intifada* was raising Israel's costs of maintaining control over occupied territories. Secretary of State James Baker also pressed Israel to reassess its policies: "Lay aside, once and for all, the unrealistic vision of a greater Israel," he implored. "Forswear annexation. Stop settlement activity. . . . Reach out to the Palestinians as neighbors who deserve political rights."

Gains in the Mideast Peace Process

In a major breakthrough in 1991, Arab and Israeli leaders went to a peace conference in Madrid. In September 1993, the PLO's Yasir Arafat and Israel's Prime Minister Yizhak Rabin signed an agreement for Palestinian self-rule in the Gaza Strip and the West Bank's Jericho. In 1994, Israel signed a peace accord with Jordan, further reducing the chances of another full-scale Arab-Israeli war. Radical anti-Arafat Palestinians, however, continued to stage bloody terrorist attacks on Israelis, while extremist Israelis killed Palestinians and, in November 1995, even Rabin himself. Arafat won Palestine's first national election in early 1996. But the 1996 election of a conservative Israeli government that openly rejected the "land-for-peace" concept sparked new disputes with the Palestinians. The peace process stalled.

The United States also became involved in peacekeeping efforts in East Africa. Somalia had long suffered from the effects of soil erosion and famine. When Somalia's repressive dictator was driven from power in early 1991, rival clans vied for power and public authority broke down. Gun-toting bandits stole international relief

Operation Restore Hope in Somalia

supplies. Hundreds of thousands of Somalis died. President Bush ordered more than 28,000 American troops to Somalia in December 1992 to ensure the delivery of relief aid. A United Nations peacekeeping force, including 9,000 Americans, took over in mid-1993 (see map, page 600). In early 1994 Clinton pulled all United States troops out; the United Nations peacekeepers left about a year later. The mission had saved perhaps some 250,000 lives, but Somalia reverted to violent, chaotic politics.

United States troops also found their way to Haiti. In 1990 poverty-wracked and environmentally devastated Haiti held its first free elections in decades. But the next year the Haitian army overthrew the government of Jean-Bertrand Aristide. The United States imposed economic sanctions against the Caribbean nation, causing further hardship. Tens of thousands of Haitians fled in boats for United States territory, spawning an immigration crisis. The United States demanded that the military dictators restore Aristide to power, but they balked. Then in September 1994, Clinton sent Jimmy Carter to Haiti. The former president cut a deal with the generals that gave them "honorable retirement" under a general amnesty. Soon, without seeking congressional approval, Clinton ordered United States troops to Haiti in Operation Uphold Democracy. Aristide returned. In early 1996 American forces departed, their mission to revitalize Haiti yet unfulfilled.

United States Troops to Haiti

Throughout Latin America, the Clinton administration continued to promote liberalized trade, privatized economies, orderly immigration, democratization, and the war against drugs. When politically corrupt Mexico's economy neared collapse in 1995, the United States bailed it out with large loans. As for Cuba, Clinton encouraged cultural exchanges while maintaining the punishing economic embargo.

In March 1996, after an airplane carrying members of the provocative anti-Castro group Brothers to the Rescue was shot down by Cuban fighter pilots near Cuba, Clinton pandered to the politically influential Cuban-American communities in Florida and New Jersey and signed

Helms-Burton Act and Cuba

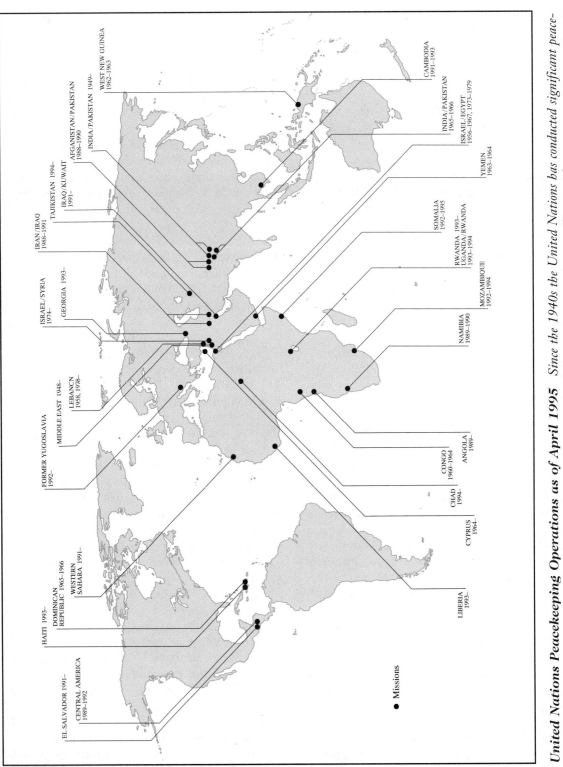

United Nations Peacekeeping Operations as of April 1995   *Since the 1940s the United Nations has conducted significant peace-keeping operations, using the contributed troops of many nations to quiet civil unrest or to monitor compliance with agreements.*   Source: Adapted from United Nations, *Yearbook of the United Nations* (New York: Special Edition, 1995).

the Helms-Burton Act. This legislation tightened the economic embargo against the Caribbean island by allowing American nationals and companies to sue in United States courts foreign companies that were using formerly American-owned properties in Cuba. The Castro government had seized these assets in the early days of the Cuban Revolution. After Canada and the European Union (both traded with Cuba) took the issue to the World Trade Organization, the Clinton administration suspended the act's provision that permitted the suing of foreign companies.

In an increasingly fragmented international system, Third World issues filled the international agenda. Clinton administration officials and

**Americans
Debate the
United States's
Role in
the World**

other internationalists spoke of America's "world responsibilities," humanitarianism, and dedication to spreading democracy abroad. Others argued that the United States had neither the money nor the ability to build or reform other peoples; instead, the United States had to accept its limitations and solve its own domestic problems first. Reasserting traditional notions of United States world leadership, Clinton dismissed such thinking as a dangerous retreat to "isolationism."

Americans divided over foreign policy issues in a host of ways, and the budget especially sparked debate. Some people worried about domestic ills such as crime and underfunded education. Decline-theorist Paul Kennedy favored reallocating some funds in the military budget ($260 billion in 1995) "to employ the tens of thousands of scientists and engineers now released from Cold War-related research to seek solutions to environmental problems." Indeed, disappointed environmentalists, predicting a bleak future of ozone-layer depletion, deforestation, polluted water, and global warming, appealed for greater United States activism.

Conservative nationalists demanded less United States cooperation with the United Nations, which they condemned as too expensive, inefficient, and challenging to American sovereignty. Defenders of the world body praised its positive role in the Persian Gulf War and its successful calming of civil wars in El Salvador, Mozambique, Cambodia, and Guatemala. The United Nations also conducted important peacekeeping functions in Africa and the Middle East. Yet the United Nations became strapped for funds for peacekeeping, in part because by 1998 the United States owed the organization $1.5 billion in unpaid contributions.

Laborers in declining industries protested NAFTA and other trade agreements that cost them jobs. Women, such as those who attended the International Conference on Women in Beijing in 1995, lobbied for a major American commitment to combat gender discrimination. Seventy percent of the world's poor were women, and women worldwide earned 30 to 40 percent less than their male counterparts for the same work. Military veterans and families of missing-in-action (MIA) soldiers protested Clinton's 1996 decision to open full diplomatic relations with Vietnam, while American businesses such as Otis and Pepsico welcomed the new economic opportunities there. Human-rights observers criticized Clinton's preference for expanding trade rather than pressing for human rights in relations with China. In mid-1994, moreover, the United States and the United Nations responded too late to the Hutus' calculated genocide against the Tutsis in Rwanda, where between 500,000 and 1 million Tutsis were butchered in a ghastly display of ethnic rivalry.

 Conclusion

Since 1945 the United States has been at odds with the Third World. The United States usually stood with its European Cold War allies to resist decolonization and denounced the preference of many Third World nations for nonalignment in the Cold War. And the globalist perspective of the United States prompted Americans to interpret many Third World troubles as Cold War conflicts, inspired if not directed by Soviet-backed communists. The intensity of the Cold War obscured for Americans the indigenous roots of most Third World troubles, as the Vietnam War attested.

Nor could the United States abide Third World nations' drive for economic independence—

for gaining control of their own raw materials and economies. Deeply intertwined in the global economy as importer, exporter, and investor, the United States read Third World challenges as threats to the American standard of living and way of life. Through foreign aid, trade and investment, CIA covert actions, diplomatic mediation, USIA propaganda, military interventions, arms sales, development projects, cultural exchanges, environmental treaties, and more, the United States has sought for a half-century to help and to discipline Third World peoples. When the Cold War ended, the Third World still remained—high on the world agenda.

Suggestions for Further Reading

For the Cold War, Soviet-American relations, Sino-American relations, and environmental issues, see Chapter 29. Many works cited in Chapter 29 include discussion of issues related to the Third World.

Third World Relations: Truman to Clinton

Richard J. Barnet, *Intervention and Revolution* (1972); Edward H. Berman, *The Influence of the Carnegie, Ford, and Rockefeller Foundations on American Foreign Policy* (1983); Scott L. Bills, *Empire and Cold War* (1990); H. W. Brands, *The Specter of Neutralism* (1989); Gabriel Kolko, *Confronting the Third World* (1988); James Mayall, ed., *The New Interventionism* (1996); Larry Minear and Thomas G. Weiss, *Humanitarian Politics* (1995); Brenda G. Plummer, *Rising Wind: Black Americans and U.S. Foreign Affairs, 1935–1960* (1996); David M. Reimers, *Still the Golden Door* (1992) (on immigration); Alvin Z. Rubenstein and Donald E. Smith, eds., *Anti-Americanism in the Third World* (1985); Paul B. Stares, *Global Habit* (1996) (on drugs); Ronald Steel, *Temptations of a Superpower* (1995); Stephen R. Weissman, *A Culture of Deference: Congress's Failure of Leadership in Foreign Policy* (1995). For global economic issues, see works cited in Chapter 29.

The CIA and Counterinsurgency

Douglas S. Blaufarb, *The Counterinsurgency Era* (1977); Peter Grose, *Gentleman Spy* (1994) (on Allen Dulles); Rhodi Jeffreys-Jones, *The CIA and American Democracy* (1989); Loch K. Johnson, *America's Secret Power* (1989); Mark Lowenthal, *U.S. Intelligence* (1984); Thomas Powers, *The Man Who Kept the Secrets* (1979); John Prados, *Presidents' Secret Wars* (1986); John Ranelagh, *The Agency* (1986); Jeffrey T. Richelson, *A Century of Spies* (1995); Jeffrey T. Richelson, *The U.S. Intelligence Community*, 3d ed. (1995); Robin Winks, *Cloak & Gown* (1987).

The Vietnam War and Southeast Asia: General

David L. Anderson, *Shadow on the White House* (1993); Loren Baritz, *Backfire* (1985); Eric M. Bergerud, *The Dynamics of Defeat* (1991); William J. Duiker, *U.S. Containment Policy and the Conflict in Indochina* (1994); Frances FitzGerald, *Fire in the Lake* (1972); William C. Gibbons, *The U.S. Government and the Vietnam War* (1986–1994); Daniel C. Hallin, *The "Uncensored War"* (1986); George C. Herring, *America's Longest War* (1996); Gary R. Hess, *Vietnam and the United States* (1990); Stanley Karnow, *Vietnam* (1991); Gabriel Kolko, *Anatomy of a War* (1986); Guenter Lewy, *America in Vietnam* (1978); Joseph G. Morgan, *The Vietnam Lobby: The American Friends of Vietnam, 1955–1975* (1997); William Shawcross, *Sideshow* (1979) (on Cambodia); Anthony Short, *The Origins of the Vietnam War* (1989); Marilyn B. Young, *The Vietnam Wars* (1991). For works on the antiwar movement, see Chapter 31.

Truman, Eisenhower, and Vietnam

David L. Anderson, *Trapped by Success* (1991); James R. Arnold, *The First Domino* (1991); Melanie Billings-Yun, *Decision Against War: Eisenhower and Dien Bien Phu, 1954* (1988); Lloyd C. Gardner, *Approaching Vietnam* (1988); Gary Hess, *The United States' Emergence as a Southeast Asian Power* (1987); Lawrence S. Kaplan et al., eds., *Dien Bien Phu and the Crisis of Franco-American Relations* (1990); David G. Marr, *Vietnam 1945* (1995); Andrew Rotter, *The Path to Vietnam* (1987); Stein Tonnesson, *The Vietnamese Revolution of 1945* (1991).

Kennedy, Johnson, Vietnam, and the Third World

LeRoy Ashby and Rod Gramer, *Fighting the Odds* (1994) (on Senator Frank Church); David M. Barrett, *Uncertain Warriors* (1993); Larry Berman, *Lyndon Johnson's War* (1989); Larry Berman, *Planning a Tragedy* (1982); James A. Bill, *George Ball* (1997); Larry Cable, *Unholy Grail* (1991); Charles DeBenedetti and Charles Chatfield, *An American Ordeal* (1990) (on antiwar movement); David L. DiLeo, *George Ball, Vietnam, and the Rethinking of Containment* (1991); Lloyd C. Gardner, *Pay Any Price* (1995); George C. Herring, *LBJ and Vietnam* (1994); Michael H. Hunt, *Lyndon Johnson's War* (1996); George McT. Kahin, *Intervention* (1986); Diane Kunz, ed., *The Diplomacy of the Crucial Decade* (1994); Thomas G. Paterson, ed., *Kennedy's Quest for Victory* (1989); William Prochnau, *Once upon a Distant War* (1995) (on journalists); Gerald T. Rice, *The Bold Experiment: JFK's Peace Corps* (1985); Deborah Shapley, *Promise and Power* (1993) (on Robert McNamara); Kevin Sim and Michael Bilton, *Four Hours in My Lai* (1992); Melvin Small, *Johnson, Nixon and the Doves* (1988); Brian VanDerMark, *Into the Quagmire* (1991); Randall B. Woods, *Fulbright* (1995).

The Vietnam War: Military Aspects

Robert Buzzanco, *Masters of War: Military Dissent and Politics in the Vietnam Era* (1996); Jeffrey J. Clarke, *United States Army in*

Vietnam (1988); Mark Clodfelter, *The Limits of Power* (1989) (on bombing); Phillip B. Davidson, *Vietnam at War* (1988); Ronald H. Spector, *After Tet: The Bloodiest Year in Vietnam* (1992); Ronald H. Spector, *United States Army in Vietnam* (1983).

Legacy and Lessons of the Vietnam War

John Hellman, *American Myth and the Legacy of Vietnam* (1986); Herbert Hendin and Ann P. Haas, *Wounds of War: The Psychological Aftermath of Combat in Vietnam* (1984); Ole R. Holsti and James Rosenau, *American Leadership in World Affairs: Vietnam and the Breakdown of Consensus* (1984); David Levy, *The Debate over Vietnam* (1991); Myra MacPherson, *Long Time Passing* (1984); Norman Podhoretz, *Why We Were in Vietnam* (1982); Earl C. Ravenal, *Never Again* (1978); Harrison E. Salisbury, ed., *Vietnam Reconsidered* (1984); Harry G. Summers, Jr., *On Strategy* (1982).

Latin America: General

Cole Blasier, *Hovering Giant* (1974); David W. Dent, ed., *U.S.-Latin American Policymaking* (1995); Guy Gugliotta and Jeff Leen, *Kings of Cocaine* (1989); Lester Langley, *America and the Americas* (1989); Abraham F. Lowenthal, ed., *Exporting Democracy* (1991); Abraham F. Lowenthal, *Partners in Conflict: The United States and Latin America*, rev. ed. (1990); Donald J. Mabry, ed., *The Latin American Narcotics Trade and U.S. National Security* (1989); Brenda G. Plummer, *Haiti and the United States* (1992); W. Dirk Raat, *Mexico and the United States* (1992); Stephen G. Rabe, *Eisenhower and Latin America* (1988); Stephen G. Rabe, *The Road to OPEC: United States Relations with Venezuela* (1982); William F. Sater, *Chile and the United States* (1990); Peter H. Smith, *Talons of the Eagle . . .* (1996). Books on Cuba and the missile crisis are cited in Chapter 29.

Central America and Panama

Cynthia J. Arnson, *Crossroads* (1989) (on Ronald Reagan); Morris J. Blachman et al., eds., *Confronting Revolution* (1986); Kevin Buckley, *Panama* (1991); John Coatsworth, *Central America and the United States* (1994); Kenneth M. Coleman and George C. Herring, eds., *Understanding the Central American Crisis* (1991); Michael Conniff, *Panama and the United States* (1992); John Dinges, *Our Man in Panama* (1990); Theodore Draper, *A Very Thin Line: the Iran-Contra Affairs* (1991); Piero Gleijeses, *Shattered Hope* (1991) (on Guatemala); J. Michael Hogan, *The Panama Canal in American Politics* (1986); Richard Immerman, *The CIA in Guatemala* (1982); Michael Klare and Peter Kornbluh, eds., *Low Intensity Warfare* (1988); Walter LaFeber, *Inevitable Revolutions* (1993); Walter LaFeber, *The Panama Canal* (1989); Anthony Lake, *Somoza Falling* (1989); Robert A. Pastor, *Whirlpool* (1992); Robert A. Pastor, *Condemned to Repetition* (1987) (on Nicaragua); Peter Dale Scott and Jonathan Marshall, *Cocaine Politics* (1991); Christian Smith, *Resisting Reagan: the U.S.-Central America Peace Movement* (1996); Thomas W. Walker, ed., *Revolution and Counterrevolution in Nicaragua* (1991).

Middle East

James A. Bill, *The Eagle and the Lion* (1988) (on Iran); William J. Burns, *Economic Aid and American Policy Toward Egypt, 1955–1981* (1985); Michael J. Cohen, *Palestine and the Great Powers, 1945–1948* (1983); Mark Gasiorowski, *U.S. Foreign Policy and the Shah* (1991); Peter L. Hahn, *The United States, Great Britain, and Egypt, 1945–1956* (1991); Burton I. Kaufman, *The Arab Middle East and the United States* (1996); Diane Kunz, *The Economic Diplomacy of the Suez Crisis* (1991); George Lenczowski, *The Middle East in World Affairs*, 4th ed. (1980); William Roger Louis and Roger Owen, eds., *Suez 1956* (1989); Aaron D. Miller, *Search for Security* (1980); Donald Neff, *Warriors at Suez* (1981); William B. Quandt, *Peace Process* (1993); Cheryl A. Rubenberg, *Israel and the American National Interest* (1986); David Schoenbaum, *The United States and the State of Israel* (1993); Gary Sick, *October Surprise* (1991) (on Iranian hostage crisis); Steven L. Spiegel, *The Other Arab-Israeli Conflict* (1985); William Stivers, *America's Confrontation with Revolutionary Change in the Middle East* (1986); Robert W. Stookey, *America and the Arab States* (1975); Daniel Yergin, *The Prize* (1991) (on oil).

Persian Gulf War

Deborah Amos, *Lines in the Sand* (1992); Lawrence Freedman and Efraim Karsh, *The Gulf Conflict, 1990–1991* (1993); Stephen Graubard, *Mr. Bush's War* (1992); John MacArthur, *Second Front: Censorship and Propaganda in the Gulf War* (1992); John Mueller, *Policy and Opinion in the Gulf War* (1994); Joseph S. Nye, Jr., and Roger K. Smith, eds., *After the Storm* (1992); Michael Palmer, *Guardians of the Gulf* (1992); Jean Edward Smith, *George Bush's War* (1992); Philip M. Taylor, *War and the Media* (1992).

Africa

Pauline H. Baker, *The United States and South Africa: The Reagan Years* (1989); Thomas Borstelmann, *Apartheid's Reluctant Uncle* (1993); Christopher Coker, *The United States and South Africa, 1968–1985* (1986); David N. Gibbs, *The Political Economy of Third World Intervention* (1991) (on Congo crisis); Jeffrey Lefebvre, *Arms for the Horn* (1992) (on Ethiopia and Somalia); Richard D. Mahoney, *JFK: Ordeal in Africa* (1983); Thomas J. Noer, *Cold War and Black Liberation* (1985); Peter J. Schraeder, *United States Policy Toward Africa* (1994); Jonathan Stevenson, *Losing Mogadishu* (1995) (on Somalia).

Asia

H. W. Brands, *India and the United States* (1989); Kenton J. Clymer, *Question for Freedom* (1995) (on India's independence); Nick Cullather, *Illusions of Influence* (1994) (on the Philippines); Audrey R. Kahin and George McT. Kahin, *Subversion as Foreign Policy* (1995) (on Indonesia); Stanley Karnow, *In Our Image* (1989) (on the Philippines); Robert J. McMahon, *Colonialism and Cold War* (1981) (on Indonesia); Dennis Merrill, *Bread and the Ballot* (1990) (on India). Works on United States relations with China and Japan are cited in Chapter 29.

CHAPTER

31

Reform and Conflict:
A Turbulent Era
1961–1974

I
n 1964 politics and civil rights were in the forefront of the news and inextricably tied together. It was a presidential election year, and when the Democrats convened to pick a presidential candidate, they discovered how politically volatile the civil rights issue could be. Two delegations had arrived from Mississippi, demanding to be seated. One was all-white; the other was largely African-American and called itself the Mississippi Freedom Democratic Party (MFDP). Arguing that the state's regular Democratic organization was vehemently segregationist, the MFDP asked the convention to honor its credentials.

In Mississippi, as a result of phony literacy tests, economic intimidation, and violence, less than 7 percent of the black population could vote. In 1963, civil rights activists conducted their own "freedom vote," and a year later the MFDP ran candidates for Congress. The same year, more than a thousand northern students traveled south to Mississippi to work for the Freedom Summer Project, registering voters and organizing protests against segregation. In response, white vigilantes bombed and burned two dozen black churches, and three civil rights workers— one black and two white—were murdered by sheriff's deputies in Philadelphia, Mississippi.

It was in this context that the Democratic Party's credentials committee met on August 22, 1964, to hear the contesting delegations. The hearings were nationally televised. Speaking for the MFDP was Fannie Lou Hamer, a forty-six-year-old African-American field secretary for the

Student Nonviolent Coordinating Committee (SNCC). Hamer was the twentieth child of sharecropper parents. By the time she was thirteen she was picking three to four hundred pounds of cotton a day on a plantation in Sunflower County.

In the early 1960s, Fannie Lou Hamer began to envision a better future through the direct action of the civil rights movement. In 1962, she lost her job when she attempted to register to vote. The next year, Hamer was arrested with five other SNCC volunteers and brutally assaulted by police swinging blackjacks. By 1964, she had become a field worker for SNCC, known for her courage and inspiring speeches and singing.

At the Democratic convention, Hamer spoke to the credentials committee and the television audience. She described being beaten in jail because she and others "wanted to register, to become first-class citizens." She demanded that the MFDP—those who had fought for freedom—be seated, not those who opposed it. If "the Freedom Party is not seated now I question America," she said.

The MFDP did not receive justice from the Democratic Party. Offered a consolation prize of two seats, the MFDP refused. "We didn't come all this way for no two seats," Hamer said. In this election year, President Johnson was unwilling to alienate powerful southern white politicians by seating the civil rights delegation, but his action threw into question the Democrats' commitment to racial equality. Civil rights had become the most important political issue in the country; it also threatened to destroy the New Deal coalition.

The civil rights movement was a dynamic motive force in America society in the 1960s, giving birth in subsequent years to the antiwar movement, the New Left, and a resurgent feminist movement, not to mention the environmental movement and equality movements for other minorities. The civil rights movement also energized the presidential politics of John F. Kennedy and Lyndon B. Johnson. Kennedy's call for a New Frontier had inspired liberals, idealists, and brave young activists to work to eliminate poverty, segregation, and voting rights abuses. But Americans' dreams were shattered on November 22, 1963, when President Kennedy was assassinated in Dallas.

Lyndon Johnson, who asked for national unity in the wake of the Kennedy assassination, was a strong leader who presided over what he called the Great Society. His administration produced a flood of legislation, including civil rights laws, anti-poverty measures, and the Medicare program. But amid these liberal triumphs, anger and social tension intermittently flared into violence. Beginning with Kennedy's assassination in 1963, ten years of bloodshed—race riots, the murders of other political and civil rights leaders, and the war in Vietnam—shattered the optimism of the Kennedy and Johnson eras.

The perceived excesses of the 1960s, added to snowballing white opposition to the civil rights movement, prompted many Americans to shift to the right politically. In 1968, Richard M. Nixon was elected president, but his presidency polarized the nation still further. The presidencies of Nixon's two immediate predecessors had ended tragically: Dallas and Vietnam were the sites of their undoings. A third location, the Watergate apartment complex in Washington, D.C., would become Richard Nixon's downfall.

Civil Rights and the New Frontier

President John F. Kennedy was, as the writer Norman Mailer observed, "our leading man." Young, handsome, and vigorous, the new chief executive was the first president born in the twentieth century. Kennedy had a genuinely inquiring mind, and as a patron of the arts he brought wit and sophistication to the White House.

In a departure from the Eisenhower administration's staid, conservative image, the new president surrounded himself with young men of intellectual verve who proclaimed that they had fresh ideas for invigorating the nation; the writer David Halberstam called them "the best and the brightest" (Kennedy appointed only one woman to a significant position). Secretary of Defense Robert McNamara (age forty-four) had been an assistant professor at Harvard at twenty-four and later the whiz-kid

"The Best and the Brightest"

president of the Ford Motor Company. Kennedy's special assistant for national security affairs, McGeorge Bundy (age forty-one) had become a Harvard dean at thirty-four with only a bachelor's degree. Kennedy himself was only forty-three, and his brother Robert, the attorney general, was thirty-five.

Kennedy's ambitious program, the New Frontier, promised more than the president could deliver: an end to racial discrimination, federal aid to education, medical care for the elderly, and government action to halt the recession the country was suffering. Only eight months into his first year, it was evident that Kennedy lacked the ability to move a Congress dominated by conservative Republicans and southern Democrats.

The New Frontier

Struggling to appease conservative members of Congress, the new president pursued civil rights with a notable lack of vigor. Kennedy did establish the President's Committee on Equal Employment Opportunity to eliminate racial discrimination in government hiring. But he waited until late 1962 before honoring a 1960 campaign pledge to issue an executive order forbidding segregation in federally subsidized housing. Meanwhile, he appointed five die-hard segregationists to the federal bench in the Deep South. The struggle for racial equality was the most important domestic issue of the time, and Kennedy's performance disheartened civil rights advocates.

Despite President Kennedy's lack of support, African-American civil rights activists in the early 1960s continued their struggle through the tactic of nonviolent civil disobedience. Volunteers organized by the Southern Christian Leadership Conference (SCLC), headed by Reverend Martin Luther King, Jr., deliberately violated segregation laws by sitting in at whites-only lunch counters, libraries, and bus stations in the South. The Congress of Racial Equality (CORE) initiated the Freedom Rides in May 1961: an integrated group of thirteen people boarded a bus in Washington, D.C., and traveled into the South, where they

SCLC, CORE, and SNCC

braved attacks by white mobs for daring to desegregate interstate transportation. Meanwhile, black students in the South joined the Student Nonviolent Coordinating Committee (SNCC). These young people walked the dusty back roads of Mississippi and Georgia, encouraging African-Americans to resist segregation and register to vote.

As the civil rights movement gained momentum, President Kennedy gradually made a commitment to first-class citizenship for blacks. In 1962 he ordered U.S. marshals to protect James Meredith, the first African-American student to attend the University of Mississippi. And in June 1963 Kennedy finally requested legislation to outlaw racial discrimination in employment and racial segregation in public accommodations. When more than 250,000 people, black and white, gathered at the Lincoln Memorial for a March on Washington that August, they did so with the knowledge that President Kennedy was at last on their side.

March on Washington

The television nightly news programs brought the civil rights struggles into Americans' homes. The story was sometimes grisly. In 1963 Medgar Evers, director of the NAACP in Mississippi, was gunned down in his own driveway. The same year police in Birmingham, Alabama, attacked nonviolent civil rights demonstrators, including children, with snarling dogs, fire hoses, and cattle prods. Then, two horrifying events helped to convince reluctant politicians that action on civil rights was long overdue. In September white terrorists exploded a bomb during Sunday morning services at Birmingham's Sixteenth Street Baptist Church. Sunday school was in session, and four black girls were killed. A little more than two months later, John Kennedy was assassinated in Dallas.

The first dreadful flash of Kennedy's shooting clattered over newsroom Teletype machines across the country at 1:34 P.M. Eastern Standard Time, November 22, 1963. Broadcast immediately on radio and television, the news was soon on the streets. Time stopped for Americans, and they experienced what psychologists call flashbulb memory,

The Kennedy Assassination

• *Important Events* •

1960   John F. Kennedy elected president

1961   President's Commission on the Status of
Women established

1962   Students for a Democratic Society issues Port
Huron Statement
Baker v. *Carr* establishes "one person, one
vote" principle

1963   Betty Friedan's *The Feminine Mystique* published
Civil rights advocates march on Washington
Baptist church in Birmingham, Alabama,
bombed
Kennedy assassinated; Lyndon B. Johnson
becomes president

1964   Economic Opportunity Act allocates funds to
fight poverty
Civil Rights Act outlaws discrimination in
jobs and public accommodations
Twenty-fourth Amendment outlaws the poll
tax in federal elections
Riots break out in first of the "long hot
summers"
Fannie Lou Hamer speaks on behalf of
Mississippi Freedom Democratic Party at
Democratic convention
Free Speech Movement begins at Berkeley
Johnson elected president

1965   Malcolm X assassinated
Voting Rights Act allows federal supervision
of voting registration
Medicare program established
Elementary and Secondary Education Act
provides federal aid to education
Watts race riot leaves thirty-four dead

1966   National Organization for Women (NOW)
founded
Miranda v. *Arizona* requires police to inform
suspects of their rights

1967   Race riots erupt in Newark, Detroit, and
other cities
Twenty-fifth Amendment establishes the
order of presidential succession

1968   U.S.S. *Pueblo* captured by North Korea
Tet offensive causes fear of losing Vietnam War
Martin Luther King, Jr., assassinated
African-Americans riot in 168 cities and towns
Civil Rights Act bans discrimination in housing
Antiwar protests escalate
Robert F. Kennedy assassinated
Violence erupts at Democratic convention
Richard M. Nixon elected president

1969   Stonewall riot sparked by police harassment
of homosexuals
400,000 gather at Woodstock festival
Moratorium Day calls for end to Vietnam War

1970   United States invades Cambodia
Students killed at Kent State and Jackson
State Universities
Environmental Protection Agency created

1971   *Pentagon Papers* published
Twenty-sixth Amendment extends vote to
eighteen-year-olds
Swann v. *Charlotte-Mecklenberg* upholds
North Carolina desegregation plan

1972   Nixon visits China and Soviet Union
Congress approves Equal Rights Amendment
"Plumbers" break into Watergate
Nixon reelected

1973   Watergate burglars tried
Senator Sam Ervin chairs Watergate hearings
White House aides John Ehrlichman and
H. R. Haldeman resign
Roe v. *Wade* legalizes abortion
War Powers Act passed
Spiro Agnew resigns; Nixon appoints Gerald
R. Ford vice president
"Saturday Night Massacre" provokes public
outcry

1974   Supreme Court orders Nixon to release
White House tapes
House Judiciary Committee votes to impeach
Nixon
Nixon resigns; Ford becomes president
Ford pardons Nixon
Freedom of Information Act passed over
Ford's veto

the freeze-framing of an exceptionally emotional event down to the most incidental detail.

Historians have wondered what John Kennedy would have accomplished had he lived. Although his legislative achievements were meager, he inspired genuine idealism in Americans. When Kennedy exhorted Americans in his inaugural address to "Ask not what your country can do for you; ask what you can do for your country," tens of thousands volunteered to spend two years of their lives in the Peace Corps. Kennedy also promoted a sense of national purpose through his vigorous support of the space program.

In recent years, writers have drawn attention to Kennedy's recklessness in world events, such as authorizing CIA attempts to assassinate Cuba's leader Fidel Castro. They also

Kennedy in Retrospect

have criticized his timidity in civil rights. It is clear, however, that Kennedy had begun to grow as president during his last few months in office. He made a moving appeal for racial equality and called for reductions in Cold War tensions. And in a peculiar way he accomplished more in death than in life. In the post-assassination atmosphere of grief and remorse, Lyndon Johnson pushed through Congress practically the entire New Frontier agenda.

 ## The Great Society and the Triumph of Liberalism

In the aftermath of the assassination, President Johnson resolved to unite the country behind the unfulfilled legislative program of the martyred president. More than that, he wanted to realize Roosevelt's and Truman's unmet goals. He called his new program the Great Society.

Johnson made civil rights his top legislative priority. "No memorial oration or eulogy," he told a joint session of Congress five days after the assassination, "could more elo-

Civil Rights Act of 1964

quently honor President Kennedy's memory than the earliest passage of the civil rights bill." Within months Johnson had signed into law the Civil Rights Act of 1964, which

outlawed discrimination on the basis of race, color, religion, sex, or national origin, not only in public accommodations but also in employment. The act also authorized the government to withhold funds from public agencies that discriminated on the basis of race, and it empowered the attorney general to guarantee voting rights and end school segregation. In 1964 African-Americans gained two additional victories. First, the president appointed an Equal Employment Opportunity Commission to investigate and judge complaints of job discrimination. Second, the states ratified the Twenty-fourth Amendment to the Constitution, which outlawed the poll tax in federal elections.

Johnson enunciated another priority in his first State of the Union address: "The administration today . . . declares unconditional war on poverty." Eight months later, he signed into law the Economic Opportunity Act of 1964. The act became the opening salvo in Johnson's War on Poverty.

In the year following Kennedy's death, Johnson sought to govern by a liberal consensus, appealing to the shared values and aspirations of the majority of the nation for

Election of 1964

continued economic growth and social justice. His lopsided victory in 1964 over his conservative Republican opponent, Senator Barry Goldwater of Arizona, indicates that he succeeded. Johnson garnered 61 percent of the popular vote and the electoral votes of all but six states. Riding on Johnson's coattails, the Democrats won large majorities in both the House and the Senate. Johnson recognized that the opportunity to push through further reform had arrived, and Congress responded in 1965 and 1966 with the most sweeping reform legislation since 1935.

Three bills enacted in 1965 were legislative milestones: the Medicare program insured the elderly against medical and hospital bills; the Ele-

Voting Rights Act of 1965

mentary and Secondary Education Act provided for general federal aid to education for the first time; and the Voting Rights Act of 1965 empowered the attorney general to supervise voter registration in areas where fewer than half the minority residents of voting age were registered. In 1960 only 29 percent of the South's African-American population was registered to vote; when Johnson left office in 1969, the proportion was approaching two-thirds.

The flurry of legislation enacted into law during Johnson's presidency was staggering: establishment of the Department of Housing and Urban Development, the Department of Transportation, and the National Endowments for the Arts and Humanities; water- and air-quality improvement acts; liberalization of immigration laws; and appropriations for the most ambitious federal housing program since 1949, including rent supplements to low-income families. In 1968 Johnson signed another Civil Rights Act—his third—banning racial and religious discrimination in the sale and rental of housing. Another provision of this legislation, known as the Indian Bill of Rights, extended those constitutional protections to American Indians living under tribal self-government on reservations.

By far the most ambitious of Johnson's initiatives was the War on Poverty. Beginning with a $1 billion appropriation in 1964, the War on Poverty evolved in 1965 and 1966 to include the Job Corps, to provide marketable skills, work experience, and remedial education for young people; Project Head Start, to prepare preschoolers from low-income families for grade school; and Upward Bound, to help high-school students from low-income families to prepare for a college education. Other antipoverty programs were Legal Services for the Poor, Volunteers in Service to America (VISTA), and the Model Cities program, which channeled federal funds to upgrade employment, housing, education, and health in targeted neighborhoods.

War on Poverty

In tandem with a rising gross national product (GNP), the War on Poverty substantially alleviated hunger and suffering in the United States. Between 1965 and 1970, the GNP leaped from $685 billion to $977 billion, and federal spending for Social Security, health, welfare, and education more than doubled. Not only

Successes in Reducing Poverty

did some of this prosperity trickle down to the poor, but also—and more important—millions of new jobs were created. The result was a startling reduction in the number of poor people, from 25 percent of the population in 1962 to 11 percent in 1973 (see figure, page 610).

The period of liberal ascendancy represented by the War on Poverty was short-lived; most of the Great Society's legislative achievements occurred in 1964, 1965, and 1966. Disillusioned with America's deepening involvement in Vietnam and upset by the violence of urban race riots (see page 611), many of Johnson's allies began to reject both him and his liberal consensus.

One branch of government however, maintained the liberal tradition: the Supreme Court. Under the intellectual and moral leadership of Chief Justice Earl Warren, the Court in the 1960s was disposed by political conviction and a belief in judicial activism to play a central role in the resurgence of liberalism. In 1962 the Court began handing down a series of landmark decisions. *Baker* v. *Carr* (1962) and subsequent rulings established that the principle of "one person, one vote" must prevail at both the state and national levels. This decision required the reapportionment of state legislatures so that each representative would serve the same number of constituents. The Court also outlawed required prayers and Bible reading in public schools, explaining that such practices imposed an "indirect coercive pressure upon religious minorities."

The Warren Court

The Court also attacked the legal underpinning of McCarthyism, ruling in 1965 that a person need not register with the government as a member of a subversive organization. In *Griswold* v. *Connecticut* (1965), the Court ruled that a state law prohibiting the use of contraceptives by married couples violated "a marital right of privacy" and was unconstitutional. The Court upheld the Civil Rights Act of 1964 and the Voting Rights Act of 1965. In other rulings that particularly upset conservatives, the Court decreed that books, magazines, and films could not be banned as obscene

Civil Rights Rulings

Poverty in America for Whites, African Americans, and All Races, 1959–1974

——— All Races	········ Whites	——— African Americans	— — — No Statistics Available

Poverty in America for Whites, African Americans, and All Races, 1959–1974 Because of rising levels of economic prosperity, combined with the impact of Great Society programs, the percentage of Americans living in poverty in 1974 was half as high as in 1959. African-Americans were still far more likely than white Americans to be poor. In 1959, more than half of all blacks (55.1 percent) were poor; in 1974, the figure remained high (30.3 percent). The government did not record data on African-American poverty for the years 1960 through 1965.

unless they were found to be "utterly without redeeming social value."

Perhaps most controversial of all was the Court's transformation of the criminal justice system. Beginning with *Gideon* v. *Wainwright* (1963), the Court ruled that a poor person charged with a felony had the right to a state-appointed lawyer. In *Escobedo* v. *Illinois* (1964), it decreed that the accused had a right to counsel during interrogation and a right to remain silent. *Miranda* v.

Arizona (1966) established that police had to inform criminal suspects that they had these rights and that any statements they made could be used against them.

Despite conservatives' demands for Warren's removal, constitutional historians consider him one of the two most influential chief justices in the nation's history (the other was John Marshall). Whether or not one approved of the decisions of the Warren Court (which ended with Warren's retirement in 1969), its effect on the American people is undeniable.

Civil Rights Disillusionment, Race Riots, and Black Power

Even while the civil rights movement was winning important victories in the mid-1960s, some activists began to grumble that the federal government was not to be trusted. The Mississippi Freedom Democratic Party felt betrayed by Lyndon Johnson and the Democrats in 1964, and evidence suggested that the Federal Bureau of Investigation was hostile to the civil rights movement. Indeed, it turned out that at least one FBI informant not only was a member of the Ku Klux Klan but also was involved in the bombing of Birmingham's Sixteenth Street Baptist Church in 1963. FBI Director J. Edgar Hoover was a racist, activists charged, and they were disturbed by rumors (later confirmed) that Hoover had wiretapped and bugged Martin Luther King, Jr.'s hotel rooms and planted allegations in the newspapers about his sexual improprieties.

The year 1964 witnessed the first of the "long hot summers" of race riots in northern cities. In Harlem and Rochester in New York, and in several cities in New Jersey, brutal actions by white police officers sparked riots in black neighborhoods. African-Americans deeply resented the unnecessary force that police sometimes used.

Explosion of Black Anger

Whites wondered why African-Americans were venting their frustration violently at a time when they were making real progress in the civil rights struggle. The civil rights movement however, had focused mostly on the South, to abolish Jim Crow and black disfranchisement. In the North, African-Americans could vote, but the median income of northern blacks was little more than half that of northern whites, and their unemployment rate was twice as high: Many African-American families, particularly those headed by women, lived in perpetual poverty. The primary assistance program, Aid to Families with Dependent Children (AFDC), failed to provide payments that would meet a family's expenses for rent, utilities, and food.

Northern blacks, surveying the economic and civil rights gains of the 1960s, wondered when they, too, would benefit from the Great Society. Concentrated in the inner cities, they looked around the ghettos in which they lived and knew their circumstances were deteriorating. Their neighborhoods were more segregated than ever; in increasing numbers during the 1960s, whites had responded to the continuing black migration from the South by fleeing to the suburbs. And as inner-city neighborhoods became all black, so did the neighborhood schools.

If 1964 was fiery and violent, 1965 was even more so. In August, an altercation between blacks and police sparked rioting in the Watts section of Los Angeles; thirty-four people were killed. Other cities exploded in riots between 1966 and 1968. In stark contrast to the white-instigated riots of 1919 and 1943, the riots of the 1960s were started by blacks angry over their joblessness and lack of opportunity. The anger was vented through the looting and burning of white-owned stores.

The Watts Race Riot

In 1968 the National Advisory Commission on Civil Disorders, chaired by Governor Otto Kerner of Illinois, released a report blaming white racism for the riots: "The nation is rapidly moving toward two increasingly separate Americas . . . a white society principally located in suburbs . . . and a Negro society largely concentrated within large central cities."

Clearly, many blacks, especially in the North, were beginning to question whether the nonviolent civil rights movement was serving their needs. In 1963 Martin Luther King, Jr., had appealed to whites' humanitarian instincts in his "I Have a Dream" speech. Now another voice was beginning to be heard, one that urged blacks to seize their freedom "by any means necessary." It was the voice of Malcolm X, a one-time pimp and street hustler who had converted while in prison to the Nation of Islam faith, commonly known as the Black Muslims.

A small sect that espoused black pride and separatism from white society, the Black Muslims

Malcolm X, as chief spokesperson for the Black Muslims, espoused African-American pride and separatism from white society and urged blacks to defend themselves with violence if necessary. Martin Luther King, Jr., preached nonviolence and racial integration. Still, these men agreed on many things. Their common goal was freedom and dignity for all black people in the United States. In 1964 King and Malcolm X met at the United States Capitol and enjoyed a few words together. Wide World Photos.

condemned "the white devil" as the chief source of evil in the world and exhorted blacks to lead sober lives and practice thrift. By the early 1960s Malcolm X had become the Black Muslims' chief spokesperson, and his advice was straightforward: "If someone puts a hand on you, send him to the cemetery."

Malcolm X

Malcolm X was murdered in early 1965. His assassins were Black Muslims who believed he had betrayed their cause, because he said he had met whites who were not devils and had expressed cautious support for the nonviolent civil rights move-

ment. Still, for both blacks and whites, Malcolm X symbolized black defiance and self-respect.

A year after Malcolm X's death, Stokely Carmichael, the chairman of the Student Nonviolent Coordinating Committee (SNCC), called on African-Americans to assert "Black Power." To be truly free from white oppression, Carmichael believed, blacks had to elect black candidates, organize their own schools, and control their own institutions. Several influential organizations that had previously been committed to racial integration and nonviolence embraced Black Power. SNCC in 1966 and the Congress of Racial Equality (CORE) in 1967 purged their white members and repudiated integration, arguing that black people needed power, not white friendship.

Black Power

To many white Americans, one of the most fearsome of the new groups was the Black Panther Party. Blending black nationalism and revolutionary communism, the Panthers dedicated themselves to destroying both capitalism and "the military arm of our oppressors," the police in the ghettos. The Panthers carried rifles in homage to Mao Zedong's revolutionary slogan: "Power flows from the barrel of a gun." What particularly worried white parents was that some of their own children agreed with the Panthers. Called the New Left, this vocal subset of the baby-boom generation set out to "change the system."

The New Left and the Counterculture

"I'm tired of reading history," Mario Savio, a graduate student at the University of California, complained in a letter to a friend in 1964. "I want to make it." Within a few months Savio realized his ambition as a leader of the campus Free Speech movement. After teaching in SNCC's Mississippi Freedom Summer Project, Savio and others returned to Berkeley convinced that the power structure that dominated blacks' lives also controlled the bureaucratic machinery of the university.

In fact, the University of California was a model university in 1964, with a worldwide reputation for excellence and public service. Its chancellor, the economist Clark Kerr, had likened the "multiversity" with its many separate colleges and research institutes to a big business. The largest single campus in the country, with tens of thousands of students, Berkeley had become hopelessly impersonal by the 1960s.

Free Speech Movement

The struggle at Berkeley began when the university administration yielded to pressure from political conservatives and banned recruitment by civil rights and antiwar organizations in Sproul Plaza, the students' traditional gathering place. Militant students defied Kerr's ban; the administration suspended them or had them arrested. In December the Free Speech Movement seized and occupied the main administration building. Governor Pat Brown dispatched state police to Berkeley, and more than eight hundred people were arrested.

The willingness of those in positions of authority to mobilize the police against unruly but not violent students was shocking and radicalizing to many young people. Having grown up comfortable and even indulged, they soon found themselves treated like criminals for questioning what they considered a criminal war in Vietnam and racial injustice in their own country. Within a few years, student activism would spread to hundreds of other campuses.

Students for a Democratic Society and the New Left

In 1963, another group of students had met in Port Huron, Michigan, to found Students for a Democratic Society (SDS). Like their leaders Tom Hayden and Al Haber, most SDS members were white, middle-class college students. In their platform, the Port Huron Statement, they condemned racism, poverty in the midst of plenty, and the Cold War. SDS sought nothing less than the revitalization of democracy by taking power from the corporations, the military, and the politicians and returning it to the people.

Inspired by the Free Speech Movement and SDS, a minority of students allied themselves with the New Left. Though united in their hatred of racism and the Vietnam War, the New Left divided along philosophical and political lines. Some radicals were Marxists, others black nationalists, anarchists, or pacifists. Some believed in pursuing social change through negotiation; others were revolutionaries.

By calling into question the basic foundations of American society, the New Left indirectly gave rise to a phenomenon called the counterculture.

Countercultural Revolution

Exhorted by Timothy Leary—a former Harvard instructor and advocate of expanded consciousness through use of LSD and other mind-altering drugs—to "turn on, tune in, drop out," millions of students experimented with marijuana and hallucinogenic drugs. Their political outrage, drug experiences, and experiments with communal living persuaded them that they lived in a new era unconnected to the past.

Rock 'n' Roll

Music more than anything else expressed the countercultural assault on the status quo. Bob Dylan promised revolutionary answers "blowin' in the wind," and young people cheered Jimi Hendrix, who sang of life in a drug-induced "purple haze." Like sex and drugs, the music of the 1960s represented a quest to redefine reality and create a more just and joyful society. Rock festivals became cultural watersheds. In 1969 at Woodstock in upstate New York, more than 400,000 people ignored or reveled in days of rain and mud, without shelter and without violence. A number of them began to dream of a peaceful "Woodstock nation" based on love, drugs, and rock music.

Some young people tried to construct alternative ways of life. In the Haight-Ashbury section of San Francisco, "flower children" created an urban subculture as distinctive as that of any Chinatown or Little Italy. "Hashbury" inspired numerous other communal-living experiments. The counterculture represented only a small proportion of American youth. But to middle-class parents, hippies seemed to be everywhere.

Most disturbing to parents were the casual sexual mores that young people were adopting. In 1960 the government approved the birth-control

Sexuality

pill, and use of the pill accelerated among young people. For many young people, living together no longer equaled living in sin; and as attitudes toward premarital sex changed, so did notions about homosexuality and sex roles.

The militancy of the 1960s helped inspire the gay rights movement. Homosexuals had long feared that disclosing their sexual orientation would mean losing not only their jobs but even their friends and families. That attitude began to change in June 1969, when police raided a gay bar, the Stonewall Inn, in New York City's Greenwich Village. In the ensuing riot the police were greeted with a volley of beer bottles. The Stone-

Gay Rights Movement

wall riot, as historian John D'Emilio has written, "marked a critical divide in the politics and consciousness of homosexuals and lesbians. A small, thinly spread reform effort suddenly grew into a large, grass-roots movement for liberation."

As the slogan "Make Love, Not War" suggests, the New Left and the counterculture discovered a common cause as the war in Vietnam escalated. Students held teach-ins—open forums for discussion of the war by students, professors, and guest speakers—and anti-war marches and demonstrations became a widespread protest tactic (see map). Some young men fled the draft by moving abroad; others protested at local draft board offices.

By this time, however, growing numbers of Americans, young and old, had quit believing

Antiwar Protests

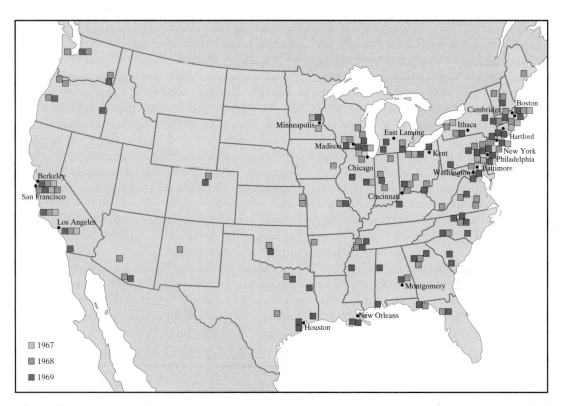

Disturbances on College and University Campuses, 1967–1969   *Students on campuses from coast to coast protested against the Vietnam War. Some protests were peaceful; others erupted into violent confrontations between protesters and police and army troops.*

their elected leaders. President Johnson claimed the United States was fighting for honorable reasons, but people wondered what goal could justify the murder of Vietnamese women and children.

1968: A Year of Protest, Violence, and Loss

As stormy and violent as the years from 1963 through 1967 had been, many Americans still tried to downplay the nation's distress in the hope that it would go away. But in 1968 a series of shocks hit them harder than ever. The first jolt came in January 1968, when the USS *Pueblo*, a navy intelligence ship, was captured by North Korea. A week later came the Tet offensive (see page 590), and for the first time many Americans believed that they might lose the war.

Controversy over the war deepened within the Democratic Party, and two candidates rose to challenge Johnson for the 1968 presidential nomination. One, Senator Eugene McCarthy of Minnesota, entered the New Hampshire primary on March 12 solely to contest Johnson's war policies; he won twenty of New Hampshire's twenty-four convention delegates. Soon another Democrat, Senator Robert F. Kennedy of New York, brother of the dead president entered the fray. Then, on March 31, President Johnson went on national television to announce a scaling-down of the bombing in North Vietnam and his decision not to run for reelection.

Less than a week later, James Earl Ray a white man, shot and killed Martin Luther King, Jr., in Memphis. The murder touched off massive grief and rage in the nation's ghettos. Riots erupted in 168 cities and towns, including the looting and burning of white businesses. Thirty-four blacks and five whites died in the violence. The terror provoked a white backlash. Tough talk was the response from Chicago's mayor Richard Daley, who ordered police to shoot to kill arsonists.

Assassination of Martin Luther King, Jr.

Gallup polls in April and May reported Robert Kennedy to be the front-running Democratic presidential candidate, and in June he won the Cal-ifornia primary. That night, after Kennedy addressed his supporters, a man stepped forward with a .22-caliber revolver and fired. Sirhan Sirhan the assassin, was an Arab nationalist who despised Kennedy for his unwavering support of Israel.

Assassination of Robert Kennedy

Violence erupted again in August at the Democratic national convention in Chicago. The Democrats were divided over the war, and thousands of antiwar protesters and members of the zany and anarchic Youth International Party (Yippies) had traveled to Chicago. The Chicago police force was still in the psychological grip of Mayor Daley's shoot-to-kill directive. Twelve thousand police were assigned to twelve-hour shifts, and another twelve thousand army troops were on call with rifles, bazookas, and flame throwers. They attacked in front of the Hilton Hotel, wading into the ranks of demonstrators, reporters, and TV camera operators. Throughout the nation, viewers watched as club-swinging police beat protesters to the ground.

Violence at the Democratic Convention

The Democratic convention nominated Vice President Hubert Humphrey for president and Senator Edmund Muskie of Maine for vice president. Like Johnson and Kennedy before him, Humphrey was both an unstinting supporter of the Vietnam War and a political liberal. The Republicans selected Richard M. Nixon as their presidential nominee; his running mate was the tough-talking Governor Spiro Agnew of Maryland. Another tough-talking governor, George C. Wallace of Alabama, ran as the nominee of the American Independent party. Wallace was a segregationist, a proponent of reducing North Vietnam to rubble with nuclear weapons, and an advocate of "law and order."

When the votes were tabulated, Nixon emerged the winner, by the slimmest of margins. Wallace collected nearly 10 million votes, or almost 14 percent of the total, the best performance by a third party since 1924. His strong showing made Nixon a minority president, elected

Election of 1968

with 43 percent of the popular vote. Moreover, the Democrats maintained control of the House (243 to 192) and the Senate (58 to 42).

Still, the 1968 election was a triumph for conservatism, for the combined vote for Nixon and Wallace was 57 percent. The war, and especially support for civil rights and welfare for the poor, hurt the Democrats. In 1968, Humphrey received 97 percent of the black vote but only 35 percent of the white vote. Among the defectors from the New Deal coalition were northern blue-collar ethnic voters. "In city after city," one observer noted, "racial conflicts had destroyed the old alliance. The New Deal had unraveled block by block."

Unraveling of the New Deal Coalition

Rebirth of Feminism

Another liberation movement gained momentum during the turbulence of the 1960s. The women's rights movement had languished after the adoption of the Nineteenth Amendment in 1920. But in the 1960s feminism was reborn. Many women were dissatisfied with their lives, and in 1963 they found a voice with the publication of Betty Friedan's *The Feminine Mystique*. According to Friedan, women across the country were deeply troubled by "the problem that has no name." Most women had grown up believing that "all they had to do was devote their lives from earliest girlhood to finding a husband and bearing children." The problem was that this "mystique of feminine fulfillment" left many wives and mothers feeling empty and incomplete.

President Kennedy appointed only one woman to a policymaking post in his administration, but she proved to be an effective advocate of women's rights. Esther Peterson served as assistant secretary of labor and director of the Women's Bureau. In 1961, at her urging, Kennedy established the first President's Commission on the Status of Women. Its report, *American Women*

National Organization for Women

(1963), argued that every obstacle to women's full participation in society ought to be removed. But little federal action resulted from the release of *American Women*, and the government was failing to enforce the gender-equality provisions of the Civil Rights Act of 1964. The need for action inspired the founding in 1966 of the National Organization for Women (NOW). In the reform tradition, NOW battled for "equal rights in partnership with men" by lobbying for legislation and testing laws in the courts.

Not long after NOW's formation, a new generation of radical feminists emerged. Most radical feminists were white and well educated; they had been raised in the era of sexual liberation, taking for granted liberation from unwanted pregnancy. The intellectual ferment of their movement produced a new feminist literature. Radical feminists focused not only on legal barriers but also on cultural assumptions and traditions. In the process they introduced the term *sexism* to signify a phenomenon far more pervasive than lack of legal equality, and they challenged everything from women's economic and political inequality to sexual double standards and sex-role stereotypes.

Unlike NOW, the radical feminists also practiced direct action, such as picketing the 1968 Miss America contest in Atlantic City. One woman auctioned off an effigy of Miss America: "Gentlemen, I offer you the 1969 model. . . . She walks. She talks. She smiles on cue. *And* she does the housework." Into the "freedom trash can" the pickets dumped false eyelashes, curlers, girdles, and *Playboy* magazine to protest the prevailing view of women as domestic servants and sex objects.

"Personal Politics"

Many radical feminists had joined the struggles for black civil rights and against the Vietnam War only to find that they were second-class citizens expected to make coffee, take minutes, and even provide sexual favors. Many of these feminists organized consciousness-raising groups to discuss matters such as homosexuality, abortion, and power relationships in romance and marriage. The issue of homosexuality caused a split in the women's movement. In 1969 and 1970

NOW forced lesbians to resign from the organization. The rift was healed in 1971, largely because lesbians as well as gay men had begun to fight back.

For working women in the 1960s, the most pressing problems were sex discrimination in employment, meager professional opportunities, un-

Working Women's Burdens

equal pay for equal work, lack of adequate daycare for children, and prohibitions against abortion. The main cause of this pay disparity was "occupational segregation" throughout the labor force. Because many women with college educations earned less than men with eighth-grade educations, it was natural that two of the most important women's goals of the 1960s were equal job opportunity and equal pay for equal work.

Despite opposition and setbacks, women were making impressive gains. They entered professional schools in record numbers: from 1969 to 1973,

Women's Educational and Professional Gains

the number of women law students almost quadrupled, and the number of women medical students more than doubled. Under Title IX of the Educational Amendments of 1972, female college athletes gained the right to the same financial support as male athletes. The same year, Congress approved the Equal Rights Amendment (ERA) and sent it to the states for ratification. (The ERA stated: "Equality of rights under the law shall not be denied or abridged by the United States or by any State on account of sex.") It fell three states shy of the three-fourths majority needed for adoption.

The Supreme Court also ruled on several issues essential to women. In its 1973 decision in *Roe* v. *Wade* the Court struck down laws that made abortion a crime. The Court

Roe* v. *Wade

at this time also addressed sex discrimination. In a 1971 ruling (*Reed* v. *Reed*), it held that legislation differentiating between the sexes "must be reasonable, not arbitrary," and in 1973 (*Frontiero* v. *Richardson*) the justices went a step further in declaring that job-related classifications

based on sex, like those based on race, were "inherently suspect." These victories gave women new confidence in the 1970s.

Nixon and the Persistence of Chaos

Richard Nixon's presidency was born in chaos. Bloody confrontations occurred at Berkeley, Wisconsin, Cornell, Harvard, and scores of other colleges and universities in 1969. In October three hundred Weathermen—an SDS splinter group—raced through Chicago's downtown district, smashing windows and attacking police officers in a deluded attempt to incite armed class struggle. A month later a half-million people assembled peacefully at the Washington Monument on Moratorium Day to call for an end to the Vietnam War.

If 1969 was bloody and turbulent, 1970 proved to be even more so. President Nixon appeared on television on April 30 to announce that the United

Kent State and Jackson State

States had launched an "incursion" into Cambodia. Antiwar protest escalated. On May 4, National Guardsmen in Ohio fired into a crowd of fleeing students at Kent State University, killing four young people. Ten days later, police and state highway patrolmen armed with automatic weapons blasted a women's dormitory at Jackson State, an all-black university in Mississippi, killing two students and wounding nine others. The police claimed they had been shot at, but no evidence of sniping could be found.

Many Americans, though disturbed by the increasing ferocity of campus confrontations, felt more personally endangered by street crime. Sales of pistols, burglar alarms, and bulletproof vests soared. Conservatives accused liberals and the Supreme Court of causing the crime wave by coddling criminals.

This new wave of riots, protests, and violent crime convinced Nixon that the nation was plunging into anarchy. Worried that the antiwar move-

Politics of Divisiveness

ment was communist inspired, he ordered the FBI, the CIA, the National Security Agency, and the Defense Intelligence Agency in mid-1970 to formulate a coordinated attack on "internal threats." Meanwhile, the administration also worked to put the Democratic Party on the defensive. For the 1970 elections, the Republicans sought to portray the Democrats as "radical liberals who . . . excuse disorder, tolerate crime . . . and undercut the President's foreign policy." The effort failed as the Democrats gained seats in the House and the Republicans lost eleven state governorships.

Nixon's fortunes declined further in 1971. In June the *New York Times* began to publish the *Pentagon Papers*, a top-secret Defense Department study of the Vietnam War.

Stagflation

Nixon also had to contend with inflation, a problem not entirely of his making. Lyndon Johnson's policy of "guns and butter"—massive deficit financing to support both the Vietnam War and the Great Society—had fueled inflation. By early 1971 the United States was suffering from a 5.3 percent inflation rate and a 6 percent unemployment rate. The word *stagflation* would shortly be coined to describe this coexistence of economic recession (stagnation) and inflation.

Nixon shocked both critics and allies by declaring in early 1971 that "I am now a Keynesian." (According to the British economist John Maynard Keynes, governments could stimulate economic growth in the private sector by means of "pump priming," or deficit financing.) Nixon's budget for fiscal 1971 would have a built-in deficit of $23 billion. Then in August, in an effort to correct the nation's balance-of-payments deficit, Nixon announced that he would devalue the dollar and allow it to "float" in international money markets. Finally, to curb inflation, the president froze prices, wages, and rents for ninety days and set limits on subsequent increases. Nixon's commitment to these controversial wage and price controls buckled the next year under pressure from businesses and unions.

Wage and price controls were just one facet of what surprised observers called Nixon's "great turn-

about" from outspoken conservative to pragmatic liberal. Another was his announcement in 1971 that he would travel to the People's Republic of China, a communist enemy Nixon had denounced for years. It was clear that the president was preparing for the 1972 presidential election.

 Nixon's Southern Strategy and the Election of 1972

Political observers believed that President Nixon would have a hard time running for reelection on his first-term record. Having urged Americans to "lower our voices," he had ordered Vice President Agnew to denounce the press and student protesters. Having espoused unity, he had practiced the politics of polarization. Having campaigned as a fiscal conservative, he had authorized near-record budget deficits. And having promised peace, he had widened the war in Southeast Asia.

During Nixon's first term, the Democrats dominated both houses of Congress, and Congress's accomplishments were more despite Nixon than because of him. Congress in-

Liberal Legislative Victories

creased Social Security payments and food-stamp funding and established the Occupational Safety and Health Administration to reduce hazards in the workplace. Moreover, in 1971 the states quickly ratified the Twenty-sixth Amendment, which extended the vote to eighteen-year-olds.

The environmental movement also bore fruit during Nixon's first term. Alerted to ecological hazards by Rachel Carson's *Silent Spring* (1962), Americans began to heed warnings of

Environmental Issues

impending disaster due to unregulated population and economic growth. Environmental tragedies such as a 1969 oil spill that fouled the beaches and killed wildlife in Santa Barbara, California, spurred citizen action. The Environmental Defense Fund (founded in 1967) successfully fought the use of DDT, and Greenpeace (founded in 1969) protested radioactive poisoning from nuclear-bomb testing. And although President

Nixon was personally unsympathetic to the environmental movement, he acknowledged the movement's political appeal by reluctantly agreeing to the establishment of the Environmental Protection Agency in 1970 and by signing into law the Clean Air Act (1970), Clean Water Act (1972), and Pesticide Control Act (1972).

In his campaign for reelection, Nixon employed a "southern strategy" of political conservatism. A product of the Sunbelt, he was acutely aware of the growing political power of that conservative region. He thus appealed to the "Silent Majority." And as in the 1970 congressional elections, Nixon equated the Republican Party with law and order and the Democrats with permissiveness, crime, drugs, pornography, the hippie lifestyle, student radicalism, black militancy, feminism, homosexuality, and dissolution of the family. Moreover, Attorney General John Mitchell had courted southern white voters by trying to delay school desegregation in Mississippi and to prevent extension of the 1965 Voting Rights Act.

Nixon's "Southern Strategy"

The southern strategy also guided Nixon's nomination of Supreme Court justices. After appointing Warren Burger, a conservative federal judge, to succeed Earl Warren as chief justice, Nixon had selected two southerners to serve as associate justices, one of whom was a segregationist. When the Senate declined to confirm either nominee, Nixon protested angrily. By 1972, however, the president had managed to appoint three more conservatives to the Supreme Court. Ironically, the new appointees did not always vote as Nixon would have wished. In *Swann* v. *Charlotte-Mecklenberg* (1971), the justices had upheld a desegregation plan that required massive cross-town busing. An unsympathetic Nixon proposed that Congress pass a busing moratorium, and he appeared on television to denounce busing as a reckless and extreme remedy for segregation.

Nixon and the Supreme Court

Though Nixon campaigned in 1972 by assuming the role of world statesman—he traveled to China and the Soviet Union—it was the inept campaign of the Democratic nominee, Senator George McGovern of South Dakota, that handed victory to the Republicans. When McGovern endorsed a $30 billion cut in the defense budget, people began to fear that he would reduce the United States to a second-rate power. McGovern's proposals split the Democrats between his supporters—antiwar activists, African-Americans, feminists, young militants—and old-guard urban bosses, labor leaders, white southerners, and growing numbers of blue-collar workers.

Election of 1972

Nixon's victory in November was overwhelming: he polled 47 million votes, more than 60 percent of the votes cast. McGovern won just one state, Massachusetts, and the District of Columbia. In addition to the South, Nixon carried such traditional Democratic constituencies as blue-collar workers, Catholics, and white ethnics. Only blacks, Jews, and low-income voters stuck by the Democratic candidate. Despite Nixon's landslide, the Democrats retained control of both houses of Congress.

Nixon's Landslide Victory

Little noticed during the campaign was a break-in at the Watergate apartment-office complex in Washington, D.C., on June 17, 1972. A watchman telephoned the police to report an illegal late-night entry into the building. At 2:30 A.M., police arrested five men who were attaching listening devices to telephones in the offices of the Democratic National Committee. The men had cameras and had been rifling through files.

Watergate Break-in

One of those arrested was James W. McCord, a former CIA employee who had become security coordinator of the Committee to Re-Elect the President (CREEP). The other four were anti-Castro Cubans from Miami who had worked with the CIA before. Unknown to the police, two other men had been in the Watergate building at the time of the break-in. One was E. Howard Hunt, a one-time CIA agent who had become a White House consultant. The other was G. Gordon Liddy, a former

FBI agent serving on CREEP's staff. What were these men trying to find in the Democrats' offices? Most important, who had ordered the break-in?

 ## Watergate and Nixon's Resignation

The Watergate fiasco had actually begun in 1971, when the White House established not only CREEP but the Special Investigations Unit, known familiarly as the "Plumbers," to stop the leaking of secret government documents to the press. After publication of the *Pentagon Papers*, the Plumbers burglarized the office of Daniel Ellsberg's psychiatrist in an attempt to discredit Ellsberg, who had leaked the top-secret report to the press. It was the Plumbers who broke into the Democratic National Committee's headquarters to photograph documents and install wiretaps; money raised by CREEP was used to pay the Plumbers' expenses both before and after the break-ins.

The arrest of the Watergate burglars generated furious activity in the White House. Incriminating documents were shredded; E. Howard Hunt's name was expunged from the White House telephone directory; and President Nixon ordered his chief of staff, H. R. Haldeman, to discourage the FBI's investigation into the burglary on the pretext that it might compromise national security. Nixon also authorized CREEP "hush-money" payments in excess of $460,000 to keep Hunt and others from implicating the White House in the crime.

White House Cover-up

Because of successful White House efforts to cover up the scandal, the break-in was almost unnoticed by the electorate. Had it not been for the diligent efforts of reporters, government special prosecutors, federal judges, and members of Congress, President Nixon might have succeeded in disguising his involvement in Watergate. Slowly, however, the tangle of lies and distortions began to unravel. In early 1973, U.S. District Judge John Sirica tried the burglars, one of

Watergate Hearings and Investigations

whom implicated his superiors in CREEP and at the White House. From May until November, the Senate Select Committee on Campaign Practices, chaired by Senator Sam Ervin of North Carolina, heard testimony from White House aides. John W. Dean III, the White House counsel, acknowledged not only that there had been a cover-up but that the president had directed it. Another aide revealed that Nixon had had a taping system installed in his White House office and that conversations about Watergate had been recorded.

Nixon feigned innocence. In April 1973 he tried to distance himself from the cover-up by announcing the resignations of his two chief White House aides, John Ehrlichman and H. R. Haldeman. The administration then appointed Archibald Cox, a Harvard law professor with a reputation for uncompromising integrity, to fill the new position of special Watergate prosecutor. But when Cox sought in October to obtain the White House tapes by means of a court order, Nixon decided to have him fired. Both Attorney General Elliot Richardson and his deputy resigned rather than carry out the dismissal order. It thus fell to the third ranking person in the Department of Justice to fire Cox. The public outcry provoked by the so-called Saturday Night Massacre compelled the president to agree to the appointment of a new special prosecutor, Leon Jaworski. When Nixon still refused to surrender the tapes, Jaworski took him to court.

Saturday Night Massacre

In the same month as the Saturday Night Massacre, the Nixon administration was stung by another scandal. Vice President Spiro Agnew resigned after pleading no contest to charges of income-tax evasion and acceptance of bribes. Under the provisions of the Twenty-fifth Amendment, ratified in 1967 after President Kennedy's assassination, Nixon nominated Gerald R. Ford, the House minority leader from Michigan, to replace Agnew.

Agnew's Resignation

Throughout 1973 and 1974, enterprising reporters uncovered more details of the break-in, the hush money, and the various people from Nixon on down who had taken part in the cover-up. White

How do historians know that President Richard M. Nixon was guilty of obstructing justice in the Watergate affair? That evidence lies in the Watergate tapes. Nixon is pictured here sitting with what he claimed were the full transcripts of the tape recordings made in the White House. But Nixon's version was filled with gaps. What was missing was the tape recording of a specific White House conversation on June 23, 1972, which proved that Nixon had instigated a cover-up and obstructed justice almost from the outset of the scandal. That day, Nixon was recorded ordering his top aide to stop the Federal Bureau of Investigation's inquiry into the Watergate break-in. The Central Intelligence Agency, Nixon thundered, should call the FBI, claim that the

break-in was a secret spy operation, and say, "'Don't go further into this case[,] period'!"

Historians have long wondered what other information the tapes might reveal. Some historians have sued for access to the tapes, but for twenty-one years, Nixon and his family succeeded in keeping them private. In 1996, however, the Nixon estate, the National Archives and Records Administration, and Stanley I. Kutler, a history professor at the University of Wisconsin, reached an agreement that calls for almost three thousand hours of tapes to be made public over the next several years. "All of us," Kutler said, "who believe in open government and full disclosure of history are winners." Photo: Nixon Presidential Materials Project.

House aides and CREEP subordinates began to go on trial, and Nixon was cited as an "unindicted co-conspirator." *Washington Post* reporters Carl Bernstein and Bob Woodward found an informant, known as "Deep Throat," who provided damning information about Nixon and his aides. As Nixon's protestations of innocence became less credible, his hold on the tapes became more tenuous. In late April 1974 the president finally released an edited transcript of the tapes.

The edited transcripts, however, had a lot of gaps. They swayed neither the public nor the House Judiciary Committee, which had begun to draft articles of impeachment against the president. Nixon still was trying to hang onto the original tapes when the Supreme Court in July, in *U.S. v. Nixon*, unanimously ordered him to surrender the recordings to Judge Sirica. At about the same time, the Judiciary Committee conducted nationally televised hearings.

After several days of testimony, the committee voted for impeachment on three of five counts: obstruction of justice through the payment of hush money to witnesses, lying, and withholding of evidence; defiance of a congressional subpoena of the tapes; and use of the CIA, the FBI, and the Internal Revenue Service to deprive Americans of their constitutional rights of privacy and free speech. On August 5 the president finally handed over the complete tapes, which he knew would condemn him. Four days later he became the first president to resign from office. The first substantive act of his successor, Gerald Ford, was to pardon Nixon. When the pardon was announced, some people concluded that Ford and Nixon had struck a deal.

The Watergate scandal prompted the reform of abuses that predated the Nixon administration. The

Nixon's Resignation

executive's usurpation of legislative prerogatives, which historian Arthur M. Schlesinger, Jr., called "the imperial presidency," dated from Franklin D. Roosevelt's administration.

To rein in presidents, Congress enacted the War Powers Act (1973) and the Congressional Budget and Impoundment Control Act (1974).

Post-Watergate Restrictions on Executive Power

The former law mandated that "in every possible instance" the president must consult with Congress before sending American troops into foreign wars. Under this law the president could commit American troops abroad for no more than sixty days, after which he had to obtain congressional approval. The latter law prohibited the impounding of federal money. In 1972 and 1974, Congress made modest attempts to reduce campaign fundraising abuses, setting ceilings on campaign contributions and expenditures for congressional and presidential elections. Finally, to aid citizens who were victims of dirty-tricks campaigns, in 1974 Congress strengthened the Freedom of Information Act of 1966.

 Conclusion

The thirteen years coinciding with the presidencies of John Kennedy, Lyndon Johnson, and Richard Nixon were a period of increasing disillusionment in the United States. As historian James T. Patterson observed, the period had begun with "grand expectations" about the attainability of "the Good Life." But riots in cities, violence on campus, diminished respect for government leaders, and growing economic uncertainty had shattered Americans' illusions and supplanted earlier hopes for peaceful social change.

In 1961, John F. Kennedy challenged Americans to "pay any price, bear any burden, meet any hardship" to defend freedom and inspire the world. Twelve years later, Richard M. Nixon echoed that rhetoric: "Let us pledge to make these four years the best four years in America's history, so that on its 200th birthday America will be as young

and vital as when it began, and as bright a beacon of hope for all the world." By the time of the bicentennial celebration in 1976, however, America seemed more bruised and battered than vital and young.

Suggestions for Further Reading

The 1960s

David Burner, *Making Peace with the 60s* (1996); David Chalmers, *And the Crooked Places Made Straight: The Struggle for Social Change in the 1960s* (1991); David Farber, *The Age of Great Dreams* (1994); David Farber, ed., *The Sixties* (1994); Godfrey Hodgson, *America in Our Time* (1976); Allen J. Matusow, *The Unraveling of America: A History of Liberalism in the 1960s* (1984); James T. Patterson, *Grand Expectations: The United States, 1945–1974* (1996); Tom Shachtman, *Decade of Shocks: Dallas to Watergate, 1963–1974* (1983); Barbara L. Tischler, ed., *Sights on the Sixties* (1992).

The Kennedy Administration

Irving Bernstein, *Promises Kept: John F. Kennedy's New Frontier* (1991); James Giglio, *The Presidency of John F. Kennedy* (1991); David Halberstam, *The Best and the Brightest* (1972); Christopher Matthews, *Kennedy and Nixon: The Rivalry That Shaped Postwar America* (1996); Herbert S. Parmet, *J.F.K.—The Presidency of John F. Kennedy* (1983); Thomas C. Reeves, *A Question of Character* (1991); Arthur M. Schlesinger, Jr., *Robert Kennedy and His Times* (1978); Arthur M. Schlesinger, Jr., *A Thousand Days: John F. Kennedy in the White House* (1965); Gary Wills, *The Kennedy Imprisonment* (1982).

The Kennedy Assassination

Edward Jay Epstein, *Legend: The Secret World of Lee Harvey Oswald* (1978); Henry Hurt, *Reasonable Doubt* (1985); Gerald Posner, *Case Closed* (1993); Anthony Summers, *Conspiracy* (1980).

The Johnson Administration and the Great Society

Irving Bernstein, *Guns or Butter: The Presidency of Lyndon Johnson* (1996); Paul K. Conkin, *Big Daddy from the Pedernales: Lyndon Baines Johnson* (1986); Doris Kearns, *Lyndon Johnson and the American Dream* (1976); Sar A. Levitan and Robert Taggart, *The Promise of Greatness* (1976); Charles Murray, *Losing Ground: American Social Policy, 1950–1980* (1983); James T. Patterson, *America's Struggle Against Poverty, 1900–1994*, rev. ed. (1994); John E. Schwarz, *America's Hidden Success: A Reassessment of Twenty Years of Public Policy* (1983); Irwin Unger, *The Best of Intentions: The Triumph and Failure of the Great Society Under Kennedy, Johnson, and Nixon* (1996).

Civil Rights, Black Power, and Urban Riots

Taylor Branch, *Parting the Waters: America in the King Years, 1954–1963* (1988); Clayborne Carson, *In Struggle: SNCC and the Black Awakening of the 1960s* (1981); William H. Chafe, *Civilities and Civil Rights: Greensboro, North Carolina, and the Black Struggle for Freedom* (1980); David L. Chappell, *Inside Agitators: White Southerners in the Civil Rights Movement* (1996); John Dittmer, *Local People: The Struggle for Civil Rights in Mississippi* (1994); Sidney Fine, *Violence in the Model City: . . . the Detroit Riot of 1967* (1989); David J. Garrow, *Bearing the Cross: Martin Luther King, Jr., and the Southern Christian Leadership Conference* (1986); Gerald Horne, *Fire This Time: The Watts Uprising and the 1960s* (1996); Malcolm X and Alex Haley, *The Autobiography of Malcolm X* (1965); August Meier and Elliott Rudwick, *CORE* (1973); Kay Mills, *This Little Light of Mine: The Life of Fannie Lou Hamer* (1993); Charles M. Payne, *I've Got the Light of Freedom: The Organizing Tradition and the Mississippi Freedom Struggle* (1995); Mark Stern, *Calculating Visions: Kennedy, Johnson, and Civil Rights* (1992).

The Warren Court

Gerald Dunne, *Hugo Black and the Judicial Revolution* (1977); G. Theodore Mitau, *Decade of Decision: The Supreme Court and the Constitutional Revolution, 1954–1964* (1967); Bernard Schwartz, *Super Chief: Earl Warren and His Supreme Court* (1983); G. Edward White, *Earl Warren* (1982).

The New Left and Protest for Peace and Justice

Terry H. Anderson, *The Movement and the Sixties* (1995); Wini Breines, *Community and Organization in the New Left, 1962–1968*, rev. ed. (1989); Charles DeBenedetti, *An American Ordeal: The Antiwar Movement of the Vietnam Era* (1990); Tom Engelhardt, *The End of Victory Culture: Cold War America and the Disillusioning of a Generation* (1995); Todd Gitlin, *The Sixties* (1987); Maurice Isserman, *If I Had a Hammer . . . : The Death of the Old Left and the Birth of the New Left* (1987); Peter B. Levy, *The New Left and Labor in the 1960s* (1994); James Miller, *"Democracy Is in the Streets": From Port Huron to the Siege of Chicago* (1987); Kirkpatrick Sale, *The Green Revolution: The American Environmental Movement, 1962–1992* (1993); Tom Wells, *The War Within: America's Battle over Vietnam* (1994).

The Counterculture

Stanley Booth, *Dance with the Devil: The Rolling Stones and Their Times* (1984); Morris Dickstein, *Gates of Eden: American Culture in the Sixties* (1977); Tim Miller, *The Hippies and American Values* (1991); Philip Norman, *Shout! The Beatles in Their Generation* (1981); Charles Perry, *The Haight-Ashbury* (1984); Jay Stevens, *Storming Heaven: LSD and the American Dream* (1987); Jon Weiner, *Come Together: John Lennon in His Time* (1984); Tom Wolfe, *The Electric Kool-Aid Acid Test* (1968).

The Rebirth of Feminism

Alice Echols, *Daring to Be Bad: Radical Feminism in America, 1965–1975* (1989); Sara Evans, *Personal Politics* (1978); Jo Freeman, *The Politics of Women's Liberation* (1975); David J. Garrow, *Liberty and Sexuality: The Right to Privacy and the Making of Roe v. Wade* (1994); Cynthia Harrison, *On Account of Sex: The Politics of Women's Issues, 1945–1968* (1988); Judith Hole and Ellen Levine, *Rebirth of Feminism* (1971); Robin Morgan, ed., *Sisterhood Is Powerful* (1970); Gayle Graham Yates, *What Women Want: The Ideas of the Movement* (1975).

Year of Shocks: 1968

David Caute, *The Year of the Barricades* (1988); Lewis Chester et al., *An American Melodrama: The Presidential Campaign of 1968* (1969); David Farber, *Chicago '68* (1988); Ronald Fraser et al., *1968: A Student Generation in Revolt* (1988); Charles Kaiser, *1968 in America* (1988).

Richard M. Nixon and the Resurgence of Conservatism

Stephen E. Ambrose, *Nixon*, 3 vols. (1987–1991); William C. Berman, *Right Turn: From Nixon to Bush* (1994); Mary C. Brennan, *Turning Right in the Sixties: The Conservative Capture of the GOP* (1995); Dan T. Carter, *The Politics of Rage: George Wallace, the Origins of the New Conservatism, and the Transformation of American Politics* (1995); Robert Alan Goldberg, *Barry Goldwater* (1995); Roger Morris, *Richard Milhous Nixon* (1990); Herbert S. Parmet, *Richard Nixon and His America* (1990); James A. Reichley, *Conservatives in an Era of Change: The Nixon and Ford Administrations* (1981); Tom Wicker, *One of Us* (1991); Garry Wills, *Nixon Agonistes* (1970).

Watergate

Jim Hougan, *Secret Agenda: Watergate, Deep Throat and the CIA* (1984); Stanley I. Kutler, *The Wars of Watergate* (1990); J. Anthony Lukas, *Nightmare: The Underside of the Nixon Years* (1976); Kim McQuaid, *The Anxious Years: America in the Vietnam-Watergate Era* (1989); Arthur M. Schlesinger, Jr., *The Imperial Presidency* (1973); Michael Schudson, *Watergate in American Memory* (1992); Theodore H. White, *Breach of Faith* (1975); Bob Woodward and Carl Bernstein, *The Final Days* (1976); Bob Woodward and Carl Bernstein, *All the President's Men* (1974).

CHAPTER

32

The End of the Postwar Boom: Stagflation, Immigration, and the Resurgence of Conservatism
1974–1989

Nguyet Thu Ha was twenty-two years old when South Vietnam capitulated to North Vietnamese and Vietcong forces in 1975. She had never before spent a night away from her parents; but North Vietnamese soldiers were fighting close to her home, so she fled, taking along her four younger brothers and sisters and a six-year-old nephew whose distraught parents had entrusted him to Ha for safekeeping. The six were loaded onto a fishing ship dangerously overcrowded with refugees. After stops at Guam and a refugee camp in Arkansas, Nguyet Ha and the children came to Kansas City, Missouri.

Nguyet Ha got a job working seven days a week as a hotel housekeeper, and at night she taught herself to sew, making shirts and dresses. She next worked as a waitress, saving her tips to buy a house. Within eight months, she had saved enough for a down payment on a $16,000 house; she paid off the mortgage in three years. She married and had two daughters of her own, and in 1989 she bought a Laundromat, five adjoining lots, and a vacant building to house her relatives, should they be allowed to emigrate to the United States. Ha also earned two associate of arts degrees and was hired as a paraprofessional at Northeast High School, a magnet school for law and public service, in Kansas City.

What sustained Nguyet Thu Ha was her dream of bringing her entire family to Kansas City. For ten years, she attempted to bring her mother and four older siblings to the United States. (Her father was dead.) Then she received a call from the Immigration and Naturalization Service: Ha's mother, two brothers, a sister-in-law, and a niece would be arriving in a couple of days at Kansas City International Airport.

Nguyet Thu Ha and her family were part of the "new immigration," which began in the early 1970s, when record numbers of immigrants came to the United States from Asia, Mexico, Central and South America, and the Caribbean. Unlike earlier immigrants, most of the new arrivals were people of color, and race proved to be both a barrier and a spur to success for the new immigrants. Almost 70 percent of the newcomers settled in six states: California, Florida, Texas, New York, New Jersey, and Illinois. They redefined urban areas such as Los Angeles, Chicago, and Miami, where nearly three-quarters of city residents spoke a language other than English at home.

Although well-wishers often were on hand to greet the newcomers, the history of the nation's treatment of people of color did not augur well for them. Most found only low-paying jobs, and some suffered hostility and even violence from native-born Americans. Nevertheless, they persevered, pursuing their dreams in a country that was changing racially and ethnically.

The 1970s and 1980s were a time of wrenching economic, political, and social change in the United States. First, the new immigration touched millions of people's lives, immigrant and non-immigrant alike. Second, the postwar economic boom ended, and the 1973 Arab oil embargo made Americans realize that the United States was not a fortress that could stand alone, its survival depended upon imported oil. Recessions also became more frequent, the rate of economic growth slowed, and the "discomfort index" (the unemployment rate plus the inflation rate) rose. Third, in response to these real changes, there was a resurgence of conservatism, both political and cultural. Fourth, economic inequality and social polarization grew, especially in the 1980s, widening the gap between rich and poor, between whites and people of color, and between the suburbs and the inner cities.

Filled with uncertainty, Americans in the 1970s reeled under the one-two punch of *stagflation*. First, there was economic *stag*nation. Unemployment was on the upswing, particularly in heavy industry. Americans saw once-proud automobile and steel plants close. As a result of such "deindustrialization," many jobs were jeopardized while others disappeared forever. Second, there was *inflation*. As soaring prices eroded the purchasing power of workers' paychecks, people raided their savings. The 1970s was the first decade since the Great Depression in which Americans' purchasing power declined. Women and people of color were particularly hard hit, for they usually were the last hired and the first laid off. Even when they had jobs, they were paid less than white men, and experts pointed to the growing "feminization" and "blackening" of poverty.

The era's resurgent conservative movement must be understood within the context of America's economic woes and social changes. Conservatives doubted that government had the capacity to serve the people, let alone solve major problems. In the 1970s they worked to repeal the social welfare system. California voters approved a 1978 tax-cutting referendum called Proposition 13, which reduced property taxes and put stringent limits on state spending for social programs. Nearly a score of other states imposed similar ceilings on taxes and expenditures. On the national level, conservatives lobbied for a constitutional amendment to prohibit federal budget deficits. Perhaps most significant, tax revolts became political vehicles for conservatve candidates to win elections.

Moreover, a new conservative political alignment took place in the 1970s and 1980s. Joining the political and economic conservatives were social and cultural conservatives, especially evangelical Christians, who believed they had a moral obligation to enter politics on the side of "a pro-life, pro-traditional family, pro-moral position." President Ronald Reagan appealed to both wings of the movement, and his 1980 presidential victory revealed that conservatism had become the dominant mood of the nation.

Ronald Reagan was a popular president. Although unemployment rose between 1981 and

1983, the economy then rebounded, and by 1984 Reagan's policies had helped lower inflation and interest rates as well as unemployment. Reagan's victory in 1984 was never in doubt, but his forty-nine-state sweep convinced some observers that he had transformed American politics by forging a conservative coalition that could dominate for years. Still, his programs provoked severe criticism. Liberal opponents lambasted his economic policies ("Reaganomics") as favoring the rich and penalizing the poor. Most people, however, did not blame Reagan. Indeed, he became what some called a Teflon-coated president—nothing stuck to him.

Reagan's favorable image was tarnished by the Iran-contra scandal in late 1986, and his influence diminished during his final two years in office. Still, when the voters went to the polls in November 1988, the nation was at peace, and both unemployment and inflation were at low levels. George Bush, Reagan's vice president, was the beneficiary of the Reagan legacy and, as the Republican presidential candidate, rode it to victory.

The Energy Crisis and End of the Economic Boom

It was evident in the early 1970s that the United States was beginning to suffer economic decline. Five recessions between 1969 and 1990 reflected the nation's economic woes. America's economic vulnerability was especially revealed by the 1973 Arab oil embargo. At the time, the country was importing one-third of its oil supplies. Even be-

The Organization of Petroleum Exporting Countries (OPEC) raised oil prices several times in the 1970s. Each increase fueled the rise of inflation in the United States; and Americans, who had expected cheap energy to last forever, saw their expectations dashed. Long lines at the gas pumps were a reminder that an era of easy abundance had passed.   Don Wright in the *Miami News*, 1976, Tribune Media Services.

• *Important Events* •

1974 OPEC oil prices increase Nixon resigns; Gerald Ford becomes president Ford creates WIN program to fight inflation Equal Credit Opportunity Act equalizes loan and credit card terms for men and women	**1981** AIDS first observed in United States Prime interest rate reaches 21.5 percent Congress approves Reagan's budget and tax cuts Reagan breaks air traffic controllers strike Economic recession; unemployment hits 8 percent
1975 Nuclear accident occurs at Brown's Ferry Antibusing agitation erupts in Boston Economic recession hits nation	**1982** Unemployment reaches 10 percent
1976 Hyde Amendment cuts off Medicaid funds for abortions Jimmy Carter elected president	**1983** More than half of adult women work outside the home ERA dies for lack of ratification
1978 *Bakke* v. *University of California* outlaws quotas but upholds affirmative action California voters approve Proposition 13	**1984** Reagan reelected
	1985 Gramm-Rudman bill calls for balanced budget by 1991
1979 Three Mile Island nuclear accident raises fears of meltdown Moral Majority established Federal Reserve Board tightens money supply American hostages seized in Iran	**1986** Tax Reform Act lowers personal income taxes Immigration Reform and Control (Simpson-Rodino) Act provides amnesty to undocumented workers Iran-contra scandal breaks Republicans lose control of Senate
1980 Economic recession recurs Race riots break out in Miami and Chattanooga Ronald Reagan elected president Republicans gain control of Senate	**1988** *Understanding AIDS* mailed to 107 million households Reagan travels to the Soviet Union George Bush elected president

fore the embargo, the United States had suffered occasional shortages of natural gas, heating oil, and gasoline. But the American people, who had grown up on inexpensive and abundant energy, made few efforts to conserve; they drove big cars and lived in poorly insulated homes.

In 1973, however, the American people had to deal with the oil price increases ordered by the Organization of Petroleum Exporting Countries (OPEC). Oil prices rose 350 percent that year. As Americans grappled with the economic, social, and political costs of the price hikes, multinational oil companies prospered: their profits jumped 70 percent in 1973

OPEC Price Increases Fuel Inflation

and another 40 percent in 1974. Meanwhile, the boost in the price of imported oil reverberated through the entire economy. Inflation jumped from 3 percent in 1972 to a frightening 11 percent in 1974.

Recession hit the auto industry in 1973 and deepened in 1974. In Detroit, General Motors laid off 38,000 workers indefinitely—6 percent of its domestic work force—and put another 48,000 on leave for up to ten days at a time. Sales of gas-guzzling American autos plummeted as consumers rushed to purchase energy-efficient foreign subcompacts from Japan and Europe. Like Ford and Chrysler, GM was stuck with mostly large-car

Auto Industry Recession

assembly plants. Moreover, there was an accelerator effect because the ailing American auto companies quit buying steel, glass, rubber, and tool-and-die products. And as the recession in the auto industry spread, other manufacturers began laying off experienced employees with seniority.

Unlike earlier postwar recessions, this one did not fade away in a year or two. Part of the reason was inflation. In the earlier recessions, Republican as well as Democratic administrations had held to a policy of neo-Keynesianism. To minimize the swings in the business cycle, they had manipulated federal policies—both fiscal policies (taxes and government spending) and monetary policies (interest rates and the money supply). They hoped by so doing to keep employment up and inflation down. Beginning in the 1970s, however, joblessness and prices both began to rise sharply. Policies designed to correct one problem seemed only to worsen the other.

Even in the best of times, the economy would have been hard pressed to produce jobs for the millions of baby boomers who joined the labor market in the 1970s. As it

The Shifting Occupational Structure

was, economic activity created 27 million additional jobs during the decade, a remarkable increase of 32 percent. But deindustrialization was causing a shift in the occupational structure. As heavy industries collapsed, laid-off workers took jobs in fast-food restaurants, all-night gas stations, and convenience stores—but at half of their former wages and without healthcare benefits. Workers who once had held high-paying blue-collar jobs saw their middle-class standard of living slipping away from them.

A central economic problem was a slowing of growth in productivity—the average output of goods per hour of labor. Be-

Lagging Productivity

tween 1947 and 1965 American industrial productivity had increased an average of 3.3 percent a year, raising manufacturers' profits and lowering the cost of products to consumers. From 1966 to 1970 annual productivity growth averaged only 1.5 percent; it fell further between 1971 and 1975 and reached a mere

0.2 percent between 1976 and 1980. Economists blamed lack of business investment in state-of-the-art technology, declining educational standards, the shift from an industrial to a service economy, and an alleged erosion of the work ethic. Whatever the causes, American goods cost more than those of foreign competitors.

The lag in productivity was not matched by a decrease in workers' expectations. Wage increases regularly exceeded production increases, and some economists blamed the raises for inflation. Indeed, wages that went up seldom came down again. Managers of the nation's basic industries—steel, autos, rubber—complained that the automatic cost-of-living adjustments in their labor contracts left them little margin to restrain price hikes.

Another spur to inflation was easy credit. Fearing scarcity, many people went on a buying spree; between 1975 and 1979, household and

Easy Credit and Inflation

business borrowing more than tripled (from $94 billion to $328 billion). More people had credit cards. The credit explosion helped bid up the price of everything, from houses to gold.

Every expert had a scapegoat to blame for the nation's economic doldrums. Labor leaders cited foreign competition and called for protective tariffs. Some businesspeople and economists blamed the cost of obeying federal health and safety laws and pollution controls. They urged officials to abolish the Environmental Protection Agency and the Occupational Safety and Health Administration. They also pressed for deregulation of the oil, airline, and trucking industries on the theory that competition would drive prices down. Above all, critics attacked the federal government's massive spending programs and mounting national debt.

President Ford's Response to the Economic Crisis

By the time Gerald R. Ford became president in 1974, OPEC price increases had pushed the inflation rate to 11 percent. Appalled, Ford created Whip Inflation Now (WIN), a voluntary program that encouraged businesses, consumers, and workers to save energy and organize grassroots anti-inflation efforts. In the 1974 congressional elections, voters responded to WIN, Watergate, and Ford's pardon of Nixon by giving the Democrats forty-three additional seats in the House and four in the Senate.

Ford's response to inflation was to curb federal spending and encourage the Federal Reserve Board to raise its interest rates to banks, thus tightening credit. But these actions prompted a recession—only this time it was the worst in forty years. Unemployment jumped to 8.5 percent in 1975 and, because the economy had stagnated, the federal deficit for the fiscal year 1976–1977 hit a record $60 billion.

Ford devised no lasting solutions to the energy crisis, but the crisis seemed to pass when OPEC ended the embargo—and the incentive to prevent future shortages dissolved as well. The energy crisis, however, did intensify public debate over nuclear power. For the sake of energy independence, advocates asserted, the United States had to rely more on nuclear energy. Environmental activists countered that the risk of nuclear accident was too great and that there was no safe way to store nuclear waste. Accidents in the nuclear power reactors at Brown's Ferry, Alabama (1975), and Three Mile Island, Pennsylvania (1979), gave credence to the activists' argument. By 1979, however, ninety-six reactors were under construction throughout the nation, and thirty more were on order.

The Energy Crisis and Nuclear Power

In the 1970s, the combined effects of the energy crisis, stagflation, and the flight of industry and the middle class to the suburbs and the Sunbelt were producing fiscal disaster in the nation's cities. Not since 1933 had a major American city gone bankrupt. But New York City was near financial collapse by late 1975. President Ford vowed "to veto any bill that has as its purpose a federal bail-out of New York City," but he relented after the Senate and House Banking Committees approved loan guarantees, and the city was saved. Other Frostbelt cities were also in trouble, saddled with growing welfare rolls, deindustrialization, and a declining tax base. In 1978 Cleve-

land became the first major city to default since the Great Depression.

Throughout Ford's term, relatively little was accomplished. Congress asserted itself and enjoyed new power. Ford almost routinely vetoed its bills, but Congress often overrode his vetoes. For the first time in the nation's history, furthermore, neither the president nor the vice president had been popularly elected. One of Ford's first acts as president had been to select Nelson Rockefeller, former governor of New York, as his vice president. But Republican prospects for retaining the presidency in the 1976 election seemed gloomy.

Gerald Ford's Presidency

 ## The Carter Presidency

While Ford struggled with a Democratic Congress, the Democratic party geared up for the presidential election of 1976. Against the background of Watergate secrecy and corruption, one candidate in particular promised honesty and openness. "I will never lie to you," pledged Jimmy Carter, an obscure former one-term governor of Georgia. When this born-again Christian promised voters efficiency and decency in government, they believed him. Carter arrived at the convention with more than enough delegates to win the nomination; he chose Senator Walter Mondale of Minnesota as his running mate.

Carter and the Election of 1976

Neither Carter nor President Ford, the Republican nominee, inspired much interest, and on election day only 54 percent of the electorate bestirred itself to vote. But as one political commentator observed, the vote nationwide was "fractured to a marked degree along the fault line separating the haves and have-nots." Although Carter won nearly 90 percent of the African- and Mexican-American vote, he squeaked to victory by a slim 1.7 million votes out of 80 million cast. Ford's appeal was strongest among middle- and upper-middle-class white voters.

Carter's most noteworthy domestic accomplishments were in energy, transportation, and conservation policy. To encourage domestic pro-duction of oil, he phased in de-control of oil prices. To moderate the social effects of the energy crisis, he called for a windfall-profits tax on excessive profits resulting from de-control, and for grants to the poor and elderly for the purchase of heating fuel. Carter also deregu-lated the airline, trucking, and railroad industries and persuaded Congress to ease federal control of banks. His administration established a $1.6 bil-lion "superfund" to clean up abandoned chemical-waste sites, and created two free-standing departments—the Departments of Energy and Education. Finally, he placed more than 100 mil-lion acres of Alaskan land under the federal gov-ernment's protection as national parks, national forests, and wildlife refuges.

Carter's Accomplish-ments

Despite these accomplishments, Carter failed to inspire Americans, and he alienated Demo-cratic Party members. Elected as an outsider, he remained one throughout his presidency. Moreover, Carter's support of deregulation and his opposition to wage and price controls and gasoline rationing ran counter to liberal Demo-cratic principles. Seeing inflation as a greater threat to the nation's economy than either recession or unemployment, Carter announced that his top pri-ority would be "to discipline the growth of govern-ment spending," even though doing so would add to the jobless rolls. But inflation continued to rise.

Carter's Flagging Popularity

Carter's problems were not entirely of his own making. In 1979 the shah of Iran's government fell to revolutionary forces. When the shah was ad-mitted to the United States for medical treatment, mobs seized the American embassy in Teheran and held fifty-two Americans as hostages for 444 days. The new Iranian government also cut off oil sup-plies to the United States. The same year OPEC raised its prices again, and the cost of crude oil nearly doubled. As Americans waited in long lines at gasoline pumps, public approval of the presi-dent reached a new low.

Carter also inherited political problems. In the wake of Vietnam and Watergate, power temporar-ily had shifted from the White House to Capi-tol Hill. Meanwhile, Congress was filling up with political newcomers, unaccustomed to reflex obedience to established leadership. It thus seemed that party discipline was a thing of the past. In addition, Capitol Hill was crawling with lobbyists from special-interest groups. In 1980, there were 2,765 political-action committees (PACs), more than four times as many as in 1974.

Decline of Presidential Authority

By 1980 the economy was in a shambles. In-flation had jumped in 1979 to over 13 percent, and traders around the world had lost confidence in the dollar, causing unprecedented increases in the price of gold. To steady the dollar and curb in-flation, the Federal Reserve Board took drastic measures. First, the board cut the money supply—partly by selling Treasury securities to take money out of circulation—thus forcing borrowers to bid up interest rates sufficiently to dampen the econ-omy and reduce inflation. Second, it raised the rate at which the Federal Reserve loaned money to banks. As a result, mortgage-interest rates leaped beyond 15 percent, and the prime lending rate (the rate charged to businesses) hit an all-time high of 20 percent. Inflation fell, but only to 12 percent.

Worse still, by 1980 the nation was in a full-fledged recession. The 1980 unemployment rate of 7.5 percent, combined with the 12 percent in-flation rate, had produced a staggeringly high "discomfort index" of just under 20 percent (see figure, page 631). In 1976 Carter had gibed at the incum-bent president, Gerald Ford, by saying, "Anything you don't like about Washing-ton, I suggest you blame on him." In 1980 many Americans blamed Carter for the problems that beset the country.

Economic Discomfort in 1980

Ronald Reagan and the Election of 1980

In the 1970s, political and economic conservatives joined forces with cultural and religious conserva-tives and thereby changed the political landscape.

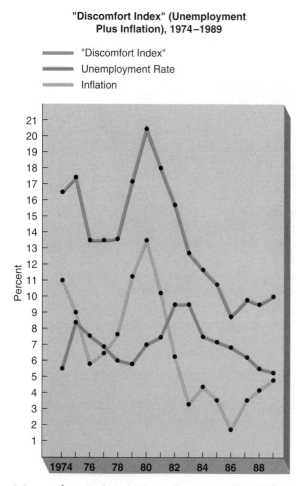

"Discomfort Index" (Unemployment Plus Inflation), 1974–1989

- "Discomfort Index"
- Unemployment Rate
- Inflation

Discomfort Index (Unemployment Plus Inflation), 1974–1989 Americans' economic discomfort (unemployment plus inflation) directly determined their political behavior. When the "discomfort index" was high in 1976 and 1980, Americans voted for a change in presidents. When the economic discomfort declined in 1984 and 1988, Ronald Reagan and George Bush were the political beneficiaries. Source: Adapted from *Economic Report of the President, 1992* (Washington, D.C., U.S. Government Printing Office, 1992), pp. 340, 365.

Resurgence of Conservatism

In 1979 Reverend Jerry Falwell, a radio-TV minister from Lynchburg, Virginia, helped to found the Moral Majority, which advocated what it called "family values," including opposition to abortion rights and homosexuality. The Moral Majority quickly registered between 2 and 3 million new voters, started a newspaper, and bought daily time on 140 radio stations. Together with conservative think tanks like the Hoover Institution and conservative magazines like *National Review*, these church groups formed a flourishing network of potential supporters for conservative candidates. By the late 1970s, conservatism was becoming a potent political force.

A Shifting Population

The 1980 federal census provided additional insights into the reasons for conservatism's resurgence in the United States. The census indicated that since 1970 there had been both a 24 percent increase in the more politically conservative elderly population and a significant movement of people from the politically liberal Frostbelt states of the Northeast and Midwest to the more conservative Sunbelt states of the South and West (see map, page 632). The internal migration led in 1982 to a shift of seventeen seats in the House of Representatives from the Frostbelt to the Sunbelt.

Reagan as the Republican Candidate

In the Republican primaries of 1980, Ronald Reagan, a former movie actor and two-term governor of California, triumphed easily over Representative John Anderson and former CIA director George Bush. His appeal to the voters was much broader than experts had predicted. He promised economy in government and a balanced budget, and he committed himself to "supply-side" economics, or tax reductions to businesses to encourage capital investment. Although Reagan planned to slash federal spending, he also pledged to cut income taxes and boost the defense budget. Reagan declared that he now opposed legalized abortion, and his stand against the Equal Rights Amendment (ERA) recommended him to the "profamily" movement.

Election of 1980

Reagan's candidacy united the old right wing with the new. And on election day, voters gave Reagan and his running mate George Bush 51 percent of the vote to 41 percent for Carter and almost 7 percent for Anderson. The vote was an affirmation of Reagan's conservatism and a signal of the

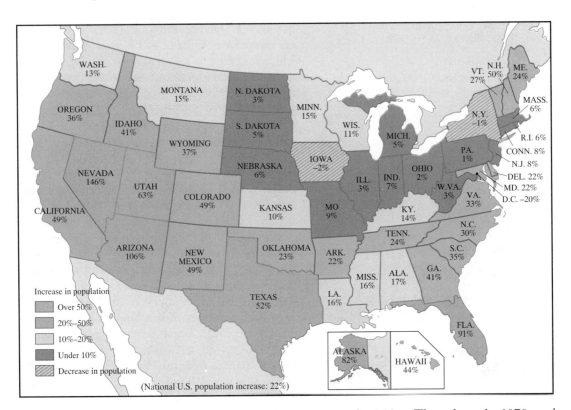

WASH. 13%

MONTANA 15%

N. DAKOTA 3%

MINN. 15%

OREGON 36%

IDAHO 41%

S. DAKOTA 5%

WIS. 11%

MICH. 5%

WYOMING 37%

NEBRASKA 6%

IOWA –2%

VT. 27%   N.H. 50%   ME. 24%

N.Y. –1%

MASS. 6%

R.I. 6%

CONN. 8%

N.J. 8%

PA. 1%

ILL. 3%   IND. 7%   OHIO 2%   W.VA. 3%

DEL. 22%

MD. 22%

D.C. –20%

VA. 33%

NEVADA 146%

UTAH 63%

COLORADO 49%

KANSAS 10%

MO 9%

KY. 14%

CALIFORNIA 49%

ARIZONA 106%

NEW MEXICO 49%

OKLAHOMA 23%

ARK. 22%

TENN. 24%

N.C. 30%

S.C. 35%

MISS. 16%   ALA. 17%

GA. 41%

TEXAS 52%

LA. 16%

FLA. 91%

Increase in population

Over 50%

20%–50%

10%–20%

Under 10%

Decrease in population

ALASKA 82%

HAWAII 44%

(National U.S. population increase: 22%)

The Continued Shift to the Sunbelt in the 1970s and 1980s   *Throughout the 1970s and 1980s, Americans continued to leave economically declining areas of the North and East in pursuit of opportunity in the Sunbelt.*

nation's deep dissatisfaction with Jimmy Carter's management of both the economy and foreign policy. As startling as Reagan's victory was the capture of eleven Senate seats by Republican candidates, giving the Republicans a majority in that house. Republicans also gained thirty-three seats in the House.

"Reaganomics"

Upon taking office, President Reagan immediately launched a double-barreled attack on problems in the economy. First, he asked Congress to cut billions from domestic programs, including Medicare and Medicaid, food stamps, welfare subsidies for the working poor, and school meals.

Congress endorsed most of Reagan's demands. Reagan soon initiated a second round of budget cuts, resulting among other things in the trimming of a million food-stamp recipients from government rolls.

Tax cuts were the second facet of Reagan's economic plan. A fervent believer in supply-side economics, he called for reductions in the income taxes of the affluent and of corporations in order to stimulate savings and investments. New capital would be invested, the argument went, and would produce new plants, new jobs, and new products. As prosperity returned, the profits at the top would "trickle down" to the middle classes and even to the poor. Congress responded with a five-year, $750 billion tax cut, the largest ever in American history, featuring a 25 per-

Tax Cuts

cent reduction in personal income taxes over three years. Other provisions increased business investment tax credits and depreciation allowances and lowered the maximum tax on income from 70 to 50 percent. The wealthy gained the most from these tax cuts.

A third item occupied Reagan's agenda: a vigorous assault on federal environmental, health, and safety regulations that, Reagan believed, excessively reduced business profits and discouraged economic growth. The president appointed opponents of the regulations to enforce them. Reagan officials explained that slackened enforcement was necessary to reduce business costs and make American goods competitive in world markets, but environmentalists countered that such policies invited disaster, such as toxic-waste poisoning or nuclear reactor accidents.

Weakened Environmental Enforcement

Hard times hit labor unions in the 1980s. Faced with recession and unemployment, union negotiators had to settle for less than they were accustomed to receiving. American workers who ratified contracts during the first three months of Reagan's term settled for pay increases averaging only 2.2 percent, the biggest drop in wage settlements since the government began collecting such data in 1954. Unions had suffered large membership losses when unemployment hit heavy industry, and their efforts to unionize the high-growth electronics and service sectors of the economy were failing.

Hard Times for Labor Unions

Reagan made the unions' hard times worse. He presided over the government's busting of the Professional Air Traffic Controllers Organization (PATCO) during the union's 1981 strike. His appointees to the National Labor Relations Board consistently voted against labor and for management. Despite Reagan's anti-labor posture, many union families responded positively to his genial personality, espousal of old-fashioned values, and vigorous anticommunist rhetoric.

Reagan enjoyed two notable economic successes during his first two years in office. First, the inflation rate plummeted, falling from 12 percent in 1980 to less than 7 percent in 1982. Oil led the way in price declines; after eight years OPEC had at last increased its oil production. In 1981 oil prices fell as world oil production exceeded demand by 2 million barrels a day. Second, as inflation fell, so too did the cost of borrowing money. Interest rates for bank loans, which had stood at a record high of 21.5 percent in early 1981, dropped to 10.5 percent by 1983.

Falling Inflation

But there was also a second, more sobering, explanation for the decline in inflation. By mid-1981 the nation was mired in a recession that not only persisted but deepened. During the last three months of the year, the GNP fell 5 percent. With declining economic activity, unemployment soared to 8 percent, the highest level in almost six years. By late 1982, unemployment had reached 10 percent, the highest rate since 1940. Among African-Americans, the unemployment rate reached 20 percent. Many of the unemployed were blue-collar workers in ailing "smokestack industries" such as autos, steel, and rubber. Reagan and his advisers had promised that supply-side economics would produce demand-side results and that consumers would lift the economy out of the recession by spending their tax cuts. But as late as April 1983, unemployment still stood at 10 percent. Agriculture, too, was faltering and near collapse. Farmers suffered from floods, droughts, and burdensome debts incurred at high interest rates. Many lost their property through mortgage foreclosures and farm auctions. Others filed for bankruptcy.

Rising Unemployment

As the recession deepened in 1982, poverty rose to its highest level since 1965. The Bureau of the Census reported that the number of Americans living in poverty increased from 26 million in 1979 to 34 million in 1982. The largest single category of poor families consisted of households headed by women (36 percent). With one exception, poverty continued its rise in 1983, returning to the level that had prevailed before the enactment of President Johnson's Great Society. That exception

Resurgence of Poverty

was the elderly; politicians had begun paying attention to this vocal and rapidly growing population.

President Reagan had announced that his administration would halt the expansion of social and health programs but would retain a "safety net" for the "truly needy." But he went back on this promise. Facing a budget deficit in excess of $200 billion in mid-1982, Reagan had three choices. First, he could cut back on his rearmament plans to spend $1.7 trillion over five years. This he refused to do; in fact, the budget he signed raised defense spending another 13 percent. Second, he could suspend or reduce the second installment of his tax cut. This choice, too, he found unacceptable. Third, he could—and did—cut welfare and social programs, pushing through Congress further cuts in Medicare and Medicaid, food stamps, federal pensions, and government-guaranteed home mortgages. Nevertheless, in the absence of budget cuts in other areas, or higher taxes, the federal debt continued to grow.

Reagan Triumphant: The Election of 1984

In 1984 the GNP rose 7 percent, the sharpest increase since 1951, and midyear unemployment fell to a four-year low of 7 percent. The economy

Reagan's Reelection Assets

was heating up, but without sparking inflation. Indeed, inflation (4 percent in 1984) fell to its lowest level since 1967. A second factor in Reagan's favor was people's perception of him as a strong leader in foreign as well as national affairs. Third, Reagan was the enthusiastic choice of political conservatives of all kinds across the country. Patriotism was back in style, and so were traditional values.

Aiding Reagan was the Democrats' failure to field a convincing alternative. The Democratic nominee—former vice president Walter Mondale—did not inspire Americans, and his policies seemed dated and out of step with the nation's conservatism. Adding to Mondale's woes was the disarray of the Democratic Party; it had fragmented into separate caucuses of union members,

African-Americans, women, Jews, homosexuals, Hispanics, and other groups. Each caucus had its own agenda. The one bright spot for Mondale was his selection of Representative Geraldine Ferraro of New York as the first woman vice-presidential candidate of a major political party. Ferraro showed herself to be an intelligent, indefatigable campaigner.

Mondale wanted to debate the federal deficit, but Reagan preferred to invoke the theme of leadership and rely on slogans. Mondale chastised Reagan

Reagan's 1984 Victory

for the mounting deficit, which had reached $175 billion in fiscal year 1984. But when Mondale announced that he would raise taxes to cut the deficit, he lost votes. Voters in 1984 had a clear choice, and in every state but Minnesota—Mondale's home state—they chose the Republican ticket. The election returns were the most convincing evidence yet that the nation had shifted to the right. The only groups still loyal to the Democratic ticket were African-Americans, Hispanics, Jews, and the poor. Reagan scored solid victories with all other voting groups, including young people, whites in both North and South, high-school and college graduates, and Catholics as well as Protestants.

In the 1930s, Franklin Roosevelt and his New Dealers forged a coalition that controlled national politics for more than thirty years. Reagan's victory seemed to shatter that coalition. At a minimum the victory reflected a growing reaction against the liberalized moral standards associated with the Democratic Party. Many Democrats held conservative views on welfare, abortion, homosexuality, and other social issues, and they switched their votes to Ronald Reagan and the Republican Party.

People of Color and New Immigrants

Poverty was a growing problem in the 1970s and 1980s, particularly for people of color. Joblessness plagued blacks, Native Americans, and Hispanics, as well as new immigrants. African-Americans made up a disproportionate share of the poor. The overall poverty rate was 13 percent by 1980, but among blacks it was 33 percent and among Hispanics 26 percent, compared with 10 percent for whites. These figures had barely changed by the end of Ronald Reagan's presidency in 1989.

The weight of poverty fell most heavily on children, especially African-American children, almost half of whom lived below the poverty line. A 1981 Children's Defense Fund survey reported that black children in the United States were four times more likely than whites to be born into poverty, twice as likely to drop out of school before twelfth grade, three times as likely to be unemployed, and five times as likely to be murdered. Many children lived in poor families headed by single women who earned meager incomes as domestic servants, laundresses, and kitchen helpers, supplemented by welfare assistance.

Some whites and even other blacks grumbled that poor blacks were responsible for their own poverty. But the job market was far different in the 1970s and 1980s from that of twenty-five, fifty, or seventy-five years before. During periods of rapid industrialization, unskilled European immigrants and black migrants from the South had been able to find blue-collar jobs. Beginning in the 1970s, fewer such jobs were available; demand was greatest for skilled workers such as computer operators, bank tellers, secretaries, and bookkeepers. Most jobless people could not qualify.

Declining Job Opportunities for African-Americans

But a historical anomaly was at work. For even as the plight of the African-American poor worsened, the black middle class expanded. The number of black college students increased from 282,000 in 1966 to more than 1 million in 1980; by 1980, about one-third of all black high-school graduates were going on to college, the same proportion as among white youths. By 1990, the number of black college students had increased further to 1.3 million. At least at the upper levels of black society, the dream of equality was being realized.

African-American Middle Class

But as middle-class African-Americans made gains, resentful whites complained that they were being victimized by "reverse discrimination." To meet federal affirmative-action requirements, some schools and companies had established quotas for minorities and women; in some cases the standards were lower than those for whites. When Allan Bakke, a white man, was denied admission to medical school, he sued on the grounds that black applicants less qualified than he had been admitted. In a 5-to-4 ruling in 1978, the Supreme Court outlawed quotas but upheld the principle of affirmative action, explaining that race or ethnicity could be counted as "a 'plus' in a particular applicant's file" (*Bakke* v. *University of California*). Eleven years later, however, the Court ruled that past discrimination did not "justify a rigid racial quota" and that white workers could sue to reopen affirmative-action cases settled in federal courts years earlier (*Richmond* v. *Croson, Martin* v. *Wilks*).

White Backlash

White anger over affirmative action and busing combined with the effects of stagflation to produce an upsurge in racism. In Boston, where busing provoked numerous riots, a group of white students attacked a black passerby outside city hall. "Get the nigger; kill him," they shouted as they ran at him with the sharp end of a flagstaff flying an American flag. Racial tension rose in cities across the nation.

African-Americans were tense, and they showed their anger more openly than in the past. Charles Silberman wrote in *Criminal Violence, Criminal Justice* (1978) that "black Americans have discovered that fear runs the other way, that whites are intimidated by their very presence. . . . The taboo against expression of antiwhite anger is breaking down, and 350 years of festering hatred has come spilling out." That hatred erupted several times in 1980, most notably in Miami and Chattanooga, after all-white juries acquitted whites in the killings of blacks. Miami's three days of rioting left eighteen dead and four hundred injured.

Black Anger

African-American civil rights leaders denounced not only the judicial system but also the executive branch headed by President Ronald Reagan. Appointments were one issue: whereas 12 percent of President Jimmy Carter's high-level appointees had been black and 12 percent women, Reagan's were 4 percent black and 8 percent women. (Reagan did appoint four women to his cabinet and made history by appointing Sandra Day O'Connor the first woman associate justice of the Supreme Court.) Moreover, Reagan's civil rights chief in the Justice Department opposed busing and affirmative action, and he was criticized for lax enforcement of fair housing laws and laws banning sexual and racial discrimination in federally funded education programs.

Every bit as angry as African-Americans were Native Americans. Their new militancy burst into the headlines in 1969, when a small group of In-

Native American Militancy

dians seized Alcatraz Island in San Francisco Bay. Arguing that an 1868 Sioux treaty entitled them to possession of unused federal lands, the group occupied the island until mid-1971. Two years later, members of the militant American Indian Movement (AIM), demanding the rights guaranteed Indians in treaties with the United States, seized eleven hostages and a trading post on the Pine Ridge Reservation at Wounded Knee, South Dakota, where troops of the Seventh Cavalry had massacred three hundred Sioux in 1890. Their seventy-one-day confrontation with federal marshals ended with a government agreement to examine the treaty rights of the Oglala Sioux.

White society posed more than a cultural threat to Indians. Four in ten Native Americans were unemployed, and nine out of ten lived in substandard housing. Often, being an Indian also meant being unhealthy. Native Americans suffered the highest incidence of tuberculosis, alcoholism, and suicide of any ethnic group in the United States.

Since 1924, Indians have had dual legal status as United States citizens and as members of tribal nations subject to special treaty agreements with the United States. Their dual status has proved a curse, in

Indian Suits for Lost Lands

large part because the government found it easier to breach its treaty commitments. In 1946 Congress established the Indian Claims Commission to compensate Indians for lands stolen from

them. Under the legislation, lawyers for the Native American Rights Fund and other groups scored notable victories. In 1980, for example, the Supreme Court ordered the government to pay $106 million plus interest to the Lakota nation for the Black Hills of South Dakota, stolen when gold was found there in the 1870s. Nevertheless, corporations and government agencies continued to covet Indian lands and disregard Indian religious beliefs: a coal company strip-mined a portion of the Hopi Sacred Circle, which according to tribal religion is the source of all life.

As Indians fought to regain old rights, Hispanic-Americans struggled to make a place for themselves. An inflow of immigrants unequaled

Hispanic-Americans

since the turn of the century coupled with a high birth rate made Hispanic peoples America's fastest-growing minority by the 1970s. Of the more than 20 million Hispanics living in the United States in the 1970s, 8 million were Mexican-Americans concentrated in California, Texas, Arizona, New Mexico, and Colorado. Several million Puerto Ricans, Cubans, Dominicans, and other immigrants from the Caribbean also lived in the United States, clustered principally on the East Coast.

These officially acknowledged Hispanic-Americans were joined by millions of undocumented workers, or illegal aliens. Beginning in the mid-1960s, large numbers of poverty-stricken Mexicans began to cross the poorly guarded 2,000-mile border. The movement north continued in the 1970s and 1980s. By 1990, one out of three Los Angelenos and Miamians would be Hispanic, as would be 48 percent of the population of San Antonio and 70 percent of El Paso.

Poverty awaited many of these new immigrants, as it had previous groups of newcomers. Like earlier groups, Hispanics faced a language barrier. Most inner-city schools did not provide bilingual education for Spanish-speaking students. And the larger the Hispanic population has become, the more widespread has been the discrimination.

Most of these new Americans preferred their family-centered culture to Anglo culture and, for that reason, resisted assimilation. "We want to be

How do historians know the extent of the illegal immigration to the United States? In truth, historians do not know precisely how large it has been. The most reliable data come from the United States Census Bureau's reports, but even the Census Bureau concedes that it can only estimate the extent of illegal immigration. In 1992, an estimated 3.4 million immigrants lived illegally in the United States. Academic demographers have contributed to historical understanding through their analyses of government statistics. Philip Martin and Elizabeth Midgley studied recent immigration to the United States and concluded that at least 1 million people move to the United States each year, of whom some 300,000 are undocumented immigrants The photograph below captures the image that many have of illegal immigrants crossing the border from Mexico; highway crossings such as this one have caused numerous deaths. But as statistics show, this stereotype is misleading. Illegal immigrants, for example, come from all over the world, not merely from Mexico, Central America, the Caribbean, or Asia. There also are sizable contingents from Ireland, Poland, Israel, and Iran. Source: Data from Philip Martin and Elizabeth Midgley, "Immigration to the United States: Journey to an Uncertain Destination," *Population Bulletin* 49 (September 1994): 1–46. Photo: Don Bartletti, *LA Times.*

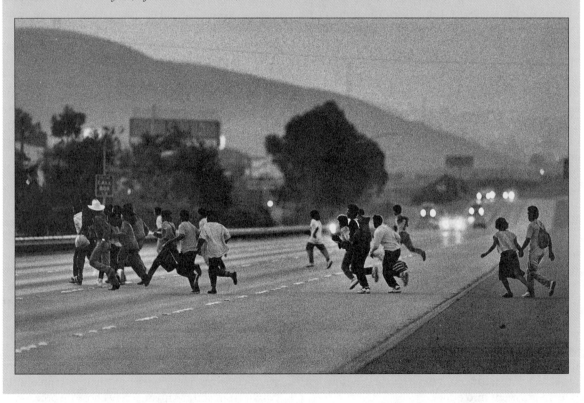

Hispanic Cultural Pride

here," explained Daniel Villanueva, a TV executive in Los Angeles, "but without losing our language and our culture. They are a richness, a treasure that we don't care to lose."

Like other minorities, Hispanics wanted political power—"brown power." Cesar Chavez's United Farm Workers was the first Hispanic interest group to gain national attention. The militant Brown Berets also attracted notice for their efforts to provide meals to preschoolers and courses in Chicano studies and consciousness raising to older students. And throughout the 1970s the Mexican-American political party La Raza Unida was a potent force in the Southwest and in East Los Angeles. Still, the group that was becoming the nation's largest minority exercised a disproportionately small share of political power.

During the 1970s and 1980s people of color immigrated to the United States in record numbers from Indochina, Mexico, Central and South America, and the Caribbean. Between 1970 and 1980 the United States absorbed more than 4 million immigrants and refugees and uncounted numbers of illegal aliens. In the 1980s, the number of immigrants surpassed the historic high mark of 8.7 million set between 1900 and 1909. Many of the new immigrants came in family units, and women and children accounted for two-thirds of all legal immigrants. Among the newcomers, Asian-Americans seemed to be the most successful.

New Influx of Immigrants

The arrival of so many newcomers put pressure on Congress to curtail the flow and perhaps offer amnesty to aliens already living illegally in the United States. In 1978 Congress authorized a comprehensive reexamination of America's immigration policy. Eight years later Congress passed the Immigration Reform and Control (Simpson-Rodino) Act, which provided amnesty to undocumented workers who had arrived before 1982. The act's purpose was to discourage illegal immigration by imposing sanctions on employers who hired undocumented workers, but it failed to stem the flow of people fleeing Mexico's economic woes. In 1988 the number of new immigrants from Mexico approached the record numbers reached before the reform law went into effect.

Immigration Reform

Feminism, Antifeminism, and Women's Lives

Women scored some impressive victories in the 1970s. In 1974, Congress passed the Equal Credit Opportunity Act, which enabled women to get bank loans and obtain credit cards on the same terms as men. In the field of criminal law, many states revised their statutes on rape, prohibiting defense lawyers from discrediting rape victims by revealing their previous sexual experience. Perhaps most significant were women's gains from affirmative action in hiring. As mandated by the Civil Rights Act of 1964 and the establishment of the Equal Employment Opportunity Commission, women and people of color applying for jobs had to receive the same consideration as white males.

Still, women continued to encounter opposition in their struggle for gender equality. Particularly formidable was the antifeminist or "profamily" movement, which contended that men should lead and women should follow, especially within the family, and that women should stay home and raise children. The conservative backlash against feminism became an increasingly powerful political force in the United States, especially in the Republican Party. In defense of the patriarchal, or father-led, family, antifeminists campaigned against the Equal Rights Amendment, the gay rights movement, and abortion on demand.

Antifeminist Movement

Antifeminists blamed the women's movement for the country's spiraling divorce rate; they charged that feminists would jettison their husbands and even their children in their quest for job fulfillment and gender equality. Although the number of divorces almost tripled from 1960 to 1976, often the decision to divorce was made not by the wives but by the husbands. According to Barbara Ehrenreich, a feminist scholar, men started walking out on their families in large numbers in the 1950s, well before the rebirth of feminism. Tired of fulfilling the role of husband, father, and financial provider, many men came to see their wives as the agent of their entrapment; in "flight from commitment," they chose divorce.

Antifeminists successfully stalled ratification of the Equal Rights Amendment, which—after quickly passing thirty-five state legislatures—died in 1983, three states short when the time limit expired. Phyllis Schlafly's "Stop ERA" campaign claimed that the ERA would abolish alimony and legalize homosexual

Equal Rights Amendment

marriages. Schlafly refused to acknowledge gender-based discrimination and derided ERA advocates as "bitter women seeking a constitutional cure for their personal problems."

Many conservative women also participated in the anti-abortion or "prolife" movement, which sprang up almost overnight in the wake of the Supreme Court's 1973 decision in *Roe* v. *Wade*. Along with Catholics, Mormons, and other religious opponents of abortion, the anti-abortion movement supported the Hyde Amendment, the successful legislative effort of Representative Henry Hyde of Illinois in 1976 to cut off most Medicaid funds for abortions.

Feminists fought back, assailing Reagan for failing to reverse "the feminization of poverty" and for approving cuts in food stamps and school meals. The Reagan adminis-

Women Opponents of Reagan's Conservatism

tration's opposition to federally subsidized childcare and the feminist goal of "comparable worth" also drew their ire. Because of occupational segregation, 80 percent of all working women in 1985 were concentrated in low-paying "female" occupations such as clerking, selling, teaching, and waitressing. Recognizing this, feminists supplemented their earlier rallying cry of "equal pay for equal work" with a call for "equal pay for jobs of comparable worth." Why, women asked, should a grade-school teacher earn less than an electrician, if the two jobs require comparable training and skills and involve comparable responsibilities? In the 1970s, female workers still took home only 60 cents to every male worker's dollar; by 1990, the figure had risen to 71 cents.

Activists in the women's struggle had to acknowledge certain harsh realities. One was the tight job market created by the economic recessions of the 1970s and 1980s.

Increased Burdens on Women

Other problems included a rising divorce rate, which left increasing numbers of women and their children with lower standards of living, and a high teenage pregnancy rate. The tandem of divorce and teenage pregnancy meant that a progressively smaller proportion of America's children lived with two parents. Many women also had to contend with what came to be called "the Superwoman Squeeze." According to a report by the Worldwatch Institute, most working wives and mothers "retained an unwilling monopoly on unpaid labor at home." Combining housework and outside employment, wives worked 71 hours a week; husbands worked 55 hours a week. By 1983, 51 percent of adult women were working outside the home.

A Polarized People: American Society in the 1980s

The United States became an increasingly polarized society in the 1980s. The rich got richer, while the poor sank deeper into despair (see figure). Indeed, by 1989 the top 1 percent (834,000 households with $5.7 trillion in net worth) was worth more than the bottom 90 percent (84 million households with $4.8 trillion in net worth).

By the end of the 1980s, as many Americans were living in poverty as had been living in poverty in 1964, when President Johnson declared war on poverty. But the poor themselves were somewhat different.

Increasing Inequality

The poverty of the 1980s, explained the authors of a 1988 report of the Social Science Research Council, "is found less among the elderly and people living in nonurban areas and more among children living with one parent—in households headed principally by young women." As inequality grew, the gap widened between affluent whites and poor blacks, Indians, and Hispanics, and between the suburbs and the inner cities. And as inequality increased, so too did social pathology. Violent crime, particularly homicides and gang warfare, grew alarmingly, as did school dropout rates, crime rates, and child abuse.

Poverty resulted not only from discrimination based on race and gender, but also from economic recessions and from the changing structure of the labor market. As dein-

Changing Job Market

dustrialization took hold, the job market shifted from high-paying, unionized, blue-collar jobs to low-paying service

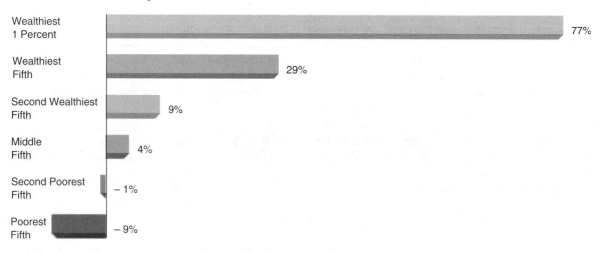

While the Rich Got Richer in the 1980s, the Poor Got Poorer

Percentage Increase in Pretax Income from 1977–1989

Wealthiest 1 Percent	77%
Wealthiest Fifth	29%
Second Wealthiest Fifth	9%
Middle Fifth	4%
Second Poorest Fifth	– 1%
Poorest Fifth	– 9%

While the Rich Got Richer in the 1980s, the Poor Got Poorer   Between 1977 and 1989, the richest 1 percent of American families reaped most of the gains from economic growth. In fact, the average pretax income of families in the top percentage rose 77 percent. At the same time, the typical family saw its income edge up only 4 percent. And the bottom 40 percent of families had actual declines in income.   Source: Data from the *New York Times*, March 5, 1992.

jobs. Minimum-wage employment burgeoned in fast-food restaurants, but such jobs meant a substantial drop in workers' standard of living. Indeed, by 1990, although 40 percent of the nation's poor were working, few had full-time, year-round jobs. At the same time, social workers reported that more and more of the nation's homeless were families.

About a third of the homeless were former psychiatric patients who found themselves living on the streets after hospitals emptied their psychiatric wards in a burst of enthusiasm for "deinstitutionalization." By 1985, 80 percent of the total number of beds in state mental hospitals had been eliminated on the premise that small neighborhood programs would be more responsive than large state hospitals to people's needs. Few provisions were made for medical treatment, and these troubled people increasingly found that they had nowhere to go except the street.

Another cause of homelessness was drug use. Mired in hopelessness, poverty-stricken men and women tried to find forgetfulness in hard drugs,

Drugs and Violence

especially cocaine and its derivative crack, which first struck New York City's poorest neighborhoods in 1985. Crack's legacy included destroyed families, abused children, and drug dealers too young for a driver's license but with access to submachine guns and other state-of-the-art firearms. Gang shootouts over drugs were deadly: the toll in Los Angeles in 1987 was 387 deaths; more than half of the victims were innocent bystanders.

Another lethal byproduct of the 1980s drug epidemic was the spread of AIDS. First observed in the United States in 1981, AIDS is a disease trans-

AIDS

mittable through the sharing of intravenous needles by drug users or through the exchange of infected body fluids, often during sexual contact. Caused by a virus that attacks cells in the immune system, AIDS makes its victims susceptible to deadly infections and cancers. In the

For this family, which includes a one-week-old baby, homelessness came suddenly. Home had been a squalid motor inn in North Bergen, New Jersey, but the board of health condemned the motel and the police put the family out on the street. In 1988, as many as a million people were homeless.   Eugene Richards/Magnum.

United States, AIDS initially was linked to the sexual practices of male homosexuals, but the disease spread to heterosexuals. Of the 57,000 AIDS cases reported between 1981 and 1988, nearly 32,000 resulted in death. But because it takes several years for symptoms to appear, the worst had not yet revealed itself. A 1988 study reported that half of the gay men in San Francisco would develop AIDS and another 25 percent would develop the AIDS-related complex within about nine years of infection.

AIDS—along with other sexually transmitted diseases such as genital herpes and chlamydia—affected Americans' sexual behavior. Caution replaced the mores of the "sexual revolution." "Safe sex" campaigns urged the use of condoms. For years Americans had pretended the disease was limited to promiscuous homosexuals and drug addicts. But as writers, artists, athletes, actors, and relatives and friends died, people began to confront the horrifying epidemic.

Nonetheless, AIDS divided communities. Conservative Protestant sects joined the Roman Catholic Church in warning that condom advertising implicitly sanctioned contraception and encouraged promiscuity. Sex education should not be offered in the schools, they contended, citing their deep belief that any sexual activity other than heterosexual matrimonial monogamy was wrong. Gay men expected little assistance from the conservative executive branch, but they were partly wrong. In 1988 the federal government mailed a booklet entitled *Understanding AIDS* to 107 million households. Nevertheless, AIDS continued to be one of several unsolved social problems dividing the nation in the 1980s.

 Reagan's Second Term and the Election of 1988

Despite Ronald Reagan's overwhelming reelection victory in 1984, for much of 1985 the president was on the defensive. One reason was the mounting

Mounting Fiscal Deficit

fiscal deficit. Though a fiscal conservative, Reagan presided over the greatest deficit budgets in the nation's history. During the fiscal years 1982 through 1986, tax reductions and spiraling defense budgets caused the national debt to grow by $955 billion. Overall, Reagan oversaw the accumulation of more new debt than all previous presidents put together throughout America's history. In response, Reagan and the Congress reluctantly agreed to the 1985 Gramm-Rudman bill, which called for a balanced federal budget by fiscal 1991 through a gradual reduction of the annual deficit. The deficit did drop, but for the three fiscal years from 1987 to 1989, it still totaled $457 billion.

During his second term, Reagan was successful in confronting other challenges. After Warren Burger's decision to retire from the Supreme Court, he nominated William Rehnquist to serve as chief justice and Antonin Scalia to fill Rehnquist's seat; the Senate confirmed both choices. Another victory was the Tax Reform Act of 1986, which lowered personal income taxes while closing some flagrant loopholes and eliminating 6 million poor people from the tax rolls.

But midway through his second term, Reagan encountered problems that endangered his historical reputation. First, the Republicans lost control of the Senate, stripping the president of a crucial power base. Second, from Lebanon came a bizarre story that the president's national security adviser had traveled to Iran with a Bible, a cake, and a planeload of weapons seeking the release of Americans held hostage in the Middle East. "No comment," Reagan told reporters, but as details of the Iran-contra scandal surfaced, half of the people in the country believed that Reagan was lying about his lack of involvement in the Iran-contra scandal.

Iran-Contra Scandal

On a personal level, President Reagan had taken on the appearance of a tired, bumbling old man. "Who's in Charge Here?" asked a *Time* magazine headline. The Iran-contra hearings focused attention on President Reagan's "hands-off" management style. Some observers argued that Reagan was unengaged and uninformed. Donald T. Regan described his experience: "In the four years that I served as Secretary of the Treasury I never saw President Reagan alone and never discussed economic philosophy or fiscal and monetary policy with him one-on-one."

Reagan's Decline

Reagan's problems continued in 1987 and 1988. Congress overrode his veto of a massive highway-construction bill, and twice his choices for the Supreme Court failed to win confirmation by the Senate. Still, as the 1988 elections approached, there was also some excellent political and economic news for Republicans. First, Reagan had moderated his anti-Soviet rhetoric and in 1988, to the applause of most Americans, had traveled to the Soviet Union—the first American president to visit Moscow since Richard Nixon in 1972. Second—and of greater importance to voters—after the economic recession of 1981 and 1982, the United States had embarked on a six-year business recovery. The discomfort index, which had risen alarmingly in the 1970s and early 1980s, dropped to more comfortable levels in the later 1980s. And although unemployment dropped to a decade-low 5.4 percent in April 1988, it did so without refueling inflation.

Continuing Economic Recovery

The Reagan administration pointed to the economy as proof of the success of supply-side economics. Critics retorted that Reagan's policy of pursuing massive tax cuts while greatly increasing the defense budget was just another form of Keynesianism—deficit financing to stimulate the economy. But the average American, caring little about this kind of debate, was content to enjoy the economic recovery. It was true that the poor had little to rejoice over and that Americans viewed the economic future with uncertainty. But it was also true that in the 1980s most Americans had jobs and were living very comfortably.

Had Reagan been allowed by the Constitution to run for a third term, he probably would have ridden the economic boom to victory. But the 1988 election was for his successor, and the competition in both parties was intense. On the Republican side the candidates included Vice President George Bush, Senate minority leader Bob Dole, and Pat Robertson, a television evangelist. Bush emerged with the nomination after bitter Republican infighting in state primaries.

George Bush

On the Democratic side, the race narrowed to a two-person contest between Michael Dukakis, under whose governorship Massachusetts had seemed a model of economic recovery and welfare reform, and Jesse Jackson, a former colleague of Reverend Martin Luther King, Jr., who had moved to Chicago to organize economic and educational programs for the poor. An eloquent preacher, Jackson campaigned on his dream of forming a "Rainbow Coalition" of the "rejected"—African-Americans, women, Hispanics, the disabled. Jackson was the first African-American to win mass support in seeking the presidential nomination of a major political party.

Both Bush and Dukakis avoided serious debate of the issues: drugs, environmental collapse, poverty, rising medical and educational costs, childcare, and the fiscal and trade deficits. Despite the gravity of the problems, the candidates relied on clichés and negative campaigning. Television dominated the presidential election as never before. Bush aimed his appeals at the "Reagan Democrats" by pushing emotional "hot buttons" such as "patriotism" and the death penalty. A Republican advertisement for television appealed to racism and fear by accusing Dukakis of being soft on crime for furloughing Willie Horton, a black convict.

Presidential Campaign of 1988

But with America at peace and inflation and unemployment both low, Bush's victory was seldom in doubt. His margin over Dukakis was substantial: 53 percent of the popular vote to 46 percent. The election confirmed that the "Solid South," once a Democratic stronghold, had become

Bush's Victory in 1988

solidly Republican. Bush won every state in the region. In both South and North, race was a key factor, as it had been in every presidential election since 1964: for twenty-five years, the Republican vote had been almost exclusively white, and almost all blacks had voted Democratic.

Many Americans seemed unconcerned as they confronted the new decade. College students in the 1990s, unlike many of their predecessors in the 1960s, aspired to join the system. They yearned not to save the world but to scramble up the corporate ladder. Baby boomers and their younger sisters and brothers reported frustration in their efforts to replicate their parents' standard of living, particularly because of high housing costs.

But polls in 1989 reported that Americans were generally happy with their lives. Many expressed pleasure with the new toys and comforts in their lives. Especially impressive was the widespread use of videocassette recorders (VCRs) and personal computers. From 1980 to 1984, movie rentals for VCRs soared from 26 million to 304 million. Meanwhile, the phenomenal spread of computers revolutionized not only communications but also people's workplaces and lifestyles. In 1981, the number of personal computers in use in America numbered 2 million; in 1988, the figure was 45 million.

Conclusion

The United States changed in fundamental ways between 1974 and 1989. The spread of technological developments was part of that change. So, too, was the new immigration, which in the 1970s and 1980s not only swelled tremendously but shifted in origin. People came from Mexico, Central and South America, and the Caribbean, as well as from the Philippines, Korea, Taiwan, and India. Refugees of the Vietnam War also arrived.

Another change was the country's shift to the right politically. The champion of this change was President Ronald Reagan, whose supporters included both economic and social conservatives and both Republicans and disillusioned Democrats. Despite Reagan's successes, when he left office in

1989, the country faced unsolved economic, social, and political issues of great importance. "Ronald Reagan leaves no Vietnam War, no Watergate, no hostage crisis," reported the *New York Times*. "But he leaves huge question marks—and much to do." First, inequality had escalated in the 1980s, as the poor got poorer and the rich got richer. Second, the rise of the federal debt continued unabated. Third, the effects of mismanagement and outright fraud were beginning to show in certain industries, forcing the federal government to consider massive bailouts.

When George Bush was inaugurated as the forty-first president of the United States on January 20, 1989, the American people prepared to greet not only a new presidency but also a new decade. It was clear that Americans and their leaders would have to make difficult economic, social, and political choices in the 1990s.

Suggestions for Further Reading

Deficits, Deindustrialization, and Other Economic Woes

Barry Bluestone and Bennett Harrison, *The Deindustrialization of America* (1982); Richard Feldman and Michael Betzold, *End of the Line: Autoworkers and the American Dream* (1988); Robert Heilbroner and Peter Bernstein, *The Debt and the Deficit* (1989); John P. Hoerr, *And the Wolf Finally Came: The Decline of the American Steel Industry* (1988); Gregory Pappas, *The Magic City: Unemployment in a Working-Class Community* (1989).

The Ford and Carter Administrations

John Dumbrell, *The Carter Presidency* (1993); John Robert Greene, *The Presidency of Gerald R. Ford* (1995); Erwin C. Hargrove, *Jimmy Carter as President* (1989); Charles O. Jones, *The Trusteeship Presidency: Jimmy Carter and the United States Congress* (1988); Burton I. Kaufman, *The Presidency of James Earl Carter, Jr.* (1993); A. James Reichley, *Conservatives in an Age of Change: The Nixon and Ford Administrations* (1981).

Women and Children's Struggles

Marian Wright Edelman, *Families in Peril* (1987); Barbara Ehrenreich, *The Hearts of Men: American Dreams and the Flight from Commitment* (1983); David T. Ellwood, *Poor Support: Poverty in the American Family* (1988); Susan Faludi, *Backlash: The Undeclared War Against American Women* (1991); Sylvia Ann Hewlett, *When the Bough Breaks: The Cost of Neglecting Our Children* (1991); Arlie Russell Hochschild, *The Second Shift:*

Working Parents and the Revolution at Home (1989); Rebecca E. Klatch, *Women of the New Right* (1987); Kristin Luker, *Abortion and the Politics of Motherhood* (1984); Maggie Scarf, *Unfinished Business: Pressure Points in the Lives of Women* (1980); Winifred D. Wandersee, *On the Move: American Women in the 1970s* (1988).

People of Color and New Immigrants

John Crewdson, *The Tarnished Door: The New Immigrants and the Transformation of America* (1983); Leslie W. Dunbar, ed., *Minority Report: What Has Happened to Blacks, Hispanics, American Indians, and Other Minorities in the Eighties* (1984); Reynolds Farley and Walter R. Allen, *The Color Line and the Quality of Life in America* (1987); Nancy Foner, ed., *New Immigrants in New York* (1987); Ronald P. Formisano, *Boston Against Busing* (1991); Troy R. Johnson. *The Occupation of Alcatraz Island: Indian Self-Determination and the Rise of Indian Activism* (1996); Joane Nagel, *American Indian Ethnic Revival: Red Power and the Resurgence of Identity and Culture* (1996); David M. Reimers, *Still the Golden Door: The Third World Comes to America* (1985); Sanford J. Ungar, *Fresh Blood: The New Immigrants* (1995); William Julius Wilson, *The Truly Disadvantaged: The Inner City, the Underclass, and Public Policy* (1987).

The New Conservatism and the Election of 1980

William C. Berman, *America's Right Turn* (1994); Alan Crawford, *Thunder on the Right* (1980); Thomas Byrne Edsall, *The New Politics of Inequality* (1984); Jack W. Germond and Jules Witcover, *Blue Smoke and Mirrors: How Reagan Won and Why Carter Lost the Election of 1980* (1981); Godfrey Hodgson, *The World Turned Right Side Up: A History of the Conservative Ascendancy in America* (1996); Gillian Peele, *Revival and Reaction* (1984).

Ronald Reagan and His Presidency

Lou Cannon, *President Reagan* (1991); Paul D. Erickson, *Reagan Speaks: The Making of an American Myth* (1985); Mark Hertsgaard, *On Bended Knee: The Press and the Reagan Presidency* (1988); Haynes Johnson, *Sleepwalking Through History: America in the Reagan Years* (1991); Jane Mayer and Doyle McManus, *Landslide: The Unmaking of the President, 1984–1988* (1988); Michael Schaller, *Reckoning with Reagan* (1992); Larry M. Schwab, *The Illusion of a Conservative Reagan Revolution* (1991); David Thelen, *Becoming Citizens in an Age of Television: How Americans Challenged the Media and Seized Political Initiative During the Iran-Contra Debate* (1996); John Kenneth White, *The New Politics of Old Values* (1988); Garry Wills, *Reagan's America* (1987).

"Reaganomics"

Joan Claybrook, *Retreat from Safety: Reagan's Attack on America's Health* (1984); Benjamin Friedman, *Day of Reckoning: The Consequences of American Economic Policy Under Reagan and After* (1988); Jonathan Lash, *A Season of Spoils: The Story of the Reagan Administration's Attack on the Environment* (1984); Robert Lekachman, *Greed Is Not Enough: Reaganomics* (1982); William A. Niskanen, *Reaganomics* (1988); Charles Noble, *Liberalism at*

Work: The Rise and Fall of OSHA (1986); Kevin Phillips, *The Politics of Rich and Poor* (1990); Lawrence J. White, *The S & L Debacle* (1991).

A Polarized Society in the 1980s

Chandler Davidson, *Race and Class in Texas Politics* (1990); Michael Harrington, *The New American Poverty* (1984); Katherine S. Newman, *Declining Fortunes: The Withering of the American Dream* (1993); Randy Shilts, *And the Band Played On: Politics, People and the AIDS Epidemic* (1987); Studs Terkel, *The Great Divide* (1988); Edward N. Wolff, *Top Heavy: A Study of Increasing Inequality in America* (1995).

Presidential Politics: The Elections of 1984 and 1988

Sidney Blumenthal, *Pledging Allegiance: The Last Campaign of the Cold War* (1990); Richard Ben Cramer, *What It Takes* (1992); Thomas Byrne Edsall and Mary D. Edsall, *Chain Reaction: The Impact of Race, Rights, and Taxes on American Politics* (1991); Thomas Ferguson and Joel Rogers, *Right Turn: The Decline of the Democrats and the Future of American Politics* (1986); Marshall Frady, *Jesse: The Life and Pilgrimage of Jesse Jackson* (1996); Jack W. Germond and Jules Witcover, *Wake Us When It's Over: Presidential Politics of 1984* (1985); Peter Goldman and Tom Mathews, *The Quest for the Presidency: The 1988 Campaign* (1989).

CHAPTER

33

Anxiety and Anger: America in the 1990s

Chase Smith, age three, and his two-year-old brother, Colton, were eating powdered doughnuts as their mother Edye Smith drove them to the American Kids daycare center in downtown Oklahoma City. When they kissed Edye goodbye at the daycare center on the second floor of the Alfred P. Murrah Federal Building, they left powdered sugar on her cheeks. As Edye turned to walk back to her car, Colton called out and ran to give her a big hug. "I love you, Mommy." Not to be outdone, Chase did likewise. It was Wednesday morning, April 19, 1995.

Jumping into her car, Edye Smith hurried to her job as a secretary at the Internal Revenue Service five blocks away. What awaited Edye was a birthday party—her own. Knowing that she would be twenty-three in two days, her coworkers had bought a cake to celebrate. Edye was just about to slice the cake when she heard a blast and felt the building shake. From the window, she could see smoke rising.

Edye, her mother (who also worked for the Internal Revenue Service), and other workers in the downtown area soon flooded into the streets. As they got closer to the area of the blast, they sensed the worst. They walked past dead bodies and saw bloodied children huddled with rescue workers. When they could not find the boys, Edye's brother, Daniel Coss, a police officer, took up the search. Several hours later, he identified Colton at a temporary morgue set up near the rubble; then he located Chase's body at the medical examiner's office. Chase and Colton Smith were buried together, holding hands in a small white coffin.

This was the worst act of terrorism in United States history. One hundred sixty-eight children, women, and men were killed in the blast. They were in or near the Murrah Building at 9:02 that morning, when a yellow rental truck containing a homemade two-ton bomb of fuel oil and ammonium nitrate fertilizer exploded.

Americans were dazed, saddened, and angry. In the aftermath of the tragedy, they called in to radio talk shows to denounce the bombers and express their sorrow for the victims and their families. Some callers suggested that the Oklahoma City bombing was a government plot to discredit the "Patriot movement" in America. Others compared it to the tragedy in Waco, Texas, in 1993, when the FBI led an assault on the compound of a religious sect known as the Branch Davidians, a fire broke out, and some eighty people died. "If anyone is responsible for the bombing," explained a woman caller in Richmond, Virginia, "it's the mainstream press for covering up the real story about Waco and the horrible things the Government, [President] Bill Clinton and [Attorney General] Janet Reno did to those women and children." A climate of fear and hatred was growing, and some critics blamed the radio talk shows for fueling people's dark suspicions and anger.

At first, most Americans wanted to think that the bomb had come from abroad, perhaps set off by terrorists from the Middle East. But a charred piece of truck axle located two blocks from the explosion, with the vehicle identification number still legible, seemed to prove otherwise. Arrested was Timothy McVeigh, a native-born white American and an army veteran of the Persian Gulf War. He apparently hated the federal government, which he condemned for betraying the American people and the Constitution. The conflagration at Waco had agitated McVeigh; he saw it as deliberate slaughter by the Federal Bureau of Investigation.

In 1997, McVeigh was convicted and given a death sentence. In a separate trial, Terry Nichols— a former army buddy of McVeigh—received a life sentence after being convicted of conspiracy and involuntary manslaughter.

Investigations following the tragedies in Waco and Oklahoma City uncovered networks of Militiamen, Patriots, tax resisters, and various Aryan-supremacist groups. Computer-literate "patriots" used the Internet to rally support for their view that the federal government had to be resisted or even overthrown because it was controlled not by the people but by Zionists, corrupt politicians, cultural elitists, the Russians, the United Nations, and other "sinister" forces.

It was not just the far right, however, that was politically disaffected in the 1990s. People of far more moderate beliefs also abjured political participation. Americans were disgusted with negative political advertisements, and many did not know where to turn to make real political choices in their lives. They rejected the Democratic Party for having lost touch with their cultural and moral values, and they rejected the Republicans for failing to represent their economic and social needs.

In 1989, as the political scientist James MacGregor Burns concluded his multivolume history of the United States, he was discouraged by what he saw. What the nation needed, he wrote, was "creative and transforming leadership" that would mobilize the country and "carry through great projects." Surely in the 1990s the challenges were there, but would the presidential leadership be there to meet them?

From 1989 to 1993, America's presidential leader was George W. Bush. Bush had a rough ride as president. With victory in the Persian Gulf War in 1991, his popularity rating in the polls soared to 89 percent, tied with the high set by Harry S Truman in June 1945 after the surrender of Germany. Bush's reelection in 1992 seemed guaranteed. The president, however, had already sown the seeds of his own defeat. Bush had proclaimed in 1988, "Read my lips: no new taxes," but he betrayed that pledge in 1990 when he agreed to a tax hike as part of a tradeoff to reduce the spiraling fiscal deficit.

The early 1990s was a time of economic stagnation and deepening poverty. By 1992, several million Americans had joined the unemployment rolls, and factory employment was skidding to its lowest level since the recession of 1982. And the number of poor people in America reached the highest level since 1964.

Bush's greatest handicap as president was his inability to give American voters a sure sense of who he was and what remedies he would prescribe for the economy, which had slipped into a recession in 1990 and 1991. He also seemed perplexed and without a plan when Los Angeles erupted in race rioting in 1992.

Americans sensed that 1992 was an important election year. The Cold War was over. The economy was in trouble. Anti-incumbent sentiment was on the rise. In fact, in 1992 the American people saw the most successful third-party campaign in eighty years. H. Ross Perot, a multibillionaire who spoke plain language and said he could fix the deficit, garnered 19 percent of the popular vote. But the winner and president-elect was the Democratic candidate, Governor Bill Clinton of Arkansas.

Born in 1946—the first baby boomer president—Bill Clinton hoped, said an ally, "to modernize liberalism so it could sell again." As president, however, Clinton alienated both liberals and conservatives. He failed to deliver on healthcare reform, and his "Don't ask, don't tell" policy for gays in the military angered homosexuals as well as the military. And throughout his administration, Clinton battled charges of unethical behavior.

As Clinton's public approval rating plummeted, Republican conservatives under the leadership of Representative Newt Gingrich of Georgia launched an assault to win control of government, beginning with Congress. In 1994, "the Republican revolution" was triumphant; the Republicans won control of both houses of Congress for the first time since 1954. But the Republicans failed to enact most of their agenda.

Just two years after the Republicans' historic 1994 triumph, it seemed possible that Bill Clinton could make a political comeback. The Republican candidate in 1996 was Bob Dole, the Senate majority leader from Kansas. Dole's political vision was vague, and he did not inspire the voters. For his part, Clinton stole some of the conservative thunder by moving to the right himself, declaring that the "era of big government" was over, and running as a budget-balancing cultural conservative. The voters seemed to be listening, and Clinton won reelection.

President Clinton had promised that his administration would build "a bridge to the twenty-first century, wide enough and strong enough to take us to America's best days." The building of this bridge to the future, Clinton hoped, would serve as the basis of his historical legacy.

Economic and Social Anxieties: The Presidency of George W. Bush

In the 1990s, public apathy, even disgust, grew as Americans witnessed gridlock in the federal government. Instead of compromise and negotiated solutions, there was partisanship and stalemate; Republican president George W. Bush and the Democratic Congress seemed unable to work together or agree on anything. Bush vetoed thirty-seven bills during his presidency, only one of which was overridden.

Decisive presidential leadership might have broken the gridlock, but Bush was a political chameleon. Once a supporter of family planning and a woman's right to an abortion, he had switched his position and denounced abortion as murder. In the 1980 Republican primaries, he had dismissed Ronald Reagan's "supply-side" economic ideas as "voodoo economics," but he quickly endorsed these policies when he became Reagan's running mate in 1980. He thus seemed to lack firm convictions of his own. Still, when President Bush was inaugurated in 1989, the future appeared bright. There had been six straight years of economic growth, and both unemployment and inflation were low.

Bush's Political Shifts

Soon, however, the economy took a nosedive, and Bush's inactivity on the home front revealed the shallowness of his inaugural call for a "kinder, gentler nation." In 1989 Bush vetoed an increase in the minimum wage. And he did seem uncaring when he defended tax breaks for the rich but opposed extending relief payments to the long-term unemployed. In October 1990 alone, the president's popularity plummeted 25 points. Kevin Phillips, a political analyst, wrote that Bush's "dithering" over domestic issues was responsible for the decline.

• *Important Events* •

1989	George Bush becomes president Bush vetoes increase in minimum wage
1990	Clean Air Act reauthorization requires reduction in emission of pollutants Bush-Congress budget agreement raises taxes; Bush reneges on "no new taxes" pledge Americans with Disabilities Act prohibits discrimination Recession begins; personal incomes fall
1991	Persian Gulf War Anita Hill testifies at Senate hearings to confirm Clarence Thomas's Supreme Court nomination Thomas is confirmed
1992	Los Angeles riots erupt Bill Clinton and George Bush win nominations California pays employees with IOUs Clinton elected president H. Ross Perot's third-party candidacy wins one-fifth of the vote Bush pardons former government officials in Iran-contra scandal Twenty-seventh Amendment prohibits future midterm congressional pay raises
1993	Clinton becomes president Hillary Rodham Clinton heads task force on healthcare reform Clinton lifts restrictions on abortion counseling

	Clinton's proposal to lift ban on homosexuals in the military stirs controversy Congress approves the North American Free Trade Agreement Branch Davidian compound burns in Waco, Texas, killing at least 80 people Clinton appoints Ruth Bader Ginsburg to the Supreme Court Motor-voter and family-leave acts become law Gun control laws require a waiting period for handguns and ban the sale of assault weapons
1994	Clinton appoints Stephen Breyer to the Supreme Court Clinton signs crime bill into law Republican candidates for Congress offer voters the "Contract with America" Republicans win the House and Senate
1995	Bombing of federal building in Oklahoma City kills 168 people
1996	Telecommunications Act allows telephone and cable companies to compete Freedom to Farm Act mandates phaseout of federal subsidies to farmers Convictions in the first of several Whitewater trials Clinton signs welfare act eliminating Aid to Families with Dependent Children Clinton reelected
1997	Madeleine Albright becomes first woman confirmed as Secretary of State

In the fall of 1990, Bush earned high praise for assembling the multinational force stationed in Saudi Arabia. And the Persian Gulf War (1991) temporarily saved his floundering presidency. Still, Bush's inaction on healthcare, unemployment, and other pressing domestic concerns drew mounting criticism. Bush's slogan, "First, do no harm," reflected his aversion to government action to solve economic and social problems. Moreover, Bush's advisers believed that he would win reelection easily in 1992 by riding the wave of approval generated from the successful war with Iraq.

Bush's domestic problems began in 1990, when he betrayed the pledge he had made at the 1988

"First, Do No Harm"

Republican convention: "Read my lips: no new taxes." During the 1990 bud-get summit with Congress, the White House agreed to a tax increase in exchange for the acquiescence of congressional Democrats in budget cuts. Many applauded Bush's action as responsible leadership, but soon the television news began running the videotape of Bush's "Read my lips" statement, and questioning whether the president could be trusted in the future.

"Read My Lips: No New Taxes"

As a candidate in 1988, Bush had promised that he would be the "environmental president" as well as the the "education president"; but he failed in both areas. While Bush accepted high praise for signing the 1990 reauthorization of the Clean Air Act, which required limits on emissions of sulfur dioxide and nitrogen oxides, he gutted enforcement of the act by establishing the Council on Competitiveness. The council declared that environmental regulations should be eliminated because they slowed economic growth and cost jobs. In addition, the Justice Department overruled the Environmental Protection Agency when it sought to have large corporate polluters prosecuted. In education, President Bush announced that, by the year 2000, American students would be second to none in science and mathematics. His administration, however, did little to support education reform, other than argue for government vouchers that parents could use to pay tuition at public or private schools of their choice.

Lack of Support for Environment and Education

The president's credibility also suffered during the confirmation hearings of Clarence Thomas, nominated in the fall of 1991 to serve on the Supreme Court. Few people believed that this inexperienced federal judge was, as Bush put it, the "best man for the job." But Thomas, an African-American, was highly conservative. He opposed affirmative action in hiring, believed in returning prayer to the schools, and opposed abortion. Bush's nomination of a black conservative was a clever but cynical po-

Nomination of Clarence Thomas to the Supreme Court

litical move. One opponent, Eleanor Holmes Norton, the African-American congressional delegate from Washington, D.C., denounced the choice as "calculated . . . to mute the expected reaction to yet another conservative nominee."

Despite the opposition, it seemed that Thomas would be confirmed. In October, however, the nation was electrified by the testimony of Anita Hill, an African-American law professor at the University of Oklahoma, who charged that Thomas had sexually harassed her when she worked for him in the early 1980s. Thomas was confirmed by the Senate, but Hill's testimony—and the Senate's disregard of it—so angered women that many thousands vowed to oppose the Republican Party in 1992.

Social ills that had plagued the United States in the 1980s persisted unabated into the new decade: AIDS, homelessness, drug and alcohol addiction, racism and inequality, poverty among children, the day-to-day struggles of single-parent families. In the 1990s, however, economic and social problems that once had afflicted only the poor now touched the lives of the middle classes, who saw their standard of living decline.

Persistent Social Problems

One group, however, made real progress in 1990. That year, President Bush signed the Americans with Disabilities Act, which banned job discrimination, in companies with twenty-five or more employees, against the blind, deaf, mentally retarded, and physically impaired as well as against those who are H.I.V. positive or have cancer. The act, which covered 87 percent of all wage earners, also required that "reasonable accommodations," such as wheelchair ramps, be made available to people with disabilities.

Americans with Disabilities Act

In the year following the signing of the Americans with Disabilities Act, panic struck the White House. The occasion was the election to the Senate of a Democrat whose campaign included the advocacy of a national health insurance system. At the time there were few incentives to control healthcare costs, and with the spread of expen-

Healthcare Problems

sive technologies, medical expenses were rising rapidly. Still worse, some 33 million Americans, about 13 percent of the population, had no health insurance at all. Three-fourths of these people were employed but worked at minimum-wage jobs that did not provide health benefits. Additional tens of millions had such limited coverage that they constantly were at risk of financial devastation.

Also fueling Americans' anxieties were the growing numbers of job layoffs, some of them temporary but many of them permanent. Sensing that economic recovery would be slow, businesses were hesitant to take back workers even if the economy did pick up. In a practice called "outsourcing," companies stopped making their components and began ordering them from factories in states and countries where wages were far lower and benefit packages nonexistent. Other businesses replaced workers with computers and other machines, not only to cut costs but also to increase productivity. Throughout the nation, numerous industries were deciding whether to reduce labor costs by opting for technology, outsourcing, or moving their plants to Mexico, South Korea, and other low-wage countries.

"Downsizing" and "Outsourcing"

By mid-1990 there was no doubt the United States was mired in a recession. American businesses were eliminating tens of thousands of jobs. "The recession that won't go away," *Newsweek* reported in November 1991, "has average Americans spooked and politicians running scared." And a poll that month showed that for the first time in Bush's presidency, less than a majority of the voters (47 pecent) were inclined to reelect him in 1992.

American Voters and the Election of 1992

Prior to the 1992 presidential election, the Republican Party had been on a roll. From 1968 through 1988, the Republicans had captured the White House five times by building a coalition of ideologically diverse constituencies. First, there were economic conservatives who had always voted Republican. Second, there were cultural conservatives, particularly fundamentalist and evangelical Christians who advocated "family values." Third, there were the "Reagan Democrats," blue-collar workers and one-time Democrats who had supported Bush in 1988 as Reagan's heir. Fourth, there were white voters in the South, where Republican growth had been impressive since the 1960s. Fifth, there were young Americans between eighteen and thirty who had come of age politically during the Reagan years. Last were the antitax and antigovernment voters of America's ever-growing suburbs. In the 1980s what had held the Republican coalition together were economic growth, anticommunism, and Ronald Reagan. In 1992, these three factors were absent.

As the 1992 presidential election neared, Republicans from all parts of the country pleaded with the White House to take action on the economy. Between 1989 and 1992, the economy had grown slowly or not at all; the gross national product averaged an increase of only 0.7 percent a year, the worst showing since the Great Depression of the 1930s. Even for Americans with jobs, personal income was stagnant. In fact, in 1991 median household incomes fell by 3.5 percent.

A Stagnant Economy

Even worse off were some city and state governments that faced bankruptcy. The state of California, out of money in mid-1992, paid its workers and bills in IOUs. A series of "tax revolts," beginning with Proposition 13 in 1978, had cut property taxes. But California was not alone; some thirty states were in serious financial difficulty in the 1990s. Businesses, too, were deeply burdened with debt. And as companies tottered, the American people were anxious about their jobs. The president, however, seemed out of touch with the American people, and in a poll taken in January 1992 eight of ten Americans rated the economy as "fairly bad" or "very bad."

But the Democrats had problems of their own, particularly in the 102nd Congress, which they

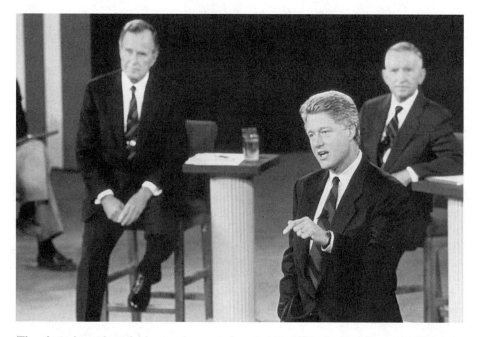

The televised presidential debates took on an informal air in 1992. At this debate at the University of Richmond, George Bush (left) and Ross Perot (right) listen while Bill Clinton speaks. In the debates, Clinton used the talk-show format to his advantage, demonstrating his ability to connect with people.   Agence France Presse/Corbis-Bettmann.

controlled. The most blatant scandal involved the House bank, where representatives wrote thousands of bad checks, all of which the bank covered at no fee. The Senate angered the public with ethical violations by several of its members who did favors for Charles Keating, who had plundered a large California savings and loan association, causing many unsuspecting small investors to lose their savings. Many Americans also blamed Congress for the gridlock in Washington. And people were upset when members of Congress voted themselves a pay raise. (In 1992, the necessary number of states ratified the new Twenty-seventh Amendment to the Constitution to prohibit midterm congressional pay raises.)

Scandals in Congress

In 1992 the Democrats nominated Governor Bill Clinton of Arkansas for president. Clinton was a baby boomer whose message was mixed. He emphasized the need to move people off welfare, and he called for more police officers on the streets and for capital punishment. But he also advocated greater public investment in building roads, bridges, and communications infrastructure; universal access to apprenticeship programs and college educations; basic healthcare for all Americans; and a shift of funds from defense to civilian programs. Clinton's running mate, Tennessee senator Albert Gore, was also a baby boomer, a white southerner, a Baptist, and a moderate Democrat. Gore appealed to environmentalists as the author of a bestselling book, *Earth in the Balance: Ecology and the Human Spirit* (1992).

Bill Clinton

Clinton was not Bush's only opponent. In April 1992, Ross Perot, who had amassed a fortune in the computer industry, announced on a television call-in show that he would run for president if voters in all fifty states put his name on the ballot. Many people responded to Perot's candidacy, convinced that he had the answers.

Ross Perot

While Clinton and Bush fought for the nominations of their respective parties, riots erupted in Los Angeles. The violence came after a

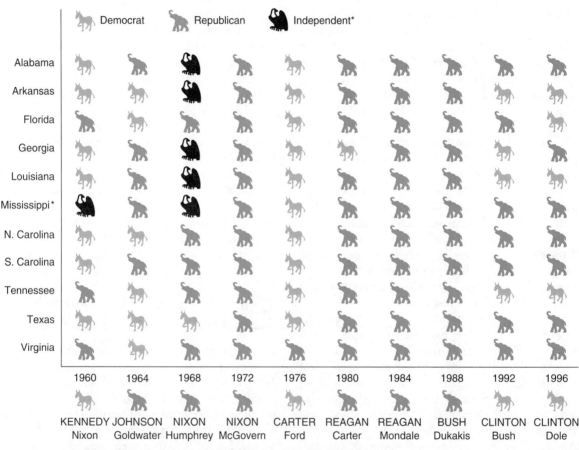

Southern States in Presidential Elections, 1960–1996

*Mississippi Voters elected Harry Byrd in 1960. In 1968, George Wallace carried Alabama, Arkansas, Georgia, Louisiana, and Mississippi.

Southern States in Presidential Elections, 1960–1996 *A major shift in modern American political history occurred in the 1960s and 1970s. In those years, the once-solid Democratic South became Republican in presidential elections; in 1972 Richard M. Nixon won every state in the region. In the aftermath of the Watergate scandal, a southern Democrat, Jimmy Carter of Georgia, won all but one state in the South. But the Republicans' ascendancy returned in 1980, when Ronald Reagan won every southern state but Georgia. And in 1984 and 1988, the Republican ticket handily won all of the South. Even though a southerner, Bill Clinton of Arkansas, won the presidential elections of 1992 and 1996, the Republican tickets led by George Bush and Bob Dole still managed to carry a majority of states in the region.*

Los Angeles Riots

California jury had discounted videotaped evidence and acquitted four police officers charged with beating Rodney King, an African-American motorist pulled over after a high-speed chase. Forty-four people died during the rioting, and entire blocks of houses and stores went up in flames, leaving $1 billion in charred ruins. President Bush paid a two-day trip to Los Angeles and advocated emergency aid, but he missed an opportunity to take a bold step in addressing the nation's urban and racial problems. He gave no civil rights talks, and he avoided meeting with the nation's mayors. It seemed to increasing numbers of voters that President Bush did not really care.

At the Republican convention in August, the president assumed the identity of guardian of "family values." The convention itself was dominated

The 1992 Republican Convention

by cultural conservatives, one of whom called for a "religious war" and a "cultural war" against the nation's internal enemies, including homosexuals. The party renominated George Bush and Dan Quayle, but in his acceptance speech the president had little new to offer.

The Bush-Quayle election strategy featured negative campaigning, particularly attacks on Bill Clinton's character. Clinton's Vietnam draft status (he had pulled strings to avoid military service) and his alleged extramarital affairs led to his being caricatured as "Slick Willie," a draft-dodger, and a ladies' man. During the campaign, Bush said the issue was "trust," and he asked whether the American people could trust Clinton's international leadership.

On November 3, the American people voted to make a change. The Clinton-Gore ticket swept all of New England and the West Coast and much

Clinton's Victory

of the industrial heartland of the Middle West. It also made inroads into the South (see figure), recaptured many "Reagan Democrats," and ran well in the suburbs. Simply put, the Republican coalition failed. The Democrats thus won 43 percent

of the vote, while the Republican ticket gained 37 percent. Perot's 19 percent of the vote reflected the public's dissatisfaction with both major parties.

Voters also changed the Congress. The party distribution remained about the same, with the Democrats in control of both houses, but four more women were sent to the Senate and nineteen more to the House. Voters also elected more African-American and Hispanic-American representatives. Many of the first-term members of Congress were—like Clinton—in their forties with advanced degrees, no military service, and considerable experience in politics at the state level.

One of Bush's last decisions as president smacked of the discredited past. Just before leaving office, the president pardoned Reagan's secretary of defense Caspar Wein-

Bush's Pardon of Iran-Contra Officials

berger and other Iran-contra figures who had been indicted on felony counts for lying to Congress and obstructing a congressional inquiry. Had nothing been learned from the Watergate scandal, asked the *Washington Post* columnist David Broder.

 Bill Clinton, Newt Gingrich, and Political Stalemate

President Bill Clinton was one of the most paradoxical presidents in American history. In a 1996 story for the *New York Times*, journalist Todd S. Purdum observed of Clinton: "One of the biggest, most talented, articulate, intelligent, open, colorful characters ever to inhabit the White House [Clinton] can also be an undisciplined, fumbling, obtuse, defensive, self-justifying rogue. . . . He is esentially sunny, yet capable of black cloudbursts of thundering rage. . . . He is breathtakingly bright while capable of doing really dumb things."

Clinton's immediate goal as president was to mobilize the nation to pull itself out of its economic, social, and political doldrums. He named to his cabinet a mix of seasoned politicos, young politicians, intellectuals, women, and minorities. In his inaugural address, he called on Americans to "take more responsibility, not only for ourselves and our families, but for our communities and our country." One of Clinton's first acts was to overturn Bush's "gag rule," which had prohibited abortion counseling in clinics that received federal funds. And he appointed his wife, Hillary Rodham Clinton, to draft a plan for healthcare reform.

Clinton soon ran into trouble, however, by acting on a campaign pledge to lift the ban on homosexuals in the armed forces. Military leaders and Republicans harshly criticized the proposal. Seeing that the American people were evenly divided on the issue, and fearful of losing support for his economic proposals, Clinton delayed a decision for months. Finally, he accepted a "Don't ask, don't tell" compromise that prohibited discrimination against gays in the military as long as they did not reveal their homosexuality; if their sexual orientation became known, however, they would be discharged "for the good of the service." The compromise alienated liberals, conservatives, the military, and the gay community.

The Issue of Gays in the Military

In 1993, the economy drew the president's close scrutiny. The economic plan that Clinton sent to Congress in February called for higher taxes for the middle class, a 10 percent surtax on individuals with taxable incomes over $250,000, an energy tax, and a higher corporate tax. Clinton promised to end business deductions for expense accounts, such as memberships in country clubs. He also proposed to cut government spending through a smaller defense budget and a downsized bureaucracy, and he offered an immediate stimulus to the economy through public works projects.

Clinton's Economic Proposals

Interest-group lobbyists wasted no time in attacking Clinton's economic plan. Republicans protested that Clinton was not cutting back enough on spending, and other critics hammered him for going back on his campaign pledge to provide tax relief for middle-class Americans. The president fought back, arguing that all Americans must pay to clean up the mess the deficit-spending Republicans had left them.

Congress killed Clinton's economic stimulus proposal but passed other requests, including the "motor-voter" act, which enabled people to register to vote when they applied for drivers' licenses, and the Family and Medical Leave Act, which required employers to grant workers unpaid family or medical leave of up to twelve weeks. Clinton also signed into law measures dealing with the sale of firearms. The Brady bill (1993) required a short waiting period before the sale of a handgun; a second law banned the sale of assault weapons. And in 1994, Clinton, with the help of three Republican senators who broke with their party, secured the enactment of a $30.2 billion crime bill. The new law provided funds for building more prisons and increasing the size of urban police forces. And in 1993, with considerable opposition from his own party and organized labor, Clinton secured congressional approval of the North American Free Trade Agreement. The Senate also approved the nominations of Ruth Bader Ginsburg, a women's rights advocate and federal appeals court judge, and Stephen Breyer, a federal judge from Massachusetts, to replace retiring justices Byron White and Harry Blackmun.

Clinton's Legislative Successes

Clinton's appointments bolstered the moderate wing of the Supreme Court. In *U.S.* v. *Virginia* (1996), the Court held that the Virginia Military Institute could not exclude women, because to do so would violate the constitutional guarantee of "equal protection of the laws"; thus separate-but-equal was unconstitutional whether based on race or gender. Also in 1996, in a landmark gay rights case (*Romer* v. *Evans*), the Court ruled unconstitutional a Colorado amendment that nullified civil rights protections for homosexuals.

During Clinton's presidency, the annual fiscal deficit began to shrink. Because of reduced spending and higher taxes, the federal deficit declined by some $83 billion during Clinton's first fiscal year in office. The president touted the accomplishment but could not take credit alone. The economy rebounded in 1993, outperforming estimates,

Declining Fiscal Deficit

increasing tax revenues, and cutting interest on the federal debt. Spending for healthcare and for Social Security fell below estimates. Not only did the decline in the fiscal deficit continue, but in early 1998 President Clinton submitted a balanced budget to Congress.

Despite the president's legislative accomplishments, it became apparent that Clinton's healthcare plan and welfare proposals would determine his success or failure on the domestic front. Almost everyone—liberal and conservative, Democrat and Republican—agreed that the nation's healthcare system was in crisis and that its welfare system was a failure. Different constituencies, with vastly different solutions, led to gridlock rather than legislation.

The failure to deliver on healthcare was Clinton's major defeat, and it was one he shared with First Lady Hillary Rodham Clinton, who cochaired the president's task force on healthcare reform. In trying to transform healthcare "in one bite," Clinton himself later conceded, he had "overestimated how much the system could change." Opposed to substantive reform were powerful interests, including corporations, the insurance industry, and small business. Most important of all, Clinton had been elected a minority president in 1992 and thus lacked the political clout of a leader with a clear mandate from the people.

Clinton's Defeat on Healthcare Reform

President Clinton's honeymoon in office was brief. People protested higher taxes and showed impatience with the slowness of his plan to revive the economy. Critics charged that Clinton backed down when pressed and was unwilling to take risks. Liberals complained that he was too conservative, conservatives that he was too liberal. Public relations gaffes and late-hour White House abandonment of controversial appointees raised doubts about the president's management ability.

In 1993, a scandal dating back to the mid-1980s also began to dog the Clintons. The scandal involved the failed Madison Guaranty Savings and Loan and the Whitewater Development Company. Then-Governor Bill Clinton and Hillary Clinton had been partners in the Whitewater Company with James McDougal, who was indicted for conspiracy and mail fraud, along with his wife Susan and Governor Jim Guy Tucker, Clinton's successor in Arkansas. In 1994, Webb Hubbell, former managing partner of the law firm in which Hillary Clinton had worked and a close friend whom President Clinton had appointed deputy attorney general, entered a plea agreement with the special prosecutor investigating Whitewater. In return for his cooperation in the ongoing investigation, Hubbell was allowed to plead guilty to one count of tax evasion and one count of mail fraud. A Senate committee also launched an investigation into Whitewater, including the role of the Clintons.

Whitewater Indictments and Investigations

Meanwhile, Republicans were taking control of Congress. In 1992, American voters had thrown the incumbent out of the White House. Two years later, an angry electorate focused on the Democratic-controlled Congress. Conservative Republicans led by Representative Newt Gingrich of Georgia were prepared to exploit the anger. As part of a strategy to break America's habit of sending Democrats to the House, the Gingrich forces drafted a tentative legislative agenda. Then in September 1994, more than three hundred Republican candidates for the House stood on the steps of the United States Capitol and proclaimed their endorsement of the "Contract with America." An ambitious document, the ten-point contract called for a balanced-budget amendment to the Constitution; a presidential line-item veto; the prohibition of welfare payments to unmarried mothers under eighteen and a two-years-and-out limit on welfare benefits; more prisons and longer prison sentences; a $500-per-child tax credit; increased defense spending; a reduced capital gains tax; and congressional term limits.

"Contract with America"

Using the "Contract with America" as a focal point of the campaign, the Republican Party scored one of the most smashing victories in American

The 1994 Congressional Elections

political history, winning both houses of Congress for the first time since 1954. Not a single Republican incumbent lost, and many newcomers were elected, 73 in the House alone. Gingrich became Speaker of the House, and Bob Dole of Kansas became majority leader of the Senate.

When the 104th Congress convened in January 1995, the Republicans set out to reverse more than sixty years of federal dominance and to dismantle the welfare state. A year later, however, "the Republican Revolution" had stalled on Capitol Hill. Political stalemate gripped the government. Twice, in 1995 and 1996, failure to enact routine appropriations bills caused the government to close most of its offices. The American people were disgruntled; some were angry. And as the 1996 election approached, hostility to the government was both widespread and intense.

Disgruntled Americans: Anger and Apathy

In mid-1996 federal agents in Arizona arrested twelve members of a paramilitary group called the Viper Militia for plotting to blow up government buildings in Phoenix. Later that year, five Viper Militia members pleaded guilty to illegally conspiring to make explosive devices. The home of one militia member had yielded several hundred pounds of ingredients for ammonium nitrate bombs, like the one used in Oklahoma City in 1995. Office workers in Phoenix were terrified.

Terrorism, which to Americans had seemed remote and foreign, now seemed nearby and homegrown. But while terrorism was relatively new to the American experience, hostility to the government was not. In fact, the American Revolution was an antigovernment movement directed against George III and his rule in the colonies. And, as the historian Michael Kazin has noted, "Throughout American history groups on the right and the left have seen the Fed-

Americans' History of Hostility to Government

eral Government as an alien force, inimical to their interests." Such groups have shared certain articles of faith: the government has betrayed the people, its leaders are corrupt, and the Constitution has been subverted. In the 1990s increasing numbers of Americans seemed to share this outlook.

For many Americans, the roots of their hostility to the federal government were planted in the 1960s during the Vietnam War. That tumultuous decade bequeathed two antigovernment legacies to American politics. One was a leftist critique of government as an instrument of the ruling classes. The other was a libertarian critique calling for freedom from government restraints. Student radicals in the 1960s opposed the draft and demanded the right to smoke marijuana. Conservatives in the 1990s railed against taxes and proclaimed the unfettered right to own handguns and assault weapons.

Legacies of the 1960s

Building on the disillusionment of the 1960s, subsequent decades have deepened Americans' distrust of the federal government. In the 1970s, the Watergate scandal and Richard Nixon's resignation from the presidency convinced many that politics was inherently corrupt. In the 1980s, the administration of Ronald Reagan added the Iran-contra scandal to the public's concerns about government corruption and cover-ups. And in the 1990s, Bill Clinton's White House was tainted by a variety of special investigations and trials, as well as by allegations about his character.

In quite a different way, President Ronald Reagan also fueled hostility to the government. In his inaugural address in 1981, Reagan asserted that "government is not the solution to our problem; government *is* the problem." Reagan's contribution to antigovernment sentiment in America was twofold. First, even though he was the head of the government, his rhetoric continued to be staunchly antigovernment. Second, the Reagan administration—aided by a fiscally irresponsible Congress—bequeathed an enormous federal debt to future generations.

During the Reagan years, the debt increased from just under $1 trillion to almost $3 trillion.

How do historians know that militia and similar far-right groups have grown and spread in the United States in the 1990s? Investigators from civil rights and human rights organizations, as well as from governmental agencies, have identified networks of Klansmen, skinheads, tax resisters, Militiamen, Patriots, and Freemen, and members of Aryan supremacist groups such as Christian Identity and the Order. One of the most reliable investigative sources is the Southern Poverty Law Center, which, in its Klanwatch Intelligence Report (winter 1997) year-end edition for 1996 (see below), identified 241 white supremacist hate groups in the United States. Another important source is the Anti-

Defamation League of the B'nai B'rith; its chief investigator, Kenneth S. Stern, is the author of a definitive study, A Force upon the Plain: The American Militia Movement and the Politics of Hate (1996).

Historians can also turn to the daily media for information about hate groups. In 1996, for example, newspapers ran frequent stories about an epidemic of suspicious fires at black churches across the South. In the first half of the year, there were more than thirty such fires; in a case in South Carolina, Klansmen pleaded guilty to arson.   Photo: Klanwatch.

When George Bush left office in 1993, the debt had climbed to $4.4 trillion. Massive federal funds were needed to pay the interest on the debt, not to mention to fund entitlement programs

Growing Federal Debt

such as Social Security, Medicare, and veterans' benefits. Thus when Bill Clinton took office in 1993, not much money was available to finance his program objectives: healthcare; investments in roads, technologies, and training; increased spending for children and the poor.

Americans in the 1990s also faced economic uncertainties, such as wage stagnation and job insecurity caused by downsizing. Some Americans blamed their plight on job competition from immigrants, and they condemned affirmative action for giving what they perceived to be an unfair advantage to African-Americans and to women. Anti-immigration sentiment found political expression in the 1990s. Politicians decried what they called the "flood" or the "invasion" of new immigrants. And in 1994, voters in California approved Proposition 187, a ballot initiative to cut off social services to illegal aliens.

It was clear that American voters were deeply alienated from politics. They had had their fill of negative attack advertisements and political "dirty tricks." They expressed disgust not only with the presidency and Congress but also with political parties, special-interest groups, and the press. They found few politicians to admire or even trust.

Clearly, the media had changed American politics. Television dominated family life, and most Americans got their news from television. For

Television's Influence

some, this meant not ABC News or CNN but rather *A Current Affair* or *Hard Copy*. People seemed inattentive to political issues. "Given the increasing domination of television as the key medium of public discourse," the political scientist James Fishkin observed, "the primary process has become a dual of attack ads and sound bites fighting for the attention of an inattentive public."

Many in the public were pitifully uninformed. A survey in 1996 asked for the name of the vice president of the United States; four in ten did not

Americans' Political Ignorance

know or got it wrong. Two out of three could not name the person who represented them in the House of Representatives. And, the survey found, less knowledgeable Americans were much more likely to be cynical about government and to believe that actions by the federal government invariably make every problem worse.

Misinformed or not, angry American voters wanted changes. And although the Republican 104th Congress they elected in 1994 under Gin-

grich's leadership failed with much of its legislative program, it did recast the American political debate. Many Democrats conceded that the government could not solve all problems and needed to be shrunk. Federalism was back in fashion, and both Congress and the president urged returning power to the states. Sacred cows from the New Deal and the Great Society, such as Social Security and Medicare, were under scrutiny as never before. Civil rights issues seemingly became of secondary political importance to both major parties.

As the 1996 election neared, some political observers predicted that angry voters would send Bill Clinton back to Arkansas and put a conservative Republican in the White

Women Voters

House. But these pundits overlooked an essential segment of the electorate: women. For years, political scholars had identified a "gender gap" in voting behavior: women were more likely than men to vote Democratic. In the mid-1990s, women tended to view the 104th Congress as hostile to measures essential to family welfare. The gender gap thus threatened to become a chasm.

"Women are still bigger believers in government," explained Andrew Kohut, a veteran pollster, in 1996. "Women are stronger environmentalists, more critical of business and less critical of government. This drives their party preferences. . . ." Issues like health insurance, daycare for children, and education were very important to women. They were also concerned about the future of safety net programs and generally believed that the government should do more to help families. Looking to the 1996 elections, Democrats hoped that women could do for them what "angry white men" had done for the Republicans in 1994.

 ## Clinton Fights Back: The Election of 1996

Clinton's chances of being returned to the White House were enhanced by the performance of congressional Republicans. The Gingrich-led 104th Congress made voters even angrier than Clinton had made them in his first two years. For one thing, the "Contract with America" called for cuts

in programs that were especially beneficial to the middle class. People worried about Medicare and Medicaid, aid to education and college loans, highway construction and farm subsidies, Social Security and veterans' benefits. When the Republicans attempted to turn over to the states responsibility for child nutrition programs, including school lunches, the Democrats resisted and the public was on their side. Republicans later repeated the mistake in pushing to cut spending for education and to repeal decades of environmental and occupational safety legislation.

The Republicans also made a mistake when they used the threat of a federal government shutdown as a bargaining chip in their quest for a balanced budget by the year 2002.

Government Shutdowns

When the government closed its doors in 1995 and 1996, the public was inconvenienced and angry. Most Americans perceived the Congress as ideologically inflexible but tended to see Clinton as moderate and "reasonable." Congress did, however, pass several significant acts, including the line item veto, which allowed the president to cut specific spending items from the federal budget. Of far-reaching influence, the Telecommunications Act of 1996 made sweeping changes in federal law, allowing telephone companies and cable companies to compete, deregulating cable rates, and permitting media companies to own more television and radio stations.

As campaigns for the 1996 elections took shape, Republicans focused on Bill Clinton and the "character" issue. The special prosecutor investigating Whitewater began to produce indictments and even convictions. The president gave videotaped testimony, but in 1996 the McDougals and Governor Tucker were found guilty.

Hint of Scandal in the White House

Hillary Clinton testified before a Senate committee investigating Whitewater. She could not explain how long-lost law-firm billing records from Little Rock, which had been subpoenaed by the committee, disappeared for two years before surfacing in the family quarters of the White House. Republican anger erupted in mid-1996 when the Clinton administration acknowledged that in 1993 and 1994, on orders from the White House, the Federal Bureau of Investigation had sent over the confidential records of some nine hundred Republicans. The White House said it was a mistake; others thought it smelled of an earlier scandal, Watergate.

Among the Republican hopefuls in 1996 was Senator Bob Dole of Kansas. Dole, the Senate majority leader, had served in Congress for thirty-five years, and many Republicans, believing that he had earned his party's presidential nomination, cast their votes for him.

The Campaigns Unfold

Bill Clinton was reelected with 49 percent of the popular vote. Although he did not achieve his goal of winning a majority of the vote, he easily defeated Dole (41 percent) and Ross Perot (8 percent), who again had run as an independent (see map). Although the Republicans lost the contest

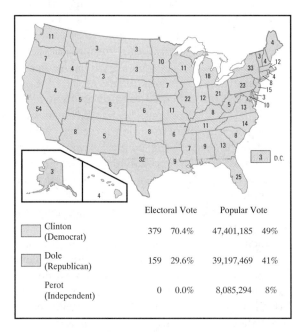

	Electoral Vote		Popular Vote	
Clinton (Democrat)	379	70.4%	47,401,185	49%
Dole (Republican)	159	29.6%	39,197,469	41%
Perot (Independent)	0	0.0%	8,085,294	8%

Presidential Election, 1996 *Although Bill Clinton did not win a majority of the vote, he came close at 49 percent, winning thirty-one states to nineteen for Bob Dole. Ross Perot, with 8 percent of the vote, was less of a factor than in 1992, when he had earned 19 percent of the vote. Despite Clinton's victory, the Republicans retained control of both houses of Congress.*

From the beginning of the American republic, all secretaries of state had been men. This changed in 1997, when Madeleine Albright, the ambassador to the United Nations, was nominated by President Clinton to be the secretary of state. Immediately after being sworn in, Secretary Albright traveled to trouble spots around the world. Here she is speaking at her first press conference. Corbis-Bettman.

for the White House, they retained control of both houses of Congress.

In 1996 Clinton ran as a conservative, calling for a balanced budget and family values such as "fighting for the family-leave law or the assault-weapons ban or the Brady Bill or the V-chip for parents or trying to keep tobacco out of the hands of kids." Clinton also called for an end to federal welfare "as we know it." And in 1996, he signed two laws that repealed New Deal benefits that had been in existence for sixty years. One act eliminated the section of the Social Security Act of 1935 that provided Aid to Families with Dependent Children (AFDC). The other, the Freedom to Farm Act, authorized the phasing out of agricultural subsidy payments to farmers, thus ending the farm support program in existence since the New Deal.

Despite Clinton's success at the polls, the stench of scandal—both political and personal—hung over his administration. First Lady Hillary Rodham Clinton was in the middle of several con-troversies, including the 1993 firing of the White House travel office staff. The suicide of the deputy White House counsel and former law partner of Hillary Clinton raised questions. The Clintons received some relief when the Little Rock, Arkansas, Whitewater grand jury ended its work in May 1998 with only one additional indictment. By then, however, the Whitewater special prosecutor, Kenneth Starr, was focusing on an offshoot of a sexual harassment lawsuit against Bill Clinton.

The alleged harassment incident dated back to Clinton's days as governor of Arkansas. During Starr's probe, rumors surfaced about a sexual relationship between Clinton and a White House intern named Monica Lewinsky. In January 1998 both Lewinsky and Clinton gave depositions in the sexual misconduct case (*Jones* v *Clinton*) in which they denied having sexual relations with one another. Also in January, Linda Tripp, a friend

Hints of a Sex Scandal

of Ms. Lewinsky, turned over to the special prosecutor approximately twenty hours of taped telephone conversations between herself and Lewinsky. In these conversations, Lewinsky talked about having an affair with the president. Toward the end of the month, Clinton addressed the nation and said, "I did not have sexual relations with that woman, Ms. Lewinsky."

Thoughout the spring and summer, Starr subpoenaed numerous witnesses, including White House staffers, secret service agents, and Lewinsky's mother to appear before the grand jury. Americans were enjoying economically prosperous times and often appeared indifferent about the president's personal life. Many disagreed with Starr's tactics. Still, Starr persisted, as did the question of whether Clinton had obstructed justice by asking Lewinsky to lie about the relationship. The question also remained as to whether the president had committed perjury in his deposition.

By late summer, many people, including representatives and senators, were wanting Starr to complete his work and submit a report to Congress. Starr, however, was not finished. He and Lewinsky's

A Deepening Investigation

lawyers struck a deal in which she received immunity from prosecution in exchange for her testimony. She admitted having a sexual relationship with the president. Less than two weeks later, Bill Clinton became the first American president to be required to give testimony before a grand jury. Reports of Clinton's testimony alleged that he acknowledged an "improper" relationship with Lewinsky. Later, in a brief address to the nation, he admitted to inappropriate behavior but avoided the words sexual relationship. The president's words and manner failed to convey a sense of contrition. Some members of Congress spoke of impeachment, others talked of some form of official censure; all awaited Starr's report.

The wait ended on September 10, 1998. On that Thursday, the Starr referral, as the report was now being called, and boxes of supporting evidence were delivered to the House of Representatives. The next day House members by a vote of 363 to 63 agreed to release Starr's entire 445 page

document via the internet. Over the next few days, millions of people accessed the various web sites on which the report was posted. Millions more obtained details about Starr's findings from newspapers, television, and radio. The referral was full of lurid details about a sexual relationship between Clinton and Lewinsky that began in 1995 and ended in 1997. It also contained what Starr deemed to be eleven grounds for the impeachment of President Clinton.

After a more than four-year investigation of the president and the expenditure of approximately $40 million, the special prosecutor based

Impeachment, Censure, or Resignation?

his case for impeachment on grounds which in one way or another were tied to a dismissed civil case (*Jones* v *Clinton*) or the attempt to cover up the affair between Clinton and Lewinsky. The possible grounds for impeachment listed by Starr focused on the president lying under oath and obstructing justice. For members of the House of Representatives and the American people, a basic question had to be answered. Did the offensives delineated by the special prosecutor constitute "high crimes and misdemeanors" or did they simply reflect reprehensible behavior? The latter could lead to an official congressional censure of President Clinton or possibly his resignation. Should a majority of the members of the House of Representatives decide that "high crimes and misdemeanors" had been committed, impeachment or resignation were distinct possibilities. And despite early talk of a bipartisan approach to the crisis, it was, with the November congressional elections approaching, becoming increasingly partisan. The Clinton presidency appeared crippled and his party's prospects for regaining control of the House of Representatives were waning.

 Conclusion

Throughout American history, the closing decade of a century has been a time of turbulence and transformation. In the 1690s, as the colonists struggled to adjust to the Navigation Acts that governed their membership in the far-flung British mercantile empire, King William's War pitted the French and their Indian allies against British-Americans, and accusations of witchcraft in Massachusetts revealed political disorder and a society in stress. In the 1790s, a new republic with a new constitution confronted the Whiskey Rebellion, the Alien and Sedition Acts, the rise of partisan political parties, and entanglement in Europe's wars. The 1890s witnessed devastating depression, agrarian revolt, burgeoning cities, bloody labor strikes, the emergence of corporate giants, the onset of a major reform movement, and a new empire abroad that anti-imperialists considered a violation of United States principles.

As the twenty-first century beckoned, the later 1990s, too, promised to be a period of adjustment for Americans. As in prior centuries, Americans had lost faith in their government; confidence in government, which was expressed by 76 percent of Americans in 1964, had plummeted to 19 percent by 1996. And as people lost confidence in the government, the conservative movement that had germinated in the 1970s remained very much alive. Indeed, in becoming the first Democrat since Franklin Roosevelt to be reelected, Clinton had run as an anti–New Deal candidate.

Many Americans looked toward the new century with apprehension. Some, however, thought of the nation's enduring legacy. In a poem he read at Bill Clinton's second inauguration, Miller Williams evoked America's history. Titled "Of History and Hope," his poem called upon Americans to remember their heritage of justice and compassion, of freedom and equality, and to convey that heritage to the children, who are the future:

> All this in the hands of children, eyes already set
> on a land we can never visit—it isn't there yet—
> but looking through their eyes, we can see
> what our long gift to them may come to be
> If we can truly remember, they will not forget.

Suggestions for Further Reading

The Bush Administration

Donald L. Bartlett and James B. Steele, *America: What Went Wrong?* (1992); Colin Campbell and Bert A. Rockman, eds., *The* *Bush Presidency* (1991); Michael Duffy and Don Goodgame, *Marching in Place: The Status Quo Presidency of George Bush* (1992); Dilys M. Hill and Phil Williams, eds., *The Bush Presidency* (1994).

Politics and the Election of 1992

Alan Ehrenhalt, *The United States of Ambition: Politicians, Power, and the Pursuit of Office* (1991); William Greider, *Who Will Tell the People: The Betrayal of American Democracy* (1992); Kathleen Hall Jamieson, *Dirty Politics* (1992); Kevin Phillips, *The Politics of Rich and Poor* (1990); Gerald Posner, *Citizen Perot* (1996); Ray A. Teixeira, *The Disappearing American Voter* (1992); George F. Will, *Restoration: Congress, Term Limits and the Recovery of Deliberative Democracy* (1992).

The Clinton Administration

Haynes Johnson and David S. Broder, *The System: The American Way of Politics at the Breaking Point* (1996); David Maraniss, *First in His Class: A Biography of Bill Clinton* (1995); Roger Morris, *Partners in Power: The Clintons and Their America* (1996); Richard Reeves, *Running in Place: How Bill Clinton Disappointed America* (1996); James B. Stewart, *Blood Sport: The President and His Adversaries* (1996); Martin Walker, *The President We Deserve* (1996); Bob Woodward, *The Agenda: Inside the Clinton White House* (1994).

American Society in the 1990s

Sheldon Danziger and Peter Gottschalk, *American Unequal* (1996); Robert H. Frank and Philip J. Cook, *The Winner-Take-All Society* (1995); Herbert J. Gans, *The War Against the Poor* (1995); David M. Gordon, *Fat and Mean: The Corporate Squeeze of Working Americans and the Myth of Managerial "Downsizing"* (1996); Jennifer L. Hochschild, *Facing Up to the American Dream: Race, Class, and the Soul of the Nation* (1995); Jonathan Kozol, *Amazing Grace: The Lives of Children and the Conscience of a Nation* (1995); Katherine S. Newman, *Declining Fortunes: The Withering of the American Dream* (1993); New York Times, *The Downsizing of America* (1996); Michael D. Yates, *Longer Hours, Fewer Jobs* (1994).

Disgruntled Americans: Political Apathy and Antigovernment Movements

Stephen Ansolabehere and Shanto Iyengar, *Going Negative: How Attack Ads Shrink and Polarize the Electorate* (1995); Sara Diamond, *Roads to Dominion: Right-Wing Movements and Political Power in America* (1995); E. J. Dionne, Jr., *Why Americans Hate Politics* (1991); James Fallows, *Breaking the News: How the Media Undermine American Democracy* (1996); Thomas Ferguson, *Golden Rule: The Investment Theory of Party Competition and the Logic of Money-Driven Political Systems* (1995); William Martin, *With God on Our Side: The Rise of the Religious Right in America* (1996); Larry J. Sabato and Glenn R. Simpson, *Dirty Little Secrets: The Persistence of Corruption in American Politics* (1996); Robert J. Samuelson, *The Good Life and Its Discontents: The American Dream in an*

Age of Entitlements (1995); Kenneth S. Stern, *A Force upon the Plain: The American Militia Movement and the Politics of Hate* (1996).

The Election of 1994: "The Republican Revolution"

Dan Balz and Ronald Brownstein, *Storming the Gates: Protest Politics and the Republican Revival* (1996); Elizabeth Drew, *Showdown: The Struggle Between the Gingrich Congress and the Clinton White House* (1996); David Frum, *Dead Right* (1994); David Maraniss and Michael Weisskopf, *"Tell Newt to Shut Up!"* (1996).

The 1996 Election and the Future of American Politics

E. J. Dionne, Jr., *They Only Look Dead: Why Progressives Will Dominate the Next Political Era* (1996); James S. Fishskin, *The Voice of the People: Public Opinion and Democracy* (1995); Jake H. Thompson, *Bob Dole* (1994); Michael Tomasky, *Left for Dead: The Life, Death, and Possible Resurrection of Progressive Politics in America* (1996); Ben J. Wattenberg, *Values Matter Most: How Republicans or Democrats or a Third Party Can Win and Renew the American Way of Life* (1995); Jacob Weisberg, *In Defense of Government: The Fall and Rise of Public Trust* (1996); Bob Woodward, *The Choice* (1996).

Historical Reference Books by Subject:
Encyclopedias, Dictionaries, Atlases, Chronologies, and Statistics

American History: General

Gorton Carruth, ed., *The Encyclopedia of American Facts and Dates* (1993); *Dictionary of American History* (1976) and Joan Hoff and Robert H. Ferrell, eds., *Supplement* (1996); Eric Foner and John A. Garraty, eds., *The Reader's Companion to American History* (1991); Bernard Grun, *The Timetables of History* (1991); *International Encyclopedia of the Social Sciences* (1968–); Richard B. Morris and Jeffrey B. Morris, eds., *Encyclopedia of American History* (1996); Harry Ritter, *Dictionary of Concepts in History* (1986); Arthur M. Schlesinger, Jr., ed., *The Almanac of American History* (1983); Lawrence Urdang, ed., *The Timetables of American History* (1996); U.S. Bureau of the Census, *Historical Statistics of the United States* (1975).

American History: General, Twentieth Century

John D. Buenker and Edward R. Kantowicz, eds., *Historical Dictionary of the Progressive Era, 1890–1920* (1988); Robert H. Ferrell and John S. Bowman, eds., *The Twentieth Century: An Almanac* (1984); George H. Gallup, *The Gallup Poll: Public Opinion, 1935–1971* (1972), *1972–1977* (1978), and annual reports (1979–); Stanley Hochman and Eleanor Hochman, *A Dictionary of Contemporary American History* (1993); Stanley I. Kutler, ed., *Encyclopedia of the United States in the Twentieth Century* (1995); Peter B. Levy, *Encyclopedia of the Reagan-Bush Years* (1996); James S. Olson, *Historical Dictionary of the 1920s* (1988); Thomas Parker and Douglas Nelson, *Day by Day: The Sixties* (1983).

American History: General Atlases and Gazetteers

Geoffrey Barraclough, ed., *The Times Atlas of World History* (1994); Rodger Doyle, *Atlas of Contemporary America* (1994); Robert H. Ferrell and Richard Natkiel, *Atlas of American History* (1987); Edward W. Fox, *Atlas of American History* (1964); Archie Hobson, *The Cambridge Gazetteer of the United States and Canada* (1996); Eric Homberger, *The Penguin Historical Atlas of North America* (1995); Kenneth T. Jackson and James T. Adams, *Atlas of American History* (1978); Catherine M. Mattson and Mark T. Mattson, *Contemporary Atlas of the United States* (1990); National Geographic Society, *Historical Atlas of the United States* (1994); U.S. Department of the Interior, *National Atlas of the United States* (1970). Other atlases are listed under specific categories.

American History: General Biographies

Lucian Boia, ed., *Great Historians of the Modern Age* (1991); John S. Bowman, *The Cambridge Dictionary of American Biography* (1995); *Current Biography* (1940–); *Dictionary of American Biography* (1928–); John Garraty and Jerome L. Sternstein, eds., *The Encyclopedia of American Biography* (1996); *National Cyclopedia of American Biography* (1898–). Other biographical works appear under specific categories.

African Americans

Molefi Asante and Mark T. Mattson, *Historical and Cultural Atlas of African-Americans* (1991); John N. Ingham, *African-American Business Leaders* (1993); Bruce Kellner, *The Harlem Renaissance* (1984); Rayford W. Logan and Michael R. Winston, eds., *The Dictionary of American Negro Biography* (1983); W. A. Low and Virgil A. Clift, eds., *Encyclopedia of Black America* (1981); Sharon Harley, *The Timetables of African-American History* (1995); Darlene C. Hine et al., eds., *Black Women in White America* (1994); Charles D. Lowery and John F. Marszalek, eds., *Encyclopedia of African-American Civil Rights* (1992); Randall M. Miller and John D. Smith, eds., *Dictionary of Afro-American Slavery* (1997); Larry G. Murphy et al., eds., *Encyclopedia of African American*

Religions (1993); Harry A. Ploski and James Williams, eds., *The Negro Almanac* (1989); Dorothy C. Salem, ed., *African American Women* (1993).

American Revolution and Colonies

Richard Blanco and Paul Sanborn, eds., *The American Revolution* (1993); Lester J. Cappon, ed., *Atlas of Early American History: The Revolutionary Era, 1760–1790* (1976); Jacob E. Cooke, ed., *Encyclopedia of the American Colonies* (1993); John M. Faragher, ed., *The Encyclopedia of Colonial and Revolutionary America* (1990); Jack P. Greene and J. R. Pole, eds., *The Blackwell Encyclopedia of the American Revolution* (1991); Douglas W. Marshall and Howard H. Peckham, *Campaigns of the American Revolution* (1976); Gregory Palmer, ed., *Biographical Sketches of Loyalists of the American Revolution* (1984); John W. Raimo, ed., *Biographical Directory of American Colonial and Revolutionary Governors, 1607–1789* (1980); *Rand-McNally Atlas of the American Revolution* (1974); Seymour I. Schwartz, *The French and Indian War, 1754–1763* (1995).

Architecture

William D. Hunt, Jr., ed., *Encyclopedia of American Architecture* (1980).

Asian Americans

Hyung-Chan Kim, ed., *Dictionary of Asian American History* (1986); Brian Niiya, ed., *Japanese American History* (1993). See also "Immigration and Ethnic Groups."

Business and the Economy

Christine Ammer and Dean S. Ammer, *Dictionary of Business and Economics* (1983); Douglas Auld and Graham Bannock, *The American Dictionary of Economics* (1983); Michael J. Freeman, *Atlas of World Economy* (1991); Douglas Greenwald, *Encyclopedia of Economics* (1982); John N. Ingham, *Biographical Dictionary of American Business Leaders* (1983); John N. Ingham and Lynne B. Feldman, *Contemporary American Business Leaders* (1990); William H. Mulligan, Jr., ed., *A Historical Dictionary of American Industrial Language* (1988); Glenn G. Munn, *Encyclopedia of Banking and Finance* (1973); Paul Paskoff, ed., *Encyclopedia of American Business History and Biography* (1989); Glenn Porter, *Encyclopedia of American Economic History* (1980); Richard Robinson, *United States Business History, 1602–1988* (1990); Malcolm Warner, ed., *International Encyclopedia of Business and Management* (1996). See also "African Americans" and "Transportation."

Cities and Towns

Charles Abrams, *The Language of Cities: A Glossary of Terms* (1971); John L. Androit, ed., *Township Atlas of the United States* (1979); David J. Bodenhamer and Robert J. Barrows, eds., *The Encyclopedia of Indianapolis* (1994); Melvin G. Holli and Peter d'A. Jones, eds., *Biographical Dictionary of American Mayors, 1820–1980: Big City Mayors* (1981); Kenneth T. Jackson, ed., *Encyclopedia of New York City* (1995); Ory M. Nergal, ed., *The Encyclopedia of American Cities* (1980); David D. Van Tassel and John J. Grabowski, eds., *The Dictionary of Cleveland Biography* (1996); David D. Van Tassel and John J. Grabowski, eds., *The Encyclopedia of Cleveland History* (1987). See also "Politics and Government."

Civil War and Reconstruction

Mark M. Boatner III, *The Civil War Dictionary* (1988); Richard N. Current, ed., *Encyclopedia of the Confederacy* (1993); John T. Hubbell and James W. Geary, eds., *Biographical Dictionary of the Union* (1995); Kenneth C. Martis, *The Historical Atlas of the Congresses of the Confederate States of America: 1861–1865* (1994); James M. McPherson, ed., *The Atlas of the Civil War* (1994); Mark E. Neely, Jr., *The Abraham Lincoln Encyclopedia* (1982); Craig L. Symonds, *A Battlefield Atlas of the Civil War* (1983); Hans L. Trefousse, *Historical Dictionary of Reconstruction* (1991); U.S. War Department, *The Official Atlas of the Civil War* (1958); Jon L. Wakelyn, ed., *Biographical Dictionary of the Confederacy* (1977); Ezra J. Warner and W. Buck Yearns, *Biographical Register of the Confederate Congress* (1975); Steven E. Woodworth, ed., *The American Civil War* (1996). See also "South" and "Politics and Government."

Constitution, Supreme Court, and Judiciary

David Bradley and Shelly F. Fishkin, eds., *The Encyclopedia of Civil Rights* (1997); Congressional Quarterly, *The Supreme Court A to Z* (1994); Kermit L. Hall, ed., *The Oxford Companion to the Supreme Court of the United States* (1992); Richard F. Hixson, *Mass Media and the Constitution* (1989); Robert J. Janosik, ed., *Encyclopedia of the American Judicial System* (1987); John W. Johnson, ed., *Historic U.S. Court Cases, 1690–1990* (1992); Arthur S. Leonard, ed., *Sexuality and the Law* (1993); Leonard W. Levy et al., eds., *Encyclopedia of the American Constitution* (1986); Fred R. Shapiro, *The Oxford Dictionary of American Legal Quotations* (1993); Melvin I. Urofsky, ed., *The Supreme Court Justices* (1994). See also "Politics and Government."

Crime, Violence, Police, and Prisons

William G. Bailey, *Encyclopedia of Police Science* (1994); Sanford H. Kadish, ed., *Encyclopedia of Crime and Justice* (1983); Marilyn D. McShane and Frank P. Williams III, eds., *Encyclopedia of American Prisons* (1995); Michael Newton and Judy Ann Newton, *Racial and Religious Violence in America* (1991); Michael Newton and Judy Newton, *The Ku Klux Klan* (1990); Carl Sifakis, *Encyclopedia of Assassinations* (1990); Carl Sifakis, *The Encyclopedia of American Crime* (1982).

Culture and Folklore

Hennig Cohen and Tristam Potter Coffin, eds., *The Folklore of American Holidays* (1987); Richard M. Dorson, ed., *Handbook of American Folklore* (1983); Robert L. Gale, *A Cultural Encyclopedia of the 1850s in America* (1993); Robert L. Gale, *The Gay Nineties in America* (1992); M. Thomas Inge, ed., *Handbook of American Popular Culture* (1979–1981); Wolfgang Mieder et al., eds., *A Dictionary of American Proverbs* (1992); J. F. Rooney, Jr., et al., eds., *This Remarkable Continent: An Atlas of United States and Canadian Society and Cultures* (1982); Jane Stern and Michael Stern, *Encyclopedia of Pop Culture* (1992); Justin Wintle, ed., *Makers of Nineteenth Century Culture, 1800–1914* (1982). See also "Entertainment," "Mass Media and Journalism," "Music," and "Sports."

Education and Libraries

Lee C. Deighton, ed., *The Encyclopedia of Education* (1971); Joseph C. Kiger, ed., *Research Institutions and Learned Societies* (1982); John F. Ohles, ed., *Biographical Dictionary of American Educators* (1978); Wayne A. Wiegard and Donald E. Davis, Jr., eds., *Encyclopedia of Library History* (1994).

Entertainment

Tim Brooks and Earle Marsh, *The Complete Directory to Prime Time Network and Cable TV Shows, 1946–Present* (1995); Barbara N. Cohen-Stratyner, *Biographical Dictionary of Dance* (1982); John Dunning, *Tune in Yesterday* (radio) (1967); Larry Langman and Edgar Borg, *Encyclopedia of American War Films* (1989); Larry Langman and David Ebner, *Encyclopedia of American Spy Films* (1990); *Notable Names in the American Theater* (1976); Andrew Sarris, *The American Cinema: Directors and Directions, 1929–1968* (1968); Anthony Slide, *The American Film Industry* (1986); Anthony Slide, *The Encyclopedia of Vaudeville* (1994); Evelyn M. Truitt, *Who Was Who on Screen* (1977); Don B. Wilmeth and Tice L. Miller, eds., *The Cambridge Guide to American Theatre* (1993). See also "Culture and Folklore," "Mass Media and Journalism," "Music," and "Sports."

Environment and Conservation

André R. Cooper, ed., *Cooper's Comprehensive Environmental Desk Reference* (1996); Forest History Society, *Encyclopedia of American Forest and Conservation History* (1983); Irene Franck and David Brownstone, *The Green Encyclopedia* (1992); Robert J. Mason and Mark T. Mattson, *Atlas of United States Environmental Issues* (1990); Robert Paehlke, ed., *Conservation and Environmentalism* (1995); World Resources Institute, *Environmental Almanac* (1992).

Exploration: From Columbus to Space

Silvio A. Bedini, ed., *The Christopher Columbus Encyclopedia* (1992); Michael Cassutt, *Who's Who in Space* (1987); W. P. Cumming et al., *The Discovery of North America* (1972); William Goetzmann and Glyndwr Williams, *The Atlas of North American Exploration* (1992); Clive Holland, *Arctic Exploration and Development* (1993); Adrian Johnson, *America Explored* (1974); Kenneth Nebenzahl, *Atlas of Columbus and the Great Discoveries* (1990). See also "Science and Technology."

Foreign Relations

Thomas S. Arms, *Encyclopedia of the Cold War* (1994); Gerard Chaliand and Jean-Pierre Rageau, *Strategic Atlas* (1990); Alexander DeConde, ed., *Encyclopedia of American Foreign Policy* (1978); Margaret B. Denning and J. K. Sweeney, *Handbook of American Diplomacy* (1992); Graham Evans and Jeffrey Newnham, eds., *The Dictionary of World Politics* (1990); John E. Findling, *Dictionary of American Diplomatic History* (1989); Chas. W. Freeman, Jr., *The Diplomat's Dictionary* (1997); Michael Kidron and Ronald Segal, *The State of the World Atlas* (1995); Bruce W. Jentleson and Thomas G. Paterson, eds., *Encyclopedia of U.S. Foreign Relations* (1997); Warren F. Kuehl, ed., *Biographical Dictionary of Internationalists* (1983); Edward Lawson, *Encyclopedia of Human Rights* (1991); Jack C. Plano and Roy Olton, eds., *The International Relations Dictionary* (1988). See also "Peace Movements and Pacifism," "Politics and Government," "Military and Wars," and specific wars.

Immigration and Ethnic Groups

James P. Allen and Eugene J. Turner, *We the People: An Atlas of America's Ethnic Diversity* (1988); Gerald

Chaliand and Jean-Pierre Rageau, *The Penguin Atlas of Diasporas* (1995); Francesco Cordasco, ed., *Dictionary of American Immigration History* (1990); Judy B. Litoff and Judith McDonnell, eds., *European Immigrant Women in the United States* (1994); Sally M. Miller, ed., *The Ethnic Press in the United States* (1987); Stephan Thernstrom, ed., *Harvard Encyclopedia of American Ethnic Groups* (1980). See also "Asian Americans," "Jewish Americans," and "Latinos."

Jewish Americans

American Jewish Yearbook (1899–); Jack Fischel and Sanford Pinsker, eds., *Jewish-American History and Culture* (1992); Geoffrey Wigoder, *Dictionary of Jewish Biography* (1991). See also "Immigration and Ethnic Groups."

Labor

Ronald L. Filippelli, *Labor Conflict in the United States* (1990); Gary M. Fink, ed., *Biographical Dictionary of American Labor* (1984); Gary M. Fink, ed., *Labor Unions* (1977); Philip S. Foner, *First Facts of American Labor* (1984).

Latinos

Nicolás Kanellos, ed., *The Hispanic-American Almanac* (1993); Nicolás Kanellos, ed., *Reference Library of Hispanic America* (1993); Matt S. Meier, *Mexican-American Biographies* (1988); Matt S. Meier, *Notable Latino Americans* (1997); Matt S. Meier and Feliciano Rivera, *Dictionary of Mexican American History* (1981); Joseph C. Tardiff and L. Mpho Mabunda, eds., *Dictionary of Hispanic Biography* (1996). See also "Immigration and Ethnic Groups."

Literature

James T. Callow and Robert J. Reilly, *Guide to American Literature* (1976–1977); *Dictionary of Literary Biography* (1978–); Eugene Ehrlich and Gorton Carruth, *The Oxford Illustrated Literary Guide to the United States* (1982); Jon Tuska and Vicki Piekarski, *Encyclopedia of Frontier and Western Fiction* (1983). See also "Culture and Folklore," "The South," and "Women."

Mass Media and Journalism

Robert V. Hudson, *Mass Media* (1987); Joseph P. McKerns, ed., *Biographical Dictionary of American Journalism* (1989); William H. Taft, ed., *Encyclopedia of Twentieth-Century Journalists* (1986). See also "Constitution, Supreme Court, and Judiciary," "Entertainment," and "Immigration and Ethnic Groups."

Medicine and Nursing

Rima D. Apple, ed., *Women, Health, and Medicine in America* (1990); Vern L. Bullough et al., eds., *American Nursing: A Biographical Dictionary* (1988); Martin Kaufman et al., eds., *Dictionary of American Nursing Biography* (1988); Martin Kaufman et al., eds., *Dictionary of American Medical Biography* (1984); George L. Maddox, ed., *The Encyclopedia of Aging* (1987).

Military and Wars

William M. Arkin et al., *Encyclopedia of the U.S. Military* (1990); Charles D. Bright, ed., *Historical Dictionary of the U.S. Air Force* (1992); Andre Corvisier, ed., *A Dictionary of Military History* (1994); R. Ernest Dupuy and Trevor N. Dupuy, *The Harper Encyclopedia of Military History* (1993); John E. Jessup, ed., *Encyclopedia of the American Military* (1994); Kenneth Macksey and William Woodhouse, *The Penguin Encyclopedia of Modern Warfare* (1992); Franklin D. Margiotta, ed., *Brassey's Encyclopedia of Naval Forces and Warfare* (1996); James I. Matray, ed., *Historical Dictionary of the Korean War* (1991); Stanley Sandler, ed., *The Korean War* (1995); Roger J. Spiller and Joseph G. Dawson III, eds., *Dictionary of American Military Biography* (1984); Jerry K. Sweeney, ed., *A Handbook of American Military History* (1996); Peter G. Tsouras et al., *The United States Army* (1991); U.S. Military Academy, *The West Point Atlas of American Wars, 1689–1953* (1959); Bruce W. Watson et al., eds., *United States Intelligence* (1990); *Webster's American Military Biographies* (1978); Bruce W. Watson and Susan M. Watson, *The United States Air Force* (1992); Bruce W. Watson and Susan M. Watson, *The United States Navy* (1991). See also "American Revolution and Colonies," "Civil War and Reconstruction," "Vietnam War," and "World War II."

Music

John Chilton, *Who's Who of Jazz* (1972); Donald Clarke, ed., *The Penguin Encyclopedia of Popular Music* (1989); Edward Jablonski, *The Encyclopedia of American Music* (1981); Roger Lax and Frederick Smith, *The Great Song Thesaurus* (1984); Philip D. Morehead, *The New International Dictionary of Music* (1993); Austin Sonnier, Jr., *A Guide to the Blues* (1994). See also "Culture and Folklore" and "Entertainment."

Native Americans and Indian Affairs

Gretchen M. Bataille, ed., *Native American Women* (1992); Michael Coe et al., *Atlas of Ancient America* (1986); Mary B. Davis, ed., *Native America in the Twentieth Century* (1994); Frederick J. Dockstader, *Great*

North American Indians (1977); *Handbook of North American Indians* (1978–); Sam D. Gill and Irene F. Sullivan, *Dictionary of Native American Mythology* (1992); J. Norman Heard et al., *Handbook of the American Frontier: Four Centuries of Indian-White Relationships* (1987–); Bruce E. Johnson and Donald A. Grinde, *The Encyclopedia of Native American Biography* (1997); Barry Klein, ed., *Reference Encyclopedia of the American Indian* (1993); Francis P. Prucha, *Atlas of American Indian Affairs* (1990); Paul Stuart, *Nation Within a Nation: Historical Statistics of American Indians* (1987); Helen H. Tanner, ed., *Atlas of Great Lakes Indian History* (1987); Carl Waldman, *Encyclopedia of Native American Tribes* (1988); Carl Waldman, *Atlas of the North American Indian* (1985).

The New Deal and Franklin D. Roosevelt

Otis L. Graham, Jr., and Meghan R. Wander, eds., *Franklin D. Roosevelt: His Life and Times* (1985); James S. Olson, ed., *Historical Dictionary of the New Deal* (1985). See also "Politics and Government."

Peace Movements and Pacifism

Harold Josephson et al., eds., *Biographical Dictionary of Modern Peace Leaders* (1985); Ervin Laszlo and Jong Y. Yoo, eds., *World Encyclopedia of Peace* (1986); Robert S. Meyer, *Peace Organizations Past and Present* (1988); Nancy L. Roberts, *American Peace Writers, Editors, and Periodicals* (1991). See also "Military and Wars" and specific wars.

Politics and Government: General

Erik W. Austin and Jerome M. Clubb, *Political Facts of the United States Since 1789* (1986); *The Columbia Dictionary of Political Biography* (1991); Jack P. Greene, ed., *Encyclopedia of American Political History* (1984); Leon Hurwitz, *Historical Dictionary of Censorship in the United States* (1985); Edwin V. Mitchell, *An Encyclopedia of American Politics* (1968); Philip Rees, *Biographical Dictionary of the Extreme Right Since 1890* (1991); Charles R. Ritter et al., *American Legislative Leaders, 1850–1910* (1989); William Safire, *Safire's Political Dictionary* (1978); Robert Scruton, *A Dictionary of Political Thought* (1982); Jay M. Shafritz, *The HarperCollins Dictionary of American Government and Politics* (1992). See also "Cities and Towns," "Constitution, Supreme Court, and Judiciary," "States," and the following sections.

Politics and Government: Congress

Donald C. Brown et al., eds., *The Encyclopedia of the United States Congress* (1995); Stephen G. Christianson, *Facts About the Congress* (1996); Congressional Quarterly, *Biographical Directory of the American Congress, 1774–1996* (1997); Congressional Quarterly, *Congress and the Nation, 1945–1984* (1965–1985); Kenneth C. Martis, *Historical Atlas of Political Parties in the United States Congress, 1789–1989* (1989); Kenneth C. Martis, *Historical Atlas of United States Congressional Districts, 1789–1983* (1982); Joel H. Silbey, ed., *Encyclopedia of the American Legislative System* (1994).

Politics and Government: Election Statistics

Congressional Quarterly, *Guide to U.S. Elections* (1975); L. Sandy Maisel, ed., *Political Parties and Elections in the United States* (1991); Richard M. Scammon et al., eds., *America Votes* (1956–); Harold W. Stanley and Richard G. Niemi, *Vital Statistics on American Politics* (1990); G. Scott Thomas, *The Pursuit of the White House* (1987).

Politics and Government: Parties

Earl R. Kruschke, *Encyclopedia of Third Parties in the United States* (1991); George T. Kurian, ed., *The Encyclopedia of the Republican Party and The Encyclopedia of the Democratic Party* (1996); Edward L. Schapsmeier and Frederick H. Schapsmeier, eds., *Political Parties and Civic Action Groups* (1981). See also other listings for "Politics and Government."

Politics and Government: Presidency and Executive Branch

Henry F. Graff, *The Presidents* (1996); Bernard S. Katz and C. Daniel Vencill, eds., *Biographical Dictionary of the United States Secretaries of the Treasury, 1789–1995* (1996); Richard S. Kirkendall, ed., *The Harry S Truman Encyclopedia* (1989); Leonard W. Levy and Louis Fisher, eds., *Encyclopedia of the American Presidency* (1993); Merrill D. Peterson, ed., *Thomas Jefferson: A Reference Biography* (1986); Lyn Ragsdale, *Vital Statistics on the Presidency* (1995); Robert A. Rutland, ed., *James Madison and the American Nation* (1994); Robert Sobel, ed., *Biographical Directory of the United States Executive Branch, 1774–1977* (1977). See other categories for various presidents.

Politics and Government: Radicalism and the Left

Mari Jo Buhle et al., eds., *The American Radical* (1994); Mari Jo Buhle et al., eds., *Encyclopedia of the American Left* (1998); David DeLeon, ed., *Leaders of the 1960s* (1994); Bernard K. Johnpoll and Harvey Klehr, eds., *Biographical Dictionary of the American Left* (1986).

Religion and Cults

Henry Bowden, *Dictionary of American Religious Biography* (1993); S. Kent Brown et al., eds., *Historical Atlas of Mormonism* (1995); John T. Ellis and Robert Trisco, *A Guide to American Catholic History* (1982); Edwin Gaustad and Philip L. Barlow, *New Historical Atlas of Religion in America* (1998); Samuel S. Hill, Jr., ed., *Encyclopedia of Religion in the South* (1984); Bill J. Leonard, *Dictionary of Baptists in America* (1994); Donald Lewis, ed., *A Dictionary of Evangelical Biography* (1995); Charles H. Lippy and Peter W. Williams, eds., *Encyclopedia of the American Religious Experience* (1988); J. Gordon Melton, *The Encyclopedia of American Religions* (1987); J. Gordon Melton, *Biographical Dictionary of American Cult and Sect Leaders* (1986); J. Gordon Melton, *The Encyclopedic Handbook of Cults in America* (1992); Mark A. Noll and Nathan O. Hatch, eds., *Eerdmans Handbook to Christianity in America* (1983); Arthur C. Piepkorn, *Profiles in Belief: The Religious Bodies of the United States and Canada* (1977–1979); Paul J. Weber and W. Landis Jones, *U.S. Religious Interest Groups* (1994). See also "African Americans."

Science and Technology

James W. Cortada, *Historical Dictionary of Data Processing* (1987); Clark A. Elliott, *Biographical Index to American Science: The Seventeenth Century to 1920* (1990); Charles C. Gillispie, ed., *Dictionary of Scientific Biography* (1970–); National Academy of Sciences, *Biographical Memoirs* (1877–); Roy Porter, ed., *The Biographical Dictionary of Scientists* (1994). See also "Exploration."

Social History and Reform

Mary K. Cayton et al., eds., *Encyclopedia of American Social History* (1993); Wayne R. Dynes, ed., *Encyclopedia of Homosexuality* (1990); Louis Filler, *Dictionary of American Social Change* (1982); Louis Filler, *A Dictionary of American Social Reform* (1963); Robert S. Fogarty, *Dictionary of American Communal and Utopian History* (1980); Joseph M. Hawes and Elizabeth I. Nybakken, eds., *American Families* (1991); David Hey, ed., *The Oxford Companion to Local and Family History* (1996); Harold M. Keele and Joseph C. Kiger, eds., *Foundations* (1984); Mark E. Lender, *Dictionary of American Temperance Biography* (1984); Patricia M. Melvin, ed., *American Community Organizations* (1986); Randall M. Miller and Paul A. Cimbala, eds., *American Reform and Reformers* (1996); Roger S. Powers and William B. Vogele, eds., *Protest, Power, and Change* (1996); Alvin J. Schmidt, *Fraternal Organizations* (1980); Peter N. Stearns, ed., *Encyclopedia of Social History* (1993); Walter I. Trattner, *Biographical Dictionary of Social Welfare in America* (1986); Alden Whitman, ed., *American Reformers* (1985). See also "Crime, Violence, Police, and Prisons."

South

Edward L. Ayers and Brad Mittendorf, eds., *The Oxford Book of the American South* (1997); Robert Bain et al., eds., *Southern Writers* (1979); Kenneth Coleman and Charles S. Gurr, eds., *Dictionary of Georgia Biography* (1983); William S. Powell, ed., *Dictionary of North Carolina Biography* (1979–1996); David C. Roller and Robert W. Twyman, eds., *The Encyclopedia of Southern History* (1979); Walter P. Webb et al., eds., *The Handbook of Texas* (1952, 1976); Charles R. Wilson and William Ferris, eds., *Encyclopedia of Southern Culture* (1986). See also "Civil War and Reconstruction," "Politics and Government," and "States."

Sports

Peter C. Bjarkman, ed., *Encyclopedia of Major League Baseball Team Histories* (1991); Ralph Hickok, *The Encyclopedia of North American Sports History* (1991); Zander Hollander, *The NBA's Official Encyclopedia of Pro Basketball* (1981); Frank G. Menke and Suzanne Treat, *The Encyclopedia of Sports* (1977); *The NFL's Official Encyclopedic History of Professional Football* (1977); David L. Porter, *Biographical Dictionary of American Sports: Baseball* (1987), *Basketball and Other Indoor Sports* (1989), *Football* (1987), and *Outdoor Sports* (1988); David L. Porter, ed., *Biographical Dictionary of American Sports: 1989–1992 Supplement* (1992) and *1992–1995 Supplement* (1995); Paul Soderberg et al., *The Big Book of Halls of Fame in the United States and Canada* (1977); David Wallechinsky, *The Complete Book of the Summer Olympics* (1996); David Wallechinsky, *The Complete Book of the Winter Olympics* (1993). See also "Culture and Folklore."

States

Gary Alampi, ed., *Gale State Rankings Reporter* (1994); Roy R. Glashan, comp., *American Governors and Gubernatorial Elections, 1775–1978* (1979); John Hoffmann, ed., *A Guide to the History of Illinois* (1991); Edith R. Hornor, *Almanac of the Fifty States* (1993); Joseph E. Kallenback and Jessamine S. Kallenback, *American State Governors, 1776–1976* (1977); Joseph N. Kane et al., eds., *Facts About the States* (1994); John E. Kleber et al., eds., *The Kentucky Encyclopedia* (1992); Thomas A. McMullin and Marie Mullaney, *Biographical Directory of the Governors of the United States, 1983–1987* (1988) and

1988–1993 (1994); Marie Mullaney, *Biographical Directory of the Governors of the United States 1988–1994* (1994); Thomas J. Noel, *Historical Atlas of Colorado* (1994); John W. Raimo, ed., *Biographical Directory of the Governors of the United States, 1978–1983* (1985); James W. Scott and Ronald L. De Lorme, *Historical Atlas of Washington* (1988); Benjamin F. Shearer and Barbara S. Shearer, *State Names, Seals, Flags, and Symbols* (1994); Robert Sobel and John W. Raimo, eds., *Biographical Directory of the Governors of the United States, 1789–1978* (1978); Richard W. Wilkie and Jack Tager, eds., *Historical Atlas of Massachusetts* (1991). See also "Politics and Government," "South," and "West and Frontier."

Transportation

Keith L. Bryant, ed., *Railroads in the Age of Regulation, 1900–1980* (1988); Rene De La Pedraja, *A Historical Dictionary of the U.S. Merchant Marine and Shipping Industry* (1994); Robert L. Frey, ed., *Railroads in the Nineteenth Century* (1988). See also "Business and the Economy."

Vietnam War

John S. Bowman, ed., *The Vietnam War: An Almanac* (1986); Stanley I. Kutler, ed., *Encyclopedia of the Vietnam War* (1996); James S. Olson, ed., *Dictionary of the Vietnam War* (1988); Harry G. Summers, Jr., *Vietnam War Almanac* (1985). Also see "Peace Movements and Pacifism" and "Military and Wars."

West and Frontier

William A. Beck and Ynez D. Haase, *Historical Atlas of the American West* (1989); Doris O. Dawdy, *Artists of the American West* (1974–1984); J. Norman Heard, *Handbook of the American Frontier* (1987); Howard R. Lamar, ed., *The Reader's Encyclopedia of the American West* (1977); Clyde A. Milner III et al., eds., *The Oxford History of the American West* (1994); Jay Robert Nash, *Encyclopedia of Western Lawmen and Outlaws* (1992); Doyce B. Nunis, Jr., and Gloria R. Lothrop, eds., *A Guide to the History of California* (1989); Charles Phillips and Alan Axelrod, eds., *Encyclopedia of the American West* (1996); Dan L. Thrapp, *The Encyclopedia of Frontier Biography* (1988–1994); David Walker, *Biographical Directory of American Territorial Governors* (1984). See also "Literature" and "Native Americans and Indian Affairs."

Women

Anne Gibson and Timothy Fast, *The Women's Atlas of the United States* (1986); Karen Greenspan, *The Timetables of Women's History* (1996); Maggie Humm, *The Dictionary of Feminist Theory* (1990); Edward T. James et al., *Notable American Women, 1607–1950* (1971); Lina Mainiero, ed., *American Women Writers* (1979–1982); Wilma Mankiller et al., *The Reader's Companion to U.S. Women's History* (1998); Kirstin Olsen, *Chronology of Women's History* (1994); Barbara G. Shortridge, *Atlas of American Women* (1987); Barbara Sicherman and Carol H. Green, eds., *Notable American Women, The Modern Period* (1980); Helen Tierney, ed., *Women's Studies Encyclopedia* (1991); Angela H. Zophy and Frances M. Kavenik, eds., *Handbook of American Women's History* (1990). See also "African Americans," "Immigration and Ethnic Groups," "Medicine and Nursing," and "Native Americans and Indian Affairs."

World War I

Arthur Banks, *A Military History Atlas of the First World War* (1975); Martin Gilbert, *Atlas of World War I* (1994); Holger H. Herwig and Neil M. Heyman, *Biographical Dictionary of World War I* (1982); George T. Kurian, *Encyclopedia of the First World War* (1990); Stephen Pope and Elizabeth-Anne Wheal, *The Dictionary of the First World War* (1995); Anne C. Venzon, *The United States in the First World War* (1995). See also "Military and Wars."

World War II

Marcel Baudot et al., eds., *The Historical Encyclopedia of World War II* (1980); David G. Chandler and James Lawton Collins, Jr., eds., *The D-Day Encyclopedia* (1993); I. C. B. Dear and M. R. D. Foot, eds., *The Oxford Companion to World War II* (1995); Simon Goodenough, *War Maps: Great Land Battles of World War II* (1988); Robert Goralski, *World War II Almanac* (1981); John Keegan, ed., *The Times Atlas of the Second World War* (1989); George T. Kurian, *Encyclopedia of the Second World War* (1991); Norman Polmer and Thomas B. Allen, *World War II: America at War* (1991); Louis L. Snyder, *Louis L. Snyder's Historical Guide to World War II* (1982); U.S. Military Academy, *Campaign Atlas to the Second World War: Europe and the Mediterranean* (1980); Peter Young, ed., *The World Almanac Book of World War II* (1981). See also "Military and Wars."

Documents

DECLARATION OF INDEPENDENCE IN CONGRESS, JULY 4, 1776

When, in the course of human events, it becomes necessary for one people to dissolve the political bonds which have connected them with another, and to assume, among the powers of the earth, the separate and equal station to which the laws of nature and of nature's God entitle them, a decent respect to the opinions of mankind requires that they should declare the causes which impel them to the separation.

We hold these truths to be self-evident: That all men are created equal; that they are endowed by their Creator with certain unalienable rights; that among these are life, liberty, and the pursuit of happiness; that, to secure these rights, governments are instituted among men, deriving their just powers from the consent of the governed; that whenever any form of government becomes destructive of these ends, it is the right of the people to alter or to abolish it, and to institute new government, laying its foundation on such principles, and organizing its powers in such form, as to them shall seem most likely to effect their safety and happiness. Prudence, indeed, will dictate that governments long established should not be changed for light and transient causes; and accordingly all experience hath shown that mankind are more disposed to suffer, while evils are sufferable, than to right themselves by abolishing the forms to which they are accustomed. But when a long train of abuses and usurpations, pursuing invariably the same object, evinces a design to reduce them under absolute despotism, it is their right, it is their duty, to throw off such government, and to provide new guards for their future security. Such has been the patient sufferance of these colonies; and such is now the necessity which constrains them to alter their former systems of government. The history of the present King of Great Britain is a history of repeated injuries and usurpations, all having in direct object the establishment of an absolute tyranny over these states. To prove this, let facts be submitted to a candid world.

He has refused his assent to laws, the most wholesome and necessary for the public good.

He has forbidden his governors to pass laws of immediate and pressing importance, unless suspended in their operation till his assent should be obtained; and, when so suspended, he has utterly neglected to attend to them.

He has refused to pass other laws for the accommodation of large districts of people, unless those people would relinquish the right of representation in the legislature, a right inestimable to them, and formidable to tyrants only.

He has called together legislative bodies at places unusual, uncomfortable, and distant from the depository of their public records, for the sole purpose of fatiguing them into compliance with his measures.

He has dissolved representative houses repeatedly, for opposing, with manly firmness, his invasions on the rights of the people.

He has refused for a long time, after such dissolutions, to cause others to be elected; whereby the legislative powers, incapable of annihilation, have returned to the people at large for their exercise; the state remaining, in the mean time, exposed to all the dangers of invasions from without and convulsions within.

He has endeavored to prevent the population of these states; for that purpose obstructing the laws for naturalization of foreigners; refusing to pass others to encourage their migration hither, and raising the conditions of new appropriations of lands.

He has obstructed the administration of justice, by refusing his assent to laws for establishing judiciary powers.

He has made judges dependent on his will alone, for the tenure of their offices, and the amount and payment of their salaries.

He has erected a multitude of new offices, and sent hither swarms of officers to harass our people and eat out their substance.

He has kept among us, in times of peace, standing armies, without the consent of our legislatures.

He has affected to render the military independent of, and superior to, the civil power.

He has combined with others to subject us to a jurisdiction foreign to our constitution, and unacknowledged by our laws, giving his assent to their acts of pretended legislation:

For quartering large bodies of armed troops among us;

For protecting them, by a mock trial, from punishment for any murders which they should commit on the inhabitants of these states;

For cutting off our trade with all parts of the world;

For imposing taxes on us without our consent;

For depriving us, in many cases, of the benefits of trial by jury;

For transporting us beyond seas, to be tried for pretended offenses;

For abolishing the free system of English laws in a neighboring province, establishing therein an arbitrary government, and enlarging its boundaries, so as to render it at once an example and fit instrument for introducing the same absolute rule into these colonies;

For taking away our charters, abolishing our most valuable laws, and altering fundamentally the forms of our governments;

For suspending our own legislatures, and declaring themselves invested with power to legislate for us in all cases whatsoever.

He has abdicated government here, by declaring us out of his protection and waging war against us.

He has plundered our seas, ravaged our coasts, burned our towns, and destroyed the lives of our people.

He is at this time transporting large armies of foreign mercenaries to complete the works of death, desolation, and tyranny already begun with circumstances of cruelty and perfidy scarcely paralleled in the most barbarous ages, and totally unworthy the head of a civilized nation.

He has constrained our fellow-citizens, taken captive on the high seas, to bear arms against their country, to become the executioners of their friends and brethren, or to fall themselves by their hands.

He has excited domestic insurrection among us, and has endeavored to bring on the inhabitants of our frontiers the merciless Indian savages, whose known rule of warfare is an undistinguished destruction of all ages, sexes, and conditions.

In every stage of these oppressions we have petitioned for redress in the most humble terms; our repeated petitions have been answered only by repeated injury. A prince, whose character is thus marked by every act which may define a tyrant, is unfit to be the ruler of a free people.

Nor have we been wanting in our attentions to our British brethren. We have warned them, from time to time, of attempts by their legislature to extend an unwarrantable jurisdiction over us. We have reminded them of the circumstances of our emigration and settlement here. We have appealed to their native justice and magnanimity; and we have conjured them, by the ties of our common kindred, to disavow these usurpations, which would inevitably interrupt our connections and correspondence. They, too, have been deaf to the voice of justice and of consanguinity. We must, therefore, acquiesce in the necessity which denounces our separation, and hold them, as we hold the rest of mankind, enemies in war, in peace friends.

We, therefore, the representatives of the United States of America, in General Congress assembled, appealing to the Supreme Judge of the world for the rectitude of our intentions, do, in the name and by the authority of the good people of these colonies, solemnly publish and declare, that these United Colonies are, and of right ought to be, FREE AND INDEPENDENT STATES; that they are absolved from all allegiance to the British crown, and that all political connection between them and the state of Great Britain is, and ought to be, totally dissolved; and that, as free and independent states, they have full power to levy war, conclude peace, contract alliances, establish commerce, and do all other acts and things which independent states may of right do. And for the support of this declaration, with a firm reliance on the protection of Divine Providence, we mutually pledge to each other our lives, our fortunes, and our sacred honor.

JOHN HANCOCK
and fifty-five others

CONSTITUTION OF THE UNITED STATES OF AMERICA AND AMENDMENTS*

Preamble

We the people of the United States, in order to form a more perfect union, establish justice, insure domestic tranquillity, provide for the common defense, promote the general welfare, and secure the blessings of liberty to ourselves and our posterity, do ordain and establish this Constitution for the United States of America.

Article I

Section 1 All legislative powers herein granted shall be vested in a Congress of the United States, which shall consist of a Senate and a House of Representatives.

---

*Passages no longer in effect are printed in italic type.

Section 2   The House of Representatives shall be composed of members chosen every second year by the people of the several States, and the electors in each State shall have the qualifications requisite for electors of the most numerous branch of the State Legislature.

No person shall be a Representative who shall not have attained to the age of twenty-five years, and been seven years a citizen of the United States, and who shall not, when elected, be an inhabitant of that State in which he shall be chosen.

Representatives and direct taxes shall be apportioned among the several States which may be included within this Union, according to their respective numbers, *which shall be determined by adding to the whole number of free persons, including those bound to service for a term of years and excluding Indians not taxed, three-fifths of all other persons.* The actual enumeration shall be made within three years after the first meeting of the Congress of the United States, and within every subsequent term of ten years, in such manner as they shall by law direct. The number of Representatives shall not exceed one for every thirty thousand, but each State shall have at least one Representative; *and until such enumeration shall be made, the State of New Hampshire shall be entitled to choose three, Massachusetts eight, Rhode Island and Providence Plantations one, Connecticut five, New York six, New Jersey four, Pennsylvania eight, Delaware one, Maryland six, Virginia ten, North Carolina five, South Carolina five, and Georgia three.*

When vacancies happen in the representation from any State, the Executive authority thereof shall issue writs of election to fill such vacancies.

The House of Representatives shall choose their Speaker and other officers; and shall have the sole power of impeachment.

Section 3   The Senate of the United States shall be composed of two Senators from each State, *chosen by the legislature thereof,* for six years; and each Senator shall have one vote.

Immediately after they shall be assembled in consequence of the first election, they shall be divided as equally as may be into three classes. The seats of the Senators of the first class shall be vacated at the expiration of the second year, of the second class at the expiration of the fourth year, and of the third class at the expiration of the sixth year, so that one-third may be chosen every second year; *and if vacancies happen by resignation or otherwise, during the recess of the legislature of any State, the Executive thereof may make temporary appointments until the next meeting of the legislature, which shall then fill such vacancies.*

No person shall be a Senator who shall not have attained to the age of thirty years, and been nine years a citizen of the United States, and who shall not, when elected, be an inhabitant of that State for which he shall be chosen.

The Vice-President of the United States shall be President of the Senate, but shall have no vote, unless they be equally divided.

The Senate shall choose their other officers, and also a President *pro tempore*, in the absence of the Vice-President, or when he shall exercise the office of President of the United States.

The Senate shall have the sole power to try all impeachments. When sitting for that purpose, they shall be on oath or affirmation. When the President of the United States is tried, the Chief Justice shall preside: and no person shall be convicted without the concurrence of two-thirds of the members present.

Judgment in cases of impeachment shall not extend further than to removal from the office, and disqualification to hold and enjoy any office of honor, trust or profit under the United States: but the party convicted shall nevertheless be liable and subject to indictment, trial, judgment and punishment, according to law.

Section 4   The times, places and manner of holding elections for Senators and Representatives shall be prescribed in each State by the legislature thereof; but the Congress may at any time by law make or alter such regulations, except as to the places of choosing Senators.

The Congress shall assemble at least once in every year, and such meeting *shall be on the first Monday in December, unless they shall by law appoint a different day.*

Section 5   Each house shall be the judge of the elections, returns and qualifications of its own members, and a majority of each shall constitute a quorum to do business; but a smaller number may adjourn from day to day, and may be authorized to compel the attendance of absent members, in such manner, and under such penalties, as each house may provide.

Each house may determine the rules of its proceedings, punish its members for disorderly behavior, and with the concurrence of two-thirds, expel a member.

Each house shall keep a journal of its proceedings, and from time to time publish the same, excepting such parts as may in their judgment require secrecy; and the yeas and nays of the members of either house on any question shall, at the desire of one-fifth of those present, be entered on the journal.

Neither house, during the session of Congress, shall, without the consent of the other, adjourn for more than three days, nor to any other place than that in which the two houses shall be sitting.

Section 6   The Senators and Representatives shall receive a compensation for their services, to be ascertained by law and paid out of the treasury of the United States. They shall in all cases except treason, felony and breach of the peace, be privileged from arrest during their attendance at the session of their respective houses, and in going to and returning from the same; and for any speech or debate in either house, they shall not be questioned in any other place.

No Senator or Representative shall, during the time for which he was elected, be appointed to any civil office under the authority of the United States, which shall have been created, or the emoluments whereof shall have been increased, during such time; and no person holding any office under the United States shall be a member of either house during his continuance in office.

Section 7   All bills for raising revenue shall originate in the House of Representatives; but the Senate may propose or concur with amendments as on other bills.

Every bill which shall have passed the House of Representatives and the Senate, shall, before it become a law, be presented to the President of the United States; if he approve he shall sign it, but if not he shall return it with objections to that house in which it originated, who shall enter the objections at large on their journal, and proceed to reconsider it. If after such reconsideration two-thirds of that house shall agree to pass the bill, it shall be sent, together with the objections, to the other house, by which it shall likewise be reconsidered, and, if approved by two-thirds of that house, it shall become a law. But in all such cases the votes of both houses shall be determined by yeas and nays, and the names of the persons voting for and against the bill shall be entered on the journal of each house respectively. If any bill shall not be returned by the President within ten days (Sundays excepted) after it shall have been presented to him, the same shall be a law, in like manner as if he had signed it, unless the Congress by their adjournment prevent its return, in which case it shall not be a law.

Every order, resolution, or vote to which the concurrence of the Senate and House of Representatives may be necessary (except on a question of adjournment) shall be presented to the President of the United States; and before the same shall take effect, shall be approved by him, or being disapproved by him, shall be repassed by two-thirds of the Senate and House of Representatives, according to the rules and limitations prescribed in the case of a bill.

Section 8   The Congress shall have power

To lay and collect taxes, duties, imposts, and excises, to pay the debts and provide for the common defense and general welfare of the United States; but all duties, imposts and excises shall be uniform throughout the United States;

To borrow money on the credit of the United States;

To regulate commerce with foreign nations, and among the several States, and with the Indian tribes;

To establish an uniform rule of naturalization, and uniform laws on the subject of bankruptcies throughout the United States;

To coin money, regulate the value thereof, and of foreign coin, and fix the standard of weights and measures;

To provide for the punishment of counterfeiting the securities and current coin of the United States;

To establish post offices and post roads;

To promote the progress of science and useful arts by securing for limited times to authors and inventors the exclusive right to their respective writings and discoveries;

To constitute tribunals inferior to the Supreme Court;

To define and punish piracies and felonies committed on the high seas and offenses against the law of nations;

To declare war, grant letters of marque and reprisal, and make rules concerning captures on land and water;

To raise and support armies, but no appropriation of money to that use shall be for a longer term than two years;

To provide and maintain a navy;

To make rules for the government and regulation of the land and naval forces;

To provide for calling forth the militia to execute the laws of the Union, suppress insurrections, and repel invasions;

To provide for organizing, arming, and disciplining the militia, and for governing such part of them as may be employed in the service of the United States, reserving to the States respectively the appointment of the officers, and the authority of training the militia according to the discipline prescribed by Congress;

To exercise exclusive legislation in all cases whatsoever, over such district (not exceeding ten miles square) as may, by cession of particular States, and the acceptance of Congress, become the seat of government of the

United States, and to exercise like authority over all places purchased by the consent of the legislature of the State, in which the same shall be, for erection of forts, magazines, arsenals, dockyards, and other needful buildings; — and

To make all laws which shall be necessary and proper for carrying into execution the foregoing powers, and all other powers vested by this Constitution in the government of the United States, or in any department or officer thereof.

Section 9   The migration or importation of such persons as any of the States now existing shall think proper to admit shall not be prohibited by the Congress prior to the year 1808; but a tax or duty may be imposed on such importation, not exceeding $10 for each person.

The privilege of the writ of habeas corpus shall not be suspended, unless when in cases of rebellion or invasion the public safety may require it.

No bill of attainder or ex post facto law shall be passed.

No capitation, or other direct, tax shall be laid, unless in proportion to the census or enumeration herein before directed to be taken.

No tax or duty shall be laid on articles exported from any State.

No preference shall be given by any regulation of commerce or revenue to the ports of one State over those of another; nor shall vessels bound to, or from, one State, be obliged to enter, clear, or pay duties in another.

No money shall be drawn from the treasury, but in consequence of appropriations made by law; and a regular statement and account of the receipts and expenditures of all public money shall be published from time to time.

No title of nobility shall be granted by the United States: and no person holding any office of profit or trust under them, shall, without the consent of the Congress, accept of any present, emolument, office, or title, of any kind whatever, from any king, prince, or foreign state.

Section 10   No State shall enter into any treaty, alliance, or confederation; grant letters of marque and reprisal; coin money; emit bills of credit; make anything but gold and silver coin a tender in payment of debts; pass any bill of attainder, ex post facto law, or law impairing the obligation of contracts, or grant any title of nobility.

No State shall, without the consent of Congress, lay any imposts or duties on imports or exports, except what may be absolutely necessary for executing its inspection laws: and the net produce of all duties and imposts, laid by any State on imports or exports, shall be for the use of the treasury of the United States; and all such laws shall be subject to the revision and control of the Congress.

No State shall, without the consent of Congress, lay any duty of tonnage, keep troops or ships of war in time of peace, enter into any agreement or compact with another State, or with a foreign power, or engage in war, unless actually invaded, or in such imminent danger as will not admit of delay.

Article II

Section 1   The executive power shall be vested in a President of the United States of America. He shall hold his office during the term of four years, and, together with the Vice-President, chosen for the same term, be elected as follows:

Each State shall appoint, in such manner as the legislature thereof may direct, a number of electors, equal to the whole number of Senators and Representatives to which the State may be entitled in the Congress; but no Senator or Representative, or person holding an office of trust or profit under the United States, shall be appointed an elector.

The electors shall meet in their respective States, and vote by ballot for two persons, of whom one at least shall not be an inhabitant of the same State with themselves. And they shall make a list of all the persons voted for, and of the number of votes for each; which list they shall sign and certify, and transmit sealed to the seat of government of the United States, directed to the President of the Senate. The President of the Senate shall, in the presence of the Senate and House of Representatives, open all the certificates, and the votes shall then be counted. The person having the greatest number of votes shall be the President, if such number be a majority of the whole number of electors appointed; and if there be more than one who have such majority, and have an equal number of votes, then the House of Representatives shall immediately choose by ballot one of them for President; and if no person have a majority, then from the five highest on the list said house shall in like manner choose the President. But in choosing the President the votes shall be taken by States, the representation from each State having one vote; a quorum for this purpose shall consist of a member or members from two-thirds of the States, and a majority of all the States shall be necessary to a choice. In every case, after the choice of the President, the person having the greatest number of votes of the electors shall be the Vice-President. But if there should remain two or more who have equal votes, the Senate shall choose from them by ballot the Vice-President.

The Congress may determine the time of choosing the electors and the day on which they shall give their votes; which day shall be the same throughout the United States.

No person except a natural-born citizen, *or a citizen of the United States at the time of the adoption of this Constitution*, shall be eligible to the office of President; neither shall any person be eligible to that office who shall not have attained to the age of thirty-five years, and been fourteen years a resident within the United States.

In cases of the removal of the President from office or of his death, resignation, or inability to discharge the powers and duties of the said office, the same shall devolve on the Vice-President, and the Congress may by law provide for the case of removal, death, resignation, or inability, both of the President and Vice-President, declaring what officer shall then act as President, and such officer shall act accordingly, until the disability be removed, or a President shall be elected.

The President shall, at stated times, receive for his services a compensation, which shall neither be increased nor diminished during the period for which he shall have been elected, and he shall not receive within that period any other emolument from the United States, or any of them.

Before he enter on the execution of his office, he shall take the following oath or affirmation:—"I do solemnly swear (or affirm) that I will faithfully execute the office of the President of the United States, and will to the best of my ability preserve, protect and defend the Constitution of the United States."

Section 2 The President shall be commander in chief of the army and navy of the United States, and of the militia of the several States, when called into the actual service of the United States; he may require the opinion, in writing, of the principal officer in each of the executive departments, upon any subject relating to the duties of their respective offices, and he shall have power to grant reprieves and pardons for offenses against the United States, except in cases of impeachment.

He shall have power, by and with the advice and consent of the Senate, to make treaties, provided two-thirds of the Senators present concur; and he shall nominate, and by and with the advice and consent of the Senate, shall appoint ambassadors, other public ministers and consuls, judges of the Supreme Court, and all other officers of the United States, whose appointments are not herein otherwise provided for, and which shall be established by law: but Congress may by law vest the appointment of such inferior officers, as they think proper, in the President alone, in the courts of law, or in the heads of departments.

The President shall have power to fill up all vacancies that may happen during the recess of the Senate, by granting commissions which shall expire at the end of their next session.

Section 3 He shall from time to time give to the Congress information of the state of the Union, and recommend to their consideration such measures as he shall judge necessary and expedient; he may, on extraordinary occasions, convene both houses, or either of them, and in case of disagreement between them, with respect to the time of adjournment, he may adjourn them to such time as he shall think proper; he shall receive ambassadors and other public ministers; he shall take care that the laws be faithfully executed, and shall commission all the officers of the United States.

Section 4 The President, Vice-President and all civil officers of the United States shall be removed from office on impeachment for, and on conviction of, treason, bribery, or other high crimes and misdemeanors.

Article III

Section 1 The judicial power of the United States shall be vested in one Supreme Court, and in such inferior courts as the Congress may from time to time ordain and establish. The judges, both of the Supreme and inferior courts, shall hold their offices during good behavior, and shall, at stated times, receive for their services a compensation which shall not be diminished during their continuance in office.

Section 2 The judicial power shall extend to all cases, in law and equity, arising under this Constitution, the laws of the United States, and treaties made, or which shall be made, under their authority;—to all cases affecting ambassadors, other public ministers and consuls;—to all cases of admiralty and maritime jurisdiction;—to controversies to which the United States shall be a party;—to controversies between two or more States;—*between a State and citizens of another State;*—between citizens of different States;—between citizens of the same State claiming lands under grants of different States, and between a State, or the citizens thereof, and foreign states, citizens or subjects.

In all cases affecting ambassadors, other public ministers and consuls, and those in which a State shall be party, the Supreme Court shall have original jurisdiction. In all the other cases before mentioned, the Supreme Court shall have appellate jurisdiction, both as to law and fact, with such exceptions, and under such regulations, as the Congress shall make.

The trial of all crimes, except in cases of impeachment, shall be by jury; and such trial shall be held in the State where said crimes shall have been committed; but when not committed within any State, the trial shall be at such place or places as the Congress may by law have directed.

Section 3   Treason against the United States shall consist only in levying war against them, or in adhering to their enemies, giving them aid and comfort. No person shall be convicted of treason unless on the testimony of two witnesses to the same overt act, or on confession in open court.

The Congress shall have power to declare the punishment of treason, but no attainder of treason shall work corruption of blood, or forfeiture except during the life of the person attainted.

Article IV

Section 1   Full faith and credit shall be given in each State to the public acts, records, and judicial proceedings of every other State. And the Congress may by general laws prescribe the manner in which such acts, records, and proceedings shall be proved, and the effect thereof.

Section 2   The citizens of each State shall be entitled to all privileges and immunities of citizens in the several States.

A person charged in any State with treason, felony, or other crime, who shall flee from justice, and be found in another State, shall on demand of the executive authority of the State from which he fled, be delivered up, to be removed to the State having jurisdiction of the crime.

No person held to service or labor in one State, under the laws thereof, escaping into another, shall, in consequence of any law or regulation therein, be discharged from such service or labor, but shall be delivered up on claim of the party to whom such service or labor may be due.

Section 3   New States may be admitted by the Congress into this Union; but no new State shall be formed or erected within the jurisdiction of any other State; nor any State be formed by the junction of two or more States, or parts of States, without the consent of the legislatures of the States concerned as well as of the Congress.

The Congress shall have power to dispose of and make all needful rules and regulations respecting the territory or other property belonging to the United States; and nothing in this Constitution shall be so construed as to prejudice any claims of the United States, or of any particular State.

Section 4   The United States shall guarantee to every State in this Union a republican form of government, and shall protect each of them against invasion; and on application of the legislature, or of the executive (when the legislature cannot be convened), against domestic violence.

Article V

The Congress, whenever two-thirds of both houses shall deem it necessary, shall propose amendments to this Constitution, or, on the application of the legislatures of two-thirds of the several States, shall call a convention for proposing amendments, which, in either case, shall be valid to all intents and purposes, as part of this Constitution, when ratified by the legislatures of three-fourths of the several States, or by conventions in three-fourths thereof, as the one or the other mode of ratification may be proposed by the Congress; provided *that no amendments which may be made prior to the year one thousand eight hundred and eight shall in any manner affect the first and fourth clauses in the ninth section of the first article*; and that no State, without its consent, shall be deprived of its equal suffrage in the Senate.

Article VI

All debts contracted and engagements entered into, before the adoption of this Constitution, shall be as valid against the United States under this Constitution, as under the Confederation.

This Constitution, and the laws of the United States which shall be made in pursuance thereof; and all treaties made, or which shall be made, under the authority of the United States, shall be the supreme law of the land; and the judges in every State shall be bound thereby, anything in the Constitution or laws of any State to the contrary notwithstanding.

The Senators and Representatives before mentioned, and the members of the several State legislatures, and all executive and judicial officers, both of the United States and of the several States, shall be bound by oath or affirmation to support this Constitution; but no religious test shall ever be required as a qualification to any office or public trust under the United States.

Article VII

The ratification of the conventions of nine States shall be sufficient for the establishment of this Constitution between the States so ratifying the same.

Done in Convention by the unanimous consent of the States present, the seventeenth day of September in the year of our Lord one thousand seven hundred and eighty-seven and of the Independence of the United States of America the twelfth. In witness whereof we have hereunto subscribed our names.

GEORGE WASHINGTON
and thirty-seven others

Amendments to the Constitution*

Amendment I

Congress shall make no law respecting an establishment of religion, or prohibiting the free exercise thereof; or abridging the freedom of speech, or of the press; or the right of the people peaceably to assemble, and to petition the government for a redress of grievances.

Amendment II

A well-regulated militia being necessary to the security of a free State, the right of the people to keep and bear arms shall not be infringed.

Amendment III

No soldier shall, in time of peace, be quartered in any house without the consent of the owner, nor in time of war, but in a manner to be prescribed by law.

Amendment IV

The right of the people to be secure in their persons, houses, papers, and effects, against unreasonable searches and seizures, shall not be violated, and no warrants shall issue but upon probable cause, supported by oath or affirmation, and particularly describing the place to be searched, and the persons or things to be seized.

Amendment V

No person shall be held to answer for a capital, or otherwise infamous crime, unless on a presentment or indictment of a grand jury, except in cases arising in the land or naval forces, or in the militia, when in actual service in time of war or public danger; nor shall any person be subject for the same offense to be twice put in jeopardy of life or limb; nor shall be compelled in any criminal case to be a witness against himself, nor be deprived of life, liberty, or property, without due process of law; nor shall private property be taken for public use without just compensation.

Amendment VI

In all criminal prosecutions, the accused shall enjoy the right to a speedy and public trial, by an impartial jury of the State and district wherein the crime shall have been committed, which district shall have been previously ascertained by law, and to be informed of the nature and cause of the accusation; to be confronted with the witnesses against him; to have compulsory process for obtaining witnesses in his favor, and to have the assistance of counsel for his defense.

Amendment VII

In suits at common law, where the value in controversy shall exceed twenty dollars, the right of trial by jury shall be preserved, and no fact tried by a jury shall be otherwise reexamined in any court of the United States, than according to the rules of the common law.

Amendment VIII

Excessive bail shall not be required, nor excessive fines imposed, nor cruel and unusual punishments inflicted.

Amendment IX

The enumeration in the Constitution, of certain rights, shall not be construed to deny or disparage others retained by the people.

Amendment X

The powers not delegated to the United States by the Constitution, nor prohibited by it to the States, are reserved to the States respectively, or to the people.

Amendment XI

[Adopted 1798]

The judicial power of the United States shall not be construed to extend to any suit in law or equity, commenced or prosecuted against one of the United States by citizens of another State, or by citizens or subjects of any foreign state.

Amendment XII

[Adopted 1804]

The electors shall meet in their respective States, and vote by ballot for President and Vice-President, one of whom, at least, shall not be an inhabitant of the same State with themselves; they shall name in their ballots the person voted for as President, and in distinct ballots the person voted for as Vice-President, and they shall make distinct lists of all persons voted for as President, and of all persons voted for as Vice-President, and of the num-

---

*The first ten Amendments (the Bill of Rights) were adopted in 1791.

ber of votes for each, which lists they shall sign and certify, and transmit sealed to the seat of government of the United States, directed to the President of the Senate;—the President of the Senate shall, in the presence of the Senate and House of Representatives, open all the certificates and the votes shall then be counted;—the person having the greatest number of votes for President shall be the President, if such number be a majority of the whole number of electors appointed; and if no person have such majority, then from the persons having the highest numbers not exceeding three on the list of those voted for as President, the House of Representatives shall choose immediately, by ballot, the President. But in choosing the President, the votes shall be taken by States, the representation from each State having one vote; a quorum for this purpose shall consist of a member or members from two-thirds of the States, and a majority of all the States shall be necessary to a choice. And if the House of Representatives shall not choose a President whenever the right of choice shall devolve upon them, before *the fourth day of March* next following, then the Vice-President shall act as President, as in the case of the death or other constitutional disability of the President.

The person having the greatest number of votes as Vice-President shall be the Vice-President, if such number be a majority of the whole number of electors appointed; and if no person have a majority, then from the two highest numbers on the list the Senate shall choose the Vice-President; a quorum for the purpose shall consist of two-thirds of the whole number of Senators, and a majority of the whole number shall be necessary to a choice. But no person constitutionally ineligible to the office of President shall be eligible to that of Vice-President of the United States.

Amendment XIII

[Adopted 1865]

Section 1   Neither slavery nor involuntary servitude, except as a punishment for crime whereof the party shall have been duly convicted, shall exist within the United States, or any place subject to their jurisdiction.

Section 2   Congress shall have power to enforce this article by appropriate legislation.

Amendment XIV

[Adopted 1868]

Section 1   All persons born or naturalized in the United States, and subject to the jurisdiction thereof, are citizens of the United States and of the State wherein they reside. No State shall make or enforce any law which shall

abridge the privileges or immunities of citizens of the United States; nor shall any State deprive any person of life, liberty, or property, without due process of law; nor deny to any person within its jurisdiction the equal protection of the laws.

Section 2   Representatives shall be apportioned among the several States according to their respective numbers, counting the whole number of persons in each State, excluding Indians not taxed. But when the right to vote at any election for the choice of Electors for President and Vice-President of the United States, Representatives in Congress, the executive and judicial officers of a State, or the members of the legislature thereof, is denied to any of the male inhabitants of such State, being twenty-one years of age and citizens of the United States, or in any way abridged, except for participation in rebellion, or other crime, the basis of representation therein shall be reduced in the proportion which the number of such male citizens shall bear to the whole number of male citizens twenty-one years of age in such State.

Section 3   No person shall be a Senator or Representative in Congress, or Elector of President and Vice-President, or hold any office, civil or military, under the United States, or under any State, who, having previously taken an oath, as a member of Congress, or as an officer of the United States, or as a member of any State legislature, or as an executive or judicial officer of any State, to support the Constitution of the United States, shall have engaged in insurrection or rebellion against the same, or given aid or comfort to the enemies thereof. Congress may, by a vote of two-thirds of each house, remove such disability.

Section 4   The validity of the public debt of the United States, authorized by law, including debts incurred for payment of pensions and bounties for services in suppressing insurrection or rebellion, shall not be questioned. But neither the United States nor any State shall assume or pay any debt or obligation incurred in aid of insurrection or rebellion against the United States, or any claim for the loss of emancipation of any slave; but all such debts, obligations, and claims shall be held illegal and void.

Section 5   The Congress shall have power to enforce, by appropriate legislation, the provisions of this article.

Amendment XV

[Adopted 1870]

Section 1   The right of citizens of the United States to vote shall not be denied or abridged by the United

States or by any State on account of race, color, or previous condition of servitude.

Section 2 The Congress shall have power to enforce this article by appropriate legislation.

Amendment XVI

[Adopted 1913]

The Congress shall have power to lay and collect taxes on incomes, from whatever source derived, without apportionment among the several States, and without regard to any census or enumeration.

Amendment XVII

[Adopted 1913]

Section 1 The Senate of the United States shall be composed of two Senators from each State, elected by the people thereof, for six years; and each Senator shall have one vote. The electors in each State shall have the qualifications requisite for electors of [voters for] the most numerous branch of the State legislatures.

Section 2 When vacancies happen in the representation of any State in the Senate, the executive authority of such State shall issue writs of election to fill such vacancies: Provided, that the Legislature of any State may empower the executive thereof to make temporary appointments until the people fill the vacancies by election as the Legislature may direct.

Section 3 This amendment shall not be so construed as to affect the election or term of any Senator chosen before it becomes valid as part of the Constitution.

Amendment XVIII

[Adopted 1919; Repealed 1933]

Section 1 After one year from the ratification of this article the manufacture, sale, or transportation of intoxicating liquors within, the importation thereof into, or the exportation thereof from the United States and all territory subject to the jurisdiction thereof, for beverage purposes, is hereby prohibited.

Section 2 The Congress and the several States shall have concurrent power to enforce this article by appropriate legislation.

Section 3 This article shall be inoperative unless it shall have been ratified as an amendment to the Constitution by the legislatures of the several States, as provided by the Constitution, within seven years from the date of the submission thereof to the States by the Congress.

Amendment XIX

[Adopted 1920]

Section 1 The right of citizens of the United States to vote shall not be denied or abridged by the United States or by any State on account of sex.

Section 2 The Congress shall have power to enforce this article by appropriate legislation.

Amendment XX

[Adopted 1933]

Section 1 The terms of the President and Vice-President shall end at noon on the 20th day of January, and the terms of Senators and Representatives at noon on the 3rd day of January, of the years in which such terms would have ended if this article had not been ratified; and the terms of their successors shall then begin.

Section 2 The Congress shall assemble at least once in every year, and such meeting shall begin at noon on the 3d day of January, unless they shall by law appoint a different day.

Section 3 If, at the time fixed for the beginning of the term of the President, the President-elect shall have died, the Vice-President-elect shall become President. If a President shall not have been chosen before the time fixed for the beginning of his term, or if the President-elect shall have failed to qualify, then the Vice-President-elect shall act as President until a President shall have qualified; and the Congress may by law provide for the case wherein neither a President-elect nor a Vice-President-elect shall have qualified, declaring who shall then act as President, or the manner in which one who is to act shall be selected, and such persons shall act accordingly until a President or Vice-President shall have qualified.

Section 4 The Congress may by law provide for the case of the death of any of the persons from whom the House of Representatives may choose a President whenever the right of choice shall have devolved upon them, and for the case of the death of any of the persons from whom the Senate may choose a Vice-President whenever the right of choice shall have devolved upon them.

Section 5 Sections 1 and 2 shall take effect on the 15th day of October following the ratification of this article.

Section 6 This article shall be inoperative unless it shall have been ratified as an amendment to the Constitution by the Legislatures of three-fourths of the several States within seven years from the date of its submission.

Amendment XXI

[Adopted 1933]

Section 1 The eighteenth article of amendment to the Constitution of the United States is hereby repealed.

Section 2 The transportation or importation into any State, Territory, or Possession of the United States for delivery or use therein of intoxicating liquors, in violation of the laws thereof, is hereby prohibited.

Section 3 This article shall be inoperative unless it shall have been ratified as an amendment to the Constitution by conventions in the several States, as provided in the Constitution, within seven years from the date of submission thereof to the States by the Congress.

Amendment XXII

[Adopted 1951]

Section 1 No person shall be elected to the office of President more than twice, and no person who has held the office of President, or acted as President, for more than two years of a term to which some other person was elected President shall be elected to the office of President more than once. But this article shall not apply to any person holding the office of President when this article was proposed by the Congress, and shall not prevent any person who may be holding the office of President, or acting as President, during the term within which this article becomes operative from holding the office of President or acting as President during the remainder of such term.

Section 2 This article shall be inoperative unless it shall have been ratified as an amendment to the Constitution by the legislatures of three-fourths of the several States within seven years from the date of its submission to the States by the Congress.

Amendment XXIII

[Adopted 1961]

Section 1 The District constituting the seat of Government of the United States shall appoint in such manner as the Congress may direct:

A number of electors of President and Vice-President equal to the whole number of Senators and Representatives in Congress to which the District would be entitled if it were a State, but in no event more than the least populous State; they shall be in addition to those appointed by the States, but they shall be considered for the purposes of the election of President and Vice-President, to be electors appointed by a State; and they shall meet in the District and perform such duties as provided by the twelfth article of amendment.

Section 2 The Congress shall have the power to enforce this article by appropriate legislation.

Amendment XXIV

[Adopted 1964]

Section 1 The right of citizens of the United States to vote in any primary or other election for President or Vice-President, for electors for President or Vice-President, or for Senator or Representative in Congress, shall not be denied or abridged by the United States or any State by reason of failure to pay any poll tax or other tax.

Section 2 The Congress shall have the power to enforce this article by appropriate legislation.

Amendment XXV

[Adopted 1967]

Section 1 In case of the removal of the President from office or of his death or resignation, the Vice-President shall become President.

Section 2 Whenever there is a vacancy in the office of the Vice-President, the President shall nominate a Vice-President who shall take office upon confirmation by a majority vote of both Houses of Congress.

Section 3 Whenever the President transmits to the President pro tempore of the Senate and the Speaker of the House of Representatives his written declaration that he is unable to discharge the powers and duties of his office, and until he transmits to them a written declaration to the contrary, such powers and duties shall be discharged by the Vice-President as Acting President.

Section 4 Whenever the Vice-President and a majority of either the principal officers of the executive departments or of such other body as Congress may by law provide, transmit to the President pro tempore of the Senate and the Speaker of the House of Representatives their written declaration that the President is unable to discharge the powers and duties of his office, the Vice-President shall immediately assume the powers and duties of the office as Acting President.

Thereafter, when the President transmits to the President pro tempore of the Senate and the Speaker of the House of Representatives his written declaration that no inability exists, he shall resume the powers and duties of his office unless the Vice-President and a majority of either the principal officers of the executive department[s] or of such other body as Congress may by law provide, transmit within four days to the President pro tempore of the Senate and the Speaker of the House of Representatives their written declaration that the President is unable to discharge the powers and duties of his office. Thereupon Congress shall decide the issue, assembling within forty-eight hours for that purpose if not in session. If the Congress, within twenty-one days after receipt of the latter written declaration, or, if Congress is not in session, within twenty-one days after Congress is required to assemble, determines by two-thirds vote of both Houses that the President is unable to discharge the powers and duties of his office, the Vice-President shall continue to discharge the same as Acting President; otherwise, the President shall resume the powers and duties of his office.

Amendment XXVI

[Adopted 1971]

Section 1 The right of citizens of the United States, who are eighteen years of age or older, to vote shall not be denied or abridged by the United States or by any State on account of age.

Section 2 The Congress shall have power to enforce this article by appropriate legislation.

Amendment XXVII

[Adopted 1992]

No law, varying the compensation for the services of the Senators and Representatives, shall take effect, until an election of Representatives shall have intervened.

The American People and Nation: A Statistical Profile

Population of the United States

Year	Number of States	Population	Percent Increase	Population Per Square Mile	Percent Urban/ Rural	Percent Male/ Female	Percent White/ Non-white	Persons Per House-hold	Median Age
1790	13	3,929,214		4.5	5.1/94.9	NA/NA	80.7/19.3	5.79	NA
1800	16	5,308,483	35.1	6.1	6.1/93.9	NA/NA	81.1/18.9	NA	NA
1810	17	7,239,881	36.4	4.3	7.3/92.7	NA/NA	81.0/19.0	NA	NA
1820	23	9,638,453	33.1	5.5	7.2/92.8	50.8/49.2	81.6/18.4	NA	16.7
1830	24	12,866,020	33.5	7.4	8.8/91.2	50.8/49.2	81.9/18.1	NA	17.2
1840	26	17,069,453	32.7	9.8	10.8/89.2	50.9/49.1	83.2/16.8	NA	17.8
1850	31	23,191,876	35.9	7.9	15.3/84.7	51.0/49.0	84.3/15.7	5.55	18.9
1860	33	31,443,321	35.6	10.6	19.8/80.2	51.2/48.8	85.6/14.4	5.28	19.4
1870	37	39,818,449	26.6	13.4	25.7/74.3	50.6/49.4	86.2/13.8	5.09	20.2
1880	38	50,155,783	26.0	16.9	28.2/71.8	50.9/49.1	86.5/13.5	5.04	20.9
1890	44	62,947,714	25.5	21.2	35.1/64.9	51.2/48.8	87.5/12.5	4.93	22.0
1900	45	75,994,575	20.7	25.6	39.6/60.4	51.1/48.9	87.9/12.1	4.76	22.9
1910	46	91,972,266	21.0	31.0	45.6/54.4	51.5/18.5	88.9/11.1	4.54	24.1
1920	48	105,710,620	14.9	35.6	51.2/48.8	51.0/49.0	89.7/10.3	4.34	25.3
1930	48	122,775,046	16.1	41.2	56.1/43.9	50.6/49.4	89.8/10.2	4.11	26.4
1940	48	131,669,275	7.2	44.2	56.5/43.5	50.2/49.8	89.8/10.2	3.67	29.0
1950	48	150,697,361	14.5	50.7	64.0/36.0	49.7/50.3	89.5/10.5	3.37	30.2
1960	50	179,323,175	18.5	50.6	69.9/30.1	49.3/50.7	88.6/11.4	3.33	29.5
1970	50	203,302,031	13.4	57.4	73.6/26.4	48.7/51.3	87.6/12.4	3.14	28.0
1980	50	226,542,199	11.4	64.0	73.7/26.3	48.6/51.4	85.9/14.1	2.75	30.0
1990	50	248,718,301	9.8	70.3	75.2/24.8	48.7/51.3	83.9/16.1	2.63	32.8
1995*	50	263,034,000*	5.1	70.7	NA	48.8/51.2	83.0/17.0	2.65	34.3

NA = Not available.
*Population in 1997 = 268, 921, 733.

Vital Statistics

| Year | Birth Rate* | Death Rate* | Life Expectancy in Years | | | | | Marriage Rate | Divorce Rate |
			Total Population	White Females	Nonwhite Females	White Males	Nonwhite Males		
1790	NA	NA	NA	NA	NA	NA	NA	NA	NA
1800	55.0	NA	NA	NA	NA	NA	NA	NA	NA
1810	54.3	NA	NA	NA	NA	NA	NA	NA	NA
1820	55.2	NA	NA	NA	NA	NA	NA	NA	NA
1830	51.4	NA	NA	NA	NA	NA	NA	NA	NA
1840	51.8	NA	NA	NA	NA	NA	NA	NA	NA
1850	43.3	NA	NA	NA	NA	NA	NA	NA	NA
1860	44.3	NA	NA	NA	NA	NA	NA	NA	NA
1870	38.3	NA	NA	NA	NA	NA	NA	NA	NA
1880	39.8	NA	NA	NA	NA	NA	NA	NA	NA
1890	31.5	NA	NA	NA	NA	NA	NA	NA	NA
1900	32.3	17.2	47.3	48.7	33.5	46.6	32.5	NA	NA
1910	30.1	14.7	50.0	52.0	37.5	48.6	33.8	NA	NA
1920	27.7	13.0	54.1	55.6	45.2	54.4	45.5	12.0	1.6
1930	21.3	11.3	59.7	63.5	49.2	59.7	47.3	9.2	1.6
1940	19.4	10.8	62.9	66.6	54.9	62.1	51.5	12.1	2.0
1950	24.1	9.6	68.2	72.2	62.9	66.5	59.1	11.1	2.6
1960	23.7	9.5	69.7	74.1	66.3	67.4	61.1	8.5	2.2
1970	18.4	9.5	70.8	75.6	69.4	68.0	61.3	10.6	3.5
1980	15.9	8.8	73.7	78.1	73.6	70.7	65.3	10.6	5.2
1990	16.6	8.6	75.4	79.4	75.2	72.7	67.0	9.8	4.7
1994	15.3	8.8	75.7	79.6	75.8	73.2	67.5	9.1	4.6

Data per one thousand for Birth, Death, Marriage, and Divorce rates.

NA = Not available. *Data for 1800, 1810, 1830, 1850, 1870, and 1890 for whites only.

Immigrants to the United States

Immigration Totals by Decade			
Years	Number	Years	Number
1820–1830	151,824	1911–1920	5,735,811
1831–1840	599,125	1921–1930	4,107,209
1841–1850	1,713,251	1931–1940	528,431
1851–1860	2,598,214	1941–1950	1,035,039
1861–1870	2,314,824	1951–1960	2,515,479
1871–1880	2,812,191	1961–1970	3,321,677
1881–1890	5,246,613	1971–1980	4,493,314
1891–1900	3,687,546	1981–1990	7,338,062
1901–1910	8,795,386	1991–1994	4,509,852
		Total	61,503,866

Major Sources of Immigrants by Country or Region (in thousands)

Period	Asia[a]	Germany	Mexico	Italy	Great Britain (UK)[b]	Ireland	Canada	Austria and Hungary	Soviet Union (Russia)	Caribbean	Central America and South America	Norway and Sweden
1820–1830	—	8	5	—	27	54	2	—	—	4	—	—
1831–1840	—	152	7	2	76	207	14	—	—	12	—	1
1841–1850	—	435	3	2	267	781	42	—	—	14	4	14
1851–1860	42	952	3	9	424	914	59	—	—	11	2	21
1861–1870	65	787	2	12	607	436	154	8	3	9	1	109
1871–1880	124	718	5	56	548	437	384	73	39	14	1	211
1881–1890	70	1,453	2[c]	307	807	655	393	354	213	29	3	568
1891–1900	75	505	1[c]	652	272	388	3	593	505	33	2	321
1901–1910	324	341	50	2,046	526	339	179	2,145	1,597	108	25	440
1911–1920	247	144	219	1,110	341	146	742	896	921	123	59	161
1921–1930	112	412	459	455	340	211	925	64	62	75	58	166
1931–1940	17	114	22	68	32	11	109	11	1	16	14	9
1941–1950	37	227	61	58	139	20	172	28	—	50	43	21
1951–1960	153	478	300	185	203	48	378	104	—	123	136	45
1961–1970	428	191	454	214	214	33	413	26	2	470	359	33
1971–1980	1,588	74	640	129	137	11	170	16	39	741	430	10
1981–1990	2,738	92	2,336	67	160	32	182	25	58	872	930	15
1991–1994	1,315	43	1,400	49	77	47	88	13	193	333	505	8
Total	7,334	7,126	5,970	5,422	5,196	4,772	4,408	4,356	3,637	3,036	2,575	2,154

Notes: Numbers for periods are rounded. Dash indicates less than one thousand; [a]Includes Middle East; [b]Since 1925, includes England, Scotland, Wales, and Northern Ireland data; [c]No data available for 1886–1894.

The American Worker

Year	Total Number of Workers	Males as Percent of Total Workers	Females as Percent of Total Workers	Married Women as Percent of Female Workers	Female Workers as Percent of Female Population	Percent of Labor Force Unemployed	Percent of Workers in Labor Unions
1870	12,506,000	85	15	NA	NA	NA	NA
1880	17,392,000	85	15	NA	NA	NA	NA
1890	23,318,000	83	17	14	19	4 (1894 = 18)	NA
1900	29,073,000	82	18	15	21	5	3
1910	38,167,000	79	21	25	25	6	6
1920	41,614,000	79	21	23	24	5 (1921 = 12)	12
1930	48,830,000	78	22	29	25	9 (1933 = 25)	11.6
1940	53,011,000	76	24	36	27	15 (1944 = 1)	26.9
1950	62,208,000	72	28	52	31	5.3	31.5
1960	69,628,000	67	33	55	38	5.5	31.4
1970	82,771,000	62	38	59	43	4.9	27.3
1980	106,940,000	58	42	55	52	7.1	21.9
1990	125,840,000	55	45	54	58	5.6	16.1
1995	132,304,000	54	46	55	59	5.6	15.5

NA = Not available.

The American Economy

Year	Gross National Product (GNP) (in $ billions)	Steel Production (in tons)	Automobiles Registered	New Housing Starts	Foreign Trade (in millions of dollars) Exports	Imports
1790	NA	NA	NA	NA	20	23
1800	NA	NA	NA	NA	71	91
1810	NA	NA	NA	NA	67	85
1820	NA	NA	NA	NA	70	74
1830	NA	NA	NA	NA	74	71
1840	NA	NA	NA	NA	132	107
1850	NA	NA	NA	NA	152	178
1860	NA	13,000	NA	NA	400	362
1870	7.4[a]	77,000	NA	NA	451	462
1880	11.2[b]	1,397,000	NA	NA	853	761
1890	13.1	4,779,000	NA	328,000	910	823
1900	18.7	11,227,000	8,000	189,000	1,499	930
1910	35.3	28,330,000	458,300	387,000 (1918 = 118,000)	1,919	1,646
1920	91.5	46,183,000	8,131,500	247,000 (1925 = 937,000)	8,664	5,784
1930	90.7	44,591,000	23,034,700	330,000 (1933 = 93,000)	4,013	3,500
1940	100.0	66,983,000	27,465,800	603,000 (1944 = 142,000)	4,030	7,433
1950	286.5	96,836,000	40,339,000	1,952,000	9,997	8,954
1960	506.5	99,282,000	61,682,300	1,365,000	19,659	15,093
1970	1,016.0	131,514,000	89,279,800	1,434,000	42,681	40,356
1980	2,819.5	111,835,000	121,601,000	1,292,000	220,626	244,871
1990	5,764.9	98,906,000	143,550,000	1,193,000	394,030	485,453
1995	7,237.5	104,930,000	133,930,000[c]	1,354,000	584,742	743,445

[a]Figure is average for 1869–1878.
[b]Figure is average for 1879–1888.
[c]Figure for 1994.
NA = Not available.

Federal Budget Outlays and Debt

Year	Defense[a]	Veterans Benefits[a]	Income Security[a]	Social Security[a]	Health and Medicare[a]	Education[ad]	Net Interest Payments[a]	Federal Debt (dollars)
1790	14.9	4.1[b]	NA	NA	NA	NA	55.0	75,463,000[c]
1800	55.7	.6	NA	NA	NA	NA	31.3	82,976,000
1810	48.4 (1814: 79.7)	1.0	NA	NA	NA	NA	34.9	53,173,000
1820	38.4	17.6	NA	NA	NA	NA	28.1	91,016,000
1830	52.9	9.0	NA	NA	NA	NA	12.6	48,565,000
1840	54.3 (1847: 80.7)	10.7	NA	NA	NA	NA	.7	3,573,000
1850	43.8	4.7	NA	NA	NA	NA	1.0	63,453,000
1860	44.2 (1865: 88.9)	1.7	NA	NA	NA	NA	5.0	64,844,000
1870	25.7	9.2	NA	NA	NA	NA	41.7	2,436,453,000
1880	19.3	21.2	NA	NA	NA	NA	35.8	2,090,909,000
1890	20.9 (1899: 48.6)	33.6	NA	NA	NA	NA	11.4	1,222,397,000
1900	36.6	27.0	NA	NA	NA	NA	7.7	1,263,417,000
1910	45.1 (1919: 59.5)	23.2	NA	NA	NA	NA	3.1	1,146,940,000
1920	37.1	3.4	NA	NA	NA	NA	16.0	24,299,321,000
1930	25.3	6.6	NA	NA	NA	NA	19.9	16,185,310,000
1940	17.5 (1945: 89.4)	6.0	16.0	.3	.5	20.8	9.4	42,967,531,000
1950	32.2	20.3	9.6	1.8	.6	.6	11.3	256,853,000,000
1960	52.2	5.9	8.0	12.6	.9	1.0	7.5	290,525,000,000
1970	41.8	4.4	8.0	15.5	6.2	4.4	7.3	308,921,000,000
1980	22.7	3.6	14.6	20.1	9.4	5.4	8.9	909,050,000,000
1990	23.9	2.3	11.7	19.8	12.4	3.1	14.7	3,206,564,000,000
1995	17.9	2.5	14.5	22.1	18.1	3.6	15.3	5,207,298,000,000[e]

[a]Figures represent percentage of total federal spending for each category. Not included are categories of transportation, commerce, and housing.

[b]1789–1791 figure.

[c]1791 figure.

[d]Includes training, employment, and social services.

[e]1996 figure.

NA = Not available.

The Fifty States, District of Columbia, and Puerto Rico

State	Date of Admission (with Rank)	Capital City	Population (1995) (with Rank)	Racial/Ethnic Distribution (1995)	Per Capita Personal Income (1995) (with Rank)	Total Area in Square Miles (with Rank)
Alabama (AL)	Dec. 14, 1819 (22)	Montgomery	4,253,000 (22)	White: 3,140,000; Black: 1,083,000; Hispanic: 29,000; Asian: 33,000	$18,781 (41)	52,423 (30)
Alaska (AK)	Jan. 3, 1959 (49)	Juneau	604,000 (48)	White: 477,000; Black: 26,000; Hispanic: 22,000; Asian: 29,000; Native American: 102,000	$24,182 (10)	656,424 (1)
Arizona (AZ)	Feb. 14, 1912 (48)	Phoenix	4,218,000 (23)	White: 3,606,000; Black: 123,000; Hispanic: 853,000; Asian: 91,000; Native American: 251,000	$20,421 (35)	114,006 (6)
Arkansas (AR)	June 15, 1836 (25)	Little Rock	2,484,000 (33)	White: 2,047,000; Black: 386,000; Hispanic: 27,000; Asian: 26,000	$17,429 (49)	53,182 (29)
California (CA)	Sept. 9, 1850 (31)	Sacramento	31,589,000 (1)	White: 25,701,000; Black: 2,512,000; Hispanic: 9,143,000; Asian: 3,908,000; Native American: 277,000	$23,699 (12)	163,707 (3)
Colorado (CO)	Aug. 1, 1876 (38)	Denver	3,747,000 (25)	White: 3,431,000; Black: 156,000; Hispanic: 511,000; Asian: 89,000; Native American: 34,000	$23,449 (16)	104,100 (8)
Connecticut (CT)	Jan. 9, 1788 (5)	Hartford	3,275,000 (28)	White: 2,915,000; Black: 293,000; Hispanic: 258,000; Asian: 60,000	$30,303 (1)	5,544 (48)
Delaware (DE)	Dec. 7, 1787 (1)	Dover	717,000 (46)	White: 570,000; Black: 132,000; Hispanic: 22,000; Asian: 14,000	$24,124 (11)	2,489 (49)
District of Columbia (DC)	U.S. Capital, Dec. 1, 1800*	Washington (coextensive with DC)	554,000 (not ranked)	White: 185,000; Black: 384,000; Hispanic: 35,000; Asian: 16,000	$32,274*	68*
Florida (FL)	Mar. 3, 1845 (27)	Tallahassee	14,166,000 (4)	White: 11,867,000; Black: 2,073,000; Hispanic: 1,948,000; Asian: 231,000	$22,916 (20)	65,756 (22)
Georgia (GA)	Jan. 2, 1788 (4)	Atlanta	7,201,000 (10)	White: 5,025,000; Black: 1,955,000; Hispanic: 144,000; Asian: 109,000	$21,278 (28)	59,441 (24)
Hawai'i (HI)	Aug. 21, 1959 (50)	Honolulu	1,187,000 (40)	White: 499,000; Black: 36,000; Hispanic: 106,000; Asian: 679,000	$24,738 (9)	10,932 (43)
Idaho (ID)	July 3, 1890 (43)	Boise	1,163,000 (41)	White: 1,118,000; Black: 5,000; Hispanic: 74,000; Asian: 15,000; Native American: 18,000	$19,264 (38)	83,574 (14)
Illinois (IL)	Dec. 3, 1818 (21)	Springfield	11,830,000 (6)	White: 9,603,000; Black: 1,843,000; Hispanic: 1,086,000; Asian: 383,000	$24,763 (8)	57,918 (25)
Indiana (IN)	Dec. 11, 1816 (19)	Indianapolis	5,803,000 (14)	White: 5,275,000; Black: 476,000; Hispanic: 122,000; Asian: 55,000	$21,273 (29)	36,420 (38)
Iowa (IA)	Dec. 28, 1846 (29)	Des Moines	2,842,000 (30)	White: 2,763,000; Black: 57,000; Hispanic: 45,000; Asian: 33,000	$21,012 (30)	56,276 (26)
Kansas (KS)	Jan. 29, 1861 (34)	Topeka	2,565,000 (32)	White: 2,365,000; Black: 159,000; Hispanic: 116,000; Asian: 50,000	$21,825 (23)	82,282 (15)
Kentucky (KY)	June 1, 1792 (15)	Frankfort	3,860,000 (24)	White: 3,535,000; Black: 286,000; Hispanic: 23,000; Asian: 24,000	$18,612 (43)	40,411 (37)

The Fifty States, District of Columbia,
and Puerto Rico (continued)

State	Date of Admission (with Rank)	Capital City	Population (1995) (with Rank)	Racial/Ethnic Distribution (1995)	Per Capita Personal Income (1995) (with Rank)	Total Area in Square Miles (with Rank)
Louisiana (LA)	Apr. 30, 1812 (18)	Baton Rouge	4,342,000 (21)	White: 2,909,000; Black: 1,371,000; Hispanic: 109,000; Asian: 60,000	$18,827 (39)	51,843 (31)
Maine (ME)	Mar. 15, 1820 (23)	Augusta	1,241,000 (39)	White: 1,217,000; Black: 5,000; Hispanic: 9,000; Asian: 8,000; Native American: 6,000	$20,527 (34)	35,387 (39)
Maryland (MD)	Apr. 28, 1788 (7)	Annapolis	5,042,000 (19)	White: 3,500,000; Black: 1,368,000; Hispanic: 158,000; Asian: 196,000	$25,927 (5)	12,407 (42)
Massachusetts (MA)	Feb. 6, 1788 (6)	Boston	6,074,000 (13)	White: 5,445,000; Black: 340,000; Hispanic: 342,000; Asian: 180,000	$26,994 (3)	10,555 (44)
Michigan (MI)	Jan. 26, 1837 (26)	Lansing	9,549,000 (8)	White: 7,958,000; Black: 1,417,000; Hispanic: 242,000; Asian: 140,000; Native American: 61,000	$23,551 (15)	96,705 (11)
Minnesota (MN)	May 11, 1858 (32)	Saint Paul	4,610,000 (20)	White: 4,344,000; Black: 104,000; Hispanic: 68,000; Asian: 113,000; Native American: 58,000	$23,118 (19)	86,943 (12)
Mississippi (MS)	Dec. 10, 1817 (20)	Jackson	2,697,000 (31)	White: 1,688,000; Black: 952,000; Hispanic: 18,000; Asian: 17,000	$16,531 (50)	48,434 (32)
Missouri (MO)	Aug. 10, 1821 (24)	Jefferson City	5,324,000 (16)	White: 4,629,000; Black: 581,000; Hispanic: 71,000; Asian: 56,000	$21,627 (26)	69,709 (21)
Montana (MT)	Nov. 8, 1889 (41)	Helena	870,000 (44)	White: 798,000; Black: 2,000; Hispanic: 15,000; Asian: 6,000; Native American: 55,000	$18,482 (44)	147,046 (4)
Nebraska (NE)	Mar. 1, 1867 (37)	Lincoln	1,637,000 (37)	White: 1,550,000; Black: 64,000; Hispanic: 53,000; Asian: 17,000; Native American: 14,000	$21,703 (25)	77,358 (16)
Nevada (NV)	Oct. 3, 1864 (36)	Carson City	1,530,000 (38)	White: 1,281,000; Black: 100,000; Hispanic: 195,000; Asian: 70,000; Native American: 27,000	$25,013 (7)	110,567 (7)
New Hampshire (NH)	June 21, 1788 (9)	Concord	1,148,000 (42)	White: 1,109,000; Black: 7,000; Hispanic: 13,000; Asian: 14,000	$25,151 (6)	9,351 (46)
New Jersey (NJ)	Dec. 18, 1787 (3)	Trenton	7,945,000 (9)	White: 6,405,000; Black: 1,156,000; Hispanic: 898,000; Asian: 356,000	$28,858 (2)	8,722 (47)
New Mexico (NM)	Jan. 6, 1912 (47)	Santa Fe	1,685,000 (36)	White: 1,460,000; Black: 32,000; Hispanic: 686,000; Asian: 25,000; Native American: 159,000	$18,055 (47)	121,598 (5)
New York (NY)	July 26, 1788 (11)	Albany	18,136,000 (3)	White: 14,025,000; Black: 3,249,000; Hispanic: 2,372,000; Asian: 846,000; Native American: 57,000	$26,782 (4)	54,471 (27)
North Carolina (NC)	Nov. 21, 1789 (12)	Raleigh	7,195,000 (11)	White: 5,378,000; Black: 1,594,000 Hispanic: 100,000; Asian: 88,000 Native American: 90,000	$20,604 (33)	53,821 (28)
North Dakota (ND)	Nov. 2, 1889 (39)	Bismarck	641,000 (47)	White: 600,000; Black: 4,000; Hispanic: 5,000; Asian: 5,000; Native American: 28,000	$18,663 (42)	70,704 (19)
Ohio (OH)	Mar. 1, 1803 (17)	Columbus	11,151,000 (7)	White: 9,806,000; Black: 1,253,000; Hispanic: 170,000; Asian: 122,000	$22,021 (21)	44,828 (34)

The Fifty States, District of Columbia, and Puerto Rico (continued)

State	Date of Admission (with Rank)	Capital City	Population (1995) (with Rank)	Racial/Ethnic Distribution (1995)	Per Capita Personal Income (1995) (with Rank)	Total Area in Square Miles (with Rank)
Oklahoma (OK)	Nov. 16, 1907 (46)	Oklahoma City	3,278,000 (27)	White: 2,699,000; Black: 244,000; Hispanic: 106,000; Asian: 52,000; Native American: 276,000	$18,152 (46)	69,903 (20)
Oregon (OR)	Feb. 14, 1859 (33)	Salem	3,141,000 (29)	White: 2,929,000; Black: 54,000; Hispanic: 151,000; Asian: 111,000; Native American: 47,000	$21,736 (24)	98,386 (9)
Pennsylvania (PA)	Dec. 12, 1787 (2)	Harrisburg	12,072,000 (5)	White: 10,768,000; Black: 1,167,000; Hispanic: 297,000; Asian: 185,000	$23,279 (18)	46,058 (33)
Puerto Rico (PR)	Ascension 1898; Common-wealth Status 1952	San Juan	3,720,000*	White: >1,000; Black: >1,000; Hispanic: 3,621,000; Asian: >1,000	$6,360*	3,427*
Rhode Island (RI)	May 29, 1790 (13)	Providence	990,000 (43)	White: 927,000; Black: 44,000; Hispanic: 58,000; Asian: 25,000	$23,310 (17)	1,545 (50)
South Carolina (SC)	May 23, 1788 (8)	Columbia	3,673,000 (26)	White: 2,561,000; Black: 1,131,000; Hispanic: 40,000; Asian: 31,000	$18,788 (40)	32,008 (40)
South Dakota (SD)	Nov. 2, 1889 (40)	Pierre	729,000 (45)	White: 663,000; Black: 3,000; Hispanic: 7,000; Asian: 5,000; Native American: 62,000	$19,506 (37)	77,121 (17)
Tennessee (TN)	June 1, 1796 (16)	Nashville	5,256,000 (17)	White: 4,327,000; Black: 845,000; Hispanic: 42,000; Asian: 46,000	$20,376 (36)	42,149 (36)
Texas (TX)	Dec. 29, 1845 (28)	Austin	18,724,000 (2)	White: 15,814,000; Black: 2,251,000; Hispanic: 5,260,000; Asian: 461,000	$20,654 (32)	268,601 (2)
Utah (UT)	Jan. 4, 1896 (45)	Salt Lake City	1,951,000 (34)	White: 1,843,000; Black: 14,000; Hispanic: 106,000; Asian: 54,000; Native American: 33,000	$18,223 (45)	84,904 (13)
Vermont (VT)	Mar. 4, 1791 (14)	Montpelier	585,000 (49)	White: 570,000; Black: 2,000; Hispanic: 4,000; Asian: 4,000; Native American: 2,000	$20,927 (31)	9,615 (45)
Virginia (VA)	June 25, 1788 (10)	Richmond	6,618,000 (12)	White: 5,127,000; Black: 1,284,000 Hispanic: 193,000; Asian: 220,000	$25,597 (14)	42,777 (35)
Washington (WA)	Nov. 11, 1889 (42)	Olympia	5,431,000 (15)	White: 4,915,000; Black: 164,000; Hispanic: 291,000; Asian: 318,000; Native American: 101,000	$23,639 (13)	71,302 (18)
West Virginia (WV)	June 20, 1863 (35)	Charleston	1,828,000; (35)	White: 1,756,000; Black: 54,000; Hispanic: 10,000; Asian: 11,000	$17,915 (48)	24,231 (41)
Wisconsin (WI)	May 29, 1848 (30)	Madison	5,123,000 (18)	White: 4,750,000; Black: 288,000; Hispanic: 118,000; Asian: 76,000; Native American: 45,000	$21,839 (22)	65,499 (23)
Wyoming (WY)	July 10, 1890 (44)	Cheyenne	480,000 (50)	White: 467,000; Black: 4,000; Hispanic: 31,000; Asian: 4,000; Native American: 12,000	$21,321 (27)	97,818 (10)

*Not ranked.

Presidential Elections

Year	Number of States	Candidates	Parties	Popular Vote	% of Popular Vote	Electoral Vote	% Voter Partici- pation[b]
1789	11	**George Washington**	No party			69	
		John Adams	designations			34	
		Other candidates				35	
1792	15	**George Washington**	No party			132	
		John Adams	designations			77	
		George Clinton				50	
		Other candidates				5	
1796	16	**John Adams**	Federalist			71	
		Thomas Jefferson	Democratic-Republican			68	
		Thomas Pinckney	Federalist			59	
		Aaron Burr	Democratic-Republican			30	
		Other candidates				48	
1800	16	**Thomas Jefferson**	Democratic-Republican			73	
		Aaron Burr	Democratic-Republican			73	
		John Adams	Federalist			65	
		Charles C. Pinckney	Federalist			64	
		John Jay	Federalist			1	
1804	17	**Thomas Jefferson**	Democratic-Republican			162	
		Charles C. Pinckney	Federalist			14	
1808	17	**James Madison**	Democratic-Republican			122	
		Charles C. Pinckney	Federalist			47	
		George Clinton	Democratic-Republican			6	
1812	18	**James Madison**	Democratic-Republican			128	
		DeWitt Clinton	Federalist			89	
1816	19	**James Monroe**	Democratic-Republican			183	
		Rufus King	Federalist			34	
1820	24	**James Monroe**	Democratic-Republican			231	
		John Quincy Adams	Independent Republican			1	

Presidential Elections (continued)

Year	Number of States	Candidates	Parties	Popular Vote	% of Popular Vote	Electoral Vote	% Voter Participation[b]
1824	24	**John Quincy Adams**	Democratic-Republican	108,740	30.5	84	26.9
		Andrew Jackson	Democratic-Republican	153,544	43.1	99	
		Henry Clay	Democratic-Republican	47,136	13.2	37	
		William H. Crawford	Democratic-Republican	46,618	13.1	41	
1828	24	**Andrew Jackson**	Democratic	647,286	56.0	178	57.6
		John Quincy Adams	National Republican	508,064	44.0	83	
1832	24	**Andrew Jackson**	Democratic	688,242	54.5	219	55.4
		Henry Clay	National Republican	473,462	37.5	49	
		William Wirt	Anti-Masonic	101,051	8.0	7	
		John Floyd	Democratic			11	
1836	26	**Martin Van Buren**	Democratic	765,483	50.9	170	57.8
		William H. Harrison	Whig			73	
		Hugh L. White	Whig	739,795	49.1	26	
		Daniel Webster	Whig			14	
		W. P. Mangum	Whig			11	
1840	26	**William H. Harrison**	Whig	1,274,624	53.1	234	80.2
		Martin Van Buren	Democratic	1,127,781	46.9	60	
1844	26	**James K. Polk**	Democratic	1,338,464	49.6	170	78.9
		Henry Clay	Whig	1,300,097	48.1	105	
		James G. Birney	Liberty	62,300	2.3		
1848	30	**Zachary Taylor**	Whig	1,360,967	47.4	163	72.7
		Lewis Cass	Democratic	1,222,342	42.5	127	
		Martin Van Buren	Free Soil	291,263	10.1		
1852	31	**Franklin Pierce**	Democratic	1,601,117	50.9	254	69.6
		Winfield Scott	Whig	1,385,453	44.1	42	
		John P. Hale	Free Soil	155,825	5.0		
1856	31	**James Buchanan**	Democratic	1,832,955	45.3	174	78.9
		John C. Frémont	Republican	1,339,932	33.1	114	
		Millard Fillmore	American	871,731	21.6	8	
1860	33	**Abraham Lincoln**	Republican	1,865,593	39.8	180	81.2
		Stephen A. Douglas	Democratic	1,382,713	29.5	12	
		John C. Breckinridge	Democratic	848,356	18.1	72	
		John Bell	Constitutional Union	592,906	12.6	39	
1864	36	**Abraham Lincoln**	Republican	2,206,938	55.0	212	73.8
		George B. McClellan	Democratic	1,803,787	45.0	21	

Presidential Elections (continued)

Year	Number of States	Candidates	Parties	Popular Vote	% of Popular Vote	Electoral Vote	% Voter Participation[b]
1868	37	**Ulysses S. Grant**	Republican	3,013,421	52.7	214	78.1
		Horatio Seymour	Democratic	2,706,829	47.3	80	
1872	37	**Ulysses S. Grant**	Republican	3,596,745	55.6	286	71.3
		Horace Greeley	Democratic	2,843,446	43.9	a	
1876	38	**Rutherford B. Hayes**	Republican	4,036,572	48.0	185	81.8
		Samuel J. Tilden	Democratic	4,284,020	51.0	184	
1880	38	**James A. Garfield**	Republican	4,453,295	48.5	214	79.4
		Winfield S. Hancock	Democratic	4,414,082	48.1	155	
		James B. Weaver	Greenback-Labor	308,578	3.4		
1884	38	**Grover Cleveland**	Democratic	4,879,507	48.5	219	77.5
		James G. Blaine	Republican	4,850,293	48.2	182	
		Benjamin F. Butler	Greenback-Labor	175,370	1.8		
		John P. St. John	Prohibition	150,369	1.5		
1888	38	**Benjamin Harrison**	Republican	5,477,129	47.9	233	79.3
		Grover Cleveland	Democratic	5,537,857	48.6	168	
		Clinton B. Fisk	Prohibition	249,506	2.2		
		Anson J. Streeter	Union Labor	146,935	1.3		
1892	44	**Grover Cleveland**	Democratic	5,555,426	46.1	277	74.7
		Benjamin Harrison	Republican	5,182,690	43.0	145	
		James B. Weaver	People's	1,029,846	8.5	22	
		John Bidwell	Prohibition	264,133	2.2		
1896	45	**William McKinley**	Republican	7,102,246	51.1	271	79.3
		William J. Bryan	Democratic	6,492,559	47.7	176	
1900	45	**William McKinley**	Republican	7,218,491	51.7	292	73.2
		William J. Bryan	Democratic; Populist	6,356,734	45.5	155	
		John C. Wooley	Prohibition	208,914	1.5		
1904	45	**Theodore Roosevelt**	Republican	7,628,461	57.4	336	65.2
		Alton B. Parker	Democratic	5,084,223	37.6	140	
		Eugene V. Debs	Socialist	402,283	3.0		
		Silas C. Swallow	Prohibition	258,536	1.9		
1908	46	**William H. Taft**	Republican	7,675,320	51.6	321	65.4
		William J. Bryan	Democratic	6,412,294	43.1	162	
		Eugene V. Debs	Socialist	420,793	2.8		
		Eugene W. Chafin	Prohibition	253,840	1.7		
1912	48	**Woodrow Wilson**	Democratic	6,296,547	41.9	435	58.8
		Theodore Roosevelt	Progressive	4,118,571	27.4	88	
		William H. Taft	Republican	3,486,720	23.2	8	
		Eugene V. Debs	Socialist	900,672	6.0		
		Eugene W. Chafin	Prohibition	206,275	1.4		

Presidential Elections (continued)

Year	Number of States	Candidates	Parties	Popular Vote	% of Popular Vote	Electoral Vote	% Voter Participation[b]
1916	48	**Woodrow Wilson**	Democratic	9,127,695	49.4	277	61.6
		Charles E. Hughes	Republican	8,533,507	46.2	254	
		A. L. Benson	Socialist	585,113	3.2		
		J. Frank Hanly	Prohibition	220,506	1.2		
1920	48	**Warren G. Harding**	Republican	16,143,407	60.4	404	49.2
		James M. Cox	Democratic	9,130,328	34.2	127	
		Eugene V. Debs	Socialist	919,799	3.4		
		P. P. Christensen	Farmer-Labor	265,411	1.0		
1924	48	**Calvin Coolidge**	Republican	15,718,211	54.0	382	48.9
		John W. Davis	Democratic	8,385,283	28.8	136	
		Robert M. La Follette	Progressive	4,831,289	16.6	13	
1928	48	**Herbert C. Hoover**	Republican	21,391,993	58.2	444	56.9
		Alfred E. Smith	Democratic	15,016,169	40.9	87	
1932	48	**Franklin D. Roosevelt**	Democratic	22,809,638	57.4	472	56.9
		Herbert C. Hoover	Republican	15,758,901	39.7	59	
		Norman Thomas	Socialist	881,951	2.2		
1936	48	**Franklin D. Roosevelt**	Democratic	27,752,869	60.8	523	61.0
		Alfred M. Landon	Republican	16,674,665	36.5	8	
		William Lemke	Union	882,479	1.9		
1940	48	**Franklin D. Roosevelt**	Democratic	27,307,819	54.8	449	62.5
		Wendell L. Wilkie	Republican	22,321,018	44.8	82	
1944	48	**Franklin D. Roosevelt**	Democratic	25,606,585	53.5	432	55.9
		Thomas E. Dewey	Republican	22,014,745	46.0	99	
1948	48	**Harry S Truman**	Democratic	24,179,345	49.6	303	53.0
		Thomas E. Dewey	Republican	21,991,291	45.1	189	
		J. Strom Thurmond	States' Rights	1,176,125	2.4	39	
		Henry A. Wallace	Progressive	1,157,326	2.4		
1952	48	**Dwight D. Eisenhower**	Republican	33,936,234	55.1	442	63.3
		Adlai E. Stevenson	Democratic	27,314,992	44.4	89	
1956	48	**Dwight D. Eisenhower**	Republican	35,590,472	57.6	457	60.6
		Adlai E. Stevenson	Democratic	26,022,752	42.1	73	
1960	50	**John F. Kennedy**	Democratic	34,226,731	49.7	303	62.8
		Richard M. Nixon	Republican	34,108,157	49.5	219	
1964	50	**Lyndon B. Johnson**	Democratic	43,129,566	61.1	486	61.7
		Barry M. Goldwater	Republican	27,178,188	38.5	52	
1968	50	**Richard M. Nixon**	Republican	31,785,480	43.4	301	60.6
		Hubert H. Humphrey	Democratic	31,275,166	42.7	191	
		George C. Wallace	American Independent	9,906,473	13.5	46	

Presidential Elections (continued)

Year	Number of States	Candidates	Parties	Popular Vote	% of Popular Vote	Electoral Vote	% Voter Participation[b]
1972	50	**Richard M. Nixon**	Republican	47,169,911	60.7	520	55.2
		George S. McGovern	Democratic	29,170,383	37.5	17	
		John G. Schmitz	American	1,099,482	1.4		
1976	50	**James E. Carter**	Democratic	40,830,763	50.1	297	53.5
		Gerald R. Ford	Republican	39,147,793	48.0	240	
1980	50	**Ronald W. Reagan**	Republican	43,899,248	50.8	489	52.6
		James E. Carter	Democratic	35,481,432	41.0	49	
		John B. Anderson	Independent	5,719,437	6.6	0	
		Ed Clark	Libertarian	920,859	1.1	0	
1984	50	**Ronald W. Reagan**	Republican	54,455,075	58.8	525	53.1
		Walter F. Mondale	Democratic	37,577,185	40.6	13	
1988	50	**George H. W. Bush**	Republican	48,901,046	53.4	426	50.2
		Michael S. Dukakis	Democratic	41,809,030	45.6	111[c]	
1992	50	**William J. Clinton**	Democratic	44,908,233	43.0	370	55.0
		George H. W. Bush	Republican	39,102,282	37.4	168	
		H. Ross Perot	Independent	19,741,048	18.9	0	
1996	50	**William J. Clinton**	Democratic	47,401,054	49.2	379	49.0
		Robert J. Dole	Republican	39,197,350	40.7	159	
		H. Ross Perot	Reform	8,085,285	8.4	0	
		Ralph Nader	Green	684,871	0.7	0	

Candidates receiving less than 1 percent of the popular vote have been omitted. Thus the percentage of popular vote given for any election year may not total 100 percent.

Before the passage of the Twelfth Amendment in 1804, the Electoral College voted for two presidential candidates; the runner-up became vice president.

Before 1824, most presidential electors were chosen by state legislatures, not by popular vote.

[a]Greeley died shortly after the election; the electors supporting him then divided their votes among minor candidates.

[b]Percent of voting-age population casting ballots.

[c]One elector from West Virginia cast her Electoral College presidential ballot for Lloyd Bentsen, the Democratic party's vice-presidential candidate.

Presidents and Vice Presidents

1. President	**George Washington**	1789–1797
Vice President	John Adams	1789–1797
2. President	**John Adams**	1797–1801
Vice President	Thomas Jefferson	1797–1801
3. President	**Thomas Jefferson**	1801–1809
Vice President	Aaron Burr	1801–1805
Vice President	George Clinton	1805–1809
4. President	**James Madison**	1809–1817
Vice President	George Clinton	1809–1813
Vice President	Elbridge Gerry	1813–1817
5. President	**James Monroe**	1817–1825
Vice President	Daniel Tompkins	1817–1825
6. President	**John Quincy Adams**	1825–1829
Vice President	John C. Calhoun	1825–1829
7. President	**Andrew Jackson**	1829–1837
Vice President	John C. Calhoun	1829–1833
Vice President	Martin Van Buren	1833–1837
8. President	**Martin Van Buren**	1837–1841
Vice President	Richard M. Johnson	1837–1841
9. President	**William H. Harrison**	1841
Vice President	John Tyler	1841
10. President	**John Tyler**	1841–1845
Vice President	None	
11. President	**James K. Polk**	1845–1849
Vice President	George M. Dallas	1845–1849
12. President	**Zachary Taylor**	1849–1850
Vice President	Millard Fillmore	1849–1850
13. President	**Millard Fillmore**	1850–1853
Vice President	None	
14. President	**Franklin Pierce**	1853–1857
Vice President	William R. King	1853–1857
15. President	**James Buchanan**	1857–1861
Vice President	John C. Breckinridge	1857–1861
16. President	**Abraham Lincoln**	1861–1865
Vice President	Hannibal Hamlin	1861–1865
Vice President	Andrew Johnson	1865
17. President	**Andrew Johnson**	1865–1869
Vice President	None	
18. President	**Ulysses S. Grant**	1869–1877
Vice President	Schuyler Colfax	1869–1873
Vice President	Henry Wilson	1873–1877
19. President	**Rutherford B. Hayes**	1877–1881
Vice President	William A. Wheeler	1877–1881
20. President	**James A. Garfield**	1881
Vice President	Chester A. Arthur	1881
21. President	**Chester A. Arthur**	1881–1885
Vice President	None	
22. President	**Grover Cleveland**	1885–1889
Vice President	Thomas A. Hendricks	1885–1889
23. President	**Benjamin Harrison**	1889–1893
Vice President	Levi P. Morton	1889–1893
24. President	**Grover Cleveland**	1893–1897
Vice President	Adlai E. Stevenson	1893–1897
25. President	**William McKinley**	1897–1901
Vice President	Garret A. Hobart	1897–1901
Vice President	Theodore Roosevelt	1901
26. President	**Theodore Roosevelt**	1901–1909
Vice President	Charles Fairbanks	1905–1909
27. President	**William H. Taft**	1909–1913
Vice President	James S. Sherman	1909–1913
28. President	**Woodrow Wilson**	1913–1921
Vice President	Thomas R. Marshall	1913–1921
29. President	**Warren G. Harding**	1921–1923
Vice President	Calvin Coolidge	1921–1923
30. President	**Calvin Coolidge**	1923–1929
Vice President	Charles G. Dawes	1925–1929
31. President	**Herbert C. Hoover**	1929–1933
Vice President	Charles Curtis	1929–1933
32. President	**Franklin D. Roosevelt**	1933–1945
Vice President	John N. Garner	1933–1941
Vice President	Henry A. Wallace	1941–1945
Vice President	Harry S Truman	1945
33. President	**Harry S Truman**	1945–1953
Vice President	Alben W. Barkley	1949–1953
34. President	**Dwight D. Eisenhower**	1953–1961
Vice President	Richard M. Nixon	1953–1961
35. President	**John F. Kennedy**	1961–1963
Vice President	Lyndon B. Johnson	1961–1963
36. President	**Lyndon B. Johnson**	1963–1969
Vice President	Hubert H. Humphrey	1965–1969
37. President	**Richard M. Nixon**	1969–1974
Vice President	Spiro T. Agnew	1969–1973
Vice President	Gerald R. Ford	1973–1974
38. President	**Gerald R. Ford**	1974–1977
Vice President	Nelson A. Rockefeller	1974–1977

Presidents and Vice Presidents (continued)

39. President	**James E. Carter**	1977–1981	41. President	**George H. W. Bush**	1989–1993
Vice President	Walter F. Mondale	1977–1981	Vice President	J. Danforth Quayle	1989–1993
40. President	**Ronald W. Reagan**	1981–1989	42. President	**William J. Clinton**	1993–
Vice President	George H. W. Bush	1981–1989	Vice President	Albert Gore	1993–

Party Strength in Congress

Period	Congress	House Majority Party		House Minority Party		Others	Senate Majority Party		Senate Minority Party		Others	Party of President	
1789–91	1st	Ad	38	Op	26		Ad	17	Op	9		F	Washington
1791–93	2nd	F	37	DR	33		F	16	DR	13		F	Washington
1793–95	3rd	DR	57	F	48		F	17	DR	13		F	Washington
1795–97	4th	F	54	DR	52		F	19	DR	13		F	Washington
1797–99	5th	F	58	DR	48		F	20	DR	12		F	J. Adams
1799–1801	6th	F	64	DR	42		F	19	DR	13		F	J. Adams
1801–03	7th	DR	69	F	36		DR	18	F	13		DR	Jefferson
1803–05	8th	DR	102	F	39		DR	25	F	9		DR	Jefferson
1805–07	9th	DR	116	F	25		DR	27	F	7		DR	Jefferson
1807–09	10th	DR	118	F	24		DR	28	F	6		DR	Jefferson
1809–11	11th	DR	94	F	48		DR	28	F	6		DR	Madison
1811–13	12th	DR	108	F	36		DR	30	F	6		DR	Madison
1813–15	13th	DR	112	F	68		DR	27	F	9		DR	Madison
1815–17	14th	DR	117	F	65		DR	25	F	11		DR	Madison
1817–19	15th	DR	141	F	42		DR	34	F	10		DR	Monroe
1819–21	16th	DR	156	F	27		DR	35	F	7		DR	Monroe
1821–23	17th	DR	158	F	25		DR	44	F	4		DR	Monroe
1823–25	18th	DR	187	F	26		DR	44	F	4		DR	Monroe
1825–27	19th	Ad	105	J	97		Ad	26	J	20		C	J. Q. Adams
1827–29	20th	J	119	Ad	94		J	28	Ad	20		C	J. Q. Adams
1829–31	21st	D	139	NR	74		D	26	NR	22		D	Jackson
1831–33	22nd	D	141	NR	58	14	D	25	NR	21	2	D	Jackson
1833–35	23rd	D	147	AM	53	60	D	20	NR	20	8	D	Jackson
1835–37	24th	D	145	W	98		D	27	W	25		D	Jackson
1837–39	25th	D	108	W	107	24	D	30	W	18	4	D	Van Buren
1839–41	26th	D	124	W	118		D	28	W	22		D	Van Buren
1841–43	27th	W	133	D	102	6	W	28	D	22	2	W	W. Harrison
												W	Tyler
1843–45	28th	D	142	W	79	1	W	28	D	25	1	W	Tyler
1845–47	29th	D	143	W	77	6	D	31	W	25		D	Polk
1847–49	30th	W	115	D	108	4	D	36	W	21	1	D	Polk
1849–51	31st	D	112	W	109	9	D	35	W	25	2	W	Taylor
												W	Fillmore
1851–53	32nd	D	140	W	88	5	D	35	W	24	3	W	Fillmore
1853–55	33rd	D	159	W	71	4	D	38	W	22	2	D	Pierce
1855–57	34th	R	108	D	83	43	D	40	R	15	5	D	Pierce
1857–59	35th	D	118	R	92	26	D	36	R	20	8	D	Buchanan
1859–61	36th	R	114	D	92	31	D	36	R	26	4	D	Buchanan
1861–63	37th	R	105	D	43	30	R	31	D	10	8	R	Lincoln
1863–65	38th	R	102	D	75	9	R	36	D	9	5	R	Lincoln

Party Strength in Congress (continued)

Period	Congress	House Majority Party		House Minority Party		Others	Senate Majority Party		Senate Minority Party		Others	Party of President	
1865–67	39th	U	149	D	42		U	42	D	10		R	Lincoln
												R	A. Johnson
1867–69	40th	R	143	D	49		R	42	D	11		R	A. Johnson
1869–71	41st	R	149	D	63		R	56	D	11		R	Grant
1871–73	42nd	R	134	D	104	5	R	52	D	17	5	R	Grant
1873–75	43rd	R	194	D	92	14	R	49	D	19	5	R	Grant
1875–77	44th	D	169	R	109	14	R	45	D	29	2	R	Grant
1877–79	45th	D	153	R	140		R	39	D	36	1	R	Hayes
1879–81	46th	D	149	R	130	14	D	42	R	33	1	R	Hayes
1881–83	47th	D	147	R	135	11	R	37	D	37	1	R	Garfield
												R	Arthur
1883–85	48th	D	197	R	118	10	R	38	D	36	2	R	Arthur
1885–87	49th	D	183	R	140	2	R	43	D	34		D	Cleveland
1887–89	50th	D	169	R	152	4	R	39	D	37		D	Cleveland
1889–91	51st	R	166	D	159		R	39	D	37		R	B. Harrison
1891–93	52nd	D	235	R	88	9	R	47	D	39	2	R	B. Harrison
1893–95	53rd	D	218	R	127	11	D	44	R	38	3	D	Cleveland
1895–97	54th	R	244	D	105	7	R	43	D	39	6	D	Cleveland
1897–99	55th	R	204	D	113	40	R	47	D	34	7	R	McKinley
1899–1901	56th	R	185	D	163	9	R	53	D	26	8	R	McKinley
1901–03	57th	R	197	D	151	9	R	55	D	31	4	R	McKinley
												R	T. Roosevelt
1903–05	58th	R	208	D	178		R	57	D	33		R	T. Roosevelt
1905–07	59th	R	250	D	136		R	57	D	33		R	T. Roosevelt
1907–09	60th	R	222	D	164		R	61	D	31		R	T. Roosevelt
1909–11	61st	R	219	D	172		R	61	D	32		R	Taft
1911–13	62nd	D	228	R	161	1	R	51	D	41		R	Taft
1913–15	63rd	D	291	R	127	17	D	51	R	44	1	D	Wilson
1915–17	64th	D	230	R	196	9	D	56	R	40		D	Wilson
1917–19	65th	D	216	R	210	6	D	53	R	42		D	Wilson
1919–21	66th	R	240	D	190	3	R	49	D	47		D	Wilson
1921–23	67th	R	301	D	131	1	R	59	D	37		R	Harding
1923–25	68th	R	225	D	205	5	R	51	D	43	2	R	Coolidge
1925–27	69th	R	247	D	183	4	R	56	D	39	1	R	Coolidge
1927–29	70th	R	237	D	195	3	R	49	D	46	1	R	Coolidge
1929–31	71st	R	267	D	167	1	R	56	D	39	1	R	Hoover
1931–33	72nd	D	220	R	214	1	R	48	D	47	1	R	Hoover
1933–35	73rd	D	310	R	117	5	D	60	R	35	1	D	F. Roosevelt
1935–37	74th	D	319	R	103	10	D	69	R	25	2	D	F. Roosevelt
1937–39	75th	D	331	R	89	13	D	76	R	16	4	D	F. Roosevelt
1939–41	76th	D	261	R	164	4	D	69	R	23	4	D	F. Roosevelt
1941–43	77th	D	268	R	162	5	D	66	R	28	2	D	F. Roosevelt
1943–45	78th	D	218	R	208	4	D	58	R	37	1	D	F. Roosevelt

Party Strength in Congress (continued)

Period	Congress	House Majority Party		House Minority Party		Others	Senate Majority Party		Senate Minority Party		Others	Party of President	
1945–47	79th	D	242	R	190	2	D	56	R	38	1	D	Truman
1947–49	80th	R	245	D	188	1	R	51	D	45		D	Truman
1949–51	81st	D	263	R	171	1	D	54	R	42		D	Truman
1951–53	82nd	D	234	R	199	1	D	49	R	47		D	Truman
1953–55	83rd	R	221	D	211	1	R	48	D	47	1	R	Eisenhower
1955–57	84th	D	232	R	203		D	48	R	47	1	R	Eisenhower
1957–59	85th	D	233	R	200		D	49	R	47		R	Eisenhower
1959–61	86th	D	284	R	153		D	65	R	35		R	Eisenhower
1961–63	87th	D	263	R	174		D	65	R	35		D	Kennedy
1963–65	88th	D	258	R	117		D	67	R	33		D	Kennedy
												D	L. Johnson
1965–67	89th	D	295	R	140		D	68	R	32		D	L. Johnson
1967–69	90th	D	246	R	187		D	64	R	36		D	L. Johnson
1969–71	91st	D	245	R	189		D	57	R	43		R	Nixon
1971–73	92nd	D	254	R	180		D	54	R	44	2	R	Nixon
1973–75	93rd	D	239	R	192	1	D	56	R	42	2	R	Nixon
1975–77	94th	D	291	R	144		D	60	R	37	3	R	Ford
1977–79	95th	D	292	R	143		D	61	R	38	1	D	Carter
1979–81	96th	D	276	R	157		D	58	R	41	1	D	Carter
1981–83	97th	D	243	R	192		R	53	D	46	1	R	Reagan
1983–85	98th	D	267	R	168		R	55	D	45		R	Reagan
1985–87	99th	D	253	R	182		R	53	D	47		R	Reagan
1987–89	100th	D	258	R	177		D	55	R	45		R	Reagan
1989–91	101st	D	259	R	174		D	54	R	46		R	Bush
1991–93	102nd	D	267	R	167	1	D	56	R	44		R	Bush
1993–95	103rd	D	258	R	176	1	D	56	R	44		D	Clinton
1995–97	104th	R	230	D	204	1	R	52	D	48		D	Clinton
1997–99	105th	R	227	D	207	1	R	55	D	45		D	Clinton

AD = Administration; AM = Anti-Masonic; C = Coalition; D = Democratic; DR = Democratic-Republican; F = Federalist; J = Jacksonian; NR = National Republican; Op = Opposition; R = Republican; U = Unionist; W = Whig. Figures are for the beginning of first session of each Congress, except the 93rd, which are for the beginning of the second session.

Justices of the Supreme Court

	Term of Service	Years of Service	Life Span
John Jay	1789–1795	5	1745–1829
John Rutledge	1789–1791	1	1739–1800
William Cushing	1789–1810	20	1732–1810
James Wilson	1789–1798	8	1742–1798
John Blair	1789–1796	6	1732–1800
Robert H. Harrison	1789–1790	—	1745–1790
James Iredell	1790–1799	9	1951–1799
Thomas Johnson	1791–1793	1	1732–1819
William Paterson	1793–1806	13	1745–1806
*John Rutledge**	1795	—	1739–1800
Samuel Chase	1796–1811	15	1741–1811
Oliver Ellsworth	1796–1800	4	1745–1807
Bushrod Washington	1798–1829	31	1762–1829
Alfred Moore	1799–1804	4	1755–1810
John Marshall	1801–1835	34	1755–1835
William Johnson	1804–1834	30	1771–1834
H. Brockholst Livingston	1806–1823	16	1757–1823
Thomas Todd	1807–1826	18	1765–1826
Joseph Story	1811–1845	33	1779–1845
Gabriel Duval	1811–1835	24	1752–1844
Smith Thompson	1823–1843	20	1768–1843
Robert Trimble	1826–1828	2	1777–1828
John McLean	1829–1861	32	1785–1861
Henry Baldwin	1830–1844	14	1780–1844
James M. Wayne	1835–1867	32	1790–1867
Roger B. Taney	1836–1864	28	1777–1864
Philip P. Barbour	1836–1841	4	1783–1841
John Catron	1837–1865	28	1786–1865
John McKinley	1837–1852	15	1780–1852
Peter V. Daniel	1841–1860	19	1784–1860
Samuel Nelson	1845–1872	27	1792–1873
Levi Woodbury	1845–1851	5	1789–1851
Robert C. Grier	1846–1870	23	1794–1870
Benjamin R. Curtis	1851–1857	6	1809–1874
John A. Campbell	1853–1861	8	1811–1889
Nathan Clifford	1858–1881	23	1803–1881
Noah H. Swayne	1862–1881	18	1804–1884
Samuel F. Miller	1862–1890	28	1816–1890
David Davis	1862–1877	14	1815–1886
Stephen J. Field	1863–1897	34	1816–1899
Salmon P. Chase	1864–1873	8	1808–1873
William Strong	1870–1880	10	1808–1895
Joseph P. Bradley	1870–1892	22	1813–1892
Ward Hunt	1873–1882	9	1810–1886
Morrison R. Waite	1874–1888	14	1816–1888
John M. Harlan	1877–1911	34	1833–1911
William B. Woods	1880–1887	7	1824–1887
Stanley Mathews	1881–1889	7	1824–1889
Horace Gray	1882–1902	20	1828–1902
Samuel Blatchford	1882–1893	11	1820–1893
Lucius Q. C. Lamar	1888–1893	5	1825–1893
Melville W. Fuller	1888–1910	21	1833–1910
David J. Brewer	1890–1910	20	1837–1910
Henry B. Brown	1890–1906	16	1836–1913
George Shiras, Jr.	1892–1903	10	1832–1924
Howell E. Jackson	1893–1895	2	1832–1895
Edward D. White	1894–1910	16	1845–1921
Rufus W. Peckham	1895–1909	14	1838–1909
Joseph McKenna	1898–1925	26	1843–1926
Oliver W. Holmes	1902–1932	30	1841–1935
William D. Day	1903–1922	19	1849–1923
William H. Moody	1906–1910	3	1853–1917
Horace H. Lurton	1910–1914	4	1844–1914
Charles E. Hughes	1910–1916	5	1862–1948
Willis Van Devanter	1911–1937	26	1859–1941
Joseph R. Lamar	1911–1916	5	1857–1916
Edward D. White	1910–1921	11	1845–1921
Mahlon Pitney	1912–1922	10	1858–1924
James C. McReynolds	1914–1941	26	1862–1946
Louis D. Brandeis	1916–1939	22	1856–1941
John H. Clarke	1916–1922	6	1857–1945
William H. Taft	1921–1930	8	1857–1930
George Sutherland	1922–1938	15	1862–1942
Pierce Butler	1922–1939	16	1866–1939
Edward T. Sanford	1923–1930	7	1865–1930
Harlan F. Stone	1925–1941	16	1872–1946
Charles E. Hughes	1930–1941	11	1862–1948
Owen J. Roberts	1930–1945	15	1875–1955
Benjamin N. Cardozo	1932–1938	6	1870–1938
Hugo L. Black	1937–1971	34	1886–1971
Stanley F. Reed	1938–1957	19	1884–1980
Felix Frankfurter	1939–1962	23	1882–1965
William O. Douglas	1939–1975	36	1898–1980
Frank Murphy	1940–1949	9	1890–1949
Harlan F. Stone	1941–1946	5	1872–1946
James F. Byrnes	1941–1942	1	1879–1972

Justices of the Supreme Court (continued)

	Term of Service	Years of Service	Life Span		Term of Service	Years of Service	Life Span
Robert H. Jackson	1941–1954	13	1892–1954	Thurgood Marshall	1967–1991	24	1908–1993
Wiley B. Rutledge	1943–1949	6	1894–1949	*Warren C. Burger*	1969–1986	17	1907–1995
Harold H. Burton	1945–1958	13	1888–1964	Harry A. Blackmun	1970–1994	24	1908–1998
Fred M. Vinson	1946–1953	7	1890–1953	Lewis F. Powell, Jr.	1972–1987	15	1907–1998
Tom C. Clark	1949–1967	18	1899–1977	*William H. Rehnquist*	1972–	—	1924–
Sherman Minton	1949–1956	7	1890–1965	John P. Stevens III	1975–	—	1920–
Earl Warren	1953–1969	16	1891–1974	Sandra Day O'Connor	1981–	—	1930–
John Marshall Harlan	1955–1971	16	1899–1971	Antonin Scalia	1986–	—	1936–
William J. Brennan, Jr.	1956–1990	34	1906–1977	Anthony M. Kennedy	1988–	—	1936–
Charles E. Whittaker	1957–1962	5	1901–1973	David H. Souter	1990–	—	1939–
Potter Stewart	1958–1981	23	1915–1985	Clarence Thomas	1991–	—	1948–
Byron R. White	1962–1993	31	1917–	Ruth Bader Ginsburg	1993–	—	1933–
Arthur J. Goldberg	1962–1965	3	1908–1990	Stephen Breyer	1994–	—	1938–
Abe Fortas	1965–1969	4	1910–1982				

*Appointed and served one term, but not confirmed by the Senate.

Note: Chief justices are in italics.

Index